Personal Financial Planner...
at the end of each new text!

Students! Pay special attention to the Personal Financial Planner sheets located at the very end of this text: fill them in, rip them out (check out the perforated pages), and keep them with you to continue financial success and refer back to long after the course has ended.

Each sheet correlates with topics within the text, and asks you to think about your own financial plan and record your steps. With spaces to write your own plan details, and questions regarding future steps for your plan - these sheets are perfect for homework and/or personal reference!

Icons in the margins of the chapters denote which sheets are linked to the appropriate sections, and list the sheet numbers and titles. You can flip ahead to work the sheets right then, or save them to work all together at a later point.

Is there a better time to start your personal financial plan than right now?

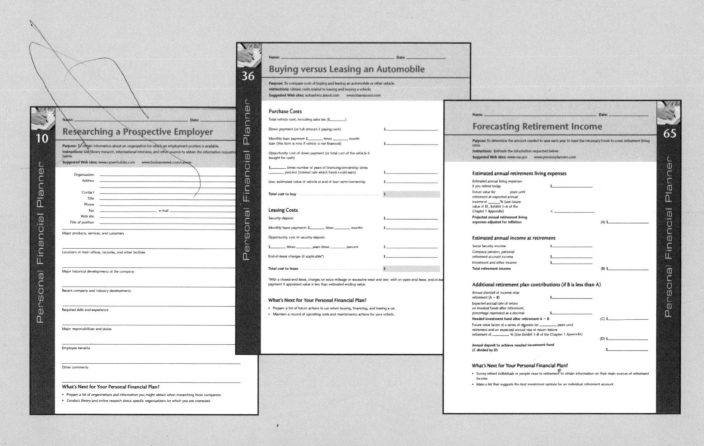

Personal Finance

EIGHTH EDITION

JACK R. KAPOOR
College of DuPage

LES R. DLABAY
Lake Forest College

ROBERT J. HUGHES
Dallas County Community Colleges

McGraw-Hill
Irwin

Boston   Burr Ridge, IL   Dubuque, IA   Madison, WI   New York   San Francisco   St. Louis
Bangkok   Bogotá   Caracas   Kuala Lumpur   Lisbon   London   Madrid   Mexico City
Milan   Montreal   New Delhi   Santiago   Seoul   Singapore   Sydney   Taipei   Toronto

McGraw-Hill
Irwin

PERSONAL FINANCE
Published by McGraw-Hill/Irwin, a business unit of The McGraw-Hill Companies, Inc., 1221 Avenue of the Americas, New York, NY, 10020. Copyright © 2007 by The McGraw-Hill Companies, Inc. All rights reserved. No part of this publication may be reproduced or distributed in any form or by any means, or stored in a database or retrieval system, without the prior written consent of The McGraw-Hill Companies, Inc., including, but not limited to, in any network or other electronic storage or transmission, or broadcast for distance learning.

Some ancillaries, including electronic and print components, may not be available to customers outside the United States.

This book is printed on acid-free paper.

3 4 5 6 7 8 9 0 DOW/ DOW 0 9 8 7

ISBN: 978-0-07-310671-7
MHID 0-07-310671-2

Publisher: *Stephen M. Patterson*
Senior sponsoring editor: *Michele Janicek*
Developmental editor II: *Jennifer V. Rizzi*
Marketing manager: *Julie Phifer*
Lead producer, Media technology: *Kai Chiang*
Lead project manager: *Mary Conzachi*
Production supervisor: *Gina Hangos*
Lead designer: *Matthew Baldwin*
Senior photo research coordinator: *Jeremy Cheshareck*
Photo researcher: *Teri Stratford*
Lead media project manager: *Becky Szura*
Senior supplement producer: *Carol Loreth*
Cover design: *Pam Verros*
Cover images: *©Corbis Images*
Typeface: *10/12 Times Roman*
Compositor: *Cenveo*
Printer: *R. R. Donnelley*

Library of Congress Cataloging-in-Publication Data

Kapoor, Jack R., 1937-
    Personal finance / Jack R. Kapoor, Les R. Dlabay, Robert J. Hughes.—8th ed.
        p. cm. — (The McGraw-Hill/Irwin series in finance, insurance, and real estate)
    Includes bibliographical references and index.
    ISBN-13: 978-0-07-310671-7 (alk. paper)
    ISBN-10: 0-07-310671-2 (alk. paper)
    1. Finance, Personal. I. Dlabay, Les R. II. Hughes, Robert James, 1946-III. Title. IV.
Series.
    HG179.K37 2007
    332.024—dc22

                                                            2005044580

www.mhhe.com

The McGraw-Hill/Irwin Series in Finance, Insurance, and Real Estate
Stephen A. Ross
Franco Modigliani Professor of Finance and Economics
Sloan School of Management
Massachusetts Institute of Technology
Consulting Editor

To my father, Ram Kapoor, and the memory of my mother, Sheila; my wife, Theresa; and my children, Karen, Kathryn, and Dave

To my mother, Mary Dlabay, and the memory of my father, Les; my wife, Linda; and my children, Carissa and Kyle

To my mother, Barbara Y. Hughes; and my wife, Peggy

About the Authors

Jack R. Kapoor, *College of DuPage*

Jack Kapoor is a professor of business and economics in the Business and Technology Division of the College of DuPage, Glen Ellyn, Illinois, where he has taught business and economics since 1969. He received his BA and MS from San Francisco State College and his EdD from Northern Illinois University. He previously taught at Illinois Institute of Technology's Stuart School of Management, San Francisco State University's School of World Business, and other colleges. Professor Kapoor was awarded the Business and Technology Division's Outstanding Professor Award for 1999–2000. He served as an assistant national bank examiner for the U.S. Treasury Department and has been an international trade consultant to Bolting Manufacturing Co., Ltd., Bombay, India.

Dr. Kapoor is known internationally as a coauthor of several textbooks, including *Business: A Practical Approach* (Rand McNally), *Business* (Houghton Mifflin), *Business and Personal Finance* (Glencoe), and *Focus on Personal Finance* (McGraw-Hill). He served as a content consultant for the popular national television series *The Business File: An Introduction to Business* and developed two full-length audio courses in business and personal finance. He has been quoted in many national newspapers and magazines, including *USA Today, U.S. News & World Report,* the *Chicago Sun-Times, Crain's Small Business,* the *Chicago Tribune,* and other publications.

Dr. Kapoor has traveled around the world and has studied business practices in capitalist, socialist, and communist countries.

Les R. Dlabay, *Lake Forest College*

Sharing resources with the less fortunate is an ongoing financial goal of Les Dlabay, professor of business at Lake Forest College, Lake Forest, Illinois. Through child sponsorship programs, world hunger organizations, and community service activities, he believes the extensive wealth in our society should be used to help others. In addition to writing several textbooks, Dr. Dlabay teaches various international business courses. His "hobbies" include collecting cereal packages from over 100 countries and paper currency from 200 countries, which are used to teach about economic, cultural, and political aspects of foreign business environments. Professor Dlabay also uses many field research activities with his students, conducting interviews, surveys, and observations of business activities.

Robert J. Hughes, *Dallas County Community Colleges*

Financial literacy! Only two words, but Bob Hughes, professor of business at Dallas County Community Colleges, believes that these two words can literally change people's lives. Whether you want to be rich or just manage the money you have, the ability to analyze financial decisions and gather financial information are skills that can always be improved. In addition to writing several textbooks, Dr. Hughes has taught personal finance, introduction to business, business math, small business management, small business finance, and accounting since 1972. He also served as a content consultant for two popular national television series, *It's Strictly Business* and *Dollars & Sense: Personal Finance for the 21st Century,* and is the lead author for a business math project utilizing computer-assisted instruction funded by the ALEKS Corporation. He received his BBA from Southern Nazarene University and his MBA and EdD from the University of North Texas. His hobbies include writing, investing, collecting French antiques, art, and travel.

Preface

"Double your money in five years"
"Eliminate your credit card debt"
"Obtain your dream job"
"Travel to a different country each year"
"Cut your automobile insurance rates by one-third"

This book *cannot* promise you any of these. However, we CAN promise you the opportunity, along with your efforts, to achieve these and many other personal financial goals.

While technology, the global economy, and other social trends are changing the financial planning environment, many fundamentals remain constant. Your ability to make informed choices related to spending, saving, borrowing, and investing continues to be the foundation of long-term financial security.

A Framework for Decision Making

Each day we are surrounded by new choices for shopping and other activities. Money choices can be intense; however, *Personal Finance,* Eighth Edition, offers many tools to cope with these situations. The steps of the financial planning decision-making process are introduced in Chapter 1. This step-by-step approach will help you identify and evaluate choices as well as understand the consequences of your decisions in terms of opportunity costs.

New Content and Features to This Edition

With a continued emphasis on technology, real-world decision making, and practical advice from financial planning professionals, this edition of *Personal Finance* provides you with a strong foundation for your current and future personal economic activities. In addition, many topics and instructional features have been added or enhanced to better serve both students and instructors.

Each day, personal financial planning activities are affected by changing influences in our society and the economy. As a result, we attempt to continually update our material so you are well prepared for facing all financial situations. Just to get an idea of the expanded coverage in this eighth edition of *Personal Finance,* the table that follows on pages viii–xiii highlights some of our additions. These improvements are in addition to revised and up-

dated foundation material provided for understanding personal finance.

Acknowledgments

We express our deepest appreciation for the efforts of the colleagues who provided extensive comments for this edition that contributed to the quality of the book you are using.

Tim Alzheimer, *Montana State University*

Jerry Belloit, *Clarion University of Pennsylvania*

Howard Bohnen, *St. Cloud State University*

Sugato Chakravarty, *Purdue University*

R. C. Grimm, *Grove City College*

Randy Guttery, *University of North Texas*

David Haeberle, *Indiana University*

Randy Ice, *University of Central Oklahoma*

John Ledgerwood, *Bethune Cookman College*

Chan Lee, *Minnesota State University*

Armand Picou, *University of Central Arkansas*

David Schalow, *California State University—San Bernadino*

Many talented professionals at McGraw-Hill Higher Education have contributed to the development of *Personal Finance,* Eighth Edition. We are especially grateful to Michele Janicek, Jennifer Rizzi, Mary Conzachi, Gina Hangos, Matt Baldwin, Becky Szura, and Carol Loreth.

We would also like to thank Anne Gleason, University of Central Oklahoma, for revising the Test Bank, and for revising all of the questions in the self-study tutor software on the student CD-ROM; Ken Mark, Kansas City Kansas Community College, for revising the PowerPoint Presentation, and Samira Hussein, Johnson County Community College, for creating the additional Instructor's Manual cases.

In addition, Jack Kapoor expresses special appreciation to Theresa and Dave Kapoor, Kathryn Thumme, and Karen Tucker for their typing, proofreading, and research assistance. Finally, we thank our wives and families for their patience, understanding, encouragement, and love throughout the years since we started this project.

A Note of Appreciation

Thousands of students at hundreds of colleges and universities throughout the world have used the previous editions of *Personal Finance*. We are honored that professors and students have chosen our text to learn about personal financial decision making. A text should always be evaluated by the people who use it. We welcome your comments, suggestions, and questions. Finally, we truly hope that, as a result of studying personal finance, you will have a fulfilling life that brings economic prosperity along with satisfying personal relationships.

Jack R. Kapoor
kapoorj@cdnet.cod.edu

Les R. Dlabay
dlabay@lfc.edu

Robert J. Hughes
bhughes@dcccd.edu

Coverage

Chapters	Selected Topics of Interest	Benefits to Users
PART ONE Planning Your Personal Finances		
Chapter 1 Personal Finance Basics and the Time Value of Money	*New case:* "Now What Should I Do?"	Provides an integrated awareness of the various elements of personal financial planning.
	New material: "Advice from a Pro" box feature on Goal-Setting Guidelines	Expands main text material to provide additional coverage of setting personal financial goals.
	New feature: Time Value of Money Financial Planning Calculation box	Presents an overview of six different methods for calculating time value of money.
Chapter 2 Financial Aspects of Career Planning	*New case:* "Which Job? Are You Sure?"	Provides students with an opportunity to evaluate employment situations in relation to financial factors.
	New feature: Entrepreneurial career options box	Offers foundation knowledge of additional career options related to starting and operating a business.
	Updated feature: Online career planning box	Summarizes actions and Web sites related to researching, applying for, and evaluating employment opportunities using the Internet.
	Expanded material: Résumé alternatives, including a targeted application letter and career portfolio	Creates awareness about actions that may be taken in the job application process for a person to distinguish one's self from other candidates.
Chapter 3 Money Management Strategy: Financial Statements and Budgeting	*New activity:* Addition of ratio analysis problem within "Financial Planning Calculations" box	Application problem that allows students to evaluate the current status of a personal financial situation.
	New material: Discussion of daily money managers who specialize in helping older person with day-to-day personal finances	These financial planning professionals provide assistance to people with special needs with their bill paying, banking, budgeting, taxes, and other personal financial activities.
	New section: Expanded material to show relationship between money management and financial goals	Connects personal financial statements and budgets to savings activities and long-term financial security.

Chapters	Selected Topics of Interest	Benefits to Users
Chapter 4 Planning Your Tax Strategy	*New Visual:* An exhibit provides a comparison of the three main 1040 forms	Develops an awareness of the relationship between a person's tax situation and the required federal tax form.
	New material: Electronic tax filing procedure	Creates a basic understanding of e-filing for federal income taxes.
	Expanded material: guidelines for evaluating tax services	Provides a list of factors to consider when considering the use of a tax preparation service.

PART TWO Managing Your Personal Finances

Chapters	Selected Topics of Interest	Benefits to Users
Chapter 5 Financial Services: Savings Plans and Payment Accounts	*New visual:* Type of a Financial Institutions	Presents the relationship between the various types of financial institutions and online banking activities.
	Updated material: U.S. savings bonds	Discusses recent changes in interest calculations, purchasing procedures, and bond choices that are available to savers.
	New feature: Highlighted content with recommended actions to avoid identity theft	Allows for a personal assessment of financial activities in an effort to avoid identity theft.
Chapter 6 Introduction to Consumer Credit	*New visual:* Top Consumer Complaint Categories	Provides a research for readers to use if they need to file a complaint.
	New Boxed Feature: Compulsive Shopping	Allows for personal assessment of the individual shopping patterns of the readers, and where to seek help if needed.
	Updated Material: Credit Card Fraud	Discusses recent changes in various schemes of credit card fraud (including telemarketing and phishing), and the steps the reader can take if it happens to them.
	Updated Material: Loans	Discusses recent changes in loans, and how your credit can effect your ability to receive one.
Chapter 7 Choosing a Source of Credit: the Costs of Credit Alternatives	*New Boxed Feature:* To Choose It, First Decide How You Plan to Use It	Suggests actions that may be taken to plan to the best of ones ability before taking the efforts to apply for a loan.
	Expanded Coverage: Cost of Credit	Updated and expanded information on all of the various costs of credit, and how to avoid some common pitfalls.
	New Boxed Feature: Money Management in Cyberspace	Suggests actions and provides research to help the reader get started on many areas of credit management.

PART THREE Making Your Purchasing Decisions

Chapters	Selected Topics of Interest	Benefits to Users
Chapter 8 Consumer Purchasing Strategies and Legal Protection	*New case:* "Online Car Buying"	Provides an analysis of a situation related to information gathering, comparing prices, and finalizing an online motor vehicle purchase.
	New content organization: Automobile buying coverage	Integration of motor vehicle buying into research-based approach for making purchases.
	New material: coverage of "phishing" and "pharming"	Offers a foundation of these high-tech scams that use spam, pop-up messages, viruses, worms, and e-mail attachments to deceive consumers.

Chapters	Selected Topics of Interest	Benefits to Users
Chapter 9 The Housing Decision: Factors and Finances	*New feature:* Advice from a Pro: Appealing Your Property Taxes	Suggests actions that may be taken to protest high property taxes.
	New material: Coverage of interest-only mortgages	Presents a basic awareness of these popular, recently developed mortgages with potential financial dangers.

PART FOUR Insuring Your Resources

Chapters	Selected Topics of Interest	Benefits to Users
Chapter 10 Property and Motor Vehicle Insurance	*Simplified coverage:* Condenses discussion of homeowner policies	Delivers a clearer overview of the main types of home insurance policies.
	New material: Filing an Auto Insurance Claim . . . or Not?	Provides guidelines to determine the financial benefits of whether to report minor auto accident claims in your insurance company.
Chapter 11 Health, Disability, and Long-Term Care Insurance	*New case:* The Digital Hospital	Provides an analysis of the way technology is improving the lives of today's patients, doctors and hospital systems–and how these issues might impact the reader or the reader's loved ones.
	New content: Organization	For better flow of topics of interest to the reader.
	New boxed feature: Health Insurance Hell	Presents some common health insurer scams that readers should be on the look out for.
Chapter 12 Life Insurance	*Updated coverage:* Life Insurance Policies	Presents all of the policies that someone will need to review before deciding on purchasing one.
	Updated coverage: Determining Life Insurance Needs	Delivers some steps the reader should work through and consider before choosing a policy.

PART FIVE Investing Your Financial Resources

Chapters	Selected Topics of Interest	Benefits to Users
Chapter 13 Investing Fundamentals	*New case:* "An Investment Plan That May Have You Shouting 'Yahoo!'"	Describes how a young couple uses the Internet to obtain the information needed to establish an investment program.
	New material: The Risk–Return Trade-off.	Explains different types of risks associated with conservative and more speculative investments.
	New material: Evaluating your tolerance for risk	Discusses personal factors that affect an investor's tolerance for risk.
	New material: Calculating rate of return	Illustrates how to calculate rate of return on investments and then describes why the information is useful.
	Expanded coverage: Asset allocation and diversification	Describes the importance of diversification and provides a suggested asset allocation for a young investor (Exhibit 13–3).
Chapter 14 Investing in Stocks	*New case:* "Investing the 'Big Apple' Way"	Describes how one investor begun an investment program after touring the financial district in New York City and visiting the NYSE Web site.
	Expanded coverage: Date of record for dividend payments	Provides a new example (Eli Lilly) and a discussion about the importance of dates connected with dividend payments.

Chapters	Selected Topics of Interest	Benefits to Users
PART FIVE Investing Your Financial Resources continued		
	New example: Dividends and dollar appreciation of stock value	Shows how dividends and an increase in value can provide a financial return for an investment in Boeing stock.
	Expanded coverage: Stock splits	Discusses why corporations split their stock. This material also stresses that there are no guarantees that a stock will go up after a split because a corporation's capitalization and earnings remain the same—see Exhibit 14–3.
	New examples: Evaluating a Stock Issue	New and current examples of information that can be used to evaluate a stock issue are provided in this major section.
	New material: Price/earnings to growth ratio and dividend payout ratio	Discusses these two new, additional calculations and how they can help investors evaluate a stock investment.
	Expanded coverage: Efficient market hypothesis and fundamental theory	Provides additional information on these investment theories.
	Expanded coverage: Long-term and short-term investment techniques	Adds new material on dividend reinvestments, direct investments, and the risk of day trading.
Chapter 15 Investing in Bonds	*New case*: "Bonds: To Buy or Not to Buy—That's The Real Question!"	Describes how one couple decided (with the help of a financial planner) to invest in bonds in order to use the concept of asset allocation.
	New examples: Throughout Chapter 15	Provides new examples throughout the chapter to illustrate current interest rates, conditions in the economy, and current tax rates that affect tax-free investments.
	New Exhibit: Financial Suggestions for Bond Investors	Provides specific reasons why investors should choose bonds (Exhibit 15–1).
	New material: Bond laddering	Discusses the concept of building a bond ladder to balance risk and return.
	Expanded coverage: Web sites for bond investors	Provides additional Web sites that provide information about corporate and government bonds.

Chapters	Selected Topics of Interest	Benefits to Users
PART FIVE Investing Your Financial Resources continued		
Chapter 16 Investing in Mutual Funds	*New case*: "The Tale of Two Mutual Fund Investors"	Describes the differences between two different mutual fund investors—one that does no research and another who uses research to help make investment decisions.
	New material: Mutual fund scandals	The "Advice from a Pro" feature describes the effect of the recent mutual fund scandal on individual investors.
	The *Expanded coverage*: Exchange-traded funds (ETFs)	Provides additional coverage on why investors may want to consider ETFs as an investment alternative.
	New material: Types of funds	Defines three new types of funds—large-cap funds, socially responsible funds, and index bond funds.
	Expanded coverage: Managed funds versus index funds	Provides additional information and performance data describing the differences between managed funds and indexed funds.
	New material: Financial Planning Case	Allows students to use the information provided in Exhibit 16-5 to research a possible investment in the T. Rowe Price Equity-Income fund.
Chapter 17 Investing in Real Estate and Other Investment Alternatives	New examples throughout the chapter	Provides new example of the housing boom of 2005, and the jump in new home sales. How can you benefit from this boom? How boomers are driving second-home prices sky high in California, Nevada, and Arizona.
	New box: Real Estate: Avoid the Burn	A few troubling signs of the real estate market top are emerging. The bull market in residential real estate shows signs of age in 2005.
	New box on REITs	REITs outlook has turned bearish, but keen-eyed investors may still find some good buys that perform well.
	New box: Just How Precious Will Gold Get?	Gold prices are up 75 percent since early 2001. The rise of Asia is boosting gold prices. Will gold's joy ride last indefinitely? Is it time to buy?
	New box: Cashing In on Abe	Collecting old letters and documents is not only fun but can also be good investment. Is it smart to invest in collectibles?
	New box: Prices for Early Computers Are on the Rise	Prices of the first 1970s-era computers have soared in recent years. Are computer collectibles for everyone? Is it a good investment for you?

Personal Finance continues to provide instructors and students with features and materials to create a learning environment that can be adapted to any educational setting.

Personal Financial Planner sheets

New to this edition, the PFP sheets that correlate with sections of the text are now conveniently located at the end of the text! Each perforated worksheet asks students to work through the application and record their own personal financial plan answers. These sheets apply concepts learned to students' personal situation and serve as a road map to their personal financial future. Students can fill them out, rip them out, submit them for homework, and keep them filed in a safe spot for future reference!

Also new to this edition's sheets, key Web sites are provided to help students research and devise their personal financial plan, and the "What's Next for Your Personal Financial Plan?" section at the end of each sheet challenges students to use their responses to plan the next level, as well as foreshadow upcoming concepts.

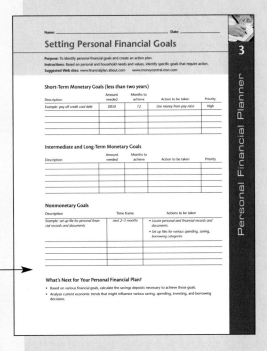

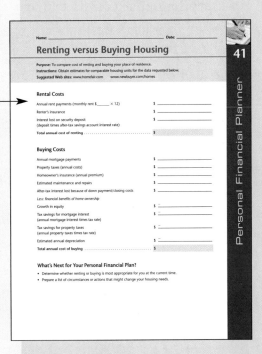

Key Concept

A short summary of why this chapter is important. Also, what students can expect to learn from it and apply to their own personal financial plan.

Digital Study Tools

A "cheat-sheet" to the many online and Student CD assets available free with this edition. Students can refer back to this list when preparing for quizzes and exams and use the items on this list for assistance in creating their own financial plan! This section is also a helpful road map for online courses and telecourses.

---

2 Financial Aspects of Career Planning

Key Concept

Employment opportunities are influenced by economic, social, and technological factors. Effective career planning requires careful analysis of yourself, the job market, and potential employers. Connecting your abilities and skills to the needs of prospective employers is the foundation of a successful job search.

Digital Study Tools

Online Learning Center Study Tools for This Chapter
- Multiple-choice quiz
- Flashcards
- eLearning sessions
- Crossword puzzle
- Personal Finance Online: Careers and Résumés

Student CD Study Tools for This Chapter
- Self-study software
- Narrated PowerPoint
- Personal financial planning software: Worksheets 6–13

www.mhhe.com/kdh

Learning Objectives

1 Describe the activities associated with career planning and advancement.
2 Evaluate the factors that influence employment opportunities.
3 Implement employment search strategies.
4 Assess the financial and legal concerns related to obtaining employment.
5 Analyze the techniques for career growth and advancement.

Learning Objectives

A summary of learning objectives is presented at the start of each chapter. These objectives are highlighted at the start of each major section in the chapter and appear again in the end-of-chapter summary. The learning objectives are also used to organize the end-of-chapter questions, problems, and exercises, as well as materials in the *Instructor's Manual, Test Bank,* and *Student Resource Manual.*

Opening Case

Each chapter starts with a new or revised opening case and related discussion questions to introduce the chapter content with a real-world situation. These compelling and realistic cases help show the relevance of the chapter's material and involve students in the content.

Questions

After each *Opening Case,* a set of questions headed "What Actions Should Be Taken?" probes students' thinking about the next step the characters in the case should take to solve their dilemma. "What about Your Situation?" questions ask students to apply the case situation to their own life.

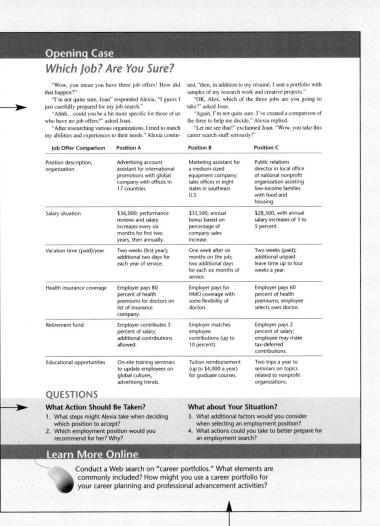

Opening Case

Which Job? Are You Sure?

"Wow, you mean you have three job offers! How did that happen?"

"I'm not quite sure, Joan" responded Alexia, "I guess I just carefully prepared for my job search."

"Ahhh…could you be a bit more specific for those of us who have no job offers?" asked Joan.

"After researching various organizations, I tried to match my abilities and experiences to their needs." Alexia continued, "then, in addition to my résumé, I sent a portfolio with samples of my research work and creative projects."

"OK, Alex, which of the three jobs are you going to take?" asked Joan.

"Again, I'm not quite sure. I've created a comparison of the three to help me decide," Alexia replied.

"Let me see that!" exclaimed Joan. "Wow, you take this career search stuff seriously!"

Job Offer Comparison	Position A	Position B	Position C
Position description, organization	Advertising account assistant for international promotions with global company with offices in 17 countries.	Marketing assistant for a medium-sized equipment company; sales offices in eight states in southeast U.S.	Public relations director in local office of national nonprofit organization assisting low-income families with food and housing.
Salary situation	$36,000; performance reviews and salary increases every six months for first two years, then annually.	$33,500; annual bonus based on percentage of company sales increase.	$28,500, with annual salary increases of 3 to 5 percent.
Vacation time (paid)/year	Two weeks (first year); additional two days for each year of service.	One week after six months on the job; two additional days for each six months of service.	Two weeks (paid); additional unpaid leave time up to four weeks a year.
Health insurance coverage	Employer pays 80 percent of health premiums for doctors on list of insurance company.	Employer pays for HMO coverage with some flexibility of doctors.	Employer pays 60 percent of health premiums; employee selects own doctor.
Retirement fund	Employer contributes 5 percent of salary; additional contributions allowed.	Employer matches employee contributions (up to 10 percent).	Employer pays 2 percent of salary; employee may make tax-deferred contributions.
Educational opportunities	On-site training seminars to update employees on global cultures, advertising trends.	Tuition reimbursement (up to $4,000 a year) for graduate courses.	Two trips a year to seminars on topics related to nonprofit organizations.

QUESTIONS

What Action Should Be Taken?

1. What steps might Alexia take when deciding which position to accept?
2. Which employment position would you recommend for her? Why?

What about Your Situation?

3. What additional factors would you consider when selecting an employment position?
4. What actions could you take to better prepare for an employment search?

Learn More Online

Conduct a Web search on "career portfolios." What elements are commonly included? How might you use a career portfolio for your career planning and professional advancement activities?

Learn More Online

This section provides a starting point to research issues touched on in the opening case and asks students to document their findings.

Boxed features are used in each chapter to build student interest and highlight important topics. Three different types of boxed features are used.

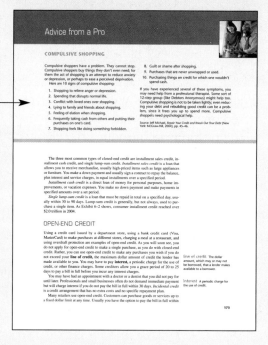

Advice from a Pro

Each box presents a personal finance issue and tips from the field that students can relate to their own personal financial situation.

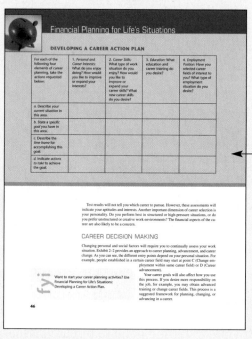

Financial Planning for Life's Situations

This box offers information that can assist students when faced with special situations and unique financial planning decisions. Many emphasize the use of Internet sources.

Financial Planning Calculations

This feature presents more than 90 mathematical applications relevant to personal financial situations.

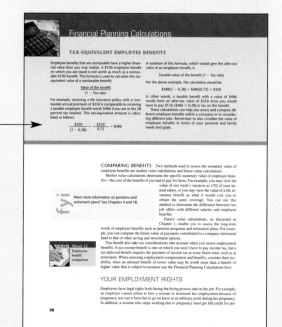

Margin notes provide connections to supplementary information. While the Did You Know? feature provides interesting statistics and tips in personal financial planning. The Concept Check feature provides an ongoing assessment tool.

Key Terms

Key terms appear in bold type with margin definitions and are also listed at the end of each chapter with page references.

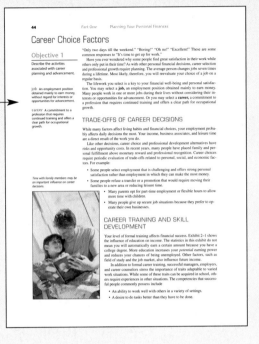

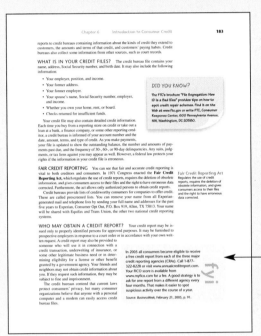

FYI

FYI boxes include helpful hints and activities, referring students to where they can find additional information on the Web regarding a topic being discussed in the narrative of the chapter.

Did You Know?

Each chapter contains several *Did You Know?* features with facts, information, and financial planning assistance.

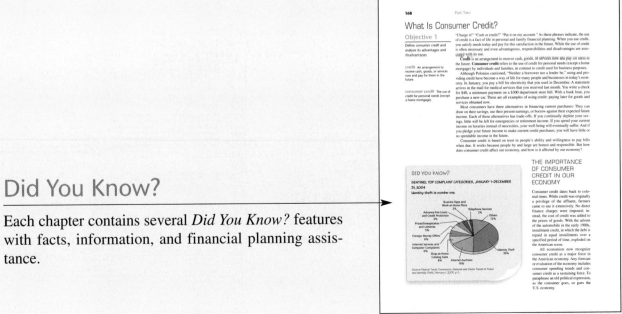

Concept Check

The *Concept Check* at the end of each major section provides questions to help students assess their knowledge of the main ideas covered in that section. The new Action Application section contains short exercises that ask the student to apply the concepts learned.

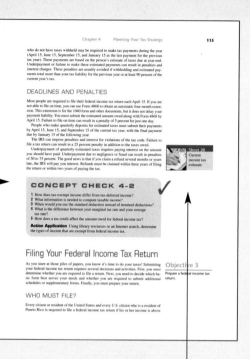

Personal Financial Planner

The integrated use of the *Personal Financial Planner,* located at the end of the book, is highlighted with a PFP graphic in the margin. This visual, near the text material needed to complete each Personal Financial Planner worksheet, helps students better integrate this instructional supplement into the teaching–learning process.

Financial Planning Problems

With more added to this edition, these problems allow students to apply their quantitative analysis of personal financial decisions.

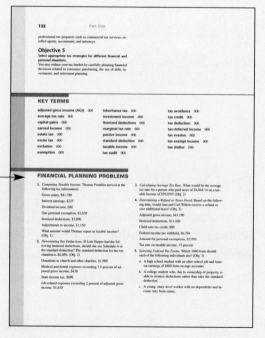

A variety of end-of-chapter features are offered to support the concepts presented throughout each chapter.

Financial Planning Activities

The *Financial Planning Activities* provide ways to research and apply financial planning topics.

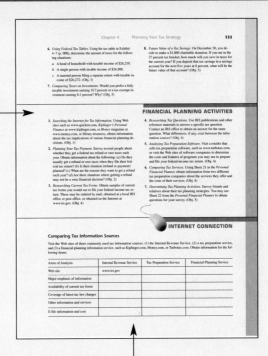

Internet Connection

This end-of-chapter Web exercise asks students to apply newly learned concepts to real-life situations by surfing the Web for data. Directions are given to help guide the way, and spaces are provided for students to record their findings for reference or for a class project.

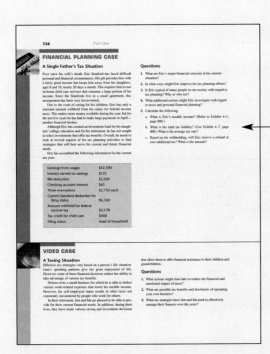

Financial Planning Case

Students are given a hypothetical personal finance dilemma and data to work through to practice concepts they have learned from the chapter. A series of questions reinforces that they have successfully mastered the chapter topics.

Each chapter concludes with a Video Case presenting a real-world situation. The Continuing Case allows analysis for an ongoing household situation.

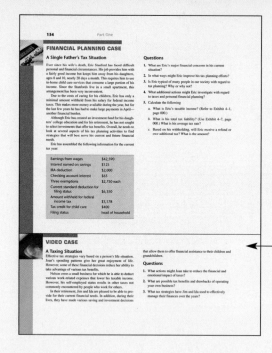

Video Case

In connection with the *Dollars & Sense* videos, a *Video Case,* at the end of every chapter, builds upon a particular topic and provides questions to support how it relates to the chapter concepts.

Your Personal Financial Planner in Action

This feature provides long- and short-term financial planning activities, per the concepts learned within the chapter, and links each to relevant *Personal Financial Planner* sheets (located at the end of the book) and Web sites for further personal financial planning.

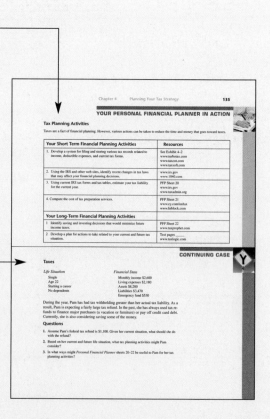

Continuing Case

Appearing at the end of each chapter, this feature allows students to apply course concepts in a life situation. This feature encourages students to evaluate the changes that affect a family and then respond to the resulting shift in needs, resources, and priorities through the questions at the end of each case.

SUPPLEMENTS

Few textbooks provide the innovative and practical instructional resources for both students and teachers. The comprehensive teaching–learning package for *Personal Finance* includes the following:

For Students

Student CD-ROM (ISBN 0073199524)—Available with each new text, this rich resource includes:

- *Personal Financial Planning Software* consisting of a Windows-based, computerized version of the *Personal Financial Planner* and other financial tools for handling personal finance calculations allows you to work through the sheets with the computer and print and/or save your personal financial plan for future reference.
- *Self-Study Tutor* with 50 to 75 multiple-choice and true–false questions per chapter, created by Anne Gleason, University of Central Oklahoma, students can prep for exams and test their knowledge of one chapter or a number of chapters by using questions specifically written for this edition. All questions are different from the end-of-chapter text problems.
- *New! Narrated Student PowerPoint* Created by Anne Gleason, University of Central Oklahoma, exclusively for students. Each chapter's slides follow the chapter topics and provide steps and explanations for how to solve those topics using real-life examples. Because each student learns differently, a quick click on each slide causes the slide to "talk through" its contents with the student!
- *Personal Financial Planner,* the electronic sheets in the *Personal Financial Planner* workbook that is packaged free with each new textbook.
- *Links* to the book Web site, Personal Finance Online, and others—a click away from additional study resources.

Personal Financial Planner comes free with each new copy of the text. Located at the end of the text, this valuable learning tool consists of 78 worksheets for creating and implementing a personal financial plan. Icons appear in each chapter indicating which worksheet relates to a particular topic.

For Instructors

The **Instructor's CD-ROM** provides the instructor with one resource for all supplementary material, including the *Instructor's Manual, Test Bank* computerized testing software, PowerPoint, and related Web links: (ISBN 0073199508)

- The *Instructor's Manual* includes a "Course Planning Guide" with instructional strategies, course projects, and supplementary resource lists. The "Chapter Teaching Materials" section of the *Instructor's Manual* provides a chapter overview, the chapter objectives with summaries, introductory activities, and detailed lecture outlines with teaching suggestions. This section also includes concluding activities, ready-to-duplicate quizzes, supplementary lecture materials and activities, and answers to concept checks, end-of-chapter questions, problems, and cases. A print version of the *Instructor's Manual* (0073199540) is also available.

- The *Test Bank,* revised by Anne Gleason, University of Central Oklahoma, consists of almost 2,000 true–false, multiple-choice, and essay questions. These test items are organized by the learning objectives for each chapter. This resource also includes answers, section references, and an indication of difficulty level.

- *Computerized Testing Software*—McGraw-Hill's EZ Test is a flexible and easy-to-use electronic testing program. The program allows instructors to create tests from book-specific items. It accommodates a wide range of question types, and instructors may add their own questions. Multiple versions of the test can be created, and any test can be exported for use with course management systems such as WebCT, BlackBoard, or PageOut. EZ Test Online is a new service and gives you a place to easily administer your EZ Test–created exams and quizzes online. The program is available for Windows and Macintosh environments.

- The *PowerPoint Presentation System,* created by Ken Mark, Kansas City Kansas Community College, found on the Instructor's CD-ROM and the Online Learning Center, offers more than 300 visual presentations that may be edited and manipulated to fit a particular course format.

Videos There are a total of 19 video segments that are each 5–10 minutes long that correspond to the end-of-chapter *Video Case* feature in the text (one for each chapter.) Also included are ten 30-minute videos that help to visually illustrate important personal finance concepts in potential real-life situations. Developed by Coastline Community College, these videos can be used with multiple chapters at any time during the course. For a list of videos and their descriptions, please see the *Instructor's Manual.* (Video: 0073199516, DVD: 0073227757)

TECHNOLOGY TO ENHANCE FINANCIAL DECISION MAKING

Online Learning Center (OLC): Online Support at www.mhhe.com/kdh

The Online Learning Center (OLC) contains FREE access to additional Web-based study and teaching aids created for this text, such as:

Student Support

Self-Study Quizzes
With the new self-study program, students can test their knowledge of one chapter or a number of chapters by using self-grading questions written specifically for this text. There are at least 10 questions per chapter.

Be sure to check out the other helpful features found on the OLC as you read the text including key-term flashcards and links to *Personal Finance Online* study problems.

Teaching Support

Along with having access to all of the same material your students can view on the book's OLC, you also have password-protected access to the *Instructor's Manual, Solutions* to end-of-chapter problems, *Instructor's PowerPoint,* and teaching notes to *Personal Finance Online.*

Personal Finance Online—Located within the OLC, *Personal Finance Online* is an exclusive Web tool from McGraw-Hill/Irwin. This value-added site enables faculty and students to engage in personal finance exercises and activities using the Internet. This site provides over 50 exercises for 11 different key personal finance topics and allows students to complete exercises and discussion questions that draw on recent articles, company reports, government data, and other Web-based resources. There are also password-protected teaching notes to assist you with classroom integration of the material.

OLCs can be delivered in multiple ways—through the textbook Web site (www.mhhe.com/kdh), through PageOut (see below), or within a course management system like Blackboard, WebCT, TopClass, and eCollege. Ask your campus representative for more details.

Personal Finance Telecourse

Personal Finance Telecourse If you teach personal finance as a telecourse, this text is a perfect fit! A telecourse program is available from Coastline Community College titled *Dollars & Sense: Personal Finance for the 21st Century* that is based on the Kapoor, Dlabay, and Hughes text. The program includes 26 thirty-minute videotapes, which you purchase directly from Coast by contacting Lynn Dahnke, Marketing Director, Coast Learning Systems, 11460 Warner Ave., Fountain Valley, CA 92708, (800) 547-4748 or www.CoastLearning.org. The course also has a *Telecourse Study Guide* (ISBN 0073198641) available that connects the videos to the text. To make sure your students receive the text and telecourse study guide package, order through McGraw-Hill/Irwin.

PACKAGE OPTIONS

You may also package your text with a variety of other learning tools that are available for your students:

McGraw-Hill's Homework Manager and Homework Manager Plus

Are you looking for a way to spend less time grading and to have more flexibility with the problems you assign as homework and tests? McGraw-Hill's *Homework Manager* is an exciting new package option developed for this text! *Homework Manager* is a Web-based tool for instructors and students for delivering, answering, and grading end-of-chapter problems and tests, and providing a limitless supply of self-graded practice for students.

All of the book's applicable end-of-chapter questions and problems are loaded into *Homework Manager,* and instructors can choose to assign the exact problems as stated in the book, or algorithmic versions of them so each student has a unique set of variables for the problems. You create the assignments and control parameters such as whether you want your students to receive hints, whether this is a graded assignment or practice, etc. The test bank is also available in *Homework Manager,* giving you the ability to use those questions for online tests. Both the problems and the tests are automatically graded, and the results are stored in a private grade book, which is created when you set up your class. Detailed results let you see at a glance how each student does on an assignment or an individual problem—you can even see how many tries it took the student to solve it. If you order this special package, students will receive a *Homework Manager User's Guide* and an access code packaged with their text.

An enhanced version of McGraw-Hill's *Homework Manager* is also available through the *Homework Manager Plus* package option. If you order the text packaged with *HM Plus,* your students will receive *Homework Manager* as described above, but with an integrated online text included. When students are in *Homework Manager* and need more help to solve a problem, there will be a link that takes them to the section of the text online that explains the concept they are struggling with. All of McGraw-Hill's media assets, such as videos, narrated lectures, and additional online quizzing, are also integrated at the appropriate places of the online text to provide students with a full learning experience. If you order this special package, students will receive the *HM Plus* card packaged with their text, which gives them access to all of these products, as well as an online *Homework Manager User's Guide.*

McGraw-Hill's *Homework Manager* is powered by Brownstone.

Student Resource Manual

The *Student Resource Manual with Readings and Cases* allows students to review and apply text concepts. Each chapter contains a chapter overview, a pretest, self-guided study questions, a posttest, problems, applications, cases, and recent articles from *BusinessWeek*. Together, these exercises reinforce important text concepts and offer students additional opportunities to use their critical thinking and writing skills. (ISBN 0073199494)

BusinessWeek

Your students can subscribe to 15 weeks of *BusinessWeek* for a specially priced rate of $8.25 in addition to the price of the text. Students will receive a passcode card shrink-wrapped with their new text. The card directs students to a Web site where they enter the code and then gain access to *BusinessWeek*'s registration page to enter address info and set up their print and online subscription.

The Wall Street Journal

Your students can subscribe to *The Wall Street Journal* for 15 weeks at a specially priced rate of $20.00 in addition to the price of the text. Students will receive a "How to Use the *WSJ*" handbook plus a passcode card shrink-wrapped with the text. The card directs students to a Web site where they enter the code and then gain access to the *WSJ* registration page to enter address info and set up their print and online subscription, and also set up their subscription to Dow Jones Interactive online for the 15-week period.

Brief Contents

Contents

2

Managing Your Personal Finances

3

Making Your Purchasing Decisions

4

Insuring Your Resources

5
Investing Your Financial Resources

6
Controlling Your Financial Future

Personal Finance

EIGHTH EDITION

1

Personal Finance Basics and the Time Value of Money

Key Concept

Each year, over a million people declare bankruptcy. And, Americans lose more than $1.2 billion in fraudulent investments. Both of these common difficulties occur due to poor personal financial planning. To effectively manage your personal finances: save regularly . . . earn honestly . . . spend wisely . . . give generously.

Digital Study Tools

Online Learning Center Study Tools for This Chapter

- Multiple-choice quiz
- Flashcards
- eLearning sessions
- Crossword puzzle
- Personal Finance Online: Time Value of Money

Student CD Study Tools for This Chapter

- Self-study software
- Narrated PowerPoint
- Personal financial planning software: Worksheets 1–5

www.mhhe.com/kdh

Learning Objectives

1 Analyze the process for making personal financial decisions.

2 Develop personal financial goals.

3 Assess personal and economic factors that influence personal financial planning.

4 Determine personal and financial opportunity costs associated with personal financial decisions.

5 Identify strategies for achieving personal financial goals for different life situations.

Now What Should I Do...?

When Nina opened the letter from her aunt, she discovered a wonderful surprise. "My aunt has given me a gift of $10,000!"

"Why would she do that?" asked Kevin.

"I guess her investments have increased in value by much more than she needs. And she wants to share it with family members," Nina responded. "I wonder what I should do with the money?"

"Oh, I have some suggestions for you . . ." Kevin said.

"Wait a minute. When did this become *our* money?" Nina asked.

"Well, I just thought I'd offer some ideas," Kevin suggested.

After some discussion, Nina considered the following uses for the money:

Credit card debt—use a portion of the money to pay off credit card bills from her last vacation.

Savings—set aside money for a down payment on a house.

Insurance—increase coverage on her health, life, and disability insurance.

Long-term investments—invest the money in a tax-deferred retirement account.

Career training—use the money for technology certification courses to enhance her earning power.

Community donations—contribute funds to a homeless shelter and a hunger-relief organization.

"Wow, I could easily use $100,000 instead of $10,000! So what should I do?" asked Nina.

"Some financial advisers recommend not doing anything for a least six months, since you could easily spend it on things with little lasting value," warned Kevin.

"Now I'm not sure what I should do!"

QUESTIONS

What Actions Should Be Taken?

1. What additional information do you need to know about Nina before determining which areas of financial planning should be her top priority?
2. What actions do you recommend that Nina take before making a final decision about the use of these funds?

What about Your Situation?

3. What do you consider to be your main money concerns for the next six months? How about the next two years?
4. What actions might you take to make better personal financial decisions?

Learn More Online

Based on information at www.money.com, www.daveramsey.com, and Kiplinger.com, describe some advice that Nina might consider for her current and future financial planning activities.

The Financial Planning Process

Objective 1

Analyze the process for making personal financial decisions.

personal financial planning The process of managing your money to achieve personal economic satisfaction.

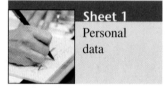

Sheet 1
Personal data

Everywhere people are talking about money. When it comes to handling your finances, are you an *explorer,* someone who is always searching through uncharted areas? Are you a *passenger,* just along for the ride on the money decision-making trip of life? Or are you a researcher, seeking answers to the inevitable money questions of life?

Most people want to handle their finances so that they get full satisfaction from each available dollar. Typical financial goals include such things as a new car, a larger home, advanced career training, contributions to charity, extended travel, and self-sufficiency during working and retirement years. To achieve these and other goals, people need to identify and set priorities. Financial and personal satisfaction are the result of an organized process that is commonly referred to as *personal money management* or *personal financial planning.*

Personal financial planning is the process of managing your money to achieve personal economic satisfaction. This planning process allows you to control your financial situation. Every person, family, or household has a unique financial position, and any financial activity therefore must also be carefully planned to meet specific needs and goals.

A comprehensive financial plan can enhance the quality of your life and increase your satisfaction by reducing uncertainty about your future needs and resources. The specific advantages of personal financial planning include

- Increased effectiveness in obtaining, using, and protecting your financial resources throughout your lifetime.

- Increased control of your financial affairs by avoiding excessive debt, bankruptcy, and dependence on others for economic security.

- Improved personal relationships resulting from well-planned and effectively communicated financial decisions.

- A sense of freedom from financial worries obtained by looking to the future, anticipating expenses, and achieving your personal economic goals.

We all make hundreds of decisions each day. Most of these decisions are quite simple and have few consequences. Some are complex and have long-term effects on our personal and financial situations. While everyone makes decisions, few people consider how to make better decisions. As Exhibit 1–1 shows, the financial planning process is a logical, six-step procedure: (1) determining your current financial situation, (2) developing financial goals, (3) identifying alternative courses of action, (4) evaluating alternatives, (5) creating and implementing a financial action plan, and (6) reviewing and revising the plan.

STEP 1: DETERMINE YOUR CURRENT FINANCIAL SITUATION

In this first step, you will determine your current financial situation regarding income, savings, living expenses, and debts. Preparing a list of current asset and debt balances and amounts spent for various items gives you a foundation for financial planning activities. The personal financial statements discussed in Chapter 3 will provide the information needed to match your goals with your current income and potential earning power.

> **Step 1 Example** Within the next two months, Kent Mullins will complete his undergraduate studies with a major in international studies. He has worked part-time in various sales jobs. He has a small savings fund ($1,700) and over $8,500 in student loans. What additional information should Kent have available when planning his personal finances?

Exhibit **1-1**

The financial planning process

STEP 2: DEVELOP YOUR FINANCIAL GOALS

You should periodically analyze your financial values and goals. This activity involves identifying how you feel about money and why you feel that way. Are your feelings about money based on factual knowledge or on the influence of others? Are your financial priorities based on social pressures, household needs, or desires for luxury items? How will economic conditions affect your goals and priorities? The purpose of this analysis is to differentiate your needs from your wants.

Specific financial goals are vital to financial planning. Others can suggest financial goals for you; however, *you* must decide which goals to pursue. Your financial goals can range from spending all of your current income to developing an extensive savings and investment program for your future financial security.

> **Step 2 Example**   Kent Mullins has several goals, including paying off his student loans, obtaining an advanced degree in global business management, and working in Latin America for a multinational company. What other goals might be appropriate for Kent?

STEP 3: IDENTIFY ALTERNATIVE COURSES OF ACTION

Developing alternatives is crucial when making decisions. Although many factors will influence the available alternatives, possible courses of action usually fall into these categories:

Financial choices require periodic evaluation.

- *Continue the same course of action.* For example, you may determine that the amount you have saved each month is still appropriate.
- *Expand the current situation.* You may choose to save a larger amount each month.
- *Change the current situation.* You may decide to use a money market account instead of a regular savings account.
- *Take a new course of action.* You may decide to use your monthly savings budget to pay off credit card debts.

Not all of these categories will apply to every decision; however, they do represent possible courses of action. For example, if you want to stop working full time to go to school, you must generate several alternatives under the category "Take a new course of action."

Creativity in decision making is vital to effective choices. Considering all of the possible alternatives will help you make more effective and satisfying decisions. For instance, most people believe they must own a car to get to work or school. However, they should consider other alternatives such as public transportation, carpooling, renting a car, shared ownership of a car, or a company car.

Remember, when you decide not to take action, you elect to "do nothing," which can be a dangerous alternative.

> **Step 3 Example**   Kent Mullins has several options available for the near future. He could work full time and save for graduate school; he could go to graduate school full time by taking out an additional loan; or he could go to school part time and work part time. What additional alternatives might he consider?

STEP 4: EVALUATE YOUR ALTERNATIVES

You need to evaluate possible courses of action, taking into consideration your life situation, personal values, and current economic conditions. How will the ages of dependents affect your saving goals? How do you like to spend leisure time? How will changes in interest rates affect your financial situation?

opportunity cost What a person gives up by making a choice.

CONSEQUENCES OF CHOICES   Every decision closes off alternatives. For example, a decision to invest in stock may mean you cannot take a vacation. A decision to go to school full time may mean you cannot work full time. **Opportunity cost** is what you give up by making a choice. This cost, commonly referred to as the trade-off of a decision, cannot always be measured in dollars. It may refer to the money you forgo by attending school rather than working, but it may also refer to the time you spend shopping around to compare brands for a major purchase. In either case, the resources you give up (money or time) have a value that is lost.

Decision making will be an ongoing part of your personal and financial situation. Thus, you will need to consider the lost opportunities that will result from your decisions. Since decisions vary based on each person's situation and values, opportunity costs will differ for each person.

EVALUATING RISK   Uncertainty is a part of every decision. Selecting a college major and choosing a career field involve risk. What if you don't like working in this field or cannot obtain employment in it? Other decisions involve a very low degree of risk, such as putting money in an insured savings account or purchasing items that cost only a few dollars. Your chances of losing something of great value are low in these situations.

In many financial decisions, identifying and evaluating risk is difficult (see Exhibit 1–2). The best way to consider risk is to gather information based on your experience and the experiences of others and to use financial planning information sources.

FINANCIAL PLANNING INFORMATION SOURCES
When you travel, you often need a road map. Traveling the path of financial planning requires a different kind of map. Relevant information is required at each stage of the decision-making process. This book provides the foundation you need to make appropriate personal financial planning decisions. Changing personal, social, and economic conditions will require that you continually supplement and update your knowledge. Exhibit 1–3 offers an overview of the informational resources available when making personal financial decisions.

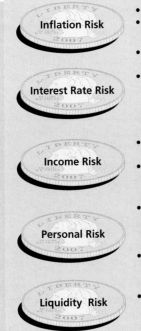

Various risks should be considered when making financial decisions.

Many personal financial planning information sources are available to assist you. See Appendix 1 on page 31.

Step 4 Example   As Kent Mullins evaluates his alternative courses of action, he must consider his income needs for both the short term and the long term. He should also assess career opportunities with his current skills and his potential with advanced training. What risks and trade-offs should Kent consider?

Inflation Risk
- Rising prices cause lost buying power.
- Decide whether to buy something now or later. If you buy later, you may have to pay more.

Interest Rate Risk
- Changing interest rates affect your costs (when you borrow) and your benefits (when you save or invest).
- Borrowing at a low interest rate when interest rates are rising can be to your advantage. But if you save when interest rates are dropping, you will earn a lower return with a six-month savings certificate than with a certificate having a longer maturity.

Income Risk
- The loss of a job could be the result of such things as changes in consumer spending.
- Individuals who face the risk of unemployment need to save while employed or acquire skills they can use to obtain a different type of work.

Personal Risk
- Many factors can create a less than desirable situation. Purchasing a certain brand or from a certain store may create the risk of having to obtain repairs at an inconvenient location.
- Personal risk may also take the form of the health risks, safety risks, or additional costs associated with various purchases or financial decisions.

Liquidity Risk
- Some savings and investments have potential for higher earnings. However, they may be more difficult to convert to cash or to sell without significant loss in value.

Exhibit **1-2**

Types of risk

Exhibit **1–3**

Financial planning
information sources

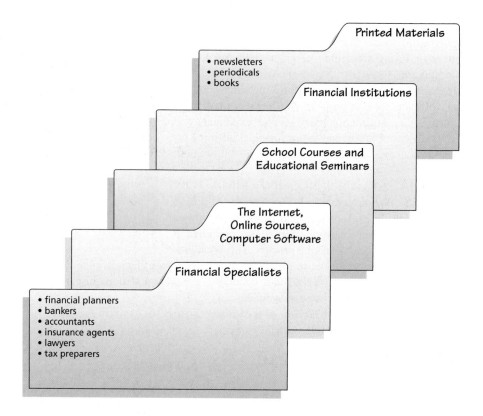

STEP 5: CREATE AND IMPLEMENT YOUR FINANCIAL ACTION PLAN

Sheet 2
Financial
institutions
and advisers

This step of the financial planning process involves developing an action plan that identifies ways to achieve your goals. For example, you can increase your savings by reducing your spending or by increasing your income through extra time on the job. If you are concerned about year-end tax payments, you may increase the amount withheld from each paycheck, file quarterly tax payments, or shelter current income in a tax-deferred retirement program. As you achieve your short-term or immediate goals, the goals next in priority will come into focus.

To implement your financial action plan, you may need assistance from others. For example, you may use the services of an insurance agent to purchase property insurance or the services of an investment broker to purchase stocks, bonds, or mutual funds.

DID YOU KNOW?

The main sources from which people get their money advice are financial professionals, friends and family, printed materials from work, newspapers and magazines, the Internet, and television and radio.

Step 5 Example   Kent Mullins has decided to work full time for a few years while he (1) pays off his student loans, (2) saves money for graduate school, and (3) takes a couple of courses in the evening and on weekends. What are the benefits and drawbacks of this choice?

STEP 6: REVIEW AND REVISE YOUR PLAN

Financial planning is a dynamic process that does not end when you take a particular action. You need to regularly assess your financial decisions. You should do a complete review of your finances at least once a year. Changing personal, social, and economic factors may require more frequent assessments.

When life events affect your financial needs, this financial planning process will provide a vehicle for adapting to those changes. Regularly reviewing this decision-making process will help you make priority adjustments that will bring your financial goals and activities in line with your current life situation.

Step 6 Example   Over the next 6 to 12 months, Kent Mullins should reassess his financial, career, and personal situations. What employment opportunities or family circumstances might affect his need or desire to take a different course of action?

CONCEPT CHECK 1–1

1 What are the main elements of every decision we make?
2 What are some risks associated with financial decisions?
3 What are some common sources of financial planning information?
4 Why should you reevaluate your actions after making a personal financial decision?

Action Application   Prepare a list of potential risks involved with making various personal and financial decisions. What actions might be taken to investigate and reduce these risks?

Developing Personal Financial Goals

Since the United States is one of the richest countries in the world, it is difficult to understand why so many Americans have money problems. The answer seems to be the result of two main factors. The first is poor planning and weak money management habits in areas such as spending and the use of credit. The other factor is extensive advertising, selling efforts, and product availability. Achieving personal financial satisfaction starts with clear financial goals.

Objective 2

Develop personal financial goals.

TYPES OF FINANCIAL GOALS

Two factors commonly influence your financial aspirations for the future. The first is the time frame in which you would like to achieve your goals. The second is the type of financial need that drives your goals.

TIMING OF GOALS   What would you like to do tomorrow? Believe it or not, that question involves goal setting. *Short-term goals* are goals to be achieved within the next year or so, such as saving for a vacation or paying off small debts. *Intermediate goals* have a time frame of two to five years. *Long-term goals* involve financial plans that are more than five years off, such as retirement savings, money for children's college educations, or the purchase of a vacation home.

Long-term goals should be planned in coordination with short-term and intermediate ones. Setting and achieving short-term goals is the basis for achieving long-term goals. For example, saving for a down payment to buy a house is a short-term goal that can be a foundation for a long-term goal: owning your own home.

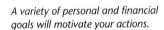
A variety of personal and financial goals will motivate your actions.

GOAL-SETTING GUIDELINES FROM CNN/MONEY

What are your top three financial objectives? Most people, when asked that question, answer with general goals, such as "achieving financial security." CNN/Money offers a framework for financial goal setting.

First, focus on a few main financial objectives. Make a list of all the things that you'd need to feel secure, happy, or fulfilled. This action will allow you to better achieve what is most important to you. Be ready for conflict. Decide which goals can be delayed or ignored. Paying for an auto repair may take money from your retirement savings. You can use "The Prioritizer" at www.money.com to help you rank the items in order of importance.

Next, start working on the financial aspects. Money deposited in savings or investment accounts will start to in-crease in value. For example, if you put aside the cost of a single candy bar (about 65 cents) each day, invested in a tax-deferred account paying 5 percent a year compounded monthly, those savings would grow to $3,073 in just 10 years and to $16,470 in 30 years.

Finally, be prepared for change. Your needs and desires will change as you age. Efforts to identify the financial goals that matter most to you will make sure that you get what you want most. Be sure to: (1) decide which goals take priority and (2) work toward the lesser goals only after the primary ones are being addressed.

CNN/Money offers a savings calculator and other financial planning tools at www.money.com

---

Goal frequency is another ingredient in the financial planning process. Some goals, such as vacations or money for gifts, may be set annually. Other goals, such as a college education, a car, or a house, occur less frequently.

GOALS FOR DIFFERENT FINANCIAL NEEDS A goal of obtaining increased career training is different from a goal of saving money to pay a semiannual auto insurance premium. *Consumable-product goals* usually occur on a periodic basis and involve items that are used up relatively quickly, such as food, clothing, and entertainment. Such purchases, if made unwisely, can have a negative effect on your financial situation.

Durable-product goals usually involve infrequently purchased, expensive items such as appliances, cars, and sporting equipment; these consist of tangible items. In contrast, many people overlook *intangible-purchase goals*. These goals may relate to personal relationships, health, education, and leisure. Goal setting for these life circumstances is also necessary for your overall well-being.

GOAL-SETTING GUIDELINES

An old saying goes, "If you don't know where you're going, you might end up somewhere else and not even know it." Goal setting is central to financial decision making. Your financial goals are the basis for planning, implementing, and measuring the progress of your spending, saving, and investing activities. Exhibit 1–4 offers typical goals and financial activities for various life situations.

Your financial goals should be stated to take the following factors into account:

1. *Financial goals should be realistic.* Financial goals should be based on your income and life situation. For example, it is probably not realistic to expect to buy a new car each year if you are a full-time student.

> ### DID YOU KNOW?
>
> A survey conducted by the Consumer Federation of America (CFA) estimates that over 60 million American households will probably fail to realize one or more of their major life goals largely due to a lack of a comprehensive financial plan. In households with annual incomes of less than $100,000, savers who say they have financial plans report about twice as much savings and investments as savers without plans.

Exhibit **1-4**   Financial goals and activities for various life situations

Common Financial Goals and Activities		
• Obtain appropriate career training. • Create an effective financial recordkeeping system. • Develop a regular savings and investment program.	• Accumulate an appropriate emergency fund. • Purchase appropriate types and amounts of insurance coverage. • Create and implement a flexible budget.	• Evaluate and select appropriate investments. • Establish and implement a plan for retirement goals. • Make a will and develop an estate plan.

Life Situation	Specialized Financial Activities
Young, single (18–35)	• Establish financial independence. • Obtain disability insurance to replace income during prolonged illness. • Consider home purchase for tax benefit.
Young couple with children under 18	• Carefully manage the increased need for the use of credit. • Obtain an appropriate amount of life insurance for the care of dependents. • Use a will to name guardian for children.
Single parent with children under 18	• Obtain adequate amounts of health, life, and disability insurance. • Contribute to savings and investment fund for college. • Name a guardian for children and make other estate plans.
Young dual-income couple, no children	• Coordinate insurance coverage and other benefits. • Develop savings and investment program for changes in life situation (larger house, children). • Consider tax-deferred contributions to retirement fund.
Older couple (+50), no dependent children at home	• Consolidate financial assets and review estate plans. • Obtain health insurance for postretirement period. • Plan retirement housing, living expenses, recreational activities, and part-time work.
Mixed-generation household (elderly individuals and children under 18)	• Obtain long-term health care insurance and life/disability income for care of younger dependents. • Use dependent care service if needed. • Provide arrangements for handling finances of elderly if they become ill. • Consider splitting of investment cost, with elderly getting income while alive and principal going to surviving relatives.
Older (+50), single	• Make arrangement for long-term health care coverage. • Review will and estate plan. • Plan retirement living facilities, living expenses, and activities.

CREATING FINANCIAL GOALS

Based on your current situation or expectations for the future, create two financial goals—one short term and one long term—using the following guidelines:

Goal-Setting Actions	Short-Term Goal	Long-Term Goal
Step 1. Create realistic goals based on your life situation.		
Step 2. State your goals in specific, measurable terms.		
Step 3. Describe the time frame for accomplishing your goals.		
Step 4. Indicate an action to be taken to achieve your goals.		

Sheet 3
Setting personal financial goals

2. *Financial goals should be stated in specific, measurable terms.* Knowing exactly what your goals are will help you create a plan designed to achieve them. For example, the goal of "Accumulate $5,000 in an investment fund within three years" is a clearer guide to planning than the goal of "Put money into an investment fund."

3. *Financial goals should have a time frame.* In the preceding example, the goal is to be achieved in three years. A time frame helps you measure your progress toward your financial goals.

4. *Financial goals should indicate the type of action to be taken.* Your financial goals are the basis for the various financial activities you will undertake. For example, "Reduce credit card debt" will usually mean decreased use of credit.

The Financial Planning for Life's Situations: Creating Financial Goals box (above) gives you an opportunity to set financial goals.

CONCEPT CHECK 1-2

1 What are examples of long-term goals?

2 What are the four main characteristics of useful financial goals?

Action Application Ask friends, relatives, and others about their short-term and long-term financial goals. What are some of the common goals for various personal situations?

Influences on Personal Financial Planning

Many factors influence daily financial decisions, ranging from age and household size to interest rates and inflation. Three main elements affect financial planning activities: life situation, personal values, and economic factors.

Objective 3

Assess personal and economic factors that influence personal financial planning.

LIFE SITUATION AND PERSONAL VALUES

People in their 20s spend money differently than those in their 50s. Personal factors such as age, income, household size, and personal beliefs influence your spending and saving patterns. Your life situation or lifestyle is created by a combination of factors.

As our society changes, different types of financial needs evolve. Today people tend to get married at a later age, and more households have two incomes. Many households are headed by single parents. More than 2 million women provide care for both dependent children and parents. We are also living longer; over 80 percent of all Americans now living are expected to live past age 65.

Try out your ability to set financial goals. Use Financial Planning for Life's Situations: Creating Financial Goals on page 12.

As Exhibit 1–5 shows, the **adult life cycle**—the stages in the family and financial needs of an adult—is an important influence on your financial activities and decisions. Your life situation is also affected by marital status, household size, and employment, as well as events such as

adult life cycle The stages in the family situation and financial needs of an adult.

- Graduation (at various levels of education).
- Engagement and marriage.
- The birth or adoption of a child.
- A career change or a move to a new area.

- Dependent children leaving home.
- Changes in health.
- Divorce.
- Retirement.
- The death of a spouse, family member, or other dependent.

In addition to being defined by your family situation, you are defined by your **values**—the ideas and principles that you consider correct, desirable, and important. Values have a direct influence on such decisions as spending now versus saving for the future or continuing school versus getting a job.

values Ideas and principles that a person considers correct, desirable, and important.

ECONOMIC FACTORS

Daily economic activities are another important influence on financial planning. In our society, the forces of supply and demand play an important role in setting prices. **Economics** is the study of how wealth is created and distributed. The economic environment includes various institutions, principally business, labor, and government, that must work together to satisfy our needs and wants.

economics The study of how wealth is created and distributed.

While various government agencies regulate financial activities, the Federal Reserve System, our nation's central bank, has significant responsibility in our economy. *The Fed,* as it is called, is concerned with maintaining an adequate money supply. It achieves this by influencing borrowing, interest rates, and the buying or selling of government securities. The Fed attempts to make adequate funds available for consumer spending and business expansion while keeping interest rates and consumer prices at an appropriate level.

GLOBAL INFLUENCES   The global marketplace influences financial activities. Our economy is affected by both the financial activities of foreign investors and

Exhibit **1–5**

Life situation influences on
your financial decisions

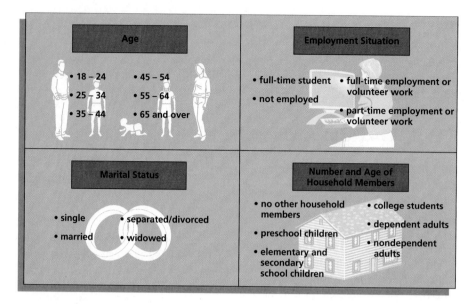

competition from foreign companies. American businesses compete against foreign companies for the spending dollars of American consumers.

When the level of exports of U.S.-made goods is lower than the level of imported goods, more U.S. dollars leave the country than the dollar value of foreign currency coming into the United States. This reduces the funds available for domestic spending and investment. Also, if foreign companies decide not to invest their dollars in the United States, the domestic money supply is reduced. This reduced money supply may cause higher interest rates.

ECONOMIC CONDITIONS

Newspapers and business periodicals regularly publish current economic statistics. Exhibit 1–6 provides an overview of some economic indicators that influence financial decisions. Your personal financial decisions are most heavily influenced by consumer prices, consumer spending, and interest rates.

inflation A rise in the general level of prices.

1. Consumer Prices **Inflation** is a rise in the general level of prices. In times of inflation, the buying power of the dollar decreases. For example, if prices increased 5 percent during the last year, items that cost $100 one year ago would now cost $105. This means it now takes more money to buy the same amount of goods and services.

The main cause of inflation is an increase in demand without a comparable increase in supply. For example, if people have more money to spend because of pay increases or borrowing but the same amounts of goods and services are available, the increased demand can bid up prices for those goods and services.

Inflation is most harmful to people living on fixed incomes. Due to inflation, retired people and others whose incomes do not change are able to afford smaller amounts of goods and services.

Inflation can also adversely affect lenders of money. Unless an adequate interest rate is charged, amounts repaid by borrowers in times of inflation have less buying power than the money they borrowed. If you pay 10 percent interest on a loan and the inflation rate is 12 percent, the dollars you pay the lender have lost buying power. For this reason, interest rates rise in periods of high inflation.

The rate of inflation varies. During the late 1950s and early 1960s, the annual inflation rate was in the 1 to 3 percent range. During the late

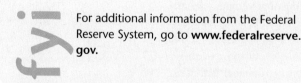

For additional information from the Federal Reserve System, go to **www.federalreserve. gov.**

Exhibit **1-6**   Changing economic conditions and financial decisions

Economic Factor	What It Measures	How It Influences Financial Planning
Consumer prices	The value of the dollar; changes in inflation.	If consumer prices increase faster than your income, you are unable to purchase the same amount of goods and services; higher consumer prices will also cause higher interest rates.
Consumer spending	The demand for goods and services by individuals and households.	Increased consumer spending is likely to create more jobs and higher wages; high levels of consumer spending and borrowing can also push up consumer prices and interest rates.
Interest rates	The cost of money; the cost of credit when you borrow; the return on your money when you save or invest.	Higher interest rates make buying on credit more expensive; higher interest rates make saving and investing more attractive and discourage borrowing.
Money supply	The dollars available for spending in our economy.	Interest rates tend to decline as more people save and invest; but higher saving (and lower spending) may also reduce job opportunities.
Unemployment	The number of people without employment who are willing and able to work.	People who are unemployed should reduce their debt level and have an emergency savings fund for living costs while out of work; high unemployment reduces consumer spending and job opportunities.
Housing starts	The number of new homes being built.	Increased home building results in more job opportunities, higher wages, more consumer spending, and overall economic expansion.
Gross domestic product (GDP)	The total value of goods and services produced within a country's borders, including items produced with foreign resources.	The GDP provides an indication of a nation's economic viability, resulting in employment and opportunities for personal financial wealth.
Trade balance	The difference between a country's exports and its imports.	If a country exports more than it imports, interest rates may rise and foreign goods and foreign travel will cost more.
Dow Jones Average, S&P 500, other stock market indexes	The relative value of stocks represented by the index.	These indexes provide an indication of the general movement of stock prices.

1970s and early 1980s, the cost of living increased 10 to 12 percent annually. At a 12 percent annual inflation rate, prices double (and the value of the dollar is cut in half) in about six years. To find out how fast prices (or your savings) will double, use the *rule of 72:* Just divide 72 by the annual inflation (or interest) rate. An annual inflation rate of 8 percent, for example, means prices will double in nine years (72 ÷ 8 = 9).

More recently, the annual price increase for most goods and services as measured by the consumer price index has been in the 2 to 4 percent range. The *consumer price index (CPI),* published by the Bureau of Labor Statistics, is a measure of the average change in the prices urban consumers pay for a fixed "basket" of goods and services. For current CPI information, go to www.bls.gov.

Inflation rates can be deceptive, since the index is based on specific items calculated in a predetermined manner. Many people face *hidden* inflation since the cost of necessities (food, gas, health care), on which they spend most of their money, may rise at a higher rate than the cost of nonessential items, which could be dropping in price. This results in a reported inflation rate much lower than the actual cost-of-living increase being experienced by consumers.

2. Consumer Spending   Total demand for goods and services in the economy influences employment opportunities and the potential for income. As consumer purchasing increases, the financial resources of current and prospective employees expand. This situation improves the financial condition of many households.

In contrast, reduced spending causes unemployment, since staff reduction commonly results from a company's reduced financial resources. The financial hardships of unemployment are a major concern of business, labor, and government. Retraining programs, income assistance, and job services can help people adjust.

How are the prices of goods and services changing around the country? For the latest consumer price index, go to **www.bls.gov.**

3. Interest Rates   In simple terms, interest rates represent the cost of money. Like everything else, money has a price. The forces of supply and demand influence interest rates. When consumer saving and investing increase the supply of money, interest rates tend to decrease. However, as consumer, business, government, and foreign borrowing increase the demand for money, interest rates tend to rise.

Interest rates affect your financial planning. The earnings you receive as a saver or an investor reflect current interest rates as well as a *risk premium* based on such factors as the length of time your funds will be used by others, expected inflation, and the extent of uncertainty about getting your money back. Risk is also a factor in the interest rate you pay as a borrower. People with poor credit ratings pay a higher interest rate than people with good credit ratings. Interest rates influence many financial decisions. Current interest rate data may be obtained at www.federalreserve.gov.

Sheet 4
Monitoring current economic conditions

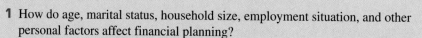

CONCEPT CHECK 1-3   ✓

1 How do age, marital status, household size, employment situation, and other personal factors affect financial planning?

2 How might the uncertainty of inflation make personal financial planning difficult?

3 What factors influence the level of interest rates?

Action Application   Using Web research and discussion with others, create an inflation rate that reflects the change in price for items commonly bought by you and your family.

Opportunity Costs and the Time Value of Money

Have you noticed that you always give up something when you make choices? In every financial decision, you sacrifice something to obtain something else that you consider more desirable. For example, you might forgo current buying to invest funds for future purchases or long-term financial security. Or you might gain the use of an expensive

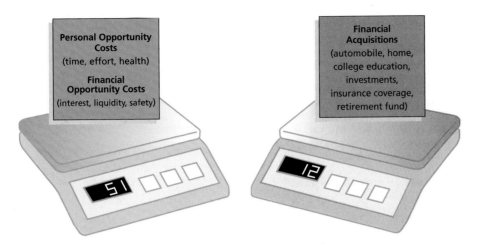

Exhibit **1–7**

Opportunity costs and financial results should be assessed when making financial decisions

item now by making credit payments from future earnings. These *opportunity costs* may be viewed in terms of both personal and financial resources (see Exhibit 1–7).

Objective 4

Determine personal and financial opportunity costs associated with personal financial decisions.

PERSONAL OPPORTUNITY COSTS

An important personal opportunity cost involves time that when used for one activity cannot be used for other activities. Time used for studying, working, or shopping will not be available for other uses. The allocation of time should be viewed like any decision: Select your use of time to meet your needs, achieve your goals, and satisfy personal values.

Other personal opportunity costs relate to health. Poor eating habits, lack of sleep, or avoiding exercise can result in illness, time away from school or work, increased health care costs, and reduced financial security. Like financial resources, your personal resources (time, energy, health, abilities, knowledge) require careful management.

FINANCIAL OPPORTUNITY COSTS

You are constantly making choices among various financial decisions. In making those choices, you must consider the **time value of money,** the increases in an amount of money as a result of interest earned. Saving or investing a dollar instead of spending it today results in a future amount greater than a dollar. Every time you spend, save, invest, or borrow money, you should consider the time value of that money as an opportunity cost. Spending money from your savings account means lost interest earnings; however, what you buy with that money may have a higher priority than those earnings. Borrowing to make a purchase involves the opportunity cost of paying interest on the loan, but your current needs may make this trade-off worthwhile.

time value of money
Increases in an amount of money as a result of interest earned.

The opportunity cost of the time value of money is also present in these financial decisions:

- Setting aside funds in a savings plan with little or no risk has the opportunity cost of potentially higher returns from an investment with greater risk.

- Having extra money withheld from your paycheck in order to receive a tax refund has the opportunity cost of the lost interest the money could earn in a savings account.

- Making annual deposits in a retirement account can help you avoid the opportunity cost of having inadequate funds later in life.

- Purchasing a new automobile or home appliance has the potential benefit of saving you money on future maintenance and energy costs.

INTEREST CALCULATIONS
Three amounts are required to calculate the time value of money for savings in the form of interest earned:

- The amount of the savings (commonly called the *principal*).
- The annual interest rate.
- The length of time the money is on deposit.

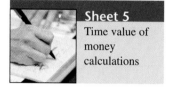

Sheet 5
Time value of money calculations

These three items are multiplied to obtain the amount of interest. Simple interest is calculated as follows:

$$\boxed{\begin{array}{c}\text{Amount}\\\text{in}\\\text{savings}\end{array}} \times \boxed{\begin{array}{c}\text{Annual}\\\text{interest}\\\text{rate}\end{array}} \times \boxed{\begin{array}{c}\text{Time}\\\text{period}\end{array}} = \boxed{\text{Interest}}$$

For example, $500 on deposit at 6 percent for six months would earn $15 ($500 × 0.06 × 6/12, or 1/2 year).

You can calculate the increased value of your money from interest earned in two ways: You can calculate the total amount that will be available later (future value), or you can determine the current value of an amount desired in the future (present value).

FUTURE VALUE OF A SINGLE AMOUNT

future value The amount to which current savings will increase based on a certain interest rate and a certain time period; also referred to as *compounding*.

Deposited money earns interest that will increase over time. **Future value** is the amount to which current savings will increase based on a certain interest rate and a certain time period. For example, $100 deposited in a 6 percent account for one year will grow to $106. This amount is computed as follows:

$$\text{Future value} = \$100 + (\$100 \times 0.06 \times 1 \text{ year}) = \$106$$

Original amount in savings   Amount of interest earned

The same process could be continued for a second, third, and fourth year, but the computations would be time consuming. Future value tables simplify the process (see Exhibit 1–8). To use a future value table, multiply the amount deposited by the factor for the desired interest rate and time period. For example, $650 at 8 percent for 10 years would have a future value of $1,403.35 ($650 × 2.159). The future value of an amount will always be greater than the original amount. As Exhibit 1–8A shows, all the future value factors are larger than 1.

Future value computations may be referred to as *compounding,* since interest is earned on previously earned interest. Compounding allows the future value of a deposit to grow faster than it would if interest were paid only on the original deposit.

The sooner you make deposits, the greater the future value will be. Depositing $1,000 in a 5 percent account at age 40 will give you $3,387 at age 65. However, making the $1,000 deposit at age 25 would result in an account balance of $7,040 at age 65.

fyi Need further explanations and exercises for future value and present value calculations? See the appendix at the end of this chapter.

FUTURE VALUE OF A SERIES OF DEPOSITS
Quite often, savers and investors make regular deposits. An *annuity* is a series of equal deposits or payments. To determine the future value of equal yearly savings deposits, use Exhibit 1–8B. For this table to be used, the deposits must earn a constant interest rate. If you deposit $50 a year at 7 percent for six years, starting at the end of the first year, you will have $357.65 at

the end of that time ($50 × 7.153). The Financial Planning Calculations box on page 21 presents examples of using future value to achieve financial goals.

PRESENT VALUE OF A SINGLE AMOUNT   Another aspect of the time value of money involves determining the current value of an amount desired in the future. **Present value** is the current value for a future amount based on a certain interest rate and a certain time period. Present value computations, also called *discounting*, allow you to determine how much to deposit now to obtain a desired total in the future.

present value The current value for a future amount based on a certain interest rate and a certain time period; also referred to as discounting.

Exhibit **1-8**

Time value of money tables (condensed)

A. Future Value of $1 (single amount)

Year	5%	6%	7%	8%	9%
5	1.276	1.338	1.403	1.469	1.539
6	1.340	1.419	1.501	1.587	1.677
7	1.407	1.504	1.606	1.714	1.828
8	1.477	1.594	1.718	1.851	1.993
9	1.551	1.689	1.838	1.999	2.172
10	1.629	1.791	1.967	2.159	2.367

B. Future Value of a Series of Annual Deposits (annuity)

Year	5%	6%	7%	8%	9%
5	5.526	5.637	5.751	5.867	5.985
6	6.802	6.975	7.153	7.336	7.523
7	8.142	8.394	8.654	8.923	9.200
8	9.549	9.897	10.260	10.637	11.028
9	11.027	11.491	11.978	12.488	13.021
10	12.578	13.181	13.816	14.487	15.193

C. Present Value of $1 (single amount)

Year	5%	6%	7%	8%	9%
5	0.784	0.747	0.713	0.681	0.650
6	0.746	0.705	0.666	0.630	0.596
7	0.711	0.665	0.623	0.583	0.547
8	0.677	0.627	0.582	0.540	0.502
9	0.645	0.592	0.544	0.500	0.460
10	0.614	0.558	0.508	0.463	0.422

D. Present Value of a Series of Annual Deposits (annuity)

Year	5%	6%	7%	8%	9%
5	4.329	4.212	4.100	3.993	3.890
6	5.076	4.917	4.767	4.623	4.486
7	5.786	5.582	5.389	5.206	5.033
8	6.463	6.210	5.971	5.747	5.535
9	7.108	6.802	6.515	6.247	5.995
10	7.722	7.360	7.024	6.710	6.418

Note: See the appendix at the end of this chapter for more complete future value and present value tables.

Present value tables (Exhibit 1–8C) can be used to make the computations. If you want $1,000 five years from now and you earn 5 percent on your savings, you need to deposit $784 ($1,000 × 0.784).

The present value of the amount you want in the future will always be less than the future value, since all of the factors in Exhibit 1–8C are less than 1 and interest earned will increase the present value amount to the desired future amount.

PRESENT VALUE OF A SERIES OF DEPOSITS   You can also use present value computations to determine how much you need to deposit so that you can take a certain amount out of the account for a desired number of years. For example, if you want to take $400 out of an investment account each year for nine years and your money is earning an annual rate of 8 percent, you can see from Exhibit 1–8D that you would need to make a current deposit of $2,498.80 ($400 × 6.247).

The formulas for calculating future and present values, as well as tables covering a wider range of interest rates and time periods, are presented in the appendix at the end of the chapter. Computer programs for calculating time value of money are also available.

CONCEPT CHECK 1-4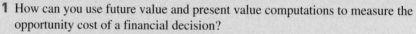

1 How can you use future value and present value computations to measure the opportunity cost of a financial decision?

2 Use the time value of money tables in Exhibit 1–8 to calculate the following:
   a. The future value of $100 at 7 percent in 10 years.
   b. The future value of $100 a year for six years earning 6 percent.
   c. The present value of $500 received in eight years with an interest rate of 8 percent.

Action Application   What is the relationship between current interest rates and financial opportunity costs? Using time value of money calculations, state one or more goals in terms of an annual savings amount and the future value of this savings objective.

Achieving Financial Goals

Objective 5

Identify strategies for achieving personal financial goals for different life situations.

Throughout life, our needs usually can be satisfied with the intelligent use of financial resources. Financial planning involves deciding how to obtain, protect, and use those resources. By using the eight major areas of personal financial planning to organize your financial activities, you can avoid many common money mistakes.

COMPONENTS OF PERSONAL FINANCIAL PLANNING

This book is designed to provide a framework for the study and planning of personal financial decisions. Exhibit 1–9 presents an overview of the eight major personal financial planning areas. To achieve a successful financial situation, you must coordinate these components through an organized plan and wise decision making.

Financial Planning Calculations

TIME VALUE OF MONEY CALCULATION METHODS

The time value of money may be calculated using a variety of techniques. When achieving specific financial goals requires regular deposits to a savings or investment account, the computation may occur in one of several ways. For example, Jonie Emerson plans to deposit $10,000 in an account for the next 10 years. She estimates these funds will earn an annual rate of 5 percent. What amount can Jonie expect to have available after 10 years?

Method	Process, Results
Formula Calculation The most basic method of calculating the time value of money involves using a formula. These are described in the appendix at the end of this chapter.	For this situation, the formula would be: $$PV(1 = i)^n = FV$$ The result sould be $$\$10,000 (1 + 0.05)^{10} = \$16,288.95$$
Time Value of Money Tables Instead of calculating with a formula, time value of money tables are available. The numeric factors presented ease the computational process.	Using the table in Exhibit 1–8A: $10,000 × Future value of $1, 5%, 10 years $10,000 × 1.629 = $16,290
Financial Calculator A variety of handheld financial calculators are programmed with various financial functions. Both future value and present value calculations may be performed using the appropriate keystrokes.	Using a financial calculator, the keystrokes would be: Amount −10000 $\boxed{PV}$ Time periods 10 $\boxed{N}$ Interest rate 5 $\boxed{I}$ Result $\boxed{FV}$ \$_____
Spreadsheet Software *Excel* and other software programs have built-in formulas for various financial computations, including time value of money.	When using a spreadsheet program, this type of calculation would require this format: $$= FV(\text{rate, periods, amount per period, single amount})$$ The results of this example would be: $$= FV(0.05, 10, 0, -10000) = \$16,288.95$$
Time Value of Money Software Various computer programs are available that specifically calculate time value of money situations. The software that accompanies this book includes a worksheet for Time Value of Money Calculations, which is shown here.	
Time Value of Money Web Sites Many time-value-of-money calculators are also available online. These Web-based programs perform calculations for the future value of savings as well as determining amounts for loan payments.	Some easy-to-use calculators for computing the time value of money and other financial computations are located at • www.kiplinger.com/tools • www.dinkytown.net • www.rbccentura.com/tools • cgi.money.cnn.com/tools

Note: The slight differences in answers are the result of rounding.

Exhibit **1-9**

Components of personal
financial planning

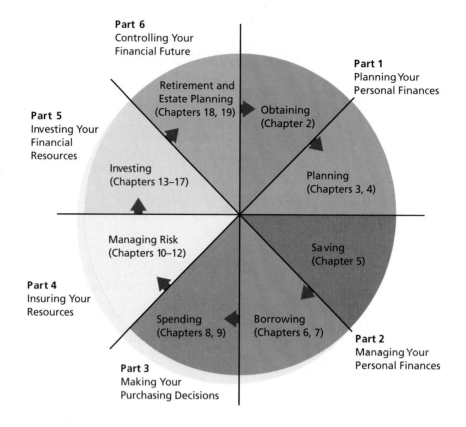

OBTAINING (CHAPTER 2)   You obtain financial resources from employment, investments, or ownership of a business. Obtaining financial resources is the foundation of financial planning, since these resources are used for all financial activities.

> **Online Sources for Obtaining**   Many guidelines for effective career planning and professional development may be obtained at www.rileyguide.com and www.monster.com

PLANNING (CHAPTERS 3, 4)   Planned spending through budgeting is the key to achieving goals and future financial security. Efforts to anticipate expenses and financial decisions can also help reduce taxes. The ability to pay your fair share of taxes—no more, no less—is vital to increasing your financial resources.

> **Online Sources for Planning**   Budgeting is an ongoing activity, and tax planning should not occur only around April 15. For assistance, go to www.money.com, www.quicken.com, and www.irs.gov.

SAVING (CHAPTER 5)   Long-term financial security starts with a regular savings plan for emergencies, unexpected bills, replacement of major items, and the purchase of special goods and services, such as a college education, a boat, or a vacation home. Once you have established a basic savings plan, you may use additional money for investments that offer greater financial growth.

liquidity The ability to readily convert financial resources into cash without a loss in value.

An amount of savings must be available to meet current household needs. **Liquidity** refers to the ability to readily convert financial resources into cash without a loss in value. The need for liquidity will vary based on a person's age, health, and family situation. Savings plans such as interest-earning checking accounts, money market accounts, and money market funds earn money on your savings while providing liquidity.

BORROWING (CHAPTERS 6, 7)

Maintaining control over your credit-buying habits will contribute to your financial goals. The overuse and misuse of credit may cause a situation in which a person's debts far exceed the resources available to pay those debts. **Bankruptcy** is a set of federal laws that allow you to either restructure your debts or remove certain debts. The people who declare bankruptcy each year may have avoided this trauma with wise spending and borrowing decisions. Chapter 7 discusses bankruptcy in detail.

The planning component of personal finance provides a foundation for other activities.

bankruptcy A set of federal laws that allow you to either restructure your debts or remove certain debts.

SPENDING (CHAPTERS 8, 9)

Financial planning is designed not to prevent your enjoyment of life but to help you obtain the things you want. Too often, however, people make purchases without considering the financial consequences. Some people shop compulsively, creating financial difficulties. You should detail your living expenses and your other financial obligations in a spending plan. Spending less than you earn is the only way to achieve long-term financial security.

MANAGING RISK (CHAPTERS 10–12)

Adequate insurance coverage is another component of personal financial planning. Certain types of insurance are commonly overlooked in financial plans. For example, the number of people who suffer disabling injuries or diseases at age 50 is greater than the number who die at that age, so people may need disability insurance more than they need life insurance. Yet surveys reveal that most people have adequate life insurance but few have disability insurance. The insurance industry is more aggressive in selling life insurance than in selling disability insurance, thus putting the burden of obtaining adequate disability insurance on you.

Many households have excessive or overlapping insurance coverage. Insuring property for more than it is worth may be a waste of money, as may both a husband and a wife having similar health insurance coverage.

INVESTING (CHAPTERS 13–17)

While many types of investment vehicles are available, people invest for two primary reasons. Those interested in *current income* select investments that pay regular dividends or interest. In contrast, investors who desire *long-term growth* choose stocks, mutual funds, real estate, and other investments with potential for increased value in the future.

DID YOU KNOW?

Research indicates that people with a financial plan (developed themselves or by a professional) had significantly higher amounts in savings than those who didn't have a plan.

You can achieve investment diversification by including a variety of assets in your *portfolio*—for example, stocks, bond mutual funds, real estate, and collectibles such as rare coins. Obtaining general investment advice is easy; however, it is more difficult to obtain specific investment advice to meet your individual needs and goals.

Online Sources for Investing   "Information is power"—this is especially true when investing. You can obtain company information and investment assistance at finance.yahoo.com, www.fool.com, and www.marketwatch.com.

RETIREMENT AND ESTATE PLANNING (CHAPTERS 18, 19)   Most people desire financial security upon completion of full-time employment. But retirement planning also involves thinking about your housing situation, your recreational activities, and possible part-time or volunteer work.

Transfers of money or property to others should be timed, if possible, to minimize the tax burden and maximize the benefits for those receiving the financial resources. A knowledge of property transfer methods can help you select the best course of action for funding current and future living costs, educational expenses, and retirement needs of dependents.

Online Sources for Retirement and Estate Planning   Whether you are 40 years or 40 minutes away from retiring, you can obtain assistance at retireplan.about.com, www.aarp.org, and www.estateplanninglinks.com.

DEVELOPING A FLEXIBLE FINANCIAL PLAN

financial plan   A formalized report that summarizes your current financial situation, analyzes your financial needs, and recommends future financial activities.

A **financial plan** is a formalized report that summarizes your current financial situation, analyzes your financial needs, and recommends future financial activities. You can create this document on your own, seek assistance from a financial planner, or use a money management software package. Exhibit 1–10 offers a framework for developing and implementing a financial plan, along with examples for several life situations.

IMPLEMENTING YOUR FINANCIAL PLAN

You must have a plan before you can implement it. However, once you have clearly assessed your current situation and identified your financial goals, what do you do next?

The most important strategy for success is to develop financial habits that contribute to both short-term satisfaction and long-term financial security, including the following:

1. Using a well-conceived spending plan will help you stay within your income while you save and invest for the future. The main source of financial difficulties is overspending.

2. Having appropriate insurance protection will help you prevent financial disasters.

3. Becoming informed about tax and investment alternatives will help you expand your financial resources.

STUDYING PERSONAL FINANCE

Within each chapter of this book are various learning devices to help you build knowledge. The *Personal Financial Planner* provides a framework for creating and implementing your financial activities. The CD-ROM and Web site (www.mhhe.com/kdh) connect you to additional resources and activities. As you move into the following chapters, we leave you with this advice:

DID YOU KNOW?

In 2004 Congress created the Financial Literacy and Education Improvement Act to promote financial education and long-term financial security in the United States. This program is administered by representatives from several federal government agencies. Additional information is available at www.treasury.gov/financialeducation and www.mymoney.gov.

Exhibit **1-10**   Financial planning in action

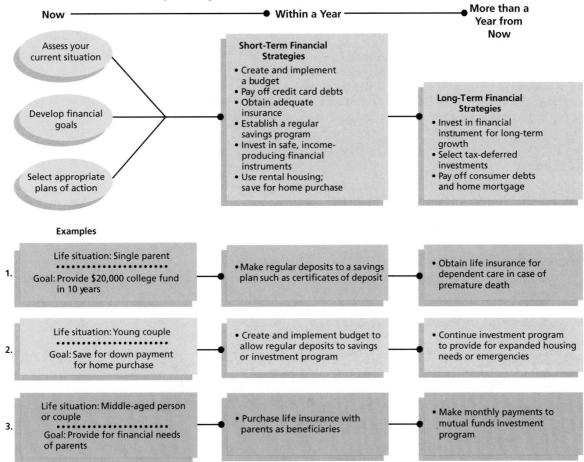

- Read and study the book carefully. Use the Concept Checks and end-of-chapter activities.
- Watch television and read newspapers and magazines for the latest personal finance information.
- Talk to others, experts and friends, who have knowledge of various money topics.
- Search the Web for answers to questions that result from your desire to know more.

Want fast access to text notes, practice quizzes, and personal finance Web sites? Go to **www.mhhe.com/kdh.**

Achieving your financial objectives requires two things: (1) a willingness to learn and (2) appropriate information sources. *You* must provide the first element; the material that follows will provide the second. For successful financial planning, know where you are now, know where you want to be, and be persistent in your efforts to get there.

CONCEPT CHECK 1-5

1 What are the main components of personal financial planning?
2 What is the purpose of a financial plan?
3 Identify some common actions taken to achieve financial goals.

Action Application Prepare a list of questions that might be asked of a financial planning professional by (1) a young person just starting out on his or her own, (2), a young couple planning for their children's education and for their own retirement, and (3) a person nearing retirement.

SUMMARY OF OBJECTIVES

Objective 1

Analyze the process for making personal financial decisions.
Personal financial planning involves the following process: (1) determine your current financial situation; (2) develop financial goals; (3) identify alternative courses of action; (4) evaluate alternatives; (5) create and implement a financial action plan; and (6) review and revise the financial plan.

Objective 2

Develop personal financial goals.
Financial goals should (1) be realistic; (2) be stated in specific, measurable terms; (3) have a time frame; and (4) indicate the type of action to be taken.

Objective 3

Assess personal and economic factors that influence personal financial planning.
Financial decisions are affected by a person's life situation (income, age, household size, health), personal values, and economic factors (prices, interest rates, and employment opportunities).

Objective 4

Determine personal and financial opportunity costs associated with personal financial decisions.
Every decision involves a trade-off with things given up. Personal opportunity costs include time, effort, and health. Financial opportunity costs are based on the time value of money. Future value and present value calculations enable you to measure the increased value (or lost interest) that results from a saving, investing, borrowing, or purchasing decision.

Objective 5

Identify strategies for achieving personal financial goals for different life situations.
Successful financial planning requires specific goals combined with spending, saving, investing, and borrowing strategies based on your personal situation and various social and economic factors.

KEY TERMS

adult life cycle 13	**future value** 18	**personal financial planning** 4
bankruptcy 23	**inflation** 14	**present value** 19
economics 13	**liquidity** 22	**time value of money** 17
financial plan 24	**opportunity cost** 6	**values** 13

FINANCIAL PLANNING PROBLEMS

(Note: Some of these problems require the use of the time value of money tables in the chapter appendix.)

1. *Calculating Future Value of Property.* Ben Collins plans to buy a house for $65,000. If that real estate is expected to increase in value by 5 percent each year, what will its approximate value be seven years from now? (Obj. 3)

2. *Using the Rule of 72.* Using the rule of 72, approximate the following amounts. (Obj. 3)

   a. If the value of land in an area is increasing 6 percent a year, how long will it take for property values to double?

   b. If you earn 10 percent on your investments, how long will it take for your money to double?

   c. At an annual interest rate of 5 percent, how long will it take for your savings to double?

3. *Determining the Inflation Rate.* In the mid-1990s, selected automobiles had an average cost of $12,000. The average cost of those same automobiles is now $15,000. What was the rate of increase for these automobiles between the two time periods? (Obj. 3)

4. *Computing Future Living Expenses.* A family spends $28,000 a year for living expenses. If prices increase by 4 percent a year for the next three years, what amount will the family need for their living expenses after three years? (Obj. 3)

5. *Calculating Earnings on Savings.* What would be the yearly earnings for a person with $6,000 in savings at an annual interest rate of 5.5 percent? (Obj. 4)

6. *Computing Time Value of Money.* Using time value of money tables, calculate the following. (Obj. 4)

   a. The future value of $450 six years from now at 7 percent.

   b. The future value of $800 saved each year for 10 years at 8 percent.

   c. The amount a person would have to deposit today (present value) at a 6 percent interest rate to have $1,000 five years from now.

   d. The amount a person would have to deposit today to be able to take out $500 a year for 10 years from an account earning 8 percent.

7. *Calculating Future Value of a Series of Amounts.* Elaine Romberg prepares her own income tax return each year. A tax preparer would charge her $60 for this service. Over a period of 10 years, how much does Elaine gain from preparing her own tax return? Assume she can earn 3 percent on her savings. (Obj. 4)

8. *Calculating Time Value of Money for Savings Goals.* If you desire to have $10,000 for a down payment for a house in five years, what amount would you need to deposit today? Assume that your money will earn 5 percent.

9. *Calculating Present Value of a Series.* Pete Morton is planning to go to graduate school in a program of study that will take three years. Pete wants to have $10,000 available each year for various school and living expenses. If he earns 4 percent on his money, how much must be deposited at the start of his studies to be able to withdraw $10,000 a year for three years?

10. *Using Time Value of Money for Retirement Planning.* Carla Lopez deposits $3,000 a year into her retirement account. If these funds have an average earning of 8 percent over the 40 years until her retirement, what will be the value of her retirement account?

11. *Calculating the Value of Reduced Spending.* If a person spends $10 a week on coffee (assume $500 a year), what would be the future value of that amount over 10 years if the funds were deposited in an account earning 4 percent?

FINANCIAL PLANNING ACTIVITIES

1. *Researching Personal Finance on the Internet.* Using Web sites such as www.money.com, www.quicken.com, or www.kiplinger.com and search engines, obtain information about commonly suggested actions related to various personal financial planning decisions. What are some of the best sources of information on the Internet to assist you with financial planning? (Obj. 1)

2. *Comparing Financial Planning Actions.* Survey friends, relatives, and others to determine the process they use when making financial decisions. How do these people measure risk when making financial decisions? (Obj. 1)

3. *Using Financial Planning Experts.* Prepare a list of financial planning specialists (investment advisers, credit counselors, insurance agents, real estate brokers, tax preparers) in your community who can assist people with personal financial planning. (Obj. 1, 3)

4. *Setting Financial Goals.* Using Sheet 3 in the *Personal Financial Planner,* create one short-term and one long-term goal for people in these life situations: *(a)* a young single person, *(b)* a single parent with a child age 8, *(c)* a married person with no children, and *(d)* a retired person. (Obj. 2)

5. *Analyzing Changing Life Situations.* Ask friends, relatives, and others how their spending, saving, and borrowing activities changed when they decided to continue their education, change careers, or have children. (Obj. 3)

6. *Researching Economic Conditions.* Use library resources, such as the *Wall Street Journal,* www.businessweek.com, or other Web sites to determine recent trends in interest rates, inflation, and other economic indicators. Information about the consumer price index (measuring changes in the cost of living) may be obtained at www.bls.gov. Report how this economic information might affect your financial planning decisions. (Obj. 3)

7. *Comparing Alternative Financial Actions.* What actions would be necessary to compare a financial planner who advertises "One Low Fee Is Charged to Develop Your Personal Financial Plan" and one that advertises "You Are Not Charged a Fee, My Services Are Covered by the Investment Company for Which I Work"? (Obj. 4, 5)

8. *Researching Financial Planning Software.* Visit software retailers to obtain information about the features and costs of various personal financial planning activities. Information about programs such as *Microsoft Money* and *Quicken* may be obtained on the Internet. (Obj. 5)

INTERNET CONNECTION

Researching Economic Conditions Affecting Financial Decisions

For these two major economic indicators, obtain current information and determine how the current trend might affect financial planning activities.

Inflation Web sources: _____

_____

_____

Current findings: _____

_____

_____

Possible influence on your financial decisions: _____

_____

_____

Interest Rates Web sources: _____

_____

_____

Current findings: _____

_____

_____

Possible influence on your financial decisions: _____

_____

_____

FINANCIAL PLANNING CASE

Triple Trouble for the "Sandwich Generation"

Until recently, Fran and Ed Blake's personal finances ran smoothly. Both have maintained well-paying jobs while raising two children. The Blakes have a daughter who is completing her freshman year of college and a son three years younger. Currently they have $22,000 in various savings and investment funds set aside for the children's education. With education costs increasing faster than inflation, they are uncertain whether this amount is adequate.

In recent months, Fran's mother has required extensive medical attention and personal care assistance. Unable to live alone, she is now a resident of a long-term care facility. The cost of this service is $2,050 a month, with annual increases of about 7 percent. While a major portion of the cost is covered by her Social Security and pension, Fran's mother is unable to cover the entire cost. Their desire to help adds to the Blakes' financial burden.

The Blakes are like millions of other Americans who have financial responsibilities for both dependent children and aging parents. Commonly referred to as the "sandwich generation," this group is squeezed on one side by the cost of raising and educating children and on the other side by the financial demands of caring for aging parents.

Finally, the Blakes, ages 47 and 43, are also concerned about saving for their own retirement. While they have consistently made annual deposits to a retirement fund, various current financial demands may force them to tap into this money.

Questions

1. What actions have the Blakes taken that would be considered wise financial planning choices?

2. What areas of financial concern do the Blakes face? What actions might be appropriate to address these concerns?

3. Using time value of money calculations (tables in the chapter appendix), compute the following:

   a. At 5 percent, what would be the value of the $22,000 education funds in three years?

   b. If the cost of long-term care is increasing at 7 percent a year, what will be the approximate monthly cost for Fran's mother eight years from now?

   c. Fran and Ed plan to deposit $1,500 a year to their retirement fund for 35 years. If they earn an average annual return of 9 percent, what will be the value of their retirement fund after 35 years?

VIDEO CASE

Your Moment of Truth

People have different attitudes toward money and financial planning. Some view spending as the ultimate purpose of making money, with nothing or very little for saving. Others, due to their family situation or age, understand the need to plan, save, and invest.

Following a logical process for developing a personal financial plan is the foundation of effective money management. By setting goals, people are able to provide a direction for the short term and long term. Specific goals can also prevent various financial planning pitfalls.

As you may already realize, different financial activities are usually appropriate for different ages. People in their 30s have many expenses; they also need to have a plan for long-term financial security. In contrast, people in their 50s need to reassess their retirement investments and start thinking about living arrangements and housing during their later years.

Questions

1. What are some common personal financial planning mistakes people make?

2. How does goal setting help a person to achieve long-term financial security?

3. What factors affect the need to take different financial actions for different ages in life, such as in your 30s, 40s, and 50s?

YOUR PERSONAL FINANCIAL PLANNER IN ACTION

Starting Your Financial Plan

Planning is the foundation for success in every aspect of life. Assessing your current financial situation, along with setting goals is the key to successful financial planning.

Your Short-Term Financial Planning Activities	Resources
1. Prepare a list of personal and financial information for yourself and family members. Also create a list of financial service organizations that you use.	PFP Sheets 1, 2 www.money.com www.kiplinger.com
2. Set financial goals related to various current and future needs.	PFP Sheet 3 http://financialplan.about.com
3. Monitor current economic conditions (inflation, interest rates) to determine possible actions to take related to your personal finances.	PFP Sheet 4 www.federalreserve.gov www.bls.gov
Your Long-Term Financial Planning Activities	
1. Based on various financial goals, calculate the savings deposits necessary to achieve those goals.	PFP Sheet 5 www.centura.com/tools
2. Identify various financial planning actions for you and other household members for the next two to five years.	Text pages 20–25 www.moneycentral.msn.com

CONTINUING CASE

Getting Started

Life Situation

Single
Age 22
Starting a career
No dependents

Financial Data:

Monthly income $2,600
Living expenses $2,180
Assets $8,200
Liabilities $3,470
Emergency fund $530

While in college, Pam Jenkins worked part-time and was never concerned about long-term financial planning. Rather than creating a budget, she used her checkbook and savings account (which usually had a very low balance) to handle her financial needs.

After completing college, Pam began her career as a sales representative for a clothing manufacturer located in California. After one year, her assets consist of a 1999 automobile, a television set, some electronic entertainment equipment, and clothing and other personal belongs, with a total value of about $8,200.

Questions

1. List various personal financial decisions that Pam might be thinking about at this point in her life.

2. What are some short-term, intermediate, and long-term financial goals that Pam might want to develop?

3. Explain which sections of *Personal Financial Planner* sheets 1–5 could be useful for Pam?

APPENDIX: The Time Value of Money: Future Value and Present Value Computations

"If I deposit $10,000 today, how much will I have for a down payment on a house in five years?"

"Will $2,000 saved each year give me enough money when I retire?"

"How much must I save today to have enough for my children's college education?"

The *time value of money,* more commonly referred to as *interest,* is the cost of money that is borrowed or lent. Interest can be compared to rent, the cost of using an apartment or other item. The time value of money is based on the fact that a dollar received today is worth more than a dollar that will be received one year from today, because the dollar received today can be saved or invested and will be worth more than a dollar a year from today. Similarly, a dollar that will be received one year from today is currently worth less than a dollar today.

The time value of money has two major components: future value and present value. *Future value* computations, which are also referred to as *compounding,* yield the amount to which a current sum will increase based on a certain interest rate and period of time. *Present value,* which is calculated through a process called *discounting,* is the current value of a future sum based on a certain interest rate and period of time.

In future value problems, you are given an amount to save or invest and you calculate the amount that will be available at some future date. With present value problems, you are given the amount that will be available at some future date and you calculate the current value of that amount. Both future value and present value computations are based on basic interest rate calculations.

Interest Rate Basics

Simple interest is the dollar cost of borrowing or the earnings from lending money. The interest is based on three elements:

- The dollar amount, called the *principal.*
- The *rate of interest.*
- The amount of *time.*

The formula for computing interest is

$$\text{Interest} = \text{Principal} \times \text{Rate of interest} \times \text{Time}$$

The interest rate is stated as a percentage for a year. For example, you must convert 12 percent to either 0.12 or 12/100 before doing your calculations. The time element must also be converted to a decimal or fraction. For example, three months would be shown as either 0.25 or 1/4 of a year. Interest for 2 1/2 years would involve a time period of 2.5.

EXAMPLE A

Suppose you borrow $1,000 at 5 percent and will repay it in one payment at the end of one year. Using the simple interest calculation, the interest is $50, computed as follows:

$$\$50 = \$1,000 \times 0.05 \times 1 \text{ (year)}$$

EXAMPLE B

If you deposited $750 in a savings account paying 8 percent, how much interest would you earn in nine months? You would compute this amount as follows:

$$\text{Interest} = \$750 \times 0.08 \times 1/4 \text{ (or 0.75 of a year)}$$

$$= \$45$$

SAMPLE PROBLEM 1

How much interest would you earn if you deposited $300 at 6 percent for 27 months? *(Answers to sample problems are on page 36)*

SAMPLE PROBLEM 2

How much interest would you pay to borrow $670 for eight months at 12 percent?

Future Value of a Single Amount

The future value of an amount consists of the original amount plus compound interest. This calculation involves the following elements:

$$FV = \text{Future value}$$

$$PV = \text{Present value}$$

$$i = \text{Interest rate}$$

$$n + \text{Number of time periods}$$

The formula for the future value of a single amount is

$$FV = PV(1 = i)^n$$

EXAMPLE C

The future value of $1 at 10 percent after three years is $1.33. This amount is calculated as follows:

$$\$1.33 = \$1.00(1 + 0.10)^3$$

Future value tables are available to help you determine compounded interest amounts (see Exhibit 1–A on page 37). Looking at Exhibit 1–A for 10 percent and three years, you can see that $1 would be worth $1.33 at that time. For other amounts, multiply the table factor by the original amount.

This may be viewed as follows:

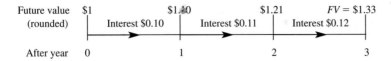

| Future value (rounded) | $1 | | $1.10 | | $1.21 | | FV = $1.33 |
| After year | 0 | Interest $0.10 | 1 | Interest $0.11 | 2 | Interest $0.12 | 3 |

EXAMPLE D

If your savings of $400 earn 12 percent, compounded *monthly,* over a year and a half, use the table factor for 1 percent for 18 time periods. The future value of this amount is $478.40, calculated as follows:

$$\$478.40 = \$400 \, (1.196)$$

SAMPLE PROBLEM 3

What is the future value of $800 at 8 percent after six years?

SAMPLE PROBLEM 4

How much would you have in savings if you kept $200 on deposit for eight years at 8 percent, compounded *semiannually?*

Future Value of a Series of Equal Amounts (an Annuity)

Future value may also be calculated for a situation in which regular additions are made to savings. The following formula is used:

$$FV = \text{Annuity} \, \frac{(1 + i)^n - 1}{i}$$

This formula assumes that (1) each deposit is for the same amount, (2) the interest rate is the same for each time period, and (3) the deposits are made at the end of each time period.

EXAMPLE E

The future value of three $1 deposits made at the end of the next three years, earning 10 percent interest, is $3.31. This is calculated as follows:

$$\$3.31 = \$1 \, \frac{(1 + 0.10)^3 - 1}{0.10}$$

This may be viewed as follows:

Future value (rounded)			$1		$2.10		FV = $3.31
		Deposit $1		Deposit $1		Deposit $1	
		Interest 0		Interest $0.10		Interest $0.21	
After year	0		1		2		3

Using Exhibit 1–B on page 38 you can find this same amount for 10 percent for three time periods. To use the table for other amounts, multiply the table factors by the annual deposit.

EXAMPLE F

If you plan to deposit $40 a year for 10 years, earning 8 percent compounded annually, use the table factor for 8 percent for 10 time periods. The future value of this amount is $579.48, calculated as follows:

$$\$579.48 = \$40(14.487)$$

SAMPLE PROBLEM 5

What is the future value of an annual deposit of $230 earning 6 percent for 15 years?

SAMPLE PROBLEM 6

What amount would you have in a retirement account if you made annual deposits of $375 for 25 years earning 12 percent, compounded annually?

Present Value of a Single Amount

If you want to know how much you need to deposit now to receive a certain amount in the future, use the following formula:

$$PV = \frac{1}{(1 + i)^n}$$

EXAMPLE G

The present value of $1 to be received three years from now based on a 10 percent interest rate is $0.75. This amount is calculated as follows:

$$\$0.75 = \frac{\$1}{(1 + 0.10)^3}$$

This may be viewed as follows:

Present value tables are available to assist you in this process (see Exhibit 1–C on page 39. Notice that $1 at 10 percent for three years has a present value of $0.75. For amounts other than $1, multiply the table factor by the amount involved.

EXAMPLE H

If you want to have $300 seven years from now and your savings earn 10 percent, compounded *semiannually,* use the table factor for 5 percent for 14 time periods. In this situation, the present value is $151.50, calculated as follows:

$$\$151.50 = \$300(0.505)$$

SAMPLE PROBLEM 7

What is the present value of $2,200 earning 15 percent for eight years?

SAMPLE PROBLEM 8

To have $6,000 for a child's education in 10 years, what amount should a parent deposit in a savings account that earns 12 percent, compounded *quarterly?*

Present Value of a Series of Equal Amounts (an Annuity)

The final time value of money situation allows you to receive an amount at the end of each time period for a certain number of periods. This amount is calculated as follows:

$$PV = \text{Annuity} \; \frac{1 - \dfrac{1}{(1 + i)^n}}{i}$$

EXAMPLE I

The present value of a $1 withdrawal at the end of the next three years would be $2.49, calculated as follows:

$$\$2.49 = \$1 \left[\frac{1 - \dfrac{1}{(1 + 0.10)^3}}{0.10} \right]$$

This may be viewed as follows:

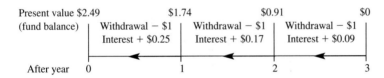

This same amount appears in Exhibit 1–D on page 40 for 10 percent and three time periods. To use the table for other situations, multiply the table factor by the amount to be withdrawn each year.

EXAMPLE J

If you wish to withdraw $100 at the end of each year for 10 years from an account that earns 14 percent, compounded annually, what amount must you deposit now? Use the table factor for 14 percent for 10 time periods. In this situation, the present value is $521.60, calculated as follows:

$$\$521.60 = \$100(5.216)$$

SAMPLE PROBLEM 9

What is the present value of a withdrawal of $200 at the end of each year for 14 years with an interest rate of 7 percent?

SAMPLE PROBLEM 10

How much would you have to deposit now to be able to withdraw $650 at the end of each year for 20 years from an account that earns 11 percent?

Using Present Value to Determine Loan Payments

Present value tables can also be used to determine installment payments for a loan as follows:

$$\frac{\text{Amount borrowed}}{\text{Present value of a series table factor (Exhibit 1–D)}} = \text{Loan payment}$$

EXAMPLE K

If you borrow $1,000 with a 6 percent interest rate to be repaid in three equal payments at the end of the next three years, the payments will be $374.11. This is calculated as follows:

$$\frac{\$1,000}{2.673} = \$374.11$$

SAMPLE PROBLEM 11

What would be the annual payment amount for a $20,000, 10-year loan at 7 percent?

Answers to Sample Problems

1. $300 × 0.06 × 2.25 years (27 months) = $40.50.
2. $670 × 0.12 × 2/3 (of a year) = $53.60.
3. $800(1.587) = $1,269.60. (Use Exhibit 1–A, 8%, 6 periods.)
4. $200(1.873) = $374.60. (Use Exhibit 1–A, 4%, 16 periods.)
5. $230(23.276) = $5,353.48. (Use Exhibit 1–B, 6%, 15 periods.)
6. $375(133.33) = $49,998.75. (Use Exhibit1–B, 12%, 25 periods.)
7. $2,200(0.327) = $719.40. (Use Exhibit 1–C, 15%, 8 periods.)
8. $6,000(0.307) = $1,842. (Use Exhibit 1–C, 3%, 40 periods.)
9. $200(8.745) = $1,749. (Use Exhibit 1–D, 7%, 14 periods.)
10. $650(7.963) = $5,175.95. (Use Exhibit 1–D, 11%, 20 periods.)
11. $20,000/7.024 = $2,847.38. (Use Exhibit 1–D, 7%, 10 periods.)

Exhibit **1-A**   Future value (compounded sum) of $1 after a given number of time periods

Period	1%	2%	3%	4%	5%	6%	7%	8%	9%	10%	11%
1	1.010	1.020	1.030	1.040	1.050	1.060	1.070	1.080	1.090	1.100	1.110
2	1.020	1.040	1.061	1.082	1.103	1.124	1.145	1.166	1.188	1.210	1.232
3	1.030	1.061	1.093	1.125	1.158	1.191	1.225	1.260	1.295	1.331	1.368
4	1.041	1.082	1.126	1.170	1.216	1.262	1.311	1.360	1.412	1.464	1.518
5	1.051	1.104	1.159	1.217	1.276	1.338	1.403	1.469	1.539	1.611	1.685
6	1.062	1.126	1.194	1.265	1.340	1.419	1.501	1.587	1.677	1.772	1.870
7	1.072	1.149	1.230	1.316	1.407	1.504	1.606	1.714	1.828	1.949	2.076
8	1.083	1.172	1.267	1.369	1.477	1.594	1.718	1.851	1.993	2.144	2.305
9	1.094	1.195	1.305	1.423	1.551	1.689	1.838	1.999	2.172	2.358	2.558
10	1.105	1.219	1.344	1.480	1.629	1.791	1.967	2.159	2.367	2.594	2.839
11	1.116	1.243	1.384	1.539	1.710	1.898	2.105	2.332	2.580	2.853	3.152
12	1.127	1.268	1.426	1.601	1.796	2.012	2.252	2.518	2.813	3.138	3.498
13	1.138	1.294	1.469	1.665	1.886	2.133	2.410	2.720	3.066	3.452	3.883
14	1.149	1.319	1.513	1.732	1.980	2.261	2.579	2.937	3.342	3.797	4.310
15	1.161	1.346	1.558	1.801	2.079	2.397	2.759	3.172	3.642	4.177	4.785
16	1.173	1.373	1.605	1.873	2.183	2.540	2.952	3.426	3.970	4.595	5.311
17	1.184	1.400	1.653	1.948	2.292	2.693	3.159	3.700	4.328	5.054	5.895
18	1.196	1.428	1.702	2.026	2.407	2.854	3.380	3.996	4.717	5.560	6.544
19	1.208	1.457	1.754	2.107	2.527	3.026	3.617	4.316	5.142	6.116	7.263
20	1.220	1.486	1.806	2.191	2.653	3.207	3.870	4.661	5.604	6.727	8.062
25	1.282	1.641	2.094	2.666	3.386	4.292	5.427	6.848	8.623	10.835	13.585
30	1.348	1.811	2.427	3.243	4.322	5.743	7.612	10.063	13.268	17.449	22.892
40	1.489	2.208	3.262	4.801	7.040	10.086	14.974	21.725	31.409	45.259	65.001
50	1.645	2.692	4.384	7.107	11.467	18.420	29.457	46.902	74.358	117.390	184.570

Period	12%	13%	14%	15%	16%	17%	18%	19%	20%	25%	30%
1	1.120	1.130	1.140	1.150	1.160	1.170	1.180	1.190	1.200	1.250	1.300
2	1.254	1.277	1.300	1.323	1.346	1.369	1.392	1.416	1.440	1.563	1.690
3	1.405	1.443	1.482	1.521	1.561	1.602	1.643	1.685	1.728	1.953	2.197
4	1.574	1.630	1.689	1.749	1.811	1.874	1.939	2.005	2.074	2.441	2.856
5	1.762	1.842	1.925	2.011	2.100	2.192	2.288	2.386	2.488	3.052	3.713
6	1.974	2.082	2.195	2.313	2.436	2.565	2.700	2.840	2.986	3.815	4.827
7	2.211	2.353	2.502	2.660	2.826	3.001	3.185	3.379	3.583	4.768	6.276
8	2.476	2.658	2.853	3.059	3.278	3.511	3.759	4.021	4.300	5.960	8.157
9	2.773	3.004	3.252	3.518	3.803	4.108	4.435	4.785	5.160	7.451	10.604
10	3.106	3.395	3.707	4.046	4.411	4.807	5.234	5.696	6.192	9.313	13.786
11	3.479	3.836	4.226	4.652	5.117	5.624	6.176	6.777	7.430	11.642	17.922
12	3.896	4.335	4.818	5.350	5.936	6.580	7.288	8.064	8.916	14.552	23.298
13	4.363	4.898	5.492	6.153	6.886	7.699	8.599	9.596	10.699	18.190	30.288
14	4.887	5.535	6.261	7.076	7.988	9.007	10.147	11.420	12.839	22.737	39.374
15	5.474	6.254	7.138	8.137	9.266	10.539	11.974	13.590	15.407	28.422	51.186
16	6.130	7.067	8.137	9.358	10.748	12.330	14.129	16.172	18.488	35.527	66.542
17	6.866	7.986	9.276	10.761	12.468	14.426	16.672	19.244	22.186	44.409	86.504
18	7.690	9.024	10.575	12.375	14.463	16.879	19.673	22.091	26.623	55.511	112.460
19	8.613	10.197	12.056	14.232	16.777	19.748	23.214	27.252	31.948	69.389	146.190
20	9.646	11.523	13.743	16.367	19.461	23.106	27.393	32.429	38.338	86.736	190.050
25	17.000	21.231	26.462	32.919	40.874	50.658	62.669	77.388	95.396	264.700	705.640
30	29.960	39.116	50.950	66.212	85.850	111.070	143.370	184.680	237.380	807.790	2,620.000
40	93.051	132.780	188.880	267.860	378.720	533.870	750.380	1,051.700	1,469.800	7,523.200	36,119.000
50	289.000	450.740	700.230	1,083.700	1,670.700	2,566.200	3,927.400	5,998.900	9,100.400	70,065.000	497,929.000

Exhibit **1-B**   Future value (compounded sum) of $1 paid in at the end of each period of a given number of time periods (an annuity)

Period	1%	2%	3%	4%	5%	6%	7%	8%	9%	10%	11%
1	1.000	1.000	1.000	1.000	1.000	1.000	1.000	1.000	1.000	1.000	1.000
2	2.010	2.020	2.030	2.040	2.050	2.060	2.070	2.080	2.090	2.100	2.110
3	3.030	3.060	3.091	3.122	3.153	3.184	3.215	3.246	3.278	3.310	3.342
4	4.060	4.122	4.184	4.246	4.310	4.375	4.440	4.506	4.573	4.641	4.710
5	5.101	5.204	5.309	5.416	5.526	5.637	5.751	5.867	5.985	6.105	6.228
6	6.152	6.308	6.468	6.633	6.802	6.975	7.153	7.336	7.523	7.716	7.913
7	7.214	7.434	4.662	7.898	8.142	8.394	8.654	8.923	9.200	9.487	9.783
8	8.286	8.583	8.892	9.214	9.549	9.897	10.260	10.637	11.028	11.436	11.859
9	9.369	9.755	10.159	10.583	11.027	11.491	11.978	12.488	13.021	13.579	14.164
10	10.462	10.950	11.464	12.006	12.578	13.181	13.816	14.487	15.193	15.937	16.722
11	11.567	12.169	12.808	13.486	14.207	14.972	15.784	16.645	17.560	18.531	19.561
12	12.683	13.412	14.192	15.026	15.917	16.870	17.888	18.977	20.141	21.384	22.713
13	13.809	14.680	15.618	16.627	17.713	18.882	20.141	21.495	22.953	24.523	26.212
14	14.947	15.974	17.086	18.292	19.599	21.015	22.550	24.215	26.019	27.975	30.095
15	16.097	17.293	18.599	20.024	21.579	23.276	25.129	27.152	29.361	31.772	34.405
16	17.258	18.639	20.157	21.825	23.657	25.673	27.888	30.324	33.003	35.950	39.190
17	18.430	20.012	21.762	23.698	25.840	20.213	30.840	33.750	36.974	40.545	44.501
18	19.615	21.412	23.414	25.645	28.132	30.906	33.999	37.450	41.301	45.599	50.396
19	20.811	22.841	25.117	27.671	30.539	33.760	37.379	41.446	46.018	51.159	56.939
20	22.019	24.297	26.870	29.778	33.066	36.786	40.995	45.762	51.160	57.275	64.203
25	28.243	32.030	36.459	41.646	47.727	54.865	63.249	73.106	84.701	98.347	114.410
30	34.785	40.588	47.575	56.085	66.439	79.058	94.461	113.280	136.310	164.490	199.020
40	48.886	60.402	75.401	95.026	120.800	154.760	199.640	259.060	337.890	442.590	581.830
50	64.463	84.579	112.800	152.670	209.350	290.340	406.530	573.770	815.080	1,163.900	1,668.800

Period	12%	13%	14%	15%	16%	17%	18%	19%	20%	25%	30%
1	1.000	1.000	1.000	1.000	1.000	1.000	1.000	1.000	1.000	1.000	1.000
2	2.120	2.130	2.140	2.150	2.160	2.170	2.180	2.190	2.200	2.250	2.300
3	3.374	3.407	3.440	3.473	3.506	3.539	3.572	3.606	3.640	3.813	3.990
4	4.779	4.850	4.921	4.993	5.066	5.141	5.215	5.291	5.368	5.766	6.187
5	6.353	6.480	6.610	6.742	6.877	7.014	7.154	7.297	7.442	8.207	9.043
6	8.115	8.323	8.536	8.754	8.977	9.207	9.442	9.683	9.930	11.259	12.756
7	10.089	10.405	10.730	11.067	11.414	11.772	12.142	12.523	12.916	15.073	17.583
8	12.300	12.757	13.233	13.727	14.240	14.773	15.327	15.902	16.499	19.842	23.858
9	14.776	15.416	16.085	16.786	17.519	18.285	19.086	19.923	20.799	25.802	32.015
10	17.549	18.420	19.337	20.304	21.321	22.393	23.521	24.701	25.959	33.253	42.619
11	20.655	21.814	23.045	24.349	25.733	27.200	28.755	30.404	32.150	42.566	56.405
12	24.133	25.650	27.271	29.002	30.850	32.824	34.931	37.180	39.581	54.208	74.327
13	28.029	29.985	32.089	34.352	36.786	39.404	42.219	45.244	48.497	68.760	97.625
14	32.393	34.883	37.581	40.505	43.672	47.103	50.818	54.841	59.196	86.949	127.910
15	37.280	40.417	43.842	47.580	51.660	56.110	60.965	66.261	72.035	109.690	167.290
16	42.753	46.672	50.980	55.717	60.925	66.649	72.939	79.850	87.442	138.110	218.470
17	48.884	53.739	59.118	65.075	71.673	78.979	87.068	96.022	105.930	173.640	285.010
18	55.750	61.725	68.394	75.836	84.141	93.406	103.740	115.270	128.120	218.050	371.520
19	63.440	70.749	78.969	88.212	98.603	110.290	123.410	138.170	154.740	273.560	483.970
20	72.052	80.947	91.025	102.440	115.380	130.030	146.630	165.420	186.690	342.950	630.170
25	133.330	155.620	181.870	212.790	249.210	292.110	342.600	402.040	471.980	1,054.800	2,348.800
30	241.330	293.200	356.790	434.750	530.310	647.440	790.950	966.700	1,181.900	3,227.200	8,730.000
40	767.090	1,013.700	1,342.000	1,779.100	2,360.800	3,134.500	4,163.210	5,529.800	7,343.900	30,089.000	120,393.000
50	2,400.000	3,459.500	4,994.500	7,217.700	10,436.000	15,090.000	21,813.000	31,515.000	45,497.000	80,256.000	165,976.000

Exhibit **1-C**   Present value of $1 to be received at the end of a given number of time periods

Period	1%	2%	3%	4%	5%	6%	7%	8%	9%	10%	11%	12%
1	0.990	0.980	0.971	0.962	0.952	0.943	0.935	0.926	0.917	0.909	0.901	0.893
2	0.980	0.961	0.943	0.925	0.907	0.890	0.873	0.857	0.842	0.826	0.812	0.797
3	0.971	0.942	0.915	0.889	0.864	0.840	0.816	0.794	0.772	0.751	0.731	0.712
4	0.961	0.924	0.885	0.855	0.823	0.792	0.763	0.735	0.708	0.683	0.659	0.636
5	0.951	0.906	0.863	0.822	0.784	0.747	0.713	0.681	0.650	0.621	0.593	0.567
6	0.942	0.888	0.837	0.790	0.746	0.705	0.666	0.630	0.596	0.564	0.535	0.507
7	0.933	0.871	0.813	0.760	0.711	0.665	0.623	0.583	0.547	0.513	0.482	0.452
8	0.923	0.853	0.789	0.731	0.677	0.627	0.582	0.540	0.502	0.467	0.434	0.404
9	0.914	0.837	0.766	0.703	0.645	0.592	0.544	0.500	0.460	0.424	0.391	0.361
10	0.905	0.820	0.744	0.676	0.614	0.558	0.508	0.463	0.422	0.386	0.352	0.322
11	0.896	0.804	0.722	0.650	0.585	0.527	0.475	0.429	0.388	0.350	0.317	0.287
12	0.887	0.788	0.701	0.625	0.557	0.497	0.444	0.397	0.356	0.319	0.286	0.257
13	0.879	0.773	0.681	0.601	0.530	0.469	0.415	0.368	0.326	0.290	0.258	0.229
14	0.870	0.758	0.661	0.577	0.505	0.442	0.388	0.340	0.299	0.263	0.232	0.205
15	0.861	0.743	0.642	0.555	0.481	0.417	0.362	0.315	0.275	0.239	0.209	0.183
16	0.853	0.728	0.623	0.534	0.458	0.394	0.339	0.292	0.252	0.218	0.188	0.163
17	0.844	0.714	0.605	0.513	0.436	0.371	0.317	0.270	0.231	0.198	0.170	0.146
18	0.836	0.700	0.587	0.494	0.416	0.350	0.296	0.250	0.212	0.180	0.153	0.130
19	0.828	0.686	0.570	0.475	0.396	0.331	0.277	0.232	0.194	0.164	0.138	0.116
20	0.820	0.673	0.554	0.456	0.377	0.312	0.258	0.215	0.178	0.149	0.124	0.104
25	0.780	0.610	0.478	0.375	0.295	0.233	0.184	0.146	0.116	0.092	0.074	0.059
30	0.742	0.552	0.412	0.308	0.231	0.174	0.131	0.099	0.075	0.057	0.044	0.033
40	0.672	0.453	0.307	0.208	0.142	0.097	0.067	0.046	0.032	0.022	0.015	0.011
50	0.608	0.372	0.228	0.141	0.087	0.054	0.034	0.021	0.013	0.009	0.005	0.003

Period	13%	14%	15%	16%	17%	18%	19%	20%	25%	30%	35%	40%	50%
1	0.885	0.877	0.870	0.862	0.855	0.847	0.840	0.833	0.800	0.769	0.741	0.714	0.667
2	0.783	0.769	0.756	0.743	0.731	0.718	0.706	0.694	0.640	0.592	0.549	0.510	0.444
3	0.693	0.675	0.658	0.641	0.624	0.609	0.593	0.579	0.512	0.455	0.406	0.364	0.296
4	0.613	0.592	0.572	0.552	0.534	0.515	0.499	0.482	0.410	0.350	0.301	0.260	0.198
5	0.543	0.519	0.497	0.476	0.456	0.437	0.419	0.402	0.320	0.269	0.223	0.186	0.132
6	0.480	0.456	0.432	0.410	0.390	0.370	0.352	0.335	0.262	0.207	0.165	0.133	0.088
7	0.425	0.400	0.376	0.354	0.333	0.314	0.296	0.279	0.210	0.159	0.122	0.095	0.059
8	0.376	0.351	0.327	0.305	0.285	0.266	0.249	0.233	0.168	0.123	0.091	0.068	0.039
9	0.333	0.300	0.284	0.263	0.243	0.225	0.209	0.194	0.134	0.094	0.067	0.048	0.026
10	0.295	0.270	0.247	0.227	0.208	0.191	0.176	0.162	0.107	0.073	0.050	0.035	0.017
11	0.261	0.237	0.215	0.195	0.178	0.162	0.148	0.135	0.086	0.056	0.037	0.025	0.012
12	0.231	0.208	0.187	0.168	0.152	0.137	0.124	0.112	0.069	0.043	0.027	0.018	0.008
13	0.204	0.182	0.163	0.145	0.130	0.116	0.104	0.093	0.055	0.033	0.020	0.013	0.005
14	0.181	0.160	0.141	0.125	0.111	0.099	0.088	0.078	0.044	0.025	0.015	0.009	0.003
15	0.160	0.140	0.123	0.108	0.095	0.084	0.074	0.065	0.035	0.020	0.011	0.006	0.002
16	0.141	0.123	0.107	0.093	0.081	0.071	0.062	0.054	0.028	0.015	0.008	0.005	0.002
17	0.125	0.108	0.093	0.080	0.069	0.060	0.052	0.045	0.023	0.012	0.006	0.003	0.001
18	0.111	0.095	0.081	0.069	0.059	0.051	0.044	0.038	0.018	0.009	0.005	0.002	0.001
19	0.098	0.083	0.070	0.060	0.051	0.043	0.037	0.031	0.014	0.007	0.003	0.002	0
20	0.087	0.073	0.061	0.051	0.043	0.037	0.031	0.026	0.012	0.005	0.002	0.001	0
25	0.047	0.038	0.030	0.024	0.020	0.016	0.013	0.010	0.004	0.001	0.001	0	0
30	0.026	0.020	0.015	0.012	0.009	0.007	0.005	0.004	0.001	0	0	0	0
40	0.008	0.005	0.004	0.003	0.002	0.001	0.001	0.001	0	0	0	0	0
50	0.002	0.001	0.001	0.001	0	0	0	0	0	0	0	0	0

Exhibit **1-D**   Present value of $1 received at the end of each period for a given number of time periods (an annuity)

Period	1%	2%	3%	4%	5%	6%	7%	8%	9%	10%	11%	12%
1	0.990	0.980	0.971	0.962	0.952	0.943	0.935	0.926	0.917	0.909	0.901	0.893
2	1.970	1.942	1.913	1.886	1.859	1.833	1.808	1.783	1.759	1.736	1.713	1.690
3	2.941	2.884	2.829	2.775	2.723	2.673	2.624	2.577	2.531	2.487	2.444	2.402
4	3.902	3.808	3.717	3.630	3.546	3.465	3.387	3.312	3.240	3.170	3.102	3.037
5	4.853	4.713	4.580	4.452	4.329	4.212	4.100	3.993	3.890	3.791	3.696	3.605
6	5.795	5.601	5.417	5.242	5.076	4.917	4.767	4.623	4.486	4.355	4.231	4.111
7	6.728	6.472	6.230	6.002	5.786	5.582	5.389	5.206	5.033	4.868	4.712	4.564
8	7.652	7.325	7.020	6.733	6.463	6.210	5.971	5.747	5.535	5.335	5.146	4.968
9	8.566	8.162	7.786	7.435	7.108	6.802	6.515	6.247	5.995	5.759	5.537	5.328
10	9.471	8.983	8.530	8.111	7.722	7.360	7.024	6.710	6.418	6.145	5.889	5.650
11	10.368	9.787	9.253	8.760	8.306	7.887	7.499	7.139	6.805	6.495	6.207	5.938
12	11.255	10.575	9.954	9.385	8.863	8.384	7.943	7.536	7.161	6.814	6.492	6.194
13	12.134	11.348	10.635	9.986	9.394	8.853	8.358	7.904	7.487	7.103	6.750	6.424
14	13.004	12.106	11.296	10.563	9.899	9.295	8.745	8.244	7.786	7.367	6.982	6.628
15	13.865	12.849	11.939	11.118	10.380	9.712	9.108	8.559	8.061	7.606	7.191	6.811
16	14.718	13.578	12.561	11.652	10.838	10.106	9.447	8.851	8.313	7.824	7.379	6.974
17	15.562	14.292	13.166	12.166	11.274	10.477	9.763	9.122	8.544	8.022	7.549	7.102
18	16.398	14.992	13.754	12.659	11.690	10.828	10.059	9.372	8.756	8.201	7.702	7.250
19	17.226	15.678	14.324	13.134	12.085	11.158	10.336	9.604	8.950	8.365	7.839	7.366
20	18.046	16.351	14.877	13.590	12.462	11.470	10.594	9.818	9.129	8.514	7.963	7.469
25	22.023	19.523	17.413	15.622	14.094	12.783	11.654	10.675	9.823	9.077	8.422	7.843
30	25.808	22.396	19.600	17.292	15.372	13.765	12.409	11.258	10.274	9.427	8.694	8.055
40	32.835	27.355	23.115	19.793	17.159	15.046	13.332	11.925	10.757	9.779	8.951	8.244
50	39.196	31.424	25.730	21.482	18.256	15.762	13.801	12.233	10.962	9.915	9.042	8.304

Period	13%	14%	15%	16%	17%	18%	19%	20%	25%	30%	35%	40%	50%
1	0.885	0.877	0.870	0.862	0.855	0.847	0.840	0.833	0.800	0.769	0.741	0.714	0.667
2	1.668	1.647	1.626	1.605	1.585	1.566	1.547	1.528	1.440	1.361	1.289	1.224	1.111
3	2.361	2.322	2.283	2.246	2.210	2.174	2.140	2.106	1.952	1.816	1.696	1.589	1.407
4	2.974	2.914	2.855	2.798	2.743	2.690	2.639	2.589	2.362	2.166	1.997	1.849	1.605
5	3.517	3.433	3.352	3.274	3.199	3.127	3.058	2.991	2.689	2.436	2.220	2.035	1.737
6	3.998	3.889	3.784	3.685	3.589	3.498	3.410	3.326	2.951	2.643	2.385	2.168	1.824
7	4.423	4.288	4.160	4.039	3.922	3.812	3.706	3.605	3.161	2.802	2.508	2.263	1.883
8	4.799	4.639	4.487	4.344	4.207	4.078	3.954	3.837	3.329	2.925	2.598	2.331	1.922
9	5.132	4.946	4.772	4.607	4.451	4.303	4.163	4.031	3.463	3.019	2.665	2.379	1.948
10	5.426	5.216	5.019	4.833	4.659	4.494	4.339	4.192	3.571	3.092	2.715	2.414	1.965
11	5.687	5.453	5.234	5.029	4.836	4.656	4.486	4.327	3.656	3.147	2.752	2.438	1.977
12	5.918	5.660	5.421	5.197	4.988	4.793	4.611	4.439	3.725	3.190	2.779	2.456	1.985
13	6.122	5.842	5.583	5.342	5.118	4.910	4.715	4.533	3.780	3.223	2.799	2.469	1.990
14	6.302	6.002	5.724	5.468	5.229	5.008	4.802	4.611	3.824	3.249	2.814	2.478	1.993
15	6.462	6.142	5.847	5.575	5.324	5.092	4.876	4.675	3.859	3.268	2.825	2.484	1.995
16	6.604	6.265	5.954	5.668	5.405	5.162	4.938	4.730	3.887	3.283	2.834	2.489	1.997
17	6.729	6.373	6.047	5.749	5.475	5.222	4.988	4.775	3.910	3.295	2.840	2.492	1.998
18	6.840	6.467	6.128	5.818	5.534	5.273	5.033	4.812	3.928	3.304	2.844	2.494	1.999
19	6.938	6.550	6.198	5.877	5.584	5.316	5.070	4.843	3.942	3.311	2.848	2.496	1.999
20	7.025	6.623	6.259	5.929	5.628	5.353	5.101	4.870	3.954	3.316	2.850	2.497	1.999
25	7.330	6.873	6.464	6.097	5.766	5.467	5.195	4.948	3.985	3.329	2.856	2.499	2.000
30	7.496	7.003	6.566	6.177	5.829	5.517	5.235	4.979	3.995	3.332	2.857	2.500	2.000
40	7.634	7.105	6.642	6.233	5.871	5.548	5.258	4.997	3.999	3.333	2.857	2.500	2.000
50	7.675	7.133	6.661	6.246	5.880	5.554	5.262	4.999	4.000	3.333	2.857	2.500	2.000

2 Financial Aspects of Career Planning

www.mhhe.com/kdh

Digital Study Tools

Online Learning Center Study Tools for This Chapter

- Multiple-choice quiz
- Flashcards
- eLearning sessions
- Crossword puzzle
- Personal Finance Online: Careers and Résumés

Student CD Study Tools for This Chapter

- Self-study software
- Narrated PowerPoint
- Personal financial planning software: Worksheets 6–13

Key Concept

Employment opportunities are influenced by economic, social, and technological factors. Effective career planning requires careful analysis of yourself, the job market, and potential employers. Connecting your abilities and skills to the needs of prospective employers is the foundation of a successful job search.

Learning Objectives

1 Describe the activities associated with career planning and advancement.

2 Evaluate the factors that influence employment opportunities.

3 Implement employment search strategies.

4 Assess the financial and legal concerns related to obtaining employment.

5 Analyze the techniques for career growth and advancement.

Which Job? Are You Sure?

"Wow, you mean you have three job offers! How did that happen?"

"I'm not quite sure, Joan" responded Alexia, "I guess I just carefully prepared for my job search."

"Ahhh…could you be a bit more specific for those of us who have no job offers?" asked Joan.

"After researching various organizations, I tried to match my abilities and experiences to their needs." Alexia contin-ued, "then, in addition to my résumé, I sent a portfolio with samples of my research work and creative projects."

"OK, Alex, which of the three jobs are you going to take?" asked Joan.

"Again, I'm not quite sure. I've created a comparison of the three to help me decide," Alexia replied.

"Let me see that!" exclaimed Joan. "Wow, you take this career search stuff seriously!"

Job Offer Comparison	Position A	Position B	Position C
Position description, organization	Advertising account assistant for international promotions with global company with offices in 17 countries.	Marketing assistant for a medium-sized equipment company; sales offices in eight states in southeast U.S.	Public relations director in local office of national nonprofit organization assisting low-income families with food and housing.
Salary situation	$36,000; performance reviews and salary increases every six months for first two years, then annually.	$33,500; annual bonus based on percentage of company sales increase.	$28,500, with annual salary increases of 3 to 5 percent.
Vacation time (paid)/year	Two weeks (first year); additional two days for each year of service.	One week after six months on the job; two additional days for each six months of service.	Two weeks (paid); additional unpaid leave time up to four weeks a year.
Health insurance coverage	Employer pays 80 percent of health premiums for doctors on list of insurance company.	Employer pays for HMO coverage with some flexibility of doctors.	Employer pays 60 percent of health premiums; employee selects own doctor.
Retirement fund	Employer contributes 5 percent of salary; additional contributions allowed.	Employer matches employee contributions (up to 10 percent).	Employer pays 2 percent of salary; employee may make tax-deferred contributions.
Educational opportunities	On-site training seminars to update employees on global cultures, advertising trends.	Tuition reimbursement (up to $4,000 a year) for graduate courses.	Two trips a year to seminars on topics related to nonprofit organizations.

QUESTIONS

What Action Should Be Taken?

1. What steps might Alexia take when deciding which position to accept?
2. Which employment position would you recommend for her? Why?

What about Your Situation?

3. What additional factors would you consider when selecting an employment position?
4. What actions could you take to better prepare for an employment search?

Learn More Online

Conduct a Web search on "career portfolios." What elements are commonly included? How might you use a career portfolio for your career planning and professional advancement activities?

Career Choice Factors

Objective 1

Describe the activities associated with career planning and advancement.

job An employment position obtained mainly to earn money, without regard for interests or opportunities for advancement.

career A commitment to a profession that requires continued training and offers a clear path for occupational growth.

"Only two days till the weekend." "Boring!" "Oh no!" "Excellent!" These are some common responses to "It's time to get up for work."

Have you ever wondered why some people find great satisfaction in their work while others only put in their time? As with other personal financial decisions, career selection and professional growth require planning. The average person changes jobs seven times during a lifetime. Most likely, therefore, you will reevaluate your choice of a job on a regular basis.

The lifework you select is a key to your financial well-being and personal satisfaction. You may select a **job,** an employment position obtained mainly to earn money. Many people work in one or more jobs during their lives without considering their interests or opportunities for advancement. Or you may select a **career,** a commitment to a profession that requires continued training and offers a clear path for occupational growth.

TRADE-OFFS OF CAREER DECISIONS

While many factors affect living habits and financial choices, your employment probably affects daily decisions the most. Your income, business associates, and leisure time are a direct result of the work you do.

Like other decisions, career choice and professional development alternatives have risks and opportunity costs. In recent years, many people have placed family and personal fulfillment above monetary reward and professional recognition. Career choices require periodic evaluation of trade-offs related to personal, social, and economic factors. For example:

- Some people select employment that is challenging and offers strong personal satisfaction rather than employment in which they can make the most money.

- Some people refuse a transfer or a promotion that would require moving their families to a new area or reducing leisure time.

    - Many parents opt for part-time employment or flexible hours to allow more time with children.

    - Many people give up secure job situations because they prefer to operate their own businesses.

Time with family members may be an important influence on career decisions.

CAREER TRAINING AND SKILL DEVELOPMENT

Your level of formal training affects financial success. Exhibit 2–1 shows the influence of education on income. The statistics in this exhibit do not mean you will automatically earn a certain amount because you have a college degree. More education increases your *potential* earning power and reduces your chances of being unemployed. Other factors, such as field of study and the job market, also influence future income.

In addition to formal career training, successful managers, employers, and career counselors stress the importance of traits adaptable to varied work situations. While some of these traits can be acquired in school, others require experiences in other situations. The competencies that successful people commonly possess include

- An ability to work well with others in a variety of settings.

- A desire to do tasks better than they have to be done.

Earning a professional or doctorate
degree could be worth $2.8 million
in income over 40 years:

Exhibit **2–1**

Education and income

Source: Employment Policy
Foundation analysis of Bureau of Labor
Statistics (BLS) Current Population
Survey.

**Two-year
vocational
degree**

$1.5 million

**Bachelor's
degree**

$2 million

**Master's
degree**

$2.3 million

**Professional
or doctorate
degree**

$2.8 million

- An interest in reading a wide variety of materials.
- A willingness to cope with conflict and adapt to change.
- An awareness of accounting, finance, and marketing fundamentals.
- A knowledge of technology and computer software as well as basic Web site design and e-commerce skills.
- An ability to solve problems creatively in team settings.
- A knowledge of research techniques and library resources.
- Well-developed written and oral communication skills.
- An understanding of both their own motivations and the motivations of others.

These competencies give people flexibility, making it easy to move from one organization to another and to successfully change career fields. What actions are you taking to develop these traits?

PERSONAL FACTORS

You may identify a satisfying career using guidance tests that measure abilities, interests, and personal qualities. Aptitude tests, interest inventories, and other types of career assessment tests are available at school career counseling offices and online.

Aptitudes are natural abilities that people possess. The ability to work well with numbers, problem-solving skills, and physical dexterity are examples of aptitudes.

Interest inventories determine the activities that give you satisfaction. These instruments measure qualities related to various types of work. People with strong social tendencies may be best suited for careers that involve dealing with people, while people with investigative interests may be best suited for careers in research areas.

DID YOU KNOW?

Prospective workers who are most desirable possess technical skills (such as computer use and financial analysis), have the ability to communicate effectively, and work well in team settings.

DEVELOPING A CAREER ACTION PLAN

For each of the following four elements of career planning, take the actions requested below:	1. *Personal and Career Interests:* What do you enjoy doing? How would you like to improve or expand your interests?	2. *Career Skills:* What type of work situation do you enjoy? How would you like to improve or expand your career skills? What new career skills do you desire?	3. *Education:* What education and career training do you desire?	4. *Employment Position:* Have you selected career fields of interest to you? What type of employment situation do you desire?
a. Describe your *current situation* in this area.				
b. State a *specific goal* you have in this area.				
c. Describe the *time frame* for accomplishing this goal.				
d. Indicate *actions to take* to achieve the goal.				

Test results will not tell you which career to pursue. However, these assessments will indicate your aptitudes and interests. Another important dimension of career selection is your personality. Do you perform best in structured or high-pressure situations, or do you prefer unstructured or creative work environments? The financial aspects of the career are also likely to be a concern.

CAREER DECISION MAKING

Changing personal and social factors will require you to continually assess your work situation. Exhibit 2–2 provides an approach to career planning, advancement, and career change. As you can see, the different entry points depend on your personal situation. For example, people established in a certain career field may start at point C (Change employment within same career field) or D (Career advancement).

Your career goals will also affect how you use this process. If you desire more responsibility on the job, for example, you may obtain advanced training or change career fields. This process is a suggested framework for planning, changing, or advancing in a career.

Want to start your career planning activities? Use Financial Planning for Life's Situations: Developing a Career Action Plan.

Exhibit **2-2**

Stages of career planning and advancement

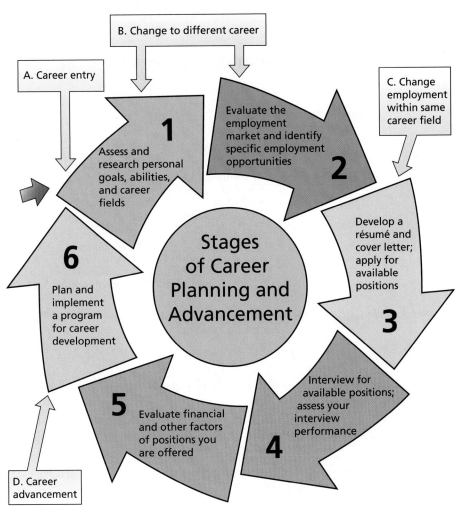

CONCEPT CHECK 2-1 ✔

1 How does a *job* differ from a *career?*
2 What opportunity costs are associated with career decisions?
3 What skills would be of value in most employment situations?

Action Application Interview several people about influences on their current employment situation. How did various personal, economic, and social factors affect their career choices and professional development?

Career Opportunities: Now and in the Future

Your job search should start with an assessment of the career choice factors shown in Exhibit 2–3.

SOCIAL INFLUENCES

Various demographic and geographic trends influence employment opportunities. Demographic trends affecting the job market include the following:

Objective 2

Evaluate the factors that influence employment opportunities.

Exhibit 2-3

Factors influencing your career opportunities

CAREER OPPORTUNITIES ARE BASED ON...

Social Influences
- Demographic trends
- Geographic trends

Economic Conditions
- Interest rates
- Inflation
- Consumer demand

Industry Trends
- Foreign competition
- Changing uses of technology

- An increase in the number of working parents expands the demand for food service and child care.

- An increase in leisure time among some segments of the population results in an increased interest in personal health, physical fitness, and recreational products and services.

- An increase in the number of older people raises the demand for travel services, health care, and retirement facilities.

- An increased demand for additional employment training increases career opportunities for teachers and trainers within business organizations.

In considering geographic areas, be sure to assess salary levels. Average incomes are high in such metropolitan areas as Boston, New York, and Chicago; however, the prices of food, housing, and other living expenses are also high.

What appears to be a big salary may actually mean a lower standard of living than in a geographic area with lower salaries and lower living costs.

Need to compare geographic cost-of-living differences for various cities? Go to **www.erieri.com.**

For example, in recent years, the cost of living for a single employee earning $30,000 annually was 60 percent higher in the District of Columbia than the national city average. In contrast, the cost of living in Fayetteville, Arkansas, was only 90 percent of the national city average.

To compare living costs and salaries in different cities, you may use the following "Geographic Buying Power" formula:

City 1
City 2
$$\frac{\text{Index number} \times \text{Salary}}{\text{Index number}} = \$ \text{ buying power}$$

For example,

Chicago
Omaha
$$\frac{123 \times \$30,000}{93.3} = \$39,550$$

A person earning $30,000 in Omaha, Nebraska, would need to earn $39,550 in Chicago to have comparable buying power.

ECONOMIC CONDITIONS

High interest rates, price increases, or decreased demand for goods and services can affect career opportunities. While you cannot eliminate the effects of economic factors on employment trends, these factors affect some businesses more than others. For example, high interest rates reduce employment in housing-related industries, since people are less likely to buy homes when interest rates are high.

DID YOU KNOW?

In recent years, nearly 80 percent of new jobs in the U.S. economy occurred in companies with fewer than 100 employees.

TRENDS IN INDUSTRY AND TECHNOLOGY

Two factors have caused a decline in manufacturing employment in our economy. First, increased competition from companies in Asia, Europe, and other regions has reduced demand for American-made products. Second, automated production methods have decreased the need for many entry-level employees in factories.

While career opportunities have dwindled in some sectors of our economy, opportunities in other sectors have grown. Service industries that are expected to have the greatest employment potential for the 21st century include

- *Computer technology*—systems analysts, computer operators, Web site developers, network operations managers, and repair personnel and service technicians for data processing equipment.
- *Health care*—medical assistants, physical therapists, home health workers, biotech analysts, laboratory technicians, registered nurses, and health care administrators.
- *Business services*—Web consultants, foreign language translators, employee benefit managers, operations consultants, and research data analysts.
- *Social services*—child care workers, elder care coordinators, family counselors, and social service agency administrators.
- *Sales and retailing*—Web promotion producers, marketing representatives, and sales managers with technical knowledge in the areas of electronics, medical products, and financial services.
- *Hospitality and food services*—resort and hotel administrators, food service managers, online customer service representatives, and meeting planners.

Salary information for various career fields in various geographic areas may be obtained at **www.salary.com**.

- *Management and human resources*—clerical supervisors, recruiters, interviewers, employee benefit administrators, and employment service workers.
- *Education*—corporate trainers, special education teachers, adult education instructors, educational administrators, and teachers for elementary, secondary, and postsecondary schools.
- *Financial services*—risk assessment managers, actuaries, e-commerce accountants, investment brokers, and others with a knowledge of accounting and taxes.

Future business demands will include expanded reading and communication skills. More and more employees are being called on to read scientific and technical journals and financial reports and to write speeches and journal articles. Your career success is likely to depend on communication skills, computer skills, and the ability to communicate in more than one language.

Sheet 6
Career area research sheet

ENTREPRENEURIAL CAREER OPTIONS

People start their own business for two main reasons: (1) reduced career opportunities in their field and (2) a desire for greater control of their work environment. Over 20 million people in the United States operate their own businesses. These range from home-based sales and consulting services to small manufacturing enterprises and technology support.

GETTING STARTED
If you are planning to start a business, consider three main issues. First, become knowledgeable about your product or service. Next, identify potential customers, select an appropriate location, and study competitors. Finally, consider your financial sources. Most entrepreneurs use a combination of personal funds and loans.

QUALITIES OF SUCCESSFUL ENTREPRENEURS
Would running your own business be an appropriate career for you? That depends on your personality and abilities. Are you a highly motivated, confident individual? Do you have the ability to manage different phases of a business? Are you someone who enjoys challenges and is willing to take risks?

In addition, skills commonly viewed as vital for entrepreneurial success include:

- Sales and marketing knowledge.
- Effective written and oral communication ability.
- An understanding of accounting and financial management of cash flows.
- An ability of motivate and coordinate the work of others.

- Efficient management of your time.
- A creative vision for success.

BUSINESS PLAN ELEMENTS
The foundation for success is a business plan, which is used to communicate the vision and purpose of an enterprise. Since the business plan contains detailed financial projections, product information, and a marketing plan, this document is a vital tool for business planning and operations. Web sites with information on business plans include www.bplans.com, www.businessplans.org, and entrepreneurs.about.com

E-COMMERCE OPTIONS
No longer is an office, store, or factory necessary. Instead, sellers or services can serve customers through online transactions. Technology has reduced barriers to entry for new competitors in many industries. In the past, an entrepreneur would have to rent a store, hire employees, obtain inventory, and advertise when starting a business. Now, a person can begin operations with a computer. Contacting suppliers, promoting the company, and filling orders can all occur online.

To obtain assistance about starting a business, contact a lawyer, local banker, accountant, or insurance agent. Additional information about running your own business may be obtained from the Small Business Administration (www.sba.gov), the Association for the Self-Employed (www.nase.org), Startup Journal (www.startupjournal.com), and SCORE (www.score.org).

CONCEPT CHECK 2-2

1 What are some demographic and economic factors that affect career opportunities?

2 How does technology affect available employment positions?

Action Application Based on a Web search or library resources, obtain articles, employment data projections, and other information about the careers with the most future potential. Prepare a report or visual presentation (slides, poster, or video) communicating the types of careers likely to be most in demand in the future.

Employment Search Strategies

Objective 3

Implement employment search strategies.

Most people have heard about job applicants who send out hundreds of résumés with very little success, while others get several offers. What are the differences between these two groups? The answer usually involves an ability to expand one's experiences and use job search techniques effectively.

OBTAINING EMPLOYMENT EXPERIENCE

A common concern among people seeking employment is a lack of work experience. Many opportunities are available to obtain work-related training.

PART-TIME EMPLOYMENT   Summer and part-time work can provide experience along with the chance to see if you enjoy a particular career field. The increased use of temporary employees has opened up opportunities to obtain experience in different career areas. More and more workers are taking advantage of temporary job assignments as a channel to a full-time position. Working as a "temp" can give you valuable experience as well as contacts in various fields of employment.

VOLUNTEER WORK   Involvement in community organizations and government agencies can provide excellent opportunities to acquire skills, establish good work habits, and make contacts. Volunteering to work at the gift shop of a museum, for example, gives you experience in retailing. You may participate in a recycling project, assist at a senior citizens' center, or help supervise youth activities at a park district. These activities will help you obtain organizational skills.

Community activities can provide experience as well as career contacts.

INTERNSHIPS   In very competitive fields, an internship will give you the experience you need to obtain employment. During an internship, you can make contacts about available jobs. Applying for an internship is similar to applying for a job. Most colleges and universities offer cooperative education and internships as part of their academic programs.

CAMPUS PROJECTS   Class assignments and campus activities are frequently overlooked as work-related experience. You can obtain valuable career skills on campus from experience in

- Managing, organizing, and coordinating people and activities as an officer or a committee chairperson of a campus organization.
- Public speaking in class, campus, and community presentations.
- Goal setting, planning, supervising, and delegating responsibility in community service and class projects.
- Financial planning and budgeting gained from organizing fund-raising projects, managing personal finances, and handling funds for campus organizations.
- Conducting research for class projects, community organizations, and campus activities.

USING CAREER INFORMATION SOURCES

Career planning and advancement, like other financial decisions, are enhanced by the use of current and relevant information. Exhibit 2–4 provides an overview of the main sources of career information.

LIBRARY MATERIALS   Most school and community libraries have extensive career information sources. The *Occupational Outlook Handbook* covers all aspects of career planning and job search and provides detailed information on jobs in various career clusters. Other helpful government resources related to careers are the *Dictionary of Occupational Titles* and the *Occupational Outlook Quarterly*.

Exhibit **2-4**

Career information sources

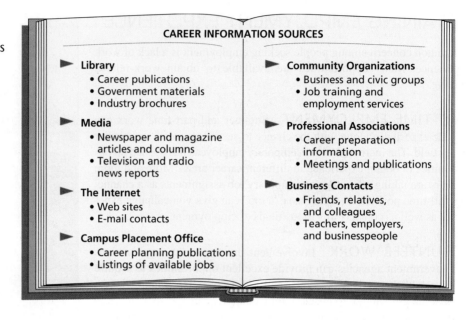

CAREER INFORMATION SOURCES

► **Library**
- Career publications
- Government materials
- Industry brochures

► **Media**
- Newspaper and magazine articles and columns
- Television and radio news reports

► **The Internet**
- Web sites
- E-mail contacts

► **Campus Placement Office**
- Career planning publications
- Listings of available jobs

► **Community Organizations**
- Business and civic groups
- Job training and employment services

► **Professional Associations**
- Career preparation information
- Meetings and publications

► **Business Contacts**
- Friends, relatives, and colleagues
- Teachers, employers, and businesspeople

MASS MEDIA CAREER INFORMATION   Most newspapers offer articles and columns about job searches and career trends. Newspapers, television reports, and radio reports also provide useful information about economic and social influences on careers.

WORLD WIDE WEB   The Internet offers a variety of information sources related to job opportunities, preparing a résumé, interviewing, and other career planning topics. See the Financial Planning for Life's Situations box on page 53 for additional information on using the Web for career planning.

 Career trends can be obtained online with the *Occupational Outlook Handbook* at www.bls.gov.oco and the *Occupational Outlook Quarterly* at **www.bls.gov/opub/ooq/ooq home.htm.**

CAREER DEVELOPMENT OFFICE   Your school probably has a career planning and placement service. This office will have materials on various career planning topics and can assist you in creating a résumé and preparing for an interview.

COMMUNITY ORGANIZATIONS   Every community has business and civic groups you can use in your career search. Public meetings featuring industry leaders and business owners provide opportunities to become acquainted with local businesspeople.

PROFESSIONAL ASSOCIATIONS   All professions have organizations to promote their career areas. These organizations include the American Marketing Association, the Independent Insurance Agents of America, the American Society of Women Accountants, and the National Association of Realtors. The *Encyclopedia of Associations* as well as a Web search can help you identify organizations representing careers that interest you.

BUSINESS CONTACTS   Professional contacts can advise you about career preparation and job opportunities. Friends, relatives, people you meet through community and professional organizations, and people you meet through school, work, church, or other activities are all potential business contacts.

networking The process of making and using contacts for obtaining and updating career information.

    Networking is the process of making and using contacts to obtain and update career information. Campus organizations, sports, and lectures can provide valuable contacts. Every person you talk to is a potential career contact who may provide career assistance.

ONLINE CAREER PLANNING

The Internet has changed the career planning process. While researching potential employment is a common use, other online activities are also affecting the way job seekers apply and interview for jobs.

CAREER PLANNING ASSISTANCE

For tips on preparing a résumé and dressing for an interview, go to www.jobhuntersbible.com, www.career journal.com, www.rileyguide.com, and jobsearch.about. com.

IDENTIFYING EMPLOYMENT OPPORTUNITIES

To research career trends and employment opportunities, go to Web sites such as www.ajb.dni.us, campus.monster. com, and www.careerbuilder.com.

POSTING YOUR RÉSUMÉ ON THE WEB

When creating a résumé for online distribution, keep the format simple and avoid e-mail attachments that some computer systems may be unable to open. Many Web sites exist for posting résumés; some of the most popular ones include www.careerpath.com, www.hotjobs.com, and www.monster.com.

CYBERINTERVIEWS

A preliminary interview may take place via e-mail. Some organizations conduct screening interviews using video conferencing. Others require that you post preliminary interview responses online. These "e-interviews" may involve questions such as: "Would you rather have structure or flexibility in your work?" and "What approach do you use to solve difficult problems?" You may be asked to respond online about your background and experience. Additional information about online interviews is available at www.careerbuilder.com and www.jobtrak.com.

SALARY AND BENEFIT INFORMATION

Comparisons of salary levels and employee benefits for various careers may be accessed at www.salary.com, salary.money.cnn.com, www.bls.gov/ncs/ebs, and www. benefitnews.com.

ONLINE CAREER ADVANCEMENT

Online courses to expand your career skills, along with information from professional organizations, may be accessed at www.ama.org (the American Marketing Association) and with a Web search for "online courses."

For effective networking: (1) prepare and practice a 30-second summary of your abilities and experience; (2) volunteer for committees and events of professional organizations; and (3) ask questions to get others to talk about themselves and their experiences.

Although contacts may not be able to hire you, if jobs are available they might refer you to the right person. They can also help you get an **informational interview,** a meeting at which you gather information about a career or an organization. When planning and using informational interviews, consider the following:

informational interview
A company visit or meeting at which one gathers information about a career or an organization.

- Prepare a list of industries and organizations for which you would like to work. Talk to family, friends, coworkers, and others for names of people you might contact.

- Prepare a list of open-ended questions that will help you obtain information about current trends in the industry and potential employment opportunities.

- Make an appointment for a 20-minute meeting; emphasize to the person that the meeting is for information only.

- Try to interact with the person at his or her place of work to gain better awareness of the work environment.

- Follow up with a thank-you note, and, if possible, send some information (such as an article) that might be of interest to your contact.

An e-mail informational "interview" may be used in some settings. Be sure your questions are open-ended and are focused on various career and industry topics. Send your e-mail request to a specific person.

Sheet 7
Making career
contacts

IDENTIFYING JOB OPPORTUNITIES

Before you apply for employment, you need to identify job openings that match your interests and abilities.

JOB ADVERTISEMENTS   Advertisements in newspapers and professional periodicals can be valuable sources of available positions. Newspapers such as the *Wall Street Journal,* the *New York Times,* the *Chicago Tribune,* and the *Los Angeles Times* have job listings covering a wide geographic area. You should also check local and regional newspapers. For opportunities in a specific career field, refer to specialized publications such as *Advertising Age, Marketing News,* the *Journal of Accountancy,* and *American Banker.* Since 80 to 90 percent of available jobs are not advertised to the general public, other job search techniques are critical.

CAREER FAIRS   Career fairs, commonly held on campuses and at convention centers, offer an opportunity to contact several firms in a short time span. Be prepared to quickly communicate your potential contributions to an organization. By making yourself memorable to the recruiter, you are likely to be called for a follow-up interview. Additional information on career fairs may be obtained at www.careerfairs.com.

EMPLOYMENT AGENCIES   Another possible source of job leads is employment agencies. These for-profit organizations match job hunters with prospective employers. Often the hiring company pays the fee charged by the employment agency; however, be careful when you are asked to pay a fee and have no guarantee of a job. Be sure you understand any contracts before signing them.

Government-supported employment services are also available. Contact your state employment service or your state department of labor for further information.

JOB CREATION   After researching a particular company or industry, present how your abilities would contribute to that organization. **Job creation** involves developing an employment position that matches your skills with the needs of an organization.

As you develop skills in areas you enjoy, you may be able to create a demand for your services. For example, a person who enjoyed researching business and economic trends was hired by a major corporation to make presentations for its managers at various company offices. Or people with an ability to design promotions and advertising might be hired by a nonprofit organization that needs to enhance its public visibility.

OTHER JOB SEARCH METHODS   Your ability to locate existing and potential employment positions is limited only by your imagination and initiative. Commonly overlooked sources of jobs include the following:

- Visit companies where you would like to work, and make face-to-face contacts. Create an impression that you are someone who can contribute. Calling or visiting before 8 a.m. or after 4 p.m. increases your chance of talking to someone who is not busy.
- Successful organizations continually look for quality employees. Telephone directories and Web searches can provide names of organizations that employ people with your qualifications.
- Search the Web for information about potential jobs and organizations that may be in search of someone with your abilities and skills.
- Talk with alumni who work in your field. Graduates who are familiar with your school and major can help you focus your career search.

DID YOU KNOW?

Campus recruiters estimate that only 20 to 30 percent of job candidates prepare for an interview.

job creation The development of an employment position that matches your skills with the needs of an organization.

DID YOU KNOW?

The first 30 seconds of a job interview are crucial. In that brief time, a judgment is usually made to determine your potential for a specific position and for success within the organization.

fyi Applying for a job or internship? The appendix for this chapter offers additional information on résumés, cover letters, and interviews.

To improve your job search efforts, work as many hours a week *getting* a job as you expect to work each week *on* the job. Maintaining an ongoing relationship with contacts can be a valuable source of information about future career opportunities.

APPLYING FOR EMPLOYMENT

Many qualified people never get the job they deserve without a presentation of skills and experiences. This process usually involves three elements.

1. The **résumé,** a summary of education, training, experience, and qualifications, provides prospective employers with an overview of your potential contributions to an organization.
2. A **cover letter** is the correspondence you send with a résumé to communicate your interest in a job and to obtain an interview.
3. The *interview* is the formal meeting used to discuss your qualifications in detail.

résumé A summary of a person's education, training, experience, and other job qualifications.

cover letter A letter that accompanies a résumé and is designed to express interest in a job and obtain an interview.

CONCEPT CHECK 2-3 ✓

1 How can a person obtain employment-related experiences without working in a job situation?
2 What types of career information sources can be helpful in identifying job opportunities?
3 How does the information in a cover letter differ from the information in a résumé?

Action Application Arrange an informational interview at a local company or with a business contact you have made. Prepare questions related to needed skills in this employment field, current trends for the industry, and future prospects for this career area.

Financial and Legal Aspects of Employment

"We would like you to work for us." When offered an employment position, you should examine a range of factors. Carefully assess the organization, the specific job, and the salary and other benefits.

ACCEPTING AN EMPLOYMENT POSITION

Before accepting a position, do additional research about the job and the company. Request information about your specific duties and job expectations. If someone currently has a similar position, ask to talk to that person. If you are replacing a person who is no longer with the company, obtain information about the circumstances of that person's departure.

THE WORK ENVIRONMENT   Investigate the work environment. The term *corporate culture* refers to management styles, work intensity, dress codes, and social interactions within an organization. For example, some companies have rigid lines of communication, while others have an open-door atmosphere. Are the values, goals, and lifestyles of current employees similar to yours? If not, you may find yourself in an uncomfortable situation.

Consider company policies and procedures for salary increases, evaluations of employees, and promotions. Talking with current workers can help you obtain this information.

Objective 4

Assess the financial and legal concerns related to obtaining employment.

FACTORS AFFECTING SALARY   Your initial salary will be influenced by your education and training, company size, and salaries for comparable positions. To ensure a fair starting salary, talk to people in similar positions and research salary levels. In addition, make sure you clearly understand company procedures and policies for raises. In recent years, increased emphasis has been placed on team results for salary increases and on rewards for expanded learning.

Performance quality and work responsibilities are the main influences on salary advances. Meet regularly with your supervisor to obtain performance evaluations and suggestions for professional growth. Communicate your desire for increased work responsibilities and greater financial rewards. Meeting and exceeding organizational expectations will usually result in salary increases.

EVALUATING EMPLOYEE BENEFITS

Escalating health care costs, changing family situations, and concerns about retirement have increased the attention given to supplementary compensation benefits.

> **DID YOU KNOW?**
>
> About 70 percent of all professionals find positions through personal contacts and networking. Responding to job ads accounts for about 15 percent of jobs.

MEETING EMPLOYEE NEEDS   In recent years, nonsalary employee benefits have expanded to meet the needs of different life situations. The increasing number of two-income and single-parent households has resulted in a greater need for child care benefits and leaves of absence. The need for elder care benefits for employees with dependent parents or grandparents has also increased. Other common employee benefits designed to meet varied life situation needs include:

- Flexible work schedules.
- Work-at-home arrangements.
- Legal assistance.
- Counseling for health, emotional, and financial needs.
- Exercise and fitness programs.

Such benefits not only enhance the quality of employees' lives but are profitable for organizations because happier, healthier employees miss fewer workdays and have a higher level of productivity.

cafeteria-style employee benefits Programs that allow workers to base their job benefits on a credit system and personal needs.

Cafeteria-style employee benefits are programs that allow workers to base their job benefits on a credit system and personal needs. Flexible selection of employee benefits has become common. A married employee with children may opt for increased life and health insurance, while a single parent may use benefit credits for child care services. The Financial Planning for Life's Situations box on page 57 can help you plan benefits for different life situations. Like any financial decision, employee benefits involve a trade-off, or opportunity cost.

Many organizations offer *flexible spending plans,* also called *expense reimbursement accounts.* This arrangement allows you to set aside part of your salary for paying medical or dependent care expenses. These funds are not subject to income or Social Security taxes. However, money not used for the specified purpose is forfeited. Therefore, you must carefully plan the amount to be designated for a flexible spending plan.

In a similar manner, a *medical-spending account (MSA)* allows people who are self-employed or work for a company with 50 or fewer employees the opportunity to pay health care costs with pretax dollars. The MSA has two components: (1) health insurance coverage with a high deductible and (2) a tax-deferred savings account for paying medical expenses. Money in this ac-

Confused by health care benefits? Chapter 11 discusses medical and disability insurance in more detail.

Financial Planning for Life's Situations

SELECTING EMPLOYEE BENEFITS

Commonly recommended employee benefits for various life situations are shown here:

Single, No Children	Young Family	Single Parent	Married, No Children	Mixed-Generation Household
• Disability income insurance • Health insurance • Retirement program • Educational assistance, such as tuition reimbursement	• Comprehensive health insurance • Life insurance • Child care services	• Health insurance • Life insurance • Disability income insurance • Dependent care benefits	• Health insurance • Retirement program • Maternity coverage and parental leave (young couple) • Long-term health care (older couple)	• Health and disability insurance • Child care services • Elder care benefits

Based on your current life situation or expectations for the future, list the employee benefits that would be most important to you.

Life Situation	Desired Employee Benefits

count may be taken out for other uses; however, the funds are then taxed, along with an additional 15 percent tax penalty. While MSAs have tax-saving implications, the high deductible may not be affordable for many households.

When matching dependent health care needs and medical insurance plans, consider the following:

• Types of services available and location of health care providers.

• Direct costs (insurance premiums) to you.

• Anticipated out-of-pocket costs (deductibles and coinsurance amounts).

As people live longer, profit-sharing plans and retirement programs are increasing in importance. In addition to Social Security benefits, some employers contribute to a pension plan. *Vesting* is the point at which retirement payments made by the organization on your behalf belong to you even if you no longer work for the organization. Vesting schedules vary, but all qualified plans (those for which an employer may deduct contributions to the plan for tax purposes) must (1) be 100 percent vested on completion of five years of service or (2) have 20 percent vesting after three years and full vesting, in stages, after seven years. Vesting refers only to the employer's pension contributions; employee contributions belong to the employees regardless of the length of their service with the organization.

Workers are commonly allowed to make personal contributions to company-sponsored retirement programs. These plans usually involve a variety of investments, making it easy for employees to create a diversified portfolio for their retirement funds.

Child care facilities provided by employers create improved career flexibility.

57

Financial Planning Calculations

TAX-EQUIVALENT EMPLOYEE BENEFITS

Employee benefits that are nontaxable have a higher financial value than you may realize. A $100 employee benefit on which you are taxed is not worth as much as a nontaxable $100 benefit. This formula is used to calculate the *tax-equivalent value* of a nontaxable benefit:

$$\frac{\text{Value of the benefit}}{(1 - \text{Tax rate})}$$

For example, receiving a life insurance policy with a nontaxable annual premium of $350 is comparable to receiving a taxable employee benefit worth $486 if you are in the 28 percent tax bracket. This tax-equivalent amount is calculated as follows:

$$\frac{\$350}{(1 - 0.28)} = \frac{\$350}{0.72} = \$486$$

A variation of this formula, which would give the *after-tax value* of an employee benefit, is

$$\text{Taxable value of the benefit } (1 - \text{Tax rate})$$

For the above example, the calculation would be

$$\$486(1 - 0.28) = \$486(0.72) = \$350$$

In other words, a taxable benefit with a value of $486 would have an after-tax value of $350 since you would have to pay $136 ($486 × 0.28) in tax on the benefit.

These calculations can help you assess and compare different employee benefits within a company or in considering different jobs. Remember to also consider the value of employee benefits in terms of your personal and family needs and goals.

COMPARING BENEFITS Two methods used to assess the monetary value of employee benefits are market value calculations and future value calculations.

Market value calculations determine the specific monetary value of employee benefits—the cost of the benefits if you had to pay for them. For example, you may view the value of one week's vacation as 1/52 of your annual salary, or you may view the value of a life insurance benefit as what it would cost you to obtain the same coverage. You can use this method to determine the difference between two job offers with different salaries and employee benefits.

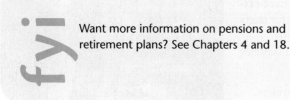

Want more information on pensions and retirement plans? See Chapters 4 and 18.

Future value calculations, as discussed in Chapter 1, enable you to assess the long-term worth of employee benefits such as pension programs and retirement plans. For example, you can compare the future value of payments contributed to a company retirement fund to that of other saving and investment options.

You should also take tax considerations into account when you assess employment benefits. A *tax-exempt* benefit is one on which you won't have to pay income tax, but a *tax-deferred* benefit requires the payment of income tax at some future time, such as at retirement. When assessing employment compensation and benefits, consider their taxability, since an untaxed benefit of lower value may be worth more than a benefit of higher value that is subject to taxation (see the Financial Planning Calculations box).

Sheet 12

Employees benefit comparison

YOUR EMPLOYMENT RIGHTS

Employees have legal rights both during the hiring process and on the job. For example, an employer cannot refuse to hire a woman or terminate her employment because of pregnancy, nor can it force her to go on leave at an arbitrary point during her pregnancy. In addition, a woman who stops working due to pregnancy must get full credit for previous service, accrued retirement benefits, and accumulated seniority. Other employment rights include the following:

- A person may not be discriminated against in the employment selection process on the basis of age, race, color, religion, sex, marital status, national origin, or mental or physical disabilities.
- Minimum-wage and overtime pay legislation apply to individuals in certain work settings.
- Worker's compensation (for work-related injury or illness), Social Security, and unemployment insurance are required benefits.

> **DID YOU KNOW?**
>
> More and more employers are using credit reports as hiring tools. Federal law requires that job applicants be told if credit histories are being used in the hiring process.

CONCEPT CHECK 2-4

1 How does a person's life situation determine the importance of certain employee benefits?

2 What methods can be used to measure the monetary value of employee benefits?

Action Application Talk to people employed in various types of organizations. Prepare a list of the most common types of employee benefits received by workers.

Long-Term Career Development

A job is for today, but a career can be for a lifetime. Will you always enjoy the work you do today? Will you be successful in the career you select? These questions cannot be answered right away; however, certain skills and attitudes can lead to a fulfilling work life.

Every day you can perform duties that contribute to your career success. Communicating and working well with others will enhance your chances for financial advancement and promotion. Flexibility and openness to new ideas will expand your abilities, knowledge, and career potential.

Develop efficient work habits. Use lists, goal setting, and time management techniques. Combine increased productivity with quality. All of your work activities should reflect your best performance. This extra effort will be recognized and rewarded.

Finally, learn to anticipate problems and areas for action. Creativity and a willingness to assist others can help the entire organization and contribute to your work enjoyment and career growth.

Objective 5

Analyze the techniques for career growth and advancement.

TRAINING OPPORTUNITIES

Many technology-work situations did not exist a few years ago. Many of the job skills you will need in the future have yet to be created. Your desire for increased education is a primary determinant of your career success and financial advancement. Continue to learn about new technology and the global economy.

Various methods for updating and expanding your knowledge are available. Formal methods include company programs, seminars offered by professional organizations, and graduate and advanced college courses. Many companies encourage and pay for continuing education.

Informal methods for updating and expanding your knowledge include reading and discussion with colleagues. Newspapers, news magazines, business periodicals, professional journals, and Web sites offer a wealth of information on business, economic, and social trends. Informal meetings with coworkers and associates from other companies

Career training can take place in both formal and informal settings.

mentor An experienced employee who serves as a teacher and counselor for a less experienced person in a career field.

Sheet 13
Career development and advancement

are a valuable source of current career information.

CAREER PATHS AND ADVANCEMENT

As with other financial decisions, career choices must be reevaluated in light of changing values, goals, economic conditions, and social trends. As Exhibit 2–5 shows, you will evolve through a series of career stages, each with specific tasks and challenges. A successful technique for coping with the anxieties associated with career development is to gain the support of an established person in your field. A **mentor** is an experienced employee who serves as a teacher and counselor for a less experienced person in a career field. A relationship with a mentor can provide such benefits as personalized training, access to influential people, and emotional support during difficult times.

Your efforts to attract a mentor start with excellent performance. Show initiative, be creative, and be alert to meeting the needs of others. Maintain visibility and display a desire to learn and grow by asking questions and volunteering for new assignments.

A prospective mentor should be receptive to assisting others and to helping them grow in both the technical and social areas of a career. Many organizations have formal mentor programs with an experienced employee assigned to oversee the career development of a new employee. Some mentor relationships involve retired individuals who desire to share their knowledge and experience.

CHANGING CAREERS

At some time in their lives, most workers change jobs. About 10 million career moves occur each year. People change jobs to obtain a better or different position within the same career field or to move into a new career field. Changing jobs may be more difficult than selecting the first job. Unless their present situation is causing mental stress or physical illness, most people are unwilling to exchange the security of an existing position for the uncertainty of an unfamiliar one.

The following may be indications that it is time to move on:

- Low motivation toward your current work.

- Physical or emotional distress caused by your job.

- Consistently poor performance evaluations.

- A lack of social interactions with coworkers.

- Limited opportunity for salary or position advancement.

- A poor relationship with your superior.

A decision to change careers may require minor alterations in your life (such as going from retail sales to industrial sales), or it may mean extensive retraining and starting at an entry level in a new field. As with every other financial decision, no exact formula

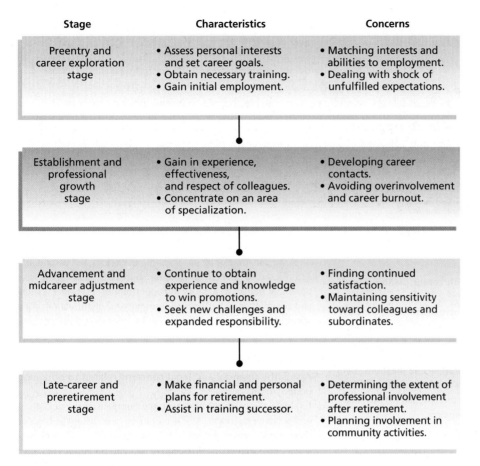

Stage	Characteristics	Concerns
Preentry and career exploration stage	• Assess personal interests and set career goals. • Obtain necessary training. • Gain initial employment.	• Matching interests and abilities to employment. • Dealing with shock of unfulfilled expectations.
Establishment and professional growth stage	• Gain in experience, effectiveness, and respect of colleagues. • Concentrate on an area of specialization.	• Developing career contacts. • Avoiding overinvolvement and career burnout.
Advancement and midcareer adjustment stage	• Continue to obtain experience and knowledge to win promotions. • Seek new challenges and expanded responsibility.	• Finding continued satisfaction. • Maintaining sensitivity toward colleagues and subordinates.
Late-career and preretirement stage	• Make financial and personal plans for retirement. • Assist in training successor.	• Determining the extent of professional involvement after retirement. • Planning involvement in community activities.

Exhibit **2-5**

Stages of career development: characteristics and concerns

exists for deciding whether you should make a career change. However, follow these guidelines. First, carefully assess the financial and personal costs and benefits of changing careers in relation to your needs and goals and those of your household. Giving up benefits such as health insurance may be costly to a family, but the expanded career opportunities in a new field may be worth the trade-off. Then determine whether a career change will serve your needs and goals and those of other household members.

In many industries, job security is a thing of the past. Company mergers, downsizing, and economic conditions may result in forced career changes. Layoffs cause emotional and financial stress for individuals and families. To cope with job termination while seeking new employment, counselors recommend that you

- Maintain appropriate eating, sleep, and exercise habits.

- Get involved in family and community activities; new career contacts are possible anywhere.

- Improve your career skills through personal study, formal classes, or volunteer work.

- Target your job search to high-growth industries or small businesses.

- Consider opportunities with nonprofit organizations, government agencies, temporary employment, or consultant work.

- Target your skills and experience to the needs of an organization.

CONCEPT CHECK 2-5

1 What types of activities would you recommend for people who desire career advancement and professional growth?

2 What factors should a person consider before changing jobs or career fields?

Action Application Create a list of competencies, skills, and technical abilities that you would like to develop over the next few years. What actions will you take to obtain those proficiencies?

SUMMARY OF OBJECTIVES

Objective 1

Describe the activities associated with career planning and advancement.

Career planning and advancement involve the following stages and activities: (1) assess and research personal goals, abilities, and career fields; (2) evaluate the employment market and identify specific employment opportunities; (3) develop a résumé and cover letter for use in applying for available positions; (4) interview for available positions; (5) evaluate financial and other elements of the positions you are offered; and (6) plan and implement a program for career development.

Objective 2

Evaluate the factors that influence employment opportunities.

Consider the selection of a career in relation to personal abilities, interests, experience, training, and goals; social influences affecting employment, such as demographic trends; changing economic conditions; and industrial and technological trends.

Objective 3

Implement employment search strategies.

For successful career planning and development, consider doing the following. Obtain employment or related experiences by working part-time or by participating in campus and community activities. Use career information sources to learn about employment fields and identify job opportunities. Prepare a résumé and cover letter that effectively present your qualifications for a specific employment position. Practice interview skills that project enthusiasm and competence.

Objective 4

Assess the financial and legal concerns related to obtaining employment.

Evaluate the work environment and compensation package of prospective employers. Assess employee benefits on the basis of their market value, future value, and taxability and your personal needs and goals. Prospective and current employees have legal rights with regard to fair hiring practices and equal opportunity on the job.

Objective 5

Analyze the techniques for career growth and advancement.

Informal and formal education and training opportunities are available to foster professional development and facilitate career changes.

KEY FORMULAS

Page	Topic	Formula
48	Geographic buying power	Geographic Buying Power $= \dfrac{\text{City 1}}{\text{City 2}} \dfrac{\text{Index number} \times \text{Salary}}{\text{Index number}}$ *Example:* $= \dfrac{123 \times 50{,}000}{98.8}$ $= \$62{,}247$
58	Tax-equivalent employee benefits	Tax-equivalent of a nontaxable benefit $= \dfrac{\text{Value of the benefit}}{(1 - \text{Tax rate})}$ *Example:* $= \dfrac{\$1{,}250}{(1 - 0.28)}$ $= \$1{,}736$

FINANCIAL PLANNING PROBLEMS

1. *Determining the Future Value of Education.* Jenny Franklin estimates that as a result of completing her master's degree, she will earn $6,000 a year more for the next 40 years. (Obj. 1)

    a. What would be the total amount of these additional earnings?

    b. What would be the *future value* of these additional earnings based on an annual interest rate of 6 percent? (Use Table 1–B in the Chapter 1 Appendix.)

2. *Comparing Living Costs.* Brad Edwards is earning $42,000 a year in a city located in the Midwest. He is interviewing for a position in a city with a cost of living 12 percent higher than where he currently lives. What would be the minimum salary he would need at his new job to maintain the same standard of living? (Obj. 2)

3. *Calculating Future Value of Salary.* During a job interview, Pam Thompson is offered a salary of $23,000. The company gives annual raises of 6 percent. What would be Pam's salary during her fifth year on the job? (Obj. 3)

4. *Computing Future Value.* Calculate the future value of a retirement account in which you deposit $2,000 a year for 30 years with an annual interest rate of 8 percent. (Use the tables in the Chapter 1 Appendix.) (Obj. 4)

5. *Comparing Taxes for Employee Benefits.* Which of the following employee benefits has the greater value? Use the formula given in the Financial Planning Calculations box on page 58 to compare these benefits. (Assume a 28 percent tax rate.) (Obj. 4)

    a. A nontaxable pension contribution of $4,300 or the use of a company car with a taxable value of $6,325.

    b. A life insurance policy with a taxable value of $450 or a nontaxable increase in health insurance coverage valued at $340.

6. *Comparing Employment Offers.* Bill Mason is considering two job offers. Job 1 pays a salary of $36,500 with $4,500 of nontaxable employee benefits. Job 2 pays a salary of $34,700 and $6,120 of nontaxable benefits. Which position would have the higher monetary value? Use a 28 percent tax rate. (Obj. 4)

FINANCIAL PLANNING ACTIVITIES

1. *Researching Career Planning Activities.* Interview a person who recently made a major career change. What personal and economic factors influenced this decision? What specific career planning activities did the person use? (Obj. 1)

2. *Comparing Career Alternatives.* Using Sheet 6 in the *Personal Financial Planner,* research two careers you might consider. Compare employment requirements, duties on the job, and future potential. (Obj. 2)

3. *Searching Employment Opportunities on the Internet.* Using Web sites such at www.ajb.dni.us or www.career-mosiac.com (or Web search engines), obtain information about positions available in your areas of interest. (Obj. 3)

4. *Searching the Web for Benefit Information.* Using a Web search or the library, obtain information about various employee benefits such as health insurance, retirement plans, child care, life insurance, and tuition reimbursement. (Obj. 4)

5. *Analyzing Employee Benefits.* Using Sheet 12 in the *Personal Financial Planner,* obtain information about various employee benefits from current or prospective employers. (Obj. 4)

6. *Obtaining Career Advancement Information.* Talk with several people employed in various types of careers (large company, international business, individual entrepreneur, nonprofit, or government). Prepare an outline or other visual presentation describing the training and professional development activities they have found most valuable. (Obj. 5)

7. *Creating a Personal Data Sheet.* Using Sheet 8 in the *Personal Financial Planner,* plan the content and format for a résumé that you might use in the near future. (Ch. Appendix.)

8. *Preparing for an Interview.* Based on library research, a Web search, and experiences of others, obtain information about effective interviewing techniques. Prepare a video that presents appropriate and inappropriate actions one might take when preparing for and participating in an interview. (Ch. Appendix.)

INTERNET CONNECTION

Comparing Online Career Advice

Conduct an Internet search to locate two Web sites that provide information on some career planning topic, such as résumés, interviews, career portfolios, or changing careers.

Career Planning Topic _____

Web site 1: _____

Summary of findings _____

_____

_____

_____

Web site 2: _____

Summary of findings _____

_____

_____

_____

What similarities and differences exist in the advice given by these Web sites? How might this information assist you in your career planning activities?

FINANCIAL PLANNING CASE

Economic Uncertainty and Cyber Job Hunting

Lower consumer spending. High-level corporate mismanagement. Overspeculation in technology companies. Political instability in many areas of the world.

These factors and others resulted in higher levels of unemployment. Uncertainty of employment in many sectors of the economy also created financial turmoil in many households.

Matt Khan has worked for Collins Technology since finishing college. His professional growth in the organization was impressive. Matt developed new systems to reduce costs and also trained new managers in his division. He also was a product development team leader working with people from manufacturing, sales, finance, and human resources.

However, the stability of Matt's position has changed as new quality control software took over some of the tasks that he supervised. As several of the other managers were let go or reassigned to other locations, Matt realized that his future was uncertain. When faced with the possibility of a job loss, financial advisers recommend various actions:

- Review household spending and set priorities.
- Increase savings to have money in an emergency fund.

- Make plans for continuation of health care coverage.
- Reduce the use of credit.

When Matt decided to look for new employment opportunities, he realized that this job search would be different than seven years ago. While networking is still important, *e-networking* using e-mail and online bulletin boards will be crucial. While his résumé may be distributed by traditional mail, Matt will also need to have scannable, plain text, and e-mail versions of his résumé.

Questions

1. What actions could Matt take to ensure future employment potential?

2. Based on information at www.rileyguide.com and www.monster.com, describe actions Matt might take to assess and apply for employment positions using the Internet.

3. What would you recommend to Matt to minimize his financial difficulties while in transition between jobs?

The Job Search

After completing various courses and obtaining some work experience, Debra Chin decided to obtain a job for which she had prepared. A marketing position was the focus of Debra's job search.

Debra's preparation included her academic studies and jobs in various fields. In addition, she took a variety of actions to identify and research available jobs.

Questions

1. For Debra, you, and others, what factors commonly affect a person's career goal?

2. Describe skills and experiences that create the foundation for a person's preparation for various careers.

3. What career information sources might be valuable when researching and applying for employment positions?

4. What would you recommend when preparing for an interview?

YOUR PERSONAL FINANCIAL PLANNER IN ACTION

Planning Your Career

Your selection of a career and professional development activities will influence many aspects of your life, including financial resource availability, leisure time, living location, and acquaintances.

Your Short-Term Financial Planning Activities	Resources
1. Explore various career areas in relation to your interests, abilities, and goals.	PFP Sheets 6, 7 www.mapping-your-future.org at www.ajb.dni.us www.hotjobs.com
2. Develop a résumé and sample cover letter for use in a job search.	PFP Sheets 8, 9 www.monster.com www.rileyguide.com www.careerjournal.com
3. Research prospective employers and develop a strategy for effective interviewing.	PFP Sheets 10, 11 www.jobhuntersbible.com www.careerbuilder.com www.businessweek.com/careers
Your Long-Term Financial Planning Activities	
1. Analyze employee benefits based on your current and possible future financial needs.	PFP Sheet 12 www.benefitnews.com www.dol.gov/ebsa
2. Develop a plan of action for professional development. Consider starting your own business.	PFP Sheet 13 www.sba.gov www.inc.com www.startupjournal.com

CONTINUING CASE

Career Decisions

Life Situation

Single
Age 22
Starting a career
No dependents

Financial Data

Monthly income $2,600
Living expenses $2,180
Assets $8,200
Liabilities $3,470
Emergency fund $530

In her current employment position, as a sales representative for a clothing manufacturer, Pam encounters a variety of interesting daily activities. While her work is not directly related to her fields of study in college, she does make use of various communication, research, technology, and financial analysis skills. Pam especially enjoys the interaction with clients and helping them select inventory and plan various retail promotions.

Pam's income is based on commission, which can result in uncertainty in her personal financial planning. When consumer spending is strong, she earns a good income. However, when buying activities slow, Pam feels the stress of extra effort to generate an income to cover basic living expenses.

Questions

1. Identify the positive and negative aspects of Pam's current career situation.

2. What are some actions you might suggest Pam consider related to current and future career development activities?

3. Describe how Pam might use various sections of *Personal Financial Planner* sheets 6–13 for her current and future career planning activities.

2 APPENDIX: Résumés, Cover Letters, and Interviews

Developing a Résumé

Every business must present its product or service to potential customers in an effective manner. In the same way, you must market yourself to prospective employers by developing a résumé, creating a letter to obtain an interview, and interviewing for available positions.

RÉSUMÉ ELEMENTS

A résumé is a summary of your education, training, experience, and other job qualifications. This personal-information sheet is vital in your employment search. The main components of a résumé are as follows.

1. THE PERSONAL DATA SECTION Start with your name, address, and telephone number. Both a school and home address and telephone number may be appropriate. Do not include your birth date, sex, height, and weight in a résumé unless they apply to specific job qualifications.

2. THE CAREER OBJECTIVE SECTION Be sure to clearly focus your objective to each specific employment situation. A vague career objective will be meaningless to a prospective employer, and one that is too specific might prevent you from being considered for another position within the organization. Your career objective may be omitted from the résumé and best communicated in your cover letter. As an alternative, consider a "Summary" section with a synopsis of your distinctive capabilities.

3. THE EDUCATION SECTION This section should include dates, schools attended, fields of study, and degrees earned. Courses directly related to your career field may be highlighted. If your grade point average is exceptionally high, include it to demonstrate your ability to excel.

4. THE EXPERIENCE SECTION In this section, list organizations, dates of involvement, and responsibilities for all previous employment, work-related school activities, and community service. Highlight computer skills, technical abilities, and other specific competencies that are in demand by organizations. Use action verbs to communicate how your experience and talents will benefit the organization (see Exhibit 2–A). Focus this information on results and accomplishments, not characteristics.

5. THE RELATED INFORMATION SECTION List honors or awards to communicate your ability to produce quality work. List other interests and activities if they relate to your career. However, avoid a long list of hobbies and other interests, which can give the impression that work is not your top priority.

Exhibit **2-A**

Action verbs to effectively communicate career-related experiences

- Achieved...
- Administered...
- Coordinated...
- Created...
- Designed...
- Developed...
- Directed...
- Edited...
- Initiated...
- Implemented...

- Managed...
- Monitored...
- Organized...
- Planned...
- Produced...
- Researched...
- Summarized...
- Supervised...
- Trained...
- Updated...

6. THE REFERENCES SECTION   In this section, list people who can verify your skills and competencies. These individuals may be teachers, previous employers, supervisors, or business colleagues. Be sure to obtain permission from the people you plan to use as references. References are usually not included in a résumé; however, you will need to have this information available when a prospective employer requests it.

DID YOU KNOW?

The executive search firm of Christian and Timbers reported that almost a quarter of 7,000 resumes were inaccurate, with most exaggerating easy-to-check details such as years on a job and college degrees. As a result, most companies conduct background checks to verify information.

TYPES OF RÉSUMÉS

Three commonly used types of résumés are the chronological résumé, the functional résumé, and the targeted résumé. The *chronological résumé* (see Exhibit 2–B) presents your education, work experience, and other information in a reverse-time sequence (the most recent item first). This type of résumé is most appropriate for people with a continuous school and work record. Many people find it to be the best vehicle for presenting their career qualifications.

The *functional résumé* (see Exhibit 2–C) is suggested for people with diverse skills and time gaps in their experience. This résumé emphasizes your abilities and skills in categories such as communication, supervision, project planning, human relations, and research. Each section provides information about experiences and qualifications rather than dates, places, and job titles. This type of résumé is especially appropriate if you are changing careers or your most recent experiences are not directly related to the available position.

You may want to develop a *targeted résumé,* that is, a résumé for a specific job. Such a résumé highlights the capabilities and experiences most appropriate to the available position. The format may be similar to the chronological or functional résumé except it includes a very specific career objective. The targeted résumé takes extra time and research to prepare; however, this effort increases your opportunity for obtaining an interview.

E-résumés, used when applying for a job online, should consider the following factors:

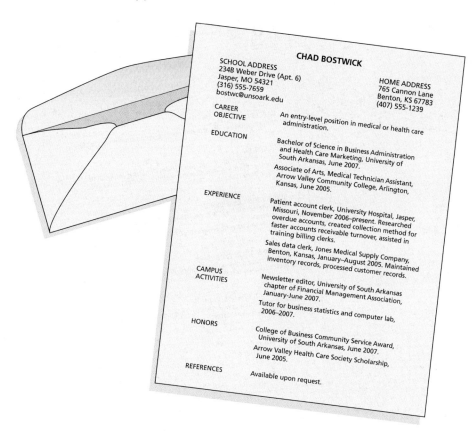

Exhibit **2-B**

A chronological résumé

CHAD BOSTWICK

SCHOOL ADDRESS
234B Weber Drive (Apt. 6)
Jasper, MO 54321
(316) 555-7659
bostwc@unsoark.edu

HOME ADDRESS
765 Cannon Lane
Benton, KS 67783
(407) 555-1239

CAREER OBJECTIVE
An entry-level position in medical or health care administration.

EDUCATION
Bachelor of Science in Business Administration and Health Care Marketing, University of South Arkansas, June 2007.

Associate of Arts, Medical Technician Assistant, Arrow Valley Community College, Arlington, Kansas, June 2005.

EXPERIENCE
Patient account clerk, University Hospital, Jasper, Missouri, November 2006–present. Researched overdue accounts, created collection method for faster accounts receivable turnover, assisted in training billing clerks.

Sales data clerk, Jones Medical Supply Company, Benton, Kansas, January–August 2005. Maintained inventory records, processed customer records.

CAMPUS ACTIVITIES
Newsletter editor, University of South Arkansas chapter of Financial Management Association, January–June 2007.

Tutor for business statistics and computer lab, 2006–2007.

HONORS
College of Business Community Service Award, University of South Arkansas, June 2007.

Arrow Valley Health Care Society Scholarship, June 2005.

REFERENCES
Available upon request.

- Keep the format simple; avoid bold type, underlines, italics, and tabs.
- Do not use attached files that may be difficult to open.
- Résumés posted on the Internet may be viewed by your current employer, whom you may not want to know about your job search.
- An Internet résumé is less personal than a printed one or a phone call; most jobs are obtained offline through ads, job fairs, and networking.

RÉSUMÉ PREPARATION

No formula exists for preparing an effective résumé; however, a résumé must be presented in a professional manner. Many candidates are disqualified due to poor résumés. Personal computers and laser printers make the résumé design process easier. Many photocopy businesses specialize in preparing and reproducing résumés.

Limit your résumé to one page. Send a two-page résumé only if you have enough material to fill three pages; then use the most valid information to prepare an impressive two-page presentation.

Use a format that highlights how your experiences will contribute to the company's needs. Underline or italicize items, if appropriate. Remember, résumés are usually skimmed very quickly; some companies use scanners to check for key words related to education and technical expertise.

Words and phrases that commonly impress prospective employers include "foreign language skills," "computer experience," "achievement," "research experience," "flexible," "team projects," and "overseas study" or "overseas experience."

For best results, seek guidance in preparing and evaluating your résumé. Counselors, the campus placement office, and friends may find errors and suggest improvements.

Sheet 8
Résumé worksheet

Exhibit **2-C**

A functional résumé

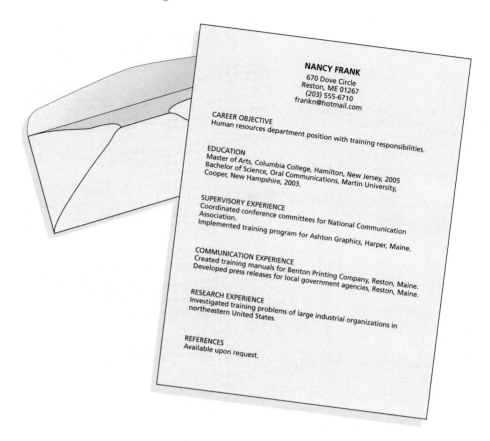

NANCY FRANK
670 Dove Circle
Reston, ME 01267
(203) 555-6710
frankn@hotmail.com

CAREER OBJECTIVE
Human resources department position with training responsibilities.

EDUCATION
Master of Arts, Columbia College, Hamilton, New Jersey, 2005
Bachelor of Science, Oral Communications, Martin University,
Cooper, New Hampshire, 2003.

SUPERVISORY EXPERIENCE
Coordinated conference committees for National Communication
Association.
Implemented training program for Ashton Graphics, Harper, Maine.

COMMUNICATION EXPERIENCE
Created training manuals for Benton Printing Company, Reston, Maine.
Developed press releases for local government agencies, Reston, Maine.

RESEARCH EXPERIENCE
Investigated training problems of large industrial organizations in
northeastern United States.

REFERENCES
Available upon request.

RÉSUMÉ DELIVERY METHODS

Traditionally, résumés have been mailed or hand delivered. When presenting a résumé in person, you have an opportunity to observe the company environment and make a positive impression about your career potential. Electronic résumé delivery may be done by fax, by e-mail, or posting on Web sites such as www.monster.com and www.resumemailman.com.

RÉSUMÉ ALTERNATIVES

Thousands of résumés are sent each day. To stand out, applicants have tried various creative approaches. Employers report receiving résumés in the form of comic strips, "wanted" posters, advertisements, and menus; résumés attached to balloons, pizzas, and plants; and résumés on video and CD-ROMs. Some of these efforts were effective; however, most employers view them as frivolous. A creative approach may be appropriate in fields such as advertising, journalism, photography, and public relations.

TARGETED APPLICATION LETTER   Instead of a résumé, some career counselors recommend a *targeted application letter* describing specific experiences and accomplishments. After researching a position and company, communicate how your specific skills will benefit the organization. Within your letter, present a bulleted list with short descriptions of your specific experiences that relate to the available position.

CAREER PORTFOLIO   You might also create a *career portfolio* containing tangible evidence of your experience and competencies. This printed or digital presentation (on Web site or CD-ROM) could include:

- Résumé, cover letter, answers to sample interview questions, and letters of recommendation.
- Sample reports, presentation materials, photos, research findings, and published articles from school projects or other activities.
- Web site designs, creative works from school activities or previous employment, such as product designs, ads, packages, promotions, video clips, sales results, and financial data.
- News articles of community activities or other experiences in which you have participated.

Need additional information about preparing a résumé? Go to **www.monster.com.**

A professionally prepared career portfolio can effectively communicate your initiative and distinctiveness.

Creating a Cover Letter

Your résumé must be targeted to a specific organization and job. A *cover letter* is designed to express your interest in a job and help you obtain an interview. This letter accompanies your résumé and usually consists of an introductory paragraph, one or two development paragraphs, and a concluding paragraph.

INTRODUCTION

The introductory paragraph should get the reader's attention. Indicate your reason for writing by referring to the job or type of employment in which you are interested. Communicate what you have to offer the company based on your experience and qualifications. If applicable, mention the name of the person who referred you to this organization.

DEVELOPMENT

The development section should highlight the aspects of your background that specifically qualify you for the job. Refer the employer to your résumé for more details. At this point, elaborate on experiences and training. Connect your skills and background to specific organizational needs.

CONCLUSION

The concluding paragraph should request action from the employer. Ask for the opportunity to discuss your qualifications and potential with the employer in more detail; in other words, get an interview! Include information to make contacting you convenient, such as telephone numbers and the times when you are available. Close your letter by summarizing how you can benefit the organization.

You should create a personalized cover letter (see Exhibit 2–D) for each position for which you apply. A poorly prepared cover letter usually guarantees rejection. Be sure to address your correspondence to the appropriate person in the organization.

A résumé and cover letter are your ticket to the interview. You may possess outstanding qualifications and career potential, but you need an interview to communicate this information. The time, effort, and care you take to present yourself on paper will help you achieve your career goal.

Sheet 9
Planning a cover letter

Exhibit **2-D**

Sample cover letter

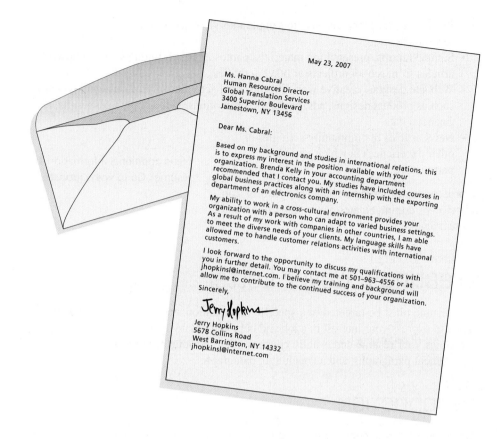

May 23, 2007

Ms. Hanna Cabral
Human Resources Director
Global Translation Services
3400 Superior Boulevard
Jamestown, NY 13456

Dear Ms. Cabral:

Based on my background and studies in international relations, this is to express my interest in the position available with your organization. Brenda Kelly in your accounting department recommended that I contact you. My studies have included courses in global business practices along with an internship with the exporting department of an electronics company.

My ability to work in a cross-cultural environment provides your organization with a person who can adapt to varied business settings. As a result of my work with companies in other countries, I am able to meet the diverse needs of your clients. My language skills have allowed me to handle customer relations activities with international customers.

I look forward to the opportunity to discuss my qualifications with you in further detail. You may contact me at 501–963–4556 or at jhopkinsl@internet.com. I believe my training and background will allow me to contribute to the continued success of your organization.

Sincerely,

Jerry Hopkins

Jerry Hopkins
5678 Collins Road
West Barrington, NY 14332
jhopkinsl@internet.com

The Job Interview

"Why should we hire you?" This may be an unexpected question; however, you may need to answer it. The interview phase of job hunting is limited to candidates who possess the specific qualifications the employer wants. Being invited for an interview puts you closer to receiving a job offer.

PREPARING FOR THE INTERVIEW

Prepare for your interview by obtaining additional information about your prospective employer. The best sources of company information include

- Library resources such as annual reports or recent articles.
- Internet searches of company and industry information.
- Observations during company visits.
- Observations of company products in stores or other places.
- Informal interviews with current and past employees.
- Discussions with people knowledgeable about the company or industry.

Sheet 10
Researching a prospective employer

During your research, try to obtain information about the company's past and current activities. Facts about its operations, competitors, recent successes, planned expansion, and personnel policies will be helpful when you discuss your potential contributions to the company.

Another preinterview activity is preparing questions such as

- What training opportunities are available to employees who desire advancement?
- What qualities do your most successful employees possess?

- What do your employees like best about working here?
- What actions of competitors are likely to affect the company in the near future?

Also, prepare questions about your specific interests and about the particular organization with which you are interviewing. Request information about company policies and employee benefits.

Successful interviewing requires practice. By using a video recorder or working with friends, you can develop the confidence needed for effective interviewing. Work to organize ideas, speak clearly and calmly, and communicate enthusiasm. Prepare specific answers regarding your strengths. Many campus organizations and career placement offices offer opportunities for practice by conducting mock interviews. Prepare concise answers for specific questions (see Exhibit 2–E) explaining how your experience will contribute to the future of the company. If appropriate, plan to bring photos or other evidence of your past efforts.

Sheet 11
Preparing for
an interview

As you get ready for the interview, keep in mind that proper dress and grooming are important. Current employees are the best source of information about how to dress. In general, dress more conservatively than employees do. A business suit is usually appropriate for both men and women. Avoid trendy and casual styles, and don't wear too much jewelry. Confirm the time and location of the interview. Take copies of your résumé, your reference list, and a small notebook for writing down ideas during the interview. Plan to arrive about 10 minutes earlier than your appointed time.

THE INTERVIEW PROCESS

A *screening interview* is an initial, usually brief, meeting with applicants that reduces the pool of job candidates. In the screening interview, interviewees are processed on the basis of overall impression and a few general questions. Screening interviews may be conducted on college campuses by corporate recruiters. Success qualifies you for closer consideration by the employer.

Organizations are expanding the use of online screening interviews in which applicants provide basic personal and background information. In addition, these "e-interviews" may ask you to respond to questions such as "Would you rather have structure or flexibility in your work?" and "What approach do you use to solve difficult problems?" Computerized interviewing may also be used to test an applicant's ability in job-related situations such as those that a bank teller or retail clerk might encounter.

Once you are judged to be a strong candidate for a job, your next interview can last from one hour to several days. The *selection interview,* which is reserved for the finalists in the job search, may involve a series of activities, including responses to questions, meetings with several people on the staff, and a seminar presentation.

The first part of the selection interview usually occurs in an informal setting. This arrangement is designed to help you relax and to establish rapport. Next, a brief discussion of the available position may take place. The main part of the interview involves questions to assess your abilities, potential, and personality. Interviews may include situations or questions to determine how you react under pressure. Remain calm. Answer clearly in a controlled manner. In the last portion of the interview, you are usually given an opportunity to ask questions.

DID YOU KNOW?

In *situational interviewing,* candidates for a sales position may be asked to interact with a potential customer. This and other hypothetical circumstances require the prospective employee to resolve a problematic situation that might happen on the job.

Exhibit **2-E**
Common interview
questions

Education and Training Questions

What education and training qualify you for this job?

Why are you interested in working for this company?

In addition to going to school, what activities have helped you to expand your interests and knowledge?

What did you like best about school?

What did you like least?

Work and Other Experience Questions

In what types of situations have you done your best work?

Describe the supervisors who motivated you most.

Which of your past accomplishments are you most proud of?

Have you ever had to coordinate the activities of several people?

Describe some people whom you have found difficult to work with.

Describe a situation in which your determination helped you achieve a specific goal.

What situations frustrate you?

Other than past jobs, what experiences have helped prepare you for this job?

What methods do you consider best for motivating employees?

Personal Qualities Questions

What are your major strengths?

What are your major weaknesses? What have you done to overcome your weaknesses?

What do you plan to be doing 5 or 10 years from now?

Which individuals have had the greatest influence on you?

What traits make a person successful?

How well do you communicate your ideas orally and in writing?

How would your teachers and your past employers describe you?

What do you do in your leisure time?

How persuasive are you in presenting ideas to others?

An interviewer *cannot* ask:

- Where you were born.
- Your age.
- If you have any disabilities.
- About marital status, religion, or responsibility for children.

However, an interviewer *can* ask:

- If you are a U.S. citizen.
- You to prove you are over 18.
- If you have the physical ability to perform the job for which you have applied.
- If there are any days or times when you can't work.

The use of *behavioral interviewing* is expanding to better evaluate an applicant's on-the-job potential. In these situations, prospective employees are asked how they might handle various work situations. Behavioral interview questions typically begin with "describe" or "tell me about . . ." to encourage interviewees to better explain their work style.

Most interviewers conclude the selection interview by telling you when you can expect to hear from the company. While waiting, consider doing two things. First, send a follow-up letter within a day or two expressing your appreciation for the opportunity to interview. If you don't get the job, this thank-you letter can make a positive impression that improves your chances for future consideration. Second, do a self-evaluation of your interview performance. Write down the areas that you could improve. Try to remember the questions you were asked that were different from what you expected.

Finally, the more interviews you have, the better you will present yourself. And the more interviews you have, the better the chance of being offered a job.

3 Money Management Strategy: Financial Statements and Budgeting

Digital Study Tools

Online Learning Center Study Tools for This Chapter

- Multiple-choice quiz
- Flashcards
- eLearning sessions
- Crossword puzzle
- Personal Finance Online: Personal Financial Statements and Budgeting

Student CD Study Tools for This Chapter

- Self-study software
- Narrated PowerPoint
- Personal financial planning software: Worksheets 14–19

Key Concept

The average person in the United States saves less than three cents of every dollar earned. This lack of saving results in not having adequate funds for long-term financial security. Effectively planning your spending and saving decisions provides a foundation for wise money management today and financial prosperity in the future.

Learning Objectives

1 Recognize relationships among financial documents and money management activities.

2 Design a system for maintaining personal financial records.

3 Develop a personal balance sheet and cash flow statement.

4 Create and implement a budget.

5 Relate money management and savings activities to achieving financial goals.

A Little Becomes a Lot

Can you imagine saving 25 cents a week and having it grow to over $30,000?

As hard as that may be to believe, that's exactly what Ken Lopez was able to do. Putting aside a quarter a week starting in second grade, he built up a small savings account. These funds were then invested in various stocks and mutual funds.

While in college, Ken was able to pay for his education while continuing to save between $50 and $100 a month. He closely monitored spending. Ken realized that the few dollars here and there for snacks and other minor purchases quickly add up.

Today, at age 27, Ken works as a customer service manager for an online sales division of a retailing company. He lives with his wife, Alicia, and their two young children. The family's spending plan allows for all their needs and also includes regularly saving and investing for the children's education and for retirement.

Recently, Ken was asked by a coworker, Brian, "How come you and Alicia never seem to have financial stress in your household?"

Ken replied, "Do you know where your money is going each month?"

"Not really," was Brian's response.

"You'd be surprised by how much is spent on little things you might do without," Ken responded.

"I guess so. I just don't want to have to go around with a notebook writing down every amount I spend," Brian said in a troubled voice.

"Well, you have to take some action if you want your financial situation to change," Ken said in an encouraging voice.

Brian conceded with, "All right, what would you recommend?"

QUESTIONS

What Actions Should Be Taken?

1. What money management behaviors did Ken practice that most people neglect?
2. What additional goals might be appropriate for Ken, Alicia, and their children?

What about Your Situation?

3. Are your money management activities more like Ken's or Brian's?
4. What actions might you take to better control your spending and to increase your saving?

Learn More Online

Based on information at www.quicken.com, www.moneymanagement.org, or www.asec.org, describe money management and financial planning advice that would be appropriate for Brian and others to follow.

Planning for Successful Money Management

Objective 1

Recognize relationships among financial documents and money management activities.

money management
Day-to-day financial activities necessary to manage current personal economic resources while working toward long-term financial security.

"Each month I have too much month and not enough money. If the month were only 20 days long, budgeting would be easy." Most of us have heard a comment like this when it comes to budgeting and money management.

Your daily spending and saving decisions are at the center of financial planning. You must coordinate these decisions with your needs, goals, and personal situation. When people watch a baseball or football game, they usually know the score. In financial planning, knowing the score is also important.

Maintaining financial records and planning your spending are essential to successful personal financial management. The time and effort you devote to these recordkeeping activities will yield benefits. **Money management** refers to the day-to-day financial activities necessary to manage current personal economic resources while working toward long-term financial security.

OPPORTUNITY COST AND MONEY MANAGEMENT

Consumers can choose from more than 25,000 items in a supermarket, more than 11,000 periodicals, and as many as 500 cable television stations. Daily decision making is a fact of life, and trade-offs are associated with each choice made. Selecting an alternative means you give up something else. In terms of money management decisions, examples of trade-off situations, or *opportunity costs,* include the following:

- Spending money on current living expenses reduces the amount you can use for saving and investing for long-term financial security.
- Saving and investing for the future reduce the amount you can spend now.
- Buying on credit results in payments later and reduces the amount of future income available for spending.
- Using savings for purchases results in lost interest earnings and an inability to use savings for other purposes.
- Comparison shopping can save you money and improve the quality of your purchases but uses up something of value you cannot replace: your time.

As you plan and implement various money management activities, you need to assess financial and personal costs and benefits associated with financial decisions.

Exhibit **3-1**   Money management activities

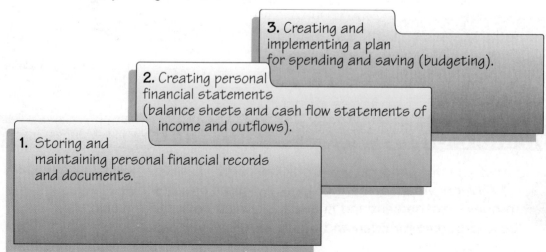

3. Creating and implementing a plan for spending and saving (budgeting).

2. Creating personal financial statements (balance sheets and cash flow statements of income and outflows).

1. Storing and maintaining personal financial records and documents.

COMPONENTS OF MONEY MANAGEMENT

As Exhibit 3–1 shows, three major money management activities are interrelated. First, personal financial records and documents are the foundation of systematic resource use. These provide written evidence of business transactions, ownership of property, and legal matters. Next, personal financial statements enable you to measure and assess your financial position and progress. Finally, your spending plan, or *budget,* is the basis for effective money management.

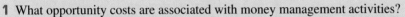

CONCEPT CHECK 3-1

1 What opportunity costs are associated with money management activities?
2 What are the three major money management activities?

Action Application Talk to several people regarding wise and poor money management actions they have taken in their lives.

A System for Personal Financial Records

Today, computers seem to be generating more paperwork than ever. Much of that paperwork relates to financial matters. Invoices, credit card statements, insurance policies, and tax records are the basis of financial recordkeeping and personal economic choices.

An organized system of financial records provides a basis for

- Handling daily business affairs, including payment of bills on time.

- Planning and measuring financial progress.

- Completing required tax reports.

- Making effective investment decisions.

- Determining available resources for current and future buying.

As Exhibit 3–2 shows, most financial records are kept in one of three places: a home file, a safe deposit box, or a home computer. A home file should be used to keep records for current needs and documents with limited value. Your home file may be a series of folders, a cabinet with several drawers, or even a cardboard box. Whatever method you use, it is most important that your home file be organized to allow quick access to required documents and information.

Important financial records and valuable articles should be kept in a location that provides better security than a home file. A **safe deposit box** is a private storage area at a financial institution with maximum security for valuables and difficult-to-replace documents. Access to the contents of a safe deposit box requires two keys. One key is issued to you; the other is kept by the financial institution where the safe deposit box is located. Items commonly kept in a safe deposit box include stock certificates, contracts, a list of insurance policies, and valuables such as rare coins and stamps. These documents may also be kept in a fireproof home safe.

Objective 2

Design a system for maintaining personal financial records.

safe deposit box A private storage area at a financial institution with maximum security for valuables.

DID YOU KNOW?

In the United States, people keep various documents and valuables in 30 million safe deposit boxes in banks and other financial institutions. While these boxes are usually very safe, each year a few people lose the contents of their safe deposit boxes through theft, fire, or natural disasters. Such losses are usually, but not always, covered by the financial institution's insurance.

Exhibit **3-2** Where to keep your financial records

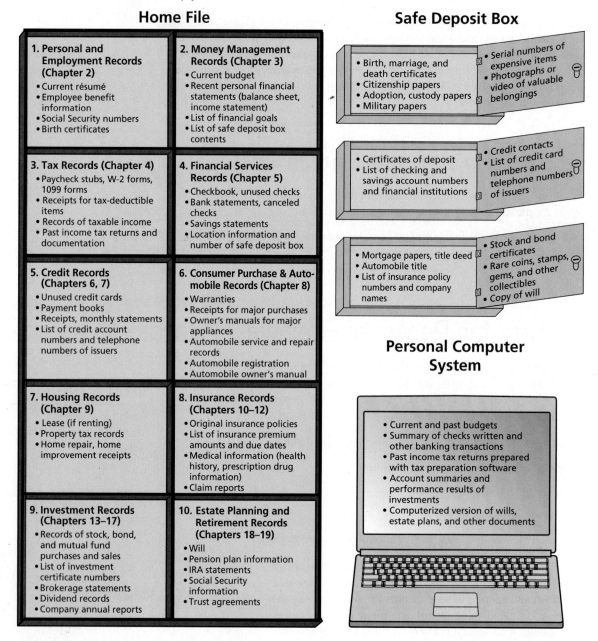

Home File

1. Personal and Employment Records (Chapter 2)
- Current résumé
- Employee benefit information
- Social Security numbers
- Birth certificates

2. Money Management Records (Chapter 3)
- Current budget
- Recent personal financial statements (balance sheet, income statement)
- List of financial goals
- List of safe deposit box contents

3. Tax Records (Chapter 4)
- Paycheck stubs, W-2 forms, 1099 forms
- Receipts for tax-deductible items
- Records of taxable income
- Past income tax returns and documentation

4. Financial Services Records (Chapter 5)
- Checkbook, unused checks
- Bank statements, canceled checks
- Savings statements
- Location information and number of safe deposit box

5. Credit Records (Chapters 6, 7)
- Unused credit cards
- Payment books
- Receipts, monthly statements
- List of credit account numbers and telephone numbers of issuers

6. Consumer Purchase & Automobile Records (Chapter 8)
- Warranties
- Receipts for major purchases
- Owner's manuals for major appliances
- Automobile service and repair records
- Automobile registration
- Automobile owner's manual

7. Housing Records (Chapter 9)
- Lease (if renting)
- Property tax records
- Home repair, home improvement receipts

8. Insurance Records (Chapters 10–12)
- Original insurance policies
- List of insurance premium amounts and due dates
- Medical information (health history, prescription drug information)
- Claim reports

9. Investment Records (Chapters 13–17)
- Records of stock, bond, and mutual fund purchases and sales
- List of investment certificate numbers
- Brokerage statements
- Dividend records
- Company annual reports

10. Estate Planning and Retirement Records (Chapters 18–19)
- Will
- Pension plan information
- IRA statements
- Social Security information
- Trust agreements

Safe Deposit Box

- Birth, marriage, and death certificates
- Citizenship papers
- Adoption, custody papers
- Military papers
- Serial numbers of expensive items
- Photographs or video of valuable belongings

- Certificates of deposit
- List of checking and savings account numbers and financial institutions
- Credit contacts
- List of credit card numbers and telephone numbers of issuers

- Mortgage papers, title deed
- Automobile title
- List of insurance policy numbers and company names
- Stock and bond certificates
- Rare coins, stamps, gems, and other collectibles
- Copy of will

Personal Computer System

- Current and past budgets
- Summary of checks written and other banking transactions
- Past income tax returns prepared with tax preparation software
- Account summaries and performance results of investments
- Computerized version of wills, estate plans, and other documents

Sheet 14
Financial documents and records

The number of financial records and documents may seem overwhelming; however, they can easily be organized into 10 categories (see Exhibit 3–2). These groups correspond to the major topics covered in this book. You may not need to use all of these records and documents at present. As your financial situation changes, you will add others.

How long should you keep personal finance records? The answer to this question differs for various documents. Records such as birth certificates, wills, and Social Security data should be kept permanently. Records on property and investments should be kept as long as you own these items. Federal tax laws dictate the length of time you should keep tax-related information. Copies of tax returns and supporting data should be saved for six years. Normally, an audit will go back only three years; however, under certain circumstances, the Internal Revenue Service may request information from six years back. Financial experts also recommend keeping documents related to the purchase and sale of real estate indefinitely.

CONCEPT CHECK 3-2

1 What are the benefits of an organized system of financial records and documents?

2 What suggestions would you give for creating a system for organizing and storing financial records and documents?

3 What influences the length of time you should keep financial records and documents?

Action Application Outline a system for filing and maintaining personal financial records. What are some of the goals of your system?

Personal Financial Statements Measure Financial Progress

Every journey starts somewhere. You need to know where you are before you can go somewhere else. Personal financial statements tell you the starting point of your financial journey.

Most of the financial documents we have discussed come from financial institutions, business organizations, or the government. Two documents that you create yourself, the personal balance sheet and the cash flow statement, are called *personal financial statements*. These reports provide information about your current financial position and present a summary of your income and spending. The main purposes of personal financial statements are to

- Report your current financial position in relation to the value of the items you own and the amounts you owe.

- Measure your progress toward your financial goals.

- Maintain information about your financial activities.

- Provide data you can use when preparing tax forms or applying for credit.

Objective 3

Develop a personal balance sheet and cash flow statement.

THE PERSONAL BALANCE SHEET: WHERE ARE YOU NOW?

The current financial position of an individual or a family is a common starting point for financial planning. A **balance sheet,** also called a *net worth statement* or *statement of financial position,* reports what you own and what you owe. You prepare a personal balance sheet to determine your current financial position using the following process:

balance sheet A financial statement that reports what an individual or a family owns and owes; also called a *net worth statement.*

| Item of value (what you own) | − | Amounts owed (what you owe) | = | Net worth (your wealth) |

For example, if your possessions are worth $4,500 and you owe $800 to others, your net worth is $3,700.

assets Cash and other property with a monetary value.

liquid assets Cash and items of value that can easily be converted to cash.

STEP 1: LISTING ITEMS OF VALUE   Available cash and money in bank accounts combined with other items of value are the foundation of your current financial position. **Assets** are cash and other tangible property with a monetary value. The balance sheet for Rose and Edgar Gomez (Exhibit 3–3) lists their assets under four categories:

1. **Liquid assets** are cash and items of value that can easily be converted to cash. Money in checking and savings accounts is liquid and is available to the Gomez family for current spending. The cash value of their life insurance may be borrowed if needed. While assets other than liquid assets can also be converted into cash, the process is not quite as easy.

2. *Real estate* includes a home, a condominium, vacation property, or other land that a person or family owns.

Exhibit **3-3**   Creating a personal balance sheet

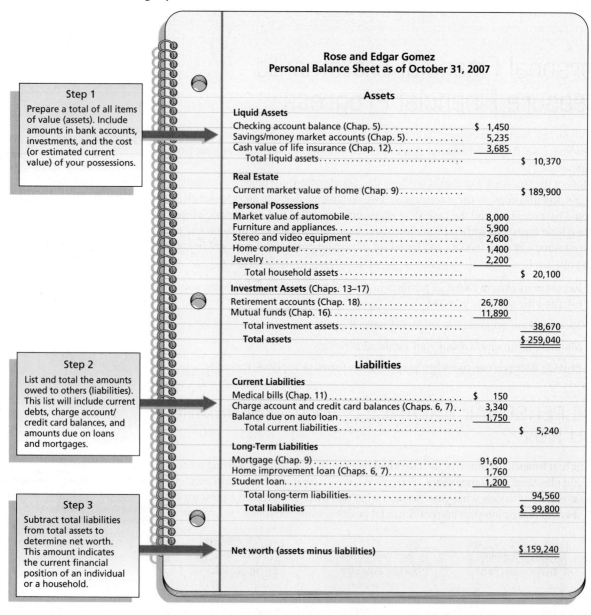

Step 1
Prepare a total of all items of value (assets). Include amounts in bank accounts, investments, and the cost (or estimated current value) of your possessions.

Step 2
List and total the amounts owed to others (liabilities). This list will include current debts, charge account/ credit card balances, and amounts due on loans and mortgages.

Step 3
Subtract total liabilities from total assets to determine net worth. This amount indicates the current financial position of an individual or a household.

Rose and Edgar Gomez
Personal Balance Sheet as of October 31, 2007

Assets

Liquid Assets
Checking account balance (Chap. 5)	$ 1,450	
Savings/money market accounts (Chap. 5)	5,235	
Cash value of life insurance (Chap. 12)	3,685	
Total liquid assets		$ 10,370

Real Estate
Current market value of home (Chap. 9)	$ 189,900

Personal Possessions
Market value of automobile	8,000	
Furniture and appliances	5,900	
Stereo and video equipment	2,600	
Home computer	1,400	
Jewelry	2,200	
Total household assets		$ 20,100

Investment Assets (Chaps. 13–17)
Retirement accounts (Chap. 18)	26,780	
Mutual funds (Chap. 16)	11,890	
Total investment assets		38,670
Total assets		**$ 259,040**

Liabilities

Current Liabilities
Medical bills (Chap. 11)	$ 150	
Charge account and credit card balances (Chaps. 6, 7)	3,340	
Balance due on auto loan	1,750	
Total current liabilities		$ 5,240

Long-Term Liabilities
Mortgage (Chap. 9)	91,600	
Home improvement loan (Chaps. 6, 7)	1,760	
Student loan	1,200	
Total long-term liabilities		94,560
Total liabilities		**$ 99,800**

Net worth (assets minus liabilities)	**$ 159,240**

Note: Various asset and liability items are discussed in the chapters listed next to them.

3. *Personal possessions* are a major portion of assets for most people. Included in this category are automobiles and other personal belongings. While these items have value, they may be difficult to convert to cash. You may decide to list your possessions on the balance sheet at their original cost. However, these values probably need to be revised over time, since a five-year-old television set, for example, is worth less now than when it was new. Thus, you may wish to list your possessions at their current value (also referred to as *market value*). This method takes into account the fact that such things as a home or rare jewelry may increase in value over time. You can estimate current value by looking at ads for the selling price of comparable automobiles, homes, or other possessions. Or you may use the services of an appraiser.

4. *Investment assets* are funds set aside for long-term financial needs. The Gomez family will use their investments for such things as financing their children's education, purchasing a vacation home, and planning for retirement. Since investment assets usually fluctuate in value, the amounts listed should reflect their value at the time the balance sheet is prepared.

STEP 2: DETERMINING AMOUNTS OWED
Looking at the total assets of the Gomez family, you might conclude that they have a strong financial position. However, their debts must also be considered. **Liabilities** are amounts owed to others but do not include items not yet due, such as next month's rent. A liability is a debt you owe now, not something you may owe in the future. Liabilities fall into two categories:

> ### DID YOU KNOW?
> According to the Bureau of the Census, U.S. Department of Commerce, the most common assets held by households are motor vehicles, homes, savings accounts, U.S. savings bonds, certificates of deposit, mutual funds, stocks, corporate bonds, and retirement accounts.

liabilities Amounts owed to others.

1. Current liabilities are debts you must pay within a short time, usually less than a year. These liabilities include such things as medical bills, tax payments, insurance premiums, cash loans, and charge accounts.

2. Long-term liabilities are debts you do not have to pay in full until more than a year from now. Common long-term liabilities include auto loans, educational loans, and mortgages. A *mortgage* is an amount borrowed to buy a house or other real estate that will be repaid over a period of 15, 20, or 30 years. Similarly, a home improvement loan may be repaid to the lender over the next 5 to 10 years.

current liabilities Debts that must be paid within a short time, usually less than a year.

long-term liabilities Debts that are not required to be paid in full until more than a year from now.

The debts listed in the liability section of a balance sheet represent the amount owed at the moment; they do not include future interest payments. However, each debt payment is likely to include a portion of interest. Chapters 6 and 7 discuss the cost of borrowing further.

STEP 3. COMPUTING NET WORTH
Your **net worth** is the difference between your total assets and your total liabilities. This relationship can be stated as

net worth The difference between total assets and total liabilities.

$$\text{Assets} - \text{Liabilities} = \text{Net worth}$$

Net worth is the amount you would have if all assets were sold for the listed values and all debts were paid in full. Also, total assets equal total liabilities plus net worth. The balance sheet of a business is commonly expressed as

$$\text{Assets} = \text{Liabilities} + \text{Net worth}$$

As Exhibit 3–3 shows, Rose and Edgar Gomez have a net worth of $159,240. Since very few people, if any, liquidate all assets, the amount of net worth has a more practical purpose: It provides a measurement of your current financial position.

A person may have a high net worth but still have financial difficulties. Having many assets with low liquidity means not having the cash available to pay current expenses.

insolvency The inability to pay debts when they are due because liabilities far exceed the value of assets.

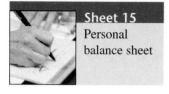

Sheet 15
Personal balance sheet

Insolvency is the inability to pay debts when they are due; it occurs when a person's liabilities far exceed available assets. Bankruptcy, discussed in Chapter 7, may be an alternative for a person in this position.

You can increase your net worth in various ways, including

- Increasing your savings.
- Reducing spending.
- Increasing the value of investments and other possessions.
- Reducing the amounts you owe.

Remember, your net worth is *not* money available for use but an indication of your financial position on a given date.

EVALUATING YOUR FINANCIAL POSITION

To assess your financial progress, see Financial Planning Calculations: Ratios for Evaluating Financial Progress on page 85.

A personal balance sheet helps you measure progress toward financial goals. Your financial situation improves if your net worth increases each time you prepare a balance sheet. It will improve more rapidly if you are able to set aside money each month for savings and investments. As with net worth, the relationship among various balance sheet items can give an indication of your financial position.

THE CASH FLOW STATEMENT: WHERE DID YOUR MONEY GO?

cash flow The actual inflow and outflow of cash during a given time period.

Each day, financial events can affect your net worth. When you receive a paycheck or pay living expenses, your total assets and liabilities change. **Cash flow** is the actual inflow and outflow of cash during a given time period. Income from employment will probably represent your most important *cash inflow;* however, other income, such as interest earned on a savings account, should also be considered. In contrast, payments for items such as rent, food, and loans are *cash outflows.*

cash flow statement A financial statement that summarizes cash receipts and payments for a given period.

A **cash flow statement,** also called a *personal income and expenditure statement* (Exhibit 3–4 on page 86), is a summary of cash receipts and payments for a given period, such as a month or a year. This report provides data on your income and spending patterns, which will be helpful when preparing a budget. A checking account can provide information for your cash flow statement. Deposits to the account are your *inflows;* checks written are your *outflows.* Of course, in using this system, when you do not deposit the entire amounts received, you must also note the spending of undeposited amounts in your cash flow statement.

The process for preparing a cash flow statement is

| Total cash received during the time period | − | Cash outflows during the time period | = | Cash surplus or deficit |

TAX CREDITS VERSUS TAX DEDUCTIONS

Many people confuse *tax credits* with *tax deductions.* Is one better than the other? A tax *credit,* such as eligible child care or dependent care expenses, results in a dollar-for-dollar reduction in the amount of taxes owed. A *tax deduction,* such as an itemized deduction in the form of medical expenses, mortgage interest, or charitable contributions, reduces the taxable income on which your taxes are based.

Here is how a $100 tax credit compares with a $100 tax deduction:

As you might expect, tax credits are less readily available than tax deductions. To qualify for a $100 child care tax credit, you may have to spend $500 in child care expenses. In some situations, spending on deductible items may be more beneficial than qualifying for a tax credit. A knowledge of tax law and careful financial planning will help you use both tax credits and tax deductions to maximum advantage.

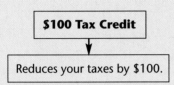

> **$100 Tax Credit**
>
> Reduces your taxes by $100.

> **$100 Tax Deduction**
>
> Reduces your taxable income by $100. The amount of your tax reduction depends on your tax bracket. Your taxes will be reduced by $15 if you are in the 15 percent tax bracket and by $28 if you are in the 28 percent tax bracket.

full dollar effect in lowering taxes, whereas a *deduction* reduces the taxable income on which the tax liability is computed. (See the Financial Planning Calculations box, above.)

Low-income workers can benefit from the *earned-income credit (EIC).* This federal tax regulation, for working parents with taxable income under a certain amount ($34,458 in 2005), can result in a tax credit of more than $2,600. Families that do not earn enough to owe federal income taxes are also eligible for the EIC. When these families file a tax return and attach Schedule EIC, they receive a check from the IRS for the amount of their credit.

Recent tax credits also included:

- Foreign tax credit to avoid double taxation on income taxes paid to another country.

- Retirement tax credit to encourage investment contributions to individual and employer-sponsored retirement plans by low- and middle-income taxpayers.

- Adoption tax credit to cover expenses when adopting a child under age 18.

- Hope Scholarship and Lifetime Learning tax credits to help offset college education expenses.

MAKING TAX PAYMENTS

You will make your payment of income taxes to the federal government in one of two ways: through payroll withholding or through estimated tax payments.

WITHHOLDING   The pay-as-you-go system requires an employer to deduct federal income tax from your pay and send it to the government. The withheld amount is

Exhibit **4-3**

W-2 form

a Control number		
	OMB No. 1545-0008	

b Employer's identification number	**1** Wages, tips, other compensation	**2** Federal income tax withheld
37 - 19876541	23,972.09	2,678.93

c Employer's name, address, and ZIP code	**3** Social security wages	**4** Social security tax withheld
	23,972.09	1,725.99
Information Data, Inc.	**5** Medicare wages and tips	**6** Medicare tax withheld
9834 Collins Blvd.		
Benton, NJ 08734	**7** Social security tips	**8** Allocated tips

d Employee's social security number	**9** Advance EIC payment	**10** Dependent care benefits
123-45-6789		

e Employee's name, address, and ZIP code	**11** Nonqualified plans	**12** Benefits included in box 1
	13 See Instrs. for box 13	**14** Other
Barbara Victor		
124 Harper Lane		
Parmont, NJ 07819		

15 Statutory employee	Deceased	Pension plan	Legal rep.	Hshld. emp.	Subtotal	Deferred compensation
☐	☐	☐	☐	☐	☐	☐

16 State	Employer's state I.D. No.	**17** State wages, tips, etc.	**18** State income tax	**19** Locality name	**20** local wages, tips, etc.	**21** Local income tax
	37 - 19876541					

(1)   Department of the Treasury—Internal Revenue Service

Form **W-2** **Wage and Tax Statement**
Copy B To Be Filed With Employee's FEDERAL Tax Return

This information is being furnished to the Internal Revenue Service.

based on the number of exemptions and the expected deductions claimed on the W-4 form. For example, a married person with children would have less withheld than a single person with the same salary, since the married person will owe less tax at year-end.

After the end of the year, you will receive a W-2 form (see Exhibit 4–3), which reports your annual earnings and the amounts that have been deducted for federal income tax, Social Security, and, if applicable, state income tax. A copy of the W-2 form is filed with your tax return to document your earnings and the amount you have paid in taxes. The difference between the amount withheld and the tax owed is either the additional amount you must pay or the refund you will receive.

Many taxpayers view an annual tax refund as a "windfall," extra money they can count on each year. However, these taxpayers are forgetting the opportunity cost of withholding excessive amounts. Others view their extra tax withholding as "forced savings." However, a payroll deduction plan for savings could serve the same purpose and would enable them to earn the interest instead of giving the government an interest-free loan.

Students and low-income individuals may file for exemption from withholding if they paid no federal income tax last year and do not expect to pay any in the current year. Dependents may not be exempt from withholding if they have any unearned income and if their total gross income will exceed $500. Being exempt from withholding results in not having to file for a refund and allows you to make more use of your money during the year. However, even if federal income tax is not withheld, Social Security taxes will still be deducted.

ESTIMATED PAYMENTS   People with income from savings, investments, independent contracting, royalties, and lump-sum payments from pensions or retirement plans have their earnings reported on Form 1099. People in these situations and others who do not have taxes withheld may be required to make tax payments during the year (April 15, June 15, September 15, and January 15 as the last payment for the previous tax year). These payments are based on the person's estimate of taxes due at year-end. Underpayment or failure to make these estimated payments can result in penalties and interest charges. These penalties are usually avoided if withholding and estimated payments total more than your tax liability for the previous year or at least 90 percent of the current year's tax.

DEADLINES AND PENALTIES

Most people are required to file their federal income tax return each April 15. If you are not able to file on time, you can use Form 4868 to obtain an automatic four-month extension. This extension is for the 1040 form and other documents, but it does not delay your payment liability. You must submit the estimated amount owed along with Form 4868 by April 15. Failure to file on time can result in a penalty of 5 percent for just one day.

People who make quarterly deposits for estimated taxes must submit their payments by April 15, June 15, and September 15 of the current tax year, with the final payment due by January 15 of the following year.

The IRS can impose penalties and interest for violations of the tax code. Failure to file a tax return can result in a 25 percent penalty in addition to the taxes owed.

Underpayment of quarterly estimated taxes requires paying interest on the amount you should have paid. Underpayment due to negligence or fraud can result in penalties of 50 to 75 percent. The good news is that if you claim a refund several months or years late, the IRS will pay you interest. Refunds must be claimed within three years of filing the return or within two years of paying the tax.

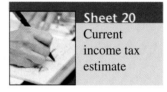

Sheet 20
Current income tax estimate

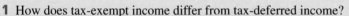

CONCEPT CHECK 4-2 ✓

1 How does tax-exempt income differ from tax-deferred income?
2 What information is needed to compute taxable income?
3 When would you use the standard deduction instead of itemized deductions?
4 What is the difference between your marginal tax rate and your average tax rate?
5 How does a tax credit affect the amount owed for federal income tax?

Action Application Using library resources or an Internet search, determine the types of income that are exempt from federal income tax.

Filing Your Federal Income Tax Return

As you stare at those piles of papers, you know it's time to do your taxes! Submitting your federal income tax return requires several decisions and activities. First, you must determine whether you are required to file a return. Next, you need to decide which basic form best serves your needs and whether you are required to submit additional schedules or supplementary forms. Finally, you must prepare your return.

Objective 3

Prepare a federal income tax return.

WHO MUST FILE?

Every citizen or resident of the United States and every U.S. citizen who is a resident of Puerto Rico is required to file a federal income tax return if his or her income is above

Your family situation affects your tax filing status.

a certain amount. The amount is based on the person's *filing status* and other factors such as age. For example, single persons under 65 had to file a return on April 15, 2005 (for tax year 2004), if their gross income exceeded $7,950, single persons over 65 had to file if their gross income exceeded $9,150. The amount at which you are required to file will change each year based on changes in the standard deduction and in the allowed personal exemptions. If your gross income is less than this amount but taxes were withheld from your earnings, you will need to file a return to obtain a refund.

Your filing status is affected by such factors as marital status and dependents. The five filing status categories are as follows:

- *Single*—never-married, divorced, or legally separated individuals with no dependents.

- *Married, filing joint return*—combines the income of a husband and a wife.

- *Married, filing separate returns*—each spouse is responsible for his or her own tax. Under certain conditions, a married couple can benefit from this filing status.

- *Head of household*—an unmarried individual or a surviving spouse who maintains a household (paying for more than half of the costs) for a child or a dependent relative.

- *Qualifying widow or widower*—an individual whose spouse died within the past two years and who has a dependent; this status is limited to two years after the death of the spouse.

In some situations, you may have a choice of filing status. In such cases, compute your taxes under the available alternatives to determine the most advantageous filing status.

WHICH TAX FORM SHOULD YOU USE?

Although about 400 federal tax forms and schedules exist, you have a choice of three basic forms when filing your income tax (see Exhibit 4–4). Recently about 20 percent of taxpayers used Form 1040EZ or Form 1040A; about 60 percent used the regular Form 1040. Your decision in this matter will depend on your type of income, the amount of your income, the number of your deductions, and the complexity of your tax situation. Most tax preparation software programs will guide you in selecting the appropriate 1040 form.

COMPLETING THE FEDERAL INCOME TAX RETURN

The major sections of Form 1040 (see Exhibit 4–5) correspond to tax topics discussed in the previous sections of this chapter:

1. *Filing status and exemptions.* Your tax rate is determined by your filing status and allowances for yourself, your spouse, and each person you claim as a dependent.

2. *Income.* Earnings from your employment (as reported by your W-2 form) and other income, such as savings and investment income, are reported in this section of Form 1040.

3. *Adjustments to income.* As discussed later in the chapter, if you qualify, you may deduct contributions (up to a certain amount) to an

> ### DID YOU KNOW?
>
> The Internal Revenue Service oversees more than 17,000 pages of laws and regulations with about 500 different tax forms.

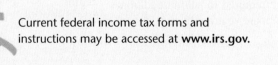

fyi

Current federal income tax forms and instructions may be accessed at **www.irs.gov.**

Exhibit **4-4**   Selecting a 1040 form

FORM 1040EZ

You may use Form 1040EZ if:

• You are single or married filing a joint return, under age 65, and claim no dependents.

• Your income consisted only of wages, salaries, and tips and not more than $1,500 of taxable interest.

• Your taxable income is less than $100,000.

• You do not itemize deductions or claim any adjustments to income or any tax credits.

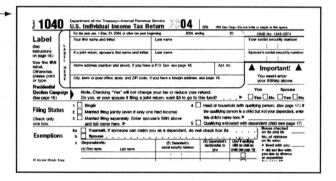

FORM 1040A

This form would be used by people who have less that $100,000 in taxable income from wages, salaries, tips, unemployment compensation, interest, or dividends and use the standard deduction. With Form 1040A, you can also take deductions for individual retirement account (IRA) contributions and a tax credit for child care and dependent care expenses. If you qualify for either Form 1040EZ or Form 1040A, you may wish to use one of them to simplify filing your tax return. You may not want to use either the Form 1040EZ or Form 1040A if Form 1040 allows you to pay less tax.

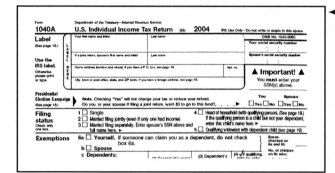

FORM 1040

Form 1040 is an expanded version of Form 1040A that includes sections for all types of income. You are required to use this form if your income is over $50,000 or if you can be claimed as a dependent on your parents return _and_ you had interest or dividends over a set limit.

Form 1040 allows you to itemize your deductions. You can list various allowable expenses (medical costs, home mortgage interest, real estate property taxes) that will reduce taxable income and the amount you owe the government. You should learn about all the possible adjustments to income, deductions, and tax credits for which you may qualify.

FORM 1040X

This form is used to amend a previously filed tax return. If you discover income that was not reported, or if you find additional deductions, you should file Form 1040X to pay the additional tax or obtain a refund.

individual retirement account (IRA) or other qualified retirement program.

4. *Tax computation.* In this section, your adjusted gross income is reduced by your itemized deductions (see Exhibit 4–6 on page 120) or by the standard deduction for your tax situation. In addition, an amount is deducted for each exemption to arrive at your taxable income. That income is the basis for determining the amount of your tax (see Exhibit 4–7 on page 121).

5. *Tax credits.* Any tax credits for which you qualify are subtracted at this point.

6. *Other taxes.* Any special taxes, such as self-employment tax, are included at this point.

7. *Payments.* Your total withholding and other payments are indicated in this section.

Exhibit **4-5** Federal income tax return—Form 1040

Form 1040 Department of the Treasury—Internal Revenue Service
U.S. Individual Income Tax Return (P) IRS Use Only—Do not write or staple in this space.

For the year Jan. 1–Dec. 31, 2004, or other tax year beginning ending , 20 OMB No. 1545-0074

Label (See instructions on page 16.)
Use the IRS label. Otherwise, please print or type.

Your first name and initial: Edward L. Last name: Rameriz
Your social security number: 123 45 6789

If a joint return, spouse's first name and initial: Marge S. Last name: Rameriz
Spouse's social security number: 123 54 9876

Home address (number and street). If you have a P.O. box, see page 16. Apt. no.: 8734 Conner Lane

City, town or post office, state, and ZIP code. If you have a foreign address, see page 16.: Collins, IA 51733

▲ **Important!** ▲ You **must** enter your SSN(s) above.

Presidential Election Campaign (See page 16.)
Note. Checking "Yes" will not change your tax or reduce your refund.
Do you, or your spouse if filing a joint return, want $3 to go to this fund? ▶ You [ ] Yes [ ] No Spouse [ ] Yes [ ] No

Filing Status Check only one box.
1 [ ] Single
2 [X] Married filing jointly (even if only one had income)
3 [ ] Married filing separately. Enter spouse's SSN above and full name here. ▶
4 [ ] Head of household (with qualifying person). (See page 17.) If the qualifying person is a child but not your dependent, enter this child's name here. ▶
5 [ ] Qualifying widow(er) with dependent child (see page 17)

Exemptions
6a [X] Yourself. If someone can claim you as a dependent, do not check box 6a
b [X] Spouse
Boxes checked on 6a and 6b: 2
c Dependents:

(1) First name Last name	(2) Dependent's social security number	(3) Dependent's relationship to you	(4) ✓ if qualifying child for child tax credit (see page 18)
John Rameriz	987 65 4321	Son	[ ]
Sandy Rameriz	789 56 1234	Daughter	[ ]

If more than four dependents, see page 18.

No. of children on 6c who: • lived with you 2 • did not live with you due to divorce or separation (see page 18)
Dependents on 6c not entered above
Add numbers on lines above ▶ 4

d Total number of exemptions claimed

Income
Attach Form(s) W-2 here. Also attach Forms W-2G and 1099-R if tax was withheld.
If you did not get a W-2, see page 19.
Enclose, but do not attach, any payment. Also, please use Form 1040-V.

7 Wages, salaries, tips, etc. Attach Form(s) W-2 ... 7 | 54,492
8a Taxable interest. Attach Schedule B if required ... 8a | 280
b Tax-exempt interest. Do not include on line 8a ... 8b
9a Ordinary dividends. Attach Schedule B if required ... 9a
b Qualified dividends (see page 20) ... 9b
10 Taxable refunds, credits, or offsets of state and local income taxes (see page 20) ... 10
11 Alimony received ... 11
12 Business income or (loss). Attach Schedule C or C-EZ ... 12
13 Capital gain or (loss). Attach Schedule D if required. If not required, check here ▶ [ ] ... 13 | 360
14 Other gains or (losses). Attach Form 4797 ... 14
15a IRA distributions ... 15a b Taxable amount (see page 22) ... 15b
16a Pensions and annuities ... 16a b Taxable amount (see page 22) ... 16b
17 Rental real estate, royalties, partnerships, S corporations, trusts, etc. Attach Schedule E ... 17
18 Farm income or (loss). Attach Schedule F ... 18
19 Unemployment compensation ... 19
20a Social security benefits ... 20a b Taxable amount (see page 24) ... 20b
21 Other income. List type and amount (see page 24) ... 21
22 Add the amounts in the far right column for lines 7 through 21. This is your **total income** ▶ 22 | 55,132

Adjusted Gross Income
23 Educator expenses (see page 26) ... 23
24 Certain business expenses of reservists, performing artists, and fee-basis government officials. Attach Form 2106 or 2106-EZ ... 24 | 2,000
25 IRA deduction (see page 26) ... 25
26 Student loan interest deduction (see page 28) ... 26
27 Tuition and fees deduction (see page 29) ... 27
28 Health savings account deduction. Attach Form 8889 ... 28
29 Moving expenses. Attach Form 3903 ... 29
30 One-half of self-employment tax. Attach Schedule SE ... 30
31 Self-employed health insurance deduction (see page 30) ... 31
32 Self-employed SEP, SIMPLE, and qualified plans ... 32
33 Penalty on early withdrawal of savings ... 33
34a Alimony paid b Recipient's SSN ▶ ... 34a
35 Add lines 23 through 34a ... 35 | 2,000
36 Subtract line 35 from line 22. This is your **adjusted gross income** ▶ 36 | 53,132

For Disclosure, Privacy Act, and Paperwork Reduction Act Notice, see page 75. Cat No 12599G Form **1040**

1. Your marriage and household situation will affect your taxable income and tax rate.

2. Your earnings and other sources of income will be reported in this section.

3. Adjusted gross income results from certain deductions and will be used as a basis for computing other deductions.

8. *Refund or amount you owe.* If your payments exceed the amount of income tax you owe, you are entitled to a refund. If the opposite is true, you must make an additional payment. Taxpayers who want their refunds sent directly to a bank record the necessary account information directly on Form 1040, 1040A, or 1040EZ.

9. *Your signature.* Forgetting to sign a tax return is one of the most common filing errors.

FILING STATE INCOME TAX RETURNS

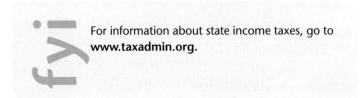

For information about state income taxes, go to **www.taxadmin.org.**

All but seven states (Alaska, Florida, Nevada, South Dakota, Texas, Washington, and Wyoming) have a state income tax. In most states, the tax rate ranges from 1 to 10 percent and is based on some aspect of your federal income tax return, such as adjusted gross income or taxable income. For further information about the income tax in your state, contact the state department of revenue.

Exhibit **4-5 continued**

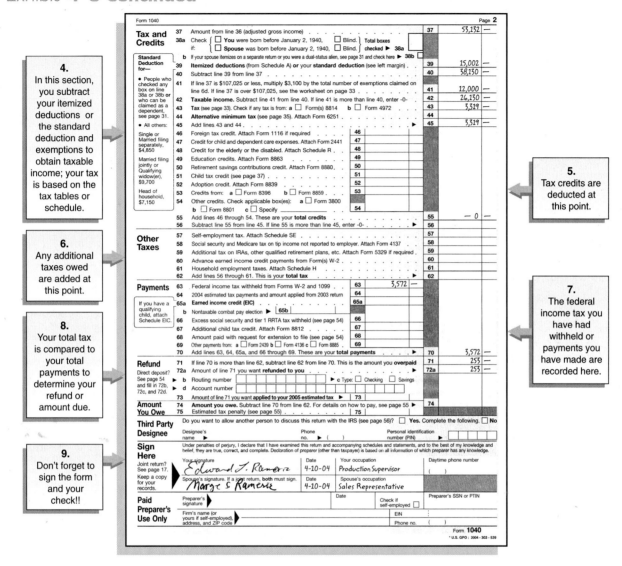

Note: These forms were used in a recent year; the current forms may not be exactly the same. Obtain current income tax forms and current tax information from your local IRS office, post office, public library, or at www.irs.gov.

States usually require income tax returns to be filed when the federal income tax return is due. For help in planning your tax activities, see Exhibit 4–8 on page 122.

CONCEPT CHECK 4-3

1 In what ways does your filing status affect preparation of your federal income tax return?

2 What factors affect your choice of a 1040 form?

Action Application Create a visual presentation (video or slides) that demonstrates actions a person might take to reduce errors when filing a federal tax return.

Exhibit **4-6** Schedule A for itemized deductions—Form 1040

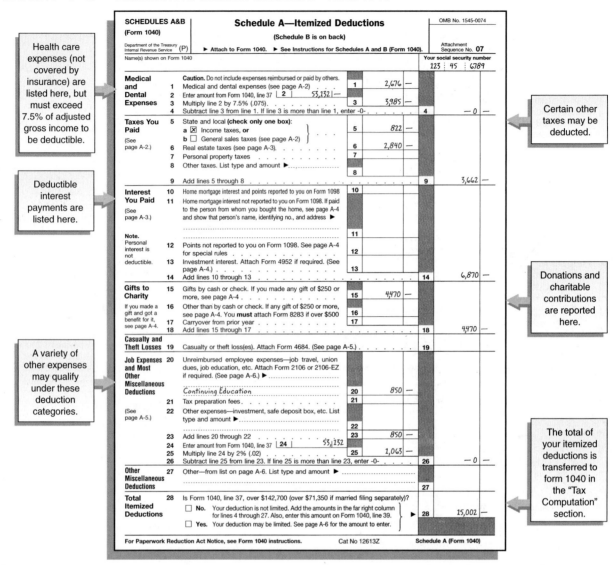

Tax Assistance and the Audit Process

Objective 4

Identify tax assistance sources.

In the process of completing your federal income tax return, you may seek additional information or assistance. After filing your return, you may be identified for a tax audit. If this happens, several policies and procedures protect your rights.

TAX INFORMATION SOURCES

As with other aspects of personal financial planning, many resources are available to assist you with your taxes. The IRS offers a wide variety of services to taxpayers. Libraries and bookstores offer books and other publications that are updated annually.

IRS SERVICES   If you wish to do your own tax return or just to expand your knowledge of tax regulations, the IRS has several methods of assistance:

Exhibit **4-7**   Tax tables and tax rate schedules

Tax Table

If line 42 (taxable income) is—		And you are—			
At least	But less than	Single	Married filing jointly	Married filing separately	Head of a household
					Your tax is—
26,000					
26,000	26,050	3,546	3,189	3,546	3,394
26,050	26,100	3,554	3,196	3,554	3,401
26,100	26,150	3,561	3,204	3,561	3,409
26,150	26,200	3,569	3,211	3,569	3,416
26,200	26,250	3,576	3,219	3,576	3,424
26,250	26,300	3,584	3,226	3,584	3,431
26,300	26,350	3,591	3,234	3,591	3,439
26,350	26,400	3,599	3,241	3,599	3,446
26,400	26,450	3,606	3,249	3,606	3,454
26,450	26,500	3,614	3,256	3,614	3,461
26,500	26,550	3,621	3,264	3,621	3,469
26,550	26,600	3,629	3,271	3,629	3,476
26,600	26,650	3,636	3,279	3,636	3,484
26,650	26,700	3,644	3,286	3,644	3,491
26,700	26,750	3,651	3,294	3,651	3,499
26,750	26,800	3,659	3,301	3,659	3,506
26,800	26,850	3,666	3,309	3,666	3,514
26,850	26,900	3,674	3,316	3,674	3,521
26,900	26,950	3,681	3,324	3,681	3,529
26,950	27,000	3,689	3,331	3,689	3,536

* This column must also be used by a qualifying widow(er).

Tax Rate Schedules

Schedule Y-1—If your filing status is Married filing jointly or Qualifying widow(er)

If your taxable income is:		The tax is:		of the amount over—
Over—	But not over—			
$0	$14,300	.... 10%		$0
14,300	58,100	$1,430.00 + 15%		14,300
58,100	117,250	8,000.00 + 25%		58,100
117,250	178,650	22,787.50 + 28%		117,250
178,650	319,100	39,979.50 + 33%		178,650
319,100	....	86,328.00 + 35%		319,100

 Use **only** if your taxable income (Form 1040, line 41) is $100,000 or more. If less, use the **Tax Table.** Even though you cannot use the Tax Rate Schedules below if your taxable income is less than $100,000, all levels of taxable income are shown so taxpayers can see the tax rate that applies to each level.

Note: These were the federal income tax rates for a recent year. Current rates may vary due to changes in the tax code and adjustments for inflation. Obtain current income tax booklets from your local IRS office, post office, bank, public library, or at www.irs.gov.

1. *Publications.* The IRS offers hundreds of free booklets and pamphlets. You can obtain these publications at a local IRS office, by mail request, or by a telephone call to the office listed in your tax packet or your local telephone directory. Especially helpful is *Your Federal Income Tax* (IRS Publication 17). You may obtain IRS publications and tax forms by calling 1-800-TAX-FORM, online at www.irs.gov, or by fax at 703-368-9694.

2. *Recorded messages.* The IRS Tele-Tax system allows you access to about 150 telephone tax tips covering everything from filing requirements to reporting gambling income. Your push-button phone gives you 24-hour-a-day access to this recorded information. Telephone numbers can be found in your tax packet or your telephone directory, or call 1-800-829-4477.

3. *Phone hot line.* You can obtain information about specific problems through an IRS-staffed phone line. The appropriate telephone number is listed in your local telephone directory, or call 1-800-829-1040. You are not asked to give your name when you use this service, so your questions are anonymous.

4. *Walk-in service.* You can visit your local or district IRS office to obtain assistance with your taxes. More than 500 of these facilities are available to taxpayers. Be aware, however, that information IRS employees provide is not always reliable. Various studies in recent years have reported incorrect answers over 30 percent of the time. You are still liable for taxes owed even if you based your calculations on information provided by IRS employees.

5. *CD-ROM.* The Internal Revenue Service also sells a CD-ROM with over 2,000 tax forms and publications.

In addition, the IRS has videos, free speakers for community groups, and teaching materials for schools to assist taxpayers.

Exhibit **4-8**

Tax-planner calendar

January	February	March
• Establish a recordkeeping system for your tax information. • If you expect a refund, file your tax return for the previous year. • Make your final estimated quarterly payment for the previous year for income not covered by withholding.	• Check to make sure you received W-2 and 1099 forms from all organizations from which you had income during the previous year; these should have been received by January 31; if not, contact the organization.	• Organize your records and tax information in preparation for filing your tax return; if you expect a refund, file as soon as possible.

April	May	June
• April 15 is the deadline for filing your federal tax return; if it falls on a weekend, you have until the next business day (usually Monday). • If necessary, file for an automatic extension for filing your tax forms.	• Review your tax return to determine whether any changes in withholding, exemptions, or marital status have not been reported to your employer.	• The second installment for estimated tax is due June 15 for income not covered by withholding.

July	August	September
• With the year half over, consider or implement plans for a personal retirement program such as an IRA or a Keogh.	• Tax returns are due August 15 for those who received the automatic four-month extension.	• The third installment for estimated tax is due September 15 for income not covered by withholding.

October	November	December
• Determine the tax benefits of selling certain investments by year-end. • Prepare a preliminary tax form to determine the most advantageous filing status.	• Make any last-minute changes in withholding by your employer to avoid penalties for too little withholding. • Determine if you qualify for an IRA; if so, consider opening one.	• Determine if it would be to your advantage to make payments for next year before December 31 of the current year. • Decide if you can defer income for the current year until the following year.

Note: Children born before the end of the year give you a full-year exemption, so plan accordingly!

TAX PUBLICATIONS   Each year, several tax guides are published and offered for sale. These publications include *J. K. Lasser's Your Income Tax, The Ernst & Young Tax Guide,* and *Consumer Reports Books Guide to Income Tax Preparation.* You can purchase them online or at local stores.

THE INTERNET   As with other personal finance topics, extensive information may be found on the Internet. The Internal Revenue Service (www.irs.gov) is a good starting point. Personal finance magazines, such as *Kiplinger's Personal Finance* and *Money,* as well as other financial planning information services, offer a variety of tax information. In addition, the Web sites of companies that sell tax software and tax-related organizations can be useful.

TAX PREPARATION SOFTWARE

Today, most taxpayers use personal computers for tax recordkeeping and tax form preparation. A spreadsheet program can be helpful in maintaining and updating income and expense data. Software packages such as *TaxCut* and *TurboTax* allow you to complete needed tax forms and schedules to either print for mailing or file online.

Using tax software can save you 10 or more hours when preparing your Form 1040 and accompanying schedules. When selecting tax software, consider the following factors:

1. Your personal situation—are you employed or operate your own business?
2. Special tax situations with regard to types of income, unusual deductions, and various tax credits.
3. Features in the software, such as "audit check," future tax planning, and filing your federal and state tax forms online.
4. Technical aspects, such as the hardware and operating system requirements, and online support that is provided.
5. Purchase location—will you buy from a local store or from an online retailer?

Software can reduce tax return preparation time and effort.

ELECTRONIC FILING

In recent years, the IRS has made online filing easier and less expensive. Through the Free File Alliance, online tax preparation and e-filing is available free to millions of taxpayers. This partnership between the IRS and the tax software industry encourages more e-filing. The online filing process involves the following steps:

STEP 1   Go to the "Free File" page at www.irs.gov and click "Start Now" to view the various Free File companies.

STEP 2   Determine your eligibility with a particular company. A brief description of the criteria for each is provided. Some companies limit service to taxpayers in certain states; others target filers by age (younger than 21 or older than 61). Many of the services are limited to lower-income taxpayers, and some offer: "No restrictions. Everyone qualifies." A "Guide Me to a Service" option is available to help you narrow down the possible companies offering free preparation and e-filing for you.

STEP 3   Next, connect to the company's Web site to begin the preparation of your tax return.

STEP 4   Finally, use the company's online software to prepare your return. Your federal tax return is then filed electronically and your tax data is stored at the vendor's site. Taxpayers who do not qualify for the Free File Alliance program may still be able to file online for a nominal fee. You don't have to purchase the software; simply go to the software company's Internet site and pay a fee to use the tax program.

Taxpayers who use the Free File Alliance are cautioned to be careful consumers. A company may attempt to sell other financial products to inexperienced taxpayers, such

DID YOU KNOW?

Electronically filed federal income tax returns have an accuracy rate of 99 percent, compared to 81 percent for paper returns. Most electronic filing programs do your calculations and signal potential errors before you file.

as expensive refund anticipation loans. Also, taxpayers using the free file service must be aware that their state tax return might not be included in the free program.

Telefile is a file-by-phone system that has been tested in various geographic areas. It allows taxpayers to call a toll-free number, using a touch-tone phone, to file their tax returns. A follow-up written or voice "signature" confirmation is required.

TAX PREPARATION SERVICES

Over 40 million U.S. taxpayers pay someone to do their income taxes. The fee for this service can range from $40 at a tax preparation service for a simple return to more than $2,000 to a certified public accountant for a complicated return.

TYPES OF TAX SERVICES

Doing your own taxes may not be desirable, especially if you have sources of income other than salary. The sources available for professional tax assistance include the following:

- Tax services range from local, one-person operations to national firms with thousands of offices, such as H&R Block.
- Enrolled agents—government-approved tax experts—prepare returns and provide tax advice. You may contact the National Association of Enrolled Agents at 1-800-424-4339 for information about enrolled agents in your area.
- Many accountants offer tax assistance along with other business services. A certified public accountant (CPA) with special training in taxes can help with tax planning and the preparation of your annual tax return.
- Attorneys usually do not complete tax returns; however, you can use an attorney's services when you are involved in a tax-related transaction or when you have a difference of opinion with the IRS.

EVALUATING TAX SERVICES

When planning to use a tax preparation service, consider these factors:

- What training and experience does the tax professional possess?
- How will the fee be determined? (Avoid preparers who earn a percentage of your refund.)
- Does the preparer suggest you report various deductions that might be questioned?
- Will the preparer represent you if your return is audited?
- Is tax preparation the main business activity, or does it serve as a front for selling other financial products and services?

Additional information about tax preparers may be obtained at the Web sites for the National Association of Enrolled Agents (www.naea.org) and the National Association of Tax Professionals (www.natptax.com).

TAX SERVICE WARNINGS

Even if you hire a professional tax preparer, you are responsible for supplying accurate and complete information. Hiring a tax preparer will not guarantee that you pay the *correct* amount. A study conducted by *Money* magazine of 41 tax preparers reported fees ranging from $375 to $3,600, with taxes due ranging from $31,846 to $74,450 for the same fictional family. If you owe more tax because your return contains errors or you have made entries that are not allowed, it is your responsibility to pay that additional tax, plus any interest and penalties.

Beware of tax preparers and other businesses that offer your refund in advance. These "refund anticipation loans" frequently charge very high interest rates for this type of consumer credit. Studies reveal interest rates sometimes exceeding 300 percent (on an annualized basis).

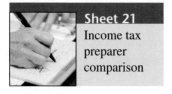

Sheet 21

Income tax preparer comparison

WHAT IF YOUR RETURN IS AUDITED?

The Internal Revenue Service reviews all returns for completeness and accuracy. If you make an error, your tax is automatically refigured and you receive either a bill or a refund. If you make an entry that is not allowed, you will be notified by mail. A **tax audit** is a detailed examination of your tax return by the IRS. In most audits, the IRS requests more information to support the entries on your tax return. Be sure to keep accurate records to support your return. Keep receipts, canceled checks, and other evidence to prove amounts that you claim. Avoiding common filing mistakes (see Exhibit 4–9) helps to minimize your chances of an audit.

tax audit A detailed examination of your tax return by the Internal Revenue Service.

WHO GETS AUDITED?   About 1 percent of all tax filers—1.4 million people—are audited each year. While the IRS does not reveal its basis for auditing returns, several indicators are evident. People who claim large or unusual deductions increase their chances of an audit.

Tax advisers suggest including a brief explanation or a copy of receipts for deductions that may be questioned. Individuals with high incomes who report large losses due to tax shelters or partnerships, or who have had their tax returns questioned in the past, may also be targeted for an audit.

TYPES OF AUDITS   The simplest and most common type of audit is the *correspondence audit*. This mail inquiry requires you to clarify or document minor questions about your tax return. You usually have 30 days to provide the requested information.

The *office audit* requires you to visit an IRS office to clarify some aspect of your tax return. This type of audit usually takes an hour or two.

Exhibit 4–9   How to avoid common filing errors

- Organize all tax-related information for easy access.
- Follow instructions carefully. Many people deduct total medical and dental expenses rather than the amount of these expenses that exceeds 7.5 percent of adjusted gross income.
- Use the proper tax rate schedule or tax table column.
- Be sure to claim the correct number of exemptions and the correct amounts of standard deductions.
- Consider the alternative minimum tax that may apply to your situation. Be sure to pay self-employment tax and tax on early IRA withdrawals.
- Check your arithmetic and accuracy of software data entry several times.
- Sign your return (both spouses must sign a joint return), or the IRS won't process it.
- Be sure to include the correct Social Security number(s) and to record amounts on the correct lines.
- Attach necessary documentation, such as your W-2 forms and required supporting schedules.
- Make the check payable to "U.S. Treasury."
- Put your Social Security number, the tax year, and a daytime telephone number on your check—and be sure to sign the check!
- Keep a copy of your return.
- Put the proper postage on your mailing envelope.
- Finally, check everything again—and file on time! Care taken when you file your income tax can result in "many happy returns."

The *field audit* is more complex. An IRS agent visits you at your home, your business, or the office of your accountant so you have access to records. A field audit may be done to verify whether an individual has an office in the home as claimed.

The IRS also conducts more detailed audits for about 50,000 taxpayers. These range from random requests to document various tax return items to line-by-line reviews by IRS employees.

YOUR AUDIT RIGHTS   When you receive an audit notice, you have the right to request time to prepare. Also, you can ask the IRS for clarification of items being questioned. When you are audited, use the following suggestions:

- Decide whether you will bring your tax preparer, accountant, or lawyer.
- Be on time for your appointment; bring only relevant documents.
- Present tax records and receipts in a logical, calm, and confident manner; maintain a positive attitude.
- Make sure the information you present is consistent with the tax law.
- Keep your answers aimed at the auditor's questions. Answer questions clearly and completely. Be as brief as possible; you can never tell an auditor too little.

People under stress tend to talk too much. IRS auditors are trained to create silence and listen in case the taxpayer blurts out damaging information. The five best responses to questions during an audit are "Yes," "No," "I don't recall," "I'll have to check on that," and "What specific items do you want to see?"

If you disagree with the results of an audit, you may request a conference at the Regional Appeals Office. Although most differences of opinion are settled at this stage, some taxpayers take their cases further. A person may go to the U.S. tax court, the U.S. claims court, or the U.S. district court. Some tax disputes have gone to the U.S. Supreme Court.

> **DID YOU KNOW?**
>
> Federal income taxes are considered to be a *progressive tax,* in which a person is taxed an increasing proportion of income as income rises. In contrast, a *regressive tax* takes a smaller percentage from those with high income than from those with lower income. Sales taxes are considered to be regressive.

CONCEPT CHECK 4-4

1 What are the main sources available to help people prepare their taxes?
2 What actions can reduce the chances of an IRS audit?
3 What appeal process do taxpayers have if they disagree with an audit decision of the IRS?

Action Application Conduct an Internet search to obtain additional information about e-filing procedures.

Tax Planning Strategies

Objective 5

Select appropriate tax strategies for different financial and personal situations.

Most people want to pay their fair share of taxes—no more, no less. They do this by practicing **tax avoidance,** the use of legitimate methods to reduce one's taxes. In contrast, **tax evasion** is the use of illegal actions to reduce one's taxes. To minimize taxes owed, follow these guidelines:

- If you expect to have the *same* or a *lower* tax rate next year, *accelerate deductions* into the current year. Pay real estate property taxes or make your January mortgage payment in December. Make charitable donations by December 31.

Exhibit **4–10**   Special tax situations

Business in your home	• You may deduct any ordinary and necessary expenses related to starting and maintaining your business, including a portion of your rent or mortgage if that portion of your home is used exclusively for business.
	• It must be your principal place of business. (Individuals who are employed elsewhere and claim an office at home are likely to be challenged by the IRS on this deduction.)
Divorced persons	• Child support payments have no tax consequences. They are neither deductible by the payer nor included in the recipient's income.
	• Alimony is tax deductible by the payer and must be included as income by the recipient.
	• Exemptions for children are generally claimed by the parent who has custody for a longer period during the tax year.
Single parents	• A single parent may claim "head of household" filing status, which has greater advantages than "single" status.
	• Working parents may qualify for a child care tax credit.
	• Low-income families may qualify for the earned-income credit (EIC).
Retired persons	• Individuals over age 59½ may withdraw tax-deferred funds from a retirement plan without penalty. Of course, these funds must be reported as ordinary income.
	• As of 2005, retirees with total incomes, including Social Security, exceeding $44,000 (couples) and $34,000 (others) pay income tax on up to 85 percent of their Social Security benefits. Those with incomes between $25,000 and $34,000 (singles) or $32,000 and $44,000 (couples) continue to be taxed on up to 50 percent of their benefits.

Note: Individual circumstances and changes in the tax laws can affect these examples.

• If you expect to have a *lower* or the *same* tax rate next year, *delay the receipt of income* until next year. This means income will be taxed at a lower rate or at a later date.

• If you expect to have a *higher* tax rate next year, consider *delaying deductions,* since they will have a greater benefit. A $1,000 deduction at 28 percent lowers your taxes $280; at 33 percent, your taxes are lowered $330.

• If you expect to have a *higher* tax rate next year, *accelerate the receipt of income* to have it taxed at the current lower rate.

tax avoidance The use of legitimate methods to reduce one's taxes.

tax evasion The use of illegal actions to reduce one's taxes.

As Exhibit 4–10 shows, people in different life situations can take advantage of various tax rules. When considering financial decisions in relation to your taxes, remember that purchasing, investing, and retirement planning are the areas most heavily affected by tax laws.

CONSUMER PURCHASING

The buying decisions most directly affected by taxes are the purchase of a residence, the use of credit, and job-related expenses.

PLACE OF RESIDENCE   Owning a home is one of the best tax shelters. Both real estate property taxes and interest on the mortgage are deductible (as itemized deductions) and thus reduce your taxable income. While renting may seem less expensive than owning, the after-tax cost of owning a home often makes owning financially advantageous. Chapter 9 presents specific calculations for comparing renting and buying.

CONSUMER DEBT Current tax laws allow homeowners to borrow for consumer purchases. You can deduct interest on loans (of up to $100,000) secured by your primary or secondary home up to the actual dollar amount you have invested in it—the difference between the market value of the home and the amount you owe on it. These *home equity loans,* which are *second mortgages,* are discussed in greater detail in Chapters 6 and 9. Current tax laws allow you to use that line of credit to buy a car, consolidate credit card or other debts, or finance other personal expenses. Some states place restrictions on home equity loans. A person may also claim a deduction for interest expense on qualified education loans.

JOB-RELATED EXPENSES As previously mentioned, certain work expenses, such as union dues, some travel and education costs, and business tools, may be included as itemized deductions. Job search expenses are also deductible if you incur them when seeking employment in your current occupational category. Such expenses may include transportation to interviews, résumé preparation and duplication, and employment agency or career counseling fees. Remember, only the portion of these expenses that exceeds 2 percent of adjusted gross income is deductible. Expenses related to finding your first job or obtaining work in a different field are not deductible.

HEALTH CARE EXPENSES *Flexible spending account (FSA),* also called health savings accounts and expense reimbursement accounts, allow you to reduce your taxable income when paying for medical expenses or child care costs. Workers are allowed to put pretax dollars into these employer-sponsored programs. These "deposits" result in a lower taxable income. Then, the funds in the FSA may be used to pay for various medical expenses and dependent care costs.

A drawback of the FSA is that any account funds must be used to pay for expenses incurred before year's end or the money is lost. As a result, before December 31, you should make sure your funds are all spent with additional medical tests or eye exams. Participants in these plans are also encouraged to carefully plan potential medical and dependent care spending for the upcoming year.

INVESTMENT DECISIONS

A major area of tax planning involves the wide variety of decisions related to investing.

TAX-EXEMPT INVESTMENTS Interest income from municipal bonds, which are issued by state and local governments, and other tax-exempt investments is not subject to federal income taxes. While municipal bonds have lower interest rates than other investments, the *after-tax* income may be higher. For example, if you are in the 27 percent tax bracket, earning $100 of tax-exempt income would be worth more to you than earning $125 in taxable investment income. The $125 would have an after-tax value of $91: $125 less $34 (27 percent of $125) for taxes. Interest on EE savings bonds is exempt from federal income tax if it is used to pay tuition at a college, university, or qualified technical school. Chapter 5 gives further details.

TAX-DEFERRED INVESTMENTS Although, from a tax standpoint, tax-deferred investments, whose income will be taxed at a later date, are less beneficial than tax-exempt investments, they also have financial advantages. According to basic opportunity cost, paying a dollar in the future instead of today gives you the opportunity to invest (or spend) it now. Examples of tax-deferred investments include

- *Tax-deferred annuities,* usually issued by insurance companies. These investments are discussed in Chapter 19.

- *Section 529 savings plans* are state-run, tax-deferred plans to set aside money for a child's education. The 529 is like a prepaid tuition plan in which you invest to cover future education costs. The 529 plans differ from state to state.

- *Retirement plans* such as IRA, Keogh, or 401(k) plans. The next section discusses the tax implications of these plans.

Capital gains, profits from the sale of a capital asset such as stocks, bonds, or real estate, are also tax deferred; you do not have to pay the tax on these profits until the asset is sold. In recent years, *long-term* capital gains (on investments held more than a year) have been taxed at a lower rate. Certain assets, however, such as art, antiques, stamps, and other collectibles, are still taxed at the pre-1997 capital gains rate—28 percent.

Short-term capital gains (on investments held for less than a year) are taxed as ordinary income (see the Financial Planning Calculations box on page 130). Taxpayers in the lowest tax bracket have lower capital gains tax rates for both short-term and long-term investments.

The sale of an investment for less than its purchase price is, of course, *a capital loss.* Capital losses can be used to offset capital gains and up to $3,000 of ordinary income. Unused capital losses may be carried forward into future years to offset capital gains or ordinary income up to $3,000 per year.

Capital gains of $500,000 on the sale of a home may be excluded by a couple filing a joint return ($250,000 for singles). This exclusion is allowed each time a taxpayer sells or exchanges a principal residence—however, only once every two years.

Owning a business can result in various tax benefits.

capital gains Profits from the sale of a capital asset such as stocks, bonds, or real estate.

SELF-EMPLOYMENT   Owning your own business has certain tax advantages. Self-employed persons may deduct expenses such as health and life insurance as business costs. However, business owners have to pay self-employment tax (Social Security) in addition to the regular tax rate.

CHILDREN'S INVESTMENTS   In past years, parents made investments on their children's behalf and listed the children as owners. This process, known as *income shifting,* attempted to reduce the taxable income of parents by shifting the ownership of investments to children in lower tax brackets. A child under 14 with investment income of more than $1,500 is taxed at the parent's top rate. For investment income under $1,500, the child receives a deduction of $750 and the next $750 is taxed at his or her own rate, which is probably lower than the parent's rate. This income-shifting restriction does not apply to children 14 and older, so it is possible to take advantage of income shifting with them.

RETIREMENT PLANS

A major tax strategy of benefit to working people is the use of tax-deferred retirement plans such as individual retirement arrangements (IRAs), Keogh plans, and 401(k) plans.

TRADITIONAL IRA   When IRAs were first established, every working person was allowed to deduct up to $2,000 per year for IRA contributions. The contributions to and earnings from these accounts are not taxed until they are withdrawn. Today the regular IRA deduction is available only to people who do not participate in

For additional tax planning suggestions, go to **www.quicken.com/taxes.**

fyi.

SHORT-TERM AND LONG-TERM CAPITAL GAINS

You will pay a lower tax rate on the profits from stocks and other investments if you hold the asset for more than 12 months. As of 2005, a taxpayer in the 28 percent tax bracket would pay $280 in taxes on a $1,000 short-term capital gain (assets held for less than a year). However, that same taxpayer would pay only $150 on the $1,000 (a 15 percent capital gains tax) if the investment were held for more than a year.

	Short-Term Capital Gain (assets held less than a year)	Long-Term Capital Gain (assets held a year or more)
Capital gain	$1,000	$1,000
Capital gains tax rate	28%	15%
Capital gains tax	$280	$150
Tax savings		$130

employer-sponsored retirement plans or who have an adjusted gross income under a certain amount. As of 2005, the IRA contribution limit was $4,000. Older workers, age 50 and over, were allowed to contribute up to $4,500 as a "catch up" to make up for lost time saving for retirement.

In general, amounts withdrawn from deductible IRAs are included in gross income. An additional 10 percent penalty is usually imposed on withdrawals made before age 59½ unless the withdrawn funds are on account of death or disability, for medical expenses, or for qualified higher education expenses.

ROTH IRA   The Roth IRA also allows a $3,000 annual contribution, which is not tax deductible; however, the earnings on the account are tax free after five years. The funds from the Roth IRA may be withdrawn before age 59½ if the account owner is disabled, or for the purchase of a first home ($10,000 maximum). Like the regular IRA, the Roth IRA is limited to people with an adjusted gross income under a certain amount.

Deductible IRAs provide tax relief up front as contributions reduce current taxes. However, taxes must be paid when the withdrawals are made from the deductible IRA. In contrast, the Roth IRA does not have immediate benefits, but the investment grows in value on a tax-free basis. Withdrawals from the Roth IRA are exempt from federal and state taxes.

Sheet 22
Tax planning
activities

EDUCATION IRA   The Education Savings Account is designed to assist parents in saving for the college education of their children. Once again, the annual contribution (limited to $2,000) is not tax deductible and is limited to taxpayers with an adjusted gross income under a certain amount. However, as with the Roth IRA, the earnings accumulate tax free.

KEOGH PLAN   If you are self-employed and own your own business, you can establish a Keogh plan. This retirement plan, also called an HR10 plan, may combine a profit-sharing plan and a pension plan of other investments purchased by the employee. In general, with a Keogh, people may contribute 25 percent of their annual income, up to a maximum of $30,000, to this tax-deferred retirement plan.

401(K) PLAN   The part of the tax code called 401(k) authorizes a tax-deferred retirement plan sponsored by an employer. This plan allows you to contribute a greater tax-deferred amount ($15,000 in 2006) than you can contribute to an IRA. Older workers, age 50 and over, are allowed to contribute up to $14,000. However, most companies set a limit on your contribution, such as 15 percent of your salary. Many employers provide a matching contribution in their 401(k) plans. For example, a company may contribute 50 cents for each $1 contributed by an employee. This results in an immediate 50 percent return on your investment.

Tax planners advise people to contribute as much as possible to a Keogh or 401(k) plan since (1) the increased value of the investment accumulates on a tax-free basis until the funds are withdrawn and (2) contributions reduce your adjusted gross income for computing your current tax liability. Chapter 18 discusses retirement plans in greater detail.

CHANGING TAX STRATEGIES

Someone once said that "death and taxes are the only certainties of life." Changing tax laws seem to be another certainty. Each year, the IRS modifies the tax form and filing procedures. In addition, Congress frequently passes legislation that changes the tax code. These changes require that you regularly determine how to take best advantage of the tax laws for personal financial planning. Finally, carefully consider changes in your personal situation and your income level. You should carefully monitor your personal tax strategies to best serve both your daily living needs and your long-term financial goals.

CONCEPT CHECK 4-5

1 How does tax avoidance differ from tax evasion?
2 What common tax-saving methods are available to most individuals and households?

Action Application Talk to several people about the benefits and drawbacks of receiving a federal tax refund each year.

SUMMARY OF OBJECTIVES

Objective 1
Describe the importance of taxes for personal financial planning.
Tax planning can influence spending, saving, borrowing, and investing decisions. A knowledge of tax laws and maintenance of accurate tax records allow you to take advantage of appropriate tax benefits. An awareness of income taxes, sales taxes, excise taxes, property taxes, estate taxes, inheritance taxes, gift taxes, and Social Security taxes is vital for successful financial planning.

Objective 2
Calculate taxable income and the amount owed for federal income tax.
Taxable income is determined by subtracting adjustments to income, deductions, and allowances for exemptions from gross

income. Your total tax liability is based on the published tax tables or tax schedules, less any tax credits.

Objective 3
Prepare a federal income tax return.
The major sections of Form 1040 require you to calculate (1) your filing status, (2) exemptions, (3) income from all sources, (4) adjustments to your income, (5) standard deduction or itemized deductions, (6) tax credits for which you qualify, (7) other taxes you owe, (8) amounts you have withheld or paid in advance, and (9) your refund or the additional amount you owe.

Objective 4
Identify tax assistance sources.
The main sources of tax assistance are IRS services and publications, other publications, the Internet, computer software, and

professional tax preparers such as commercial tax services, enrolled agents, accountants, and attorneys.

Objective 5
Select appropriate tax strategies for different financial and personal situations.
You may reduce your tax burden by carefully planning financial decisions related to consumer purchasing, the use of debt, investments, and retirement planning.

KEY TERMS

adjusted gross income (AGI)   109

average tax rate   112

capital gains   129

earned income   108

estate tax   106

excise tax   106

exclusion   109

exemption   111

inheritance tax   107

investment income   108

itemized deductions   109

marginal tax rate   112

passive income   108

standard deduction   109

taxable income   107

tax audit   125

tax avoidance   126–127

tax credit   112

tax deduction   109

tax-deferred income   109

tax evasion   126–127

tax-exempt income   109

tax shelter   109

FINANCIAL PLANNING PROBLEMS

1. *Computing Taxable Income.* Thomas Franklin arrived at the following tax information:

   Gross salary, $41,780

   Interest earnings, $225

   Dividend income, $80

   One personal exemption, $2,650

   Itemized deductions, $3,890

   Adjustments to income, $1,150

   What amount would Thomas report as taxable income? (Obj. 1)

2. *Determining Tax Deductions.* If Lola Harper had the following itemized deductions, should she use Schedule A or the standard deduction? The standard deduction for her tax situation is $6,050. (Obj. 2)

   Donations to church and other charities, $1,980

   Medical and dental expenses exceeding 7.5 percent of adjusted gross income, $430

   State income tax, $690

   Job-related expenses exceeding 2 percent of adjusted gross income, $1,610

3. *Calculating Average Tax Rate.* What would be the average tax rate for a person who paid taxes of $4,864.14 on a taxable income of $39,870? (Obj. 2)

4. *Determining a Refund or Taxes Owed.* Based on the following data, would Ann and Carl Wilton receive a refund or owe additional taxes? (Obj. 2)

   Adjusted gross income, $43,190

   Itemized deductions, $11,420

   Child care tax credit, $80

   Federal income tax withheld, $6,784

   Amount for personal exemptions, $7,950

   Tax rate on taxable income, 15 percent

5. *Selecting Federal Tax Forms.* Which 1040 form should each of the following individuals use? (Obj. 3)

   a. A high school student with an after-school job and interest earnings of $480 from savings accounts.

   b. A college student who, due to ownership of property, is able to itemize deductions rather than take the standard deduction.

   c. A young, entry-level worker with no dependents and income only from salary.

6. *Using Federal Tax Tables.* Using the tax table in Exhibit 4–7 (p. 121), determine the amount of taxes for the following situations:

   a. A head of household with taxable income of $26,210.

   b. A single person with taxable income of $26,888.

   c. A married person filing a separate return with taxable income of $26,272. (Obj. 3)

7. *Comparing Taxes on Investments.* Would you prefer a fully taxable investment earning 10.7 percent or a tax-exempt investment earning 8.1 percent? Why? (Obj. 5)

8. *Future Value of a Tax Savings.* On December 30, you decide to make a $1,000 charitable donation. If you are in the 28 percent tax bracket, how much will you save in taxes for the current year? If you deposit that tax savings in a savings account for the next five years at 8 percent, what will be the future value of that account? (Obj. 5)

FINANCIAL PLANNING ACTIVITIES

1. *Searching the Internet for Tax Information.* Using Web sites such as www.quicken.com, *Kiplinger's Personal Finance* at www.kiplinger.com, or *Money* magazine at www.money.com, or library resources, obtain information about the tax implications of various financial planning decisions. (Obj. 1)

2. *Planning Your Tax Payment.* Survey several people about whether they get a federal tax refund or owe taxes each year. Obtain information about the following: (*a*) Do they usually get a refund or owe taxes when they file their federal tax return? (*b*) Is their situation (refund or payment) planned? (*c*) What are the reasons they want to get a refund each year? (*d*) Are there situations where getting a refund may not be a wise financial decision? (Obj. 2)

3. *Researching Current Tax Forms.* Obtain samples of current tax forms you would use to file your federal income tax return. These may be ordered by mail, obtained at a local IRS office or post office, or obtained on the Internet at www.irs.gov. (Obj. 4)

4. *Researching Tax Questions.* Use IRS publications and other reference materials to answer a specific tax question. Contact an IRS office to obtain an answer for the same question. What differences, if any, exist between the information sources? (Obj. 4)

5. *Analyzing Tax Preparation Software.* Visit a retailer that sells tax preparation software, such as www.turbotax.com, or visit the Web sites of software companies to determine the costs and features of programs you may use to prepare and file your federal income tax return. (Obj. 4)

6. *Comparing Tax Services.* Using Sheet 21 in the *Personal Financial Planner,* obtain information from two different tax preparation companies about the services they offer and the costs of their services. (Obj. 4)

7. *Determining Tax Planning Activities.* Survey friends and relatives about their tax planning strategies. You may use Sheet 22 from the *Personal Financial Planner* to obtain questions for your survey. (Obj. 5)

INTERNET CONNECTION

Comparing Tax Information Sources

Visit the Web sites of three commonly used tax information sources: (1) the Internal Revenue Service, (2) a tax preparation service, and (3) a financial planning information service, such as Kiplinger.com, Money.com, or Turbotax.com. Obtain information for the following items:

Areas of Analysis	Internal Revenue Service	Tax Preparation Service	Financial Planning Service
Web site	www.irs.gov		
Major emphasis of information			
Availability of current tax forms			
Coverage of latest tax law changes			
Other information and services			
E-file information and cost			

FINANCIAL PLANNING CASE

A Single Father's Tax Situation

Ever since his wife's death, Eric Stanford has faced difficult personal and financial circumstances. His job provides him with a fairly good income but keeps him away from his daughters, ages 8 and 10, nearly 20 days a month. This requires him to use in-home child care services that consume a large portion of his income. Since the Stanfords live in a small apartment, this arrangement has been very inconvenient.

Due to the costs of caring for his children, Eric has only a minimal amount withheld from his salary for federal income taxes. This makes more money available during the year, but for the last few years he has had to make large payments in April—another financial burden.

Although Eric has created an investment fund for his daughters' college education and for his retirement, he has not sought to select investments that offer tax benefits. Overall, he needs to look at several aspects of his tax planning activities to find strategies that will best serve his current and future financial needs.

Eric has assembled the following information for the current tax year:

Earnings from wages	$42,590
Interest earned on savings	$125
IRA deduction	$2,000
Checking account interest	$65
Three exemptions	$2,750 each
Current standard deduction for filing status	$6,350
Amount withheld for federal income tax	$3,178
Tax credit for child care	$400
Filing status	Head of household

Questions

1. What are Eric's major financial concerns in his current situation?
2. In what ways might Eric improve his tax planning efforts?
3. Is Eric typical of many people in our society with regard to tax planning? Why or why not?
4. What additional actions might Eric investigate with regard to taxes and personal financial planning?
5. Calculate the following
   a. What is Eric's taxable income? (Refer to Exhibit 4–1, page 108.)
   b. What is his total tax liability? (Use Exhibit 4–7, page 121.) What is his average tax rate?
   c. Based on his withholding, will Eric receive a refund or owe additional tax? What is the amount?

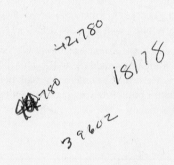

VIDEO CASE

A Taxing Situation

Effective tax strategies vary based on a person's life situation. Joan's spending patterns give her great enjoyment of life. However, some of these financial decisions reduce her ability to take advantage of various tax benefits.

Nelson owns a small business for which he is able to deduct various work-related expenses that lower his taxable income. However, his self-employed status results in other taxes not commonly encountered by people who work for others.

In their retirement, Jim and Ida are pleased to be able to provide for their current financial needs. In addition, during their lives, they have made various saving and investment decisions that allow them to offer financial assistance to their children and grandchildren.

Questions

1. What actions might Joan take to reduce the financial and emotional impact of taxes?
2. What are possible tax benefits and drawbacks of operating your own business?
3. What tax strategies have Jim and Ida used to effectively manage their finances over the years?

YOUR PERSONAL FINANCIAL PLANNER IN ACTION

Tax Planning Activities

Taxes are a fact of financial planning. However, various actions can be taken to reduce the time and money that goes toward taxes.

Your Short Term Financial Planning Activities	Resources
1. Develop a system for filing and storing various tax records related to income, deductible expenses, and current tax forms.	See Exhibit 4–2 (p. 111) www.turbotax.com www.taxcut.com www.taxsoft.com
2. Using the IRS and other Web sites, identify recent changes in tax laws that may affect your financial planning decisions.	www.irs.gov www.1040.com
3. Using current IRS tax forms and tax tables, estimate your tax liability for the current year.	PFP Sheet 20 www.irs.gov www.taxadmin.org
4. Compare the cost of tax preparation services.	PFP Sheet 21 www.ey.com/us/tax www.hrblock.com
Your Long-Term Financial Planning Activities	
1 Identify saving and investing decisions that would minimize future income taxes.	PFP Sheet 22 www.taxprophet.com
2 Develop a plan for actions to take related to your current and future tax situation.	Text pages 126–131 www.taxlogic.com

CONTINUING CASE

Taxes

Life Situation

Single
Age 22
Starting a career
No dependents

Financial Data

Monthly income $2,600
Living expenses $2,180
Assets $8,200
Liabilities $3,470
Emergency fund $530

During the year, Pam has had tax withholding greater than her actual tax liability. As a result, Pam is expecting a fairly large tax refund. In the past, she has always used tax refunds to finance major purchases (a vacation or furniture) or pay off credit card debt. Currently, she is also considering saving some of the money.

Questions

1. Assume Pam's federal tax refund is $1,100. Given her current situation, what should she do with the refund?

2. Based on her current and future life situation, what tax planning activities might Pam consider?

3. In what ways might *Personal Financial Planner* sheets 20–22 be useful to Pam for her tax planning activities?

5 Financial Services: Savings Plans and Payment Accounts

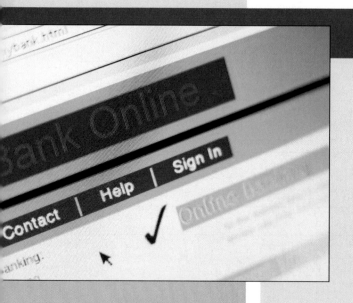

Digital Study Tools

Online Learning Center Study Tools for This Chapter

- Multiple-choice quiz
- Flashcards
- eLearning sessions
- Crossword puzzle
- Personal Finance Online: Personal Financial Statements & Budgeting

Student CD Study Tools for This Chapter

- Self-study software
- Narrated PowerPoint
- Personal financial planning software: Worksheets 23–28

Key Concept

Assessing financial services will help you minimize banking fees and maximize interest earned on deposited funds. The use of online banking provides the convenience of quickly comparing financial institutions along with conducting banking transactions from any location at any time of the day or night.

Learning Objectives

1 Analyze factors that affect the selection and use of financial services.

2 Compare the types of financial institutions.

3 Compare the costs and benefits of various savings plans.

4 Identify the factors used to evaluate different savings plans.

5 Compare the costs and benefits of different types of payment accounts.

Online Banking: "Press 1 to Withdraw Cash, Press 2 to Deposit, Press 3 for Higher Fees"

"Wow! My account balance is a little lower than I expected," commented Lisa Cross as she reviewed her monthly bank statement. "Wait a minute! There's nearly $20 in fees for ATM withdrawals and other service charges," she cried out.

Many people do not realize the amount they pay each month for various bank fees. These charges result from various services that give customers convenience, reliability, and safety.

"Oh no! I also went below the minimum balance required for my *free* checking account," Lisa groaned. "That cost me $7.50!"

Lisa is not alone in her frustration with fees paid for financial services. While careless money management caused many of these charges, others could be reduced or eliminated by comparing costs at various financial institutions.

Many consumers are also upset with slow customer service and long waits in lines. These drawbacks have caused many customers to consider the use of online banking services.

Whether using the Internet services of your current financial institution or starting an account with a "Web" bank, you can gain faster access to your account. Other benefits may also be present. Often, costs of online banking services are lower than in traditional settings. Online banking can also mean access to an expanded array of financial services. For example, some online bank accounts include low-cost, online investment trading and instant loan approval.

Lisa believes that online banking services provide her with an opportunity to better control her financial service costs. However, she also has concerns about introductory low costs, privacy, and security of transaction information.

QUESTIONS

What Actions Should Be Taken?

1. What benefits might Lisa gain when using online banking services?
2. What factors should Lisa consider when selecting various banking services?

What About Your Situation?

3. How well informed are you regarding (a) online banking services, (b) certificates of deposit and other savings plans, and (c) checking accounts and other payment methods?
4. What actions might you take to better understand the concerns associated with using online banking?

Learn More Online

Based on information at www.bankrate.com, describe how you could minimize various banking fees.

A Cash Management Strategy

Objective 1

Analyze factors that affect the selection and use of financial services.

More than 20,000 banks, savings and loan associations, credit unions, and other financial institutions provide a variety of services for your payment and savings needs. Today a trip to "the bank" may mean a visit to a credit union, an automatic teller machine in a shopping mall, or transferring funds on the Web.

While some financial decisions relate directly to goals, your daily activities require various financial services. Exhibit 5–1 provides an overview of financial services for managing cash flows and moving toward specific financial goals.

In addition to separate services, many financial institutions offer *account aggregation,* in which customers access a private online banking site. You are able to view deposit accounts, investments, credit cards, loans, mortgages, rewards programs, and individual retirement accounts. With account aggregation, you can view the account status and the history of payments and charges, and complete various banking transactions.

MEETING DAILY MONEY NEEDS

Buying groceries, paying the rent, and other routine spending activities require a cash management plan.

MANAGING CASH   Cash, check, credit card, or automatic teller machine (ATM) card are the common payment choices. While most people desire ease of payment, they must also consider fees and the potential for impulse buying and overspending. For example, in recent years ATM fees have risen from nothing to $1 or $2 per cash withdrawal and even higher charges for balance inquiries. If you are charged two $1 transaction fees a week and could invest your money at 5 percent, this convenience will cost you more than $570 over a five-year period.

Common mistakes made when managing current cash needs include

- Overspending as a result of impulse buying and using credit cards.

Exhibit 5–1

Financial services for managing cash flow

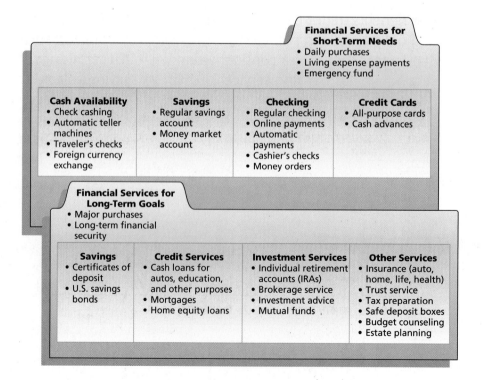

- Having insufficient liquid assets (cash, checking account) to pay current bills.
- Using savings or borrowing to pay for current expenses.
- Failing to put unneeded funds in an interest-earning savings account or investment plan to achieve long-term goals.

SOURCES OF QUICK CASH No matter how carefully you manage your money, there may be times when you will need more cash than you currently have available. To cope with that situation, you have two basic choices: liquidate savings or borrow. A savings account, certificate of deposit, mutual fund, or other investment may be accessed when you need funds. Or a credit card cash advance or a personal loan may be appropriate. Remember, however, that both using savings and increasing borrowing reduce your net worth and your potential to achieve long-term financial security.

Information on various financial services is available from many sources.

TYPES OF FINANCIAL SERVICES

Banks and other financial institutions offer services to meet a variety of needs. These services fall into four main categories.

1. SAVINGS Safe storage of funds for future use is a basic need for everyone. These services, commonly referred to as *time deposits,* include money in savings accounts and certificates of deposit. Selection of a savings plan is commonly based on the interest rate earned, liquidity, safety, and convenience, which are discussed later in the chapter.

2. PAYMENT SERVICES The ability to transfer money to other parties is a necessary part of daily business activities. Checking accounts and other payment methods, commonly called *demand deposits,* are also covered later in the chapter.

Sheet 23
Planning the use of financial services

3. BORROWING Most people use credit at some time during their lives. Credit alternatives range from short-term accounts, such as credit cards and cash loans, to long-term borrowing, such as a home mortgage. Chapters 6 and 7 discuss the types and costs of credit.

4. OTHER FINANCIAL SERVICES Insurance protection, investment for the future, real estate purchases, tax assistance, and financial planning are additional services you may need for successful financial management. With some financial plans, someone else manages your funds. A **trust** is a legal agreement that provides for the management and control of assets by one party for the benefit of another. This type of arrangement is most commonly created through a commercial bank or a lawyer. Parents who want to set aside certain funds for their children's education may use a trust. The investments and money in the trust are managed by a bank, and the necessary amounts go to the children for their educational expenses. Trusts are covered in more detail in Chapter 19.

trust A legal agreement that provides for the management and control of assets by one party for the benefit of another.

To simplify the maze of financial services and to attract customers, many financial institutions offer all-in-one accounts. An **asset management account,** also called a *cash management account,* provides a complete financial services program for a single fee. Investment brokers and other financial institutions offer this all-purpose account, which usually includes a checking account, an ATM card, a credit card, online banking, as well as a line of credit for obtaining quick cash loans. These accounts also provide access to

asset management account An all-in-one account that includes savings, checking, borrowing, investing, and other financial services for a single fee; also called a *cash management account.*

stock, bond, mutual fund, and other types of investments. Asset management accounts are offered by companies such as American Express (www.americanexpress.com) and Charles Schwab (www.schwab.com).

ELECTRONIC BANKING

Banking by telephone, home computer, and other online services continues to expand, with 24-hour access to various transactions (see Exhibit 5–2). Most banks and other financial institutions have "cyber" branches that provide the following:

1. *Direct deposit* of paychecks and government payments is used by a major portion of our society. Funds are deposited electronically and available automatically for your use.

2. *Automatic payments* transfer funds for rent, mortgage, utilities, loan payment, and investment deposits without writing a check. Be sure to check your bank statement regularly to ensure that correct amounts have been deducted.

3. Access to an **automatic teller machine (ATM),** also called a *cash machine,* allows banking and other types of transactions such as buying bus passes, postage stamps, and gift certificates. To minimize ATM fees, compare several financial institutions, use your bank's ATM to avoid surcharges, and withdraw larger amounts to avoid fees on several small transactions.

automatic teller machine (ATM) A computer terminal used to conduct banking transactions.

Exhibit **5-2**

Electronic banking services

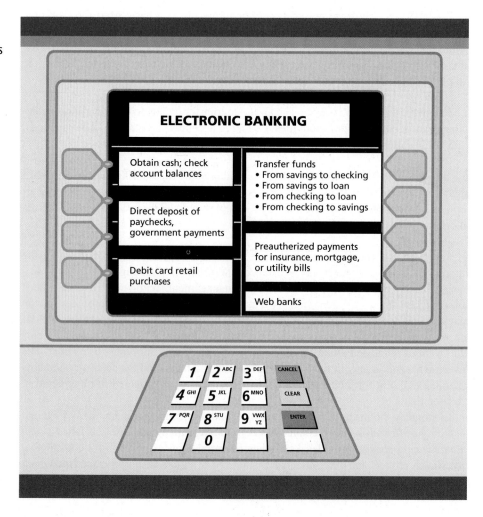

4. A **debit card,** or *cash card,* activates ATM transactions and may also be used to make purchases. A debit card is in contrast to a *credit card,* since you are spending your own funds rather than borrowing additional money.

Electronic banking services are commonly available at many locations.

A lost or stolen debit card can be expensive. If you notify the financial institution within two days of the lost card, your liability for unauthorized use is $50. After that, you can be liable for up to $500 of unauthorized use for up to 60 days. Beyond that, your liability is unlimited. However, some card issuers use the same rules for lost or stolen debit cards as for credit cards: a $50 maximum. Of course, you are not liable for unauthorized use, such as a con artist using your account number to make a purchase. Remember to report the fraud within 60 days of receiving your statement to protect your right not to be charged for the transaction.

5. *Online banking* is commonly available through the Web site of a financial institution. Making transfers among accounts, viewing balances, and authorizing payments are some of the many online banking activities.

Often, this service includes *account aggregation,* with access to all of your accounts. You can view and implement various payment, savings, loan, and investment transactions.

debit card A plastic access card used in computerized banking transactions; also called a *cash card* or *ATM card.*

OPPORTUNITY COSTS OF FINANCIAL SERVICES

When making decisions about spending and saving, consider the trade-off between current satisfaction and long-term financial security. Consider the opportunity cost—what you give up—when you evaluate, select, and use financial services. Common trade-offs related to financial services include the following:

- Higher returns of long-term savings and investment plans may be achieved at the cost of *low liquidity,* the inability to obtain your money quickly.

- The convenience of a 24-hour automatic teller machine or a bank branch office near your home or place of work should be considered against service fees.

- The "no-fee" checking account that requires a non-interest-bearing $500 minimum balance means lost interest of nearly $400 at 6 percent compounded over 10 years.

You should evaluate costs and benefits in both monetary and personal terms to choose the financial services that best serve your needs.

> **DID YOU KNOW?**
>
> According to the 2004 Community Bank Competitiveness Survey, published in the ABA Banking Journal, over 60 percent of the bankers reported observing an increase in the offering of free checking.

FINANCIAL SERVICES AND ECONOMIC CONDITIONS

Changing interest rates, rising consumer prices, and other economic factors also influence financial services. For successful financial planning, be aware of the current trends and future prospects for interest rates (see Exhibit 5–3). You can learn about these trends and prospects by reading *Wall Street Journal* (www.wsj.com), the business section of

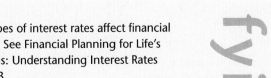

What types of interest rates affect financial services? See Financial Planning for Life's Situations: Understanding Interest Rates page 143

fyi

Exhibit **5-3**

Changing interest rates and decisions related to financial services

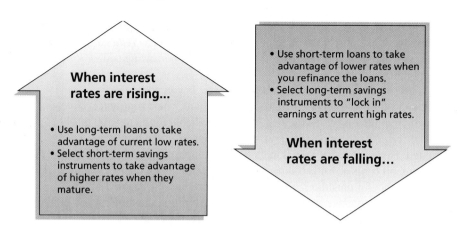

When interest rates are rising...

- Use long-term loans to take advantage of current low rates.
- Select short-term savings instruments to take advantage of higher rates when they mature.

- Use short-term loans to take advantage of lower rates when you refinance the loans.
- Select long-term savings instruments to "lock in" earnings at current high rates.

When interest rates are falling...

daily newspapers, and business periodicals such as *BusinessWeek* (www.business week.com), *Forbes* (www.forbes.com), and *Fortune* (www.fortune.com).

CONCEPT CHECK 5-1

1 What is the relationship between financial services and overall financial planning?

2 What are the major categories of financial services?

3 What financial services are available through electronic banking systems?

4 Why shouldn't you select financial services only on the basis of monetary factors?

5 How do changing economic conditions affect the use of financial services?

Action Application Survey several people to determine awareness and use of online banking services.

Financial Institutions

Objective 2

Compare the types of financial institutions.

Many businesses, such as insurance companies, investment brokers, and credit card companies, have become involved in financial services previously limited to banks. Companies such as General Motors, Sears, and AT&T now issue or sponsor credit cards. Banks have also expanded their competitive efforts by opening offices that specialize in financial services such as investments, insurance, or real estate.

Despite changes in the banking environment, many familiar financial institutions still serve your needs. Most of these institutions have expanded their services. As Exhibit 5–4 shows, financial institutions fall into two major categories along with extended service and online organizations.

DEPOSIT INSTITUTIONS

The financial institutions that most people use serve as intermediaries between suppliers (savers) and users (borrowers) of funds. These deposit-type institutions include commercial banks, savings and loan associations, mutual savings banks, and credit unions.

COMMERCIAL BANKS

commercial bank A financial institution that offers a full range of financial services to individuals, businesses, and government agencies.

COMMERCIAL BANKS A **commercial bank** offers a full range of financial services, including checking, savings, and lending, along with many other services. Commercial banks are organized as corporations, with individual investors (stockhold-

Financial Planning for Life's Situations

UNDERSTANDING INTEREST RATES

When people discuss higher or lower interest rates, they could be talking about one of many types. Some interest rates refer to the cost of borrowing by a business; others refer to the cost of buying a home. Your awareness of various types of interest rates can help you plan your spending, saving, borrowing, and investing. The accompanying table describes some commonly reported interest rates and gives their *annual average* for selected years.

Using the business section of a newspaper, the *Wall Street Journal,* the Web site of the Federal Reserve System (www.federalreserve.gov), or other business information sources, obtain current numbers for some or all of these interest rates. How might the current trend in interest rates affect your financial decisions?

	1975	1980	1985	1990	1995	2000	2004	Current
Prime rate—an indication of the rate banks charge large corporations	7.85%	15.26%	9.93%	10.01%	8.83%	9.23%	4.34%	____%
Discount rate—the rate financial institutions are charged to borrow funds from Federal Reserve banks	6.25	11.77	7.69	6.98	5.21	5.73	2.34	____
T-bill rate—the yield on short-term (13-week) U.S. government debt obligations	5.78	11.43	7.48	7.51	5.51	5.66	1.37	____
Treasury bond rate—the yield on long-term (20-year) U.S. government debt obligations	8.19	11.39	10.97	8.55	6.96	6.23	5.04	____
Mortgage rate—the amount individuals are paying to borrow for the purchase of a new home	9.00	12.66	11.55	10.13	7.95	8.06	5.84	____
Corporate bond rate—the cost of borrowing for large U.S. corporations	8.83	11.94	11.37	9.32	7.59	7.62	5.63	____
Certificate of deposit rate—the rate for six-month time deposits at savings institutions	6.89	12.99	8.25	8.17	5.93	6.59	1.74	____

Source: Federal Reserve Statistical Release: *Selected Interest Rates* (H-15), www.federalreserve.gov.

ers) contributing the capital the banks need to operate. National banks are chartered by the federal government and state banks by state governments. State-chartered banks are usually subject to fewer restrictions than federally chartered banks.

In recent years, some banks have opened full-service branch offices in grocery stores. These are truly "financial supermarkets," offering everything from automatic teller machines and loans to safe deposit boxes.

SAVINGS AND LOAN ASSOCIATIONS
While the commercial bank traditionally served businesses and individuals with large amounts of money, the **savings and loan association (S&L)** specialized in savings accounts and loans for mortgages.

savings and loan association (S&L) A financial institution that traditionally specialized in savings accounts and mortgage loans.

143

Exhibit 5-4

Types of financial institutions

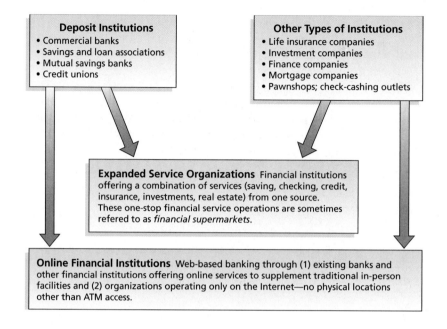

Deposit Institutions
• Commercial banks
• Savings and loan associations
• Mutual savings banks
• Credit unions

Other Types of Institutions
• Life insurance companies
• Investment companies
• Finance companies
• Mortgage companies
• Pawnshops; check-cashing outlets

Expanded Service Organizations Financial institutions offering a combination of services (saving, checking, credit, insurance, investments, real estate) from one source. These one-stop financial service operations are sometimes refered to as *financial supermarkets*.

Online Financial Institutions Web-based banking through (1) existing banks and other financial institutions offering online services to supplement traditional in-person facilities and (2) organizations operating only on the Internet—no physical locations other than ATM access.

Today, savings and loan associations also offer checking accounts, specialized savings plans, loans to businesses, and other investment and financial planning services.

mutual savings bank A financial institution that is owned by depositors and specializes in savings accounts and mortgage loans.

MUTUAL SAVINGS BANKS   A **mutual savings bank** is owned by depositors and, like the traditional savings and loan association, specializes in savings accounts and mortgage loans. Mutual savings banks are located mainly in the northeastern United States. Unlike the profits of other types of financial institutions, the profits of a mutual savings bank go to the depositors, paying higher rates on savings.

credit union A user-owned, nonprofit, cooperative financial institution that is organized for the benefit of its members.

CREDIT UNIONS   A **credit union** is a user-owned, nonprofit, cooperative financial institution. Traditionally, credit union members had to have a common bond such as work, church, or community affiliation. As the common bond restriction was loosened, the membership of credit unions increased. Today more than 80 million people belong to over 9,000 credit unions in the United States.

Credit unions offer a low-cost alternative for financial services. For additional information about credit unions, go to **www.cuna.org**.

Each year, surveys conducted by consumer organizations and others report lower fees for checking accounts, lower loan rates, and higher levels of user satisfaction for credit unions compared to other financial institutions. Most credit unions offer credit cards, mortgages, home equity loans, direct deposit, cash machines, safe deposit boxes, and investment services.

OTHER FINANCIAL INSTITUTIONS

Financial services are also available from institutions such as life insurance companies, investment companies, finance companies, mortgage companies, pawnshops, and check-cashing outlets.

LIFE INSURANCE COMPANIES   While the main purpose of life insurance is to provide financial security for dependents, many life insurance policies contain savings and investment features. Chapter 12 discusses these policies. In recent years, life insurance companies have expanded their financial services to include investment and retirement planning.

INVESTMENT COMPANIES   Investment companies, also referred to as *mutual funds,* offer banking-type services. A common service of these organizations is the **money market fund,** a combination savings–investment plan in which the investment company uses your money to purchase a variety of short-term financial instruments. Unlike accounts at most banks, savings and loan associations, and credit unions, investment company accounts are not covered by federal deposit insurance. Investors in money market funds are usually allowed to write a limited number of checks, providing the convenience of liquidity.

FINANCE COMPANIES   Making loans to consumers and small businesses is the main function of finance companies. These loans have short and intermediate terms with higher rates than most other lenders charge. Some finance companies have expanded their activities to offer other financial planning services.

MORTGAGE COMPANIES   Mortgage companies are organized primarily to provide loans to purchase homes. Chapter 9 discusses the activities of mortgage companies.

PAWNSHOPS   Pawnshops make loans based on the value of tangible possessions such as jewelry or other valuable items. Many low- and moderate-income families use these organizations to obtain cash loans quickly. Pawnshops charge higher fees than other financial institutions.

CHECK-CASHING OUTLETS   Most financial institutions will not cash a check unless the person has an account. The more than 6,000 check-cashing outlets (CCOs) charge anywhere from 1 to 20 percent of the face value of a check; the average cost is between 2 and 3 percent. However, for a low-income family, that can be a significant portion of the total household budget (see the Financial Planning for Life's Situations box on page 146).

   CCOs offer a variety of services, including electronic tax filing, money orders, private postal boxes, utility bill payment, and the sale of bus and subway tokens. You can usually obtain these services for less at other locations.

Credit unions can offer a low-cost alternative for financial services.

money market fund A savings-investment plan offered by investment companies, with earnings based on investments in various short-term financial instruments.

> **DID YOU KNOW?**
>
> According to a study conducted by the U.S. Public Interest Research Group (www.uspirg.org), credit unions charge the lowest fees among financial institutions.

COMPARING FINANCIAL INSTITUTIONS

The basic concerns of a financial services customer are simple:

- Where can I get the best return on my savings?
- How can I minimize the cost of checking and payments services?
- Will I be able to borrow money when I need it?

   As you use financial services, decide what you want from the organization that will serve your needs. With the financial marketplace constantly changing, you must assess the various services and other factors before selecting an organization (see Exhibit 5–5).

   The services the financial institution offers are likely to be a major factor. Personal service is important to many customers. Convenience may be provided by business hours, branch offices, automatic teller machines, and online service. Convenience and service have a cost, so be sure to compare fees and other charges at several financial institutions.

> **DID YOU KNOW?**
>
> 7-Eleven is expanding into a wide range of financial services. The electronic kiosks in their stores will allow cashing of paychecks, paying utility bills, and obtaining money orders.

BEWARE OF HIGH-COST FINANCIAL SERVICES

Would you pay $8 to cash a $100 check? Or pay $20 to borrow $100 for two weeks? Many people without ready access to financial services (especially low-income consumers) commonly use the services of check-cashing outlets, pawnshops, payday loan stores, and rent-to-own centers. Offers of "quick cash" and "low payments" attract consumers without a bank account or credit cards.

PAWNSHOPS
Even during times of economic prosperity, thousands of consumers are increasingly in need of small loans—usually $50 to $75, to be repaid in 30 to 45 days. Pawnshops have become the "neighborhood bankers" and the "local shopping malls," since they provide both lending and retail shopping services, selling items that owners do not redeem. While states regulate the interest rates charged by pawnshops, 3 percent a month or higher is common.

PAYDAY LOANS
Many consumer organizations warn of increased use of *payday loans,* also referred to as *cash advances, check advance loans, postdated check loans,* and *delayed deposit loans.* Desperate borrowers pay annual interest rates of as much as 780 percent and more to obtain needed cash from payday loan companies. These enterprises have increased to more than 8,000. The most common users of payday loans are workers who have become trapped by debts run up by free spending or have been driven into debt by misfortune.

In a typical payday loan, a consumer writes a personal check for $115 to borrow $100 for 14 days. The payday lender agrees to hold the check until the next payday. This $15 finance charge for the 14 days translates into an annual percentage rate of 391 percent. Some consumers "roll over" their loans, paying another $15 for the $100 loan for the next 14 days. After a few rollovers, the finance charge can exceed the amount borrowed. The Chicago Department of Consumer Services has reported annual rates ranging from 659 to 1,300 percent for some payday loans.

RENT-TO-OWN CENTERS
Years ago, people who rented furniture and appliances found few deluxe items available. Today rental businesses offer big-screen televisions, seven-piece cherrywood bedroom sets, and personal computers. The rental-purchase industry is defined as stores that lease products to consumers who can own the item if they complete a certain number of monthly or weekly payments.

In Wisconsin, more than 10,000 customers of the Rent-A-Center chain became part of a class action lawsuit seeking refunds of finance charges for rented merchandise. The suit accused the rental chain of illegally charging interest rates as high as 100 percent to rent televisions and other appliances, often to customers in low-income areas. The rental agreements were disguised as leases to get around a Wisconsin law that requires disclosure of any credit sale interest rate above 5 percent.

Finally, you should consider safety factors and interest rates. Obtain information about earnings you will receive on savings and checking accounts and the rate you will pay for borrowed funds. Most financial institutions have deposit insurance to protect customers against losses; however, not all of them are insured by federal government programs. Investigate the type of protection you will have.

Your selection of a financial institution should be based on valid information. Never assume that one will provide a better interest rate or service than another. You need to compare banks, savings and loan associations, and credit unions with other providers of financial services.

Exhibit 5-5

How should you choose a financial institution?

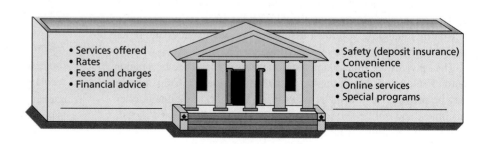

- Services offered
- Rates
- Fees and charges
- Financial advice

- Safety (deposit insurance)
- Convenience
- Location
- Online services
- Special programs

Savings Plans

As Chapter 3 emphasized, a savings program is needed to achieve financial goals. Evaluation of various savings plans is the starting point of this process. An overview of savings alternatives is presented in Exhibit 5–6.

Objective 3

Compare the costs and benefits of various savings plans.

REGULAR SAVINGS ACCOUNTS

Regular savings accounts, traditionally called *passbook accounts,* usually involve a low or no minimum balance. Today, instead of a passbook showing deposits and withdrawals, savers receive a monthly or quarterly statement with a summary of transactions.

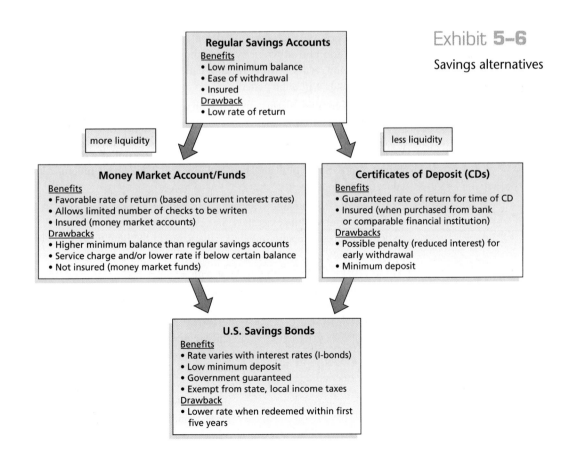

Exhibit **5–6**

Savings alternatives

share account A regular savings account at a credit union.

A regular savings account usually allows you to withdraw money as needed. Banks, savings and loan associations, and other financial institutions offer regular savings accounts. At a credit union, these savings plans are called **share accounts.**

CERTIFICATES OF DEPOSIT

certificate of deposit (CD) A savings plan requiring that a certain amount be left on deposit for a stated time period to earn a specified interest rate.

Higher earnings are commonly available to savers when they leave money on deposit for a set time period. A **certificate of deposit (CD)** is a savings plan requiring that a certain amount be left on deposit for a stated time period (ranging from 30 days to five or more years) to earn a specific rate of return. These time deposits can be an attractive and a safe savings alternative. However, most financial institutions impose a penalty for early withdrawal of CD funds.

TYPES OF CDS   Financial institutions offer certificates of deposit with a variety of features:

1. *Rising-rate* or *bump-up CDs* may have higher rates at various intervals, such as every six months. However, beware of ads that highlight a higher rate in the future. This rate may be in effect only for the last couple of months for an 18- or 24-month CD. Also, some bump-ups may require a rather large minimum investment.

2. *Indexed CDs* have earnings based on the stock market. In times of strong stock performance, your CD earnings can be higher than those on other CDs. At other times, however, you may earn no interest and may even lose part of your savings. A CD based on the consumer price index can result in higher returns as inflation increases.

3. *Callable CDs* start with higher rates and usually have long-term maturities, as high as 10 to 15 years. These savings plans also have the benefit of federal deposit insurance. However, the bank may "call" the account after a stipulated period, such as one or two years, if interest rates drop. When the call option is exercised, the saver receives the original investment principal and any interest that has been earned. Remember, don't be drawn in by the high initial rate on a callable CD; it could change in a few years. Also, if it is not called, you may not have the flexibility to withdraw funds without a penalty.

4. *Global CDs* combine higher interest with a hedge on future changes in the dollar compared to other currencies. As exchange rates change, your earnings can fluctuate. A weaker U.S. dollar (compared to a given foreign currency) can result in a higher return on your savings. In contrast, a stronger dollar will result in a lower rate of return. Some global CDs offered by U.S. banks have federal deposit insurance; others do not.

5. *Promotional CDs* attempt to attract savers with gifts or special rates. A Colorado bank once offered Rolex watches, archery equipment, and Zodiac inflatable boats in lieu of interest. Be sure to balance the value of the item against the lost interest.

MANAGING CDS   When saving with a CD or *rolling over* a CD (buying a new one at maturity), carefully assess all earnings and costs. Do not allow your financial institution to automatically roll over your money into another CD for the same term. If interest rates have dropped, you might consider a shorter maturity. Or if you believe rates are at a peak and you won't need the money for some time, obtain a CD with a longer term.

Consider creating a CD *portfolio* with CDs maturing at different times, for example, $2,000 in a three-month CD, $2,000 in a six-month CD, $2,000 in a one-year CD, and $2,000 in a two-year

Want to compare the rates on CDs around the country? Information may be obtained at **www.bankrate.com.**

CD. This will give you some degree of liquidity and flexibility when you reinvest your funds.

Don't hesitate to buy CDs by mail or online from a financial institution in another state. You might earn as much as a full percentage point higher than with your local bank. Also, when interest rates stay low, consider other savings alternatives such as savings bonds, mutual funds, and government securities. Current information about CD rates at various financial institutions may be obtained at www.bankrate.com.

MONEY MARKET ACCOUNTS AND FUNDS

To meet consumer demand for higher savings rates, a savings plan with a floating interest rate was created. A **money market account** is a savings account that requires a minimum balance and has earnings based on market interest rates. Money market accounts allow you to write a limited number of checks to make large payments or to transfer money to other accounts. Since money market accounts may impose a fee when you go below the required minimum balance, usually $1,000, consider a regular savings account or a payroll deduction savings plan.

money market account A savings account offered by banks, savings and loan associations, and credit unions that requires a minimum balance and has earnings based on market interest rates.

Both money market accounts and money market funds offer earnings based on current interest rates, and both have minimum-balance restrictions and allow check writing. The major difference is in safety. Money market *accounts* at banks and savings and loan associations are covered by federal deposit insurance. This is not true of money market *funds,* which are a product of investment companies. Since money market funds invest mainly in short-term (less than a year) government and corporate securities, however, they are usually quite safe.

U.S. SAVINGS BONDS

Years ago, the low return on savings bonds made their purchase a patriotic act rather than a wise saving choice. In recent years, however, the Treasury Department has offered various programs to make buying savings bonds more attractive.

EE BONDS Series EE bonds (called Patriot Bonds after the September 11, 2001, terrorist attacks) may be purchased for amounts ranging from $25 to $5,000 (face values of $50 to $10,000, respectively). Electronic EE bonds are purchased at face value, for example you pay $50 for a $50 bond. These bonds may be purchased in amounts of $25 or more.

EE bonds increase in value every month, as interest accrues monthly and compounds semiannually. If you redeem EE Bonds before five years; you forfeit the latest three months of interest; after five years, you are not penalized. A bond must be held for one year before it can be cashed.

EE bonds purchased between May 1997 and April 30, 2005, earned market-based interest. Since that time, a fixed interest rate has been paid. Series EE bonds continue to earn interest for 30 years, well beyond the time at which the face value is reached. The main tax advantages of Series EE bonds are that (1) the interest earned is exempt from state and local taxes and (2) you do not have to pay federal income tax on earnings until the bonds are redeemed.

Redeemed Series EE bonds may be exempt from federal income tax if the funds are used to pay tuition and fees at a college, university, or qualified technical school for yourself or a dependent. The bonds must be purchased by an individual who is at least 24 years old, and they must be issued in the names of one or both parents. These provisions have been designed to

> **DID YOU KNOW?**
>
> In South Korea, special chips in cell phones are used to pay for purchases at vending machines. The Octopus Card in Hong Kong has a radio-frequency chip for use in making payments at a wide range of businesses.

assist low- and middle-income households; people whose incomes exceed a certain amount do not qualify for the exemption.

HH BONDS   Series HH bonds are *current-income* bonds, which earn interest every six months. The interest is deposited electronically to your bank account. This interest is taxed as current income. The semiannual interest payments of HH bonds make them a popular source of retirement income.

You can redeem your HH bonds at any time after six months from the issue date. The value of HH bonds doesn't change, so when redeemed, you get back your original investment. HH bonds were available in denominations of $500, $1,000, $5,000, and $10,000. As of 2004, investors are no longer able to reinvest HH bonds or exchange EE bonds for HH bonds.

I BONDS   The I bond earns a combined rate consisting of (1) a fixed rate for the life of the bond and (2) an inflation rate that changes twice a year. Every six months, a new, fixed base rate is set for new bonds. The additional interest payment is recalculated twice a year, based on the current annual inflation rate. I bonds are sold in the same denominations as EE bonds, but are purchased at face value, not at a discount. Also, as with EE bonds, the minimum holding period is one year.

A person may purchase up to $15,000 ($30,000 maturity face) of U.S. savings bonds a year. This amount applies to any person, so parents may buy an additional $15,000 in each child's name. Banks and other financial institutions sell U.S. savings bonds; they may also be purchased online. Lost, stolen, or destroyed savings bonds will be replaced by the government free of charge. Additional information and current value calculations for savings bonds values may be obtained at www.savingsbonds.gov.

Sheet 24
Using savings to achieve financial goals

For the latest rates and information on U.S. savings bonds, go to **www.savingsbonds.gov.**

CONCEPT CHECK 5-3

1 What are the main types of savings plans offered by financial institutions?
2 How does a money market *account* differ from a money market *fund?*
3 What are the benefits of U.S. savings bonds?

Action Application Conduct online research to obtain past and current data on various interest rates (such as prime rate, T-bill rate, mortgage rate, corporate bond rate, and 6-month CD rate). Information may be obtained at www.federal reserve.gov and other Web sites. How do these rates affect various personal financial decisions?

Evaluating Savings Plans

Objective 4

Identify the factors used to evaluate different savings plans.

rate of return The percentage of increase in the value of savings as a result of interest earned; also called *yield.*

Your selection of a savings plan will be influenced by various factors, as shown in Exhibit 5–7.

RATE OF RETURN

Earnings on savings can be measured by the **rate of return,** or *yield,* the percentage of increase in the value of your savings from earned interest. For example, a $100 savings account that earned $5 after a year would have a rate of return, or yield, of 5 percent.

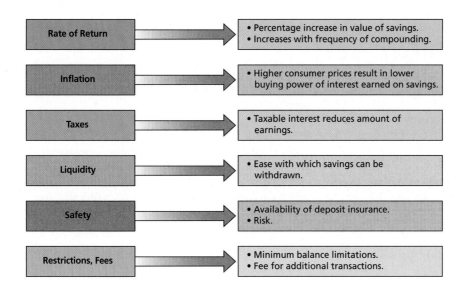

Exhibit **5-7**

Selecting a savings plan

- **Rate of Return** → • Percentage increase in value of savings.
  • Increases with frequency of compounding.
- **Inflation** → • Higher consumer prices result in lower buying power of interest earned on savings.
- **Taxes** → • Taxable interest reduces amount of earnings.
- **Liquidity** → • Ease with which savings can be withdrawn.
- **Safety** → • Availability of deposit insurance.
  • Risk.
- **Restrictions, Fees** → • Minimum balance limitations.
  • Fee for additional transactions.

This rate of return was determined by dividing the interest earned ($5) by the amount in the savings account ($100).

COMPOUNDING   The yield on your savings usually will be greater than the stated interest rate. **Compounding** refers to interest that is earned on previously earned interest. Each time interest is added to your savings, the next interest amount is computed on the new balance in the account. Future value and present value calculations, introduced in Chapter 1, take compounding into account.

compounding A process that calculates interest based on previously earned interest.

The more frequent the compounding, the higher your rate of return will be. For example, $100 in a savings account that earns 6 percent compounded annually will increase $6 after a year. But the same $100 in a 6 percent account compounded daily will earn $6.19 for the year. Although this difference may seem slight, large amounts held in savings for long periods of time will result in far higher differences (see Exhibit 5–8).

	Compounding Method			
End of Year	**Daily**	**Monthly**	**Quarterly**	**Annually**
1	$10,832.78	$10,830.00	$10,824.32	$10,800.00
2	11,743.91	11,728.88	11,716.59	11,664.00
3	12,712.17	12,702.37	12,682.41	12,597.12
4	13,770.82	13,756.66	13,727.85	13,604.89
5	14,917.62	14,898.46	14,859.46	14,693.28
Annual yield	8.33%	8.30%	8.24%	8.00%

Exhibit **5-8**

Compounding frequency affects the savings yield

Shorter compounding periods result in higher yields. This chart shows the growth of $10,000, five-year CDs paying the same rate of 8 percent, but with different compounding methods.

TRUTH IN SAVINGS   The *Truth in Savings* law (Federal Reserve Regulation DD) requires financial institutions to disclose the following information on savings account plans:

- Fees on deposit accounts.
- The interest rate.
- The annual percentage yield (APY).
- Other terms and conditions of the savings plan.

ANNUAL PERCENTAGE YIELD

The Truth in Savings law, which took effect in 1993, requires that financial institutions report in advertisements, if a rate is quoted, and to savings plan customers the annual percentage yield (APY). The formula for APY is

$$APY = 100 [(1 + Interest/Principal)^{365/days\ in\ term} - 1]$$

The *principal* is the amount of funds on deposit. *Interest* is the total dollar amount earned during the term on the principal. *Days in term* is the actual number of days over which interest is earned.

When the number of days in the term is 365 (that is, where the stated maturity is 365 days) or where the account does not have a stated maturity, the APY formula is simply

$$APY = 100 (Interest/Principal)$$

APY provides a consistent comparison for savings plans with different interest rates, different compounding frequencies, and different time periods. APY may be easily viewed in terms of a $100 deposit for a 365-day year. For example, an APY of 6.5 percent would mean $6.50 interest for a year.

---

annual percentage yield (APY) The percentage rate expressing the total amount of interest that would be received on a $100 deposit based on the annual rate and frequency of compounding for a 365-day period.

Truth in Savings (TIS) defines **annual percentage yield (APY)** as the percentage rate expressing the total amount of interest that would be received on a $100 deposit based on the annual rate and frequency of compounding for a 365-day period. This law defines a year as 365 days rather than 360, 366, or some other number. TIS eliminates the confusion caused by the more than 8 million variations of interest calculation methods previously used by financial institutions. APY reflects the amount of interest a saver should expect to earn. (See the Financial Planning Calculations box above for additional information on APY.)

In addition to setting the formula for computing the annual percentage yield, Truth in Savings (1) requires disclosure of fees and APY earned on any statements provided to customers, (2) establishes rules for advertising deposit accounts, and (3) restricts the method of calculating the balance on which interest is paid. Financial institutions are also required to calculate interest on the full principal balance in the account each day.

INFLATION

The rate of return you earn on your savings should be compared with the inflation rate. When the inflation rate was over 10 percent, people with money in savings accounts earning 5 or 6 percent were experiencing a loss in the buying power of that money. In general, as the inflation rate increases, the interest rates offered to savers also increase. This gives you an opportunity to select a savings option that will minimize the erosion of your dollars on deposit.

TAX CONSIDERATIONS

Like inflation, taxes reduce interest earned on savings. For example, a 10 percent return for a saver in a 28 percent tax bracket means a real return of 7.2 percent (the Financial Planning Calculations feature on page 153 shows how to compute the after-tax savings rate of return). As discussed in Chapter 4 and discussed further in Part 5, several tax-exempt and tax-deferred savings plans and investments can increase your real rate of return.

Also, remember that taxes usually are not withheld from savings and investment income. Consequently, you may owe additional taxes at year-end as a result of earnings on savings.

Financial Planning Calculations

AFTER-TAX SAVINGS RATE OF RETURN

The taxability of interest on your savings reduces your real rate of return. In other words, you lose some portion of your interest to taxes. This calculation consists of the following steps:

1. Determine your top tax bracket for federal income taxes.
2. Subtract this rate, expressed as a decimal, from 1.0.
3. Multiply the result by the yield on your savings account.
4. This number, expressed as a percentage, is your after-tax rate of return.

For example,

1. You are in the 28 percent tax bracket.
2. $1.0 - 0.28 = 0.72$.
3. If the yield on your savings account is 6.25 percent, $0.0625 \times 0.72 = 0.045$.
4. Your after-tax rate of return is 4.5 percent.

You may use the same procedure to determine the *real rate of return* on your savings based on inflation. For example, if you are earning 6 percent on savings and inflation is 5 percent, your real rate of return (after inflation) is 5.7 percent: $0.06 \times (1 - 0.05) = 0.057$.

LIQUIDITY

Liquidity allows you to withdraw your money on short notice without a loss of principal or fees. Some savings plans impose penalties for early withdrawal or have other restrictions. With certain types of savings certificates and accounts, early withdrawal may be penalized by a loss of interest or a lower earnings rate.

You should consider the degree of liquidity you desire in relation to your savings goals. To achieve long-term financial goals, many people trade off liquidity for a higher return.

SAFETY

Most savings plans at banks, savings and loan associations, and credit unions are insured by agencies affiliated with the federal government. This protection prevents a loss of money due to the failure of the insured institution.

While a few financial institutions have failed in recent years, savers with deposits covered by federal insurance have not lost any money. Depositors of failed organizations have either been paid the amounts in their accounts or have had the accounts taken over by a financially stable institution.

The Federal Deposit Insurance Corporation (FDIC) administers separate insurance funds: the Bank Insurance Fund and the Savings Association Insurance Fund (SAIF). Credit unions may obtain deposit insurance through the National Credit Union Association (NCUA). Some state-chartered credit unions have opted for a private insurance program.

The FDIC insures deposits of up to $100,000 per person per financial institution; a joint account is considered to belong proportionally to each name on the account. For example, if you have a $70,000 individual account and an $80,000 joint account with a relative in the same financial institution, $10,000 of your savings will not be covered

Concerned or confused about federal deposit insurance? Additional information is available at **www.fdic.gov.**

by federal deposit insurance ($70,000 plus one-half of $80,000 exceeds the $100,000 limit). However, by using combinations of individual, joint, and trust accounts in different financial institutions, it is possible to have federal deposit insurance cover amounts that exceed $100,000. Remember, the maximum coverage of federal deposit insurance is based on each depositor, not on each account. The best advice is to never keep more than $100,000 in one financial institution. Be careful, however, since different branch offices count as the same institution. Also, mergers in the financial service industry may bring accounts from different banks together. Consideration is being given to increasing FDIC coverage to take inflation into account.

Since not all financial institutions have federal deposit insurance, investigate this matter when you are selecting a savings plan. Additional information on the regulation and consumer protection aspects of financial institutions is included in Appendix B.

RESTRICTIONS AND FEES

Sheet 25
Savings plan comparison

Other limitations can affect your choice of a savings program. For example, there may be a delay between the time interest is earned and the time it is added to your account. This means it will not be available for your immediate use. Also, some institutions charge a transaction fee for each deposit or withdrawal.

In the past, some financial institutions had promotions offering a "free" gift when a certain savings amount was deposited. To receive this gift, you had to leave your money on deposit for a certain time period, or you may have received less interest, since some of the earnings were used to cover the cost of the "free" items. Economists tell us that "there is no such thing as a free lunch"; the same holds true for toasters and television sets.

CONCEPT CHECK 5-4

1 When would you prefer a savings plan with high liquidity over one with a high rate of return?
2 What is the relationship between compounding and the future value of an amount?
3 How do inflation and taxes affect earnings on savings?

Action Application Contact local financial institutions to determine current rates earned on money market accounts and other savings plans. Compare these rates with similar accounts that you research online.

Payment Methods

Objective 5

Compare the costs and benefits of different types of payment accounts.

While check writing still accounts for a major portion of consumer transactions, various electronic payment methods are now more commonly used (Exhibit 5–9).

ELECTRONIC PAYMENTS

Transactions not involving cash, checks, or credit cards have expanded with technology, improved security, and increased consumer acceptance.

DEBIT CARD TRANSACTIONS   Most retail stores, restaurants, and other businesses accept check cards issued by Visa and MasterCard. When the debit card transaction is processed, the amount of the purchase is deducted from your checking account.

Most debit cards can be used two ways: (1) with your signature, like a credit card, and (2) with your personal identification number (PIN), like an ATM card. While the second method provides more security, many financial institutions charge a fee for this

Exhibit **5-9**   Payment alternatives

Electronic Payments	Checking Accounts	Other Payment Methods
• Debit (cash, check) cards • Online payments, transfer • Stored-value (prepaid) cards • Smart cards ("electronic wallet")	• Regular checking account • Activity checking account • Interest-earning checking account	• Certified check • Cashier's check • Money order • Traveler's checks

type of use. The signature method is more profitable for banks since these are processed like credit card transactions with fees paid by the retailer.

ONLINE PAYMENTS   Banks and Internet companies are serving as third parties to facilitate online bill payments. Some of these include www.paypal.com, www.checkfree.com, and www.paytrust.com. When using these services, be sure to consider the monthly charge as well as online security and customer service availability.

Also on the Web are "cyber cash" services designed to serve as financial intermediaries. These organizations create their own *e-money* that serves as a medium of exchange for online transactions; one example is www.cybercash.com.

STORED-VALUE CARDS   Prepaid cards for telephone service, transit fares, highway tolls, laundry service, and school lunches are common. While some of these stored-value cards are disposable, others can be reloaded with an additional amount.

SMART CARDS   These "electronic wallets" are similar to other ATM cards. However, their imbedded microchip stores prepaid amounts as well as information with account balances, transaction records, insurance information, and medical history.

TYPES OF CHECKING ACCOUNTS

With a major portion of business transactions conducted by check, a checking account is a necessity for most people. Checking accounts fall into three major categories: regular checking accounts, activity accounts, and interest-earning checking accounts.

Financial institutions offer their services at convenient locations.

REGULAR   CHECKING   ACCOUNTS   *Regular checking accounts* usually have a monthly service charge that you may avoid by keeping a minimum balance in the account. Some financial institutions will waive the monthly fee if you keep a certain amount in savings. Avoiding the monthly service charge can be beneficial. For example, a monthly fee of $7.50 results in $90 a year. However, you lose interest on the minimum-balance amount in a non-interest-earning account.

ACTIVITY ACCOUNTS   *Activity accounts* charge a fee for each check written and sometimes a fee for each deposit, in addition to a monthly service charge. However, you do not have to maintain a minimum balance. An activity account is most appropriate for people who write only a few checks each month and are unable to maintain the required minimum balance.

DID YOU KNOW?

Electronic check conversion (ECC) systems in stores process paper checks just like electronic payments. The check is run through an ECC reader to obtain the necessary data. Once processed, the paper check is marked "void" and returned to the customer.

share draft account An interest-bearing checking account at a credit union.

INTEREST-EARNING CHECKING ACCOUNTS *Interest-earning checking accounts,* sometimes called *NOW accounts* (NOW stands for *negotiable order of withdrawal*), usually require a minimum balance. If the account balance goes below this amount, you may not earn interest and will likely incur a service charge.

The **share draft account** is an interest-earning checking account at a credit union. Credit union members write checks, called *share drafts,* against their account balances.

Sheet 26
Payment account comparison

EVALUATING CHECKING ACCOUNTS

Would you rather have a checking account that pays interest and requires a $1,000 minimum balance or an account that doesn't pay interest and requires a $300 minimum balance? This decision requires evaluating factors such as restrictions, fees and charges, interest, and special services (see Exhibit 5–10).

RESTRICTIONS The most common limitation on checking accounts is the amount you must keep on deposit to earn interest or avoid a service charge. Until recently, financial institutions also placed various restrictions on the holding period for deposited checks; that is, they required a period of time for checks to clear before you were allowed to use the funds. The Expedited Funds Availability Act requires that funds from local checks be available within two business days and funds from out-of-town checks be withheld for no more than five business days.

FEES AND CHARGES Nearly all financial institutions require a minimum balance or impose service charges for checking accounts. When using an interest-bearing

Exhibit 5–10

Checking account selection factors

CHECKING ACCOUNT SELECTION FACTORS

Restrictions	Fees and Charges
• Minimum balance	• Monthly fee
• Federal deposit insurance	• Fees for each check or deposit
• Hours and location of branch offices	• Printing of checks
• Holding period for deposited checks	• Fee to obtain canceled check copy
	• Overdraft, stop-payment order, certified check fee
	• Fees for preauthorized bill payment, fund transfer, or home banking activity

Special Services	Interest
• Direct deposit of payroll and government checks	• Interest rate
• 24-hour teller machines	• Minimum deposit to earn interest
• Overdraft protection	• Method of compounding
• Banking at home	• Portion of balance used to compute interest
• Discounts or free checking for certain groups (students, senior citizens, employees of certain companies)	• Fee charged for falling below necessary balance to earn interest
• Free or discounted services, such as traveler's checks	

Financial Planning for Life's Situations

ARE YOU AVOIDING IDENTITY THEFT?

People who put their Social Security and driver's license numbers on their checks are making identity theft fairly easy. With one check, a con artist could know your Social Security, driver's license, and bank account numbers as well as your address, phone number, and perhaps even a sample of your signature.

An attorney had his wallet stolen. Within a week, the thieves ordered an expensive monthly cell phone package, applied for a VISA credit card, had a credit line approved to buy a Gateway computer, and received a PIN number from the Department of Motor Vehicles DMV to change his driving record information online.

Identity fraud can range from passing bad checks and using stolen credit cards to theft of another person's total financial existence. The following quiz can help you avoid becoming one of the more than 1,000 people who each day have their identities stolen by con artists.

Which of the Following Actions Have You Taken to Avoid Identity Theft?	Yes	No	Action Needed
1. I only have my initials and last name on my checks so a person will not know how I sign my checks.			
2. I do not put the full account number on my checks when paying a bill, only the last four numbers.			
3. I have my work phone and a P.O. Box (if applicable) on my checks instead of home information.			
4. I do not put my Social Security number on any document unless it is legally required.			
5. I shred or burn financial information containing account or Social Security numbers.			
6. I use passwords other than maiden names.			
7. I do not mail bills from my home mailbox, especially if it is out by the street.			
8. I check my credit report once or twice a year to make sure it is correct.			
9. I ask to have my name removed from mailing lists operated by credit agencies and companies offering credit promotions.			
10. I have a photocopy of the contents of my wallet (both sides of each item) as a record to cancel accounts if necessary.			

If you are a victim of identity theft, take the following actions:

- File a police report immediately in the area where it was stolen. This proves you were diligent and is a first step toward an investigation (if there ever is one).

- Call the three national credit reporting organizations *immediately* to place a fraud alert on your name and Social Security number. The numbers are Equifax I-800-525-6285, Experian (formerly TRW) I-888-397-3742, and Trans Union I-800-680-7289.

- Contact the Social Security Administration fraud line at 1-800-269-0271.

Additional information on financial privacy and identity theft is available at www.identitytheft.org, www.idfraud.org, www.privacyrights.org, and www.pirg.org/calpirg/consumer/privacy.

checking account, compare your earnings with any service charge or fee. Also, consider the cost of lost or reduced interest due to the need to maintain the minimum balance.

Checking account fees have increased in recent years. Items such as check printing, overdraft fees, and stop-payment orders have doubled or tripled in price at some financial institutions. Some institutions will "bait" you with fancy checks at a low price and then charge a much higher price when you reorder. You may be able to purchase checks at a lower cost from a mail-order or online company.

INTEREST   As discussed earlier, the interest rate, the frequency of compounding, and the interest computation method will affect the earnings on your checking account.

SPECIAL SERVICES   Financial institutions are attempting to reduce the paper and postage costs associated with checking accounts. One solution is to not return canceled checks to customers. The financial institution then uses microfilm to store checks and provides customers with detailed statements summarizing the checks written. If a customer requests a copy of a canceled check, the institution reproduces the copy from its microfilm file for a fee.

overdraft protection An automatic loan made to checking account customers to cover the amount of checks written in excess of the available balance in the checking account.

   Overdraft protection is an automatic loan made to checking account customers for checks written in excess of the available balance. This service is convenient but costly. Most overdraft plans make loans based on $50 or $100 increments. An overdraft of just $1 might trigger a $50 loan and corresponding finance charges of perhaps 18 percent. But overdraft protection can be less costly than the fee charged for a check you write when you do not have enough money on deposit to cover it. That fee may be $20 or more. Many financial institutions will allow you to cover checking account overdrafts with an automatic transfer from a savings account for a nominal fee.

   Beware of checking accounts that offer several services (safe deposit box, traveler's checks, low-rate loans, and travel insurance) for a single monthly fee. This may sound like a good value; however, financial experts observe that such accounts benefit only a small group of people who make constant use of the services in the package.

Sheet 27
Checking/
payment
account cost
analysis

MANAGING YOUR CHECKING ACCOUNT

Obtaining and using a checking account involves several activities.

OPENING A CHECKING ACCOUNT   First, decide the owner of the account. Only one person is allowed to write checks on an *individual account*. A *joint account* has two or more owners. Both an individual account and a joint account require a signature card. This document is a record of the official signatures of the person or persons authorized to write checks on the account.

MAKING DEPOSITS   A *deposit ticket* is used for adding funds to your checking account. On this document, you list the amounts of cash and checks being deposited. Each check you deposit requires an *endorsement*—your signature on the back of the check—to authorize the transfer of the funds into your account. The three common endorsement forms are:

- A *blank endorsement* is just your signature, which should only be used when you are actually depositing or cashing a check, since a check could be cashed by anyone once it has been signed.

- A *restrictive endorsement* consists of the words *for deposit only,* followed by your signature, which is especially useful when you are depositing checks.

- A *special endorsement* allows you to transfer a check to someone else with the words *pay to the order of,* followed by the name of the other person and then your signature.

WRITING CHECKS   Before writing a check, record the information in your check register and deduct the amount of the check from your balance. Many checking account customers use duplicate checks to maintain a record of their current balance.

The procedure for proper check writing has the following steps: (1) record the date; (2) write the name of the person or organization receiving the payment; (3) record the amount of the check in figures; (4) write the amount of the check in words (checks for less than a dollar should be written as "only 79 cents," for example, and cross out the word *dollars* on the check); (5) sign the check; (6) note the reason for payment.

A *stop-payment order* may be necessary if a check is lost or stolen. Most banks do not honor checks with "stale" dates, usually six months old or older. The fee for a stop-payment commonly ranges from $10 to $20. If several checks are missing or you lose your checkbook, closing the account and opening a new one is likely to be less costly than paying several stop-payment fees.

RECONCILING YOUR CHECKING ACCOUNT   Each month you will receive a *bank statement* summarizing deposits, checks paid, interest earned, and fees such as service charges and printing of checks. The balance reported on the statement will usually differ from the balance in your checkbook. Reasons for a difference include checks that have not yet cleared, deposits not received by the bank, and interest earned.

To determine the correct balance, prepare a *bank reconciliation* to account for differences between the bank statement and your checkbook balance. The steps to take in this process are as follows:

Sheet 28
Checking
account
reconciliation

1. Compare the checks written with those reported as paid on the statement. Use the canceled checks, or compare your check register with the check numbers reported on the bank statement. *Subtract* from the *bank statement balance* the total of the checks written but not yet cleared.

2. Determine whether any deposits are not on the statement; *add* the amount of the outstanding deposits to the *bank statement balance.*

3. *Subtract* fees or charges on the bank statement, ATM withdrawals, and other automatic payments from your *checkbook balance.*

4. *Add* any interest earned to your *checkbook balance.*

At this point, the revised balances for both the checkbook and the bank statement should be the same. If the two do not match, check your math; make sure every check and deposit was recorded correctly. See the Financial Planning Calculations box on page 160 for additional details on the bank reconciliation process.

DID YOU KNOW?

The Check Clearing for the 21st Century Act (known as Check 21) shortens the processing time of checks using electronic systems. The actual paper check will no longer be processed.

OTHER PAYMENT METHODS

While personal checks are the most common payment form, other methods are available. A *certified check* is a personal check with guaranteed payment. The amount of the check is deducted from your balance when the financial institution certifies the check. A *cashier's check* is a check of a financial institution. You may purchase one by paying the amount of the check plus a fee. You may purchase a *money order* in a similar manner from financial institutions, post offices, and stores. Certified checks, cashier's checks, and money orders allow you to make a payment that the recipient knows is valid.

Traveler's checks allow you to make payments when you are away from home. This payment form requires you to sign each check twice. First, you sign the traveler's checks when you purchase them. Then, to identify you as the authorized person, you sign them again as you cash them. Electronic traveler's checks, in the form of a prepaid travel card, are also available. The card allows travelers visiting other nations to get local currency from an ATM.

Financial Planning Calculations

RECONCILING YOUR CHECKING ACCOUNT

The process of comparing your checkbook balance to the bank statement is vital for determining any errors that may have occurred. Use the following steps to reconcile your account.

The Bank Statement			Your Checkbook	
Balance on current bank statement	$	643.96	Current balance in your checkbook	$ 295.91

	Date	Amount		
Step 1.			**Step 3.**	
Add up outstanding checks (checks that you have written but have not yet cleared the banking system) and withdrawals still outstanding.	10-4	70.00	Subtract total of fees or other charges listed on bank statement	$ −15.75
	10-6	130.00		
	10-7	111.62		
			Subtract ATM withdrawals, debit card payments, and other automatic payments	$ −100.00
Subtract the total	$	−311.62	**Step 4.**	
			Add interest earned.	$ +2.18
Step 2.	Date	Amount		
Add up deposits in transit (deposits that have been made but are not reported on the current statement).	10-2	60.00	Add direct deposits.	$ +300.00
	10-5	90.00		
Add the total.	$	+150.00		
☐ Adjusted bank balance	$	482.34	Adjusted checkbook balance	$ 482.34

CONCEPT CHECK 5-5

1 What factors are commonly considered when selecting a checking account?

2 Are checking accounts that earn interest preferable to regular checking accounts? Why or why not?

Action Application Observe customers making payments in a retail store. How often are cash, checks, credit cards, or cash cards used?

SUMMARY OF OBJECTIVES

Objective 1

Analyze factors that affect the selection and use of financial services.

Financial products such as savings plans, checking accounts, loans, trust services, and electronic banking are used for managing daily financial activities. Technology, opportunity costs, and economic conditions affect the selection and use of financial services.

Objective 2

Compare the types of financial institutions.

Commercial banks, savings and loan associations, mutual savings banks, credit unions, life insurance companies, investment companies, finance companies, mortgage companies, pawnshops, and check-cashing outlets may be compared on the basis of services offered, rates and fees, safety, convenience, and special programs available to customers.

Objective 3

Compare the costs and benefits of various savings plans.

Commonly used savings plans include regular savings accounts, certificates of deposit, money market accounts, money market funds, and U.S. savings bonds.

Objective 4

Identify the factors used to evaluate different savings plans.

Savings plans may be evaluated on the basis of rate of return, inflation, tax considerations, liquidity, safety, restrictions, and fees.

Objective 5

Compare the costs and benefits of different types of payment accounts.

Electronic payment methods include debit card transactions, online payments, stored-value cards, and smart cards. Regular checking accounts, activity accounts, and interest-earning checking accounts can be compared with regard to restrictions (such as a minimum balance), fees and charges, interest, and special services. Other payment alternatives include certified checks, cashier's checks, money orders, and traveler's checks.

KEY FORMULAS

Page	Topic	Formula
152	Annual percentage yield (APY)	$APY = 100\,[(1 + \text{Interest/Principal})^{365/\text{days in term}} - 1]$
		Principal = The amount of funds on deposit
		Interest = The total dollar amount earned on the principal
		Days in term = The actual number of days in the term of the account
	When the number of days in the term is 365 or where the account does not have a stated maturity, the APY formula is simply	$APY = 100\,(\text{Interest/Principal})$
		Example:
		$100\left[\left(1 + \dfrac{\$56.20}{\$1{,}000}\right)^{\frac{365}{365}} - 1\right] = 0.0562 = 5.62\%$
153	After-tax rate of return	Interest rate $\times$ (1 − Tax rate)
		Example:
		$0.05 \times (1 - 0.28) = 0.036 = 3.6\%$

KEY TERMS

annual percentage yield (APY) 152	compounding 151	rate of return 150
asset management account 139	credit union 144	savings and loan association 143
automatic teller machine (ATM) 140	debit card 141	share account 148
certificate of deposit (CD) 148	money market account 149	share draft account 156
commercial bank 142	money market fund 145	trust 139
	mutual savings bank 144	
	overdraft protection 158	

FINANCIAL PLANNING PROBLEMS

1. *Determining Savings Goals.* What would be common savings goals for a person who buys a five-year CD paying 5.5 percent instead of an 18-month savings certificate paying 4.75 percent? (Obj. 4)

2. *Computing Future Value.* What would be the value of a savings account started with $500, earning 6 percent (compounded annually) after 10 years? (Obj. 5)

3. *Calculating Present Value.* Brenda Young desires to have $10,000 eight years from now for her daughter's college fund. If she will earn 7 percent (compounded annually) on her money, what amount should she deposit now? Use the present value of a single amount calculation. (Obj. 5)

4. *Computing Future Value of Annual Deposits.* What amount would you have if you deposited $1,500 a year for 30 years at 8 percent (compounded annually)? (Use the Chapter 1 appendix.) (Obj. 5)

5. *Comparing Taxable and Tax-Free Yields.* With a 28 percent marginal tax rate, would a tax-free yield of 7 percent or a taxable yield of 9.5 percent give you a better return on your savings? Why? (Obj. 5)

6. *Computing APY.* What would be the annual percentage yield for a savings account that earned $56 in interest on $800 over the past 365 days? (Obj. 5)

7. *Calculating Opportunity Cost.* What is the annual opportunity cost of a checking account that requires a $350 minimum balance to avoid service charges? Assume an interest rate of 6.5 percent. (Obj. 5)

8. *Comparing Costs of Checking Accounts.* What would be the net *annual* cost of the following checking accounts? (Obj. 5)

   a. Monthly fee, $3.75; processing fee, $0.25 cents per check; checks written, an average of 22 a month.

   b. Interest earnings of 6 percent with a $500 minimum balance; average monthly balance, $600; monthly service charge of $15 for falling below the minimum balance, which occurs three times a year (no interest earned in these months).

9. *Computing Checking Account Costs.* Based on the following information, determine the true balance in your checking account. (See pages 158–160.)

   Balance in your checkbook, $356

   Balance on bank statement, $472

   Service charge and other fees, $15

   Interest earned on the account, $4

   Total of outstanding checks, $187

   Deposits in transit, $60

FINANCIAL PLANNING ACTIVITIES

1. *Researching Financial Services.* Using the World Wide Web or library resources, obtain information about new developments in financial services. How have technology, changing economic conditions, and new legislation affected the types and availability of various saving and checking financial services? (Obj. 1)

2. *Monitoring Economic Conditions.* Research current economic conditions (interest rates, inflation) using the *Wall Street Journal*, other library resources, or Web sites. Based on current economic conditions, what actions would you recommend to people who are saving and borrowing money? (Obj. 1)

3. *Comparing Financial Institutions.* Collect advertisements and promotional information from several financial institutions, or locate the Web sites of financial institutions such as Wells Fargo Bank (www.wellsfargo.com) and Bank of

FINANCIAL PLANNING ACTIVITIES CONTINUED

America (www.bankamerica.com). Create a list of factors that a person might consider when comparing costs and benefits of various savings plans and checking accounts. (Obj. 2)

4. *Obtaining Opinions about Financial Services.* Survey several people to determine awareness and use of various financial services such as online banking, "smart cards," and check-writing software. (Obj. 2)

5. *Comparing Savings Plans.* Collect advertisements from several financial institutions with information about the savings plans they offer. (You may do this using the Web sites of various financial institutions.) Using Sheet 25 in the *Personal Financial Planner,* compare the features and potential earnings of two or three savings plans. (Obj. 3, 4)

6. *Comparing Checking Accounts.* Using Sheets 26 and 27 in the *Personal Financial Planner,* compare the features and

costs of checking accounts at two different financial institutions. Online searches of bank Web sites may be useful. (Obj. 5)

7. *Analyzing Check-Writing Software.* Visit software retailers to obtain information about the features in various personal computer programs used for maintaining a checking account. Information about programs such as *Microsoft Money* and *Quicken* may be obtained on the Internet. (Obj. 5)

8. *Researching Checking Accounts.* Several states require that banks offer basic checking accounts. For example, in Illinois, New York, New Jersey, and Minnesota, check services with minimal fees must be made available for consumers making a limited number of transactions. Obtain information about the availability of these types of *life-line* accounts in your area. (Obj. 5)

INTERNET CONNECTION

Comparing Online Payment Systems

Compare the online bill payment services for (1) a bank, (2) a bill payment service (such as www.bills.com or www.paytrust.com), and (3) money management software.

	Online Bank	Internet Payment Service	Software (*MS Money, Quicken*)
Name, Web site			
Description of online payment services; types of payments			
Cost (per month or per transaction)			
Security measures			
Potential concerns			

FINANCIAL PLANNING CASE

Checking Out Financial Services

Carla and Ed Johnson have separate checking accounts. Each pays part of the household and living expenses. Carla pays the mortgage and telephone bill, while Ed pays for food and utilities and makes the insurance and car payments. This arrangement allows them the freedom to spend whatever extra money they have each month without needing to explain their actions to each other. Carla and Ed believe their separate accounts have minimized disagreements about money. Since both spend most of their money each month, they have low balances in their checking accounts. For Carla this results in a monthly charge totaling $15.

In the same financial institution where Carla has her checking account, the Johnsons have $600 in a passbook savings account that earns 2.2 percent interest. If the savings account balance exceeded $1,000, they would earn 3.15 percent. If the balance stayed above $1,000, they would not have to pay the monthly service charge on Carla's checking account. The financial institution has a program that moves money from checking to savings. This program would allow the Johnsons to increase their savings and work toward a secure financial future.

Ed has his checking account at a bank that offers an electronic banking system allowing a customer to obtain cash at many locations 24 hours a day. Ed believes this feature is valuable when cash is needed to cover business expenses and

CONTINUED

personal spending. For an additional monthly fee, the bank would also provide Ed with a credit card, a safe deposit box, and a single monthly statement summarizing all transactions.

While most people plan their spending for living expenses, few plan their use of financial services. Therefore, many people are charged high fees for checking accounts and earn low interest on their savings. Despite a wide choice of financial institutions and services, you can learn to compare their costs and benefits. Your awareness of financial services and your ability to evaluate them are vital skills for a healthy personal economic future.

Questions

1. Which financial services are most important to Carla and Ed Johnson?

2. What efforts are the Johnsons currently making to assess their use of financial services in relation to their other financial activities?

3. How should the Johnsons assess their needs for financial services? On what bases should they compare financial services?

4. What should the Johnsons do to improve their use of financial services?

VIDEO CASE

You Can Bank On It

Today, many people are writing fewer checks than in the past. Increases in the use of online payments, debit cards, and other electronic banking services are resulting in different types of transactions appearing on your bank statement. However, monitoring the correct balance in your account is still a necessary activity.

Anita recently realized that she had written checks for more than the amount in her account. She expected her next paycheck to be deposited earlier. To avoid various charges for "bouncing"

a check, the service representative at Anita's bank recommended that she take advantage of overdraft protection.

Questions

1. What fees and deductions may be commonly overlooked when balancing your checking account?

2. What are potential benefits of an "overdraft protection" service for your checking account?

3. What costs should Anita consider before deciding to use the "overdraft protection" service?

YOUR PERSONAL FINANCIAL PLANNER IN ACTION

Selecting Savings and Payment Services

The use of payment services and savings programs influences other aspects of financial planning. Attempts to minimize banking fees while maximizing earnings on funds are common objectives.

Your Short-Term Financial Planning Activities	Resources
1. Identify various financial services needed for savings, payment, and money management activities. Identify financial institutions that you might use to obtain these services.	PFP Sheet 23 www.bankrate.com www.creditunion.coop www.wachovia.com
2. Compare the rates of return, fees, and other factors for different savings plans that you might use to meet your financial goals.	PFP Sheets 24, 25 www.fdic.gov www.savingsbonds.gov
3. Compare the features and costs of checking and check card services at various financial institutions.	PFP Sheets 26, 27 www.bankrate.com www.checkfree.com

CONTINUED

Your Long-Term Financial Planning Activities	Resources
1. Identify savings decisions that would best help you achieve long-term financial goals.	www.clevelandsaves.org www.asec.org www.centura.com/tools
2. List the economic conditions (inflation, current interest rates) and personal factors related to the costs and benefits of financial services that you should monitor as your personal life situation changes over time.	Text pages 141–142, 143 www.federalreserve.gov www.bis.gov

CONTINUING CASE

Banking Services

Life Situation	Financial Data	
Recently married couple	Monthly income	$5,840
Pam, 26	Living expenses	$3,900
Josh, 28	Assets	$13,500
Renting an apartment	Liabilities	$4,800
	Emergency fund	$1,000

Pam Jenkins recently married Josh Brock. Pam continues to work as a sales representative for a clothing manufacturer, and her monthly income has averaged $2,840 a month over the past year. Josh is employed as a computer programmer and earns $3,000 a month. Their combined monthly income allows them to live comfortably. Yet they have been unable to save any money for emergencies.

According to Josh, "It's hard to believe, but we don't even have a savings account because we spend almost everything we make." Every month, they deposit each of their paychecks in separate checking accounts. Josh pays the rent and makes the car payment. Pam buys the groceries and pays the utilities. They use the money left over to purchase new clothes and the other "necessities" for enjoying life.

Questions

1. What is the minimum amount that the Brocks should have in an emergency fund? What actions might be taken to increase the amount in this fund?

2. What other money management and financial planning activities would you recommend for the Brocks?

3. Which of *Personal Financial Planner* sheets 23–28 could be useful for planning and using financial services by Pam and Josh?

6 Introduction to Consumer Credit

Key Concept

Understanding the advantages and disadvantages of consumer credit as well as the types of credit that are available will enable you to make wise decisions regarding credit, now and in the future.

Digital Study Tools

Online Learning Center Study Tools for This Chapter

- Multiple-choice quiz
- Flashcards
- eLearning sessions
- Crossword puzzle
- Personal Finance Online: The Cost of Credit and Credit Management

Student CD Study Tools for This Chapter

- Self-study software
- Narrated PowerPoint
- Personal financial planning software: Worksheet 29

www.mhhe.com/kdh

Learning Objectives

1. Define *consumer credit* and analyze its advantages and disadvantages.

2. Differentiate among various types of credit.

3. Assess your credit capacity and build your credit rating.

4. Describe the information creditors look for when you apply for credit.

5. Identify the steps you can take to avoid and correct credit mistakes.

6. Describe the laws that protect you if you have a complaint about consumer credit.

Don't Let Crooks Steal Your Identity: How to Protect Yourself—and Your Credit Rating

In 2004 Consumer Sentinel, the complaint database developed and maintained by the Federal Trade Commission, received over 635,000 consumer fraud and identity theft complaints. Consumers reported losses from fraud of more than $547 million.

Identity theft is the fastest-growing financial crime. One of the first things the FBI discovered about the September 11 hijackers was that as many as half a dozen were using credit cards and driver's licenses with identities lifted from stolen or forged passports.

If you care at all about the privacy of your financial information—your credit history, your portfolio, your charge card numbers—you can protect yourself from criminals determined to exploit that information. The theft can be as simple as someone pilfering your credit card number and charging merchandise to your account. Or it can be as elaborate as a crook using your name, birth date, and Social Security number to take over your credit card and bank accounts, or set up new ones.

If your identity has been snatched, you're first likely to learn about it when checks start bouncing or a collection agency begins calling. The damage isn't so much in dollars, since the financial institutions are liable for the unauthorized charges. Rather, the fallout includes a checkered credit history, which could prevent you from getting a mortgage or a job, and the countless phone calls and piles of paperwork you'll need to go through to set the records straight. Guarding against identity theft is much like locking the door and activating the burglar alarm when you leave your home. By and large, the crime is a low-tech operation, despite well-publicized instances of hackers breaking into Web sites and stealing millions of credit card numbers. Usually, someone fishes a bank statement or credit card offer out of your trash, or a dishonest employee peeks at your personnel file.

To protect yourself, keep your Social Security number in a secure place and never carry it around with you. Provide your Social Security number only when necessary. Instead, try to use other forms of identification. Ignore e-mail requests for your personal financial information. Shred your discarded financial records and any preapproved credit card applications. And check your credit report regularly, because credit-card companies don't have to honor fraud alerts.

Finally, protect your identity by giving it a lower profile. For example, remove your name from junk mail and telemarketing lists by going to the Direct Marketing association's Web site at www.thedma.org/consumers/privacy.html. Call 1-888-567-8688 to stop receiving preapproved credit card offers.

QUESTIONS

What Actions Should Be Taken?

1. What steps can you take to thwart identity thieves?
2. What actions might you take to ensure that your credit cards and other financial information is secure?

What about Your Situation?

3. What are several methods that crooks use to steal your identity?
4. How do you discover that someone has stolen your identity?

Source: Larry Armstrong, "Don't Let Crooks Steal Your Identity: How to Protect Yourself—and Your Credit Rating," *BusinessWeek*, November 19, 2001, pp. 134–36; Ann Tergesen, "The Price of ID Protection," *BusinessWeek*, November 29, 2004, pp. 136–137; and Federal Trade Commission, *National and State Trends in Fraud and Identity Theft*, February 1, 2005, p. 2.

Learn More Online

Based on the National Fraud Information Center Web site at www.fraud.org and www.consumer.gov/sentinel Web site, describe (*a*) other types of ID theft scams that should be avoided and (*b*) useful Web sources for learning about consumer credit.

What Is Consumer Credit?

Objective 1

Define *consumer credit* and analyze its advantages and disadvantages.

credit An arrangement to receive cash, goods, or services now and pay for them in the future.

consumer credit The use of credit for personal needs (except a home mortgage).

"Charge it!" "Cash or credit?" "Put it on my account." As these phrases indicate, the use of credit is a fact of life in personal and family financial planning. When you use credit, you satisfy needs today and pay for this satisfaction in the future. While the use of credit is often necessary and even advantageous, responsibilities and disadvantages are associated with its use.

Credit is an arrangement to receive cash, goods, or services now and pay for them in the future. **Consumer credit** refers to the use of credit for personal needs (except a home mortgage) by individuals and families, in contrast to credit used for business purposes.

Although Polonius cautioned, "Neither a borrower nor a lender be," using and providing credit have become a way of life for many people and businesses in today's economy. In January, you pay a bill for electricity that you used in December. A statement arrives in the mail for medical services that you received last month. You write a check for $40, a minimum payment on a $300 department store bill. With a bank loan, you purchase a new car. These are all examples of using credit: paying later for goods and services obtained now.

Most consumers have three alternatives in financing current purchases: They can draw on their savings, use their present earnings, or borrow against their expected future income. Each of these alternatives has trade-offs. If you continually deplete your savings, little will be left for emergencies or retirement income. If you spend your current income on luxuries instead of necessities, your well-being will eventually suffer. And if you pledge your future income to make current credit purchases, you will have little or no spendable income in the future.

Consumer credit is based on trust in people's ability and willingness to pay bills when due. It works because people by and large are honest and responsible. But how does consumer credit affect our economy, and how is it affected by our economy?

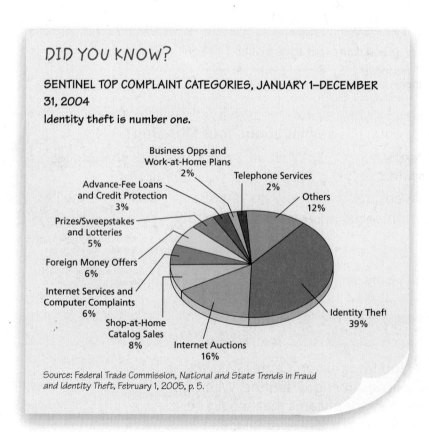

THE IMPORTANCE OF CONSUMER CREDIT IN OUR ECONOMY

Consumer credit dates back to colonial times. While credit was originally a privilege of the affluent, farmers came to use it extensively. No direct finance charges were imposed; instead, the cost of credit was added to the prices of goods. With the advent of the automobile in the early 1900s, installment credit, in which the debt is repaid in equal installments over a specified period of time, exploded on the American scene.

All economists now recognize consumer credit as a major force in the American economy. Any forecast or evaluation of the economy includes consumer spending trends and consumer credit as a sustaining force. To paraphrase an old political expression, as the consumer goes, so goes the U.S. economy.

The aging of the baby boom generation has added to the growth of consumer credit. This generation currently represents about 30 percent of the population but holds nearly 60 percent of the outstanding debt. The people in this age group have always been disproportionate users of credit, since consumption is highest as families are formed and homes are purchased and furnished. Thus, while the extensive use of debt by this generation is nothing new, the fact that it has grown rapidly has added to overall debt use.

USES AND MISUSES OF CREDIT

Using credit to purchase goods and services may allow consumers to be more efficient or more productive or to lead more satisfying lives. There are many valid reasons for using credit. A medical emergency may leave a person strapped for funds. A homemaker returning to the workforce may need a car. It may be possible to buy an item now for less money than it will cost later. Borrowing for a college education is another valid reason. But it probably is not reasonable to borrow for everyday living expenses or finance a Corvette on credit when a Ford Focus is all your budget allows.

"Shopaholics" and young adults are most vulnerable to misusing credit. College students are a prime target for credit card issuers, and issuers make it very easy for students to get credit cards. Wendy Leright, a 25-year-old teacher in Detroit, knows this all too well. As a college freshman, she applied for and got seven credit cards, all bearing at least an 18.9 percent interest rate and a $20 annual fee. Although unemployed, she used the cards freely, buying expensive clothes for herself, extravagant Christmas presents for friends and family, and even a one-week vacation in the Bahamas. "It got to a point where I didn't even look at the price tag," she said. By her senior year, Wendy had amassed $9,000 in credit card debt and couldn't make the monthly payments of nearly $200. She eventually turned to her parents to bail her out. "Until my mother sat me down and showed me how much interest I had to pay, I hadn't even given it a thought. I was shocked," Wendy said. "I would have had to pay it off for years."[1]

Using credit increases the amount of money a person can spend to purchase goods and services now. But the trade-off is that it decreases the amount of money that will be available to spend in the future. However, many people expect their incomes to increase and therefore expect to be able to make payments on past credit purchases and still make new purchases.

Here are some questions you should consider before you decide how and when to make a major purchase, for example, a car:

- Do I have the cash I need for the down payment?
- Do I want to use my savings for this purchase?
- Does the purchase fit my budget?
- Could I use the credit I need for this purchase in some better way?
- Could I postpone the purchase?
- What are the opportunity costs of postponing the purchase (alternative transportation costs, a possible increase in the price of the car)?
- What are the dollar costs and the psychological costs of using credit (interest, other finance charges, being in debt and responsible for making a monthly payment)?

If you decide to use credit, make sure the benefits of making the purchase now (increased efficiency or productivity, a more satisfying life, etc.) outweigh the costs (financial and psychological) of using credit. Thus, credit, when effectively used, can help you have more and enjoy more. When misused, credit can result in default, bankruptcy, and loss of creditworthiness.

THINK FIRST. If you decide to use credit, make sure the benefits of making the purchase now outweigh the costs of using credit.

ADVANTAGES OF CREDIT

Consumer credit enables people to enjoy goods and services now—a car, a home, an education, help in emergencies—and pay for them through payment plans based on future income.

Credit cards permit the purchase of goods even when funds are low. Customers with previously approved credit may receive other extras, such as advance notice of sales and the right to order by phone or to buy on approval. In addition, many shoppers believe it is easier to return merchandise they have purchased on account. Credit cards also provide shopping convenience and the efficiency of paying for several purchases with one monthly payment.

Credit is more than a substitute for cash. Many of the services it provides are taken for granted. Every time you turn on the water tap, flick the light switch, or telephone a friend, you are using credit.

It is safer to use credit, since charge accounts and credit cards let you shop and travel without carrying a large amount of cash. You need a credit card to make a hotel reservation, rent a car, and shop by phone. You may also use credit cards for identification when cashing checks, and the use of credit provides you with a record of expenses.

The use of credit cards can provide up to a 50-day "float," the time lag between when you make the purchase and when the lender deducts the balance from your checking account when the payment is due. This float, offered by many credit card issuers, includes a grace period of 20 to 25 days. During the grace period, no finance charges are assessed on current purchases if the balance is paid in full each month within 25 days after billing.

Some large corporations, such as General Electric Company and General Motors Corporation, issue their own Visa and MasterCard and offer rebates on purchases. For example, every time you make a purchase with the GM MasterCard, 5 percent of the purchase price is set aside for you in a special GM Card Rebate account. When you are ready to buy or lease a GM car or truck, you just cash in your rebate at the GM dealership. Similarly, with an AT&T MasterCard, you can earn a cash bonus of up to 5 percent based on your total purchases during the year. In the late 1990s, however, some corporations began to eliminate these cards.

Platinum credit cards offered by American Express provide emergency medical evacuation for travelers. In 1994 Stephen Bradley of New York was vacationing in tiny, isolated Coruripe, Brazil. He ate something that made him gravely ill. With no doctor nearby, a friend frantically called American Express about its guarantee to arrange emergency medical evacuation and treatment for Platinum Card users. AmEx moved fast: It lined up a car to rush Bradley to the nearest large town, managed to book a room in a sold-out hotel, and sent a doctor there to make a house call. The physician even accompanied Bradley's travel partner, Richard Laermer, to a local pharmacy for medicine. "When we went home to see our doctor, he told us she had saved Steve's life," recalls Laermer. "For the last five years we have been indebted to Platinum." Merrill Lynch and Company has introduced a new card with many of the same benefits, but with a lower annual fee.[2] The accompanying Financial Planning for Life's Situations feature describes what American Express and other card issuers have planned for the big spenders.

Finally, credit indicates stability. The fact that lenders consider you a good risk usually means you are a responsible individual. However, if you do not repay your debts in a timely manner, you will find that credit has many disadvantages.

DISADVANTAGES OF CREDIT

Perhaps the greatest disadvantage of using credit is the temptation to overspend, especially during periods of inflation. It seems easy to buy today and pay tomorrow using cheaper dollars. But continual overspending can lead to serious trouble.

THIS BLACK CARD GIVES YOU CARTE BLANCHE

A real T-shirt-and-jeans kind of guy, Peter H. Shankman certainly doesn't look like a high roller, but American Express Co. knows better. After he was snubbed by salesmen at a Giorgio Armani boutique on Fifth Avenue in New York recently, the 31-year-old publicist saw "an unbelievable attitude reversal" at the cash register when he whipped out his black AmEx Centurion card. In June a Radio Shack cashier refused the card, thinking it was a fake. "'Trust me,' I said. 'Run the card,'" recalls the chief executive of Geek Factory Inc., a public-relations and marketing firm. "I could buy a Learjet with this thing."

An exaggeration, perhaps. But AmEx's little black card is decidedly the "It" card for big spenders. Launched in late 1999, Centurion is given out by invitation only to customers who spend at least $150,000 a year on other AmEx cards and meet other requirements. The chosen cardholders pay an annual fee of $2,500, raised from $1,000 two years ago.

Although AmEx has spent zilch on promotion, some would-be customers go to absurd lengths to get what they see as a must-have status symbol. Hopefuls have written poems to plead their case. Others say they'll pay the fee but swear not to use the card—they want it just for show. "Every week I get phone calls or letters, often from prominent people, asking me for the card," says AmEx's head of consumer cards, Alfred F. Kelly Jr.

Who, he won't say. In fact, AmEx deliberately builds an air of mystery around the sleek card, keeping hush-hush such details as the number of cards in circulation. Analysts say AmEx earns back many times what it spends on perks for black card customers in both marketing buzz and fees.

The card is now being flattered by imitators. In April, Merrill Lynch & Co. and MBNA Corp. launched a black-colored Visa card with a credit limit of up to $250,000. The card offers bonus points that can be used to pay for brokerage charges—or a night at the Ritz. "Our goal wasn't to come out with a me-too card," says Peter Barsoom, director of card payments for Merrill Lynch. "Our clients needed a better card in their wallet." J. P. Morgan Chase & Co. is sizing up its own version. Says Jamie Dimon, the bank's chief operating officer and president, "We may want to try to outdo that at some point."

Basic services on the Centurion card include a personal travel counselor and concierge, available 24/7. Beyond that, almost anything goes. Feel like shopping at Bergdorf Goodman or Saks Fifth Avenue at midnight? No problem. Traveling abroad in first class? Take a pal—the extra ticket is free.

The royal treatment often requires elaborate planning. One AmEx concierge arranged a bachelor party for 25, which involved a four-day trip that included 11 penthouse suites, travel by private jet, and meet-and-greet with an owner of the Sacramento Kings basketball team. The tab was more than $300,000.

How did Shankman, who says his firm has no business dealings with AmEx, earn his card? All the travel and entertainment charges he racks up hosting his clients prompted AmEx to send it to him. It arrived in December, along with a 43-page manual. Recently, Shankman sought reservations for Spice Market, an often-overbooked restaurant in Manhattan, to impress a friend. He called his concierge. "Half an hour later it was done," says Shankman. Membership does have its privileges.

Source: Mara Der Hovanesian, "This Black Card Gives You Carte Blanche," *BusinessWeek*, August 9, 2004, p. 54.

Whether or not credit involves security (something of value to back the loan), failure to repay a loan may result in loss of income, valuable property, and your good reputation. It can even lead to court action and bankruptcy. Misuse of credit can create serious long-term financial problems, damage to family relationships, and a slowing of progress toward financial goals. Therefore, you should approach credit with caution and avoid using it more extensively than your budget permits.

Although credit allows more immediate satisfaction of needs and desires, it does not increase total purchasing power. Credit purchases must be paid for out of future income; therefore, credit ties up the use of future income. Furthermore, if your income does not increase to cover rising costs, your ability to repay credit commitments will diminish. Before buying goods and services on credit, consider whether they will have lasting value, whether they will increase your personal satisfaction during present and future income periods, and whether your current income will continue or increase.

Finally, credit costs money. It is a service for which you must pay. Paying for purchases over a period of time is more costly than paying for them with cash. Purchasing with credit rather than cash involves one very obvious trade-off: the fact that it will cost more due to monthly finance charges and the compounding effect of interest on interest.

SUMMARY: ADVANTAGES AND DISADVANTAGES OF CREDIT

The use of credit provides immediate access to goods and services, flexibility in money management, safety and convenience, a cushion in emergencies, a means of increasing resources, and a good credit rating if you pay your debts back in a timely manner. But remember, the use of credit is a two-sided coin. An intelligent decision as to its use demands careful evaluation of your current debt, your future income, the added cost, and the consequences of overspending.

CONCEPT CHECK 6-1

1 How might consumers protect themselves against identity theft?
2 What is consumer credit?
3 Why is consumer credit important to our economy?
4 What are the uses and misuses of credit?
5 What are the advantages and disadvantages of credit?

Action Application Using Web research and discussions with family members and friends, prepare a list of advantages and disadvantages of using credit.

Types of Credit

Objective 2

Differentiate among various types of credit.

closed-end credit One-time loans that the borrower pays back in a specified period of time and in payments of equal amounts.

open-end credit A line of credit in which loans are made on a continuous basis and the borrower is billed periodically for at least partial payment.

Two basic types of consumer credit exist: closed-end credit and open-end credit. With **closed-end credit,** you pay back one-time loans in a specified period of time and in payments of equal amounts. With **open-end credit,** loans are made on a continuous basis and you are billed periodically for at least partial payment. Exhibit 6–1 shows examples of closed-end and open-end credit.

CLOSED-END CREDIT

Closed-end credit is used for a specific purpose and involves a specified amount. Mortgage loans, automobile loans, and installment loans for purchasing furniture or appliances are examples of closed-end credit. An agreement, or contract, lists the repayment terms: the number of payments, the payment amount, and how much the credit will cost. Closed-end payment plans usually involve a written agreement for each credit purchase. A down payment or trade-in may be required, with the balance to be repaid in equal weekly or monthly payments over a period of time. Generally, the seller holds title to the merchandise until the payments have been completed.

Exhibit 6-1

Examples of closed-end and open-end credit

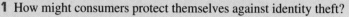

Closed-End Credit	Open-End Credit
• Mortgage loans	• Cards issued by department stores, bank
• Automobile loans	cards (Visa, MasterCard)
• Installment loans (installment sales contract, installment cash credit, single lump-sum credit)	• Travel and entertainment cards (Diners Club, American Express)
	• Overdraft protection

COMPULSIVE SHOPPING

Compulsive shoppers have a problem. They cannot stop. Compulsive shoppers buy things they don't even need; for them the act of shopping is an attempt to reduce anxiety or depression, or perhaps to ease a perceived deprivation.

Here are 10 signs of compulsive shopping:

1. Shopping to relieve anger or depression.
2. Spending that disrupts normal life.
3. Conflict with loved ones over shopping.
4. Lying to family and friends about shopping.
5. Feeling of elation when shopping.
6. Frequently taking cash from others and putting their purchases on one's card.
7. Shopping feels like doing something forbidden.
8. Guilt or shame after shopping.
9. Purchases that are never unwrapped or used.
10. Purchasing things on credit for which one wouldn't spend cash.

If you have experienced several of these symptoms, you may need help from a professional therapist. Some sort of 12-step group (like Debtors Anonymous) might help too. Compulsive shopping is not to be taken lightly; even reducing your debt and rebuilding good credit can be a problem, since it frees you up to spend more. Compulsive shoppers need psychological help.

Source: Jeff Michael, *Repair Your Credit and Knock Out Your Debt* (New York: McGraw-Hill, 2004), pp. 45–46.

The three most common types of closed-end credit are installment sales credit, installment cash credit, and single lump-sum credit. *Installment sales credit* is a loan that allows you to receive merchandise, usually high-priced items such as large appliances or furniture. You make a down payment and usually sign a contract to repay the balance, plus interest and service charges, in equal installments over a specified period.

Installment cash credit is a direct loan of money for personal purposes, home improvements, or vacation expenses. You make no down payment and make payments in specified amounts over a set period.

Single lump-sum credit is a loan that must be repaid in total on a specified day, usually within 30 to 90 days. Lump-sum credit is generally, but not always, used to purchase a single item. As Exhibit 6–2 shows, consumer credit reached over $2.0 trillion in 2004.

OPEN-END CREDIT

Using a credit card issued by a department store, using a bank credit card (Visa, MasterCard) to make purchases at different stores, charging a meal at a restaurant, and using overdraft protection are examples of open-end credit. As you will soon see, you do not apply for open-end credit to make a single purchase, as you do with closed-end credit. Rather, you can use open-end credit to make any purchases you wish if you do not exceed your **line of credit,** the maximum dollar amount of credit the lender has made available to you. You may have to pay **interest,** a periodic charge for the use of credit, or other finance charges. Some creditors allow you a grace period of 20 to 25 days to pay a bill in full before you incur any interest charges.

line of credit The dollar amount, which may or may not be borrowed, that a lender makes available to a borrower.

You may have had an appointment with a doctor or a dentist that you did not pay for until later. Professionals and small businesses often do not demand immediate payment but will charge interest if you do not pay the bill in full within 30 days. *Incidental credit* is a credit arrangement that has no extra costs and no specific repayment plan.

interest A periodic charge for the use of credit.

Many retailers use open-end credit. Customers can purchase goods or services up to a fixed dollar limit at any time. Usually you have the option to pay the bill in full within

Exhibit 6-2

Volume of consumer credit

All economists now recognize consumer credit as a major force in the American economy.

Source: *Statistical Abstract of the United States 2004–2005,* Table 1184, p. 747, and http://www.federalreserve.gov, April 11, 2005.

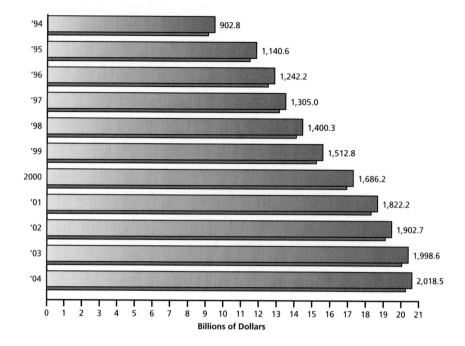

30 days without interest charges or to make set monthly installments based on the account balance plus interest.

revolving check credit A prearranged loan from a bank for a specified amount; also called a *bank line of credit.*

Many banks extend **revolving check credit.** Also called a *bank line of credit,* this is a prearranged loan for a specified amount that you can use by writing a special check. Repayment is made in installments over a set period. The finance charges are based on the amount of credit used during the month and on the outstanding balance.

CREDIT CARDS

Credit cards are extremely popular. According to a recent *American Banker* survey, 8 out of 10 U.S. households carry one or more credit cards. Two out of three households have at least one retail credit card, 56 percent have one or more Visa cards, and 47 percent have at least one MasterCard.

One-third of all credit card users generally pay off their balances in full each month. These cardholders are often known as *convenience users.* Others are borrowers; they carry balances beyond the grace period and pay finance charges. As Exhibit 6–3 illustrates, consumers use almost 1.5 billion credit cards to buy clothing, meals, vacations, gasoline, groceries, doctor visits, and other goods and services on credit.

While cash advances on credit cards can look attractive, remember that interest usually accrues from the moment you accept the cash, and you must also pay a transaction fee. One cash advance could cost you the money you were saving for a birthday gift for that special someone.

About 25,000 financial institutions participate in the credit card business, and the vast majority of them are affiliated with Visa International or the Interbank Card Association, which issues MasterCard. The Financial Planning for Life's Situations box on page 176 provides a few helpful hints for choosing a credit card.

Cobranding is the linking of a credit card with a business trade name offering "points" or premiums toward the purchase of a product or service. Cobranding has become increasingly popular since the success of General Motors Corporation's

DID YOU KNOW?

Americans will charge more than $2.0 trillion on their credit cards in the year 2005. The average cardholder has more than nine credit cards, including bank, retail, gasoline, and telephone cards.

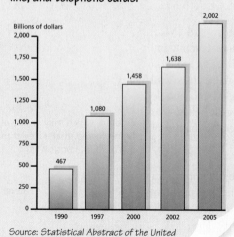

Source: *Statistical Abstract of the United States, 2004–2005,* Table 1185, p. 747.

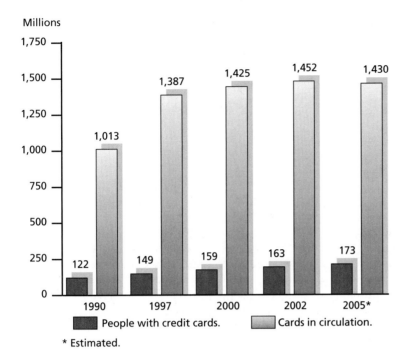

Exhibit **6-3**

Credit card holders and credit cards held

About 173 million people use almost 1.5 billion credit cards to buy goods and services.

Source: *Statistical Abstract of the United States 2004–2005*, Table 1185, p. 747.

credit card, launched in 1992. Cobranded credit cards offer rebates on products and services such as health clubs, tax preparation services from H&R Block, and gasoline purchases. Banks are realizing that cobranded credit cards help build customer loyalty. *Smart cards,* the ultimate plastic, embedded with a computer chip that can store 500 times the data of a credit card, are on their way.

Smart cards combine credit cards, a driver's license, a health care ID with your medical history and insurance information, frequent-flier miles, and telephone cards. A single smart card, for example, can be used to buy an airline ticket, store it digitally, and track frequent-flier miles. In the near future, smart cards will provide a crucial link between the World Wide Web and the physical world.

At Florida State University, smart cards have become practically indispensable. Students use smart cards to pay tuition, buy meals in the cafeteria, borrow library books, rent videos, and gain access to dormitories and online study groups.

Don't confuse credit cards with debit cards. Debit cards are often called *bank cards, ATM cards, cash cards,* and *check cards.* Although they may look alike, the **debit card,** as the name implies, electronically subtracts from your account at the moment you buy goods or services, while the credit card extends credit and delays your payment. Debit cards are most commonly used at automatic teller machines, but they are increasingly being used to purchase goods at point-of-sale terminals in stores and service stations. It is estimated that in 2005, over 25.5 billion transactions worth $1.2 trillion took place with 283 million debit cards.[3]

You are never responsible for charges on a debit card you haven't accepted. If you report a lost or stolen debit card within two days, federal regulations limit your liability to $50. After two days, your liability is limited to $50 plus any amount resulting from your failure to notify the issuer. If your debit card is lost or stolen, you must work directly with the issuer.

debit card Electronically subtracts the amount of a purchase from the buyer's account at the moment the purchase is made.

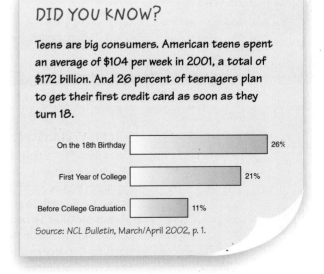

DID YOU KNOW?

Teens are big consumers. American teens spent an average of $104 per week in 2001, a total of $172 billion. And 26 percent of teenagers plan to get their first credit card as soon as they turn 18.

On the 18th Birthday	26%
First Year of College	21%
Before College Graduation	11%

Source: NCL Bulletin, March/April 2002, p. 1.

CHOOSING A CREDIT CARD?

When choosing a credit card, it pays to shop around. Follow these suggestions to select the card that best meets your needs.

1. Department stores and gasoline companies are good places to obtain your first credit card. Pay your bills in full and on time, and you will begin to establish a good credit history.

2. Bank cards are offered through banks and savings and loan associations. Fees and finance charges vary considerably (from 8 to 21.6 percent), so shop around.

3. If you usually pay your bills in full, try to deal with a financial institution with an interest-free grace period, which is the time after a purchase has been made and before a finance charge is imposed, typically 20 to 30 days.

4. If you're used to paying monthly installments, look for a card with a low monthly finance charge. Be sure you understand how that finance charge is calculated.

5. Consider obtaining a card from an out-of-state financial institution if it offers better terms than those offered locally.

6. Be aware of some credit cards that offer "no fee" or low interest but start charging interest from the day you purchase an item.

7. Watch out for credit cards that do not charge annual fees but instead charge a "transaction fee" each time you use the card.

8. If you're paying only the minimum amounts on your monthly statement, you need to plan your budget more carefully. The longer it takes for you to pay off a bill, the more interest you pay. The finance charges you pay on an item could end up being more than the item is worth.

9. With a grace period of 25 days, you actually get a free loan when you pay bills in full each month.

10. To avoid delays that may result in finance charges, follow the card issuer's instructions as to where, how, and when to make bill payments.

11. If you have a bad credit history and problems getting a credit card, look for a savings institution that will give you a secured credit card if you open a savings account. Your line of credit will be determined by the amount you have on deposit.

12. Beware of offers of easy credit. No one can guarantee to get you credit.

13. Think twice before making a 900 number telephone call for a credit card. You will pay from $2 to $50 for the 900 call and may never receive a credit card.

14. Be aware of credit cards offered by "credit repair" companies or "credit clinics." These firms may also offer to clean up your credit history for a fee. But remember, only time and good credit habits will repair your credit report if you have a poor credit history.

15. If you don't have a list of your credit issuers' telephone numbers, you may be able to obtain them by calling the 800 number directory assistance at 1-800-555-1212.

16. Travel and entertainment (T&E) cards often charge higher annual fees than most credit cards. Usually you must make payment in full within 30 days of receiving your bill or typically no further purchases will be approved on the account.

17. Often additional credit cards on your account for a spouse or child (over 18) are available with a minimum additional fee or no fee at all.

18. Be aware that debit cards are not credit cards but simply a substitute for a check or cash. The amount of the sale is subtracted from your checking account.

Sources: American Institute of Certified Public Accountants; U.S. Office of Consumer Affairs; Federal Trade Commission.

PROTECTING YOURSELF AGAINST DEBIT/CREDIT CARD FRAUD

Dead Man Walking is the title of a movie, but it's also the nickname for a man arrested by postal inspectors. Using a bizarre twist on mail fraud and credit card fraud, Michael Dantorio was accused of using personal information from at least 17 deceased persons across the country to acquire credit cards in their names, resulting in fraudulent charges of over $60,000. Hence his nickname, "Dead Man Walking."

Dantorio relied on the use of several private mailboxes. He filed false changes of address for the deceased individuals and directed the credit cards to his private mailboxes. Once he received the cards, he lost no time in running up huge charges. If you have recently lost a loved one, be on the lookout for crooks who try to take advantage when you are most vulnerable.

In a country where consumers owe more than $2.0 trillion on their credit cards, estimates of $3 billion to $4 billion in credit fraud losses—just two to three one-thousandths of 1 percent—may not seem all that terrible. But it *is* terrible for victims of fraud. Though they may be protected financially, they are forced to endure major inconvenience. Many fraud victims are devastated emotionally. The negative effects can linger for years. Moreover, all of us pay the costs of credit card fraud through higher prices, higher interest rates, and increased inconvenience.

How can you protect yourself against credit card fraud? You can take several measures:

- Sign your new cards as soon as they arrive.
- Treat your cards like money. Store them in a secure place.
- Shred anything with your account number before throwing it away.
- Don't give your card number over the phone or online unless you initiate the call.
- Don't write your card number on a postcard or the outside of an envelope.
- Remember to get your card and receipt after a transaction, and double-check to be sure it's yours.
- If your billing statement is incorrect or your credit cards are lost or stolen, notify your card issuers immediately.
- If you don't receive your billing statement, notify the company immediately.

The Internet has joined the telephone and television as an important part of our lives. Every day, more consumers use the Internet for financial activities like investing, banking, and shopping.

When you make purchases online, make sure your transactions are secure, your personal information is protected, and your fraud sensors are sharpened. Although you can't control fraud or deception on the Internet, you can take steps to recognize it, avoid it, and report if it does occur. Here's how:

- *Use a secure browser,* software that encrypts or scrambles the purchase information you send over the Internet, to guard the security of your online transactions. Most computers come with a secure browser already installed. You can also download some browsers for free over the Internet.
- *Keep records of your online transactions.* Read your e-mail. Merchants may send you important information about your purchases.
- *Review your monthly bank and credit card statements* for any billing errors or unauthorized purchases. Notify your credit card issuer or bank immediately if your credit card or checkbook is lost or stolen.
- *Read the policies of Web sites you visit,* especially the disclosures about a site's security, its refund policies, and its privacy policy on collecting and using your personal information. Some Web sites' disclosures are easier to find than others; look at the bottom of the home page, on order forms, or in the "About" or "FAQs" section of a site. If you can't find a privacy policy, consider shopping elsewhere.

Credit card companies spend hundreds of millions of dollars to promote their credit cards. The average cardholder has more than nine credit cards.

DID YOU KNOW?

Credit card offers are one of the top 10 telemarketing frauds.

2004 Telemarketing Frauds

1. Prizes/sweepstakes
2. Credit card offers
3. Scholarship/educational grants
4. Advance fee loans
5. Magazine sales scams
6. Lotteries/lottery clubs
7. Work-at-home schemes
8. Buyers' clubs
9. Travel/vacations
10. Phishing

Source: NCL Bulletin, January/February 2005, p. 4.

DID YOU KNOW?

OPTING OUT
You can stop preapproved credit card offers by calling 1-888-567-8688.

WHAT'S "PHISHING"?

Regulatory agencies have published a brochure, *Internet Pirates Are Trying to Steal Your Information,* to assist you in identifying and preventing a new type of Internet fraud known as "phishing." With this type of scam, you receive fraudulent e-mail messages that appear to be from your financial institution. The messages often appear authentic and may include the institution's logo and marketing slogans.

These messages usually describe a situation that requires immediate attention and state that your accounts will be terminated unless you verify your personal information by clicking on a provided Web link. The Web link then takes you to a screen that asks for confidential information, including:

- account numbers,
- Social Security numbers,
- passwords,
- place of birth, or
- other information used to identify you.

Those perpetrating the fraud then use this information to access your accounts or assume your identity.

The brochure advises consumers:

- If you're not sure the e-mail is legitimate, go to the company's site by typing in a Web address that you know is authentic.
- If you think the e-mail message might be fraudulent, *do not* click on any embedded link within the e-mail. The link may contain a virus.
- Do not be intimidated by e-mails that warn of dire consequences for not following the sender's instructions.
- If you do you fall victim to a phishing scam, act immediately to protect yourself by alerting your financial institution, placing fraud alerts on your credit files, and monitoring your account statements closely.
- Report suspicious e-mails or calls from third parties to the Federal Trade Commission, either through the Internet at www.consumer.gov/idtheft or by calling 1-877-IDTHEFT.

The brochure is on the Office of the Comptroller of the Currency's Web site, www.occ.gov/consumer/phishing.htm.

Source: Federal Trade Commission, www.ftc.gov, April 2005.

- *Keep your personal information private.* Don't disclose personal information— your address, telephone number, Social Security number, or e-mail address—unless you know who's collecting the information, why they're collecting it, and how they'll use it.
- *Give payment information only to businesses you know and trust* and only in appropriate places such as electronic order forms.
- *Never give your password to anyone online,* even your Internet service provider.
- *Do not download files sent to you by strangers or click on hyperlinks from people you don't know.* Opening a file could expose your computer system to a virus.[4]

The accompanying Financial Planning for Life's Situations box describes what *phishing* is and what you can do to protect yourself.

TRAVEL AND ENTERTAINMENT (T&E) CARDS   T&E cards are really not credit cards, because the monthly balance is due in full. However, most people think of Diners Club or American Express cards as credit cards because they don't pay the moment they purchase goods or services. Recently, American Express began issuing credit cards also.

HOME EQUITY LOANS   A **home equity loan** is based on the difference between the current market value of your home and the amount you still owe on your mortgage. With such a loan, you can borrow up to $100,000 or more on your home. Depending on the value of the home, you can borrow up to 85 percent of its appraised value, less the

home equity loan A loan based on the current market value of a home less the amount still owed on the mortgage.

Financial Planning Calculations

HOW MUCH CAN YOU BORROW WITH A HOME EQUITY LOAN?

Depending on your income and the equity in your home, you can apply for a line of credit for anywhere from $10,000 to $250,000 or more.

Some lenders let you borrow only up to 75 percent of the value of your home, less the amount of your first mortgage. At some banks you may qualify to borrow up to 85 percent! This higher lending limit may make the difference in your ability to get the money you need for home improvements, education, or other expenses.

Use the following chart to calculate your home loan value, which is the approximate amount of your home equity line of credit.

	Example	Your Home
Approximate market value of your home	$100,000	$ _____
Multiply by .75	×.75	×.75
Approximate loan value	75,000	_____
Subtract balance due on mortgage(s)	50,000	_____
Approximate credit limit available	$25,000	$ _____

In the above example, your "credit limit available" home loan value see table above (the amount for which you could establish your account) is $25,000. Once your ac-

count is established, you can write a check for any amount you need up to $25,000.

In choosing a home equity loan,

1. Find out if your lending institution protects you against rising interest rates.
2. Compare the size of your lender's fee with those of other institutions.
3. Find out if your lender charges an inactivity fee.
4. Make sure high annual fees and other costs do not outweigh the tax advantage of a home equity loan, especially if you are borrowing only a small amount.
5. Be careful of interest-only payments on home equity loans.
6. Find out whether your lender has the right to change the terms and conditions of your loan or to terminate your loan.
7. Make sure that all of the interest you hope to finally deduct on your home equity loan is in fact deductible.
8. Carefully evaluate your reasons for using the equity in your home for loans.
9. Know the full costs and risks of home equity loans before you make a commitment to a lending institution.

Sources: Household Bank, F.S.B., *Home Equity Loan Guide,* August 1991, p. 3; American Institute of CPAs, *Home Equity Loans: A Consumer's Guide,* n.d.

---

amount you still owe on your mortgage. The interest you pay on a home equity loan is tax deductible, unlike interest on other types of loans.

A home equity loan is usually set up as a revolving line of credit, typically with a variable interest rate. A *revolving line of credit* is an arrangement whereby borrowings are permitted up to a specified limit and for a stated period, usually 5 to 10 years. Once the line of credit has been established, you draw from it only the amount you need at any one time (see the Financial Planning Calculations box). Today many lenders offer home equity lines of credit. But your home is probably your largest asset. You should use the home equity loan only for major items such as education, home improvements, or medical bills and not for daily expenses or to buy a boat, new car, or to pay for a cruise. *Remember, if you miss payments on a home equity loan, you can lose your home.* Furthermore, when you sell your home, you probably will be required to pay off your equity line in full. If you plan to sell your house in the near future, consider whether annual fees to maintain the account and other costs of setting up an equity credit line make sense.

DID YOU KNOW?

Launched in 1997, the Consumer Sentinel collects information about consumer fraud and identity theft from the FTC and over 150 other organizations. The database is available to law enforcement agencies across the nation and throughout the world for use in their investigations.

Source: Federal Trade Commission, *National and State Trends in Fraud and Identity Theft: January–December 2004,* February 1, 2005.

179

CONCEPT CHECK 6-2

1 What are the two main types of consumer credit?
2 What is a debit card?
3 What is a home equity loan?

Action Application   Research three credit card companies. List their fees and any advantages they offer. Record your findings.

Measuring Your Credit Capacity

Objective 3

Assess your credit capacity and build your credit rating.

The only way to determine how much credit you can assume is to first learn how to make an accurate and sensible personal or family budget. Budgets, as you learned in Chapter 3, are simple, carefully considered spending plans. With budgets, you first provide for basic necessities such as rent or mortgage, food, and clothing. Then you provide for items such as home furnishings and other heavy, more durable goods.

CAN YOU AFFORD A LOAN?

Before you take out a loan, ask yourself whether you can meet all of your essential expenses and still afford the monthly loan payments. You can make this calculation in two ways. One is to add up all of your basic monthly expenses and then subtract this total from your take-home pay. If the difference will not cover the monthly payment and still leave funds for other expenses, you cannot afford the loan.

A second and more reliable method is to ask yourself what you plan to give up to make the monthly loan payment. If you currently save a portion of your income that is greater than the monthly payment, you can use these savings to pay off the loan. But if you do not, you will have to forgo spending on entertainment, new appliances, or perhaps even necessities. Are you prepared to make this trade-off? Although it is difficult to precisely measure your credit capacity, you can follow certain rules of thumb.

GENERAL RULES OF CREDIT CAPACITY

DEBT PAYMENTS–TO–INCOME RATIO   The debt payments–to–income ratio is calculated by dividing your monthly debt payments (not including house payment, which is a long-term liability) by your net monthly income. Experts suggest that you spend no more than 20 percent of your net (after-tax) income on consumer credit payments. Thus, as Exhibit 6–4 shows, a person making $1,068 per month after taxes should spend no more than $213 on credit payments per month.

The 20 percent estimate is the maximum; however, 15 percent is much better. The 20 percent estimate is based on the average family, with average expenses; it does not take major emergencies into account. If you are just beginning to use credit, you should not consider yourself safe if you are spending 20 percent of your net income on credit payments.

DEBT-TO-EQUITY RATIO   The debt-to-equity ratio is calculated by dividing your total liabilities by your net worth. In calculating this ratio, do not include the value of your home and the amount of its mortgage. If your debt-to-equity ratio is about 1— that is, if your consumer installment debt roughly equals your net worth (not including your home or the mortgage)—you have probably reached the upper limit of debt obligations.

Monthly gross income	$1,500
Less:	
All taxes	270
Social Security	112
Monthly IRA contribution	50
Monthly net income	$1,068
Monthly installment credit payments:	
Visa	25
MasterCard	20
Discover card	15
Education loan	—
Personal bank loan	—
Auto loan	153
Total monthly payments	$ 213
Debt payments–to–income ratio ($213/$1,068)	19.94%

Exhibit **6–4**

How to calculate debt payments–to–income ratio

Spend no more than 20 percent of your net (after-tax) income on credit payments.

The debt-to-equity ratio for business firms in general ranges between 0.33 and 0.50. The larger this ratio, the riskier the situation for lenders and borrowers. Of course, you can lower the debt-to-equity ratio by paying off debts.

None of the above methods is perfect for everyone; the limits given are only guidelines. Only you, based on the money you earn, your current obligations, and your financial plans for the future, can determine the exact amount of credit you need and can afford. You must be your own credit manager.

Keep in mind that you adversely affect your credit capacity if you cosign a loan for a friend or a relative.

Sheet 29
Consumer credit usage patterns

COSIGNING A LOAN

What would you do if a friend or a relative asked you to cosign a loan? Before you give your answer, make sure you understand what cosigning involves. Under a recent Federal Trade Commission rule, creditors are required to give you a notice to help explain your obligations. The cosigner's notice says,

> You are being asked to guarantee this debt. Think carefully before you do. If the borrower doesn't pay the debt, you will have to. Be sure you can afford to pay if you have to, and that you want to accept this responsibility.
>
> You may have to pay up to the full amount of the debt if the borrower does not pay. You may also have to pay late fees or collection costs, which increase this amount.
>
> The creditor can collect this debt from you without first trying to collect from the borrower. The creditor can use the same collection methods against you that can be used against the borrower, such as suing you, garnishing your wages, etc. If this debt is ever in default, that fact may become a part of *your* credit record.

COSIGNERS OFTEN PAY   Some studies of certain types of lenders show that as many as three of four cosigners are asked to wholly or partially repay the loan. That statistic should not surprise you. When you are asked to cosign, you are being asked to take a risk that a professional lender will not take. The lender would not require a cosigner if the borrower met the lender's criteria for making a loan.

In most states, if you do cosign and your friend or relative misses a payment, the lender can collect the entire debt from you immediately without pursuing the borrower first. Also, the amount you owe may increase if the lender decides to sue to collect. If the lender wins the case, it may be able to take your wages and property.

IF YOU DO COSIGN   Despite the risks, at times you may decide to cosign. Perhaps your child needs a first loan or a close friend needs help. Here are a few things to consider before you cosign:

1. Be sure you can afford to pay the loan. If you are asked to pay and cannot, you could be sued or your credit rating could be damaged.

2. Consider that even if you are not asked to repay the debt, your liability for this loan may keep you from getting other credit you want.

3. Before you pledge property such as your automobile or furniture to secure the loan, make sure you understand the consequences. If the borrower defaults, you could lose the property you pledge.

4. Check your state law. Some states have laws giving you additional rights as a cosigner.

5. Request that a copy of overdue-payment notices be sent to you so that you can take action to protect your credit history.

BUILDING AND MAINTAINING YOUR CREDIT RATING

If you apply for a charge account, credit card, car loan, personal loan, or mortgage, your credit experience, or lack of it, will be a major consideration for the creditor. Your credit experience may even affect your ability to get a job or buy life insurance. A good credit rating is a valuable asset that should be nurtured and protected. If you want a good rating, you must use credit with discretion: Limit your borrowing to your capacity to repay, and live up to the terms of your contracts. The quality of your credit rating is entirely up to you.

In reviewing your creditworthiness, a creditor seeks information from a credit bureau. Most creditors rely heavily on credit reports in considering loan applications.

credit bureau A reporting agency that assembles credit and other information about consumers.

CREDIT BUREAUS   **Credit bureaus** or Consumer Reporting Agencies (CRAs) collect credit and other information about consumers. There are three major credit bureaus: Experian Information Solutions (formerly TRW, Inc.), Trans Union Credit Information Company, and Equifax Services, Inc. Each bureau maintains over 200 million credit files on individuals based on over 2½ billion items of information received each month from lenders. In addition, several thousand regional credit bureaus collect credit information about consumers. These firms sell the data to creditors that evaluate credit applications.

The Federal Trade Commission receives more consumer complaints about credit bureaus than about any other industry, on average 12,000 a year. A common complaint involves mixups between people with identical surnames. However, the accuracy of credit reports has improved recently, due primarily to public outcry and the threat of stricter federal laws.

LOOK BEFORE YOU LEAP. Before taking out a loan, a consumer examines her credit report.

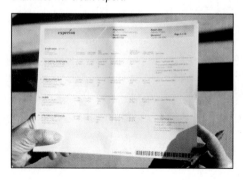

WHO PROVIDES DATA TO CREDIT BUREAUS?   Credit bureaus obtain their data from banks, finance companies, merchants, credit card companies, and other creditors. These sources regularly send reports to credit bureaus containing information about the kinds of credit they extend to customers, the amounts and terms of that credit, and customers' paying habits. Credit bureaus also collect some information from other sources, such as court records.

WHAT IS IN YOUR CREDIT FILES?

The credit bureau file contains your name, address, Social Security number, and birth date. It may also include the following information:

- Your employer, position, and income.
- Your former address.
- Your former employer.
- Your spouse's name, Social Security number, employer, and income.
- Whether you own your home, rent, or board.
- Checks returned for insufficient funds.

Your credit file may also contain detailed credit information. Each time you buy from a reporting store on credit or take out a loan at a bank, a finance company, or some other reporting creditor, a credit bureau is informed of your account number and the date, amount, terms, and type of credit. As you make payments, your file is updated to show the outstanding balance, the number and amounts of payments past due, and the frequency of 30-, 60-, or 90-day delinquencies. Any suits, judgments, or tax liens against you may appear as well. However, a federal law protects your rights if the information in your credit file is erroneous.

> **DID YOU KNOW?**
>
> The FTC's brochure "File Segregation: New ID Is a Bad IDea" provides tips on how to spot credit repair schemes. Find it on the Web at www.ftc.gov or write FTC, Consumer Response Center, 600 Pennsylvania Avenue, NW, Washington, DC 20580.

FAIR CREDIT REPORTING

You can see that fair and accurate credit reporting is vital to both creditors and consumers. In 1971 Congress enacted the **Fair Credit Reporting Act,** which regulates the use of credit reports, requires the deletion of obsolete information, and gives consumers access to their files and the right to have erroneous data corrected. Furthermore, the act allows only authorized persons to obtain credit reports.

Credit bureaus provide lists of creditworthy consumers for companies to offer credit. These are called prescreened lists. You can remove your name from all Experian-generated mail and telephone lists by sending your full name and addresses for the past five years to Experian, Consumer Opt Out, P.O. Box 919, Allen, TX 75013. Your name will be shared with Equifax and Trans Union, the other two national credit reporting systems.

Fair Credit Reporting Act
Regulates the use of credit reports, requires the deletion of obsolete information, and gives consumers access to their files and the right to have erroneous data corrected.

WHO MAY OBTAIN A CREDIT REPORT?

Your credit report may be issued only to properly identified persons for approved purposes. It may be furnished to prospective employers in response to a court order or in accordance with your own written request. A credit report may also be provided to someone who will use it in connection with a credit transaction, underwriting of insurance, or some other legitimate business need or in determining eligibility for a license or other benefit granted by a government agency. Your friends and neighbors may not obtain credit information about you. If they request such information, they may be subject to fine and imprisonment.

The credit bureaus contend that current laws protect consumers' privacy, but many consumer organizations believe that anyone with a personal computer and a modem can easily access credit bureau files.

fyi

In 2005 all consumers became eligible to receive a free credit report from each of the three major credit reporting agencies (CRAs). Call 1-877-322-8228 or visit **www.annualcreditreport.com.** Your FICO score is available from **www.myfico.com** for a fee. A good strategy is to ask for one report from a different agency every four months. That makes it easier to spot suspicious activity over the course of a year.

Source: *BusinessWeek,* February 21, 2005, p. 91.

Exhibit 6-5

Sample dispute letter

The law requires credit card companies to correct inaccurate or incomplete information in your credit report.

Date

Your Name
Your Address
Your City, State, Zip Code

Complaint Department
Name of Credit Reporting Agency
Address
City, State, Zip Code

Dear Sir or Madam:

I am writing to dispute the following information in my file. The items I dispute are also encircled on the attached copy of the report I received. (Identify item(s) disputed by name of source, such as creditor or tax court, and identify type of item, such as credit account, judgment, etc.)

This item is (inaccurate or incomplete) because (describe what is inaccurate or incomplete and why). I am requesting that the item be deleted (or request another specific change) to correct the information.

Enclosed are copies of (use this sentence if applicable and describe any enclosed documentation, such as payment records, court documents) supporting my position. Please reinvestigate this (these) matter(s) and (delete or correct) the disputed item(s) as soon as possible.

Sincerely,
Your name
Enclosures: (List what you are enclosing)

Source: Federal Trade Commission, April 2005.

TIME LIMITS ON ADVERSE DATA   Most of the information in your credit file may be reported for only seven years. If you have declared personal bankruptcy, however, that fact may be reported for 10 years. After 7 or 10 years, a credit reporting agency can't disclose the information in your credit file unless you are being investigated for a credit application of $75,000 or more or for an application to purchase life insurance of $150,000 or more.

INCORRECT INFORMATION IN YOUR CREDIT FILE   Credit bureaus are required to follow reasonable procedures to ensure that subscribing creditors report information accurately. However, mistakes may occur. Your file may contain erroneous data or records of someone with a name similar to yours. When you notify the credit bureau that you dispute the accuracy of its information, it must reinvestigate and modify or remove inaccurate data. You should give the credit bureau any pertinent data you have concerning an error. If you contest an item on your credit report, the reporting agency must remove the item unless the creditor verifies that the information is accurate (see Exhibit 6–5).

If you are denied credit, insurance, employment, or rental housing based on the information in the report, you can get a copy of your credit report free within 60 days of your request. You should review your credit files every year even if you are not planning to apply for a big loan. Married women and young adults should make sure that all accounts for which they are individually and jointly liable are listed in their credit files.

Exhibit **6-6**   What if you are denied credit?

Steps you can take if you are denied credit.

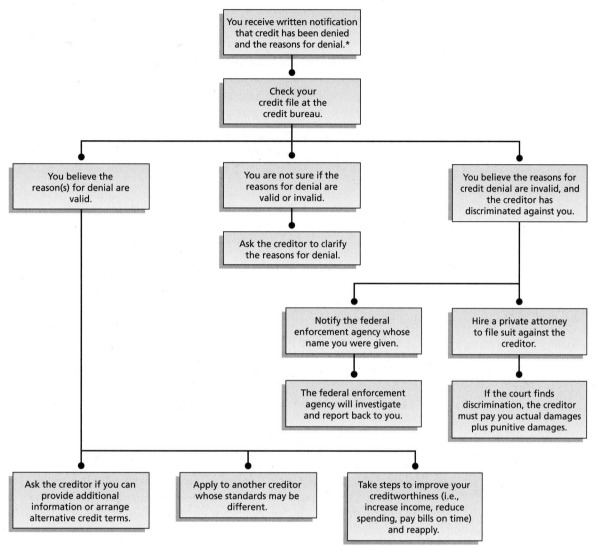

*If a creditor receives no more than 150 applications during a calendar year, the disclosures may be oral.

Source: Reprinted courtesy of Office of Public Information, Federal Reserve Bank of Minneapolis, Minneapolis, MN 55480.

WHAT ARE THE LEGAL REMEDIES?   Any consumer reporting agency or user of reported information that willfully or through negligence fails to comply with the provisions of the Fair Credit Reporting Act may be sued by the affected consumer. If the agency or the user is found guilty, the consumer may be awarded actual damages, court costs, and attorneys' fees and, in the case of willful noncompliance, punitive damages as allowed by the court. The action must be brought within two years of the occurrence or within two years after the discovery of material and willful misrepresentation of information. An unauthorized person who obtains a credit report under false pretenses may be fined up to $5,000, imprisoned for one year, or both. The same penalties apply to anyone who willfully provides credit information to someone not authorized to receive it.

Exhibit 6–6 outlines the steps you can take if you are denied credit.

CONCEPT CHECK 6-3

1 What are the general rules for measuring credit capacity?
2 What can happen if you cosign a loan?
3 What can you do to build and maintain your credit rating?
4 What is the Fair Credit Reporting Act?
5 How do you correct erroneous information in your credit file?
6 What are your legal remedies if a credit reporting agency engages in unfair reporting practices?

Action Application Talk to a person who has cosigned a loan. What experiences did this person have as a cosigner?

Applying for Credit

A SCENARIO FROM THE PAST

Objective 4

Describe the information creditors look for when you apply for credit.

Mary and John Jones have a joint income that is more than enough for them to make payments on their dream house. Yet they are turned down for a mortgage loan. The lender says Mary might become pregnant and leave her job.

In fact, however, it is illegal for a creditor to ask or assume anything about a woman's childbearing plans. It is even illegal to discourage the Joneses from applying for a loan because Mary is of childbearing age. Also, the lender must fully acknowledge Mary's income.

When you are ready to apply for credit, you should know what creditors think is important in deciding whether you are creditworthy. You should also know what they cannot legally consider in their decisions. The **Equal Credit Opportunity Act (ECOA)** starts all credit applicants off on the same footing. It states that race, color, age, sex, marital status, and certain other factors may not be used to discriminate against you in any part of a credit dealing. Credit rights of women are protected under the ECOA. Women should build and protect their own credit histories, using the checklist shown in the Financial Planning for Life's Situations box on page 187.

Equal Credit Opportunity Act (ECOA) Bans discrimination in the extension of credit on the basis of race, color, age, sex, marital status, and other factors.

WHAT CREDITORS LOOK FOR: THE FIVE Cs OF CREDIT MANAGEMENT[5]

When a lender extends credit to its customers, it recognizes that some customers will be unable or unwilling to pay for their purchases. Therefore, lenders must establish policies for determining who will receive credit. Most lenders build their credit policies around the *five Cs of credit:* **character, capacity, capital, collateral,** and **conditions** (see the Financial Planning for Life's Situations box on page 190).

Character is the borrower's attitude toward credit obligations. Most credit managers consider character the most important factor in predicting whether you will make timely payments and ultimately repay your loan.

Capacity is your financial ability to meet credit obligations, that is, to make regular loan payments as scheduled in the credit agreement. Therefore, the lender checks your salary statements and other sources of income, such as dividends and interest. Your other financial obligations and monthly expenses are also considered before credit is approved.

Capital refers to your assets or net worth. Generally, the greater your capital, the greater your ability to repay a loan. The lender determines your net worth by requiring

character The borrower's attitude toward his or her credit obligations.

capacity The borrower's financial ability to meet credit obligations.

capital The borrower's assets or net worth.

Financial Planning for Life's Situations

WOMEN'S CHECKLIST FOR BUILDING AND PROTECTING THEIR CREDIT HISTORIES

It is simple and sensible to build and protect your own credit history. Here are some steps to get you started.

IF YOU ARE SINGLE:

- Open a checking or savings account, or both.
- Apply for a local department store card.
- Take out a small loan from your bank. Make timely payments.

IF YOU ARE ALREADY MARRIED:

- Establish credit in your maiden name or your first name.
- Open your own accounts.
- Try to have separate credit card accounts in your own name.
- Review your joint accounts.
- Make sure that creditors report your credit history to credit bureaus in both names.

IF YOU ARE GETTING MARRIED:

- Write to your creditors and ask them to continue maintaining your credit file separately.
- You can choose to use your first name and your maiden name (Sue Smith), your first name and your husband's last name (Sue Jones), or your first name and a combined last name (Sue Smith-Jones).
- Once you have picked a name, use it consistently.

IF YOU HAVE RECENTLY BEEN SEPARATED OR DIVORCED:

- Close all of your joint accounts. Your credit record could suffer if your ex-partner is delinquent.
- Meet your creditors and clear your credit record if your ex-partner has hurt your credit rating.

IF YOU ARE WIDOWED:

- Notify all creditors and tell them whether you or the executor of the estate will handle payment.
- Transfer all existing joint loans to your name alone. You may also want to renegotiate repayment terms.
- Transfer joint credit card accounts to your name alone or reapply for new accounts.
- Seek professional advice, if needed.

And remember that a creditor *cannot*:

1. Refuse you individual credit in your own name if you are creditworthy.
2. Require a spouse to cosign a loan. Any creditworthy person can be your cosigner if one is required.
3. Ask about your birth control practices or family plans or assume that your income will be interrupted to have children.
4. Consider whether you have a telephone listing in your own name.

A creditor *must*:

5. Evaluate you on the same basis as applicants who are male or who have a different marital status.
6. Consider income from part-time employment.
7. Consider reliable alimony, child support, or separate-maintenance payments.
8. Consider the payment history of all joint accounts that accurately reflect your credit history.
9. Report the payment history on an account if you use the account jointly with your spouse.
10. Disregard information on accounts if you can prove that it does not reflect your ability or willingness to repay.

Source: Reprinted courtesy of Office of Public Information, Federal Reserve Bank of Minneapolis, Minneapolis, MN 55480.

---

you to complete certain credit application questions (see Exhibit 6–7). You must authorize your employer and financial institutions to release information to confirm the claims made in the credit application.

Collateral is an asset that you pledge to a financial institution to obtain a loan. If you fail to honor the terms of the credit agreement, the lender can repossess the collateral and then sell it to satisfy the debt.

Conditions refer to general economic conditions that can affect your ability to repay a loan. The basic question focuses on security—of both your job and the firm that employs you.

collateral A valuable asset that is pledged to ensure loan payments.

conditions The general economic conditions that can affect a borrower's ability to repay a loan.

Exhibit **6–7**

Sample credit application questions

- Amount of loan requested.
- Proposed use of the loan.
- Your name and birth date.
- Social Security and driver's license numbers.
- Present and previous street addresses.
- Present and previous employers and their addresses.
- Present salary.
- Number and ages of dependents.
- Other income and sources of other income.
- Have you ever received credit from us?

- If so, when and at which office?
- Checking account number, institution, and branch.
- Savings account number, institution, and branch.
- Name of nearest relative not living with you.
- Relative's address and telephone number.
- Your marital status.
- Information regarding joint applicant: same questions as above.

Creditors use different combinations of the five Cs to reach their decisions. Some creditors set unusually high standards, and others simply do not make certain kinds of loans. Creditors also use different kinds of rating systems. Some rely strictly on their own instinct and experience. Others use a credit-scoring or statistical system to predict whether an applicant is a good credit risk. They assign a certain number of points to each characteristic that has proven to be a reliable sign that a borrower will repay. Then they rate the applicant on this scale.

Typical questions in a credit application appear in Exhibit 6–7. The information in your credit report is used to calculate your FICO credit score—a number generally between 350 and 850 that rates how risky a borrower is. The higher the score, the less risk you pose to creditors. Your FICO score is available from www.myfico.com for a fee. Free credit reports do not contain your credit score. Exhibit 6–8 shows a numerical depiction of your creditworthiness and how you can improve your credit score. In addition, during the loan application process, the lender may evaluate many of the following criteria to determine whether you are a good credit risk.

AGE   Eugene and Ethel Esposito, a retired couple, and many older people have complained that they were denied credit because they were over a certain age or that, when they retired, their credit was suddenly cut off or reduced.

The ECOA is very specific about how a person's age may be used in credit decisions. A creditor may ask about your age, but if you're old enough to sign a binding contract (usually 18 or 21 years old, depending on state law), a creditor may not

- Turn you down or decrease your credit because of your age.
- Ignore your retirement income in rating your application.
- Close your credit account or require you to reapply for it because you have reached a certain age or retired.
- Deny you credit or close your account because credit life insurance or other credit-related insurance is not available to people of your age.

PUBLIC ASSISTANCE   You may not be denied credit because you receive Social Security or public assistance. But, as with age, certain information related to this source of income could have a bearing on your creditworthiness.

HOUSING LOANS   The ECOA covers your application for a mortgage or a home improvement loan. It bans discrimination due to characteristics such as your race,

Exhibit **6-8**   TransUnion personal credit score

The higher your FICO score, the less risk you pose to creditors.

 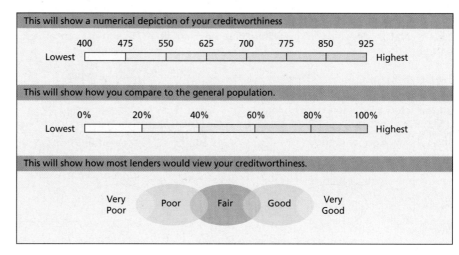

color, or sex or to the race or national origin of the people in the neighborhood where you live or want to buy your home. Creditors may not use any appraisal of the value of your property that considers the race of the people in your neighborhood.

WHAT IF YOUR APPLICATION IS DENIED?

ASK QUESTIONS IF YOUR APPLICATION IS DENIED
If you receive a notice that your application has been denied, the ECOA gives you the right to know the specific reasons for denial. If the denial is based on a credit report, you are entitled to know the specific information in the credit report that led to it. After you receive this information from the creditor, you should contact the local credit bureau to find out what information it reported. The bureau cannot charge you a disclosure fee if you ask for a copy of your credit report within 60 days of being notified of a denial based on a credit report. You may ask the bureau to investigate any inaccurate or incomplete information and correct its records.

How can I improve my credit score? A credit score is a snapshot of the contents of your credit report at the time it is calculated. The first step in improving your score is to review your credit report to ensure it is accurate. Long-term, responsible credit behavior is the most effective way to improve future scores. Pay bills on time, lower balances, and use credit wisely to improve your score over time.

fyi

CONCEPT CHECK 6-4 ✓

1 What is the Equal Credit Opportunity Act?
2 What are the five Cs of credit?
3 What can you do if your credit application is denied?

Action Application Visit www.myfico.com and learn how calculators can help you make important decisions about borrowing money, debt payoff, and savings. Which choices will help you reach your goals?

Avoiding and Correcting Credit Mistakes

Has a department store's computer ever billed you for merchandise that you returned to the store or never received? Has a credit company ever charged you for the same item twice or failed to properly credit a payment on your account?

Objective 5

Identify the steps you can take to avoid and correct credit mistakes.

Financial Planning for Life's Situations

THE FIVE Cs OF CREDIT

Here is what lenders look for in determining your credit-worthiness.

CREDIT HISTORY

1. Character: Will you repay the loan?	Yes	No
Do you have a good attitude toward credit obligations?	—	—
Have you used credit before?	—	—
Do you pay your bills on time?	—	—
Have you ever filed for bankruptcy?	—	—
Do you live within your means?	—	—

STABILITY

How long have you lived at your present address? ___ yrs.

Do you own your home? ___ ___

How long have you been employed by your present employer? ___ yrs.

INCOME

2. Capacity: Can you repay the loan?

Your salary and occupation? $ ____; ____

Place of occupation? _____

How reliable is your income? Reliable ___; Not reliable ___

Any other sources of income? $ _____

EXPENSES

Number of dependents? _____

Do you pay any alimony or child support? Yes ___; No ___

Current debts? $ _____

NET WORTH

3. Capital: What are your assets and net worth?

What are your assets? $ _____

What are your liabilities? $ _____

What is your net worth? $ _____

LOAN SECURITY

4. Collateral: What if you don't repay the loan?

What assets do you have to secure the loan? (Car, home, furniture?) _____

What sources do you have besides income? (Savings, stocks, bonds, insurance?) _____

JOB SECURITY

5. Conditions: What general economic conditions can affect your repayment of the loan?

How secure is your job? Secure ___; Not secure ___

How secure is the firm you work for? Secure ___; Not secure ___

Source: Adapted from William M. Pride, Robert J. Hughes, and Jack R. Kapoor, *Business,* 8th ed. (Boston: Houghton Mifflin, 2005), pp. 590–592.

Fair Credit Billing Act (FCBA) Sets procedures for promptly correcting billing mistakes, refusing to make credit card payments on defective goods, and promptly crediting payments.

The best way to maintain your credit standing is to repay your debts on time. But complications may still occur. To protect your credit and save your time, money, and future credit rating, you should learn how to correct any mistakes and misunderstandings that crop up in your credit accounts. If a snag occurs, first try to deal directly with the creditor. The credit laws can help you settle your complaints.

The **Fair Credit Billing Act (FCBA),** passed in 1975, sets procedures for promptly correcting billing mistakes, refusing to make credit card or revolving credit payments on defective goods, and promptly crediting your payments.

The act defines a billing error as any charge for something you did not buy or for something bought by a person not authorized to use your account. Also included among billing errors is any charge that is not properly identified on your bill (that is, for an amount different from the actual purchase price) or that was entered on a date other than the purchase date. A billing error may also be a charge for something you did not accept on delivery or was not delivered according to agreement.

Billing errors also include errors in arithmetic; failure to reflect a payment or other credit to your account; failure to mail the statement to your current address, provided you notified the creditor of an address change at least 20 days before the end of the billing period; and questionable items, or items about which you need additional information.

IN CASE OF A BILLING ERROR

If you think your bill is wrong or you want more information about it, follow these steps. First, notify the creditor *in writing* within 60 days after the bill was mailed. A telephone call will not protect your rights. Be sure to write to the address the creditor lists for billing inquiries. Give the creditor your name and account number, say that you believe the bill contains an error, and explain what you believe the error to be. State the suspected amount of the error or the item you want explained. Then pay all the parts of the bill that are not in dispute. While waiting for an answer, you do not have to pay the disputed amount or any minimum payments or finance charges that apply to it.

The creditor must acknowledge your letter within 30 days, unless it can correct your bill sooner. Within two billing periods, but in no case longer than 90 days, either your account must be corrected or you must be told why the creditor believes the bill is correct. If the creditor made a mistake, you need not pay any finance charges on the disputed amount. Your account must be corrected, and you must be sent an explanation of any amount you still owe.

If no error is found, the creditor must promptly send you an explanation of the reasons for that determination and a statement of what you owe, which may include any finance charges that have accumulated and any minimum payments you missed while you were questioning the bill. Exhibit 6–9 summarizes the steps in resolving a billing dispute, and Exhibit 6–9A shows a sample letter to dispute a billing error.

YOUR CREDIT RATING DURING THE DISPUTE

A creditor may not threaten your credit rating while you are resolving a billing dispute. Once you have written about a possible error, a creditor is prohibited from giving out information that would damage your credit reputation to other creditors or credit bureaus. And until your complaint has been answered, the creditor may not take any action to collect the disputed amount.

Beware of credit repair. There is nothing credit repair can repair in your credit reports that you can't repair yourself. Visit this Web site: **www.consumercreditrepair.com/.**

After explaining the bill, the creditor may report you as delinquent on the amount in dispute and take action to collect if you do not pay in the time allowed. Even so, you can still disagree in writing. Then the creditor and the credit bureau must report that you have challenged your bill and give you the name and address of each recipient of information about your account. When the matter has been settled, the creditor must report the outcome to each recipient of the information. Remember, you may also place your version of the dispute in your credit record.

DEFECTIVE GOODS OR SERVICES

Your new sofa arrives with only three legs. You try to return it, but no luck. You ask the merchant to repair or replace it; still no luck. The Fair Credit Billing Act provides that

Exhibit **6-9**   Steps in the process of resolving a billing dispute   *A creditor may not threaten your credit rating while you are resolving a billing dispute.*

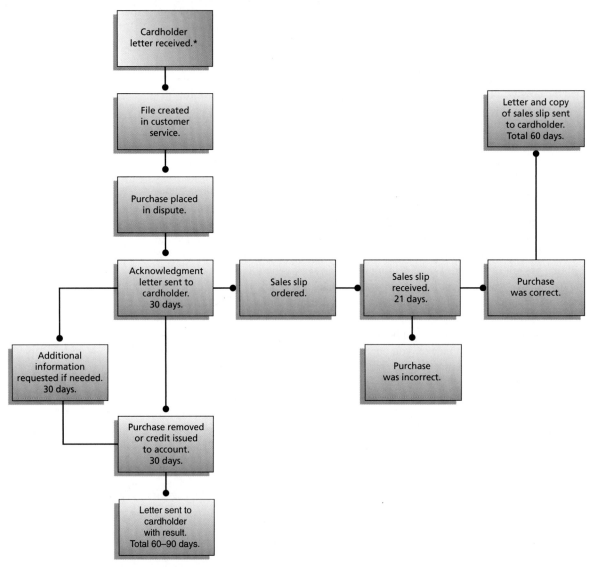

*Exhibit 6–9A shows a sample letter to dispute a billing error.
Source: Courtesy of Charge-It-System, Billing Errors Section, *Cardholder Tips,* March 1992, n.p.

you may withhold payment on any damaged or shoddy goods or poor services that you have purchased with a credit card as long as you have made a sincere attempt to resolve the problem with the merchant.

IDENTITY CRISIS: WHAT TO DO IF YOUR IDENTITY IS STOLEN

"I don't remember charging those items. I've never even been in that store." Maybe you never charged those goods and services, but someone else did—someone who used your name and personal information to commit fraud. When impostors take your name, Social Security number, credit card number, or some other piece of your personal information for their use, they are committing a crime. As you learned from the chapter opening case, identity theft is the fastest-growing financial crime.

Date

Your Name
Your Address
Your City, State, Zip Code
Your Account Number

Name of Creditor
Billing Inquiries
Address
City, State, Zip Code

Dear Sir or Madam:

I am writing to dispute a billing error in the amount of $_____ on my
account. The amount is inaccurate because (describe the problem).
I am requesting that the error be corrected, that any finance and other
charges related to the disputed amount be credited as well, and that
I receive an accurate statement.

Enclosed are copies of (use this sentence to describe any enclosed
information, such as sales slips, payment records) supporting my
position. Please investigate this matter and correct the billing error
as soon as possible.

Sincerely,
Your name
Enclosures: (List what you are enclosing)

Exhibit 6-9A

A sample letter to dispute a billing error

Write to the creditor at the address given for "billing inquiries," not the address for sending your payments.

Source: Federal Trade Commission, April 2005.

The biggest problem is that you may not know your identity has been stolen until you notice that something is amiss: You may get bills for a credit card account you never opened, your credit report may include debts you never knew you had, a billing cycle may pass without you receiving a statement, or you may see charges on your bills that you didn't sign for, didn't authorize, and know nothing about.

If someone has stolen your identity, the Federal Trade Commission recommends that you take three actions immediately:

1. *Contact the fraud departments of each of the three major credit bureaus* (see the table that follows). Tell them to flag your file with a fraud alert, including a statement that creditors should call you for permission before they open any new accounts in your name.

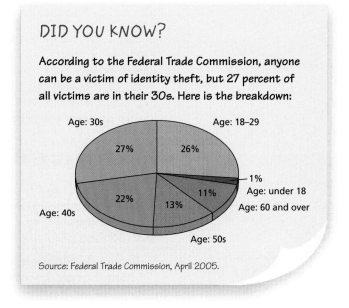

DID YOU KNOW?

According to the Federal Trade Commission, anyone can be a victim of identity theft, but 27 percent of all victims are in their 30s. Here is the breakdown:

Age: 30s — 27%
Age: 18–29 — 26%
Age: under 18 — 1%
Age: 60 and over — 11%
Age: 50s — 13%
Age: 40s — 22%

Source: Federal Trade Commission, April 2005.

	To Report Fraud	To Order Credit Report	Web Site
Equifax	1-800-525-6285	1-800-685-1111	www.equifax.com
Experian	1-888-397-3742	1-888-EXPERIAN	www.experian.com
Trans Union	1-800-680-7289	1-800-916-8800	www.transunion.com

PROTECTING YOURSELF
If someone steals your identity, contact credit bureaus, the creditors, and file a police report immediately.

2. *Contact the creditors for any accounts that have been tampered with or opened fraudulently.* Ask to speak with someone in the security or fraud department, and follow up in writing.

3. *File a police report.* Keep a copy in case your creditors need proof of the crime.

To prevent an identity thief from picking up your trash to capture your personal information, tear or shred your charge receipts, copies of credit applications, insurance forms, bank checks and statements, expired charge cards, and credit offers you get in the mail.

If you believe an identity thief has accessed your bank accounts, checking account, or ATM card, close the accounts immediately. When you open new accounts, insist on password-only access. If your checks have been stolen or misused, stop payment. If your ATM card has been lost, stolen, or otherwise compromised, cancel the card and get another with a new personal identification number (PIN).

If, after taking all these steps, you are still having identity problems, stay alert to new instances of identity theft. Notify the company or creditor immediately, and follow up in writing. Also, contact the Privacy Rights Clearinghouse, which provides information on how to network with other identity theft victims. Call 619-298-3396 or visit www.privacyrights.org.

The U.S. Secret Service has jurisdiction over financial fraud cases. Although the service generally investigates cases where the dollar loss is substantial, your information may provide evidence of a larger pattern of fraud that requires its involvement. Contact your local field office.

 The Federal Trade Commission maintains the Identity Theft Data Clearinghouse and provides information to identify theft victims. You can call toll-free 1-877-ID-THEFT or visit **www.consumer.gov/idtheft.**

The Social Security Administration may issue you a new Social Security number if you still have difficulties after trying to resolve problems resulting from identity theft. Unfortunately, however, there is no guarantee that a new Social Security number will resolve your problems. Call the Social Security Administration at 1-800-772-1213.

Finally, you can file a complaint with the Federal Trade Commission (FTC) through a toll-free consumer help line at 1-877-FTC-HELP; by mail at Consumer Response Center, Federal Trade Commission, 600 Pennsylvania Ave., NW, Washington, DC 20580; or at its Web site, www.ftc.gov, using the online complaint form. Although the FTC cannot resolve individual problems for consumers, it can act against a company if it sees a pattern of possible law violations.

CONCEPT CHECK 6-5

1 What is the Fair Credit Billing Act?

2 What must you do to protect your rights if a billing error occurs?

3 What happens to your credit rating during the billing dispute?

4 What can you do if your identity is stolen?

Action Application Visit the Identity Theft Resource Center at www.idtheftcenter.org. List the steps you can take to reduce the chance of ID theft.

Complaining about Consumer Credit

Objective 6
Describe the laws that protect you if you have a complaint about consumer credit.

If you have a complaint about credit, first try to solve your problem directly with the creditor. Only if that fails should you use more formal complaint procedures. This section describes how to file a complaint with the federal agencies responsible for administering consumer credit protection laws.

COMPLAINTS ABOUT BANKS

If you have a complaint about a bank in connection with any of the federal credit laws, or if you think any part of your business with a bank has been handled in an unfair or deceptive way, you may get advice and help from the Federal Reserve System. You don't need to have an account at the bank to file a complaint. (See Exhibit 6–10.)

PROTECTION UNDER CONSUMER CREDIT LAWS

You may also take legal action against a creditor. If you decide to file a lawsuit, there are important consumer credit laws you should know about.

TRUTH IN LENDING AND CONSUMER LEASING ACTS

If a creditor fails to disclose information required under the Truth in Lending Act or the Consumer Leasing Act, gives inaccurate information, or does not comply with the rules regarding credit cards or the right to cancel them, you may sue for actual damages, that is, any money loss you suffer. Class action suits are also permitted. A class action suit is a suit filed on behalf of a group of people with similar claims.

EQUAL CREDIT OPPORTUNITY ACT

If you think you can prove that a creditor has discriminated against you for any reason prohibited by the ECOA, you may sue for actual damages plus punitive damages (that is, damages for the fact that the law has been violated) of up to $10,000.

COMPLAINT FORM   **Federal Reserve System**

Name _____   Name of Bank _____

Address _____   Address _____

     Street   City   State   Zip

City   State   Zip

Daytime telephone _____   Account number (if applicable) _____
     (include area code)

The complaint involves the following service: Checking Account ☐   Savings Account ☐   Loan ☐

Other: Please specify _____

I have attempted to resolve this complaint directly with the bank: No ☐   Yes ☐

     If "No", an attempt should be made to contact the bank and resolve the complaint.

     If "Yes", name of person or department contacted is _____

                                               Date

MY COMPLAINT IS AS FOLLOWS (Briefly describe the events in the order in which they happened, including specific dates and the bank's actions to which you object. Enclose copies of any pertinent information or correspondence that may be helpful. Do not send us your only copy of any document):   .

_____

_____

_____

_____

_____

_____

This information is solicited under the Federal Trade Commission Improvement Act. Providing the information is voluntary, complete information is necessary to expedite investigation of your complaint. Routine use of the information may include disclosing it to bank(s) or others involved or to other governmental agencies as deemed appropriate.

Date _____   Signatures _____

_____

Exhibit 6–10

Complaint form to report violations of federal credit laws

Source: Board of Governors of the Federal Reserve System.

FAIR CREDIT BILLING ACT   A creditor that fails to comply with the rules applying to the correction of billing errors automatically forfeits the amount owed on the item in question and any finance charges on it, up to a combined total of $50, even if the bill was correct. You may also sue for actual damages plus twice the amount of any finance charges.

FAIR CREDIT REPORTING ACT   You may sue any credit reporting agency or creditor for violating the rules regarding access to your credit records and correction of errors in your credit file. You are entitled to actual damages plus any punitive damages the court allows if the violation is proven to have been intentional.

CONSUMER CREDIT REPORTING REFORM ACT   An unfavorable credit report can force you to pay a higher interest rate on a loan or cost you a loan, an insurance policy, an apartment rental, or even a job offer. The **Consumer Credit Reporting Reform Act** of 1997 places the burden of proof for accurate credit information on the credit reporting agency rather than on you. Under this law, the creditor must certify that disputed data are accurate. If a creditor or the credit bureau verifies incorrect data, you can sue for damages. The federal government and state attorneys general can also sue creditors for civil damages.

Consumer Credit Reporting Reform Act
Places the burden of proof for accurate credit information on the credit reporting agency.

Exhibit 6–11 summarizes the major federal consumer credit laws. The Federal Reserve System has set up a separate office, the Division of Consumer and Community Affairs, in Washington to handle consumer complaints. Contact the director of this division in Washington, DC 20551. This division also writes regulations to carry out the consumer credit laws, enforces these laws for state-chartered banks that are members of the Federal Reserve System, and helps banks comply with these laws.

YOUR RIGHTS UNDER CONSUMER CREDIT LAWS

If you believe you have been refused credit due to discrimination, you can do one or more of the following:

1. Complain to the creditor. Let the creditor know you are aware of the law.

2. File a complaint with the government. You can report any violations to the appropriate government enforcement agency (see Exhibit 6–12). Although the agencies use complaints to decide which companies to investigate, they cannot handle private cases. When you are denied credit, the creditor must give you the name and address of the appropriate agency to contact.

For an overview of consumer credit law, with links to key primary and secondary sources, visit Cornell University's Web site at **www.law.cornell.edu.**

3. If all else fails, sue the creditor. You have the right to bring a case in a federal district court. If you win, you can recover your actual damages and punitive damages of up to $10,000. You can also recover reasonable attorneys' fees and court costs. A private attorney can advise you on how to proceed.

CONCEPT CHECK 6-6

1 What federal laws protect you if you have a complaint regarding consumer credit?

2 What are your rights under the consumer credit laws?

Action Application Use the Internet to obtain information about consumer credit protection laws.

Exhibit **6-11**   Summary of federal consumer credit laws

Act (date effective)	Major Provisions
Truth in Lending Act (July 1, 1969)	Provides specific cost disclosure requirements for the annual percentage rate and the finance charges as a dollar amount.
	Requires disclosure of other loan terms and conditions.
	Regulates the advertising of credit terms.
	Provides the right to cancel a contract when certain real estate is used as security.
(January 25, 1971)	Prohibits credit card issuers from sending unrequested cards; limits a cardholder's liability for unauthorized use of a card to $50.
(October 1, 1982)	Requires that disclosures for closed-end credit (installment credit) be written in plain English and appear apart from all other information.
	Allows a credit customer to request an itemization of the amount financed if the creditor does not automatically provide it.
Fair Credit Reporting Act (April 24, 1971)	Requires disclosure to consumers of the name and address of any consumer reporting agency that supplied reports used to deny credit, insurance, or employment.
	Gives consumers the right to know what is in their files, have incorrect information reinvestigated and removed, and include their versions of a disputed item in the file.
	Requires credit reporting agencies to send the consumer's version of a disputed item to certain businesses or creditors.
	Sets forth identification requirements for consumers wishing to inspect their files.
	Requires that consumers be notified when an investigative report is being made.
	Limits the amount of time certain information can be kept in a credit file.
Fair Credit Billing Act (October 28, 1975)	Establishes procedures for consumers and creditors to follow when billing errors occur on periodic statements for revolving credit accounts.
	Requires creditors to send a statement setting forth these procedures to consumers periodically.
	Allows consumers to withhold payment for faulty or defective goods or services (within certain limitations) when purchased with a credit card.
	Requires creditors to promptly credit customers' accounts and to return overpayments if requested.
Equal Credit Opportunity Act (October 28, 1975)	Prohibits credit discrimination based on sex and marital status.
	Prohibits creditors from requiring women to reapply for credit upon a change in marital status.
	Requires creditors to inform applicants of acceptance or rejection of their credit application within 30 days of receiving a completed application.
	Requires creditors to provide a written statement of the reasons for adverse action.
(March 23, 1977)	Prohibits credit discrimination based on race, national origin, religion, age, or the receipt of public assistance.
(June 1, 1977)	Requires creditors to report information on an account to credit bureaus in the names of both husband and wife if both use the account and both are liable for it.
Fair Debt Collection Practices Act (March 20, 1978)	Prohibits abusive, deceptive, and unfair practices by debt collectors.
	Establishes procedures for debt collectors contacting a credit user.
	Restricts debt collector contacts with a third party.
	Specifies that payment for several debts be applied as the consumer wishes and that no money be applied to a debt in dispute.
Consumer Credit Reporting Reform Act (September 30, 1997)	Places the burden of proof for accurate credit information on credit issuers rather than on consumers.
	Requires creditors to certify that disputed credit information is accurate.
	Requires "credit repair" companies to give consumers a written contract that can be canceled within three business days.
	Requires the big three credit bureaus (Experian, Equifax, and Trans Union) to establish a joint toll-free system that allows consumers to call and remove their names permanently from all prescreened lists.
	Places the maximum cost of a credit report at $8; however, indigent persons, welfare recipients, unemployed persons, and jobhunters can get one free report annually.
Fair and Accurate Credit Transactions Act (April 28, 2003)	Requires the Federal Trade Commission to issue proposed rules to address identity theft concerns.
	Defines identity theft as a fraud committed or attempted using the identifying information of another person without lawful authority.
	Requires credit reporting agencies to develop and implement reasonable requirements for what information can be considered a consumer's proof of identity.

Sources: *Managing Your Credit,* rev. ed. (Prospect Heights, IL: Money Management Institute, Household Financial Services, 1988), p. 36, © Household Financial Services, Prospect Heights, IL; *Banking Legislation & Policy,* Federal Reserve Bank of Philadelphia, April–June 1997, pp. 3–4; Federal Trade Commission, www.ftc.gov, March 2005.

Exhibit **6-12**   Federal government agencies that enforce consumer credit laws

If you think you've been discriminated against by:	You may file a complaint with the following agency:
Consumer reporting agencies, creditors and others not listed below.	Federal Trade Commission Consumer Response Center—FCRA Washington, DC 20580 877-382-4357
National banks, federal branches/agencies of foreign banks (word "National" or initials "N.A." appear in or after bank's name).	Office of the Comptroller of the Currency Compliance Management, Mail Stop 6-6 Washington, DC 20219 800-613-6743
Federal Reserve System member banks (except national banks, and federal branches/agencies of foreign banks).	Federal Reserve Board Division of Consumer & Community Affairs Washington, DC 20551 202-452-3693
Savings associations and federally chartered savings banks (word "Federal" or initials "F.S.B." appear in federal institution's name).	Office of Thrift Supervision Consumer Complaints Washington, DC 20552 800-842-6929
Federal credit unions (words "Federal Credit Union" appear in institution's name).	National Credit Union Administration 1775 Duke Street Alexandria, VA 22314 703-519-4600
State-chartered banks that are not members of the Federal Reserve System.	Federal Deposit Insurance Corporation Consumer Response Center, 2345 Grand Avenue, Suite 100 Kansas City, Missouri 64108-2638 877-275-3342
Air, surface, or rail common carriers regulated by former Civil Aeronautics Board or Interstate Commerce Commission.	Department of Transportation Office of Financial Management Washington, DC 20590 202-366-1306

Source: Federal Trade Commission, www.ftc.gov, May 2005.

SUMMARY OF OBJECTIVES

Objective 1
Define *consumer credit* **and analyze its advantages and disadvantages.**
Consumer credit is the use of credit by individuals and families for personal needs. Among the advantages of using credit are the ability to purchase goods when needed and pay for them gradually, the ability to meet financial emergencies, convenience in shopping, and establishment of a credit rating. Disadvantages are that credit costs money, encourages overspending, and ties up future income.

Objective 2
Differentiate among various types of credit.
Closed-end and open-end credit are two types of consumer credit. With closed-end credit, the borrower pays back a one-time loan in a stated period of time and with a specified number of payments. With open-end credit, the borrower is permitted to take loans on a continuous basis and is billed for partial payments periodically.

Objective 3
Assess your credit capacity and build your credit rating.
Two general rules for measuring credit capacity are the debt payments–to–income ratio and the debt-to-equity ratio. In reviewing your creditworthiness, a creditor seeks information from one of the three national credit bureaus or a regional credit bureau.

Objective 4
Describe the information creditors look for when you apply for credit.
Creditors determine creditworthiness on the basis of the five Cs: character, capacity, capital, collateral, and conditions.

Objective 5
Identify the steps you can take to avoid and correct credit mistakes.
If a billing error occurs on your account, notify the creditor in writing within 60 days. If the dispute is not settled in your favor,

you can place your version of it in your credit file. You may also withhold payment on any defective goods or services you have purchased with a credit card as long as you have attempted to resolve the problem with the merchant.

Objective 6
Describe the laws that protect you if you have a complaint about consumer credit.

If you have a complaint about credit, first try to deal directly with the creditor. If that fails, you can turn to the appropriate

consumer credit law. These laws include the Truth in Lending Act, the Consumer Leasing Act, the Equal Credit Opportunity Act, the Fair Credit Billing Act, the Fair Credit Reporting Act, the Consumer Credit Reporting Reform Act, and the Fair and Accurate Credit Transactions Act.

KEY TERMS

capacity   186

capital   186

character   186

closed-end credit   172

collateral   187

conditions   187

consumer credit   168

Consumer Credit Reporting
   Reform Act   196

credit   168

credit bureau   182

debit card   175

Equal Credit Opportunity Act
   (ECOA)   186

Fair Credit Billing Act (FCBA)   190

Fair Credit Reporting Act   183

home equity loan   178

interest   173

line of credit   173

open-end credit   172

revolving check credit   174

FINANCIAL PLANNING PROBLEMS

1. *Calculating the Amount for a Home Equity Loan.* A few years ago, Michael Tucker purchased a home for $100,000. Today the home is worth $150,000. His remaining mortgage balance is $50,000. Assuming Michael can borrow up to 80 percent of the market value of his home, what is the maximum amount he can borrow? (Obj. 2)

2. *Determining the Debt Payments–to–Income Ratio.* Louise McIntyre's monthly gross income is $2,000. Her employer withholds $400 in federal, state, and local income taxes and $160 in Social Security taxes per month. Louise contributes $80 per month for her IRA. Her monthly credit payments for Visa, MasterCard, and Discover cards are $35, $30, and $20, respectively. Her monthly payment on an automobile loan is $285. What is Louise's debt payments–to–income ratio? Is Louise living within her means? Explain. (Obj. 3)

3. *Calculating the Debt-to-Equity Ratio.* Robert Thumme owns a $140,000 townhouse and still has an unpaid mortgage of $110,000. In addition to his mortgage, he has the following liabilities:

Visa	$ 565
MasterCard	480
Discover card	395
Education loan	920
Personal bank loan	800
Auto loan	4,250
Total	$7,410

Robert's net worth (not including his home) is about $21,000. This equity is in mutual funds, an automobile, a

coin collection, furniture, and other personal property. What is Robert's debt-to-equity ratio? Has he reached the upper limit of debt obligations? Explain. (Obj. 3)

4. *Calculating the Net Worth and Determining a Safe Credit Limit.*

   a. Calculate your net worth based on your present assets and liabilities.

   b. Refer to your net worth statement and determine your safe credit limit. Use the debt payments–to–income and debt-to-equity formulas. (Obj. 3)

5. *Calculating Debt Payments–to–Income Ratio.* Kim Lee is trying to decide whether she can afford a loan she needs in order to go to chiropractic school. Right now Kim is living at home and works in a shoe store, earning a gross income of $820 per month. Her employer deducts a total of $145 for taxes from her monthly pay. Kim also pays $95 on several credit card debts each month. The loan she needs for chiropractic school will cost an additional $120 per month. Help Kim make her decision by calculating her debt payments–to–income ratio with and without the college loan. (Remember the 20 percent rule.) (Obj. 3)

6. *Using Credit Cards as an Identification.* Dinesh D'Souza flew to New York to attend his brother's wedding. Knowing that his family would be busy, he did not ask anyone to meet him at the airport. Instead, he planned to rent a car to use while in New York. He has no nationally known credit cards but is prepared to pay cash for the rental car. The car rental agency refuses to rent him a car, even though it has several cars available. Why do you think Dinesh is unable to rent a car? (Obj. 4)

7. *Determining What Creditors Look for in Approving Loans.* Jim Moniz, a recent college graduate, has accepted a teaching position at Hubbleville High School. Jim moved to Hubbleville and applied for a car loan at First National Bank. He had never used credit or obtained a loan. The bank notified him that it will not approve the loan unless he has a cosigner. On what basis has the bank denied Jim credit? (Obj. 4)

8. *Analyzing Feasibility of a Loan.* Fred Reinero has had a student loan, two auto loans, and three credit cards. He has always made timely payments on all obligations. He has a savings account of $2,400 and an annual income of $25,000. His current payments for rent, insurance, and utilities are about $1,100 per month. Fred has accumulated $12,800 in an individual retirement account. Fred's loan application asks for $10,000 to start up a small restaurant with some friends. Fred will not be an active manager; his partner will run the restaurant. Will he get the loan? Explain your answer. (Obj. 4)

9. Carl's house payment is $1,050 per month and his car payment is $385 per month. If Carl's take-home pay is $2,800 per month, what percentage does Carl spend on his home and car? (Obj. 4)

FINANCIAL PLANNING ACTIVITIES

1. *Determining Whether or Not to Use Credit.* Survey friends and relatives to determine the process they used in deciding whether or not to use credit to purchase an automobile or a major appliance. What risks and opportunity costs did they consider? (Obj. 1)

2. *Analyzing Opportunity Costs Using Credit.* Think about the last three major purchases you made. (Obj. 1)

   a. Did you pay cash? If so, why?

   b. If you paid cash, what opportunity costs were associated with the purchase?

   c. Did you use credit? If so, why?

   d. What were the financial and psychological opportunity costs of using credit?

3. *Comparing Reasons for Using Credit.* Prepare a list of similarities and differences in the reasons the following individuals might have for using credit. (Obj. 2)

   a. A teenager.

   b. A young adult.

   c. A growing family of four.

   d. A retired couple.

4. *Using the Internet to Obtain Information about Credit Cards.* Choose one of the following organizations and visit its Web site. Then prepare a report that summarizes the information the organization provides. How could this information help you in choosing your credit card?

   a. Credit Card Network—provides information on credit card rates. (www.creditnet.com)

   b. Federal Trade Commission—provides information on how to regain financial health, uses and misuses of credit cards, and many other related topics. (www.ftc.gov) (Obj. 2)

5. *Using your Home Equity to Obtain a Loan.* Visit your local financial institutions, such as commercial banks, federal savings banks, and credit unions, to obtain information about getting a home equity loan. Compare their requirements for the loan. (Obj. 2)

6. *Determining Whether to Cosign a Loan.* Talk to a person who has cosigned a loan. What experiences did this person have as a cosigner? (Obj. 3)

7. *Determining Net Worth and Credit Capacity.* What changes might take place in your personal net worth during different stages of your life? How might these changes affect your credit capacity? (Obj. 4)

8. *Assessing How Lenders Determine Creditworthiness.* Survey credit representatives such as bankers, managers of credit departments in retail stores, managers of finance companies, credit union officers, managers of credit bureaus, and savings and loan officers. Ask what procedures they follow in granting or refusing a loan. Write a report of your survey. (Obj. 4)

9. *Analyzing Credit-Related Problems.* Bring to class examples of credit-related problems of individuals or families. Suggest ways in which these problems might be solved. (Obj. 5)

10. *Evaluating Creditors and Seeking Help with Credit-Related Problems.* Compile a list of places a person can call to report dishonest credit practices, get advice and help with credit problems, and check out a creditor's reputation before signing a contract. (Obj. 6)

INTERNET CONNECTION

Researching Credit Reports and Scores

Credit bureaus gather your personal information and sell it to creditors, employers, insurers, and others. Obtain current information and learn how credit bureaus perform their functions.

Credit Reports Web sources: _____
_____
_____
_____
_____

Current findings: _____
_____
_____
_____
_____

Possible influence on your credit report: _____
_____
_____
_____
_____

Credit Scores Web sources: _____
_____
_____
_____
_____

Current findings: _____
_____
_____
_____
_____

How can you improve your credit score? _____
_____
_____
_____
_____

FINANCIAL PLANNING CASE

A Hard Lesson on Credit Cards

Parents of college students, beware: The empty-nest syndrome you're experiencing may end up as empty-wallet syndrome. The moment your kids step on campus, they become highly sought-after credit card customers. To establish relationships they hope will extend well beyond the college years, card marketers are offering students everything from free T-shirts to chances to win airline tickets as enticements to sign up. As a result, college students now have heavy credit card debts. Some 14 percent have balances of $3,000 to $7,000, and 10 percent owe amounts exceeding $7,000, according to Nellie Mae, a nonprofit student loan provider in Braintree, Massachusetts.

"Students who have no history with credit are being handed it on a silver platter," say Gerri Detweiler, education adviser for Debt Counselors of America, a consumer advocacy group in Rockville, Maryland. As long as they are over 18, students can get a card without asking mom or dad to cosign. But when they get into trouble, they often go running to their folks for help. Jason Britton did—and then some. Now 21 and a senior at Georgetown University in Washington, Britton racked up $21,000 in debt on 16 cards over four years. "When I first started, my attitude was: 'I'll get a job after college to pay off all my debt,'" he says. He realized he dug himself into a hole when he couldn't meet the minimum monthly payments. Now he works three part-time jobs, and his parents are helping him pay his tuition and loans.

Questions

1. Why should parents of college students beware?
2. How do credit card marketers entice college students?
3. Where do students turn for help when they get into debt trouble?

Source: Adapted from Marcia Vickers, "A Hard Lesson on Credit Cards," *BusinessWeek,* March 15, 1999, p. 107. Reprinted from the March 15, 1999, issue of *BusinessWeek* by special permission. © 1999 McGraw-Hill Companies, Inc.

VIDEO CASE

Consumer Credit

How does the use of credit affect your financial plan? What types of credit are available to you? How do you obtain credit? What factors do lenders consider before extending credit? How do you improve your chances of obtaining the credit you need?

A young woman faces the above questions. She is tempted to buy clothing that she really likes but knows she can't afford. However, when she makes the decision to use her credit card, she suddenly goes on a shopping spree. She joins most consumers who have a limited understanding of consumer credit and the pros and cons of using it.

Credit is *not* free money. In addition to repaying the amount she charged, she must pay an additional expense in interest until the full balance is repaid.

When used responsibly, credit is a valuable financial tool. When used excessively, credit can destroy financial plans.

Questions

1. What are the pros and cons of using credit cards?
2. What suggestions might you offer the young woman regarding the use of her credit card?
3. Assuming the young woman does not pay the full balance, which type of credit card would you recommend for her?

YOUR PERSONAL FINANCIAL PLANNER IN ACTION

Establishing and Maintaining a Credit Record

The wise use of credit requires knowledge of the process for establishing credit. In addition, you should develop an awareness of credit reports and the legal rights associated with using consumer credit

Your Short-Term Financial Planning Activities	Resources
1. Prepare an inventory of current credit balances and monthly payments.	PFP Sheet 29 http://credit.about.com www.bankrate.com www.banx.com
2. Review your credit file for current accuracy of information.	www.myfico.com www.equifax.com www.experian.com www.transunion.com
3. Become familiar with consumer credit laws that may relate to various aspects of your use of credit.	www.ftc.gov www.federalreserve.gov
Your Long-Term Financial Planning Activities	
1. Describe actions you may take to reduce your credit balances (if applicable).	www.ncfe.org www.profina.org
2. Create a plan for spending that provides for using credit at an appropriate level.	Text pages 169–172 www.mymoney.gov

CONTINUING CASE

Obtaining Credit

Life Situation

Recently married couple
Pam, 26
Josh, 28
Renting an apartment

Financial Data

Monthly income	$5,840
Assets	$13,500
Living expenses	$3,900
Liabilities	$4,800
Emergency fund	$1,000

The buying activities of the Brocks often involve the use of credit cards. Over the past two years, they have increased the amount owed on their various charge cards. These accounts are used for various purchases when they both run out of money near the end of the month.

Questions

1. If you were Pam or Josh, how would you go about paying off your credit card debts and other liabilities?

2. What attitudes and actions might the Brocks develop to better make use of credit and to avoid long-term financial difficulties?

3. Explain how *Personal Financial Planner* sheet 29 might help the Brocks plan their use of credit.

7 Choosing a Source of Credit: The Costs of Credit Alternatives

Key Concept

Understanding the costs involved in obtaining credit will give you the tools to acquire the best source of credit.

www.mhhe.com/kdh

Digital Study Tools

Online Learning Center Study Tools for This Chapter

- Multiple-choice quiz
- Flashcards
- eLearning sessions
- Crossword puzzle
- Personal Finance Online: The Cost of Credit and Credit Management

Student CD Study Tools for This Chapter

- Self-study software
- Narrated PowerPoint
- Personal financial planning software: Worksheets 30–31

Learning Objectives

1 Analyze the major sources of consumer credit.

2 Determine the cost of credit by calculating interest using various interest formulas.

3 Develop a plan to manage your debts.

4 Evaluate various private and governmental sources that assist consumers with debt problems.

5 Assess the choices in declaring personal bankruptcy.

Opening Case

The Perils of Plastic

After getting a couple of low-rate credit card offers each week for months, Saundra Williams decided last fall to see if she could do better than the 18.5 percent annual interest rate on her cards. When she called to bargain, she thought she was doing well when Citibank promptly offered her a menu of fixed or variable rates, including a nifty 10.9 percent. But Bank of America did even better, slashing her rate to 9.9 percent and hiking her credit line to boot. "I was astounded at all of the options they offered me," says Williams, an assistant professor at North Carolina State University in Raleigh. "I never heard of negotiating a rate." Negotiate with a credit card company? It would have been unthinkable a few years ago. But it's happening. For many of the players in the industry, times are tough. Now that they've saturated the American public with plastic, they're finding it hard to expand. As more and more customers pay off balances each month—"freeloading" in industry parlance—card companies are working harder than ever before to squeeze out a buck.

Miss a payment by a few days? You could be slapped with a $29 late charge, up from an average of $13 just three years ago. And, to drive home the point, your interest rate could be jacked up as an added penalty, perhaps to as high as 30 percent. Don't use the card much? You might see an inactivity fee and then get tagged with a closing fee if you cut the card up. "We call it a 'fee frenzy,'" says Robert B. McKinley, chief executive of CardWeb.com Inc., an industry tracking service. But such soak-the-customer tactics can backfire. First USA, which now boasts some 50 million customers, has lost millions of them in the last two years, cutting its total outstanding card loans by 1 percent, to $69.4 billion last year. Bank officials blame consumer anger over such practices as ratcheting up loan rates above 19 percent from introductory 3.9 percent rates, if the borrower paid late just twice in six months. "We lost many of our best customers," said William P. Boardman, vice chairman of First USA parent, Bank One Corp.

Many credit card issuers are pursuing wealthy customers just as feverishly. American Express is offering the Centurion charge card—which must be paid off monthly—to holders of its high-end Platinum card. The jet-black Centurion, offered by invitation only, carries a whopping $2,500 annual fee. That gets you upgrades on jet travel and a personal counselor for travel needs. And you get special privileges at Neiman Marcus and Saks Fifth Avenue, with such amenities as private shopping hours. AmEx officials won't say how many of these cards—which they call a "niche product"—they expect to sell. Remember, membership does have its privileges.

QUESTIONS

What Actions Should Be Taken?

1. What action(s) can be taken to avoid paying late charges and other penalties?
2. Would you recommend that your family and friends negotiate the interest rate for their credit cards?

What about Your Situation?

3. What actions might you take to see if you can lower the interest rate charged on your credit card(s)?
4. Is it prudent for you to become a "freeloader"? Explain your situation.
5. Would you pay a $2,500 annual fee to obtain a prestigious credit card? Why or why not?

Sources: Adapted from Joseph Weber and Ann Therese Palmer, "The Perils of Plastic," *BusinessWeek*, February 14, 2000, p. 127; and Mara Der Hovanesian, "This Black Card Gives Your Carte Blanche," *BusinessWeek*, August 9, 2004, p. 54.

Learn More Online

Based on information at www.cardWeb.com, a Web site maintained by Card Web.com Inc., an industry tracking service, describe other examples of "fee frenzy."

Sources of Consumer Credit

Objective 1

Analyze the major sources of consumer credit.

Credit costs got you down? Well, you are not alone. Credit costs money; therefore, always weigh the benefits of buying an item on credit now versus waiting until you have saved enough money to pay cash. We can all get into credit difficulties if we do not understand how and when to use credit.

Financial and other institutions, the sources of credit, come in all shapes and sizes. They play an important role in our economy, and they offer a broad range of financial services. By evaluating your credit options, you can reduce your finance charges. You can reconsider your decision to borrow money, discover a less expensive type of loan, or find a lender that charges a lower interest rate.

Before deciding whether to borrow money, ask yourself these three questions: Do I need a loan? Can I afford a loan? Can I qualify for a loan? We discussed the affordability of loans and the qualifications required to obtain loans in the last chapter. Here we wrestle with the first question.

You should avoid credit in two situations. The first situation is one in which you do not need or really want a product that will require financing. Easy access to installment loans or possession of credit cards sometimes encourages consumers to make expensive purchases they later regret. The solution to this problem is simple: After you have selected a product, resist any sales pressure to buy immediately and take a day to think it over.

The second situation is one in which you can afford to pay cash. Consider the trade-offs and opportunity costs involved. Paying cash is almost always cheaper than using credit. In fact, some stores even offer a discount for payment in cash.

WHAT KIND OF LOAN SHOULD YOU SEEK?

As discussed in the last chapter, two types of credit exist: closed-end and open-end credit. Because installment loans may carry a lower interest rate, they are the less expensive credit option for loans that are repaid over a period of many months or years. However, because credit cards usually provide a float period—a certain number of days during which no interest is charged—they represent the cheaper way to make credit purchases that are paid off in a month or two. Also, once you have a credit card, using it is always easier than taking out an installment loan. An alternative to a credit card is a travel and entertainment (T&E) card, such as an American Express or Diners Club card. A T&E card requires full payment of the balance due each month but does not impose a finance charge. Annual fees, however, can be high.

In seeking an installment loan, you may think first of borrowing from a bank or a credit union. However, less expensive credit sources are available.

INEXPENSIVE LOANS
Parents or family members are often the source of the least expensive loans. They may charge you only the interest they would have earned had they not made the loan—as little as the 3 percent they would have earned on a passbook account. Such loans, however, can complicate family relationships. All loans to or from family members should be in writing and state the interest rate, if any, repayment schedule, and the final payment date.

Also relatively inexpensive is money borrowed on financial assets held by a lending institution, for example, a bank certificate of deposit or the cash value of a whole life insurance policy. The interest rate on such loans typically ranges from 7 to 10 percent. But the trade-off is that your assets are tied up until you have repaid the loan.

MEDIUM-PRICED LOANS
Often you can obtain medium-priced loans from commercial banks, federal savings banks (Savings and Loan Associations), and credit unions. New-car loans, for example, may cost 8 to 12 percent; used-car loans and home improvement loans may cost slightly more.

Financial Planning Calculations

CASH ADVANCES

A cash advance is a loan billed to your credit card. You can obtain a cash advance with your credit card at a bank or an automated teller machine (ATM) or by using checks linked to your credit card account.

Most cards charge a special fee when a cash advance is taken out. The fee is based on a percentage of the amount borrowed, usually about 2 or 3 percent.

Some credit cards charge a minimum cash advance fee, as high as $5. You could get $20 in cash and be charged $5, a fee equal to 25 percent of the amount you borrowed.

Most cards do not have a grace period on cash advances. This means you pay interest every day until you repay the cash advance, even if you do not have an outstanding balance from the previous statement.

On some cards, the interest rate on cash advances is higher than the rate on purchases. Be sure you check the details on the contract sent to you by the card issuer.

Here is an example of charges that could be imposed for a $200 cash advance that you pay off when the bill arrives:

Cash advance fee = $4 (2% of $200)

Interest for one month = $3 (1.5% APR on $200)

Total cost for one month = $7 ($4 + $3)

In comparison, a $200 purchase on a card with a grace period could cost $0 if paid off promptly in full.

The bottom line: It is usually much more expensive to take out a cash advance than to charge a purchase to your credit card. Use cash advances only for real emergencies.

Source: A pamphlet provided by the office of Public Responsibility, American Express Company and Consumer Action, San Francisco, CA 94105. (n.p; n.d.)

Borrowing from credit unions has several advantages. These institutions provide free credit life insurance, are generally sympathetic to borrowers with legitimate payment problems, and provide personalized service. Credit unions can now offer the same range of consumer loans that banks and other financial institutions do. Over 80 million Americans belong to credit unions, and the number of credit union members has been growing steadily. Over 10,000 credit unions exist in the United States today.[1]

EXPENSIVE LOANS   Though convenient to obtain, the most expensive loans available are from finance companies, retailers, and banks through credit cards. Finance companies often lend to people who cannot obtain credit from banks or credit unions. Typically, the interest ranges from 12 to 25 percent. If you are denied credit by a bank or a credit union, you should question your ability to afford the higher rate a loan company charges.

For helpful articles related to costs of credit and choosing sources of credit, visit the Federal Trade Commission Web site at **www.ftc.gov.**

Check cashers, finance companies, and others make small, short-term, high-rate loans called payday loans, cash advance loans, check advance loans, postdated check loans, or deferred deposit check loans. Such loans secured by a personal check are extremely expensive. Suppose you write a personal check for $115 to borrow $100 for 14 days. The lender agrees to hold the check until your next payday, when you redeem the check by paying the $115 in cash. Your cost of this loan is a $15 finance charge that amounts to a whopping 391 percent annual percentage rate (APR).

Borrowing from car dealers, appliance stores, department stores, and other retailers is also relatively expensive. The interest rates retailers charge are usually similar to those charged by finance companies, frequently 20 percent or more.

Banks lend funds not only through installment loans but also through cash advances on MasterCard or Visa cards. (See the Financial Planning Calculations box, above.) According to Stephen Brobeck, executive director of the Consumer Federation of America in Washington, DC, the average household has more than 10 credit cards and owes $9,000 on them. More than 3 billion credit card solicitations are mailed to consumers each year.[2] See the Financial Planning for Life's Situations feature for

TO CHOOSE IT, FIRST DECIDE HOW YOU PLAN TO USE IT

Many bank cards offer added value through enhancements such as discounts on merchandise, rebates on purchases, travel and accident insurance, frequent-flier mileage, emergency card replacement, donations to nonprofit groups, and 24-hour customer service. The trick to finding the bank card that's right for you is to balance the benefits with the right price. You should consider interest rates and fees based on how you plan to use the card.

- *Annual fee.* If you plan to pay your balance in full each month, shop for a card that has a grace period and carries no annual fee, or a low annual fee, even if the trade-off is a higher interest rate. You plan to pay little or no interest anyway. Gold or platinum cards often charge $100 or more in annual fees.

- *Low rates.* If you prefer to stretch out repayment, aim for a card with a lower interest rate. In general, lower-interest-rate cards tend to have tougher credit approval requirements, may not offer a grace period, and often have slightly higher annual fees. But if you qualify, the money you save on interest is likely to offset a higher fee.

- *Variable rates.* Some credit cards promote variable interest rates tied to an index like the *Wall Street Journal* "prime rate." You may benefit from lower interest rates when the index is low, but remember that when the index rises, you'll pay the higher rate even on purchases you've already made.

- *Grace period.* Not all credit cards offer a grace period. When you use such a card, the bank begins charging you interest on the day you make the purchase or the day the purchase is recorded on your account. Try to pay off your balance in full each month to maintain the grace period and avoid paying interest.

- *Cash advance fees.* Most automated teller machine (ATM) cards charge a special fee when you take a cash advance. Usually the fee is about 3 to 3.5 percent of the amount borrowed.

- *Currency conversion fees.* These are fees charged when you use the credit card in a foreign country.

Many banks impose late fees even when payment arrives a day after the due date. Some banks charge a set fee, such as $15 or $35, while others charge a percentage, such as 5 percent, of the minimum payment due.

Most cards assess an over-credit-limit fee. For instance, if you charge $400 over your limit and the penalty is 5 percent, you will pay a $20 fee in addition to interest charges. A few companies charge lost-card replacement fees, usually $5 or $10.

Some credit card issuers allow you to skip a payment without a penalty. While this sounds like the bank is giving you a break, you will be charged interest during this period and will owe more in interest than you did before.

Once you decide on the right combination of features and price, you can begin shopping. Federal law requires that every mail solicitation, "take one" application, and application brochure carry a special box listing the interest rate, annual fee, length of grace period, and other fees. This will allow you to easily compare the costs of different card plans.

Sources: American Bankers Association; *Annual Credit Card Survey 2002* (San Francisco: Consumer Action, March 2002); *Choosing and Using Credit Cards* (Washington, DC: Federal Trade Commission, January 1999). © American Bankers Association. Reprinted with permission.

guidance in choosing the card that is right for you. Credit card cobranding has become increasingly popular with banks and industries. Cobranded credit cards, such as the Yahoo! Visa card will make shopping over the Internet easier and faster. Yahoo! will designate Visa as its "preferred card" and will promote Visa throughout its Web sites and to online merchants worldwide.

One type of loan from finance companies is currently less expensive than most other credit. Loans of this kind, which often can be obtained at a rate of under 4 percent, are available from the finance companies of major automakers—General Motors Acceptance Corporation, Ford Motor Credit Corporation, and others. But a car dealer that offers you such a rate may be less willing to discount the price of the car or throw in free options.

Exhibit 7–1 summarizes the major sources of consumer credit: commercial banks, consumer finance companies, credit unions, life insurance companies, and savings and loan associations. This exhibit attempts to generalize the information and give an average picture of each source regarding the type of credit available, lending policies, and customer services. Due to the dramatic fluctuations in interest rates in recent years, it is

Exhibit **7–1**   Sources of consumer credit

Credit Source	Type of Loan	Lending Policies
Commercial banks	Single-payment loan Personal installment loans Passbook loans Check-credit loans Credit card loans Second mortgages	• Seek customers with established credit history. • Often require collateral or security. • Prefer to deal in large loans, such as vehicle, home improvement, and home modernization, with the exception of credit card and check-credit plans. • Determine repayment schedules according to the purpose of the loan. • Vary credit rates according to the type of credit, time period, customer's credit history, and the security offered. • May require several days to process a new credit application.
Consumer finance companies	Personal installment loans Second mortgages	• Often lend to consumers without established credit history. • Often make unsecured loans. • Often vary rates according to the size of the loan balance. • Offer a variety of repayment schedules. • Make a higher percentage of small loans than other lenders. • Maximum loan size limited by law. • Process applications quickly, frequently on the same day the application is made.
Credit unions	Personal installment loans Share draft–credit plans Credit card loans Second mortgages	• Lend to members only. • Make unsecured loans. • May require collateral or cosigner for loans over a specified amount. • May require payroll deductions to pay off loan. • May submit large loan applications to a committee of members for approval. • Offer a variety of repayment schedules.
Life insurance companies	Single-payment or partial-payment loans	• Lend on cash value of life insurance policy. • No date or penalty on repayment. • Deduct amount owed from the value of policy benefit if death or other maturity occurs before repayment.
Federal savings banks (savings and loan associations)	Personal installment loans (generally permitted by state-chartered savings associations) Home improvement loans Education loans Savings account loans Second mortgages	• Will lend to all creditworthy individuals. • Often require collateral. • Loan rates vary depending on size of loan, length of payment, and security involved.

Consumer credit is available from several types of sources. *Which sources seem to offer the widest variety of loans?*

no longer possible to provide a common range of annual percentage rates for each source of credit. Check with your local lender for current interest rates. Study and compare the differences to determine which source can best meet your needs and requirements.

Today borrowing and credit are more complex than ever. As more and more types of financial institutions offer financial services, your choices of what and where to borrow will widen. The Internet may be used to compare interest rates for different loan sources and credit cards. Shopping for credit is just as important as shopping for an automobile, furniture, or major appliances.

CONCEPT CHECK 7-1

1 Why did First USA parent Bank One Corp. lose many of its best customers?
2 What are the major sources of consumer credit?
3 What are some advantages and disadvantages of securing a loan from a credit union? From a finance company?

Action Application Research any three lending institutions. List the types of loans offered and their lending policies.

The Cost of Credit

Objective 2

Determine the cost of credit by calculating interest using various interest formulas.

Truth in Lending law A federal law that requires creditors to disclose the annual percentage rate (APR) and the finance charge as a dollar amount.

finance charge The total dollar amount paid to use credit.

annual percentage rate (APR) The percentage cost (or relative cost) of credit on a yearly basis. The APR yields a true rate of interest for comparison with other sources of credit.

The **Truth in Lending law** of 1969 was a landmark piece of legislation. For the first time, creditors were required to state the cost of borrowing as a dollar amount so that consumers would know exactly what the credit charges were and thus could compare credit costs and shop for credit.

If you are thinking of borrowing money or opening a credit account, your first step should be to figure out how much it will cost you and whether you can afford it. Then you should shop for the best terms. Two key concepts that you should remember are the finance charge and the annual percentage rate.

FINANCE CHARGE AND ANNUAL PERCENTAGE RATE (APR)

Credit costs vary. If you know the finance charge and the annual percentage rate (APR), you can compare credit prices from different sources. Under the Truth in Lending law, the creditor must inform you, in writing and before you sign any agreement, of the finance charge and the APR.

The **finance charge** is the total dollar amount you pay to use credit. It includes interest costs and sometimes other costs such as service charges, credit-related insurance premiums, or appraisal fees.

For example, borrowing $100 for a year might cost you $10 in interest. If there is also a service charge of $1, the finance charge will be $11. The **annual percentage rate (APR)** is the percentage cost (or relative cost) of credit on a yearly basis. The APR is your key to comparing costs, regardless of the amount of credit or how much time you have to repay it.

Suppose you borrow $100 for one year and pay a finance charge of $10. If you can keep the entire $100 for the whole year and then pay it all back at once, you are paying an APR of 10 percent:

Amount Borrowed	Month Number	Payment Made	Loan Balance
$100	1	$0	$100
	2	0	100
	3	0	100
	.	.	.
	.	.	.
	.	.	.
	.	.	.
	12	100 (plus $10 interest)	0

On average, you had full use of $100 throughout the year. To calculate the average use, add the loan balance during the first and last month, then divide by 2:

$$\text{Average balance} = \frac{\$100 + \$100}{2} = \$100$$

But if you repay the $100 and the finance charge (a total of $110) in 12 equal monthly payments, you don't get use of the $100 for the whole year. In fact, as shown next, you get use of less and less of that $100 each month. In this case, the $10 charge for credit amounts to an APR of 18.5 percent.

Amount Borrowed	Month Number	Payment Made	Loan Balance
$100	1	$ 0	$100.00
	2	8.33	91.67
	3	8.33	83.34
	4	8.33	75.01
	5	8.33	66.68
	6	8.33	58.35
	7	8.33	50.02
	8	8.33	41.69
	9	8.33	33.36
	10	8.33	25.03
	11	8.33	16.70
	12	8.33	8.37

Note that you are paying 10 percent interest on $100 even though you had use of only $91.67 during the second month, not $100. During the last month, you owed only $8.37 (and had use of $8.37), but the $10 interest is for the entire $100. As calculated in the previous example, the average use of the money during the year is $100 + $8.37 ÷ 2, or $54.18.

The Financial Planning Calculations box on page 212 shows how to calculate the APR. All creditors—banks, stores, car dealers, credit card companies, and finance companies—must state the cost of their credit in terms of the finance charge and the APR. The law does not set interest rates or other credit charges, but it does require their disclosure so that you can compare credit costs and tackle the trade-offs.

THE ARITHMETIC OF THE ANNUAL PERCENTAGE RATE (APR)

There are two ways to calculate the APR: using an APR formula and using the APR tables. The APR tables are more precise than the formula. The formula, given below, only approximates the APR:

$$r = \frac{2 \times n \times I}{P(N + 1)}$$

where

r = Approximate APR

n = Number of payment periods in one year (12, if payments are monthly; 52, if weekly)

I = Total dollar cost of credit

P = Principal, or net amount of loan

N = Total number of payments scheduled to pay off the loan

Let us compare the APR when the $100 loan is paid off in one lump sum at the end of the year and when the same loan is paid off in 12 equal monthly payments. The stated annual interest rate is 10 percent for both loans.

Using the formula, the APR for the lump-sum loan is

$$r = \frac{2 \times 1 \times \$10}{\$100(1 + 1)} = \frac{\$20}{\$100(2)} = \frac{\$20}{\$200} = 0.10$$

or 10 percent.

Using the formula, the APR for the monthly payment loan is

$$r = \frac{2 \times 12 \times \$10}{\$100(12 + 1)} = \frac{\$240}{\$100(13)} = \frac{\$240}{\$1,300}$$

= 0.1846, or 18.46 percent (rounded to 18.5 percent).

TACKLING THE TRADE-OFFS

When you choose your financing, there are trade-offs between the features you prefer (term, size of payments, fixed or variable interest, or payment plan) and the cost of your loan. Here are some of the major trade-offs you should consider.

TERM VERSUS INTEREST COSTS   Many people choose longer-term financing because they want smaller monthly payments. But the longer the term for a loan at a given interest rate, the greater the amount you must pay in interest charges. Consider the following analysis of the relationship between the term and interest costs.

A COMPARISON   Even when you understand the terms a creditor is offering, it's easy to underestimate the difference in dollars that different terms can make. Suppose you're buying a $7,500 used car. You put $1,500 down, and you need to borrow $6,000. Compare the following three credit arrangements:

	APR	Length of Loan	Monthly Payment	Total Finance Charge	Total Cost
Creditor A	14%	3 years	$205.07	$1,382.52	$7,382.52
Creditor B	14	4 years	163.96	1,870.08	7,870.08
Creditor C	15	4 years	166.98	2,015.04	8,015.04

How do these choices compare? The answer depends partly on what you need. The lowest-cost loan is available from creditor A. If you are looking for lower monthly payments, you could repay the loan over a longer period of time. However, you would have to pay more in total costs. A loan from creditor B—also at a 14 percent APR, but for four years—would add about $488 to your finance charge.

If that four-year loan were available only from creditor C, the APR of 15 percent would add another $145 to your finance charges. Other terms, such as the size of the down payment, will also make a difference. Be sure to look at all the terms before you make your choice.

LENDER RISK VERSUS INTEREST RATE   You may prefer financing that requires low fixed payments with a large final payment or only a minimum of up-front cash. But both of these requirements can increase your cost of borrowing because they create more risk for your lender.

If you want to minimize your borrowing costs, you may need to accept conditions that reduce your lender's risk. Here are a few possibilities.

Variable Interest Rate   A variable interest rate is based on fluctuating rates in the banking system, such as the prime rate. With this type of loan, you share the interest rate risks with the lender. Therefore, the lender may offer you a lower initial interest rate than it would with a fixed-rate loan.

A Secured Loan   If you pledge property or other assets as collateral, you'll probably receive a lower interest rate on your loan.

Up-Front Cash   Many lenders believe you have a higher stake in repaying a loan if you pay cash for a large portion of what you are financing. Doing so may give you a better chance of getting the other terms you want. Of course, by making a large down payment, you forgo interest that you might earn in a savings account.

A Shorter Term   As you have learned, the shorter the period of time for which you borrow, the smaller the chance that something will prevent you from repaying and the lower the risk to the lender. Therefore, you may be able to borrow at a lower interest rate if you accept a shorter-term loan, but your payments will be higher.

In the next section, you will see how the above-mentioned trade-offs can affect the cost of closed-end and open-end credit.

CALCULATING THE COST OF CREDIT

simple interest Interest computed on principal only and without compounding.

The two most common methods of calculating interest are compound and simple interest formulas. Perhaps the most basic method is the simple interest calculation. Simple interest on the declining balance, add-on interest, bank discount, and compound interest are variations of simple interest.

When you choose your financing, there are trade-offs between the features you prefer and the cost of your loan.

SIMPLE INTEREST   **Simple interest** is the interest computed on principal only and without compounding; it is the dollar cost of borrowing money. This cost is based on three elements: the amount borrowed, which is called the *principal;* the rate of interest; and the amount of time for which the principal is borrowed.

You can use the following formula to find simple interest:

$$\text{Interest} = \text{Principal} \times \text{Rate of interest} \times \text{Time}$$

or

$$I = P \times r \times T$$

Example 1   Suppose you have persuaded a relative to lend you $1,000 to purchase a laptop computer. Your relative agreed to charge only 5 percent interest, and you

agreed to repay the loan at the end of one year. Using the simple interest formula, the interest will be 5 percent of $1,000 for one year, or $50, since you have the use of $1,000 for the entire year:

$$I = \$1,000 \times 0.05 \times 1$$

$$= \$50$$

Using the APR formula discussed earlier,

$$APR = \frac{2 \times n \times I}{P(N+1)} = \frac{2 \times 1 \times \$50}{\$1,000(1+1)} = \frac{\$100}{\$2,000} = 0.05, \text{ or } 5 \text{ percent}$$

Note that the stated rate, 5 percent, is also the annual percentage rate.

SIMPLE INTEREST ON THE DECLINING BALANCE

When more than one payment is made on a simple interest loan, the method of computing interest is known as the **declining balance method.** Since you pay interest only on the amount of the original principal that you have not yet repaid, the more frequent the payments, the lower the interest you will pay. Most credit unions use this method for their loans.

declining balance method A method of computing interest when more than one payment is made on a simple interest loan.

Example 2 Using simple interest on the declining balance to compute interest charges, the interest on a 5 percent, $1,000 loan repaid in two payments, one at the end of the first half-year and another at the end of the second half-year, would be $37.50, as follows:

First payment:

$$I = P \times r \times T$$

$$= \$1,000 \times 0.05 \times \tfrac{1}{2}$$

$$= \$25 \text{ interest plus } \$500, \text{ or } \$525$$

Second payment:

$$I = P \times r \times T$$

$$= \$500 \times 0.05 \times \tfrac{1}{2}$$

$$= \$12.50 \text{ interest plus the remaining balance of } \$500, \text{ or } \$512.50$$

Total payment on the loan:

$$\$525 + \$512.50 = \$1,037.50$$

Using the APR formula,

$$APR = \frac{2 \times n \times I}{P(N+1)} = \frac{2 \times 2 \times \$37.50}{\$1,000(2+1)} = \frac{\$150}{\$3,000} = 0.05, \text{ or } 5 \text{ percent}$$

Note that using simple interest under the declining balance method, the stated rate, 5 percent, is also the annual percentage rate. The add-on interest, bank discount, and compound interest calculation methods differ from the simple interest method as to when, how, and on what balance interest is paid. For these methods, the real annual rate, or the annual percentage rate, differs from the stated rate.

add-on interest method A method of computing interest in which interest is calculated on the full amount of the original principal.

ADD-ON INTEREST

With the **add-on interest method,** interest is calculated on the full amount of the original principal. The interest amount is immediately added to the original principal, and payments are determined by dividing principal plus interest by the number of payments to be made. When only one payment is required, this method produces the same APR as the simple interest method. However, when two or more payments are to be made, the add-on method results in an effective rate of interest that is higher than the stated rate.

Example 3   Consider again the two-payment loan in Example 2. Using the add-on method, interest of $50 (5 percent of $1,000 for one year) is added to the $1,000 borrowed, giving $1,050 to be repaid—half (or $525) at the end of the first half-year and the other half at the end of the second half-year.

Even though your relative's stated interest rate is 5 percent, the real interest rate is

$$\text{APR} = \frac{2 \times n \times I}{P(N+1)} = \frac{2 \times 2 \times \$50}{\$1,000(2+1)} = \frac{\$200}{\$3,000} = 0.066, \text{ or 6.6 percent}$$

Note that using the add-on interest method means that no matter how many payments you are to make, the interest will always be $50. As the number of payments increases, you have use of less and less credit over the year. For example, if you make four quarterly payments of $262.50, you have use of $1,000 during the first quarter, about $750 during the second quarter, about $500 during the third quarter, and about $250 during the fourth and final quarter. Therefore, as the number of payments increases, the true interest rate, or APR, also increases.

COST OF OPEN-END CREDIT   As discussed earlier, open-end credit includes credit cards, department store charge cards, and check overdraft accounts that allow you to write checks for more than your actual balance. You can use open-end credit again and again until you reach a prearranged borrowing limit. The Truth in Lending law requires that open-end creditors let you know how the finance charge and the APR will affect your costs.

First, creditors must tell you how they calculate the finance charge. Creditors use various systems to calculate the balance on which they assess finance charges. Some creditors add finance charges after subtracting payments made during the billing period; this is called the **adjusted balance method.** Other creditors give you no credit for payments made during the billing period; this is called the **previous balance method.** Under the third—and the fairest—method, the **average daily balance method,** creditors add your balances for each day in the billing period and then divide by the number of days in the period. The average daily balance may include or exclude new purchases during the billing period.

Here is how some different methods of calculating finance charges affect the cost of credit:

adjusted balance method
The assessment of finance charges after payments made during the billing period have been subtracted.

previous balance method
A method of computing finance charges that gives no credit for payments made during the billing period.

average daily balance method   A method of computing finance charges that uses a weighted average of the account balance throughout the current billing period.

	Average Daily Balance (*including* new purchases)	Average Daily Balance (*excluding* new purchases)
Monthly rate	1½%	1½%
APR	18%	18%
Previous balance	$400	$400
New purchases	$50 on 18th day	$50 on 18th day
Payments	$300 on 15th day (new balance = $100)	$300 on 15th day (new balance = $100)
Average daily balance	$270*	$250**
Finance charge	$4.05 (1½% × $270)	$3.75 (1½% × $250)

*To figure average daily balance (*including* new purchases):
($400 × 15 days) + ($100 × 3 days) + ($150 × 12 days) ÷ 30 days =
($6,000 + $300 + $1,800) ÷ 30 = $8,100 ÷ 30 days = $270

**To figure average daily balance (*excluding* new purchases):
($400 × 15 days) + ($100 × 15 days) ÷ 30 days =
($6,000 + $1,500) ÷ 30 = $7,500 ÷ 30 days = $250

	Adjusted Balance	Previous Balance
Monthly rate	1½%	1½%
APR	18%	18%
Previous balance	$400	$400
Payments	$300	$300
Average daily balance	N/A	N/A
Finance charge	$1.50 (1½% × $100)	$6.00 (1½% × $400)

Sheet 30
Credit card/charge account comparison

As the example shows, the finance charge varies for the same pattern of purchases and payments. Furthermore, some creditors use a *two-cycle average daily balance* method, which may *include* or *exclude* new purchases. Instead of using the average daily balance for one billing cycle, as described above, these creditors use the average daily balance for *two* consecutive billing cycles.

Second, creditors must tell you when finance charges on your credit account begin, so that you know how much time you have to pay your bills before a finance charge is added. Some creditors, for example, give you a 20- to 25-day grace period to pay your balance in full before imposing a finance charge. But in most cases, the grace period applies only if you have no outstanding balance on your card. Therefore, if you want to take advantage of the interest-free period on your card, you must pay your bill in full every month.

All credit card issuers must include the following key pieces of information with their applications for credit cards. Look for a box similar to the one on page 217 for information about interest rates, fees, and other terms for the card you are considering.

The Truth in Lending law does not set rates or tell the creditor how to make interest calculations. It requires only that the creditor tell you the method that will be used. You should ask for an explanation of any terms you don't understand.

COST OF CREDIT AND EXPECTED INFLATION

Borrowers and lenders, are less concerned about dollars, present or future, than about the goods and services those dollars can buy—that is, their purchasing power.

Inflation erodes the purchasing power of money. Each percentage point increase in inflation means a decrease of approximately 1 percent in the quantity of goods and services you can purchase with a given quantity of dollars. As a result, lenders, seeking to protect their purchasing power, add the expected rate of inflation to the interest rate they charge. You are willing to pay this higher rate because you expect inflation to enable you to repay the loan with cheaper dollars.

For example, if a lender expects a 4 percent inflation rate for the coming year and desires an 8 percent return on its loan, it will probably charge you a 12 percent nominal or stated rate (a 4 percent inflation premium plus an 8 percent "real" rate).

Return to Example 1, in which you borrowed $1,000 from your relative at the bargain rate of 5 percent for one year. If the inflation rate was 4 percent during that year, your relative's real rate of return was only 1 percent (5 percent stated interest minus 4 percent inflation rate) and your "real" cost was not $50 but only $10 ($50 minus $40 inflation premium).

Annual percentage rate (APR) for purchases	2.9% until 11/1/2006 after that, **14.9%.**
Other APRs	Cash-advance APR: 15.9%.
	Balance-transfer APR: 15.9%.
	Penalty rate: 23.9% See explanation below.*
Variable-rate information	Your APR for purchase transactions may vary. The rate is determined monthly by adding 5.9% to the prime rate.**
Grace period for repayment of balances for purchases	25 days on average, if each month payment is received in full by the payment due date.
Method of computing the balance for purchases	Average daily balance (excluding new purchases).
Annual fees	None.
Minimum finance charge	$.50.
Transaction fee for purchases	Transaction fee for the purchase of wire transfers, person-to-person money transfers, money orders, bets, lottery tickets, and casino gaming chips: 3% of each such purchase (minimum $5).
Transaction fee for ATM cash advances	3% of the amount advanced (minimum $5).
Balance-transfer fee	3% of the amount transferred (minimum $5, maximum $40).
Late-payment fee	$29.
Over-the-credit-limit fee	$29.

*Explanation of penalty: If your payment arrives more than 10 days late two times within a six-month period, the penalty rate will apply.
**The prime rate used to determine your APR is the rate published in the *Wall Street Journal* on the 10th day of the prior month.

COST OF CREDIT AND TAX CONSIDERATIONS   Before the Tax Reform Act of 1986, the interest you paid on consumer credit reduced your taxable income. The new law did not affect the deductibility of home mortgage interest, but now you can no longer deduct interest paid on consumer loans.

AVOID THE MINIMUM MONTHLY PAYMENT TRAP
The "minimum monthly payment" is the smallest amount you can pay and still be a cardholder in good standing. Banks often encourage you to make the minimum payment, such as 2 percent of your outstanding balance or $20, whichever is greater. Some statements refer to the minimum as the "cardholder amount due." But that is not the total amount you owe.

Consider the following examples. In each example, the minimum payment is based on ⅟₃₆ of the outstanding balance or $20, whichever is greater.

Example 1   You are buying new books for college. If you spend $500 on textbooks using a credit card charging 19.8 percent interest and make only the minimum payment, it will take you more than 2½ years to pay off the loan, adding $150 in interest charges to the cost of your purchase. The same purchase on a credit card charging 12 percent interest will cost only $78 extra.

Look before you leap! Pay the credit card balance in full every month and avoid the minimum monthly payment trap.

Example 2   You purchase a $2,000 stereo system using a credit card with 19 percent interest and a 2 percent minimum payment. If you pay just the minimum every month, it will take you 265 months—over 22 years—to pay off the debt and will cost you nearly $4,800 in interest payments. Doubling the amount paid each month to 4 percent of the balance owed would allow you to shorten the payment time to 88 months from 265 months—or 7 years as opposed to 22 years—and save you about $3,680.

Example 3   You charge $2,000 in tuition and fees on a credit card charging 18.5 percent interest. If you pay off the balance by making the minimum payment each month, it will take you more than 11 years to repay the debt. By the time you have paid off the loan, you will have spent an extra $1,934 in interest alone—almost the actual cost of your tuition and fees. Again, to be prudent, pay off the balance as quickly as possible.

WHEN THE REPAYMENT IS EARLY: THE RULE OF 78s

rule of 78s A mathematical formula to determine how much interest has been paid at any point in a loan term.

Creditors sometimes use tables based on a mathematical formula called the **rule of 78s,** also called *the sum of the digits,* to determine how much interest you have paid at any point in a loan. This formula favors lenders and dictates that you pay more interest at the beginning of a loan, when you have the use of more of the money, and pay less and less interest as the debt is reduced. Because all of the payments are the same in size, the part going to pay back the amount borrowed increases as the part representing interest decreases.

The laws of several states authorize the use of the rule of 78s as a means of calculating finance charge rebates when you pay off a loan early. The Truth in Lending law requires that your creditor disclose whether or not you are entitled to a rebate of the finance charge if you pay off the loan early. Loans for a year or less, however, usually do not allow for a finance charge rebate. Read the accompanying Financial Planning Calculations boxes to learn how to use the rule of 78s and other methods of determining the cost of credit.

CREDIT INSURANCE

credit insurance Any type of insurance that ensures repayment of a loan in the event the borrower is unable to repay it.

Credit insurance ensures the repayment of your loan in the event of death, disability, or loss of property. The lender is named the beneficiary and directly receives any payments made on submitted claims.

There are three types of credit insurance: credit life, credit accident and health, and credit property. The most commonly purchased type of credit insurance is credit life insurance, which provides for the repayment of the loan if the borrower dies. According to the Consumer Federation of America and the National Insurance Consumer Organization, most borrowers don't need credit life insurance. Those who don't have life insurance can buy term life insurance for less. Term life insurance is discussed in Chapter 12.

Credit accident and health insurance, also called *credit disability insurance,* repays your loan in the event of a loss of income due to illness or injury. Credit property insurance provides coverage for personal property purchased with a loan. It may also insure collateral property, such as a car or furniture. However, premiums for such coverages are quite high.

Financial Planning Calculations

THE RULE OF 78s

HOW TO USE THE RULE OF 78s

The first step is to add up all the digits for the number of payments scheduled. For a 12-installment loan, add the numbers 1 through 12:

$$1 + 2 + 3 + 4 + 5 + 6 + 7 + 8 + 9 + 10 + 11 + 12 = 78$$

The answer—"the sum of the digits"—explains how the rule was named. One might say that the total interest is divided into 78 parts for payment over the term of the loan.

In the first month, before making any payments, you have the use of the whole amount borrowed, and therefore you pay 12/78 of the total interest in the first payment, in the second month, you still have the use of 11 parts of the loan and pay 11/78 of the interest; in the third, 10/78; and so on down to the final installment, 1/78.

Adding all the numbers in a series of payments is rather tedious. We can arrive at the answer quickly by using this formula:

$$\frac{N}{2} \times (N + 1)$$

N is the number of payments. For a 12-month loan, it looks like this:

$$\frac{12}{2} \times (12 + 1) = 6 \times 13 = 78$$

A LOAN FOR KAREN AND MIKE

Let us suppose that Karen and Mike borrow $3,000 from the National Bank to redecorate their home. Interest comes to $225, and the total of $3,225 is to be paid in 15 equal installments of $215.

Using the rule of 78s, we can determine how much of each installment represents interest. We add all the numbers from 1 through 15:

$$\frac{15}{2} \times (15 + 1) = 7.5 \times 16 = 120$$

Total interest is divided into 120 parts The first payment will include 15 parts of the total interest, or 15/120

$$\left(\frac{\$225}{120} \times 15 = \$28.13\right)$$

the second, 14/120

$$\left(\frac{\$225}{120} \times 14 = \$26.25\right)$$

and so on.

Notice in the following table that the interest decreases with each payment and the repayment of the amount borrowed increases with each payment:

Payment Number	Interest	Reduction of Debt	Total Payment
1	$28.13	$186.87	$215.00
2	26.25	188.75	215.00
3	24.37	190.63	215.00
4	22.50	192.50	215.00
5	20.63	194.37	215.00
6	18.75	196.25	215.00
7	16.87	198.13	215.00
8	15.00	200.00	215.00
9	13.13	201.87	215.00
10	11.25	203.75	215.00
11	9.37	205.63	215.00
12	7.50	207.50	215.00
13	5.63	209.37	215.00
14	3.75	211.25	215.00
15	1.87	213.13	215.00
	$225.00	$3,000.00	$3,225.00

HOW MUCH IS THE REBATE?

Now let's assume Karen and Mike want to pay off the loan with the fifth payment. We know the total interest is divided into 120 parts. To find out how many parts will be rebated, we add up the numbers for the remaining 10 installments, which will be prepaid:

$$\frac{10}{2} \times (10 + I) = 5 \times 11 = 55$$

Now we know that 55/120 of the interest will be deducted as a rebate; it amounts to $103.12:

$$\frac{55}{120} \times \$225 = \frac{\$12,375}{120} = \$103.12$$

We see that Karen and Mike do not save two-thirds of the interest (which would be $150) by paying off the loan in one-third of the scheduled time. But the earlier they repay the loan the higher the portion of interest they do save. The rule of 78s favors lenders.

Source: *The Rule of 78s* (Philadelphia: Federal Reserve Bank of Philadelphia).

OTHER METHODS OF DETERMINING THE COST OF CREDIT

BANK DISCOUNT METHOD

When the *bank discount rate* method is used, interest is calculated on the amount to be paid back and you receive the difference between the amount to be paid back and the interest amount. For instance, if your relative lends you $1,000 less $50 (interest at 5 percent), you receive $950.

Example 1. Using the APR formula, you find the true interest rate, or the annual percentage rate, is 5.263 percent, not the stated 5 percent:

$$\text{APR} = \frac{2 \times n \times I}{P(N + 1)} = \frac{2 \times 1 \times \$50}{\$950(1 + 1)} = \frac{\$100}{\$1,900}$$

$$= 0.05263, \text{ or } 5.263 \text{ percent}$$

COMPOUND INTEREST

Unlike simple interest, *compound interest* is the interest paid on the original principal *plus* the accumulated interest. With interest compounding, the greater the number of periods for which interest is calculated, the more rapidly the amount of interest on interest and interest on principal builds.

Annual compounding means there is only *one* period annually for the calculation of interest. With such compounding, interest charges on a *one-year* loan are identical whether they are figured on a simple interest basis or on an annual compound basis. However, a new interest formula, based on the simple interest formula, must be used if there is annual compounding for two or more years or compounding with more than one compound period per year.

A compact formula that describes compound interest calculations is

$$F = P(1 + r)^T$$

where

F = Total future repayment value of a loan (principal *plus* total accumulated or compound interest)
P = Principal
r = Rate of interest per year, or annual interest rate
T = Time in years

Before the compound interest formula can be used for *multiple*-period compounding, two important adjustments must be made.

First, adjust the *annual* interest rate (r) to reflect the number of compounding periods per year. For example, a 5 percent annual rate of interest, compounded half-yearly, works out to 2.5 percent (5 percent divided by 2) per half-year.

Second, adjust the time factor (T), which is measured in years, to reflect the *total* number of compounding periods. For example, your loan for one year compounded half-yearly works out to two compound periods (1 year multiplied by 2 compounding periods per year) over the length of the loan.

Example 2. Suppose your relative compounds interest semiannually and you make two payments, six months apart. Using the compound interest formula, here is the annual percentage rate:

$$F = P(1 + r)^T$$

$$F = \$1,000[1 + (0.05/2)]^{1 \times 2}$$

$$= \$1,000(1 + 0.025)^2$$

$$= \$1,000(1.050625)$$

$$= \$1,050.625$$

That is, you are paying $50.63 in interest for a one-year, $1,000 loan. Now, using the APR formula, you find the APR is 6.75 percent:

$$\text{APR} = \frac{2 \times n \times I}{P(N + 1)}$$

$$= \frac{2 \times 2 \times \$50.63}{\$1,000(2 + 1)}$$

$$= \frac{\$202.52}{\$3,000}$$

$$= 0.0675, \text{ or } 6.75 \text{ percent}$$

If your relative chose to compound interest daily (365 compounding periods per year), the solution to this problem would be quite complicated. A calculator or a compound interest table can make interest calculations more manageable.

The following table summarizes the effects on the APR when the interest on a one-year, $1,000 loan is calculated using the simple interest, declining balance, add-on interest, bank discount, and compound interest methods:

Method	Amount Borrowed	Stated Interest	Total Interest	Number of Payments	APR
Simple interest*	$1,000	5%	$50.00	1	5.00%
Declining balance*	1,000	5	37.50	2	5.00
Add-on*	1,000	5	50.00	2	6.60
Bank discount	1,000(–50)	5	50.00	1	5.26
Compound interest	1,000	5	50.63	2	6.75

*Discussed in the chapter.

CONCEPT CHECK 7-2

1 Distinguish between the finance charge and the annual percentage rate.

2 What are the three variations of the simple interest formula?

3 Distinguish among the adjusted balance, previous balance, and average daily balance methods of calculating the cost of open-end credit.

4 What is the rule of 78s?

Action Application Use the Internet to obtain information about the costs of closed-end and open-end credit.

Sheet 31
Consumer loan comparison

Managing Your Debts

A sudden illness or the loss of your job may make it impossible for you to pay your bills on time. If you find you cannot make your payments, contact your creditors at once and try to work out a modified payment plan with them. If you have paid your bills promptly in the past, they may be willing to work with you. Do not wait until your account is turned over to a debt collector. At that point, the creditor has given up on you.

Automobile loans present special problems. Most automobile financing agreements permit your creditor to repossess your car anytime you are in default on your payments. No advance notice is required. If your car is repossessed and sold, you will still owe the difference between the selling price and the unpaid debt, plus any legal, towing, and storage charges. Try to solve the problem with your creditor when you realize you will not be able to meet your payments. It may be better to sell the car yourself and pay off your debt than to incur the added costs of repossession.

If you are having trouble paying your bills, you may be tempted to turn to a company that claims to offer assistance in solving debt problems. Such companies may offer debt consolidation loans, debt counseling, or debt reorganization plans that are "guaranteed" to stop creditors' collection efforts. Before signing with such a company, investigate it. Be sure you understand what services the company provides and what they will cost you. Do not rely on verbal promises that do not appear in your contract. Also, check with the Better Business Bureau and your state or local consumer protection office. It may be able to tell you whether other consumers have registered complaints about the company.

A constant worry for a debtor who is behind in payments is the fear of debt collection agencies. However, as you will see in the next section, a federal agency protects certain legal rights that you possess in your dealings with such agencies.

DEBT COLLECTION PRACTICES

The Federal Trade Commission enforces the **Fair Debt Collection Practices Act (FDCPA),** which prohibits certain practices by agencies that collect debts for creditors. The act does not apply to creditors that collect debts themselves. While the act does not erase the legitimate debts consumers owe, it does regulate the ways debt collection agencies do business. Exhibit 7–2 summarizes the steps you may take if a debt collector calls.

WARNING SIGNS OF DEBT PROBLEMS

Bill Kenney, in his early 30s, has a steady job with an annual income of $50,000. Bill, his wife, and their two children enjoy a comfortable life. A new car is parked in the driveway of their home, which is furnished with

Objective 3

Develop a plan to manage your debts.

DID YOU KNOW?

Citibank offers booklets on personal money management for young people. Visit their Web site at www.credit-ed.citibank.com.

Fair Debt Collection Practices Act (FDCPA) A federal law, enacted in 1978, that regulates debt collection activities.

Drowning in a sea of debt can turn your American dream into a living nightmare.

Exhibit **7-2**   What to do if a debt collector calls

The Federal Trade Commission enforces the Fair Debt Collection Practices Act. The law dictates how and when a debt collector may contact you.

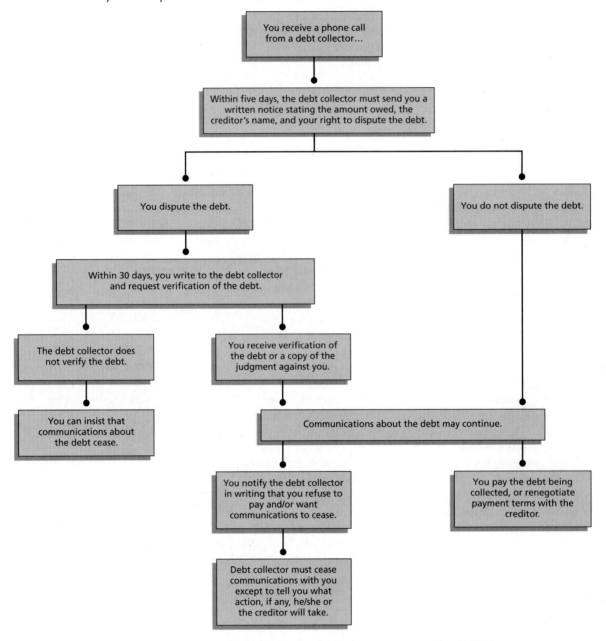

Source: Reprinted courtesy of Office of Public Information, Federal Reserve Bank of Minneapolis, Minneapolis, MN 55480.

such amenities as a six-burner gourmet stove, a subzero freezer, and a large-screen high-definition television set.

However, Bill Kenney is in debt. He is drowning in a sea of bills, with most of his income tied up in repaying debts. Foreclosure proceedings on his home have been instituted, and several stores have court orders to repossess practically every major appliance

Reason for Default	Primary or Contributing Cause of Default (percent of cases)
Excessive use of credit	39
Unemployment/reduced income	24
Poor money management	15
Divorce/separation	8
Medical expenses	7
Other	7

Source: Consumer Credit Counseling Service of the Gulf Coast Area, www.nfcc.org, April 12, 2005.

Exhibit **7-3**

Why consumers don't pay

Excessive use of credit and loss of income due to unemployment are the major reasons consumers don't pay.

in it. His current car payment is overdue, and three charge accounts at local stores are several months delinquent.

This case is neither exaggerated nor isolated. Unfortunately, a large number of people are in the same floundering state. These people's problem is immaturity. Mature consumers have certain information; they demonstrate self-discipline, control their impulses, and use sound judgment; they accept responsibility for money management; and they are able to postpone and govern expenditures when overextension of credit appears likely. As Exhibit 7–3 shows, excessive use of credit is the most common reason consumers are unable to pay their bills on time.

Referring to overindebtedness as the nation's number one family financial problem, a nationally noted columnist on consumer affairs lists the following as frequent reasons for indebtedness:

1. *Emotional problems,* such as the need for instant gratification, as in the case of a man who can't resist buying a costly suit or a woman who impulsively purchases an expensive dress in a trendy department store.

2. *The use of money to punish,* such as a husband who buys a new car without consulting his wife, who in turn buys a diamond watch to get even.

3. *The expectation of instant comfort* among young couples who assume that by use of the installment plan, they can have immediately the possessions their parents acquired after years of work.

4. *Keeping up with the Joneses,* which is more apparent than ever, not only among prosperous families but among limited-income families too.

5. *Overindulgence of children,* often because of the parents' own emotional needs, competition with each other, or inadequate communication regarding expenditures for the children.

6. *Misunderstanding or lack of communication among family members.* For example, a salesperson visited a Memphis family to sell them an expensive freezer. Although the freezer was beyond the means of this already overindebted family and too large for their needs anyway, the husband thought his wife wanted it. Not until later, in an interview with a debt counselor, did the wife relate her concern when she signed the contract; she had wanted her husband to say no.

7. *The amount of the finance charges,* which can push a family over the edge of their ability to pay, especially when they borrow from one company to pay another and these charges pyramid.

Exhibit 7–4 lists the danger signals of potential debt problems.

Running to a pawnshop for some cash is just one of the serious consequences of debt.

Exhibit **7-4**

Danger signals of potential debt problems

Seek help from your local Consumer Credit Counseling Service if you experience these danger signals.

1. Paying only the minimum balance on credit card bills each month.
2. Increasing the total balance due on credit accounts each month.
3. Missing payments, paying late, or paying some bills this month and others next month.
4. Intentionally using the overdraft or automatic loan features on checking accounts or taking frequent cash advances on credit cards.
5. Using savings to pay routine bills such as groceries or utilities.
6. Receiving second or third payment notices from creditors.
7. Not talking to your spouse about money or talking *only* about money.
8. Depending on overtime, moonlighting, or bonuses to meet everyday expenses.
9. Using up your savings.
10. Borrowing money to pay old debts.
11. Not knowing how much you owe until the bills arrive.
12. Going over your credit limit on credit cards.
13. Having little or nothing in savings to handle unexpected expenses.
14. Being denied credit because of a negative credit bureau report.
15. Getting a credit card revoked by the issuer.
16. Putting off medical or dental visits because you can't afford them right now.

If your household is experiencing more than two of these warning signals, it's time to examine your budget for ways to reduce expenses.

Sources: *Advice for Consumers Who Use Credit* (Silver Springs, MD: Consumer Credit Counseling Service of Maryland, Inc.); *How to Be Credit Smart* (Washington, DC: Consumer Credit Education Foundation).

THE SERIOUS CONSEQUENCES OF DEBT

DID YOU KNOW?

By senior year, the average undergraduate has racked up more than $3,200 in debt, spread out over six credit cards.

Source: *U.S. News & World Report,* April 19, 2004, p. 62.

Just as the causes of indebtedness vary, so too do the other personal and family problems that frequently result from overextension of credit.

Loss of a job because of garnishment proceedings may occur in a family that has a disproportionate amount of income tied up in debts. Another possibility is that such a family is forced to neglect vital areas. In the frantic effort to rob Peter to pay Paul, skimping may seriously affect the family's health and neglect the educational needs of children. Excessive indebtedness may also result in heavy drinking, neglect of children, marital difficulties, and drug abuse. But help is available to those debtors who seek it.

See the Financial Planning for Life's Situations feature on page 225 to obtain free credit information on the Internet.

CONCEPT CHECK 7-3

1 What is the Fair Debt Collection Practices Act?
2 What are the most frequent reasons for indebtedness?
3 What are common danger signals of potential debt problems?

Action Application Ask friends, relatives, and others to share their ways to make sure they will never get into serious debt.

MONEY MANAGEMENT IN CYBERSPACE

Whether you're developing a plan for reaching your financial goals or searching for a low-interest credit card, you can look to the Internet for a world of free information. Many Web sites provide interactive worksheets that allow you to plug in personal information and obtain customized reports. Here are some suggestions.

www.bankrate.com (Bank Rate Monitor). Looking for the best credit card rates available or up-to-the-minute news on the credit industry? Then log on here. This site posts a survey of card rates and even lets you apply online for some cards.

www.ramresearch.com (RAM Research). Created by this independent bank research organization, the site contains everything you ever wanted to know about credit cards. It includes a database of 10,000 financial institutions, and news and statistics on the credit industry.

www.aaii.org (American Association of Individual Investors). The AAII Web site covers the fundamentals of investing, with an array of subjects that will interest both the novice and the advanced investor.

www.napfa.org (National Association of Personal Financial Advisors). NAPFA offers consumer information on what to expect from a financial planner, as well as how and why to choose one. A handy search tool lets you pinpoint an adviser close to home.

www.iafp.org (International Association for Financial Planning). Check here to learn how to assess your financial situation and ways to set budget goals. The site also features a section on determining whether or not you need a financial planner.

www.money.com (*Money* magazine). This site covers virtually all topics related to money, including credit information, current money indexes, and a financial calculator.

www.consumercredit.com (American Consumer Credit Counseling, Inc.). This site is a good place to go if you have a credit problem or are heading that way.

www.nfcc.org (National Foundation for Consumer Credit). This is the home page for a network of local nonprofit organizations that provide consumer credit education and services.

Consumer Credit Counseling Services

If you are having problems paying your bills and need help, you have several options. You can contact your creditors and try to work out an adjusted repayment plan yourself, or you can check your telephone directory for a nonprofit financial counseling program to get help.

The **Consumer Credit Counseling Service (CCCS)** is a local, nonprofit organization affiliated with the National Foundation for Consumer Credit (NFCC). Branches of the CCCS provide debt counseling services for families and individuals with serious financial problems. It is not a charity, a lending institution, or a governmental or legal agency. The Consumer Credit Counseling Service is supported by contributions from banks, consumer finance companies, credit unions, merchants, and other community-minded organizations and individuals.

According to the NFCC, every year millions of consumers contact CCCS offices for help with their personal financial problems. More than 90 percent of the U.S. population has convenient access to CCCS services.

To find an office near you, check the white pages of your local telephone directory under Consumer Credit Counseling Service, or call 1-800-388-CCCS. All information is kept strictly confidential. Exhibit 7–5 reveals the characteristics of the typical CCCS client.

Objective 4

Evaluate various private and governmental sources that assist consumers with debt problems.

Consumer Credit Counseling Service (CCCS) A local, nonprofit organization that provides debt counseling services for families and individuals with serious financial problems.

225

Exhibit **7–5**

Profile of a CCCS Client

Characteristics of the Typical Client of the Consumer Credit Counseling Service	
Age:	38
Sex:	Male 43%, female 57%
Marital status:	Single 31%, married 48%
	Separated, divorced, or widowed 21%
Number in family:	3.3
Buying or own home:	38%
Average monthly gross income:	$2,562
Average total debt:	$20,045
Average number of creditors:	10.5

Source: Consumer Credit Counseling Service (Houston), www.cccsintl.org/info/stats.html, February 28, 2005.

WHAT THE CCCS DOES

Credit counselors are aware that most people who are in debt over their heads are basically honest people who want to clear up their indebtedness. Too often, the problems of such people arise from a lack of planning or a miscalculation of what they earn. Therefore, the CCCS is as concerned with preventing the problems as with solving them. As a result, its activities are divided into two parts:

Don't forget to visit a few of the money management Web sites outlined in the Financial Planning for Life's Situations: Money Management in Cyberspace box on page 225.

1. Aiding families with serious debt problems by helping them manage their money better and setting up a realistic budget and plan for expenditures.

2. Helping people prevent debt problems by teaching them the necessity of family budget planning, providing education to people of all ages regarding the pitfalls of unwise credit buying, suggesting techniques for family budgeting, and encouraging credit institutions to provide full information about the costs and terms of credit and to withhold credit from those who cannot afford to repay it.

Anyone who is overburdened by credit obligations can phone, write, or visit a CCCS office. The CCCS requires that an applicant complete an application for credit counseling and then arranges an appointment for a personal interview with the applicant.

CCCS counseling is usually free. However, when the CCCS administers a debt repayment plan, it sometimes charges a nominal fee to help defray administrative costs.

ALTERNATIVE COUNSELING SERVICES

In addition to the CCCS, universities, military bases, credit unions, local county extension agents, and state and federal housing authorities sometimes provide nonprofit counseling services. These organizations usually charge little or nothing for such assistance. You can also check with your local bank or consumer protection office to see whether it

Advice from a Pro

CHOOSING A CREDIT COUNSELOR

Credit counseling organizations provide valuable assistance to financially distressed consumers. However, some firms may be misleading you about who they are, what they do, or how much they charge. Experts advise that you ask the following questions to find the best credit counselor:

- *What services do you offer?* Look for an organization that offers budget counseling and money management classes as well as a debt-management plan.

- *Do you offer free information?* Avoid organizations that charge for information or demand details about your problem first.

- *What are your fees?* Are there set-up and/or monthly fees? A typical set-up fee is $10. If you're paying a lot more, you may be the one who's being set up.

- *How will the debt-management plan work?* What debts can be included in the plan, and will you get regular reports on your accounts?

- *Can you get my creditors to lower or eliminate my interest and fees?* If the answer is yes, contact your creditors to verify this.

- *What if I can't afford to pay you?* If an organization won't help you because you can't afford to pay, go somewhere else for help.

- *Will you help me avoid future problems?* Getting a plan for avoiding future debt is as important as solving the immediate debt problem.

- *Will we have a contract?* All verbal promises should be in writing before you pay any money.

- *Are your counselors accredited or certified?* Legitimate credit counseling firms are affiliated with the National Foundation for Credit Counseling or the Association of Independent Consumer Credit Counseling Agencies.

Check with your local consumer protection agency and the Better Business Bureau to see if any complaints have been filed about the company.

---

has a listing of reputable, low-cost financial counseling services.

Several national nonprofit organizations provide information and assist people with debt problems by phone and Internet.

- American Consumer Credit Counseling. Visit www.consumercredit.com or call 1-800-769-3571.

- InCharge Institute of America. Visit www.incharge.org or call 1-800-565-8953.

- Money Management International. Visit www.moneymanagement.org or call 1-866-899-9347.

- Myvesta. Visit www.myvesta.org or call 1-800-680-DEBT.

Typically, a counseling service will negotiate lower payments with your creditors, then make the payments using money you send to them each month. The creditor, not you, pays the cost of setting up this debt management plan (DMP). Read the Advice from a Pro feature on how to find the best credit counselor. Read the Financial Planning for Life's Situations box on page 228 to be aware of deceptive credit counseling organizations.

But what if a debtor suffers from an extreme case of financial woes? Is there any relief? The answer is yes: bankruptcy proceedings.

American Consumer Credit Counseling is a nonprofit organization helping those who have money troubles or are considering bankruptcy. Visit this organization at **www.consumercredit.com/**.

fyi

CREDIT COUNSELING IN CRISIS

The National Consumer Law Center and Consumer Federation of America's comprehensive report recently indicated that a new generation of credit counseling agencies is a serious threat to debt-burdened consumers. The study found that, unlike the previous creditor-funded counseling services, these new agencies often harm debtors with improper advice, deceptive practices, excessive fees, and abuse of their nonprofit status. "Nonprofit" credit counseling agencies are increasingly performing like profit-making enterprises and pay their executives lavishly. For example, recently American Consumer Credit Counseling paid its president $462,350 in annual salary plus over $130,000 in benefits. According to Thomas Leary, a member of the Federal Trade Commission (FTC), "some companies use their nonprofit status as a badge of trustworthiness to attract customers, who are then duped into paying large fees." For example, Mr. Leary testified that in November 2003 the commission filed a lawsuit against AmeriDebt, a large, Maryland-based credit-counseling firm. According to the FTC complaint, the firm "aggressively advertises itself as a nonprofit and dedicated to assisting consumers with their finances. AmeriDebt advertises its services as 'free' when in fact the company retains a consumer's first payment as a 'contribution.'"

Traditional credit-counseling agencies offer financial and budget counseling, debt counseling, and community education as well as debt-management plans (DMP). Newer agencies, however, force consumers only into DMPs (also known as debt consolidation plans) and charge high monthly maintenance fees. Some agencies charge as much as a full month's consolidated payment, usually hundreds of dollars, simply to establish an account.

The report recommends that Congress and the states enact laws to curb abuses by credit counseling agencies. The law should:

- Prohibit false or misleading advertising and referral fees.
- Require credit-counseling agencies to better inform consumers about fees, the sources of agency funding, suitability of DMPs for many consumers, and other options that consumers should consider, such as bankruptcy.
- Prohibit agencies from receiving a fee for service from a consumer until all her/his creditors have approved a DMP.
- Give consumers three days to cancel an agreement with a credit-counseling agency without obligation.
- Cap fees charged by agencies at $50 for enrollment or set-up. Allow only reasonable monthly charges.
- Require agencies to prominently disclose all financial arrangements with lenders or financial service providers.
- Provide consumers with the right to enforce the law in court.

Finally, the Internal Revenue Service should aggressively enforce existing standards for nonprofit credit counseling organizations, and credit counseling trade associations should set strong "best practice standards."

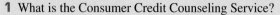

CONCEPT CHECK 7–4

1 What is the Consumer Credit Counseling Service?
2 What are the two major activities of the Consumer Credit Counseling Service?
3 What options other than the CCCS do consumers have for financial counseling?

Action Application Use an Internet search engine to find branches of the Consumer Credit Counseling Service across the country. Choose one in your area and one in another part of the country. Visit the Web sites to find out who funds the offices.

Declaring Personal Bankruptcy

Jan Watson typifies the new face of bankruptcy. A 43-year-old freelance commercial photographer from Point Reyes, California, she was never in serious financial trouble until she began incurring big medical costs last year and reached for her credit cards to pay the bills. Since Jan didn't have health insurance, her debt quickly mounted and soon reached $17,000. It was too much for her to pay off with her $25,000-a-year freelance income. Her solution: Declare personal bankruptcy and the immediate freedom it would bring from creditors' demands.

Ms. Watson's move put her in familiar company, demographically speaking. An increasing number of bankruptcy filers are well-educated, middle-class baby boomers with an overwhelming level of credit card debt. These baby boomers make up 45 percent of the adult population, but they account for 60 percent of personal bankruptcies. In that group, the people most likely to be in bankruptcy are between 35 and 44 years old (average age is 38), an age group that is usually assumed to be economically established. Increasingly, too, the bankruptcy debtor is likely to be female. Women now account for 30 percent of bankruptcy filers, up from 17 percent two decades ago.

In 1994, the U.S. Senate unanimously passed a bill that reduced the time and cost of bankruptcy proceedings. The bill strengthened creditor rights and enabled more individuals to weather bankruptcy proceedings without selling their assets.

Unfortunately, for some debtors, bankruptcy has become an acceptable tool of credit management. During the last nine years, the personal bankruptcy rate has increased 17 percent annually. According to the American Bankruptcy Institute, a record 1.6 million people declared bankruptcy in 2004, the highest rate since the U.S. bankruptcy code took effect in 1979 (see Exhibit 7–6). Bankruptcy courts have turned to regular Saturday sessions to handle the overflow.

THE U.S. BANKRUPTCY ACT OF 1978: THE LAST RESORT

Nationwide, the overwhelming majority of bankruptcies like Jan Watson's are filed under Chapter 7 of the U.S. bankruptcy code. You have two choices in declaring personal bankruptcy: Chapter 7 (a straight bankruptcy) and Chapter 13 (a wage earner plan) bankruptcy. Both choices are undesirable, and neither should be considered an easy way out.

Objective 5

Assess the choices in declaring personal bankruptcy.

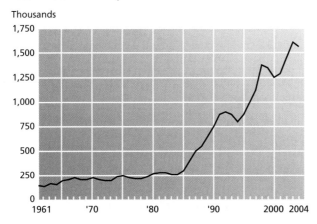

Total Personal Bankruptcies

Exhibit **7-6**

U.S. bankruptcies, 1961–2004

Source: Administrative Office of the United States Courts; www.uscourts.gov, April 14, 2005.

Chapter 7 bankruptcy
One type of personal (or straight) bankruptcy in which many debts are forgiven.

CHAPTER 7 BANKRUPTCY

In a **Chapter 7 bankruptcy,** a debtor is required to draw up a petition listing his or her assets and liabilities. The debtor submits the petition to a U.S. district court and pays a filing fee. A person filing for relief under the bankruptcy code is called a *debtor;* the term *bankrupt* is not used.

Chapter 7 is a straight bankruptcy in which many, but not all, debts are forgiven. Most of the debtor's assets are sold to pay off creditors. However, certain assets of the debtor are protected to some extent. For example, Social Security payments; unemployment compensation; limited values of your equity in a home, car, or truck; household goods and appliances; trade tools; books; and so forth are protected.

However, some creditors still try to collect. In 1997, for example, the Federal Trade Commission negotiated a settlement agreement with Sears, Roebuck and Company ensuring that Sears made full refunds totaling more than $100 million to consumers. More than 200,000 consumers whose debts were discharged in bankruptcy proceedings had been forced by Sears to continue payments or face illegal collection efforts.

The discharge of debts in Chapter 7 does not affect alimony, child support, certain taxes, fines, certain debts arising from educational loans, or debts that you fail to properly disclose to the bankruptcy court. At the request of a creditor, the bankruptcy judge may also exclude from the discharge debts resulting from loans you received by giving the lender a false financial statement. Furthermore, debts arising from fraud, embezzlement, driving while intoxicated, larceny, or certain other willful or malicious acts may also be excluded.

fyi
Is debt burden unbearable? For help, visit **DebtAdvice.org.** This Web site is maintained by the members of the National Foundation for Credit Counseling Services.

The Bankruptcy Abuse Prevention and Consumer Protection Act of 2005

On April 20, 2005, President Bush signed the Bankruptcy Abuse Prevention and Consumer Protection Act which is perhaps the largest overhaul of the Bankruptcy Code since it was enacted in 1978. Signing the bill, the president declared, "Bankruptcy should always be the last resort in our legal system. In recent years too many people have abused the bankruptcy laws. Under the new law, Americans who have the ability to pay will be required to pay back at least a portion of their debts. The law will help make credit more affordable, because when bankruptcy is less common, credit can be extended to more people at better rates. Debtors seeking to erase all debts will now have to wait eight years from their last bankruptcy before they can file again. The law will also allow us to clamp down on bankruptcy mills that make their money by advising abusers on how to game the system."

Among other provisions, the law requires that:

- The director of the Executive Office for U.S. Trustees develop a financial management training curriculum to educate individual debtors on how to better manage their finances; and test, evaluate, and report to Congress on the curriculum's effectiveness.

- Debtors complete an approved instructional course in personal financial management.

- The clerk of each bankruptcy district maintains a list of credit counseling agencies and instructional courses on personal financial management.

Furthermore, the law may require that states should develop personal finance curricula designed for use in elementary and secondary schools.

The bottom line: the new law made it more difficult for consumers to file a Chapter 7 bankruptcy and forces them into a Chapter 13 repayment plan.

Chapter 13 bankruptcy A voluntary plan that a debtor with regular income develops and proposes to a bankruptcy court.

CHAPTER 13 BANKRUPTCY

In a **Chapter 13 bankruptcy,** a debtor with a regular income proposes to a bankruptcy court a plan for extinguishing his or her debts from future earnings or other property over a period of time. In such a bankruptcy, the debtor normally keeps all or most of the property.

During the period the plan is in effect, which can be as long as five years, the debtor makes regular payments to a Chapter 13 trustee. The trustee, in turn, distributes the money to the creditors. Under certain circumstances, the bankruptcy court may approve a plan permitting the debtor to keep all property even though the debtor repays less than the full amount of the debts. Certain debts not dischargeable in Chapter 7, such as those based on fraud, may be discharged in Chapter 13 if the debtor successfully completes the plan. To file a Chapter 13 bankruptcy, a person must have regular income and not more than $250,000 in unsecured debts or $750,000 in secured debts.[3]

EFFECT OF BANKRUPTCY ON YOUR JOB AND YOUR FUTURE CREDIT

Different people have different experiences in obtaining credit after they file bankruptcy. Some find obtaining credit more difficult. Others find obtaining credit easier because they have relieved themselves of their prior debts or because creditors know they cannot file another bankruptcy case for a period of time. Obtaining credit may be easier for people who file a Chapter 13 bankruptcy and repay some of their debts than for people who file a Chapter 7 bankruptcy and make no effort to repay. The bankruptcy law prohibits your employer from discharging you simply because you have filed a bankruptcy case.

One caution: Don't confuse a personal bankruptcy with a business (or Chapter 11) bankruptcy. The Chapter 11 bankruptcy is a reorganization requested by a business and ordered by the court because a business is unable to pay its debts.

SHOULD A LAWYER REPRESENT YOU IN A BANKRUPTCY CASE?

When 29-year-old Lynn Jensen of San Gabriel, California, lost her $35,000-a-year job, she ended up filing for bankruptcy using a "how to file for bankruptcy" book because she could not afford a lawyer. Like Lynn, you have the right to file your own bankruptcy case and to represent yourself at all court hearings. In any bankruptcy case, however, you must complete and file with a bankruptcy court several detailed forms concerning your property, debts, and financial condition. Many people find it easier to complete these forms with the assistance of experienced bankruptcy counsel. In addition, you may discover that your case will develop complications, especially if you own a substantial amount of property or your creditors object to the discharge of your debts. Then you will require the advice and assistance of a lawyer.

Choosing a bankruptcy lawyer may be difficult. Some of the least reputable lawyers make easy money by handling hundreds of bankruptcy cases without adequately considering individual needs. Recommendations from those you know and trust and from employee assistance programs are most useful.

> **DID YOU KNOW?**
>
> Chapter 13 and Chapter 7 bankruptcies must be filed in federal bankruptcy court. The current filing fees are $185 for Chapter 13 and $200 for Chapter 7 bankruptcy. Attorney fees are additional and can vary widely.
>
> Source: Federal Trade Commission, *Consumer Alert*, April 2002.

WHAT ARE THE COSTS?   The monetary costs to the debtor under Chapter 13 bankruptcy include the following:

1. *Court costs.* The debtor must pay a filing fee to the clerk of the court at the time of filing his or her petition. The filing fee may be paid in up to four installments if the court grants authorization.

WHAT'S YOUR CREDIT IQ?

CREDIT-ABILITY SCORECARD

Test your credit IQ. For each question, circle the letter that best describes your credit habits.

1. **I pay my bills when they are due.**

    (A) Always   (B) Almost Always   (C) Sometimes

2. **After paying my regular bills each month, I have money left from my income.**

    (A) Yes   (B) Sometimes   (C) Never

3. **I know how much I owe on my credit cards each month before I receive my bills.**

    (A) Yes   (B) Sometimes   (C) No

4. **When I get behind in my payments, I ignore the past-due notices.**

    (A) Never or Not Applicable   (B) Sometimes   (C) Always

5. **When I need more money for my regular living expenses, I take out a loan or use my line of credit on my credit card or checking account.**

    (A) Never   (B) Sometimes   (C) Often

6. **If I want to see a copy of my credit report, I would contact . . .**

    (A) A credit reporting agency   (B) My lenders   (C) My lawyer

7. **My credit record shows that I am current on all my loans and charge accounts.**

    (A) Yes   (B) Don't know   (C) No

8. **I pay more than the minimum balance due on my credit card accounts.**

    (A) Always   B) Sometimes   (C) Never

9. **To pay off my current credit and charge card accounts, it would take me . . .**

    (A) 4 months or less   (B) 5 to 8 months   (C) Over 8 months

10. **My consumer loans (including auto loans, but not mortgage payment) and credit card bills each month average more than 20% of my take-home pay.**

    (A) No   (B) Sometimes   (C) Always

11. **If I had serious credit problems, I would contact my creditors to explain the problem.**

    (A) Yes   (B) Probably   (C) No

12. **If I default (don't repay) on a loan, that fact can stay on my credit report for . . .**

    (A) 7 years   (B) 3 years   (C) 1 year

Assign a score of 3 for each "A" answer, 2 for each "B" answer, and 1 for each "C" response. Total the score.

If you scored:

31–36	You have an excellent knowledge of credit and its responsible use.
24–30	You should take steps toward a better understanding of your personal finances and of the credit process.
18–23	You probably need to take a serious look at your personal finances; consider controlling your spending and keeping on a tight budget.
12–17	You may be heading for serious trouble; consider seeking help, such as nonprofit consumer credit counseling services.

Source: AFSA Education Foundation, *How to Be Credit Smart,* 1997.

---

2. *Attorneys' fees.* These fees are usually the largest single item of cost. Often the attorney does not require them to be paid in advance at the time of filing but agrees to be paid in installments after receipt of a down payment. Fees range between $800 and $1,200.

3. *Trustees' fees and costs.* The trustees' fees are established by the bankruptcy judge in most districts and by a U.S. trustee in certain other districts.

Although it is possible to reduce these costs by purchasing the legal forms in a local office supplies store and completing them yourself, an attorney is strongly recommended.

There are also intangible costs to bankruptcy. For example, obtaining credit in the future may be difficult, since bankruptcy reports are retained in credit bureaus for 10 years. Therefore, you should take the extreme step of declaring personal bankruptcy only when no other options for solving your financial problems exist.

Since you now know everything you ever wanted to know about consumer credit, read the Financial Planning for Life's Situations feature on page 232 to test your credit IQ.

CONCEPT CHECK 7-5

1 What is the purpose of Chapter 7 bankruptcy?
2 What is the difference between Chapter 7 and Chapter 13 bankruptcy?
3 How does bankruptcy affect your job and future credit?
4 What are the costs of declaring bankruptcy?

Action Application Use an Internet search engine to seek answers to the most frequently asked questions about Chapter 7 and Chapter 13 bankruptcy.

SUMMARY OF OBJECTIVES

Objective 1
Analyze the major sources of consumer credit.
The major sources of consumer credit are commercial banks, savings and loan associations, credit unions, finance companies, life insurance companies, and family and friends. Each of these sources has unique advantages and disadvantages.

Parents or family members are often the source of the least expensive loans. They may charge you only the interest they would have earned had they not made the loan. Such loans, however, can complicate family relationships.

Objective 2
Determine the cost of credit by calculating interest using various interest formulas.
Compare the finance charge and the annual percentage rate (APR) as you shop for credit. Under the Truth in Lending law, creditors are required to state the cost of borrowing so that you can compare credit costs and shop for credit.

For a borrower, the most favorable method of calculating the cost of open-end credit is the adjusted balance method. In this method, creditors add finance charges after subtracting payments made during the billing period. The rule of 78s favors lenders. This formula dictates that you pay more interest at the beginning of a loan, when you have the use of more money, and pay less and less interest as the debt is reduced. Because all the payments are the same size, the part going to pay back the amount borrowed increases as the part representing interest decreases.

Objective 3
Develop a plan to manage your debts.
The Fair Debt Collection Practices Act prohibits certain practices by debt collection agencies. Debt has serious consequences if a proper plan for managing it is not implemented.

Most people agree that emotional problems, the use of money to punish, the expectation of instant comfort, keeping up with the Joneses, overindulgence of children, misunderstanding or lack of communication among family members, and the amount of finance charge are common reasons for indebtedness.

Objective 4
Evaluate various private and governmental sources that assist consumers with debt problems.
If you cannot meet your obligations, contact your creditors immediately. Before signing up with a debt consolidation company, investigate it thoroughly. Better yet, contact your local Consumer Credit Counseling Service or other debt counseling organizations.

Such organizations help people manage their money better by setting up a realistic budget and plan for expenditures. These organizations also help people prevent debt problems by teaching them the necessity of family budget planning and providing education to people of all ages.

Objective 5
Assess the choices in declaring personal bankruptcy.
A debtor's last resort is to declare bankruptcy, permitted by the U.S. Bankruptcy Act of 1978. Consider the financial and other costs of bankruptcy before taking this extreme step. A debtor can declare Chapter 7 (straight) bankruptcy or Chapter 13 (wage earner plan) bankruptcy.

Some people find obtaining credit more difficult after filing bankruptcy. Others find obtaining credit easier because they have relieved themselves of their prior debts or because creditors know they cannot file another bankruptcy case for a period of time. Obtaining credit may be easier for people who file a Chapter 13 bankruptcy and repay some of their debts than for people who file a Chapter 7 bankruptcy and make no effort to repay their debts.

The Bankruptcy Abuse Prevention and Consumer Protection Act of 2005 overhauls the Bankruptcy Code and makes it more difficult for consumers to file Chapter 7 bankruptcy and forces them into a Chapter 13 repayment plan.

KEY FORMULAS

Page	Topic	Formula

212   Calculating annual percentage rate (APR)

$$APR = \frac{2 \times \text{Number of payment periods in one year} \times \text{Dollar cost of credit}}{\text{Loan amount (Total number of payments to pay off the loan} + 1)}$$

$$= \frac{2 \times n \times I}{P(N + 1)}$$

Example:

P = Principal borrowed, $100

n = number of payments in one year, 1

I = Dollar cost of credit, $8

$$APR = \frac{2 \times 1 \times \$8}{\$100(1 + 1)} = \frac{\$16}{\$200} = 0.08, \text{ or 8 percent}$$

For 12 equal monthly payments,

$$APR = \frac{2 \times 12 \times \$8}{\$100(12 + 1)} = \frac{\$192}{\$1,300} = 0.1476, \text{ or 14.76 percent}$$

213   Calculating simple interest

Interest (in dollars) = Principal borrowed $\times$ Interest rate $\times$ Length of loan in years

$$I = P \times r \times T$$

Example:

From above: $P = \$100$; $r = 0.08$; $T = 1$

$$I = \$100 \times 0.08 \times 1 = \$8$$

220   Calculating compound interest

Total future value of a loan = Principal $(1 + \text{Rate of interest})^{\text{Time in years}}$

$$F = P(1 + r)^T$$

Example:

From above: $P = \$100$; $r = 0.08$; $T = 1$

$$F = \$100(1 + 0.08)^1 = \$100(1.08) = \$108$$

KEY TERMS

1. *Calculating the Finance Charge on a Loan.* Dave borrowed $500 for one year and paid $50 in interest. The bank charged him a $5 service charge. What is the finance charge on this loan? (Obj. 2)

2. *Calculating the Annual Percentage Rate.* In problem 1, Dave borrowed $500 on January 1, 2006, and paid it all back at once on December 31, 2006. What was the APR? (Obj. 2)

3. *Calculating the Annual Percentage Rate.* If Dave paid the $500 in 12 equal monthly payments, what was the APR? (Obj. 2)

4. *Comparing the Costs of Credit Cards.* Bobby is trying to decide between two credit cards. One has no annual fee and an 18 percent interest rate, and the other has a $40 annual fee and an 8.9 percent interest rate. Should he take the card that's free or the one that costs $40? (Obj. 2)

5. *Calculating Cash Advance Fee and the Dollar Amount of Interest.* Sidney took a $200 cash advance by using checks linked to her credit card account. The bank charges a 2 percent cash advance fee on the amount borrowed and offers no grace period on cash advances. Sidney paid the balance in full when the bill arrived. What was the cash advance fee? What was the interest for one month at an 18 percent APR? What was the total amount she paid? What if she had made the purchase with her credit card and paid off the bill in full promptly? (Obj. 2)

6. *Comparing the Cost of Credit during Inflationary Periods.* Dorothy lacks cash to pay for a $600 dishwasher. She could buy it from the store on credit by making 12 monthly payments of $52.74. The total cost would then be $632.88. Instead, Dorothy decides to deposit $50 a month in the bank until she has saved enough money to pay cash for the dishwasher. One year later, she has saved $642—$600 in deposits plus interest. When she goes back to the store, she

finds the dishwasher now costs $660. Its price has gone up 10 percent, the current rate of inflation. Was postponing her purchase a good trade-off for Dorothy? (Obj. 2)

7. *Comparing Costs of Credit Using Three Calculation Methods.* You have been pricing a compact disk player in several stores. Three stores have the identical price of $300. Each store charges 18 percent APR, has a 30-day grace period, and sends out bills on the first of the month. On further investigation, you find that store A calculates the finance charge by using the average daily balance method, store B uses the adjusted balance method, and store C uses the previous balance method. Assume you purchased the disk player on May 5 and made a $100 payment on June 15. What will the finance charge be if you made your purchase from store A? From store B? From store C? (Obj. 2)

8. *Determining Interest Cost Using the Simple Interest Formula.* What are the interest cost and the total amount due on a six-month loan of $1,500 at 13.2 percent simple annual interest? (Obj. 2)

9. *Calculating the Total Cost of a Purchase, the Monthly Payment, and an APR.* After visiting several automobile dealerships, Richard selects the used car he wants. He likes its $10,000 price, but financing through the dealer is no bargain. He has $2,000 cash for a down payment, so he needs an $8,000 loan. In shopping at several banks for an installment loan, he learns that interest on most automobile loans is quoted at add-on rates. That is, during the life of the loan, interest is paid on the full amount borrowed even though a portion of the principal has been paid back. Richard borrows $8,000 for a period of four years at an add-on interest rate of 11 percent. What is the total interest on Richard's loan? What is the total cost of the car? What is the monthly payment? What is the annual percentage rate (APR)? (Obj. 2)

FINANCIAL PLANNING PROBLEMS

FINANCIAL PLANNING ACTIVITIES

1. *Determining Whether a Loan Is Needed.* Survey friends and relatives to find out what criteria they used to determine the need for credit. (Obj. 1)

2. *Comparing Costs of Loans from Various Lenders.* Prepare a list of sources of inexpensive loans, medium-priced loans, and expensive loans in your area. What are the trade-offs in obtaining a loan from an "easy" lender? (Obj. 1)

3. *Using Current Information on Obtaining the Best Credit Terms.* Choose a current issue of *Worth, Money, Kiplinger's Personal Finance Magazine,* or *BusinessWeek* and summarize an article that provides suggestions on how you can choose the best, yet least expensive, source of credit. (Obj. 2)

4. *Using the Internet to Obtain Information about the Costs of Credit.* As pointed out at the beginning of this chapter, credit costs money; therefore, you must conduct a cost/benefit analysis before making any major purchase. While most people consider credit costs, others simply ignore them and eventually find themselves in financial difficulties. To help consumers avoid this problem, each of the following organizations has a home page on the Internet:

Finance Center Inc. helps consumers save money when purchasing, financing, or refinancing a new home or a car, or making a credit card transaction. (www.financenter.com)

Debtors Anonymous offers financial counseling to debt-ridden consumers. (www.debtorsanonymous.org)

Bank Rate Monitor is America's consumer rate source for mortgages, credit cards, auto loans, home equity loans, and personal loans. (www.bankrate.com)

Choose one of the above organizations and visit its Web site. Then prepare a report that summarizes the information the organization provides. Finally, decide how this information could help you better manage your credit and its costs. (Obj. 2)

5. *Calculating the Cost of Credit Using Three APR Formulas.* How are the simple interest, simple interest on the declining balance, and add-on interest formulas used in determining the cost of credit? (Obj. 2)

6. *Handling Harassment from Debt Collection Agencies.* Your friend is drowning in a sea of overdue bills and is being ha-

rassed by a debt collection agency. Prepare a list of the steps your friend should take if the harassment continues. (Obj. 3)

7. *Seeking Assistance from the Consumer Credit Counseling Service.* Visit a local office of the Consumer Credit Counseling Service. What assistance can debtors obtain from this office? What is the cost of this assistance, if any? (Obj. 4)

8. *Assessing the Choices in Declaring Personal Bankruptcy.* What factors would you consider in assessing the choices in declaring personal bankruptcy? Why should personal bankruptcy be the choice of last resort? (Obj. 5)

INTERNET CONNECTION

Researching Credit and Debt Counseling

Challenging life situations can sometimes lead to financial hardships. Credit and debt counseling can help deal with stressful financial times.

Credit Web sources: _____

Current findings: _____
_____

Possible influence on your financial decisions: _____
_____

Debt counseling Web sources: _____

Current findings: _____
_____

Possible influence on your financial decisions: _____
_____
_____

FINANCIAL PLANNING CASE

Financing Sue's Hyundai Excel

After shopping around, Sue Wallace decided on the car of her choice, a used Hyundai Excel. The dealer quoted her a total price of $8,000. Sue decided to use $2,000 of her savings as a down payment and borrow $6,000. The salesperson wrote this information on a sales contract that Sue took with her when she set out to find financing.

When Sue applied for a loan, she discussed loan terms with the bank lending officer. The officer told her that the bank's policy was to lend only 80 percent of the total price of a used car.

Sue showed the officer her copy of the sales contract, indicating that she had agreed to make a $2,000, or 25 percent, down payment on the $8,000 car, so this requirement caused her no problem. Although the bank was willing to make 48-month loans at an annual percentage rate of 15 percent on used cars, Sue chose a 36-month repayment schedule. She believed she could afford the higher payments, and she knew she would not have to pay as much interest if she paid off the loan at a faster rate. The bank lending officer provided Sue with a copy of the Truth-in-Lending Disclosure Statement shown here.

Truth-in-Lending Disclosure Statement (Loans)

Annual Percentage Rate	Finance Charge	Amount Financed	Total of Payments, 36
The cost of your credit as a yearly rate.	The dollar amount the credit will cost you.	The amount of credit provided to you or on your behalf.	The amount you will have paid after you have made all payments as scheduled.
15%	$1,487.64	$6,000.00	$7,487.64

You have the right to receive at this time an itemization of the Amount Financed.

☒ I want an itemization.   ❑ I do not want an itemization.

Your payment schedule will be:

Number of Payments	Amount of Payments	When Payments Are Due
36	$207.99	1st of each month

Sue decided to compare the APR she had been offered with the APR offered by another bank, but the 20 percent APR of the second bank (bank B) was more expensive than the 15 percent APR of the first bank (bank A). Here is her comparison of the two loans:

	Bank A 15% APR	Bank B 20% APR
Amount financed	$6,000.00	$6,000.00
Finance charge	1,487.64	2,027.28
Total of payments	7,487.64	8,027.28
Monthly payments	207.99	222.98

The 5 percent difference in the APRs of the two banks meant Sue would have to pay $15 extra every month if she got her loan from the second bank. Of course, she got the loan from the first bank.

Questions

1. What is perhaps the most important item shown on the disclosure statement? Why?

2. What is included in the finance charge?

3. What amount will Sue receive from the bank?

4. Should Sue borrow from bank A or bank B? Why?

VIDEO CASE

Credit Problems

This video case features a couple who are dining at a fine restaurant and realize they have exceeded their credit limit on both of their credit cards. The couple seems unaware of some important warning signs of potential credit problems.

Credit counselor Joanne Budde explains the three goals of the Consumer Credit Counseling Service: to educate consumers, provide confidential counseling, and develop personalized debt management plans.

Gerri Detweiler of Debt Counselors of America states that one reason many people have credit problems is that credit is so easily available. A financial adviser explains that credit counseling may be a better alternative to bankruptcy.

Maxine Sweet of Experian states that missed payments can stay on a credit report for up to 7 years and bankruptcies for 10 years. She also advises consumers to beware of some credit re-

pair scams. Finally, financial adviser Dianne Wilkman explains how some credit counselors can negotiate with lenders to work out a repayment plan.

Questions

1. What are some important warning signs of potential credit problems? Do you believe the couple in the video are experiencing these signs?

2. What are the major functions of the Consumer Credit Counseling Service? Would you suggest the couple seek CCCS assistance? Why or why not?

3. Do you believe credit is too easily available? If so, explain and give examples.

4. Why would credit counseling be a better alternative to bankruptcy?

YOUR PERSONAL FINANCIAL PLANNER IN ACTION

Comparing Credit Sources and Costs

Credit is available from many sources. Becoming aware of the differences among financial institutions related to borrowing costs and other factors while wisely managing your debt will help you avoid financial difficulties.

Your Short-Term Financial Planning Activities	Resources
1. Evaluate your current use of credit cards. Compare various credit card offers related to APR, annual fee, grace period, and other fees.	PFP Sheet 30 www.bankrate.com www.consumer-action.org
2. Compare various credit sources for loans related to various financial needs.	PFP Sheet 31 www.eloan.com www.lendingtree.com www.finance-center.com
Your Long-Term Financial Planning Activities	
1. Investigate various actions commonly taken to avoid debt problems.	www.moneymanagement.org www.nfcc.org www.dca.org
2. Prepare a spending plan to minimize the use of credit.	Text pages 221–224 www.debtadvice.org www.kiplinger.com/tools

CONTINUING CASE

Credit Decisions

Life Situation

Recently married couple
Pam, 26
Josh, 28
Renting an apartment

Financial Data

Monthly income	$5,840
Assets	$13,500
Liabilities	$4,800
Living expenses	$3,900
Emergency fund	$1,000

In an effort to make wise use of credit, the Brocks have examined various sources that could serve their current and future financial needs. In the assessment process, they compared the APR along with various fees and potential charges.

Josh and Pam are also learning about various actions that might be useful if they encounter credit troubles. Their discussions with friends and money management advisers provided expanded knowledge of credit counseling and bankruptcy alternatives.

Questions

1. List other actions that the Brocks might consider to reduce the cost of using credit.

2. What information sources might be useful when comparing various sources of credit?

3. Explain ways in which *Personal Financial Planner* sheets 30 and 31 could be useful to the Brocks.

8

Consumer Purchasing Strategies and Legal Protection

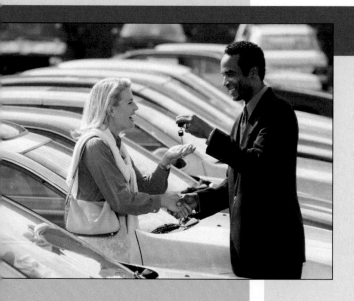

Digital Study Tools

Online Learning Center Study Tools for This Chapter

- Multiple-choice quiz
- Flashcards
- eLearning sessions
- Crossword puzzle
- Personal Finance Online: Consumer Purchase Decisions: Housing and Automobiles

Student CD Study Tools for This Chapter

- Self-study software
- Narrated PowerPoint
- Personal financial planning software: Worksheets 32–39

Key Concept

Wise buying combines understanding personal needs and wants with research to obtain relevant information about purchase alternatives. Unplanned and careless buying will reduce your long-term financial security. Impulse buying activities of a few dollars a week can cost you thousands of dollars in just a couple of years.

Learning Objectives

1 Identify strategies for effective consumer buying.

2 Implement a process for making consumer purchases.

3 Identify steps to take to resolve consumer problems.

4 Evaluate the legal alternatives available to consumers.

Online Car Buying

Mackenzie enters the auto "showroom" with a click of the mouse. Recently, she realized that the repair costs for her 11-year-old car were accelerating. So Mackenzie decided to start shopping online. She decides to start her Internet *stroll* for a vehicle by searching for small and mid-sized SUVs.

Her friends suggested that Mackenzie look at more than one type of vehicle. She was reminded that comparable models are available from various auto manufacturers.

In her online car-buying process, MacKenzie next did a price comparison. She obtained more than one price quote by using various online sources.

As a result of this experience, Mackenzie prepared an overview of her online car-buying experiences:

Online Car Buying Action	Online Activities	Web Sites Consulted
Gather information	• Review available vehicle models and options. • Evaluate operating costs and safety features.	autos.msn.com www.consumerreports.org www.caranddriver.com www.motortrend.com
Compare prices	• Identify specific make, model, and features desired. • Locate availability and specific price in your geographic area.	www.autosite.com www.edmunds.com www.kbb.com www.nada.com
Finalize purchase	• Make payment or financing arrangements. • Conduct in-person inspection. • Arrange for delivery.	www.autobytel.com www.autonation.com www.autoweb.com www.carsdirect.com

Mackenzie's next step was to make her final decision. After selecting what she plans to buy, she could finalize the purchase online and then take delivery at a local dealer. In recent years, less than 3 percent of car buyers actually purchased vehicles over the Internet, but that number is increasing. Car-buying experts strongly recommend that you make a personal examination of the vehicle before taking delivery.

QUESTIONS

What Actions Should Be Taken?

1. Based on Mackenzie's experiences, what benefits and drawbacks are associated with online car buying?
2. What additional actions might Mackenzie consider before buying a motor vehicle?

What about Your Situation?

3. Describe some of your online shopping experiences.
4. What do you consider to be the benefits and drawbacks of shopping online for motor vehicles and other items?

Learn More Online

Based on a Web search, obtain additional information to guide consumers when researching, comparing, and purchasing a motor vehicle online.

Consumer Buying Activities

Objective 1

Identify strategies for effective consumer buying.

FINANCIAL IMPLICATIONS OF CONSUMER DECISIONS

Every person making personal financial decisions is a consumer. Regardless of age, income, or household situation, we all use goods and services. Daily buying decisions involve a trade-off between current spending and saving for the future.

Various economic, social, and personal factors affect daily buying habits (see Exhibit 8–1). These factors are the basis for spending, saving, investing, and achieving personal financial goals. In very simple terms, the only way you can have long-term financial security is to not spend all of your current income. In addition, as Exhibit 8–1 shows, overspending leads to misuse of credit and financial difficulties.

Throughout your life, your buying decisions reflect many influences. You should consider opportunity costs to maximize the satisfaction you obtain from available financial resources. Commonly overlooked trade-offs when buying include

- Paying a higher price over time by using credit to buy items that you need now.
- Buying unknown, possibly poor-quality brands that are less expensive.

Exhibit 8–1

Consumer buying influences and financial implications

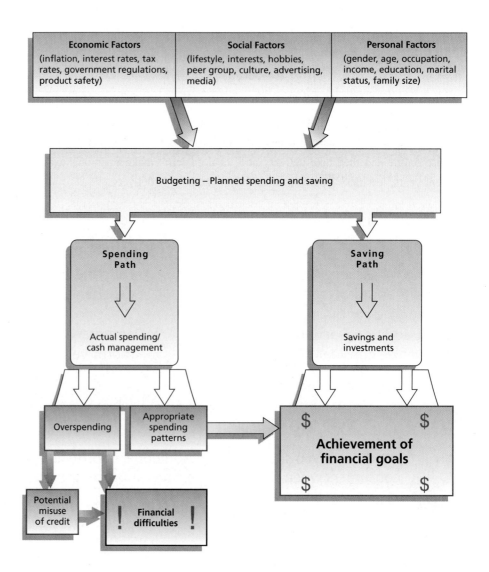

Economic Factors (inflation, interest rates, tax rates, government regulations, product safety)	Social Factors (lifestyle, interests, hobbies, peer group, culture, advertising, media)	Personal Factors (gender, age, occupation, income, education, marital status, family size)

Budgeting – Planned spending and saving

Spending Path → Actual spending/cash management

Saving Path → Savings and investments

Overspending

Appropriate spending patterns

Potential misuse of credit → ! **Financial difficulties** !

$ $ **Achievement of financial goals** $ $

- Selecting brands that may be difficult to service or repair.
- Ordering by mail or online, which saves time and money but may make it harder to return, replace, or repair purchases.
- Taking time and effort to comparison-shop to save money and obtain better after-sale service.

Your buying decisions reflect many aspects of your personality, life situation, values, and goals. Combine this fact with the complexity of the marketplace, and you can see that most purchase decisions require analysis.

PRACTICAL PURCHASING STRATEGIES

Comparison shopping is the process of considering alternative stores, brands, and prices. In contract, **impulse buying** is unplanned purchasing, which can result in financial problems. Several buying techniques are commonly suggested for wise buying.

impulse buying Unplanned buying.

TIMING PURCHASES   Certain items go on sale the same time each year. You can obtain bargains by buying winter clothing in mid- or late winter, or summer clothing in mid- or late summer. Many people save by buying holiday items and other products at reduced prices in late December and early January.

Weather reports and other news can also help you plan your purchasing. A crop failure can quickly result in higher prices for certain food products. Changing economic conditions and political difficulties around the world may result in higher prices and reduced supplies of certain products. Awareness of such situations can help you buy when prices are relatively low.

STORE SELECTION   Your decision to use a particular retailer is probably influenced by location, price, product selection, and services available. Competition and technology have changed retailing with superstores, specialty shops, and online buying. This expanded shopping environment provides consumers with greater choice, potentially lower prices, and the need to carefully consider buying alternatives.

One alternative is the **cooperative,** a nonprofit organization whose member–owners may save money on certain products or services. As discussed in Chapter 5, a credit union is an example of a financial services cooperative. Food cooperatives, usually based in a community group or church, buy grocery items in large quantities. The savings on these bulk purchases are passed on to the co-op's members in the form of lower food prices. Cooperatives have also been organized to provide less expensive child care, recreational equipment, health care, cable television, and burial services.

cooperative A nonprofit organization whose member–owners may save money on certain products or services.

BRAND COMPARISON   Food and other products come in various brands. *National-brand* products are highly advertised items available in many stores. You are probably familiar with brands such as Green Giant, Nabisco, Del Monte, Kellogg's, Kraft, Sony, Kodak, Tylenol, and Gap. Brand-name products are usually more expensive than nonbrand products, but they offer a consistency of quality for which people are willing to pay.

Store-brand and *private-label* products, sold by one chain of stores, are low-cost alternatives to famous-name products. These products have labels that identify them with a specific retail chain, such as Safeway, Kroger, A&P, Osco, Walgreen's, and Wal-Mart. Since store-brand products are frequently manufactured by the same companies that produce brand-name counterparts, these lower-cost alternatives allow consumers to save money. Private-label and store-brand items can result in extensive savings over time.

DID YOU KNOW?

Rebate redemption rates generally range from 5 percent to 80 percent, depending on the value of the rebate. Many rebates are denied due to not following instructions (missing the deadline) or not including all required items, such as a receipt, the UPC code, or the rebate form. If a rebate asks for the original receipt, don't send a photocopy.

ANALYZING CONSUMER PURCHASES

UNIT PRICING

The process for calculating and using the unit price involves the following steps:

1. Determine the common unit of measurement, such as ounces, pounds, gallons, or number of sheets (for items such as paper towels and facial tissues).

2. Divide the price by the number of common units; for example, an 8-ounce package of breakfast cereal selling for $1.52 has a unit price of 19 cents per ounce, while an 11-ounce package costing $1.98 has a unit price of 18 cents per ounce.

3. Compare the unit prices for various sizes, brands, and stores to determine the best buy for your situation.

Remember, the package with the lowest unit price may not be the best buy for you since it may contain more food than you would use before spoilage occurs.

NET PRESENT VALUE OF A CONSUMER PURCHASE

The time value of money (see Chapter 1) may be used to evaluate the financial benefits of buying home appliances and other items. For example, when you purchase a washing machine and a clothes dryer, the money you save by not driving to and using a laundromat could be considered a cash *inflow* (since money not going out is like money coming in). The cost of the appliances would be the current cash *outflow*. If the appliances have an expected life of 10 years, the *net present value* calculations might be as shown below. You can use this calculation format to assess the financial benefits of a consumer purchase by comparing the cost savings achieved by the purchase over time with the current price of the item purchased.

Step 1.	Estimated amount saved on weekly washing and drying at laundromat:	
	$4.75 times 52 weeks	$ 247.00
	Savings from not driving to laundromat: 6 miles a week at 15 cents a mile times 52 weeks	46.80
	Less: Estimated cost of hot water and electricity to operate appliances at home	−13.80
	Total annual savings	$ 280.00
Step 2.	Multiply annual savings by the present value of a series (Exhibit 1–8D in Chapter 1 or Exhibit 1–D in the appendix to Chapter 1) for 3 percent over 10 years (3 percent is the average expected return from a savings account)	8.53
		2,388.40
Step 3.	Subtract the cost of the washing machine and the clothes dryer.	−875.00
	The result is the net present value of the savings obtained by buying the appliances.*	$1,513.40

*A negative net present value would indicate that the financial aspects of the purchase are not desirable.

open dating Information about freshness or shelf life found on the package of a perishable product.

unit pricing The use of a standard unit of measurement to compare the prices of packages of different sizes.

Coupons are available online at **www.coolsavings.com, www.centsoff.com,** and **www.couponsurfer.com.**

LABEL INFORMATION Certain label information is helpful; however, other information is nothing more than advertising. Federal law requires that food labels contain information. Product labeling for appliances includes information about operating costs, to assist you in selecting the most energy-efficient models. **Open dating** describes the freshness or shelf life of a perishable product. Phrases such as "Use before May 2007" or "Not to be sold after October 8" appear on most grocery items.

PRICE COMPARISON **Unit pricing** uses a standard unit of measurement to compare the prices of packages of different sizes. To calculate the unit price, divide the price by the number of units of measurement, such as ounces, pounds, gallons, or number of sheets (for items such as paper towels and facial tissues). Then, compare the unit prices for various sizes, brands, and stores.

Coupons and rebates also provide better pricing for wise consumers. A family saving about $8 a week on their groceries by using coupons will save $416 over a year and $2,080 over five years (not counting interest). A **rebate** is a partial refund of the price of a product.

When comparing prices, remember that

- More store convenience (location, hours, sales staff) usually means higher prices.
- Ready-to-use products have higher prices.
- Large packages are usually the best buy; however, compare using unit pricing.
- "Sale" may not always mean saving money.

Exhibit 8–2 provides a summary of various wise-buying actions.

Online shopping and information sources provide consumers with convenience.

rebate A partial refund of the price of a product.

Exhibit **8-2**

Wise buying techniques: a summary

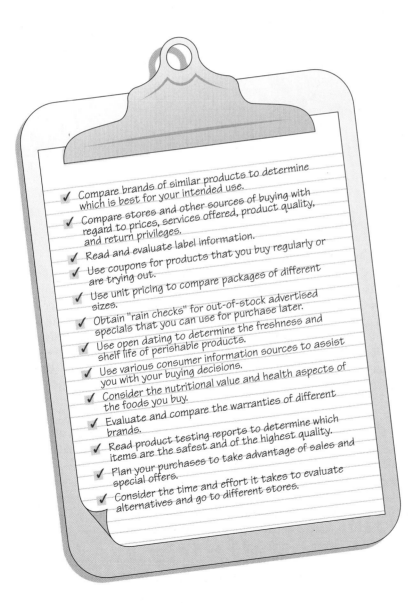

- ✔ Compare brands of similar products to determine which is best for your intended use.
- ✔ Compare stores and other sources of buying with regard to prices, services offered, product quality, and return privileges.
- ✔ Read and evaluate label information.
- ✔ Use coupons for products that you buy regularly or are trying out.
- ✔ Use unit pricing to compare packages of different sizes.
- ✔ Obtain "rain checks" for out-of-stock advertised specials that you can use for purchase later.
- ✔ Use open dating to determine the freshness and shelf life of perishable products.
- ✔ Use various consumer information sources to assist you with your buying decisions.
- ✔ Consider the nutritional value and health aspects of the foods you buy.
- ✔ Evaluate and compare the warranties of different brands.
- ✔ Read product testing reports to determine which items are the safest and of the highest quality.
- ✔ Plan your purchases to take advantage of sales and special offers.
- ✔ Consider the time and effort it takes to evaluate alternatives and go to different stores.

Financial Planning for Life's Situations

COMMON CONSUMER MYTHS

The National Association of Consumer Agency Administrators recently identified a list of misconceptions among consumers. These common myths include the following:

- "I can return my car within three days of purchase." While many people believe this (including many lawyers), there is no cooling-off period for motor vehicles.

- "My credit report information is confidential." Although wrongfully obtaining another person's credit report is a crime, there are many ways the information can be legally distributed. Recently enacted federal laws allow corporate affiliates to share most information.

- "My creditors can't call me at work." In most states, creditors (but not third-party debt collectors) can call—days, nights, weekends, and holidays—and write until the debts are repaid.

- "You can't repossess my car; it's on private property." While state laws differ, the general rule is that repossession cannot occur if it involves force, a breach of the peace, or entry into a dwelling. Vehicles in driveways and unlocked garages are usually fair game.

- "An auto lease is like a rental; if I have problems with the car or problems paying, I can just bring it back." Most leases require payments for the duration of the contract. Early termination often results in various additional charges.

- "If I lose my credit cards, I'm liable for purchases." Credit card companies perpetuate this myth in an attempt to sell "credit card protection" coverage. Federal laws limit charges on lost or stolen cards to $50. Most national credit card companies will not charge the $50 if the consumer makes a good-faith effort to notify the lender quickly of lost or stolen cards.

- "It says right here that I've won; it must be true." Fake prize notifications continue to become more convincing. Some consumers actually go to the company office to try to pick up their prizes.

Source: "Ten Top Consumer Law 'Urban Myths,'" National Association of Consumer Agency Administrators, 1010 Vermont Ave., NW, #514, Washington, DC 20005; 202–347–7395; www.nacaanet.org.

WARRANTIES

warranty A written guarantee from the manufacturer or distributor of a product that specifies the conditions under which the product can be returned, replaced, or repaired.

Sheet 32
Unit pricing worksheet

Most products come with some guarantee of quality. A **warranty** is a written guarantee from the manufacturer or distributor that specifies the conditions under which the product can be returned, replaced, or repaired. An *express warranty,* usually in written form, is created by the seller or manufacturer and has two forms: the full warranty and the limited warranty. A *full warranty* states that a defective product can be fixed or replaced during a reasonable amount of time. A *limited warranty* covers only certain aspects of the product, such as parts, or requires the buyer to incur part of the costs for shipping or repairs. An *implied warranty* covers a product's intended use or other basic understandings that are not in writing. For example, an implied *warranty of title* indicates that the seller has the right to sell the product. An implied *warranty of merchantability* guarantees that the product is fit for the ordinary uses for which it is intended: A toaster must toast bread, and a stereo must play CDs or tapes. Implied warranties vary from state to state.

USED-CAR WARRANTIES The Federal Trade Commission (FTC) requires businesses that sell used cars to place a buyer's guide sticker in the windows of cars for sale. This disclosure must state whether the car comes with a warranty and, if so, what protection the dealer will provide. If no warranty is offered, the car is sold "as is" and the dealer assumes no responsibility for any repairs, regardless of any oral claims.

About one-half of all the used cars sold by dealers come without a warranty, and if you buy such a car, you must pay for any repairs needed to correct problems. Be sure to get in writing any promises made by the salesperson.

The buyer's guide required by the FTC encourages you to have the used car inspected by a mechanic and to get all promises in writing. You also receive a list of the

14 major systems of an automobile and some of
the major problems that may occur in these systems. This list can be helpful in comparing the vehicles and warranties offered by different dealers.
FTC used-car regulations do not apply to vehicles
purchased from private owners.

Information on the used-car buyer's guide of the
Federal Trade Commission may be obtained at
www.ftc.gov.

While a used car may not have an *express war-
ranty,* most states have *implied warranties* that protect basic rights of the used-car buyer.
An implied warranty of merchantability means the product is guaranteed to do what it is
supposed to do. The used car is guaranteed to run—at least for awhile!

NEW-CAR WARRANTIES   New-car warranties provide buyers with an assurance of quality. These warranties vary in the time, mileage, and parts they cover. The
main conditions of a new-car warranty are (1) coverage of basic parts against defects;
(2) power train coverage for the engine, transmission, and drive train; and (3) the corro-
sion warranty, which usually applies only to holes due to rust, not to surface rust. Other
important conditions of a warranty are a statement regarding whether the warranty is
transferable to other owners of the car and details about the charges, if any, that will be
made for major repairs, in the form of a *deductible.*

SERVICE CONTRACTS   A **service contract** is an agreement between a business and a consumer to cover the repair costs of a product. Frequently called *extended
warranties,* they are not warranties. For a fee, they insure the buyer against losses due
to the cost of certain repairs. Automotive service contracts can cover repairs not included in the manufacturer's warranty. Service contracts range from $400 to over
$1,000; however, they do not always include everything you might expect. These con-
tracts usually cover failure of the engine cooling system; however, some contracts exclude coverage of such failures if caused by overheating.

Because of costs and exclusions, service contracts may not be a wise financial decision. You can minimize your concern about expensive repairs by setting aside a fund of
money to pay for them. Then, if you need repairs, the money to pay for them will be
available.

service contract An
agreement between a business
and a consumer to cover the
repair costs of a product.

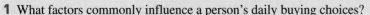

CONCEPT CHECK 8-1 ✔

1 What factors commonly influence a person's daily buying choices?
2 How are daily buying decisions related to overall financial planning?
3 What types of brands are commonly available to consumers?
4 In what situations can comparing prices help in purchasing decisions?
5 How does a service contract differ from a warranty? What rights do pur-
chasers of products have even if no written warranty exists?

Action Application   Conduct a survey regarding brand loyalty. For what products are people most brand loyal? What factors (price, location, information) may
influence their selection of another brand?

Major Consumer Purchases:
Buying Motor Vehicles

Objective 2

Shopping decisions should be based on a specific decision-making process. Exhibit 8–3
presents effective steps for purchasing a motor vehicle.

Implement a process for
making consumer purchases.

Exhibit 8-3

A research-based approach for purchasing a motor vehicle

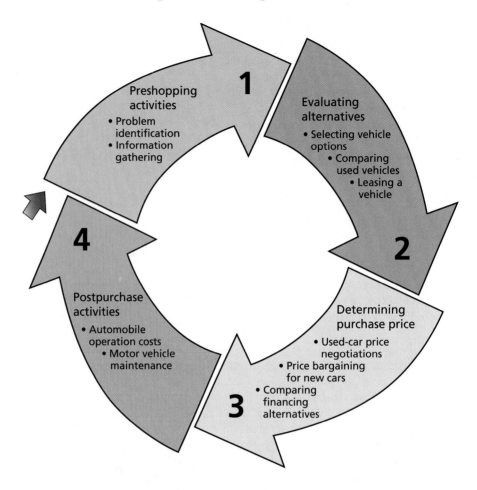

1 Preshopping activities
- Problem identification
- Information gathering

2 Evaluating alternatives
- Selecting vehicle options
- Comparing used vehicles
- Leasing a vehicle

3 Determining purchase price
- Used-car price negotiations
- Price bargaining for new cars
- Comparing financing alternatives

4 Postpurchase activities
- Automobile operation costs
- Motor vehicle maintenance

PHASE 1—PRESHOPPING ACTIVITIES

Sheet 33
Consumer purchase comparison

First, define your needs and obtain relevant product information. These activities are the foundation for buying decisions to help you achieve your goals.

PROBLEM IDENTIFICATION   Effective decision making should start with an open mind. Some people always buy the same brand when another brand at a lower price would also serve their needs or when another brand at the same price may provide better quality. A narrow view of the problem is a weakness in problem identification. You may think the problem is "I need to have a car," when the real problem is "I need transportation."

Consumers face an extensive number of buying choices each day.

INFORMATION GATHERING   Information is power. The better informed you are, the better buying decisions you will make. Some people spend little time gathering and evaluating buying information. At the other extreme are people who spend much time obtaining consumer information. While information is necessary for wise purchasing, too much information can create confusion and frustration. Common information sources include:

- *Personal contacts* allow you to learn about product performance, brand quality, and prices from others.
- *Business organizations* offer advertising, product labels, and packaging that provide information about price, quality, and availability.

- *Media information* (television, radio, newspapers, magazines, Web sites) can provide valuable with purchasing advice.

- *Independent testing organizations* provide information about the quality of products and services, as Consumers Union does each month in *Consumer Reports.*

Underwriters Laboratories (UL) tests products for electrical and fire safety. Items with the UL symbol provide consumers with an assurance that the product has met safety standards.

- *Government agencies,* local, state, and federal, provide publications, toll-free telephone numbers, Web sites, and community programs.

- *Online sources* offer extensive information and shopping suggestions. When buying an automobile, the Internet can be a valuable tool. Basic information about car buying may be obtained at www.edmunds.com. www.caranddriver.com, www.autoweb.com, www.autoconnect.com, and carpoint.msn.com. Consumers Union (www.ConsumerReports.org) offers a computerized car cost data service. Finally, car-buying services, such as www.acscorp.com, www.autobytel.com, and www.autoadvisor.com, allow you to order your vehicle online.

PHASE 2—EVALUATION OF ALTERNATIVES

Most purchasing decisions have several acceptable alternatives. Ask yourself: Is it possible to delay the purchase or to do without the item? Should I pay for the item with cash or buy it on credit? Which brands should I consider? How do the price, quality, and service compare at different stores? Is it possible to rent the item instead of buying it? Considering such alternatives will result in more effective purchasing decisions.

Sheet 34 Current and future transportation needs

Research shows that prices can vary for all types of products. For a camera, prices may range from under $200 to well over $500. The price of aspirin may range from less than $1 to over $3 for 100 five-grain tablets. While differences in quality and attributes may exist among the cameras, the aspirin are the same in quantity and quality.

Many people view comparison shopping as a waste of time. While this may be true in some situations, comparison shopping can be beneficial when: (1) buying expensive or complex items; (2) buying items that you purchase often; (3) comparison shopping can be done easily, such as with advertisements, catalogs, or online; (4) different sellers offer different prices and services; and (5) product quality or prices vary greatly.

SELECTING VEHICLE OPTIONS
Optional equipment for cars may be viewed in three categories: (1) *mechanical devices* to improve performance, such as a larger engine, the transmission, power steering, power brakes, and cruise control; (2) *convenience options,* including power seats, air conditioning, stereo systems, power locks, rear window defoggers, and tinted glass; and (3) *aesthetic features* that add to the vehicle's visual appeal, such as metallic paint, special trim, and upholstery.

COMPARING USED VEHICLES
The average used car costs about $10,000 less than the average new car. Common sources of used vehicles include:

- New-car dealers offer late-model vehicles and may give you a warranty, which usually means higher prices than at other sources.

- Used-car dealers usually have older vehicles. Warranties, if offered, will be limited. However, lower prices may be available.

- Individuals selling their own cars can be a bargain if the vehicle was well maintained. Few consumer protection regulations apply to private-party sales. Caution is suggested.

CONSUMER BUYING MATRIX

Buying alternatives may be evaluated on the basis of personal values and goals; available time and money; costs and benefits; and specific needs with regard to product size, quality, quantity, and features. Presented here is a buying matrix that may be used to evaluate alternatives.

Item _Notebook Computer_

Information Sources/Comments _Consumer magazine/brand C slow compared to others tested; Friend/brand B performs well_

Attribute	Weight	Alternatives					
		Brand A Price $1,325		Brand B Price $1,200		Brand C Price $1,050	
		Rating (1-10)	Weighted Score	Rating (1-10)	Weighted Score	Rating (1-10)	Weighted Score
Step 2 →							
● Features	.3	6	1.8	8	2.4	10	3
● Performance	.4	9	3.6	7	2.8	5	2
● Design	.1	8	.8	8	.8	7	.7
● Warranty	.2	9	1.8	6	1.2	4	.8
■ Totals	1.0	●	8.0	●	7.2	●	6.5

Step 1 (Attribute rows: Features, Performance, Design, Warranty)
Step 4 (Totals)
Step 3

In this example, a consumer is using the following steps to evaluate the purchase of one of three brands of notebook computers.

Step 1.
Identify attributes such as features, performance, design, and warranty, and assign a weight based on the importance of each attribute.

Step 2.
Select the brands to be evaluated.

Step 3.
Rate (from 1 to 10) each brand based on the attributes identified in step 1. Multiply the rating number by the weight. For example, in this example, brand A received a rating of 6 for "features," giving a weighted score of 1.8 (6 × .3).

Step 4.
Total and assess the results. Besides this numeric evaluation, consider other factors such as price, store reputation, and your personal situation.

As you research a consumer purchase, identify the attributes that are important to you. Helpful sources for this task are friends who own the product, salespeople, periodicals such as *Consumer Reports,* and various Web sites. The specific attributes will vary depending on the product or service. When buying a cordless telephone, for example, you might consider sound quality, ring loudness, number memory, and the range of use. You might assess a microwave oven on the basis of size, ease of operation, power settings, and exterior finish. And you are likely to select a provider of services based on training, experience, and reputation.

- Auctions and dealers sell automobiles previously owned by businesses, auto rental companies, and government agencies.

- Used-car superstores, such as CarMax, offer a large inventory of previously owned vehicles.

- Online used-car businesses, such as www.dealernet.com and www.americasautomall.com.

Certified, preowned (CPO) vehicles are nearly new cars that come with the original manufacturer's guarantee of quality. The rigorous inspection and repair process means a higher price than other used vehicles. CPO programs were originally created to create demand for the many low-mileage vehicles returned at the end of a lease.

The appearance of a used car can be deceptive. A well-maintained engine may be inside a body with rust; a clean, shiny exterior may conceal major operational problems. Therefore, conduct a used-car inspection as outlined in Exhibit 8–4. Have a trained and trusted mechanic of *your* choice check the car to estimate the costs of potential repairs. This service will help you avoid surprises.

LEASING A MOTOR VEHICLE   *Leasing* is a contractual agreement with monthly payments for the use of an automobile over a set time period, typically three, four, or five years. At the end of the lease term, the vehicle is usually returned to the leasing company.

The main advantages of leasing include (1) only a small cash outflow may be required for the security deposit, whereas buying can require a large down payment; (2) monthly lease payments are usually lower than monthly financing payments; (3) the lease agreement provides detailed records for business purposes; and (4) you are usually able to obtain a more expensive vehicle, more often.

> **DID YOU KNOW?**
>
> Every year, over 450,000 people buy used vehicles with mileage gauges rolled back. According to the National Highway Traffic Safety Administration, consumers pay an average of $2,336 more than they should for vehicles with fraudulent mileage totals.

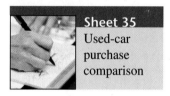

Sheet 35
Used-car purchase comparison

Exhibit **8–4**   Checking out a used car

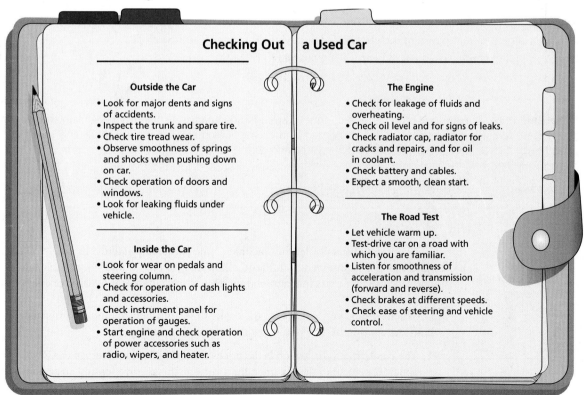

Checking Out a Used Car

Outside the Car
- Look for major dents and signs of accidents.
- Inspect the trunk and spare tire.
- Check tire tread wear.
- Observe smoothness of springs and shocks when pushing down on car.
- Check operation of doors and windows.
- Look for leaking fluids under vehicle.

Inside the Car
- Look for wear on pedals and steering column.
- Check for operation of dash lights and accessories.
- Check instrument panel for operation of gauges.
- Start engine and check operation of power accessories such as radio, wipers, and heater.

The Engine
- Check for leakage of fluids and overheating.
- Check oil level and for signs of leaks.
- Check radiator cap, radiator for cracks and repairs, and for oil in coolant.
- Check battery and cables.
- Expect a smooth, clean start.

The Road Test
- Let vehicle warm up.
- Test-drive car on a road with which you are familiar.
- Listen for smoothness of acceleration and transmission (forward and reverse).
- Check brakes at different speeds.
- Check ease of steering and vehicle control.

BUYING VERSUS LEASING AN AUTOMOBILE

To compare the costs of purchasing and leasing a vehicle, use the following framework.

Purchase Costs	Example	Your Figures	Leasing Costs	Example	Your Figures
Total vehicle cost, including sales tax ($22,000)			Security deposit ($370)		
Down payment (or full amount if paying cash)	$ 2,000	$____	Monthly lease payments: $300 × 48-month length of lease	$17,760	$____
Monthly loan payment: $469.70 × 48-month length of financing (this item is zero if vehicle is not financed)	22,545	____	Opportunity cost of security deposit: $300 security deposit × 4 years × 3 percent	36	____
Opportunity cost of down payment (or total cost of the vehicle if it is bought for cash): $2,000 × 4 years of financing/ ownership × 3 percent	240	____	End-of-lease charges (if applicable)*	800	____
Less: Estimated value of vehicle at end of loan term/ ownership period	−6,000	____	Total cost to lease	$18,596	____
Total cost to buy	$18,785	____			

*With a closed-end lease, charges for extra mileage or excessive wear and tear; with an open-end lease, end-of-lease payment if appraised value is less than estimated ending value.

AVOIDING LEASE TRAPS

When considering a lease agreement for a motor vehicle, beware of the following common pitfalls:

- Not knowing the total cost of the agreement, including the cost of the vehicle, not just the monthly payment.
- Making a larger up-front payment than is required or paying unnecessary add-on costs.
- Negotiating the monthly payment rather than the capitalized cost of the vehicle.
- Not having the value of any trade-in vehicle reflected in the lease.
- Signing a contract you don't understand.

Compare monthly payments and other terms among several leasing companies. People have been known to pay over $24,000 to lease a vehicle worth only $20,000 at the start of the lease agreement. Comparison of leasing terms is available at Web sites such as www.leasesource.com and www.carinfo.com.

Major drawbacks of leasing include (1) no ownership interest in the vehicle; (2) a need to meet requirements similar to qualifying for credit; and (3) possible additional costs incurred for extra mileage, certain repairs, turning the car in early, or even a move to another state.

When leasing, you arrange for the dealer to sell the vehicle through a financing company. As a result, be sure you know the true cost, including

1. The *capitalized cost,* which is the price of the vehicle. The average car buyer pays about 92 percent of the list price for a vehicle; the average leasing arrangement has a capitalized cost of 96 percent of the list price.

2. The *money factor,* which is the interest rate being paid on the capitalized cost.

3. The monthly payment and number of payments.

4. The *residual value* is the expected value of the vehicle at the end of the lease.

After the final payment, you may choose to return, keep, or sell the vehicle. If the current market value is greater than the residual value, you may be able to sell it for a profit. If the residual value is less than the market value (which is the typical case), returning the vehicle to the leasing company is usually the best decision.

Sheet 36
Buying vs. leasing an automobile

PHASE 3—DETERMINING PURCHASE PRICE

Once you've done your research and evaluations, other activities and decisions will be necessary. Products such as real estate or automobiles may be purchased using price negotiation. Negotiation may also be used in other buying situations to obtain a lower price or additional features. Two vital factors in negotiation are (1) having all the necessary information about the product and buying situation and (2) dealing with a person who has the authority to give you a lower price or additional features, such as the owner or store manager.

USED-CAR PRICE NEGOTIATION   Begin to determine a fair price by checking newspaper ads for the prices of comparable vehicles. Other sources of current used-car prices are *Edmund's Used Car Prices* (www.edmunds.com) and the *Kelley Blue Book* (www.kbb.com).

A number of factors influence the basic price of a used car. The number of miles the car has been driven, along with features and options, affects price. A low-mileage car will have a higher price than a comparable car with high mileage. The condition of the vehicle and the demand for the model also affect price.

PRICE BARGAINING FOR NEW CARS   An important new-car price information source is the *sticker price,* printed on the vehicle with the suggested retail price. This label presents the base price of the car with costs of added features. The dealer's cost, or *invoice price,* is an amount less than the sticker price. The difference between the sticker price and the dealer's cost is the range available for negotiation. This range is larger for full-size, luxury cars with more options; subcompacts usually do not have a wide negotiation range. Information about dealer's cost is available from sources such as *Edmund's New Car Prices* (www.edmunds.com) and *Consumer Reports* (www. ConsumerReports.org).

Set-price dealers use no-haggling car selling, with prices presented to be accepted or rejected as stated. *Car-buying services* are businesses that help buyers obtain a specific new car at a reasonable price. Also referred to as an *auto broker,* these businesses offer desired models with options for prices ranging between $50 and $200 over the dealer's cost. First, the auto broker charges a small fee for price information on desired models. Then, if you decide to buy a car, the auto broker arranges the purchase with a dealer near your home.

To prevent confusion in determining the true price of the new car, do not mention a trade-in vehicle until the cost of the new car has been settled. Then ask how much the dealer is willing to pay for your old car. If the offer price is not acceptable, sell the old car on your own. A typical negotiating conversation might go like this:

Customer: "I'm willing to give you $15,600 for the car. That's my top offer."
Auto salesperson: "Let me check with my manager." After returning, "My manager says $16,200 is the best we can do."
Customer: (who should be willing to walk out at this point): "I can go to $15,650."
Auto salesperson: "We have the car you want, ready to go. How about $15,700?"

If the customer agrees, the dealer has gotten $100 more than the customer's "top offer!"

Other sales techniques you should avoid include:

- *Lowballing,* when quoted a very low price that increases when add-on costs are included at the last moment.
- *Highballing,* when offered a very high amount for a trade-in vehicle, with the extra amount made up by increasing the new-car price.
- When asked "How much can you afford per month?" be sure to also ask how many months.
- "A small deposit will hold this vehicle for you." Never leave a deposit unless you are ready to buy a vehicle or are willing to lose that amount.
- "Your price is only $100 above our cost." However, many hidden costs may have been added in to get the dealer's cost.
- Beware of sales agreements with preprinted amounts. Cross out numbers you believe are not appropriate for your purchase.

COMPARING FINANCING ALTERNATIVES   You may pay cash; however, most people buy cars on credit. Auto loans are available from banks, credit unions, consumer finance companies, and other financial institutions. Many lenders will *preapprove* you for a certain loan amount, which separates financing from negotiating the price of the car. Until the new-car price is set, you should not indicate that you intend to use the dealer's credit plan.

The lowest interest rate or the lowest payment does not necessarily mean the best credit plan. Also consider the loan length. Otherwise, after two or three years, the value of your car may be less than the amount you still owe; this situation is referred to as *upside-down* or *negative equity.* If you default on your loan or sell the car at this time, you will have to pay the difference. A larger down payment can reduce this risk.

Automobile manufacturers frequently offer opportunities for low-interest financing. They may offer rebates at the same time, giving buyers a choice between a rebate and a low-interest loan. Carefully compare low-interest financing and the rebate (see Exhibit 8–5). Special rebates are sometimes offered to students, teachers, credit union members, real estate agents, and other groups.

The annual percentage rate (APR) is the best indicator of the true cost of credit. The federal Truth in Lending law requires that the APR be clearly stated in advertising and other communications. Low payments may seem to be a good deal, but they mean you will be paying longer and your total finance charges will be higher. Consider both the APR and the finance charge when comparing credit terms of different lenders. Additional auto financing information may be obtained at www.bankrate.com, www.carfinance.com, and www.quicken.com.

Sheet 37
Comparing cash and credit for major purchases

Exhibit **8–5**

Comparing rebates and special financing: an example

	AUTO MANUFACTURER FINANCING	FINANCIAL INSTITUTION FINANCING (BANK, CREDIT UNION)
ANNUAL PERCENTAGE RATE	2.9%	6.0%
VEHICLE PRICE	$17,500	$17,500
DOWN PAYMENT	$ 2,500	$ 2,500
MANUFACTURER'S REBATE	—	$ 1,500
LOAN AMOUNT	$15,000	$13,500
TERM OF LOAN	60 MONTHS	60 MONTHS
MONTHLY PAYMENT	$ 269.00	$ 262.00
TOTAL PAYMENT (NOT INCLUDING DOWN PAYMENT)	$16,140	$15,720
TOTAL SAVINGS USING FINANCIAL INSTITUTION, $420		

PHASE 4—POSTPURCHASE ACTIVITIES

Maintenance and ownership costs are associated with most purchases. Correct use can result in improved performance and fewer repairs. When you need repairs not covered by a warranty, follow a pattern similar to that used when making the original purchase. Investigate, evaluate, and negotiate a variety of servicing options.

In the past, when major problems occurred with a new car and the warranty didn't solve the difficulty, many consumers lacked a course of action. As a result, all 50 states and the District of Columbia enacted *lemon laws* that require a refund for the vehicle after the owner has made repeated attempts to obtain servicing. These laws apply to situations in which a person has made four attempts to get the same problem corrected or situations in which the vehicle has been out of service for more than 30 days within 12 months of purchase or the first 12,000 miles. The terms of the state laws vary; for details go to www.lemonlawamerica.com.

AUTOMOBILE OPERATION COSTS
Over your lifetime, you can expect to spend more than $200,000 on automobile-related expenses. Your driving costs will vary based on two main factors: the size of your automobile and the number of miles you drive. These costs involve two categories:

Fixed Ownership Costs	Variable Operating Costs
Depreciation	Gasoline and oil
Interest on auto loan	Tires
Insurance	Maintenance and repairs
License, registration, taxes, and fees	Parking and tolls

The largest fixed expense associated with a new automobile is *depreciation,* the loss in the vehicle's value due to time and use. Since money is not paid out for depreciation, many people do not consider it an expense. However, this decreased value is a cost that owners incur. Well-maintained vehicles and certain high-quality, expensive models, such as BMW and Lexus, depreciate at a slower rate.

Costs such as gasoline, oil, and tires increase with the number of miles driven. Planning expenses is easier if the number of miles you drive is fairly constant. Unexpected trips and vehicle age will increase such costs.

Awareness of the total cost of owning and operating an automobile can help your overall financial planning. An automobile expense record should include the dates of odometer readings. Recording your mileage each time you buy gas will allow you to compute fuel efficiency. For tax-deductible travel, the Internal Revenue Service requires specific information about the mileage, locations, dates, and purposes of trips. Use a notebook to keep records of regular operating expenses such as gas, oil, parking, and tolls. Also, consider keeping files on maintenance, repair, and replacement part costs. Finally, keep a record of infrequent expenditures such as insurance payments and license and registration fees.

Sheet 38
Auto ownership and operation costs

MOTOR VEHICLE MAINTENANCE
People who sell, repair, or drive automobiles for a living stress the importance of regular care. While owner's manuals and articles suggest mileage or time intervals for certain servicing, more frequent oil changes or tune-ups can minimize major repairs and maximize vehicle life. Exhibit 8–6 offers suggested maintenance areas to consider.

Exhibit 8-6

Extended vehicle life with
proper maintenance

- Get regular oil changes.
- Check fluids (brake, power steering, transmission).
- Inspect hoses and belts for wear.
- Get a tune-up (new spark plugs, fuel filter, air filter) 12,000–15,000 miles.
- Check and clean battery cables and terminals.
- Check tire pressures regularly.

- Check spark plug wires after 50,000 miles.
- Flush radiator and service transmission every 25,000 miles.
- Keep lights, turn signals, and horn in good working condition.
- Check muffler and exhaust pipes.
- Check tires for wear; rotate tires every 7,500 miles.
- Check condition of brakes.

AUTOMOBILE SERVICING SOURCES   The various businesses that offer automobile maintenance and repair service include:

- Car dealers provide a service department with a wide range of car care services. Service charges at a car dealer may be higher than those of other repair businesses.
- Service stations can provide convenience and reasonable prices for routine maintenance and repairs. However, the number of full-service stations has declined in recent years.
- Independent auto repair shops can service your vehicle at fairly competitive prices. Since the quality of these repair shops can vary, talk with previous customers.
- Mass merchandise retailers, such as Sears and Wal-Mart, may emphasize the sale of tires and batteries, as well as brakes, oil changes, and tune-ups.
- Specialty shops offer brakes, tires, automatic transmissions, and oil changes at a reasonable price with fast service.

Regular maintenance can reduce future repair costs and increase the vehicle's life.

To avoid unnecessary expenses, be aware of the common repair frauds presented in Exhibit 8–7. Remember to deal with reputable auto service businesses. Be sure to get a written, detailed estimate in advance as well as a detailed, paid receipt for the service completed. Studies of consumer problems consistently rank auto repairs as one of the top consumer ripoffs. Many people avoid problems and minimize costs by working on their own vehicles.

CONCEPT CHECK 8-2

1 What are the major sources of consumer information?
2 What actions are appropriate when buying a used car?
3 When might leasing a motor vehicle be appropriate?
4 What maintenance activities could increase the life of your vehicle?

Action Application Compare the prices charged by different automotive service locations for a battery, tune-up, oil change, and tires.

Resolving Consumer Complaints

Objective 3

Identify steps to take to resolve consumer problems.

Most customer complaints result from defective products, low quality, short product lives, unexpected costs, deceptive pricing, and poor repairs. These problems are most commonly associated with the following products and services:

Exhibit **8-7**

Common auto repair scams

The majority of automobile servicing sources are fair and honest. Sometimes, however, consumers waste dollars when they fall prey to the following tricks:

- When checking the oil, the attendant puts the dipstick only partway down and then shows you that you need oil.

- An attendant cuts a fan belt or punctures a hose. Watch carefully when someone checks under your hood.

- A garage employee puts some liquid on your battery and then tries to convince you that it is leaking and you need a new battery.

- Removing air from a tire instead of adding air to it can make an unwary driver open to buying a new tire or paying for an unneeded patch on a tire that is in perfect condition.

- The attendant puts grease near a shock absorber or on the ground and then tells you your present shocks are dangerous and you need new ones.

- You are charged for two gallons of antifreeze with a radiator flush when only one gallon was put in.

Dealing with reputable businesses and a basic knowledge of your automobile are the best methods of avoiding deceptive repair practices.

- Motor vehicle purchases, repairs
- Mail-order purchases
- Magazine subscriptions
- Work-at-home, business opportunities
- Landlord–tenant relations
- Investment scams
- Telemarketing
- Computers, home electronics
- Health clubs, diet programs
- Online auctions
- Home remodeling, home repairs

- Credit card promotions, practices
- Contests, sweepstakes, phony prizes
- Dry cleaning, laundry companies
- Travel services, travel packages
- Rent-to-own companies
- Slamming (switching phone service to another carrier without permission)
- Cramming (telephoning customers for services never ordered)
- Spamming (unsolicited e-mail messages)

Federal consumer agencies estimate annual consumer losses from fraudulent business activities at $10 billion to $40 billion for telemarketing and mail order, $3 billion for credit card fraud and credit "repair" scams, and $10 billion for investment swindles.

Most people do not anticipate or have problems with their purchases. Since problems do arise, however, it's best to be prepared for them. The process for resolving differences between buyers and sellers includes the steps presented in Exhibit 8–8. To help ensure success when you make a complaint, keep a file of receipts, names of people you talked to, dates of attempted repairs, copies of letters you wrote, and costs incurred. Written documents can help to resolve a problem in your favor. An automobile owner kept detailed records and receipts for all gasoline purchases, oil changes, and repairs. When a warranty dispute occurred, the owner was able to prove proper maintenance and received a refund for the defective vehicle.

Consumer scams can be very creative. For various examples, see Financial Planning for Life's Situations: Beware of These Common (and Not So Common) Frauds on page 258.

BEWARE OF THESE COMMON (AND NOT SO COMMON) FRAUDS

Foreign Scams. Many people have received a letter or e-mail from a Nigerian bank or other foreign source promising all or part of $30 million. The letter requested the recipient's bank account number so the money could be transferred. There was another catch: To receive the fortune, the recipient would have to pay between $15,000 and $1 million in taxes—in advance! Fourteen people, none of them U.S. residents, sent checks totaling about $20 million.

Disaster-Related Fraud. A variety of scams surfaced after the September 11 tragedy. Phony charities solicited funds for families of the victims. Fraudulent telemarketers told consumers that donations would be made to recovery and rescue efforts if they purchased magazines or other products.

Credit Repair. Companies offer to clean up the credit reports of consumers with poor credit histories. After paying hundreds of dollars, consumers find out these companies can do nothing to improve their credit reports.

Automatic Debit Scams. Automatic debiting of your checking account can be a legitimate payment method. However, many fraudulent telemarketers use this technique to take money from a person's checking account. *Do not* give out checking account information unless you are familiar with the company.

Fraudulent Diet Products and Health Claims. Americans spend an estimated $6 billion a year on fraudulent diet products such as "The Amazing Skin Patch Melts Away Body Fat," "Lose Weight While You Sleep," and "Lose All the Weight You Can for Just $99." Spotting false health claims may be as easy as being cautious of phrases such as "scientific breakthrough," "miraculous cure," "exclusive product," "secret ingredient," or "ancient remedy." Common health fraud schemes occur in the areas of cancer, HIV-AIDS, and arthritis.

Magazine Subscription Scams. Beware of telephone sales pitches for "free," "prepaid," or "special" magazine offers. One consumer received a call stating that the company had prepaid seven magazine subscriptions for 60 months. All that would be required would be a "small" weekly service fee of $3.43. The magazines would cost nearly $900 over five years.

Toll-Free Scams. Calls to 800, 888, and 877 numbers are almost always free. However, there are some exceptions. Companies that provide audio entertainment or information services may charge for calls to toll-free numbers, but only if they follow the Federal Trade Commission's 900-number rule.

Bogus "Campus Card." Consumer protection offices in 20 states warned about "campus cards" available for a $25 fee. These prepaid debit cards were being promoted as "required" for many services and privileges at whichever college or university the student decided to attend. While the company appeared to be affiliated with the school, it was actually a for-profit business.

Internet Pyramid Scheme. The Council of Better Business Bureaus issued an alert about an "international program of wealth distribution" called "Pentagono" or "Future Strategies International." The plan, based in Italy and promoted on the Internet, advertised that consumers could receive up to $116,000 for an initial investment of about $120. Participants were asked to purchase three certificates and sell those to three other people. For everyone to profit in the scheme, there had to be a never-ending supply of potential and willing participants.

Phishing. This high-tech scam uses spam or pop-up messages to deceive you into revealing your credit card number, bank account information, Social Security number, passwords, or other sensitive information. Never disclose personal data online to a questionable source.

Pharming. Pharming involves computer viruses or worms. Malicious software or an e-mail attachment plants the virus or worm in the user's computer or in a server that directs traffic on the Internet. Even if you type in the correct address of a Web site, the software sends you to a bogus one. Computer users are encouraged to keep antivirus and anti-spyware programs up to date.

Fraudulent Hotline. The attorney general in Missouri obtained a court order to shut down a fraudulent consumer telemarketing "hotline" that was being used to divert inquiries and complaints about a vacation company from legitimate consumer protection agencies.

Further information about various frauds and deceptive business practices is available at www.fraud.org and www.ftc.gov.

STEP 1: RETURN TO PLACE OF PURCHASE

Most consumer complaints are resolved at the original sales location. Since most business firms are concerned about their reputations, they usually honor legitimate com-

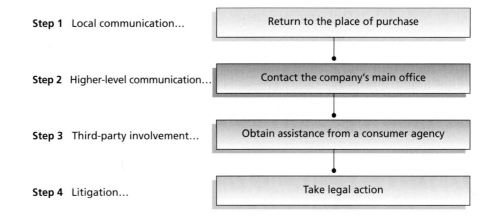

Exhibit **8-8**

Suggested steps for resolving consumer complaints

Step 1 Local communication...   Return to the place of purchase

Step 2 Higher-level communication...   Contact the company's main office

Step 3 Third-party involvement...   Obtain assistance from a consumer agency

Step 4 Litigation...   Take legal action

plaints. As you talk with the salesperson, customer service person, or store manager, avoid yelling, threatening a lawsuit, or demanding unreasonable action. In general, a calm, rational, yet persistent approach is recommended.

STEP 2: CONTACT COMPANY HEADQUARTERS

Express your dissatisfaction to the corporate level if a problem is not resolved at the local store. A letter or e-mail like the one in Exhibit 8–9 may be appropriate. You can obtain addresses of companies you may wish to contact from the *Consumer's Resource Handbook,* published by the federal government; Standard & Poor's *Register of Corporations, Directors, and Executives;* Dun & Bradstreet's *Million Dollar Directory;* or other reference books available at your library. The Web sites of major companies also offer a method to communicate with these organizations; see www.hoovers.com.

Most consumer complaints are resolved by contacting the place of purchase.

You can obtain a company's consumer hotline number by using a directory of toll-free numbers or calling 1-800-555-1212, the toll-free information number. Many companies print the toll-free hotline number on product packages. Studies reveal that most consumer complaints made to company toll-free numbers are resolved on the first contact.

STEP 3: OBTAIN CONSUMER AGENCY ASSISTANCE

If you do not receive satisfaction from the company, several consumer, business, and government organizations are available. These include national organizations specializing in issues such as automobile safety, health care, and nutrition, and local organizations that handle complaints, conduct surveys, and provide legal assistance.

The Better Business Bureaus are a network of offices that resolve complaints against local merchants. Better Business Bureaus are sponsored by local business organizations, and companies are not obligated to respond to the complaints. The Better Business Bureau in your area can be of value before you make a purchase. Its files will tell you about the experiences of others who dealt with a firm with which you are planning to do business.

Mediation involves the use of a third party to settle grievances. In mediation, an impartial person—the *mediator*—tries to resolve a conflict between a customer and a business through discussion and negotiation. Mediation is a nonbinding process. It can save time and money compared to other dispute settlement methods.

mediation The attempt by an impartial third party to resolve a difference between two parties through discussion and negotiation.

Exhibit **8-9**   Sample complaint letter

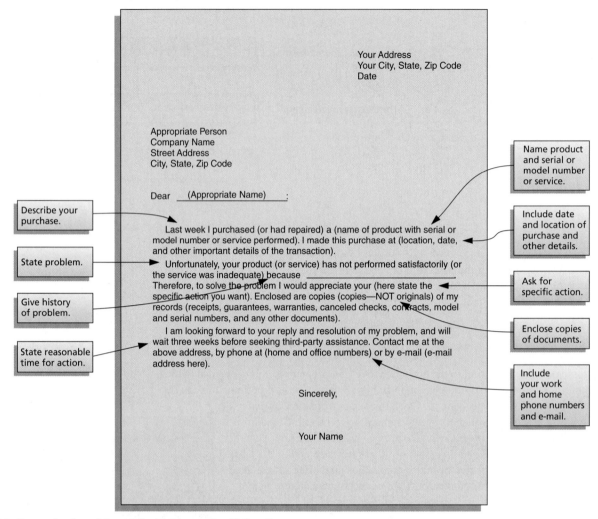

Note: Keep copies of your letter and all related documents and information.
Source: *Consumer's Resource Handbook* (www.pueblo.gsa.gov).

arbitration The settlement of a difference by a third party whose decision is legally binding.

DID YOU KNOW?

An AARP study reports that just over half of consumers (52 percent) said they would go back to the source when they have a complaint about a product or service. A third (34 percent) would report the company to the Better Business Bureau, while fewer than one in five (17 percent) said they would contact the manufacturer or company headquarters.

Arbitration is the settlement of a difference by a third party—the *arbitrator*—whose decision is legally binding. After both sides agree to the arbitration process, each side presents its case to the arbitrator. Arbitrators are selected from volunteers trained for this purpose. Most major automobile manufacturers and many industry organizations have arbitration programs to resolve consumer complaints.

A vast network of government agencies is also available. Problems with local restaurants or food stores may be handled by a city or county health department. Every state has agencies to handle problems involving deceptive advertising, fraudulent business practices, banking, insurance companies, and utility rates.

Federal agencies available to help resolve consumer difficulties and provide information are listed in Appendix B. When you are uncertain about which agency to use, contact your U.S. representative in Washington, DC. This office can help channel your concern to the appropriate consumer protection agency.

STEP 4: TAKE LEGAL ACTION

The next section discusses various legal actions available to resolve consumer problems.

CONCEPT CHECK 8-3

1 What are common causes of consumer problems and complaints?

2 How can most consumer complaints be resolved?

3 How does arbitration differ from mediation?

Action Application Conduct online research to determine the most common sources of consumer complaints.

Legal Options for Consumers

What should you do if all of the previously mentioned avenues of action fail to bring about a resolution of a consumer complaint? One of the following legal actions may be appropriate.

Objective 4

Evaluate the legal alternatives available to consumers.

SMALL CLAIMS COURT

Every state has a court system to settle minor disagreements. In **small claims court,** a person may file a claim involving amounts below a set dollar limit. The maximum varies from state to state, ranging from $500 to $10,000; most states have a limit of between $1,500 and $3,000. The process usually takes place without a lawyer, although in many states attorneys are allowed in small claims court.

To make best use of small claims court, experts suggest the following tips:

- Become familiar with the court's location, procedures, and filing fees (usually from $5 to $50).

- Observe other cases to learn more about the process.

- Present your case in a polite, calm, and concise manner.

- Submit evidence such as photographs, contracts, receipts, and other documents.

- Use witnesses who can testify on your behalf.

While obtaining a favorable judgment in small claims court may be easy, the collection process is frequently difficult. Since the defendant may not appear, you may have to pay a sheriff to serve a court order or use a collection agency to get your money.

DID YOU KNOW?

Without realizing it, many consumers sign contracts with provisions that stipulate arbitration as the method to resolve disputes. As a result, consumers face various risks, including rules vastly different from a jury trial, higher costs for the arbitrator's time, and selection of an arbitrator by the defendant.

small claims court A court that settles legal differences involving amounts below a set limit and employs a process in which the litigants usually do not use a lawyer.

class-action suit A legal action taken by a few individuals on behalf of all the people who have suffered the same alleged injustice.

CLASS-ACTION SUITS

Occasionally a number of people have the same complaint—for example, people who were injured by a defective product, customers who were overcharged by a utility company, or travelers who were cheated by a tour business. Such people may qualify for a class-action suit. A **class-action suit** is a legal action taken by a few individuals on behalf of all the people who have suffered the

Interested in learning more about small claims court? Go to **www.nolo.com** or **www.lawguru.com**.

same alleged injustice. These people, called a *class,* are represented by one lawyer or by a group of lawyers working together.

Once a situation qualifies as a class-action suit, all of the affected parties must be notified of the suit. At this point, a person may decide not to participate in the class-action suit and instead file an individual lawsuit. If the court ruling is favorable to the class, the funds awarded may be divided among all the people involved, used to reduce rates in the future, or assigned to public funds for government use. Recent class-action suits included auto owners who were sold unneeded replacement parts for their vehicles and a group of investors who sued a brokerage company for unauthorized buy-and-sell transactions that resulted in high commission charges.

DID YOU KNOW?

A class-action suit can be expensive. After winning $2.19 in back interest, Dexter J. Kamilewicz also noted a $91.33 "miscellaneous deduction" on his mortgage escrow account. This charge was his portion for lawyers he never knew he hired to win a class-action suit.

Sheet 39
Legal services cost comparison

legal aid society One of a network of publicly supported community law offices that provide legal assistance to consumers who cannot afford their own attorney.

USING A LAWYER

When small claims court or a class-action suit is not appropriate, you may seek the services of an attorney. The most common sources of available lawyers are referrals from people you know, the local branch of the American Bar Association, and telephone directory listings. Lawyers advertise in newspapers, on television, and in other media. Be aware that impressive advertising does not mean competent legal counsel.

Deciding when to use a lawyer is difficult. In general, straightforward legal situations such as appearing in small claims court, renting an apartment, or defending yourself on a minor traffic violation usually do not require legal counsel. But for more complicated matters, such as writing a will, settling a real estate purchase, or suing for injury damages caused by a product, it is probably wise to obtain the services of an attorney.

When selecting a lawyer, you should consider several questions. Is the lawyer experienced in your type of case? Will you be charged on a flat fee basis, at an hourly rate, or on a contingency basis? Is there a fee for the initial consultation? How and when will you be required to make payment for services?

OTHER LEGAL ALTERNATIVES

The cost of legal services can be a problem, especially for low-income consumers. A **legal aid society** is one of a network of publicly supported community law offices that provide legal assistance to people who cannot afford their own attorney. These community agencies provide this assistance at a minimal cost or without charge.

Prepaid legal services provide unlimited or reduced-fee legal assistance for a set fee. Some of these programs provide certain basic services, such as telephone consultation and preparation of a simple will, for an annual fee ranging from $50 to $150 or more. More complicated legal assistance requires an additional fee, usually at a reduced rate. Other programs do not charge an advance fee but allow members to obtain legal services at discount rates. In general, prepaid legal programs are designed to prevent minor troubles from becoming complicated legal problems. Legal questions may be researched online at www.nolo.com.

PERSONAL CONSUMER PROTECTION

While many laws, agencies, and legal tools are available to protect your rights, none will be of value unless you use them. (See Financial Planning for Life's Situations: Is It Legal? on page 263) Consumer protection experts suggest that to prevent being taken in by deceptive business practices, you should

IS IT LEGAL?

The following situations are common problems for consumers. How would you respond to the question at the end of each situation?

	Yes	No
1. A store advertised a bottle of shampoo as "the $1.79 size, on sale for 99¢" If the store never sold the item for $1.79 but the manufacturer's recommended price was $1.79, was this a legitimate price comparison?	___	___
2. You purchase a stereo system for $650. Two days later, the same store offers the same item for $425. Is this legal?	___	___
3. You receive an unordered sample of flower seeds in the mail. You decide to plant them to see how well they will grow in your yard. A couple of days later, you receive a bill for the seeds. Do you have to pay for the seeds?	___	___
4. A store has a "going out of business sale—everything must go" sign in its window. After six months, the sign is still there. Is this a deceptive business practice?	___	___
5. A 16-year-old injured while playing ball at a local park is taken to a hospital for medical care. The parents refuse to pay the hospital since they didn't request the service. Can the parents be held legally responsible for the charges?	___	___
6. You purchase a shirt for a friend. The shirt doesn't fit, but when you return it to the store, you are offered an exchange since the store policy is no cash refunds. Is this legal?	___	___
7. A manufacturer refuses to repair a motorcycle that is still under warranty. The manufacturer can prove that the motorcycle was used improperly. If this is true, must the manufacturer honor the warranty?	___	___
8. An employee of a store incorrectly marks the price of an item at a lower amount. Is the store obligated to sell the item at the lower price?	___	___

Circumstances, interpretations of the law, and store policies, as well as state and local laws, can affect the above situations. The generally accepted answers are *no* for 1, 3, 7, and 8; *yes* for 2, 4, 5, and 6.

1. Do business only with reputable companies with a record of satisfying customers.

2. Avoid signing contracts and other documents you do not understand.

3. Be cautious about offerings that seem too good to be true—they probably are!

4. Compare the cost of buying on credit with the cost of paying cash; also, compare the interest rates the seller offers with those offered by a bank or a credit union.

5. Avoid rushing to get a good deal; successful con artists depend on impulse buying.

CONCEPT CHECK 8-4

1 In what types of situations would small claims court and class-action suits be helpful?

2 Describe some situations in which you might use the services of a lawyer.

Action Application Interview someone who has had a consumer complaint. What was the basis of the complaint? What actions did the person take? Was the complaint resolved in a satisfactory manner?

SUMMARY OF OBJECTIVES

Objective 1

Identify strategies for effective consumer buying.
Various economic, social, and personal factors influence daily buying decisions. Overspending and poor money management are frequent causes of overuse of credit and other financial difficulties. Timing purchases, comparing stores and brands, using label information, computing unit prices, and evaluating warranties are common strategies for effective purchasing.

Objective 2

Implement a process for making consumer purchases.
A research-based approach to consumer buying involves (1) preshopping activities, such as problem identification and information gathering; (2) evaluating alternatives; (3) determining the purchase price; and (4) postpurchase activities, such as proper operation and maintenance.

Objective 3

Identify steps to take to resolve consumer problems.
Most consumer problems can be resolved by following these steps: (1) Return to the place of purchase; (2) contact the company's main office; (3) obtain assistance from a consumer agency; and (4) take legal action.

Objective 4

Evaluate the legal alternatives available to consumers.
Small claims court, class-action suits, the services of a lawyer, legal aid societies, and prepaid legal services are legal means for handling consumer problems that cannot be resolved through communication with the business involved or through the help of a consumer protection agency.

KEY TERMS

arbitration   260

class-action suit   261

cooperative   243

impulse buying   243

legal aid society   262

mediation   259

open dating   244

rebate   244

service contract   247

small claims court   261

unit pricing   244

warranty   246

FINANCIAL PLANNING PROBLEMS

1. *Analyzing Influences on Consumer Buying.* Use advertisements, recent news articles, and personal observations to point out the economic, social, and personal factors that influence the purchases of people in the following life situations. (Obj. 1)

   a. A retired person.

   b. A single parent with children ages 5 and 9.

   c. A dual-income couple with no children.

   d. A person with a dependent child and a dependent parent.

2. *Calculating Future Value.* You can purchase a service contract for all of your major appliances for $160 a year. If the appliances are expected to last for 10 years and you earn 5 percent on your savings, what would be the future value of the amount you will pay for the service contract? (Obj. 1)

3. *Comparing Buying Alternatives.* Tammy Monahan is considering the purchase of a home entertainment center. The product attributes she plans to consider and the weights she gives to them are as follows:

Portability	.1
Sound projection	.6
Warranty	.3

   Tammy related the brands as follows:

	Portability	Sound Projection	Warranty
Brand A	6	8	7
Brand B	9	6	8
Brand C	5	9	6

   Using the consumer buying matrix (p. 250), conduct a quantitative product evaluation rating for each brand. What other factors is Tammy likely to consider when making her purchase? (Obj. 2)

4. *Researching Consumer Purchases.* Using the consumer buying matrix (p. 250), analyze a consumer purchase you

plan to make sometime in the future. What factors affected the selection of the attributes and weights you chose for this purchase analysis? (Obj. 2)

5. *Calculating the Cost of Credit.* John Walters is comparing the cost of credit to the cash price of an item. If John makes a $60 down payment and pays $32 a month for 24 months, how much more will that amount be than the cash price of $685? (Obj. 2)

6. *Computing Unit Prices.* Calculate the unit price of each of the following items: (Obj. 2)

Item	Price	Size		Unit Price
Motor oil	$1.95	2.5	quarts	_____ cents/quart
Cereal	2.17	15	ounces	_____ cents/ounces
Canned fruit	0.89	13	ounces	_____ cents/ounces
Facial tissue	2.25	300	tissues	_____ cents/100 tissues
Shampoo	3.96	17	ounces	_____ cents/ounces

7. *Calculating the Present Value of a Consumer Purchase.* What would be the net present value of a microwave oven that costs $159 and will save you $68 a year in time and food away from home? Assume an average return on your savings of 4 percent for five years. (Obj. 2)

8. *Computing Net Present Value.* Use the feature Financial Planning Calculations: Analyzing Consumer Purchases (p. 244) to analyze a past or a future purchase. (Obj. 1)

9. *Comparing Automobile Purchases.* Based on financial and opportunity costs, which of the following do you believe would be the wiser purchase? (Obj. 2)

Vehicle 1: A three-year-old car with 45,000 miles, costing $6,700, and requiring $385 of immediate repairs.

Vehicle 2: A five-year-old car with 62,000 miles, costing $4,500, and requiring $760 of immediate repairs.

10. *Calculating Motor Vehicle Operating Costs.* Using Sheet 38 in the *Personal Financial Planner,* calculate the approximate yearly operating cost of the following vehicle. (Obj. 2)

Annual depreciation, $2,500

Annual mileage, 13,200

Current year's loan interest, $650

Miles per gallon, 24

Insurance, $680

License and registration fees, $65

Average gasoline price, $2.18 per gallon

Oil changes/repairs, $370

Parking/tolls, $420

FINANCIAL PLANNING ACTIVITIES

1. *Obtaining Consumer Information.* Using an Internet search, library resources, or a survey of acquaintances, determine the major factors people consider when (*a*) buying food, (*b*) selecting a store at which to shop, and (*c*) using information from advertisements. (Obj. 1)

2. *Comparing Consumer Information Sources.* Obtain a recent issue of *Consumer Reports* (or go to www.ConsumerReports.org) to evaluate and compare different brands of a product. Also obtain information on this product from people who sell this item and those who have recently purchased it. Compare the information received from these sources. (Obj. 2)

3. *Evaluating Consumer Information Sources.* Develop guidelines that consumers could use to evaluate different sources of consumer information (advertising, salespeople, friends, government publications, Internet sites). Consider the (*a*) objectivity, (*b*) accuracy, (*c*) clarity, and (*d*) usefulness of these sources. Prepare a video or other visual presentation to communicate your guidelines. (Obj. 2)

4. *Researching Consumer Information on the Internet.* Locate Web sites that would provide you with useful information when buying various consumer products. (Obj. 2)

5. *Comparing Used Cars.* Use Sheet 35 in the *Personal Financial Planner* to compare different sources of used motor vehicles. (Obj. 2)

6. *Searching the Internet for Transportation Information.* Using various search engines, identify Web sites that could assist consumers with evaluating and comparing automobile prices. (Obj. 2)

7. *Evaluating Motor Vehicle Leases.* Use Sheet 36 in the *Personal Financial Planner* to compare the costs of buying and leasing a motor vehicle. (Obj. 2)

8. *Identifying and Solving Consumer Problems.* Collect magazine or newspaper advertisements that appear to be "too good to be true." Why are these ads deceptive? Should government agencies take action against any of the companies presenting these ads? (Additional information about common frauds may be obtained at www. fraud.org.) (Obj. 3)

9. *Comparing Legal Services.* Prepare a survey of legal services available to students and others in your community. Use Sheet 39 in the *Personal Financial Planner* to compare the fees and services provided by lawyers and other sources of legal assistance. (Obj. 4)

INTERNET CONNECTION

Obtaining Consumer Protection Assistance

A variety of local, state, and federal government agencies provide consumer information and assistance. In addition, many other organizations also exist to provide consumer assistance. Conduct a Web search to locate a local, state, and federal agency or organization available to assist consumers.

Consumer Assistance Agency, Organization	Local (city or county) Agency	State Agency	Federal Agency
Name of agency, organization			
Phone			
Web address			
Main purpose, services provided			
Types of assistance provided; types of consumer problems			
Publications, or other information provided online			

FINANCIAL PLANNING CASE

As Amie Carver finished her workday, she realized that she needed a birthday gift for her mother. Her time and energy level did not allow store shopping. However, she knew of several online sites with items her mother would like.

A few months ago, the many online shopping Web sites overwhelmed Amie. But today she was able to locate three that would be useful. On one Web site (www.gifts-for-mom.com), Amie saw a sweater her mother would probably like. "This looks very nice," she thought. "And it's quite reasonably priced."

Amie placed an order online using her credit card. Within a week, she received it. But when she opened the package, she noticed the style of the sweater was different than it looked online. "Oh no, this isn't what I wanted," she thought.

Amie checked online to find out how to return the item. She discovered that she could send the sweater back for a refund. While the company would pay the return postage, Amie was not refunded the original shipping and handling charges.

Later that day, Amie saw a table lamp for sale online. "This is a nice gift for Mother," she thought. After putting the item in her online shopping cart, she received a message notice that the item would not be available for four to six weeks. Frustrated by her online and catalog shopping experiences, Amie was not sure what to do next.

With more than 60 percent of all Internet users buying something online, there will be problems. One study revealed that one in five survey respondents had a problem with online shopping. The two most common concerns were that they paid for something and didn't get it, or paid for something and got something different from what was expected. While consumers have a strong concern about being charged for something they never agreed to, only a small percentage of online shoppers have this problem.

When shopping online, consumer experts warn shoppers to consider all costs associated with the purchase and delivery. Some online shopping Web sites charge a "restocking" fee for an item that is returned. Most will also make the consumer pay for the shipping when returning a product. Studies also reveal that most shopping Web sites either do not include their return policies or hide them in the fine print.

Questions

1. What benefits and drawbacks are associated with online shopping?

2. Based on information at www.consumer.gov, describe advice that could help when shopping online.

3. What actions might a consumer take before making an online purchase?

4. Based on a Web search, obtain additional information on actions available to consumers who are dissatisfied with an online purchase or other buying situation.

VIDEO CASE

Mediation: The Courtroom Alternative

Legal action can be expensive and may not provide the results desired. While various legal alternatives are available to resolve financial and consumer problems, mediation can be appropriate in certain situations.

In the mediation process, the parties are allowed to present their cases without the services of a lawyer. The person hired to resolve a dispute usually charges a fee far less than the costs of using the court system. The time and cost savings associated with mediation are important benefits of this legal process.

Questions

1. What are benefits of mediation?

2. In what types of situations might the use of mediation be appropriate?

3. How do the three types of mediators differ in their approaches to resolving a dispute?

4. Conduct a Web search to obtain additional information about the use of mediation to resolve consumer and financial disputes.

YOUR PERSONAL FINANCIAL PLANNER IN ACTION

Comparison Shopping and Buying Motor Vehicles

Daily buying actions such as comparing prices, evaluating brands, and avoiding fraud allow you to wisely use resources for both current living expenses and long-term financial security.

Your Short-Term Financial Planning Activities	Resources
1. Compare the use of cash and credit, and various brands, for the purchase of a major consumer item you may need in the near future.	PFP Sheets 33, 37 www.ConsumerReports.org www.pricescan.com www.bbbonline.org
2. Conduct a unit pricing comparison at several stores.	PFP Sheet 32 www.consumer.gov
3. Determine current transportation needs related to new and used motor vehicles and compare buying and leasing options.	PFP Sheets 34, 35, 36 http://autoadvice.about.com www.centura.com/tools www.kbb.com www.leasesource.com

(Continued)

Your Long-Term Financial Planning Activities	
1. Determine buying guidelines for major purchases (appliances, furniture, home entertainment equipment). Identify brands, store locations, and savings plans to avoid buying on credit.	www.consumer.gov www.pueblo.gsa.gov www.consumerworld.org
2. Identify and compare various legal services available for use.	PFP Sheet 39 www.ftc.gov www.fraud.org www.nolo.com
3. Identify motor vehicles that would provide the lowest operating and insurance costs.	PFP Sheet 38 www.consumerreports.org www.autobytel.com www.carsafety.org

CONTINUING CASE

Purchasing Choices

Life Situation

Young married couple
Pam, 30
Josh, 32
Two children, ages 1 and 3

Financial Data

Monthly income	$3,600
Assets	$33,850
Living expenses	$3,125
Liabilities	$1,520

The Brocks now have two preschool-age children. Their household income has declined with Pam providing full-time care for the children. To compensate for their lower monthly income, Pam and Josh have cut back to only spend money on basics. As a result of this action, the Brocks have managed to pay down their liabilities over the past four years.

The Brocks are considering purchasing a second automobile. Currently, Pam must drive Josh to the train station (creating many inconveniences for her and the children) if she wants to use the car for various business and education activities.

Questions

1. What major factors could affect the Brocks' spending habits?

2. What transportation alternatives should the Brocks consider? If they decide that they need a second motor vehicle, how should they finance it?

3. Describe how various elements of *Personal Financial Planner* sheets 32–39 could be useful to the Brocks when making various purchasing decisions?

9 The Housing Decision: Factors and Finances

Digital Study Tools

Online Learning Center Study Tools for This Chapter

- Multiple-choice quiz
- Flashcards
- eLearning sessions
- Crossword puzzle
- Personal Finance Online: Consumer Purchase Decisions: Housing and Automobiles

Student CD Study Tools for This Chapter

- Self-study software
- Narrated PowerPoint
- Personal financial planning software: Worksheets 40–45

Key Concept

Selection of housing is affected by a person's financial situation, individual needs, and desired location. While many people take out a 30-year mortgage, paying off the loan faster can save thousands of dollars. In most situations, paying an additional $25 a month can shorten your loan by 8 years or more and save you over $10,000 in interest.

Learning Objectives

1 Evaluate available housing alternatives.

2 Analyze the costs and benefits associated with renting.

3 Implement the home-buying process.

4 Calculate the costs associated with purchasing a home.

5 Develop a strategy for selling a home.

The Paperless Home Purchase

When Jamie Covington bought her first home, she did so without ever meeting in person with a mortgage broker or the title insurance representative. She was one of the first home buyers to conduct her real estate transaction completely online.

The process started with viewing homes on Web sites of various real estate companies and those listed online with various newspapers in her area. Later, Jamie went out to see several of the properties she was considering. The financing process involved several online activities, including:

- The prequalification process to determine the amount of mortgage for which Jamie was eligible.
- Comparing mortgage rates among various lenders both in her area and around the country.
- The mortgage application process, in which Jamie was approved for her mortgage within a few hours.

The final negotiations involved a series of e-mail exchanges. Once the buyer and seller agreed on a price, next came the *closing,* which was conducted completely online. The bank providing Jamie's mortgage prepared the closing documents and sent them electronically over the Internet to the closing agent, who brought them up on a specially equipped computer screen.

Jamie signed the documents on the screen. The deed was scanned and delivered by computer image. All completed documents were forwarded to the appropriate parties, with Jamie receiving a CD-ROM with copies of all files.

The Electronic Signature in Global and National Commerce Act allowed this process to take place. This law recognizes an *electronic signature* as "an electronic sound, symbol, or process, attached to or logically associated with a contract or other record and executed or adopted by a person with the intent to sign the record."

The time needed for the postclosing process is also reduced. Recording the documents and issuing the title insurance policy usually takes 45 days. Online, the process was complete in a few days. This process can result in lower closing costs. Various financial experts estimate that online closings could save businesses and home buyers several hundred dollars.

QUESTIONS

What Actions Should Be Taken?

1. What are some possible concerns associated with the online home buying activities experienced by Jamie?
2. What actions would be appropriate by Jamie to minimize these potential concerns?

What about Your Situation?

3. How can online activities be used in the housing rental process?
4. What aspects of online home buying might be appropriate for your future use?

Learn More Online

Based on a Web search to obtain additional information on electronic home buying, what other advice would you offer when using the Internet for various phases of the home-buying process?

Housing Alternatives

Objective 1

Evaluate available housing alternatives.

As you walk around various neighborhoods, you are likely to see a variety of housing types. When you assess housing alternatives, you need to identify the factors that will influence your choice.

YOUR LIFESTYLE AND YOUR CHOICE OF HOUSING

While the concept of *lifestyle*—how you spend your time and money—may seem intangible, it materializes in consumer purchases. Every buying decision is a statement about your lifestyle. Your lifestyle, needs, desires, and attitudes are reflected in your choice of a place to live. For example, some people want a kitchen large enough for family gatherings. Career-oriented people may want a lavish bathroom or a home spa where they can escape the pressures of work. As you select housing, you might consider the alternatives in Exhibit 9–1.

While personal preferences are the foundation of a housing decision, financial factors will modify the final choice. A budget and other financial records discussed in Chapter 3 can help you evaluate your income, living costs, and other financial obligations to determine an appropriate amount for your housing expenses.

OPPORTUNITY COSTS OF HOUSING CHOICES

Although the selection of housing is usually based on life situation and financial factors, you should also consider what you might have to give up. While the opportunity costs of your housing decision will vary, some common trade-offs include

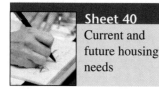

Sheet 40
Current and future housing needs

Exhibit **9–1**

Housing for different life situations

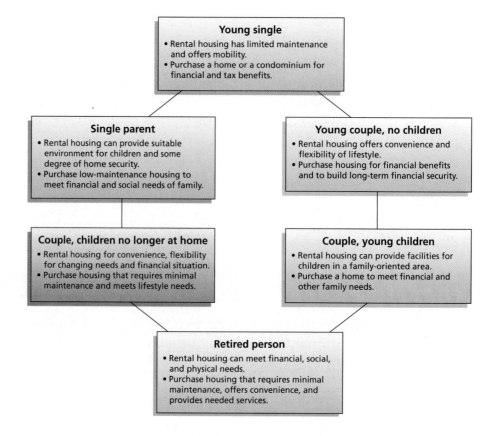

Young single
- Rental housing has limited maintenance and offers mobility.
- Purchase a home or a condominium for financial and tax benefits.

Single parent
- Rental housing can provide suitable environment for children and some degree of home security.
- Purchase low-maintenance housing to meet financial and social needs of family.

Young couple, no children
- Rental housing offers convenience and flexibility of lifestyle.
- Purchase housing for financial benefits and to build long-term financial security.

Couple, children no longer at home
- Rental housing for convenience, flexibility for changing needs and financial situation.
- Purchase housing that requires minimal maintenance and meets lifestyle needs.

Couple, young children
- Rental housing can provide facilities for children in a family-oriented area.
- Purchase a home to meet financial and other family needs.

Retired person
- Rental housing can meet financial, social, and physical needs.
- Purchase housing that requires minimal maintenance, offers convenience, and provides needed services.

- The interest earnings lost on the money used for a down payment on a home or the security deposit for an apartment.

- The time and cost of commuting to work when you live in an area that offers less expensive housing or more living space.

- The loss of tax advantages and equity growth when you rent a city apartment to be close to your work.

- The time and money you spend when you repair and improve a lower-priced home.

- The time and effort involved when you have a home built to your personal specifications.

For additional housing information from various government agencies, see Appendix B at the end of the book.

Like every other financial choice, a housing decision requires consideration of what you give up in time, effort, and money.

RENTING VERSUS BUYING HOUSING

Living in a mobile society affects the decision as to whether to rent or buy your housing. Your choice of residence should be analyzed based on lifestyle and financial factors. Exhibit 9–2 can help you assess various housing alternatives.

Sheet 41
Renting versus buying housing

For many young people, renting may be preferable for now. However, if you plan to live in the same area for several years and believe real estate prices will increase, owning your home should be considered.

Some people who are financially able to buy a home may choose to rent to avoid the time and money commitment required to maintain a house. If you continue to rent, be sure to invest your savings so you can easily buy a home should the situation arise. Long-term renting may also be appropriate for people not able to maintain a home because of physical limitations.

As you can see in the Financial Planning Calculations feature on page 275 the choice between renting and buying usually is not clear-cut. In general, renting is less costly in the short run, but home ownership usually has long-term financial advantages.

HOUSING INFORMATION SOURCES

As with other consumer purchases, housing information is available. Start your data search with basic resources such as this book and books available in libraries. Consult the real estate section of your newspaper for articles about renting, buying, financing, remodeling, and other housing topics. Other helpful information sources are friends, real estate agents, and government agencies (see Appendix B).

The Internet has become an important source of housing information. In addition to providing home-buying tips and mortgage rates, real estate and rental Web sites can be used to investigate available housing in an area.

CONCEPT CHECK 9-1

1 How does a person's employment and household situation influence the selection of housing?

2 What are some common opportunity costs associated with the selection of housing?

Action Application Based on personal observation and analysis of advertisements, prepare a list of various housing alternatives available in your geographic area.

Exhibit **9-2**

Evaluating housing
alternatives

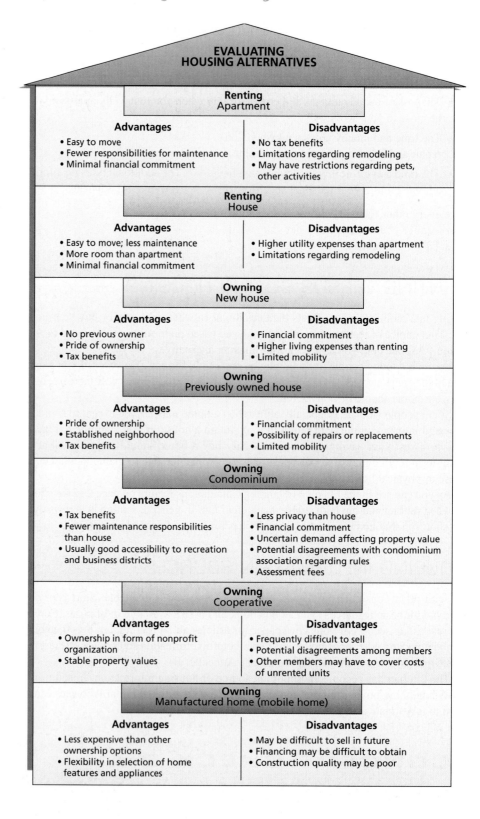

Renting Your Residence

Are you interested in a "2-bd. garden apt, a/c, crptg, mod bath, lndry, sec $850"? Not
sure? Translated, this means a two-bedroom garden apartment (at or below ground

Financial Planning Calculations

RENTING VERSUS BUYING YOUR PLACE OF RESIDENCE

Comparing the costs of renting and buying involves consideration of a variety of factors. The following framework and example provide a basis for assessing these two housing alternatives. The apartment in the example has a monthly rent of $700, and the home costs $85,000. A 28 percent tax rate is assumed.

Although the numbers in this example favor buying, remember that in any financial decision, calculations provide only part of the answer. You should also consider your needs and values and assess the opportunity costs associated with renting and buying.

	Example	Your Figures
Rental Costs		
Annual rent payments	$ 8,400	$_____
Renter's insurance	170	_____
Interest lost on security deposit (amount of security deposit times after-tax savings account interest rate)	80	_____
Total annual cost of renting	$ 8,650	_____
Buying Costs		
Annual mortgage payments	$10,500	_____
Property taxes (annual costs)	2,000	_____
Homeowner's insurance (annual premium)	400	_____
Estimated maintenance and repairs (1%)	850	_____
After-tax interest lost on down payment and closing costs	1,030	_____
Less (financial benefits of home ownership):		
Growth in equity	−264	=_____
Tax savings for mortgage interest (annual mortgage interest times tax rate)	−2,866	=_____
Tax savings for property taxes (annual property taxes times tax rate)	−560	=_____
Estimated annual appreciation (3%)*	−2,550	=_____
Total annual cost of buying	$ 8,540	_____

*This is a nationwide average; actual appreciation of property will vary by geographic area and economic conditions.

level) with air conditioning, carpeting, a modern bath, and laundry facilities. An $850 security deposit is required.

At some point in your life, you are likely to rent your place of residence. You may rent when you are first on your own or later in life when you want to avoid the activities required to maintain your own home. About 35 percent of U.S. households live in rental units.

As a tenant, you pay for the right to live in a residence owned by someone else. Exhibit 9–3 presents the activities involved in finding and living in a rental unit.

Objective 2

Analyze the costs and benefits associated with renting.

Exhibit 9-3

Housing rental activities

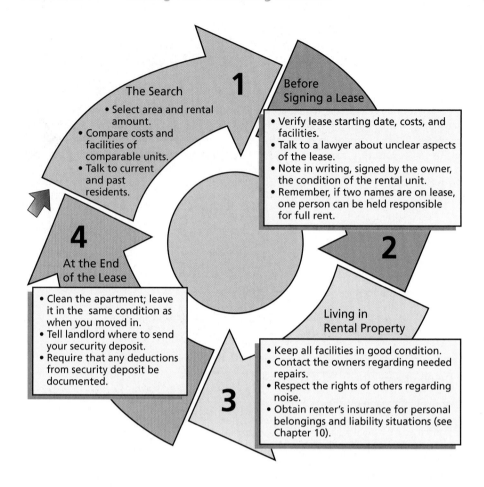

1

The Search

- Select area and rental amount.
- Compare costs and facilities of comparable units.
- Talk to current and past residents.

Before Signing a Lease

- Verify lease starting date, costs, and facilities.
- Talk to a lawyer about unclear aspects of the lease.
- Note in writing, signed by the owner, the condition of the rental unit.
- Remember, if two names are on lease, one person can be held responsible for full rent.

2

4

At the End of the Lease

- Clean the apartment; leave it in the same condition as when you moved in.
- Tell landlord where to send your security deposit.
- Require that any deductions from security deposit be documented.

Living in Rental Property

- Keep all facilities in good condition.
- Contact the owners regarding needed repairs.
- Respect the rights of others regarding noise.
- Obtain renter's insurance for personal belongings and liability situations (see Chapter 10).

3

SELECTING A RENTAL UNIT

An apartment is the most common type of rental housing. Apartments range from modern, luxury units with extensive recreational facilities to simple one- and two-bedroom units in quiet neighborhoods.

If you need more room, you should consider renting a house. The increased space will cost more, and you will probably have some responsibility for maintaining the property. If you need less space, you may rent a room in a private house.

The main sources of information on available rental units are newspaper ads, real estate and rental offices, and people you know. When comparing rental units, consider the factors presented in Exhibit 9–4.

Most people rent their housing at some stage in their lives.

ADVANTAGES OF RENTING

The three main advantages of renting are mobility, fewer responsibilities, and lower initial costs.

MOBILITY   Renting offers mobility when a location change is necessary or desirable. A new job, a rent increase, the need for a larger apartment, or the desire to live in a different community can make relocation necessary. Moving is easier when you are renting than when you own a home. After you have completed school and started your career, renting makes it easier for job transfers.

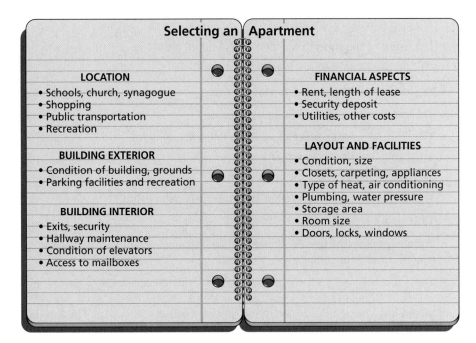

Exhibit 9–4

Selecting an apartment

FEWER RESPONSIBILITIES   Renters have fewer responsibilities than home-owners since they usually do not have to be concerned with maintenance and repairs. However, they are expected to do regular household cleaning. Renters also have fewer financial concerns. Their main housing costs are rent and utilities, while homeowners incur expenses related to property taxes, property insurance, and upkeep.

LOWER INITIAL COSTS   Taking possession of a rental unit is less expensive than buying a home. While new tenants usually pay a security deposit, a new home buyer is likely to have a down payment and closing costs of several thousand dollars.

DISADVANTAGES OF RENTING

Renting has few financial benefits, may impose a restricted lifestyle, and involves legal details.

FEW FINANCIAL BENEFITS   Renters do not enjoy the financial advantages homeowners do. Tenants cannot take tax deductions for mortgage interest and property taxes or benefit from the increased value of real estate. They are subject to rent increases over which they have little control.

RESTRICTED LIFESTYLE   Renters are generally limited in the types of activities they can pursue in their place of residence. Noise from a stereo system or parties may be monitored closely. Tenants are often subject to restrictions regarding pets and decorating the property.

LEGAL DETAILS   Most tenants sign a **lease,** a legal document that defines the conditions of a rental agreement. This document provides the following information:

- A description of the property, including the address.
- The name and address of the owner/landlord (the *lessor*).
- The name of the tenant (the *lessee*).

lease A legal document that defines the conditions of a rental agreement.

- The effective date of the lease.

- The length of the lease.

- The amount of the security deposit.

- The amount and due date of the monthly rent.

- The location at which the rent must be paid.

- The date and amount due of charges for late rent payments.

- A list of the utilities, appliances, furniture, or other facilities that are included in the rental amount.

- The restrictions regarding certain activities (pets, remodeling).

- The tenant's right to sublet the rental unit.

- The charges for damages or for moving out of the rental unit later (or earlier) than the lease expiration date.

- The conditions under which the landlord may enter the apartment.

Standard lease forms include conditions you may not want to accept. The fact that a lease is printed does not mean you must accept it as is. Negotiate with the landlord about lease terms you consider unacceptable.

Some leases give you the right to *sublet* the rental unit. Subletting may be necessary if you must vacate the premises before the lease expires. Subletting allows you to have another person take over rent payments and live in the rental unit.

Most leases are written, but oral leases are also valid. With an oral lease, one party must give a 30-day written notice to the other party before terminating the lease or imposing a rent increase.

A lease provides protection to both landlord and tenant. The tenant is protected from rent increases during the lease term unless the lease contains a provision allowing an increase. In most states, the tenant cannot be locked out or evicted without a court hearing. The lease gives the landlord the right to take legal action against a tenant for nonpayment of rent or destruction of property.

fyi

Signing a lease? Additional information may be obtained at **www.nolo.com**.

DID YOU KNOW?

Renter's insurance is one of the most overlooked expenses of apartment dwellers. Damage or theft of personal property (clothing, furniture, stereo equipment, jewelry) usually is not covered by the landlord's insurance policy.

COSTS OF RENTING

A *security deposit* is usually required when you sign a lease. This money is held by the landlord to cover the cost of any damages done to the rental unit during the lease period. The security deposit is usually one month's rent.

Several state and local governments require that the landlord pay interest on a security deposit. After you vacate the rental unit, your security deposit should be refunded within a reasonable time. Many states require that it be returned within 30 days of the end of the lease. If money is deducted from your security deposit, you have the right to an itemized list of the cost of repairs.

As a renter, you will incur other living expenses besides monthly rent. For many apartments, water is covered by the rent; however, other utilities may not be covered. If you rent a house, you will probably pay for heat, electricity, water, and telephone. When you rent, you should obtain insurance coverage for your personal property. Renter's insurance is discussed in Chapter 10.

Sheet 42
Apartment rental comparison

The Home-Buying Process

Many people dream of having a place of residence they can call their own. Home ownership is a common financial goal. Exhibit 9–5 presents the process for achieving this goal.

Objective 3

Implement the home-buying process.

STEP 1: DETERMINE HOME OWNERSHIP NEEDS

In the first phase of the home-buying process, you should consider the benefits and drawbacks of this major financial commitment. Also, evaluate different types of housing units and determine the amount you can afford.

EVALUATE OWNING YOUR PLACE OF RESIDENCE

What Are the Benefits of Home Ownership?   Whether you purchase a house, a condominium, or a manufactured home, you can enjoy the pride of ownership, financial benefits, and lifestyle flexibility of home ownership.

1. *Pride of ownership.* Having a place to call their own is a primary motive of many home buyers. Stability of residence and a personalized living location can be important.
2. *Financial benefits.* One financial benefit is the deductibility of mortgage interest and real estate tax payments for federal income taxes. A potential benefit is increases in the value of the property. Finally, homeowners in most states may be able to borrow against the equity in their homes. *Equity* is the home value less the amount owed on the mortgage.
3. *Lifestyle flexibility.* While renting gives you mobility, home ownership gives you more opportunity to express individuality. Homeowners have greater freedom than renters in decorating their dwellings and entertaining guests.

Various professionals are available to assist you when buying a home.

What Are the Drawbacks of Home Ownership?   The American dream of buying one's own home does not guarantee a glamorous existence. This investment can result in financial uncertainty, limited mobility, and higher living costs.

1. *Financial uncertainty.* Among the financial uncertainties associated with buying a home is obtaining money for a down payment. Obtaining mortgage financing may be a problem due to your personal situation or current economic conditions. Finally, changing property values in an area can affect your financial investment.

Exhibit **9-5**

The home-buying process

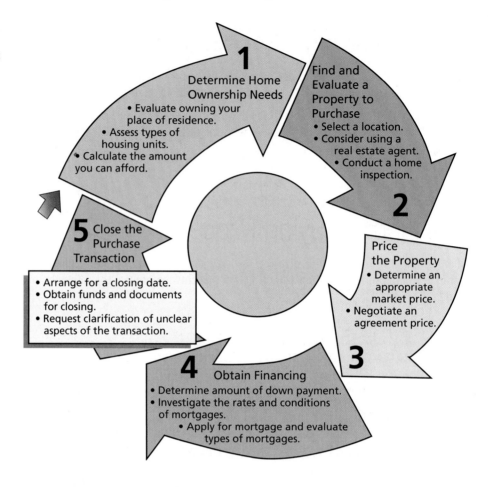

2. *Limited mobility.* Home ownership does not provide ease of changing living location as does renting. If changes in your situation make it necessary to sell your home, doing so may be difficult. High interest rates and other factors can result in a weak demand for housing.

3. *Higher living costs.* Owning your place of residence can be expensive. The homeowner is responsible for maintenance and costs of repainting, repairs, and home improvements.

Real estate taxes are a major expense of homeowners. Higher property values and higher tax rates mean higher real estate taxes. Higher taxes affect homeowners more directly than renters, who pay them in the form of higher rent. It is harder for homeowners to counter the effects of high taxes by moving to less expensive housing.

Home ownership allows you the flexibility to decorate as you desire.

ASSESS TYPES OF HOUSING AVAILABLE
Seven common options are available to home buyers:

1. *Single-family dwellings* are the most popular form of housing. These residences include previously owned houses, new houses, and custom-built houses. Older houses may be preferred by people who want a certain style and quality of housing.

2. *Multiunit dwellings,* dwellings with more than one living unit, include duplexes and townhouses. A *duplex* is a building that contains two separate homes. A *townhouse* contains two, four, or six single-family living units.

Advice From A Pro

APPEALING YOUR PROPERTY TAXES

Property taxes vary from area to area. Generally, real estate taxes range from 2 to 4 percent of the market value of the property. Taxes are based on the *assessed value,* the amount that your local government determines your property to be worth for tax purposes.

Assessed values normally are lower than the market value, often only about half. A home with a market value of $180,000 may be assessed at $90,000. If the tax rate is $60 per $1,000 of assessed value, this would result in annual taxes of $5,400 ($90,000 divided by $1,000 times $60). This rate is 6 percent of the assessed value but only 3 percent of the market value.

While higher home values are desired, this increase also means higher property assessments. Quickly increasing property taxes are frustrating, but there are actions you can take:

1. *Know the appeal deadline.* Call your local assessor's office for this information. You will probably have between 14 and 90 days to initiate your appeal. Late requests will most likely not be accepted. Send your appeal by certified mail to have proof that you met the deadline, and keep copies of all documents.

2. *Check for mistakes.* The assessment office may have incorrect information. Obvious mistakes may include incorrect square footage or an assessment may report a home with four bedrooms when there are only three.

3. *Determine what issues to emphasize.* A property tax appeal can be based on a mistake in the assessment criteria or a higher assessment than comparable homes. Note any items that negatively affect the value of your home. For example, a bridge is no longer in operation near your home, making your house much less accessible—and less valuable. If a garage has been taken down to increase garden space, the home's value likely would be less. Sometimes simply pointing out the facts can lower an assessment.

Compare your assessment with homes of the same size, age, and general location. This information may be obtained at the assessor's office. Consider obtaining comparisons on 5 to 10 homes. Use this comparative data to build your case.

4. *Prepare for the hearing.* Gather your evidence and prepare an organized presentation. Photos of comparable properties may be useful. A spreadsheet can make it easy for the hearing officials to view your evidence. Suggest a specific corrected assessment, and give your reasons.

Observe the hearing of another person to become familiar with the process. Most important, stay calm and professional.

Sources: Jenny C. McCune, "Protesting Your Property Assessment," www.bankrate.com, May 14, 2004; "How to Beat Back Those Ever-Rising Property Taxes," *Consumer Reports Money Advisor,* February 2005, pp. 1, 4–5.

---

3. **Condominiums** are individually owned housing units in a building with several units. Individual ownership does not include the common areas, such as hallways, outside grounds, and recreational facilities. These areas are owned by the condominium association, which is run by the people who own the housing units. The condominium association oversees the management and operation of the housing complex. Condominium owners are charged a monthly fee to cover the maintenance, repairs, improvements, and insurance for the building and common areas. A condominium is not a type of building structure; it is a legal form of home ownership.

4. **Cooperative housing** is a form of housing in which a building containing a number of units is owned by a nonprofit organization whose members rent the units. Buying a membership in the co-op gives a person the right to rent a housing unit. The living units of a co-op, unlike condominiums, are owned not by the residents but by the co-op. Rents in a co-op can increase quickly if living units become vacant, since the remaining residents must cover the maintenance costs of the building.

5. **Manufactured homes** are housing units that are fully or partially assembled in a factory and then moved to the living site. There are two basic types of manufactured

condominium An individually owned housing unit in a building with several such units.

cooperative housing A form of housing in which a building containing a number of housing units is owned by a nonprofit organization whose members rent the units.

manufactured home A housing unit that is fully or partially assembled in a factory before being moved to the living site.

homes. One type is the *prefabricated home,* with components built in a factory and then assembled at the housing site. With this type of housing, mass production can keep building costs lower.

6. *Mobile homes* are a second type of manufactured home. Since very few mobile homes are moved from their original sites, the term is not completely accurate. These housing units are typically less than 1,000 square feet in size; however, they usually offer the same features as a conventional house—fully equipped kitchens, fireplaces, cathedral ceilings, and whirlpool baths. The site for a mobile home may be either purchased or leased in a development specifically designed for such housing units.

   The safety of mobile homes is continually debated. Fires occur no more frequently in these housing units than in other types of homes. But due to the construction of mobile homes, a fire spreads faster than in conventional houses. Manufacturers' standards for the fire safety of mobile homes are higher than in the past. Still, when a fire occurs in a mobile home, the unit is often completely destroyed. This type of housing is also vulnerable to wind.

   Another common concern about mobile homes is their tendency to depreciate in value. When this occurs, an important benefit of home ownership is eliminated. Depreciation may make it difficult to obtain financing to purchase a mobile home.

7. *Building a home* is another option. Some people want a home built to their specifications. Before you begin such a project, be sure you possess the necessary knowledge, money, and perseverance. When choosing a contractor to coordinate the project, consider the following:

- Does the contractor have the experience needed to handle the type of building project you require?
- Does the contractor have a good working relationship with the architect, materials suppliers, electricians, plumbers, carpenters, and other personnel needed to complete the project?
- What assurance do you have about the quality of materials?
- What arrangements must be made for payments during construction?
- What delays in the construction process will be considered legitimate?
- Is the contractor licensed and insured?
- Is the contractor willing to provide names, addresses, and phone numbers of satisfied customers?
- Have local consumer agencies received any complaints about this contractor?

Your written contract should include a time schedule, cost estimates, a description of the work, and a payment schedule.

DETERMINE HOW MUCH YOU CAN AFFORD
As you determine how much of your budget you will spend on a home, consider the price of the house along with its size and quality.

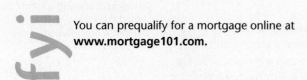

You can prequalify for a mortgage online at **www.mortgage101.com.**

Price and Down Payment The amount you can spend is affected by funds available for a down payment, your income, and your current living expenses. Other factors you should consider are current mortgage rates, the potential future value of the property, and your ability to make monthly mortgage, tax, and insurance payments. To determine how much you can afford to spend on a home, have a loan officer at a mortgage company or other financial institution *prequalify* you. This service is provided without charge.

Size and Quality   You may not get all the features you want in your first home, but financial advisers suggest you get into the housing market by purchasing what you can afford. As you move up in the housing market, your second or third home can include more of the features you want.

Ideally, the home you buy will be in good condition. In certain circumstances, you may be willing to buy a *handyman's special,* a home that needs work and that you are able to get at a lower price because of its condition. You will then need to put more money into the house for repairs and improvements or to invest *sweat equity* by doing some of the work yourself. Home improvement information and assistance are available from hardware stores and other home product retailers.

> **DID YOU KNOW?**
>
> In addition to location, the value of a home is commonly affected by the square footage, number of complete bathrooms, number of bedrooms, a modern kitchen, presence of a garage, a basement, a deck, central air conditioning, a fireplace, and a lake, river, or pond within 300 feet of the house.

STEP 2: FIND AND EVALUATE A PROPERTY TO PURCHASE

Next, you should select a location, consider using the services of a real estate agent, and conduct a home inspection.

SELECTING A LOCATION   An old adage among real estate people is that the three most important factors to consider when buying a home are *location, location,* and *location!* Perhaps you prefer an urban, a suburban, or a rural setting. Or perhaps you want to live in a small town or in a resort area. In selecting a neighborhood, compare your values and lifestyle with those of current residents.

Be aware of **zoning laws,** restrictions on how the property in an area can be used. The location of businesses and the anticipated construction of industrial buildings or a highway may influence your buying decision.

Before buying a home, be sure to inspect all aspects of the property you are considering.

zoning laws Restrictions on how the property in an area can be used.

If you have or plan to have a family, you should assess the school system. Educators recommend that schools be evaluated on program variety, achievement level of students, percentage of students who go on to college, dedication of faculty members, facilities, school funding, and involvement of parents. Homeowners without children also benefit from strong schools, since the educational advantages of a community help maintain property values.

USING A REAL ESTATE AGENT   A real estate agent can help you assess your housing needs and determine the amount you can afford to spend. Real estate agents have information about areas of interest and what housing is available to buy.

The main services a real estate agent provides include (1) presenting your offer to the seller, (2) negotiating a settlement price, (3) assisting you in obtaining financing, and (4) representing you at the closing. A real estate agent will also recommend lawyers, insurance agents, home inspectors, and mortgage companies to serve your needs.

Since the seller of the home usually pays the real estate agent's commission, the buyer may not incur a direct cost. However, this expense may be reflected in the price paid for the home. In some states, the agent could be working for the seller. In others, the agent may be working for the buyer, the seller, or as a *dual agent,* working for both the buyer and the seller. When dual agency exists, some states require that buyers sign a disclosure acknowledging that they are aware the agent is working for both buyer and seller.

Many states now have *buyer agents* who represent the buyer's interests. In these situations, the buyer agent may be paid by either the seller or the buyer.

Exhibit **9-6**   Conducting a home inspection

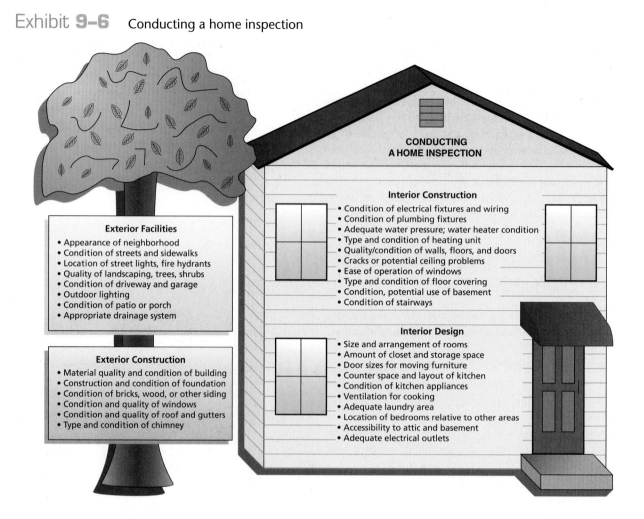

CONDUCTING A HOME INSPECTION

Exterior Facilities
- Appearance of neighborhood
- Condition of streets and sidewalks
- Location of street lights, fire hydrants
- Quality of landscaping, trees, shrubs
- Condition of driveway and garage
- Outdoor lighting
- Condition of patio or porch
- Appropriate drainage system

Exterior Construction
- Material quality and condition of building
- Construction and condition of foundation
- Condition of bricks, wood, or other siding
- Condition and quality of windows
- Condition and quality of roof and gutters
- Type and condition of chimney

Interior Construction
- Condition of electrical fixtures and wiring
- Condition of plumbing fixtures
- Adequate water pressure; water heater condition
- Type and condition of heating unit
- Quality/condition of walls, floors, and doors
- Cracks or potential ceiling problems
- Ease of operation of windows
- Type and condition of floor covering
- Condition, potential use of basement
- Condition of stairways

Interior Design
- Size and arrangement of rooms
- Amount of closet and storage space
- Door sizes for moving furniture
- Counter space and layout of kitchen
- Condition of kitchen appliances
- Ventilation for cooking
- Adequate laundry area
- Location of bedrooms relative to other areas
- Accessibility to attic and basement
- Adequate electrical outlets

CONDUCTING A HOME INSPECTION   Before reaching your decision about a specific home, conduct a complete evaluation of the property. An evaluation by a trained home inspector can minimize future problems. Do not assume everything is in proper working condition just because someone lives there now. Being cautious and determined will save you headaches and unplanned expenses. Exhibit 9–6 presents a detailed format for inspecting a home. A home purchase agreement may include the right to have various professionals (roofer, plumber, electrician) inspect the property.

Some states, cities, and lenders require inspection documents. The mortgage company will usually conduct an *appraisal* to determine the fair market value of the property. An appraisal is not a detailed inspection.

STEP 3: PRICE THE PROPERTY

After you have selected a home, determine an offer price and negotiate a final buying price.

DETERMINING THE HOME PRICE   What price should you offer for the home? The main factors to consider are recent selling prices in the area, current demand for housing, the length of time the home has been on the market, the owner's need to sell, financing options, and features and condition of the home. Each of these factors can

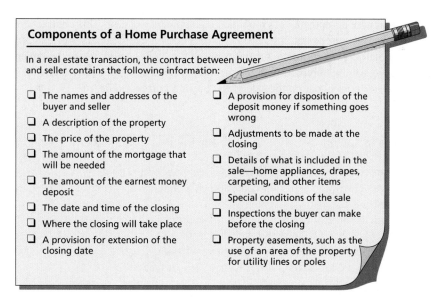

Source: *Homeownership: Guidelines for Buying and Owning a Home* (Richmond, VA: Federal Reserve Bank of Richmond).

Exhibit 9-7

The components of a home purchase agreement

affect your offer price. For example, you will have to offer a higher price in times of low interest rates and high demand for homes. On the other hand, a home that has been on the market for over a year could mean an opportunity to offer a lower price. The services of a real estate agent or an appraiser can assist you in assessing the current value of the home.

Your offer will be in the form of a *purchase agreement,* or contract (see Exhibit 9–7). This document constitutes your legal offer to purchase the home. Your first offer price usually will not be accepted.

NEGOTIATING THE PURCHASE PRICE

If your initial offer is accepted, you have a valid contract. If your offer is rejected, you have several options, depending on the seller. A *counteroffer* from the owner indicates a willingness to negotiate a price settlement. If the counteroffer is only slightly lower than the asking price, you are expected to move closer to that price with your next offer. If the counteroffer is quite a bit off the asking price, you are closer to the point where you might split the difference to arrive at the purchase price. If no counteroffer is forthcoming, you may wish to make another offer to see whether the seller is willing to do any negotiating.

In times of high demand for housing, negotiating may be minimized; this situation is referred to as a *seller's market,* since the current homeowner is likely to have several offers for the property. In contrast, when home sales are slow, a *buyer's market* exists and a lower price is likely.

When you buy a previously owned home, your negotiating power is based on current market demand and the current owner's need to sell. When you buy a new home, a slow market may mean lower prices or an opportunity to obtain various amenities (fireplace, higher-quality carpeting) from the builder at a lower cost.

Once a price has been agreed on, the purchase contract becomes the basis for the real estate transaction. As part of the offer, the buyer must present **earnest money,** a portion of the purchase price deposited as evidence of good faith to show that the purchase offer is serious. At the closing of the home purchase, the earnest money is applied toward the down payment. This money is usually returned if the sale cannot be completed due to circumstances beyond the buyer's control.

earnest money A portion of the price of a home that the buyer deposits as evidence of good faith to indicate a serious purchase offer.

Home purchase agreements often contain a *contingency clause*. This contract condition states that the agreement is binding only if a certain event occurs. For example, a real estate contract may stipulate that the contract will not be valid unless the buyer obtains financing for the purchase within a certain period of time, or it may make the purchase of a home contingent on the sale of the buyer's current home.

CONCEPT CHECK 9-3

1 What are the advantages and disadvantages of owning a home?
2 What guidelines can be used to determine the amount to spend for a home purchase?
3 How can the quality of a school system benefit even homeowners in a community who do not have school-age children?
4 What services are available to home buyers from real estate agents?
5 How does a *seller's* market differ from a *buyer's* market?

Action Application Talk with a real estate agent about the process involved in selecting and buying a home. Obtain information about housing prices in your area and the services the agent provides.

The Finances of Home Buying

Objective 4

Calculate the costs associated with purchasing a home.

After you have decided to purchase a specific home and have agreed on a price, you will probably obtain a loan. Financing a home purchase requires obtaining a mortgage, an awareness of types of mortgages, and settling the real estate transaction.

STEP 4: OBTAIN FINANCING

DETERMINE AMOUNT OF DOWN PAYMENT The amount of cash available for a down payment will affect the size of the mortgage loan you require. A large down payment, such as 20 percent or more, will make it easier for you to obtain a mortgage.

Personal savings, pension plan funds, sales of investments or other assets, and assistance from relatives are the most common sources of a down payment. Parents can help their children purchase a home by giving them a cash gift or a loan, depositing money with the lender to reduce the interest rate on the loan, cosigning the loan, or acting as co-mortgagors.

Private mortgage insurance (PMI) is usually required if the down payment is less than 20 percent. This coverage protects the lender from financial loss due to default. PMI charges, which the borrower pays, vary depending on the amount of the down payment. These costs may be paid in full at closing or are sometimes financed over the life of the mortgage, depending on the type of financing.

After building up 20 percent equity in a home, a home buyer should contact the lender to cancel PMI. The Homeowners Protection Act of 1998 requires that a PMI policy be terminated automatically when a homeowner's equity reaches 22 percent of the property value at the time the mortgage was executed. Homeowners can request termination earlier if they can provide proof that the equity in the home has grown to 20 percent of the current market value. Additional information is available at www.privatemi.com.

QUALIFYING FOR A MORTGAGE Do you have funds for a down payment? Do you earn enough to make mortgage payments while covering other living expenses? Do you have a good credit rating? Unless you pay cash for a home, a favorable response to these questions is necessary.

A **mortgage** is a long-term loan on a specific piece of property such as a home or other real estate. Payments on a mortgage are usually made over 15, 20, or 30 years. Banks, savings and loan associations, credit unions, and mortgage companies are the most common home financing sources. *Mortgage brokers* can help home buyers obtain financing, since they are in contact with several financial institutions. A mortgage broker may charge higher fees than a lending institution with which you deal directly.

To qualify for a mortgage, you must meet criteria similar to those for other loans. The home you buy serves as security, or *collateral,* for the mortgage. The major factors that affect the affordability of your mortgage are your income, other debts, the amount available for a down payment, the length of the loan, and current mortgage rates. The results calculated in Exhibit 9–8 are (*a*) the monthly mortgage payment you can afford, (*b*) the mortgage amount you can afford, and (*c*) the home purchase price you can afford.

The procedures in Exhibit 9–8 include the following:

mortgage A long-term loan on a specific piece of property such as a home or other real estate.

DID YOU KNOW?

A hybrid adjustable rate mortgage resembles a fixed-rate mortgage in the initial years of the loan. The "five-one" hybrid, for example, offers a fixed rate for the first 5 years and then adjusts annually for the next 25 years.

1. Indicate your monthly gross income.
2. Multiply your monthly gross income by 0.33 (or 0.38 if you have other debts, such as an auto loan). Lenders commonly use 33 and 38 percent as guidelines to determine the amount most people can comfortably afford for housing.

Exhibit **9–8**   Housing affordability and mortgage qualification amounts

		Example A	Example B
Step 1:	Determine your monthly gross income (annual income divided by 12).	$48,000 ÷ 12	$48,000 ÷ 12
Step 2:	With a down payment of at least 10 percent, lenders use 33 percent of monthly gross income as a guideline for PITI (principal, interest, taxes, and insurance) and 38 percent of monthly gross income as a guideline for PITI plus other debt payments.	$ 4,000 × .38 $ 1,520	$ 4,000 × .33 $ 1,320
Step 3:	Subtract other debt payments (e.g., payments on an auto loan) and an estimate of the monthly costs of property taxes and homeowner's insurance.	−380 −300	— −300
(a) Affordable monthly mortgage payment		$ 840	$1,020
Step 4:	Divide this amount by the monthly mortgage payment per $1,000 based on current mortgage rates—an 8 percent, 30-year loan, for example (see Exhibit 9–9)—and multiply by $1,000.	÷ $ 7.34 × $1,000	÷ $ 7.34 × $1,000
(b) Affordable mortgage amount		$114,441	$138,965
Step 5:	Divide your affordable mortgage amount by 1 minus the fractional portion of your down payment (e.g., 1 − .1 with a 10 percent down payment).	÷ .9	÷ .9
(c) Affordable home purchase price		$127,157	$154,405

Note: The two ratios lending institutions use (step 2) and other loan requirements may vary based on a variety of factors, including the type of mortgage, the amount of the down payment, your income level, and current interest rates.

3. After subtracting the monthly debt payments and an estimate of the monthly cost for property taxes and homeowner's insurance, you arrive at your *affordable monthly mortgage payment (a)*.

4. Divide (*a*) by the factor from Exhibit 9–9, based on your mortgage term (in years) and rate. Then multiply your answer by $1,000 to convert your figure to thousands of dollars. This gives you your *affordable mortgage amount (b)*. Exhibit 9–9 provides the factors for determining the amount you need to pay back $1,000 over 15, 20, 25, or 30 years based on various interest rates.

5. To obtain your *affordable home purchase price (c)*, divide (*b*) by the amount you will be financing, such as 0.9 when you make a 10 percent down payment.

These sample calculations are typical of those most financial institutions use; the actual qualifications for a mortgage may vary by lender and by the type of mortgage. Your credit record, job stability, and assets can increase the amount of the mortgage. In addition, current mortgage interest rates will affect the amount of the mortgage loan for which you qualify.

The mortgage loan for which you can qualify is larger when interest rates are low than when they are high. For example, a person who can afford a monthly mortgage payment of $700 will qualify for a 30-year loan of

$130,354 at 5 percent	$95,368 at 8 percent
$116,667 at 6 percent	$86,956 at 9 percent
$105,263 at 7 percent	$79,726 at 10 percent

As interest rates rise, fewer people are able to afford the cost of an average-priced home.

points Prepaid interest charged by a lending institution for the mortgage; each discount point is equal to 1 percent of the loan amount.

EVALUATING POINTS   When you compare costs at several mortgage companies, the interest rate you are quoted is not the only factor to consider. The required down payment and the points charged will affect the interest rate. **Points** are prepaid in-

---

Sheet 43
Housing affordability and mortgage qualification

Exhibit 9–9

Mortgage payment factors (principal and interest factors per $1,000 of loan amount)

Term Rate	30 Years	25 Years	20 Years	15 Years
5.0%	$5.37	$5.85	$6.60	$7.91
5.5	5.68	6.14	6.88	8.17
6.0	6.00	6.44	7.16	8.43
6.5	6.32	6.67	7.45	8.71
7.0	6.65	7.06	7.75	8.98
7.5	6.99	7.39	8.06	9.27
8.0	7.34	7.72	8.36	9.56
8.5	7.69	8.05	8.68	9.85
9.0	8.05	8.39	9.00	10.14
9.5	8.41	8.74	9.32	10.44
10.0	8.78	9.09	9.65	10.75
10.5	9.15	9.44	9.98	11.05
11.0	9.52	9.80	10.32	11.37
11.5	9.90	10.16	10.66	11.68
12.0	10.29	10.53	11.01	12.00

terest charged by the lender. Each *discount point* is equal to 1 percent of the loan amount and should be viewed as a premium you pay for obtaining a lower mortgage rate. In deciding whether to take a lower rate with more points or a higher rate with fewer points, do the following:

1. Determine the difference between the monthly payments you will make for two different situations.

2. Determine the difference between the points charged for the two different rates or at two different lenders.

3. Divide the result in step 2 by the result in step 1. This will tell you how many months it will take for the lower monthly payment to offset the higher cost of the points.

If you plan to live in your home longer than the time calculated in step 3, paying the points and taking the lower mortgage rate is probably the best action. This decision will, however, be affected by the amount of funds available to pay the points at the time of closing. If you plan to sell your home sooner than the time calculated in step 3, the higher mortgage rate with fewer discount points may be better. Online research may be used to compare current mortgage rates and to apply for a mortgage.

> **DID YOU KNOW?**
>
> Among different lenders, interest rates on a 30-year mortgage may vary up to a full percentage point within a single geographic region.

THE APPLICATION PROCESS

Applying for a mortgage involves three main phases:

1. After completing the mortgage application, a meeting between lender and borrower is scheduled. The borrower presents evidence of employment, income, ownership of assets, and amounts of existing debts. At this point, most lenders charge an application fee of between $100 and $300.

2. The lender obtains a credit report and verifies other aspects of the borrower's application and financial status.

3. The mortgage is either approved or denied. The decision is based on the potential borrower's credit and financial history and an evaluation of the home, including its location, condition, and value. This process will indicate the maximum mortgage for which you qualify. This amount may not be loaned on every house you are considering.

The loan commitment is the financial institution's decision to provide the funds needed to purchase a specific property. At this point, the purchase contract for the home becomes legally binding. The approved mortgage application usually *locks in* an interest rate for 30 to 60 days.

FIXED-RATE, FIXED-PAYMENT MORTGAGES

As Exhibit 9–10 on page 291 shows, fixed-rate, fixed-payment mortgages are one of the two major types of mortgages.

Conventional Mortgages   The **conventional mortgage** usually has equal payments over 15, 20, or 30 years based on a fixed interest rate. This mortgage offers home buyers certainty about future loan payments. The mortgage payments are set at a level that allows **amortization** of the loan; that is, the balance owed is reduced with each payment. Since the amount borrowed is large, the payments made during the early years of the mortgage are applied mainly to interest, with only small reductions in the principal of the loan. As the amount owed declines, the monthly payments have an increasing impact on the loan balance. Near the end of the mortgage term, nearly all of each payment is applied to the balance.

For example, a $75,000, 30-year, 10 percent mortgage would have monthly payments of $658.18. The payments would be divided as follows:

conventional mortgage A fixed-rate, fixed-payment home loan with equal payments over 15, 20, or 30 years.

amortization The reduction of a loan balance through payments made over a period of time.

	Interest	Principal	Remaining Balance
For the first month	$625.00 ($75,000 × 0.10 × ½)	$ 33.18	$74,966.82 ($75,000 − $33.18)
For the second month	624.72 ($74,966.82 × 0.10 × ½)	33.46	74,933.36 ($74,966.82 − $33.46)
For the 360th month	5.41	649.54	–0–

In the past, many conventional mortgages were *assumable.* This feature allowed a home buyer to continue with the seller's original agreement. Assumable mortgages were especially attractive if the mortgage rate was lower than market interest rates at the time of the sale. Today, due to volatile interest rates, few assumable mortgages are offered.

Government Financing Programs   *Government financing programs* include loans insured by the Federal Housing Authority (FHA) and loans guaranteed by the Veterans Administration (VA). These government agencies do not provide the mortgage money; rather, they help home buyers obtain low-interest, low-down-payment loans.

What are the current mortgage rates in my area? This information may be obtained at **www.bankrate.com, www.hsh.com,** and **www.interest.com** as well as from local financial institutions.

To qualify for an FHA-insured loan, a person must meet certain conditions related to the down payment and fees. Most low- and middle-income people can qualify for the FHA loan program. The minimum down payment starts at 3 percent and varies depending on the loan size. This lower down payment makes it easier for a person to purchase a home. FHA-insured loans have interest rates slightly lower than market interest rates, since the FHA's involvement reduces the risk for the lending institution. The borrower is required to pay a fee for insurance that protects the lender from financial loss due to default. Despite the protection given the lender, the lower-than-market interest rate can result in extra prepaid interest as a condition of the loan.

The VA-guaranteed loan program assists eligible armed services veterans with home purchases. As with the FHA program, the funds for VA loans come from a financial institution or a mortgage company, with the risk reduced by government participation. A VA loan can be obtained without a down payment.

Both FHA-insured loans and VA-guaranteed loans can be attractive financing alternatives and are assumable by future owners when the house is sold to qualifying individuals. Both impose limits on the amount one can borrow, and a backlog of processing applications and approving loans may occur during periods of high demand.

Balloon Mortgages   The high mortgage rates of the early 1980s (Exhibit 9–11) on page 292 led to innovative lending plans for home buyers. One such plan is the **balloon mortgage,** which has fixed monthly payments and a very large final payment, usually after three, five, or seven years. This financing plan is designed for people who wish to buy a home during periods of high interest rates but expect to be able to refinance the loan or sell the home before or when the balloon payment is due. Most balloon mortgages allow conversion to a conventional mortgage (for a fee) if certain conditions are met.

balloon mortgage A home loan with fixed monthly payments and a large final payment, usually after three, five, or seven years.

ADJUSTABLE-RATE, VARIABLE-PAYMENT MORTGAGES   As noted in Exhibit 9–10, adjustable-rate, variable-payment mortgages are a major category of financing available to home buyers.

Adjustable-Rate Mortgages   The **adjustable-rate mortgage (ARM),** also referred to as a *flexible-rate mortgage* or a *variable-rate mortgage,* has an interest rate that increases or decreases during the life of the loan. When mortgage rates were at record

adjustable-rate mortgage (ARM) A home loan with an interest rate that can change during the mortgage term due to changes in market interest rates; also called a *flexible-rate mortgage* or a *variable-rate mortgage.*

Exhibit **9-10**   Types of mortgage loans

Loan Type	Benefits	Drawback
FIXED-RATE, FIXED-PAYMENT		
1. Conventional 30-year mortgage.	• Fixed monthly payments for 30 years provide certainty of principal and interest payments.	• Higher initial rates than adjustables.
2. Conventional 15- or 20-year mortgage.	• Lower rate than 30-year fixed; faster equity buildup and quicker payoff of loan.	• Higher monthly payments.
3. FHA/VA fixed-rate mortgage (30-year and 15-year).	• Low down payment requirements and fully assumable with no prepayment penalties.	• May require additional processing time.
4. "Balloon" loan (3–10-year terms).	• May carry discount rates and other favorable terms, particularly when the home seller provides the loan.	• At the end of the 3–10-year term, the entire remaining balance is due in a lump-sum or "balloon" payment, forcing the borrower to find new financing.
ADJUSTABLE-RATE, VARIABLE-PAYMENT		
5. Adjustable-rate mortgage (ARM)—payment changes on 1-year, 3-year, and 5-year schedules.	• Lower initial rates than fixed-rate loans, particularly on the 1-year adjustable. Generally assumable by new buyers. Offers possibility of future rate and payment decreases. Loans with rate "caps" may protect borrowers against increases in rates. Some may be convertible to fixed-rate plans.	• Shifts far greater interest rate risk onto borrowers than fixed-rate loans. May push up monthly payments in future years.
6. Graduated-payment mortgage (GPM)—payment increases by prearranged increments during first 5 to 7 years, then levels off.	• Allows buyers with marginal incomes to qualify. Higher incomes over next 5–7 years expected to cover gradual payment increases. May be combined with adjustable-rate mortgage to further lower initial rate and payment.	• May have higher annual percentage rate (APR) than standard fixed-rate or adjustable-rate loans. May involve negative amortization—increasing debt owed by lender. Income may not increase as expected.
7. Growing-equity mortgage (GEM)—contributes rising portions of monthly payments to payoff of principal debt. Typically pays off in 15–18 years rather than 30.	• Lower up-front payments, quicker loan payoff than conventional fixed-rate or adjustable-rate loans.	• May have higher effective rates and higher down payments than other loans in the marketplace.

highs, many people took out variable-rate home loans, expecting rates would eventually go down. ARMs usually have a lower initial interest rate than fixed-rate mortgages; however, the borrower, not the lender, bears the risk of future interest rate increases.

Exhibit **9-11**

Mortgage rates through
the years

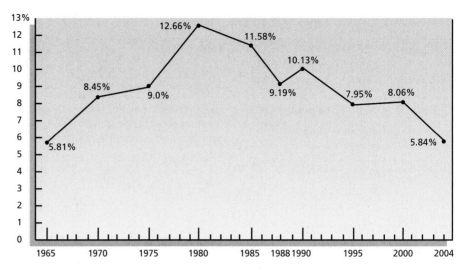

Source: Board of Governors of the Federal Reserve System.

rate cap A limit on the
increases and decreases in the
interest rate charged on an
adjustable-rate mortgage.

payment cap A limit on the
payment increases for an
adjustable-rate mortgage.

DID YOU KNOW?

By taking out a 15-year instead of a 30-
year mortgage, a home buyer borrowing
$200,00 can save over $150,000 in interest over the life of the loan. The faster equity growth with the shorter mortgage is
also a benefit. A 15-year mortgage may not
make sense for everyone, since the additional monthly payment may be needed to
pay off credit cards or for other living
expenses.

Sheet 44
Mortgage
company
comparison

A **rate cap** restricts the amount by which the interest rate can increase or decrease during the ARM term. This limit prevents the borrower from having to pay an interest rate significantly higher than the one in the original agreement. Most rate caps limit increases (or decreases) in the mortgage rate to one or two percentage points in a year and to no more than five points over the life of the loan.

A **payment cap** keeps the payments on an adjustable-rate mortgage at a given level or limits the amount to which those payments can rise. When mortgage payments do not rise but interest rates do, the amount owed can increase in months in which the mortgage payment does not cover the interest owed. This increased loan balance, called *negative amortization,* means the amount of the home equity is decreasing instead of increasing. As a result of these increases in the amount owed, the borrower usually has to make payments for a period longer than planned. Beware: Some adjustable-rate mortgages may stretch out as long as 40 years.

Consider several factors when you evaluate adjustable-rate mortgages: (1) determine the frequency of and restrictions on allowed changes in interest rates; (2) consider the frequency of and restrictions on changes in the monthly payment; (3) investigate the possibility that the loan will be extended due to negative amortization, and find out whether the mortgage agreement limits the amount of negative amortization; (4) find out what index the lending institution will use to set the mortgage interest rate over the term of the loan.

A lending institution will revise the rate for an adjustable-rate mortgage based on changes in the rates on U.S. Treasury securities, the Federal Home Loan Bank Board's mortgage rate index, or its own cost-of-funds index. Studies reveal that an ARM can be less costly over the life of a mortgage as long as interest rates remain fairly stable.

Convertible ARMs allow the home buyer to change an adjustable-rate mortgage to a fixed-rate mortgage during a certain period, such as the time between the second and fifth year of the loan. A conversion fee, typically between $250 and $500, must be paid to obtain a fixed rate, usually 0.25 to 0.50 percent higher than the current rates for conventional 30-year mortgages.

Graduated-Payment Mortgages   A **graduated-payment mortgage** is a financing agreement in which payments rise to different levels every 5 or 10 years during the term of the loan. In the early years, the loan payments could lead to a negative amortization with an increase in the amount owed. This type of mortgage is especially beneficial for people who anticipate increases in income in the future.

graduated-payment mortgage A home financing agreement in which payments rise to different levels every 5 or 10 years during the loan term.

Growing-Equity Mortgages   A **growing-equity mortgage** provides for increases in payments that allow the amount owed to be paid off more quickly. With such a mortgage, a person would be able to pay off a 30-year home loan in 15 to 18 years. A growing-equity mortgage may be desired by individuals who want to build equity in their homes quickly.

growing-equity mortgage A home loan agreement that provides for payment increases to allow the amount owed to be paid off more quickly.

OTHER FINANCING METHODS   To assist first-time home buyers, builders and financial institutions offer financing plans to make the purchase easier.

Buy-Downs   A **buy-down** is an interest rate subsidy from a home builder or a real estate developer that reduces the mortgage payments during the first few years of the loan. This assistance is intended to stimulate sales among home buyers who cannot afford conventional financing. After the buy-down period, the mortgage payments increase to the level that would have existed without the financial assistance.

buy-down An interest rate subsidy from a home builder or a real estate developer that reduces a home buyer's mortgage payments during the first few years of the loan.

Shared Appreciation Mortgages   The **shared appreciation mortgage (SAM)** is an arrangement in which the borrower agrees to share the increased value of the home with the lender when the home is sold. This agreement provides the home buyer with a below-market interest rate and lower payments than a conventional loan. To obtain these conditions, the borrower typically must agree to give the lending institution 30 to 50 percent of the home's appreciation when the home is sold or after a set number of years. Shared appreciation agreements are also common when parents provide financial assistance to their children for the purchase of a home.

shared appreciation mortgage (SAM) A home loan agreement in which the borrower agrees to share the increased value of the home with the lender when the home is sold.

Second Mortgages   A **second mortgage,** more commonly called a *home equity loan,* allows a homeowner to borrow on the paid-up value of the property. Traditional second mortgages allow a homeowner to borrow a lump sum against the equity and repay it in monthly installments. Recently, lending institutions have offered a variety of home equity loans, including a line of credit program that allows the borrower to obtain additional funds. You need to be careful when using a home equity line of credit. This revolving credit plan can keep you continually in debt as you request new cash advances.

second mortgage A cash advance based on the paid-up value of a home; also called a *home equity loan.*

A home equity loan makes it possible to deduct the interest on consumer purchases on your federal income tax return. However, it creates the risk of losing the home if required payments on both the first and second mortgages are not made. To help prevent this financial disaster, some states restrict the use of home equity loans. Be cautious of home equity loans for amounts that exceed 100 percent of your equity in the home.

Reverse Mortgages   Programs are available to assist people who have a high equity in their homes and need cash. **Reverse mortgages** provide elderly homeowners with tax-free income in the form of a loan that is paid back (with interest) when the home is sold or the homeowner dies. You must be 62 to qualify. These financing plans, also called *home equity conversion mortgages,* have two main formats. A *reverse mortgage annuity* guarantees the homeowner a monthly income for life. In contrast, a reverse mortgage may have a *set term,* at the end of which the loan would be due. This format is likely to offer a higher monthly income; however, an elderly person faces the prospect of having to sell the home before he or she desires to do so. Reverse mortgages are increasing in availability through both government programs and private lending institutions.

reverse mortgage A loan based on the equity in a home, that provides elderly homeowners with tax-free income and is paid back with interest when the home is sold or the homeowner dies.

refinancing The process of obtaining a new mortgage on a home to get a lower interest rate.

Sheet 45
Mortgage refinance analysis

Refinancing   During the term of your mortgage, you may want to **refinance** your home, that is, obtain a new mortgage on your current home at a lower interest rate. Before taking this action, be sure the costs of refinancing do not offset the savings of a lower interest rate. Refinancing is most advantageous when you can get a rate 2 or 3 percent lower than your current rate and when you plan to own your present home for at least two more years. Divide the costs of refinancing by the amount saved each month to determine the time you need to cover your costs. Also, be sure to consider the tax deductibility of refinancing costs. Another financing decision involves making extra payments on your mortgage (see the Financial Planning for Life's Situations feature on page 295).

STEP 5: CLOSE THE PURCHASE TRANSACTION

Before finalizing the transaction, do a *walk-through* to inspect the condition and facilities of the home you plan to buy. You can use a digital camera to collect evidence for any last-minute items you may need to negotiate.

The *closing* involves a meeting among the buyer, seller, and lender of funds, or representatives of each party, to complete the transaction. Documents are signed, last-minute details are settled, and appropriate amounts are paid. A number of expenses are incurred at the closing. The **closing costs,** also referred to as *settlement costs,* are the fees and charges paid when a real estate transaction is completed (see Exhibit 9–12).

Title insurance is one closing cost. This coverage has two phases. First, the title company defines the boundaries of the property being purchased and conducts a search to determine whether the property is free of claims such as unpaid real estate

> **DID YOU KNOW?**
>
> *An interest-only mortgage* allows a home buyer to have lower payments for the first few years of the loan. During that time, none of the mortgage payment goes toward the loan amount. Once the interest-only period ends, the payment rises to include both principal and interest. Remember, the higher payments are based on the amount of the original loan since no principal has been paid. Interest-only mortgages can be especially dangerous if the value of the property declines.

closing costs Fees and charges paid when a real estate transaction is completed; also called *settlement costs.*

taxes. Second, during the mortgage term, the title company protects the owner and the lender against financial loss resulting from future defects in the title and from other unforeseen property claims not excluded by the policy.

Also due at closing time is the deed recording fee. The **deed** is the document that transfers ownership of property from one party to another. With a *warranty deed,* the seller guarantees the title is good. This document certifies that the seller is the true owner of the property, there are no claims against the title, and the seller has the right to sell the property.

Mortgage insurance is another possible closing cost. If required, mortgage insurance protects the lender from loss resulting from a mortgage default.

The Real Estate Settlement Procedures Act (RESPA) helps home buyers understand the closing process and closing costs. This legislation requires that loan applicants be given certain information, including an estimate of the closing costs, before the actual closing. Obtaining this information as early as possible will allow you to plan for the closing costs. Information on RESPA is available online at www.hud.gov.

At the closing and when you make your monthly payments, you will probably deposit money to be used for home expenses. For example, the lender will require that you have property insurance. An **escrow account** is money, usually deposited with the lending institution, for the payment of property taxes and homeowner's insurance. This account protects the lender from financial loss due to unpaid real estate taxes or damage from fire or other hazards.

As a new home buyer, you might also consider purchasing an agreement that gives you protection against defects in the home. *Implied warranties* created by state laws may cover some problem areas; other repair costs can occur. Home builders and real estate sales companies offer warranties to buyers. Coverage offered commonly provides

title insurance Insurance that, during the mortgage term, protects the owner or the lender against financial loss resulting from future defects in the title and from other unforeseen property claims not excluded by the policy.

deed A document that transfers ownership of property from one party to another.

escrow account Money, usually deposited with the lending financial institution, for the payment of property taxes and homeowner's insurance.

SHOULD YOU PAY OFF YOUR MORTGAGE EARLY?

If you have a mortgage, you might consider paying it off early. Make sure the mortgage does not include a *prepayment penalty,* a fee you pay for the privilege of retiring a loan early. Most mortgages do not include this penalty. Before paying off your mortgage early, however, consider the tax deductions you may lose and your lost earnings on the money you use to retire this debt.

Instead of paying off your entire mortgage early, consider paying an additional amount each month—for example, $25. Since this amount will be applied to the loan principal, you will save interest and pay off the mortgage in a shorter time than the contracted period. Paying an additional $25 a month on a $75,000, 30-year, 10 percent mortgage will save you over $34,000 in interest and enable you to pay off the loan in less than 25 years.

Beware of organizations that promise to help you make additional payments on your mortgage. This is something you could do on your own, and they are likely to charge you a fee for doing it. In addition, these organizations frequently collect money from you every two weeks but make a payment only once a month, which gives them the use of thousands of *your* dollars to invest for *their* gain.

protection against structural, wiring, plumbing, heating, and other mechanical defects. Most home warranty programs have many limitations.

In addition, a new homeowner may purchase a service contract from a real estate company such as Century 21 or Remax. This agreement warrants appliances, plumbing, air conditioning and heating systems, and other items for one year. As with any service contract, you must decide whether the coverage provided and the chances of repair expenses justify the cost.

Exhibit 9–12 Common closing costs

At the transaction settlement of a real estate purchase and sale, the buyer and seller will encounter a variety of expenses that are commonly referred to as *closing costs.*

	Cost Range Encountered	
	By the Buyer	**By the Seller**
Title search fee	$50–$150	—
Title insurance	$100–$600	$100–$600
Attorney's fee	$50–$700	$50–$700
Property survey	—	$100–$400
Appraisal fee	$100–$300	—
Recording fees; transfer taxes	$15–$30	$15–$30
Credit report	$25–$75	—
Termite inspection	$50–$150	—
Lender's origination fee	1–3% of loan amount	—
Reserves for home insurance and property taxes	Varies	—
Interest paid in advance (from the closing date to the end of the month) and "points"	Varies	—
Real estate broker's commission	—	5–7% of purchase price

Note: The amounts paid by the buyer are in addition to the down payment.

295

HOME BUYING: A SUMMARY

For most people, buying a home is the most expensive decision they will undertake. As a reminder, Exhibit 9–13 provides an overview of the major elements to consider when making this critical financial decision.

CONCEPT CHECK 9-4

1 What are the main sources of money for a down payment?
2 What factors affect a person's ability to qualify for a mortgage?
3 How do changing interest rates affect the amount of mortgage a person can afford?
4 How do discount points affect the cost of a mortgage?
5 Under what conditions might an adjustable-rate mortgage be appropriate?
6 When might refinancing a mortgage be advisable?
7 How do closing costs affect a person's ability to afford a home purchase?

Action Application Conduct Web research on various types of mortgages and current rates.

Selling Your Home

Objective 5

Develop a strategy for selling a home.

Most people who buy a home will eventually be on the other side of a real estate transaction. Selling your home requires preparing it for selling, setting a price, and deciding whether to sell it yourself or use a real estate agent.

PREPARING YOUR HOME FOR SELLING

The effective presentation of your home can result in a fast and financially favorable sale. Real estate salespeople recommend that you make needed repairs and paint worn exterior and interior areas. Clear the garage and exterior areas of toys, debris, and old vehicles, and keep the lawn cut and the leaves raked. Keep the kitchen and bathroom clean. Avoid offensive odors by removing garbage and keeping pets and their areas clean. Remove excess furniture and dispose of unneeded items to make the house, closets, and storage areas look larger. When showing your home, open drapes and turn on lights to give it a pleasant atmosphere. This effort will give your property a positive image and make it attractive to potential buyers.

DETERMINING THE SELLING PRICE

appraisal An estimate of the current value of a property.

Putting a price on your home can be difficult. You risk not selling it immediately if the price is too high, and you may not get a fair amount if the price is too low. An **appraisal,** an estimate of the current value of the property, can provide a good indication of the price you should set. An asking price is influenced by recent selling prices of comparable homes in your area, demand in the housing market, and available financing based on current mortgage rates.

The home improvements you have made may or may not increase the selling price. A hot tub or an exercise room may have no value for potential buyers. Among the most desirable improvements are energy-efficient features, a remodeled kitchen, an additional or remodeled bathroom, added rooms and storage space, a converted basement, a fireplace, and an outdoor deck or patio.

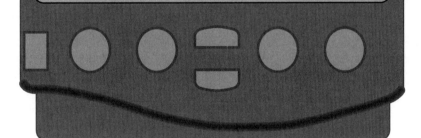

- **Location.** Consider the community and geographic region. A $150,000 home in one area may be an average-priced house, while in another part of the country it may be fairly expensive real estate. The demand for homes is largely affected by the economy and the availability of jobs.
- **Down payment.** While making a large down payment reduces your mortgage payments, you will also need the funds for closing costs, moving expenses, repairs, or furniture.
- **Mortgage application.** When applying for a home loan, you will usually be required to provide copies of recent tax returns, a residence and employment history, information about bank and investment accounts, a listing of debts, and evidence of auto and any real estate ownership.
- **Points.** You may need to select between a higher rate with no discount points and a lower rate requiring points paid at closing.
- **Closing costs.** Settlement costs can range from 2 to 6 percent of the loan amount. This means you could need as much as $6,000 to finalize a $100,000 mortgage; this amount is in addition to your down payment.
- **PITI.** Your monthly payment for principal, interest, taxes, and insurance is an important budget item. Beware of buying "too much house" and not having enough for other living expenses.
- **Maintenance costs.** As any homeowner will tell you, owning a home can be expensive. Set aside funds for repair and remodeling expenses.

Exhibit **9-13**

The main elements of buying a home

The time to think about selling your home is when you buy it and every day you live there. Daily maintenance, timely repairs, and home improvements will increase the future sales price.

SALE BY OWNER

Each year, over 10 percent of home sales are made by the home's owners. If you decide to sell your home without using a real estate professional,

DID YOU KNOW?

An appraisal is likely to cost between $200 and $300. This expense can help people selling a home on their own to get a realistic view of the property's value.

price the home and advertise it through local newspapers and with an information sheet describing it in detail. Obtain a listing sheet from a real estate office as an example of the information to include on your flier. Distribute the sheet at stores and in other public areas.

When selling your home on your own, obtain information about the availability of financing and financing requirements. This information will help you and potential buyers to determine whether a sale is possible. Use the services of a lawyer or title company to assist you with the contract, the closing, and other legal matters.

Require potential buyers to provide their names, addresses, telephone numbers, and background information, and show your home only by appointment. As a security measure, show it only when two or more adults are at home. Selling your own home can save you several thousand dollars in commission, but it requires an investment of time and effort.

fyi

Selling your home on your own? Various Internet sources are available to help, such as **www.owners.com**.

LISTING WITH A REAL ESTATE AGENT

You may decide to sell your home with the assistance of a real estate agent. These businesses range from firms owned by one person to nationally franchised companies. Primary selection factors should be the real estate agent's knowledge of the community and the agent's willingness to actively market your home.

Your real estate agent will provide you with various services. These services include suggesting a selling price, making potential buyers and other agents aware of your home, providing advice on features to highlight, conducting showings of your home, and handling the financial aspects of the sale. A real estate agent can also help screen potential buyers to determine whether they will qualify for a mortgage.

Discount real estate brokers are available to assist sellers who are willing to take on certain duties and want to reduce selling costs. Companies such as Save More Real Estate and Help-U-Sell Real Estate charge a flat fee or 1 to 2 percent of the selling price instead of the customary 6 percent.

CONCEPT CHECK 9-5

1 What actions are recommended when planning to sell your home?
2 What factors affect the selling price of a home?
3 What should you consider when deciding whether to sell your home on your own or use the services of a real estate agent?

Action Application Visit a couple of homes for sale. What features do you believe would appeal to potential buyers? What efforts were made to attract potential buyers to the open houses?

SUMMARY OF OBJECTIVES

Objective 1
Evaluate available housing alternatives.
Your needs, life situation, and financial resources are the major factors that influence your selection of housing. Assess renting and buying alternatives in terms of their financial and opportunity costs.

Objective 2
Analyze the costs and benefits associated with renting.
The main advantages of renting are mobility, fewer responsibilities, and lower initial costs. The main disadvantages of renting are few financial benefits, a restricted lifestyle, and legal concerns.

Objective 3
Implement the home-buying process.
Home buying involves five major stages: (1) determining home ownership needs, (2) finding and evaluating a property to pur-

chase, (3) pricing the property, (4) financing the purchase, and (5) closing the real estate transaction.

Objective 4
Calculate the costs associated with purchasing a home.
The costs associated with purchasing a home include the down payment; mortgage origination costs; closing costs such as a deed fee, prepaid interest, attorney's fees, payment for title insurance, and a property survey; and an escrow account for homeowner's insurance and property taxes.

Objective 5
Develop a strategy for selling a home.
When selling a home, you must decide whether to make certain repairs and improvements, determine a selling price, and choose between selling the home yourself and using the services of a real estate agent.

KEY TERMS

adjustable-rate mortgage (ARM)   290

amortization   289

appraisal   296

balloon mortgage   290

buy-down   293

closing costs   294

condominium   281

conventional mortgage   289

cooperative housing   281

deed   294

earnest money   285

escrow account   294

graduated-payment mortgage   293

growing-equity mortgage   293

lease   277

manufactured home   281

mortgage   287

payment cap   292

points   288

rate cap   292

refinancing   294

reverse mortgage   293

second mortgage   293

shared appreciation mortgage (SAM)   293

title insurance   294

zoning laws   283

FINANCIAL PLANNING PROBLEMS

1. *Determining Appropriate Housing.* What type of housing would you suggest for people in the following life situations? (Obj. 1)

   a. A single parent with two school-age children.

   b. A two-income couple without children.

   c. A person with both dependent children and a dependent parent.

   d. A couple near retirement with grown children.

2. *Comparing Renting and Buying.* Based on the following data, would you recommend buying or renting?

Rental Costs	Buying Costs
Annual rent, $7,380	Annual mortgage payments, $9,800 ($9,575 is interest)
Insurance, $145	
Security deposit, $650	Property taxes, $1,780
	Insurance/maintenance, $1,050
	Down payment/closing costs, $4,500
	Growth in equity, $225
	Estimated annual appreciation, $1,700

Assume an after-tax savings interest rate of 6 percent and a tax rate of 28 percent. (Obj. 2)

3. *Analyzing the Buy-versus-Rent Decision.* Use the buy-versus-rent analysis on page 275 to compare two residences you might consider. (Obj. 2)

4. *Estimating a Monthly Mortgage Payment.* Estimate the affordable monthly mortgage payment, the affordable mortgage amount, and the affordable home purchase price for the following situation (see Exhibit 9–8). (Obj. 4)

Monthly gross income, $2,950

Down payment to be made—15 percent of purchase price

Other debt (monthly payment), $160

Monthly estimate for property taxes and insurance, $210

30-year loan at 8 percent.

5. *Calculating Monthly Mortgage Payments.* Based on Exhibit 9–9, what would be the monthly mortgage payments for each of the following situations?

 a. $40,000, 15-year loan at 11.5 percent.

 b. $76,000, 30-year loan at 9 percent.

 c. $65,000, 20-year loan at 10 percent.

What relationship exists between the length of the loan and the monthly payment? How does the mortgage rate affect the monthly payment? (Obj. 4)

6. *Comparing Total Mortgage Payments.* Which mortgage would result in higher total payments? (Obj. 4)

Mortgage A: $985 a month for 30 years

Mortgage B: $780 a month for 5 years and $1,056 for 25 years

7. *Evaluating a Refinance Decision.* Kelly and Tim Jones plan to refinance their mortgage to obtain a lower interest rate. They will reduce their mortgage payments by $56 a month. Their closing costs for refinancing will be $1,670. How long will it take them to cover the cost of refinancing? (Obj. 4)

8. *Future Value of an Amount Saved.* You estimate that you can save $3,800 by selling your home yourself rather than using a real estate agent. What would be the future value of that amount if invested for five years at 7 percent? (Obj. 5)

FINANCIAL PLANNING ACTIVITIES

1. *Comparing Housing Alternatives.* Interview several people about the factors that influenced their current residence. (Obj. 1)

2. *Comparing Rental Situations.* Using Sheet 42 in the *Personal Financial Planner,* compare the costs, facilities, and features of apartments and other rental housing in your area. You may obtain this information through newspaper advertisements, rental offices, or online searches. (Obj. 2)

3. *Comparing Home-Buying Alternatives.* Visit the sales office for a condominium, a new home, and a mobile home. Based on the information obtained, prepare a written or an oral presentation comparing the benefits and potential concerns of these housing alternatives. (Obj. 3)

4. *Comparing Types of Mortgages.* Talk with people who have different types of mortgages. What suggestions do they offer about obtaining home financing? What were their experiences with closing costs when they purchased their homes? (Obj. 4)

5. *Comparing Mortgage Companies.* Using Sheet 44 in the *Personal Financial Planner,* contact several mortgage companies and other financial institutions to obtain information about current mortgage rates, application fees, and the process for obtaining a mortgage. (Obj. 4)

INTERNET CONNECTION

Comparing Mortgage Rates Online

Using the three Web sites listed (or others of your choice), obtain the following information.

Mortgage Rate Web Site	www.bankrate.com	www.hsh.com	www.bestrate.com
What is the current rate for a 30-year, fixed-rate mortgage in your geographic area?			
What is the rate for a 15-year, fixed-rate mortgage?			
What is the rate for an adjustable-rate mortgage?			
What is the recent trend (up, down, stable) for mortgage rates?			
What do you believe to be the future prospect for mortgage rates (up, down, stable)?			
In addition to rate information, what additional services are provided on this Web site?			

FINANCIAL PLANNING CASE

Housing Decisions

When Mark and Valerie Bowman first saw the house, they didn't like it. However, it was a dark, rainy day. They viewed the house more favorably on their second visit, which they had expected to be a waste of time. Despite cracked ceilings, the need for a paint job, and a kitchen built in the 1960s, the Bowmans saw a potential to create a place they could call their own.

Beth Franklin purchased her condominium six years ago. She obtained a mortgage rate of 8.25 percent, a very good rate then. Recently, when interest rates dropped, Beth was considering refinancing her mortgage at a lower rate.

Matt and Peggy Zoran had been married for five years and were still living in an apartment. Several of the Zorans' friends had purchased homes recently. However, Matt and Peggy were not sure they wanted to follow this example. Although they liked their friends' homes and had viewed photographs of homes currently on the market, they also liked the freedom from maintenance responsibility they enjoyed as renters.

Questions

1. How could the Bowmans benefit from buying a home that needed improvements?

2. How might Beth Franklin have found out when mortgage rates were at a level that would make refinancing her condominium more affordable?

3. Although the Zorans had good reasons for continuing to rent, what factors might make it desirable for an individual or a family to buy a home?

VIDEO CASE

The Home-Buying Process

After renting for awhile, Janet and Jeff are now planning to buy their first home. They believe the time has come to take a big step forward in their housing choice.

City or suburbs? Condominium or townhouse? Existing home or new construction? Conventional mortgage or FHA? Fixed-rate mortgage or ARM?

"Wow, this gets a bit confusing," exclaimed Jeff.

"I'm sure we'll be able to get through this," responded Janet.

While they are a bit overwhelmed by this decision, Janet and Jeff also know that many information sources and housing professionals are available to assist them.

Questions

1. What factors commonly influence renters to buy a home?

2. How can Janet and Jeff determine how much they can afford when buying a home?

3. What professionals will be most useful to Janet and Jeff when buying a home?

4. Are Janet and Jeff financially qualified to purchase a home? What factors will influence the decision to grant them a mortgage?

YOUR PERSONAL FINANCIAL PLANNER IN ACTION

Selecting and Financing Housing

Housing represents a major budget expenditure. This area of financial planning requires careful analysis of needs along with a comparison of the costs and benefits of housing alternatives.

Your Short-Term Financial Planning Activities	Resources
1. Compare your current housing situation with your housing needs and financial situation	PFP Sheet 40 http://homebuying.about.com http://houseandhome.msn.com www.mymoney.gov www.hud.gov
2. Conduct an analysis to compare renting and buying of housing	PFP Sheet 41 www.homefair.com www.newbuyer.com
3. Compare various rental alternatives as needed	PFP Sheet 42 http://apartments.about.com
4. Determine your housing and mortgage affordability, and compare various sources of mortgages	PFP Sheet 43, 44 www.centura.com/tools http://loan.yahoo.com/m/ http://nt.mortgage101.com www.bankrate.com www.hsh.com
Your Long-Term Financial Planning Activities	
1. Monitor changing interest rates and assess refinancing alternatives	PFP Sheet 45 www.interest.com www.mortgage-net.com
2. Develop a plan for assessing housing needs and costs in the future.	Text pages 272–275 www.realestatejournal.com www.hud.gov/buying/rvrsmort.cfm

CONTINUING CASE

Housing Decisions

Life Situation	*Financial Data*	
Young married couple	Monthly income	$3,600
Pam, 30	Assets	$33,850
Josh, 32	Living expenses	$3,125
Two children, ages 1 and 3	Liabilities	$1,520

Housing needs are changing for the Brocks as their family increases in size. At present, they pay $750 in rent for a two-bedroom apartment. To purchase a home for a comparable monthly payment, the Brocks would have to relocate farther from Josh's place of employment. With a second car and public transportation available, Pam and Josh are starting to consider this home purchase.

Questions

1. Based on a monthly income of $3,600, an estimated $240 per month for property taxes and homeowner's insurance, a current mortgage interest rate of 6 percent, and a down payment of at least 10 percent, what would it cost the Brocks to purchase a home?

2. What tax advantages will the Brocks realize by purchasing a home rather than renting?

3. Explain which sections of *Personal Financial Planner* sheets 40–45 could be useful to the Brocks when assessing their housing situation.

10 Property and Motor Vehicle Insurance

Key Concept

Adequate insurance coverage for your home, personal property, and automobile protects you from loss of your most valuable tangible assets. Planning an insurance program requires balancing potential financial risks with the cost of obtaining insurance coverage.

Digital Study Tools

Online Learning Center Study Tools for This Chapter

- Multiple-choice quiz
- Flashcards
- eLearning sessions
- Crossword puzzle
- Personal Finance Online: Risk Management: Property and Casualty Insurance

Student CD Study Tools for This Chapter

- Self-study software
- Narrated PowerPoint
- Personal financial planning software: Worksheets 46–50

www.mhhe.com/kdh

Learning Objectives

1 Develop a risk management plan using insurance.

2 Discuss the importance of property and liability insurance.

3 Explain the insurance coverages and policy types available to homeowners and renters.

4 Analyze factors that influence the amount of coverage and cost of home insurance.

5 Identify the important types of automobile insurance coverages.

6 Evaluate factors that affect the cost of automobile insurance.

On the Road to Higher Auto Insurance Rates?

"Should we take my car on the trip, or your van?

When Elise asked this question, she started thinking about not only their upcoming vacation to California but also their auto insurance coverages and costs.

"California is a long trip. The van has over 130,000 miles, and is in good condition," replied Mark. "It would be more comfortable for the four of us, but it might not be as reliable as your car."

"I'm not sure. Do we have the right types of insurance coverage?" Elise asked. "Do we need towing or car rental coverage? What about the loss limit for our bodily injury liability?"

"Wait a minute, this is supposed to be a vacation not an insurance planning seminar," Mark commented.

"But we need to consider these sometime," Elise responded.

"OK, OK. We seem to be fairly well covered," replied Mark. "Our auto club membership takes care of towing,

and we have 50/100 bodily injury coverage. The state only requires 20/40."

"Those are only minimum legal amounts," noted Elise. "We could easily have an accident that could result in much higher claims. We should consider 100/300. Also, we seem to be paying a lot for our auto insurance."

With auto insurance rates increasing in some areas by 8 to 11 percent annually, Elise and Mark, like many others, desire to lower their auto insurance costs.

Mark asked, "How about checking online for possible insurance discounts or companies that offer lower rates?"

Elise warned, "Be careful that those companies provide appropriate claim service. And don't forget, if you think our rates are high now, wait a couple of years, when our children start driving!"

"Maybe we can save some money on our trip if we sleep in the car," Mark suggested. "In that case, we'd better take the van!"

QUESTIONS

What Actions Should Be Taken?

1. What additional auto insurance coverage should Mark and Elise consider?
2. What actions would you recommend to Mark and Elise to better understand their auto insurance coverages?

What about Your Situation?

3. How would you assess your current situation regarding adequate auto insurance coverages?
4. What benefits and drawbacks are associated with buying auto insurance online?

Learn More Online

Based on information at personalinsure.about.com and www.iii.org, describe some advice that could help a person better understand various auto insurance coverages.

Insurance and Risk Management: An Introduction

Objective 1

Develop a risk management plan using insurance.

insurance Protection against possible financial loss.

insurance company A risk-sharing firm that assumes financial responsibility for losses that may result from an insured risk.

insurer An insurance company.

policy A written contract for insurance.

premium The amount of money a policyholder is charged for an insurance policy.

insured A person covered by an insurance policy.

policyholder A person who owns an insurance policy.

risk Chance or uncertainty of loss; also used to mean "the insured."

peril The cause of a possible loss.

hazard A factor that increases the likelihood of loss through some peril.

Insurance involves property and people. By providing protection against the risks of financial uncertainty and unexpected losses, insurance makes it possible to plan for the future.

WHAT IS INSURANCE?

Insurance is protection against possible financial loss. Although many types of insurance exist, they all have one thing in common: They give you the peace of mind that comes from knowing that money will be available to meet the needs of your survivors, pay medical expenses, protect your home and belongings, and cover personal or property damage caused by you when driving.

Life insurance replaces income that would be lost if the policyholder died. Health insurance helps meet medical expenses when the policyholder becomes ill. Automobile insurance helps cover property and personal damage caused by the policyholder's car. Home insurance covers the policyholder's place of residence and its associated financial risks, such as damage to personal property and injuries to others.

Insurance is based on the principle of *pooling risks,* in which thousands of policyholders pay a small sum of money (*premium*) into a central pool. The pool is then large enough to meet the expenses of the small number of people who actually suffer a loss.

An **insurance company,** or **insurer,** is a risk-sharing firm that agrees to assume financial responsibility for losses that may result from an insured risk. A person joins the risk-sharing group (the insurance company) by purchasing a **policy** (a contract). Under the policy, the insurance company agrees to assume the risk for a fee (the **premium**) that the person (the **insured** or the **policyholder**) pays periodically.

Insurance can provide protection against many risks of financial uncertainty and unexpected losses. The financial consequences of failing to obtain the right amount and type of insurance can be disastrous.

TYPES OF RISKS

You face risks every day. You can't cross the street without some danger that you'll be hit by a car. You can't own property without taking the chance that it will be lost, stolen, damaged, or destroyed. Insurance companies offer financial protection against such dangers and losses by promising to compensate the insured for a relatively large loss in return for the payment of a much smaller but certain expense called the *premium.*

Risk, peril, and *hazard* are important terms in insurance. While in popular use these terms tend to be interchangeable, each has a distinct, technical meaning in insurance terminology.

Basically, **risk** is uncertainty or lack of predictability. In this instance, it refers to the uncertainty as to loss that a person or a property covered by insurance faces. Insurance companies frequently refer to the insured person or property as the *risk.*

Peril is the cause of a possible loss. It is the contingency that causes someone to take out insurance. People buy policies for financial protection against perils such as fire, windstorms, explosions, robbery, accidents, and premature death.

Hazard increases the likelihood of loss through some peril. For example, defective house wiring is a hazard that increases the likelihood of the peril of fire.

The most common risks are classified as personal risks, property risks, and liability risks. *Personal risks* are the uncertainties surrounding loss of income or life due to premature death, illness, disability, old age, or unemployment. *Property risks* are the uncertainties of direct or indirect losses to personal or real property due to fire, windstorms, accidents, theft, and other hazards. *Liability risks* are possible losses due to negligence resulting in bodily injury or property damage to others. Such harm or damage could be caused by an automobile, professional misconduct, injury suffered on one's property, and so on.

Personal risks, property risks, and liability risks are types of **pure risk,** or *insurable risk,* since there would be a chance of loss only if the specified events occurred. Pure risks are accidental and unintentional risks for which the nature and financial cost of the loss can be predicted.

A **speculative risk** is a risk that carries a chance of either loss or gain. Starting a small business that may or may not succeed is an example of speculative risk. So is gambling. Most speculative risks are considered to be uninsurable.

RISK MANAGEMENT METHODS

Risk management is an organized strategy for protecting assets and people. It helps reduce financial losses caused by destructive events. Risk management is a long-range planning process. People's risk management needs change at various points in their lives. If you understand risks and how to manage them, you can provide better protection for yourself and your family. In this way, you can reduce your financial losses and thereby improve your chances for economic, social, physical, and emotional well-being. Since you will probably be unable to afford to cover all risks, you need to understand how to obtain the best protection you can afford.

Most people think of risk management as buying insurance. However, insurance is not the only method of dealing with risk; in certain situations, other methods may be less costly. Four general risk management techniques are commonly used.

1. RISK AVOIDANCE   You can avoid the risk of an automobile accident by not driving. General Motors can avoid the risk of product failure by not introducing new cars. Risk avoidance would be practiced in both instances, but at a very high cost. You might have to give up your job, and General Motors might lose out to competitors that introduce new models.

In some situations, however, risk avoidance is practical. At the personal level, people avoid risks by not smoking or by not walking through high-crime neighborhoods. At the business level, jewelry stores avoid losses through robbery by locking their merchandise in vaults. Obviously, no person or business can avoid all risks.

2. RISK REDUCTION   While avoiding risks completely may not be possible, reducing risks may be a cause of action. You can reduce the risk of injury in an auto accident by wearing a seat belt. You can install smoke alarms and fire extinguishers to protect life and reduce potential fire damage. You can reduce the risk of illness by eating a balanced diet and exercising.

3. RISK ASSUMPTION   Risk assumption means taking on responsibility for the loss or injury that may result from a risk. Generally, it makes sense to assume a risk when the potential loss is small, when risk management has reduced the risk, when insurance coverage is expensive, and when there is no other way to obtain protection. For instance, you might decide not to purchase collision insurance on an older car. Then, if an accident occurs, you will bear the costs of fixing the car.

Self-insurance is the process of establishing a monetary fund to cover the cost of a loss. Self-insurance does not eliminate risks; it only provides means for covering losses. Many people self-insure by default, not by choice.

pure risk A risk in which there is only a chance of loss; also called *insurable risk.*

speculative risk A risk in which there is a chance of either loss or gain.

self-insurance The process of establishing a monetary fund to cover the cost of a loss.

Exhibit **10–1**   Examples of risks and risk management strategies

Risks		Strategies for Reducing Financial Impact		
Personal Events	**Financial Impact**	**Personal Resources**	**Private Sector**	**Public Sector**
Disability	Loss of one income Loss of services Increased expenses	Savings, investments Family observing safety precautions	Disability insurance	Disability insurance Social Security
Illness	Loss of one income Catastrophic hospital expenses	Health-enhancing behavior	Health insurance Health maintenance organizations	Military health care Medicare, Medicaid
Death	Loss of one income Loss of services Final expenses	Estate planning Risk reduction	Life insurance	Veteran's life insurance Social Security survivor's benefits
Retirement	Decreased income Unplanned living expenses	Savings Investments Hobbies, skills Part-time work	Retirement and/or pensions	Social Security Pension plan for government employees
Property loss	Cost to repair damage to property Repair or replacement cost of theft	Property repair and upkeep Security plans	Automobile insurance Homeowner's insurance Flood insurance (joint program with government)	Flood insurance (joint program with business)
Liability	Claims and settlement costs Lawsuits and legal expenses Loss of personal assets and income	Observing safety precautions Maintaining property	Homeowner's insurance Automobile insurance Malpractice insurance	State-operated insurance plans

4. RISK SHIFTING   The most common method of dealing with risk is to shift, or transfer, it to an insurance company or some other organization. Insurance is the protection against loss afforded by the purchase of an insurance policy from an insurance company.

Exhibit 10–1 summarizes various risks and appropriate strategies for managing them.

PLANNING AN INSURANCE PROGRAM

Because all people have their own needs and goals, many of which change over the years, a personal insurance program should be tailored to those changes. In the early years of marriage, when the family is growing, most families need certain kinds of insurance protection. This protection may include property insurance on an apartment or a house, life and disability insurance for wage earners and caretakers of dependents, and adequate health insurance for the whole family.

Later, when the family has a higher income and a different financial situation, protection needs will change. There might be a long-range provision for the children's education, more life insurance to match higher income and living standards, and revised health insurance protection. Still later, when the children have grown and are on their

Exhibit **10-2**

Creating a personal insurance program

own, retirement benefits will be a consideration, further changing the family's personal insurance program.

The Financial Planning for Life's Situations feature on page 310 suggests several guidelines to follow in planning your insurance program. Exhibit 10–2 outlines the steps in developing a personal insurance program.

STEP 1: SET INSURANCE GOALS
In managing risks, your goals are to minimize personal, property, and liability risks. Your insurance goals should define what to do to cover the basic risks present in your life situation. Covering the basic risks means providing a financial resource to cover costs resulting from a loss.

Suppose your goal is to buy a new car. You must plan to make the purchase and to protect yourself against financial losses from accidents. Auto insurance on the car lets you enjoy the car without worrying that an auto accident might leave you worse off, financially and physically, than before.

Each individual has unique goals. Income, age, family size, lifestyle, experience, and responsibilities influence the goals you set, and the insurance you buy must reflect those goals. In general, financial advisers say that a basic risk management plan must set goals to reduce

- Potential loss of income due to the premature death, illness, accident, or unemployment of a wage earner.

- Potential loss of income and extra expense resulting from the illness, disability, or death of a spouse.

- Additional expenses due to the injury, illness, or death of other family members.

HOW CAN YOU PLAN AN INSURANCE PROGRAM?

Did you:	Yes	No
1. Seek advice from a competent and reliable insurance adviser?	☐	☐
2. Determine what insurance you need to provide your family with sufficient protection if you die?	☐	☐
3. Consider what portion of the family protection is met by Social Security and by group insurance?	☐	☐
4. Decide what other needs insurance must meet (funeral expenses, savings, retirement annuities, etc.)?	☐	☐
5. Decide what types of insurance best meet your needs?	☐	☐
6. Plan an insurance program and implement it except for periodic reviews of changing needs and changing conditions?	☐	☐
7. Avoid buying more insurance than you need or can afford?	☐	☐
8. Consider dropping one policy for another that provides the same coverage for less money?	☐	☐

Note: *Yes* answers reflect wise actions for insurance planning.

- Potential loss of real or personal property due to fire, theft, or other hazards.
- Potential loss of income, savings, and property due to personal liability.

STEP 2: DEVELOP A PLAN TO REACH YOUR GOALS Planning is a sign of maturity, a way of taking control of life instead of letting life happen to you. What risks do you face? Which risks can you afford to take without having to back away from your goals? What resources—public programs, personal assets, family, church, or private risk-sharing plans—are available to you?

To understand and use the resources at your command, you need good information. In terms of insurance, this means a clear picture of the available insurance, the reliability of different insurers, and the comparative costs of the coverage needed.

STEP 3: PUT YOUR PLAN INTO ACTION As you carry out your plan, obtain financial and personal resources, budget them, and use them to reach risk management goals. If, for example, you find the insurance protection you have is not enough to cover your basic risks, you may purchase additional coverage, change the kind of insurance coverage, restructure your budget to cover additional insurance costs, and strengthen your savings or investment programs to reduce long-term risk.

The best risk management plans have flexibility. Savings accounts or other cash, for example, should be available as emergency funds for unexpected financial problems. The best plans are also flexible enough to allow you to respond to changing life situations. Your goal should be an insurance program that expands (or contracts) with changing protection needs.

To put your risk management plan to work, you must answer four basic questions: (1) What should be insured, (2) for how much, (3) what kind of insurance should I buy, and (4) from whom?

STEP 4: REVIEW YOUR RESULTS   Evaluate your insurance plan periodically, at least every two or three years or whenever your family circumstances change. Among the questions you should ask yourself are: Does it work? Does it adequately protect my plans and goals? An effective risk manager consistently checks the outcomes of decisions and is alert to changes that may reduce the effectiveness of the current risk management plan.

A young working couple may be entirely happy with their life and health insurance coverage. When they add an infant to the family, a review of protection is appropriate. Suddenly the risk of financial catastrophe to the family (should one or both parents die or become disabled) is much greater.

The needs of a single person differ from those of a family, a single parent, a couple, or a group of unrelated adults living in the same household. While these people face similar risks, their financial responsibility to others differs greatly. In each case, the vital question is: Have I provided the financial resources and risk management strategy needed to take care of my basic responsibilities for my own well-being and the well-being of others?

Sheet 46
Current insurance policies and needs

CONCEPT CHECK 10-1

1 What is the purpose of insurance?
2 How are the most common risks classified?
3 What is the difference between pure risk and speculative risk?
4 What are the methods of managing risk?
5 What are the steps in planning your personal insurance coverage?

Action Application   Locate Web sites that provide useful information for selecting and comparing various insurance coverages.

Property and Liability Insurance

Major disasters have caused catastrophic amounts of property loss in the United States. In recent years, hurricanes, tornadoes, and floods in various areas have caused billions of dollars of damage.

Since most people invest large amounts of money in their homes and motor vehicles, protecting these assets from loss is a great concern. Each year, homeowners and renters lose billions of dollars from more than 3 million burglaries, 500,000 fires, and 200,000 instances of damage from other hazards. The cost of injuries and property damage caused by automobiles is also very great. Most people use insurance to reduce their chances of economic loss from these risks.

The price you pay for home and automobile insurance may be viewed as an investment in financial protection against these losses. Although the costs of home and automobile insurance may seem high, the financial losses from which insurance protects you are much higher. Property and liability insurance offer protection from financial losses that may arise from a wide variety of situations.

The main types of risks related to a home and an automobile are (1) property damage or loss and (2) your responsibility for injuries to others or damage to the property of others.

POTENTIAL PROPERTY LOSSES

Houses, automobiles, furniture, clothing, and other personal belongings are a substantial financial commitment. Property owners face two basic types of risks. The first is

Objective 2

Discuss the importance of property and liability insurance.

Property owners face a variety of risks.

physical damage caused by hazards such as fire, wind, water, and smoke. These hazards can cause destruction of your property or temporary loss of its use. For example, if a windstorm causes a large tree branch to break your automobile windshield, you lose the use of the vehicle while it is being repaired. The second type of risk property owners face is *loss of use* due to robbery, burglary, vandalism, or arson.

LIABILITY PROTECTION

In a wide variety of circumstances, a person may be judged legally responsible for bodily injuries or property damages. For example, if a child walks across your property, falls, and sustains severe injuries, the child's family may be able to recover substantial damages from you as a result of the injuries. If you accidentally damage a rare painting while assisting a friend with home repairs, the friend may take legal action against you to recover the cost of the painting.

liability Legal responsibility for the financial cost of another person's losses or injuries.

Liability is legal responsibility for the financial cost of another person's losses or injuries. Your legal responsibility is commonly caused by **negligence,** failure to take ordinary or reasonable care. Doing something in a careless manner, such as improperly supervising children at a swimming pool or failing to remove items from a frequently used staircase, may be ruled as negligence in a liability lawsuit.

negligence Failure to take ordinary or reasonable care in a situation.

Despite taking great care, a person may still be held liable in a situation. **Strict liability** is present when a person is held responsible for intentional or unintentional actions. **Vicarious liability** occurs when a person is held responsible for the actions of another person. If the behavior of a child causes financial or physical harm to others, the parent may be held responsible; if the activities of an employee cause damage, the employer may be held responsible.

strict liability A situation in which a person is held responsible for intentional or unintentional actions.

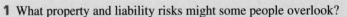
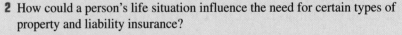

CONCEPT CHECK 10-2 ✔

vicarious liability A situation in which a person is held legally responsible for the actions of another person.

1 What property and liability risks might some people overlook?
2 How could a person's life situation influence the need for certain types of property and liability insurance?

Action Application Talk to a financial planner or an insurance agent about the financial difficulties faced by people who lack adequate home and auto insurance. What common property and liability coverages do many people overlook?

Home and Property Insurance

Objective 3

Explain the insurance coverages and policy types available to homeowners and renters.

Your home and personal belongings are probably a major portion of your assets. Whether you rent your dwelling or own a home, property insurance is vital. **Homeowner's insurance** is coverage for your place of residence and its associated financial risks, such as damage to personal property and injuries to others (see Exhibit 10–3).

HOMEOWNER'S INSURANCE COVERAGES

homeowner's insurance Coverage for a place of residence and its associated financial risks.

A homeowner's policy provides coverages for the house and other structures, additional living expenses, personal property, personal liability and related coverages, and specialized coverages.

HOUSE AND OTHER STRUCTURES   The main component of homeowner's insurance is protection against financial loss due to damage or destruction to a house or other structures. Your dwelling and attached structures are covered for fire and

other hazards. Detached structures on the property, such as a garage, toolshed, or gazebo, are also protected. The coverage also includes trees, shrubs, and plants.

ADDITIONAL LIVING EXPENSES

If damage from a fire or other event prevents the use of your home, *additional living expense coverage* pays for the cost of living in a temporary location while your home is being repaired. Some policies limit additional living expense coverage to 10 to 20 percent of the home's coverage and limit payments to a maximum of six to nine months; other policies pay the full cost incurred for up to a year.

PERSONAL PROPERTY

Your household belongings, such as furniture, appliances, and clothing, are covered for damage or loss up to a portion of the insured value of the home, usually 55, 70, or 75 percent. For example, a home insured for $80,000 might have $56,000 (70 percent) of coverage for household belongings.

Personal property coverage commonly has limits for the theft of certain items, such as $1,000 for jewelry, $2,000 for firearms, and $2,500 for silverware. Items with a value exceeding these limits can be protected with a **personal property floater,** which covers the damage or loss of a specific item of high value. A floater requires a detailed description of the item and periodic appraisals to verify the current value. This coverage protects the item regardless of location; thus, the item is insured while you are traveling or transporting it.

Floaters to protect home computers and related equipment are recommended. This additional coverage can prevent financial loss due to damage or loss of your computer. Contact your insurance agent to determine whether the equipment is covered against damage from mischievous pets, spilled drinks, dropping, or power surges.

Personal property coverage usually provides protection against the loss or damage of articles taken with you when away from home. For example, possessions taken on vacation or used while at school are usually covered up to a policy limit. Property that you rent, such as some power tools or a rug shampoo machine, is insured while in your possession.

In the event of damage or loss of property, you must be able to prove both ownership and value. A **household inventory** is a list or other documentation of personal belongings, with purchase dates and cost information. You can get a form for such an inventory from an insurance agent. Exhibit 10–4 provides a reminder of the items you should include in the inventory. For items of special value, you should have receipts, serial numbers, brand names, model names, and written appraisals of value.

personal property floater
Additional property insurance to cover the damage or loss of a specific item of high value.

household inventory A list or other documentation of personal belongings, with purchase dates and cost information.

Exhibit 10-3   Home insurance coverage

House and other structures   **Personal property**   **Loss of use/additional living expenses while home is uninhabitable**   **Personal liability and related coverages**

Expensive personal property items may require additional insurance coverage.

Your household inventory can include photographs or a video recording of your home and contents. Make sure the closet and storage area doors are photographed open. On the backs of the photographs, indicate the date and the value of the objects. Regularly update your inventory, photos, and appraisal documents. Keep a copy of each document in a secure location such as a safe deposit box.

PERSONAL LIABILITY AND RELATED COVERAGES   Each day, you face the risk of financial loss due to injuries to others or damage to property for which you are responsible. The following are examples of this risk:

Exhibit **10-4**   Household inventory contents

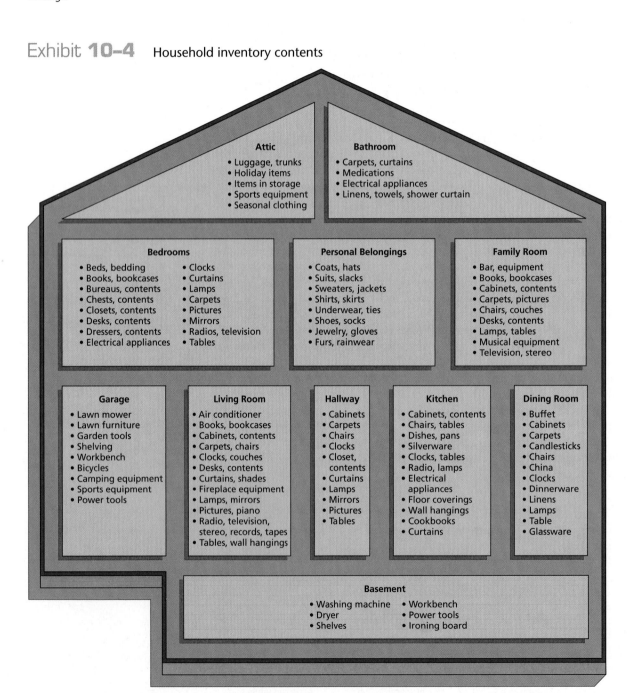

- A neighbor or guest falls on your property, resulting in permanent disability.
- A spark from burning leaves on your property starts a fire that damages a neighbor's roof.
- A member of your family accidentally breaks an expensive glass statue while at another person's house.

Sheet 47
Home inventory

In each of these situations, you could be held responsible for the costs incurred. The personal liability component of a homeowner's policy protects you from financial losses resulting from legal action or claims against you or family members due to damages to the property of others. This coverage includes the cost of legal defense.

Not all individuals who come to your property are covered by your liability insurance. While a babysitter or others who assist you occasionally are probably covered, regular employees, such as a housekeeper or a gardener, may require worker's compensation coverage.

Additional information about conducting a home inventory may be obtained at **www.iii.org** or **www.homestore.com.**

Most homeowner's policies provide a basic personal liability coverage of $100,000, but additional amounts are frequently recommended. An **umbrella policy,** also called a *personal catastrophe policy,* supplements your basic personal liability coverage. This added protection covers you for personal injury claims such as libel, slander, defamation of character, and invasion of property. Extended liability policies are sold in amounts of $1 million or more and are useful for individuals with substantial net worth. If you are a business owner, you may need other types of liability coverage.

umbrella policy
Supplementary personal liability coverage; also called a *personal catastrophe policy.*

Medical payments coverage pays the costs of minor accidental injuries on your property and minor injuries caused by you, family members, or pets away from home. Settlements under medical payments coverage are made without determining fault. This protection allows fast processing of small claims, generally up to $5,000. Suits for more severe personal injuries are covered by the personal liability portion of the homeowner's policy. Medical payments coverage does not cover the people who live in the home being insured.

medical payments coverage Home insurance that pays the cost of minor accidental injuries on one's property.

Should you or a family member accidentally damage another person's property, the *supplementary coverage* of homeowner's insurance will pay for these minor mishaps. This protection is usually limited to $500 or $1,000. Again, payments are made regardless of fault. Any property damage claims for greater amounts would require action under the personal liability coverage.

SPECIALIZED COVERAGES

Homeowner's insurance usually does not cover losses from floods and earthquakes. People living in areas with these two risks need special coverage. In various communities, the National Flood Insurance Program makes flood insurance available. This protection is separate from the homeowner's policy. An insurance agent or the Federal Emergency Management Agency of the Federal Insurance Administration (see Appendix B) can give you additional information about this coverage. Fewer than half of the people who live in flood-prone areas have this coverage.

Earthquake insurance can be obtained as an **endorsement,** or addition of coverage, to the homeowner's policy. Since the most severe earthquakes occur in the Pacific Coast region, most insurance against this risk is bought in that region. Remember, however, that every state is vulnerable to earthquakes and this insurance coverage is available in all areas. Lenders frequently require insurance against both floods and earthquakes for a mortgage to buy a home in areas with these risks.

endorsement An addition of coverage to a standard insurance policy.

Exhibit **10-5**   Types of home insurance policies

The policies below cover perils provided for in the basic and broad forms, including		
Basic Form (HO–1)	• Fire, lightning • Windstorm, hail • Explosion • Riot or civil commotion • Aircraft • Vehicles	• Smoke • Vandalism or malicious mischief • Theft • Glass breakage • Volcanic eruption
Broad Form (HO–2)	Covers all basic-form risks, plus • Falling objects • Weight of ice, snow, or sleet • Discharge of water or steam	• Tearing apart of heating system or appliance • Freezing • Accidental damage from electrical current
Special Form (All risk) (HO–3)	Covers all basic and broad-form risks, plus any other risks except those specifically excluded from the policy, such as • Flood • War • Earthquake • Nuclear accidents	
Tenants Form (HO–4)	Covers personal belongings against the risks covered by the basic and broad forms of the homeowner's policies	
Comprehensive Form (HO–5)	Expands coverage of HO–3 to include endorsements for items such as replacement cost coverage on contents and guaranteed replacement cost coverage on buildings	
Condominium Form (HO–6)	Covers personal belongings and additions to the living unit	
Country Home Form (HO–7)	For nonfarm business rural residents with coverage on agricultural buildings and equipment	
Modified Coverage Form (HO–8)	This older-home policy covers residences with high replacement cost relative to current market value. For example, decorative woodwork in a Victorian home would be very costly to duplicate; coverage pays for the restoration of property, but not necessarily with the same materials as used in the original. The other major coverages of each policy are • Personal liability • Medical payments for guests on the property • Additional living expenses	

Note: HO–1 and HO–2 policies are no longer sold in most areas.

RENTER'S INSURANCE

For people who rent, home insurance coverages include personal property protection, additional living expenses coverage, and personal liability and related coverages. Protection against financial loss due to damage or loss of personal property is the main component of renter's insurance. Often renters believe they are covered under the insurance policy of the building owner. In fact, the building owner's property insurance does not cover tenants' personal property unless the building owner can be proven liable. If

Certain personal property is specifically excluded from the coverage provided by homeowner's insurance:

- Articles separately described and specifically insured, such as jewelry, furs, boats, or expensive electronic equipment.
- Animals, birds, or fish.
- Motorized land vehicles, except those used to service an insured's residence, that are not licensed for road use.
- Any device or instrument for the transmission and recording of sound, including any accessories or antennas, while in or on motor vehicles. This includes stereo tape players, stereo tapes, and citizens' band radios.
- Aircraft and parts.
- Property of roomers, boarders, and other tenants who are not related to any insured.
- Property contained in an apartment regularly rented or held for rental to others by any insured.
- Property rented or held for rental to others away from the residence premises.
- Business property in storage, or held as a sample, or for sale, or for delivery after sale.
- Business property pertaining to business actually conducted on the residence premises.
- Business property away from the residence premises.

Exhibit 10–6

Not everything is covered

faulty wiring causes a fire and damages a tenant's property, the renter may be able to collect for damages from the building owner.

The personal belongings of students in college housing are usually covered (up to certain amount) on the home insurance policies of their parents. However, if living off campus or owning many expensive items, a separate policy should be considered. Renter's insurance is relatively inexpensive and provides protection from financial loss due to many of the same risks covered in homeowner's policies.

HOME INSURANCE POLICY FORMS

Until the mid-1950s, a homeowner had to buy separate coverage for fire, theft, and other risks. Then the insurance industry developed a series of package policies as shown in Exhibit 10–5. Some property is excluded from most home insurance (see Exhibit 10–6).

Manufactured housing units and mobile homes usually qualify for insurance coverage with conventional policies. However, certain mobile homes may require a special arrangement and higher rates since their construction makes them more prone to fire and wind damage. The cost of mobile home insurance coverage is most heavily affected by location and by the method used to attach the housing unit to the ground. This type of property insurance is quite expensive; a $20,000 mobile home can cost as much to insure as a $60,000 house.

In addition to the property and liability risks previously discussed, home insurance policies include coverage for

- Credit card fraud, check forgery, and counterfeit money.

> **DID YOU KNOW?**
>
> While more than 9 out of 10 home-owners have property insurance, only about 4 out of 10 renters are covered.

> **DID YOU KNOW?**
>
> Computers and other equipment used in a home-based business are not usually covered by a home insurance policy. Contact your insurance agent to obtain needed coverage.

- The cost of removing damaged property.
- Emergency removal of property to protect it from damage.
- Temporary repairs after a loss to prevent further damage.
- Fire department charges in areas with such fees.

CONCEPT CHECK 10-3

1 What main coverages are included in home insurance policies?
2 What is the purpose of personal liability coverage?
3 How does renter's insurance differ from other home insurance policies?

Action Application To assist yourself or someone else who rents, contact an insurance agent to obtain information about the cost of renter's insurance.

Home Insurance Cost Factors

Objective 4

Analyze factors that influence the amount of coverage and cost of home insurance.

coinsurance clause A policy provision that requires a homeowner to pay for part of the losses if the property is not insured for the specified percentage of the replacement value.

actual cash value (ACV) A claim settlement method in which the insured receives payment based on the current replacement cost of a damaged or lost item, less depreciation.

Insurance premiums are affected by claims in your area.

Studies reveal that as many as two-thirds of homes in the United States are not insured or are underinsured. Financial losses caused by fire, theft, wind, and other risks amount to billions of dollars each year. Since most homeowners have a mortgage on their property, their lending institutions usually require insurance. When purchasing insurance, you can get the best value by selecting the appropriate coverage amount and being aware of factors that affect insurance costs.

HOW MUCH COVERAGE DO YOU NEED?

Several factors affect the insurance coverage needed for your home and property (see Exhibit 10–7). Your insurance protection should be based on the amount needed to rebuild or repair your house, not the amount you paid for it. As construction costs rise, you should increase the amount of coverage. In recent years, most insurance policies have had a built-in inflation clause that increases coverage as property values increase.

In the past, most homeowner's policies contained a provision requiring that the building be insured for at least 80 percent of the replacement value. Under this **coinsurance clause,** the homeowner would have to pay for part of the losses if the property was not insured for the specified percentage of the replacement value. Few companies still use coinsurance, most require full coverage.

If you are financing a home, the lending institution will require you to have property insurance in an amount that covers its financial investment. Remember, too, that the amount of insurance on your home will determine the coverage on the contents. Personal belongings are generally covered up to an amount ranging from 55 to 75 percent of the insurance amount on the dwelling.

Insurance companies base claim settlements on one of two methods. Under the **actual cash value (ACV)** method, the payment you receive is based on the current replacement cost of a damaged or lost item less depreciation. This means you would get $180 for a five-year-old television set that cost you $400 and had an estimated life of eight years if the same set now costs $480. Your settlement amount is determined by taking the current cost of $480 and subtracting five years of depreciation from it—$300 for five years at $60 a year.

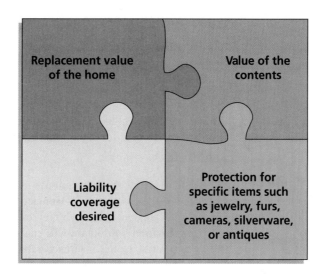

Exhibit **10-7**

Determining the amount of home insurance you need

Under the **replacement value** method for settling claims, you receive the full cost of repairing or replacing a damaged or lost item; depreciation is not considered. However, many companies limit the replacement cost to 400 percent of the item's actual cash value. Replacement value coverage costs about 10 to 20 percent more than ACV coverage.

replacement value A claim settlement method in which the insured receives the full cost of repairing or replacing a damaged or lost item.

FACTORS THAT AFFECT HOME INSURANCE COSTS

The main influences on the premium paid for home and property insurance are the location of the home, the type of structure, the coverage amount and policy type, discounts, and differences among insurance companies.

Sheet 48 Determining needed property insurance

LOCATION OF HOME   The location of the residence affects insurance rates. So do the efficiency of the fire department, distance from the fire station, the available water supply, and the frequency of thefts in the area. If more claims have been filed in an area, home insurance rates for people living there will be higher. Weather events such as a hailstorm or a hurricane also affect insurance costs.

TYPE OF STRUCTURE   The type of home and the construction materials influence the costs of insurance coverage. A brick house, for example, would cost less to insure than a similar house made of wood. However, earthquake coverage is more expensive for a brick home than for a wood dwelling. Stronger, more wind-resistant home construction can reduce insurance costs in Florida, and provide greater protection against hurricane damage. Also, the age and style of the house can create potential risks and increase insurance costs.

COVERAGE AMOUNT AND POLICY TYPE   The policy you select and the financial limits of coverage affect the premium you pay. It costs more to insure a $150,000 home than a $100,000 home. The comprehensive form of homeowner's policy costs more than a tenant's policy.

The *deductible* amount in your policy also affects the cost of your insurance. If you increase the amount of your deductible, your premium will be lower since the company will pay out less in claims. The most common deductible amount is $250. Increasing the deductible from $250 to $500 or $1,000 can reduce the premium 15 percent or more.

DID YOU KNOW?

In some areas, a home could be automatically rejected for insurance coverage if it has had two or three claims of any sort in the past three years. Homes that have encountered water damage, storm damage, and burglaries are most vulnerable to rejection.

REDUCING HOME INSURANCE COSTS

HOME INSURANCE DISCOUNTS   Most companies offer incentives that reduce home insurance costs. Your premium may be lower if you have smoke detectors or a fire extinguisher. Deterrents to burglars, such as dead bolt locks or an alarm system, can also save you money. Some companies offer home insurance discounts to policyholders who are nonsmokers or may give a discount for being "claim free" for a certain number of years.

COMPANY DIFFERENCES   Studies show that you can save more than 30 percent on homeowner's insurance by comparing companies. Contact both insurance agents who work for one company and independent agents who represent several. The information you obtain will enable you to compare rates. Home insurance rates may be compared using information from Web sites such as www.insuremarket.com.

The Insurance Information Institute, **www.iii.org**, can provide you with additional information related to home and auto insurance.

Don't select a company on the basis of price alone. Also consider service and coverage. Not all companies settle claims in the same way. For example, a number of homeowners had two sides of their houses dented by hail. Since the type of siding used in these houses was no longer available, all of the siding had to be replaced. Some insurance companies paid for complete replacement of the siding, while others paid only for replacement of the damaged areas. State insurance commissions, other government agencies, and consumer organizations can provide information about the reputations of insurance companies. *Consumer Reports* (www.Consumer Reports.org) regularly publishes a satisfaction index of property insurance companies.

Sheet 49
Apartment/
home
insurance
comparison

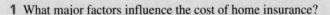
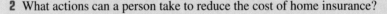

CONCEPT CHECK 10-4

1 What major factors influence the cost of home insurance?
2 What actions can a person take to reduce the cost of home insurance?

Action Application Conduct Web research or contact an insurance agent to determine the natural disasters that occur most frequently in your geographic area. What actions could be taken to reduce the financial risk of these natural disasters?

Automobile Insurance Coverages

Objective 5

Identify the important types of automobile insurance coverages.

financial responsibility law State legislation that requires drivers to prove their ability to cover the cost of damage or injury caused by an automobile accident.

Each year, motor vehicle crashes cost over $150 billion in lost wages and medical costs. The National Traffic Safety Administration estimates that alcohol use is a factor in over 60 percent of automobile accidents. Such accidents result in thousands of highway deaths and injuries and over $30 billion in costs. These automobile accidents create a risk that affects many people financially and emotionally. Automobile insurance cannot eliminate the costs of automobile accidents; however, it does reduce the financial impact.

A **financial responsibility law** is state legislation that requires drivers to prove their ability to cover the cost of damage or injury caused by an automobile accident. All states have such laws to protect the public from physical harm and property damage losses caused by drivers. When injuries or significant property damage occur in an accident, the drivers involved are required to file a report with the state and to show financial re-

State	Liability Limits	State	Liability Limits
Alabama*	20/40/10	Montana*	25/50/10
Alaska*	50/100/25	Nebraska*	25/50/25
Arizona*	15/30/10	Nevada*	15/30/10
Arkansas*	25/50/25	New Hampshire	25/50/25
California*	15/30/5	New Jersey*	15/30/5
Colorado*	25/50/15	New Mexico*	25/50/10
Connecticut*	20/40/10	New York*†	25/50/10
Delaware*	15/30/10	North Carolina*	30/60/25
District of Columbia*	25/50/10	North Dakota*	25/50/25
Florida*	10/20/10	Ohio*	12.5/25/7.5
Georgia*	25/50/25	Oklahoma*	25/50/25
Hawaii*	20/40/10	Oregon*	25/50/10
Idaho*	25/50/15	Pennsylvania*	15/30/5
Illinois*	20/40/15	Rhode Island*	25/50/25
Indiana*	25/50/10	South Carolina*	15/30/10
Iowa*	20/40/15	South Dakota*	25/50/25
Kansas*	25/50/10	Tennessee	25/50/10
Kentucky*	25/50/10	Texas*	20/40/15
Louisiana*	10/20/10	Utah*	25/50/15
Maine*	50/100/25	Vermont*	20/50/10
Maryland*	20/40/15	Virginia	25/50/20
Massachusetts*	20/40/5	Washington*	25/50/10
Michigan*	20/40/10	West Virginia*	20/40/10
Minnesota*	30/60/10	Wisconsin	25/50/10
Mississippi	25/50/25	Wyoming*	25/50/20
Missouri*	25/50/10		

*State with compulsory automobile liability insurance.
†50/100 in cases where injury results in death.

Exhibit **10-8**

Automobile financial responsibility/compulsory insurance minimum limits (as of 2000)

Source: Insurance Information Institute (www.iii.org).

sponsibility. As of 2003, over 45 states had compulsory automobile insurance laws. In other states, most people meet the financial responsibility requirement by buying insurance, since very few have the financial resources to meet this legal requirement on their own. Exhibit 10–8 presents each state's minimum limits for financial responsibility. These amounts represent the minimum state requirement; higher coverage is recommended to protect the financial assets of individuals.

The main coverages provided by automobile insurance fall into two categories: bodily injury coverages and property damage coverages (see Exhibit 10–9). Other coverages include wage loss insurance, towing service, accidental death, and car rental when a vehicle is undergoing repairs due to an accident.

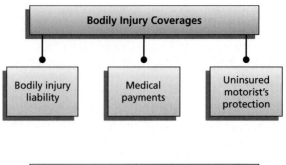

Exhibit **10-9**

Two major categories of automobile insurance

Exhibit **10-10**

Automobile liability insurance coverage

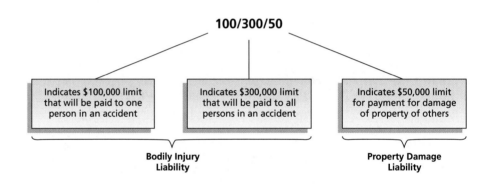

MOTOR VEHICLE BODILY INJURY COVERAGES

Most money automobile insurance companies pay in claims goes for expenses of injury lawsuits, medical expenses, and related legal costs. The main bodily injury coverages are bodily injury liability, medical payments coverage, and uninsured motorist's protection. No-fault systems in a number of states have influenced the process of settling bodily injury claims.

bodily injury liability
Coverage for the risk of financial loss due to legal expenses, medical costs, lost wages, and other expenses associated with injuries caused by an automobile accident for which the insured was responsible.

BODILY INJURY LIABILITY   **Bodily injury liability** covers the risk of financial loss due to legal expenses, medical expenses, lost wages, and other expenses associated with injuries caused by an automobile accident for which you were responsible. This insurance protects you from extensive financial losses.

Bodily injury liability is usually expressed as a split limit, such as 50/100 or 100/300. These amounts represent thousands of dollars of coverage. The first number (see Exhibit 10–10) is the limit for claims that can be paid to one person; the second number is the limit for each accident; the third number is discussed in the section on property damage coverages. With 100/300 bodily injury coverage, for example, a driver would have a limit of $100,000 for claims that could be paid to one person in an accident. In addition, there would be a $300,000 limit for all bodily injury claims from a single accident.

MEDICAL PAYMENTS COVERAGE   While bodily injury liability pays for the costs of injuries to persons who were not in your automobile, **medical payments**

coverage covers the costs of health care for people who were injured in your automobile, including yourself. This protection covers friends, carpool members, and others who ride in your vehicle. Medical payments insurance also provides medical benefits if you or a member of your family is struck by an automobile or injured while riding in another person's automobile.

UNINSURED MOTORIST'S PROTECTION
If you are in an accident caused by a person without insurance, **uninsured motorist's protection** covers the cost of injuries to you and your family; in most states, however, it does not cover property damage. This insurance also provides protection against financial losses due to injuries caused by a hit-and-run driver or by a driver who has insufficient coverage to cover the cost of your injuries. *Underinsured motorist's coverage* provides financial protection when another driver has insurance but less coverage than needed to cover the financial damages brought on you.

NO-FAULT INSURANCE
Difficulties and high costs of settling claims for medical expenses and personal injuries resulted in the creation of the **no-fault system,** in which drivers involved in accidents collect medical expenses, lost wages, and related injury costs from their own insurance companies. The system is intended to provide fast, smooth methods of paying for damages without taking the legal action frequently necessary to determine fault.

In 1971, Massachusetts was the first state to implement no-fault insurance. As of 2003, nearly 30 states had some variation of the system. While no-fault automobile insurance was intended to reduce the time and cost associated with the settlement of automobile injury cases, this has not always been the result. One reason for continued difficulties is that no-fault systems vary from state to state. Some no-fault states set limits on medical expenses, lost wages, and other claim settlements, while other states allow lawsuits under certain conditions, such as permanent paralysis or death. Some states include property damage in no-fault insurance. Drivers should investigate the coverages and implications of no-fault insurance in their states.

MOTOR VEHICLE PROPERTY DAMAGE COVERAGES

Three coverages protect you from financial loss due to damage of property of others and damage to your vehicle: (1) property damage liability, (2) collision, and (3) comprehensive physical damage. (See the accompanying Financial Planning for Life's Situation feature on page 324.)

PROPERTY DAMAGE LIABILITY
When you damage the property of others, **property damage liability** protects you against financial loss. This coverage applies mainly to other vehicles; however, it also includes damage to street signs, lampposts, buildings, and other property. Property damage liability protects you and others covered by your policy when driving another person's automobile with permission. The policy limit for property damage liability is commonly stated with your bodily injury coverages. The last number in 50/100/25 and 100/300/50, for example, is for property damage liability ($25,000 and $50,000, respectively).

COLLISION
When your automobile is involved in an accident, **collision** insurance pays for the damage to the automobile regardless of fault. However, if another driver caused the accident, your insurance company may try to recover the repair costs

medical payments coverage Automobile insurance that covers medical expenses for people injured in one's car.

uninsured motorist's protection Automobile insurance coverage for the cost of injuries to a person and members of his or her family caused by a driver with inadequate insurance or by a hit-and-run driver.

no-fault system An automobile insurance program in which drivers involved in accidents collect medical expenses, lost wages, and related injury costs from their own insurance companies.

property damage liability Automobile insurance coverage that protects a person against financial loss when that person damages the property of others.

collision Automobile insurance that pays for damage to the insured's car when it is involved in an accident.

DID YOU KNOW?

A global positioning system (GPS) and other technology are being used to encourage safer driving and reduce auto insurance costs. In Britain, one insurance company adjusts premiums each month based on a driver's braking and acceleration habits. The Car Chip (www.carchip.com) allows parents to monitor the speed and braking actions of young drivers.

Financial Planning for Life's Situations

ARE YOU COVERED?

Often people believe their insurance will cover various financial losses. For each of the following situations, name the type of home or automobile insurance that would protect you.

1. While you are on vacation, clothing and other personal belongings are stolen. _____

2. Your home is damaged by fire, and you have to live in a hotel for several weeks. _____

3. You and members of your family suffer injuries in an automobile accident caused by a hit-and-run driver. _____

4. A delivery person is injured on your property and takes legal action against you. _____

5. Your automobile is accidentally damaged by some people playing baseball. _____

6. A person takes legal action against you for injuries you caused in an automobile accident. _____

7. Water from a local lake rises and damages your furniture and carpeting. _____

8. Your automobile needs repairs because you hit a tree. _____

9. You damaged a valuable tree when your automobile hit it, and you want to pay for the damage. _____

10. While riding with you in your automobile, your nephew is injured in an accident and incurs various medical expenses. _____

Answers: (1) Personal property coverage of home insurance; (2) additional living expenses of home insurance; (3) uninsured motorist's protection; (4) personal liability coverage of home insurance; (5) comprehensive physical damage; (6) bodily injury liability; (7) flood insurance—requires coverage separate from home insurance; (8) collision; (9) property damage liability of automobile insurance; (10) medical payments.

---

for your vehicle through the other driver's property damage liability. The insurance company's right to recover the amount it pays for the loss from the person responsible for the loss is called *subrogation*.

The amount you can collect with collision insurance is limited to the retail value of the automobile at the time of the accident. This amount is usually based on the figures provided by some appraisal service such as the *Official Used Car Guide* of the National Automobile Dealers Association (www.nada.org). If you have an automobile with many add-on features or one that is several years old and has been restored, you should obtain a documented statement of its condition and value before an accident occurs.

comprehensive physical damage Automobile insurance that covers financial loss from damage to a vehicle caused by a risk other than a collision, such as fire, theft, glass breakage, hail, or vandalism.

COMPREHENSIVE PHYSICAL DAMAGE   Another protection for your automobile involves financial losses from damage caused by a risk other than a collision. **Comprehensive physical damage** covers you for risks such as fire, theft, glass breakage, falling objects, vandalism, wind, hail, flood, tornado, lightning, earthquake, avalanche, or damage caused by hitting an animal. Certain articles in your vehicle, such as some radios and stereo equipment, may be excluded from this insurance. These articles may be protected by the personal property coverage of your home insurance. Like collision insurance, comprehensive coverage applies only to your car, and claims are paid without considering fault. (See Financial Planning Calculations: Claim Settlements and Deductibles on page 325.)

OTHER AUTOMOBILE INSURANCE COVERAGES

In addition to basic bodily injury and property damage coverages, other protection is available. *Wage loss insurance* will reimburse you for any salary or income lost due to injury in an automobile accident. Wage loss insurance is usually required in states with a no-fault insurance system; in other states, it is available on an optional basis.

CLAIM SETTLEMENTS AND DEDUCTIBLES

Both collision and comprehensive coverage are commonly sold with a *deductible* to help reduce insurance costs. If a broken windshield costs $250 to replace and you have a $100 deductible on your comprehensive coverage, the insurance company will pay $150 of the damages.

Deductibles keep insurance premiums lower by reducing the number of small claims companies pay. Going from full-coverage comprehensive insurance to a $100 deductible may reduce the cost of that coverage by as much as 40 percent.

Towing and emergency road service coverage pays for the cost of breakdowns and mechanical assistance. This coverage can be especially beneficial on long trips or during inclement weather. Towing and road service coverage pays for the cost of getting the vehicle to a service station or starting it when it breaks down on the highway, not for the cost of repairs. If you belong to an automobile club, your membership may include towing coverage. Purchasing duplicate coverage as part of your automobile insurance could be a waste of money. Rental reimbursement coverage pays for a rental car if your vehicle is stolen or is in the shop for repairs after an accident.

CONCEPT CHECK 10-5

1 What is the purpose of financial responsibility laws?
2 What are the main coverages included in most automobile insurance policies?
3 What is no-fault insurance?
4 How does collision coverage differ from comprehensive physical damage coverage?

Action Application Survey several people to determine the types and amounts of automobile insurance coverage they have. Do most of them have adequate coverage?

Automobile Insurance Costs

The average household spends more than $1,200 for auto insurance each year. Automobile insurance premiums reflect the amounts insurance companies pay for injury and property damage claims. Your automobile insurance is directly related to coverage amounts and factors such as the vehicle, your place of residence, and your driving record.

AMOUNT OF COVERAGE

"How much coverage do I need?" This question affects the amount you pay for insurance. Our legal environment and increasing property values influence coverage amounts.

LEGAL CONCERNS As discussed earlier, every state has laws that require or encourage automobile liability insurance coverage. Since very few people can afford to pay an expensive court settlement with personal assets, most drivers buy automobile liability insurance.

Objective 6

Evaluate factors that affect the cost of automobile insurance.

DID YOU KNOW?

The foods and drinks that were reported as the most common distractions in auto accidents: coffee, hot soup, tacos, chili-covered foods, hamburgers, chicken, jelly- or cream-filled doughnuts, and soft drinks. These are in addition to other common driving disruptions such as cell phones and other electronic devices, shaving, cosmetics, and reading.

Auto insurance premiums are affected by a person's driving record, claims, and the type of vehicle.

In the past, bodily injury liability coverage of 10/20 was considered adequate. In fact, some states still use these amounts as their minimum limits for financial responsibility. However, in recent injury cases, some people have been awarded millions of dollars; thus, legal and insurance advisers now recommend 100/300. As discussed earlier in this chapter, an umbrella policy can provide additional liability coverage of $1 million or more.

PROPERTY VALUES   Just as medical expenses and legal settlements have increased, so has the cost of vehicles. Therefore, a policy limit of more than $10,000 for property damage liability is appropriate; $50,000 or $100,000 is usually suggested.

AUTOMOBILE INSURANCE PREMIUM FACTORS

Several factors influence the premium you pay for automobile insurance. The main factors are vehicle type, rating territory, and driver classification.

AUTOMOBILE TYPE   The year, make, and model of your motor vehicle strongly influence automobile insurance costs. Expensive replacement parts and complicated repairs due to body style contribute to higher rates. Also, certain makes and models are stolen more often than others.

rating territory The place of residence used to determine a person's automobile insurance premium.

RATING TERRITORY   In most states, your **rating territory** is the place of residence used to determine your automobile insurance premium. Various geographic locations have different costs due to differences in the number of claims made. For example, fewer accidents and less vandalism occur in rural areas than in large cities. New York City, Los Angeles, and Chicago have the highest incidence of automobile theft.

driver classification A category based on the driver's age, sex, marital status, driving record, and driving habits; used to determine automobile insurance rates.

DRIVER CLASSIFICATION   You are compared with other drivers to set your automobile insurance premium. **Driver classification** is a category based on the driver's age, sex, marital status, driving record, and driving habits; drivers' categories are used to determine automobile insurance rates. In general, young drivers (under 25) and those over 70 have more frequent and severe accidents. As a result, they pay higher premiums.

Accidents and traffic violations influence your driver classification. A poor driving record increases your insurance costs. Finally, you pay less for insurance if you do not drive to work than if you use your automobile for business. Belonging to a carpool instead of driving to work alone can reduce insurance costs.

Your credit history may also be considered when applying for auto insurance. While some states limit the use of credit scoring in auto insurance, the practice is common in other areas.

The number of claims you file with your insurance company also affects your premiums. Expensive liability settlements or extensive property damage will increase your rates. If you have many expensive claims or a poor driving record, your company may cancel your policy, making it difficult for you to obtain coverage from another company. To deal with this problem, every state has an **assigned risk pool** consisting of people who are unable to obtain automobile insurance. Some of these people are assigned to each insurance company operating in the state. They pay several times the normal rates, but they do get coverage. Once they establish a good driving record, they can reapply for insurance at regular rates.

assigned risk pool Consists of people who are unable to obtain automobile insurance due to poor driving or accident records and must obtain coverage at high rates through a state program that requires insurance companies to accept some of them.

FILING AN AUTO INSURANCE CLAIM . . . OR NOT?

You quickly back out of your driveway, late for a meeting. A short mental lapse and BANG . . . you hit a post at the end of your driveway. The damage seems minor. Should you report it to your insurance company?

As you answer this question, consider the following:

1. *Are you required to file all damages?* Some insurance companies require that all accidents be reported. This provision prevents a driver from missing hidden damages.

2. *Was someone else involved in the accident?* Insurance companies strongly encourage filing a claim when others are involved. Reporting the situation to your insurance company is especially important when a person appears to be injured in the accident.

3. *How much is your deductible?* If your collision deductible is $500 and you have $600 of damage, not reporting the claim might be appropriate. Remember, higher deductibles will reduce your insurance costs, but will also increase the amount you have to pay when a claim is filed. Be sure to put aside money in savings for those situations.

4. *What about other recent claims?* If you have an accident-free record for several years, a claim may be an appropriate action. However, several claims in a short time period may significantly increase your rates or result in difficulty obtaining coverage in the future.

While no one plans to have an auto accident, more than 18 million occur each year. If you are involved in an auto accident, take the following actions:

- Stop your vehicle. Turn off the engine. Stay at the accident scene. Try to remain calm.

- Seek medical assistance for anyone with injuries; DO NOT MOVE an injured person.

- Obtain names and contact information of others involved in the accident and witnesses. Take notes regarding the circumstances of the accident.

- Report the accident to the police; obtain a copy of the accident report. File any necessary reports with state government agencies.

- Discuss the accident only with the police; do not admit any fault or liability.

Source: *Kiplinger Personal Finance;* personalinsure.about.com

REDUCING AUTOMOBILE INSURANCE PREMIUMS

Methods for lowering automobile insurance costs include comparing companies and taking advantage of commonly offered discounts.

COMPARING COMPANIES Rates and service vary among automobile insurance companies. Among companies in the same area, premiums can vary as much as 100 percent. If you relocate, don't assume your present company will offer the best rates in your new living area. Rates may be compared online at www.insuremarket.com.

Also consider the service the local insurance agent provides. Will this company representative be available to answer questions, change coverages, and handle claims as needed? You can check a company's reputation for handling automobile insurance claims and other matters with sources such as *Consumer Reports* or your state insurance department. Several states publish information with sample auto insurance rates for different companies to help consumers save money. The address and contact information of your state insurance regulator may be found online.

Sheet 50
Automobile insurance costs comparison

PREMIUM DISCOUNTS The best way to keep your rates down is to establish and maintain a safe driving record. Taking steps to avoid accidents and traffic violations will mean lower automobile insurance premiums. In addition, most insurance compa-

DID YOU KNOW?

To reduce driving accidents among teens, some parents have installed an in-car monitoring device that records seat belt use, engine speed, and tire traction. The device also beeps when preset limits for speed, braking, or sharp turns are violated.

nies offer various discounts. Drivers under 25 can qualify for reduced rates by completing a driver training program or maintaining good grades in school. When young drivers are away at school without a car, families are likely to get reduced premiums since the student will not be using the vehicle on a regular basis.

Installing security devices such as a fuel shutoff switch, a second ignition switch, or an alarm system will decrease your chances of theft and lower your insurance costs. Being a non-smoker can qualify you for lower automobile insurance premiums. Discounts are also offered for participating in a carpool and insuring two or more vehicles with the same company. Ask your insurance agent about other methods for lowering your automobile insurance rates.

Increasing the amount of deductibles will result in a lower premium. Also, some people believe an old car is not worth the amount paid for collision and comprehensive coverages and therefore dispense with them. However, before doing this, be sure to compare the value of your car for getting you to school or work with the cost of these coverages.

If you change your driving habits, get married, or alter your driving status in other ways, be sure to notify the insurance company. Premium savings can result. Also, some employers make group automobile insurance available to workers. Before you buy a motor vehicle, find out which makes and models have the lowest insurance costs. This information can result in a purchasing decision with many financial benefits.

CONCEPT CHECK 10-6 ✔

1 What factors influence how much a person pays for automobile insurance?
2 What actions can a person take to reduce the cost of automobile insurance?

Action Application Search the Web or talk to an insurance agent to obtain suggestions for reducing automobile insurance costs.

SUMMARY OF OBJECTIVES

Objective 1
Develop a risk management plan using insurance.
The four general risk management techniques are risk avoidance, risk reduction, risk assumption, and risk shifting. In planning a personal insurance program, set your goals, make a plan to reach your goals, put your plan into action, and review your results.

Objective 2
Discuss the importance of property and liability insurance.
Owners of homes and automobiles face the risks of (1) property damage or loss and (2) legal actions by others for the costs of injuries or property damage. Property and liability insurance offer protection from financial losses that may arise from a wide variety of situations faced by owners of homes and users of automobiles.

Objective 3
Explain the insurance coverages and policy types available to homeowners and renters.
Homeowner's insurance includes protection for the building and other structures, additional living expenses, personal property, and personal liability. Renter's insurance includes the same coverages excluding protection for the building and other structures, which is the concern of the building owner. The main types of home insurance policies are the basic, broad, special, tenants, comprehensive, condominium, country home, and modified coverage forms. These policies differ in the risks and property they cover.

Objective 4
Analyze factors that influence the amount of coverage and cost of home insurance.
The amount of home insurance coverage is determined by the replacement cost of your dwelling and personal belongings. The

cost of home insurance is influenced by the location of the home, the type of structure, the coverage amount, the policy type, discounts, and insurance company differences.

Objective 5
Identify the important types of automobile insurance coverages.
Automobile insurance is used to meet states' financial responsibility laws and to protect drivers against financial losses associated with bodily injury and property damage. The major types of automobile insurance coverages are bodily injury liability, medical payments, uninsured motorist's, property damage liability, collision, and comprehensive physical damage.

Objective 6
Evaluate factors that affect the cost of automobile insurance.
The cost of automobile insurance is affected by the amount of coverage, automobile type, rating territory, driver classification, differences among insurance companies, and premium discounts.

KEY TERMS

actual cash value (ACV)   318
assigned risk pool   326
bodily injury liability   322
coinsurance clause   318
collision   323
comprehensive physical
   damage   324
driver classification   326
endorsement   315
financial responsibility law   320
hazard   306
homeowner's insurance   312
household inventory   313

insurance   306
insurance company   306
insured   306
insurer   306
liability   312
medical payments coverage   315
negligence   312
no-fault system   323
peril   306
personal property floater   313
policy   306
policyholder   306
premium   306

property damage liability   323
pure risk   307
rating territory   326
replacement value   319
risk   306
self-insurance   307
speculative risk   307
strict liability   312
umbrella policy   315
uninsured motorist's
   protection   323
vicarious liability   312

FINANCIAL PLANNING PROBLEMS

1. *Calculating Property Loss Claim Coverage.* Most home insurance policies cover jewelry for $1,000 and silverware for $2,500 unless items are covered with additional insurance. If $3,500 worth of jewelry and $3,800 worth of silverware were stolen from a family, what amount of the claim would not be covered by insurance? (Obj. 2)

2. *Computing Actual Cash Value Coverage.* What amount would a person with actual cash value (ACV) coverage receive for two-year-old furniture destroyed by a fire? The furniture would cost $1,000 to replace today and had an estimated life of five years. (Obj. 3)

3. *Determining Replacement Cost.* What would it cost an insurance company to replace a family's personal property that originally cost $18,000? The replacement costs for the items have increased 15 percent. (Obj. 3)

4. *Calculating a Coinsurance Claim.* If Carissa Dalton has a $130,000 home insured for $100,000, based on the 80 percent coinsurance provision, how much would the insurance company pay on a $5,000 claim? (Obj. 4)

5. *Determining the Claim Amount (with Deductibles).* For each of the following situations, what amount would the insurance company pay? (Obj. 3)

   a. Wind damage of $785; the insured has a $500 deductible.

   b. Theft of a stereo system worth $1,300; the insured has a $250 deductible.

   c. Vandalism that does $375 of damage to a home; the insured has a $500 deductible.

6. *Calculating Auto Liability Claim Coverage.* Becky Fenton has 25/50/10 automobile insurance coverage. If two other people are awarded $35,000 each for injuries in an auto accident in which Becky was judged at fault, how much of this judgment would the insurance cover? (Obj. 5)

7. *Determining a Property Damage Liability Claim.* Kurt Simmons has 50/100/15 auto insurance coverage. One evening he lost control of his vehicle, hitting a parked car and damaging a storefront along the street. Damage to the parked car was $5,400, and damage to the store was

$12,650. What amount will the insurance company pay for the damages? What amount will Kurt have to pay? (Obj. 5)

8. *Calculating Future Value of Insurance Savings.* Beverly and Kyle Nelson currently insure their cars with separate companies, paying $450 and $375 a year. If they insured both cars with the same company, they would save 10 percent on the annual premiums. What would be the future value of the annual savings over 10 years based on an annual interest rate of 6 percent? (Obj. 6)

FINANCIAL PLANNING ACTIVITIES

1. *Determining Insurance Coverages.* Survey friends and relatives to determine the types of insurance coverages they have. Also, obtain information about the process used to select these coverages. (Obj. 1)

2. *Developing a Personal Insurance Plan.* Outline a personal insurance plan with the following phases: *(a)* identify personal, financial, and property risks; *(b)* set goals you might achieve when obtaining needed insurance coverages; and *(c)* describe actions you might take to achieve these insurance goals. (Obj. 1)

3. *Analyzing Insurance Coverages.* Talk to a financial planner or an insurance agent about the financial difficulties faced by people who lack adequate home and auto insurance. What common coverages do many people overlook? (Obj. 2)

4. *Maintaining a Household Inventory.* Survey several people about their household inventory records. In the event of damage or loss, would they be able to prove the value of their personal property and other belongings? (Obj. 3)

5. *Comparing Home Insurance Costs.* Contact two or three insurance agents to obtain information about home or renter's insurance. Use Sheet 49 in the *Personal Financial Planner* to compare the coverages and costs. (Obj. 4)

6. *Analyzing Home Insurance Policies.* Examine a homeowner's or renter's insurance policy. What coverages does the policy include? Does the policy contain unclear conditions or wording? (Obj. 4)

7. *Reducing Home Insurance Costs.* Talk to several homeowners about the actions they take to reduce the cost of their home insurance. Locate Web sites that offer information about reducing home insurance costs. Prepare a video or other visual presentation to communicate your findings. (Obj. 4)

8. *Comparing Auto Insurance Costs.* Contact two or three insurance agents to obtain information about automobile insurance. Use Sheet 50 in the *Personal Financial Planner* to compare costs and coverages for various insurance companies. (Obj. 6)

INTERNET CONNECTION

Updating Home and Motor Vehicle Insurance Information

Current information on (1) home/renter's insurance and (2) automobile insurance is vital for obtaining appropriate coverage at a fair price. For each of these two types of insurance, conduct a Web search to locate current information for the requested items.

Information Needs	Home/Renter's Insurance	Automobile Insurance
Address for Web site providing insurance information		
Sponsors or advertisers for the Web site		
Main features of the Web site		
Suggestions offered for selecting appropriate coverage		

Information Needs	Home/Renter's Insurance	Automobile Insurance
Type of insurance rate information provided on this Web site		
Suggestions for obtaining lower insurance premiums		
Other insurance information provided on the Web site		

FINANCIAL PLANNING CASE

We Rent, So Why Do We Need Insurance?

"Have you been down in the basement?" Nathan asked his wife, Erin, as he entered their apartment.

"No, what's up?" responded Erin.

"It's flooded because of all that rain we got last weekend!" he exclaimed.

"Oh no! We have the extra furniture my mom gave us stored down there. Is everything ruined?" Erin asked.

"The couch and coffee table are in a foot of water; the loveseat was the only thing that looked OK. Boy, I didn't realize the basement of this building wasn't waterproof. I'm going to call our landlady to complain."

As Erin thought about the situation, she remembered that when they moved in last fall, Kathy, their landlady, had informed them that her insurance policy covered the building but not the property belonging to each tenant. Because of this, they had purchased renter's insurance. "Nathan, I think our renter's insurance will cover the damage. Let me give our agent a call."

When Erin and Nathan purchased their insurance, they had to decide whether they wanted to be insured for cash value or for replacement costs. Replacement was more expensive, but it meant they would collect enough to go out and buy new household items at today's prices. If they had opted for cash value, the couch Erin's mother had paid $1,000 for five years ago would be worth less than $500 today.

Erin made the call and found out their insurance did cover the furniture in the basement, and at replacement value after

they paid the deductible. The $300 they had invested in renter's insurance last year was well worth it!

Not every renter has as much foresight as Erin and Nathan. Fewer than 4 in 10 renters have renter's insurance. Some aren't even aware they need it. They may assume they are covered by the landlord's insurance, but they aren't. This mistake can be costly.

Think about how much you have invested in your possessions and how much it would cost to replace them. Start with your stereo equipment or the color television and DVD player that you bought last year. Experts suggest that people who rent start thinking about these things as soon as they move into their first apartment. Your policy should cover your personal belongings and provide funds for living expenses if you are dispossessed by a fire or other disaster.

Questions

1. Why is it important for people who rent to have insurance?

2. Does the building owner's property insurance ever cover the tenant's personal property?

3. What is the difference between cash value and replacement value?

4. When shopping for renter's insurance, what coverage features should you look for?

VIDEO CASE

Selecting Insurance Coverage

An auto accident can take place at any time. Just when you least expect it, a minor "fender bender" can disrupt your daily routine. In addition, without proper insurance coverage, an accident can put a strain on your financial resources.

In our daily activities, personal injuries can happen. While most people have some type of medical insurance coverage, injuries can have other financial implications.

Many burglaries of personal property occur each day. Most people do not believe that this type of loss will happen to them.

Renters often overlook insurance coverage for their household belongings.

Questions

1. What types of financial losses are commonly covered by automobile liability insurance? What mistakes can occur when buying this coverage?

2. What are potential benefits of disability insurance?

3. What are some reasons renters overlook property insurance?

YOUR PERSONAL FINANCIAL PLANNER IN ACTION

Obtaining Home and Auto Insurance

Creation of an insurance plan, including appropriate coverage for your home, personal property, and motor vehicles, helps to avoid financial difficulties.

Your Short-Term Financial Planning Activities	Resources
1. List current and needed insurance coverages.	PFP Sheet 46, 48 www.insurance.about.com www.insure.com www.iii.org
2. (a) Prepare an inventory of personal belongings. (b) Compare the cost of homeowner's or renter's insurance from two or more companies.	PFP Sheet 47, 49 www.quicken.com/insurance www.insweb.com
3. Compare the cost of auto insurance from two or more companies	PFP Sheet 50 http://personalinsure.about.com www.insquote
Your Long-Term Financial Planning Activities	
1. Identify buying decisions that could reduce your future home and auto insurance costs.	Text pages 320, 327–328 www.iiaa.com
2. Develop a plan to monitor changes in your life situation that would affect the need to change home or auto insurance coverages.	Text pages 318–319, 325–326 www.ircweb.org

CONTINUING CASE

Property Insurance

Life Situation
Pam, 36
Josh, 38
Three children, ages 9, 7, and 4

Financial Data
Monthly income $4,300
Assets $150,850
Living expenses $4,075
Liabilities $99,520

Both Pam and Josh Brock are pleased with their lives and various family activities. They now have three children, are enjoying their home, and are more financially secure than six years ago. Yet the Brocks still have financial needs they must address.

Several changes have affected their financial planning. The value of their home has increased due to inflation and home improvements. They have purchased a used car to meet additional transportation needs. These situations must be considered in relation to insurance needs for the Brock household.

Questions

1. How should the Brocks determine whether they have enough insurance coverage for their home?

2. What factors should the Brocks consider in deciding whether to purchase collision insurance coverage for their used car?

3. Describe the possible use of *Personal Financial Planner* sheets 46–50 by the Brocks.

11

Health, Disability, and Long-Term Care Insurance

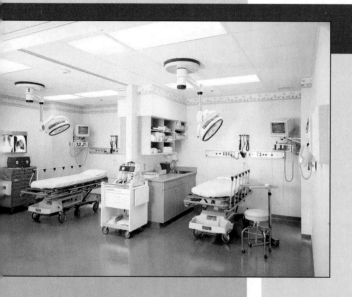

Key Concept

Knowing how to determine the type of health, disability, and long-term care insurance that you need can help you meet your financial goals even when dealing with unexpected medical costs or the inability to work.

Digital Study Tools

Online Learning Center Study Tools for This Chapter

- Multiple-choice quiz
- Flashcards
- eLearning sessions
- Crossword puzzle
- Personal Finance Online: Health Insurance Fundamentals

Student CD Study Tools for This Chapter

- Self-study software
- Narrated PowerPoint
- Personal financial planning software: Worksheets 51–52

www.mhhe.com/kdh

Learning Objectives

1 Explain why the costs of health insurance and health care have been increasing.

2 Define *health insurance* and *disability income insurance* and explain their importance in financial planning.

3 Analyze the benefits and limitations of the various types of health care coverage.

4 Evaluate private sources of health insurance and health care.

5 Appraise the sources of government health care programs.

6 Recognize the need for disability income insurance.

The Digital Hospital

Peter A. Gross has been a doctor for 40 years, rising up the ranks to become the chairman of internal medicine at Hackensack University Medical Center in Hackensack, New Jersey. But one day this winter, a homeless man checked into the hospital with HIV, and Gross made a decision that could have seriously harmed his patient. He chose to give the patient an HIV drug, tapping a request into a hospital computer and zapping it off to the two-year-old digital drug-order entry system. Moments later he got back a message he never would have received before the system was in place: a warning that the drug could mix dangerously with an antidepressant the patient was already taking. Gross got on the phone to figure out the problem, eventually asking the man's psychiatrist to reduce the dosage of his antidepressant. "There's no way I would have picked that up." Gross says. "It was totally unexpected."

Scenes like this are unfolding across the country, providing a glimpse into the potential of information technology to transform the health care industry. Hackensack is one of the nation's most aggressive tech adopters. Millions of dollars in investments have paid for projects well beyond the online drug system that tipped off Gross. Doctors can tap an internal Web site to examine X rays from a PC anywhere. Patients can use 37-inch plasma TVs in their rooms to surf the Net for information about their medical conditions. There's even a life-size robot, Mr. Rounder, that doctors can control from their laptops at home. They direct the digital doc, complete with white lab coat and stethoscope, into hospital rooms and use two-way video to discuss patients' conditions.

Whimsical? Maybe, but Hackensack's results are perfectly serious. Patient mortality rates are down. Quality of care is up. At the same time, productivity is rising. While these are early days and plenty of hurdles remain, the hospital has no doubts that its technology investments are making the difference. "We could never become a top hospital unless we were tops in tech," says John P. Ferguson, the hospital's chief executive.

QUESTIONS

What Action Should Be Taken?

1. If you or your loved ones were checked into a hospital, would you want the digital doc to play a vital role in the treatment? Why or why not?
2. Would you support the high-tech initiatives now being undertaken by hospitals in the United States? In your opinion, are such efforts safe and cost-effective?

What about Your Situation?

3. If you were hospitalized, would you surf the Net for information about your medical conditions?
4. Do you believe the digital hospital, complete with Mr. Rounder the robot, is the health care industry's future?

Source: Timothy J. Mullaney and Arlene Weintraub, "The Digital Hospital," *BusinessWeek*, March 28, 2005, pp. 77–81.

Learn More Online

Visit *Business Week* online at www.businessweek.com/extras and learn more about the future of the digital hospital. See how the people and the machines are turning Hackensack University Medical Center into a digital hospital. Other Web sites to visit: www.medconsumer.com, www.patientadvocate.org, and www.carecounsel.com.

Health Care Costs

Objective 1

Explain why the costs of health insurance and health care have been increasing.

Health insurance is one way people protect themselves against economic losses due to illness, accident, or disability. Health coverage is available through private insurance companies, service plans, health maintenance organizations, and government programs.

Employers often offer health insurance, called *group health insurance*, as part of an employee benefits package, and health care providers sell it to individuals.

Affordable health care has become one of the most important social issues of our time. News broadcasts abound with special reports on "America's health care crisis" or politicians demanding "universal health insurance."

HIGH MEDICAL COSTS

What do an aging and overweight population, the cost of prescription drugs, the growing number of uninsured, and advancements in medical technology have in common? These and other factors all add up to rising health costs. The United States has the highest per capita medical expenditures of any country in the world. We spend twice as much on health care as the average for the 24 industrialized countries in Europe and North America. The average per employee cost for health care was $7,761 in 2005. It seems that, year after year, there is a third sure thing for U.S. citizens besides death and taxes: higher health costs.

Health care costs were estimated at $1.92 trillion in 2005 (see Exhibit 11–1). Since 1993, health care spending as a percentage of gross domestic product (GDP) has remained relatively constant at 13.6 percent, except in 1997, when it fell to 13.4 percent, and in 2005, when it increased to 15.7 percent (see Exhibit 11–2). The latest projections from The Centers of Medicare and Medicaid Services show that over the next 10 years annual health care spending is expected to grow to over $2.8 trillion, or 17.4 percent of GDP. Yet 45 million people, or 15.6 percent of our population, have no health insurance.[1]

RAPID INCREASE IN MEDICAL EXPENDITURES
Since federally sponsored health care began in 1965, U.S. health care expenditures rose from $41.6 billion, or about 6 percent of GDP, to over $1.9 trillion in 2005, about 15.7 percent of GDP (see Exhibit 11–2).

HIGH ADMINISTRATIVE COSTS
In the United States, administrative costs consume nearly 26 percent of health care dollars, compared to 1 percent under Canada's socialized system. These costs include activities such as enrolling beneficiaries in a health plan, paying health insurance premiums, checking eligibility, obtaining authorizations for specialist referrals, and filing reimbursement claims. More than 1,100 different insurance forms are now in use in the United States.

WHY DOES HEALTH CARE COST SO MUCH?

The high and rising costs of health care are attributable to many factors, including

- The use of sophisticated, expensive technologies.
- Duplication of tests and sometimes duplication of technologies that yield similar results.

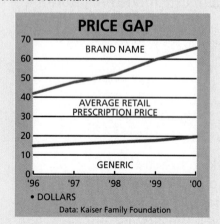

DID YOU KNOW?

Americans spent a staggering $172 billion on medicines in 2001. Meanwhile, on average, a generic prescription runs $46 less than a brand name.

PRICE GAP

BRAND NAME

AVERAGE RETAIL PRESCRIPTION PRICE

GENERIC

'96   '97   '98   '99   '00

• DOLLARS

Data: Kaiser Family Foundation

Source: *BusinessWeek,* May 27, 2002, p. 66.

Exhibit **11-1**   U.S. national health expenditures, 1960–2005

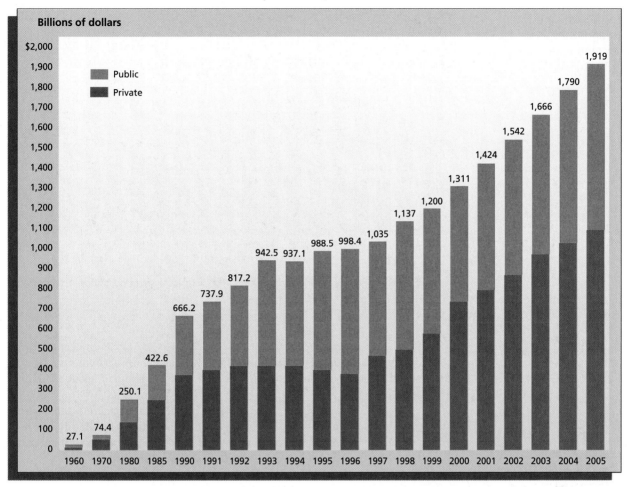

Sources: U.S. Department of Health and Human Services, The Centers for Medicare and Medicaid Services; *Statistical Abstract of the United States, 2004–2005*, Table 116, p. 93; *BusinessWeek*, January 10, 2005, p. 115.

- Increases in the variety and frequency of treatments, including allegedly unnecessary tests.
- The increasing number and longevity of elderly people.
- Regulations that result in cost shifting rather than cost reduction.
- The increasing number of accidents and crimes that require emergency medical services.
- Limited competition and restrictive work rules in the health care delivery system.
- Labor intensiveness and rapid average earnings growth for health care professionals and executives.
- Using more expensive medical care than necessary, such as going to an emergency room with a bad cold.
- Built-in inflation in the health care delivery system.
- Aging baby boomers, use of more health care services, whether they're going to the doctor more often, or snapping up pricier drugs, from Celebrex to Viagra.
- Other major factors that cost billions of dollars each year, including fraud, administrative waste, malpractice insurance, excessive surgical procedures, a wide range of prices for similar services, and double health coverage.

Exhibit **11-2**

U.S. health care
expenditures as a
percentage of GDP,
1970–2010

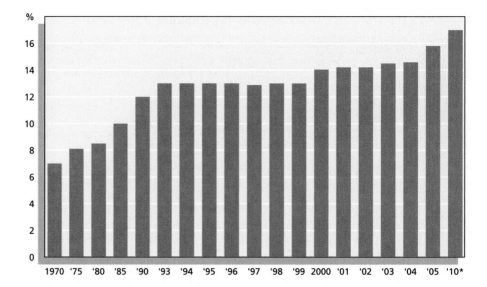

*Estimated.
Sources: U.S. Department of Health and Human Services, The Centers for Medicare and Medicaid Services, April 2005.

According to the General Accounting Office, fraud and abuse account for nearly 10 percent of all dollars spent on health care. In 2005, that was a loss of about $25 billion to Medicare.

Because third parties—private health insurers and government—pay such a large part of the nation's health care bill, hospitals, doctors, and patients often lack the incentive to make the most economical use of health care services.

WHAT IS BEING DONE ABOUT THE HIGH COSTS OF HEALTH CARE?

In the private sector, concerned groups such as employers, labor unions, health insurers, health care professionals, and consumers have undertaken a wide range of innovative activities to contain the costs of health care. These activities include

- Programs to carefully review health care fees and charges and the use of health care services.

- The establishment of incentives to encourage preventive care and provide more services out of hospitals, where this is medically acceptable.

- Involvement in community health planning to help achieve a better balance between health needs and health care resources.

- The encouragement of prepaid group practices and other alternatives to fee-for-service arrangements.

- Community health education programs that motivate people to take better care of themselves.

- Physicians encouraging patients to pay cash for routine medical care and lab tests.

DID YOU KNOW?

A visit to the emergency room for non-emergency care can cost $383 vs. $60 for a doctor's appointment. And the average cost of a 30-day supply of a brand-name drug costs $71, compared to $22 for a generic equivalent.

Source: Blue Cross Blue Shield of Illinois, Spring 2005.

The use of sophisticated and expensive technologies is one of the major reasons for the rising costs of health care.

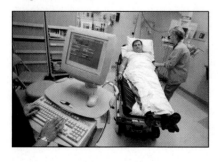

WHAT CAN YOU DO TO REDUCE PERSONAL HEALTH CARE COSTS?

The best way to avoid the high cost of illness is to stay well. The prescription is the same as it has always been:

1. Eat a balanced diet and keep your weight under control.

2. Avoid smoking and don't drink to excess.

3. Get sufficient rest, relaxation, and exercise.

4. Drive carefully and watch out for accident and fire hazards in the home.

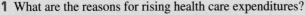

CONCEPT CHECK 11-1

1 What are the reasons for rising health care expenditures?
2 What are various groups doing to curb the high costs of health care?
3 What can individuals do to reduce health care costs?

Action Application Create a list of personal actions that you can take to reduce the costs of health care.

Health Insurance and Financial Planning

Although the United States spent over $1.9 trillion on health care in 2005 (see Exhibit 11–1), the number of Americans without basic health insurance has been growing. In this wealthy country of over 285 million people, 45 million citizens have no health insurance. Two-thirds of uninsured persons are either full-time workers or family members of full-time employees.

According to recent government reports, two-thirds of uninsured pregnant women fail to receive adequate prenatal care. Among children, 40 percent fail to receive basic childhood vaccinations, 25 percent don't see a doctor even once a year, and 31 percent in low-income families lack health coverage.

A growing number of college students have been uninsured due to the growth of an older student population not covered by family policies. Today 40 percent of college students are older than 25.

Objective 2

Define *health insurance* and *disability income insurance* and explain their importance in financial planning.

WHAT IS HEALTH INSURANCE?

Health insurance is a form of protection to alleviate the financial burdens individuals suffer from illness or injury. According to The Centers for Medicare and Medicaid Services, health insurance includes both medical expense insurance and disability income insurance.

HEALTH INSURANCE   Health insurance, like other forms of insurance, reduces the financial burden of risk by dividing losses among many individuals. It works in the same way as life insurance, homeowner's insurance, and automobile insurance. You pay the insurance company a specified premium, and the company guarantees you some degree of financial protection. Like the premiums and benefits of other types

DID YOU KNOW?

GENERICS BRING PRICES DOWN STEEPLY

Generics reduce drug prices by 80% on average within three years on the market.

100% 90% 80% 70% 60% 50% 40% 30% 20% 10% 0

1 YEAR   2 YEARS   3 YEARS

Source: PRIME Institute, University of Minnesota, AARP Bulletin, April 2002, p. 6.

of insurance, the premiums and benefits of health insurance are figured on the basis of average experience. To establish rates and benefits, insurance company actuaries rely on general statistics that tell them how many people in a certain population group will become ill and how much their illnesses will cost.

Medical expense insurance and disability income insurance, discussed in the last section, are an important part of your financial planning. To safeguard your family's economic security, both protections should be a part of your overall insurance program.

There are many ways individuals or groups of individuals can obtain health insurance protection. Planning a health insurance program takes careful study because the protection should be shaped to the needs of the individual or family. For many families, the task is simplified because the group health insurance they obtain at work already provides a foundation for their coverage.

GROUP HEALTH INSURANCE   Group plans comprise about 90 percent of all the health insurance issued by health and life insurance companies. Most of these plans are employer sponsored, and the employer often pays part or most of their cost. Group insurance will cover you and your immediate family. Group insurance seldom requires evidence that you are insurable, if you enroll when you first become eligible for coverage.

The *Health Insurance Portability and Accountability Act of 1996 (HIPA)* legislates new federal standards for health insurance portability, nondiscrimination in health insurance, and guaranteed renewability. The law provides tax breaks for long-term care insurance, authorizes various government agencies to investigate Medicare/Medicaid fraud and abuses, and permits establishing experimental *medical savings accounts (MSAs).* The MSA allowed small businesses and self-employed people to open medical savings accounts for the first time in 1997. The law permitted 750,000 people to open tax-free MSAs for routine health care costs and to buy high-deductible health insurance for major medical expenses.

This landmark legislation gives millions of workers the comfort of knowing that if they change jobs, they need not lose their health insurance. For example, a parent with a sick child can move from one group plan to another without lapses in health insurance and without paying more than other employees for coverage. In addition to providing health care portability, this law created a stable source of funding for fraud control activities.

The protection group insurance provides varies from plan to plan. The plan may not cover all of your health insurance needs; therefore, you will have to consider supplementing it with individual health insurance.

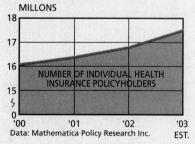

DID YOU KNOW?

RISING TIDE

As costs rise and employer-based health plans are pared back, more people are signing up for individual policies.

MILLIONS

NUMBER OF INDIVIDUAL HEALTH INSURANCE POLICYHOLDERS

'00   '01   '02   '03 EST.

Data: Mathematica Policy Research Inc.

Source: *BusinessWeek,* September 13, 2004, p. 61.

INDIVIDUAL HEALTH INSURANCE   Individual health insurance covers either one person or a family. If the kind of health insurance you need is not available through a group or if you need coverage in addition to the coverage a group provides, you should obtain an individual policy—a policy tailored to your particular needs—from the company of your choice. This requires careful shopping, because coverage and cost vary from company to company. For example, the premiums for similar coverage can vary up to 50 percent for the same person, according to Mark Gurda, president of Castle Group Health in Northbrook, Illinois. Moreover, the rules and regulations vary from state to state.

Find out what your group insurance will pay for and what it won't. Make sure you have enough insurance, but don't waste money by overinsuring.

SUPPLEMENTING YOUR GROUP INSURANCE   A sign that your group coverage needs supplementing would be its failure to provide benefits for the major portion of your medical care bills, mainly hospital, doctor, and surgical charges. If, for example, your group policy will pay only $500 per day toward a hospital room and the cost in your area is $1,000, you should look for an individual policy that covers most of the remaining amount. Similarly, if your group policy will pay only about half the going rate for surgical procedures in your area, you need individual coverage for the other half.

In supplementing your group health insurance, consider the health insurance benefits your employer-sponsored plan provides for family members. Most group policy contracts have a **coordination of benefits (COB)** provision. The COB is a method of integrating the benefits payable under more than one health insurance plan so that the benefits received from all sources are limited to 100 percent of allowable medical expenses.

If you have any questions about your group plan, you should be able to get answers from your employer, union, or association. If you have questions about an individual policy, talk with your insurance company representative.

> **coordination of benefits (COB)** A method of integrating the benefits payable under more than one health insurance plan.

MEDICAL COVERAGE AND DIVORCE

Medical coverage of nonworking spouses is a concern when couples divorce. Under federal law, coverage under a former spouse's medical plan can be continued for 36 months if the former spouse works for a company with 20 or more employees.

Premiums will be totally paid by the individual and can run as high as $7,000 annually. If there are children and the custodial parent doesn't work, the working parent usually can still cover the children under an employer's group plan.

The federal *Consolidated Omnibus Budget Reconciliation Act of 1986 (COBRA)* requires many employers to offer employees and dependents who would otherwise lose group health insurance the option to continue their group coverage for a set period of time. Employees of private companies and state and local governments are covered by this law; employees of the federal government and religious institutions are not.

CONCEPT CHECK 11-2

1 What is health insurance, and what is its purpose?
2 What are group health and individual health insurance?
3 What is a coordination of benefits provision?

Action Application Ask someone in a human resource office of an organization for information on the health insurance provided as an employee benefit.

Types of Health Insurance Coverage

With today's high cost of health care, it makes sense to be as fully insured as you can afford. Combining the group plan available where you work with the individual policies insurance companies offer will enable you to put together enough coverage to give you peace of mind. A good health insurance plan should

- Offer basic coverage for hospital and doctor bills.
- Provide at least 120 days' hospital room and board in full.

Objective 3

Analyze the benefits and limitations of the various types of health care coverage.

- Provide at least a $1 million lifetime maximum for each family member.
- Pay at least 80 percent for out-of-hospital expenses after a yearly deductible of $500 per person or $1,000 per family.
- Impose no unreasonable exclusions.
- Limit your out-of-pocket expenses to no more than $3,000 to $5,000 a year, excluding dental, optical, and prescription costs.

Several types of health insurance coverage are available under group and individual policies.

TYPES OF MEDICAL COVERAGE

hospital expense insurance Pays part or all of hospital bills for room, board, and other charges.

HOSPITAL EXPENSE INSURANCE   **Hospital expense insurance** pays part or the full amount of hospital bills for room, board, and other charges. Frequently a maximum amount is allowed for each day in the hospital, up to a maximum number of days. More people have hospital insurance than any other kind of health insurance.

surgical expense insurance Pays part or all of the surgeon's fees for an operation.

SURGICAL EXPENSE INSURANCE   **Surgical expense insurance** pays part or the full amount of the surgeon's fees for an operation. A policy of this kind usually lists a number of specific operations and the maximum fee allowed for each. The higher the maximum fee allowed in the policy, the higher the premium charged. People often buy surgical expense insurance in combination with hospital expense insurance.

physician expense insurance Provides benefits for doctors' fees for nonsurgical care, X rays, and lab tests.

PHYSICIAN EXPENSE INSURANCE   **Physician expense insurance** helps pay for physician's care that does not involve surgery. Like surgical expense insurance, it lists maximum benefits for specific services. Its coverage may include visits to the doctor's office, X rays, and lab tests. This type of insurance is usually bought in combination with hospital and surgical insurance. The three types of insurance combined are called **basic health insurance coverage.**

basic health insurance coverage Combination of hospital expense insurance, surgical expense insurance, and physician expense insurance.

major medical expense insurance Pays most of the costs exceeding those covered by the hospital, surgical, and physician expense policies.

MAJOR MEDICAL EXPENSE INSURANCE   **Major medical expense insurance** protects against the large expenses of a serious injury or a long illness. It adds to the protection offered by basic health insurance coverage. The costs of a serious illness can easily exceed the benefits under hospital, surgical, and physician expense policies. Major medical pays the bulk of the additional costs. The maximum benefits payable under major medical insurance are high—up to $1 million. Because major medical insurance offers such a wide range of benefits and provides high maximums, it contains two features to help keep the premium within the policyholder's means.

deductible An amount the insured must pay before benefits become payable by the insurance company.

One of these features is a **deductible** provision that requires the policyholder to pay a basic amount before the policy benefits begin—for example, the first $500 per year under an individual plan and a lesser amount under a group plan. (Sometimes part or all of the deductible amount is covered by the benefits of a basic hospital and surgical plan.) The other feature is a **coinsurance** provision that requires the policyholder to share expenses beyond the deductible amount. Many policies pay 75 or 80 percent of expenses above the deductible amount; the policyholder pays the rest.

coinsurance A provision under which both the insured and the insurer share the covered losses.

stop-loss A provision under which an insured pays a certain amount, after which the insurance company pays 100 percent of the remaining covered expenses.

Some major medical policies contain a **stop-loss** provision. This requires the policyholder to pay up to a certain amount, after which the insurance company pays 100 percent of all remaining covered expenses. Typically, the out-of-pocket payment is between $4,000 and $6,000.

comprehensive major medical insurance A type of major medical insurance that has a very low deductible and is offered without a separate basic plan.

COMPREHENSIVE MAJOR MEDICAL INSURANCE   **Comprehensive major medical insurance** is a type of major medical insurance that has a very low deductible amount, often $200 or $300, and is offered without a separate basic plan. This all-inclusive health insurance helps pay hospital, surgical, medical, and other bills.

Many major medical policies have specific maximum benefits for certain expenses, such as hospital room and board and the cost of surgery.

HOSPITAL INDEMNITY POLICIES   A **hospital indemnity policy** pays benefits only when you are hospitalized, but these benefits, stipulated in the policy, are paid to you in cash and you can use the money for medical, nonmedical, or supplementary expenses. While such policies have limited coverage, their benefits can have wide use. The hospital indemnity policy is not a substitute for basic or major medical protection but a supplement to it. Many people buy hospital indemnity policies in the hope that they will make money if they get sick, but the average benefit return does not justify the premium cost.

hospital indemnity policy
Pays stipulated daily, weekly, or monthly cash benefits during hospital confinement.

DENTAL EXPENSE INSURANCE   *Dental expense insurance* provides reimbursement for the expenses of dental services and supplies and encourages preventive dental care. The coverage normally provides for oral examinations (including X rays and cleanings), fillings, extractions, inlays, bridgework, and dentures, as well as oral surgery, root canal therapy, and orthodontics.

VISION CARE INSURANCE   A recent development in health insurance coverage is *vision care insurance.* An increasing number of insurance companies and prepayment plans are offering this insurance, usually to groups.

Vision and eye health problems are second among the most prevalent chronic health care concerns, affecting 140 million Americans. Good vision care insurance should cover diagnosing and treating eye diseases such as glaucoma, periodic eye examinations, eyeglasses, contact lenses, and eye surgery.

In considering vision and dental coverages, you should analyze their costs and benefits. Sometimes these coverages cost more than they are worth.

OTHER INSURANCE POLICIES
Dread disease, trip accident, death insurance, and cancer policies, which are usually sold through the mail, in newspapers and magazines, or by door-to-door salespeople working on commission, are notoriously poor values. Their appeal is based on unrealistic fears, and a number of states have prohibited their sale. Such policies provide coverage only for specific conditions and are no substitute for comprehensive insurance. To protect yourself from health insurance scams, read the accompanying Financial Planning for Life's Situations feature on page 344.

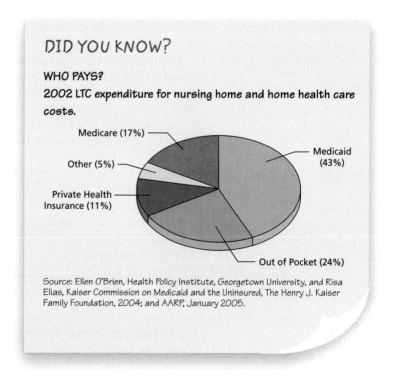

DID YOU KNOW?

WHO PAYS?
2002 LTC expenditure for nursing home and home health care costs.

Medicare (17%)
Other (5%)
Private Health Insurance (11%)
Medicaid (43%)
Out of Pocket (24%)

Source: Ellen O'Brien, Health Policy Institute, Georgetown University, and Risa Elias, Kaiser Commission on Medicaid and the Uninsured, The Henry J. Kaiser Family Foundation, 2004; and AARP, January 2005.

LONG-TERM CARE INSURANCE

Long-term care insurance (LTC), virtually unknown 25 years ago, is growing faster than any other form of insurance in the country. *Long-term care* is day-in, day-out assistance that you might need if you ever have an illness or a disability that lasts a long time and leaves you unable to care for yourself. You may or may not need lengthy care in a nursing home, but you may need help at home with daily activities such as dressing, bathing, and doing household chores.

long-term care insurance (LTC) Provides day-in, day-out care for long-term illness or disability.

HEALTH COVERAGE HELL

Regulators say some unscrupulous health insurers and medical discounters are hoodwinking consumers. A few popular topics:

FAKE POLICIES
Targeting individuals, small businesses, and the self-employed, these scams hawk professional-sounding plans with ultra-low rates using slick marketing, many claiming to be exempt from state laws. Since 2001, just five bogus insurers have left more than 85,000 people with at least $85 million in unpaid medical claims. Florida alone has shut down more than 200 unauthorized operators in the past two years.

CUT-RATE PLANS
These supercheap medical plans are often marketed as if they were insurance, offering "group coverage" for as little as $89.95 a month. But often their advertised networks don't exist. Because state insurance regulators in most states have no jurisdiction over noninsurance products, they're hard to patrol. Montana issued 15 cease-and-desist orders in the past six weeks against such discount plans.

ASSOCIATIONS
Regulators say that some health insurers market policies through associations that claim they're independent but often aren't. Their alleged independence often exempts them from state insurance laws, allowing big, unexpected rate hikes. An estimated 6 million individuals are covered by such association group insurers. Some of these associations, however, insist they are entirely legitimate.

DISCOUNT DRUG CARDS
Preying primarily on the elderly confused about new Medicare prescription drug benefits, a rash of drug card scams has hit at least 11 states since the new Medicare law went into effect on June 1, 2004. The Federal Trade Commission recently sued one company for allegedly attempting to steal more than $10 million from the checking accounts of 90,000 people.

Source: Brian Grow, "It's Enough to Make You Sick," *BusinessWeek*, September 13, 2004, pp. 58–62.

In 2005, about 9 million men and women over age 65 were estimated to need long-term care. The number is expected to increase to 12 million by the year 2020. Most of these older Americans will be cared for at home; family members and friends are the sole caregivers for 70 percent of the elderly population. A 2002 study by Americans for Long-Term Care Security (ALTCS) found that one out of five Americans over age 50 is at risk of needing some form of long-term care within the next 12 months. The same study revealed that more than half of the U.S. population will need long-term care during their lives.[2]

Long-term care can be very expensive. As a national average, a year in a nursing home can cost $62,000. In some regions, it can cost as much as $90,000. Bringing an aide into your home just three times a week to help with dressing, bathing, preparing meals, and similar household chores can easily cost $1,700 a month.

The annual premium for LTC policies can range from under $1,000 up to $16,000, depending on your age and the choices you make. The older you are when you enroll, the higher your annual premium. Typically, individual insurance plans are sold to the 50-to-80 age group, pay benefits for a maximum of two to six years, and carry a dollar limit on the total benefits they will pay (see the Advice from a Pro feature on page 345).

The number of policies in effect has more than doubled since 1990, to about 9 million. About 120 insurance companies cover 12 percent of people age 65 and over. But long-term care insurance is not for everyone; it is rarely recommended for people under 60. If you are over 60, you may consider it if you wish to protect your assets, but if you have substantial wealth ($1 million or more), or very little (less than $150,000), the premium can be a waste of money.[3] However, if your employer pays the premium, the

To receive a free copy of *A Shopper's Guide to Long-Term Care Insurance,* visit the National Association of Insurance Commissioners Web site at **www.naic.org.** *Long-Term Care Insurance: Understanding Your Options* is available free by writing to AARP Fulfillment, 601 E St. NW, Washington, DC 20049.

WHAT YOU NEED TO ASK ABOUT LONG-TERM CARE INSURANCE

DAILY BENEFIT
What is the maximum amount per day the insurance will pay? You probably want at least $100. An extra 5 percent inflation option helps protect against rising health costs, but premiums will be higher.

BENEFIT PERIOD
How long will you be covered? Typical policies range from two to six years. But nearly all claims are for three years or less.

POLICY LIMIT
What's the maximum dollar amount your policy will pay out? A four-year policy at $100 a day will pay up to $146,000.

ELIMINATION PERIOD
It's really just the deductible—how long you will pay for care before coverage kicks in. It can be between 30 and 90 days. The shorter the period, the higher the premium.

BENEFIT LIMITS
How much coverage will you get if you stay at home, rather than enter a nursing home? How sick must you be before making a claim? Who makes that determination?

INSURER SAFETY
You may pay premiums for 30 years before making a claim. Will your insurer still be around? Check rating services such as A.M. Best (ambest.com), Standard & Poor's (www.standardandpoors.com), or Weiss Ratings (weissratings.com) to learn how solid your insurance company is today.

Source: Howard Gleckman, "Providing for Your Own Care," *BusinessWeek*, July 12, 2004, p. 93.

Health Insurance Portability and Accountability Act of 1996 treats a long-term care premium as a tax-deductible expense for the employer.

Explore services available in your community to help meet long-term care needs. Care given by family members can be supplemented by visiting nurses, home health aides, friendly visitor programs, home-delivered meals, chore services, adult day care centers, and respite services for caregivers who need a break from daily responsibilities.

These services are becoming more widely available. Some or all of them may be found in your community. Your local area Agency on Aging or Office on Aging can help you locate the services you need. Call the Eldercare Locator at 1-800-677-1116 to locate your local office.

The Financial Planning for Life's Situations box on page 346 can help you compare the features of long-term care policies.

MAJOR PROVISIONS IN A HEALTH INSURANCE POLICY

All health insurance policies have certain provisions in common. Be sure you understand what

DID YOU KNOW?

THE NEW HEALTH PRIVACY RULE
On April 14, 2003, federal law protected your medical information. Here are some provisions:

- Health care providers and insurers must have a written privacy policy—and give it to patients.
- Patients will be allowed to see and obtain copies of their own records and request changes.
- Those who illegally obtain or disclose health information will face a fine of up to $250,000 and up to 10 years in prison.
- Employers that self-insure must maintain a firewall to prevent those processing employee health claims from sharing medical information with others at the company.
- Health care providers and insurers must say when they're using patient information for marketing purposes. Patients have the right to nix future marketing from a source after an initial solicitation.

Source: *BusinessWeek*, November 19, 2001.

LONG-TERM CARE POLICY CHECKLIST

The following checklist will help you compare LTC policies you may be considering:

	Policy A	Policy B
1. What services are covered?		
Skilled care	___	___
Intermediate care	___	___
Custodial care	___	___
Home health care	___	___
Adult day care	___	___
Other	___	___
2. How much does the policy pay per day?		
For skilled care	___	___
For intermediate care	___	___
For custodial care	___	___
For home health care	___	___
For adult day care	___	___
3. How long will benefits last?		
In a nursing home for:		
Skilled nursing care	___	___
Intermediate nursing care	___	___
Custodial care	___	___
At home	___	___
4. Does the policy have a maximum lifetime benefit? If so, what is it?		
For nursing home care	___	___
For home health care	___	___
5. Does the policy have a maximum length of coverage for each period of confinement? If so, what is it?		
For nursing home care	___	___
For home health care	___	___
6. How long must I wait before preexisting conditions are covered?	___	___
7. How many days must I wait before benefits begin?		
For nursing home care	___	___
For home health care	___	___

	Policy A	Policy B
8. Are Alzheimer's disease and other organic mental and nervous disorders covered?	___	___
9. Does this policy require:		
Physician certification of need?	___	___
An assessment of activities of daily living?	___	___
A prior hospital stay for:		
Nursing home care?	___	___
Home health care?	___	___
A prior nursing home stay for home health care coverage?	___	___
Other	___	___
10. Is the policy guaranteed renewable?	___	___
11. What is the age range for enrollment?	___	___
12. Is there a waiver-of-premium provision:		
For nursing home care?	___	___
For home health care?	___	___
13. How long must I be confined before premiums are waived?	___	___
14. Does the policy offer an inflation adjustment feature? If so:		
What is the rate of increase?	___	___
How often is it applied?	___	___
For how long?	___	___
Is there an additional cost?	___	___
15. What does the policy cost:		
Per year?	___	___
With inflation feature	___	___
Without inflation feature	___	___
Per month?		
With inflation feature	___	___
Without inflation feature	___	___
16. Is there a 30-day free look?	___	___

Source: *Guide to Long-Term Care Insurance* (Washington, DC: Health Insurance Association of America, 1994), pp. 11–12.

your policy covers. Even the most comprehensive policy may be of little value if a provision in small print limits or denies benefits.

An insurance company usually allows you a minimum of 10 days to review your health insurance policy, so be sure to check the major provisions that affect your coverage. Deductible, coinsurance, and stop-loss provisions were discussed under major medical expense insurance. Other major provisions are described in the following sections.

ELIGIBILITY   The eligibility provision defines who is entitled to benefits under the policy. Age, marital status, and dependency requirements are usually specified in this provision. For example, foster children usually are not automatically covered under the family contract, but stepchildren may be. Check with your insurance company to be sure.

ASSIGNED BENEFITS   When you assign benefits, you sign a paper allowing your insurance company to make payments to your hospital or doctor. Otherwise, the payments will be made to you when you turn in your bills and claim forms to the company.

INTERNAL LIMITS   A policy with internal limits will pay only a fixed amount for your hospital room no matter what the actual rate is, or it will cover your surgical expenses only to a fixed limit no matter what the actual charges are. For example, if your policy has an internal limit of $200 per hospital day and you are in a $300-a-day hospital room, you will have to pay the difference.

COPAYMENT   **Copayment** is a type of cost sharing. Most major medical plans define copayment as the amount the patient must pay for medical services after the deductible has been met. You pay a flat dollar amount each time you receive a covered medical service. Copayments of $5 to $10 for prescriptions and $5 to $15 for doctors' office visits are common. The amount of copayment does not vary with the cost of service.

copayment A provision under which the insured pays a flat dollar amount each time a covered medical service is received after the deductible has been met.

SERVICE BENEFITS   In a service benefits provision, insurance benefits are expressed in terms of entitlement to receive specified hospital or medical care rather than entitlement to receive a fixed dollar amount for each procedure. Service benefits are always preferable to a coverage stated in dollar amounts.

BENEFIT LIMITS   The benefit limits provision defines the maximum benefits possible, in terms of either a dollar amount or a number of days in the hospital. Many policies today have benefit limits ranging from $250,000 to unlimited payments.

EXCLUSIONS AND LIMITATIONS   The exclusions and limitations provision specifies the conditions or circumstances for which the policy does not provide benefits. For example, the policy may exclude coverage for preexisting conditions, cosmetic surgery, or routine checkups.

COORDINATION OF BENEFITS   As discussed earlier, the coordination of benefits provision prevents you from collecting benefits from two or more group policies that would in total exceed the actual charges. Under this provision, the benefits from your own and your spouse's policies are coordinated to allow you up to 100 percent payment of your covered charges.

GUARANTEED RENEWABLE   With this policy provision, the insurance company cannot cancel a policy unless you fail to pay premiums when due. Also, it cannot raise premiums unless a rate increase occurs for all policyholders in that group.

CANCELLATION AND TERMINATION   This provision explains the circumstances under which the insurance company can terminate your health insurance policy. It also explains your right to convert a group contract into an individual contract.

WHICH COVERAGE SHOULD YOU CHOOSE?

Now that you are familiar with the types of health insurance available and some of their major provisions, how do you choose one? The most important thing to understand is that the more money you can pay for health insurance, the more coverage you can get.

For medical insurance, you have three choices. You can buy (1) basic, (2) major medical, or (3) both basic and major medical. If your budget is very limited, it is a toss-up between choosing a basic plan or a major medical plan. In many cases, either plan will handle a major share of your hospital and doctor bills. In the event of an illness involving catastrophic costs, however, you will need the protection a major medical policy offers. Ideally, you should get a basic plan and a major medical supplementary plan or a comprehensive major medical policy that combines the values of both these plans in a single policy.

The medical costs of giving birth can be high. However, most people have the basic health insurance coverage to minimize out-of-pocket costs.

HEALTH INSURANCE TRADE-OFFS

The benefits of health insurance policies differ, and the differences can have a significant impact on your premiums. Consider the following trade-offs.

REIMBURSEMENT VERSUS INDEMNITY   A reimbursement policy provides benefits based on the actual expenses you incur. An indemnity policy provides specified benefits, regardless of whether the actual expenses are greater or less than the benefits.

INTERNAL LIMITS VERSUS AGGREGATE LIMITS   A policy with internal limits stipulates maximum benefits for specific expenses, such as the maximum reimbursement for daily hospital room and board. Other policies may limit only the total amount of coverage, such as $1 million major expense benefits, or may have no limits.

DEDUCTIBLES AND COINSURANCE   The cost of a health insurance policy can be greatly affected by the size of the deductible (the amount you must pay toward medical expenses before the insurance company pays), the degree of coinsurance, and the share of medical expenses you must pay (for example, 20 percent).

OUT-OF-POCKET LIMIT   A policy that limits the total of the coinsurance and deductibles you must pay (for example, $2,000) will limit or eliminate your financial risk, but it will also increase the premium.

BENEFITS BASED ON REASONABLE AND CUSTOMARY CHARGES   A policy that covers "reasonable and customary" medical expenses limits reimbursement to the usual charges of medical providers in an area and helps prevent overcharging.

HEALTH INFORMATION ONLINE

Recent studies indicate that consumers are seeking information on health and health care online to supplement traditional medical counsel. Many legitimate providers of reliable health and medical information, including the federal Food and Drug Administration, are taking advantage of the Web's popularity by offering brochures and

THE BEST MEDICAL WEB SITES

The Net is awash in medical information. The hard part is finding advice you can trust. Some sites display symbols indicating that they are committed to quality standards set by organizations such as the Utilization Review Accreditation Commission (URAC) or Health on the Net Foundation (HON). But the acronyms don't tell you everything. HON sites are largely self-policing, for example. And some good, smaller sites can't afford the more thorough URAC accreditation. What's more, many sites have vested interests—sponsorship by clinics specializing in a particular treatment, say, or by drugmakers whose products are recommended on the site. To learn more, always click the "about us" tab, and make sure the articles were written or vetted by medical professionals. While you're at it, check to see when the information was last updated. Such caveats aside, there is much credible health information on the Net. Here are some sites worth adding to your "favorites" list.

Web Site/Sponsor	Highlights	Quibbles
WWW.NLM.NIH.GOV National Library of Medicine, part of the government's National Institutes of Health	Home to health sites such as Medline Plus, a patient-friendly location for looking up drugs and medical conditions. Gives the latest health news and a link for info on clinical trials in your area. Check out MEDLINE/PubMed, where you can research citations and summaries of articles in medical journals.	Getting the full text of an article cited on MEDLINE/PubMed can be a chore.
WWW.NIMH.NIH.GOV National Institute of Mental Health, part of the National Institutes of Health	Comprehensive and authoritative source of information on mental disorders and treatments. Posts breaking news and information about clinical trials.	After the initial screens, this mostly text site lacks color and razzle-dazzle.
WWW.4WOMAN.GOV U.S. Health & Human Services Dept.	Well-organized info on everything from breast-feeding to menopause, as well as news about women's health. Many reports on the site are available in Spanish.	Bland compared with chatty but less authoritative women's sites.
WWW.MAYOCLINIC.COM Mayo Foundation for Medical Education & Research, an affiliate of Mayo Clinic of Rochester, Minn.	Comprehensive site guides patients who are weighing treatment options. Tools let you calculate everything from body mass index to pregnancy due date. Doctors at the Mayo Clinic and Mayo Medical School contribute to and review articles, except those on drugs, herbs, and supplements, which are licensed from outside sources.	None.
WWW.NATIONALHEALTH COUNCIL.ORG A nonprofit made up of voluntary health agencies, professional associations, and medical nonprofits and businesses	One-stop directory of links to groups like the American Cancer Society, the American Heart Assn., and the National Hospice & Palliative Care Organization. The council serves as a lobbying/advocacy organization for health agencies, with positions posted clearly on the site.	Contains little original content.
WWW.YOURDISEASERISK. HARVARD.EDU Harvard Center for Cancer Prevention, at the Harvard School of Public Health	Readers can fill out online questionnaires for a quick assessment of their risk for diabetes, heart disease, osteoporosis, stroke, and various cancers. The site ranks your risk. It also throws in tips on lowering risk and praise for what the user is doing right.	There's no posting date on individual articles; the entire site was updated in June 2004.

continued

Web Site/Sponsor	Highlights	Quibbles
WWW.DRUGDIGEST.ORG Express Scripts, a major pharmacy-benefits manager	Allows users to check for potential interactions between the drugs they use, as well as with food and alcohol. Also lets users compare side effects of different drugs. Site tells whether a generic is available, provides a picture of the pill, and cites uses for the medication.	Though it tracks 5,000 drugs, over-the-counter meds, and supplements, it's not all-inclusive.
WWW.QUESTDIAGNOS-TICS.COM Quest Diagnostics, a leading diagnostics-testing company	Its health library offers information on medical tests, medications, support groups, and general health topics. There's also a list of frequently ordered tests where you can find out how a test is performed and its risks.	None.
WWW.ONCOLINK.COM Abramson Cancer Center of the University of Pennsylvania	Its library provides physician summaries of the journal articles that have influenced the standard of care for various types of cancer, as well as free access to the table of contents and abstracts from many cancer-related journals. There are also reviews of books and videos for cancer patients, recent news, and accessible background info on cancer and treatment options.	The clinical trials link refers patients only to trials at the University of Pennsylvania cancer center.

For more information on useful medical Web sites, go to www.businessweek.com/execlife.
Source: Carol Marie Cropper, *BusinessWeek,* August 30, 2004, p. 152.

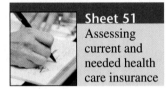

Sheet 51
Assessing current and needed health care insurance

in-depth information on specific topics at their Web sites. The Financial Planning for Life's Situations feature on pages 349–350 lists some good health care Web sites.

CONCEPT CHECK 11-3

1 What are several types of health insurance coverage available under group and individual policies?
2 What are the major provisions of a health insurance policy?
3 How do you decide which coverage to choose?
4 How can you analyze the costs and benefits of your health insurance policy?

Action Application Prepare a list of provisions in a health insurance policy that are important to you.

Private Sources of Health Insurance and Health Care

Objective 4

Evaluate private sources of health insurance and health care.

Health insurance is available from more than 800 private insurance companies. Moreover, service plans such as Blue Cross/Blue Shield, health maintenance organizations, preferred provider organizations, government programs such as Medicare, fraternal organizations, and trade unions provide health insurance.

PRIVATE INSURANCE COMPANIES

Insurance companies sell health insurance through either group or individual policies. Of these two types, group health insurance represents about 90 percent of all medical expense insurance and 80 percent of all disability income insurance.

The policies insurance companies issue provide for payment either directly to the insured for reimbursement of expenses incurred or, if assigned by the insured, to the provider of services.

Most private insurance companies sell health insurance policies to employers, who in turn offer them as fringe benefits to employees and employees' dependents. The premiums may be partially paid by employers. The Health Insurance Portability and Accountability Act, as discussed earlier, requires employers to keep detailed records of all employees and dependents covered by the company's health plan. Employers must be able to provide certificates of coverage for any employee covered since July 1, 1996.

HOSPITAL AND MEDICAL SERVICE PLANS

Blue Cross and Blue Shield are statewide organizations similar to commercial health insurance companies. Each state has its own Blue Cross and Blue Shield. The Blues plans play an important role in providing private health insurance to millions of Americans.

Blue Cross plans provide *hospital care benefits* on essentially a "service-type" basis. Through a separate contract with each member hospital, Blue Cross reimburses the hospital for covered services provided to the insured.

Blue Shield plans provide benefits for *surgical and medical services* performed by physicians. The typical Blue Shield plan provides benefits similar to those provided under the benefit provisions of hospital-surgical policies issued by insurance companies.

During the 1970s and 1980s, increasing health care costs spurred the growth of managed care. **Managed care** refers to prepaid health plans that provide comprehensive health care to members. Managed care is offered by health maintenance organizations, preferred provider organizations, exclusive provider organizations, point-of-service plans, and traditional indemnity insurance companies.

A recent industry survey estimated that 85 percent of employed Americans are enrolled in some form of managed care. Managed care companies now provide information that helps you better manage your health care needs. Health plans have launched Internet programs that allow you to access medical research, support groups, and professional advice, and to exchange e-mail with health care providers. The best-known managed care plans are health maintenance organizations (HMOs) and preferred provider organizations (PPOs), which offer a wide range of preventive services.

HEALTH MAINTENANCE ORGANIZATIONS (HMOS)

Prepaid managed care is designed to make the provision of health care services cost-effective by controlling their use. Health maintenance organizations are an alternative to basic and major medical insurance plans. A **health maintenance organization (HMO)** is a health insurance plan that directly employs or contracts with selected physicians, surgeons, dentists, and optometrists to provide health care services in exchange for a fixed, prepaid monthly premium. HMOs operate on the premise that maintaining health through preventive care will minimize future medical problems.

The preventive care HMOs provide includes periodic checkups, screening programs, diagnostic testing, and immunizations. HMOs also provide a comprehensive range of other health care services. These services are divided into two categories: basic and supplemental. *Basic health services* include inpatient, outpatient, maternity, mental health, substance abuse, and emergency care. *Supplemental services* include vision, hearing, and pharmaceutical care, which are usually available for an additional fee.

Your membership in a typical HMO should cover office visits, routine checkups, hospital and surgical care, eye exams, laboratory and X-ray services, hemodialysis for kidney failure, and mental health services. See the Financial Planning for Life's Situations feature on page 352 for tips on how to choose and use an HMO.

Blue Cross An independent, nonprofit membership corporation that provides protection against the cost of hospital care.

Blue Shield An independent, nonprofit membership corporation that provides protection against the cost of surgical and medical care.

managed care Prepaid health plans that provide comprehensive health care to members.

health maintenance organization (HMO) A health insurance plan that provides a wide range of health care services for a fixed, prepaid monthly premium.

Financial Planning for Life's Situations

TIPS ON USING AND CHOOSING AN HMO

HOW TO USE AN HMO

When you first enroll in an HMO, you must choose a plan physician (family practitioner, internist, pediatrician, or obstetrician-gynecologist) who provides or arranges for all of your health care services. It is extremely important that you receive your care through the plan physician. If you don't, you are responsible for the cost of the service rendered.

The only exceptions to the requirement that care be received through the plan physician are medical emergencies. A medical emergency is a sudden onset of illness or a sudden injury that would jeopardize your life or health if not treated immediately. In such instances, you may use the facilities of the nearest hospital emergency room. All other care must be provided by hospitals and doctors under contract with the HMO.

HOW TO CHOOSE AN HMO

If you decide to enroll in an HMO, you should consider these additional factors:

1. *Accessibility.* Since you must use plan providers, it is extremely important that they be easily accessible from your home or office.

2. *Convenient office hours.* Your plan physician should have convenient office hours.

3. *Alternative physicians.* Should you become dissatisfied with your first choice of a physician, the HMO should allow you the option to change physicians.

4. *Second opinions.* You should be able to obtain second opinions.

5. *Type of coverage.* You should compare the health care services offered by various HMOs, paying particular attention to whether you will incur out-of-pocket expenses or copayments.

6. *Appeal procedures.* The HMO should have a convenient and prompt system for resolving problems and disputes.

7. *Price.* You should compare the prices various HMOs charge, to ensure that you are getting the most services for your health care dollar.

WHAT TO DO WHEN AN HMO DENIES TREATMENT OR COVERAGE

- *Get it in writing.* To better defend your case, ask for a letter detailing the clinical reasons your claim was denied and the name and medical expertise of the HMO staff member responsible.

- *Know your rights.* The plan document or your HMO's member services department will tell you how experimental treatments are defined and covered and how the appeals process works.

- *Keep records.* Make copies of any correspondence, including payments and any reimbursements. Also, keep a written log of all conversations relevant to your claim.

- *Find advocates.* Enlist the help of your doctor, employer, and state insurance department to lobby your case before the HMO.

Source: Reprinted from *BusinessWeek*, May 19, 1997, by special permission. © 1999 McGraw-Hill Companies, Inc.

In the new millennium, HMOs are coming under fire from patients, doctors, unions, and federal and state governments. Since 1998, 27 states have passed limited patients' rights bills that allow patients to appeal medical decisions to external review boards. This brings to 38 the number of states with such appeals programs. In addition, 7 states, led by Texas, have passed laws giving patients the right to sue HMOs, and 26 more are considering them. Responding to new state laws that could cost millions of dollars in lawsuits, some managed care companies are paying for medical services and procedures they previously rejected.

Because patients dislike restrictions on which doctors they can see, they have stampeded out of HMOs. Just 23 percent of workers are covered by HMOs today versus 31 percent in 1996, according to the Kaiser Family Foundation, which studies health care. By contrast, 70 percent now use less restrictive preferred provider organizations or point-of-service plans, up from 42 percent. The result: Americans have gained some patients' rights, but at the expense of giving providers more leeway to push through price increases.[4]

PREFERRED PROVIDER ORGANIZATIONS (PPOs)

A **preferred provider organization (PPO)** is a group of doctors and hospitals that agree to provide health care at rates approved by the insurer. In return, PPOs expect prompt payment and the opportunity to serve an increased volume of patients. The premiums for PPOs are slightly higher than those for HMOs. An insurance company or your employer contracts with a PPO to provide specified services at predetermined fees to PPO members.

Preferred provider organizations combine the best elements of the fee-for-service and HMO systems. PPOs offer the services of doctors and hospitals at discount rates or give breaks in copayments and deductibles. PPOs provide their members with essentially the same benefits HMOs offer. However, while HMOs require members to seek care from HMO providers only (except for emergency treatment), PPOs allow members to use a preferred provider—or another provider for a higher copayment—each time a medical need arises. This combination of allowing free choice of physicians and low-cost care makes PPOs popular.

The **exclusive provider organization (EPO)** is the extreme form of the PPO. Services rendered by nonaffiliated providers are not reimbursed. Therefore, if you belong to an EPO, you must receive your care from affiliated providers or pay the entire cost yourself. Providers typically are reimbursed on a fee-for-service basis according to a negotiated discount or fee schedule.

A **point-of-service plan (POS),** sometimes called an *HMO-PPO hybrid* or *open-ended HMO,* combines characteristics of both HMOs and PPOs. POSs use a network of selected, contracted, participating providers. Employees select a primary care physician, who controls referrals for medical specialists. If you receive care from a plan provider, you pay little or nothing, as in an HMO, and do not file claims. Medical care provided by out-of-plan providers will be reimbursed, but you must pay significantly higher copayments and deductibles. Hybrid plans are useful if you want to try managed care but don't want to be locked into a network of doctors. A drawback is that they cost more than HMOs.

The distinction among HMOs, PPOs, EPOs, and POSs is becoming blurred. As cost reduction pressures mount and these alternative delivery systems try to increase their market share, each tries to make its system more attractive. The evolution of health care plans will likely continue so that it will become increasingly difficult to characterize a particular managed care delivery system as adhering to any particular model.

preferred provider organization (PPO) A group of doctors and hospitals that agree to provide health care at rates approved by the insurer.

exclusive provider organization (EPO) Renders medical care from affiliated health care providers.

point-of-service plan (POS) A network of selected contracted, participating providers; also called an *HMO-PPO hybrid* or *open-ended HMO.*

HOME HEALTH CARE AGENCIES

Home health care providers furnish and are responsible for the supervision and management of preventive medical care in a home setting in accordance with a medical order. Rising hospital care costs, new medical technology, and the increasing number of elderly and infirm people have helped make home care one of the fastest-growing areas of the health care industry.

Spending on home health care has been growing at an annual rate of about 20 percent over the past few years. This rapid growth reflects (1) the increasing proportion of older people in the U.S. population, (2) the lower costs of home health care compared to the costs of institutional health care, (3) insurers' active support of home health care, and (4) Medicare's promotion of home health care as an alternative to institutionalization.

Home health care consists of home health agencies, home care aide organizations, and hospices. Recently the National Association for Home Care identified over 20,000 home care institutions in the United States. These agencies provide services to over 8 million people with an acute illness, a long-term medical condition, a permanent disability, or a terminal illness.[5]

HMOs are based on the premise that preventive medical services will minimize future medical problems.

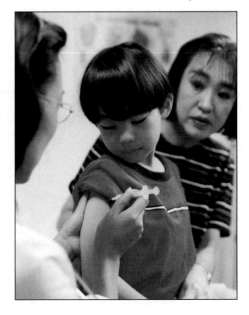

EMPLOYER SELF-FUNDED HEALTH PLANS

Certain types of health insurance coverage are made available by plans that employers, labor unions, fraternal societies, or communities administer. Usually these groups provide the amount of protection a specific group of people desires and can afford.

Self-funded groups must assume the financial burden if medical bills are greater than the amount covered by premium income. While private insurance companies have the assets needed in such situations, self-funded plans often do not. The results can be disastrous.

NEW HEALTH CARE ACCOUNTS

Health savings accounts (HSAs), which Congress authorized in 2003, are the newest addition to the alphabet soup of health insurance available to American workers. Now you and your employer must sort through HSAs, health reimbursement accounts (HRAs), and flexible spending accounts (FSAs). Each has its own rules about how money is spent, how it can be saved, and how it is taxed.

How do FSAs, HRAs, and HSAs differ? FSAs allow you to contribute pretax dollars to an account managed by your employer. You use the money for health care spending but forfeit anything left over at the end of the year.

HRAs are tied to high-deductible policies. They are funded *solely* by your employer and give you a pot of money to spend on health care. You can carry over unspent money from year to year, but you lose the balance if you switch jobs. Premiums tend to be lower than for traditional insurance but higher than for HSAs. You can invest the funds in stocks, bonds, and mutual funds. The money grows tax-free but can be spent only on health care. And it's your money. Any unspent funds stay in your account year to year, and you take it all with you if you leave the company.

HSAs allow you to contribute money to a tax-free account that can be used for out-of-pocket health care expenses if you buy high-deductible health insurance policies to cover catastrophic expenses. In 2006 up to 75 percent of U.S. employers are expected to offer HSAs as a major weapon in the fight against rising health care costs. Read the accompanying Financial Planning for Life's Situations feature on page 355 to learn how HSAs will work.

In addition to the private sources of health insurance and health care discussed in this section, government health care programs cover over 45 million people. The next section discusses these programs.

CONCEPT CHECK 11-4

1 What are the major sources of health insurance and health care?
2 What are Blue Cross and Blue Shield plans? What benefits does each plan provide?
3 What are the differences among HMOs, PPOs, EPOs, and POSs?
4 What are home health care agencies?
5 What are employer self-funded health plans?

Action Application Visit the National Health Information Center's Web site at nhic-nt.health.org. Describe in a two-page report the types of health insurance and health care available to consumers.

Government Health Care Programs

Public opinion polls consistently show that Americans are unhappy with the nation's health care system. Increasingly, businesses and citizens have been calling for some kind of national health program.

Financial Planning for Life's Situations

HSAs: How They Work

1. Your company offers a health insurance policy with an *annual deductible* of at least $1,000.

2. You can put *pretax dollars* into an HSA each year, up to the amount of the deductible—but no more than $5,150 for family coverage or $2,600 for individual coverage.

3. You withdraw the money from your HSA tax-free, but it can only go for your *family's medical expenses.* After the deductible and copays are met, insurance still typically *covers 80 percent* of health costs.

4. HSA plans are required to have maximum *out-of-pocket spending limits,* $5,000 for individuals, $10,000 for families. That's when your company's insurance kicks in again at 100 percent coverage.

5. Your *company can match* part or all of your HSA contributions if it wishes, just as it does with 401(k)s.

6. You can invest your HSA in stocks, bonds, or mutual funds. *Unused money remains* in your account at the end of the year and *grows tax free.*

7. You can also take your HSA with you if you if *change jobs or retire.*

8. To help you *shop for health care* now that you're spending your own money, employers say they will give you detailed information about prices and quality of doctors and hospitals in your area.

Source: Howard Gleckman, "Your New Health Plan," *BusinessWeek,* November 8, 2004, p. 98.

Federal and state governments offer health coverage in accordance with laws that define the premiums and benefits they can offer. Specific requirements as to age, occupation, length of service, and family income may be used to determine eligibility for coverage. Two sources of government health insurance are Medicare and Medicaid.

Objective 5

Appraise the sources of government health care programs.

MEDICARE

Medicare, established in 1965, is a federal health insurance program for people 65 or older, people of any age with permanent kidney failure, and people with certain disabilities. The program is administered by The Centers for Medicare and Medicaid Services (formerly known as the Health Care Financing Administration). Local Social Security Administration offices take applications for Medicare, assist beneficiaries in filing claims, and provide information about the program.

Originally, Medicare had two parts: hospital insurance (Part A) and medical insurance (Part B). In December 2003, the Medicare Prescription Drug, Improvement and Modernization Act created the Medicare Advantage program (Part C) and Medicare prescription drug benefit program (Part D).

Medicare *hospital insurance* (Part A) helps pay for inpatient hospital care, inpatient care in a skilled nursing facility, home health care, and hospice care. Hospital insurance is financed from a portion of the Social Security tax. Part A pays for all covered services for inpatient hospital care after you pay a single annual deductible ($912 in 2005). Most people over 65 are eligible for free Medicare hospital insurance.

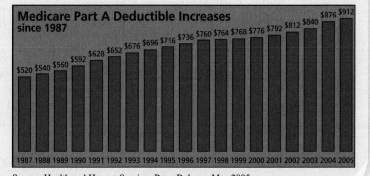

DID YOU KNOW?

Medicare Part A Deductible Increases since 1987

$520 (1987), $540 (1988), $560 (1989), $592 (1990), $628 (1991), $652 (1992), $676 (1993), $696 (1994), $716 (1995), $736 (1996), $760 (1997), $764 (1998), $768 (1999), $776 (2000), $792 (2001), $812 (2002), $840 (2003), $876 (2004), $912 (2005)

Source: Health and Human Services Press Release, May 2005.

Medicare *medical insurance* helps pay for doctors' services and a variety of other medical services and supplies not covered by hospital insurance. Each year, as soon as you meet the annual medical insurance deductible, medical insurance will pay 80 percent of the approved charges for the covered services that you receive during the rest of the year. In 2005 the annual deductible was $110 and the monthly premium was $78.20. Starting in 2007, people with Medicare who have higher incomes will pay higher premiums for Medicare Part B coverage. Voluntary medical insurance is financed from the monthly premiums paid by people who have enrolled in it and from general federal revenues. You must sign up for Part B coverage.

The Balanced Budget Act of 1997 created the new Medicare + Choice program. The act expands managed care options by encouraging wider availability of HMOs and allows other types of health plans to participate in Medicare. It gives you the option to remain in the original Medicare (Parts A and B) or to enroll in a Medicare + Choice plan. The Medicare Prescription, Drug Improvement and Modernization Act of 2003 renamed the Medicare + Choice program as Medicare Advantage (Part C). This new plan may be less expensive than the original Medicare. The plan is run by private health care providers who receive a set amount from Medicare for your health care regardless of how many or how few services you use.

The new law also provides Medicare beneficiaries with prescription drug discounts (Part D). This voluntary, comprehensive Medicare drug coverage became effective on January 1, 2006. Most seniors will pay about $35 per month for this new drug benefit and pay a copayment or coinsurance for each prescription. As with Medicare Part B enrollment, there is a penalty for not enrolling in the Medicare drug benefit in the first six months that you are eligible. People with the lowest incomes will pay no premiums or deductibles and small or no copayments.

DID YOU KNOW?

MEDICARE—BEFORE AND AFTER

1965: Medicare enacted into law. By 1969, Medicare represents about 0.7 percent of gross domestic product.

2004: Medicare provides benefits to 41.7 million elderly and disabled. Total cost of $308.9 billion. Represents 2.6 percent of gross domestic product.

2006: Prescription drug coverage (Medicare Part D) takes full effect (results from Medicare Modernization Act of 2003).

2020: Part A Hospital Insurance trust fund reserves projected to be depleted. (Program will be able to pay 79 percent of benefits.)

2035: Total Medicare costs (including prescription drug coverage) projected to represent 7.5 percent of gross domestic product.

MENDING MEDICARE   Without changes, the nation's multibillion-a-year system for providing health care to seniors is projected to go broke in 2008. That's decades before Social Security could exhaust its trust fund, but before 80 million baby boomers start collecting Medicare benefits. Medicare is a much smaller program, but due to a combination of rising health care costs and a growing elderly population, Medicare spending will soar at a faster rate than Social Security, from 12 percent of the budget in 1999 to more than 27 percent by 2030. "With all due respect for all the hoopla over Social Security, Medicare is a far more important and more difficult issue," says Brandeis University health policy expert Stuart H. Altman. "Anything we do still leaves a huge gap between the available money and the program's cost."[6]

Exhibit 11–3 compares features of different Medicare options.

For health care information, counseling, and assistance with Medicare, managed care, Medigap insurance, and long-term care insurance, visit the State of New York Web site at **hiicap.state.ny.us.**

WHAT IS NOT COVERED BY MEDICARE?   Although Medicare is very helpful for meeting medical costs, it does not cover everything. In addition to the deductibles and coinsurance mentioned earlier, Medicare does not cover some medical expenses at all, including

Exhibit **11-3**   A comparison of various Medicare plans

	Current Options	New Options (Medicare and Choice)	Plan Description
Original Medicare	✓	✓	• You choose your health care providers. • Medicare pays your providers for covered services. • Most beneficiaries choose Medicare supplemental insurance to cover deductible and copayments.
Medicare health maintenance organization (HMO)	✓	✓	• You must live in the plan's service area. • You agree to use the plan's network of doctors, hospitals, and other health providers, except in an emergency. • Medicare pays the HMO to provide all medical services.
Preferred provider organization (PPO)		✓	• Works like an HMO, except you have the choice to see a health provider out of the network. • If you do see an out-of-network provider, you will pay a higher cost.
Provider-sponsored organization (PSO)		✓	• Works like a Medicare HMO, except the networks are managed by health care providers (doctors and hospitals) rather than an insurance company.
Private fee for service		✓	• Medicare pays a lump sum to a private insurance health plan. • Providers can bill more than what the plan pays; you are responsible for paying the balance. • The plan may offer more benefits than original Medicare.

Source: *Medicare & You* (Washington, DC: The Centers for Medicare and Medicaid Services, 2005).

- Accupuncture.
- Care in a skilled nursing facility (SNF) beyond 100 days per benefit period.
- Skilled nursing care in facilities not approved by Medicare.
- Intermediate and custodial nursing care (the kind many nursing home residents need).
- Most screening tests, vaccinations, and some diabetic supplies.
- Private-duty nursing.
- Routine checkups, dental care, most immunizations, cosmetic surgery, routine foot care, eyeglasses, and hearing aids.
- Care received outside the United States except in Canada and Mexico, and then only in limited circumstances.
- Services Medicare does not consider medically necessary.
- Physician charges above Medicare's approved amount. The government has a fee schedule for physician charges and places limits on charges in excess of the

Medicare-approved amount when the physician does not accept Medicare's approved amount as payment in full.

For a more complete description of Medicare coverage and costs, ask your local Social Security Administration office for a copy of *The Medicare Handbook.* For more information, call the Medicare Hotline at 1-800-633-4227.

MEDIGAP   Medicare was never intended to pay all medical costs. To fill the gap between Medicare payments and medical costs not covered by Medicare, many companies sell medigap insurance policies. **Medigap** or **MedSup insurance** is not sold or serviced by the federal government or state governments. Contrary to the claims made by some advertising and insurance agents, Medicare supplement insurance is not a government-sponsored program.

Most states now have 10 standardized Medicare supplement policies, designated by the letters *A* through *J*. These standardized policies make it easier to compare the costs of policies issued by different insurers. All Medicare policies must cover certain gaps in Medicare coverage, such as the daily coinsurance amount for hospitalization. In addition to the basic benefits that must now be included in all newly issued Medicare supplement policies in most states, you should consider other policy features.

> **medigap (MedSup) insurance** Supplements Medicare by filling the gap between Medicare payments and medical costs not covered by Medicare.

MEDICAID

Title XIX of the Social Security Act provides for a program of medical assistance to certain low-income individuals and families. In 1965 the program, known as *Medicaid,* became federal law.

Medicaid is administered by each state within certain broad federal requirements and guidelines. Financed by both state and federal funds, it is designed to provide medical assistance to groups or categories of persons who are eligible to receive payments under one of the cash assistance programs such as Aid to Families with Dependent Children and Supplemental Security Income. The states may also provide Medicaid to medically needy individuals, that is, to persons who fit into one of the categories eligible for public assistance. But is the middle class mooching off Medicaid? Read the accompanying Financial Planning for Life's Situations feature on page 359.

Many members of the Medicaid population are also covered by Medicare. Where such dual coverage exists, most state Medicaid programs pay for the Medicare premiums, deductibles, and copayments and for services not covered by Medicare. Medicaid differs from Medicare because eligibility for Medicaid depends on having very low income and assets. Once a person is eligible, Medicaid provides more benefits than does Medicare. Because Medicaid coverage is so comprehensive, people using it do not need to purchase supplemental insurance.

To qualify for federal matching funds, state programs must include inpatient hospital services; outpatient hospital services; laboratory and X-ray services; skilled nursing and home health services for individuals age 21 and older; family planning services; early and periodic screening, diagnosis, and treatment for individuals under 21; and physicians' services in the home, office, hospital, nursing home, or elsewhere.

> **DID YOU KNOW?**
>
> You can call 1-800-HHS-TIPS to report fraud and abuse in Medicare and Medicaid programs.

FIGHT AGAINST MEDICARE/ MEDICAID FRAUD AND ABUSE

Nearly 70 percent of consumers believe the Medicare program would not go broke if fraud and abuse were eliminated. Moreover, nearly 80 percent are not aware of any efforts to reduce health care fraud and abuse. In 1997 President Clinton introduced the Medicare/Medicaid Anti-Waste, Fraud and Abuse

MOOCHING OFF MEDICAID

Blame the middle class for many of Medicaid's problems. Harsh as that sounds, the state-run medical-care programs originally designed to help poor mothers and their children now increasingly pay for nursing home care for seniors. While many of those seniors are genuinely poor, others are not. They have simply shifted their savings and assets to relatives—faking poverty and getting Medicaid and taxpayers to shoulder their long-term nursing home costs. While this may be legal, it is surely not moral. It is also fiscally ruinous. President Bush's budgetary proposal to cut $60 billion out of Medicaid over the next decade is driven in part by the explosion in nursing home costs. Tightening up Medicaid eligibility rules, as well as expanding the long-term care insurance market, can save a portion of those cuts for those who deserve it: the truly poor.

Check out the numbers. Medicaid costs already absorb 22 percent of state budgets, twice the portion spent on higher education. Only about 9 percent of those enrolled in Medicaid are seniors, but they claimed 26 percent of the program's budget, almost all nursing home expenses. Medicaid already pays more than 60 percent of the country's bill for nursing homes. And this can only get worse as baby boomers start to retire.

Is it time for state and federal governments to step up? Savings are supposed to pay for a person's old age, not be given to children, leaving taxpayers to pick up the burden. Demand for assets-shifting is so great in retirement communities that lawyers provide ready assistance. Virginia plans to examine financial statements for the six years before people apply for Medicaid, up from the current three. Other states should follow suit.

Source: *BusinessWeek,* February 21, 2005, p. 96.

Act, which established tough new requirements for health care providers that wish to participate in the Medicare/Medicaid program.

The Financial Planning for Life's Situations feature on page 360 provides some consumer tips on health and disability insurance.

GOVERNMENT CONSUMER HEALTH INFORMATION WEB SITES

With more than 60 central World Wide Web sites on eight separate Web domains, the Department of Health and Human Services (HHS) maintains one of the richest and most reliable sources of information on the Internet (www.hhs.gov). HHS documents on the Web include information on health issues, research-related data, and access to HHS services, including interactive sites. Major HHS health information Web sites include the following.

HEALTHFINDER Healthfinder includes links to more than 1,250 Web sites, including over 250 federal sites and 1,000 state, local, not-for-profit, university, and other consumer health resources. Topics are organized in a subject index. With more than 7 million hits in its first two months of operation, Healthfinder is currently rated fifth among consumers' favorite Web sites on the "Web 100" list (www.hhs.gov).

Serving Health Insurance Needs of Elders (SHINE) is a volunteer organization that provides free counseling and assistance regarding Medicare, Medicaid, and supplemental health insurance to seniors and their families. Visit SHINE at **www.mfaaa.org/shine/shine.html**.

fyi

MEDLINEPLUS MEDLINEplus, the world's most extensive collection of published medical information, is coordinated by the National Library of Medicine. Originally designed for health professionals and researchers, MEDLINEplus is also valuable for students and for those seeking more specific information about health care (www.nlm.nih.gov/medlineplus).

359

CONSUMER TIPS ON HEALTH AND DISABILITY INSURANCE

1. If you pay your own premiums directly, try to arrange to pay them on an annual or quarterly basis rather than a monthly basis. It is cheaper.

2. Policies should be delivered to you within 30 days. If not, contact your insurer and find out, in writing, why. If a policy is not delivered in 60 days, contact the state department of insurance.

3. When you receive a policy, take advantage of the free-look provision. You have 10 days to look it over and obtain a refund if you decide it is not for you.

4. Unless you have a policy with no internal limits, read over your contract every year to see whether its benefits are still in line with medical costs.

5. Don't replace a policy because you think it is out of date. Switching may subject you to new waiting periods and new exclusions. Rather, add to what you have if necessary.

6. On the other hand, don't keep a policy because you've had it a long time. You don't get any special credit from the company for being an old customer.

7. Don't try to make a profit on your insurance by carrying overlapping coverages. Duplicate coverage is expensive. Besides, most group policies now contain a coordination of benefits clause limiting benefits to 100 percent.

8. Use your health emergency fund to cover small expenses.

9. If you're considering the purchase of a dread disease policy such as cancer insurance, understand that it is supplementary and will pay for only one disease. You should have full coverage before you consider it. Otherwise, it's a gamble.

10. Don't lie on your insurance application. If you fail to mention a preexisting condition, you may not get paid. You can usually get paid even for that condition after one or two years have elapsed if you have had no treatment for the condition during that period.

11. Keep your insurance up to date. Some policies adjust to inflation better than others. Some insurers check that benefits have not been outdistanced by inflation. Review your policies annually.

12. Never sign a health insurance application (such applications are lengthy and detailed for individually written policies) until you have recorded full and complete answers to every question.

Source: Health Insurance Association of America.

NIH HEALTH INFORMATION PAGE This Web site provides a single access point to the consumer health information resources of the National Institutes of Health, including the NIH Health Information Index, NIH publications and clearinghouses, and the Combined Health Information Database (www.nih.gov).

CONCEPT CHECK 11-5

1 What are the two sources of government health insurance?
2 What benefits do Part A and Part B of Medicare provide?
3 What is medigap, or MedSup, insurance?

Action Application Visit www.medicare.gov and describe the changes that have been made in the hospital and medical insurance provided by Medicare.

Disability Income Insurance

Objective 6

Recognize the need for disability income insurance.

Because you feel young and healthy now, you may overlook the very real need for disability income insurance. Disability income insurance protects your most valuable asset: your ability to earn income. People are more likely to lose their incomes due to disability than to death. The fact is that for all age groups, disability is more likely than death.

Disability income insurance provides regular cash income lost by employees as the result of an accident or illness. Disability income insurance is probably the most neglected form of available insurance protection. Many people who insure their houses, cars, and other property fail to insure their most valuable resource: their earning power. Disability can cause even greater financial problems than death. In fact, disability is often called "the living death." Disabled persons lose their earning power while continuing to incur normal family expenses. In addition, they often face huge expenses for the medical treatment and special care their disabilities require.

If you are between ages 35 and 65, your chances of being unable to work for 90 days or more due to a disabling illness or injury are greater than your chances of dying. To be more specific, at age 40 you face a 12 percent chance of dying before reaching age 65 and a 19 percent chance of having at least one disability lasting 90 days or longer.[7] If you have no disability income protection, you are betting that you will not become disabled, and that could be a very costly bet.

The probability of a male becoming temporarily or permanently disabled between ages 20 and 30 is 1.3 percent, but between ages 20 and 60 it increases to 19.1 percent. Females are less prone to disability during their lifetimes and have only a 15.3 percent chance of becoming disabled between 20 and 60 years of age.[8]

disability income insurance Provides payments to replace income when an insured person is unable to work.

DEFINITION OF DISABILITY

Disability has several definitions. Some policies define it simply as the inability to do your regular work. Others have stricter definitions. For example, a dentist who is unable to do his or her regular work because of a hand injury but can earn income through related duties, such as teaching dentistry, would not be considered permanently disabled under certain policies.

Good disability plans pay when you are unable to work at your regular job; poor disability plans pay only when you are unable to work at any job. A good disability plan will also make partial disability payments when you return to work on a part-time basis.

DID YOU KNOW?

- One in three working Americans will become disabled for 90 days or more before age 65.
- The average disability absence is 2 1/2 years.
- More than 80 percent of working Americans don't have disability income insurance or aren't covered adequately.

DISABILITY INSURANCE TRADE-OFFS

Following are some important trade-offs you should consider in purchasing disability income insurance.

WAITING OR ELIMINATION PERIOD   Benefits don't begin on the first day you become disabled. Usually there is a waiting or elimination period of between 30 and 90 days. Some waiting periods may be as long as 180 days. Generally, disability income policies with longer waiting periods have lower premiums. If you have substantial savings to cover three to six months of expenses, the reduced premiums of a policy with a long waiting period may be attractive. But if you need every paycheck to cover your bills, you are probably better off paying the higher premium for a short waiting period. Short waiting periods, however, are very expensive.

Chances of becoming disabled are greater in professions that involve physical risks.

DURATION OF BENEFITS   The maximum time a disability income policy will pay benefits may be a few years, to age 65, or for life. You should seek a policy that pays benefits for life. If you became permanently disabled, it would be financially disastrous if your benefits ended at age 55 or 65.

AMOUNT OF BENEFITS   You should aim for a benefit amount that, when added to your other income, will equal 60 to 70 percent of your gross pay. Of course, the greater the benefits, the greater the cost.

ACCIDENT AND SICKNESS COVERAGE   Consider both accident and sickness coverage. Some disability income policies will pay only for accidents, but you want to be insured for illness, too.

GUARANTEED RENEWABILITY   Ask for noncancelable and guaranteed renewable coverage. Either coverage will protect you against your insurance company dropping you if your health becomes poor. The premium for these coverages is higher, but the coverages are well worth the extra cost. Furthermore, look for a disability income policy that waives premium payments while you are disabled.

See whether you qualify for a lower premium if you agree to forgo part of your monthly benefit when Social Security, company retirement benefits, or worker's compensation benefits begin. Most disability income policies coordinate their benefits with these programs.

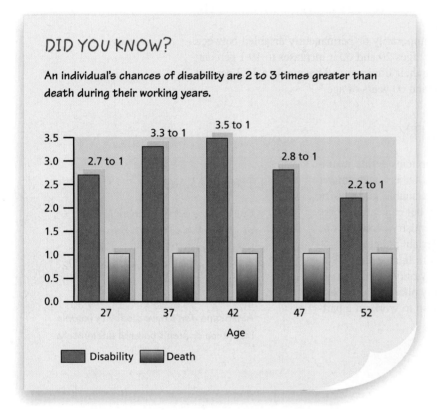

DID YOU KNOW?

An individual's chances of disability are 2 to 3 times greater than death during their working years.

SOURCES OF DISABILITY INCOME

Before you buy disability income insurance, remember that you may already have some form of such insurance. This coverage may come to you through your employer, Social Security, or worker's compensation.

EMPLOYER   Many, but not all, employers provide disability income protection for their employees through group insurance plans. Your employer may have some form of wage continuation policy that lasts a few months or an employee group disability plan that provides long-term protection. In most cases, your employer will pay part or all of the cost of this plan.

SOCIAL SECURITY   Most salaried workers in the United States participate in the Social Security program. In this program, your benefits are determined by your salary and by the number of years you have been covered under Social Security. Your dependents also qualify for certain benefits. However, Social Security has strict rules. You must be totally disabled for 12 months or more, and you must be unable to do *any* work.

WORKER'S COMPENSATION   If your accident or illness occurred at your place of work or resulted from your type of employment, you could be entitled to worker's compensation benefits in your state. Like Social Security benefits, these benefits are determined by your earnings and work history.

Other possible sources of disability income include Veterans Administration pension disability benefits, civil service disability benefits for government workers, state vocational rehabilitation benefits, state welfare benefits for low-income people, Aid to Families with Dependent Children, group union disability benefits, automobile insurance that provides benefits for disability from an auto accident, and private insurance programs such as credit disability insurance, which covers loan payments when you are disabled. Exhibit 11–4 will help you identify the sources and amount of income available to you if you become disabled.

The availability and extent of these and other disability income sources vary widely in different parts of the country. Be sure to look into such sources carefully before calculating your need for additional disability income insurance.

> **DID YOU KNOW?**
>
> Average 2005 monthly Social Security benefits for a disabled worker were $895 ($1,497 for a disabled worker with a spouse and a child).
>
> Source: www.ssa.gov, January 2005.

DETERMINING YOUR DISABILITY INCOME INSURANCE REQUIREMENTS

Once you have found out what your benefits from the numerous public and private disability income sources would be, you should determine whether those benefits are sufficient to meet your disability income needs. If the sum of your disability benefits approaches your after-tax income, you can safely assume that should disability strike, you'll be in good shape to pay your day-to-day bills while recuperating.

You should know how long you would have to wait before the benefits begin (the waiting or elimination period) and how long they would be paid (the benefit period).

What if, as is often the case, Social Security and other disability benefits are not sufficient to support your family? In that case, you may want to consider buying disability income insurance to make up the difference.

Don't expect to insure yourself for your full salary. Most insurers limit benefits from all sources to no more than 70 to 80 percent of your take-home pay. For example, if you earn $400 a week, you could be eligible for disability insurance of about $280 to $320 a week. You will not need $400, because while you are disabled, your work-related expenses will be eliminated and your taxes will be far lower or may even be zero.

The Financial Planning for Life's Situations box on page 364 shows you how to compare different features among disability income policies.

Sheet 52
Disability income insurance needs

Exhibit **11–4**

Disability income worksheet

How much income will you have available if you become disabled?			
	Monthly Amount	**After Waiting:**	**For a Period of:**
Sick leave or short-term disability	_____	_____	_____
Group long-term disability	_____	_____	_____
Social Security	_____	_____	_____
Other government programs	_____	_____	_____
Individual disability insurance	_____	_____	_____
Credit disability insurance	_____	_____	_____
Other income:	_____	_____	_____
Savings	_____	_____	_____
Spouse's income	_____	_____	_____
Total monthly income while disabled:	$_____		

Financial Planning for Life's Situations

DISABILITY INCOME POLICY CHECKLIST

Every disability income policy may have different features. The following checklist will help you compare policies you may be considering.

	Policy A	Policy B
1. How is disability defined?		
Inability to perform your own job?	——	——
Inability to perform any job?	——	——
2. Does the policy cover		
Accident?	——	——
Illness?	——	——
3. Are benefits available		
For total disability?	——	——
For partial disability?	——	——
Only after total disability?	——	——
Without a prior period of total disability?	——	——
4. Are full benefits paid, whether or not you are able to work, for loss of		
Sight?	——	——
Speech?	——	——
Hearing?	——	——
Use of limbs?	——	——

	Policy A	Policy B
5. What percentage of your income will the maximum benefit replace?	——	——
6. Is the policy noncancelable, guaranteed renewable, or conditionally renewable?	——	——
7. How long must you be disabled before premiums are waived?	——	——
8. Is there an option to buy additional coverage, without evidence of insurability, at a later date?	——	——
9. Does the policy offer an inflation adjustment feature?	——	——
If so, what is the rate of increase?	——	——
How often is it applied?	——	——
For how long?	——	——

	Policy A		Policy B	
10. What does the policy cost?	With Inflation Feature	Without Inflation Feature	With Inflation Feature	Without Inflation Feature
For a waiting period of —— days and (30–180)	——————	——————	——————	——————
For a benefit period of —————— 1 yr.–lifetime?	——————	——————	——————	——————
Total	——————	——————	——————	——————

Source: Health Insurance Association of America, Washington, DC.

CONCEPT CHECK 11-6

1 What is disability income insurance?
2 What are the three main sources of disability income?
3 How can you determine the amount of disability income insurance you need?

Action Application List the benefits in your employee benefit package, such as health insurance, disability income insurance, and life insurance.

SUMMARY OF OBJECTIVES

Objective 1

Explain why the costs of health insurance and health care have been increasing.

Health care costs, except during 1994–1996, have gone up faster than the rate of inflation. Among the reasons for high and rising health care costs are the use of expensive technologies, duplication of tests and sometimes technologies, increases in the variety and frequency of treatments, unnecessary tests, the increasing number and longevity of elderly people, regulations that shift rather than reduce costs, the increasing number of accidents and crimes requiring emergency services, limited competition and restrictive work rules in the health care delivery system, rapid earnings growth among health care professionals, built-in inflation in the health care delivery system, and other factors.

Objective 2

Define *health insurance* and *disability income insurance* and explain their importance in financial planning.

Health insurance is protection that provides payment of benefits for a covered sickness or injury. Disability income insurance protects a person's most valuable asset: the ability to earn income.

Health insurance and disability income insurance are two protections against economic losses due to illness, accident, or disability. Both protections should be a part of your overall insurance program to safeguard your family's economic security.

Disability can cause even greater financial problems than death. In fact, disability is often called "the living death." Disabled persons lose their earning power while continuing to incur normal family expenses. In addition, they often face huge expenses for the medical treatment and special care their disabilities require.

Objective 3

Analyze the benefits and limitations of the various types of health care coverage.

Five basic types of health insurance are available under group and individual policies: hospital expense insurance, surgical expense insurance, physician's expense insurance, major medical expense insurance, and comprehensive major medical insurance. The benefits and limitations of each policy differ. Ideally, you should get a basic plan and a major medical supplementary plan, or a comprehensive major medical policy that combines the values of both of these plans in a single policy.

Major provisions of a health insurance policy include eligibility requirements, assigned benefits, inside limits, copayment, service benefits, benefit limits, exclusions and limitation, coordination of benefits, guaranteed renewability, and cancellation and termination.

Objective 4

Evaluate private sources of health insurance and health care.

Health insurance and health care are available from private insurance companies, hospital and medical service plans such as Blue Cross/Blue Shield, health maintenance organizations (HMOs), preferred provider organizations (PPOs), exclusive provider organizations (EPOs), point-of-service plans (POSs), home health care agencies, and employer self-funded health plans.

Objective 5

Appraise the sources of government health care programs.

The federal and state governments offer health coverage in accordance with laws that define the premiums and benefits. Two well-known government health programs are Medicare and Medicaid.

Objective 6

Recognize the need for disability income insurance.

Disability income insurance provides regular cash income lost by employees as the result of an accident or illness. Sources of disability income insurance include the employer, Social Security, worker's compensation, the Veterans Administration, the federal and state governments, unions, and private insurance.

KEY TERMS

basic health insurance coverage   342

Blue Cross   351

Blue Shield   351

coinsurance   342

comprehensive major medical insurance   342

coordination of benefits (COB)   341

copayment   347

deductible   342

disability income insurance   361

exclusive provider organization (EPO)   353

health maintenance organization (HMO)   351

hospital expense insurance   342

hospital indemnity policy   343

long-term care insurance (LTC)   343

major medical expense insurance   342

managed care   351

medigap (MedSup) insurance   358

physician expense insurance   342

point-of-service plan (POS)   353

preferred provider organization (PPO)   353

stop-loss   342

surgical expense insurance   342

FINANCIAL PLANNING PROBLEMS

1. *Calculating the Effect of Inflation on Health Care Costs.* As of 1995, per capita spending on health care in the United States was about $3,600. If this amount increased by 5 percent a year, what would be the amount of per capita spending for health care in 10 years? (Obj. 1)

2. *Calculating the Amount of Reimbursement from an Insurance Company.* The Kelleher family has health insurance coverage that pays 80 percent of out-of-hospital expenses after a $500 deductible per person. If one family member has doctor and prescription medication expenses of $1,100, what amount would the insurance company pay? (Obj. 3)

3. *Comparing the Costs of a Regular Health Insurance Policy and an HMO.* A health insurance policy pays 65 percent of physical therapy costs after a $200 deductible. In contrast, an HMO charges $15 per visit for physical therapy. How much would a person save with the HMO if he or she had 10 physical therapy sessions costing $50 each? (Obj. 4)

4. Sarah's comprehensive major medical health insurance plan at work has a deductible of $750. The policy pays 85 percent of any amount above the deductible. While on a hiking trip, she contracted a rare bacterial disease. Her medical costs for treatment, including medicines, tests, and a six-day hospital stay, totaled $8,893. A friend told her that she would have paid less if she had a policy with a stop-loss feature that capped her out-of-pocket expenses at $3,000. Was her friend correct? Show your computations. Then determine which policy would have cost Sarah less and by how much.

5. *Calculating the Amount of Disability Benefits.* Georgia Braxton, a widow, has take-home pay of $600 a week. Her disability insurance coverage replaces 70 percent of her earnings after a four-week waiting period. What amount would she receive in disability benefits if an illness kept Georgia off work for 16 weeks? (Obj. 6)

FINANCIAL PLANNING ACTIVITIES

1. *Identifying Financial Resources Needed to Pay for Health Care Services.* List health care services that you and other members of your family have used during the past year. Assign an approximate dollar cost to each of these services, and identify the financial resources (savings, health insurance, government sources, etc.) you used to pay for them. (Obj. 1)

2. *Using Current Information to Obtain Costs of Health Care.* Choose a current issue of *Consumer Reports, Money, BusinessWeek,* or *Kiplinger's Personal Finance* and summarize an article that updates the costs of health care. How might you use this information to reduce your health care costs? (Obj. 1)

3. *Comparing Major Provisions in a Health Care Insurance Policy.* Obtain sample health insurance policies from insurance agents or brokers, and analyze the policies for definitions, coverages, exclusions, limitations on coverage, and amounts of coverage. In what ways are the policies similar? In what ways do they differ? (Obj. 3)

4. *Using the Internet to Obtain Information about Various Types of Health Insurance Coverages.* Visit the following Department of Health and Human Services Web sites to gather information about various types of health insurance coverages. Prepare a summary report on how this information may be useful to you. (Obj. 5)

   a. Healthfinder (www.healthfinder.gov)

   b. MEDLINE (www.medline.gov)

INTERNET CONNECTION

Health Insurance Statistics

The U.S. Census Bureau collects a wide variety of data about the people and economy of the United States. Health insurance coverage is one of the many surveys the Bureau completes each year.

Locate the Health Insurance section of the U.S. Census Bureau Web site. Then complete the worksheet on page 367.

Key Words:

_____

_____

_____

_____

_____

(CONTINUED)

U.S. Census Bureau Web site address:	
For what year is the most recent health insurance coverage survey presented?	
In the most recent health insurance survey, how many people in the U.S. were without health insurance coverage?	
What populations (age or race) are less likely to have health insurance?	
How many children under the age of 18 have no health insurance according to the most recent health insurance survey?	

FINANCIAL PLANNING CASES

Giving Power to the Patient

Kimberly Salzbrunn of Oswego, Illinois, is on the cutting edge of a dramatic change in health care. Since January, she has taken her two-year-old son Jacob to the doctor three times for chronic breathing problems, purchased five prescriptions, and spent a recent Saturday in the emergency room. She has not yet had to pay for any of it out of her own pocket.

So far, she's paid her bills—$358—by drawing down $1,500 that her employer, Budget Rent-A-Car, is putting aside for her health care this year. She can use the money for her own medical needs, or those of Jacob or her husband, Dan. Preventive care is 100 percent covered, though doctors must be in the network.

If the Salzbrunns use up their $1,500, they must pay health care expenses themselves until they hit a $2,000 deductible. If they don't spend the entire $1,500 this year, what is left will be added to their account in future years.

Salzbrunn, a 34-year-old job-training specialist, is one of tens of thousands of Americans with what's known as consumer-driven, or defined-contribution, health care. Her plan is run by Definity Health of Minneapolis, one of two players—Lumenos of Alexandria, Virginia, is the other. About 50 companies offer these plans, including defense contractor Raytheon and chipmaker Intel.

So far, 12 percent of Budget's staff—625 workers—is participating in the plan. Budget won't disclose how much workers kick in, but it's 20 percent less than the preferred provider organization (PPO) and 10 percent more than the HMO options.

With health care costs poised to double in five years, companies have no choice but to find alternatives. If employees like those at Budget continue to express satisfaction with consumer-driven plans, they're likely to get a lot of company—very soon.

Questions

1. Why did Kimberly Salzbrunn not have to pay from her own pocket even though she has taken her two-year-old son to the doctor three times, purchased five prescriptions, and spent a day in the emergency room?

2. What will happen when the Salzbrunns use up their $1,500? What if they don't use their $1,500 this year?

3. What is the name for this kind of a health plan?

Source: Laura Cohn, "Giving Power to the Patient," *Business-Week,* May 6, 2002, p. 102.

Making Sense of Medicare

Eugenio Costa, 65, received a 100-page booklet from Uncle Sam called *Medicare and You 2002.* It doesn't have much of a plot, but it might be the most important reading he does this year.

For seniors or their adult children, the booklet outlines the choices Medicare recipients face in the fast-changing world of health care. But Medicare is mind-numbingly complicated, and it is too easy to get lost in a maze of options.

Eugenio is fully aware, however, that Medicare, Medicare HMO (Medicare + Choice), or medigap do not cover long-term nursing home or at-home care. For that, he will have to buy private insurance, which can cost thousands of dollars a year if he signs up now.

All of these choices allow seniors to tailor a plan to their needs. But it also makes picking insurance much more complicated. Eugenio knows that a mistake can be costly in terms of both health and money.

(CONTINUED)

Questions

1. What factors should Eugenio Costa consider in making the choice among various types of Medicare, medigap, or HMO health care insurance policies?

2. Visit the following Web sites for Medicare resources to obtain general information, guides on buying medigap or HMO coverage, and price quotations with insurance company ratings on medigap insurance carriers.

General Information
Medicare
1-800-633-4227
www.medicare.gov

ElderCare Locator
1-800-677-1116
Guides on Buying Medigap or HMO Coverage
Medicare Rights Center
www.medicarerights.org
United Seniors Health Cooperative
www.ushc-online.org
Quotes and Ratings on Medigap Carriers
Weiss Rating
1-800-289-9222
www.weissratings.com
Quotesmith.com
1-800-566-9393
www.quotesmith.com

VIDEO CASE

Health and Disability Insurance

This video case features a young couple, Kathy and Ted. Ted, 28, is in a hospital, where he faces several surgeries, chemotherapy, radiation therapy, and possibly a bone marrow transplant. Ted runs marathons, works out for an hour five to six times a week, and eats the kind of diet the health experts recommended. Ted and Kathy never thought they would get seriously ill, because they were young and healthy. If Ted's employer had not provided health insurance as a benefit, they would have never bought it.

Mike Lugo, a registered health underwriter, states that indemnity health insurance plans are expensive. However, such plans have no restrictions and pay the most generous amount when a claim is made.

Alan Puzarne of Blue Shield of California explains that his organization offers PPO products for both individuals and groups. Amanda O'Connor, Marketing Director for Kaiser Permanente Health Maintenance Organization, states that an HMO is a less expensive health insurance option, considering the benefits received.

Dr. Thomas Rice, Professor and Chair, Department of Health Services, UCLA School of Public Health, explains differences among HMOs, PPOs, and POS plans. He states that indemnity health insurance is very expensive; therefore, fewer and fewer people have such insurance. Finally, a medical doctor explains several reasons for the high cost of medical care.

Questions

1. What are the major differences among HMOs, PPOs, POSs, and indemnity health insurance plans?

2. Why is the health insurance decision an important one?

3. What are some reasons for the high cost of medical care?

YOUR PERSONAL FINANCIAL PLANNER IN ACTION

Comparing Health Insurance Plans

Changing programs and regulations influence your ability to be properly covered for health care and disability insurance coverage. Awareness of policy types, coverages, and limitations will help you plan this phase of your financial plan.

Short-Term Financial Planning Activities	Resources
1. Assess your current habits that could improve your health and reduce medical costs.	www.webmd.com www.healthfinder.gov www.healthseek.com
2. Analyze current health insurance coverage in relation to family and household needs.	PFP Sheet 51 www.quicken.com/insurance www.healthchoices.org www.ncqa.org
3. Compare the cost of health insurance programs available from various sources.	http://personalinsure.about.com www.insure.com
4. Evaluate your need for expanded disability insurance.	PFP Sheet 52 www.life-line.org www.disability-insurance-center.com

(CONTINUED)

Long-Term Financial Planning Activities	Resources
1. Identify possible future needs for supplemental Medicare and long-term care insurance coverages..	www.longtermcareinsurance.org www.ssa.gov www.medicare.gov www.naic.org
2. Develop a plan for reducing health care and medical insurance costs.	Text pages 336–339 www.ahip.org www.mib.com

CONTINUING CASE

Health Insurance

Life Situation
Pam, 36
Josh, 38
Three children, ages 9, 7, and 4

Financial Data
Monthly income $4,300
Living expenses $4,075
Assets $150,850
Liabilities $99,520

The Brocks are assessing their health insurance coverages. Since Josh's current employer offers him only 30 days of sick leave, they need to consider this factor when assessing disability insurance plans.

Since Pam's work activities have varied, the family is dependent on Josh's health insurance. In recent weeks, his company is considering several types of plans. These alternatives include traditional health insurance programs and HMOs, with a wide variety of coverage and cost differences.

Questions

1. When considering disability income insurance, what length of waiting period and duration of benefits should the Brocks consider?

2. What types of health insurance coverages would be recommended for the Brocks?

3. How might the Brocks use *Personal Financial Planner* sheets 51 and 52 to select health and disability insurance?

12 Life Insurance

PRIMERICA LIFE INSURANCE COMPANY

Executive Offices: Home Office: Boston, Massachusetts
3120 Breckinridge Boulevard, Duluth, Georgia 30099-0001

CHILDREN'S TERM INSURANCE RIDER

have issued this Rider as a part of the Policy to which it is attached. Any benefits under th
provisions of this Rider and the Policy. In case of conflict between this Rider and th
r will control.

ill pay to the Beneficiary
t of due proof

POLICY FACT SHEET

This Fact Sheet provides important information about your insurance
rage as of 04/21/1999, as well as identification and reference cards.
f you have any questions about your policy, please do not
our toll-free Client Services line.

Policyowner:
Insured:

Key Concept

Life insurance helps protect the people who depend on you. Deciding whether you need it and choosing the right policy take time, research, and careful thought.

Digital Study Tools

Online Learning Center Study Tools for This Chapter

- Multiple-choice quiz
- Flashcards
- eLearning sessions
- Crossword puzzle
- Personal Finance Online: Life Insurance Fundamentals

Student CD Study Tools for This Chapter

- Self-study software
- Narrated PowerPoint
- Personal financial planning software: Worksheets 53–54

www.mhhe.com/kdh

Learning Objectives

1 Define *life insurance* and describe its purpose and principle.

2 Determine your life insurance needs.

3 Distinguish between the two types of life insurance companies and analyze various types of life insurance policies these companies issue.

4 Select important provisions in life insurance contracts.

5 Create a plan to buy life insurance.

6 Recognize how annuities provide financial security.

Variable Life Insurance

Variable life insurance, the best-selling form of life insurance since 1999 when measured by dollars paid, may be anything but a solid protection. The falling stock market in the late 1990s eroded its value. Thousands of policyholders faced the choice of paying higher premiums, reducing their death benefit, or letting their policies lapse. "Variable life has the potential to be a time bomb," says Robert Cohen, an independent insurance agent in Farmington, Massachusetts.

Consider the case of a Wisconsin couple in their 30s with young children who bought a variable life policy in 1997 with a death benefit of $620,000. Their scheduled premium payments rose in 2002 from $676 a month to $905. They had put a total of $57,000 into the policy, but the combination of high fees and the poor performance of their investments, which were split between large-cap and midcap equity funds, left the policy's cash value at only $28,000, said Thomas Batterman at Vigil Trust & Financial Advocacy in Wausau, Wisconsin, a financial adviser the couple hired to evaluate the policy.

Batterman advised the couple to let the policy lapse. He said they should stop paying the premiums and consider another type of insurance. By letting it lapse, the remaining cash value should fund the death benefit for three or four years. If they surrendered the policy immediately, they would get the existing cash value minus a surrender penalty of $6,300 and they would have to pay taxes on the remaining $21,700. "The risks of these policies are very hard to understand," Batterman says.

Indeed, variable life is full of twists and turns. There are two kinds of policies: variable whole life and, the most popular, variable universal life. Both let you invest part of your premium in mutual fund–like investment pools called subaccounts, which often include a broad selection of funds from major fund companies. The key difference is that variable whole life policies require fixed premiums, while variable universal life policies let you vary your payments.

Variable life policies demand multiple fees. Besides mortality charges, they typically include a broker's sales charge (which can be 4 percent or more at the time of purchase), an administrative fee, state and federal premium taxes, and fund management fees. These charges often eat up the entire first year's premium and much of the second year's as well. "It's such a confusing type of contract, I don't think even some lawyers understand how it works," says George Cushing, a Boston estate lawyer.

Variable life policyholders can take their policies to their insurance agents and ask for updated analyses of performance. For a second opinion, it's a good idea to hire an independent financial planner to review your policy. The National Association of Personal Financial Advisors (1-800-366-2732 or www.napfa.org) can give referrals. Another option is the Consumer Federation of America, which has an insurance-evaluation service run by James Hunt, former Vermont state insurance commissioner. It costs $50 for the first policy. Details are available at www.consumerfed.org.

QUESTIONS

What Action Should Be Taken?

1. What choices do thousands of variable life insurance policyholders now face?
2. What is the major reason for variable life policies to be vulnerable and undesirable?

What about Your Situation?

3. What is Thomas Batterman's advice for the young Wisconsin couple who bought a variable life insurance policy in 1997?

Source: Adapted from Geoffrey Smith, "Variable Life Insurance Variables," *BusinessWeek,* April 8, 2002, pp. 78–79.

Learn More Online

Visit the National Association of Personal Financial Advisors Web site at www.napfa.org. What sources are listed at this site where you can get additional information about variable life insurance?

Life Insurance: An Introduction

Objective 1

Define *life insurance* and describe its purpose and principle.

Even though it is impossible to put a price on your life, you probably own some life insurance—through a group plan where you work, as a veteran, or through a policy you bought. Perhaps you are considering the purchase of additional life insurance to keep pace with inflation or cover your growing family. If so, you should prepare for that purchase by learning as much as possible about life insurance and how it can help you meet your needs.

Most American families face substantial loss when one spouse dies unexpectedly. Unfortunately, 45 percent of widows and 37 percent of widowers say their spouse had been inadequately insured. Life for the surviving spouse becomes a financial struggle (see Video Case for this chapter).

Life insurance is one of the most important and expensive purchases you may ever make. Deciding whether you need it and choosing the right policy from dozens of options take time, research, and careful thought. This chapter will help you make decisions about life insurance. It describes what life insurance is and how it works, the major types of life insurance coverage, and how you can use life insurance to protect your family.

Consumer awareness of life insurance has changed little over the years. Life insurance is still more often sold than bought. In other words, while most people actively seek to buy insurance for their property and health, they avoid a life insurance purchase until an agent approaches them. Still, recently, over 39.6 million policies, with face value of over $2.8 trillion, were sold in one year. Eight out of ten households now have life insurance. At the beginning of 2003, 396 million policies were in force, with a total value of $16.4 trillion.

You can receive a free *Life Insurance Buyer's Guide* from the National Association of Insurance Commissioners. Visit their Web site at **www.naic.org.** The guide helps you get the most for your money and answers questions about buying life insurance, deciding how much is needed, and finding the right kind of insurance.

WHAT IS LIFE INSURANCE?

Life insurance is neither mysterious nor difficult to understand. It works in the following manner. A person joins a risk-sharing group (an insurance company) by purchasing a contract (a policy). Under the policy, the insurance company promises to pay a sum of money at the time of the policyholder's death to the person or persons (the beneficiaries) selected by him or her. In the case of an endowment policy, the money is paid to the policyholder (the insured) if he or she is alive on the future date (the maturity date) named in the policy. The insurance company makes this promise in return for the insured's agreement to pay it a sum of money (the premium) periodically.

THE PURPOSE OF LIFE INSURANCE

Most people buy life insurance to protect someone who depends on them from financial losses caused by their death.

Most people buy life insurance to protect someone who depends on them from financial losses caused by their death. That someone could be the nonworking spouse and children of a single-income family. It could be the wife or husband of a two-income family. It could be an aging parent. It could be a business partner or a corporation.

Life insurance proceeds may be used to

- Pay off a home mortgage or other debts at the time of death.
- Provide lump-sum payments through an endowment to children when they reach a specified age.
- Provide an education or income for children.

- Make charitable bequests after death.
- Provide a retirement income.
- Accumulate savings.
- Establish a regular income for survivors.
- Set up an estate plan.
- Make estate and death tax payments.

Life insurance is one of the few ways to provide liquidity at the time of death.

THE PRINCIPLE OF LIFE INSURANCE

The principle of home insurance, discussed in Chapter 10, can be applied to the lives of persons. From records covering many years and including millions of lives, mortality tables have been prepared to show the number of deaths among various age groups during any year. In the 1950s, the life insurance industry developed and the National Association of Insurance Commissioners (NAIC) approved a mortality table known as the Commissioners 1958 Standard Ordinary (CSO) Mortality Table. In 1980 the NAIC approved a new Standard Ordinary Mortality Table based on experience during 1970–1975. Unlike the 1958 CSO table, which combined the mortality experience of males and females, the 1980 CSO table separates the experience by sex.

HOW LONG WILL YOU LIVE?

No one really knows how long a particular individual will live. But life expectancy in the United States has been steadily increasing since 1900. For example, in 1900 the life expectancy of a man was 46.3 years and of a woman 48.3 years. By 1998, life expectancy had increased to 74.5 years for white males and 80.0 for white females. Exhibit 12–1 shows the most recent life expectancy table, issued in 2000 by the National Center for Health Statistics. The life expectancy shown does not indicate the age at which a person has the highest probability of dying. For example, the exhibit shows that the life expectancy of a black male at age 30 is 40.6 years. This does not mean 30-year-old black males will probably die at age 70.6 years. It means 40.6 is the average number of additional years black males alive at age 30 may expect to live.

CONCEPT CHECK 12-1

1 How can the Internet help you create a life insurance plan?
2 What is the meaning of life insurance?
3 What is the purpose of life insurance?
4 What is the principle of life insurance?
5 What do life expectancy tables indicate?

Action Application Interview relatives and friends to determine why they purchased life insurance. Prepare an essay summarizing your findings.

Determining Your Life Insurance Needs

You should consider a number of factors before you buy life insurance. These factors include your present and future sources of income, other savings and income protection, group life insurance, group annuities (or other pension benefits), net worth, and Social Security. First, however, you should determine whether you *need* life insurance.

Objective 2
Determine your life insurance needs.

Exhibit **12-1**   Expectation of life and expected deaths by race, sex, and age: 1998

Age (Years)	Total	Expectation of Life in Years				Total	Expected Deaths per 1,000 Alive at Specified Age*			
		White		Black			White		Black	
		Male	Female	Male	Female		Male	Female	Male	Female
At birth	76.7	74.5	80.0	67.6	74.8	7.21	6.48	5.42	15.79	12.85
1	76.3	74.0	79.4	67.7	74.8	0.55	0.49	0.44	1.16	0.90
2	75.3	73.0	78.5	66.8	73.8	0.36	0.36	0.28	0.67	0.52
3	74.3	72.1	77.5	65.8	72.9	0.26	0.25	0.21	0.52	0.44
4	73.4	71.1	76.5	64.9	71.9	0.21	0.21	0.17	0.42	0.29
5	72.4	70.1	75.5	63.9	70.9	0.20	0.20	0.15	0.39	0.31
6	71.4	69.1	74.5	62.9	69.9	0.19	0.19	0.14	0.37	0.27
7	70.4	68.1	73.5	61.9	69.0	0.18	0.18	0.13	0.34	0.24
8	69.4	67.1	72.5	60.9	68.0	0.17	0.17	0.13	0.30	0.22
9	68.4	66.2	71.6	60.0	67.0	0.15	0.15	0.12	0.25	0.20
10	67.4	65.2	70.6	59.0	66.0	0.13	0.13	0.11	0.21	0.19
11	66.4	64.2	69.6	58.0	65.0	0.14	0.13	0.12	0.20	0.18
12	65.5	63.2	68.6	57.0	64.0	0.18	0.19	0.14	0.29	0.19
13	64.5	62.2	67.6	56.0	63.0	0.27	0.31	0.19	0.48	0.23
14	63.5	61.2	66.6	55.0	62.1	0.39	0.47	0.26	0.74	0.27
15	62.5	60.2	65.6	54.1	61.1	0.52	0.65	0.33	1.02	0.32
16	61.5	59.3	64.6	53.1	60.1	0.64	0.81	0.40	1.28	0.38
17	60.6	58.3	63.7	52.2	59.1	0.73	0.94	0.44	1.52	0.43
18	59.6	57.4	62.7	51.3	58.1	0.80	1.04	0.45	1.74	0.49
19	58.7	56.4	61.7	50.4	57.2	0.85	1.11	0.44	1.93	0.54
20	57.7	55.5	60.8	49.5	56.2	0.89	1.18	0.42	2.16	0.61
21	56.8	54.6	59.8	48.6	55.2	0.94	1.26	0.41	2.40	0.69
22	55.8	53.6	58.8	47.7	54.3	0.97	1.30	0.40	2.57	0.76
23	54.9	52.7	57.8	46.8	53.3	0.98	1.30	0.41	2.65	0.82
24	53.9	51.8	56.8	45.9	52.4	0.97	1.27	0.42	2.65	0.86
25	53.0	50.8	55.9	45.1	51.4	0.96	1.23	0.44	2.62	0.91
26	52.0	49.9	54.9	44.2	50.5	0.95	1.20	0.46	2.61	0.97
27	51.1	49.0	53.9	43.3	49.5	0.96	1.19	0.48	2.61	1.04
28	50.1	48.0	52.9	42.4	48.6	0.98	1.21	0.51	2.64	1.11
29	49.2	47.1	52.0	41.5	47.6	1.03	1.25	0.54	2.71	1.20
30	48.2	46.1	51.0	40.6	46.7	1.08	1.31	0.57	2.78	1.30
31	47.3	45.2	50.0	39.7	45.7	1.13	1.37	0.61	2.86	1.40
32	46.3	44.3	49.1	38.8	44.8	1.19	1.44	0.66	2.96	1.51
33	45.4	43.3	48.1	38.0	43.9	1.27	1.52	0.72	3.10	1.65
34	44.4	42.4	47.1	37.1	42.9	1.35	1.60	0.79	3.26	1.80

Age (Years)	Expectation of Life in Years					Expected Deaths per 1,000 Alive at Specified Age*				
		White		Black			White		Black	
	Total	Male	Female	Male	Female	Total	Male	Female	Male	Female
35	43.5	41.5	46.2	36.2	42.0	1.44	1.69	0.86	3.43	1.96
36	42.6	40.5	45.2	35.3	41.1	1.53	1.79	0.93	3.62	2.12
37	41.6	39.6	44.2	34.4	40.2	1.63	1.90	1.00	3.85	2.29
38	40.7	38.7	43.3	33.6	39.3	1.74	2.03	1.07	4.15	2.48
39	39.8	37.7	42.3	32.7	38.4	1.88	2.19	1.15	4.50	2.70
40	38.8	36.8	41.4	31.9	37.5	2.03	2.36	1.24	4.88	2.93
41	37.9	35.9	40.4	31.0	36.6	2.18	2.54	1.34	5.29	3.16
42	37.0	35.0	39.5	30.2	35.7	2.35	2.73	1.44	5.76	3.42
43	36.1	34.1	38.5	29.4	34.8	2.53	2.94	1.55	6.32	3.69
44	35.2	33.2	37.6	28.5	33.9	2.73	3.17	1.67	6.96	3.97
45	34.3	32.3	36.7	27.7	33.1	2.95	3.42	1.80	7.71	4.30
46	33.4	31.4	35.7	26.9	32.2	3.20	3.71	1.95	8.52	4.65
47	32.5	30.5	34.8	26.2	31.4	3.47	4.01	2.13	9.31	4.99
48	31.6	29.6	33.9	25.4	30.5	3.75	4.33	2.35	10.01	5.32
49	30.7	28.8	32.9	24.7	29.7	4.04	4.66	2.60	10.65	5.65
50	29.8	27.9	32.0	23.9	28.8	4.36	5.03	2.88	11.34	6.01
51	29.0	27.0	31.1	23.2	28.0	4.73	5.44	3.19	12.16	6.43
52	28.1	26.2	30.2	22.5	27.2	5.13	5.90	3.51	13.06	6.93
53	27.2	25.3	29.3	21.8	26.4	5.58	6.43	3.85	14.02	7.51
54	26.4	24.5	28.4	21.1	25.6	6.10	7.04	4.23	15.04	8.15
55	25.5	23.7	27.6	20.4	24.8	6.69	7.76	4.66	16.08	8.84
56	24.7	22.9	26.7	19.7	24.0	7.36	8.58	5.16	17.19	9.59
57	23.9	22.0	25.8	19.0	23.2	8.09	9.47	5.71	18.49	10.39
58	23.1	21.3	25.0	18.4	22.5	8.88	10.42	6.30	20.06	11.26
59	22.3	20.5	24.1	17.8	21.7	9.73	11.44	6.93	21.85	12.20
60	21.5	19.7	23.3	17.1	21.0	10.68	12.56	7.65	23.87	13.24
61	20.7	18.9	22.5	16.5	20.2	11.74	13.84	8.48	25.92	14.35
62	20.0	18.2	21.6	16.0	19.5	12.88	15.26	9.36	27.72	15.44
63	19.2	17.5	20.8	15.4	18.8	14.07	16.82	10.28	29.04	16.45
64	18.5	16.8	20.1	14.9	18.1	15.29	18.48	11.23	29.98	17.41
65	17.8	16.1	19.3	14.3	17.4	16.51	20.16	12.19	30.64	18.28
70	14.3	12.8	15.6	11.5	14.1	25.51	31.60	19.41	43.07	28.47
75	11.3	10.0	12.2	9.2	11.3	37.99	47.05	30.07	61.44	41.10
80	8.6	7.5	9.1	7.1	8.7	59.23	73.21	49.50	86.29	60.15

*Based on the proportion of cohorts who are alive at the beginning of an indicated age interval who will die before reaching the end of that interval. For example, out of every 1,000 people alive and exactly 50 years old at the beginning of the period, between 4 and 5 (4.44) will die before reaching their 51st birthdays.

Sources: U.S. National Center for Health Statistics, *Vital Statistics of the United States,* annual; *National Vital Statistics Report* 47, no. 28; and U.S. Census Bureau, *Statistical Abstract of the United States, 2001,* p. 74; and unpublished data.

DO YOU NEED LIFE INSURANCE?

If your death would cause financial stress for your spouse, children, parents, or anyone else you want to protect, you should consider purchasing life insurance. Your stage in the life cycle and the type of household you live in will influence this decision. Single persons living alone or with their parents usually have little or no need for life insurance. Consider Brian Brickman, 28, a bachelor who does not smoke, is in excellent health, and has no dependents. Brian owns a $100,000 condominium with a $90,000 mortgage. Since his employer provides a $100,000 group term life policy, he needs no additional life insurance. Larry Lucas, 32, and his wife, Liz, 30, are professionals, each earning $45,000 a year. The Lucases have no dependents. This two-earner couple may have a moderate need for life insurance, especially if they have a mortgage or other large debts. Households with small children usually have the greatest need for life insurance.

DETERMINING YOUR LIFE INSURANCE OBJECTIVES

Before you consider types of life insurance policies, you must decide what you want your life insurance to do for you and your dependents.

First, how much money do you want to leave to your dependents should you die today? Will you require more or less insurance protection to meet their needs as time goes on?

Second, when would you like to be able to retire? What amount of income do you believe you and your spouse would need then?

Third, how much will you be able to pay for your insurance program? Are the demands on your family budget for other living expenses likely to be greater or lower as time goes on?

When you have considered these questions and developed some approximate answers, you are ready to select the types and amounts of life insurance policies that will help you accomplish your objectives.

Once you have decided what you want your life insurance to accomplish, the next important decision is how much to buy.

A professional life insurance agent can help you determine the right amount of insurance you need.

ESTIMATING YOUR LIFE INSURANCE REQUIREMENTS

How much life insurance should you carry? This question is important for every person who owns or intends to buy life insurance. Because of the various factors involved, the question cannot be answered by mathematics alone. Nevertheless, an insurance policy puts a price on the life of the insured person. Therefore, methods are needed to estimate what that price should be.

There are four general methods for determining the amount of insurance you may need: the easy method, the DINK method, the "nonworking" spouse method, and the "family need" method.

THE EASY METHOD   Simple as this method is, it is remarkably useful. It is based on the insurance agent's rule of thumb that a "typical family" will need approximately 70 percent of your salary for seven years before they adjust to the financial consequences of your death. In other words, for a simple estimate of your life insurance needs, just multiply your current gross income by 7 (7 years) and 0.70 (70 percent). For example:

$30,000 current income × 7 = $210,000; $210,000 × 0.70 = $147,000

Your figures:

$_____ current income × 7 = $_____ × 0.70 = $_____

This method assumes your family is "typical." You may need more insurance if you have four or more children, if you have above-average family debt, if any member of your family suffers from poor health, or if your spouse has poor employment potential. On the other hand, you may need less insurance if your family is smaller.

THE DINK (DUAL INCOME, NO KIDS) METHOD

If you have no dependents and your spouse earns as much as or more than you do, you have simple insurance needs. All you need to do is ensure that your spouse will not be unduly burdened by debts should you die. Here is an example of the DINK method:

	Example	Your Figures
Funeral expenses	$ 5,000	$_____
One-half of mortgage	60,000	_____
One-half of auto loan	7,000	_____
One-half of credit card balance	1,500	_____
One-half of personal debt	1,500	_____
Other debts	1,000	_____
Total insurance needs	$76,000	$_____

This method assumes your spouse will continue to work after your death. If your spouse suffers poor health or is employed in an occupation with an uncertain future, you should consider adding an insurance cushion to see him or her through hard times.

THE "NONWORKING" SPOUSE METHOD

Insurance experts have estimated that extra costs of up to $10,000 a year may be required to replace the services of a homemaker in a family with small children. These extra costs may include the cost of a housekeeper, child care, more meals out, additional carfare, laundry services, and so on. They do not include the lost potential earnings of the surviving spouse, who often must take time away from the job to care for the family.

InsureMarket, a Web site run by Quicken, has some good life insurance worksheets and advice. You can save price quotes for later retrieval.

To estimate how much life insurance a homemaker should carry, multiply the number of years before the youngest child reaches age 18 by $10,000. For example:

10 years × $10,000 = $100,000

Your figures:

_____ years × $10,000 = $_____

If there are teenage children, the $10,000 figure can be reduced. If there are more than two children under age 13, or anyone in the family suffers poor health or has special needs, the $10,000 figure should be adjusted upward.

THE "FAMILY NEED" METHOD

The first three methods assume you and your family are "typical" and ignore important factors such as Social Security and your liquid assets. Exhibit 12–2 provides a detailed worksheet for making a thorough estimation of your life insurance needs.

Although this method is quite thorough, you may believe it does not address all of your special needs. If so, you should obtain further advice from an insurance expert or a financial planner.

As you determine your life insurance needs, don't forget to consider the life insurance you may already have. You may have ample coverage through your employer and through any mortgage and credit life insurance you have purchased.

In our dynamic economy, inflation and interest rates change often. Therefore, experts recommend that you reevaluate your insurance coverage every two years. Be sure to update your insurance whenever your situation changes substantially. For example, the birth of another child or an increase in your home mortgage can boost your insurance needs.

Sheet 53
Determining life insurance needs

Exhibit **12–2**

A worksheet to calculate your life insurance needs

Sources: Metropolitan Life Insurance Company, *About Life Insurance*, February 1997, p. 3; *The TIAA Guide to Life Insurance Planning for People in Education* (New York: Teachers Insurance and Annuity Association, January 1997), p. 3.

1. Five times your personal yearly income	_____ (1)
2. Total approximate expenses above and beyond your daily living costs for you and your dependents (e.g., tuition, care for a disabled child or parent) amount to	_____ (2)
3. Your emergency fund (3 to 6 months of living expenses) amounts to	_____ (3)
4. Estimated amount for your funeral expenses (U.S. average is $5,000 to $10,000)	+ _____ (4)
5. Total estimate of your family's financial needs (add lines 1 through 4)	= _____ (5)
6. Your total liquid assets (e.g., savings accounts, CDs, money market funds, existing life insurance both individual and group, pension plan death benefits, and Social Security benefits	− _____ (6)
7. Subtract line 6 from line 5 and enter the difference here.	= _____ (7)

The net result (line 7) is an estimate of the shortfall your family would face upon your death. Remember, these are just rules of thumb. For a complete analysis of your needs, consult a professional.

CONCEPT CHECK 12-2

1 How do you determine the need for life insurance?
2 What determines your life insurance objectives?
3 What are the four methods of estimating your life insurance requirements?

Action Application Analyze the four methods of determining life insurance requirements. Which method is best and why?

Types of Life Insurance Companies and Policies

TYPES OF LIFE INSURANCE COMPANIES

You can purchase the new or extra life insurance you need from two types of life insurance companies: stock life insurance companies, owned by shareholders, and mutual life insurance companies, owned by their policyholders. About 95 percent of U.S. life insurance companies are stock companies, and about 5 percent are mutuals.

Stock companies generally sell **nonparticipating** (or *nonpar*) policies, while mutual companies specialize in the sale of **participating** (or *par*) policies. A participating policy has a somewhat higher premium than a nonparticipating policy, but a part of the premium is refunded to the policyholder annually. This refund is called the *policy dividend*.

There has been long and inconclusive debate about whether stock companies or mutual companies offer less expensive life insurance. You should check with both stock and mutual companies to determine which type offers the best policy for your particular needs at the lowest price.

If you wish to pay exactly the same premium each year, you should choose a nonparticipating policy with its guaranteed premiums. However, you may prefer life insurance whose annual price reflects the company's experience with its investments, the health of its policyholders, and its general operating costs, that is, a participating policy.

Nevertheless, as with other forms of insurance, price should not be your only consideration in choosing a life insurance policy. You should consider the financial stability, reliability, and service the insurance company provides. Currently about 1,700 life insurance companies in the United States sell life insurance.

Objective 3

Distinguish between the two types of life insurance companies and analyze various types of life insurance policies these companies issue.

nonparticipating policy Life insurance that does not provide policy dividends; also called a *nonpar policy.*

participating policy Life insurance that provides policy dividends; also called a *par policy.*

TYPES OF LIFE INSURANCE POLICIES

Both mutual insurance companies and stock insurance companies sell two basic types of life insurance: temporary and permanent insurance. Temporary insurance can be term, renewable term, convertible term, or decreasing term insurance. Permanent insurance is known by different names, including *whole life, straight life, ordinary life,* and *cash value life insurance.* As you will learn in the next section, permanent insurance can be limited payment, variable, adjustable, or universal life insurance. Other types of insurance policies—group life and credit life insurance—are generally temporary forms of insurance. Exhibit 12–3 shows the types of policies issued recently, and Exhibit 12–4 shows major types and subtypes of life insurance.

An excellent source of information about all types of topics in life insurance is available on the CNN/Money Web site at **money.cnn.com/pf/101/lessons.**

TERM LIFE INSURANCE

Term insurance is protection for a specified period of time, usually 1, 5, 10, or 20 years or up to age 70. A term insurance policy pays a benefit only if you die during the period it covers. If you stop paying the premiums, the insurance stops. Term insurance is therefore sometimes called *temporary life insurance.*

Term insurance is a basic, "no frills" form of life insurance and is the best value for most consumers. The premiums for people in their 20s and 30s are less expensive than those for whole life insurance, discussed in the next section. According to Jack Dolan, associate director of media relations for the American Council of Life Insurers, "Term insurance is growing more popular as consumers use the low cost to bulk up on coverage. But whole life is the type of policy people hold on to."[1]

term insurance Life insurance protection for a specified period of time; sometimes called *temporary life insurance.*

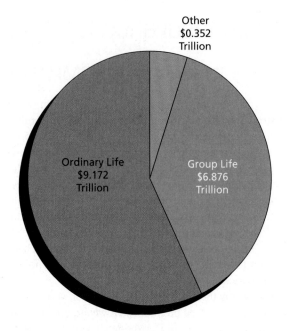

You need insurance coverage most while you are raising young children. Although
term life insurance premiums increase as you get older, you can reduce your coverage
as your children grow up and your assets (the value of your savings, investments, home,
autos, etc.) increase.

Here are various options in choosing your term insurance.

RENEWABILITY OPTION   The coverage of term insurance ends at the conclusion of the term, but you can continue it for another term if you have a renewability
option. For example, the term insurance of the Teachers Insurance and Annuity
Association is renewable at your option for successive five-year periods to age 70 without medical reexamination. Level premiums are paid during each five-year period. The
premiums increase every five years.

MULTIYEAR LEVEL TERM (OR STRAIGHT TERM)   *Multiyear term life*
is a relatively new policy. It guarantees that you will pay the same premium for the life
of your policy.

CONVERSION OPTION   If you have convertible term insurance, you can exchange it for a whole life policy without a medical examination and at a higher premium. The premium for the whole life policy stays the same for the rest of your life.

Exhibit **12-4**

Major types and subtypes
of life insurance

Term (temporary)	Whole, Straight, or Ordinary Life	Other Types
• Term	• Limited payment	• Group life
• Renewable term	• Single premium	• Credit life
• Multiyear level term	• Modified life	
• Convertible term	• Variable life	
• Decreasing term	• Adjustable life	
	• Universal life	
	• Variable universal life	

Advice from a Pro

RETURN OF PREMIUM POLICIES

For those who see term life insurance as a losing proposition—live and you lose the money you paid in, die and, well, you're dead—an old insurance product is back. Called return of premium (ROP) or money-back term, these policies refund every penny paid in premiums if you outlive the 15-, 20-, or 30-year term of the policy.

There is a catch. The policies cost more—perhaps 30 percent to 50 percent more for a 30-year policy—than traditional term life. A healthy 35-year-old man might pay $550 annually for a basic $500,000, 30-year term policy versus $810 for one with the ROP feature. You can get policies for a shorter term, but they cost so much more—sometimes six or seven times as much as simple term—that Byron Udell, CEO of insurance brokerage AccuQuote, advises against them. American General Life & Accident Insurance is the biggest player in this field, but ROPs are also offered by Fidelity & Guaranty Life Insurance, United of Omaha Life Insurance, and Federal Kemper Life Assurance.

Does an ROP policy make sense? That depends on your answer to two questions: Would you earn more buying a cheaper term policy and investing the savings? Are you likely to cancel before the 30 (or however many) years are up?

In the example above, the ROP would cost $260 more each year than regular term insurance but would return $24,300 in premiums at the end of 30 years. That amounts to an annualized return of 6.6 percent, and it's tax-free because you're just getting back your own money. For someone looking for a conservative investment, such a policy could make sense, says Charles Hais, manager of the insurance department at Brecek & Young Advisors, a Cincinnati brokerage.

But remember, you get that return only if you pay the premiums for the entire 30 years. If you drop the policy before (most buyers of term life do), you'll get less, or perhaps nothing, in return for those higher premiums. "A company generally counts on people dropping the policies—in order to pay the money to those who don't," says James Hunt, a life insurance actuary for the Consumer Federation of America.

If you've decided to use insurance as an investment vehicle, you ought to check out universal, variable universal, and whole life policies as well. These other types of insurance usually cost even more. But because they pay interest or dividends or allow you to invest in mutual funds, they have the potential for higher returns.

Source: Carol Marie Cropper, "Premiums You Can Retrieve," *BusinessWeek,* May 10, 2004, p. 114.

Consider this option if you want cash-value life insurance and can't afford it now but expect to do so in the future.

DECREASING TERM INSURANCE Term insurance is also available in a form that pays less to the beneficiary as time passes. The insurance period you select might depend on your age or on how long you decide you will need the coverage. For example, a decreasing term contract for 25 years might be appropriate as coverage of a mortgage loan balance on a house, because the coverage will decrease as the balance on the mortgage decreases. You could get the same result by purchasing annual renewable term policies of diminishing amounts during the period of the mortgage loan. An annual renewable policy would offer more flexibility to change coverage if you were to sell or remortgage the house. Mortgage insurance, therefore, is a form of decreasing term insurance, decreasing to keep pace with the principal balance on your mortgage loan. Recently a 35-year-old person buying a $100,000, 20-year decreasing term policy from the Teachers Insurance and Annuity Association would pay a first-year premium of $141.

RETURN OF PREMIUM Return of premium (ROP), or money-back term policies refund every penny you paid in premiums if you outlive the 15-, 20-, or 30-year term of the policy. However, ROP policies cost 30 percent to 50 percent more than traditional term life. Does an ROP policy make sense for you? Read the accompanying Advice from a Pro feature.

If you want to compare rates and avoid a high-pressure pitch for permanent insurance, contact a low-load, no-commission insurer. One life insurance adviser recommends

whole life policy An insurance plan in which the policyholder pays a specified premium each year for as long as he or she lives; also called a *straight life policy, cash-value life policy,* or *ordinary life policy.*

cash value The amount received after giving up a life insurance policy.

either USAA Life & Health Insurance Company (1-800-531-8000) or Ameritas Life Insurance Corporation (1-800-552-3553); both give quotes over the phone.

WHOLE LIFE INSURANCE

The most common type of permanent life insurance is the **whole life policy** (also called a *straight life policy,* a *cash-value life policy,* or an *ordinary life policy*), for which you pay a specified premium each year for as long as you live. In return, the insurance company promises to pay a stipulated sum to the beneficiary when you die. The amount of your premium depends primarily on the age at which you purchase the insurance.

One important feature of the whole life policy is its cash value. **Cash value** (or *cash surrender value*) is an amount which increases each year, that you receive if you give up the insurance. Hence, cash-value policies provide a death benefit *and* a savings account. Insurance salespeople often emphasize the "forced savings" aspect of cash-value insurance. A table in the whole life policy enables you to tell exactly how much cash value the policy has at any given time (see Exhibit 12–5).

Cash-value policies may make sense for people who intend to keep the policies for the long term or for people who must be forced to save. But you should not have too low a death benefit just because you would like the savings component of a cash-value life policy. Experts suggest that you explore other savings and investment strategies before investing your money in a permanent life insurance policy.

The insurance company accumulates a substantial reserve during the early years of the whole life policy to pay the benefits in the later years, when your chances of dying are greater. At first, the annual premium for whole life insurance is higher than that for term insurance. However, the premium for a whole life policy remains constant throughout your lifetime, whereas the premium for a term policy increases with each renewal.

Several types of whole life insurance have been developed to meet different objectives. A few of the more popular types are discussed next.

LIMITED PAYMENT POLICY

One type of whole life policy is called the *limited payment policy.* With this plan, you pay premiums for a stipulated period, usually 20 or 30 years, or until you reach a specified age, such as 60 or 65 (unless your death occurs earlier). Your policy then becomes "paid up," and you remain insured for life. The company will pay the face amount of the policy at your death. Because the premium payment period for a limited payment policy is shorter than that for a whole life policy, the annual premium is higher. For example, recently a 35-year-old person buying a $25,000, 20-payment life policy at a preferred risk rate from the Teachers Insurance and Annuity Association (TIAA) would pay a $236.25 premium during the first year. In contrast, the premium for an ordinary life policy would be $183.50 for the same coverage. How do you qualify for preferred risk rates? See the accompanying Financial Planning for Life's Situations feature on page 384.

A special form of the limited payment plan is the single-premium policy. In this type of contract, you make only one very large premium payment.

VARIABLE LIFE INSURANCE POLICY

The cash values of a *variable life* insurance policy fluctuate according to the yields earned by a separate fund, which can be a stock fund, a money market fund, or a bond fund. A minimum death benefit is guaranteed, but the death benefit can rise above that minimum depending on the earnings of the dollars invested in the separate fund. Hence, policyholders, not insurance companies, assume the investment risk. The premium payments for a variable life policy are fixed.

When you purchase a variable life policy, you assume the risk of poor investment performance. Therefore, the cash value of a variable life policy is not guaranteed. (Remember the Wisconsin couple from the opening case?) Life insurance agents selling

Plan and Additional Benefits	Amount	Premium	Years Payable
Whole life (premiums payable to age 90)	$10,000	$229.50	55
Waiver of premium (to age 65)		4.30	30
Accidental death (to age 70)	10,000	7.80	35

A premium is payable on the policy date and every 12 policy months thereafter. The first premium is $241.60.

Explanation for Table of Guaranteed Values: To cancel the policy in the 10th year, the insured would get $1,719 in savings (cash value). He or she could use the $1,719 to purchase a $3,690 paid-up life policy or purchase an extended term policy that would be in effect for 19 years and 78 days.

Table of Guaranteed Values

End of Policy Year	Cash or Loan Value	Paid-up Insurance	Extended Term Insurance	
			Years	Days
1	$14	$30	0	152
2	174	450	4	182
3	338	860	8	65
4	506	1,250	10	344
5	676	1,640	12	360
6	879	2,070	14	335
7	1,084	2,500	16	147
8	1,293	2,910	17	207
9	1,504	3,300	18	177
10	1,719	3,690	19	78
11	1,908	4,000	19	209
12	2,099	4,300	19	306
13	2,294	4,590	20	8
14	2,490	4,870	20	47
15	2,690	5,140	20	65
16	2,891	5,410	20	66
17	3,095	5,660	20	52
18	3,301	5,910	20	27
19	3,508	6,150	19	358
20	3,718	6,390	19	317
Age 60	4,620	7,200	18	111
Age 65	5,504	7,860	16	147

Paid-up additions and dividend accumulations increase the cash values; indebtedness decreases them.

Direct Beneficiary: Helen M. Benson, wife of the insured
Owner: Thomas A. Benson, the insured
Insured: Thomas A. Benson   **Age and Sex:** 37 Male
Policy Date: November 1, 2006   **Policy Number:** 000/00
Date of Issue: November 1, 2006

Exhibit **12-5**

An example of guaranteed cash value

Source: *Sample Life Insurance Policy* (Washington, DC: American Council of Life Insurance, n.d.), p. 2.

GUIDELINES FOR PREFERRED RATES

Do you qualify for preferred rates? These guidelines are used to determine preferred rates; standard rates are higher.

Blood Profile. All favorable values for cholesterol, triglycerides, and lipids.

Blood Pressure. May not exceed 140/90.

Urinalysis. No abnormal findings. Presence of nicotine will disqualify the applicant for no-tobacco rates.

Personal History. No history of or current treatment for high blood pressure, cancer, diabetes, mental or nervous disorders, or disorders of the heart, lungs, liver, or kidneys.

Build. Weight may not exceed 115 percent of average for height.

Driving. No convictions for reckless driving or driving under the influence of alcohol or drugs in the past five years; no more than three moving violations in the past three years; no more than one moving violation in the past six months.

Family History. No family history (natural parents and siblings) of death from heart disease, cardiovascular impairments, cancer, or diabetes prior to age 60.

Source: Ameritas Life Insurance Corporation.

---

variable life policies must be registered representatives of a broker-dealer licensed by the National Association of Securities Dealers and registered with the Securities and Exchange Commission. If you are interested in a variable life policy, be sure your agent gives you a prospectus that includes an extensive disclosure about the policy.

ADJUSTABLE LIFE INSURANCE POLICY The *adjustable life* insurance policy is another relatively recent type of whole life insurance. You can change such a policy as your needs change. For example, if you want to increase or decrease your coverage, you can change either the premium payments or the period of coverage.

UNIVERSAL LIFE Subject to certain minimums, **universal life** insurance, first introduced in 1979, is designed to let you pay premiums at any time in virtually any amount. The amount of insurance can be changed more easily in a universal life policy than in a traditional policy. The increase in the cash value of a universal life policy reflects the interest earned on short-term investments. Thus, the universal life policy clearly combines term insurance and investment elements.

Like the details of other types of policies, the details of universal life policies vary from company to company. The key distinguishing features of universal life policies are explicit, separate accounting reports to policyholders of (1) the charges for the insurance element, (2) the charges for company expenses (commissions, policy fees, etc.), and (3) the rate of return on the investment (cash value) of the policy. The rate of return is flexible; it is guaranteed to be not less than a certain amount (usually 4 percent), but it may be more, depending on the insurance company's decision.

What are the differences between universal life and whole life insurance? While both policy types have cash value, universal life gives you more direct control. With universal life, you control your outlay and can change your premium without changing your coverage. Whole life, in contrast, requires you to pay a specific premium every year, or the policy will lapse. Universal life allows you access to your cash value by a policy loan or withdrawal. Whole life allows only for policy loans.

Since your primary reason for buying a life insurance policy is the insurance component, the cost of that component should

universal life A whole life policy that combines term insurance and investment elements.

DID YOU KNOW?

A Harris Interactive poll reported 8 percent of Americans bought more disability insurance and 6 percent bought or increased their life insurance within one month of September 11, 2001.

Exhibit **12-6**   Comparison of term, whole life, universal life, and variable life insurance

Type of Policy		Period Covered	Cash Value	Insurance Protection	Premium	Coverage	Comments
Temporary	**Term**						
	Level	A stated number of years, such as 1, 5, 20	None	High	Stays the same until renewal	Stays the same	Pure insurance coverage
	Decreasing	A stated number of years, such as 1, 5, 20	None	High	Stays the same	Decreases	Least expensive type of insurance
Permanent	**Whole life**						Part insurance, part savings
	Straight	Whole life	Low	Moderate	Stays the same	Stays the same	
	Limited payment	Whole life	Low	Moderate	Stays the same for a specified number of years	Stays the same	Paid up after a certain number of years
	Universal life	Varies	Low to high	Low to high	Varies	Varies	Combines renewable term insurance with a savings account paying market interest rates
	Variable life	Varies	Low to high	Low to high	Varies	Varies	Part insurance, part invest-ments in stock, bond, or money market funds

be your main consideration. Thus, universal life policies, which offer a high rate of return on the cash value but charge a high price for the insurance element, generally should be avoided.

Over the years, variations on term and whole life insurance have been developed. The details of these policies may differ among companies. Therefore, check with individual companies to determine the best policy for your needs. Exhibit 12–6 compares some important features of term, whole life, and universal life, and variable life policies.

DID YOU KNOW?

A 25-year-old can buy a $2 million, 30-year term life policy from a reputable insurer for about $1,600 a year. That same premium would buy a death benefit of only $500,000 if it were put into a variable universal life policy that has an investment feature.

Source: *BusinessWeek*, February 21, 2005, p. 89.

OTHER TYPES OF LIFE INSURANCE POLICIES

GROUP LIFE INSURANCE   In recent decades, *group life insurance* has become quite popular. A group insurance plan insures a large number of persons under the terms of a single policy without requiring medical examinations. In general, the principles that apply to other forms of insurance also apply to group insurance.

Fundamentally, group insurance is term insurance, which was described earlier. Usually the cost of group insurance is split between the employer and the employees so that the cost of insurance per $1,000 is the same for each employee, regardless of age. For older employees, the employer pays a larger portion of the costs of the group policy.

However, group life insurance is not always a good deal. Insurance advisers offer countless stories about employer-sponsored plans, or group plans offered through professional associations, offering coverage that costs 20, 50, or even 100 percent more than policies their clients could buy on the open market.

ENDOWMENT LIFE INSURANCE   *Endowment life insurance* provides coverage from the beginning of the contract to maturity and guarantees payment of a specified sum to the insured, even if he or she is still living at the end of the endowment period. The face value of the policy is paid to beneficiaries upon the death of the insured. The endowment period typically has a duration of 10 to 20 years or the attainment of a specified age.

CREDIT LIFE INSURANCE   *Credit life insurance* is used to repay a personal debt should the borrower die before doing so. It is based on the belief that "no person's debts should live after him or her." It was introduced in the United States in 1917, when installment financing and purchasing became popular. Credit life insurance policies for auto loans and home mortgages are not the best buy for the protection they offer. Instead, buy less expensive decreasing term insurance, discussed earlier. In fact, some experts claim that credit life insurance policies are the nation's biggest ripoff.

Exhibit 12–7 shows the growth of individual and group life insurance in the United States.

INDUSTRIAL LIFE INSURANCE   With industrial life insurance policies, also known as home service or debit insurance, agents collect weekly, bimonthly, or monthly premiums at the insured's home. Industrial life insurance is the least popular form, and its appeal continues to drop rapidly.

CONCEPT CHECK 12-3

1 What are the two types of life insurance companies?
2 What are the major types and subtypes of life insurance?

Action Application Research the differences in premium costs for a $100,000 whole life policy from a mutual and a stock company.

Important Provisions in a Life Insurance Contract

Objective 4

Select important provisions in life insurance contracts.

Modern life insurance policies contain numerous provisions whose terminology can be confusing. Therefore, an understanding of these provisions is very important for the insurance buyer.

Your life insurance policy is valuable only if it meets your objectives. When your objectives change, however, it may not be necessary to give up the policy. Instead, study

Exhibit **12-7**

Growth of individual and group life insurance in force in the United States

Most group life insurance contracts are issued to employers, though many are issued to unions, professional associations, and other groups.

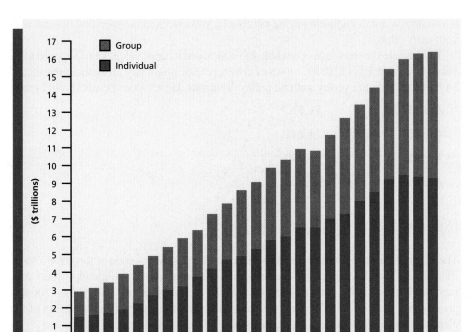

Source: *Statistical Abstract of the United States, 2004–2005,* Table 1216, p. 760.

the policy carefully and discuss its provisions with your agent. Following are some of the most common provisions.

NAMING YOUR BENEFICIARY

An important provision in every life insurance policy is the right to name your beneficiary. A **beneficiary** is a person who is designated to receive something, such as life insurance proceeds, from the insured. In your policy, you can name one or more persons as contingent beneficiaries who will receive your policy proceeds if the primary beneficiary dies at the same time or before you do.

beneficiary A person designated to receive something, such as life insurance proceeds, from the insured.

THE GRACE PERIOD

When you buy a life insurance policy, the insurance company agrees to pay a certain sum of money under specified circumstances and you agree to pay a certain premium regularly. The *grace period* allows 28 to 31 days to elapse, during which time you may pay the premium without penalty. After that time, the policy lapses if you have not paid the premium.

POLICY REINSTATEMENT

A lapsed policy can be put back in force, or reinstated, if it has not been turned in for cash. To reinstate the policy, you must again qualify as an acceptable risk, and you must pay overdue premiums with interest. There is a time limit on reinstatement, usually one or two years.

NONFORFEITURE CLAUSE

One important feature of a whole life policy is the **nonforfeiture clause.** This provision prevents the forfeiture of accrued benefits if you choose to drop the policy. For example,

nonforfeiture clause A provision that allows the insured not to forfeit all accrued benefits.

if you decide not to continue paying premiums, you can exercise specified options with your cash value.

To illustrate the workings of a whole life policy and its cash value, let us suppose a 30-year-old woman buys $30,000 worth of coverage. She might pay an annual premium of $435 for a whole life policy with no policy dividends. Here's how the cash would grow:

Age 35	$1,830
Age 40	4,260
Age 45	6,990
Age 50	9,960

INCONTESTABILITY CLAUSE

incontestability clause A provision stating that the insurer cannot dispute the validity of a policy after a specified period.

The **incontestability clause** stipulates that after the policy has been in force for a specified period (usually two years), the insurance company cannot dispute its validity during the lifetime of the insured for any reason, including fraud. One reason for this provision is that the beneficiaries, who cannot defend the company's contesting of the claim, should not be forced to suffer because of the acts of the insured.

SUICIDE CLAUSE

suicide clause A provision stating that if the insured dies by suicide during the first two years the policy is in force, the death benefit will equal the amount of the premium paid.

The **suicide clause** provides that if the insured dies by suicide during the first two years the policy is in force, the death benefit will equal the amount of the premium paid. Generally, after two years, the suicide becomes a risk covered by the policy and the beneficiaries of a suicide receive the same benefit that is payable for death from any other cause.

AUTOMATIC PREMIUM LOANS

With an automatic premium loan option, if you do not pay the premium within the grace period, the insurance company automatically pays it out of the policy's cash value if that cash value is sufficient in your whole life policy. This prevents you from inadvertently allowing the policy to lapse.

MISSTATEMENT OF AGE PROVISION

The misstatement of age provision says that if the company finds out that your age was incorrectly stated, it will pay the benefits your premiums would have bought if your age had been correctly stated. The provision sets forth a simple procedure to resolve what could otherwise be a complicated legal matter.

POLICY LOAN PROVISION

A loan from the insurance company is available on a whole life policy after the policy has been in force for one, two, or three years, as stated in the policy. This feature, known as the *policy loan provision,* permits you to borrow any amount up to the cash value of the policy. However, a policy loan reduces the death benefit by the amount of the loan plus interest if the loan is not repaid.

RIDERS TO LIFE INSURANCE POLICIES

rider A document attached to a policy that modifies its coverage.

An insurance company can change the provisions of a policy by attaching a rider to it. A **rider** is any document attached to the policy that modifies its coverage by adding or excluding specified conditions or altering its benefits. A whole life insurance policy may include a waiver of premium disability benefit, an accidental death benefit, or both.

WAIVER OF PREMIUM DISABILITY BENEFIT
Under this provision, the company waives any premiums that are due after the onset of total and permanent disability. In effect, the company pays the premiums. The disability must occur before you reach a certain age, usually 60.

The waiver of premium rider is sometimes desirable. Don't buy it, however, if the added cost will prevent you from carrying needed basic life insurance. Some insurance companies include this rider automatically in all policies issued through age 55.

ACCIDENTAL DEATH BENEFIT
Under this provision, the insurance company pays twice the face amount of the policy if the insured's death results from an accident. The accidental death benefit is often called **double indemnity.** Accidental death must occur within a certain time period after the injury, usually 90 days, and before the insured reaches a certain age, usually 60 or 65.

double indemnity A benefit under which the company pays twice the face value of the policy if the insured's death results from an accident.

The accidental death benefit is expensive. Moreover, your chances of dying in the exact manner stated in the policy are very small, so the chances that your beneficiary will collect the double payment are also small.

GUARANTEED INSURABILITY OPTION
This option allows you to buy specified additional amounts of life insurance at stated intervals without proof of insurability. Thus, even if you do not remain in good health, you can increase the amount of your insurance as your income rises. This option is desirable if you anticipate the need for additional life insurance in the future.

COST OF LIVING PROTECTION
This special rider is designed to help prevent inflation from eroding the purchasing power of the protection your policy provides. A *loss, reduction,* or *erosion of purchasing power* refers to the impact inflation has on a fixed amount of money. As inflation increases the costs of goods and services, that fixed amount will not buy as much in the future as it does today. Exhibit 12–8 shows the effects of inflation on a $100,000 life insurance policy. However, your insurance needs are likely to be smaller in later years.

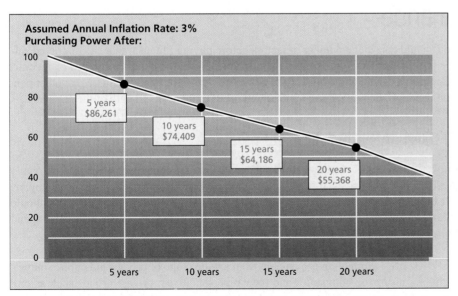

Assumed Annual Inflation Rate: 3%
Purchasing Power After:

5 years $86,261
10 years $74,409
15 years $64,186
20 years $55,368

Exhibit 12-8

Effects of inflation on a $100,000 life insurance policy

Source: *The TIAA Guide to Life Insurance Planning for People in Education* (New York: Teachers Insurance and Annuity Association, January 1997), p. 8.

ACCELERATED BENEFITS

Accelerated benefits, also known as *living benefits,* are life insurance policy proceeds paid to the terminally ill policyholder *before* he or she dies. The benefits may be provided for directly in the policies, but more often they are added by riders or attachments to new or existing policies. A representative list of insurers that offer accelerated benefits is available from the National Insurance Consumer Helpline (NICH) at 1-800-942-4242. Although more than 150 companies offer some form of accelerated benefits, not all plans are approved in all states. NICH cannot tell you whether a particular plan is approved in any given state. For more information, check with your insurance agent or your state department of insurance.

National Life Insurance, John Hancock, and Columbus Life Insurance now sell a new life insurance policy with an accelerated benefits rider that promises to pay out all or part of the death benefit should you need it for long-term care. Read the accompanying Financial Planning for Life's Situations feature on page 391 for details.

SECOND-TO-DIE OPTION

A *second-to-die life insurance* policy, also called *survivorship life,* insures two lives, usually husband and wife. The death benefit is paid when the second spouse dies. Usually a second-to-die policy is intended to pay estate taxes when both spouses die. However, some attorneys claim that with the right legal advice, you can minimize or avoid estate taxes completely.

Now that you know the various types of life insurance policies and the major provisions of and riders to such policies, you are ready to make your buying decisions.

CONCEPT CHECK 12-4

1 What are the most common provisions in life insurance contracts?
2 What is a beneficiary?
3 What is a rider?
4 What is the concept of double indemnity?

Action Application Examine your life insurance policies and the policies of other members of your family. Note the contractual provision of each policy. What does the company promise to do in return for premiums?

Buying Life Insurance

Objective 5

Create a plan to buy life insurance.

You should consider a number of factors before buying life insurance. As discussed earlier in this chapter, these factors include your present and future sources of income, other savings and income protection, group life insurance, group annuities (or other pension benefits), Social Security, and, of course, the financial strength of the company.

FROM WHOM TO BUY?

Look for insurance coverage from financially strong companies with professionally qualified representatives. It is not unusual for a relationship with an insurance company to extend over a period of 20, 30, or even 50 years. For that reason alone, you should choose carefully when deciding on an insurance company or an insurance agent. Fortunately, you have a choice of sources.

SOURCES

Protection is available from a wide range of private and public sources, including insurance companies and their representatives; private groups such as employers, labor unions, and professional or fraternal organizations; and financial institutions and manufacturers offering credit insurance.

A COMBO POLICY FOR LONG-TERM CARE: LIFE INSURANCE THAT CAN BE USED FOR NURSING HOMES

When Richard Becker and his wife, Flora, now both 68, purchased long-term care insurance in 1997, he thought of his father, who died at 94 in an assisted-living facility without benefit of such coverage. But as rates for the Pennsylvania retirees' policies soared—doubling in seven years—the couple calculated the cost of payments over the coming decades, then weighed their chances of ever collecting. "We dropped it," Becker says. This was not before they had paid in about $30,000. "It's goodbye to that," he says.

Such stories, and the 30 percent drop in sales of new long-term care insurance policies last year, have led more insurers to offer a new product: a life insurance policy with an "accelerated benefits rider" that promises to pay out all or part of the death benefit should the policyholder need it for long-term care. Depending on its terms, a $500,000 life insurance policy might pay from $200,000 to $500,000—or even $1 million—toward the costs of a nursing home, as well as, perhaps, in-home care and assisted living. That amount (plus, in some policies, interest) is later deducted from the death benefit that goes to beneficiaries when the policyholder dies.

This combined approach attempts to offer something more to people like the Beckers. "One of the main reasons people don't buy long-term care insurance is they think, 'What if I pay for all this insurance and never use it?'" says Robert Davis, president of Long-Term Care Quote, which sells such coverage. Among the companies selling the long-term care add-on are National Life Insurance, John Hancock, and Columbus Life Insurance. The feature is typically offered in conjunction with whole or universal life policies, which are more expensive than term life, since they act as savings or investment vehicles—building up cash values—as well as life insurance. Some variable universal and term policies may offer LTC riders as well.

Those who simply want the most coverage for the lowest price will do better buying a basic term life policy for the years they need life insurance (often just until their children are grown), then adding a long-term care policy as they approach middle age. The total annual cost for both products could be half the price of a whole or universal life policy with the rider. Shopping for separate policies might be easier than evaluating life insurance tied to long-term care coverage tied to an investment. And you will likely have more coverage options if you choose a stand-alone long-term care plan.

Combining the care with the death benefit in a whole or universal policy costs more, but there is a payoff either way. If you go into a nursing home, you collect. If you don't need that care, there's still cash for your heirs.

Those who want the lifelong coverage and investment features of a whole or universal policy may find that the long-term care benefit adds little extra cost. John Hancock, one of the largest sellers of long-term care insurance, charges a healthy 50-year-old man buying a $500,000 universal life policy only $333 a year more for the rider. In return, the buyer gets up to $10,000 a month in long-term care benefits until the death benefit runs out. But shop around. Prices and terms vary widely.

If you have accumulated cash value in a life insurance policy but no longer need the coverage, you might consider trading it in for a new one with the LTC rider. You can do that through a tax-free swap. If you merely cash in the old policy, you may be liable for taxes on the investment gains.

If you decide to buy a life policy with the rider, examine the long-term care benefits carefully. Does the policy pay for in-home care, assisted living, and adult day care as well as for a nursing home stay? How is the amount of coverage calculated?

Finally, make sure the company you're buying from is highly rated by A.M. Best, Fitch, Moody's, or Standard & Poor's. The last thing you need is for your insurer to become terminally ill.

Source: Carol Marie Cropper, "A Combo Policy for Long-Term Care," *BusinessWeek,* May 2, 2005, pp. 91–92.

With life expectancies going up, life insurance rates should be coming down, right? That has been the case for a decade, as term life premiums dropped by about half. But now the industry is tightening its guidelines, and that could spell a hike of 5–25 percent for many applicants. Some insurers are raising rates outright, says Bob Barney, president of Compulife Software, which provides rate comparisons.

Others are simply making it harder to qualify for their best rate. For example, American International Group has just lowered the weight cutoff from 221 pounds to 205 for a six-foot man, says Barney. A 40-year-old in the preferred-plus rate category would pay $395 a year for a $500,000, 20-year term policy, but $490 at AIG's preferred level. Insurers are also getting pickier about cholesterol levels, family history of disease, even driving records, says Byron Udell, CEO of AccuQuote. But some good news could be in the offing. State regulators are adopting a new actuarial table that takes into account longer life spans. That could offset the rate upsurge when states adopt the new numbers in 2006.[2]

RATING INSURANCE COMPANIES

Some of the strongest, most reputable insurance companies in the nation provide excellent insurance coverage at reasonable costs. In fact, the financial strength of an insurance company may be a major factor in holding down premium costs for consumers.

Locate an insurance company by checking the reputations of local agencies. Ask members of your family, friends, or colleagues about the insurers they prefer.

For a more official review, consult *Best's Agents Guide* or *Best's Insurance Reports* at your public library. Exhibit 12–9 describes the rating systems used by A. M. Best and the other big four rating agencies. As a rule, you should deal with companies rated superior or excellent. In addition, *Consumer Reports, Kiplinger's Personal Finance,* and *Money* periodically provide satisfaction ratings on various types of insurance and insurance companies. For the latest ratings, visit www.standardandpoor.com and info-seek.go.com/.

CHOOSING YOUR INSURANCE AGENT

An insurance agent handles the technical side of insurance. However, that's only the beginning. The really important

Exhibit 12-9

Rating systems of major rating agencies

You should deal with companies rated superior or excellent.

	A. M. Best	Standard & Poor's Duff & Phelps	Moody's	Weiss Research
Superior	A++	AAA	Aaa	A+
	A+			
Excellent	A	AA+	Aa1	A
	A−	AA	Aa2	A−
		AA−	Aa3	B+
Good	B++	A+	A1	B
	B+	A	A2	B−
		A−	A3	C+
Adequate	B	BBB+	Baa1	C
	B−	BBB	Baa2	C−
		BBB−	Baa3	D+
Below average	C++	BB+	Ba1	D
	C+	BB	Ba2	D−
		BB−	Ba3	E+
Weak	C	B+	B1	E
	C−	B	B2	E−
	D	B−	B3	
Nonviable	E	CCC	Caa	F
	F	CC	Ca	
		C, D	C	

Financial Planning for Life's Situations

CHECKLIST FOR CHOOSING AN INSURANCE AGENT

	Yes	No
1. Is your agent available when needed? Clients sometimes have problems that need immediate answers.	☐	☐
2. Does your agent advise you to have a financial plan? Each part of the plan should be necessary to your overall financial protection.	☐	☐
3. Does your agent pressure you? You should be free to make your own decisions about insurance coverage.	☐	☐
4. Does your agent keep up with changes in the insurance field? Agents often attend special classes or study on their own so that they can serve their clients better.	☐	☐
5. Is your agent happy to answer questions? Does he or she want you to know exactly what you are paying for with an insurance policy?	☐	☐

part of the agent's job is to apply his or her knowledge of insurance to help you select the proper kind of protection within your financial boundaries.

Not all agents are paid the same way. Some insurance companies, such as GEICO and USAA, use salaried agents. Firms such as Allstate and State Farm use primarily "captive agents," who may be salaried or paid on commission. Either way, they sell only those companies' policies. Independent agents represent multiple carriers and can offer more choices. They collect conventional commissions from insurance companies. Is one kind of agent better than another? In theory, independent agents have an edge because they're not limited to just one insurance company's products. But they may be tempted to direct consumers to companies that pay them the most. Truth is, you can get a good policy from any of the different types of insurance agents.

Choosing a good agent is among the most important steps in building your insurance program. How do you find an agent? One of the best ways to begin is by asking your parents, friends, neighbors, and others for their recommendations. However, note that you will seldom have the same agent all your life. The accompanying Financial Planning for Life's Situations feature on this page offers guidelines for choosing an insurance agent.

You may also want to investigate an agent's membership in professional groups. Agents who belong to a local Life Underwriters Association are often among the more experienced agents in their communities. A **chartered life underwriter (CLU)** is a life insurance agent who has passed a series of college-level examinations on insurance and related subjects. Such agents are entitled to use the designation CLU after their names. Other professional designations that life insurance agents may earn include Life Underwriter Training Council Fellow (LUTCF), Chartered Financial Consultant (ChFC), Certified Financial Planner (CFP), or Member of The Registry of Financial Planning Practitioners. Agents who have passed a series of examinations on property and casualty insurance are designated as *chartered property and casualty underwriters (CPCUs).*

chartered life underwriter (CLU) A life insurance agent who has passed a series of college-level examinations on insurance and related subjects.

Once you have found an agent, you must decide which policy is right for you. The best way to do this is to talk to your agent, which does not obligate you to buy insurance.

COMPARING POLICY COSTS

Each life insurance company designs the policies it sells to make them attractive and useful to many policyholders. One policy may have features another policy doesn't; one company may be more selective than another company; one company may get a better return on its investments than another company. These and other factors affect the prices of life insurance policies.

In brief, five factors affect the price a company charges for a life insurance policy: the company's cost of doing business, the return on its investments, the mortality rate it expects among its policyholders, the features the policy contains, and competition among companies with comparable policies.

Quotesmith.com has quotes from over 300 life insurance companies and details on policies available from them. It also provides ratings for the insurance companies from the major rating agencies.

The prices of life insurance policies therefore vary considerably among life insurance companies. Moreover, a particular company will not be equally competitive for all policies. Thus, one company might have a competitively priced policy for 24-year-olds but not for 35-year-olds.

interest-adjusted index
A method of evaluating the cost of life insurance by taking into account the time value of money.

Ask your agent to give you interest-adjusted indexes. An **interest-adjusted index** is a method of evaluating the cost of life insurance by taking into account the time value of money. Highly complex mathematical calculations and formulas combine premium payments, dividends, cash-value buildup, and present value analysis into an index number that makes possible a fairly accurate cost comparison among insurance companies. The lower the index number, the lower the cost of the policy. The Consumer Federation of America Insurance Group offers a computerized service for comparing policy costs. Visit them at www.consumerfed.org.

Price quote services offer convenient and free, no-obligation premium comparisons. Insurance Information Inc., in South Dennis, Massachusetts, provides free price quotes for term insurance. It will run your age, health status, and occupation through computer data banks covering about 650 different policies and send you the names of the five policies suitable for you and sold in your state. Contact this company at 1-800-472-5800. TermQuote in Dayton, Ohio, represents about 100 insurance companies, and Select Quote in San Francisco represents about 20 insurance companies. Here are the Web addresses and telephone numbers of some price quote services:

- AccuQuote (www.accuquote.com) 1-800-442-9899
- InsuranceQuote Services (www.iquote.com) 1-800-972-1104
- InstantQuote (www.instantquote.com) 1-888-223-2220
- MasterQuote (www.masterquote.com) 1-800-627-LIFE
- QuickQuote (www.quickquote.com) 1-800-867-2404
- TermQuote (www.rcinet.com/~termquote) 1-800-444-8376

These services are not always unbiased, since most sell life insurance themselves; they may recommend more coverage than you need. Ask them to quote you the rate each insurer charges most of its policyholders, not the best rate, for which few persons qualify.

The accompanying Financial Planning Calculations feature on page 395 shows how to use an interest-adjusted index to compare the costs of insurance.

OBTAINING A POLICY

A life insurance policy is issued after you submit an application for insurance and the insurance company accepts the application. The application usually has two parts. In the first part, you state your name, age, and sex, what type of policy you desire, how much insurance you want, your occupation, and so forth. In the second part, you give your medical history. While a medical examination is frequently required for ordinary policies, usually no examination is required for group insurance.

The company determines your insurability by means of the information in your application, the results of the medical examination, and the inspection report. Of all applicants, 98 percent are found to be insurable, though some may have to pay higher premiums because of an existing medical condition.

Financial Planning Calculations

DETERMINING THE COST OF INSURANCE

In determining the cost of insurance, don't overlook the time value of money. You must include as part of that cost the interest (opportunity cost) you would earn on money if you did not use it to pay insurance premiums. For many years, insurers did not assign a time value to money in making their sales presentations. Only recently has the insurance industry widely adopted interest-adjusted cost estimates.

If you fail to consider the time value of money, you may get the false impression that the insurance company is giving you something for nothing. Here is an example. Suppose you are 35 and have a $10,000 face amount, 20-year, limited-payment, participating policy. Your annual premium is $210, or $4,200 over the 20-year period. Your dividends over the 20-year payment period total $1,700, so your total net premium is $2,500 ($4,200 − $1,700). Yet the cash value of your policy at the end of 20 years is $4,600. If you disregard the interest your premiums could otherwise have earned, you might get the impression that the insurance company is giving you $2,100 more than you paid ($4,600 − $2,500). But if you consider the time value of money (or its opportunity cost), the insurance company is not giving you $2,100. What if you had in-

vested the annual premiums in a conservative stock mutual fund? At an 8 percent annual yield, your account would have accumulated to $6,180 in 20 years. Therefore, instead of having received $2,100 from the insurance company, you have paid the company $1,580 for 20 years of insurance protection:

Premiums you paid over 20 years	$4,200	
Time value of money	+1,980	($6,180 − $4,200)
Total cost	$6,180	
Cash value	−4,600	
Net cost of insurance	$1,580	($6,180 − $4,600)

Be sure to request interest-adjusted indexes from your agent; if he or she doesn't give them to you, look for another agent. As you have seen in the example, you can compare the costs among insurance companies by combining premium payments, dividends, cash value buildup, and present value analysis into an index number.

EXAMINING A POLICY

BEFORE THE PURCHASE When you buy a life insurance policy, read every word of the contract and, if necessary, ask your agent for a point-by-point explanation of the language. Many insurance companies have rewritten their contracts to make them more understandable. These are legal documents, and you should be familiar with what they promise, even though they use technical terms.

AFTER THE PURCHASE After you buy new life insurance, you have a 10-day "free-look" period during which you can change your mind. If you do so, the company will return your premium without penalty.

It's a good idea to give your beneficiaries and your lawyer a photocopy of your policy. Your beneficiaries should know where the policy is kept, because to obtain the insurance proceeds, they will have to send it to the company upon your death, along with a copy of the death certificate.

When you receive a life insurance policy, read it very carefully and ask your agent for an explanation of any provision you don't understand.

CHOOSING SETTLEMENT OPTIONS

A well-planned life insurance program should cover the immediate expenses resulting from the death of the insured. However, that is only one of its purposes. In most instances, the primary purpose of life insurance is to protect dependents against a loss of income resulting from the premature death of the primary wage earner. Thus, selecting the appropriate settlement option is an important part of designing a life insurance

395

program. The most common settlement options are lump-sum payment, limited installment payment, life income option, and proceeds left with the company.

LUMP-SUM PAYMENT   The insurance company pays the face amount of the policy in one installment to the beneficiary or to the estate of the insured. This form of settlement is the most widely used option.

LIMITED INSTALLMENT PAYMENT   This option provides for payment of the life insurance proceeds in equal periodic installments for a specified number of years after your death.

LIFE INCOME OPTION   Under the life income option, payments are made to the beneficiary for as long as she or he lives. The amount of each payment is based primarily on the sex and attained age of the beneficiary at the time of the insured's death.

PROCEEDS LEFT WITH THE COMPANY   The life insurance proceeds are left with the insurance company at a specified rate of interest. The company acts as trustee and pays the interest to the beneficiary. The guaranteed minimum interest rate paid on the proceeds varies among companies.

SWITCHING POLICIES

Sheet 54
Life insurance policy comparison

Think twice if your agent suggests that you replace the whole life or universal life insurance you already own. According to a recent study by the Consumer Federation of America, consumers lose billions of dollars each year because they don't hold their cash-value life insurance policies long enough or because they purchase the wrong policies. The author of the study, James Hunt, Vermont's former insurance commissioner, notes that half of those who buy whole or universal life policies drop them within 10 years.

Before you give up this protection, make sure you are still insurable (check medical and any other qualification requirements). Remember that you are now older than you were when you purchased your policy, and a new policy will therefore cost more. Moreover, the older policy may have provisions that are not duplicated in some of the new policies. This does not mean you should reject the idea of replacing your present policy; rather, you should proceed with caution. We recommend that you ask your agent or company for an opinion about the new proposal to get both sides of the argument.

The insurance industry is regulated by state insurance commissioners. Recently many states passed new laws to protect consumers from overzealous sales agents. The National Association of Insurance Commissioners, state regulators, and insurance companies plan to develop new standards to protect consumers.

The Financial Planning for Life's Situations feature on page 397 presents 10 important guidelines for purchasing life insurance.

CONCEPT CHECK 12-5   ✓

1 How do insurance companies price their products?
2 How do insurance companies determine your insurability?
3 What should you do in examining a policy before and after the purchase?
4 What are the four most common settlement options?
5 Should you switch life insurance policies?

Action Application List the factors that would influence you in selecting the type of settlement option.

TEN GOLDEN RULES OF BUYING LIFE INSURANCE

Remember that your need for life insurance coverage will change over time. Your income may go up or down, or your family size might change. Therefore, it is wise to review your coverage periodically to ensure that it keeps up with your changing needs.

Follow these rules when buying life insurance:	Done
1. Understand and know what your life insurance needs are before you make any purchase, and make sure the company you choose can meet those needs.	☐
2. Buy your life insurance from a company that is licensed in your state.	☐
3. Select an agent who is competent, knowledgeable, and trustworthy.	☐
4. Shop around and compare costs.	☐
5. Buy only the amount of life insurance you need and can afford.	☐
6. Ask about lower premium rates for nonsmokers.	☐
7. Read your policy and make sure you understand it.	☐
8. Inform your beneficiaries about the kinds and amount of life insurance you own.	☐
9. Keep your policy in a safe place at home, and keep your insurance company's name and your policy number in a safe deposit box.	☐
10. Check your coverage periodically, or whenever your situation changes, to ensure that it meets your current needs.	☐

Source: American Council of Life Insurance, 1001 Pennsylvania Avenue, NW, Washington, DC 20004-2599.

Financial Planning with Annuities

As you have seen so far, life insurance provides a set sum of money at your death. However, if you want to enjoy benefits while you are still alive, you might consider annuities. An annuity protects you against the risk of outliving your assets.

An **annuity** is a financial contract written by an insurance company that provides you with a regular income. Generally, you receive the income monthly, often with payments arranged to continue for as long as you live. The payments may begin at once (*immediate annuity*) or at some future date (*deferred annuity*). According to a recent Gallup Organization survey, the average owner of an annuity is a 66-year-old, retired person with an annual household income of less than $75,000. About 95 percent of annuities issued were deferred annuities. The remainder were immediate annuities used to provide retirement income. The annuity is often described as the opposite of life insurance: It pays while you live, while life insurance pays when you die.

As with the life insurance principle, discussed earlier, the predictable mortality experience of a large group of individuals is fundamental to the annuity principle. By determining the average number of years a large number of persons in a given age group will live, the insurance company can calculate the annual amount to pay to each person in the group over his or her entire life.

For example, for annuity purposes, the life expectancy of white males age 75 is 10 years (see Exhibit 12–1 on pages 374–375). Thus, if 1,000 males age 75 each pay a $10,000 premium (a total of $10 million), each is guaranteed a payment of $1,000 per year for life. Those who live beyond the 10-year average have their "excess" payments funded by those who die before 10 years have elapsed.

Objective 6

Recognize how annuities provide financial security.

annuity A contract that provides a regular income for as long as the person lives.

397

Because the annual payouts per premium amount are determined by average mortality experience, annuity contracts are more attractive for people whose present health, living habits, and family mortality experience suggest that they are likely to live longer than average. As a general rule, annuities are not advisable for people in poor health, although exceptions to this rule exist.

WHY BUY ANNUITIES?

A primary reason for buying an annuity is to give you retirement income for the rest of your life. You should fully fund your IRAs, Keoghs, and 401(k)s before considering annuities. We discuss retirement income in Chapter 18, "Starting Early: Retirement Planning."

Although people have been buying annuities for many years, the appeal of variable annuities increased during the mid-1990s due to a rising stock market. A *fixed annuity* states that the annuitant (the person who is to receive the annuity) will receive a fixed amount of income over a certain period or for life. With a *variable annuity,* the monthly payments vary because they are based on the income received from stocks or other investments.

Some of the growth in the use of annuities can be attributed to the passage of the Employee Retirement Income Security Act (ERISA) of 1974. Annuities are often purchased for individual retirement accounts (IRAs), which ERISA made possible. They may also be used in Keogh-type plans for self-employed people. As you will see in Chapter 18, contributions to both IRA and Keogh plans are tax deductible up to specified limits.

TAX CONSIDERATIONS

When you buy an annuity, the interest on the principal, as well as the interest compounded on that interest, builds up free of current income tax. The Tax Reform Act of 1986 preserves the tax advantages of annuities (and insurance) but curtails deductions for IRAs. With an annuity, there is no maximum annual contribution. Also, if you die during the accumulation period, your beneficiary is guaranteed no less than the amount invested.

Exhibit 12–10 shows the difference between an investment in an annuity and an investment in a certificate of deposit (CD). Remember, federal income tax on an annuity is deferred, whereas the tax on interest earned on a CD must be paid currently.

Exhibit **12–10**

Tax-deferred annuity versus taxable CD (a 30-year projection of performance; single deposit of $30,000)

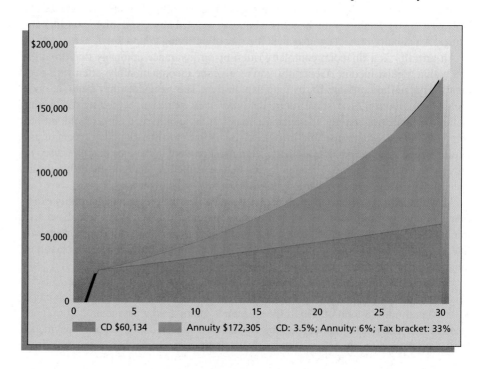

CD $60,134   Annuity $172,305   CD: 3.5%; Annuity: 6%; Tax bracket: 33%

DON'T BELIEVE THE HYPE

Have you bought a variable annuity yet? If you're a baby boomer and your answer is no, get ready for the hard sell. The promoters of these savings vehicles will prey on your insecurity about not having enough money for retirement to get you to sign up for what could be a costly investment. Even if you already have a variable annuity, someone may try to convince you to trade in your existing contract for one with new bells and whistles—in which are buried higher fees. The problem with variable annuities is they are often a high-cost answer to a problem that may have simpler, cheaper solutions, such as fully funding your tax-deferred retirement accounts or assembling a portfolio of reliable, dividend-paying stocks. Still, through September 30, 2004, variable annuity sales were $98.4 billion, about 4 percent higher than during the same period in 2003. And it's insurance salespeople, no Wall Street brokers, who are making most of the sales. Financial planners in particular have been cool to the product. Variable annuities "are tax-inefficient, difficult if not impossible to understand, and have high costs," says Warren McIntyre, a financial planner in Troy, Michigan.

Sure, potential buyers can ignore the sales fluff and dig into the fine print to figure out whether an annuity is right for them. But that can be a real slog: The prospectus for MetLife's Preference Plus Select Variable Annuity runs over 500 pages, so you know why most buyers wind up relying on a sales spiel.

The legions of sales folks are spending time and money to refine their pitches. In February, for instance, at the annual marketing conference of the National Association for Variable Annuities (NAVA) in Tucson, one session will cover, according to the program, "the hot buttons that drive baby boomers' long-term financial decisions and how to connect the benefits of variable annuities to these hot buttons." NF Communications of Walnut Creek, California, a sales training firm, offers a marketing system over the Internet that teaches salespeople how to find affluent seniors and get them to exchange annuities they own for new ones that throw off a slew of new fees. By doing so, says NF's Web site, you "can sell two to four additional annuities a month," with an average commission of $2,500 each. Commissions on these annuities run 5 percent to 7 percent, says NAVA, which, in the investment world these days, is a pretty big number.

Tax deferral was a critical selling point for many years, but now such deferral may be unwise for many investors. Here's why: If you invest your annuity in stocks, they'll produce both long-term capital gains and dividends, which right now are taxed at a maximum rate of 15 percent. But long-term gains and dividends earned in the annuity will eventually be taxed as ordinary income, usually at a much higher rate.

Annuities come with a host of fees and conditions. The average annual expense for a variable annuity in 2003 was 2.32 percent of the value, says NAVA, compared with 1.4 percent for an equity mutual fund. Another cost that may come into play if you want to break the contract is the surrender charge. That's an early withdrawal penalty, which declines over a specified period. For example, you may pay 7 percent of the annuity value to get out the first year, 6 percent the second year, and so on until it reaches zero after seven years.

As a consumer, the best way to arm yourself against the pressures of annuity marketers is to know the common sales pitches and how to respond to them. In the end, you still might want a variable annuity. But make that decision after careful consideration of the product and alternative solutions—not because someone pressured you into it.

Source: Adapted from Ellen Hoffman, "Don't Believe the Hype," *BusinessWeek*, February 7, 2005, pp. 82–84.

As with any other financial product, the advantages of annuities are tempered by drawbacks. In the case of variable annuities, these drawbacks include reduced flexibility and fees that lower investment return. Even though many of the tax benefits of variable annuities no longer exist, the hard sell continues. Read the accompanying Financial Planning for Life's Situations feature to protect yourself from what could be a costly investment.

CONCEPT CHECK 12-6

1 What is an annuity?
2 Why do people buy annuities?
3 How are annuities taxed?

Action Application Interview friends, relatives, and others who have bought annuities. Which type of annuity did they purchase, and why?

SUMMARY OF OBJECTIVES

Objective 1

Define *life insurance* and describe its purpose and principle.

Life insurance is a contract between an insurance company and a policyholder under which the company agrees to pay a specified sum to a beneficiary upon the insured's death. Most people buy life insurance to protect someone who depends on them from financial losses caused by their death. Fundamental to the life insurance principle is the predictable mortality experience of a large group of individuals.

Objective 2

Determine your life insurance needs.

In determining your life insurance needs, you must first determine your insurance objectives and then use the easy method, the DINK method, the "nonworking" spouse method, or the "family need" method. The "family need" method is recommended. You should consider a number of factors before you buy insurance, including your present and future sources of income, other savings and income protection, group life insurance, group annuities (or other pension benefits), and Social Security.

Objective 3

Distinguish between the two types of life insurance companies and analyze various types of life insurance policies these companies issue.

The two types of life insurance companies are stock companies, owned by stockholders, and mutual companies, owned by policyholders. In general, stock companies sell nonparticipating policies and mutual companies sell participating policies. The three basic types of life insurance are term, whole life, and endowment policies. Many variations and combinations of these types are available. You should check with both stock and mutual companies to determine which type offers the best policy for your particular needs at the lowest price.

Nevertheless, as with other forms of insurance, price should not be your only consideration in choosing a life insurance policy. You should also consider the financial stability, reliability, and service the insurance company provides.

Objective 4

Select important provisions in life insurance contracts.

The naming of the beneficiary, the grace period, policy reinstatement, the incontestability clause, the suicide clause, automatic premium loans, the misstatement of age provision, and the policy loan provision are important provisions in most life insurance policies. Common riders in life insurance policies are the waiver of premium disability benefit, the accidental death benefit, the guaranteed insurability option, cost of living protection, and accelerated benefits.

Objective 5

Create a plan to buy life insurance.

Before buying life insurance, consider your present and future sources of income, group life insurance, group annuities (or other pension benefits), and Social Security. Then compare the costs of several life insurance policies. Examine your policy before and after the purchase, and choose appropriate settlement options. The most common settlement options are lump-sum payment, limited installment payment, life income option, and proceeds left with the company. Online computer services provide a wealth of information about all topics related to life insurance.

Objective 6

Recognize how annuities provide financial security.

An annuity is the opposite of life insurance: It pays while you live, whereas life insurance pays when you die. An annuity provides you with a regular income during your retirement years. The Tax Reform Act of 1986 gives annuities favorable income tax treatment.

The appeal of fixed annuities has increased recently. With a fixed annuity, the annuitant receives a fixed amount of income over a certain period or for life. With a variable annuity, the monthly payments vary because they are based on the income received from stocks or other investments.

KEY TERMS

annuity 397	incontestability clause 388	suicide clause 388
beneficiary 387	interest-adjusted index 394	term insurance 379
cash value 382	nonforfeiture clause 387	universal life 384
chartered life underwriter (CLU) 393	nonparticipating policy 379	whole life policy 382
double indemnity 389	participating policy 379	
	rider 388	

1. *Calculating the Amount of Life Insurance Needed Using the Easy Method.* You are the wage earner in a "typical family," with $30,000 gross annual income. Use the easy method to determine how much life insurance you should carry. (Obj. 2)

2. *Estimating Life Insurance Needs Using the DINK Method.* You and your spouse are in good health and have reasonably secure careers. Each of you makes about $28,000 annually. You own a home with an $80,000 mortgage, and you owe $10,000 on car loans, $5,000 in personal debts, and $3,000 on credit card loans. You have no other debts. You have no plans to increase the size of your family in the near future. Estimate your total insurance needs using the DINK method. (Obj. 2)

3. *Using the "Nonworking" Spouse Method to Determine Life Insurance Needs.* Tim and Allison are married and have two children, ages 4 and 7. Allison is a "nonworking" spouse who devotes all of her time to household activities. Estimate how much life insurance Tim and Allison should carry. (Obj. 2)

4. *Comparing the Costs of Life Insurance and Various Provisions in a Life Insurance Policy.* Obtain premium rates for $25,000 whole life, universal life, and term life policies from local insurance agents. Compare the costs and provisions of these policies. (Obj. 3)

5. *Calculating Your Life Insurance Needs.* Use Exhibit 12–2 to calculate your life insurance needs. (Obj. 3)

6. *Choosing the Settlement Options.* Review the settlement options on your family's life insurance policies, and discuss with your family which option would be the best choice for them at this time. (Obj. 5)

7. *Calculating Accumulated Account Values.* Assume you have $10,000 to invest for 10 years. You can invest in a cer-

FINANCIAL PLANNING PROBLEMS

tificate of deposit at 8.5 percent or a 10-year, tax-deferred annuity at 8.5 percent. Assume a 33 percent federal tax bracket. Use Exhibit 12–10 or Exhibit 1–8 in Chapter 1 to find your accumulated account values. Which investment is better, and by how much? (Obj. 6)

8. *Calculating the Death Benefit.* You own a variable annuity that offers a death benefit equal to the greater of the account value or the total purchase payments minus withdrawals. You have made purchase payments totaling $50,000. In addition, you have withdrawn $5,000 from your account. Because of these withdrawals and investment losses, your account value is currently $40,000. If you die, what will your designated beneficiary receive?

9. *Calculating the Surrender Charge.* You purchase a variable annuity contract with a $10,000 purchase payment. The contract has a schedule of surrender charges, beginning with a 7 percent charge in the first year and declining by 1 percent each year. In addition, you are allowed to withdraw 10 percent of your contract value each year free of surrender charges. In the first year, you decide to withdraw $5,000, or one-half of your contract value of $10,000 (assuming that your contract value has not increased or decreased because of investment performance). What amount can you withdraw without surrender charges? What is the total surrender charge you will have to pay?

10. *Calculating a Mortality and Expense Risk Charge.* Your variable annuity has a mortality and expense risk charge at an annual rate of 1.25 percent of account value. Your average account value during the year is $20,000. What is your mortality and expense risk charge for the year?

11. *Calculating Administrative Fees.* Your variable annuity charges administrative fees at an annual rate of 0.15 percent of account value. Your average account value during the year is $50,000. What is the administrative fee for the year?

1. *Planning for Life Insurance.* Choose a current issue of *Money, Kiplinger's Personal Finance, Consumer Reports,* or *Worth* and summarize an article that provides information on human life expectancy and how life insurance may provide financial security. (Obj. 1)

2. *Assessing the Need for Life Insurance.* Interview relatives and friends to determine why they purchased life insurance. Prepare an essay summarizing your findings. (Obj. 1)

3. *Comparing the Methods of Determining Life Insurance Requirements.* Analyze the four methods of determining life insurance requirements. Which method is best, and why? (Obj. 2)

FINANCIAL PLANNING ACTIVITIES

4. *Comparing Premiums for Life Insurance Policies.* Choose one stock and one mutual life insurance company. Obtain and compare premiums for

   a. Term life insurance for $50,000.

   b. Whole life insurance for $50,000.

   c. Universal life insurance for $50,000.

   Prepare a summary table indicating which policy you would consider and why. (Obj. 3)

5. *Using the Internet to Obtain Information about Various Types of Life Insurance.* All major life insurance companies now maintain a Web page. Visit a few Web sites of

companies such as Metropolitan Life, New York Life, Transamerica Life, Lincoln Benefit Life, or others of your choice. Then prepare a report that summarizes the various types of insurance coverages available from these companies. (Obj. 4)

6. *Comparing the Provisions of Life Insurance Policies.* Examine your life insurance policies and the policies of other members of your family. Note the contractual provisions of each policy. What does the company promise to do in return for premiums? (Obj. 4)

7. *Using the Services Provided by State Insurance Departments.* Contact your state insurance department to get information about whether your state requires interest-adjusted cost disclosure. Prepare a summary report of your finding. (Obj. 5)

8. *Assessing the Use and Need for Annuities.* Interview friends, relatives, and others who have bought annuities. Which type of annuity did they purchase, and why? (Obj. 6)

INTERNET CONNECTION

Buying Life Insurance

Providing for the financial needs of dependents is the primary goal of a life insurance program. Comparing policy types, coverage amounts, and other provisions will help you meet this financial purpose. Visit Web sites of two reputable insurance companies of your choice and compare the following:

Company A Web address _____

Company B Web address _____

Type of Policy	Company A	Company B
20-year term insurance, $100,000		
Monthly premium		
Total premiums, 20 years		
Cash value at 20 years	None	None
Whole life insurance, $100,000		
Monthly premium		
Total premiums, 20 years		
Cash value at 20 years		

1. Which is less expensive, term insurance or whole life insurance?

_____ term _____ whole life

2. Which company would you select for your purchase of life insurance? Why?

_____
_____
_____
_____

Life Insurance for the Young Married

Jeff and Ann are both 28 years old. They have been married for three years, and they have a son who is almost two. They expect their second child in a few months.

Jeff is a teller in a local bank. He has just received a $60-a-week raise. His income is $960 a week, which, after taxes, leaves him with $3,200 a month. His company provides $50,000 of life insurance, a medical/hospital/surgical plan, and a major medical plan. All of these group plans protect him as long as he stays with the bank.

When Jeff received his raise, he decided that part of it should be used to add to his family's protection. Jeff and Ann talked to their insurance agent, who received the insurance Jeff obtained through his job. Under Social Security, they also had some basic protection against the loss of Jeff's income if he became totally disabled or if he died before the children were 18.

FINANCIAL PLANNING CASE

But most of this protection was only basic, a kind of floor for Jeff and Ann to build on. For example, monthly Social Security payments to Ann would be approximately $1,550 if Jeff died leaving two children under age 18. Yet the family's total expenses would soon be higher after the birth of the second baby. Although the family's expenses would be lowered if Jeff died, they would be at least $500 a month more than Social Security would provide.

Questions

1. What type of policy would you suggest for Jeff and Ann? Why?

2. In your opinion do Jeff and Ann need additional insurance? Why or why not?

VIDEO CASE

Life Insurance

A seven-year old boy, Dennis, is playing soccer in his driveway. People are loading boxes and furniture into a moving van, and Dennis asks his mom, Diane, why his neighbor and friend, Cathy, is moving. Diane explains to her son that Cathy is moving because her daddy died and her mommy could not afford to live in that house anymore.

The death of Diane's neighbor made her start to think: What would happen if she or her husband, Jim, died? Jim has a life insurance policy from his work, but that equals only about one year's salary. That's not enough. Diane and Jim realize they need more life insurance and contact an insurance agent to help them determine their insurance needs.

Mark Savalle, an insurance agent from New York Life Insurance Company, explains how to choose an insurance agent and an insurance company. He states that an insurance company must be rated "A" or better by Standard and Poor, Duff and Phelps, Moody's, and Weiss.

Jonathan Pond offers two reasons why it is difficult to get a good idea about how much life insurance you need. However, the need for life insurance is greatest during early years and it decreases during the middle years, when children leave the

house. In many cases, there is no need for life insurance during retirement years, when income continues even after the death of one of the spouses.

Jim and Diane meet with their insurance agent and determine how much insurance they need if Jim or Diane died. Of course, Jim's $45,000 life insurance from his employer was just not enough.

Questions

1. What triggered Jim and Diane to start thinking about life insurance?

2. How much life insurance did Jim have from his employer? Was it adequate? Explain your answer.

3. What was the couple's first step once they determined they needed more life insurance?

4. What is Mark Savalle's advice to those looking for life insurance?

5. According to Jonathan Pond, "There are two reasons why it is tough to get a good idea about how much life insurance you need." What are these reasons?

YOUR PERSONAL FINANCIAL PLANNER IN ACTION

Determining Life Insurance Needs

Providing for the financial needs of dependents is the primary goal of a life insurance program. Comparing policy types, coverage amounts, and other provisions will help you meet this financial purpose.

Your Short-Term Financial Planning Activities	Resources
1. Determine life insurance needs for your current life situation.	PFP Sheet 53 www.life-line.org www.quicken.com/insurance http://moneycentral.msn.com www.finaid.org/calculators/
2. Compare rates and coverages for different life insurance policies and companies.	PFP Sheet 54 http://personalinsure.about.com www.quickquote.com www.insure.com www.accuquote.com
3. Evaluate the use of annuities in your financial plan.	www.annuities.com http://invest-faq.com www.sec.gov
Your Long-Term Financial Planning Activities	
1. Identify information sources to monitor changes in life insurance coverages and costs offered by life insurance companies.	www.life-line.org
2. Develop a plan for reassessing life insurance needs as family and household situations change.	Text pages 373–378 www.insurance.com

CONTINUING CASE

Life Insurance

Life Situation
Pam, 36
Josh, 38
Three children, ages 9, 7, and 4

Financial Goals
Monthly income $4,300
Living expenses $4,075
Assets $150,850
Liabilities $99,520

With three dependent children, the Brocks are assessing their life insurance. Pam has $5,000 of coverage. Josh has life insurance coverage equal to approximately eight times his annual salary.

Questions

1. Do you think Pam and Josh have enough life insurance? If not, describe changes you would recommend for the Brocks.

2. Explain which sections of *Personal Financial Planner* sheets 53 and 54 could be useful to the Brocks.

13 Investing Fundamentals

Key Concept

The basic investment principles presented in this chapter, along with the information on stocks, bonds, mutual funds, real estate, and other alternatives in the remaining investment chapters, will enable you to create an investment plan that is custom-made for you.

Learning Objectives

1 Describe why you should establish an investment program.

2 Assess how safety, risk, income, growth, and liquidity affect your investment decisions.

3 Explain how asset allocation and different investment alternatives affect your investment plan.

4 Recognize the importance of your role in a personal investment program.

5 Use various sources of financial information that can reduce risks and increase investment returns.

An Investment Plan That May Have You Shouting "Yahoo!"

Think for a moment about how long it takes to save $2,400. For Noah and Clare Cardoza, it took 12 months to reach their goal of establishing a nest egg that could be used to begin an investment program. Once they obtained their goal, it was time to begin investing. That's when they realized they didn't really know anything about investing! And the worst case scenario: They could lose the $2,400 they had worked so hard to save if they didn't learn something about making investment decisions.

Twelve months ago, the Cardozas made a decision to save the money needed to start an investment program. Now, they made another decision to learn how to invest before investing their money. They began their search for educational materials by using their home computer to find investment Web sites. According to Clare, there were many sites offering investment information, but they chose the Yahoo! Finance Web site because it contained practical information on how to establish an investment program.

Although just one of many Web sites, the Yahoo! Finance site (finance.yahoo.com) is an excellent choice for beginning investors like Clare and Noah Cardoza, as well as more experienced investors. Clare and Noah began by examining the material in a section called "Investing 101." Topics in this section include (1) Getting Started in Investing, (2) Advice for a Novice, (3) Types of Investments, (4) Basic Investment Concepts & Strategies, and (5) Investment Tips. In addition to the topics explained in the "Investing 101" section, there were a glossary of investment terms and more detailed information on personal finance topics, including stocks, bonds, and mutual funds.

Both Clare and Noah quickly realized there was more to investing than just purchasing stocks, bonds, or mutual funds. While they continued to look at other Web sites, they kept coming back to Yahoo! Finance because it provided the educational tools they needed and research information they could understand. According to Noah, learning about investing was fun because it helped them make their first investment decision.

Source: Yahoo! Finance, finance.yahoo.com, April 3, 2005.

QUESTIONS

What Action Should Be Taken?

1. Why is learning about investments important for your financial success?
2. Clare and Noah Cardoza began their search for investment information by examining the Yahoo! Finance Web site. If you were seeking help to establish an investment program, where would you go?

   Many personal financial experts recommend that beginning investors establish an emergency fund and pay off credit card debt before beginning an investment program.

What about Your Situation?

3. Assuming you have credit card debt, how would you pay off the debt?
4. What steps could you take to save the money needed to establish an emergency fund and fund an investment program?

Learn More Online

Based on the information at finance.yahoo.com, describe the other types of available information that will help you learn how to establish an investment program and ultimately become a successful investor.

Preparing for an Investment Program

Objective 1

Describe why you should establish an investment program.

The old saying goes "I've been rich and I've been poor, and believe me, rich is better." While being rich doesn't guarantee happiness, the creation of wealth does provide financial security. The creation of wealth can also provide a safety net for the unexpected events and emergencies you may experience as you travel life's uncertain road. Finally, the act of saving and investing money will allow you to retire on your terms when and where you choose. Regardless of the reason, the creation of wealth is a worthy goal. And yet, just dreaming of being rich doesn't make it happen. In fact, it takes planning, research, and continued evaluation of existing investments to establish and maintain an investment program that will help you accomplish your goals.

Like many investors, Clare and Noah Cardoza, the couple in the opening case, didn't know how to evaluate investments. That's when they began to search the Internet for investment information and found the Yahoo! Finance Web site. Although one of hundreds of Web sites offering investment information, the Yahoo! Finance site provides information written in everyday language that you can understand. Why not take a look? To visit the material on the Yahoo! Finance Web site, follow these steps:

1. Type in the following Web address: finance.yahoo.com.
2. Locate the heading, "Education."
3. Click on the section titled "Investing 101."
4. Choose a topic that will help you learn about investing. It's that simple.

By studying the material contained in this Web site and following the basic investment principles presented in this chapter, along with the information on stocks, bonds, mutual funds, real estate, and other alternatives in the remaining investment chapters, you can create an investment plan that is custom-made for you.

The decision to establish an investment plan is an important first step to accomplishing your long-term financial goals. Like other decisions, the decision to start an investment plan is one you must make for yourself. No one is going to make you save the money you need to fund an investment plan. These things won't be done unless you want to do them. In fact, the *specific* goals you want to accomplish must be the driving force behind your investment plan.

ESTABLISHING INVESTMENT GOALS

While it would be nice if you could magically accumulate wealth, it takes careful planning and discipline to achieve the financial freedom you desire. For most people, the first step is to establish investment goals. Without investment goals, you cannot know what you want to accomplish.

Sheet 55
Setting investment goals

Some financial planners suggest that investment goals be stated in terms of money: By December 31, 2011, I will have total assets of $120,000. Other financial planners believe investors are more motivated to work toward goals that are stated in terms of the particular things they desire: By January 1, 2012, I will have accumulated enough money to purchase a second home in the mountains. To be useful, investment goals must be *specific* and *measurable*. They must be tailored to your particular financial needs. The following questions will help you establish valid investment goals:

1. What will you use the money for?
2. How much money do you need to satisfy your investment goals?
3. How will you obtain the money?
4. How long will it take you to obtain the money?
5. How much risk are you willing to assume in an investment program?

6. What possible economic or personal conditions could alter your investment goals?

7. Considering your economic circumstances, are your investment goals reasonable?

8. Are you willing to make the sacrifices necessary to ensure that you meet your investment goals?

9. What will the consequences be if you don't reach your investment goals?

Your investment goals are always oriented toward the future. In Chapter 1, we classified goals as short term (less than two years), intermediate (two to five years), or long term (more than five years). These same classifications are also useful in planning your investment program. For example, you may establish a short-term goal of accumulating $5,000 in a savings account over the next 18 months. You may then use the $5,000 to purchase stocks or mutual funds to help you obtain your intermediate or long-term investment goals.

PERFORMING A FINANCIAL CHECKUP

Before beginning an investment program, your personal financial affairs should be in good shape. In this section, we examine several factors you should consider before making your first investment.

WORK TO BALANCE YOUR BUDGET   Many individuals regularly spend more than they make. They purchase items on credit and then must make monthly installment payments and pay finance charges ranging between 10 and 21 percent. With this situation, it makes no sense to start an investment program until credit card and installment purchases, along with the accompanying finance charges, are reduced or eliminated. Therefore, you should limit credit purchases to only the necessities or to purchases required to meet emergencies. A good rule of thumb is to limit consumer credit payments to 20 percent of your net (after tax) income. Eventually, the amount of cash remaining after the bills are paid will increase and can be used to start a savings program or finance investments. A word of caution: Corrective measures take time.

The Consumer Credit Counseling Service offers budget counseling and educational programs. Visit their Web site at **www.cccs.net.**

OBTAIN ADEQUATE INSURANCE PROTECTION   We discussed insurance in detail in earlier chapters, and will not cover that topic again here. However, it is essential that you consider insurance needs before beginning an investment program. The types of insurance and the amount of coverage will vary from one person to the next. Before you start investing, examine the amount of your insurance coverage for life insurance, hospitalization, your home and other real estate holdings, automobiles, and any other assets that may need coverage.

START AN EMERGENCY FUND   Most financial planners suggest that an investment program should begin with the accumulation of an emergency fund. An **emergency fund** is an amount of money you can obtain quickly in case of immediate need. This money should be deposited in a savings account paying the highest available interest rate or in a money market mutual fund that provides immediate access to cash if needed.

The amount of money to be put away in the emergency fund varies from person to person. However, most financial planners agree that an amount equal to three to nine months' living expenses is reasonable. For example, Debbie Martin's monthly expenses total $1,600. Before Debbie can begin investing, she must save at least $4,800 ($1,600 × 3 months = $4,800) in a savings account or other near-cash investments to meet emergencies.

emergency fund An amount of money you can obtain quickly in case of immediate need.

HAVE ACCESS TO OTHER SOURCES OF CASH FOR EMERGENCY NEEDS   You may also want to establish a line of credit at a commercial bank, savings and loan association, credit union, or credit card company. A **line of credit** is a short-term loan that is approved before you actually need the money. Because the paperwork has already been completed and the loan has been preapproved, you can later obtain the money as soon as you need it. The cash advance provision offered by major credit card companies can also be used in an emergency. However, both lines of credit and credit cards have a ceiling, or maximum dollar amount, that limits the amount of available credit. If you have already exhausted both of these sources of credit on everyday expenses, they will not be available in an emergency.

line of credit A short-term loan that is approved before the money is actually needed.

GETTING THE MONEY NEEDED TO START AN INVESTMENT PROGRAM

Once you have established your investment goals and completed your financial checkup, it's time to start investing—assuming you have enough money to finance your investments. Unfortunately, the money doesn't automatically appear. In today's world, you must work to accumulate the money you need to start any investment program.

PRIORITY OF INVESTMENT GOALS   How badly do you want to achieve your investment goals? Are you willing to sacrifice some purchases to provide financing for your investments? The answers to both questions are extremely important. Take Rita Johnson, a 32-year-old nurse in a large St. Louis hospital. As part of a divorce settlement in 2003, she received a cash payment of almost $55,000. At first, she was tempted to spend this money on a trip to Europe, a new BMW, and new furniture. But after some careful planning, she decided to save $35,000 in a certificate of deposit and invest the remainder in a conservative mutual fund. On May 31, 2006, these investments were valued at $79,000.

As pointed out earlier in this chapter, no one can make you save money to finance your investment program. You have to *want* to do it. And *you* may be the most important part of a successful investment program. What is important to you? What do you value? Each of these questions affects your investment goals. At one extreme are people who save or invest as much of each paycheck as they can. The satisfaction they get from attaining their investment goals is more important than the more immediate satisfaction of spending their paychecks on new clothes, a meal at an expensive restaurant, or a weekend getaway. At the other extreme are people who spend everything they make and run out of money before their next paycheck. Most people find either extreme unacceptable and take a more middle-of-the-road approach. These people often spend money on the items that make their lives more enjoyable and still save enough to fund an investment program. Some suggestions to help you obtain the money you need to establish an investment program are described in the Financial Planning for Life's Situations feature on page 411.

DID YOU KNOW?

The more you make, the more challenging your investment goals can be. Here are household income levels for U.S. families.

- 9% Over $125,000
- 19% $75,000 to $125,000
- 38% Under $40,000
- 34% $40,000 to $75,000

Source: U.S. Bureau of the Census, *Statistical Abstract of the United States, 2004–2005* (Washington, DC: U.S. Government Printing Office), p. 448 (www.census.gov).

THE VALUE OF LONG-TERM INVESTMENT PROGRAMS

Should college students worry about planning for retirement? You bet! There is no better time to begin an investment program than when you are young. The reason is simple: If you start an investment program when young, let the time value of money work

OBTAINING MONEY TO ESTABLISH AN INVESTMENT PROGRAM

Ever feel like it's hard to save money? Well, you're not alone. In fact, most people—especially younger savers—often find it difficult to salt money away. Below are some suggestions for obtaining the money you need to fund an investment program.

Suggestion	Specific Actions to Take
1. Pay yourself first.	Each month, pay your monthly bills, save or invest a reasonable amount of money, and use whatever money is left over for personal expenses.
2. Take advantage of employer-sponsored retirement programs.	Sign up for a retirement program at work, because many employers will match part or all of the contributions.
3. Participate in an elective savings program.	Elect to have money withheld from your paycheck each payday and automatically deposited in a savings or investment account.
4. Make a special savings effort one or two months each year.	Many financial planners recommend that you cut back to the basics for one or two months each year.
5. Take advantage of gifts, inheritances, and windfalls.	Use money from unexpected sources to fund an investment program.

for you, and make sound investments, you won't have to worry about finances when you reach retirement age.

Unfortunately, many people never start an investment program, because they have only small sums of money. But even small sums grow over a long period of time. For example, if you invest $2,000 *each year* for 40 years at a 5 percent annual rate of return, your investment will grow to $241,600. Notice that the value of your investments increases each year because of two factors. First, it is assumed you will invest another $2,000 each year. For example, at the end of 40 years, you will have invested a total of $80,000 ($2,000 × 40 years = $80,000). Second, all investment earnings are allowed to accumulate and are added to your yearly deposits. In the above example, you earned $161,600 ($241,600 total return − $80,000 yearly contributions = $161,600 accumulated earnings).

Also, the rate of return and the length of time your money is invested do make a difference. Exhibit 13–1 shows how much your investment portfolio will be worth at the end of selected time periods and with different rates of return. As noted above, a $2,000 annual investment that earns 5 percent is worth $241,600 at the end of 40 years. But if the same $2,000 annual investment earns 12 percent each year, your investment is worth $1,534,180 at the end of the same 40-year period. The search for higher returns is one reason many investors choose stocks and mutual funds, which offer higher potential returns compared to certificates of deposit or savings accounts. Be warned: investments with higher returns are not guaranteed. In order to obtain higher returns, you must sacrifice some safety. The material in the next section will help you understand the relationship between safety and risk when choosing an investment.

The investment earnings illustrated in Exhibit 13–1 are taxable as ordinary income under current Internal Revenue Service guidelines. To avoid or postpone taxation, you may want to invest your money in a traditional individual re-

It's time! Often writing the first check to open an investment account is the hardest part.

Exhibit **13-1**

Growth rate for $2,000 invested at the end of each year at various rates of return for different time periods

Rate of Return	Balance at End of Year					
	1	5	10	20	30	40
4%	$2,000	$10,832	$24,012	$59,556	$112,170	$190,052
5	2,000	11,052	25,156	66,132	132,878	241,600
6	2,000	11,274	26,362	73,572	158,116	309,520
7	2,000	11,502	27,632	81,990	188,922	399,280
8	2,000	11,734	28,974	91,524	226,560	518,120
9	2,000	11,970	30,386	102,320	272,620	675,780
10	2,000	12,210	31,874	114,550	328,980	885,180
11	2,000	12,456	33,444	128,406	398,040	1,163,660
12	2,000	12,706	35,098	144,104	482,660	1,534,180

tirement account (IRA), a Roth IRA, a 401(k) or 403(b) retirement account offered through your employer, or one of the tax-free investments described later in the text. The details about different types of retirement accounts are presented in Chapter 18.

CONCEPT CHECK 13-1

1 How can an Internet site like Yahoo! Finance help you to become a better investor?
2 Why should an investor develop specific investment goals?
3 What factors should you consider when performing a financial checkup?
4 Explain the time value of money concept and how it affects your investment program.

Action Application Using Web research and discussion with family members, establish specific goals that will provide a foundation for your investment program.

Factors Affecting the Choice of Investments

Objective 2

Assess how safety, risk, income, growth, and liquidity affect your investment decisions.

Millions of Americans buy stocks, bonds, or mutual funds, purchase gold and silver, or make similar investments. And they all have reasons for investing their money. Some people want to supplement their retirement income when they reach age 65, while others want to become millionaires before age 40. Although each investor may have specific, individual goals for investing, all investors must consider a number of factors before choosing an investment alternative.

SAFETY AND RISK

How do you define a perfect investment? For most people, the perfect investment is one with no risk and above average returns. Unfortunately, the perfect investment does not exist, because of the relationship between safety and risk. The safety and risk factors are two sides of the same coin. *Safety* in an investment means minimal risk of loss. On the other hand, *risk* in an investment means a measure of uncertainty about the outcome.

Investments range from very safe to very risky. At one end of the investment spectrum are very safe investments that attract conservative investors. Investments in this category include government bonds, savings accounts, certificates of deposit, and certain stocks, mutual funds, and corporate bonds. Real estate may also sometimes be a very safe investment. Investors choose such investments because they know there is little chance that investments of this kind will become worthless. At the other end of the investment spectrum are speculative investments. A **speculative investment** is a high-risk investment made in the hope of earning a relatively large profit in a short time. Such investments offer the possibility of larger dollar returns, but if they are unsuccessful, you may lose most or all of your initial investment. Speculative stocks, certain bonds, some mutual funds, some real estate, commodities, options, precious metals, precious stones, and collectibles are high-risk investments. Today, it is impossible to evaluate any investment without assessing how safety relates to risk.

Sheet 56
Assessing risk
for investments

speculative investment A high-risk investment made in the hope of earning a relatively large profit in a short time.

THE RISK–RETURN TRADE-OFF

You invest your money and your investments earn money. That's the way investing is supposed to work, but there is some risk associated with all investments. In fact, you may experience two types of risks with many investments.

- First, investors often choose some investments because they provide a predictable source of income. For example, you may choose to purchase a corporate bond because the bond pays a predictable amount of interest every six months. If the corporation experiences financial difficulties, it may default on interest payments. In other words, there is a risk that you will not receive periodic income payments.

- A second type of risk associated with many investments is that an investment will decrease in value. For example, the value of Krispy Kreme stock decreased in 2005 when consumers opted for low-carb diets in place of the firm's tasty donuts. In addition to low consumer demand, the company also encountered other financial difficulties. As a result, the stock decreased 39 percent in just four months.[1]

Exhibit 13–2 lists a number of factors related to safety and risk that can affect an investor's choice of investments.

EVALUATING YOUR TOLERANCE FOR RISK
When investing, not everyone has the same tolerance for risk. In fact, some people may actually be risk averse. Typically a risk averse investor will seek investment alternatives that offer the

Less Risk and Conservative Investments	More Risk and Speculative Investments
People with no financial training or investment background	Investors with financial training and investment background
Older investors	Younger investors
Lower-income investors	Higher-income investors
Families with children	Married couples with no children or single individuals
Employees worried about job loss	Employees with secure employment positions

Exhibit **13-2**

Factors that can affect your tolerance for risk and your investment choices

least risk. For example, Ana Luna was injured in a work-related accident three years ago. After a lengthy lawsuit, she received a legal settlement totaling $420,000. As a result of the injury, she was no longer qualified to perform her old job as an assembler for an electronics manufacturer. When she thought about the future, she knew she needed to get a job, but realized she would be forced to acquire new employment skills. She also realized she had received a great deal of money that could be invested to provide a steady source of income not only for the next two years while she obtained job training but also for the remainder of her life. Having never invested before, she quickly realized her tolerance for risk was minimal. She had to conserve her $420,000 settlement. Eventually, after much discussion with professionals and her own research, she chose to save about half of her money in federally insured certificates of deposit. For the remaining half, she chose three stocks that offered a 3 percent average dividend, a potential for growth, and a high degree of safety because of the financial stability of the corporations that issued the stocks. A more risk-oriented investor might have criticized Ana's decisions as too conservative. In fact, this second type of investor might have chosen to invest in more speculative stocks that offer a greater potential for growth and increase in market value.

When people choose investments that have a higher degree of risk, they expect larger returns. Simply put, one basic rule sums up the relationship between the factors of safety and risk: *The potential return on any investment should be directly related to the risk the investor assumes.* To help you determine how much risk you are willing to assume, take the test for risk tolerance presented in the Financial Planning for Life's Situations feature at the top of page 415.

CALCULATING RETURN ON AN INVESTMENT

When you invest, you expect a return on your investment. Part of the justification for this return is because you are sacrificing immediate purchasing power. The rate of return you receive is often determined by the amount of risk you are willing to take. For example, if you purchase a one-year certificate of deposit (CD) *guaranteed* by the FDIC (Federal Deposit Insurance Corporation), your CD may earn 3 percent a year. At the end of one year, you receive your initial investment plus 3 percent interest. Another investment alternative like a mutual fund may earn 10 percent a year. In this case, you receive an additional 7 percent return when compared to the CD because you chose to invest in a mutual fund that increased in value. While most investors don't like to think about it, the mutual fund could decrease in value for a number of reasons and your original investment or any possible returns are *not guaranteed.*

rate of return The total income you receive on an investment over a specific period of time divided by the original amount invested.

Some investors often base their investment decisions on projections for rate of return. You can also use the same calculation to determine how much you actually earn on an investment over a specific period of time. To calculate **rate of return,** the total income you receive on an investment over a specific period of time is divided by the original amount invested. Assume that you invest $3,000 in a mutual fund. Also assume the mutual fund pays you $50 in dividends this year and that the mutual fund is worth $3,275 at the end of one year. Your rate of return is 10.8 percent, as illustrated below.

Step 1: Subtract the investment's initial value from the investment's value at the end of the year.

$$\$3,275 - \$3,000 = \$275$$

Step 2: Add the annual income to the amount calculated in Step 1.

$$\$50 + \$275 = \$325$$

Step 3: Divide the total dollar amount of return calculated in Step 2 by the original investment.

$$\$325 \div \$3,000 = 0.108 = 10.8\%$$

A QUICK TEST TO MEASURE INVESTMENT RISK TOLERANCE

The following quiz, adapted from one prepared by the T. Rowe Price group of mutual funds, can help you discover how comfortable you are with varying degrees of risk. Other things being equal, your risk tolerance score is a useful guide in deciding how heavily you should weight your portfolio toward safe investments versus more risk-oriented, speculative investments.

1. You're the winner on a TV game show. Which prize would you choose?

☐ $2,000 in cash (1 point).

☐ A 50 percent chance to win $4,000 (3 points).

☐ A 20 percent chance to win $10,000 (5 points).

☐ A 2 percent chance to win $100,000 (9 points).

2. You're down $500 in a poker game. How much more would you be willing to put up to win the $500 back?

☐ More than $500 (8 points).

☐ $500 (6 points).

☐ $250 (4 points).

☐ $100 (2 points).

☐ Nothing—you'll cut your losses now (1 point).

3. A month after you invest in a stock, it suddenly goes up 15 percent. With no further information, what would you do?

☐ Hold it, hoping for further gains (3 points).

☐ Sell it and take your gains (1 point).

☐ Buy more—it will probably go higher (4 points).

4. Your investment suddenly goes down 15 percent one month after you invest. Its fundamentals still look good. What would you do?

☐ Buy more. If it looked good at the original price, it looks even better now (4 points).

☐ Hold on and wait for it to come back (3 points).

☐ Sell it to avoid losing even more (1 point).

5. You're a key employee in a start-up company. You can choose one of two ways to take your year-end bonus. Which would you pick?

☐ $1,500 in cash (1 point).

☐ Company stock options that could bring you $15,000 next year if the company succeeds, but will be worthless if it fails (5 points).

Your total score: _____

SCORING

5–18 points. You are a more conservative investor. You prefer to minimize financial risks. The lower your score, the more cautious you are. When you choose investments, look for high credit ratings, well-established records, and an orientation toward stability. In stocks, bonds, and real estate, look for a focus on income.

19–30 points. You are a less conservative investor. You are willing to take more chances in pursuit of greater rewards. The higher your score, the bolder you are. When you invest, look for high overall returns. You may want to consider bonds with higher yields and lower credit ratings, the stocks of newer companies, and real estate investments that use mortgage debt.

A primer on the ABCs of investing is available from T. Rowe Price, 100 E. Pratt St., Baltimore, MD 21202 (1-800-638-5660).

Note: If an investment decreases in value, the steps used to calculate the rate of return are the same, but the answer is a negative number.

With this information, it is possible to compare the rate of return for different investment alternatives that offer more or less risk. Keep in mind that the above calculations may be calculated using projections or real numbers at the end of an investment period. If based on projections, the rate of return is only as good as the projections used in the calculations.

Often, beginning investors are afraid of the risk associated with many investments. But it helps to remember that without risk, it is impossible to obtain larger returns that really make an investment program grow. The key is to determine how much risk you are willing to assume, and then choose quality investments that offer higher returns without an unacceptably high risk. The bottom line: What is right for one investor may not be right for another. You must determine how much risk you are willing to assume. Once you have determined the amount of risk you are comfortable with, you can choose different investments that hopefully will provide the expected return.

COMPONENTS OF THE RISK FACTOR

The risk factor associated with a specific investment does change from time to time. For example, the stock of Computer Tabulating-Recording Company was once considered a high-risk investment. Then this company changed its name to IBM and eventually became a leader in the computer industry. By the early 1980s, many conservative investors were purchasing IBM stock because of its safety and earnings potential. But in the early 1990s, many of these same investors sold their IBM stock because changes in the computer industry had brought financial problems for IBM. IBM was once again considered too risky for many investors. In the late 1990s, as a result of solving many of its financial problems, IBM was once again considered an excellent choice for most investors. Today, many conservative investors again own IBM stock.

When choosing an investment, you must carefully evaluate changes in the risk factor. In fact, the overall risk factor can be broken down into five components.

INFLATION RISK   Your investments can provide a way to keep up with or stay ahead of inflation. While inflation rates have fallen sharply from the high levels of the early 1980s, the dollar is still shrinking in value. One dollar placed in a safe deposit box in the early 1980s had less than 54 cents of buying power in early 2003.[2] As defined in Chapter 1, inflation is a rise in the general level of prices.

During periods of high inflation, there is a risk that the financial return on an investment will not keep pace with the inflation rate. To see how inflation reduces your buying power, let's assume you have deposited $10,000 in the bank at 3 percent interest. At the end of one year, your money will have earned $300 in interest ($10,000 $\times$ 3% = $300). Assuming an inflation rate of 4 percent, it will cost you an additional $400 ($10,000 $\times$ 4% = $400), or a total of $10,400, to purchase the same amount of goods you could have purchased for $10,000 a year earlier. Thus, even though you earned $300, you lost $100 in purchasing power. And after paying taxes on the $300 interest, your loss of purchasing power is even greater.

INTEREST RATE RISK   The interest rate risk associated with government or corporate bonds or preferred stock is the result of changes in the interest rates in the economy. The value of these investments decreases when overall interest rates increase. In contrast, the value of these same investments rises when overall interest rates decrease. For example, suppose you purchase a $1,000 corporate bond issued by AMR, the parent company of American Airlines, that matures in 2016 and pays 9 percent interest until maturity. This means AMR will pay $90 ($1,000 $\times$ 9% = $90) each year until the maturity date in 2016. If bond interest rates for comparable bonds increase to 10 percent, the market value of your 9 percent bond will decrease. No one will be willing to purchase your bond at the price you paid for it, since a comparable bond that pays 10 percent can be purchased for $1,000. As a result, you will have to sell your bond for less than $1,000 or hold it until maturity. If you decide to sell your AMR bond, the approximate dollar price you could sell it for would be $900 ($90 $\div$ 10% = $900). This price would provide the purchaser with a 10 percent return, and you would lose $100 ($1,000 − $900 = $100) because you owned a bond with a fixed interest rate of 9 percent during a period when overall interest rates in the economy increased.

Of course, if overall interest rates declined, your bond would increase in value. Let's assume that interest rates on comparable corporate bonds declined to 7 percent. As a result, the value of your AMR bond that pays 9 percent would increase in value. The approximate price you could sell it for would be $1,286 ($90 ÷ 7% = $1,286). This price would provide the purchaser with a 7 percent return, and you would earn a profit of $286 ($1,286 − $1,000 = $286) because you owned a bond with a fixed interest rate of 9 percent during a period when overall interest rates in the economy declined.

BUSINESS FAILURE RISK   The risk of business failure is associated with investments in stock and corporate bonds. With each of these investments, you face the possibility that bad management, unsuccessful products, competition, or a host of other factors will cause the business to be less profitable than originally anticipated. Lower profits usually mean lower dividends or no dividends at all. If the business continues to operate at a loss, even interest payments and repayment of bonds may be questionable. The business may even fail and be forced to file for bankruptcy, in which case your investment may become totally worthless. Before ignoring the possibility of business failure, consider the plight of employees and investors who owned stock in Enron. Of course, the best way to protect yourself against such losses is to carefully evaluate the companies that issue the stocks and bonds you purchase. It also helps to purchase different types of investments.

A sweet deal or a sour tart? When Krispy Kreme began selling stock, investors thought it was the sweetest deal in town. A few years later the stock's value took a nosedive when consumers opted for low-carb diets.

MARKET RISK   The prices of stocks, bonds, mutual funds, and other investments may fluctuate because of the behavior of investors in the marketplace. As a result, economic growth is not as systematic and predictable as most investors might believe. Generally, a period of rapid expansion is followed by a period of recession. During periods of recession, it may be quite difficult to sell investments such as real estate. Fluctuations in the market price for stocks and bonds may have nothing to do with the fundamental changes in the financial health of corporations. Such fluctuations may be caused by political or social conditions. For example, the price of petroleum stocks may increase or decrease as a result of political activity in the Middle East. Certainly, the tragic events of September 11, 2001, caused the value of many investments to decline.

GLOBAL INVESTMENT RISK   Today more investors are investing in stocks and bonds issued by foreign firms and in global mutual funds. While we discuss these investments in more detail in the remaining investment chapters, you should know that investing in global securities creates additional risk. And yet, investing in global securities can also diversify your portfolio. For example, when the U.S. markets are in decline, other markets around the globe may be increasing. An investor can purchase stocks or bonds issued by individual foreign firms or purchase shares in a global mutual fund. For the small investor who has less than $200,000 to invest and is unaccustomed to the risks in foreign investments, global or international mutual funds offer more safety. Here are two factors to consider before taking the plunge.

First, *global investments must be evaluated just like domestic investments.* But evaluating foreign firms and global mutual funds may be difficult because reliable accounting information on foreign firms is often scarce. Of course, you can get an annual report, but you won't know whether the foreign firm uses the generally accepted accounting principles used by U.S. firms or follows its own national accounting rules.

Second, *changes in the currency exchange rate may affect the return on your investment.* The foreign currency exchange rate is applied whenever securities are bought and sold and whenever dividends are paid. For instance, if you want to purchase stock issued by a French firm, your U.S. currency must be converted into euros. And the euros you receive when you sell your shares in the foreign firm must be converted back to U.S. dollars. Your potential return is determined not only by how well your investment performs but also by whether the currency exchange rate becomes more or less favorable during the time you hold the investment.

For more information on global investments, visit the Finance Around the World feature that accompanies the Online Learning Center for this text at **www.mhhe.com/kdh**.

INVESTMENT INCOME

Investors sometimes purchase certain investments because they want a predictable source of income. The safest investments—passbook savings accounts, certificates of deposit, and securities issued by the United States government—are also the most predictable sources of income. With these investments, you know exactly what the interest rate is and how much income will be paid on a specific date.

If investment income is a primary objective, you can also choose municipal bonds, corporate bonds, preferred stocks, utility stocks, or selected common stock issues. When purchasing stocks, municipal bonds, or corporate bonds for potential income, most investors are concerned about the issuer's ability to continue making periodic interest or dividend payments. Also, repayment at maturity may be a concern for bondholders. For example, some corporations, such as ExxonMobil and General Electric, are very proud of their long record of consecutive dividend payments and will maintain that policy if at all possible.

Other investments that may provide income potential are mutual funds and real estate rental property. Although the income from mutual funds is not guaranteed, you can choose funds whose primary objective is income. Like income from mutual funds, income from rental property is not guaranteed, because the possibility of either vacancies or unexpected repair bills always exists. The more speculative investments, such as commodities, options, precious metals, gemstones, and collectibles, offer little, if any, potential for regular income.

INVESTMENT GROWTH

To investors, *growth* means their investments will increase in value. Often the greatest opportunity for growth is an investment in common stock. During the 1990s, investors found that stocks issued by corporations in the electronics, technology, energy, and health care industries provided the greatest growth potential. And yet, many corporations in those same industries encountered financial problems, lower profits or even losses, and employee layoffs during the first part of the 21st century. In fact, many firms—especially dot-coms and technology firms—failed during this same time period. Now the U.S. economy appears to be weathering the storm and shows signs of stability and even improvement. While many analysts still debate whether the recent recession is over, one factor is certain, investors still like the potential that is offered by growth investments. And yet, you should remember the relationship between risk and return that was described earlier in this section.

When purchasing growth stocks, investors often sacrifice immediate cash dividends in return for greater dollar value in the future. Companies with better than average earnings potential, sales revenues that are increasing, and managers who can solve the problems associated with rapid expansion are often considered to be growth companies. These same companies generally pay little or no dividends. For most growth companies, profits that would normally be paid to stockholders in the form of dividends are reinvested in the companies. The money the companies keep can provide at least part of the financing they need for future growth and expansion and control the cost of borrowing money. As a result, they grow at an even faster pace. Growth financed by profits reinvested in the company normally increases the dollar value of a share of stock for the investor.

Other investments that may offer growth potential include selected mutual funds and real estate. For example, many mutual funds are referred to as growth funds or aggressive growth funds because of the growth potential of the individual securities included in the fund.

Precious metals, gemstones, and collectibles are more speculative investments that offer less predictable growth potential. Investments in commodities and options are more speculative investments that usually stress immediate returns as opposed to continued long-term growth.

INVESTMENT LIQUIDITY

Liquidity is the ability to buy or sell an investment quickly without substantially affecting the investment's value. Investments range from near-cash investments to frozen investments from which it is impossible to get your money. Checking and savings accounts are very liquid because they can be quickly converted to cash. Certificates of deposit impose penalties for withdrawing money before the maturity date.

With other investments, you may be able to sell quickly, but market conditions, economic conditions, or many other factors may prevent you from regaining the amount you originally invested. For example, the owner of real estate may have to lower the asking price to find a buyer. And it may be difficult to find a buyer for investments in collectibles such as antiques and paintings.

liquidity The ability to buy or sell an investment quickly without substantially affecting the investment's value.

CONCEPT CHECK 13-2 ✓

1 Why are safety and risk two sides of the same coin?
2 In your own words, describe the risk–return trade-off.
3 What are the five components of the risk factor?
4 How do income, growth, and liquidity affect the choice of an investment?

Action Application Using Internet research and discussion with other people, determine if you prefer less risk and conservative investments or more risk and speculative investments. Explain your answer.

Asset Allocation and Investment Alternatives

By now, you are probably thinking, How can I choose the right investment for me? Good question. To help answer that question, consider the following: Since 1900, stocks have returned approximately 10 percent a year and outperformed other investment alternatives on average. By comparison, government treasury bills and government bonds have returned about 4 percent during the same period.[3] And projections by well-respected Roger Ibbotson, chairman of Ibbotson Associates, the investment consulting, software, and research firm, indicate that these same investments will perform at about the same pace between now and the year 2025.[4] Based on the above facts and projections, it would seem that everyone should invest in stocks because they offer the largest returns. In reality, stocks may have a place in every investment portfolio, but there is more to establishing a long-term, investment program than just picking a bunch of stocks. Before making the decision to purchase stocks, consider the factors of asset allocation, the time period that your investments will work for you, and your age.

Objective 3

Explain how asset allocation and different investment alternatives affect your investment plan.

ASSET ALLOCATION AND DIVERSIFICATION

Asset allocation is the process of spreading your assets among several different types of investments (sometimes referred to as asset classes) to lessen risk. While the term *asset allocation* is a fancy way of saying it, simply put, it really means that you need to diversify and avoid the pitfall of putting all your eggs in one basket—a common mistake made by investors. The diversification provided by investing in *different* asset classes provides a measure of safety and reduces risk, because a loss in one investment is

asset allocation The process of spreading your assets among several different types of investments (sometimes referred to as asset classes) to lessen risk.

Small-cap or large-cap stock? Intel started small and grew into a VERY large company because of growing demand for its technology products.

usually offset by gains from other types of investments. Typical asset classes include stocks issued by large corporations (large cap), stocks issued by medium-size corporations (midcap), stocks issued by small, rapidly growing companies (small cap), foreign stocks, bonds, and cash. Note: mutual funds can also be included as an asset class, but the typical mutual fund will invest in the above securities or a combination of the above securities.

Many financial experts argue that asset allocation is the most important factor when establishing a long-term investment program because choosing the "right mix" of assets will outperform the investment selections that individual investors make over a long period of time.[5] How difficult is it to find the right mix of asset classes? Surprisingly easy! According to noted financial expert and author William Bernstein, if you had invested your investment portfolio in the stocks and bonds that make up the widely quoted averages for U.S. large-cap stocks, small-cap U.S. stocks, foreign stocks, and high-quality U.S. bonds (25 percent in each of these asset classes), you would have beaten over 90 percent of all professional money managers and with considerably less risk over a 10 to 20 year period.[6] And Bernstein is not alone. Today, most financial experts recommend asset allocation as a valued tool that can reduce the risk associated with long-term investment programs.

The percentage of your investments that should be invested in each asset class is determined by your age, investment objectives, ability to tolerate risk, how much you can save and invest each year, the dollar value of your current investments, the economic outlook for the economy, and several other factors. Given these factors, a typical asset allocation for a 31-year-old investor is illustrated in Exhibit 13–3.

As illustrated in Exhibit 13–3, asset allocation is often expressed in percentages of different investment alternatives. For example, it was suggested that 30 percent of this investor's assets should be invested in large-cap stocks. Now the big questions! What percentage of your assets do you want to invest in stocks and bonds? What percentage of your assets do you want to put in certificates of deposit and other investment alternatives? The answers to these questions are often tied to your tolerance for risk. Remember the basic rule presented earlier in this chapter: *The potential return on any investment should be directly related to the risk the investor assumes.* Consider what happened when Susan Vaughn invested over $20,000 in stocks and mutual funds during the summer of 2001. She chose quality stock and mutual fund investments that should have done well over a long period of time. But after the tragic events of September 11, the value of her investments dropped 30 percent within a three-week period. That's when she called her broker and sold her investments. Later she admitted that she wasn't comfortable with the risk associated with investments in the stocks and mutual funds she chose. In short, the amount of risk that you are comfortable with is a very important factor when choosing where to allocate your investment dollars.

Regardless of which type of assets you choose for your investment program and the percentage you invest in each asset class, it may be necessary to adjust your asset allo-

Exhibit **13–3**

Suggested asset allocation for a young investor

The suggested investments are for an investor who is 31 years old, has current investments valued at $10,000, is committed to saving $2,400 a year, and has an average tolerance for risk.

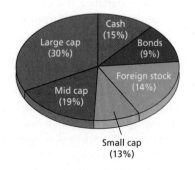

Source: Asia-Europe-Americas Bank Web site (aea-bank.com/calc/AssetAllocator.html), April 7, 2005.

cation from time to time. Often, the main reasons for making changes are because of changes in your tolerance for risk, the amount of time that your investments have to work for you, and your age.

THE TIME FACTOR   The amount of time that your investments have to work for you is another important factor when managing your investment portfolio. Return to the investment returns presented above. For over 100 years, stocks have returned approximately 10 percent a year and returned more than other investment alternatives. And yet, during the same period, there were years when stocks decreased in value.[7] The point is that if you invested at the wrong time and then couldn't wait for the investment to recover, you would lose money. Remember Susan Vaughn's decision to sell her stocks and mutual funds at a loss. Had she been willing to wait for her stock and mutual fund investments to recover, she would not have lost 30 percent of her original investment.

The amount of time you have before you need your investment money is crucial. If you can leave your investments alone and let them work for 5 to 10 years or more, then you can invest in stocks and mutual funds. On the other hand, if you need your investment money in two years, you should probably invest in short-term government bonds, highly rated corporate bonds, or certificates of deposit. By taking a more conservative approach for short-term investments, you reduce the possibility of having to sell your investments at a loss because of depressed market value or a staggering economy.

YOUR AGE   A final factor to consider when choosing an investment is your age. As mentioned earlier in this chapter, younger investors tend to invest a large percentage of their nest egg in growth-oriented investments. If their investments take a nosedive, they have time to recover. On the other hand, older investors tend to be more conservative and invest in government bonds, high-quality corporate bonds, and very safe corporate stocks or mutual funds. As a result, a smaller percentage of their nest egg is placed in growth-oriented investments. How much of your portfolio should be in growth-oriented investments? Well-known personal financial expert Suze Orman suggests that you subtract your age from 110, and the difference is the percentage of your assets that should be invested in growth investments. For example, if you are 40 years old, subtract 40 from 110, which gives you 70. Therefore, 70 percent of your assets should be invested in growth-oriented investments while the remaining 30 percent should be kept in safer, conservative investments.[8] Instead of using the number 110, some conservative financial planners suggest you begin with the number 100. Regardless of whether you use 100 or 110, the answer is only a guideline that indicates how much of your investment portfolio should be invested in growth-oriented investments or more conservative investments.

AN OVERVIEW OF INVESTMENT ALTERNATIVES

Once you have considered the risks involved when investing, asset allocation, the time factor your investments can work for you, and your age, it's time to consider which investment alternative is right for you. The remainder of this section provides a brief overview of different investment alternatives. The remaining investment chapters provide more detailed information on stocks, bonds, mutual funds, real estate, and other investment alternatives.

STOCK OR EQUITY FINANCING

Equity capital is money that a business obtains from its owners. If a business is a sole proprietorship or a partnership, it acquires equity capital when the owners invest their own money in the business. For a corporation, equity capital is provided by stockholders, who buy shares of its stock. Since all stockholders are owners, they share in the success of the corporation. This can make buying stock an attractive investment opportunity.

equity capital Money that a business obtains from its owners.

Advice from a Pro

DON'T COUNT ON SOCIAL SECURITY WHEN IT'S TIME TO RETIRE!

Lately, there has been a lot of discussion about Social Security and ways to keep the system solvent. The fact is that even with changes, the benefits you receive from Social Security will not enable you to live the "good life" once you choose to retire. If you don't believe the above statement, consider the following: According to Mary Beth Franklin, columnist for Kiplinger.com, you'll need 70 to 80 percent of your preretirement income to live comfortably in retirement. That means if you earn $50,000 a year, you will need $35,000 to $40,000 to maintain the same lifestyle you had while working.

At the present time, Social Security provides only about 55 percent of the income of a low-wage earner whose average annual earnings are under $16,000. If your earnings average $70,000, the amount you receive from Social Security will account for only 30 percent of your retirement income. And for high-income individuals that earn $150,000 a year, the percentage drops to 15 percent.

This information underscores the need to begin your own investment program. And there is no better time than now, regardless of your age. Options include contributions to an individual retirement account (IRA) or participating in an employer-sponsored retirement plan. After you have contributed the maximum allowed by the Internal Revenue Service to your IRA and employer-sponsored retirement accounts each year, you can still save and invest additional funds, using asset allocation to choose investments outside your tax-deferred accounts.

For those who don't accumulate enough money to retire, they may be forced to work longer than they would like. Another option is to continue working on a part-time basis two or three days a week. But even with these options, the prime motivation for investing now is to make sure that the decision to keep working is a choice, not a requirement.

Source: Mary Beth Franklin, "Retire in Style," Kiplinger.com, March 2005, www.kiplinger.com, April 17, 2005.

However, you should consider at least two factors before investing in stock. First, a corporation is not required to repay the money obtained from the sale of stock or to repurchase the stock at a later date. Assume you purchased 100 shares of Southwest Airlines stock. Later you decide to sell your Southwest stock. Your stock is sold to another investor, not back to the company. In many cases, a stockholder sells a stock because he or she thinks its price is going to decrease in value. The purchaser, on the other hand, buys that stock because he or she thinks its price is going to increase. This creates a situation in which either the seller or the buyer earns a profit while the other party to the transaction experiences a loss.

Second, a corporation is under no legal obligation to pay dividends to stockholders. A **dividend** is a distribution of money, stock, or other property that a corporation pays to stockholders. Dividends are paid out of earnings, but if a corporation that usually pays dividends has a bad year, its board of directors can vote to omit dividend payments to help pay necessary business expenses. Corporations may also retain earnings to make additional financing available for expansion, research and product development, or other business activities.

dividend A distribution of money, stock, or other property that a corporation pays to stockholders.

There are two basic types of stock: *common stock* and *preferred stock*. Both types have advantages and disadvantages that you should consider before deciding which to use for an investment program. A share of common stock represents the most basic form of corporate ownership. People often purchase common stock because this type of investment can provide (1) a source of income if the company pays dividends, (2) growth potential if the dollar value of the stock increases, and (3) growth potential if the company splits its common stock. Be warned: There are no guarantees that a stock's value will go up after a split.

The most important priority an investor in preferred stock enjoys is receiving cash dividends before common stockholders are paid any cash dividends. This factor is especially important when a corporation is experiencing financial problems and cannot pay cash dividends to both preferred and common stockholders. Other factors you should consider before purchasing either common or preferred stock are discussed in Chapter 14.

CORPORATE AND GOVERNMENT BONDS

There are two types of bonds an investor should consider. A **corporate bond** is a corporation's written pledge to repay a specified amount of money, along with interest. A **government bond** is the written pledge of a government or a municipality to repay a specified sum of money, along with interest. Thus, when you buy a bond, you are loaning a corporation or government entity money for a period of time. Regardless of who issues the bond, you need to consider two major questions before investing in bonds. First, will the bond be repaid at maturity? The maturity dates for most bonds range between 1 and 30 years. An investor who purchases a bond has two options: keep the bond until maturity and then redeem it, or sell the bond to another investor before maturity. In either case, the value of the bond is closely tied to the ability of the corporation or government agency to repay the bond at maturity. Second, will the corporation or government entity be able to maintain interest payments to bondholders until maturity? Bondholders normally receive interest payments every six months. Again, if a corporation or government agency cannot pay the interest on its bonds, the value of those bonds will decrease.

Receiving periodic interest payments until maturity is one method of making money on a bond investment. Investors also use two other methods that can provide more liberal returns on bond investments. Chapter 15 discusses each of these methods.

corporate bond A corporation's written pledge to repay a specified amount of money, along with interest.

government bond The written pledge of a government or a municipality to repay a specified sum of money, along with interest.

MUTUAL FUNDS

A **mutual fund** is an investment alternative chosen by people who pool their money to buy stocks, bonds, and other securities selected by professional managers employed by an investment company. Professional management is an especially important factor for investors with little or no previous experience in financial matters. Another reason investors choose mutual funds is *diversification*. Since mutual funds invest in a number of different securities, an occasional loss in one security is often offset by gains in other securities. As a result, the diversification provided by a mutual fund reduces risk.

The goals of one investor often differ from those of another. The managers of mutual funds realize this and tailor their funds to meet individual needs and objectives. As a result of all the different investment alternatives, mutual funds range from very conservative to extremely speculative investments.

Although investing money in a mutual fund provides professional management, even the best managers can make errors in judgment. The responsibility for choosing the right mutual fund is still based on the investor's evaluation of a mutual fund investment. While mutual funds offer professional management and diversification, there are at least two specific problems for mutual fund investors. First, almost all investment companies allow you to reinvest income you receive from a mutual fund during a tax year. Even though you didn't receive cash because you chose to reinvest the income, it is still taxable. Second, mutual funds buy and sell securities within the fund's portfolio on a regular basis during any tax year. At the end of the year, profits that result from the mutual fund's buying and selling activities are paid to shareholders and are taxable. Unlike investments you manage, you have no control over when the mutual fund sells securities and when you will be taxed. To postpone taxation of income and profits from mutual fund investments, you may want to consider purchasing mutual fund shares that are part of an individual retirement account or retirement plan sponsored by your employer. Chapter 16 presents more information on the different types of mutual funds, the costs involved, and techniques for evaluating mutual fund investments.

mutual fund An investment alternative chosen by people who pool their money to buy stocks, bonds, and other securities selected by professional managers employed by an investment company.

REAL ESTATE

As a rule, real estate increases in value and eventually sells at a profit, but there are no guarantees. Although many beginning investors believe real estate values increase by 10 or 15 percent a year, in reality the nationwide average annual increase is about 3 percent. This growth rate makes real estate a long-term investment and not a get-rich-quick scheme.

Success in real estate investments depends on how well you evaluate alternatives. Experts often tell would-be investors that the three most important factors when evaluating a potential real estate investment are *location, location,* and *location.* While location may be the most important factor, other factors may determine whether or not a piece of real estate is a good investment. For example, you should answer the following questions before making a decision to purchase any property:

1. Is the property priced competitively with similar properties?

2. What type of financing is available, if any?

3. How much are the taxes?

4. What is the condition of the buildings and houses in the immediate area?

5. Why are the present owners selling the property?

6. Is there a chance that the property will decrease in value?

Any investment has disadvantages, and real estate is no exception. Poor location can cause a piece of property to decrease in value. And finding a buyer can be difficult if loan money is scarce, the real estate market is in a decline, or you overpaid for the property. If you are forced to hold your investment longer than you originally planned, you must also consider taxes and loan payments. Chapter 17 presents additional information on how to evaluate a real estate investment.

OTHER INVESTMENT ALTERNATIVES

As defined earlier in this chapter, a speculative investment is a high-risk investment made in the hope of earning a relatively large profit in a short time. By its very nature, any investment may be speculative; that is, it may be quite risky. However, a true speculative investment is speculative because of the methods investors use to earn a quick profit. Typical speculative investments include

- Options
- Commodities
- Precious metals and gemstones
- Coins and stamps
- Antiques and collectibles

Without exception, investments of this kind are normally referred to as speculative for one reason or another. For example, the gold market has many unscrupulous dealers who sell worthless gold-plated lead coins to unsuspecting, uninformed investors. With any speculative investment, it is extremely important to deal with reputable dealers and recognized investment firms. It pays to be careful. While investments in this category can lead to large dollar gains, they should not be used by anyone who does not fully understand the risks involved. Chapter 14 presents information on options. Chapter 17 discusses precious metals, gemstones, and collectibles.

A PERSONAL PLAN FOR INVESTING

Earlier in this chapter, we examined how safety, risk, income, growth, and liquidity affect your investment choices. In the preceding section we looked at investment alternatives. Now let's compare the factors that affect the choice of investments with each alternative. Exhibit 13–4 ranks the alternatives in terms of safety, risk, income, growth, and liquidity.

		Factors to Be Evaluated				
	Type of Investment	Safety	Risk	Income	Growth	Liquidity
Traditional investments	Common stock	Average	Average	Average	High	Average
	Preferred stock	Average	Average	High	Average	Average
	Corporate bonds	Average	Average	High	Low	Average
	Government bonds	High	Low	Low	Low	High
	Mutual funds	Average	Average	Average	Average	Average
	Real estate	Average	Average	Average	Average	Low
Speculative investments	Options	Low	High	N/A	Low	Average
	Commodities	Low	High	N/A	Low	Average
	Precious metals, gemstones, antiques, and collectibles	Low	High	N/A	Low	Low

N/A = Not applicable.

Exhibit 13–4

Factors used to evaluate typical investment alternatives

With this type of information, it is now possible to begin building a personal plan for investing. Most people use a series of steps like those listed in Exhibit 13–5. And while each step is important, establishing investment goals (step 1), evaluating risk and potential return for each investment alternative (step 5), and continued evaluation (step 8) may be the most important. Although your investment plan may be quite different from someone else's plan, the steps in Exhibit 13–5 will help you follow through and obtain your investment goals. Often the follow-through is the most important component when it comes to developing a successful long-term investment plan. Simply put: How important are your investment goals, and are you willing to work to attain them?

1. Establish your investment goals.
2. Determine the amount of money you need to obtain your goals.
3. Specify the amount of money you currently have available to fund your investments.
4. List different investments that you want to evaluate.
5. Evaluate (a) the risk factor and (b) the potential return for all investments.
6. Reduce possible investments to a reasonable number.
7. Choose at least two different investments.
8. Continue to evaluate your investment program.

Exhibit 13–5

Steps for effective investment planning

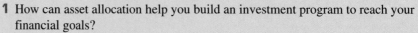

Factors That Reduce Investment Risk

Objective 4

Recognize the importance of your role in a personal investment program.

In this section, we examine the factors that can spell the difference between success and failure for an investor. We begin by considering your role in the investment process.

YOUR ROLE IN THE INVESTMENT PROCESS

Let's assume you have $25,000 to invest. Also assume your investment will earn a 10 percent return the first year. At the end of one year, you will have earned $2,500 and your investment will be worth $27,500. Not a bad return on your original investment! Now ask yourself: How long would it take to earn $2,500 if I had to work for this amount of money at a job? For some people, it might take a month; for others, it might take longer. The point is that if you want this type of return, you should be willing to work for it, but the work takes a different form than a job. When choosing an investment, the work you invest is the time it takes to research different investments so that you can make an informed decision.

Some people invest large sums of money and never research the investments they purchase. Obviously, this is a flawed approach that can lead to large dollar losses. On the other hand, an informed investor has a much better chance of choosing the types of investments that will increase in value. In fact, much of the information in the remaining investment chapters will help you learn how to evaluate different investment opportunities. But you have to be willing to work and learn if you want to be a successful investor. As you will see in the next section, evaluation doesn't stop once you make a decision to purchase an investment. It continues as long as you own the investment.

MONITOR THE VALUE OF YOUR INVESTMENTS
Would you believe that some people invest large sums of money and don't know what their investments are worth? They don't know if their investments have increased or decreased in value. They don't know if they should sell their investments or continue to hold them. A much better approach is to monitor the value of your investments. If you choose to invest in stocks, bonds, mutual funds, commodities, or options, you can determine the value of your holdings by looking at the price quotations reported on the Internet, on cable financial news programs, and in newspapers. Your real estate holdings may be compared with similar properties currently for sale in the surrounding area. Finally, you can determine the value of your precious metals, gemstones, and collectibles by checking with reputable dealers and investment firms. Regardless of which type of investment you choose, close surveillance will keep you informed of whether your investment increases

Financial Planning Calculations

MONITORING THE VALUE OF YOUR INVESTMENT

To monitor the value of their investments, many investors use a simple chart like the one illustrated here. To construct a chart like this one, place the original purchase price of your investment on the side of the chart. Then use price increments of a logical amount to show increases and decreases in dollar value.

Place individual dates along the bottom of the chart. For stocks, bonds, mutual funds, and similar investments, you may want to graph every two weeks and chart current values on, say, a Friday. For longer-term investments like real estate, you can chart current values every six months. It is

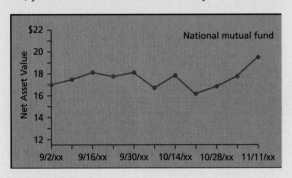

also possible to use computer software to chart the value of your investments.

In addition to graphing your stock, you can calculate the percentage of increase or decrease from one period to another period. For example, if the value of a share of Home Depot stock is $40 on January 1 and a share of the same stock is $47 on December 31, the percentage of increase is 17.5 percent, as illustrated below.

$$\$47 \text{ (ending value)} - \$40 \text{ (beginning value)} = \$7 \text{ (increase)}$$

$$\$7 \text{ (increase)} \div \$40 \text{ (beginning value)} = 0.175 = 17.5\% \text{ (percentage increase)}$$

A WORD OF CAUTION

If an investment is beginning to have a large increase or decrease in value, you should watch that investment more closely. You can still continue to chart at regular intervals, but you may want to check dollar values more frequently—in some cases, daily. You may also want to calculate the percentage of increase or decrease more frequently.

---

or decreases in value. The Financial Planning Calculations box on this page presents further information on monitoring the value of your investments.

KEEP ACCURATE AND CURRENT RECORDS   Accurate recordkeeping can help you spot opportunities to maximize profits or reduce dollar losses when you sell your investments. Accurate recordkeeping can also help you decide whether you want to invest additional funds in a particular investment. At the very least, you should keep purchase records for each of your investments that include the actual dollar cost of the investment, plus any commissions or fees you paid, along with records of income (dividends, interest payments, rental income, etc.) you receive from your investment holdings. It is also useful to keep a list of the sources of information (Internet addresses, business periodicals, research publications, etc.), along with copies of the material you used to evaluate each investment. Then, when it is time to reevaluate an existing investment, you will know where to begin your search for current information. Accurate recordkeeping is also necessary for tax purposes.

OTHER FACTORS THAT IMPROVE INVESTMENT DECISIONS

To achieve their financial goals, many people seek professional help. In many cases, they turn to stockbrokers, lawyers, accountants, bankers, or insurance agents. However, these professionals are specialists in one specific field and may not be qualified to provide the type of advice required to develop a thorough financial plan. Another source of

Wise advice! Often, investors must consult with professionals to develop an investment program.

investment help is a financial planner who has had training in securities, insurance, taxes, real estate, and estate planning. For more information on choosing a financial planner and the type of services she or he provides, you may want to review the material in Appendix A at the end of the text.

For more information about how taxes affect your investment decisions, visit the Internal Revenue Service Web site at **www.irs.gov.**

Regardless of whether you are making your own decisions or have professional help, you must consider the tax consequences of selling your investments. Taxes were covered in Chapter 4, and it is not our intention to cover them again. And yet, it is your responsibility to determine how taxes affect your investment decisions. You may want to review the material on dividend, interest, and rental income and on gains and losses that result from selling an investment. You may also want to read the material on tax-deferred investment income and retirement planning presented in Chapter 18.

CONCEPT CHECK 13-4

1 What is your role in the investment process?
2 Why should you monitor the value of your investment?
3 Assume that you have $10,000 that can be invested. Would you make your own decisions or seek professional help? Explain your answer.

Action Application Using Internet research, describe the services provided by a financial planner. How are they usually compensated?

Sources of Investment Information

Objective 5

Use various sources of financial information that can reduce risks and increase investment returns.

With most investments, more information is available than you can read and comprehend. Therefore, you must be selective in the type of information you use for evaluation purposes. With some investments, however, only a limited amount of information is available. For example, a wealth of information is available on individual stocks and mutual funds, whereas the amount of information on a metal such as cobalt or manganese may be limited to one source. Regardless of the number or availability of sources, always determine how reliable and accurate the information is. Following are sources of information you can use to evaluate present and future investments.

THE INTERNET

Today more people have access to information provided by computers located in their homes or at libraries, universities, or businesses than ever before. And this number is growing. More important, a wealth of information is available on most personal finance topics and different investment alternatives. For example, you can obtain interest rates for certificates of deposit; current price information for stocks, bonds, and mutual funds; and brokers' recommendations to buy, hold, or sell a corporation's stock. You can even trade securities online just by pushing the right button on your computer keyboard. You can also use computers and financial planning software to develop a personal financial plan.

One of the most widely used search engines in the world, Yahoo! also provides a wealth of investment info. Visit their Web site at **finance.yahoo.com.**

To use your computer to generate information you really need, you must be selective. One of the best ways to access needed information is to use a search engine. Search engines like Yahoo!, Ask Jeeves, and Google allow you to do a word search for either the personal finance topic or investment alternative that you want to explore. Federal, state, and local governments; brokerage firms and investment companies; banks and other financial institutions; and most corporations also have a home page where you can obtain valuable investment information. It is also possible to use an Internet service provider like America Online or Microsoft Network. These companies usually provide subscribers with access to a broad range of information on a variety of topics including personal finance and investments as well as a connection to the Internet. While it is impossible to list all the Internet sites related to personal finance, those listed in Exhibit 13–6 will get you started. We will examine other specific Internet sites in the remaining investment chapters. Also, read Appendix A at the end of the text for information on how to use the Internet for personal financial planning.

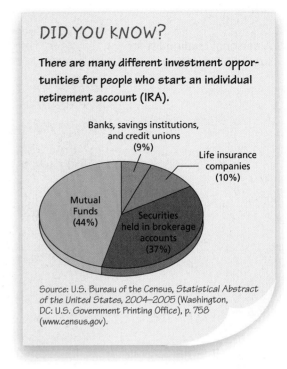

DID YOU KNOW?

There are many different investment opportunities for people who start an individual retirement account (IRA).

Banks, savings institutions, and credit unions (9%)

Life insurance companies (10%)

Mutual Funds (44%)

Securities held in brokerage accounts (37%)

Source: U.S. Bureau of the Census, *Statistical Abstract of the United States, 2004–2005* (Washington, DC: U.S. Government Printing Office), p. 758 (www.census.gov).

NEWSPAPERS AND NEWS PROGRAMS

One of the most readily available sources of information for the average investor is the financial page of a metropolitan newspaper or the *Wall Street Journal*. There you will find a summary of the day's trading on the New York Stock Exchange, the American Stock Exchange, and the Nasdaq over-the-counter market. In addition to stock coverage, most newspapers

Exhibit 13-6

Useful Internet sites for personal financial planning

These five Internet sites provide information that you can use to establish a financial plan and begin an investment program.

Sponsor and Description	Web Address
The **CNN/Money** Web site provides current financial news and material that can help investors sharpen their investment skills.	money.cnn.com
The **Kiplinger** Web site contains a number of tools to help beginners become better investors. This site also allows users to track investments and screen both stocks and mutual funds.	www.kiplinger.com
The **Money Central** Web site provides people with information about personal finance, investing, banking, financial and retirement planning, and taxes.	www.moneycentral.com
The **Motley Fool** Web site provides lighthearted but excellent educational materials if you want to learn more about financial planning and investments.	www.fool.com
The **Quicken** Web site provides information about investments, home mortgages, insurance, taxes, banking and credit, and retirement programs.	www.quicken.com

Exhibit **13–7**

A personal reading list for successful investing

While individual investors have their favorite sources for investment information, it is quite likely that most successful investors use some of the following newspapers, periodicals, and news programs on a regular basis.

Newspapers

- Metropolitan newspapers—published daily
- *The Wall Street Journal*—published Monday through Friday each week
- *USA Today*—published daily
- *The New York Times*—published daily

Television

- CNN—ongoing
- CNBC—ongoing

Business and General Periodicals

- *Barron's*—published weekly
- *Business Week*—published weekly
- *Fortune*—published twice a month
- *Forbes*—published twice a month
- *Newsweek*—published weekly
- *U.S. News & World Report*—published weekly

Personal Financial Publications

- *Kiplinger's Personal Finance Magazine*—published monthly
- *Money*—published monthly
- *Smart Money*—published monthly
- *Worth*—published monthly

provide information on mutual funds, corporate and government bonds, commodities and options, and general economic news. Detailed information on how to read price quotations for stocks, bonds, mutual funds, and other investments is presented in the remaining investment chapters.

It is also possible to obtain economic and investment information on radio or television. Many stations broadcast investment market summaries and economic information as part of their regular news programs. Cable providers like CNN and CNBC provide ongoing market coverage, investment information, and economic news. See Exhibit 13–7 for publications and news programs used by successful investors.

BUSINESS PERIODICALS AND GOVERNMENT PUBLICATIONS

Most business periodicals are published weekly, twice a month, or monthly. *Barron's, BusinessWeek, Fortune, Forbes,* and similar business periodicals provide not only general news about the overall economy but detailed financial information about individual corporations. Some business periodicals—for example, *Advertising Age* and *Business Insurance*—focus on information about the firms in a specific industry. In addition to business periodicals, more general magazines such as *U.S. News & World Report, Time,* and *Newsweek* provide investment information as a regular feature. Finally, *Money,*

Smart Money, Kiplinger's Personal Finance, Worth, and similar periodicals provide information and advice designed to improve your investment skills.

The U.S. government is the world's largest provider of information. Much of this information is of value to investors and is either free or available at minimal cost. U.S. government publications that investors may find useful include the *Federal Reserve Bulletin,* published by the Federal Reserve System, and the *Survey of Current Business,* published by the Department of Commerce.

CORPORATE REPORTS

The federal government requires corporations selling new issues of securities to disclose information about corporate earnings, assets and liabilities, products or services, and the qualifications of top management in a *prospectus* that they must give to investors. In addition to the prospectus, publicly owned corporations send their stockholders an annual report that contains detailed financial data. Annual reports contain a statement of financial position, which describes changes in assets, liabilities, and owners' equity. These reports also include an income statement, which provides dollar amounts for sales, expenses, and profits or losses. Today, most corporate financial information is available on the corporation's Web site.

INVESTOR SERVICES AND NEWSLETTERS

Many stockbrokers and financial planners mail a free monthly or quarterly newsletter to their clients. In addition, investors can subscribe to services that provide investment information. The fees for investor services generally range from $30 to $750 a year.

Five widely used services are available for investors who specialize in stocks, bonds, and mutual funds:

1. *Standard & Poor's Stock Reports.* These up-to-date reports on corporations cover such topics as recommendations, sales and earnings, prospects, recent developments, income statements, and statements of financial position.

2. *Value Line.* These reports supply detailed information about major corporations—earnings, dividends, sales, liabilities, and other financial data.

3. *Mergent.* Mergent's reports help investors evaluate potential investments in corporate securities and provide information similar to that contained in Standard & Poor's and Value Line reports.

4. *Morningstar Investment Reports.* Morningstar tracks thousands of mutual funds and issues monthly reports on safety, financial performance, and other important information that investors can use to evaluate a mutual fund.

5. *Lipper Reports.* The mutual fund information provided by Lipper is similar to Morningstar's detailed reports.

Other publications that may help you evaluate potential investments include Dun & Bradstreet's *Key Business Ratios* and *Hoover's Handbook of American Business.*

In addition to the preceding publications, each of the following securities exchanges provides information through printed materials and the Internet:

- New York Stock Exchange (www.nyse.com).
- Nasdaq market (www.nasdaq.com).
- American Stock Exchange (www.amex.com).
- Chicago Mercantile Exchange (www.cme.com).

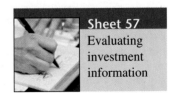

Sheet 57
Evaluating investment information

Each of these Web sites provides basic information about the exchange, offers educational material and a glossary of important terms, and describes how investors can profit from transactions through the exchange.

The preceding discussion of investor services and newsletters is not exhaustive, but it gives you some idea of the amount and scope of the information available to serious investors. Although most small investors find many of the services and newsletters described here too expensive for personal subscriptions, this information may be available from stockbrokers or financial planners. This type of information is also available at many public libraries.

CONCEPT CHECK 13-5

1 What do you think is the most readily available source of information for the average investor? Explain your answer.

2 What type of information can you obtain using the Internet?

3 Briefly describe the additional sources of information you can use to evaluate a potential investment and lessen risk.

Action Application Pick one of the Web sites mentioned in this section and describe the type of information it provides.

SUMMARY OF OBJECTIVES

Objective 1
Describe why you should establish an investment program.
Investment goals must be specific and measurable and should be classified as short term, intermediate, and long term. Before beginning an investment program, you must make sure your personal financial affairs are in order. This process begins with learning to live within your means and obtaining adequate insurance protection. The next step is the accumulation of an emergency fund equal to three to nine months' living expenses. Then, and only then, is it time to save the money needed to establish an investment program. Because of the time value of money, even small investments can grow to substantial amounts over a long period of time.

Objective 2
Assess how safety, risk, income, growth, and liquidity affect your investment decisions.
Although each investor may have specific, individual reasons for investing, all investors must consider the factors of safety, risk, income, growth, and liquidity. Especially important is the relationship between safety and risk. Keep in mind that there is risk associated with all investments. Often, investors may experience two types of risk: a risk you will not receive periodic income payments; and a risk that an investment will decrease in value. As a result, all investors must evaluate their tolerance for risk. Basically, this concept can be summarized as follows: The potential return for any investment should be directly related to the risk the investor assumes. In fact, some investors base their investment decisions on projections for rate of return. You can also use the same calculation to determine how much you actually earn on an investment over a specific period of time.

The risk factor can be broken down into five components: inflation risk, interest rate risk, business failure risk, market risk, and global investment risk. Income, growth, and liquidity may also affect your choice of investments.

Objective 3
Explain how asset allocation and different investment alternatives affect your investment plan.
Asset allocation is the process of spreading your assets among several different types of investments (sometimes referred to as asset classes) to lessen risk. Typical asset classes include large-cap stocks, midcap stocks, small-cap stocks, foreign stocks, bonds, and cash. The percentage of your investments that should be invested in each asset class is determined by your age, investment objectives, ability to tolerate risk, how much you can save and invest each year, the dollar value of your current investments, and the economic outlook for the economy.

Typical long-term investment alternatives include stocks, bonds, mutual funds, and real estate. More speculative investment alternatives include options, commodities, precious metals, gemstones, and collectibles. Before choosing a specific investment, you should evaluate all potential investments on the basis of safety, risk, income, growth, and liquidity. With all of these factors in mind, the next step is to develop a specific, personal investment plan to help you accomplish your goals.

Objective 4
Recognize the importance of your role in a personal investment program.
It is your responsibility to evaluate and to monitor the value of your investments. Accurate recordkeeping can also help you spot opportunities to maximize profits or reduce losses when you sell your investments. These same detailed records can help you decide whether you want to invest additional funds in a particular investment. To achieve their financial goals, many people seek professional help. In many cases, they turn to stockbrokers, lawyers, accountants, bankers, insurance agents, or financial planners. Finally, it is your responsibility to determine how taxes affect your investment decisions.

Objective 5

Use various sources of financial information that can reduce risks and increase investment returns.

Because more information on investments is available than most investors can read and comprehend, you must be selective in the type of information you use for evaluation purposes. Sources of information include the Internet, newspapers and news programs, business periodicals, government publications, corporate reports, and investor services.

KEY FORMULAS

Page	Topic	Formula	
414	Rate of return	Rate of return $= \dfrac{\text{Increase or decrease in value} + \text{Annual income}}{\text{Dollar amount of original investment}}$	
	Example:	Rate of return $= \dfrac{\$200 + \$50}{\$4,000}$	
		$= \dfrac{\$250}{\$4,000}$	
		$= 0.063$	
		$= 6.3\%$	
416	Interest calculation for a corporate bond	Dollar amount of annual interest	$= \text{Issue price} \times \text{Interest rate}$
	Example:	Dollar amount of annual interest	$= \$1,000 \times 7\%$
			$= \$1,000 \times 0.07$
			$= \$70$
416	Approximate market price	Approximate market price	$= \dfrac{\text{Annual interest amount}}{\text{Comparable interest rate}}$
	Example:	Approximate market price	$= \dfrac{\$80}{0.09} \quad \dfrac{\$80}{9\%}$
			$= \$888.89$

KEY TERMS

FINANCIAL PLANNING PROBLEMS

1. *Calculating the Amount for an Emergency Fund.* Beth and Bob Martin have total take-home pay of $3,200 a month. Their monthly expenses total $2,800. Calculate the minimum amount this couple needs to establish an emergency fund. How did you calculate this amount? (Obj. 1)

2. *Using the Yahoo! Finance Web Site.* Visit the Yahoo! Finance web site and describe the material contained in the Education section. To complete this activity, follow these steps: (Obj. 1)

   a. Go to finance.yahoo.com.

   b. Click on the section titled "Education."

   c. Click on the section titled "Investing 101."

   d. Click on one of the articles that are listed. Then, in a one-page report, describe how the information in the article could help you establish an investment program.

   e. Print the article for future reference.

3. *Determining the Time Value of Money.* Using Exhibit 13–1, complete the following table. Then answer the questions that follow the table. Hint: To calculate the amount of interest, subtract the amount of your total investment from the value at the end of the time period. (Obj. 1)

Annual Deposit	Rate of Return	Number of Years	Investment Value at the End of Time Period	Total Amount of Investment	Total Amount of Interest
$2,000	4%	10			
$2,000	10%	10			
$2,000	4%	20			
$2,000	10%	20			

   a. In the above situations, describe the effect that the rate of return has on the investment value at the end of the selected time period.

   b. In the above situations, describe the effect that the number of years has on the investment value at the end of the selected time period.

4. *Calculating Rate of Return.* Assume that at the beginning of the year, you purchase an investment for $6,000 that pays $80 annual income. Also assume the investment's value has increased to $6,900 by the end of the year. (Obj. 2)

   a. What is the rate of return for this investment?

   b. Is the rate of return a positive or negative number?

5. *Calculating Rate of Return.* Assume that at the beginning of the year, you purchase an investment for $8,000 that pays $100 annual income. Also assume the investment's value has decreased to $7,400 by the end of the year. (Obj. 2)

   a. What is the rate of return for this investment?

   b. Is the rate of return a positive or negative number?

6. *Determining Interest and Approximate Bond Value.* Assume that three years ago, you purchased a corporate bond that pays 9.5 percent. The purchase price was $1,000. Also assume that three years after your bond investment, comparable bonds are paying 8 percent. (Obj. 2)

   a. What is the annual dollar amount of interest that you receive from your bond investment?

   b. Assuming that comparable bonds are paying 8 percent, what is the approximate dollar price for which you could sell your bond?

   c. In your own words, explain why your bond increased or decreased in value.

7. *Analyzing Income and Growth Investments.*

   a. List three personal factors that might lead some investors to emphasize income rather than growth in their investment planning.

   b. List three personal factors that might lead some investors to emphasize growth rather than income. (Obj. 2)

8. *Using Asset Allocation to Diversify Risk.* Assume you are 59 years old, want to retire in 6 years, and currently have an investment portfolio valued at $550,000 invested in technology stocks. After talking with friends and relatives, you have decided that you have "too many eggs in one basket." Based on this information, use the asset allocation method described in this chapter and the table below to diversify your investment portfolio. Then answer the questions below. (Obj. 3)

Investment Alternative	Percentage You Would Like in This Category
Large-cap stocks	
Midcap stocks	
Small-cap stocks	
Foreign stocks	
Government bonds	
Corporate bonds	
Cash	
Other investment (specify type)	
	100%

   a. What are the advantages of asset allocation?

   b. How could the time your investments have to work for you and your age affect your asset allocation?

9. *Comparing Investment Alternatives.* Choose three of the investment alternatives presented in this chapter, then rank them from high to low on safety, risk, and liquidity. Assume that 3 is the highest score and 1 is the lowest score for each factor. Based on your ranking, which of the three alternatives would you choose for your own investment program? Why? (Obj. 3)

10. *Developing a Financial Plan.* Assume you are single and have graduated from college. Your monthly take-home pay is $2,100, and your monthly expenses total $1,800, leaving you with a monthly surplus of $300. Develop a personal plan of action for investing using the steps listed in Exhibit 13–5. (Obj. 3)

11. *Monitoring an Investment's Financial Performance.* Based on the following information, construct a graph that illustrates price movement for a share of the Davis New York Venture Mutual Fund. Note: You may want to review the material presented in the Financial Planning Calculations feature on page 427. (Obj. 4)

January	$28.70	July	$26.10
February	28.00	August	25.50
March	30.30	September	26.40
April	31.35	October	26.90
May	29.50	November	28.40
June	27.80	December	27.20

12. *Using Financial Information.* Suppose you just inherited 500 shares of General Motors stock. List five sources of information you could use to evaluate your inheritance. Beside each source, briefly state how the information it contains could help in your evaluation. (Obj. 5)

FINANCIAL PLANNING ACTIVITIES

1. *Using Investment Information.* Choose a current issue of *Kiplinger's Personal Finance* or *Money* and summarize an article that provides suggestions on how you could use your money more effectively. (Obj. 1)

2. *Planning for an Investment Program.* Assume you are 28 years old, your take-home pay totals $2,200 a month, you have monthly living expenses that total $1,200, your monthly car payment is $300, and your credit card debts total $4,900. Using the information presented in this chapter, develop a three-part plan to (a) reduce your monthly expense, (b) establish an emergency fund, and (c) save $4,000 to establish an investment program. (Obj. 1)

3. *Using the Internet to Obtain Information about Money Management.* As pointed out at the beginning of this chapter, it doesn't make sense to establish an investment program until credit card and installment purchases are reduced or eliminated. While most people are responsible and make payments when they're supposed to, some people get in trouble. To help avoid this problem, each of the following organizations has a home page on the Internet:

   Myvesta—The Financial Health Center provides information about how to manage consumer debt (http://myvesta.org).

   Equifax provides information about how you can obtain your credit report (www.equifax.com).

   Choose one of the above organizations and visit its home page. Then prepare a report that summarizes the information provided by the organization. Finally, indicate if this information could help you manage your consumer debt. (Obj. 1)

4. *Choosing Investment Alternatives.* From the investment alternatives described in this chapter, choose two specific investments you believe would help an individual who is 35 years old, is divorced, and earns $27,000 a year begin an investment program. Assume this person has $30,000 to invest at this time. As part of your recommendation, compare each of your investment suggestions on safety, risk, income, growth, and liquidity. (Obj. 2)

5. *Choosing Investment Alternatives.* Choose one of the investment alternatives presented in this chapter (stocks, bonds, mutual funds, real estate, or speculative investments) and prepare a two-page report describing why this investment would be appropriate for a woman who is 68 years old and has just lost her husband. Assume she is debt free and has inherited $175,000. (Obj. 3)

6. *Explaining the Principle of Asset Allocation.* Prepare a two-minute presentation describing why the principle of asset allocation is important when establishing an investment program. (Obj. 3)

7. *Using Financial Information to Track the Value of an Investment.* Choose one stock and one mutual fund investment. Using the Internet, the *Wall Street Journal,* or your local newspaper, track the value of both investments for a two-week period. Then construct a graph that illustrates the changes in each investment's value over the two-week period. In a one-page report, indicate whether either of the two investments would have been a good investment over the two-week time period. Explain your answer. (Obj. 4)

8. *Using Investment Information.* Assume you have established an emergency fund and have saved an additional $12,000 to fund an investment in common stock issued by SBC Corporation. Using the sources of information discussed in this chapter, go to the library and obtain information about this company. Summarize your findings in a three-page report describing SBC's current operations and the firm's past and present financial performance. Finally, indicate whether you would purchase SBC common stock based on the information in your report. (Obj. 5)

9. *Using the Internet to Obtain Investment Information.* One of the most useful Internet investment Web sites available is the Motley Fool. Visit the Motley Fool site (www.fool.com). Then describe in a two-page report the type of information available and how it could help you become a better investor. (Obj. 5)

INTERNET CONNECTION

Researching the Topics of Investment Planning and Asset Allocation

Use the Internet to research the following topics, determine the type of information that is available, and determine how it might affect your investment decisions.

Investment Planning   Web sources: _____

Type of information available: _____

Possible influence on your investment decisions: _____

_____

Asset Allocation   Web Sources: _____

Type of information available: _____

Possible influence on your investment decisions: _____

FINANCIAL PLANNING CASE

First Budget, Then Invest for Success!

Joe and Mary Garner, married 12 years, have an eight-year-old child. Six years ago, they purchased a home on which they owe about $110,000. They also owe $6,000 on their two-year-old automobile. All of their furniture is paid for, but they owe a total of $4,120 on two credit cards. Joe is employed as an engineer and makes $54,000 a year. Mary works as a part-time computer analyst and earns about $22,000 a year. Their combined monthly income after deductions is $4,520.

About six months ago, the Garners had what they now describe as a "financial meltdown." It all started one Monday afternoon when their air conditioner stopped cooling. Since their home was only six years old, they thought the repair ought to be a simple one—until the repair technician diagnosed their problem as a defective compressor. Unfortunately, the warranty on the compressor had run out about three months before the compressor broke down. According to the technician, it would cost over $1,200 to replace the compressor. At the time, they had about $2,000 in their savings account, which they had been saving for their summer vacation, and now they had to use their vacation money to fix the air conditioner.

For the Garners, the fact that they didn't have enough money to take a vacation was like a wake-up call. They realized they were now in their mid-30s and had serious cash problems. According to Joe, "We don't waste money, but there just never seems to be enough money to do the things we want to do." But according to Mary, "The big problem is that we never have enough money to start an investment program that could pay for our daughter's college education or fund our retirement."

They decided to take a "big" first step in an attempt to solve their financial problems. They began by examining their monthly expenses for the past month. Here's what they found:

Income (cash inflow)		
Joe's take-home salary	$3,150	
Mary's take-home salary	1,370	
Total income		$4,520

Cash outflows		
Monthly fixed expenses:		
Home mortgage payment, including taxes and insurance	$1,190	
Automobile loan	315	
Automobile insurance	130	
Life insurance premium	50	
Total fixed expenses		$1,685

Monthly variable expenses:		
Food and household necessities	$680	
Electricity	140	
Natural gas	75	
Water	35	
Telephone	80	
Family clothing allowance	230	
Gasoline and automobile repairs	145	
Personal and health care	150	
Recreation and entertainment	700	
Gifts and donations	300	
Minimum payment on credit cards	80	
Total variable expenses		$2,615

Total monthly expenses		**$4,300**
Surplus for savings or investments		**$220**

Once the Garners realized they had a $220 surplus each month, they began to replace the $1,200 they had taken from their savings account to pay for repairing the air conditioner. Now it was time to take the next step.

Questions

1. How would you rate the financial status of the Garners before the air conditioner broke down?

2. The Garners' take-home pay is over $4,500 a month. Yet, after all expenses are paid, there is only a $220 surplus each month. Based on the information presented in this case, what expenses, if any, seem out of line and could be reduced to increase the surplus at the end of each month?

3. Given that both Joe and Mary Garner are in their mid-30s and want to retire when they reach age 65, what type of investment goals would be most appropriate for them?

4. How does the time value of money and the asset allocation concept affect the types of long-term goals and the investments that a couple like the Garners might use to build their financial nest egg?

5. Based on the different investments described in this chapter, what specific types of investments (stocks, mutual funds, real estate, etc.) would you recommend for the Garners? Why?

VIDEO CASE

Fundamentals of Investing

Why do we spend so much time on financial planning in this course?

Good question. Now for some answers. The fact is that a personal financial course is all about planning and investing. As illustrated in the video, personal financial planning is important because it allows you to manage your money to achieve personal economic satisfaction and provides funding for your investment program. The first step is always to perform a financial checkup. Specifically, you should

1. Develop a budget and determine if you can live within it.

2. Make sure you are adequately insured.

3. Establish an emergency fund.

Once you have completed the financial checkup and made any necessary changes in your spending patterns, you can establish investment goals. Factors that influence your investment goals include your age, how long before you need the money, and your tolerance for risk.

Based on your goals, and assuming you have accumulated the money needed to fund your investment program, it's time to make some investment decisions. Most beginning investors think all they have to do is find one good investment. Unfortunately, that's not true. A much better approach is to use asset allocation to minimize your risk. A simple definition of asset allocation is putting your investment dollars into different baskets. Separate "baskets" might include cash, stocks, bonds, mutual funds, and other investment alternatives. Specific investments within each category are chosen based on the individual investor's attitude toward safety and risk. As pointed out in the video and the text, safety in an investment means minimal risk of loss, while risk in an investment means a measure of uncertainty about the outcome. Today most investors break the risk factor into different components.

In addition to analyzing the risk/reward offered by different investment alternatives, many investors research different investment alternatives by visiting a college or public library or using the Internet. Other investors choose to use a financial planner, an investment manager, or other professionals. Once a decision to purchase a specific investment is made, good investors continue to evaluate their investments by monitoring the investments' value, keeping accurate records, performing financial calculations, and revising their goals if necessary. In some cases, it is necessary to sell one investment and purchase another.

Questions

1. Assume you were just notified that you have inherited $5,000. What would you do with the money? Justify your answer.

2. Many individuals choose their own investments. Others use a financial planner, an investment manager, or other professional. Which approach seems right for you? How would you go about choosing a professional to help you make investment decisions?

3. As pointed out in the video case, an informed investor is a wise investor. Choose a specific investment alternative, and describe the types of information you could use to evaluate it. Where would you get this information?

YOUR PERSONAL FINANCIAL PLANNER IN ACTION

Developing an Investment Plan

An investment program should consider safety, current income, growth potential, liquidity, and taxes. Your ability to set financial goals and select investment vehicles is crucial to long-term financial prosperity.

Your Short-Term Financial Planning Activities	Resources
1. Set investment goals for various financial needs	PFP Sheet 55 http://beginnersinvest.about.com www.investopedia.com www.fool.com www.aaii.org
2. Assess various types of investments for market risk, inflation, interest rate risk, and liquidity	PFP Sheet 56 www.bloomberg.com www.marketwatch.com
3. Identify and evaluate investment information sources.	PFP Sheet 57 www.invest-faq.com www.nasd.com www.sec.gov
Your Long-Term Financial Planning Activities	
1. Identify saving and investing decisions that would serve your changing life situations.	www.better-investing.org www.money.com
2. Develop a plan for revising investments as family and household situations change.	Text pages 426–428 www.quicken.com

CONTINUING CASE

Investment Foundations

Life Situation
   Pam, 43
   Josh, 45
   Children ages 16, 14, and 11

Financial Data
   Monthly income $4,900
   Living expenses $4,450
   Emergency fund $5,000
   Assets $262,700
   Liabilities $84,600

With approximately 20 years to retirement, Pam and Josh Brock want to establish a more aggressive investment program to accumulate funds for their long-term financial needs. Josh does have a retirement program at work. This money, about $110,000, is invested in various conservative mutual funds.

In addition, the Brocks established their own investment program about four years ago, and today they have about $36,000 invested in conservative stocks and mutual funds. In addition to their investment program, the Brocks have accumulated $11,000 to help pay for the children's college educations. Also, they have $5,000 tucked away in a savings account that serves as the family's emergency fund. Finally, both will qualify for Social Security when they reach retirement age.

Questions

1. What would you view as the strengths and weaknesses of the Brocks' financial situation at this stage in their lives?

2. Given that Pam is 43 and Josh is 45 and they have three children who will soon begin their college educations, what investment goals would be most appropriate?

3. Describe a preliminary investment portfolio for the Brocks. Suggest *specific* investments and explain risks associated with each.

4. Describe how the Brocks might use *Personal Financial Planner* sheets 55–57 for planning investments.

14 Investing in Stocks

Key Concept

Investors who want their investments to grow often choose stocks because of the historically high returns provided by this investment alternative over a long period of time. This chapter provides the information you need to become a better stock investor.

Learning Objectives

1 Identify the most important features of common and preferred stocks.

2 Explain how you can evaluate stock investments.

3 Analyze the numerical measures that cause a stock to increase or decrease in value.

4 Describe how stocks are bought and sold.

5 Explain the trading techniques used by long-term investors and short-term speculators.

Investing the "Big Apple" Way

Back in 2003, Matt Ryan went to New York City for a long weekend. Initially, this trip was for fun and relaxation—a time to kick back and enjoy the Big Apple. Now, over three years later, Matt says the trip turned his life around. According to Matt, it all began on Saturday morning when he took a tour of the city and saw the financial district. Among other buildings, the tour guide pointed out the New York Stock Exchange (NYSE) building located at the corner of Broad and Wall Streets. Founded in 1792, the NYSE is one of the largest stock exchanges in the world, with more than 2,700 companies listed on the exchange today.

Although Matt was impressed with the memorials at Ground Zero where the twin towers once stood, the Empire State building, the theaters on Broadway, and the other sites on the guided tour, he kept thinking about the NYSE. All that money! There had to be a way for him to invest and experience part of the American dream.

Even after Matt returned home, he still remembered that large, impressive NYSE building. He still had thoughts of becoming rich overnight just by purchasing stock. It all seemed so easy, but that's when reality set in. He quickly realized he didn't know anything about stocks. Although he had $3,000 that could be used to fund an investment pro-gram, he didn't want to take chances. Even the thought of losing that much money was frightening.

According to Matt, it had taken him over two years to save his $3,000 nest egg, and he wanted to make sure he knew something about stock investing before he took the plunge. He began his search for educational materials by accessing the NYSE Web site. In the investor education section, he found basic material about investing, including information on the differences between stocks, bonds, and mutual funds. The site also described different types of stocks that could be used to obtain different investment goals. Then he learned about the steps involved when buying or selling stocks. While exploring the Web site, he also realized he could track the value of his portfolio—once he made his decision to actually buy individual stocks.

When he took the time to look at his watch, he had spent more than two-and-a-half hours just getting basic information about stocks and how the exchange worked, but still didn't have a clue about which companies represented quality investments. It seemed that he had only scratched the surface, and he still had much more to learn. But the funny thing was that he looked forward to learning more.

Source: New York Stock Exchange, www.nyse.com, April 17, 2005.

QUESTIONS

What Actions Should Be Taken?

1. Why do you think people believe stock investing is an easy way to become rich?
2. Often investors purchase stocks without learning anything about the company that issued the stock. Why is this a flawed approach?

What about Your Situation?

In order to invest money in any type of investment, you have to have some money.

3. Consider your own personal situation. Then describe the steps you should take to establish an investment program.
4. When you invest in stocks, there is a risk that you could lose part or all of your original investment. What can you do to reduce the risk involved with stock investments?

Learn More Online

Based on the information at www.nyse.com, describe the types of available information that will help you learn how to purchase stocks and become a more knowledgeable investor.

Common and Preferred Stocks

Objective 1

Identify the most important features of common and preferred stocks.

Should you invest in stocks? Well, that's a difficult question to answer! The truth is that investing in stocks offers larger potential returns than other investment alternatives, but there is more risk involved. And you should know the risks are real. You can lose part or all of your money. Matt Ryan, the investor profiled in the opening case, realized that there was more to investing than just picking a stock and sitting back and letting the profits roll in. Early on, Matt knew he had to learn something about investing before investing his $3,000 nest egg. That's when he accessed the New York Stock Exchange Web site to learn more about stocks and how the exchange helps people buy and sell stocks.

Today, investors—especially beginning investors—face two concerns when they begin an investment program. First, they don't know where to get the information they need to evaluate potential investments. In reality, more information is available than most investors can read. As crazy as it sounds, there are investors who invest in stocks without doing any research at all. Unfortunately, these same uninformed investors often lose money on their investments. As we begin this chapter, you should know that there is no substitute for quality information about a potential investment. *Simply put, good investors know something about the company before they invest their money in the company's stock.*

Second, beginning investors sometimes worry that they won't know what the information means when they do find it. Yet common sense goes a long way when evaluating potential investments. For example, consider the following questions:

1. Is an increase in sales revenues a healthy sign for a corporation? (Answer: yes)
2. Should a firm's net income increase or decrease over time? (Answer: increase)
3. Should a corporation's earnings per share increase or decrease over time? (Answer: increase)

Although the answers to these questions are obvious, you will find more detailed answers to these and other questions in this chapter. In fact, that's what this chapter is all about. We want you to learn how to evaluate a stock and to make money from your investment decisions.

Today a lot of people buy and sell stocks. Why? The most obvious answer is simple: They want larger returns than those more conservative investments offer. As pointed out in the last chapter, significant differences exist between the rates of return offered by stock investments compared to those of U.S. Treasury bills and government bonds. Although stocks have returned on average about 10 percent a year over the past 100 years—substantially more than U.S. Treasury bills or bonds—there are periods when stocks have declined in value.[1] For proof, just ask any long-term investor what happened for the three-year period beginning in 2000. And yet, projections by well-respected Roger Ibbotson, chairman of Ibbotson Associates, the investment consulting, software, and research firm, indicate that stock investments will grow at about the same pace between now and the year 2025.[2] The key to success with any investment program is often the opportunity to allow your investments to work for you over a long period of time. In short, a long-term investment program allows you to ride through the rough times and enjoy the good times. Although some short-term (higher-risk) techniques are discussed, this chapter is about long-term investing.

In this chapter, we examine stocks. There are two types of stocks: common and preferred. Since common stockholders are the actual owners of the corporation, they share in its success. But before investing your money, it helps to understand why corporations issue common stock and why investors purchase that stock.

WHY CORPORATIONS ISSUE COMMON STOCK

Corporations issue common stock to finance expansion. Corporate managers prefer selling common stock as a method of financing for several reasons.

A FORM OF EQUITY   *Important point:* Corporations don't have to repay the money a stockholder pays for stock. Generally, a stockholder may sell his or her stock to another individual. The selling price is determined by how much a buyer is willing to pay for the stock. Simply put, if the demand for a particular stock increases, the market value of the stock will increase. If the demand for a particular stock decreases, the market value of the stock will decrease. Demand for a stock changes when information about the firm or its future prospects is released to the general public. For example, information about expected sales revenues, earnings, expansions or mergers, or other important developments within the firm can increase or decrease the demand for, and ultimately the market value of, the firm's stock.

Need advice? While many people offer investment advice, the trick is to obtain quality advice you can trust.

DIVIDENDS NOT MANDATORY   *Important point:* Dividends are paid out of profits, and dividend payments must be approved by the corporation's board of directors. Dividend policies vary among corporations, but most firms distribute between 30 and 70 percent of their earnings to stockholders. However, some corporations follow a policy of smaller or no dividend distributions to stockholders. In general, these are rapidly growing firms, like Amazon (online sales), Michaels (crafts), and Staples (office supplies), that retain a large share of their earnings for research and development, expansion, or major projects. On the other hand, utility companies, such as Duke Energy and Progress Energy, and other financially secure enterprises may distribute 70 to 90 percent of their earnings. Always remember that if a corporation has had a bad year, dividend payments may be reduced or omitted.

VOTING RIGHTS AND CONTROL OF THE COMPANY   In return for the financing provided by selling common stock, management must make concessions to stockholders that may restrict corporate policies. For example, corporations are required by law to have an annual meeting at which stockholders have a right to vote, usually casting one vote per share of stock. Stockholders may vote in person or by proxy. A **proxy** is a legal form that lists the issues to be decided at a stockholders' meeting and requests that stockholders transfer their voting rights to some individual or individuals. The common stockholders elect the board of directors and must approve major changes in corporate policies. Typical changes in corporate policy include (1) an amendment of the corporate charter, (2) the sale of certain assets, (3) possible mergers, (4) the issuance of preferred stock or corporate bonds, and (5) changes in the amount of common stock.

proxy A legal form that lists the issues to be decided at a stockholders' meeting and requests that stockholders transfer their voting rights to some individual or individuals.

WHY INVESTORS PURCHASE COMMON STOCK

How do you make money by buying common stock? Basically, there are two ways: income from dividends and dollar appreciation of stock value. In addition to dividend income and dollar appreciation, a stock split may affect the value of a corporation's stock.

INCOME FROM DIVIDENDS   While the corporation's board members are under no legal obligation to pay dividends, most board members like to keep stockholders happy (and prosperous). Few things will unite stockholders into a powerful opposition force more rapidly than omitted or lowered dividends. Therefore, board members usually declare dividends if the corporation's after-tax profits are sufficient for them to do so. Since dividends are a distribution of profits, investors must be concerned about future after-tax profits. In short, how secure is the dividend?

Corporate dividends for common stock may take the form of cash, additional stock, or company products. However, the last type of dividend is extremely unusual. If the board of directors declares a cash dividend, each common stockholder receives an equal amount per share. Although dividend policies vary, most corporations pay dividends on a quarterly

tion to determine whether the new issue is financially sound and how difficult it will be to sell.

If the investment bank is satisfied that the new stock is a good risk, it will buy the stock and then resell it to its customers—commercial banks, insurance companies, pension funds, mutual funds, and the general public.

If the investment bank's analysts believe the new issue will be difficult to sell, the investment bank may agree to take the stock on a best-efforts basis, without guaranteeing that the stock will be sold. Because the corporation must take back any unsold stocks after a reasonable time, most large corporations are unwilling to accept this arrangement. If the stock issue is too large for one investment bank, a group of investment bankers may form an *underwriting syndicate*. Then each member of the syndicate is responsible for selling only a part of the new issue.

The second method used by a corporation trying to obtain financing through the primary market is to sell directly to current stockholders. You may ask, "Why would a corporation try to sell its own stock?" The most obvious reason for doing so is to avoid the investment bank's commission. Of course, a corporation's ability to sell a new stock issue without the aid of an investment bank is tied directly to investors' perception of the corporation's financial health.

The floor of the New York Stock Exchange—one of the largest securities exchanges in the world.

SECONDARY MARKETS FOR STOCKS

How do you buy or sell stock in the secondary market? To purchase common or preferred stock, you usually have to work with an employee of a brokerage firm who will buy or sell for you at a securities exchange or through the over-the-counter market.

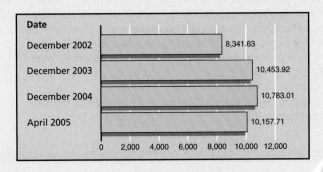

DID YOU KNOW?

The Dow Jones Industrial Average measures 30 different stocks that are considered leaders in the economy. (Closing values as of end of December, except as noted.)

Date	
December 2002	8,341.63
December 2003	10,453.92
December 2004	10,783.01
April 2005	10,157.71

Source: Yahoo! Finance, finance.yahoo.com.

SECURITIES EXCHANGES   A **securities exchange** is a marketplace where member brokers who represent investors meet to buy and sell securities. The securities sold at a particular exchange must first be listed, or accepted for trading, at that exchange. Generally, the securities issued by nationwide corporations are traded at either the New York Stock Exchange or the American Stock Exchange. The securities of regional corporations are traded at smaller, regional exchanges. These exchanges are located in Chicago, San Francisco, Philadelphia, Boston, and several other cities. The securities of very large corporations may be traded at more than one exchange. American firms that do business abroad may also be listed on foreign securities exchanges—in Tokyo, London, or Paris, for example.

The New York Stock Exchange (NYSE) is one of the largest securities exchanges in the world. This exchange lists stocks for over 2,700 corporations with a total market value of about $15 trillion.[6] The NYSE has 1,366 members, or *seats*. Most of these members represent brokerage firms that charge commissions on security trades made by their representatives for their customers. Other members are called *specialists* or *specialist firms*. A **specialist** buys *or* sells a particular stock in an effort to maintain an orderly market.

securities exchange A marketplace where member brokers who represent investors meet to buy and sell securities.

specialist Buys or sells a particular stock in an effort to maintain an orderly market.

For more information about the NYSE, visit **www.nyse.com**.

fyi

Advice from a Pro

WHO REGULATES THE SECURITIES MARKETS?

Good question! With so many news reports of corporations that are in "hot water" over financial reporting problems that range from simple mistakes and omissions to out-and-out fraud, the concerns of investors have grown over the past few years. According to the New York Stock Exchange (NYSE), a regulatory pyramid consisting of different levels exists to make sure that investors are protected. Here's a brief overview of who is watching whom.

Group 1—Congress. The U.S. Congress is at the top of the pyramid. Early on, Congress passed the Securities Act of 1933 (sometimes referred to as the Truth in Securities Act) and the Securities Exchange Act of 1934, which created the Securities and Exchange Commission (SEC). Since then, Congress has passed additional legislation, including creating the Securities Investor Protection Corporation (SIPC) to protect investors and to curb abuses.

Group 2—The Securities and Exchange Commission (SEC). Created by Congress, the SEC requires the registration of new securities and the timely and accurate release of financial information about corporations and also enforces antifraud provisions of current legislation. The SEC supervises all national exchanges, investment companies, over-the-counter brokerage firms, and just about every other organization involved in trading securities.

Group 3—Individual States. Individual states regulate securities transactions. Most of the state laws provide for

(1) registration of securities, (2) licensing of brokers and securities salespeople, and (3) prosecution of any individual who sells fraudulent stocks and bonds. These state laws are often called *blue-sky laws* because they were designed to stop the sale of securities that had nothing to back them up except the "sky."

Group 4—The NYSE and Other Self-Regulatory Organizations. The NYSE is the most active self-regulator in the securities industry and has published over 1,000 pages of rules, policies, and standards of conduct. These standards are applied to every member in the NYSE's investment community. On-site examinations and state-of-the art computer surveillance are used to detect individuals who violate the NYSE's standards of conduct.

Group 5—Individual Brokerage Firms. The foundation of the regulatory pyramid is more than 300 brokerage firms that buy and sell securities for their customers. These firms ensure that their employees are highly trained and meet rigorous ethical standards. According to the NYSE, self-regulation—the way the securities industry monitors itself to create a fair and orderly trading environment—begins here.

Source: "Stock Market Savvy: Investing for Your Future," Lifetime Learning Systems, http://www.nyse.com/pdfs/TG_Mech.pdf, 2001.

Before a corporation's stock is approved for listing on the NYSE, the corporation must meet at least three criteria:[7]

1. Its annual earnings before income taxes must be at least $10 million in the most recent three years.

2. The market value of its publicly held stock must equal or exceed $100 million.

3. At least 2,000 stockholders must each own 100 or more shares of its stock.

The American Stock Exchange (AMEX) and various regional exchanges also have listing requirements, but typically these are less stringent than the NYSE requirements. The stock of corporations that cannot meet the NYSE requirements, find it too expensive to be listed on the NYSE, or choose not to be listed on the NYSE is often traded on the American Stock Exchange, on one of the regional exchanges, or through the over-the-counter market.

over-the-counter (OTC) market A network of dealers who buy and sell the stocks of corporations that are not listed on a securities exchange.

THE OVER-THE-COUNTER MARKET
Not all securities are traded on organized exchanges. Stocks issued by several thousand companies are traded in the over-the-counter market. The **over-the-counter (OTC) market** is a network of dealers who buy and sell the stocks of corporations that are not listed on a securities exchange. Today these stocks are not really traded over the counter. The term was coined more than 100 years ago when securities were sold "over the counter" in stores and banks.

Nasdaq An electronic marketplace for approximately 3,300 different stocks.

Most over-the-counter securities are traded through Nasdaq (pronounced "nazz-dack"). **Nasdaq** is an electronic marketplace for approximately 3,300 different stocks.

In addition to providing price information, this computerized system allows investors to buy and sell shares of companies listed on Nasdaq. When you want to buy or sell shares of a company that trades on Nasdaq—say, Microsoft—your account executive sends your order into the Nasdaq computer system, where it shows up on the screen with all the other orders from people who want to buy or sell Microsoft. Then a Nasdaq dealer (sometimes referred to as a *market maker*) sitting at a computer terminal matches buy and sell orders for Microsoft. Once a match is found, your order is completed.

Nasdaq is known for its innovative, forward-looking growth companies. Although many securities are issued by smaller companies, some large firms, including Intel, Microsoft, and Cisco Systems, also trade on Nasdaq.

BROKERAGE FIRMS AND ACCOUNT EXECUTIVES

An **account executive,** or *stockbroker,* is a licensed individual who buys or sells securities for his or her clients. (Actually, *account executive* is the more descriptive title because such individuals handle all types of securities, not just stocks.) While all account executives can buy or sell stock for clients, most investors expect more from their account executives. Ideally, an account executive should provide information and advice to be used in evaluating potential investments. Many investors begin their search for an account executive by asking friends or business associates for recommendations. This is a logical starting point, but remember that some account executives are conservative while others are more risk oriented.

Before choosing an account executive, you should have already determined your financial objectives. Then you must be careful to communicate those objectives to the account executive so that he or she can do a better job of advising you. Needless to say, account executives may err in their investment recommendations. To help avoid a situation in which your account executive's recommendations are automatically implemented, you should be *actively* involved in the decisions of your investment program and you should never allow your account executive to use his or her discretion without your approval. Watch your account for signs of churning. **Churning** is excessive buying and selling of securities to generate commissions. From a total dollar return standpoint, this practice usually leaves the client worse off or at least no better off. Churning is illegal under the rules established by the Securities and Exchange Commission; however, it may be difficult to prove. Finally, keep in mind that account executives generally are not liable for client losses that result from their recommendations. In fact, most brokerage firms require new clients to sign a statement in which they promise to submit any complaints to an arbitration board. This arbitration clause generally prevents a client from suing an account executive or a brokerage firm. Above all, remember you are investing *your* money and you should make the final decisions with the help of your account executive.

account executive A licensed individual who buys or sells securities for clients; also called a *stockbroker.*

Sheet 59
Investment broker comparison

churning Excessive buying and selling of securities to generate commissions.

SHOULD YOU USE A FULL-SERVICE OR A DISCOUNT BROKERAGE FIRM?

Today a healthy competition exists between full-serve brokerage firms and discount brokerage firms. While the most obvious difference between full-service and discount firms is the amount of the commissions they charge when you buy or sell stock and other securities, there are at least three other factors to consider. First, consider how much research information is available and how much it costs. Both types of brokerage firms offer excellent research materials, but you are more likely to pay extra for information if you choose a discount brokerage firm.

Second, consider how much help you need when making an investment decision. Many full-service brokerage firms argue that you need a professional to help you make important investment decisions. While this may be true for some investors, most account executives employed by full-service brokerage firms are too busy to spend unlimited time with you on a one-on-one basis, especially if you are investing a small amount. On the other side, many discount brokerage firms argue that you alone are responsible for making your investment decisions. They are quick to point out that the most successful investors are the ones involved in their investment programs. And they argue that they have both personnel and materials dedicated to helping you learn how to become a better investor.

Finally, consider how easy it is to buy and sell stock and other securities when using either a full-service or discount brokerage firm. Questions to ask include:

1. Can I buy or sell stocks over the phone?
2. Can I trade stocks online?
3. Where is your nearest office located?
4. Do you have a toll-free telephone number for customer use?
5. How often do I get statements?
6. Is there a charge for statements, research reports, and other financial reports?
7. Are there any fees in addition to the commissions I pay when I buy or sell stocks?

COMPUTERIZED TRANSACTIONS

While many people still prefer to use telephone orders to buy and sell stocks, a growing number are using computers to complete security transactions. To meet this need, discount brokerage firms and many full-service brokerage firms allow investors to trade online. As a rule of thumb, the more active the investor is, the more sense it makes to use computers to trade online. Other reasons that justify using a computer include

1. The size of your investment portfolio.
2. The ability to manage your investments closely.
3. The capability of your computer and the software package.

While computers can make the investment process easier and faster, you should realize that *you* are still responsible for analyzing the information and making the final decision to buy or sell a security. All the computer does is provide more information and, in most cases, complete transactions more quickly and economically.

COMMISSION CHARGES

Most brokerage firms have a minimum commission ranging from $7 to $55 for buying *and* selling stock. Additional commission charges are based on the number of shares and the value of stock bought and sold.

Exhibit 14–7 shows typical commissions charged by online brokerage firms. You should realize that when you choose an online brokerage firm, you will have to make your own decisions.

Generally, full-service and discount brokerage firms charge higher commissions than those charged by online brokerage firms. As a rule of thumb, full-service brokers may charge as much as 1 to 2 percent of the transaction amount. For example, if you use a full-service brokerage firm like Merrill Lynch to purchase Verizon stock valued at $10,000, and the brokerage firm charges 1½ percent, you will pay commissions totaling $150 ($10,000 × 0.015 = $150). In return for charging higher commissions, full-service brokers usually spend more time with each client, help make investment decisions, and provide free research information.

Visit the Charles Schwab Web site at **www.schwab.com** to find out about commission charges for buying and selling stocks.

Exhibit **14-7**   Comparison of online brokers on selected factors

Account Minimum Information	Ameritrade	ShareBuilder	Harris Direct	Brown/Co	Power E*Trade
Cash account	$1,000	No minimum	$100 (6 mos after opening)	$15,000	$1,000
Margin account	$2,000	N/A	$2,000	$15,000	$2,000
Retirement account (IRA)	No fee/no minimum	No minimum	No minimum	$5,000	No fee/no minimum
Commission Schedule—Online Trades					
Market order	$10.99	$4/ShareBuilder purchase transaction (made Tuesdays). $15.95 for real-time market orders.	Trades as low as $7.95	$5 (up to 5,000 shares) +$.01/share retroactive to the first share	As low as $6.99
Limit order	$10.99	$19.95	Trades as low as $7.95	$10 (up to 5,000 shares) +$.01/share retroactive to the first share	As low as $6.99
Commission Schedule—Touchtone Phone Trades					
Market order	$14.99	N/A	Trades as low as $7.95	$5 (up to 5,000 shares) +$.01/share retroactive to the first share	As low as $6.99
Limit order	$14.99	N/A	Trades as low as $7.95	$10 (up to 5,000 shares) +$.01/share retroactive to the first share	As low as $6.99
Commission Schedule—Broker Assisted Trades					
Market order	$24.99	N/A	$40 plus applicable commission	$17 (up to 5,000 shares) +$.01/share retroactive to the first share	$45 plus applicable commission
Limit order	$29.99	N/A	$40 plus applicable commission	$17 (up to 5,000 shares) +$.01/share retroactive to the first share	$45 plus applicable commission
Fee Schedule					
Maintenance fees	$15/quarter	None	$25/quarter	N/A	$0 if certain conditions are met
Transfer fees	$25.00 (transfer out partial or IRA) $50.00 (transfer out full non-IRA)	$10 per security ($50 maximum)	$75 (outgoing)	$50 (full transfer out)	Outgoing only: $25 for partial; $60 for full transfers
IRA custodian fees	None	$25.00	$35.00 per acct per year	N/A	$0 conditioned upon your acceptance of electronic statements and confirms

Source: Motley Fool, www.fool.com, July 5, 2005.

While full-service brokerage firms usually charge higher commissions, on some occasions a discount brokerage firm may charge higher commissions. This generally occurs when the transaction is small, involving a total dollar amount of less than $1,000, and the investor is charged the discount brokerage firm's minimum commission charge.

A SAMPLE STOCK TRANSACTION

Once you and your account executive have decided on a particular transaction, it is time to execute an order to buy or sell. Today most investors either telephone their account executives or use the Internet and trade online. Let's begin by examining four types of orders used to trade stocks.

market order A request to buy or sell a stock at the current market value.

A **market order** is a request to buy or sell a stock at the current market value. Since the stock exchange is an auction market, the account executive's representative will try to get the best price available and the transaction will be completed as soon as possible.

If you buy stock listed on the New York Stock Exchange, for example, your broker transmits your order to the floor of the exchange, where a clerk gives it to a floor broker. The floor broker then goes to one of 20 trading posts at which the specific stock is traded and trades with another floor broker employed by another firm who has an order to sell. After the trade is executed, a notice is sent to the brokerage firms involved and the transaction is displayed on the stock ticker tape. Finally, your brokerage firm notifies you that your transaction is complete. Payment for stocks is generally required within three business days of the transaction. Then, in about four to six weeks, a stock certificate is sent to the purchaser of the stock, unless the securities are left with the brokerage firm for safekeeping. Today it is common practice for investors to leave stock certificates with a brokerage firm. Because the stock certificates are in the broker's care, transfers when the stock is sold are much easier. The phrase "left in the street name" is used to describe investor-owned securities held by a brokerage firm.

limit order A request to buy or sell a stock at a specified price.

A **limit order** is a request to buy or sell a stock at a specified price. When you purchase stock, a limit order ensures that you will buy at the best possible price but not above a specified dollar amount. When you sell stock, a limit order ensures that you will sell at the best possible price, but not below a specified dollar amount. For example, if you place a limit order to buy General Motors common stock for $26 a share, the stock will not be purchased until the price drops to $26 a share or lower. Likewise, if your limit order is to sell General Motors for $26 a share, the stock will not be sold until the price rises to $26 a share or higher. *Be warned:* Limit orders are executed if and when the specified price or better is reached and *all* other previously received orders have been fulfilled.

Many stockholders are certain they want to sell their stock if it reaches a specified price. A limit order does not guarantee this will be done. With a limit order, as mentioned above, orders by other investors may be placed ahead of your order. If you want to guarantee that your order will be executed, you place a special type of limit order known as a stop order. A **stop order** (sometimes called a *stop-loss order*) is an order to sell a particular stock at the next available opportunity after its market price reaches a specified amount. This type of order is used to protect an investor against a sharp drop in price and thus stop the dollar loss on a stock investment. For example, assume you purchased General Motors common stock at $26 a share. Two weeks after making your investment, General Motors is facing multiple product liability lawsuits. Fearing that the market value of your stock will decrease, you enter a stop order to sell your General Motors stock at $20. This means that if the price of the stock decreases to $20 or lower, the account executive will sell it. While a stop order does not guarantee that your stock will be sold at the price you specified, it does guarantee that it will be sold at the next available opportunity. Both limit and stop orders may be good for one day, one week, one month, or good until canceled (GTC).

stop order An order to sell a particular stock at the next available opportunity after its market price reaches a specified amount.

discretionary order An order to buy or sell a security that lets the account executive decide when to execute the transaction and at what price.

You can also choose to place a discretionary order. A **discretionary order** is an order to buy or sell a security that lets the account executive decide when to execute the transaction and at what price. Financial planners advise against using a discretionary order for two reasons. First, a discretionary order gives the account executive a great deal of authority. If the account executive makes a mistake, it is the investor who suffers the dollar loss. Second, financial planners argue that only investors (with the help of their account executives) should make investment decisions.

CONCEPT CHECK 14-4

1 What is the difference between the primary market and the secondary market?
2 Describe how stock is bought or sold in the secondary market.
3 Assume you want to purchase stock. Would you use a full-service broker or a discount broker? Would you ever trade stocks online?

Action Application Use Internet research to choose a brokerage firm that can buy and sell stocks for you. Then describe what is required to open an account. Also print out the application form.

Long-Term and Short-Term Investment Strategies

Once you purchase stock, the investment may be classified as either long term or short term. Generally, individuals who hold an investment for a long period of time are referred to as *investors*. Typically, long-term investors hold their investments for at least a year or longer. Individuals who routinely buy and then sell stocks within a short period of time are called *speculators* or *traders*.

Objective 5

Explain the trading techniques used by long-term investors and short-term speculators.

LONG-TERM TECHNIQUES

In this section, we discuss the long-term techniques of buy and hold, dollar cost averaging, direct investment programs, and dividend reinvestment programs.

BUY-AND-HOLD TECHNIQUE   Many long-term investors purchase stock and hold onto it for a number of years. When they do this, their investment can increase in value two ways. First, they are entitled to dividends if the board of directors approves dividend payments to stockholders. While stockholders can use dividends for immediate needs, another option is to reinvest the dividends in either the same stock or a different investment alternative. By reinvesting the dividends and taking advantage of the time value of money, even small amounts can increase over a long period of time. Second, the price of the stock may go up. To see the effect of an increase in stock value over a long period of time, you may want to review the sample stock transaction for Boeing Corporation illustrated in Exhibit 14–2. Over a three-year period, both dividends *and* increase in value contributed to total profits for this investment. Finally, keep in mind that corporations do split their stock for various reasons. Although there are no guarantees that a stock split will increase the value of your stock over a long period of time, it is a factor that should be considered when choosing stocks that have a history of stock splits or stocks that may split in the future.

Often an investment program can make dreams a reality!

DOLLAR COST AVERAGING   **Dollar cost averaging** is a long-term technique used by investors who purchase an equal dollar amount of the same stock at equal intervals. Assume you invest $2,000 in Johnson & Johnson's common stock each year for a period of three years. The results of your investment program are illustrated in Exhibit 14–8. Notice that when the price of the stock increased in 2005 and 2006, you purchased fewer shares. The average cost for a share of stock, determined by dividing the total investment ($6,000) by the total number of shares, is $58.42 ($6,000 ÷ 102.7 = $58.42). Other applications of dollar cost averaging occur when employees purchase

dollar cost averaging A long-term technique used by investors who purchase an equal dollar amount of the same stock at equal intervals.

Exhibit 14-8

Dollar cost averaging for Johnson & Johnson

Year	Investment	Stock Price	Shares Purchased
2004	$2,000	$50	40.0
2005	2,000	60	33.3
2006	2,000	68	29.4
Total	$6,000		102.7

shares of their company's stock through a payroll deduction plan or as part of an employer-sponsored retirement plan over an extended period of time.

Investors use dollar cost averaging to avoid the common pitfall of buying high and selling low. In the situation shown in Exhibit 14–8, you would lose money only if you sold your stock at less than the average cost of $58.42. Thus, with dollar cost averaging, you can make money if the stock is sold at a price higher than the average cost for a share of stock.

DIRECT INVESTMENT AND DIVIDEND REINVESTMENT PLANS

direct investment plan A plan that allows stockholders to purchase stock directly from a corporation without having to use an account executive or a brokerage firm.

dividend reinvestment plan A plan that allows current stockholders the option to reinvest or use their cash dividends to purchase stock of the corporation.

Today a large number of corporations offer direct investment plans. A **direct investment plan** allows you to purchase stock directly from a corporation without having to use an account executive or a brokerage firm. Similarly, a **dividend reinvestment plan** (sometimes called a DRIP) allows you the option to reinvest your cash dividends to purchase stock of the corporation. For stockholders, the chief advantage of both types of plans is that these plans enable them to purchase stock without paying a commission charge to a brokerage firm. (Note: A few companies may charge a small fee for dividend reinvestment, but the charge is less than what most brokerage firms charge.) The fees, minimum investment amounts, rules, and features for both direct investment and dividend reinvestment do vary from one corporation to the next. For example, Harley Davidson allows investors to use a direct investment plan to purchase stock, but there is a $500 minimum investment. The Harley Davidson plan also allows participants to automatically debit the money they want to invest from their bank account. AFLAC, the insurance company that made the talking duck a famous television star, allows investors to participate in its dividend reinvestment plan if they own one share of the corporation's stock. Many companies that have dividend reinvestment plans, like AFLAC, also allow participants to use direct investment to purchase additional shares.

In addition to saving the commissions that would be paid to account executives, both types of plans enable investors to purchase stock with less money than required by most brokerage firms. Both plans also allow you to purchase fractional shares of stock and are practical applications of dollar cost averaging—a topic discussed in the last section. Simply put: You buy more shares of your favorite stocks when the price is low and fewer shares when the price is high. For corporations, the chief advantage of both types of plans is that they provide an additional source of capital. As an added bonus, they are providing a service to their stockholders. A number of Web sites provide information about direct investment or dividend reinvestment plans. If you're interested, go to your favorite search engine, and type in either term or use the sites listed in the nearby FYI feature.

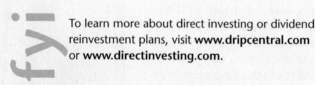

To learn more about direct investing or dividend reinvestment plans, visit **www.dripcentral.com** or **www.directinvesting.com**.

SHORT-TERM TECHNIQUES

In addition to the long-term techniques presented in the preceding section, investors sometimes use more speculative, short-term techniques. In this section, we discuss day traders, buying stock on margin, selling short, and trading in options. *Be warned: The methods presented in this section are quite risky; do not use them unless you fully understand the underlying risks.* Also, you should not use them until you have experienced success using the more traditional long-term techniques described above.

DAY TRADING
A **day trader** is an individual who buys and then later sells stocks and other securities in a very short period of time. What could be easier? Buy a stock in the morning that has a great deal of momentum because of a projected revenues jump or an increase in earnings and then sell it a few hours later the same day or in just a few days? Sounds simple! Here's the problem—*most day traders lose money!* This is a *highly* speculative practice—much like going to Las Vegas and gambling. And yet, the lure of quick profits and the success stories of a few cause people to try their luck at day trading. *Be warned: This is one of the most speculative techniques used today.* Individuals should never use day trading if they don't fully understand the risks involved and can afford to lose money if the strategy doesn't work. Other short-term techniques, including margin, selling short, and options, are sometimes used by day traders to increase profits, but with substantially more risk.

day trader An individual who buys and then later sells stocks and other securities in a very short period of time.

BUYING STOCK ON MARGIN
When buying stock on **margin,** you borrow part of the money needed to buy a particular stock. The margin requirement is set by the Federal Reserve Board and is subject to periodic change. The current margin requirement is 50 percent and a $2,000 minimum. This requirement means you may borrow up to half of the total stock purchase price as long as you have at least $2,000 in your brokerage firm account. Although margin is regulated by the Federal Reserve, margin requirements and the interest charged on the loans used to fund margin transactions may vary among brokers and dealers. Usually the brokerage firm either lends the money or arranges the loan with another financial institution. Another source of money to fund a margin transaction is a home-equity loan. This is a very speculative option, because if you lose money and can't repay the home-equity loan, you could be homeless. Investors buy on margin because doing so offers them the potential for greater profits. Exhibit 14–9 gives an example of buying stock on margin.

margin A speculative technique whereby an investor borrows part of the money needed to buy a particular stock.

As Exhibit 14–9 shows, it can be more profitable to use margin. In effect, the financial leverage (often defined as the use of borrowed funds to increase the return on an investment) allowed Paul Watson, who is single and 32 years old, to purchase a larger number of shares of stock. Since the dollar value of each share increased, Watson obtained a larger profit by buying the stock on margin.

In this example, Watson's stock did exactly what it was supposed to do: It increased in market value. His stock increased $4 per share, and he made $4,000 because he owned 1,000 shares. His actual profit would be reduced by commissions and the amount of interest his broker would charge for the margin transaction. Had the value of the stock gone down, buying on margin would have increased his loss.

If the value of a margined stock decreases to approximately one-half of the original price, you will receive a *margin call* from the brokerage firm. After the margin call, you must pledge additional cash or securities to serve as collateral for the loan. If you don't have acceptable collateral or cash, the margined stock is sold and the proceeds are used to repay the loan. The exact price at which the brokerage firm issues the margin call is determined by the amount of money you borrowed when you purchased the stock. Generally, the more money you borrow, the sooner you will receive a margin call if the value of the margined stock drops.

In addition to facing the possibility of larger dollar losses, you must pay interest on the money borrowed to purchase stock on margin. Most brokerage firms charge 1 to 3 percent above the prime rate. Normally, economists define the prime rate as the interest rate that the best business customers must pay. Interest charges can absorb the potential profits if the value of margined stock does not increase rapidly enough and the margined stocks must be held for long periods of time.

Exhibit **14-9**

A typical margin transaction

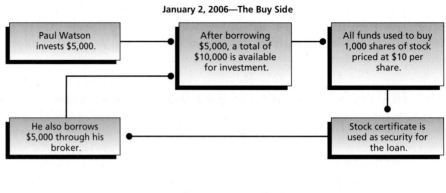

January 2, 2006—The Buy Side

Paul Watson invests $5,000. → After borrowing $5,000, a total of $10,000 is available for investment. → All funds used to buy 1,000 shares of stock priced at $10 per share.

He also borrows $5,000 through his broker. Stock certificate is used as security for the loan.

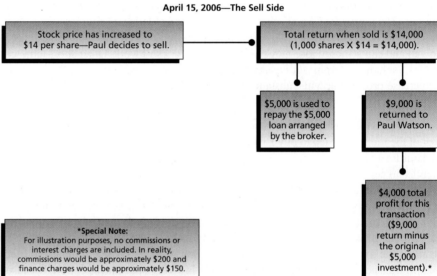

April 15, 2006—The Sell Side

Stock price has increased to $14 per share—Paul decides to sell. → Total return when sold is $14,000 (1,000 shares X $14 = $14,000).

$5,000 is used to repay the $5,000 loan arranged by the broker.

$9,000 is returned to Paul Watson.

$4,000 total profit for this transaction ($9,000 return minus the original $5,000 investment).*

*Special Note:
For illustration purposes, no commissions or interest charges are included. In reality, commissions would be approximately $200 and finance charges would be approximately $150.

selling short Selling stock that has been borrowed from a brokerage firm and must be replaced at a later date.

SELLING SHORT   Your ability to make money by buying and selling securities is related to how well you can predict whether a certain stock will increase or decrease in market value. Normally, you buy stocks and assume they will increase in value, a procedure referred to as *buying long*. But not all stocks increase in value. In fact, the value of a stock may decrease for many reasons, including lower sales, lower profits, reduced dividends, product failures, increased competition, and product liability lawsuits. With this fact in mind, you may use a procedure called *selling short* to make money when the value of a stock is expected to decrease in value. **Selling short** is selling stock that has been borrowed from a brokerage firm and must be replaced at a later date. When you sell short, you sell today, knowing you must buy, or *cover* your short transaction, at a later date. To make money in a short transaction, you must follow the steps illustrated in Exhibit 14–10.

For example, Betty Malone, who is divorced and 28 years old, believes General Motors stock is overpriced because of increased competition among automobile manufacturers and other factors. As a result, she decides to sell short 100 shares of General Motors.

As Exhibit 14–10 shows, Malone's total return for this short transaction was $700 because the stock did what it was supposed to do in a short transaction: decrease in value. A price decrease is especially important when selling short, because you must replace the stock borrowed from the brokerage firm with stock purchased (hopefully at a lower market value) at a later date. If the stock increases in value, you will lose money because you must replace the borrowed stock with stock purchased at a higher price. If the price of the General Motors stock in Exhibit 14–10 had increased from $25 to $32, Betty Malone would have lost $700.

Exhibit **14-10**   An example of selling short

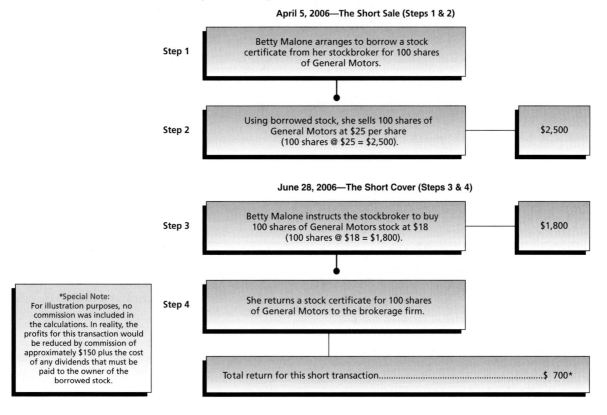

April 5, 2006—The Short Sale (Steps 1 & 2)

Step 1 — Betty Malone arranges to borrow a stock certificate from her stockbroker for 100 shares of General Motors.

Step 2 — Using borrowed stock, she sells 100 shares of General Motors at $25 per share (100 shares @ $25 = $2,500). — $2,500

June 28, 2006—The Short Cover (Steps 3 & 4)

Step 3 — Betty Malone instructs the stockbroker to buy 100 shares of General Motors stock at $18 (100 shares @ $18 = $1,800). — $1,800

Step 4 — She returns a stock certificate for 100 shares of General Motors to the brokerage firm.

*Special Note: For illustration purposes, no commission was included in the calculations. In reality, the profits for this transaction would be reduced by commission of approximately $150 plus the cost of any dividends that must be paid to the owner of the borrowed stock.

Total return for this short transaction...$ 700*

There is usually no special or extra brokerage charge for selling short, since the brokerage firm receives its regular commission when the stock is bought and sold. Before selling short, consider two factors. First, since the stock you borrow from your broker is actually owned by another investor, you must pay any dividends the stock earns before you replace the stock. After all, you borrowed the stock and then sold the borrowed stock. Eventually, dividends can absorb the profits from your short transaction if the price of the stock does not decrease rapidly enough. Second, to make money selling short, you must be correct in predicting that a stock will decrease in value. If the value of the stock increases, you lose.

TRADING IN OPTIONS   An **option** gives you the right to buy or sell a stock at a predetermined price during a specified period of time. Options are usually available for three-, six-, or nine-month periods. If you think the market price of a stock will increase during a short period of time, you may decide to purchase a call option. A *call option* is sold by a stockholder and gives the purchaser the right to *buy* 100 shares of a stock at a guaranteed price before a specified expiration date.

It is also possible to purchase a put option. A *put option* is the right to sell 100 shares of a stock at a guaranteed price before a specified expiration date. With both call and put options, you are betting that the price of the stock will increase or decrease in value before the expiration date. If this price movement does not occur before the expiration date, you lose the money you paid for your option.

Because of the increased risk involved in option trading, a more detailed discussion of how you profit or lose money with options is beyond the scope of this book. *Be warned:* Amateurs and beginning investors should stay away from options unless they fully understand all of the risks involved. For the rookie, the lure of large profits over a short period of time may be tempting, but the risks are real.

option The right to buy or sell a stock at a predetermined price during a specified period of time.

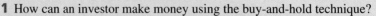

CONCEPT CHECK 14-5

1 How can an investor make money using the buy-and-hold technique?
2 What is the advantage of using dollar cost averaging?
3 Explain the difference between direct investment plans and dividend reinvestment plans.
4 Why would an investor buy stock on margin?
5 Why would an investor use the selling-short technique?

Action Application Choose a stock you would consider a quality long-term investment. Then use Internet research to determine the historical prices for the stock over the past three years. Based on this data, does the stock still warrant further evaluation for investment purposes?

SUMMARY OF OBJECTIVES

Objective 1

Identify the most important features of common and preferred stocks.

Corporations sell common stock to finance their business expansion. People invest in common stock because of dividend income and appreciation of value. There is also the *possibility* of gain through stock splits. Dividend payments to common stockholders must be approved by a corporation's board of directors. In return for providing the money needed to finance the corporation, stockholders have the right to elect the board of directors. They must also approve changes to corporate policies that include (1) an amendment to the corporate charter, (2) the sale of certain assets, (3) possible mergers, (4) the issuance of preferred stock or corporate bonds, and (5) changes in the amount of common stock. The most important priority an investor in preferred stock enjoys is receiving cash dividends before any cash dividends are paid to common stockholders. Still, dividend distributions to both preferred and common stockholders must be approved by the board of directors. To make preferred stock issues more attractive, corporations may add a cumulative feature and/or a conversion feature to these issues.

Objective 2

Explain how you can evaluate stock investments.

Depending on specific characteristics associated with a stock investment, account executives, financial planners, and investors often classify a particular stock as blue chip, income, growth, cyclical, defensive, large-cap, midcap, small-cap, or penny. A number of factors can make a share of stock increase or decrease in value. When evaluating a particular stock issue, most investors begin with the information contained in daily newspapers or on the Internet. Stock advisory services, annual reports, and information contained on the SEC Web site and in business periodicals, can all be used to help evaluate a stock investment.

Objective 3

Analyze the numerical measures that cause a stock to increase or decrease in value.

Many analysts believe that a corporation's ability or inability to generate earnings in the future may be one of the most significant factors that account for an increase or decrease in the value of a stock. Generally, higher earnings equate to higher stock value, and lower earnings equate to lower stock value. In addition to the total amount of earnings reported by the corporation, it is possible to calculate earnings per share and a price-earnings ratio to evaluate a stock investment. While both earnings per share and price-earnings ratio are historical numbers based on what a corporation has already done, it is possible to obtain earnings estimates for most corporations. Other calculations that help evaluate stock investments include dividend payout, current yield, total return, annualized holding period yield, beta, and book value. Fundamental analysis, technical analysis, and the efficient market hypothesis can also be used to explain the price movements that occur in the stock market.

Objective 4

Describe how stocks are bought and sold.

A corporation may sell a new stock issue through an investment bank or directly to current stockholders. Once the stock has been sold in the primary market, it can be sold time and again in the secondary market. In the secondary market, investors purchase stock listed on a securities exchange or traded in the over-the-counter market. Most securities transactions are made through an account executive who works for a brokerage firm. A growing number of investors are completing security transactions online. In fact, a good investment software package can help you evaluate potential investments, monitor the value of your investments, and place buy and sell orders online. Most brokerage firms charge a minimum commission for buying or selling stock. Additional commission charges are based on the number and value of the stock shares bought or sold and if you use a full-service or discount broker or trade online.

Objective 5

Explain the trading techniques used by long-term investors and short-term speculators.

Purchased stock may be classified as either a long-term investment or a speculative investment. Long-term investors typically hold their investments for at least a year or longer; speculators (sometimes referred to as *traders*) usually sell their investments within a shorter time period. Traditional trading techniques long-term investors use include the buy-and-hold technique, dollar cost averaging, direct investment plans, and dividend reinvestment plans. More speculative techniques include day trading, buying on margin, selling short, and trading in options.

KEY FORMULAS

Page	Topic	Formula
455	Earnings per share	$\text{Earnings per share} = \dfrac{\text{After-tax income}}{\text{Number of outstanding shares of common stock}}$
	Example:	$\text{Earnings per share} = \dfrac{\$11,250,000}{3,750,000}$
		$= \$3.00 \text{ per share}$
455	Price-earnings (PE) ratio	$\text{PE ratio} = \dfrac{\text{Price per share}}{\text{Earnings per share of stock}}$
	Example:	$\text{Price-earnings ratio} = \dfrac{\$54}{\$3.00}$
		$= 18$
457	Price/earnings to growth ratio (PEG)	$\text{Price/earnings to growth ratio} = \dfrac{\text{Price-earnings ratio}}{\text{Annual EPS growth}}$
	Example:	$\text{Price earnings to growth ratio} = \dfrac{20}{24\%}$
		$= 0.83$

Note: The percent sign (%) is ignored in the above calculation.

Page	Topic	Formula
456	Dividend payout	$\text{Dividend payout} = \dfrac{\text{Dividend amount}}{\text{Earnings per share}}$
	Example:	$\text{Dividend payout} = \dfrac{\$0.90}{\$1.28}$
		$= 0.70 = 70 \text{ percent}$
456	Current yield	$\text{Current yield} = \dfrac{\text{Annual income amount}}{\text{Market value}}$
	Example:	$\text{Current yield} = \dfrac{\$2.00}{\$50.00}$
		$= 0.04 = 4 \text{ percent}$

457	Total return	Total return = Current return + Capital gain
	Example:	Total return = \$120 + \$710
		= \$830

458	Annualized holding period yield	$\text{Annualized holding period yield} = \dfrac{\text{Total return}}{\text{Original investment}} \times \dfrac{1}{N}$
		N = Number of years investment is held
	Example:	$\text{Annualized holding period yield} = \dfrac{\$830}{\$2,600} \times \dfrac{1}{4}$
		$= 0.08 = 8 \text{ percent}$

459	Book value	$\text{Book value} = \dfrac{\text{Assets} - \text{Liabilities}}{\text{Number of outstanding shares of common stock}}$
	Example:	$\text{Book value} = \dfrac{\$135,000,000 - \$60,000,000}{3,750,000}$
		$= \$20 \text{ per share}$

KEY TERMS

FINANCIAL PLANNING PROBLEMS

1. *Calculating Dividend Amounts.* Betty and John Martinez own 220 shares of Exxon common stock. Exxon's quarterly dividend is $1.08 per share. What is the amount of the dividend check the Martinez couple will receive for this quarter? (Obj. 1)

2. *Determining the Number of Shares after a Stock Split.* In March, stockholders of Dress Barn Corporation approved a 2-for-1 stock split. After the split, how many shares of Dress Barn stock will an investor have if she or he owned 360 shares before the split? (Obj. 1)

3. *Calculating Total Return.* Tammy Jackson purchased 100 shares of All-American Manufacturing Company stock at $29½ a share. One year later, she sold the stock for $38 a share. She paid her broker a $34 commission when she purchased the stock and a $42 commission when she sold it. During the 12 months she owned the stock, she received $184 in dividends. Calculate Tammy's total return on this investment. (Obj. 1)

4. *Calculating Total Return.* Marie and Bob Houmas purchased 200 shares of General Electric stock for $29 a share. One year later, they sold the stock for $40 a share. They paid their broker a $130 commission when they purchased the stock and a $150 commission when they sold it. During the 12 months they owned the stock, they received $88 in dividends. Calculate the total return on this investment. (Obj. 1)

5. *Determining a Preferred Dividend Amount.* James Hayes owns Ohio Utility preferred stock. If this preferred stock issue pays 4½ percent based on a par value of $25, what is the dollar amount of the dividend for one share of Ohio Utility? (Obj. 1)

6. *Calculating the Dividend for a Cumulative Preferred Stock Issue.* Wyoming Sports Equipment issued a $3 cumulative preferred stock issue. In 2005, the firm's board of directors voted to omit dividends for both the company's common stock and its preferred stock issues. Also, the corporation's board of directors voted to pay dividends in 2006. (Obj. 1)

   a. How much did the preferred stockholders receive in 2005?

   b. How much did the common stockholders receive in 2005?

   c. How much did the preferred stockholders receive in 2006?

7. Use the Internet, the *Wall Street Journal,* or a local newspaper to find the following information for the four stocks listed below in the chart. (Obj. 2)

   Date _____

   Web site _____ or

   Newspaper name _____

Stock	Stock Symbol	52-Week High	52-Week Low	Dividend	Yield %	Close Price
Microsoft						
Toyota						
Citigroup						
Pfizer						

8. Assume you own shares in Honeywell Inc. and that the company currently earns $1.56 per share and pays quarterly dividend payments that total $0.83 a share each year. Calculate the dividend payout for Honeywell. (Obj. 3)

9. *Calculating Return on Investment.* Two years ago, you purchased 100 shares of Coca-Cola Company. Your purchase price was $41 a share, plus a total commission of $29 to purchase the stock. During the last two years, you have received the following dividend amounts: $1.03 per share for the first year and $0.91 per share the second year. Also, assume that at the end of two years, you sold your Coca-Cola stock for $52 a share minus a total commission of $34 to sell the stock. (Obj. 3)

   a. Calculate the current yield for your Coca-Cola stock at the time you purchased it.

   b. Calculate the current yield for your Coca-Cola stock at the time you sold it.

   c. Calculate the total return for your Coca-Cola investment when you sold the stock at the end of two years.

   d. Calculate the annualized holding period yield for your Coca-Cola investment at the end of the two-year period.

10. *Calculating Earnings per Share, Price-Earnings Ratio, and Book Value.* As a stockholder of Bozo Oil Company, you receive its annual report. In the financial statements, the firm has reported assets of $9 million, liabilities of $5 million, after-tax earnings of $2 million, and 750,000 outstanding shares of common stock. (Obj. 3)

    a. Calculate the earnings per share of Bozo Oil's common stock.

    b. Assuming a share of Bozo Oil's common stock has a market value of $40, what is the firm's price-earnings ratio?

    c. Calculate the book value of a share of Bozo Oil's common stock.

11. *Using Dollar Cost Averaging.* For four years, Mary Nations invested $3,000 each year in America Bank stock. The stock was selling for $34 in 2003, for $48 in 2004, $37 in 2005, and for $52 in 2006. (Obj. 5)

  a. What is Mary's total investment in America Bank?

  b. After four years, how many shares does Mary own?

  c. What is the average cost per share of Mary's investment?

12. *Using Margin.* Bill Campbell invested $4,000 and borrowed $4,000 to purchase shares in Wal-Mart. At the time of his investment, Wal-Mart stock was selling for $45 a share. (Obj. 5)

  a. If Bill paid a $30 commission, how many shares could he buy if he used *only* his own money and did not use margin?

  b. If Bill paid a $50 commission, how many shares could he buy if he used his $4,000 and borrowed $4,000 on margin to buy Wal-Mart stock?

  c. Assuming Bill did use margin, paid a $90 total commission to buy and sell his Wal-Mart stock, and sold his stock for $53 a share, how much profit did he make on his Wal-Mart investment?

13. *Selling Short.* After researching Toro common stock, Sally Jackson is convinced the stock is overpriced. She contacts her account executive and arranges to sell short 200 shares of Toro. At the time of the sale, a share of common stock has a value of $41. Three months later, Toro is selling for $34 a share, and Sally instructs her broker to cover her short transaction. Total commissions to buy and sell the stock were $74. What is her profit for this short transaction? (Obj. 5)

FINANCIAL PLANNING ACTIVITIES

1. *Surveying Investors.* Survey investors who own stock. Then explain, in a short paragraph, their reasons for owning stock. (Obj. 1)

2. *Determining the Effect of a Stock Split on a Stock's Market Value.* Use the Internet, and/or issues of the *Wall Street Journal* to locate a stock that has experienced a 2-for-1 split. (Obj. 1)

  a. What is the name of the corporation that had the 2-for-1 stock split?

  b. When did the stock split?

  c. What was the price the day before the stock split?

  d. What was the price the day after the stock split?

  e. What was the price a month after the stock split?

  f. At the end of one month, do you think the stock split was good for an individual investor?

3. *Interviewing an Account Executive.* Interview an account executive about the cumulative feature and conversion feature of preferred stock. What do these features mean to preferred stockholders? (Obj. 1)

4. *Using Research Information.* Divide a sheet of paper into three columns. In the first column, list sources of information you can use to evaluate stock investments. In the second column, state where you would find each of these sources. In the third column, describe the types of information each source would provide. (Obj. 2)

5. *Using Stock Advisory Services.* Pick a stock of interest to you and research the company at the library by examining the information contained in reports published by Mergent's, Standard & Poor's, or Value Line, or business periodicals like *BusinessWeek, Money,* or *Kiplinger's Personal Finance.* Then write a one- or two-page summary of your findings. Based on your research, would you still want to invest in this stock? Why or why not? (Obj. 2)

6. *Using the Yahoo! Finance Web Site.* Visit the Yahoo! Finance Web site and evaluate one of the corporations listed below. To complete this activity, follow these steps. (Obj. 2)

  a. Go to finance.yahoo.com.

  b. Choose one of the following three corporations, enter its stock ticker symbol (in parentheses), and click on the Go button: General Electric (GE), Johnson & Johnson (JNJ), Microsoft (MSFT).

  c. For your corporation, print out the information for the profile, 2-year chart, and analyst opinion.

  d. Based on the information included in this research report, would you invest in this corporation? Explain your answer. (Obj. 2)

7. *Using the Internet.* Choose a stock that you think would be a good investment. Then research the stock using the Internet. (Obj. 2)

  a. Based on the information contained on the corporation's investor page, would you still want to invest in the stock? Explain your answer.

  b. What other investment information would you need to evaluate the stock? Where would you obtain this information?

8. *Conducting Library Research.* Conduct library research on the fundamental theory, the technical theory, and the efficient market hypothesis described in this chapter. How do these theories explain the movements of a stock traded on the NYSE or over-the-counter market? (Obj. 3)

9. *Exploring Career Opportunities.* Prepare a list of questions you could use to interview an account executive about career opportunities in the field of finance. (Obj. 4)

10. *Using Long-Term Investment Techniques.* Interview people who have used the long-term investment techniques of buy and hold, dollar cost averaging, direct investment plan, or dividend reinvestment plan. Describe your findings. (Obj. 5)

11. *Analyzing Short-Term Investments.* Prepare a chart that describes the similarities and differences among buying stock on margin, selling short, and trading in options. (Obj. 5)

INTERNET CONNECTION

Researching Stock Investments

Visit the following Web sites and describe the type of information provided by each site.

Sponsor	Web Site	Type of Information	How Could This Site Help Me Invest?
Hoover's	www.hoovers.com		
Motley Fool	www.fool.com		
Nasdaq	www.nasdaq.com		
New York Stock Exchange	www.nyse.com		
Yahoo! Finance	finance.yahoo.com		

FINANCIAL PLANNING CASE

Research Information Available from Mergent

This chapter stressed the importance of evaluating potential investments. Now it's your turn to try your skill at evaluating a potential investment in Reebok International Ltd. Assume you could invest $10,000 in the common stock of this company. To help you evaluate this potential investment, carefully examine Exhibit 14–5, which reproduces the research report on Reebok International from Mergent. The report was published in the fall of 2004.

Questions

1. Based on the research provided by Mergent, would you buy Reebok International stock? Justify your answer.

2. What other investment information would you need to evaluate Reebok International common stock? Where would you obtain this information?

3. On Friday, April 22, 2005, Reebok International common stock was selling for $42 a share. Using a newspaper or the Internet, determine the current price for a share of Reebok common stock. Based on this information, would your Reebok investment have been profitable if you had purchased the common stock for $42 a share? (Hint: Reebok stock is listed on the New York Stock Exchange and its stock symbol is RBK.)

4. Assuming you purchased Reebok International stock on April 22, 2005, and based on your answer to question 3, would you want to hold or sell your Reebok stock? Explain your answer.

VIDEO CASE

Investing in Stocks

"If you want to be financially fit, you have to put your money to work for it to grow."

This quote says it all. For many people, investing means parking their money in a savings account and hoping the interest will add up. Although the interest may be enough to keep up with inflation, the fact remains that without a more aggressive strategy, their money will not grow. In search of higher returns, many investors turn to the stock market. Let's start with the basics:

1. When you invest in stock, you become a part owner of the corporation.

2. Your stock investment will grow if the company is prosperous and earns a profit.

3. Your stock investment can decrease in value if the company falls on hard times.

4. There are two types of stocks: common and preferred.

5. As a common stockholder, you receive dividend distributions approved by the corporation's board of directors. However, dividends are not guaranteed.

6. As a preferred stockholder, you are guaranteed to be paid dividends before common stockholders receive dividends.

While investing in stocks entails more risk, you can minimize the risk with careful planning and by learning how to research your investments. Before purchasing your first stock, you should learn as much as possible about the stock market and the company that issued the stock you want to buy. Many experts suggest that you begin the search for a stock investment by thinking about the products or services that you purchase regularly.

Then continue your search by reading investment information in magazines and newspapers or using a stock advisory service. You can also use the Internet to research stock investments. Information about the trends, fundamentals, and technical aspects of the stocks that interest you is available through Web sites like Quicken (www.quicken.com) and the Standard & Poor's site (www.standardpoor.com).

Finally, you can obtain help in making an investment decision by talking with a stockbroker. Generally, stockbrokers are classified as either full-service or discount brokers, depending on how much help they provide to clients and the amount of commissions they charge for their services.

Once you have made the decision to buy or sell, your stock is transacted on a stock exchange or the over-the-counter market. A stock market (sometimes referred to as a securities exchange) is a marketplace for buying and selling stock. Members of the exchange gather together to purchase or sell stocks for their clients.

You can also purchase or sell stocks through Nasdaq (National Association of Securities Dealers Automated Quotation system). As the name implies, Nasdaq is a computerized, electronic system that matches buy and sell orders for specific stocks.

Although it is easy to buy or sell stocks through the exchange or over-the-counter market, the responsibility for making intelligent investment decisions is still yours. You are the one who must pick the stock and decide when it is time to buy or sell.

Questions

1. You have accumulated $4,000 that you can use to start an investment program. Would you place your money in a savings account or invest in stock? Explain your answer.

2. Approximately 3,000 stocks are listed on the New York Stock Exchange, and about 4,000 stocks are traded over the counter. Assuming you decided to invest your $4,000 in two different stocks, what process would you use to identify and screen four or five potential stocks for further research and evaluation?

3. Now that you have narrowed your search down to four or five potential stock investments, what type of research information would you need to make your final decision?

YOUR PERSONAL FINANCIAL PLANNER IN ACTION

Investing in Stocks

For many investors, selection of stocks for their portfolios is an important element that helps achieve various investment goals.

Your Short-Term Financial Planning Activities	Resources
1. Identify investment goals that might be appropriate for investing in stocks for your life situation.	www.fool.com www.money.com www.bloomberg.com
2. Research a potential stock investment. Consider risk, potential growth, income, and recent market performance.	PFP Sheet 58 www.hoovers.com finance.yahoo.com www.quote.com
3. Monitor current economic conditions that may affect the value of individual stocks as well as the stock market as a whole.	www.wsj.com www.federalreserve.gov www.bls.gov
4. Compare the cost of various investment broker services.	PFP Sheet 59 www.scottrade.com www.placeatrade.com
Your Long-Term Financial Planning Activities	
1. Identify stock investing decisions that might be used for achieving long-term financial goals.	www.morningstar.com www.marketwatch.com
2. Develop a plan for investing in stocks as family and household situations change.	Text pages 467–472 www.kiplinger.com

Stock Investments

Life Situation

Pam, 43
Josh, 45
Children ages 16, 14, and 11

Financial Data

Monthly income $4,900
Assets $262,700
Liabilities $84,600
Living expenses $4,450
Emergency fund $5,000

As previously noted, the Brocks have some of their investment portfolio in conservative stocks. These equities have had very slow growth while regularly paying a small dividend.

Pam and Josh have received several e-mails recently with suggestions about various biotechnology, retailing, and environmental companies. The investment advisors believe that these industries would provide an opportunity for strong long-term financial gains.

Questions

1. According to Pam, "We both know we should have started our investment program sooner, but we always seemed to have 'emergencies' that took what extra money we had." To what extent should the Brocks invest in stocks as a major portion of their investment portfolio?

2. Research the industries recommended by the investment advisors. What are some industries and specific stocks you would recommend for the Brocks?

3. How might *Personal Financial Planner* sheets 58 and 59 be useful to the Brocks?

15 Investing in Bonds

Key Concept

By choosing corporate or government bonds, investors can use the principle of asset allocation and diversify their investment holdings. And while most bonds are conservative investments, there is still risk. This chapter provides the information you need to evaluate bond investments.

Digital Study Tools

Online Learning Center Study Tools for This Chapter

- Multiple-choice quiz
- Flashcards
- eLearning sessions
- Crossword puzzle
- Personal Finance Online: Investing in Bonds

Student CD Study Tools for This Chapter

- Self-study software
- Narrated PowerPoint
- Personal financial planning software: Worksheet 60

www.mhhe.com/kdh

Learning Objectives

1 Describe the characteristics of corporate bonds.

2 Discuss why corporations issue bonds.

3 Explain why investors purchase corporate bonds.

4 Discuss why federal, state, and local governments issue bonds and why investors purchase government bonds.

5 Evaluate bonds when making an investment.

Bonds: To Buy or Not Buy—That's the Real Question!

For Shira and Mathew Matson, stocks have always been the investment of choice. The couple, now in their early 40s, reasoned that stock investments had always outperformed other investment alternatives. So why choose any other investment?

The couple began investing when they were in their mid-20s—right after they both graduated from college. They had always appreciated the importance of personal financial management and had been dedicated to saving money each month. And their dedication and perseverance had paid off. By the end of the 1990s, their investment portfolio had grown to just over $200,000—all invested in technology stocks. Like many investors, the Matsons had enjoyed double-digit gains each year during the 1990s. But then the "bubble" burst, and they began losing money. Five years later, the value of their investment portfolio had dropped to $140,000. That's when they decided to seek professional help and made an appointment with Sally Thompson, a certified financial planner.

According to Sally, the couple was ahead of the game, because they had more money invested than many couples their age. And yet, she was surprised that they had invested *all* their money in technology stocks. According to Sally, they needed to diversify and use the principle of asset allocation to balance the risk associated with investing. While

technology stocks are one type of investment, there are others, including stocks issued by large and medium-sized corporations, foreign stocks, mutual funds, and *bonds.*

While both Shira and Mathew understood the need for different types of stock investments, they were surprised the financial planner suggested bonds for their investment portfolio. That's when Shira asked, aren't bonds for old folks who are afraid of losing their money? Sally then explained that different investments often provide a measure of safety and reduce overall risk because a loss in one investment is usually offset by gains from other types of investments. In fact, she suggested that up to 20 percent of their investment portfolio should be placed in high-quality corporate and government bonds. Still unconvinced, Mathew asked about the return for bonds. According to Sally, bonds do return less than stocks in good years, but often return more than stocks if the stock market is headed down. Then Sally used the Matson's own situation as an example: They had lost money on their stock investments for the last five years. If they had been diversified, used the principle of asset allocation, and invested some of their money in bonds, they would have reduced their losses or even made some money, depending on the amounts they invested in different investment alternatives.

QUESTIONS

What Actions Should Be Taken?

1. Over a long period of time, stocks have provided higher returns each year than bonds. With this fact in mind, why would people choose bonds?
2. What might make bonds a good investment for one person and a poor investment for another person?

What about Your Situation?

3. Talk with various people who have invested in bonds and determine their reasons for choosing bonds.
4. Discuss with other household members whether either corporate or government bonds are appropriate investment choices for you.

Learn More Online

Use one of the Internet search engines like Yahoo! or Google to find more information about bond investing.

When it comes to investing, how do bonds fit in the "big picture"? Good question. Many people believe that the best investments are always stock investments. And while stocks have traditionally returned more than other investment alternatives, bonds are often considered a safer investment when compared to stocks or mutual funds. In fact, bonds are considered a "safe harbor" in troubled economic times. Remember Shira and Mathew Matson, the couple in the opening case? At one time, they had an investment portfolio valued at more than $200,000. Not bad for a couple in their early 40s. Then the bubble burst, and five years later they had lost more than $60,000. That's when they decided to talk with a financial planner, who explained the concept of asset allocation and how bonds and other investments could diversity their investments and reduce risk at the same time.

In addition to asset allocation and diversification, investors often choose bonds because they need current income provided by bond interest payments, and they expect to be repaid when the bonds mature. Some investors even choose specific bonds because the bond's maturity date coincides with their expected future expenses. For example, you may want to pick bonds that mature when your first child begins college, because when the bonds are repaid at maturity, the money can be used to pay college tuition. We begin this chapter by describing the basic characteristics of corporate bonds that define the relationship between investors and corporations that sell bonds to obtain financing.

corporate bond A corporation's written pledge to repay a specified amount of money with interest.

Characteristics of Corporate Bonds

Objective 1

Describe the characteristics of corporate bonds.

face value The dollar amount the bondholder will receive at the bond's maturity.

maturity date For a corporate bond, the date on which the corporation is to repay the borrowed money.

Corporate Finance 101. Corporate executives often must explain to stockholders, bankers, and bondholders where the money goes.

A **corporate bond** is a corporation's written pledge to repay a specified amount of money with interest. The **face value** (sometimes referred to as par value) is the dollar amount the bondholder will receive at the bond's maturity. The usual face value of a corporate bond is $1,000, but the face value of some corporate bonds may be as high as $50,000. The total face value of all the bonds in an issue usually runs into millions of dollars. Between the time of purchase and the maturity date, the corporation pays interest to the bondholder, usually every six months, at the stated interest rate. For example, assume you purchase a $1,000 bond issued by Xerox Corporation. The interest rate for this bond is 7.125 percent. Using the following formula, you can calculate the annual interest amount for this Xerox corporate bond:

Dollar amount of annual interest = Face value × Interest rate

= $1,000 × 7.125 percent

= $1,000 × 0.07125

= $71.25

In this situation, you receive interest of $71.25 a year from Xerox. The interest is paid semiannually, or every six months, in equal ($71.25 ÷ 2 = $35.625) installments until the bond matures.

The **maturity date** of a corporate bond is the date on which the corporation is to repay the borrowed money. At the maturity date, the bondholder returns the bond to the corporation and receives cash equal to the bond's face value. Maturity dates for bonds generally range from 1 to 30 years after the date of issue. Maturities for corporate bonds may also be classified as short term (under 5 years), intermediate term (5 to 15 years), and long term (over 15 years).

The actual legal conditions for a corporate bond are described in a bond indenture. A **bond indenture** is a legal document that details all of the conditions relating to a bond issue. Often containing over 100 pages of complicated legal wording, the bond indenture remains in effect until the bonds reach maturity or are redeemed by the corporation.

Since corporate bond indentures are difficult for the average person to read and understand, a corporation issuing bonds appoints a trustee. The **trustee** is a financially independent firm that acts as the bondholders' representative. Usually the trustee is a commercial bank or some other financial institution. The corporation must report to the trustee periodically regarding its ability to make interest payments and eventually redeem the bonds. In turn, the trustee transmits this information to the bondholders along with its own evaluation of the corporation's ability to pay. If the corporation fails to live up to all the provisions in the indenture agreement, the trustee may bring legal action to protect the bondholders' interests.

bond indenture A legal document that details all of the conditions relating to a bond issue.

trustee A financially independent firm that acts as the bondholders' representative.

CONCEPT CHECK 15-1

1 If you needed information about a bond issue would you go to the library or use the Internet?

2 What is the usual face value for a corporate bond?

3 In your own words, define *maturity date* and *bond indenture.*

4 How does a trustee evaluate the provisions contained in a bond indenture?

Action Application Calculate the annual interest and the semiannual interest payment for the following corporate bond issues with a face value of $1,000.

Corporate Bond Issued By	Maturity Date	Annual Interest Rate	Annual Interest	Semiannual Interest Payment
GTE South	2026	7.00%		
Household Finance Inc.	2009	6.30		
SBC Communications	2014	5.10		

Why Corporations Sell Corporate Bonds

Let's begin this section with some basics of why corporations sell bonds. Corporations borrow when they don't have enough money to pay for major purchases—much as individuals do. Bonds can also be used to finance a corporation's ongoing business activities. In addition, corporations often sell bonds when it is difficult or impossible to sell stock. The sale of bonds can also improve a corporation's financial leverage—the use of borrowed funds to increase the corporation's return on investment. Finally, the interest paid to bond owners is a tax-deductible expense and thus can be used to reduce the taxes the corporation must pay to the federal and state governments.

Corporate bonds are often referred to as the "work horse" of corporate finance. They are used by many corporations to raise capital because it costs less to issue bonds than to sell a new stock issue. While a corporation may use both bonds and stocks to finance its activities, there are important distinctions between the two. Corporate bonds are a form of *debt financing,* whereas stock is a form of *equity financing.* Bond owners must be repaid at a future date; stockholders do not have to be repaid. Interest payments on

Objective 2

Discuss why corporations issue bonds.

bonds are required; dividends are paid to stockholders at the discretion of the board of directors. And, in the event of bankruptcy, bondholders have a claim to the assets of the corporation prior to that of stockholders. Finally, many financial managers prefer selling bonds because they retain control of the corporation since bondholders generally do not have a right to vote. On the other hand, stockholders do have a right to vote on many corporate governance issues, including the right to elect the boards of directors. Before issuing bonds, a corporation must decide what type of bond to issue and how the bond issue will be repaid.

TYPES OF BONDS

debenture A bond that is backed only by the reputation of the issuing corporation.

mortgage bond A corporate bond secured by various assets of the issuing firm.

Most corporate bonds are debentures. A **debenture** is a bond that is backed only by the reputation of the issuing corporation. If the corporation fails to make either interest payments or repayment at maturity, debenture bondholders become general creditors, much like the firm's suppliers. In the event of corporate bankruptcy, general creditors, including debenture bondholders, can claim any asset not specifically used as collateral for a loan or other financial obligation.

To make a bond issue more appealing to conservative investors, a corporation may issue a mortgage bond. A **mortgage bond** (sometimes referred to as a *secured bond*) is a corporate bond secured by various assets of the issuing firm. A first mortgage bond may be backed by a lien on a specific asset, usually real estate. A corporation can also issue bonds that are backed by stocks and other bonds that it owns and, in some cases, even its operating equipment. A general mortgage bond is secured by all the fixed assets of the firm that are not pledged as collateral for other financial obligations. A secured bond is safer than a debenture because corporate assets or collateral may be sold to repay the bondholders if the corporation defaults on interest or repayment. Because of this added security, interest rates on mortgage bonds are usually lower than interest rates on unsecured debentures.

A third type of bond a corporation may issue is called a *subordinated* debenture. A **subordinated debenture** is an unsecured bond that gives bondholders a claim secondary to that of other designated bondholders with respect to interest payments, repayment, and assets. Investors who purchase subordinated debentures usually enjoy higher interest rates than other bondholders because of the increased risk associated with this type of bond.

DID YOU KNOW?

Bond Yields for High-Quality Corporate Bonds

Source: U.S. Bureau of the Census, *Statistical Abstract of the United States, 2004–2005*, 124th ed. (Washington, DC: U.S. Government Printing Office, 2004), p. 750.

CONVERTIBLE BONDS

subordinated debenture An unsecured bond that gives bondholders a claim secondary to that of other designated bondholders with respect to interest payments, repayment, and assets.

convertible bond A bond that can be exchanged, at the owner's option, for a specified number of shares of the corporation's common stock.

A special type of bond a corporation may issue is a convertible bond. A **convertible bond** can be exchanged, at the owner's option, for a specified number of shares of the corporation's common stock. This conversion feature allows investors to enjoy the lower risk of a corporate bond but also take advantage of the speculative nature of common stock. For example, Kerr-McGee Corporation's $1,000 bond issue with a 2010 maturity date is convertible. Each bond can be converted to 16.373 shares of the company's common stock. This means you could convert the bond to common stock whenever the price of the company's common stock is $61.08 ($1,000 ÷ 16.373 = $61.08) or higher.

In reality, there is no guarantee that Kerr-McGee bondholders will convert to common stock even if the market value of the common stock does increase to $61.08 or higher. The reason for choosing not to exercise the conversion feature in this example is quite simple. As the market value of the common stock increases, the market value of the convertible bond *also* increases. By not converting to common stock, bondholders enjoy the added safety of the bond and interest income in addition to the increased market value of the bond caused by the price movement of the common stock.

The corporation gains three advantages by issuing convertible bonds. First, the interest rate on a convertible bond is often 1 to 2 percent lower than that on traditional bonds. Second, the conversion feature attracts investors who are interested in the speculative gain that conversion to common stock may provide. Third, if the bondholder converts to common stock, the corporation no longer has to redeem the bond at maturity.

Convertible bonds, like all potential investments, must be carefully evaluated. Remember, not all convertible bonds are quality investments.

PROVISIONS FOR REPAYMENT

Today most corporate bonds are callable. A **call feature** allows the corporation to call in or buy outstanding bonds from current bondholders before the maturity date. In the last part of the 20th century and the first part of the 21st century, investors saw a large number of bonds called. For bondholders who purchased bonds for income, a problem is often created when a bond paying high interest is called. For example, if your bond that pays 10 percent annual interest is called, it may be difficult for you to replace the bond with a new bond of the same quality that also pays the same 10 percent interest rate. This is especially true when overall interest rates in the economy are declining. If you choose to replace your bond, you may have to purchase a bond with a lower interest rate (and ultimately lower income from your new bond investment) or a bond with lower quality to obtain a 10 percent annual rate. Keep in mind, corporate financial managers always want to obtain financing at the lowest cost possible and won't pay more interest than they have to. The money needed to call a bond may come from the firm's profits, the sale of additional stock, or the sale of a new bond issue that has a lower interest rate.

In most cases, corporations issuing callable bonds agree not to call them for the first 5 to 10 years after the bonds have been issued. When a call feature is used, the corporation may have to pay the bondholders a *premium,* an additional amount above the face value of the bond. The amount of the premium is specified in the bond indenture; a $10 to $25 premium over the bond's face value is common.

A corporation may use one of two methods to ensure that it has sufficient funds available to redeem a bond issue. First, the corporation may establish a sinking fund. A **sinking fund** is a fund to which annual or semiannual deposits are made for the purpose of redeeming a bond issue. To retire a $54 million bond issue that matures in 2008, Scott Paper Company agreed to make annual sinking fund payments prior to maturity.

A sinking fund provision in the bond indenture is generally advantageous to bondholders. Such a provision forces the corporation to make arrangements for bond repayment before the maturity date. If the terms of the provision are not met, the trustee or bondholders may take legal action against the company.

Second, a corporation may issue serial bonds. **Serial bonds** are bonds of a single issue that mature on different dates. For example, Seaside Productions used a 20-year, $100 million bond issue to finance its expansion. None of the bonds mature during the first 10 years. Thereafter, 10 percent of the bonds mature each year until all the bonds are retired at the end of the 20-year period. A call provision can also be used to buy back bonds before the maturity date.

Detailed information about provisions for repayment, along with other vital information (including maturity date, interest rate, bond rating, call provisions, trustee, and details about security), is available from Moody's Investors Service, Standard & Poor's Corporation, and other financial service companies. Take a look at the information provided by *Mergent's Public Utility Manual* for the Cincinnati Gas & Electric Company bond illustrated in Financial Planning for Life's Situations: The "How To" of Researching a Bond.

call feature A feature that allows the corporation to call in or buy outstanding bonds from current bondholders before the maturity date.

sinking fund A fund to which annual or semiannual deposits are made for the purpose of redeeming a bond issue.

serial bonds Bonds of a single issue that mature on different dates.

Financial Planning for Life's Situations

THE "HOW TO" OF RESEARCHING A BOND

How do you find out whether or not a corporate bond is callable? Where can you find out who the trustee for a specific bond issue is? These are only two of the multitude of questions that concern investors who are trying to evaluate bond investments. Fortunately, the answers are easy to obtain if you know where to look.

Today the most readily available source of detailed information about a corporation, including information about its bond issues, is *Mergent's Manuals*. Individual subscriptions to this series of publications are too expensive for most investors, but the series is available at both college and public libraries. It includes individual manuals on industrial companies, public utilities, banks and financial institutions, and transportation companies. Each manual contains detailed information on major companies in the United States, including the company's history, operations, products, and bond issues.

The following data on a corporate bond issued by Cincinnati Gas & Electric Company will give you an idea of the contents of the "Long-Term Debt" section of a Mergent's report.

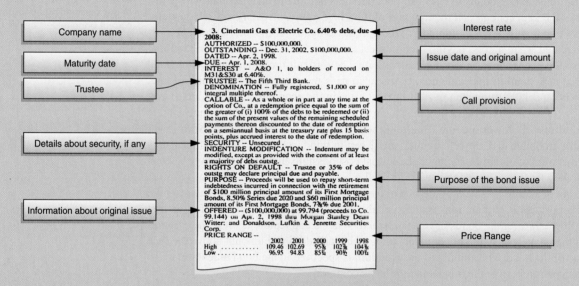

| Company name |
| Maturity date |
| Trustee |
| Details about security, if any |
| Information about original issue |

3. Cincinnati Gas & Electric Co. 6.40% debs, due 2008:
AUTHORIZED -- $100,000,000.
OUTSTANDING -- Dec. 31, 2002, $100,000,000.
DATED -- Apr. 2, 1998.
DUE -- Apr. 1, 2008.
INTEREST -- A&O 1, to holders of record on M31&S30 at 6.40%.
TRUSTEE -- The Fifth Third Bank.
DENOMINATION -- Fully registered, $1,000 or any integral multiple thereof.
CALLABLE -- As a whole or in part at any time at the option of Co., at a redemption price equal to the sum of the greater of (i) 100% of the debs to be redeemed or (ii) the sum of the present values of the remaining scheduled payments thereon discounted to the date of redemption on a semiannual basis at the treasury rate plus 15 basis points, plus accrued interest to the date of redemption.
SECURITY -- Unsecured .
INDENTURE MODIFICATION -- Indenture may be modified, except as provided with the consent of at least a majority of debs outstg.
RIGHTS ON DEFAULT -- Trustee or 35% of debs outstg may declare principal due and payable.
PURPOSE -- Proceeds will be used to repay short-term indebtedness incurred in connection with the retirement of $100 million principal amount of its First Mortgage Bonds, 8.50% Series due 2020 and $60 million principal amount of its First Mortgage Bonds, 7⅜% due 2001.
OFFERED -- ($100,000,000) at 99.794 (proceeds to Co. 99.144) on Apr. 2, 1998 thru Morgan Stanley Dean Witter; and Donaldson, Lufkin & Jenrette Securities Corp.
PRICE RANGE --

	2002	2001	2000	1999	1998
High	109.46	102.69	95⅜	102⅞	104⅛
Low	96.95	94.83	85¼	90½	100¼

| Interest rate |
| Issue date and original amount |
| Call provision |
| Purpose of the bond issue |
| Price Range |

Source: The information for the Cincinnati Gas & Electric Company corporate bond was taken from *Mergent's Public Utility Manual*, 2004, p. 908.

CONCEPT CHECK 15-2

1 Why do corporations sell bonds?

2 What are the differences among a debenture, a mortgage bond, and a subordinated debenture?

3 Why would an investor purchase a Kerr-McGee convertible bond?

4 Describe three reasons a corporation would sell convertible bonds.

5 Explain the methods corporations can use to repay a bond issue.

Action Application Use the Internet or financial publications to identify a corporation that is raising capital by selling bonds. Then describe the type of bond, the total amount of the bond issue, the interest rate for the bonds, and the maturity date.

Why Investors Purchase Corporate Bonds

In Chapters 13 and 14, we compared the historical returns provided by stocks and bonds. Stocks, with approximately a 10 percent return before adjusting for inflation, have always outdistanced the performance of bonds at a 4 percent return.[1] With this fact in mind, you may be wondering why you should consider bonds as an investment alternative. Why not just choose stocks because they provide the highest possible return of the different investment alternatives? To answer that question, you need to review the concept of asset allocation that was explained in Chapter 13. *Asset allocation* is the process of spreading your assets among several different types of investments to lessen risk. As pointed out in Chapter 13, asset allocation is a fancy way of saying that you need to avoid the pitfall of putting all of your eggs in one basket—a common mistake made by many investors. The fact is that many corporate and government bonds are safer investments and are often considered a "safe harbor" in troubled economic times. For example, many stock investors lost money during the period from 2000 to 2005 because of the economic downturn. As an alternative to leaving your money in stocks, assuming that you thought the stock market was headed for a period of decline, you could have moved money into corporate or government bonds. That's exactly what Joe Goode did in January 2000. Although his friends thought he was crazy for taking such a conservative approach, he actually avoided a prolonged downturn in the stock market. Now many of his friends wish they had made the same decision. According to Joe, he earned interest on his bond investments while preserving his investment funds for a return to the stock market when the economy rebounds. For specific suggestions to help determine whether bonds will help you achieve your financial goals, see Exhibit 15–1. Basically, investors purchase corporate bonds for three reasons: (1) interest income, (2) possible increase in value, and (3) repayment at maturity.

Objective 3

Explain why investors purchase corporate bonds.

For more information on bond investments, go to **www.investinginbonds.com**.

INTEREST INCOME

As mentioned earlier in this chapter, bondholders normally receive interest payments every six months. And, the dollar amount of interest is determined by multiplying the interest rate by the face value of the bond. In fact, because interest income is so important to bond investors, let's review this calculation. If Hertz Corporation issues a 7.40 percent bond that matures in 2011 with a face value of $1,000, the investor will receive $74 ($1,000 × 7.40% = $74) a year, paid in installments of $37 at the end of each six-month period until the bond's maturity in 2011.

Financial Need	Suggestion
1. Asset allocation	Bonds are an excellent way to diversify your portfolio and lessen risk.
2. Income for current financial needs	Generally, bonds pay interest (income) semiannually (every six months).
3. Long-term financial needs	Bonds can be purchased with maturity dates that match future financial needs.
4. Conservative investment in an economic downturn	Buy bonds with higher interest rates to lock in higher income.

Exhibit **15–1**

Financial suggestions for bond investors

Whether you are just starting your career or retired, it helps to have quality investment advice.

registered bond A bond that is registered in the owner's name by the issuing company.

bearer bond A bond that is not registered in the investor's name.

zero-coupon bond A bond that is sold at a price far below its face value, makes no annual or semiannual interest payments, and is redeemed for its face value at maturity.

The method used to pay bondholders their interest depends on whether they own registered bonds, bearer bonds, or zero-coupon bonds. A **registered bond** is registered in the owner's name by the issuing company. Generally, interest checks for registered bonds are mailed directly to the bondholder of record.

A second type of bond is a **bearer bond,** which is not registered in the investor's name. While U.S. corporations no longer issue them, bearer bonds are generally issued by corporations in foreign countries. *Be warned:* If you own a bearer bond, you can be out of luck if it is lost or stolen. Anyone—the rightful owner or a thief—can collect interest payments and the face value at maturity if he or she has physical possession of the bearer bond.

A **zero-coupon bond** is sold at a price far below its face value, makes no annual or semiannual interest payments, and is redeemed for its face value at maturity. With a zero-coupon bond, the buyer receives a return based on the bond's increased market value as its maturity date approaches. For example, assume you purchased a Waste Management zero-coupon bond for $350 in 1995 and Waste Management will pay you $1,000 when the bond matures in 2012. For holding the bond 18 years, you will receive interest of $650 ($1,000 face value − $350 purchase price = $650 interest) at maturity.

Before investing in zero-coupon bonds, you should consider at least two factors. First, even though all of the interest on these bonds is paid at maturity, the IRS requires you to report interest each year—that is, as you earn it, not when you actually receive it. Second, zero-coupon bonds are more volatile than other types of bonds. When evaluating such bonds, as in evaluating other types of bonds, the most important criterion is the quality of the issuer. It pays to be careful.

DOLLAR APPRECIATION OF BOND VALUE

Most beginning investors think that a $1,000 bond is always worth $1,000. In reality, the price of a corporate bond may fluctuate until the maturity date. Changes in overall interest rates in the economy are the primary cause of most bond price fluctuations. Today, many economists project that both long-term and short-term interest rates will increase in the near future. In reality, an increase *or* a decrease in interest rates can affect the price of a bond.

Changing bond prices that result from changes in overall interest rates in the economy are an example of interest rate risk and market risk, discussed in Chapter 13. In fact, there is an inverse relationship between a bond's market value and overall interest rates in the economy. When Hertz issued the bond mentioned earlier, the 7.40 percent interest rate was competitive with the interest rates offered by other corporations issuing bonds at that time. If overall interest rates fall, the Hertz bond will go up in market value due to its higher, 7.40 percent, interest rate. On the other hand, if overall interest rates rise, the market value of the Hertz bond will fall due to its lower, 7.40 percent, interest rate.

When a bond is selling for less than its face value, it is said to be selling at a *discount.* When a bond is selling for more than its face value, it is said to be selling at a *premium.* Generally, investors consult the Internet, the *Wall Street Journal, Barron's,* or a metropolitan newspaper to determine the price of a bond. Information on how to read bond quotations is provided later in this chapter. It is also possible to calculate a bond's approximate market value using the following formula:

$$\text{Approximate market value} = \frac{\text{Dollar amount of annual interest}}{\text{Comparable interest rate}}$$

THE RISKS ASSOCIATED WITH INVESTING IN FOREIGN BONDS

Why invest in foreign bonds? Good question! Unfortunately the answer is complicated by many factors. Usually investors choose foreign bonds because they are trying to use asset allocation to diversity their investment portfolio. In fact, many investors often choose domestic stocks, bonds, mutual funds, and even foreign bonds in an attempt to diversify their investment portfolios. And yet, two specific problems should be considered before purchasing foreign securities, according to Joshua Kennon, one of the contributors to About.com's "Your Guide to Investing for Beginners" feature.

LEGAL RIGHTS

First, foreign stocks and bonds are issued by a foreign entity such as a government, municipality, or corporation and are traded on a foreign financial market. The primary risk of a foreign security is that it is an unenforceable legal claim should the country be taken over by an extremist political movement that seizes all foreign assets. In this situation, investors do not have the same legal rights in a foreign country that they have in the United States. Is this concern justified? Just for a moment, consider the plight of the small investor who lost money in Iran after the country was taken over by a new political force.

CURRENCY EXCHANGE RISK

Second, any time you purchase a foreign bond that is bought and sold in a foreign currency, you are subject to currency risk. Simply defined, currency risk is the potential for loss due to fluctuations in exchange rates. Put another way: Changes in the currency exchange rate may turn a profit into a loss or a loss into a profit. The currency exchange rate is applied any time you buy or sell foreign securities and when interest and dividends are paid. For instance, if you want to purchase a foreign bond issued by a European firm, your U.S. dollars must be converted to euros. And the euros you receive when you sell your foreign bond must be converted back to U.S. dollars. Your potential return is determined not only by how well your investment performed, but also by whether the currency exchange rate became more or less favorable during the time you held the investment.

Source: Joshua Kennon, "The Danger of Investing in Foreign Bonds," www.about.com, May 16, 2005.

For example, assume you purchase a Verizon Global bond that pays 4 percent interest based on a face value of $1,000 with the bond's maturity in 2008. Also assume new corporate bond issues of comparable quality are currently paying 5 percent. The approximate market value is $800, as follows:

$$\text{Dollar amount of annual interest} = \$1,000 \times 4 \text{ percent}$$

$$= \$40$$

$$\text{Approximate market value} = \frac{\text{Dollar amount of annual interest}}{\text{Comparable interest rate}} = \frac{\$40}{5\%}$$

$$= \$800$$

If you purchase the Verizon Global bond for $800, you will receive $40 interest each year until the bond's maturity. You will also be repaid the $1,000 face value at maturity, which results in a $200 profit because the bond's value increased from $800 to $1,000 between the time of purchase and the maturity date.

The value of a bond may also be affected by the financial condition of the company or government unit issuing the bond, the factors of supply and demand, an upturn or downturn in the economy, and the proximity of the bond's maturity date.

BOND REPAYMENT AT MATURITY

Corporate bonds are repaid at maturity. After you purchase a bond, you have two options: You may keep the bond until maturity and then redeem it, or you may sell the bond at any time to another investor. In either case, the value of your bond is closely tied to the corporation's ability to repay its bond indebtedness. The risk of business failure and how it affects bond repayment was discussed in Chapter 13. For example, the retailer Color Tile and Carpet filed for reorganization under the provisions of the U.S. Bankruptcy Act. As a result, the bonds issued by Color Tile immediately dropped in value due to questions concerning the prospects for bond repayment at maturity. On the other hand, if a corporation establishes a reputation as an aggressive firm with excellent and innovative products, experienced and capable managers, and increasing sales and profits, the value of your bond will remain stable or even increase. Simply put: Other investors may pay more money to get a quality bond that has excellent prospects of repayment at maturity.

Some investors use a concept called "bond laddering" to help balance risk and return in an investment portfolio. To start your bond ladder, you purchase different bonds with maturities spread out over a number of years. For example, you might purchase bonds that mature in 1, 2, 3, 4, 5, 6, 7, 8, 9, and 10 years. When the first bond matures, you purchase a new bond that matures in 10 years. This new purchase continues the bond ladder. The short-term bonds provide a high degree of stability because the bonds are not very sensitive to changing interest rates. The long-term bonds provide a higher yield, but you must accept the risk that the prices of the bonds might change. By choosing bonds with different maturities, you realize greater returns than from holding only short-term bonds, but with lower risk than holding only long-term bonds. With a bond ladder, you can also take advantage of the concept of dollar-cost averaging that was discussed in Chapter 14.

A TYPICAL BOND TRANSACTION

Assume that on March 15, 1995, you purchased a 9.2 percent corporate bond issued by Borden Chemical Inc. Your cost for the bond was $920 plus a $10 commission charge, for a total investment of $930. Also, assume you held the bond until March 15, 2005,

Exhibit **15-2**

Sample corporate bond transaction for Borden Chemical Inc.

Assumptions			
Interest, 9.2 percent; maturity date, 2021; purchased March 15, 1995; sold March 15, 2005			
Costs when purchased		**Return when sold**	
1 bond @ $920	$920	1 bond @ $1,060	$1,060
Plus commission	+ 10	Minus commission	− 10
Total investment	$930	Dollar return	$1,050
Transaction summary			
Dollar return		$1,050	
Minus total investment		− 930	
Profit from bond sale		$ 120	
Plus interest ($92 for 10 years)		+ 920	
Total return on the transaction		$1,040	

when you sold it at its current market value of $1,060. Exhibit 15–2 shows the return on your investment.

After paying commissions for buying and selling your Borden Chemical bond, you experienced a capital gain of $120 because the market value of the bond increased from $930 to $1,050. The increase in the value of the bond resulted because overall interest rates in the economy declined during the 10-year period in which you owned the bond. Also, Borden Chemical's bonds will generally increase in value the closer they get to the maturity date in 2021.

You also made money on your Borden Chemical bond because of interest payments. For each of the 10 years you owned the bond, Borden Chemical paid you $92 ($1,000 × 9.2%) interest. Thus, you received interest payments totaling $920. In this example, you made a total return of $1,040, as follows:

$$\text{Total return} = \text{Current return} + \text{Capital gain}$$

$$= \$920 + \$120$$

$$= \$1,040$$

Before investing in bonds, you should remember that the price of a corporate bond can decrease and that interest payments and eventual repayment may be a problem for a corporation that encounters financial difficulties or enters bankruptcy. Also, both the interest and the capital gain are taxable. For more information on how taxation affects a bond investment see Chapter 4 of this text or visit the IRS Web site at www.irs.gov. Instead of purchasing individual bonds, some investors prefer to purchase bond funds. To help you decide whether you should purchase individual bonds or bond funds, read the Financial Planning for Life's Situations box on page 492.

THE MECHANICS OF A BOND TRANSACTION

Most bonds are sold through full-service brokerage firms, discount brokerage firms, or the Internet. If you use a full-service brokerage firm, your account executive should provide both information and advice about bond investments. As with stock investments, the chief advantage of using a discount brokerage firm or trading online is lower commissions, but you must do your own research. As you will see later in this chapter, many sources of information can be used to evaluate bond investments.

Bonds are purchased in much the same manner as stocks. Corporate bonds may be purchased in the primary market or the secondary market. (Remember, in the *primary* market, an investor purchases financial securities, via an investment bank or other representative, from the issuer of those securities. In the *secondary* market, existing financial securities are traded among investors.) The actual steps involved in purchasing a bond listed on an exchange are similar to the steps required to purchase stocks (see Chapter 14). You can also purchase corporate bonds directly from account executives who make a market or maintain an inventory for certain bonds.

Generally, if you purchase a $1,000 bond through an account executive or brokerage firm, you should expect to pay a minimum commission of between $10 and $35. If you purchase more bonds, the commission usually drops to $5 to $20 per bond. You should also expect to pay commissions when you sell bonds. If you buy or sell bonds listed on an exchange, the exchange specialist often will charge a fee for handling the transaction. This "spread" is a slight difference between the reported price for the bond and the price charged to buy the bond. The spread also affects the amount you will receive when you sell a bond listed on an exchange. This additional cost (along with the commission charged by the brokerage firm) to buy and sell bonds increases the cost of bond transactions.

Financial Planning for Life's Situations

ARE BOND FUNDS RIGHT FOR YOU?

Bond funds are an indirect way of owning bonds, debt instruments, and IOUs issued by the U.S. Treasury, corporations, or state, city, and local governments. Many financial experts recommend bond funds for small investors because these investments offer two advantages: diversification and professional management. Diversification spells safety because an occasional loss incurred with one bond issue is usually offset by gains from other bond issues in the fund. It is hard for a small investor purchasing individual bonds to achieve the level of diversification provided by a bond fund. Also, professional managers should be able to do a better job of picking bonds than individual investors. But before investing, consider three factors. First, even the best managers make mistakes. Second, it may cost more to purchase bond funds than individual bonds. Finally, rising interest rates can cause the value of an individual bond with a fixed interest rate to decline. And since bond funds are made up of individual bonds, the share value for a bond fund is likely to decline if interest rates rise. Be warned: Both long-term and short-term interest rates are projected to rise in the near future according to many economists. As with most investments, the key to making money with funds is evaluation.

EVALUATING BOND FUNDS

Martha Hernandez, a working mother with one child, received $44,000 following the death of her grandmother. After some careful planning, she decided to invest $34,000 in two high-quality corporate bond funds. She used the remaining $10,000 to pay off some credit card debts and establish an emergency fund. During the next two years, she

earned over 9 percent on her bond investments each year—not bad during a period when CDs were paying between 3 and 4 percent.

Martha's 9 percent return wasn't just luck. She began by establishing an investment goal: Find a safe investment with minimal risk. After establishing her goal, she talked with an account executive at Merrill Lynch and asked for five suggestions that would enable her to attain her goal. Of the five original suggestions, three were conservative bond funds.

Next, Martha took a crucial step that many investors forget: She decided to do her own research and not just rely on the account executive's suggestions. She used the Internet to obtain both a prospectus and an annual report for each fund. After receiving the information, she was able to determine each fund's investment objective and identify the investments each fund contained.

Then she made a trip to the library, where she analyzed the performance of each of the three bond funds in the special mutual fund editions of *BusinessWeek, Kiplinger's Personal Finance,* and *Money.* Each publication ranked the three bond funds according to the total return for different time periods and on the factors of safety and risk. Based on the account executive's suggestions and her own research, she chose the "top" two bond funds.

Martha spent almost 30 hours researching her investments, but believes the time was well spent. When you consider the amount of money she made on her bond fund investments during the first two years—over $6,000—she made over $200 an hour.

CONCEPT CHECK 15-3

1 Describe the three reasons investors purchase bonds.
2 What are the differences among a registered bond, a bearer bond, and a zero-coupon bond?
3 In what ways can interest rates in the economy affect the price of a corporate bond?
4 Why is the value of a bond closely tied to the issuing corporation's ability to repay its bond indebtedness?
5 How are corporate bonds bought and sold?

Action Application Use the Internet or library sources to identify a corporate bond that would help you obtain your financial goals. Then prepare a report that describes the corporation that issued the bond, the interest rate, the bond's current price, and why you think this bond is a good investment.

Government Bonds and Debt Securities

In addition to corporations, the U.S. government and state and local governments issue bonds to obtain financing. In this section, we discuss bonds issued by these three levels of government and look at why investors purchase these bonds.

TREASURY BILLS, NOTES, AND BONDS

Why purchase United States Treasury securities? Because they are a safe investment with little risk! The main reason investors choose U.S. government securities is that most investors consider them risk free. In fact, some financial planners refer to them as the ultimate safe investment because their quality is considered to be higher than that of any other investment. Because they are backed by the full faith and credit of the U.S. government and carry a decreased risk of default, they offer lower interest rates than corporate bonds. U.S. Treasury securities are also used by some investors to allocate their investment assets and lessen overall risk.

Today, the U.S. Treasury Department issues three principal types of securities: Treasury bills, Treasury notes, and U.S. government savings bonds. Note: Refer to Chapter 5 for a review of different types of U.S. savings bonds. (Although still available in the secondary market, another type of security—long-term Treasury bonds—is no longer issued by the Treasury Department.) At the time of publication, there are plans to begin selling bonds again in 2006. Treasury bills, notes, and savings bonds can be purchased through Treasury Direct at www.treasurydirect.gov. For more information about the Treasury Direct Web site, see Exhibit 15–3. Treasury Direct conducts auctions to sell Treasury bills and notes. Buyers interested in purchasing these securities at such auctions may bid competitively or noncompetitively. Most individual investors use noncompetitive bids once they have visited the Web site and opened an account. If they bid competitively, they must specify the rate or interest yield they are willing to accept. If they bid noncompetitively, they are willing to accept the interest rate or yield determined at auction. Treasury securities may also be purchased directly from banks or brokers, which charge a commission.

Interest paid on U.S. government securities is taxable for federal income tax purposes but is exempt from state and local taxation. Current information on prices and interest rates appears on the Internet and in the *Wall Street Journal* and other financial publications.

Without bond issues, government projects like Michigan's $88 million Hall of Justice could not be completed.

TREASURY BILLS   A *Treasury bill,* sometimes called a *T-bill,* is sold in a minimum unit of $1,000 with additional increments of $1,000 above the minimum. Although the maturity for T-bills may be as long as 1 year, the Treasury Department currently only sells T-bills with 4-week, 13-week, and 26-week maturities. Another type of bill, the cash management bill, is issued in terms usually shorter than those of other T-bills.

T-bills are discounted securities, and the actual purchase price you pay is less than the maturity value of the T-bill. Let's assume that you purchase a 26-week, $1,000 T-bill with a stated interest rate of 3 percent. To determine the discount amount ($15), multiply the maturity value by the interest rate ($1,000 × 3 percent = $30). Note: the first answer ($30) represents interest for an entire year, or 52 weeks. To determine the interest for a 26-week (one-half of a year) T-bill, it is necessary to divide the first answer by 2 ($30 ÷ 2 = $15). To determine the purchase price ($985), subtract the discount amount from the maturity value ($1,000 − $15).

Exhibit **15-3**

The Treasure Direct Web site provides information regarding United States Treasury securities

Source: www.treasurydirect.gov, May 14, 2005.

In reality, the yield on T-bills is slightly higher than the stated interest rate. In the above example, you received $15 interest on a $985 investment, which represents a 3.05 percent annual return, as follows:

$$\text{Current yield for a T-bill} = \frac{\text{Discount amount}}{\text{Purchase price}} \times 2$$

$$= \$15/\$985 \times 2$$

$$= 0.0305 = 3.05 \text{ percent}$$

The 2 in the above formula is to adjust for the fact that this T-bill has a 26-week maturity.

TREASURY NOTES   A *Treasury note* (sometimes called a T-note) is issued in $1,000 units with a maturity of more than 1 year but not more than 10 years. Typical maturities are 2, 3, 5, and 10 years. Interest rates for Treasury notes are slightly higher than those for Treasury bills, because investors must wait longer to get their money back and therefore demand more compensation in the form of higher interest. Interest for Treasury notes is paid every six months. Notes can be held until maturity or sold before maturity. Like T-bills, Treasury notes may be purchased from the U.S. Treasury by placing a competitive or noncompetitive bid in an auction.

TREASURY BONDS   As mentioned earlier in this section, the Treasury Department no longer issues Treasury bonds. However, many are still in existence and may be purchased in

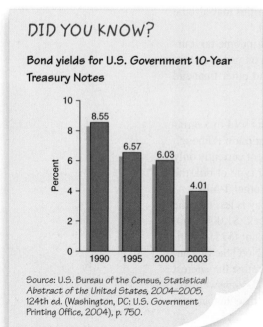

DID YOU KNOW?

Bond yields for U.S. Government 10-Year Treasury Notes

Source: U.S. Bureau of the Census, *Statistical Abstract of the United States, 2004–2005,* 124th ed. (Washington, DC: U.S. Government Printing Office, 2004), p. 750.

the secondary market through a broker or other financial institution. Therefore, basic information about Treasury bonds is provided below. A *Treasury bond* is issued in minimum units of $1,000 that have maturities ranging from 10 to 30 years. Interest rates for Treasury bonds are generally higher than those for either Treasury bills or Treasury notes. Again, the primary reason for the higher interest rates is the length of time investors must hold Treasury bonds. Like interest on Treasury notes, interest on Treasury bonds is paid every six months. Bonds can be held until maturity or sold before maturity. As mentioned earlier, the U.S. Treasury plans to begin selling 30-year bonds in 2006.

FEDERAL AGENCY DEBT ISSUES

In addition to the bonds and securities issued by the Treasury Department, debt securities are issued by federal agencies, which include the Federal National Mortgage Association (sometimes referred to as Fannie Mae), the Federal Housing Administration (FHA), the Government National Mortgage Association (sometimes referred to as Ginnie Mae), and the Federal Home Loan Mortgage Corporation (which somehow became known as Freddie Mac).

For more information on Fannie Mae investments, go to **www.fanniemae.com**.

Agency debt issues offer a slightly higher interest rate than government securities issued by the Treasury Department because of slightly higher risk when compared to Treasury securities. Their minimum denomination may be as high as $25,000. Securities issued by federal agencies have maturities ranging from 1 year to 30 years, with an average life of about 12 years. Often brokers and account executives recommend federal agency debt instruments because the interest rate is 0.50 to 1.0 percent higher than Treasury securities. However, you should know that there are differences in how interest is paid when compared to Treasury securities and that most agency debt is also callable before the maturity date. Simply put, investing in agency debt is more complicated than buying and selling Treasury securities.

STATE AND LOCAL GOVERNMENT SECURITIES

A **municipal bond,** sometimes called a *muni,* is a debt security issued by a state or local government. In the United States, there are 50 state governments. In addition, cities, counties, school districts, and special taxing districts may sell municipal bonds. Such securities are used to finance the ongoing activities of state and local governments and major projects such as airports, schools, toll roads, and toll bridges. They may be purchased directly from the government entity that issued them or through account executives.

State and local securities are classified as either general obligation bonds or revenue bonds. A **general obligation bond** is backed by the full faith, credit, and unlimited taxing power of the government that issued it. A **revenue bond** is repaid from the income generated by the project it is designed to finance.

Although both general obligation and revenue bonds are relatively safe, defaults have occurred in recent years. Generally, investment-grade corporate bonds (discussed later in this chapter) have a default rate of about 2 percent. Because of the lower risk of default, high-grade municipals rank second in quality only to securities issued by the U.S. government and government agencies.[2] Even with this fact in mind, investors should still worry about default on interest payments and eventual repayment of municipal bonds. Many people have heard the "horror" stories about investors who owned municipal bonds issued by Orange County (California) or the Washington Public Power Supply. Default rates were also high for tax-exempt bonds used to finance health care

municipal bond A debt security issued by a state or local government.

general obligation bond A bond backed by the full faith, credit, and unlimited taxing power of the government that issued it.

revenue bond A bond that is repaid from the income generated by the project it is designed to finance.

facilities in the late 1990s. Unfortunately, tax-exempt bonds used to fund other state or local government projects have also cost investors millions of dollars.

If the risk of default worries you, you can purchase insured municipal bonds. A number of states offer to guarantee payments on selected securities. Also, there are three large private insurers: MBIA Inc.(Municipal Bond Insurance Association); the Financial Security Assurance Corporation (FSA); and AMBAC Inc. (American Municipal Bond Assurance Corporation). Even if a municipal bond issue is insured, however, financial experts worry about the insurer's ability to pay off in the event of default on a large bond issue. Most advise investors to determine the underlying quality of a bond whether or not it is insured. Also, guaranteed municipal securities usually carry a slightly lower interest rate than uninsured bonds because of the reduced risk of default.

Like a corporate bond, a municipal bond may be callable by the government unit that issued it. Typically, some call protection exists. In most cases, the municipality that issues the bond agrees not to call it for the first 10 years. *Be warned:* Your municipal bond may be called if interest rates fall and the government entity that issued the bond can sell new bonds with lower rates. For example, in the late 1990s and the first part of the 21st century, thousands of municipal bondholders who purchased high-yielding municipal bonds in the late 1980s were shocked to have their bonds called. Many were counting on another 10 to 15 years of 10 percent or higher yields to finance their retirement. Although they were repaid the principal invested in the bond that was called, they faced the challenge of reinvesting their money when interest rates were at a 40-year low. If the bond is not called, the investor has two options. First, the bond may be held until maturity, in which case the investor will be repaid its face value. Second, the bond may be sold to another investor.

One of the most important features of municipal bonds is that the interest on them may be exempt from federal taxes. Whether or not the interest on municipal bonds is tax exempt often depends on how the funds obtained from their sale are used. *It is your responsibility, as an investor, to determine whether or not interest on municipal bonds is taxable.* Municipal bonds exempt from federal taxation are generally exempt from state and local taxes only in the state where they are issued. Furthermore, although the interest on municipal bonds may be exempt from taxation, a *capital gain* that results when you sell a municipal bond before maturity and at a profit may be taxable just like capital gains on other investments sold at a profit.

To some extent, the tax advantages associated with municipal bonds have diminished because current tax laws have lowered the maximum federal income tax rate for individuals. But even with the lower tax rates, municipal bonds are still popular among wealthy investors. Because of their tax-exempt status, the interest rates on municipal bonds are lower than those on taxable bonds. By using the following formula, you can calculate the *taxable equivalent yield* for a municipal security:

$$\text{Taxable equivalent yield} = \frac{\text{Tax-exempt yield}}{1.0 - \text{Your tax rate}}$$

For example, the taxable equivalent yield on a 5 percent, tax-exempt municipal bond for a person in the 28 percent tax bracket is 6.94 percent, as follows:

$$\text{Taxable equivalent yield} = \frac{0.05}{1.0 - 0.28} = 0.0694, \text{ or } 6.94 \text{ percent}$$

If this taxpayer had been in the 35 percent tax bracket, the taxable equivalent yield for a 5 percent, tax-exempt investment would increase to 7.69 percent. Once you have calculated the taxable equivalent yield, you can compare the return on tax-exempt securities with the return on taxable investments that include certificates of deposit, corporate bonds, stocks, mutual funds, and other investment alternatives. Exhibit 15–4 illustrates the yields for tax-exempt investments and their taxable equivalent yields.

The following information can be used to compare the return on tax-exempt investments with the returns offered by taxable investments. Note: Additional tax changes have been approved by Congress and will be phased in by 2010.

Tax-Exempt Yield	Equivalent Yields for Taxable Investments				
	15% Tax Rate	25% Tax Rate	28% Tax Rate	33% Tax Rate	35% Tax Rate
4%	4.71%	5.33%	5.56%	5.97%	6.15%
5	5.88	6.67	6.94	7.46	7.69
6	7.06	8.00	8.33	8.96	9.23
7	8.24	9.33	9.72	10.45	10.77
8	9.41	10.67	11.11	11.94	12.31

Exhibit **15-4**

Yields for tax-exempt investments

CONCEPT CHECK 15-4

1 What are the maturities for a Treasury bill and a Treasury note?
2 What is the difference between a general obligation bond and a revenue bond?
3 What risks are involved when investing in municipal bonds?
4 Assume a taxpayer in the 25 percent tax bracket invests in a 6 percent, tax-exempt municipal bond. Use the information in this section to find the taxable equivalent yield.

Action Application Given the information below, calculate the tax equivalent yield in the following situations.

Tax-Exempt Yield	Equivalent Yield for a Taxpayer in the 25% Tax Bracket	Equivalent Yield for a Taxpayer in the 28% Tax Bracket	Equivalent Yield for a Taxpayer in the 33% Tax Bracket
4.5%			
5.5%			
6.5%			

The Decision to Buy or Sell Bonds

One basic principle we have stressed throughout this text is the need to evaluate any potential investment. Certainly corporate *and* government bonds are no exception. Only after you have completed your evaluation should you purchase bonds. Of course, a decision to sell bonds also requires evaluation. In this section, we examine methods you can use to evaluate bond investments.

Objective 5

Evaluate bonds when making an investment.

Good advice! Serious investors turn to Moodys.com to evaluate bond issues.

THE INTERNET

Just as you can use the Internet to evaluate a stock investment, you can use much of the same financial information to evaluate a bond investment. By accessing a corporation's Web site and locating the topics "financial information," "annual report," or "investor relations," you can find many of the answers to the questions discussed in the following sections. As an added bonus, a corporation may provide more than one year's annual report on its Web site, so you can make comparisons from one year to another.

When investing in bonds, you can use the Internet in three other ways. First, you can obtain price information on specific bond issues to track your investments. Especially if you live in a small town or rural area without access to newspapers that provide bond coverage, the Internet can be a welcome source of current bond prices. Second, it is possible to trade bonds online and pay lower commissions than you would pay a full-service or discount brokerage firm. Third, you can get research about a corporation and its bond issues (including recommendations to buy or sell) by accessing specific bond Web sites. *Be warned:* Bond Web sites are not as numerous as Web sites that provide information on stocks, mutual funds, or personal financial planning. And many of the better bond Web sites charge a fee for their research and recommendations. The following Web sites provide basic and detailed information designed to make you a better bond investor:

> www.bondpage.com
>
> www.bondsonline.com
>
> www.briefing.com
>
> www.buysellbonds.com
>
> www.investinginbonds.com
>
> www.fidelity.com
>
> bonds.yahoo.com

While many of the above Web sites provide information for government bonds and debt securities, the Web sites below provide specific information about government securities issued by the Untied States government and state and local governments.

> www.emuni.com
>
> www.fmsbonds.com
>
> www.municipalbonds.com
>
> www.publicdebt.treas.gov
>
> www.treasurydirect.gov

You may also want to visit the Moody's Web site (www.moodys.com), the Standard & Poor's Web site (www.standardpoors.com), and also the Mergent Web site (www.mergent.com), to obtain detailed information about both corporate and government bonds.

Sheet 60
Evaluating corporate bonds

HOW TO READ THE BOND SECTION OF THE NEWSPAPER

Not all local newspapers contain bond quotations, but the *Wall Street Journal, Barron's,* and many metropolitan newspapers publish complete information on this subject. In

Corporate Bonds

Monday, April 18, 2005

Forty most active fixed-coupon corporate bonds

1 COMPANY (TICKER)	2 COUPON	3 MATURITY	4 LAST PRICE	5 LAST YIELD
General Motors (GM)	8.375	Jul 15, 2033	76.000	11.187
General Motors Acceptance (GM)	6.750	Jan 15, 2006	99.875	6.907
General Motors Acceptance (GM)	8.000	Nov 01, 2031	80.000	10.196
Ford Motor Credit (F)	7.000	Oct 01, 2013	86.629	9.321
Citigroup (C)	4.125	Feb 22, 2010	98.245	4.532

Exhibit **15-5**

Financial information about corporate bonds available in the *Wall Street Journal*

Source: Republished with permission of Dow Jones Inc. from the *Wall Street Journal,* April 19, 2005, p. 12; permission conveyed through Copyright Clearance Center, Inc.

1. The name of the firm is Citigroup. The "C" in parentheses is the stock symbol that can be used to obtain financial information about the company that issued this corporate bond.

2. The *coupon* is the interest rate stated on a bond. The Citigroup bond pays 4.125 percent annual interest.

3. The *maturity* is the date the issuer will repay the principal amount. For this Citigroup bond, the maturity date is February 22, 2010.

4. The *last price* paid for a Citigroup bond at the end of the day was $1,000 × 98.245%, or $982.45.

5. The *last yield* reported in the newspaper for this Citigroup bond is 4.532 percent.

bond quotations, prices are given as a percentage of the face value, which is usually $1,000. Thus, to find the actual market price for a bond, you must multiply the face value ($1,000) by the newspaper quote. For example, a price quoted as 84 means a selling price of $1,000 × 84% = $840. Purchases and sales of bonds are reported in tables like that shown at the top of Exhibit 15–5. The highlighted line in Exhibit 15–5 gives the detailed information for a Citigroup corporate bond. (The numbers in this list refer to the actual columns in the newspaper quotation.)

For government bonds, most financial publications include two price quotations. The first price quotation, or the *bid price,* is the price a dealer is willing to pay for a government security. The bid price represents the amount that a seller could receive for a government bond. The second price quotation, or the *asked price,* represents the price at which a dealer is willing to sell a government security. The asked price represents the amount for which a buyer could purchase the security. In addition to price quotations, the *Wall Street Journal, Barron's,* and many metropolitan newspapers provide information about the interest rates, maturity dates, and yields of government securities. Note: Most bonds are traded in the over-the-counter market by bond dealers and brokers around the country who trade bonds over the phone or electronically. Thus, bonds (and the prices) reported in the newspaper make up only a small portion of the bonds actually bought and sold each business day.

ANNUAL REPORTS

As pointed out earlier in this chapter, bondholders must be concerned about the financial health of the corporation or government unit that issues bonds. To understand how important financial information is when evaluating a bond issue, consider the following two questions:

- Will the bond be repaid at maturity?
- Will you receive interest payments until maturity?

While it may be difficult to answer these questions with 100 percent accuracy, the information contained in a firm's annual report is the logical starting point. Today there are three ways to obtain a corporation's annual report. First, you can either write or telephone the corporation and request an annual report. (Hint: Many corporations have 800 telephone numbers for your use.) Second, as mentioned in an earlier section, most corporations maintain a Web site that contains detailed information about their financial performance. Third, some financial publications provide a reader's service that allows you to use a toll-free telephone number or a postcard to obtain an annual report.

Regardless of how you obtain an annual report, you should look for signs of financial strength or weakness. Is the firm profitable? Are sales revenues increasing? Are the firm's long-term liabilities increasing? In fact, there are many questions you should ask before making a decision to buy a bond. To help you determine the right questions to ask when evaluating a bond issue, examine the Financial Planning Calculations feature on page 502. Also, you may want to examine the bond's rating and perform the calculations described on pages 500–503 before investing your money.

BOND RATINGS

To determine the quality and risk associated with bond issues, investors rely on the bond ratings provided by Moody's Investors Service Inc. and Standard & Poor's Corporation. Both companies rank thousands of corporate and municipal bonds.

As Exhibit 15–6 illustrates, bond ratings generally range from AAA (the highest) to D (the lowest). For both Moody's and Standard & Poor's, the first four individual categories represent investment-grade securities. Investment-grade securities are suitable for conservative investors who want a safe investment that provides a predictable source of income. Bonds in the next two categories are considered speculative in nature and are often referred to as "junk" bonds. Finally, the C and D categories are used to rank bonds where there are poor prospects of repayment or even continued payment of interest. Bonds in these categories may be in default. Although bond ratings may be flawed or inaccurate, most investors regard the work of both Moody's and Standard & Poor's as highly reliable.

Generally, U.S. government securities issued by the Treasury Department and various federal agencies are not graded because they are risk free for practical purposes. The rating of long-term municipal bonds is similar to that of corporate bonds. In addition, Moody's rates shorter-term municipal bonds maturing in less than one year with the following designations:

- **MIG 1** This designation denotes superior credit quality with minimal risk for the investor.
- **MIG 2** This designation denotes strong credit quality. Margins of protection are ample, although not as large as in the preceding group.
- **MIG 3** This designation denotes acceptable credit quality. Liquidity and cash-flow protection may be small and investors are subject to more risk.
- **SG** This designation denotes speculative-grade credit quality, and investors are subject to high risk.[3]

BOND YIELD CALCULATIONS

yield The rate of return earned by an investor who holds a bond for a stated period of time.

For a bond investment, the **yield** is the rate of return earned by an investor who holds a bond for a stated period of time. Two methods are used to measure the yield on a bond investment: the current yield and the yield to maturity.

current yield Determined by dividing the yearly dollar amount of income generated by an investment by the investment's current market value.

The **current yield** is determined by dividing the yearly dollar amount of income generated by an investment by the investment's current market value. For bonds, the following formula may help you complete this calculation:

$$\text{Current yield on a corporate bond} = \frac{\text{Annual income amount}}{\text{Current market value}}$$

Exhibit **15-6**   Description of bond ratings provided by Moody's Investors Service and Standard & Poor's Corporation

Quality	Moody's	Standard & Poor's	Description
High-grade	Aaa	AAA	Bonds that are judged to be of the best quality.
	Aa	AA	Bonds that are judged to be of high quality by all standards. Together with the first group, they comprise what are generally known as *high-grade* bonds.
Medium-grade	A	A	Bonds that possess many favorable investment attributes and are to be considered upper-medium-grade obligations.
	Baa	BBB	Bonds that are considered medium-grade obligations; i.e., they are neither highly protected nor poorly secured.
Speculative	Ba	BB	Bonds that are judged to have speculative elements; their future cannot be considered well assured.
	B	B	Bonds that generally are considered high risk.
Default	Caa	CCC	Bonds that are of poor standing.
	Ca	CC	Bonds that represent obligations that are highly speculative and vulnerable to nonpayment.
	C		Bonds that are regarded as having extremely poor prospects of attaining any real investment standing.
		C	Standard & Poor's rating given to bonds where a bankruptcy petition has been filed.
		D	Bond issues in default.

Sources: Moody's Investors Service, www.moodyseurope.com, May 15, 2005; and Standard & Poor's Corporation, *Standard & Poor's Bond Guide,* April 2005.

For example, assume you own a $1,000 General Motors bond that pays 7.2 percent interest on an annual basis until the bond's maturity on January 15, 2011. This means that each year you will receive $72 ($1,000 × 7.2% = $72). Also assume the current market price of the General Motors bond is $820. Because the current market value is less than the bond's face value, the current yield increases to 8.8 percent, as follows:

yield to maturity A yield calculation that takes into account the relationship among a bond's maturity value, the time to maturity, the current price, and the dollar amount of interest.

$$\text{Current yield} = \frac{\$72}{\$820}$$

$$= 0.088, \text{ or } 8.8 \text{ percent}$$

This calculation allows you to compare the yield on a bond investment with the yields of other investment alternatives, which include savings accounts, certificates of deposit, common stock, preferred stock, and mutual funds. Naturally, the higher the current yield, the better! A current yield of 10 percent is better than a current yield of 8.8 percent.

Information about a specific bond's current yield and yield to maturity is available at **bonds.yahoo.com.**

The **yield to maturity** takes into account the relationship among a bond's maturity value, the time to maturity, the current price, and the dollar amount of interest. The formula for calculating the yield to maturity is as follows:

Financial Planning Calculations

THE TIMES INTEREST EARNED RATIO: ONE TOOL TO HELP YOU EVALUATE BOND ISSUES

After evaluating BellSouth Corporation, Shira and Mathew Matson wanted to purchase the firm's corporate debentures. But she was concerned about the corporation's ability to make future interest payments. To determine BellSouth's ability to pay interest, she calculated a formula called the *times interest earned ratio,* illustrated below:

$$\text{Times interest earned} = \frac{\text{Operating income before interest and taxes}}{\text{Interest expense}}$$

For example, BellSouth Corporation had interest expense of $916 million and operating income before interest and taxes of $5,289 million in 2004 (the latest year for which actual figures are available at the time of this publication). The times interest earned ratio for BellSouth Corporation is 5.77 to 1, as follows:

$$\text{Times interest earned} = \frac{\$5,289 \text{ million}}{\$916 \text{ million}}$$

$$= 5.77 \text{ to } 1$$

Although the average for the times interest earned ratio varies from industry to industry, a higher number is better than a lower number. BellSouth Corporation is earning slightly over 5.77 times the amount required to pay the annual interest on its long-term notes, bonds, and other financial obligations. With a times interest earned ratio of 5.77 to 1, BellSouth could experience a "significant" drop in earnings and still meet its financial obligations.

Source: Based on information contained in BellSouth Corporation's 2004 annual report.

$$\text{Yield to maturity} = \frac{\text{Dollar amount of annual interest} + \dfrac{\text{Face value} - \text{Market value}}{\text{Number of periods}}}{\dfrac{\text{Market value} + \text{Face value}}{2}}$$

If you purchased the General Motors bond in the above example on January 15, 2005 for $820 and held the bond for six years until its maturity on January 15, 2011, the yield to maturity is 11.2 percent, as follows:

$$\text{Yield to maturity} = \frac{\$72 + \dfrac{\$1,000 - \$820}{6}}{\dfrac{\$820 + \$1,000}{2}}$$

$$= \frac{\$102}{\$910}$$

$$= 0.112, \text{ or } 11.2 \%$$

In this situation, the yield to maturity takes into account two types of return on the bond. First, you will receive interest income from the purchase date until the maturity date. Second, at maturity you will receive a payment for the face value of the bond. If you purchased the bond at a price below the face value, the yield to maturity will be greater than the stated interest rate. If you purchased the bond at a price above the face value, the yield to maturity will be less than the stated interest rate. Remember, the actual price you pay for a bond may be higher or lower than the face value because of many factors, including changes in the economy, increases or decreases in comparable interest rates on other investments, and the financial condition of the company. At least part of the reason the General Motors bond in this example is priced below the $1,000 face value is because of the corporation's lower sales on its popular sport utility vehicles, brought on by higher fuel prices. Another reason for the lower price is because the firm's bond ratings were lowered during 2005. As the bond approaches maturity (and eventual repayment at maturity) the price begins to move closer to its original face value.

The yield to maturity calculation is an annualized rate of return if the bond is held until maturity. If the bond is sold before maturity, the rate of return for the investor may be higher or lower, depending on the price the bond is sold for and the length of time the bond is held. Like the current yield, the yield to maturity allows you to compare returns on a bond investment with other investments. Also, like the current yield, the higher the yield to maturity, the better. A yield to maturity of 9 percent is better than a yield to maturity of 7 percent. One additional calculation, times interest earned, is described in the Financial Planning Calculations box on page 502.

OTHER SOURCES OF INFORMATION

Investors can use two additional sources of information to evaluate potential bond investments. First, business periodicals can provide information about the economy and interest rates and detailed financial information about a corporation or government entity that issues bonds. You can locate many of these periodicals at your college or public library or on the Internet.

Second, a number of federal agencies provide information that may be useful to bond investors in either printed form or on the Internet. Reports and research published by the Federal Reserve System (www.federalreserve.gov), the U.S. Treasury (www.treasury.gov), and the Department of Commerce (www.commerce.gov) may be used to assess the nation's economy. You can also obtain information that corporations have reported to the Securities and Exchange Commission by accessing the SEC Web site (www.sec.gov). Finally, state and local governments will provide information about specific municipal bond issues.

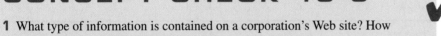

CONCEPT CHECK 15-5 ✓

1 What type of information is contained on a corporation's Web site? How could this information be used to evaluate a bond issue?

2 What is the market value for a bond with a face value of $1,000 and a newspaper quotation of 77¼?

3 How important are bond ratings when evaluating a bond issue?

4 Why should you calculate the current yield and yield to maturity on a bond investment?

5 How can business periodicals and government publications help you evaluate a bond issue?

Action Application Pick one of the Web sites mentioned in this section and describe the type of information it provides.

SUMMARY OF OBJECTIVES

Objective 1
Describe the characteristics of corporate bonds.
A corporate bond is a corporation's written pledge to repay a specified amount of money with interest. All of the details about a bond (face value, interest rate, maturity date, repayment, etc.) are contained in the bond indenture. The trustee is the bondholder's representative.

Objective 2
Discuss why corporations issue bonds.
Corporations issue bonds and other securities to pay for major purchases and to help finance their ongoing activities. Bonds may be debentures, mortgage bonds, subordinated debentures, or convertible bonds. Most bonds are callable. To ensure that the money will be available when needed to repay bonds, most cor-

porations establish a sinking fund. Corporations can also issue serial bonds that mature on different dates. A call provision can also be used to buy back bonds before the maturity date.

Objective 3
Explain why investors purchase corporate bonds.

Investors purchase corporate bonds for three reasons: (1) interest income, (2) possible increase in value, and (3) repayment at maturity. They are also an excellent way to diversify your investment portfolio. The method used to pay bondholders their interest depends on whether they own registered bonds, bearer bonds, or zero-coupon bonds. Because bonds can increase or decrease in value, it is possible to purchase a bond at a discount and hold the bond until it appreciates in value. Changes in overall interest rates in the economy are the primary causes of most bond price fluctuations. If your bond decreases in value, you can lose money on your investment. You can also choose to hold the bond until maturity and the corporation will repay the bond's face value. Corporate bonds can be bought or sold through bond exchanges or account executives who represent brokerage firms. Bonds can also be bought and sold online.

Objective 4
Discuss why federal, state, and local governments issue bonds and why investors purchase government bonds.

Bonds issued by the U.S. Treasury and federal agencies are used to finance the national debt and the ongoing activities of the federal government. Currently, the U.S. Treasury issues three prin-

cipal types of securities: Treasury bills, Treasury notes, and savings bonds. State and local governments issue bonds to finance their ongoing activities and special projects such as airports, schools, toll roads, and toll bridges. U.S. Treasury Securities can be purchased through Treasury Direct, brokerage firms, and other financial institutions. Municipal bonds are generally sold through the government entity that issued them or through account executives. One of the most important features of municipal bonds is that interest on them may be exempt from federal taxes.

Objective 5
Evaluate bonds when making an investment.

Today it is possible to trade bonds online and obtain research information via the Internet. Some local newspapers, the *Wall Street Journal,* and *Barron's* provide bond investors with information they need to evaluate a bond issue. Detailed financial information can also be obtained by requesting a printed copy of the corporation's annual report or accessing its Web site. To determine the quality of a bond issue, most investors study the ratings provided by Standard & Poor's and Moody's. Investors can also calculate a current yield and a yield to maturity to evaluate a decision to buy or sell bond issues.

The current yield is determined by dividing the annual income amount by its current market value. The yield to maturity takes into account the relationship among a bond's maturity value, the time to maturity, the current price, and the dollar amount of interest.

KEY FORMULAS

Page	Topic	Formula
482	Annual interest	Dollar amount of annual interest = Face value × Interest rate
	Example:	Dollar amount of annual interest = $1,000 × 6.75 percent
		= $1,000 × 0.0675
		= $67.50
488	Approximate market value	Approximate market value = $\dfrac{\text{Dollar amount of annual interest}}{\text{Comparable interest rate}}$
	Example:	Approximate market value = $\dfrac{\$65}{0.07}$
		= $928.57
494	Current yield for a 26-week T-bill	Current yield = $\dfrac{\text{Discount amount}}{\text{Purchase price}} \times 2$
	Example:	Current yield = $\dfrac{\$20}{\$980} \times 2$
		= 0.0408 = 4.08 percent

496	Taxable equivalent yield (25% tax rate)	$\text{Taxable equivalent yield} = \dfrac{\text{Tax-exempt yield}}{1.0 - \text{Your tax rate}}$
	Example:	$\text{Taxable equivalent yield} = \dfrac{0.04}{1.0 - 0.25}$ $= 0.0533 = 5.33 \text{ percent}$

500	Current yield on a corporate bond	$\text{Current yield} = \dfrac{\text{Annual income amount}}{\text{Current market value}}$
	Example:	$\text{Current yield} = \dfrac{\$75}{\$900}$ $= 0.0833 = 8.33 \text{ percent}$

502	Yield to maturity	$\text{Yield to maturity} = \dfrac{\text{Dollar amount of annual interest} + \dfrac{\text{Face value} - \text{Market value}}{\text{Number of periods}}}{\dfrac{\text{Market value} + \text{Face value}}{2}}$
	Example:	$\text{Yield to maturity} = \dfrac{\$60 + \dfrac{\$1,000 - \$900}{10}}{\dfrac{\$900 + \$1,000}{2}}$ $= 0.074 = 7.4 \text{ percent}$

502	Time interest earned	$\text{Times interest earned} = \dfrac{\text{Operating income before interest and taxes}}{\text{Interest expense}}$ $= \dfrac{\$4,800 \text{ million}}{\$1,066 \text{ million}}$ $= 4.50 \text{ to } 1$

KEY TERMS

bearer bond 488	face value 482	serial bonds 485
bond indenture 483	general obligation bond 495	sinking fund 485
call feature 485	maturity date 482	subordinated debenture 484
convertible bond 484	mortgage bond 484	trustee 483
corporate bond 482	municipal bond 495	yield 500
current yield 500	registered bond 488	yield to maturity 501
debenture 484	revenue bond 495	zero-coupon bond 488

FINANCIAL PLANNING PROBLEMS

1. *Calculating Interest.* Calculate the annual interest and the semiannual interest payment for the following corporate bond issues with a face value of $1,000. (Obj. 1)

Annual Interest Rate	Annual Interest Amount	Semiannual Interest Payment
5.125%		
6.25		
7.0		
7.125		

2. *Analyzing Why Investors Purchase Bonds.* In your own words, explain how each of the following factors is a reason to invest in bonds. (Obj. 3)

   a. Interest income.

   b. Possible increase in value.

   c. Repayment at maturity.

3. *Evaluating Zero-Coupon Bonds.* List the reasons investors might want to buy zero-coupon bonds. Then list the reasons investors might want to avoid zero-coupon bonds. Based on these lists, do you consider zero-coupon bonds a good alternative for your investment program? Why or why not? (Obj. 3)

4. *Determining the approximate market value for a bond.* Approximate the market value for the following $1,000 bonds. (Obj. 3)

Interest Rate When Issued	Dollar Amount of Interest for the Existing Bond	Interest Rate for Comparable Bonds Issued Today	Approximate Market Value
5%		6%	
6		5.5	
8		7	

5. *Calculating total return.* Jean Miller purchased a $1,000 corporate bond three years ago for $910. The bond pays 6 percent annual interest. Three years later, she sold the bond for $1,020. Calculate the total return for Ms. Miller's bond investment. (Obj. 3)

6. *Explaining Different Types of Treasury Securities.* Complete the following table: (Obj. 4)

	Minimum Amount	Maturity Range	How Interest Is Paid
Treasury bill			
Treasury note			
Treasury bond			

7. *Calculating the purchase price for a T-Bill.* Calculate the purchase price for a 26-week, $1,000 treasury bill with a stated interest rate of 2.5 percent. (Obj. 4)

8. *Calculating Tax-Equivalent Yield.* Assume you are in the 35 percent tax bracket and purchase a 5.12 percent, tax-exempt municipal bond. Use the formula presented in this chapter to calculate the taxable equivalent yield for this investment. (Obj.4)

9. *Using the Internet.* Use the information at bonds.yahoo.com to answer the following questions about a corporate bond. To complete this activity, follow these steps. (Obj. 5)

   a. Go to bonds.yahoo.com and click on Bond Screener.

   b. Click on Corporate and enter the information requested and click Find Bonds.

   c. Choose one of the issues listed.

   d. Using the information on the Yahoo! bond Web site, determine the current yield for this bond issue. What does the current yield calculation measure?

   e. Using the information on the Yahoo! bond Web site, what is the yield to maturity for this bond issue? What does the yield to maturity calculation measure?

   f. What is the rating for this bond? What does this rating mean?

   g. Based on your answer to the above questions, would you choose this bond for your investment portfolio? Explain your answer.

10. *Evaluating a Corporate Bond Issue.* Choose a corporate bond and use *Mergent's Industrial Manuals* and *Standard & Poor's Bond Guide* (available at your college or public library) to answer the following questions about this bond issue. (Obj. 5)

    a. What is Standard & Poor's rating for the issue?

    b. What is the purpose of the issue?

    c. Does the issue have a call provision?

    d. Who is the trustee for the issue?

    e. What collateral, if any, has been pledged as security for the issue?

    f. Based on the information you have obtained, would the bond be a good investment for you? Why or why not?

11. *Calculating current yields.* Calculate the interest amount and current yield for the following $1,000 bonds. (Obj. 5)

Interest Rate	Interest Amount	Current Market Value	Current Yield
5%		$ 870	
6.9		1,115	
4.875		815	

12. *Calculating Yields.* Assume you purchased a corporate bond at its current market price of $850 on January 1, 1999. It pays 9 percent interest and will mature on December 31, 2008, at which time the corporation will pay you the face value of $1,000. (Obj. 5)

    a. Determine the current yield on your bond investment at the time of purchase.

    b. Determine the yield to maturity on your bond investment.

FINANCIAL PLANNING ACTIVITIES

1. *Explaining the Purpose of a Bond Indenture.* Prepare a one-minute oral presentation that describes the type of information contained in a bond indenture. (Obj. 1)

2. *Investigating a New Bond Issue.* Locate an advertisement for a new bond issue in the *Wall Street Journal, Barron's,* the *New York Times,* or a local newspaper. Then go to the library or use the Internet to research the corporation or government entity that is issuing the bonds. Based on your research, prepare a two-page report on the issuer. Be sure to describe its financial condition and how it will use the money raised by selling the bonds. (Obj. 2)

3. *Interviewing an Account Executive.* Talk to an account executive or a banker about the differences among debentures, mortgage bonds, and subordinated debentures. Describe your findings. (Obj. 2)

4. *Making Investment Decisions.* Assume you just inherited 10 Kerr-McGee Corporation bonds and each bond is convertible to 16.373 shares of the corporation's common stock. (Obj. 2)

   a. What type of information would you need to help you decide whether to convert your bonds to common stock?

   b. Where would you obtain this information?

   c. Under what conditions would you convert your bonds to common stock?

   d. Under what conditions would you keep the bonds?

5. *Analyzing Why Investors Purchase Bonds.* Survey at least two investors who own either corporate or government bonds. Then answer the following questions. (Obj. 3)

   a. Why did these investors purchase the bonds?

   b. How long have they invested in bonds?

   c. Do they consider their bond issues to be conservative or speculative investments?

   d. Why did they decide to purchase bonds instead of other investments like certificates of deposit, stocks, mutual funds, or real estate?

6. *Using the Internet to Obtain Investment Information.* Use the Internet to locate the Web site for Treasury Direct (www.treasurydirect.gov). Then prepare a report that summarizes the information provided on Treasury bills, Treasury notes, and Treasury bonds. (Obj. 4)

7. *Finding Financial Information.* Using information from the local newspaper, the *Wall Street Journal,* or on the Internet, answer the following questions for one of the following bond issues. (Obj. 5)

Bond Issue	Interest Rate	Maturity Date	Current Yield	Last Price
Ford Motor Credit	7.0%	Oct. 1, 2013		
Hertz	6.350	June 15, 2010		
Alcan	5.2	Jan. 15, 2014		

8. *Analyzing Yields.* In your own words, describe what affects the current yield and the yield to maturity for a bond. (Obj. 5)

9. *Evaluating a Bond Transaction.* Choose a corporate bond that you would consider purchasing. Then, using information obtained in the library or on the Internet, answer the questions on the evaluation form presented in the *Personal Financial Planner Sheet* 60 "Evaluating Corporate Bonds" at the end of the text. Based on your research, would you still purchase this bond? Explain your answer. (Obj. 5)

INTERNET CONNECTION

Use the Internet to research the following topics, determine the types of information that is available, and determine how it might affect your investment decisions.

Corporate Bonds

Web sources: _____

_____

Type of information available: _____

_____

Possible influence on your investment decisions: _____

_____

Government and Municipal Bonds

Web sources: _____

_____

Type of information available: _____

_____

Possible influence on your investment decisions: _____

_____

FINANCIAL PLANNING CASE

A Lesson from the Past

Back in 1995, Mary Goldberg, a 34-year-old widow, got a telephone call from a Wall Street account executive who said that one of his other clients had given him her name. Then he told her his brokerage firm was selling a new corporate bond issue in New World Explorations, a company heavily engaged in oil exploration in the western United States. The bonds in this issue paid investors 11.2 percent a year. He then said that the minimum investment was $10,000 and that if she wanted to take advantage of this "once in a lifetime" opportunity, she had to move fast. To Mary, it was an opportunity that was too good to pass up, and she bit hook, line, and sinker. She sent the account executive a check—and never heard from him again. When she went to the library to research her bond investment, she found there was no such company as New World Explorations. She lost her $10,000 and quickly vowed she would never invest in bonds again. From now on, she would put her money in the bank, where it was guaranteed.

Over the years, she continued to deposit money in the bank and accumulated more than $30,000. Things seemed to be pretty much on track until one of her certificates of deposit (CDs) matured. When she went to renew the CD, the bank officer told her interest rates had fallen and current CD interest rates ranged between 2.5 and 3.5 percent. To make matters worse, the banker told Mary that only the bank's 36-month CD offered the 3.5 percent interest rate. CDs with shorter maturities paid lower interest rates.

Faced with the prospects of lower interest rates, Mary decided to shop around for higher rates. She called several local banks and got pretty much the same answer. Then a friend suggested that she talk to Peter Manning, an account executive for Citigroup Global Markets. Manning told her there were conservative corporate bonds and quality stock issues that offered higher returns. But, he warned her, these investments were *not* guaranteed. If she wanted higher returns, she would have to take some risks.

While Mary wanted higher returns, she also remembered how she had lost $10,000 investing in corporate bonds. When she told Peter Manning about her bond investment in the fictitious New World Explorations, he pointed out that she made some pretty serious mistakes. For starters, she bought the bonds over the phone from someone she didn't know, and she bought them without doing any research. He assured her that the bonds and stocks he would recommend would be issued by real companies, and she would be able to find a lot of information on each of his recommendations at the library. For starters, he suggested the following three investments:

1. AT&T Broadband corporate bond that pays 8.375 percent annual interest and matures on March 13, 2013. This bond has a current market value of $1,220 and is rated BBB.

2. John Deere Capital Corporate bond that pays 7.0 percent annual interest and matures on March 15, 2012. This bond has a current market value of $1,150 and is rated A.

3. General Electric common stock (listed on the New York Stock Exchange and selling for $36 a share with annual dividends of $0.88 per share).

Questions

1. According to Mary Goldberg, the chance to invest in New World Explorations was "too good to pass up." Unfortunately, it was too good to be true, and she lost $10,000. Why do you think so many people are taken in by get-rich-quick schemes?

2. During the first part of the 21st century, investors were forced to look for ways to squeeze additional income from their investment portfolios. Do you think investing in corporate bonds or quality stocks is the best way to increase income? Why or why not?

3. Using information obtained in the library or on the Internet, answer the following questions about Peter Manning's investment suggestions. (Hint: For the bond issues, you may want to examine *Mergent's Industrial Manuals.* For the stock issue, you can use *Mergent's Handbook of Common Stocks.*)

   a. What does the rating for the AT&T bond mean?

   b. What does the rating for the John Deere bond mean?

   c. How would you describe the common stock issued by General Electric?

4. Based on your research, which investment would you recommend to Mary Goldberg? Why?

5. Assuming you recommend one of the above investments, how much of Mary's $30,000 would you invest? What would you do with the remainder of her money?

6. Using a current newspaper, the *Wall Street Journal, Barron's,* or the Internet determine the current market value for each of the three investments suggested in this case. Based on this information, would these investments have been profitable if Mary had purchased the AT&T bond for $1,220, the John Deere bond for $1,150, or General Electric stock for $36 a share?

VIDEO CASE

Investing in Bonds

Which investment is right for you? Stocks? Certificates of deposit? Bonds? Investing your money wisely is one of the most important things you can do. But most people build their portfolios with only one thing in mind: growth. And that usually means investing in stocks. But there may be a place for bond investments in your portfolio. A bond is a loan from the bondholder to the government or corporation that issued the bond. In effect, the investor is loaning money to the bond issuer in exchange for a promise to repay the debt on the maturity date. Between the issue date and the maturity date, the government entity or corporation that issued the bond will pay the bondholder interest.

Investors often turn to bonds because of their safety, stability, and ability to produce income. U.S. Treasury bills, notes, and bonds and U.S. savings bonds are chosen because of their safety. It is also possible to purchase bonds issued by federal agencies and municipal bonds. Interest on municipal bonds, sometimes referred to as "munis," is exempt from federal and many state and local taxes. Because of their tax-free status, the interest rate on munis is often lower than that on taxable bonds. However, their tax-free status actually makes the taxable equivalent yield on these investments comparable to yields provided by taxable bonds.

The methods used to purchase bonds depends on the type of bond. Treasury bills, notes, and bonds are purchased at scheduled auctions sponsored by the federal government at different times of the year. Savings bonds, on the other hand, can be purchased on any day of the year from a financial institution. Like stocks, corporate bonds are purchased through an exchange.

Even though bonds are more conservative investments, you must still consider two risks when evaluating a bond investment: the creditworthiness of the issuer and the ability of the issuer to make interest payments and eventual repayment at maturity. Creditworthiness is often determined by a rating agency. The type of bond that a corporation issues can also affect its creditworthiness. Today corporations issue debenture bonds, mortgage bonds, and subordinated debentures. You may also want to use Web sites like Moody's (www.moodys.com) or Standard & Poor's (www.standardpoors.com) to evaluate a bond issue. To minimize risk, some investors prefer to purchase bond mutual funds.

The second risk associated with bond investing is price volatility. A bond can increase or decrease in value because of changes in interest rates. There is an inverse relationship between interest rates in the economy and the value of a specific bond with a fixed interest rate. When interest rates in the economy go down, the value of a specific bond increases. When interest rates in the economy go up, the value of a specific bond decreases. Because long-term bonds experience more interest rate fluctuations than short-term bonds, long-term bonds usually have higher interest rates and provide higher yields.

Questions

1. According to this case, investors often turn to bonds because of their safety, stability, and ability to produce income. Based on these assumptions, what type of investor would choose bonds for a portion of his or her portfolio?

2. What effect would an increase in overall interest rates have on the value of a bond with a fixed interest rate? What effect would a decrease in overall interest rates have on the value of a bond with a fixed interest rate?

3. Even though bonds are more conservative investments, they still carry risks. What are those risks? How would you go about researching an $8,000 investment in corporate bonds?

YOUR PERSONAL FINANCIAL PLANNER IN ACTION

Investing in Bonds

Inclusion of bonds in an investment portfolio can be useful for achieving various financial goals when certain life situations, business conditions, and economic trends arise.

Your Short-Term Financial Planning Activities	Resources
1. Evaluate a bond investment that might be appropriate for your various financial goals and life situation.	PFP Sheet 60 www.bonds-online.com www.investinginbonds.com
2. Compare the recent performance of various corporate bonds that could be appropriate investments for you.	bonds.yahoo.com www.moodys.com www.bloomberg.com
3. Research the recent performance of federal government and municipal bonds. Determine how these might be used in your investment portfolio.	www.publicdebt.treas.gov www.emuni.com www.invest-faq.com

Your Long-Term Financial Planning Activities	Resources
1. Identify bond investing situations that could help minimize risk.	PFP Sheet 60 www.investopedia.com
2. Develop a plan for selecting bond investments in the future.	Text pages 497–503 www.kiplinger.com

CONTINUING CASE

Bond Investments

Life Situation
   Pam, 43
   Josh, 45
   Children ages 16, 14, and 11

Financial Data
   Monthly income $4,900
   Assets $262,700
   Liabilities $84,600
   Living expenses $4,450
   Emergency fund $5,000

Bond investments have always been of interest to the Brocks as part of their investment portfolio. They believe these debt instruments can provide a secured return not available with other types of investments. However, some friends of the Brocks pointed out that bonds may not be appropriate for certain types of investment goals.

Questions

1. For what types of financial goals might the Brocks invest in bonds?

2. What types of bonds might be considered by the Brocks for their investment portfolio?

3. Describe how the Brocks could use *Personal Financial Planner* Sheet 60 for planning and implementing their investment activities?

16 Investing in Mutual Funds

Key Concept

For many investors, mutual funds have become the investment of choice. Yet even though mutual funds offer professional management and diversification, investors still need to evaluate mutual funds before investing their money.

Learning Objectives

1. Describe the characteristics of mutual fund investments.

2. Classify mutual funds by investment objective.

3. Evaluate mutual funds for investment purposes.

4. Describe how and why mutual funds are bought and sold.

The Tale of Two Mutual Fund Investors

Investor Number 1

As Bob Bittinger watched television one Saturday morning, he happened upon one of those "paid programming" shows. A well-known celebrity was telling the audience that gold coins were the ultimate safe investment. Over the next two days, Bob made his decision to purchase the gold coins, but he lost the 800 phone number. For lack of some other way to invest in gold, he decided to purchase shares in the Fidelity Select Gold mutual fund. Besides, he reasoned, shares in a mutual fund would be a better investment than purchasing individual coins because mutual funds provide diversification and professional management. And he really thought he was choosing the right investment when he invested $12,000. What could be better than a mutual fund that "specialized" in gold? His investment would be a safe choice even if other investments went down in value. All he had to do was sit back and wait for the fund to increase in value.

Investor Number 2

Karen Southworth, a single mother, had always worked hard for her money. And when it came time to invest, she did her homework. After accumulating a $5,000 emergency fund and an additional $6,000 for investment purposes, she purchased shares in the Fidelity Disciplined Equity fund based on research information available on the Morningstar and *BusinessWeek* Web sites. According to the research information, the fund manager chose large corporations that promised both revenue and profit growth. Although she researched other funds that were more aggressive, she felt comfortable with the companies in this Fidelity fund. In fact, the fund's top holdings included corporations like ExxonMobil, Citigroup, General Electric, Microsoft, and Johnson & Johnson. For Karen, the name summed it up: This was a disciplined way to invest her investment dollars.

Conclusion

Which investor do you think earned the largest return? Good news! The funds chosen by both investors had a positive return over the next 12 months. The Fidelity Disciplined Equity fund chosen by Ms. Southworth had a 9.8 percent increase for the first 12 months following her investment. The Fidelity Gold fund chosen by Mr. Bittinger had a 4.1 percent increase during the same time period. If the Fidelity Disciplined Equity fund continues to outperform the other fund, the difference in returns over a long period of time will definitely result in a lot more money in Ms. Southworth's investment portfolio. And while it is obvious that in this case the investor who did actual research earned a larger return, financial experts always recommend researching any investment before investing your money. Mutual funds are no exception.

Sources: *BusinessWeek,* www.businessweek.com, May 18, 2005; and Morningstar, www.morningstar.com, May 18, 2005.

QUESTIONS

What Actions Should Be Taken?

1. Bob Bittinger made a decision to invest in a gold fund—what he thought was a safe investment. And yet, his fund earned less money than the fund chosen by Ms. Southworth. In your opinion, what did he do wrong?
2. Was Karen Southworth just lucky? Explain your answer.

What about Your Situation?

3. In this opening case, two different styles of investors were described. Which style describes your attitude toward investing?
4. Discuss with other household members whether mutual funds are appropriate investment choices for you.

Learn More Online

Visit the Morningstar (www.morningstar.com) and *BusinessWeek* (www.businessweek.com) Web sites and describe the type of information you find that could help you evaluate a specific mutual fund like the Fidelity Disciplined Equity fund.

mutual fund An investment chosen by people who pool their money to buy stocks, bonds, and other financial securities selected by professional managers who work for an investment company.

investment company A corporation, partnership, or trust that invests the pooled monies of many investors.

If you ever thought about buying stocks or bonds but decided not to, your reasons were probably like most other people's: You didn't know enough to make a good decision, and you lacked enough money to diversify your investments among several choices. These same two reasons explain why people invest in mutual funds. By pooling your money with money from other investors, a mutual fund can do for you what you can't do on your own. Specifically, a **mutual fund** is an investment chosen by people who pool their money to buy stocks, bonds, and other financial securities selected by professional managers who work for investment companies. The Mutual Fund Education Alliance defines an **investment company** as a corporation, partnership, or trust that invests the pooled monies of many investors.[1] For a fee, an investment company invests the pooled funds of small investors in securities appropriate to a fund's investment objective. Mutual funds are an excellent choice for many individuals. In many cases, they can also be used for retirement accounts, including 401(k), 403(b), traditional individual retirement accounts, and Roth IRAs. Regardless, whether you are investing in an account subject to immediate taxation or in a retirement-type account with deferred taxation, you must be able to select the funds that will help you obtain your investment goals.

Just for a moment, think about the two investors who were profiled in the opening case. One investor, Bob Bittinger, earned just over 4 percent in 12 months. He did no research and didn't have a clue about the risks involved when investing in a gold fund. The other investor, Karen Southworth, earned almost 10 percent on her investment during the same time period. Was she just lucky? No, she did her homework before making a decision to invest any money in a mutual fund or any other type of investment. Simply put: She learned something about the fund before investing her money. As crazy as it may sound, many people never evaluate mutual fund investments. These people wouldn't buy an automobile without driving it or "kicking the tires," but they will spend the same amount of money or more on an investment without doing any research. Make no mistake about this: *Good investors evaluate an investment before purchase. The best investors continue to evaluate their investments after the purchase.*

An investment in mutual funds is based on the concept of opportunity costs, which we have discussed throughout this text. Simply put, you have to be willing to take some chances if you want to get larger returns on your investments. Before deciding whether mutual funds are the right investment for you, read the material presented in the next section.

Why Investors Purchase Mutual Funds

Objective 1

Describe the characteristics of mutual fund investments.

In the 1990s, people loved their mutual funds. With a few exceptions, investors expected and got big returns each year until the end of the 1990s. Then the bubble burst. Since 1999, many people have firsthand knowledge that the value of mutual fund shares can decline. And while some mutual funds consistently showed positive returns since 1999, many more funds lost money. Today, more funds are beginning to rebound because of an improved economy. Despite the economic problems and the poor performance over the last few years, the following statistics illustrate how important mutual fund investments are to both individuals and the nation's economy:

1. An estimated 92 million individuals in 54 million households own mutual funds in the United States.

2. The number of mutual funds grew from 361 in 1970 to over 8,000 in late 2004 and continues to increase each year.

3. At the end of 2004, the last year for which complete totals are available, the combined value of assets owned by mutual funds in the United States totaled over $8 trillion. This amount is expected to continue to increase based on long-term performance.[2]

Advice from a Pro

MUTUAL FUND SCANDALS: THE GOOD NEWS AND THE BAD

The Bottom Line: Most investors aren't affected by the scandals. Still, just the hint of scandal with an investment product that is used by so many investors causes ripples for both investors and the people who work in the mutual fund industry.

THE SCANDAL

In a nutshell, here's what happened. Back in 2003, New York Attorney General Eliot Spitzer began investigating at least four major firms in the mutual fund industry for illegal trading practices. The firms under investigation are Bank One, Janus, Bank of America, and Strong Capital, which are accused of allowing certain fund managers to trade after the close of the market. This practice is called "late trading" and is illegal under Securities and Exchange Commission (SEC) regulations because it allows a favored investor to take advantage of postmarket news or information not available to the general public. According to Spitzer, "Allowing late trading is like allowing betting on a horse race after the horses have crossed the finish line."

HOW IT AFFECTS YOU

According to Dustin Woodard, long-time financial contributor for About.com, most investors are not affected by the scandals. Even for individual shareholders with accounts with the investment companies accused of late trading, the damage was minimal. Some experts estimate that late trading may decrease a fund's overall performance by as little as 0.1 percent. And most of the companies agreed to make restitution to shareholders damaged by their late trading activities. In reality, there may be more damage to the reputation of the industry than to actual shareholders.

WHAT ACTIONS SHOULD YOU TAKE?

To put the scandals in perspective, Mr. Woodard suggests that you separate the truth from the media hype surrounding the mutual fund scandals. Then realize that investors are still investing significant amounts of money in mutual funds and that funds still have many advantages when compared to other investment alternatives. He then suggests that you may want to consider switching to, or choosing, an ethical investment company that was not involved in the late trading scandals. Investors can also be more vocal in supporting effective legislation to make sure this doesn't happen again. Finally, it never hurts to remind investment companies why they exist—to serve their shareholders, not themselves.

Sources: Dustin Woodard, "Answers to Your Mutual Fund Scandal Questions," About.com, www.about.com, May 22, 2005 and September 3, 2003; Press Release for the Office of Attorney General Eliot Spitzer, State of New York (www.oag.state.ny), May 23, 2005.

No doubt about it, the mutual fund industry is big business. And yet, you may be wondering why so many people invest in mutual funds.

The major reasons investors purchase mutual funds are *professional management* and *diversification.* Most investment companies do everything possible to convince you that they can do a better job of picking securities than you can. Investment companies do have professional fund managers with years of experience who devote large amounts of time to picking just the "right" securities for their funds' portfolios. *Be warned:* Even the best portfolio managers make mistakes. So you, the investor, must be careful!

The diversification mutual funds offer spells safety because an occasional loss incurred with one investment contained in a mutual fund is usually offset by gains from other investments in the fund. For example, consider the diversification provided in the portfolio of the AIM Blue Chip Fund, shown in Exhibit 16–1. An investment in the $2.3 billion AIM Blue Chip Fund represents ownership in at least 10 different industries, as seen in Exhibit 16–1. In addition, the companies in the fund's portfolio are often market leaders, as seen by the fund's top holdings. With almost 100 different companies included in the fund's investment portfolio, investors enjoy diversification coupled with AIM's stock selection expertise.

Big building, big expectations! People who invest in Oppenheimer Funds expect their investments to increase in value.

Exhibit **16–1** AIM Blue Chip Fund top holdings

Top Industries	% of Total Net Assets	Top Holdings	% of Total Net Assets
1. Pharmaceuticals	7.07	1. ExxonMobil Corp.	4.03
2. Systems Software	5.08	2. Johnson & Johnson	3.40
3. Industrial Conglomerates	4.97	3. General Electric Co.	3.00
4. Semiconductors	4.39	4. Microsoft Corp.	2.51
5. Integrated Oil & Gas	4.03	5. Citigroup Inc.	2.51
6. Other Diversified Financial Services	3.97	6. Wal-Mart Stores Inc.	2.31
7. Health Care Equipment	3.73	7. Procter & Gamble Co.	2.03
8. Communication Equipment	3.67	8. UnitedHealth Group Inc.	1.98
9. Computer Hardware	3.54	9. Dell Inc.	1.98
10. Hypermarkets & Super Centers	3.35	10. Tyco International Ltd.	1.97

Holdings are subject to change.
Source: AIM Investment Company, www.aiminvestments.com, May 20, 2005.

Note that the information contained in Exhibit 16–1 was taken from the fund's promotional materials at the end of May 2005. If you want more up-to-date information on the composition of investments within the fund or other information about the fund, visit its Web site at www.aimfunds.com.

CHARACTERISTICS OF MUTUAL FUNDS

Today mutual funds may be classified as either closed-end funds, exchange-traded funds, or open-end funds.

CLOSED-END, EXCHANGE-TRADED, OR OPEN-END MUTUAL FUNDS
Approximately 7 percent of all mutual funds are closed-end funds offered by investment companies. A **closed-end fund** is a mutual fund whose shares are issued by an investment company only when the fund is organized. As a result, only a certain number of shares are available to investors. After all the shares originally issued have been sold, an investor can purchase shares only from another investor who is willing to sell. Closed-end funds are actively managed by professional fund managers and shares are traded on the floors of stock exchanges or in the over-the-counter market. Like the prices of stocks, the prices of shares for closed-end funds are determined by the factors of supply and demand, by the value of stocks and other investments contained in the fund's portfolio, and by investor expectations. A special section of the *Wall Street Journal* provides information about closed-end funds.

An **exchange-traded fund (ETF)** is a fund that invests in the stocks contained in a specific stock index, like the Standard & Poor's 500 stock index, the Dow Jones Industrial average, or the Nasdaq 100 Index, and whose shares are traded on a stock exchange. With both a closed-end fund and an exchange-traded fund, an investor can purchase as little as one share of a fund, because both types are traded on a stock exchange like individual corporate stock issues. Although exchange-traded funds are similar to closed-end funds, there is an important difference. Most closed-end funds are actively managed, with portfolio managers making the selection of stocks and other securities

closed-end fund A mutual fund whose shares are issued by an investment company only when the fund is organized.

exchange-traded fund (ETF) A fund that invests in the stocks contained in a specific stock index, such as the Standard & Poor's 500 stock index, and whose shares are traded on a stock exchange.

contained in a closed-end fund. An exchange-traded fund, on the other hand, invests in the stocks included in a specific stock index. Exchange-traded funds tend to mirror the performance of the index, moving up or down as the individual stocks contained in the index move up or down. Therefore, there is less need for a portfolio manager to make investment decisions. Because of passive management, fees associated with owning shares are generally less when compared to both closed-end and open-end funds. In addition to lower fees, there are other advantages to investing in ETFs, which include

- No minimum investment amount, because shares are traded on an exchange and not purchased from an investment company, which often requires a minimum investment of $500, $1,000, or more.

- Shares can be bought or sold through a broker or online any time during regular market hours at the current price. With mutual funds, the price you pay for shares or the price you receive when you sell shares is calculated once a day—usually at the end of the trading day.

- You can use limit orders and the more speculative techniques of selling short and margin—all discussed in Chapter 14—to buy and sell ETF shares.

Although increasing in popularity, there are only about 150 exchange-traded funds.

Approximately 91 percent of all mutual funds are open-end funds. An **open-end fund** is a mutual fund whose shares are issued and redeemed by the investment company at the request of investors. Investors are free to buy and sell shares at the net asset value. The **net asset value (NAV)** per share is equal to the current market value of securities contained in the mutual fund's portfolio minus the mutual fund's liabilities divided by the number of shares outstanding:

open-end fund A mutual fund whose shares are issued and redeemed by the investment company at the request of investors.

$$\text{Net asset value} = \frac{\text{Value of the fund's portfolio} - \text{Liabilities}}{\text{Number of shares outstanding}}$$

net asset value (NAV) The current market value of the securities contained in the mutual fund's portfolio minus the mutual fund's liabilities divided by the number of shares outstanding.

For example, assume the portfolio of all investments contained in the New American Frontiers mutual fund has a current market value of $655 million. The fund also has liabilities totaling $5 million. If this mutual fund has 30 million shares outstanding, the net asset value per share is $21.67:

$$\text{Net asset value} = \frac{\text{Value of the fund's portfolio} - \text{Liabilities}}{\text{Number of shares outstanding}}$$

$$= \frac{\$655 \text{ million} - \$5 \text{ million}}{30 \text{ million shares}}$$

$$= \$21.67 \text{ per share}$$

For most mutual funds, the net asset value is calculated at the close of trading each day.

In addition to buying and selling shares on request, most open-end funds provide their investors with a wide variety of services, including payroll deduction programs, automatic reinvestment programs, automatic withdrawal programs, and the option to change shares in one fund to another fund within the same fund family—all topics discussed later in this chapter.

LOAD FUNDS AND NO-LOAD FUNDS

Before investing in mutual funds, you should compare the cost of this type of investment with the cost of other investment alternatives, such as stocks or bonds. With regard to cost, mutual funds are classified as load funds or no-load funds. A **load fund** (sometimes referred to as an *"A" fund*) is a mutual fund in which investors pay a commission every time they purchase shares. The commission, sometimes referred to as the *sales charge,* may be as high as 8½ percent of the purchase price for investments under $10,000. (This fee may decline for investments over a specified amount, say $10,000 or $25,000.)

load fund A mutual fund in which investors pay a commission (as high as 8½ percent) every time they purchase shares.

While many exceptions exist, the average load charge for mutual funds is between 3 and 5 percent. Let's assume you decide to invest $10,000 in the Davis New York Venture mutual fund. This fund charges a sales load of 4.75 percent that you must pay when you purchase shares. The dollar amount of the sales charge on your $10,000 investment is $475 ($10,000 × 4.75% = $475). After paying the $475, the amount available for investment is reduced to $9,525 ($10,000 − $475 = $9,525). The "stated" advantage of a load fund is that the fund's sales force (account executives, financial planners, or brokerage divisions of banks and other financial institutions) will explain the mutual fund to investors and offer advice as to when shares of the fund should be bought or sold.

no-load fund A mutual fund in which the individual investor pays no sales charge.

A **no-load fund** is a mutual fund in which the individual investor pays no sales charge. No-load funds don't charge commissions when you buy shares because they have no salespeople. If you want to buy shares of a no-load fund, you must deal directly with the investment company. The usual means of contact is by telephone, the Internet, or mail. You can also purchase shares in a no-load fund from many discount brokers, including Charles Schwab, Ameritrade, TD Waterhouse Securities, and E*Trade.

As an investor, you must decide whether to invest in a load fund or a no-load fund. Some investment salespeople have claimed that load funds outperform no-load funds. But many financial analysts suggest there is generally no significant difference between mutual funds that charge commissions and those that do not.[3] You should also know that investment salespeople earn more commission when they sell load funds. *Since no-load funds offer the same investment opportunities load funds offer, you should investigate them further before deciding which type of mutual fund is best for you.* Although the sales commission should not be the decisive factor, the possibility of saving a load charge of up to 8½ percent is a factor to consider. For example, suppose Barbara Harrington invests $10,000 in a mutual fund that charges an 8½ percent sales fee. Since this fee is deducted in advance, her initial $10,000 investment is reduced by $850. Simply put, she now has $9,150 that she can use to buy shares in this load fund. By comparison, Mary Hernandez decides to invest $10,000 in a no-load mutual fund. Since there is no sales fee, she can use the entire $10,000 to purchase shares in this no-load fund. Depending on the load fund's performance, it may take Barbara a year or more to "catch up" and cover the cost of the sales fee.

contingent deferred sales load A 1 to 5 percent charge that shareholders pay when they withdraw their investment from a mutual fund.

Instead of charging investors a fee when they purchase shares in a mutual fund, some mutual funds charge a **contingent deferred sales load** (sometimes referred to as a *back-end load* or a *"B" fund*). These fees range from 1 to 5 percent, depending on how long you own the mutual fund before making a withdrawal. For example, assume you withdraw $5,000 from B shares that you own in the AIM Basic Balance mutual fund within a year of your original purchase date. You must pay a 5 percent contingent deferred sales fee. Your fee is $250 ($5,000 × 5% = $250). After the fee is deducted from your $5,000 withdrawal, you will receive $4,750 ($5,000 − $250 = $4,750). *Generally,* the deferred charge declines until there is no withdrawal charge if you own the shares in the fund for more than five to seven years.

MANAGEMENT FEES AND OTHER CHARGES
In evaluating a specific mutual fund, you should consider management fees and a number of other charges. The investment companies that sponsor mutual funds charge management fees. This fee, which is disclosed in the fund's prospectus, is a fixed percentage of the fund's asset value. Typically annual management fees range between 0.25 and 2 percent of the fund's asset value. While fees vary considerably, the average is 0.5 to 1.25 percent of the fund's assets.

12b-1 fee A fee that an investment company levies to defray the costs of advertising and marketing a mutual fund and commissions paid to a broker who sold you shares in the mutual fund.

The investment company may also levy a **12b-1 fee** (sometimes referred to as a *distribution fee*) to defray the costs of advertising and marketing a mutual fund and commissions paid to a broker who sold you shares in the mutual fund. Annual 12b-1 fees are calculated on the value of a fund's assets and are generally 1 percent or less of the fund's assets per year. Note: For a fund to be called a "no-load" fund, its 12b-1 fee must not exceed 0.25 percent of its assets.

Unlike the one-time sales load fees that mutual funds charge to purchase or sell shares, the 12b-1 fee is often an ongoing fee that is charged on an annual basis. Note that 12b-1 fees can cost you a lot of money over a period of years. Assuming there is no difference in performance offered by two different mutual funds, one of which charges a 12b-1 fee while the other doesn't, choose the latter fund. The 12b-1 fee is so lucrative for investment companies that a number of them have begun selling Class C shares that often charge a higher 12b-1 fee but no sales load or contingent deferred sales fee to attract new investors. When compared to Class A shares (commissions charged when shares are purchased) and Class B shares (commissions charged when withdrawals are made over the first five to seven years), Class C shares, with their ongoing, higher 12b-1 fees, may be more expensive over a long period of time.

expense ratio All the different management fees, 12b-1 fees, if any, and additional fund operating costs for a specific mutual fund.

Together, all the different management fees, 12b-1 fees, if any, and additional fund operating costs for a specific fund are referred to as an **expense ratio.** Since it is important to keep fees and costs as low as possible, you should examine a fund's expense ratio as one more factor to consider when evaluating a mutual fund. As a guideline, many financial planners recommend that you choose a mutual fund with an expense ratio of 1 percent or less.

One good source of info about mutual funds is the Investment Company Institute at **www.ici.org.**

By now, you are probably asking yourself, "Should I purchase Class A shares, Class B shares, or Class C shares?" There are no easy answers, but your professional financial adviser or broker can help you determine which class of shares of a particular mutual fund best suits your financial needs. You can also do your own research to determine which

Fees You May Pay as a Davis Fund Shareholder (paid directly from your investment)	Class A Shares	Class B Shares	Class C Shares
Maximum sales charge (load) imposed on purchases (as a percentage of offering price)	4.75%	None	None
Maximum deferred sales charge (load) imposed on redemptions (as a percentage of the lesser of the net asset value of the shares redeemed or the total cost of such shares)	0.75%*	4.00%	1.00%
Maximum sales charge (load) imposed on reinvested dividends	None	None	None
Exchange fee	None	None	None

*As a Class A shareholder, only if you buy shares valued at $1 million or more without a sales charge and sell the shares within one year of purchase.

Davis New York Venture Fund Annual Operating Expenses (deducted from the fund's assets)	Class A Shares	Class B Shares	Class C Shares
Management fees	0.51%	0.51%	0.51%
Distribution (12b-1) fees	0.25	1.00	1.00
Other expenses	0.16	0.22	0.19
Total annual operating expenses	0.92	1.73	1.70

Expenses may vary in future years.

Exhibit **16-2**

Summary of expenses paid to invest in the Davis New York Venture mutual fund

Source: Excerpted from the Davis New York Venture Fund prospectus, December 1, 2004.

fund is right for you. Factors to consider include whether you want to invest in a load fund or no-load fund, management fees, and expense ratios. As you will see later in this chapter, a number of sources of information can help you make your investment decisions.

The investment company's prospectus must provide all details relating to management fees, sales fees, 12b-1 fees, and other expenses. Exhibit 16–2 on page 519 reproduces the summary of expenses (sometimes called a *fee table*) for the Davis New York Venture fund. Notice that this exhibit has two separate parts. The first part describes shareholder transaction expenses. For this fund, the maximum sales charge is 4.75 percent. The second part describes the fund's annual operating expenses. For this fund, the expense ratio is 0.92 percent for Class A shares. In addition, a fee table will also provide an example of what typical charges you will incur over selected time periods.

Exhibit 16–3 summarizes information for load charges, no-load charges, and Class A, Class B, and Class C shares. In addition, it reports typical contingent deferred sales loads, management fees, and 12b-1 charges.

CONCEPT CHECK 16-1

1 If you wanted to research a mutual fund, would you use the Internet or sources at the library? Why?

2 What are two major reasons investors purchase mutual funds?

3 How do a closed-end fund, an open-end fund, and an exchange-traded fund differ?

4 What are the typical sales fees charged for a load and no-load mutual funds?

5 What is the difference among Class A, B, and C shares?

6 What are the typical management fees, 12b-1 fees, and expense ratios?

Action Application Use the Internet or library sources to identify a mutual fund that you believe could help you obtain your investment goals. Then answer the following questions.

   1 What is the name of the fund?

   2 Is there a sales load? If so, how much is the charge?

   3 What is the fund's management fee?

   4 What is the fund's expense ratio?

Classifications of Mutual Funds

Objective 2

Classify mutual funds by investment objective.

The managers of mutual funds tailor their investment portfolios to the investment objectives of their customers. Usually a fund's objectives are plainly disclosed in its prospectus. For example, the objectives of the Fundamental Investors mutual fund are described as follows:

> The fund's investment objective is to achieve long-term growth of capital and income. The fund invests primarily in common stocks or securities convertible into common stocks and may invest significantly in securities of issuers domiciled outside the United States and not included in the Standard & Poor's 500 Composite Index.[4]

While it may be helpful to categorize the 8,000-plus mutual funds into different categories, note that different sources of investment information may use different categories for the same mutual fund. In most cases, the name of the category gives a pretty good clue to the types of investments included within the category. The *major* fund categories are described in alphabetical order as follows:

STOCK FUNDS

- *Aggressive growth funds* seek rapid growth by purchasing stocks whose prices are expected to increase dramatically in a short period of time. Turnover within

Type of Fee or Charge	Customary Amount
Load fund	Up to 8½ percent of the purchase.
No-load fund	No sales charge.
Contingent deferred sales load	1 to 5 percent of withdrawals, depending on how long you own the fund before making a withdrawal.
Management fee	0.25 to 2 percent per year of the fund's total assets.
12b-1 fee	Usually 1 percent or less of the fund's assets per year.
Class A shares	Commission charge when shares are purchased.
Class B shares	Commission charge when money is withdrawn during the first five to seven years.
Class C shares	No commission to buy or sell shares of a fund, but generally higher, ongoing 12b-1 fees.

Exhibit **16-3**

Typical fees associated with mutual fund investments

an aggressive growth fund is high because managers are buying and selling individual stocks of small, growth companies. Investors in these funds experience wide price swings because of the underlying speculative nature of the stocks in the fund's portfolio.

- *Equity income funds* invest in stocks issued by companies with a long history of paying dividends. The major objective of these funds is to provide income to shareholders. These funds are attractive investment choices for conservative or retired investors.

- *Global stock funds* invest in stocks of companies throughout the world, including the United States.

- *Growth funds* invest in companies expecting higher-than-average revenue and earnings growth. While similar to aggressive growth funds, growth funds tend to invest in larger, well-established companies. As a result, the prices for shares in a growth fund are less volatile compared to aggressive growth funds.

- *Index funds* invest in the same companies included in an index like the Standard & Poor's 500 stock index or Russell 3000 Index. Since fund managers pick the stocks issued by the companies included in the index, an index fund should provide approximately the same performance as the index. Also, since index funds are cheaper to manage, they often have lower management fees and expense ratios.

- *International funds* invest in foreign stocks sold in securities markets throughout the world; thus, if the economy in one region or nation is in a slump, profits can still be earned in others. Unlike global funds, which invest in stocks issued by companies in both foreign nations and the United States, a true international fund invests outside the United States.

- *Large-cap funds* invest in the stocks of companies with total capitalization of $5 billion or more.

Experience counts. A Morgan Stanley financial adviser may be able to help you achieve your financial goals.

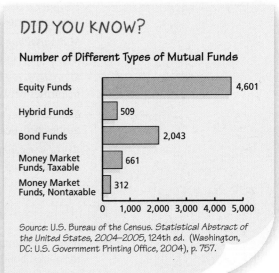

DID YOU KNOW?

Number of Different Types of Mutual Funds

Equity Funds — 4,601
Hybrid Funds — 509
Bond Funds — 2,043
Money Market Funds, Taxable — 661
Money Market Funds, Nontaxable — 312

Source: U.S. Bureau of the Census. *Statistical Abstract of the United States, 2004–2005,* 124th ed. (Washington, DC: U.S. Government Printing Office, 2004), p. 757.

Large-capitalization stocks are generally stable, well-established companies and likely to have minimal fluctuation in their value.

- *Midcap funds* invest in companies with total capitalization of $1 to $5 billion whose stocks offer more security than small-cap funds and more growth potential than funds that invest in large corporations.

For more info on mutual fund investing, go to **www.fundemail.com.**

- *Regional funds* seek to invest in stock traded within one specific region of the world, such as the European region, the Latin American region, or the Pacific region.

- *Sector funds* invest in companies within the same industry. Examples of sectors include health and biotechnology, science and technology, and natural resources.

- *Small-cap funds* invest in smaller, lesser-known companies with a total capitalization of less than $500 million. Because these companies are small and innovative, these funds offer higher growth potential. They are more speculative than funds that invest in larger, more established companies.

- *Socially responsible funds* avoid investing in companies that may cause harm to people, animals, and the environment. Typically, these funds do not invest in companies that produce tobacco, nuclear energy, or weapons or in companies that have a history of discrimination.

BOND FUNDS

- *High-yield (junk) bond funds* invest in high-yield, high-risk corporate bonds.

- *Index bond funds* invest in a sampling of bonds included in a bond index like the Lehman Brothers Aggregate Bond Index. Selection is based on bonds in the index *and* factors such as type of bond, quality, and years to maturity.

- *Intermediate corporate bond funds* invest in investment-grade corporate debt with maturities between 5 and 10 years.

- *Intermediate U.S. bond funds* invest in U.S. Treasury notes with maturities between 5 and 10 years.

- *Long-term corporate bond funds* invest in investment-grade corporate bond issues with maturities in excess of 10 years.

- *Long-term (U.S.) bond funds* invest in U.S. Treasury and U.S. zero-coupon bonds with maturities in excess of 10 years.

- *Municipal bond funds* invest in municipal bonds that provide investors with tax-free interest income.

- *Short-term corporate bond funds* invest in investment-grade bond issues with maturities between 1 and 5 years.

- *Short-term (U.S.) government bond funds* invest in U.S. Treasury issues with maturities between 1 and 5 years.

- *World bond funds* invest in bonds and other debt securities offered by foreign companies and governments.

OTHER FUNDS

- *Asset allocation funds* invest in various asset classes, including, but not limited to, stocks, bonds, and other fixed-income securities, and money market instruments. These funds seek high total return by maintaining precise amounts within each type of asset.

- *Balanced funds* invest in both stocks and bonds with the primary objectives of conserving principal, providing income, and long-term growth. Often the percentage of stocks and bonds is stated in the fund's prospectus.
- *Money market funds* invest in certificates of deposit, government securities, and other safe and highly liquid investments.

A **family of funds** exists when one investment company manages a group of mutual funds. Each fund within the family has a different financial objective. For instance, one fund may be a long-term government bond fund and another a growth fund. Most investment companies offer exchange privileges that enable shareholders to switch among the mutual funds in a fund family. For example, if you own shares in the Franklin Growth Fund, you may, at your discretion, switch to the Franklin Income Fund. Generally, investors may give instructions to switch from one fund to another within the same family either in writing, over the telephone, or via the Internet. The family-of-funds concept makes it convenient for shareholders to switch their investments among funds as different funds offer more potential, financial reward, or security. Charges for exchanges, if any, generally are small for each transaction. For funds that do charge, the fee may be as low as $5 per transaction.

family of funds A group of mutual funds managed by one investment company.

Many financial analysts suggest that the true mark of a quality mutual fund investment is the fund's ability to increase the investor's return during good times and maintain that return during bad times. To help accomplish this task, a large number of investors have turned to market timers. A **market timer** is an individual who helps investors decide when to switch their investments from one fund to another fund, usually within the same family of funds. Market timers usually charge an annual fee of 1 to 3 percent of the dollar value of the funds they manage. Early research indicates that market timers must be evaluated on their individual investment philosophy and their past performance, and it is impossible to pass judgment on *all* market timers as a group.

market timer An individual who helps investors decide when to switch their investments from one fund to another fund, usually within the same family of funds.

CONCEPT CHECK 16-2 ✔

1 How important is the investment objective as stated in a fund's prospectus?
2 Why do you think fund managers offer so many different kinds of funds?
3 What is a family of funds? How is it related to shareholder exchanges?
4 How does a market timer help people manage their mutual fund investments?

Action Application Use the Internet or library sources to identify one mutual fund in each of the three categories (stocks, bonds, and other). Describe the characteristics of the fund you select and the type of investor who would invest in that type of fund.

General Type of Fund	Name of Fund	Characteristics of Fund	Typical Investor
Stock			
Bond			
Other			

How to Decide to Buy or Sell Mutual Funds

Objective 3

Evaluate mutual funds for investment purposes.

Often the decision to buy or sell shares in mutual funds is "too easy" because investors assume they do not need to evaluate these investments. Why question what the professional portfolio managers decide to do? Yet professionals do make mistakes. The responsibility for choosing the right mutual fund rests with *you*. After all, you are the only one who knows how much risk you are willing to assume and how a particular mutual fund can help you achieve your goals.

If you think there are mutual funds designed to meet just about any conceivable investment objective, you are probably right. Hundreds of mutual funds trade daily under the headings "aggressive growth," "small-cap," and "global." Fortunately, a lot of information is available to help you evaluate a specific mutual fund. Unfortunately, you can get lost in all the facts and figures and forget your ultimate goal: to choose a mutual fund that will help you achieve your financial goals. To help you sort out all the research, statistics, and information about mutual funds and give you some direction as to what to do first, we have provided a checklist in The Financial Planning for Life's Situations feature on page 525. Let's begin with one basic question: Do you want a managed fund or an index fund?

MANAGED FUNDS VERSUS INDEXED FUNDS

Most mutual funds are managed funds. In other words, there is a professional fund manager (or team of managers) that chooses the securities that are contained in the fund. The fund manager also decides when to buy and sell securities in the fund. *Caution: Don't forget the role of the fund manager in determining a fund's success.* One important question is how long the present fund manager has been managing the fund. If a fund has performed well under its present manager over a 5-year, 10-year, or longer period, there is a strong likelihood that it will continue to perform well under that manager in the future. On the other hand, if the fund has a new manager, his or her decisions may affect the performance of the fund. Ultimately, the fund manager is responsible for the fund's success. Managed funds may be open-end funds or closed-end funds.

Instead of investing in a managed fund, some investors choose to invest in an index fund. Why? The answer to that question is simple: Over many years, the majority of managed mutual funds fail to outperform the Standard & Poor's 500 stock index. The exact statistics vary depending on the year, but on average, anywhere from 50 percent to 80 percent of managed funds are beaten by the index each year.[5] Simply put: It's hard to beat an index like the Standard & Poor's 500. If the individual securities included in an index increase in value, the index goes up. Because an index mutual fund is a mirror image of a specific index, the dollar value of a share in an index fund also increases when the index increases. Unfortunately, the reverse is true. If the index goes down, the value of a share in an index fund goes down.

The concept behind index funds is based on the efficient market hypothesis discussed in Chapter 14, which states that it is impossible to consistently beat the market without raising your risk level. John Bogle, founder of the Vanguard mutual funds, created the first index fund in 1976 as a low-cost alternative to managed mutual funds. Today, the Vanguard 500 Index fund is the largest mutual fund in the world.[6] All index funds, sometimes called "passive" funds, have managers, but they simply buy the stocks or bonds contained in the index.

A second reason why investors choose index funds is the lower expense ratio charged by these passively managed funds. The total return for any mutual fund—whether a managed fund or an index fund—is the total return on the investments contained in the fund's portfolio minus the fees an investor pays for management and other fund expenses. As mentioned earlier in this chapter, the total fees charged by a mutual fund is called the expense ratio. If a fund's expense ratio is 1.25 percent, then the fund has to earn at least that amount on its investment holdings just to break even. With very few

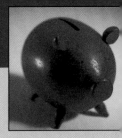

ARE YOU READY TO INVEST IN MUTUAL FUNDS?

Before beginning a mutual fund investment program, you may want to use the checklist below to determine whether you are ready to begin investing.

☐ **1. Perform a financial checkup.** Before investing, make sure your budget is balanced, you have adequate insurance protection, and you have established an emergency fund.

☐ **2. Obtain the money you need to purchase mutual funds.** Although the amount will vary, $250 to $3,000 or more is usually required to open an account with a brokerage firm or an investment company.

☐ **3. Determine your investment goals.** Without investment goals, you cannot know what you want to accomplish. For more information on the importance of goals, review the material in Chapter 13.

☐ **4. Find a fund with an objective that matches your objective.** The *Wall Street Journal, Barron's,* and personal finance magazines may help you identify funds with objectives that match your investment objectives.

☐ **5. Learn about the fund.** Once you've identified a fund with an objective that matches your objective, look for basic information about minimum investing requirements, sales fees, expense ratio, performance, and portfolio holdings.

☐ **6. Evaluate, evaluate, and evaluate any mutual fund before buying or selling.** Possible sources of more detailed information include the Internet, professional advisory services, the fund's prospectus and annual report, financial publications, and newspapers—all sources described in the remainder of this section.

exceptions, the expense ratios for index funds are lower than the expense ratios for managed funds. Typical expense ratios for an index fund are 0.50 percent or less. Index funds may be open-end funds, closed-end funds, or exchange-traded funds.

Which type of fund is best? Good question. The answer depends on which managed mutual fund you choose. If you pick a managed fund that has better performance than an index, then you made the right choice. If, on the other hand, the index (and the index fund) outperforms the managed fund—which happens 50 to 80 percent of the time, depending on the year—an index fund is a better choice. With both investments, the key is how well you can research a specific investment alternative using the sources of information that are described in the remainder of this section.

THE INTERNET

Many investors have found a wealth of information about mutual fund investments on the Internet. Basically, there are three ways to access information. First, you can obtain current market values for mutual funds by using one of the Internet Web sites, such as Yahoo! or MSN.com. The Yahoo! finance page (finance.yahoo.com) has a box where you can enter the symbol of the mutual fund you want to research. If you don't know the symbol, you can enter in the name of the mutual fund in the symbol lookup box. The Yahoo! finance Web site will respond with the correct symbol. In addition to current market values, you can obtain a price history for a mutual fund and a profile including specific holdings that the fund owns, performance data, comparative data, and research reports.

Second, most investment companies that sponsor mutual funds have a Web site. To obtain information, all you have to do is access one of the Internet search engines and type in the name of the fund. Generally, statistical information about individual funds, procedures for opening an account, promotional literature, and different investor services are provided. *Be warned:* Investment companies want you to become a shareholder. As a result, the Web sites for *some* investment companies read like a sales pitch. Read between the glowing descriptions and look at the facts before investing your money.

Finally, professional advisory services, covered in the next section, offer online research reports for mutual funds. A portion of the information available from the Morningstar Web site for the Dodge and Cox Balanced Fund is illustrated in Exhibit 16–4. Note that information about the fund symbol, current NAV, portfolio manager, and past returns is provided. It is also possible to obtain more detailed information by clicking on the appropriate button. Many investors have found that the research reports provided by companies like Morningstar Inc. (www.morningstar.com) and Lipper Analytical Inc. (www.lipperweb.com) are well worth the $5 to $10 fee charged for online services. While the information is basically the same as that in the printed reports described later in this section, the ability to obtain the information quickly without having to wait for research materials to be mailed or to make a trip to the library is a real selling point.

PROFESSIONAL ADVISORY SERVICES

A number of subscription services provide detailed information on mutual funds. Standard and Poor's Corporation, Lipper Analytical Services, Morningstar Inc. and Value Line are four widely used sources of such information. Exhibit 16–5 illustrates the type of information provided by Morningstar Inc. for the T. Rowe Price Equity-Income fund. Although the Morningstar report is just one page long, it provides a wealth of information designed to help you decide whether this is the right fund for you. Notice that the information is divided into various sections. At the top, a small box entitled

Exhibit **16–4**   Information about the Dodge and Cox Balanced Fund available from the Morningstar Web site[7]

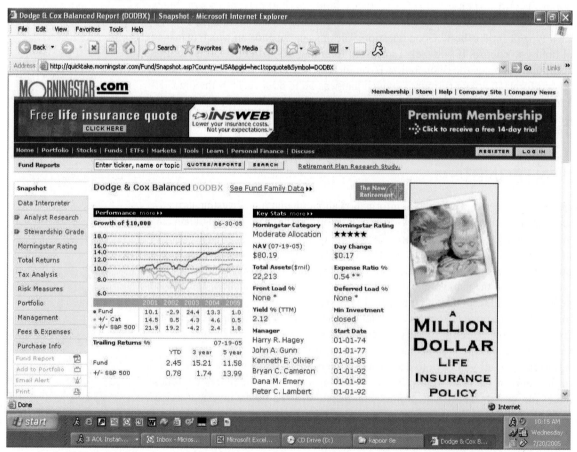

Source: Morningstar, www.morningstar.com, July 20, 2005.

Exhibit **16-5**   Mutual fund research information provided by Morningstar Inc.

T. Rowe Price Eq-Inc

	Analyst Pick	Ticker	Load	NAV	Yield	Total Assets	Mstar Category
✓		PRFDX	None	$26.08	1.6%	$18,238 mil	Large Value

Governance and Management

Stewardship Grade: B

Portfolio Manager(s)

Seasoned. Brian Rogers has managed this offering since its 1985 inception. He's backed by T. Rowe Price's deep bench of analysts. In January 2004, Rogers became T. Rowe Price's chief investment officer. He says he invests a large portion of his assets in the fund.

Strategy

This offering employs a true-blue approach to value investing. Longtime manager Brian Rogers strives to keep the fund's yield at least 25% higher than that of the S&P 500 Index, and he looks for companies trading cheaply relative to their historic price multiples. This strategy often leads him to load up on traditional value sectors, such as energy and industrial cyclicals, although he's willing to delve into growth-oriented areas such as health care, technology, and telecom when the price is right.

Performance 01-31-05

	1st Qtr	2nd Qtr	3rd Qtr	4th Qtr	Total
2000	-2.92	0.16	6.88	8.85	13.12
2001	-2.81	5.76	-8.28	7.81	1.64
2002	4.62	-7.93	-17.33	9.21	-13.04
2003	-6.02	16.82	1.49	12.90	25.78
2004	1.91	2.59	0.72	9.25	15.05

Trailing	Total Return%	+/- S&P 500	+/- Russ 1000 Vl	%Rank Cat	Growth of $10,000
3 Mo	6.01	1.03	-0.64	41	10,601
6 Mo	10.01	1.86	-1.66	37	11,001
1 Yr	11.01	4.79	-1.44	22	11,101
3 Yr Avg	7.30	4.06	-0.90	21	12,354
5 Yr Avg	8.36	10.13	2.77	17	14,940
10 Yr Avg	12.41	0.91	-0.87	19	32,214
15 Yr Avg	12.14	0.88	-0.24	16	55,771

Tax Analysis	Tax-Adj Rtn%	%Rank Cat	Tax-Cost Rat	%Rank Cat
3 Yr (estimated)	6.22	23	1.01	67
5 Yr (estimated)	6.73	20	1.50	80
10 Yr (estimated)	10.22	21	1.95	63

Potential Capital Gain Exposure: 7% of assets

Historical Profile

Return	Above Avg
Risk	Average
Rating	★★★★ Above Avg

89% 93% 93% 92% 94% 96% 96% 94%

▼ Manager Change
▽ Partial Manager Change

33.0
26.0
20.0
15.0
10.0

Growth of $10,000
— Investment Values of Fund
— Investment Values of S&P 500

Performance Quartile (within Category)

	1994	1995	1996	1997	1998	1999	2000	2001	2002	2003	2004	01-05	History
	15.98	20.01	22.54	26.07	26.32	24.81	24.67	23.65	19.79	24.16	26.59	26.08	NAV
	4.53	33.35	20.40	28.82	9.23	3.82	13.12	1.64	-13.04	25.78	15.05	-1.92	Total Return %
	3.21	-4.18	-2.55	-4.53	-19.35	-17.22	22.22	13.52	9.05	-2.89	4.18	0.52	+/-S&P 500
	6.51	-5.01	-1.24	-6.36	-6.40	-3.53	6.11	7.23	2.48	-4.25	-1.44	-0.14	+/-Russ 1000 Vl
	3.61	4.15	3.30	2.99	2.40	2.04	2.12	1.49	1.54	1.99	1.76	0.00	Income Return %
	0.92	29.20	17.10	25.83	6.83	1.78	11.00	0.15	-14.58	23.79	13.29	-1.92	Capital Return %
	8	50	47	34	71	54	31	21	12	69	23	47	Total Rtn % Rank Cat
	0.59	0.65	0.65	0.66	0.61	0.53	0.51	0.36	0.36	0.39	0.42	0.00	Income $
	0.81	0.54	0.84	2.14	1.49	1.97	2.64	1.01	0.45	0.27	0.72	0.00	Capital Gains $
	0.88	0.85	0.81	0.79	0.77	0.77	0.78	0.80	0.79	0.78	—	—	Expense Ratio %
	3.63	3.69	3.08	2.67	2.26	1.95	2.01	1.53	1.72	1.80	—	—	Income Ratio %
	36	21	25	24	23	22	22	17	15	12	—	—	Turnover Rate %
	3,204	5,215	7,818	12,771	13,495	12,321	10,187	10,128	8,954	12,167	15,947	15,946	Net Assets $mil

Rating and Risk

Time Period	Load-Adj Return %	Morningstar Rtn vs Cat	Morningstar Risk vs Cat	Morningstar Risk-Adj Rating
1 Yr	11.01			
3 Yr	7.30	+Avg	Avg	★★★★
5 Yr	8.36	+Avg	Avg	★★★★
10 Yr	12.41	+Avg	-Avg	★★★★
Incept	13.35			

Other Measures	Standard Index S&P 500	Best Fit Index Russ 1000 Vl
Alpha	4.1	-0.6
Beta	0.92	0.96
R-Squared	92	97
Standard Deviation	15.55	
Mean	7.30	
Sharpe Ratio	0.38	

Investment Style

Equity
Stock %

Portfolio Analysis 12-31-04

Share change since 09-04 Total Stocks:122

Sector	PE	Tot Ret%	% Assets
General Electric	Ind Mtrls	23.3	-1.01	2.01
J.P. Morgan Chase & Co.	Financial	19.1	-3.46	1.92
⊖ ExxonMobil	Energy	14.3	0.66	1.77
ChevronTexaco	Energy	10.2	3.60	1.74
⊕ Marsh & McLennan Compani	Financial	14.2	-1.22	1.63
⊕ Viacom B	Media	35.2	2.61	1.61
⊕ Merck	Health	10.3	-12.73	1.55
Royal Dutch Petroleum AD	Energy	—	1.90	1.42
Honeywell International	Ind Mtrls	21.7	1.61	1.42
⊖ Bank of America	Financial	12.6	-1.32	1.40
⊕ Coca-Cola	Goods	22.1	-0.36	1.38
Comcast A	Media	78.5	-3.28	1.38
⊕ New York Times A	Media	20.0	-4.71	1.35
Johnson & Johnson	Health	21.2	2.02	1.31
Union Pacific	Business	18.2	-11.38	1.30
⊕ Time Warner	Media	26.5	-7.46	1.29
Bristol-Myers Squibb	Health	16.9	-7.48	1.27
⊕ International Paper	Ind Mtrls	50.2	-6.79	1.22
Sprint	Telecom	—	-4.10	1.20
⊕ Colgate-Palmolive	Goods	21.2	3.20	1.20

Current Investment Style

Value Blnd Growth — Large / Mid / Small

Market Cap	%
Giant	37.4
Large	40.5
Mid	21.7
Small	0.4
Micro	0.0

Avg $mil: 28,686

Value Measures		Rel Category
Price/Earnings	17.31	1.12
Price/Book	2.43	1.05
Price/Sales	1.39	1.13
Price/Cash Flow	6.82	1.06
Dividend Yield %	2.16	1.09

Growth Measures	%	Rel Category
Long-Term Erngs	9.68	0.94
Book Value	0.52	0.10
Sales	0.95	0.25
Cash Flow	10.23	1.93
Historical Erngs	8.55	0.78

Profitability	%	Rel Category
Return on Equity	16.22	1.01
Return on Assets	7.44	0.91
Net Margin	9.88	0.89

Sector Weightings	% of Stocks	Rel S&P 500	3 Year High	Low
⊙ Info	19.37	0.93		
Software	0.98	0.23	1	0
Hardware	4.01	0.41	4	2
Media	8.81	2.31	9	4
Telecom	5.57	1.87	8	6
⊛ Service	37.92	0.82		
Health	10.64	0.86	11	8
Consumer	4.22	0.47	6	4
Business	3.58	0.91	6	3
Financial	19.48	0.94	20	18
Mfg	42.72	1.29		
Goods	13.67	1.42	15	11
Ind Mtrls	14.63	1.15	17	15
Energy	9.40	1.24	12	9
Utilities	5.02	1.62	5	2

Composition

		%
●	Cash	4.8
●	Stocks	93.7
●	Bonds	0.0
●	Other	1.5
	Foreign	5.1

(% of Stock)

Morningstar's Take by Christopher Davis 02-15-05

Going against the crowd has helped make this offering one of our favorites.

Veteran T. Rowe Price Equity Income manager Brian Rogers is a classic counterpuncher. When investors run from companies clouded by bad news, Rogers often gravitates to them. He is drawn to stocks with above-above average dividend yields trading cheaply relative to their historical price multiples--criteria typically met by companies suffering significant setbacks. Rogers will add to struggling picks if they fall further so long as he believes investors are overreacting to their troubles.

That was the case in last year's fourth quarter, when top holdings Merck and Marsh & McLennan slumped. The former faltered as it discontinued sales of blockbuster arthritis drug Vioxx, but Rogers believes the downside risk is minimal. And the latter suffered while its Putnam mutual fund and insurance brokerage units came under scrutiny from regulators. Rogers thought investors reacted too harshly to Marsh's travails and points to the underlying strength of insurance and consulting businesses.

Because Rogers keeps his portfolio well diversified, those troubles did little to upend returns in 2004. In fact, the fund benefited handsomely from a number of winning picks, including TXU, Verizon Communications, and ExxonMobil, propelling it to a 15% gain and a top quartile showing in the large-value category for the year.

The fund has certainly been no slouch over the long haul, either. Indeed, all of the fund's long-term trailing returns land in the category's top quartile or better. Moreover, volatility has been relatively moderate, thanks to Rogers' income-oriented approach. Rogers experience--his tenure spans nearly two decades--and the fund's modest expense ratio add to its appeal. This remains one of the large-value group's most-appealing options.

Address:	100 E Pratt St Baltimore MD 21202 800-638-5660	Minimum Purchase:	$2500	Add: $100 IRA: $1000
		Min Auto Inv Plan:	$50	Add: $50
		Sales Fees:	No-load	
Web Address:	www.troweprice.com	Management Fee:	0.57%	
Inception:	10-31-85	Actual Fees:	Mgt:0.57%	Dist:
Advisor:	T. Rowe Price Associates, Inc.	Expense Projections:	3Yr:$249	5Yr:$433 10Yr:$966
Subadvisor:	None	Income Distrib:	Quarterly	
NTF Plans:	N/A			

Source: *Morningstar Mutual Funds,* March 6, 2005, p. 94.

"Historical Profile" contains information about financial return, risk, and rating. Notice that T. Rowe Price Equity-Income is rated four stars, Morningstar's next to highest rating. The report also provides statistical information over the past 12 years. The middle section of the report provides information about performance, risk analysis, and portfolio analysis. The last section, at the very bottom, describes the investment style of the fund and information about minimum purchases and fees. Generally, this section summarizes Morningstar's research.

As you can see, the research information for this fund is pretty upbeat. However, other research firms like Standard & Poor, Lipper Analytical Services, and Value Line, as well as Morningstar Inc. will also tell you if a fund is a poor performer that offers poor investment potential.

In addition, various mutual fund newsletters provide financial information to subscribers for a fee. All of these sources are rather expensive, but their reports may be available from brokerage firms or libraries.

HOW TO READ THE MUTUAL FUNDS SECTION OF THE NEWSPAPER

Most large, metropolitan newspapers, the *Wall Street Journal,* and *Barron's* provide information about mutual funds. Typical coverage includes information about net asset value, net change, the fund family and fund name, and total return over selected time periods. The second line from the bottom of Exhibit 16–6 provides detailed information for the Hibernia Capital Appreciation fund. Each numbered entry in the list below the exhibit refers to a numbered column in the mutual fund table. Much of this same information is available on the Internet.

The letters beside the name of a specific fund can be very informative. You can find out what they mean by looking at the footnotes that accompany the newspaper's mutual

Exhibit 16-6

Financial information about mutual funds available in the *Wall Street Journal*

	1	2	3	4	5
			NET	YTD	3-YR
	FUND	NAV	CHG	%RET	%RET
	CapAppC t	21.76	0.01	−10.5	−0.9
	DivGrwA p	25.18	0.07	−5.1	4.6
	MidCapStkA p	24.93	0.02	−6.5	1.3
	MidCapStkC t	23.42	0.01	−6.7	0.5
	SmCpStA p	30.48	0.18	−10.4	2.5
Hibernia Funds					
	CapAp	18.12	0.04	−3.8	1.3
	MidCap p	15.58	0.10	−2.7	6.6

1. **FUND:** The name of the fund is the Hibernia Capital Appreciation fund.

2. **NAV** stands for net asset value. For the Hibernia Capital Appreciation fund, the NAV is $18.12 per share.

3. **NET CHG (net change)** is the difference between the price paid for the last share today and the price paid for the last share on the previous trading day. The Hibernia Capital Appreciation fund closed $0.04 higher than yesterday's closing price.

4. **YTD % RET** is the year-to-date percentage of increase or decrease for a fund. This Hibernia fund has lost 3.8 percent of its value since January 1.

5. **3-YR % RET** is the average percentage of increase or decrease over the last three years. This Hibernia fund has increased an average of 1.3 percent each year for the past three years.

Source: Republished by permission of Dow Jones Inc. from the *Wall Street Journal,* April 19, 2005, p. C14; permission conveyed through the Copyright Clearance Center, Inc.

fund quotations. Generally, "p" means a 12b-1 distribution fee is charged, "r" means a redemption charge may be made, "t" means both the p and r footnotes apply, and "s" means the fund has had a stock split or paid a dividend.

The newspaper coverage described in this section is a good means of monitoring the value of your mutual fund investments. However, other sources of information provide a more complete basis for evaluating mutual fund investments.

MUTUAL FUND PROSPECTUS

An investment company sponsoring a mutual fund must give potential investors a prospectus. According to financial experts, the prospectus is usually the first piece of information investors receive, and they should read it completely before investing. Although it may look foreboding, a commonsense approach to reading a fund's prospectus can provide valuable insights. In fact, most investors find that a fund's prospectus can provide a wealth of information. As pointed out earlier, the prospectus summarizes the fund's objective. Also, the fee table provides a summary of the fees a fund charges. In addition to information about objectives and fees, the prospectus should provide the following:

Sheet 61
Evaluating mutual fund investment information

- A statement describing the risk factors associated with the fund.
- A description of the fund's past performance.
- A statement describing the type of investments contained in the fund's portfolio.
- Information about dividends, distributions, and taxes.
- Information about the fund's management.
- Information on limitations or requirements the fund must honor when choosing investments.
- The process investors can use to buy or sell shares in the fund.
- A description of services provided to investors and fees for services, if any.
- Information about how often the fund's investment portfolio changes (sometimes referred to as its *turnover ratio*).

For help choosing a mutual fund, use the Fund Screener at **finance.yahoo.com**.

Finally, the prospectus provides information about how to open a mutual fund account with the investment company.

MUTUAL FUND ANNUAL REPORT

If you are a prospective investor, you can request an annual report by mail, through an 800 telephone number, or on the Internet. Once you are a shareholder, the investment company will send you an annual report. A fund's annual report contains a letter from the president of the investment company, from the fund manager, or both. The annual report also contains detailed financial information about the fund's assets and liabilities, statement of operations, and statement of changes in net assets. Next, the annual report includes a schedule of investments. Finally, the fund's annual report should include a letter from the fund's independent auditors that provides an opinion as to the accuracy of the fund's financial statements.

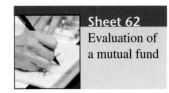

Sheet 62
Evaluation of a mutual fund

FINANCIAL PUBLICATIONS

Investment-oriented magazines such as *BusinessWeek, Forbes, Kiplinger's Personal Finance,* and *Money* are other sources of information about mutual funds. Each of these publications provides detailed information about mutual funds and ranks them on a

Exhibit **16-7** Portion of the 2005 mutual fund survey by *BusinessWeek* magazine

Personal Business Mutual Funds

Equity Fund Scoreboard

How to Use the Tables

BUSINESSWEEK RATINGS Overall ratings are based on five-year, risk-adjusted returns. They are calculated by subtracting a fund's risk-of-loss factor (see RISK) from pretax total return. Category ratings are based on risk-adjusted returns of the funds in that category. The ratings:

A	SUPERIOR	C-	BELOW AVERAGE
B+	VERY GOOD	D	POOR
B	ABOVE AVERAGE	F	VERY POOR
C	AVERAGE		

These tables list A-rated funds. For others go to http://bwnt.businessweek.com/mutual_fund
MANAGEMENT CHANGES ⚒ indicates the fund's manager has held the job at least 10 years; a ⚒ indicates a change since Dec. 31, 2003.

S&P 500 COMPARISON The pretax total returns for the Standard & Poor's 500-stock index are as follows: 2004, 10.9 %; three-year average (2002-2004), 3.6%; five-year average (2000-2004), –2.3%; 10-year average (1995-2004), 12.1%.

CATEGORY U.S. diversified funds are classified by market capitalization of the stocks in the

portfolio and by the nature of those stocks. If the average market cap is greater than $10 billion, the fund is large-cap; from $2 billion to $10 billion, mid-cap; less than $2 billion, small-cap. All-cap funds are those that don't follow a fixed-capitalization policy. Value funds are those whose stocks have price-to-earnings and price-to-book ratios lower than average for their market capitalizations. Growth funds have higher than average p-e and p-b ratios. Blend funds are those in which the ratios are about average. Hybrids mix stocks and bonds, and

FUND/SYMBOL	OVERALL RATING	CATEGORY	RATING	SIZE		FEES		2004 RETURNS (%)		
(COMPARES RISK-ADJUSTED PERFORMANCE OF EACH FUND AGAINST ALL FUNDS)		(COMPARES RISK-ADJUSTED PERFORMANCE OF FUND WITHIN CATEGORY)		ASSETS $MIL.	% CHG. 2003-2004	SALES CHARGE (%)	EXPENSE RATIO (%)	PRE-TAX	AFTER-TAX	YIELD
ABN AMRO MID CAP N CHTTX	B+	Mid-cap Blend	A	423.9	130	No load	1.34†	18.9	18.3	0.0
ABN AMRO REAL ESTATE N ARFCX	A	Real Estate	C	76.6	51	0.00 *	1.37†	33.4	32.2	1.9
AFBA FIVE STAR LARGE CAP INSTITUTIONAL AFBEX	C	Large-cap Growth	A	20.3	–1	No load	1.08	7.8	7.8	0.1
AFBA FIVE STAR USA GLOBAL INSTITUTIONAL AFGLX	C	Large-cap Growth	A	40.0	1	No load	1.08	6.6	6.6	0.4
AIM ENERGY INV. FSTEX (a) ⚒	A	Natural Resources	B	311.1	52	No load ‡	1.76†	36.6	36.6	0.0
AIM GOLD & PRECIOUS METALS INV. FGLDX (b) ⚒	A	Precious Metals	C	117.8	–18	No load ‡	1.93†	–4.9	–5.0	1.1
AIM REAL ESTATE A IARAX	A	Real Estate	B+	625.3	147	4.75	1.65†	36.0	35.1	1.4
AEGIS VALUE AVALX	A	Small-cap Value	B+	815.2	92	No load	1.50	13.5	12.7	0.0
AL FRANK VALUX	A	Mid-cap Value	B+	244.0	103	0.00 *	1.79†	15.8	15.8	0.0
ALLIANCEBERNSTEIN REAL ESTATE INV. ADV. ARSYX	A	Real Estate	B	159.3	56	No load	1.44	35.2	34.5	2.9

number of important investment criteria. Exhibit 16–7 illustrates a portion of *BusinessWeek*'s mutual fund survey for 2005.

A fund's past long-term performance is no guarantee of future success, but it may be a predictor of future performance. To gauge this variable, most annual surveys include information about a fund's total return. In Exhibit 16–7, average total returns for 1 year, 3 years, 5 years, and 10 years are reported for each fund included in the survey. Also included in the *BusinessWeek* survey is information about

- The fund's overall rating when compared with *all* other funds.
- The fund's rating when compared with funds in the same category.
- The size of the fund.
- The sales charge and expense ratio for each fund.
- Portfolio data, including turnover, percentage of cash, PE ratio, and largest holdings.
- Risk of loss factor for each fund.
- Performance for best and worst quarter.
- A toll-free telephone number for each fund.

More detailed descriptions about the information contained in each column are provided at the top of Exhibit 16–7. For a moment, choose one of the funds illustrated in

Exhibit **16-7**   Continued

possibly other assets. World funds generally include U.S. stocks; foreign funds do not. Sector and regional funds are as indicated.

SALES CHARGE Many funds take this "load" out of the initial investment, and for ratings purposes, returns are reduced by these charges. Loads may be levied on withdrawals.

EXPENSE RATIO This counts expenses as a percentage of average net assets. Footnotes indicate a 12(b)-1 plan, which uses shareholder money for marketing. The average is 1.38%.

PRETAX TOTAL RETURN A fund's net gain to investors, including reinvestment of dividends and capital gains at month-end prices.

AFTERTAX TOTAL RETURN Returns adjusted for U.S. taxes; treats all capital gains and long-term.

YIELD Income as a percent of net asset value.

HISTORY A fund's returns relative to other equity funds for, from left to right, 2000, 2001, 2002, 2003, and 2004. The numbers designate which quintile the fund was in during the period: ◼ for the top quintile, ◼ for the second, and so on. No number indicates that there are no data for that period.

TURNOVER The relative frequency of a fund's trading activity.

CASH Portion of fund not in stocks or bonds. If negative, the fund is using borrowed money.

UNTAXED GAINS Percentage of assets in portfolio that are unrealized and undistributed capital gains. A negative figure indicates losses that may offset future gains.

P-E RATIO The average price-earnings ratio of the fund derived from each stock price divided by reported per-share earnings.

TOP 10 STOCKS The percentage of fund assets that represents the 10 largest holdings. The higher the number, the more concentrated the fund, and the more dependent on the performance of a relatively small number of stocks.

LARGEST HOLDING From the latest fund reports.

RISK The risk-of-loss factor, or potential for losing money, calculated as follows: The three-month Treasury bill return is subtracted from the monthly return in each of the last 60 months. When a fund has lagged Treasury bills, the result is negative. The sum of these negative numbers is divided by the number of months. The result is a negative number, and the greater its magnitude, the higher the risk of loss.

BEST AND WORST QUARTERS Highest and lowest quarterly returns of the past five years.

AVERAGE ANNUAL TOTAL RETURNS (%)						HISTORY	PORTFOLIO DATA						RISK					TELEPHONE
3 YEARS		5 YEARS		10 YEARS		RESULTS VS.	TURNOVER	CASH	UNTAXED	P-E	TOP 10	LARGEST HOLDING	LEVEL	BEST		WORST		
PRETAX	AFTERTAX	PRETAX	AFTERTAX	PRETAX	AFTERTAX	ALL FUNDS		%	GAINS%	RATIO	STKS.%	COMPANY (% ASSETS)		QTR	% RET	QTR	% RET	
11.9	11.7	15.3	14.3	15.0	14.0	◼◼◼◼◼	Average	7	18	24	39	Readers Digest Association (5)	Average	Q2 03	30.1	Q3 02	−19.5	800-992-8151
23.9	22.4	21.3	19.5	NA	NA	◼◼◼◼◼	Very Low	1	31	31	42	Simon Property Group (5)	Very Low	Q4 04	17.0	Q3 02	−8.4	800-992-8151
1.4	1.4	1.3	1.1	NA	NA	◼◼◼◼◼	Average	5	4	21	38	American Express (5)	Average	Q2 03	20.1	Q3 01	−20.0	800-243-9865
2.3	2.3	0.9	0.7	NA	NA	◼◼◼◼◼	Low	7	−1	22	32	Microsoft (3)	Average	Q2 03	17.8	Q3 02	−21.9	800-243-9865
17.0	17.0	16.1	15.7	15.0	14.0	◼◼◼◼◼	High	NA	26	16	37	BP Amoco PLC Sponsored ADR (5)	Average	Q1 00	21.4	Q3 01	−16.9	800-347-4246
30.8	30.5	17.9	17.5	1.0	0.0	◼◼◼◼◼	Average	NA	−94	38	50	Glamis Gold (6)	High	Q1 02	33.9	Q2 04	−14.3	800-347-4246
27.2	26.3	24.0	22.7	NA	NA	◼◼◼◼◼	Average	NA	26	28	48	General Growth Properties (6)	Very Low	Q4 04	17.1	Q3 02	−6.3	800-347-4246
16.0	15.3	20.6	19.6	NA	NA	◼◼◼◼◼	Low	NA	14	NA	NA	Prime Hospitality (3)	Very Low	Q2 03	21.0	Q3 02	−9.2	800-528-3780
15.1	15.1	16.2	15.8	NA	NA	◼◼◼◼◼	Very Low	3	25	21	8	SEI Daily Income Trust Govt. Port. (3)	Average	Q2 03	31.0	Q3 02	−27.8	888-263-6443
24.7	23.5	22.1	20.5	NA	NA	◼◼◼◼◼	Average	25	23	34	45	ProLogis (7)	Very Low	Q4 04	16.5	Q3 02	−8.9	800-221-5672

Exhibit 16–7 and take a closer look at the information provided for the fund. For example, look at the Aim Energy Investor Class fund. The fund has excellent one-year performance (36.6 percent) and has also performed well for 3, 5, and 10 years. Although the expense ratio (1.76) is high, there is no sales charge. Also, the turnover ratio is "high," but the risk is average. Because of the information and statistics reported on this fund in the *BusinessWeek* annual survey, many investors would "dig" a little deeper and examine more detailed research information to determine whether this is a fund that would help them achieve their investment goals.

In addition to annual surveys like the *BusinessWeek* survey, a number of mutual fund guidebooks are available at your local bookstore or public library. You can also order these publications by phone or online. Some of the more popular publications are

1. *Fidelity Monitor Newsletter* (1-800-397-3094)
2. *IBC/Donahue Mutual Funds Almanac* (1-800-343-5413)
3. *Individual Investor's Guide to Low-Load Mutual Funds,* American Association of Individual Investors (312-280-0170)
4. *Investment Company Institute Directory of Mutual Funds* (202-326-5800)
5. *Mutual Fund Fact Book,* Investment Company Institute (202-326-5800)
6. *The Guide to No-Load Fund Investing* (703-244-1540).

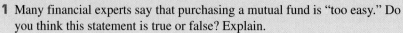

CONCEPT CHECK 16-3

1 Many financial experts say that purchasing a mutual fund is "too easy." Do you think this statement is true or false? Explain.

2 In your own words, describe the difference between a managed fund and an index fund. Which fund would you choose for your investment program?

3 How can the following help you evaluate a mutual fund?

a. The Internet   d. The prospectus

b. Professional advisory services   e. The annual report

c. Newspapers   f. Financial publications

4 Describe the type of information contained in the annual mutual fund survey published by *BusinessWeek*.

Action Application Use the Internet or library sources to report the type of fund, year-to-date (YTD) return, net asset value, and Morningstar rating for the following mutual funds. Then explain whether you think any of the funds could help you obtain your investment goals.

Fund	Fund Symbol	Type of Fund	YTD Return	Net Asset Value	Morningstar Rating
Alger Capital Appreciation	ACAAX				
Gabelli Asset	GATBX				
Franklin Balance Sheet	FRBSX				

The Mechanics of a Mutual Fund Transaction

Objective 4

Describe how and why mutual funds are bought and sold.

For many investors, mutual funds have become the investment of choice. In fact, you probably either own shares or know someone who owns shares in a mutual fund—they're that popular! They may be part of a 401(k) or 403(b) retirement account, a SEP-IRA, a Roth IRA, or a traditional IRA retirement account, all topics discussed in Chapter 18. They can also be owned outright by purchasing shares through a brokerage firm or an investment company that sponsors a mutual fund. As you will see later in this section, it's easy to purchase shares in a mutual fund. For $250 to $3,000 or more, you can open an account and begin investing. And there are other advantages that encourage investors to purchase shares in funds. Unfortunately, there are also disadvantages. Exhibit 16–8 summarizes the advantages and disadvantages of mutual fund investments.

One advantage of any investment is the opportunity to make money on it. In the next section, we examine how you can make money by investing in closed-end funds, exchange-traded funds, or open-end funds. We consider how taxes affect your mutual fund investments. Then we look at the options used to purchase shares in a mutual fund. Finally, we examine the options used to withdraw money from a mutual fund.

RETURN ON INVESTMENT

As with other investments, the purpose of investing in a closed-end fund, exchange-traded fund, or open-end fund is to earn a financial return. Shareholders in such funds can receive a return in one of three ways. First, all three types of funds pay income div-

Advantages
• Diversification.
• Professional management.
• Ease of buying and selling shares.
• Multiple withdrawal options.
• Distribution or reinvestment of income and capital gains.
• Switching privileges within the same fund family.
• Services that include toll-free telephone numbers, complete records of all transactions, and savings and checking accounts.

Disadvantages
• Purchase/withdrawal costs.
• Ongoing management fees and 12b-1 fees.
• Poor performance that may not match the Standard & Poor's 500 stock index or some other index.
• Inability to control when capital gain distributions occur and complicated tax-reporting issues.
• Potential market risk associated with all investments.
• Some sales personnel are aggressive and/or unethical.

Exhibit 16-8

Advantages and disadvantages of investing in mutual funds

idends. **Income dividends** are the earnings a fund pays to shareholders from its dividend and interest income. Second, investors may receive capital gain distributions. **Capital gain distributions** are the payments made to a fund's shareholders that result from the sale of securities in the fund's portfolio. These amounts generally are paid once a year. Note: exchange-traded funds don't usually pay end-of-the-year capital gain distributions. Third, as with stock and bond investments, you can buy shares in funds at a low price and then sell them after the price has increased. For example, assume you purchased shares in the Fidelity Stock Selector Fund at $22.00 per share and sold your shares two years later at $24.50 per share. In this case, you made $2.50 ($24.50 selling price minus $22.00 purchase price) per share. With this financial information and dollar amounts for income dividends and capital gain distributions, you can calculate a total return for your mutual fund investment. Before completing this section, you may want to examine the actual procedure used to calculate the dollar amount of total return and percentage of total return in the Financial Planning Calculations box on page 534.

When shares in a mutual fund are sold, the profit that results from an increase in value is referred to as a *capital gain*. Note the difference between a capital gain distribution and a capital gain. A capital gain distribution occurs when *the fund* distributes profits that result from *the fund* selling securities in the portfolio at a profit. On the other hand, a capital gain is the profit that results when *you* sell your shares in the mutual fund for more than you paid for them. Of course, if the price of a fund's shares goes down between the time of your purchase and the time of sale, you incur a loss.

When it comes to choosing a mutual fund, two heads are better than one.

income dividends The earnings a fund pays to shareholders from its dividend and interest income.

capital gain distributions The payments made to a fund's shareholders that result from the sale of securities in the fund's portfolio.

TAXES AND MUTUAL FUNDS

Income dividends, capital gain distributions, and financial gains and losses from the sale of closed-end, exchange-traded, or open-end funds are subject to taxation. At the end of

CALCULATING TOTAL RETURN FOR MUTUAL FUNDS

In Chapter 14, we defined total return as a value that includes not only the yearly dollar amount of income but also any increase or decrease in market value from the original purchase price of an investment. For mutual funds, you can use the following calculation to determine the dollar amount of total return:

Income dividends
+ Capital gain distributions
+ Change in share market value when sold
Dollar amount of total return

For example, assume you purchased 100 shares of Majestic Growth Fund for $12.20 per share for a total investment of $1,220. During the next 12 months, you received income dividends of $0.45 a share and capital gain distributions of $0.90. Also, assume you sold your investment at the end of 12 months for $14.40 a share. As illustrated below, the dollar amount for total return is $355:

Income dividends = 100 × $0.45 =	$ 45
Capital gain distributions = 100 × $0.90 =	+ 90
Change in share value = $14.40 − $12.20	
= $2.20 × 100 =	+ 220
Dollar amount of total return	$355

To calculate the percentage of total return, divide the dollar amount of total return by the original cost of your mutual fund investment. The percentage of total return for the above example is 29.1 percent, as follows:

$$\text{Percent of total return} = \frac{\text{Dollar amount of total return}}{\text{Original cost of your investment}}$$

$$= \frac{\$355}{\$1,220}$$

$$= 0.291, \text{ or } 29.1\%$$

each year, investment companies are required to send each shareholder a statement specifying how much he or she received in dividends and capital gain distributions. Although investment companies may provide this information as part of their year-end statement, most funds use IRS Form 1099 DIV.

The following information provides general guidelines on how mutual fund transactions are taxed:

- Income dividends are reported, along with all other dividend amounts you have received, on your federal tax return and are taxed as income

- Capital gain distributions that result from the fund selling securities in its portfolio at a profit are reported on Schedule D as part of your federal tax return and on the 1040.

- Capital gains or losses that result from your selling shares in a mutual fund are reported on Schedule D and the 1040. How long you hold the shares determines whether your gains or losses are taxed as a short-term or long-term capital gain. (See Chapter 4 for more information on capital gains and capital losses.)

Two specific problems develop with taxation of mutual funds. First, almost all investment companies allow you to reinvest income distributions and capital gain distributions from the fund in additional shares instead of receiving cash. Even though you didn't receive cash because you chose to reinvest such distributions, they are still taxable and must be reported on your federal tax return as current income. Second, when you purchase shares of stock, corporate bonds, or other investments and use the buy-and-hold technique described in Chapter 14, you decide when you

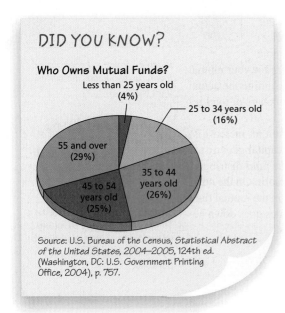

DID YOU KNOW?

Who Owns Mutual Funds?

Less than 25 years old (4%)
25 to 34 years old (16%)
35 to 44 years old (26%)
45 to 54 years old (25%)
55 and over (29%)

Source: U.S. Bureau of the Census, *Statistical Abstract of the United States, 2004–2005,* 124th ed. (Washington, DC: U.S. Government Printing Office, 2004), p. 757.

sell. Thus, you can pick the tax year when you pay tax on capital gains or deduct capital losses. Mutual funds, on the other hand, buy and sell securities within the fund's portfolio on a regular basis during any 12-month period. At the end of the year, profits that result from the mutual fund's buying and selling activities are paid to shareholders in the form of capital gain distributions. Unlike the investments that you manage, you have no control over when the mutual fund sells securities and when you will be taxed on capital gain distributions.

For more info on taxation of mutual funds, go to **www.irs.gov.**

To ensure having all of the documentation you need for tax reporting purposes, it is essential that *you* keep accurate records. The same records will help you monitor the value of your mutual fund investments and make more intelligent decisions with regard to buying and selling these investments.

PURCHASE OPTIONS

You can buy shares of a closed-end fund or exchange-traded fund through a stock exchange or in the over-the-counter market. You can purchase shares of an open-end, no-load fund by contacting the investment company that sponsors the fund. You can purchase shares of an open-end, load fund through a salesperson who is authorized to sell them, through an account executive of a brokerage firm, or directly from the investment company that sponsors the fund.

You can also purchase both no-load and load funds from mutual fund supermarkets available through discount brokerage firms. A mutual fund supermarket offers at least two advantages. First, instead of dealing with numerous investment companies that sponsor mutual funds, you can make one toll-free phone call to obtain information, purchase shares, and sell shares in a large number of mutual funds. Second, you receive one statement from the discount brokerage firm instead of receiving a statement from each investment company you deal with. One statement can be a real plus because it provides the information you need to monitor the value of your investments in one place and in the same format.

Because of the unique nature of open-end fund transactions, we will examine how investors buy and sell shares in this type of mutual fund from an investment company.

To purchase shares in an open-end mutual fund from an investment company, you may use four options: regular account transactions, voluntary savings plans, contractual savings plans, and reinvestment plans. The most popular and least complicated method of purchasing shares in an open-end fund is through a regular account transaction. When you use a regular account transaction, you decide how much money you want to invest and when you want to invest, and simply buy as many shares as possible.

The chief advantage of the voluntary savings plan is that it allows you to make smaller purchases than the minimum purchases required by the regular account method described above. At the time of the initial purchase, you declare an intent to make regular minimum purchases of the fund's shares. Although there is no penalty for not making purchases, most investors feel an "obligation" to make purchases on a periodic basis, and, as pointed out throughout this text, small monthly investments are a great way to save for long-term financial goals. For most voluntary savings plans, the minimum purchase ranges from $25 to $100 for each purchase after the initial investment. Funds try to make investing as easy as possible. Most offer payroll deduction plans, and many will deduct, upon proper shareholder authorization, a specified amount from a shareholder's bank account. Also, many investors can choose mutual funds as a vehicle to invest money that is contributed to a 401(k), 403(b), or individual retirement account. As mentioned earlier, Chapter 18 provides more information on the tax advantages of different types of retirement accounts.

Contractual savings plans require you to make regular purchases over a specified period of time, usually 10 to 20 years. These plans are sometimes referred to as *front-end load plans* because almost all of the commissions are paid in the first few years of the contract period. You will incur penalties if you do not fulfill the purchase requirements. For example, if you drop out of a contractual savings plan before completing the purchase requirements, you may sacrifice the prepaid commissions. Many financial experts and government regulatory agencies are critical of contractual savings plans. As a result, the Securities and Exchange Commission and many states have imposed new rules on investment companies offering contractual savings plans.

You may also purchase shares in an open-end fund by using the fund's reinvestment plan. A **reinvestment plan** is a service provided by an investment company in which income dividends and capital gain distributions are automatically reinvested to purchase additional shares of the fund. Most reinvestment plans allow shareholders to use reinvested money to purchase shares without having to pay additional sales charges or commissions. *Reminder:* When your dividends or capital gain distributions are reinvested, you must still report these transactions as taxable income.

All four purchase options allow you to buy shares over a long period of time. As a result, you can use the principle of *dollar cost averaging,* which was explained in Chapter 14. Dollar cost averaging allows you to average many individual purchase prices over a long period of time. This method helps you avoid the problem of buying high and selling low. With dollar cost averaging, you can make money if you sell your mutual fund shares at a price higher than their *average* purchase price.

reinvestment plan A service provided by an investment company in which shareholder income dividends and capital gain distributions are automatically reinvested to purchase additional shares of the fund.

WITHDRAWAL OPTIONS

Because closed-end funds and exchange-traded funds are listed on stock exchanges or traded in the over-the-counter market, it is possible to sell shares in such a fund to another investor. Shares in an open-end fund can be sold on any business day to the investment company that sponsors the fund. In this case, the shares are redeemed at their net asset value. All you have to do is give proper notification and the fund will send you a check. With some funds, you can even write checks to withdraw money from the fund.

In addition, most funds have provisions that allow investors with shares that have a minimum net asset value of at least $5,000 to use four options to systematically withdraw money. First, you may withdraw a specified, fixed dollar amount each month, quarter, or year until your fund has been exhausted.

A second option allows you to liquidate or "sell off" a certain number of shares each month, quarter, or year. Since the net asset value of shares in a fund varies from one period to the next, the amount of money you receive will also vary.

A third option allows you to withdraw a fixed percentage of asset growth. For example, assume you arrange to receive 60 percent of the asset growth of your investment, and the asset growth of your investment amounts to $800 in a particular investment period. For that period, you will receive a check for $480 ($800 × 60% = $480). If no asset growth occurs, no payment is made to you. Under this option, your principal remains untouched and, assuming you withdraw less than 100 percent of asset growth, your fund continues to grow.

A final option allows you to withdraw all asset growth that results from income dividends and capital gain distributions earned by the fund during an investment period. Under this option, your principal remains untouched.

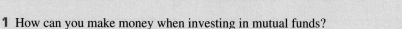

CONCEPT CHECK 16-4

1 How can you make money when investing in mutual funds?

2 What is the difference among income dividends, capital gain distributions, and capital gains?

3 How are income dividends, capital gain distributions, and capital gains reported on your federal tax return?

4 Whom would you contact to purchase a closed-end fund? An exchange-traded fund? An open-end fund?

5 What options can you use to purchase shares in a mutual fund from an investment company?

6 What options can you use to withdraw money from a mutual fund?

Action Application Use the Internet to obtain a prospectus for a specific mutual fund that you believe would be a quality long-term investment. Then describe the purchase and withdrawal options described in the fund's prospectus.

SUMMARY OF OBJECTIVES

Objective 1

Describe the characteristics of mutual fund investments.

The major reasons investors choose mutual funds are professional management and diversification. Mutual funds are also a convenient way to invest money. There are three types of mutual funds. A closed-end fund is a mutual fund whose shares are issued only when the fund is organized. An exchange-traded fund (ETF) is a fund that invests in the stocks contained in a specific stock index like the Standard & Poor's 500 stock index. Both closed-end funds and exchange-traded funds are traded on a stock exchange or in the over-the-counter market. An open-end fund is a mutual fund whose shares are sold and redeemed by the investment company at the net asset value (NAV) at the request of investors. Mutual funds are also classified as load or no-load funds. A load fund charges a commission every time you purchases shares. No commission is charged to purchase shares in a no-load fund. Mutual funds can also be classified as A shares (commissions charged when shares are purchased), B shares (commissions charged when money is withdrawn during the first five to seven years), and C shares (no commission to buy or sell shares, but higher, ongoing 12b-1 fees). Other possible fees include management fees, contingent deferred fees, and 12b-1 fees. Together all the different fees are reported as an expense ratio.

Objective 2

Classify mutual funds by investment objective.

The major categories of stock mutual funds, in terms of the types of securities in which they invest, are aggressive growth, equity income, global, growth, index, international, large-cap, midcap, regional, sector, small-cap, and socially responsible. There are also bond funds that include high-yield, index, intermediate corporate, intermediate U.S. government, long-term corporate, long-term U.S. government, municipal, short-term corporate, short-term U.S. government, and world. Finally, other funds invest in a mix of different stocks, bonds, and other investment securities that include asset allocation funds, balanced funds, and money market funds. Today many investment companies use a family-of-funds concept, which allows shareholders to switch their investments among funds as different funds offer more potential, financial reward, or security. Some investors even use a market timer to decide when to switch their investments from one fund to another fund.

Objective 3

Evaluate mutual funds for investment purposes.

The responsibility for choosing the "right" mutual fund rests with you, the investor. One of the first questions you must answer is whether you want a managed fund or an index fund. Most mutual funds are managed funds with a professional fund manager (or team of managers) who chooses the securities contained in the fund. An index fund invests in the securities that are contained in an index such as the Standard & Poor's 500 stock index. Statistically, the majority of managed mutual funds have failed to outperform index funds over many years. The information on the Internet, from professional advisory services, in newspapers, in the fund prospectus and annual report, and in financial publications can all help you evaluate a mutual fund.

Objective 4

Describe how and why mutual funds are bought and sold.

The advantages and disadvantages of mutual funds have made mutual funds the investment of choice for many investors. For $250 to $3,000 or more, you can open an account and begin investing. The shares of a closed-end fund or exchange-traded fund are bought and sold on organized stock exchanges or the over-the-counter market. The shares of an open-end fund may be purchased through a salesperson who is authorized to sell them, through an account executive of a brokerage firm, from a mutual fund supermarket, or from the investment company that sponsors the fund. The shares in an open-end fund can be sold to the investment company that sponsors the fund. Shareholders in mutual funds can receive a return in one of three ways: income dividends, capital gain distributions when the fund buys and sells securities in the fund's portfolio at a profit, and capital gains when the shareholder sells shares in the mutual fund at a higher price than the price paid. A number of purchase and withdrawal options are available.

KEY FORMULAS

Page	Topic	Formula
517	Net asset value	$\text{Net asset value} = \dfrac{\text{Value of a funds portfolio} - \text{Liabilities}}{\text{Number of shares outstanding}}$
	Example:	$\text{Net asset value} = \dfrac{\$245\text{ million} - \$5\text{ million}}{8\text{ million}}$ $= \$30\text{ per share}$

Page	Topic	Formula
534	Total return	Income dividends + Capital gain distributions + Change in market value <u>Dollar amount of total return</u>

	Example:	Dollar amount of total return	$120	Income dividends
			+ 80	Capital gain distributions
			+ 320	Change in market value
			$520	Dollar amount of total return

Page	Topic	Formula
534	Percent of total return	$\text{Percent of total return} = \dfrac{\text{Dollar amount of total return}}{\text{Original cost of investment}}$
	Example:	$\text{Percent of total return} = \dfrac{\$520}{\$4,500}$ $= 0.116, \text{ or } 11.6\%$

KEY TERMS

capital gain distributions 533
closed-end fund 516
contingent deferred sales load 518
exchange-traded fund (ETF) 516
expense ratio 519

family of funds 523
income dividends 533
investment company 514
load fund 517
market timer 523
mutual fund 514

net asset value (NAV) 517
no-load fund 518
open-end fund 517
reinvestment plan 536
12b-1 fee 518

1. *Calculating Net Asset Value.* Given the following information, calculate the net asset value for the Boston Equity mutual fund. (Obj. 1)

Total assets	$225,000,000
Total liabilities	$5,000,000
Total number of shares	4,400,000

2. *Calculating Net Asset Value.* Given the following information, calculate the net asset value for the New Empire small-cap mutual fund. (Obj. 1)

Total assets	$350,000,000
Total liabilities	$10,000,000
Total number of shares	17,000,000

3. *Calculating Sales Fees.* Jan Throng invested $15,000 in the Aim Charter mutual fund. The fund charges a 5.50 percent commission when shares are purchased. Calculate the amount of commission Jan must pay. (Obj. 1)

4. *Calculating Sales Fees.* Bill Matthews invested $9,800 in the John Hancock growth and income fund. The fund charges a 5.3 percent commission when shares are purchased. Calculate the amount of commission Bill must pay. (Obj. 1)

5. *Calculating Contingent Deferred Sales Loads.* Mary Canfield purchased the New Dimensions bond fund. While this fund doesn't charge a front-end load, it does charge a contingent deferred sales load of 4 percent for any withdrawals in the first five years. If Mary withdraws $6,000 during the second year, how much is the contingent deferred sales load? (Obj. 1)

6. *Determining Management Fees.* Mike Jackson invested a total of $8,500 in the ABC mutual fund. The management fee for this particular fund is 0.70 percent of the total asset value. Calculate the management fee Mike must pay this year. (Obj. 1)

7. *Matching Mutual Funds with Investor Needs.* This chapter classified mutual funds into different categories based on the nature of the fund's investments. Using the following information, pick a mutual fund category that you consider suitable for each investor described and justify your choice. (Obj. 2)

   a. A 25-year-old single investor with a new job that pays $30,000 a year.

   Mutual fund category _____

   Why? _____

   b. A single parent with two children who has just received a $300,000 divorce settlement, has no job, and has not worked outside the home for the past five years.

FINANCIAL PLANNING PROBLEMS

   Mutual fund category _____

   Why? _____

   c. A husband and wife who are both in their early 60s and retired.

   Mutual fund category _____

   Why? _____

8. *Finding Total Return.* Assume that one year ago, you bought 100 shares of a mutual fund for $15 per share, you received a $0.75 per-share capital gain distribution during the past 12 months, and the market value of the fund is now $18. Calculate the total return for this investment if you were to sell it now. (Obj. 4)

9. *Finding Percent of Total Return.* Given the information in question 8, calculate the percent of total return for your $1,500 investment. (Obj. 4)

10. *Finding Total Return.* Assume that one year ago, you bought 200 shares of a mutual fund for $23 per share, you received an income distribution of $0.11 cents per share and a capital gain distribution of $0.32 cents per share during the past 12 months. Also assume the market value of the fund is now $24 a share. Calculate the total return for this investment if you were to sell it now. (Obj. 4)

11. *Finding Percent of Total Return.* Given the information in question 10, calculate the percent of total return for your $4,600 investment. (Obj. 4)

12. *Using Dollar Cost Averaging.* Over a four-year period, Matt Ewing purchased shares in the Oakmark I Fund. Using the following information, answer the questions that follow. You may want to review the concept of dollar cost averaging in Chapter 14 before completing this problem. (Obj. 4)

Year	Investment Amount	Price per Share
2004	$3,000	$40 per share
2005	$3,000	$50 per share
2006	$3,000	$60 per share
2007	$3,000	$45 per share

   a. At the end of four years, what is the total amount invested?

   b. At the end of four years, what is the total number of mutual fund shares purchased?

   c. At the end of four years, what is the average cost for each mutual fund share?

FINANCIAL PLANNING ACTIVITIES

1. *Deciding if Mutual Funds Are Right for You.* Assume you are 35, are divorced, and have just received a $120,000 legal settlement. Prepare a two-page report on the major reasons you want to invest in mutual funds. (Obj. 1)

2. *Applying Terms to Mutual Fund Investments.* Using the Internet or recent newspapers, magazines, or mutual fund reports, find examples of the following concepts. (Obj. 1)

   a. The net asset value for a mutual fund.

   b. An example of a load fund.

   c. An example of a no-load fund.

   d. The management fee for a specific mutual fund.

   e. A fund that charges a contingent deferred sales load.

   f. A fund that charges a 12b-1 fee.

   g. An expense ratio.

3. *Understanding Fees Associated with Mutual Fund Investments.* Assume you are single, are 28 years old, and have decided to invest $8,000 in mutual funds. (Obj. 1)

   a. Prepare a chart that shows the typical charges for load funds, no-load funds, management fees, contingent deferred sales loads, and 12b-1 fees.

   b. Calculate the following fees for your $8,000 mutual fund investment: (1) a 5 percent load charge, (2) an annual 0.50 percent management fee, and (3) an annual 1 percent 12b-1 fee.

4. *Matching Mutual Funds with Investor Needs.* This chapter explored a number of different classifications of mutual funds. (Obj. 2)

   a. Based on your age and current financial situation, which type of mutual fund seems appropriate for your investment needs? Explain your answer.

   b. As people get closer to retirement, their investment goals often change. Assume you are now 45 and have accumulated $110,000 in a retirement account. In this situation, what type of mutual fund would you choose? Why?

   c. Assume you are now 60 years of age and have accumulated $400,000 in a retirement account. Also, assume you would like to retire when you are 65. What type of mutual funds would you choose to help you reach your investment goals? Why?

5. *Using Information to Evaluate Mutual Funds.* Obtain specific information on either the AIM Charter (symbol CHTRX) mutual fund or the AIM Basic Value (symbol GTVLX) mutual fund. Then describe how each of the following sources of information could help you evaluate one of these mutual funds. (Obj. 3)

   a. The Internet.

   b. Newspapers.

   c. The fund's prospectus.

   d. The fund's annual report.

   e. Financial publications.

   f. Professional advisory services.

   After researching one of the AIM funds, would you invest in the fund? Why or why not?

6. *Using the Yahoo! Finance Web site.* Visit the Yahoo! Finance Web site and evaluate one of the following mutual funds. To complete this activity, follow these steps. (Obj. 3)

   a. Go to finance.yahoo.com.

   b. Choose one of the following three funds, enter its symbol, and click on the "go" button: Oakmark Fund I (OAKMX), Templeton Global Bond A (TPINX), and Washington Mutual Investors Fund/A (AWSHX).

   c. Print out the information for the mutual fund that you chose to evaluate.

   d. Based on the information included in this research report, would you invest in this fund? Explain your answer.

7. *Evaluating Mutual Funds.* Choose one of the following mutual funds and use information from the Internet or newspapers, magazines, or mutual fund reports to complete the mutual fund evaluation form presented in the *Personal Financial Planner* Sheet 62 at the end of the text. Then answer the following questions. (Obj. 3)

Name of Fund	Type of Fund
Fidelity Select Electronics Fund (FSELX)	Sector fund
Highmark Balanced Fund (HMBAX)	Balanced fund
USAA S&P 500 index fund (USSPX)	Index fund

   a. Which fund did you choose?

   b. Why did you choose this fund?

   c. Do you think this fund could help you achieve your investment objectives? Explain your answer.

8. *Applying the Concept of Dollar Cost Averaging.* In a one-page report, explain how the concept of dollar cost averaging applies to the purchase options for mutual funds. (Obj. 4)

INTERNET CONNECTION

Researching Mutual Fund Investments

Visit the following Web sites and describe the types of information provided by each site. Then describe how this site could help you invest.

Sponsor	Web Site	Type of Information	How Could This Site Help Me Invest?
Bloomberg	www.bloomberg.com		
CNN/Money	www.money.com		
Motley Fool	www.fool.com		
Kiplinger	www.kiplinger.com		
Smart Money	www.smartmoney.com		

FINANCIAL PLANNING CASE

Research Information Available from Morningstar

This chapter stressed the importance of evaluating potential mutual fund investments. Now it is your turn to try your skill at evaluating a potential investment in the T. Rowe Price Equity-Income fund. Assume you could invest $10,000 in shares of this fund. To help you evaluate this potential investment, carefully examine Exhibit 16–5, which reproduces the Morningstar research report for the T. Rowe Price Equity-Income fund. The report was published in the spring of 2005.

Questions

1. Based on the research provided by Morningstar, would you buy shares in the T. Rowe Price Equity-Income fund?

2. What other investment information would you need to evaluate this fund? Where would you obtain this information?

3. On May 20, 2005, shares in the T. Rowe Price Equity-Income fund were selling for $26.19 per share. Using the Internet or a newspaper, determine the current price for a share of this fund. Based on this information, would your investment have been profitable? (Hint: The symbol for this fund is PRFDX)

4. Assuming you purchased shares in the T. Rowe Price Equity-Income fund on May 20, 2005, and based on your answer to question 3, how would you decide whether you want to hold or sell your shares? Explain your answer.

VIDEO CASE

Investing in Mutual Funds

What do long-term investments, tolerance for risk, and investment objectives have in common? Answer: They are all factors that must be considered when establishing a mutual fund investment program.

Today mutual funds are more popular than ever. Basically, a mutual fund allows you to pool your money with other investors to invest in a wide variety of investments. But before you invest, consider the following:

- Diversification and professional management are the main two advantages of mutual funds.

- You can buy shares in a closed-end or open-end mutual fund.

- Mutual funds may be front-end load funds, back-end load funds, or no-load funds.

- Over a long time period, a load fund and a no-load fund perform about the same.

- Mutual funds also charge management fees and 12b-1 fees.

For most mutual fund investors, professional management is an especially important feature. How long has the manager been the manager? Is the fund managed by one person or a group of managers? Is the fund actively or passively managed? Active management means the manager is actively buying and selling the stocks and other securities contained in the fund's portfolio. On the other hand, passive management means the manager matches the stocks and other securities in a fund with some index, like the Standard & Poor's 500 index, and uses a buy-and-hold strategy. The decision to purchase an actively managed fund or a passively managed fund is yours. Factors that may help you decide include costs and fees for each type of fund, your risk tolerance, your financial objectives, and your ability to research a fund.

To help them decide which fund is right for them, many investors begin with the fund's prospectus. A prospectus defines the fund's objective and provides information about load fees, management fees, and 12b-1 fees. The prospectus also describes the fund's performance over different time periods. Most or all of the same information contained in a printed prospectus can be found on the Web site of the investment company sponsoring the mutual fund. You can also access Web sites that contain specific information about individual mutual funds and more general education sites to help you become a better investor.

A decision to sell a mutual fund is complicated by taxation. If your money is invested as part of a 401(k), or a 403(b) retirement account, or an IRA, your investment and earnings accumulate tax free until you make withdrawals. For all other accounts, dividends and capital gains distributions are taxable. Dividends are the earnings a fund pays to shareholders from its dividend and interest income. Capital gain distributions are the payments made to a fund's shareholders that result from the sale of securities in the fund's portfolio. Even if you reinvest your dividends and capital gains in the fund, you still have to pay taxes. To determine how much tax you owe, you must keep good records. Then you can use a good software program to determine the amount of tax you owe to the IRS.

Questions

1. What factors lead investors to choose mutual fund investments?

2. When investing in mutual funds, you can choose a front-end load fund, a back-end load fund, or a no-load fund. What are the differences among the three types of funds? Does one type of fund outperform the other funds?

3. Even with professional management, investors should evaluate a mutual fund investment. Why? How would you go about evaluating a mutual fund investment?

4. What impact does taxation have on a mutual fund investment?

YOUR PERSONAL FINANCIAL PLANNER IN ACTION

Investing in Mutual Funds

Diversification through the use of mutual funds provides investors with convenience and professional management. The variety of mutual funds contributes to your ability to achieve various financial goals.

Your Short-Term Financial Planning Activities	Resources
1. Identify types of information that could help you choose a mutual fund.	PFP Sheet 61 mutualfunds.about.com biz.yahoo.com/funds www.investopedia.com/
2. Research the recent performance records and costs of a mutual fund that could be an appropriate investment for you.	PFP Sheet 62 www.money.com www.brill.com www.ibcdata.com
Your Long-Term Financial Planning Activities	
1. Identify types of mutual funds that you might use for your long-term financial goals.	www.money.com www.mfea.com
2. Develop a plan for selecting and monitoring your mutual fund portfolio.	Text pages 524–532 www.morningstar.com

Mutual Fund Investments

Life Situation
Pam, 43
Josh, 45
Children ages 16, 14, and 11

Financial Data
Monthly income $4,900
Assets $262,700
Living expenses $4,450
Liabilities $84,600
Emergency fund $5,000

In recent years, the Brocks have made extensive use of mutual funds in their investment portfolio. However, they are concerned that their selection of the funds may not be coordinated. With over 8,000 different mutual funds available, this financial marketplace is confusing.

The Brocks start the evaluation process by connecting various types of mutual funds to their investment goals. Next, they assess the past performance and management of the funds, Finally, they talk with various financial advisers and other investors to gather additional information.

Questions

1. How might Pam and Josh use mutual funds for various investment goals?

2. What types of mutual funds might be considered by the Brocks for their investment portfolio?

3. How could *Personal Financial Planner* Sheet 62 be used by the Brocks?

17 Investing in Real Estate and Other Investment Alternatives

Key Concept

Real estate investment opportunities vary widely. In order to invest your money wisely, you'll need to consider the advantages and disadvantages of each type. The risks and rewards of investing in precious metals, gems, and collectibles may help you build a diversified portfolio.

Digital Study Tools

Online Learning Center Study Tools for This Chapter

- Multiple-choice quiz
- Flashcards
- eLearning sessions
- Crossword puzzle
- Personal Finance Online

Student CD Study Tools for This Chapter

- Self-study software
- Narrated PowerPoint
- Personal financial planning software: Worksheet 77

Learning Objectives

1 Identify types of real estate investments.

2 Evaluate the advantages of real estate investments.

3 Assess the disadvantages of real estate investments.

4 Analyze the risks and rewards of investing in precious metals, gems, and collectibles.

Snapping Up Second Homes: Demographics and Wall Street's Woes Make for a Superheated Market

Want to buy a vacation home? Join the crowd. From Montauk, New York, to Monterey, California, the second-home market is on a tear. "Sales of resort condos and single-family houses around the country have been strong for the past five years, and we see no signs of slowing," says Earl Lee, president of Prudential Real Estate Affiliates in Irvine, California. Second homes in the United States sold for a record high median price of $162,000 last year, up 27 percent from 1999, according to the National Association of Realtors.

Low mortgage rates are stoking the boom, but there's more. A dreary stock market is prompting some to snap up second and even third homes to diversify their investments. Demographics is also a factor, with baby boomers hitting middle age, when people traditionally buy a second residence. In addition, a fear of flying is prompting some who used to splurge on overseas vacations to use the dough for a getaway they can reach by car.

Since September 11, the hottest second-home markets are in resort areas that are a tank full of gas from big cities. They include tony environs like the Hamptons on Long Island, as well as lesser-known areas like the Outer Banks of North Carolina, Florida's Gulf Coast, and New Hampshire's White Mountains. Resort-home prices in these areas are up 10 percent to 40 percent in the past year, local brokers say. On the Outer Banks barrier islands, prices for beach houses in upscale towns such as Duck have jumped around 25 percent since last summer, thanks to an influx of buyers from the Washington area. Similarly, Susan Spica, owner of Prudential Lake Ozark Realty in Lake Ozark, Missouri, says her company has sold more resort condos in the first five months of this year than in all of 2001, many to professional couples from nearby St. Louis and Kansas City. Meanwhile, Seaside, Florida, on the northwest Gulf Coast, is increasingly popular with families from Alabama, Georgia, and Texas.

Is it too late to find a great deal? Not necessarily. Sure, the market is frothy, but with 77 million baby boomers set to retire in the next three decades, housing in prime spots will only get pricier. And many desirable resort areas have a limited amount of land available for new development, which should keep vacation home prices firm.

A second home may be especially affordable for empty nesters who have built up equity in their primary residence. Realtors in resort areas say many recent buyers are couples who trade down to a smaller dwelling, then use the profit to finance a weekend home where they may eventually retire. That strategy has been popular since 1997, when tax laws changed so that married couples no longer have to pay capital gains tax on the first $500,000 of profit when selling their primary home.

Don't buy a resort home just because you think today's strong price gains will continue. If interest rates rise, as some economists expect, second-home demand could slow. Also, vacation homes are luxury items that owners dump in severe economic downturns. So pick a place you'll enjoy returning to often. Investment considerations should be secondary.

If you need rental income, take a hard look at what you can earn. In many of the hottest markets, rental rate hikes haven't kept pace with home prices. In the Outer Banks, buyers who rented out their homes during the summer used to count on annually grossing an amount equal to 10 percent of the purchase price, local realtors say. But with rents continuing to rise 3 percent to 5 percent annually while home prices have climbed around 25 percent in the past year, rental income is proportionally less. Also, count on paying 10 percent to 40 percent of rental income to a management agent who arranges rentals and maintenance.

Whether you rent or not will determine your mortgage payments. If you plan on keeping your vacation home to yourself, you'll obtain the same rates as you would with a first mortgage, says Keith Gumbinger, a vice president at HSH Associates, which tracks mortgage rates. If you count on rental income, you may pay up to 1 percentage point above prevailing rates for primary residences. Second-home buyers with good credit can put a 5 percent to 10 percent down payment on a vacation home, versus 3 percent to 5 percent for a primary residence.

Buying a second home can be tricky. But if you're smart about it, you'll wind up with a getaway that's also a dream investment.

Source: Susan Scherreik, "Snapping Up Second Homes: Demographics and Wall Street's Woes Make for a Superheated Market," *BusinessWeek*, June 17, 2002, p. 90.

QUESTIONS

What Actions Should Be Taken?

1. Would you buy a resort home just because you think today's strong price gains will continue?
2. In your geographical area, is it too late to find a great deal in second homes?

What about Your Situation?

3. Under what circumstances would you consider buying a vacation home?
4. If you need rental income, what special factors should you consider?

Learn More Online

Visit www.real-estate-online.com. Describe the type of real estate investment information that is available on this Web site.

Investing in Real Estate

Objective 1

Identify types of real estate investments.

direct investment
Investment in which the investor holds legal title to property.

indirect investment
Investment in which a trustee holds legal title to property on behalf of the investors.

Traditionally, Americans have invested in real estate. It is an asset that we can see, touch, and smell, and it is generally a good hedge against inflation. However, as you will see, the choices in real estate investment can be bewildering for the new investor. Furthermore, the Tax Reform Act of 1986 has lessened the appeal of investing in real estate.

Real estate investments are classified as direct or indirect. In a **direct investment,** the investor holds legal title to the property. Direct real estate investments include single-family dwellings, duplexes, apartments, land, and commercial property.

With an **indirect investment,** investors appoint a trustee to hold legal title on behalf of all the investors in the group. Limited partnerships and syndicates, real estate investment trusts, mortgages, and mortgage pools are examples of indirect real estate investments.

Exhibit 17–1 summarizes the advantages and disadvantages of the two types of investments.

DIRECT REAL ESTATE INVESTMENTS

YOUR HOME AS AN INVESTMENT   Your home is, first, a place to live; second, it is an income tax shelter if you have a mortgage on it; finally, it is a possible hedge against inflation.

Since the spring of 2001, the United States dipped into recession, suffered terrorist attacks, and watched as the stock market sputtered. Against that backdrop, the median price for single-family houses climbed 7.1 percent nationally between April 2001 and 2002, according to the National Association of Realtors (NAR). In some markets, the gains were astounding: Los Angeles, up almost 18 percent since March a year earlier; Washington, 20 percent; New York, 21 percent; and Providence, Rhode Island, 19 percent.

In today's ownership society, few investments have been so lucrative for so many as home ownership. Since 2001, extremely cheap mortgage rates have fueled a record-

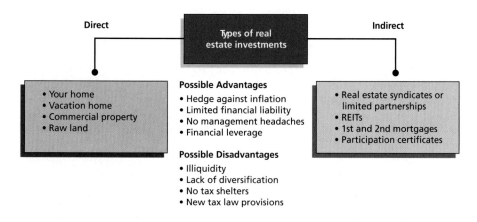

Exhibit **17-1**

Types, advantages, and disadvantages of real estate investments

setting level of home sales. Frenzied demand caused home prices to jump at rates not seen since the 1980s and generated 10 percent gains each year in housing wealth for many Americans, who quickly used refinancings or home-equity loans to convert some of the windfall into cash.

With millions of Americans still eager to get into the housing bonanza, it's no wonder signs of overheating are popping up. At building sites from Florida to California, househunters stand in line just for the chance to buy a home. Investors are flipping properties almost overnight. For some lucky folks, home values have doubled in five years. And in early 2005 the boom was in full swing. New-home sales surprised many economists by jumping 9.4 percent in February to an annual rate of 1.2 million. And starts rose to a yearly pace of 2.2 million in the month, a level not seen consistently since housing's go-go 1970s.[1]

House prices have become either a horror story or a cause for celebration—depending on whether you're buying or selling. The relentless escalation stalled only momentarily after September 11. Even San Francisco—where prices rocketed 40 percent between 1999 and 2001 and then fell as the nation's woes combined with the region's dot-com sorrows—has taken off again, say local real estate agents such as Joseph Koman. One of his clients, Tom Murphy, a journalist who lost his job in the dot-com shakeout, got six offers for his four-bedroom Victorian house. The turn-of-the-century home went for $66,000 more than its $549,000 asking price. Murphy owned a weekend house as well. As his tech stocks soared in the late 1990s, he wondered whether he should have so much money tied up in real estate. "Now I'm glad I did," he says. Can skyrocketing prices continue? Read the Financial Planning for Life's Situations: Real Estate: Avoid the Burn feature on page 548.

But anyone who lived through the 1991 recession knows that real estate can plunge in specific markets—and that declines tend to come in the very places that run up most in the boom years. Los Angeles saw prices drop 21 percent between 1991 and 1996. New York and Boston dipped, too. Ingo Winzer, president of *The Local Market Monitor,* which analyzes real estate in about 100 markets, cites San Francisco and San Jose as two areas in

DID YOU KNOW?

Home ownership in the United States soared to a historic high of 69.1 percent in 2004, up from 65.7 percent in 1997.

Source: BusinessWeek, April 11, 2005, p. 86.

DID YOU KNOW?

Home ownership is very low for people in their 20s, but it rises sharply as people enter their 30s.

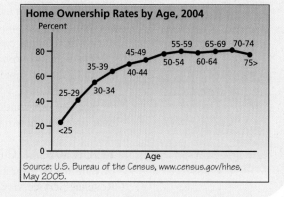

Source: U.S. Bureau of the Census, www.census.gov/hhes, May 2005.

REAL ESTATE: AVOID THE BURN

You've heard the conventional wisdom: Don't think of your house as an investment. Think of it as a place to live. But how can you not think of it as an investment when it has been such a good one lately?

The median existing home price in the United States rose to $189,000 in January 2005, up 10.5 percent year-over-year. Indeed, homes nationwide have appreciated an average of 8 percent annually in the past three years. That compares to a three-year average annual return in a typical diversified stock fund of just 5 percent. Homes in metropolitan areas on the east and west coasts have risen at a faster clip—doubling in the past five years in many markets.

Can this continue? It turns out that caution may be in order for 2005. The good news is that purchasing or owning a house remains one of the best investments you can make over the long term. Historically, the real estate market often spurts, then pauses, and sometimes even declines slightly. Prices have never really plummeted on a national basis.

Yet for three years, home-price appreciation has been running far ahead of rates of inflation, wage increases, and national economic growth. The kind of growth chalked up since 2002 is likely unsustainable, in the view of most analysts who follow the housing market. That doesn't mean home prices will crash, but they might retreat some in your region, especially if they've risen extraordinarily fast in recent years and if a downturn hits your local economy.

Even barring that, as interest rates rise, fewer people will be able to afford current home prices. That may flatten real estate prices even if demand stays robust. Overall, national home sales have cooled a degree from 2004's hottest levels, according to the National Association of Realtors (NAR). And luxury home prices in several markets, including Boston and Chicago, actually dipped in the last three months of 2004.

A few troubling signs of a real estate market top are emerging: An increasing percentage of home financings are done with adjustable-rate mortgages (ARMs), which indicates people are stretching to afford the homes they want. If rates rise quickly, buyers with short adjustment periods may face higher rates sooner than they expected. "That sets people up for a problem if something goes wrong," says David Kelly, economic adviser to Putnam Investments.

Still, if thinking of your home as an investment is practically unavoidable in this real estate market, try to make sure your decisions are sound. "If you start feeling the urge to overinvest in real estate," says Putnam's Kelly, "stop feeling and start thinking." As the bull market in residential real estate shows signs of age in 2005, that advice is worth heeding.

Source: Amey Stone, "Real Estate: Avoid the Burn," www.business-week.com, March 15, 2005.

---

danger of a fall. Real estate in both is overpriced, based on the historic ratio of local income to price, versus the nation as a whole, he says, and each has lost jobs. The same could be said for New York. Job losses eventually lead to more home sales and outward migration, increasing supply and pushing prices down. Add Boston to the watch list, says Kenneth Rosen, chairman of the Fisher Center for Real Estate at the University of California at Berkeley's Haas School of Business.

While near-term increases aren't expected to match the gains of the past, economists say demographics should then hold prices roughly in line with disposable-income gains during the coming decade. That's expected to be 5.5 percent to 6 percent, says David Berson, chief economist at Fannie Mae. Over time, prices have risen at a rate 1 percent above inflation, notes Doug Duncan, chief economist at the Mortgage Bankers Association.

Housing will continue to be a not-so-liquid investment that promises steady returns over time. Just how much depends on your timing—and location, location, location.[2]

YOUR VACATION HOME   If you have a vacation home, the after-tax cost of owning it has risen since 1987. How much depends largely on whether the Internal Revenue Service views the property as your second home or as a rental property. It is deemed a second home as long as you don't rent it for more than 14 days a year. In that case, you can write off your mortgage interest and property tax. If you rent the vacation home regularly, the size of your deductions is determined by whether you actively manage it and by the size of your income. According to one certified public accountant, "The primary reason you buy a vacation home is because you want to use it. Tax reasons . . . are way down on the list."

Boomers, in particular, are driving the second-home market with an eye toward both investment and future retirement. Debbie Bockhold, a certified public accountant in Orange County, California, and her husband, Tim, a stockbroker, plunked down $450,000 for a new vacation home—a two-bedroom condo just 15 minutes from the Strip in Las Vegas. Does she think she may be taking a gamble on housing in the city of big bets? Not at all. With other Vegas condos going for as high as $1,000 a square foot, "the price per square foot ($280) is just a great buy," Bockhold says.[3]

More second-home buyers today are blurring the line between vacation and rental properties, justifying the purchase by planning to rent it out and figuring it's sure to appreciate. But if you're really looking for an investment property, do the math. Rental income minus expenses should produce a positive cash flow, says Gayle Henderson, an agent with RE/MAX Excaliber in Scottsdale, Arizona. "Some buyers are willing to live with a shortfall if they think prices will appreciate rapidly, but that's not an ideal strategy," she says.

The National Association of Realtors reports that 36 percent of home sales in 2004 were second homes. Of those, the number of people reporting that they made the purchase primarily as an investment climbed from 20 percent in 1999 to 64 percent in 2004. That's a sign a lot more speculative buyers have come into the market, and that could be fueling a real estate bubble in some areas.

COMMERCIAL PROPERTY

The term **commercial property** refers to land and buildings that produce lease or rental income. Such property includes duplexes, apartments, hotels, office buildings, stores, and many other types of commercial establishments. After a home, the real property investment most widely favored by small investors is the duplex, fourplex, or small apartment building. Many investors have acquired sizable commercial properties by first investing in a duplex and then "trading up" to larger units as equity in the original property increases.

Under current tax laws, deductions such as mortgage interest, depreciation, property taxes, and other expenses of rental property are limited to the amount of rental income you receive. Any excess deductions are considered a passive loss and, with some exceptions, can be used only to offset income from a similar investment such as another rental property. A **passive activity** is a business or trade in which you do not materially participate, such as rental activity. **Passive loss** is the total amount of losses from a passive activity minus the total income from the passive activity.

UNDEVELOPED LAND

Since the tax law changes of 1986, popular real estate investments, such as suburban garden apartments, no longer appeal to real estate investors. Instead, these investors have been favoring more exotic property, such as undeveloped land.

If land investments have promised tremendous gains, they have also posed enormous risks. With their money riding on a single parcel, investors could end up owning overpriced cropland in the event of a building slowdown or an economic downturn. Furthermore, land usually does not produce any cash flow.

Many investors buy land with the intention of subdividing it. Purchases of this kind are speculative because they involve many risks. You must be

DID YOU KNOW?

Reasons for Buying Property in 2004

- Vacation Home (13%)
- Investment (23%)
- Primary Residence (64%)

Source: National Association of Realtors, 2005.

commercial property
Land and buildings that produce lease or rental income.

passive activity A business or trade in which the investor does not materially participate.

passive loss The total amount of losses from a passive activity minus the total income from the passive activity.

Do you want to invest in a tangible asset?

certain that water, sewers, and other utilities will be available. The most common and least expensive way to obtain water and sewer service is to hook onto existing facilities of an adjoining city or town.

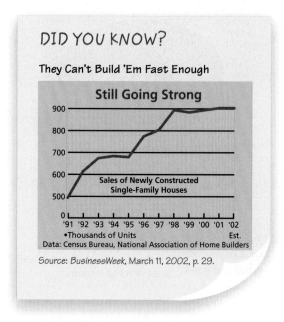

INDIRECT REAL ESTATE INVESTMENTS

Indirect real estate investments include investing in real estate syndicates, real estate investment trusts, and participation certificates.

Bernice R. Hecker, a Seattle anesthesiologist, made her first real estate investment in 1985. She joined a partnership that bought an office building in Midland, Texas. "Why real estate? Probably superstition," she said. "I wanted a tangible asset. I felt I could evaluate a piece of property much more readily" than stocks, bonds, or a cattle ranch.[4]

Dr. Hecker used a real estate syndicate, one of the three basic indirect methods of investing in real estate: (1) real estate syndicates, partnerships that buy properties; (2) real estate investment trusts (REITs), stockholder-owned real estate companies; and (3) participation certificates sold by federal and state agencies. Indirect real estate investments are sold by most brokerage firms, such as Merrill Lynch.

syndicate A temporary association of individuals or firms organized to perform a specific task that requires a large amount of capital.

REAL ESTATE SYNDICATES OR LIMITED PARTNERSHIPS   A **syndicate** is a temporary association of individuals or firms organized to perform a specific task that requires a large amount of capital.[5] The syndicate may be organized as a corporation, as a trust, or, most commonly, as a limited partnership.

The limited partnership works as follows. It is formed by a general partner, who has unlimited liability for its liabilities. The general partner then sells participation units to the limited partners, whose liability is generally limited to the extent of their initial investment, say, $5,000 or $10,000. Limited liability is particularly important in real estate syndicates because their mortgage debt obligations may exceed the net worth of the participants.

In addition to limited liability, a real estate syndicate provides professional management for its members. A syndicate that owns several properties may also provide diversification.

Traditionally, real estate syndicates have been tax shelters for the investors. However, the Tax Reform Act of 1986 limited the creativity of real estate syndicators. It hit real estate syndicates particularly hard by preventing losses from "passive" investments in partnerships from offsetting income from other sources. It also limited deductions of interest and depreciation and increased the tax on capital gains.

real estate investment trust (REIT) A firm that pools investor funds and invests them in real estate or uses them to make construction or mortgage loans.

REAL ESTATE INVESTMENT TRUSTS (REITS)   Another way to invest in real estate is the **real estate investment trust (REIT),** which is similar to a mutual fund or an investment company, and trades on stock exchanges or over the counter. Like mutual funds, REITs pool investor funds. These funds, along with borrowed funds, are invested in real estate or used to make construction or mortgage loans.

There are three types of REITs: *Equity REITs* invest in properties; *mortgage REITs* pool money

Most frequently asked questions about REITs, such as, Who invests in REITs? Why should you invest in REITs? and What should you look for before investing in a REIT? are answered on the National Association of Real Estate Investment Trusts Web site at **www.nareit.com/aboutreits.**

to finance construction loans and mortgages on developed properties; and *hybrid REITs* are combinations of mortgage and equity REITs.

Federal law requires REITs to

- Distribute at least 90 percent of their taxable annual earnings to shareholders.

- Refrain from engaging in speculative, short-term holding of real estate to sell for quick profits.

- Hire independent real estate professionals to carry out certain management activities.

- Have at least 100 shareholders; no more than half the shares may be owned by five or fewer people.

- Invest at least 75 percent of the total assets in real estate.

DID YOU KNOW?

Expensive Real Estate

- The average REIT dividend yield is 5.6%.

- That's only 0.9% above the 10-year Treasury yield.

- Over the long term, REIT dividends are 1.5% above the 10-year Treasury.

Source: National Association of Real Estate Investment Trusts; BusinessWeek, June 28, 2004, p. 140.

Recently the National Association of Real Estate Investment Trusts (NAREIT), the Washington, DC–based industry trade group, announced a $2 million ad campaign aimed at luring back investors. "There is tremendous frustration" among many REIT executives, who used to see their REITs "do nothing but go up," says Sam Zell, chairman of two of the nation's largest REITs: Equity Office Properties Trust and Equity Residential. Since 1991, about 150 REITs have gone public, and the industry's market value has soared from $13 billion to $155.3 billion.[6] (See Financial Planning for Life's Situations: The Wrong Time for REITs? on page 552)

"REITs 101: An Introductory Guide to Real Estate Investment Trusts" explains REITs and offers definitions at **www.reitnet.com/reits101.**

You may choose from among more than 300 REITs. Further information on REITs is available from the National Association of Real Estate Investment Trusts, 1129 20th Street, NW, Washington, DC 20036.

Recently, a new variation of REITs has emerged—Real Estate Operating Companies—or REOCs. REOCs' investment objective is long-term capital appreciation, while REITs seek the dividend yield. Instead of distributing 90 percent of their net annual earnings to shareholders, REOCs retain all of their cash flow for growth. Portfolio manager Michael Winer's Third Avenue Real Estate Value Fund is the only mutual fund to invest primarily in REOCs.[7]

participation certificate (PC) An equity investment in a pool of mortgages that have been purchased by a government agency, such as Ginnie Mae.

INVESTING IN FIRST AND SECOND MORTGAGES   Mortgages and other debt contracts are commonly purchased by more well-to-do investors. The purchaser of a mortgage may take on some sort of risk that is unacceptable to the financial institutions from which mortgage financing is ordinarily obtained. Perhaps the mortgage is on a property for which there is no ready market. The title to the property may not be legally clear, or the title may not be insurable. Nevertheless, many people purchase such mortgages. These investments may provide relatively high rates of return due to their special risk characteristics.

The REIT story is an economic success story. Investing in commercial real estate is a reality for all investors.

PARTICIPATION CERTIFICATES   If you want a risk-proof real estate investment, participation certificates (PCs) are for you. A **participation certificate (PC)** is an equity investment in a pool of mortgages that have been purchased by one of several government agencies. Participation certificates are sold by federal agencies such as the Government National Mortgage Association (Ginnie Mae), the Federal Home Loan Mortgage Corporation (Freddie Mac), the Federal National Mortgage Association (Fannie Mae), and the Student Loan Marketing Association (Sallie Mae). A few states issue "little siblings," such as the State of New York Mortgage Agency (Sonny Mae) and the New England Education Loan Marketing Corporation (Nellie Mae).

THE WRONG TIME FOR REITS?

As interest rates continue to rise and strength in the stock market persists, the stellar 30 percent-plus returns that investors have been enjoying from real estate investment trusts (REITs) the past few years are starting to wither. Although the sector outlook has turned decidedly bearish, keen-eyed investors may still find some good buys that perform well.

Since the start of the decade, REITs had helped assuage investors' wounds from the devastation of the Internet bubble. While the sector didn't provide the dizzying returns that the tech market did in the late 90s, the publicly traded stocks that are real estate holding companies returned 15 percent annually for five consecutive years. REITs turned in their best performances the past two years, with total returns for the Morgan Stanley REIT Index increasing 36 percent in 2003 and 32 percent in 2004.

That success was driven primarily by fund flow, experts say, as many investors who had been burned in tech stocks turned to real estate seeking income and appreciation. Yet those days likely are near an end. With the sector's strong correlation with interest rates, the Morgan Stanley REIT Index is already down more than 5 percent for the year. When rates spike, which they have lately, prices on bonds plummet—as do the returns on REITs.

REITs specializing in buying and managing mall properties are a favorite of analysts and managers in 2005 because of their economies of scale and national tenant base. Some mall-subsector REITs have seen a real improvement in fundamentals. They also have an advantage in this sector because it's difficult to add to capacity of existing malls or build new ones to compete, says Richard Cervone, portfolio manager of Putnam Investors Fund.

Investors looking to make a killing in REITs have probably missed their chance this cycle. Returns of more than 30 percent in all likelihood won't be repeated anytime soon. But for careful long-term investors looking for diversity and to keep a portion of their portfolio in real estate, REITs can still do the job.

Source: June Kim, "The Wrong Time for REITs," *BusinessWeek Online*, March 15, 2005.

Maes and Macs are guaranteed by agencies closely tied to the federal government, making them as secure as U.S. Treasury bonds and notes. At one time, you needed a minimum of $25,000 to invest in PCs. Thanks to Maes and Macs mutual funds, you now need as little as $1,000 to buy shares in a unit trust or a mutual fund whose portfolio consists entirely of these securities. Either way, you assume the role of a mortgage lender. Each month, as payments are made on the mortgages, you receive interest and principal by check, or, if you wish, the mutual fund will reinvest the amount for you.

Financial Planning for Life's Situations: Uncle Sam and His Family on page 553 describes various types of participation certificates sold by federal and state agencies.

CONCEPT CHECK 17-1 ✓

1 What are four examples of direct investments in real estate?
2 What are four examples of indirect investments in real estate?
3 What is a syndicate? A REIT? A participation certificate (PC)?

Action Application List the types of commercial property that could be attractive real estate investments in your community.

Advantages of Real Estate Investments

For many types of real estate investments, blanket statements about their investment advantages and disadvantages are not possible. However, certain types of real estate investments may possess some of the advantages discussed in this section.

UNCLE SAM AND HIS FAMILY

The government securities named Maes and Macs can offer safety and relatively high yields.

1. **Ginnie Mae—Government National Mortgage Association (GNMA).** Introduced the first mortgage-backed securities in 1970 and still dominates this market. The residential mortgage-backed securities are packaged in pools and then resold to investors as certificates ($25,000) or as shares by mutual funds. Regular payments to investors are guaranteed by the GNMA, an agency of the Department of Housing and Urban Development. Ginnie Maes are backed by the full faith and credit of the federal government. The average life of mortgages is 12 years.

2. **Freddie Mac—Federal Home Loan Mortgage Corporation (FHLMC).** Issues mortgage-backed securities similar to Ginnie Maes. The pools of fixed-rate home mortgages are made up of conventional home loans rather than mortgages insured by the FHA or the VA. The timely payment of interest and the *ultimate* payment of principal are guaranteed.

3. **Fannie Mae—Federal National Mortgage Association (FNMA).** Issues mortgage-backed securities similar to Ginnie Maes and Freddie Macs. The pools of fixed-rate home mortgages are similar to Freddie Macs but not to Ginnie Maes. Like Ginnie Maes, Fannie Maes guarantee a fair share of interest and principal *every month*. Like Ginnie Maes and Freddie Macs, newly issued Fannie Mae certificates require a minimum investment of $25,000; the older certificates (whose principal has been partially paid off) require an investment of as little as $10,000.

4. **Sallie Mae—Student Loan Marketing Association.** Created by Congress in 1972 to provide a national secondary market for government-guaranteed student loans. Issues bonds, each backed by Sallie Mae as a whole rather than as specific pools of loans. Sallie Mae bonds are considered as safe as government Treasuries. Brokers sell bonds having minimum denominations of $10,000. You can also buy shares of Sallie Mae *stock;* the corporation is government chartered but publicly owned, and its shares are traded on the New York Stock Exchange.

5. **Sonny Mae—State of New York Mortgage Agency.** Issues bonds backed by fixed-rate, single-family home mortgages and uses proceeds to subsidize below-market-rate mortgages for first-time home buyers. As with ordinary bonds, interest on Sonny Maes is paid only until the bonds mature. Sonny Maes are exempt from federal income tax, and New York State residents do not pay state income tax on them.

6. **Nellie Mae—New England Education Loan Marketing Corporation.** A nonprofit corporation created by the Commonwealth of Massachusetts. Provides a secondary market for federally guaranteed student loans issued in Massachusetts and New Hampshire. The AAA-rated Nellie Mae bonds mature in three years and are sold in minimum denominations of $5,000.

A HEDGE AGAINST INFLATION

Objective 2

Evaluate the advantages of real estate investments.

Real property equity investments usually (but not always) provide protection against purchasing power risk. In some areas, the prices of homes have increased consistently. For example, prices are rising in the Midwest and in some western areas, such as Colorado and Texas.

EASY ENTRY

You can gain entry to a shopping center or a large apartment building by investing $5,000 as a limited partner. (A limited partner's liability is restricted by the amount of his or her investment. A limited partner cannot take part in the management of the partnership.) The minimum capital requirements for the total venture may be as high as $1 million or more, which is beyond the limits of a typical real estate investor.

LIMITED FINANCIAL LIABILITY

If you are a limited partner, you are not liable for losses beyond your initial investment. This can be important if the venture is speculative and rewards are not assured. General partners, however, must bear all financial risks.

NO MANAGEMENT CONCERNS

If you have invested in limited partnerships, REITs, mortgages, or participation certificates, you need not worry about paperwork and accounting, maintenance chores, and other administrative duties.

FINANCIAL LEVERAGE

Financial leverage is the use of borrowed funds for investment purposes. It enables you to acquire a more expensive property than you could on your own. This is an advantage when property values and incomes are rising. Assume you buy a $100,000 property with no loan and then sell it for $120,000. The $20,000 gain represents a 20 percent return on your $100,000 investment. Now assume you invest only $10,000 of your own money and borrow the other $90,000 (90 percent financing). Now you have made $20,000 on your $10,000 investment, or a 200 percent return.

CONCEPT CHECK 17-2

1 What are the advantages of real estate investments?
2 How is financial leverage calculated?

Action Application Prepare a short paper describing a portfolio of real estate investments you would consider now or in the future.

Disadvantages of Real Estate Investments

Objective 3

Assess the disadvantages of real estate investments.

Real estate investments have several disadvantages. However, these disadvantages do not affect all kinds of real estate investments to the same extent.

ILLIQUIDITY

Perhaps the largest drawback of direct real estate investments is the absence of large, liquid, and relatively efficient markets for them. Whereas stocks or bonds generally can be sold in a few minutes at the market price, this is not the case for real estate. It may take months to sell commercial property or limited partnership shares.

DECLINING PROPERTY VALUES

As discussed earlier, real property investments usually provide a hedge against inflation. But during deflationary and recessionary periods, the value of such investments may decline. For example, thousands of developers, lenders, and investors have been victims of a deflation in commercial real estate that began sporadically in the early 1980s. Property values in some regions of the United States are still declining.

LACK OF DIVERSIFICATION

Diversification in direct real estate investments is difficult because of the large size of most real estate projects. REITs, Ginnie Maes, Freddie Macs, and other syndicates, however, do provide various levels of diversification.

LACK OF A TAX SHELTER

The Tax Reform Act of 1986 limits taxpayers' ability to use losses generated by real estate investments to offset income gained from other sources. Thus, investors cannot deduct their real estate losses from income generated by wages, salaries, dividends, and interest. In short, the tax shelter aspect of real estate syndicates no longer exists.

LONG DEPRECIATION PERIOD

Before the Tax Reform Act of 1986 went into effect, commercial real estate could be depreciated within 18 years. Under the accelerated cost recovery system (ACRS), adopted in 1980, an investor was allowed to use accelerated depreciation methods to recover the costs. Now investors must use the straight-line depreciation method over 27½ years for residential real estate and over 31½ years for all other types of real estate.

When you buy your own properties, you have the responsibility of maintaining them.

Other provisions of the 1986 act affect real estate investments, and all reduce the value of the tax credits for such investments. Investors are not allowed to take losses in excess of the actual amounts they invest. Furthermore, the investment tax credit has been eliminated entirely for all types of real estate except low-income housing projects.

MANAGEMENT PROBLEMS

Although investments in limited partnerships, REITs, mortgages, and participation certificates do not create management problems, buying and managing individual properties do. Along with the buildings come the responsibilities of management: finding reliable tenants, buying new carpeting, fixing the furnace when it breaks down in the middle of the night, and so on. Many people aren't willing to take on these responsibilities. "This is one reason I dislike small real estate investments," says one financial planner. "There should be a large enough amount of money that it is very important to you and you pay a lot of attention to it. Otherwise it won't work."[8]

If you believe investing in real estate is too risky or too complicated, you might want to consider other tangible investments such as gold and other precious metals, gems, and collectibles. But remember, these investments may entail both risk and reward.

CONCEPT CHECK 17-3

1 What are the disadvantages of real estate investments?
2 What depreciation method is used for residential real estate?

Action Application Talk to people who have invested in real estate. What are the disadvantages of owning real estate according to their experiences?

Investing in Precious Metals, Gems, and Collectibles

Objective 4

Analyze the risks and rewards of investing in precious metals, gems, and collectibles.

When the economy picks up, some investors predict higher inflation. Therefore, many think precious metals such as gold, platinum, and silver will regain some of their glitter. In this section, we discuss several methods for buying precious metals.

GOLD

Gold prices tend to be driven up by factors such as fear of war, political instability, and inflation. On the other hand, easing of international tensions or disinflation causes a decline in gold prices. High interest rates also depress gold prices because they make it very expensive to carry gold as an investment.

Many people have acquired gold directly. Many others have invested in gold through a number of other kinds of investments that serve a variety of purposes. Some of these investments promise quick profits at high risk, others preserve capital, and still others provide income from dividends or interest. But all of them are subject to daily gold price fluctuations. Exhibit 17–2 shows gold price fluctuations between 1976 and May 2005. Will gold prices continue to climb as they have since 2001? Read Financial Planning for Life's Situations: Just How Precious Will Gold Get?

GOLD BULLION   Gold bullion includes gold bars and wafers. The basic unit of gold bullion is 1 kilogram (32.15 troy ounces of 0.995 fine gold). Coin dealers, precious metals dealers, and some banks sell gold bullion in amounts ranging from 5 grams (16/100 of a troy ounce) to 500 ounces or more. On small bars, dealers and banks add a 5 to 8 percent premium over the pure gold bullion value; on larger bars, the premium is usually 1 to 2 percent. Gold bullion poses storage problems, and unless the gold bar or wafer remains in the custody of the bank or dealer that sells it initially, it must be reassayed (retested for fineness) before being sold.

GOLD BULLION COINS   You can avoid storage and assaying problems by investing in gold bullion coins. In the early 1980s, before South Africa's political problems intensified, South African krugerrands were the most popular gold bullion coins in the United States. Popular gold bullion coins today include Australia's kangaroo nugget, the Canadian gold maple leaf, the Mexican 50 peso, the Austrian 100 koronas, and the British sovereign. The new American eagle gold coin, the first gold bullion coin ever produced by the U.S. government, was issued in late 1986.

Exhibit **17–2**   Fluctuations in the price of gold since 1976

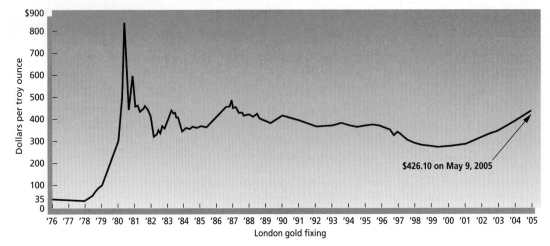

$426.10 on May 9, 2005

London gold fixing

JUST HOW PRECIOUS WILL GOLD GET?

Gold is finally getting some respect. Four years ago, when it began a steady upward march, only the hardiest gold bug believed in the glittery metal. But now, after a 75 percent climb since early 2001, gold is topping $435 an ounce, a level not seen since 1988, and the naysayers have gone to ground. "We're in a secular bull market in commodities," says Frank E. Holmes, chief executive of U.S. Global Investors Inc., a mutual fund company that's bullish on the metal. "Nobody believed oil could go to $50 a barrel. So why can't gold go to $500 an ounce?"

The fever is so intense that new competitors are vying to grab business from New York and London, traditional centers of the gold trade. Last month, the Chicago Board of Trade began offering standard 100-ounce gold futures contracts. Dubai plans to open a gold and commodity exchange next year.

In a market dominated by investors and central banks, an often-forgotten factor is demand by consumers and manufacturers. Just as with many other commodities, the rise of Asia is boosting gold prices as everyone from India's jewelry-bedecked brides to makers of computers and DVDs in China clamor for the metal.

Scarcity is driving prices higher still. Mining companies survived the doldrums after gold's plunge from nearly $900 in 1980 by pruning exploration and closing marginal mines. Even if miners step up investment, says Gregory C. Wilkins, CEO of Toronto's Barrick Gold Corp., it could be years before they dig out major new supplies.

Of course, gold's joy ride won't last indefinitely. Inflation still appears to be under control. Federal Reserve rate hikes in the months ahead could boost the dollar. And demand for gold might slip if global growth eases. Says Mark M. Zandi, chief economist for Economy.com Inc., a consulting firm in West Chester, Pennsylvania, "The bottom line is that gold prices are tilted higher, but they're not going to take off." For now, the world's gold bugs are betting he's wrong.

Source: Joseph Weber, "Just How Precious Will Gold Get?" *BusinessWeek,* November 22, 2004, p. 142.

Most brokers require a minimum order of 10 coins and charge a commission of at least 2 percent.

GOLD STOCKS   In addition to investing in gold bullion and gold bullion coins, you may invest in gold by purchasing the common stocks of gold mining companies. Among the gold mining stocks listed on U.S. stock exchanges are those of Homestake Mining (based in the United States) and Campbell Red Lake and Dome Mines (based in Canada). Because such stocks often move in a direction opposite to that of the stock market as a whole, they may provide excellent portfolio diversification. You may also wish to examine closed-end investment companies with heavy positions in gold mining stocks, such as ARA Ltd.

SILVER, PLATINUM, PALLADIUM, AND RHODIUM

Investments in silver, platinum, palladium, and rhodium, like investments in gold, are used as a hedge against inflation and as a safe haven during political or economic upheavals. During the last 70 years, silver prices ranged from a historic low of 24.25 cents an ounce in 1932, to over $50 an ounce in early 1980, and then back to less than $7.00 an ounce in May 2005.

Three lesser-known precious metals, platinum, palladium, and rhodium, are also popular investments. All have industrial uses as catalysts, particularly in automobile production. Some investors think increased car sales could mean higher prices

For some thoughts on investing in precious metals, visit **www.collectingchannel.com/cds.**

fyi

for these metals. Platinum currently sells for about $875 an ounce and palladium for about $205 an ounce. The rhodium price in May 2005 was about $1,470 per ounce.

As discussed earlier, finding storage for your precious metals can be tricky. While $20,000 in gold, for example, occupies only as much space as a thick paperback book, $20,000 in silver weighs more than 200 pounds and could require a few safe deposit boxes. Such boxes, moreover, are not insured against fire and theft.

You should remember too that unlike stocks, bonds, and other interest-bearing investments, precious metals sit in vaults earning nothing. And whether you profit on an eventual sale depends entirely on how well you call the market.

PRECIOUS STONES

Precious stones include diamonds, sapphires, rubies, and emeralds. Precious stones appeal to investors because of their small size, ease of concealment, great durability, and potential as a hedge against inflation. Inflation and investor interest in tangible assets helped increase diamond prices 40-fold between 1970 and 1980. A few lucky investors made fortunes, and brokerage and diamond firms took up the investment diamond business.

Whether you are buying precious stones to store in a safe-deposit box or to wear around your neck, there are a few risks to keep in mind. Diamonds and other precious stones are not easily turned into cash. It is difficult to determine whether you are getting a good stone. Diamond prices can be affected by the whims of De Beers Consolidated Mines of South Africa Ltd., which controls 85 percent of the world's supply of rough diamonds, and by political instability in diamond-producing countries. Moreover, you should expect to buy at retail and sell at wholesale, a difference of at least 10 to 15 percent and perhaps as much as 50 percent.

> **DID YOU KNOW?**
>
> With all diamonds, the absence of color indicates a finer grade.

The best way to know exactly what you are getting, especially if you are planning to spend more than $1,000, is to insist that your stone be certified by an independent geological laboratory, one not connected with a diamond-selling organization. (The acknowledged industry leader in this area is the Gemological Institute of America.) The certificate should list the stone's characteristics, including its weight, color, clarity, and quality of cut. The grading of diamonds, however, is not an exact science, and recent experiments have shown that when the same diamond is submitted twice to the same institute, it can get two different ratings.

Michael Roman, former chairman of the Jewelers of America, a trade group representing 12,000 retailers, stated that his group did not recommend diamonds as an investment and scoffed at the notion that local retail jewelers were realizing huge profits on diamond sales to misguided customers. He also did not believe in certification unless the stone in question was a high-grade diamond weighing at least one carat.

Despite the present rosy scenarios for precious metals and gems, the risks in trading them are sizable. Just ask investors who in 1980 bought gold at as much as $850 an ounce, platinum at $1,040 an ounce, silver at $48 an ounce, and a one-carat diamond at $62,000.

COLLECTIBLES

collectibles Rare coins, works of art, antiques, stamps, rare books, and other items that appeal to collectors and investors.

Collectibles include rare coins, works of art, antiques, stamps, rare books, sports memorabilia, rugs, Chinese ceramics, paintings, and other items that appeal to collectors and investors. Each of these items offers the knowledgeable collector/investor both pleasure and the opportunity for profit. (See Advice from a Pro: Cashing In on Abe on page 559.) Many collectors have discovered only incidentally that items they bought for their own pleasure had gained greatly in value while they owned them.

Advice from a Pro

CASHING IN ON ABE

Collecting old letters and documents is not only fun but can also be a good investment, according to a new analysis by Abraham Wyner, assistant professor of statistics at the Wharton School. He figures the annualized return from 1949 through 2002, the study period, was 10.3 percent for best-quality items, comparable to stock returns, and 9.8 percent for simple autographs. In the study's final decade, top-quality items—important documents signed by major historical figures—outperformed stocks, generating an 11.7 percent annual return, two points more than the Standard & Poor's 500 stock index.

Wyner's study, commissioned by Ardmore, Pennsylvania, dealer Steven Raab (raab-collection.com), shows it's smart to go for the best material. The top Abraham Lincoln item in Raab's inventory, a letter discussing the Civil War blockade of the South, costs $900,000, vs. $3,000 or less for a good Jimmy Carter piece. Auction house and dealer fees of about 20 percent to 50 percent will reduce real-life returns and make quick profits near-impossible. Wyner advises holding onto historical documents for a minimum of 10 years.

Source: Thane Peterson, "Cashing In on Abe," *BusinessWeek,* April 25, 2005, p. 127.

COLLECTIBLES ON THE NET
Before the era of the World Wide Web, author and antiques collector David Maloney had to search far and wide to find a 1950s cut-crystal Val St. Lambert pitcher. No one in his hometown of Frederick, Maryland, carries fancy glassware, he says, "and I would spend days driving around to yard sales and little shops." Recently, though, Maloney logged on to the Net and, in only 15 seconds, found a store in Pennsylvania that carries 40 styles of his prized crystal.

Whether you collect glassware, home-run baseballs, or Ming vases, you no longer need to travel to far-flung antiques fairs or pore over trade magazines to add to your collection. The world of collectibles is expanding onto the Web at a geometric rate, bringing unprecedented efficiency and convenience to an art collector's market. The explosion of online collecting and the success of the biggest auction site, eBay, prompted Guernsey's Auction House to open the bidding for Mark McGwire's 70th home-run baseball to online buyers as well as those in the salesroom (it went for $3 million to an anonymous phone bidder). And Sotheby's plans to set up shop on the Net for goods under $5,000.

It's easy to see why the Web has such appeal. Buyers can target obscure items with a few keystrokes, and sellers can reach a much larger, more varied market. Of course, online buyers can't kick the tires or size up dealers face to face. But so far, fraud is rare, and preventive measures are increasing.

Although you can find antique armoires and vintage cars, dealers say the Net is best suited to smaller items, such as books, coins, stamps, buttons, and textiles, that can be easily scanned for viewing and shipped by mail. There are three basic ways to go about collecting online, says Maloney, author of *Maloney's Antiques and Collectibles Resource Directory.* You can seek out specialty boutiques, such as Auntie-Dot-Com (www.auntie.com) for leads on dolls; go to auction houses such as Auction Universe (www.auctionuniverse.com); or visit virtual malls such as Buy Collectibles.com (www. buycollectibles.com).

Prices aren't necessarily cheaper on the Web, but it's much easier to compare them, and most sites don't charge a buyer's commission. To purchase an early edition of Mark Twain's *The Adventures of Tom Sawyer,* for example, use a specialty search engine, such as www.bibliofind.com, to view descriptions of dealers' inventories. The site will pro-

Many collectors have been surprised to learn that their old belongings have attained considerable value over the years.

Financial Planning for Life's Situations

ENRON COLLECTIBLES ON eBAY

Enron items are hot, with more than 1,000 sold so far on eBay. Ethics handbooks—plenty in mint condition—are big sellers. (Did you expect 'em to be dog-eared and well-read?)

Item	Price	Description
Enron *Risk Management* manual	$1,025	Tips on reorganizing expenses to improve perception of financial performance.
Enron *Code of Ethics* book	$46–$300*	64-page paperback, sections on Conflict of Interest, Securities Trades by Employees.
Enron "Retirement Planning" mug	$61–$300**	Emblazoned "Enron Retirement Planning. Tools and imagination for your future."
"Team Enron" cycling jersey	$82	Size XL, worn by a cycling team member in a Houston race.

*56 sold as of press time, January 23, 2002.
**6 sold as of press time, January 23, 2002.
Source: Sheridan Prasso, "The List: Enron Collectibles on eBay," *BusinessWeek*, February 4, 2002, p. 8.

vide details on the condition, publisher, and price of the book. Most editions of Tom Sawyer published in the 20th century sell for about $10, but a first British edition from 1898 lists for $350. Since the Net has opened up a wider market, items that probably wouldn't sell at a local antiques show can find an appropriate home.

Still, virtual collecting has drawbacks. Buyers can't examine objects for flaws or trademarks. Many knowledgeable old-time dealers aren't computer literate, while some collectors prefer the thrill of hunting in out-of-the-way junk shops. "The average person still wants to see and feel the antiques," says Terry Kovel, author of *Kovel's Antiques & Collectibles Price List.* "An awful lot of antiques purchases are emotional, because someone walks into a store and sees an object they had as a kid."

A more serious concern, perhaps, is the security risk of buying online when you don't know who's getting your cash or credit card number. But while the security risks of on-line collecting grab headlines, Kovel says fraud has been negligible. Collectors do take gambles, but for many happy hunters, the increased selection and convenience of shopping on the Web is far outweighing it dangers. Read the accompanying Financial Planning for Life's Situations: Enron Collectibles on eBay.

CAVEAT EMPTOR   Collecting can be a good investment and a satisfying hobby, but for many Americans it has recently become a financial disaster. For example, as the market for paintings by Pablo Picasso and Andy Warhol has exploded, forgeries have become a significant problem. Art experts and law enforcement officials say that a new generation of collectors is being victimized by forgeries more sophisticated, more expensive, and more difficult to detect than ever before.

Forgeries or not, art prices are booming. For example, Damien Hirst's *The Lovers*, four jars filled with cow organs in formaldehyde, sold for $229,350, and a plaster cast of the underside of a sink by Rachel Whiteread fetched $220,275. However, a single

THAT'S NOT JUNK; THAT'S EARLY TECH

Gordon Bell can hardly believe what he sees when he scrolls through the online catalog for a Christie's auction of computer memorabilia in New York. "Oh my God, the prices!" exclaims the Microsoft senior researcher, a big-time collector of computer-related books, documents, and other artifacts, most of which he has donated to the Computer History Museum in Mountain View, California. One thing that catches his eye in the 355-item "Origins of Cyberspace" catalog is a first edition of a 1617 treatise by John Napier, the Scottish mathematician whose invention of logarithms was a key advance in creating the early calculators that evolved into today's computers. The auction house figures it will go for $25,000 to $35,000. "I paid $6,000 in 1982" for a similar copy, he recalls.

Bell isn't the only connoisseur in a tizzy over the rising cachet and prices of computer memorabilia. Whether 17th-century mathematics books, mid-1940s documents connected with pioneering executives, or the first 1970s-era microcomputers, prices have soared in recent years. Apple Computer's first model, an Apple 1 introduced in 1976 for $666, now typically fetches $16,000 to $20,000 if it's in good condition, says Sellam Ismail, a curator at the Computer History Museum (computerhistory.org). Christie's estimates the most expensive item in its sale, a 1946 business plan for the first modern computer company, Electronic Control Co. of Philadelphia, will sell for $50,000 to $70,000. The company, a predecessor to today's Unisys, became famous for its Univac computers. Electronic Control's founders, John Presper Eckert and John Mauchly, were part of the team that built the ENIAC, the first "large-scale general purpose electronic digital computer," according to the Christie's catalog. It weighed 30 tons and contained 18,000 vacuum tubes.

Part of the appeal of computer collectibles is there's something for everybody's budget. Indeed, the modern computer industry is so new that key items are still widely available and inexpensive. "If you just look into it a little, you can amass a very good collection," says manufacturing consultant George Keremedjiev, who in 1990 founded the American Computer Museum (compustory.com) in Bozeman, Montana. For instance, a copy of the famous January 1975 issue of *Popular Electronics* with a story on the Altair 8800, an early kit computer that helped inspire the founding of Microsoft, still goes for $100 to $175, notes Michael Nadeau author of *Collectible Microcomputers* (Schiffer Books). Brochures for classic home computers such as the 1984 Commodore V364 can be found for $50 or less, he says, while Christie's figures "Brainiac," a 1966 "electric brain" kit designed by computing pioneer Edmund C. Berkeley, will sell for $800 to $1,200.

Classic microcomputers such as the Altair 8800, which originally retailed for about $400 as a kit and can now fetch up to $3,000, are getting pricey. But old minicomputers and mainframes can often be had for around $1,000. Patrick Finnegan, a systems administrator at Purdue University, recently paid $1,100 on eBay plus $200 for shipping for a vintage IBM mainframe that cost more than $1 million new. Storing the bulky old machines is often a collector's main expense: Pierce bought a warehouse to house his collection, considered the largest of its kind in the world outside a museum.

If you're careful, "this is a very good investment," Keremedjiev contends. Old machines are increasingly hard to find. And more people are becoming aware of the value of computer-related historical material. "I'm stunned," says Leonard Kleinrock, a University of California at Los Angeles computer science professor considered one of the founding fathers of the Internet, upon learning the value Christie's has put on some of his signed papers. It estimates a copy of his first book that he signed for Norman, a letter he sent the dealer five years ago, and other items could go for up to $3,500. In the past, Kleinrock says he never thought twice about sending his autograph to collectors who asked for it. Those days are probably as long gone as the IBM 709 mainframe.

Source: Thane Peterson, "That's Not Junk: That's Early Tech," *BusinessWeek*, February 21, 2005, p. 82.

painting, a van Gogh called *Portrait of Dr. Gachnet,* which sold for an all-time record of $82.5 million in 1990, has been up for sale privately for months. The minimum asking price: $80 million. An 1889 self-portrait believed to be the last painted by van Gogh sold for $71.5 million.

Nostalgia and limited availability will also fuel certain markets. With failed airlines and railroads becoming distant memories, count on Pan Am wing pins and Pullman porter badges to go up in value. Fanaticism, combined with a dwindling supply, will also push up prices of rock-and-roll record albums. (See the Financial Planning for Life's Situations feature, above, for more examples.)

PREVENTING FRAUD

Looking for an online investment opportunity that is "unaffected by the volatile stock market," guarantees "virtually unlimited profits," "minimizes or eliminates risk factors," and is "IRA approved"?

"Forget it," advises Jodie Bernstein, director of the Federal Trade Commission's Bureau of Consumer Protection. "Claims that an investment is IRA approved are a tip-off to a rip-off. You must be just as careful when investing in opportunities touted on the Net as you are when you make other investments. You should check out these with state securities regulators and other investment professionals." For more information about investing on the Internet, Bernstein suggests that you contact the following organizations:

- Federal Trade Commission (www.ftc.gov)
- North American Securities Administrators Association Inc. (www.nasaa.org)

- Commodity Futures Trading Commission (www.cftc.gov)
- National Association of Securities Dealers (www.nasd.com)
- Securities and Exchange Commission (www.sec.gov)
- National Association of Investors Corporation (www.better-investing.org)
- InvestorGuide (www.investorguide.com)
- InvestorWords (www.investorwords.com)
- The Motley Fool (www.fool.com)
- Alliance for Investor Education (www.investoreducation.org)
- The Online Investor (www.investhelp.com)
- National Fraud Information Center (www.fraud.org)

Rare-coin scams have increased, and many investors in rare coins have lost most of their investments as a result of fraudulent sales practices. If you are investing in coins, the Federal Trade Commission and the American Numismatic Association urge you to protect yourself by following these rules:

Sheet 77
Summary for investment activities

- Use common sense when evaluating any investment claims, and do not rush into buying.
- Make sure you know your dealer's reputation and reliability before you send money or authorize a credit card transaction.
- Do not be taken in by promises that the dealer will buy back your coins or that grading is guaranteed, unless you are confident that the dealer has the financial resources to stand behind these promises.
- Get a second opinion from another source about grade and value as soon as you receive your coins. So, before you buy, find out what remedies you will have if the second opinion differs.
- Be cautious about grading certificates, especially those furnished by coin dealers. Grading is not an exact science, and grading standards vary widely.
- Comparison shop. Visit several dealers before buying.[9]

Read the accompanying Financial Planning for Life's Situations feature on preventing fraud.

Collecting for investment purposes is very different from collecting as a hobby. Like investing in real estate or the stock market, investing in collectibles should be approached with care. Be especially careful if you buy from online auctions.

Investment counselors caution that collectibles do not provide interest or dividends, that it may be difficult to sell them at the right price on short notice, and that if they become valuable enough, they must be insured against loss or theft.

CONCEPT CHECK 17-4

1 What are several methods for buying precious metals?
2 Why do precious stones appeal to investors?
3 What are collectibles?
4 How can you protect yourself from fraudulent practices in the collectibles market?

Action Application Conduct a survey on the collecting activities of relatives and friends. Are the prices of their collections going up or down?

SUMMARY OF OBJECTIVES

Objective 1
Identify types of real estate investments.
Real estate investments are classified as direct or indirect. Direct real estate investments, in which the investor holds legal title to the property, include a home, a vacation home, commercial property, and undeveloped land. Indirect real estate investments include real estate syndicates, REITs, mortgages, and participation certificates.

Objective 2
Evaluate the advantages of real estate investments.
Real estate investments offer a hedge against inflation, easy entry, limited financial liability, no management headaches, and financial leverage.

Objective 3
Assess the disadvantages of real estate investments.
Real estate investments may have the disadvantages of illiquidity, declining values, lack of diversification, lack of a tax shelter, a long depreciation period, and management problems.

Objective 4
Analyze the risks and rewards of investing in precious metals, gems, and collectibles.
Some investors prefer to invest in precious metals such as gold, platinum, and silver; precious stones such as diamonds; or collectibles such as stamps, rare coins, works of art, antiques, rare books, and Chinese ceramics. Collectibles do not provide current income, and they may be difficult to sell quickly.

KEY TERMS

collectibles 558
commercial property 549
direct investment 546
indirect investment 546

participation certificate (PC) 551
passive activity 549
passive loss 549

real estate investment trust
  (REIT) 550
syndicate 550

FINANCIAL PLANNING PROBLEMS

1. *Calculating the Return on Investment.* Dave bought a rental property for $200,000 cash. One year later, he sold it for $240,000. What was the return on his $200,000 investment? (Obj. 2)

2. *Calculating the Return on Investment Using Financial Leverage.* Suppose Dave invested only $20,000 of his own money and borrowed $180,000 (90 percent financing). What was his return on investment? (Obj. 2)

3. *Calculating the Rate of Return on Investment.* Rani bought a rental property for $100,000 with no borrowed funds.

Later, she sold the building for $120,000. What was her return on investment? (Obj. 2)

4. *Calculating the Rate of Return of Investment Using Financial Leverage.* Suppose Shaan invested just $10,000 of his own money and had a $90,000 mortgage with an interest rate of 8.5 percent. After three years, he sold the property for $120,000. (Obj. 2)

   a. What is his profit?

   b. What is the rate of return on investment?

5. *Analyzing the Return on a Real Estate Investment.* Felice bought a duplex apartment at a cost of $150,000. Her mortgage payments on the property are $940 per month, $121 of which can be deducted from her income taxes. Her real estate taxes total $1,440 per year, and insurance costs $900 per year. She estimates that she will spend $1,000 each year *per apartment* for maintenance, replacing appliances, and other costs. The tenants will pay for all utilities. (Obj. 4)

   a. What monthly rent must she charge for each apartment to break even?

   b. What must she charge to make $2,000 in profit each year?

FINANCIAL PLANNING ACTIVITIES

1. *Using the Internet to Obtain Information about Various Types of REITs.* Many REITs now maintain Web sites. Visit a few Web sites of REIT companies discussed in this chapter and of the National Association of Real Estate Investment Trusts (NAREIT) at www. nareit.com. Then prepare a report that summarizes the various types of REITs available to investors. (Obj. 1)

2. *Assessing the Prices of Single-Family Dwellings.* Interview local real estate brokers and research current business magazines and the business section of the local newspaper to determine if the prices of single-family dwellings in your area have been increasing during the last 10 years. Prepare a written report indicating the reasons for the increase or decrease. (Obj. 1)

3. *Assessing the Investment Potential of Commercial Real Estate.* Research current commercial real estate sections of local newspapers. How many listings do you find for duplexes? For fourplexes and small apartment buildings? Prepare an analysis of the investment potential of these properties. (Obj. 1)

4. *Checking the Availability of Real Estate Limited Partnerships.* Call a few real estate and stockbrokerage firms in your area to find out if any real estate limited partnerships are available for investors. (Obj. 2)

5. *Comparing Mortgage Rates and Terms of a Loan.* Obtain duplex mortgage rates from your local commercial bank, a savings and loan association, and a credit union. Compare these rates and terms such as the down payment, loan costs (points), loan length, and maximum amount available to determine which of the three lenders offers the best financing. (Obj. 3)

6. *Checking Current Prices of Precious Metals.* Listen to business news on radio or television. What are the current quotes for an ounce of gold and an ounce of silver? Are the prices of precious metals going up or down? How do the latest prices compare with the prices quoted in the chapter? What might be some reasons for fluctuations in the prices of precious metals? (Obj. 4)

INTERNET CONNECTION

Researchinng Collectibles on the Internet

From toy trains to rare coins, collectibles appeal to hobbyists and investors alike. The Internet offers convenient buying and selling opportunities.

Use an Internet search engine to locate resources where collectors find, buy, and sell collectibles. Complete the worksheet below and answer the questions that follow.

Net Results	
List three collectibles Web sites and their addresses.	
Choose your favorite site, then list information and features offered on the site.	
List the different types of collectibles on the site.	
Find collectible toys within one of the sites you listed above. List one toy collectible, its description, and price.	
Does the site require membership in order to buy or sell collectibles? What benefits are offered to members?	

The Homes Keep Selling

When Laura and John Burgos put their house in Wayland, Massachusetts, on the market in mid-February, they didn't know how buyers would react to the $365,000 price tag—a stiff 74 percent premium over what they paid for the 1950s ranch home less than three years ago. But with 30 prospective buyers trooping through in just the first week on the market, even a realtor who is not working for the Burgoses predicts that "this house will sell in a heartbeat."

Housing, which sagged briefly during the recession, is hot again, and not just around Boston. The latest numbers from the National Association of Realtors (NAR) show that nationwide sales of existing single-family homes jumped 16 percent in January 2002, to 6.4 million homes, after declining slightly in November and December of 2001. Compared with a year earlier, prices of existing-home sales were up 10 percent, despite an economic downturn, higher unemployment, and the September 11 terrorist attacks. While some cities, such as Atlanta, Detroit, and Seattle, are still weak, markets have exploded in cities such as Washington, DC; Miami; and New York.

Is this latest housing boom sustainable or a real estate bust waiting to happen? The implications for the economy are enormous. New-home sales—more than 901,000 new single-family homes in 2001 alone—pump up homebuilders and create demand for lumber, carpeting, washing machines, furniture, and all the other things that go into homes. Perhaps more important, rising housing wealth, which increased by roughly $1 trillion in 2001, puts money into consumers' pockets by means of home-equity loans and mortgage refinancings. That in turn fuels consumer spending.

FINANCIAL PLANNING CASE

A sharp drop in housing prices, though, could hurt consumer spending as much as price hikes have helped it so far. "The importance of housing market wealth in consumption is bigger than stock market wealth," says John M. Quigley, an economist at the University of California at Berkeley who did a study on the subject. "If there is a plateau or a downturn in housing market wealth, it could come out pretty quickly in consumption."

Questions

1. What didn't Laura and John Burgos know when they put their house on the market in February 2002?

2. In what cities is the real estate market weak? Strong?

3. What are the implications for the economy when new home sales increase?

Source: Margaret Popper et al., "The Homes Keep Selling," *BusinessWeek,* March 11, 2002, pp. 26–28.

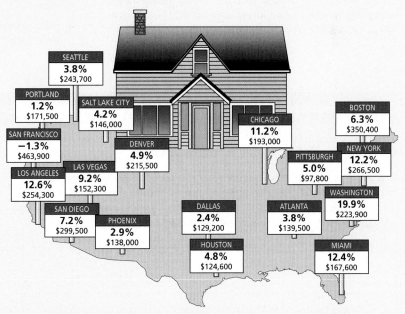

Note: One-year percentage change from fourth quarter 2000 to fourth quarter 2001 and median price of existing single-family home.
Source: From National Association of Realtors.

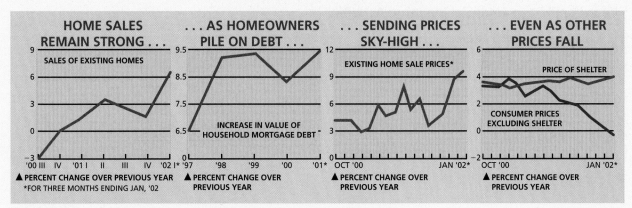

VIDEO CASE

Of REITs, Collectibles, and Art

More than half of the people interviewed on the street did not know what a REIT is! Do you? After all, REITs have been around for about 40 years. REITs are companies that own substantial amounts of properties, and their shares are traded on the New York Stock Exchange or other security exchanges—just like shares of IBM, Coca-Cola, and Microsoft.

Ralph Block from Bay Aisle Financial explains the advantages and disadvantages of investing in REITs. He cautions that while investment in REITs can be stable and provide steady income from dividends, it is not immune from market swings. For example, in the late 80s and early 90s, a lot of investors lost money, but over the long-term real estate has been a steady performing asset.

Scott Newnam of Irvine Apartment Communities in California adds diversification to the list of advantages of investing in REITs. He distinguishes between a REIT and a limited partnership. An average person can't buy into a limited partnership, but can easily invest in equity REITs, mortgage REITs, or hybrid REITs.

Other types of indirect investments in real estate, such as Ginnie Mae, Freddie Mac, Fannie Mae, and Sonny Mae, are defined and explained.

Dave Kohler discusses the investment potential in collectibles. Many people like the tangible element of investing directly in collectibles, but collecting for investment purposes is very different from collecting as a hobby. Investing in collectibles should be done with the same care and research as investing in real estate or the stock market.

Questions

1. According to Ralph Block, what are the advantages and disadvantages of investing in REITs?

2. According to Scott Newnam, what are the major differences between a REIT and a limited partnership? What is one additional benefit of investing in a REIT?

3. What are the other types of indirect investments in real estate?

4. What is Dave Kohler's advice about investing in collectibles?

YOUR PERSONAL FINANCIAL PLANNER IN ACTION

Comparing Other Types of Investments

Real estate and collectibles allow investors to achieve greater potential returns, However, these sometimes speculative ventures must be considered carefully in relation to your personal financial situation.

Your Short-Term Financial Planning Activities	Resources
1. Identify types of real estate and other investments that might serve your various financial goals and life situation.	www.hud.com www.nreionline.com www.creonline.com
2. Compare the cost of buying and operating various types of real estate investments.	www.quotes.ino.com www.kiplinger.com www.worth.com
Your Long-Term Financial Planning Activities	
1. Identify real estate and other investments that might serve you in the future.	www.ft.com www.cbot.com www.cme.com www.antiquecast.com
2. Develop a plan for selecting and monitoring real estate.	Text pages 546–552 www.nareit.com www.smartmoney.com

Other Investment Choices

Life Situation
   Pam, 43
   Josh, 45
   3 children ages 16, 14, and 11

Financial Data
   Monthly income $4,900
   Living expenses $4,450
   Assets $262,700
   Liabilities $84,600
   Emergency fund $5,000

The use of more speculative investments may be considered in certain situations. The Brocks are not sure if these would be appropriate for their portfolio. The long-term benefits of real estate and the high potential returns of other investments can be very attractive. However, the risks associated with these can create strong concerns for most investors.

Questions

1. Some financial advisors suggest that the Brocks should have been more aggressive in their investment decisions. In an effort to compensate for a late start for long-term investing, explain if Pam and Josh should consider highly speculative investments with potential for large returns.

2. Describe real estate and other speculative investments that the Brocks might consider for their portfolio.

18 Starting Early: Retirement Planning

Key Concept

Retirement planning is important because you'll probably spend many years in retirement. Properly estimating your retirement living costs and housing needs will enable you to save or invest enough money to live comfortably during retirement.

Digital Study Tools

Online Learning Center Study Tools for This Chapter

- Multiple-choice quiz
- Flashcards
- eLearning sessions
- Crossword puzzle
- Personal Finance Online: Retirement and Estate Planning

Student CD Study Tools for This Chapter

- Self-study software
- Narrated PowerPoint
- Personal financial planning software: Worksheets 63–65

Learning Objectives

1. Recognize the importance of retirement planning.
2. Analyze your current assets and liabilities for retirement.
3. Estimate your retirement spending needs.
4. Identify your retirement housing needs.
5. Determine your planned retirement income.
6. Develop a balanced budget based on your retirement income.

Just What Kind of Retiree Will You Be?

The definition of "retire," according to the dictionary, is to withdraw from action or danger. Looks like we'll have to find a new word to describe what people do when they leave a longtime employer or start drawing a pension.

According to a new poll from Harris Interactive, 95 percent of people ages 55 to 64 plan to do at least some work after they're retired. That's up from 75 percent who said the same thing in a BusinessWeek/Harris Poll just four years ago.

The latest poll, which was done for AIG SunAmerica, didn't ask people whether they'll be working because they need the money. But they don't expect what they do to be a grind: 81 percent want to continue to learn, 70 percent want to try new things, and 63 percent want a new hobby or interest.

To characterize the new lifestyles, Harris has created four categories of retirees:

- The Ageless Explorers (27 percent) are relatively wealthy and well-educated and plan active, independent lives.
- The Comfortably Contents (19 percent) indulge in a traditional retiree's lifestyle of travel, recreational activities, and relaxation.
- The Live for Todays (22 percent) share the same goals as the Explorers but are less well off and thus more dependent on a paycheck, perhaps from a part-time job.
- The Sick & Tireds (32 percent) are the least well-prepared financially or medically and are more likely to view retirement as life coming to a close.

Even so, only 22 percent of all people see retirement as a time to wind down.

Source: G. David Wallace, "Just What Kind of Retiree Will You Be?" *BusinessWeek*, June 17, 2002, p. 10.

QUESTIONS

What Actions Should Be Taken?

1. Do you agree that we need to find a new word to describe what people do when they leave a longtime employer or start drawing a pension? Explain.
2. Why do you think a higher percentage of people plan to work now than four years ago?

What about Your Situation?

3. In which category of retirees will you find yourself at retirement? Explain.
4. Do you consider yourself to be among the people who see retirement as a time to wind down?

Learn More Online

Visit the *BusinessWeek* Web site at www.businessweek.com and describe the retirement planning information that is available.

Why Retirement Planning?

Objective 1

Recognize the importance of retirement planning.

Retirement can be a rewarding phase of your life. However, a successful, happy retirement doesn't just happen; it takes planning and continual evaluation. Thinking about retirement in advance can help you anticipate future changes and gain a sense of control over the future.

The ground rules for retirement planning are changing rapidly. Reexamine your retirement plans if you hold any of these misconceptions:

- My expenses will drop when I retire.
- My retirement will last only 15 years.
- I can depend on Social Security and my company pension to pay for my basic living expenses.
- My pension benefits will increase to keep pace with inflation.
- My employer's health insurance plan and Medicare will cover my medical expenses.
- There's plenty of time for me to start saving for retirement.
- Saving just a little bit won't help.

The International Society for Retirement and Life Planning (ISRLP) is a nonprofit association to promote a holistic approach to retirement and life planning. Visit their Web site at **www.isrplan.org/**.

It is vital to engage in basic retirement planning activities throughout your working years and to update your retirement plans periodically. While it is never too late to begin sound financial planning, you can avoid many unnecessary and serious difficulties by starting this planning early. Saving now for the future requires tackling the trade-offs between spending and saving.

TACKLING THE TRADE-OFFS

Although exceptions exist, the old adage "You can't have your cake and eat it too" is particularly true in planning for retirement. For example, if you buy state-of-the-art home entertainment systems, drive expensive cars, and take extravagant vacations now, don't expect to retire with plenty of money.

Only by saving now and curtailing current spending can you ensure a comfortable retirement later. Yet saving money doesn't come naturally to many young people. Ironically, although the time to begin saving is when you are young, the people who are in the best position to save are middle-aged.

Seventy-five percent of workers expect to live as well as, if not better than, they do now when they retire, but only 20 percent of those surveyed have begun to save seriously for retirement.

DID YOU KNOW?

Happy Birthday! You're 100! Centenarians are the fastest-growing segment of our population. The second fastest is the age group 85+. Currently, there are about 40,000 centenarians in the United States, or a little more than one centenarian per 10,000 in population; 85 percent of them are women, 15 percent men.

Source: www.bumc.bu.edu/Dept/Content, May 15, 2005.

THE IMPORTANCE OF STARTING EARLY

Consider this: If from age 25 to 65 you invest $300 per month and earn an average of 9 percent interest a year, you'll have $1.4 million in your retirement fund. Waiting just 10 years until age 35 to begin your $300-a-month investing will yield about $550,000, while if you wait 20 years to begin this investment, you will have only $201,000 at age 65. Exhibit 18–1 shows how even a $2,000 annual investment earning just 4 percent will grow.

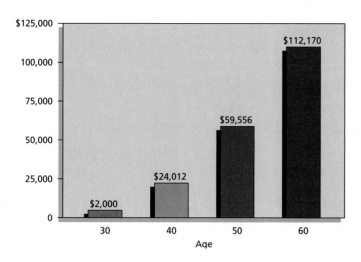

Exhibit **18-1**

It's never too early to start planning for retirement

Start young. A look at the performance of $2,000 per year of retirement plan investments over time, even at 4 percent, shows the value of starting early.

For 40 years your life, and probably your family's life, revolves around your job. One day you retire, and practically every aspect of your life changes. There's less money, more time, and no daily structure.

You can expect to spend about 16 to 25 years in retirement—too many years to be bored, lonely, and broke. You want your retirement years to be rewarding, active, and rich in new experiences. It's never too early to begin planning for retirement; some experts even suggest starting while you are in school. Be certain you don't let your 45th birthday roll by without a comprehensive retirement plan. Remember, the longer you wait, the less you will be able to shape your life in retirement.

Retirement planning has both emotional and financial components. Emotional planning for retirement involves identifying your personal goals and setting out to meet them. Financial planning for retirement involves assessing your postretirement needs and income and plugging any gaps you find. Financial planning for retirement is critical for several reasons:

1. You can expect to live in retirement for 20 years or more. At age 65, the average life expectancy is 14 years for a man and 19 years for a woman.

2. Social Security and a private pension, if you have one, are most often insufficient to cover the cost of living.

3. Inflation may diminish the purchasing power of your retirement savings. Even a 3 percent rate of inflation will cause prices to double every 24 years.

You should anticipate your retirement years by analyzing your long-range goals. What does retirement mean to you? Does it mean an opportunity to stop work and relax, or does it mean time to travel, develop a hobby, or start a second career? Where and how do you want to live during your retirement? Once you have considered your retirement goals, you are ready to evaluate their cost and assess whether you can afford them.

THE BASICS OF RETIREMENT PLANNING

Before you decide where you want to be financially, you have to find out where you are. Your first step, therefore, is to

---

DID YOU KNOW?

Retiring in Style
How much do baby boomers plan to spend annually on favorite activities?

Travel	$7,700
Home improvement	$7,000
Family outings	$3,900
Golfing	$3,500
Fishing	$2,700
Gardening	$1,500

(Amount to be spent, per retiree, by boomers who said the activity was one of their three favorites.) From a poll of 1,004 adults born between 1946 and 1961, released February 2002. Data: Harris Interactive.

Source: *BusinessWeek*, April 29, 2002, p. 16.

Exhibit **18-2**

Using a personal computer for retirement planning

It's never too early to start planning for retirement.

Source: www.dol.gov/ebsa, May 2005. U.S. Department of Labor.

General Web Sites
American Savings Education Council (www.asec.org)
Diversified Investment Advisors (www.divinvest.com)
401KAFE (www.401kafe.com)
InvestorGuide (www.investorguide.com/retirement.htm)
Longevity Game (www.northwesternmutual.com/games/longevity)
Roth IRA Web Site (www.rothira.com)
Online Planning Software
Financial Engines (www.financialengines.com)
FinancialPlanAuditors.com (www.fplanauditors.com)
Quicken.com Retirement (www.quicken.com/retirement)
Vanguard NavigatorPlus (majestic4.vanguard.com/GUIDE/DA)
Financial Calcuator Web Sites
www.kiplinger.com—Click on Retirement
www.moneymag.com—Click on Retirement
www.usnews.com—Click on Retirement Calculator
www.asec.org—Click on Ballpark Estimate Worksheet
www.nasd.com—Click on Investor Services, then Financial Calculators

analyze your current assets and liabilities. Then estimate your spending needs and adjust them for inflation. Next, evaluate your planned retirement income. Finally, increase your income by working part-time, if necessary. An attorney, for example, might teach some law courses. Recent articles and other retirement information may be accessed through online computer services. For further information, see Appendix B. Exhibit 18–2 shows some good online sources for retirement planning using a personal computer. Also, read the Financial Planning for Life's Situations feature on page 573.

CONCEPT CHECK 18-1

1 How can the Internet assist you in retirement planning?
2 Why is retirement planning important?
3 What are the four basic steps in retirement planning?

Action Application Survey friends, relatives, and other people to get their views on retirement planning. Prepare a written report of your findings.

Conducting a Financial Analysis

Objective 2

Analyze your current assets and liabilities for retirement.

As you learned in Chapter 3, your assets include everything you own that has value: cash on hand and in checking and savings accounts; the current value of your stocks, bonds, and other investments; the current value of your house, car, jewelry, and furnish-

PLANNING FOR RETIREMENT WHILE YOU ARE STILL YOUNG

Retirement probably seems vague and far off at this stage of your life. Besides, you have other things to buy right now. Yet there are some crucial reasons to start preparing now for retirement.

- You'll probably have to pay for more of your own retirement than earlier generations. The sooner you get started, the better.

- You have one huge ally—time. Let's say that you put $1,000 at the beginning of each year into an IRA from age 20 through age 30 (11 years) and then never put in another dime. The account earns 7 percent annually. When you retire at age 65 you'll have $168,514 in the account. A friend doesn't start until age 30, but saves the same amount annually for 35

years straight. Despite putting in three times as much money, your friend's account grows to only $147,913.

- You can start small and grow. Even setting aside a small portion of your paycheck each month will pay off in big dollars later.

- You can afford to invest more aggressively. You have years to overcome the inevitable ups and downs of the market.

Developing the habit of saving for retirement is easier when you are young.

Source: U.S. Department of Labor, www.dol.gov/ebsa, May 2005.

---

ings; and the current value of your life insurance and pensions. Your liabilities are everything you owe: your mortgage, car payments, credit card balances, taxes due, and so forth. The difference between the two totals is your *net worth,* a figure you should increase each year as you move toward retirement. Use Exhibit 18–3 on page 574 to calculate your net worth now and at retirement.

For more information about reverse mortgages, go to **www.aarp.org/revmort**. AARP's booklet *Home Made Money: A Consumer's Guide to Reverse Mortgages* is available online or by calling (888) 687-2277 and asking for publication D15601.

fyi

REVIEW YOUR ASSETS

Reviewing your assets to ensure they are sufficient for retirement is a sound idea. Make any necessary adjustments in your investments and holdings to fit your circumstances. In reviewing your assets, consider the following factors.

HOUSING   If you own your house, it is probably your biggest single asset. The amount tied up in your house, however, may be out of line with your retirement income. You might consider selling your house and buying a less expensive one. The selection of a smaller, more easily maintained house can also decrease your maintenance costs. The difference saved can be put into a savings account or certificates of deposit or into other income-producing investments. If your mortgage is largely or completely paid off, you may be able to get an annuity to provide you with extra income during retirement. In this arrangement, a lender uses your house as collateral to buy an annuity for you from a life insurance company. Each month, the lender pays you (the homeowner) from the annuity after deducting the mortgage interest payment. The mortgage principal, which was used to obtain the annuity, is repaid to the lender by probate after your death. This special annuity is known as a **reverse annuity mortgage (RAM)** or *equity conversion.*

Chicago-based Wells Fargo Home Mortgage (1-866-530-2424) offers a free consumers' information kit on reverse mortgages. The kit shows that the amount of money

DID YOU KNOW?

The U.S. Department of Housing and Urban Development (HUD) created the first reverse mortgage for the over-62-year-olds. Many seniors use it to supplement Social Security, meet unexpected medical expenses, make home improvements, and more. For free information, call HUD at 1-800-217-6970.

reverse annuity mortgage (RAM) A mortgage in which the lender uses the borrower's house as collateral to buy an annuity for the borrower from a life insurance company; also called an *equity conversion.*

573

Exhibit 18-3

Review your assets, liabilities, and net worth

Reviewing your assets to ensure they are sufficient for retirement is a sound idea.

Net worth: Assets of $108,800 minus liabilities of $16,300 equals $92,500.

	Sample Figures	Your Figures
Assets: What We Own		
Cash:		
Checking account	$ 800	_____
Savings account	4,500	_____
Investments:		
U.S. savings bonds (current cash-in value)	5,000	_____
Stocks, mutual funds	4,500	_____
Life insurance:		
Cash value, accumulated dividends	10,000	_____
Company pension rights:		
Accrued pension benefit	20,000	_____
Property:		
House (resale value)	50,000	_____
Furniture and appliances	8,000	_____
Collections and jewelry	2,000	_____
Automobile	3,000	_____
Other:		
Loan to brother	1,000	_____
Gross assets	**$108,800**	_____
Liabilities: What We Owe		
Current unpaid bills	$ 600	_____
Home mortgage (remaining balance)	9,700	_____
Auto loan	1,200	_____
Property taxes	1,100	_____
Home improvement loan	3,700	_____
Total liabilities	**$ 16,300**	_____

available depends on your age, the value of your home, and interest rates. For example, a 75-year-old couple with a $150,000 home in Chicago or the suburbs could receive a monthly check of about $900 for the next 10 years or $599 for as long as either partner lives in the home.

LIFE INSURANCE   You may have set up your life insurance to provide support and education for your children. Now you may want to convert some of this asset into cash or income (an annuity). Another possibility is to reduce premium payments by decreasing the face value of your insurance. This will give you extra money to spend on living expenses or invest for additional income.

Financial Planning for Life's Situations

MAKE DIVORCE A LESS TAXING TIME

Suppose you and your spouse are calling it quits. You've got two jointly owned assets—a house and a retirement account—each worth $500,000. Would it make a difference which one you walked away with? You bet. Equal division of the assets does not mean equal tax bills. "If the tax implications of a divorce settlement are not taken into account, a spouse can unwittingly end up with less, sometimes substantially less, than he or she bargained for," says Cindy Wofford, a tax attorney in Washington.

Divorcing couples should pay attention to the tax implications of retirement benefits. If the transfer of assets from one spouse to another is not done properly, the monies withdrawn from the retirement account will be subject to taxes and early withdrawal penalties.

To correctly divide retirement benefits, the couple needs to create a legal document called a qualified domestic relations order (QDRO). A QDRO helps a former spouse get his

or her fair share of a retirement account accumulated during the marriage. With a QDRO, a husband or wife can transfer some of the assets from his or her retirement account into a separate IRA account for the ex-spouse without incurring taxes and penalties. Also, remember to account for the taxes that must be paid when the retirement account is drawn down. The best way, says Ginita Wall, an accountant in San Diego who specializes in divorce settlements, is to use a 27 percent tax bracket to estimate the amount of taxes owed at retirement.

Equitably dividing assets in divorce is never easy, but you can make sure the financial nightmare doesn't continue long after the divorce is final.

Source: Condensed from Toddi Gutner, "Make Divorce a Less Taxing Time," *BusinessWeek,* April 15, 2002, p. 118.

OTHER INVESTMENTS   Evaluate any other investments you have. When you chose them, you may have been more interested in making your money grow than in getting an early return. Has the time come to take the income from your investments? You may now want to take dividends rather than reinvest them.

After thoroughly reviewing your assets, estimate your spending needs during your retirement years.

YOUR ASSETS AFTER DIVORCE

Any divorce is difficult, particularly when it comes to a division of marital assets. Your pension benefits are considered marital property, which must be divided in a divorce. "Even if a person is not ready to retire, pension benefits are considered a marital asset subject to the division of property," says Howard Sharfstein, a partner in Schulte Roth & Zabel of New York. Any retirement fund money, including a 401(k) plan or a profit-sharing plan, set aside during a marriage and the dollar growth of a pension plan during a marriage are considered marital property.

Division of pension benefits generally depends on the length of the marriage. "In a five-year marriage the percentage of one person's assets given to the spouse is usually small," says Sharfstein. "In an eight-year marriage about 25 percent of the monetary assets earned by one partner may be given to the other partner. In a marriage that lasts more than 15 years there's generally a 50-50 split of the marital assets."

Be warned: Many retirement-planning strategies accommodate the traditional husband-wife-kids family unit. But millions of nontraditional households have unique retirement needs. Nearly half of all American marriages end in divorce, creating difficulties for millions of adults thinking about their retirement years. Likewise, single parents, gays and lesbians, and individuals who choose to live together outside of marriage all have formidable retirement-planning challenges. See Financial Planning for Life's Situations: Make Divorce a Less Taxing Time for suggestions regarding retirement accounts and divorce.

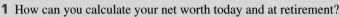

CONCEPT CHECK 18-2

1 How can you calculate your net worth today and at retirement?
2 What assets are considered marital assets?

Action Application Contact AARP at 1-800-209-8085 (or visit the AARP Web site at www.aarp.org/revmort). Ask for a free booklet, *Home Made Money*, and then prepare a report on the pros and cons of reverse mortgages.

Retirement Living Expenses

Objective 3

Estimate your retirement spending needs.

The exact amount of money you will need in retirement is impossible to predict. However, you can estimate the amount you will need by considering the changes you anticipate in your spending patterns and in where and how you live.

Your spending patterns will probably change. A study conducted by the Bureau of Labor Statistics on how families spend money shows that retired families use a greater share for food, housing, and medical care than nonretired families. Although no two families adjust their spending patterns to changes in the life cycle in the same manner, the tabulation in Exhibit 18–4 can guide you in anticipating your own future spending patterns.

The following expenses may be lowered or eliminated:

- *Work expenses.* You will no longer make payments into your retirement fund. You will not be buying gas and oil for the drive back and forth to work or for train or bus fares. You may be buying fewer lunches away from home.

- *Clothing expenses.* You will probably need fewer clothes after you retire, and your dress may be more casual.

- *Housing expenses.* If you have paid off your house mortgage by the time you retire, your cost of housing may decrease (although increases in property taxes and insurance may offset this gain).

- *Federal income taxes.* Your federal income taxes will probably be lower. No federal tax has to be paid on some forms of income, such as railroad retirement benefits and certain veterans' benefits. Under the U.S. Civil Service Retirement System, your retirement income is not taxed until you have received the amount you have invested in the retirement fund. After that, your retirement income is taxable. A retirement credit is allowed for some sources of income, such as annuities. You will probably pay taxes at a lower rate because your taxable income will be lower.

You can also estimate which of the following expenses may increase:

- *Insurance.* The loss of your employer's contribution to health and life insurance will increase your own payments. Medicare, however, may offset part of this increased expense.

- *Medical expenses.* Although medical expenses vary from person to person, they tend to increase with age.

- *Expenses for leisure activities.* With more free time, many retirees spend more money on leisure activities. You may want to put aside extra money for a retirement trip or other large recreational expenses.

Not everyone can afford to take lavish vacations. Consider your retirement goals, evaluate their cost, and assess whether you can afford them.

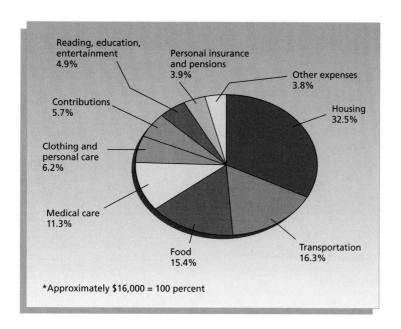

Exhibit **18-4**

How an "average" older (65+) household spends its money

Retired families spend a greater share of their income for food, housing, and medical care than nonretired families.

Source: U.S. Bureau of Labor Statistics.

Pie chart labels:
- Reading, education, entertainment 4.9%
- Personal insurance and pensions 3.9%
- Other expenses 3.8%
- Housing 32.5%
- Contributions 5.7%
- Clothing and personal care 6.2%
- Medical care 11.3%
- Food 15.4%
- Transportation 16.3%

*Approximately $16,000 = 100 percent

- *Gifts and contributions.* Many retirees who continue to spend the same amount of money on gifts and contributions find their spending in this area takes a larger share of their smaller income. Therefore, you may want to reevaluate such spending.

Using the worksheet in Exhibit 18–5, list your present expenses and estimate what these expenses would be if you were retired. To make a realistic comparison, list your major spending categories, starting with fixed expenses such as rent or mortgage payments, utilities, insurance premiums, and taxes. Then list variable expenses—food, clothing, transportation, and so on, as well as miscellaneous expenditures such as medical expenses, entertainment, vacations, gifts, contributions, and unforeseen expenses.

Be sure you have an emergency fund for unforeseen expenses. Even when you are living a tranquil life, unexpected events can occur. Build a cushion to cope with inflation. Estimate high in calculating how much the prices of goods and services will rise.

ADJUST YOUR EXPENSES FOR INFLATION

You now have a list of your likely monthly (and annual) expenses if you were to retire today. With inflation, however, those expenses will not be fixed. The potential loss of buying power due to inflation is what makes planning ahead so important. (See Exhibit 18–6.) During the 1970s and the early 1980s, the cost of living increased an average of 6.1 percent a year, though the annual increase slowed to less than 3 percent between 1983 and 2005.

To help you plan for this likely increase in your expenses, use the inflation factor table in the accompanying Financial Planning Calculations feature on page 579.

With more free time, many retirees spend more money on leisure activities.

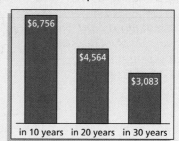

DID YOU KNOW?

The Effects of Inflation
This chart shows you what $10,000 will be worth in 10, 20, and 30 years assuming a fairly conservative 4 percent rate of inflation.

Bar chart:
- in 10 years: $6,756
- in 20 years: $4,564
- in 30 years: $3,083

Source: TIAA-CREF.

Exhibit **18-5**

Your monthly present expenses and your estimated monthly retirement expenses

Don't forget inflation in calculating the prices of goods and services in retirement.

Monthly Expenses		
Item	**Present**	**Retirement**
Fixed expenses:		
Rent or mortgage payment	$_____	$_____
Taxes	_____	_____
Insurance	_____	_____
Savings	_____	_____
Debt payment	_____	_____
Other	_____	_____
Total fixed expenses	_____	_____
Variable expenses:		
Food and beverages	_____	_____
Household operation and maintenance	_____	_____
Furnishings and equipment	_____	_____
Clothing	_____	_____
Personal	_____	_____
Transportation	_____	_____
Medical care	_____	_____
Recreation and education	_____	_____
Gifts and contributions	_____	_____
Other	_____	_____
Total variable expenses	_____	_____
Total expenses	_____	_____

Exhibit **18-6**

Even low inflation can damage purchasing power

In 25 years, at just a 3 percent annual rate of inflation, your expenses could more than double what they are today.

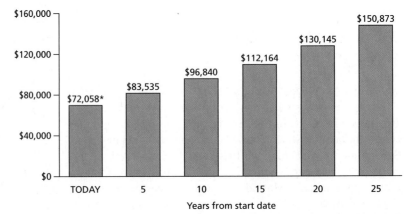

*$72,058 was the annual expenditure for individuals age 65+ with income greater than $70,000 from the U.S. Department of Labor, Bureau of Labor Statistics, Consumer Expenditures 2000 report. All other numbers were calculated based on a hypothetical 3 percent rate of inflation (historical average from 1926 through March 2003 was 3.06 percent) to show the effects of inflation over time; actual inflation rates may be more or less.
Source: Fidelity Investments, 2005.

Financial Planning Calculations

HOW MUCH INFLATION IS IN YOUR FUTURE?

ESTIMATED ANNUAL RATE OF INFLATION BETWEEN NOW AND RETIREMENT

Years to Retirement	3%	4%	5%	6%	7%	8%	9%	10%	11%	12%
5	1.2	1.2	1.3	1.3	1.4	1.5	1.5	1.6	1.7	1.8
8	1.3	1.4	1.5	1.6	1.7	1.8	2.0	2.1	2.3	2.5
10	1.4	1.5	1.6	1.8	2.0	2.2	2.4	2.6	2.8	3.1
12	1.5	1.6	1.8	2.0	2.3	2.5	2.8	3.1	3.5	3.9
15	1.6	1.8	2.1	2.4	2.8	3.2	3.6	4.2	4.8	5.5
18	1.8	2.0	2.4	2.8	3.4	4.0	4.7	5.6	6.5	7.7
20	2.0	2.2	2.7	3.2	3.9	4.7	5.6	6.7	8.1	9.6
25	2.1	2.7	3.4	4.3	5.4	6.8	8.6	10.8	13.6	17.0

1. Choose from the first column the approximate number of years until your retirement.

2. Choose an estimated annual rate of inflation. The rate of inflation cannot be predicted accurately and will vary from year to year. The 1997 inflation rate was less than 3 percent.

3. Find the inflation factor corresponding to the number of years until your retirement and the estimated annual inflation rate. (Example: 10 years to retirement combined with a 4 percent estimated annual inflation rate yields a 1.5 inflation factor.)

4. Multiply the inflation factor by your estimated retirement income and your estimated retirement expenses. (Example: $6,000 × 1.5 = $9,000.)

Total annual inflated retirement income: $_____.

Total annual inflated retirement expenses: $_____.

Sources: The above figures are from a compound interest table showing the effective yield of lump-sum investments after inflation that appeared in Charles D. Hodgman, ed., *Mathematical Tables from the Handbook of Chemistry and Physics* (Cleveland: Chemical Rubber Publishing, 1959); *Citicorp Consumer Views,* July 1985, pp. 2–3, © Citicorp, 1985; *Financial Planning Tables,* A. G. Edwards, August 1991.

CONCEPT CHECK 18-3

1 How can you estimate the amount of money you will need during retirement?
2 What expenses are likely to increase or decrease during retirement?
3 How might you adjust your expenses for inflation?

Action Application Read newspaper or magazine articles to determine what expenses are likely to increase and decrease during retirement. How might this information affect your retirement-planning decisions?

Planning Your Retirement Housing

Think about where you will want to live. If you think you will want to live in another city, it's a good idea to plan vacations now in areas you might enjoy later. When you find one that appeals to you, visit that area during various times of the year to experience the year-round climate. Meet the people. Check into available activities, transportation, and taxes. Be realistic about what you will have to give up and what you will gain.

Objective 4

Identify your retirement housing needs.

Where you live in retirement can influence your financial needs. You must make some important decisions about whether or not to stay in your present community and in your current home. Everyone has unique needs and preferences; only you can determine the location and housing that are best for you.

Consider what moving involves. Moving is expensive, and if you are not satisfied with your new location, returning to your former home may be impossible. Consider the social aspects of moving. Will you want to be near your children, other relatives, and good friends? Are you prepared for new circumstances?

TYPE OF HOUSING

Housing needs often change as people grow older. The ease and cost of maintenance and nearness to public transportation, shopping, church/synagogue, and entertainment often become more important to people when they retire.

Many housing alternatives exist, several of which were discussed in Chapter 9. Staying in their present homes, whether a single-family dwelling, a condominium, or an apartment, is the alternative preferred by most people approaching retirement. That's what John and Virginia Wolf decided to do after John took early retirement at age 47 from his job as a service manager of a Van Nuys, California, Ford dealership in the late 1970s. Even though the couple had already paid off the mortgage on their small, three-bedroom ranch house and could have moved up into a bigger or fancier place, all John wanted to do was tinker in the garage and dabble in the stock market.[1] A recent survey of over 5,000 men and women revealed that 92 percent wanted to own their homes in retirement.

DeLoma Foster of Greenville, South Carolina, has seen the future, and she wants to be prepared. DeLoma, 69, has osteoporosis, just as her mother did. Although she's not having difficulty now, she knows the debilitating bone condition eventually could make it difficult, if not impossible, to navigate steep stairs, cramped bathrooms, and narrow doorways. So two years ago, she and her husband, Clyde, a 72-year-old retired textile executive, moved into a novel type of home, one that can comfortably accommodate them no matter what disabilities old age may bring. Called a "universal design home," their residence is on the cutting edge of an architectural concept that an aging population may well embrace. The only house of its kind in the neighborhood, it has wide doors, pull-out cabinet shelves, easy-to-reach electrical switches, and dozens of other features useful for elderly persons or those with disabilities. Yet these features are incorporated into the design unobtrusively.

Apart from aesthetics, universal design is appealing because it allows people to stay in their homes as they grow older and more frail. "The overwhelming majority of people would prefer to grow old in their own homes in their own communities," says Jon Pynoos, a gerontologist at the University of Southern California in Los Angeles. Recognizing this trend, building suppliers now offer everything from lever door handles to faucets that turn on automatically when you put your hand beneath the spigot. Remodeling so far is creating the biggest demand for these products. But increasingly, contractors are building universal design homes from scratch, which generally costs less than completely retrofitting an existing house. Philip Stephen Companies in St. Paul, Minnesota, has built six universal design homes in the Southeast, ranging from a 1,240-square-foot ranch in Greer, South Carolina, that sold for $90,000 to the 2,200-square-foot home that DeLoma and Clyde bought for $190,000.

To boost demand, builders are marketing to families of all ages. In Cincinnati, Amherst Homes' sales material stresses that the wide hallways of its $300,000-to-$400,000 homes not only accommodate walkers and wheelchairs but also make it easier to carry bags of groceries and other bulky items. This new setup suits the Fosters just fine. Unlike their peers who are moving into continuing-care communities, they want to stay where they have always lived, near their three children and around people of all ages. They now have

During retirement, will you want to be near your children, grandchildren, other relatives, and good friends?

a home that can accommodate a wheelchair and even has a room for a nurse if the need arises. "We hope to be able to live here for the rest of our lives," says DeLoma Foster—in comfort and with all the touches they need to ease their daily tasks.[2]

With the many choices available, determining where to live in retirement is itself turning into a time-consuming job. (Read the Financial Planning for Life's Situations feature on page 582 regarding housing options.) But whether you want to race cars, go on a safari, or stay home to paint, the goal is to end up like Edna Cohen. "Don't feel bad if I die tomorrow," she says. "I've had a wonderful life." Who could ask for more?

Whatever retirement housing alternative you choose, make sure you know what you are signing and understand what you are buying.

AVOIDING RETIREMENT HOUSING TRAPS

Sheet 63
Retirement housing and lifestyle planning

Too many people make the move without doing enough research, and often it's a huge mistake. How can retirees avoid being surprised by hidden tax and financial traps when they move? Here are some tips from retirement specialists on how to uncover hidden taxes and other costs of a retirement area before moving:

- Write or call the local chamber of commerce to get an economic profile and details on area property taxes.
- Contact the state's tax department to find out state income, sales, and inheritance taxes and special exemptions for retirees. If your pension will be taxed by the state you're leaving, check whether the new state will give you credit for those taxes.
- Subscribe to the Sunday edition of a local newspaper.
- Call a local CPA to find out which taxes are rising.
- Check with local utilities to estimate your energy costs. Visit the area in as many seasons as possible. Talk to retirees and other local residents about costs of health care, auto insurance, food, and clothing.
- Rent for a while instead of buying immediately.

Financial Planning for Life's Situations: Dad Couldn't Live Alone on page 583 provides some guidelines in choosing an assisted-living facility.

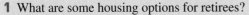

CONCEPT CHECK 18-4 ✔

1 What are some housing options for retirees?
2 How can retirees avoid retirement housing traps?

Action Application Contact assisted-living facilities, nursing homes, and continuing care communities in our area. Prepare a list of advantages and disadvantages of your housing choice.

Planning Your Retirement Income

Once you have determined your approximate future expenses, you must evaluate the sources and amounts of your retirement income. Possible sources of income for many retirees are Social Security, other public pension plans, employer pension plans, personal retirement plans, and annuities.

Objective 5

Determine your planned retirement income.

SOCIAL SECURITY

Social Security is the most widely used source of retirement income; it covers almost 97 percent of U.S. workers. Many Americans think of Social Security as benefiting only

Financial Planning for Life's Situations

HOUSING OPTIONS FOR SENIORS

Seniors and their families are confronted with a bewildering choice of housing options. Which one works best for you (or your elderly relatives) depends on your age, interests, health, and, of course, your finances.

	What Is It?	Pros	Cons	Cost*
Independent Living	Primarily a social, not a medical, setting, independent living is for active seniors who can care for themselves. It accommodates a broad range of lifestyles, often includes in-house activities, and may provide transportation to shopping and outside events. Some have dining rooms that serve one or two meals a day, though individual units have full kitchens. Some offer assisted living on site. You may rent or buy.	Resort-like ambience. Plenty of activities. No need to worry about maintenance and repairs of a home.	If you become frail or sick, you'll have to hire private aides at substantial extra cost, or you may have to move.	$1,168 to $2,234 a month.
Assisted Living	These communities are for seniors who have difficulty managing on their own. They provide a moderate level of personal care, such as assistance in bathing or taking medications. Individual units, usually rented monthly, are often efficiency-style, with limited or no cooking facilities. Resident may have to pay for extra care.	Good choice for frail elderly who can manage with some help from aides. Less costly and much more comfortable than nursing homes.	Staffs are often overworked, and it's hard to get personal attention. Management often has trouble managing medical requirements of patients. Some facilities are appropriate for residents with mild dementia, others are not.	$2,703 to $4,177 a month.
Nursing Homes	These offer a much more intense level of medical care, usually under the supervision of a doctor. Today, many nursing homes are geared to dementia patients, limited stays for rehabilitation, or patients at the end of life.	Can provide near-hospital-quality medical care for chronic illness at less cost. On-site physicians and RNs can quickly respond to changes in patients' health status.	Private rooms are expensive and often unavailable, so residents may need to share a room. Mixing mentally able patients with those suffering from dementia can create problems. Staffs are overburdened.	$172 to $248 a day.
Continuing Care Communities	Also known as life-care communities, they try to provide facilities for all stages of aging on the same campus. They usually include independent and assisted living, as well as nursing and rehab care. CCRCs charge hefty entry fees plus monthly payments. Some are operated by nonprofits or church groups, others are for-profit.	These make it easy to move between levels of care as the resident's condition changes. Seniors may maintain contact with friends as they move within the same community.	They require a major, long-term financial commitment. Residents or their families need to assess stability of the facility's ownership and management.	Entry fees $81,115 to $358,671. Monthly charges of $1,748 to $4,641.
Staying at Home	Often forgotten in the scramble for alternative housing, remaining at home, with its familiar surroundings and proximity to friends and neighbors, is the best choice for many seniors. Some senior-heavy apartment complexes are creating their own informal support systems.	Avoids wrenching change. Allows seniors to maintain a sense of independence. Care can be tailored to specific situations. Hired aides provide more personal, one-on-one care.	Finding and monitoring resources, such as shopping, transportation, and home health aides can be complex and time consuming. Renovations may be required. Not necessarily cheaper than other alternatives.	Home health aides earn about $12 to $18 an hour.

*Costs vary dramatically around the country. For instance, the annual average cost of a nursing home in New York tops $100,000, while in Jackson, Mississippi, the average is about $46,000. To compare the relative costs of various housing choices, we focused on 2003 prices in one area, the Virginia suburbs of Washington.

Source: *BusinessWeek*, July 12, 2004, p. 91.

DAD COULDN'T LIVE ALONE

He was the one who had read her bedtime stories, taught her to ride a bike, and left tooth-fairy money under her pillow. So now that her father was 87, widowed, and losing his memory, Judy Balch of Houston wanted to do the right thing. Dad couldn't live alone, and he was too healthy for a nursing home. So Balch and her husband explored four assisted-living facilities (ALFs) that provide housing as well as personal and medical services for the aging. After touring the grounds, quizzing residents, and sampling cuisines, the family settled on a top-tier, $2,800-a-month complex. Two months later, Judy Balch reports that her father is happy in his new home.

Not all consumers are as fortunate. The assisted-living industry is booming as aging Americans' quest for new housing options sends them searching for everything from residences offering minimal services to those with nursing homes attached. But the search can be full of pitfalls.

A recent General Accounting Office report found that of 60 assisted-living contracts it examined, 20 contained "language that is unclear or misleading." Furthermore, the GAO found that of 622 facilities surveyed in four states, only 65 percent provided a contract prior to the admission decision, and then only if asked. About 10 percent provide no contract at all—and no laws require them to do so. The GAO criticisms didn't end there. The agency cited one Florida contract that made a fuzzy promise to "meet your needs" as an illness progressed. The agreement then specified "changes in physical or mental condition" as reasons for immediate discharge. The GAO further found that 27 percent of the facilities it surveyed had been cited for five or more problems related to quality of care or consumer protection issues, ranging from poor hygiene to failing to notify a doctor when a resident fell.

The government is taking notice. The Senate Special Committee on Aging has asked the nation's 50 governors for details about their states' consumer protection provisions for assisted living. And more states are regulating admissions agreements.

If you're on the consumer end of a contract worth hundreds of thousands of dollars, however, you need help now. A good starting point is the federal government's Long-Term Care Ombudsman program, which can be reached via the Elder Care Locator (1-800-677-1116). With volunteers in every state, the program puts consumers in touch with agencies that can help them find ALFs—or resolve complaints against them. Checklists containing questions to ask when reviewing ALFs are available from CCAL (703-841-2333; www.ccal.org), ALFA (703-691-8100; www.alfa.org), and the American Health Care Association's National Center for Assisted Living (www.ncal.org). The American Association of Retired Persons (202-434-2277; www.aarp.org) offers a publication, *Assisted Living: Weighing the Options*.

Before choosing your option, do a self-assessment, compare fees, check personal services provided, clarify reasons for discharge, and check the owner-corporation's financial strength. Also, ask about manager and staff turnover and training. If necessary, contact your ombudsman and ask about the facility's grievance procedures.

Finally, visit your aging parent often. It's not only the right thing to do, but it will keep the staff on their toes.

Source: Adapted from Joan Oleck, "Where to Find a Helping Hand," *BusinessWeek*, July 19, 1999, pp. 132–34. Reprinted by special permission. © 1999 McGraw-Hill Companies Inc.

retired people. But it is actually a package of protection, providing retirement, survivors', and disability benefits. The package protects you and your family while you work and after you retire. Today more than 48 million people, almost one out of every six Americans, collect over $518 billion in some kind of Social Security benefit.[3] The Social Security Administration estimates that 47 percent of individuals age 65 and older would live in poverty without Social Security benefits, four times as many as live in poverty today.

Social Security should not be the only source of your retirement income, however. It should be only a small part of your plan, or you won't live a very exciting retired life. Even the Social Security Administration cautions that Social Security was never intended to provide 100 percent of retirement income.

DID YOU KNOW?

The percentage of middle-class Americans who don't believe they can count on Social Security to provide them with income for their retirements: 61 percent.
Furthermore, 20 percent say they have yet to even begin planning for the golden years.

Source: BusinessWeek, February 14, 2005, p. 10; Data: ING U.S. Financial Services.

WHEN AND WHERE TO APPLY   Most people qualify for reduced Social Security retirement benefits at age 62; widows or widowers can begin collecting Social Security benefits earlier.

Three months before you retire, apply for Social Security benefits by telephoning the Social Security office at 1-800-772-1213. The payments will not start unless you apply for them. If you apply late, you risk losing benefits.

WHAT INFORMATION WILL YOU NEED?
The Social Security office will tell you what proof you need to establish your particular case. Generally, you will be asked to provide the following:

- Proof of your age.
- Your Social Security card or Social Security number.
- Your W-2 withholding forms for the past two years.
- Your marriage license if you are applying for your spouse's benefits.
- The birth certificates of your children if you are applying for their benefits.

WHAT IF YOU RETIRE AT 62 INSTEAD OF 65?   Your Social Security benefits will be reduced if you retire before age 65. Currently there is a permanent reduction of five-ninths of 1 percent for each month you receive payments before age 65. Thus, if you retire at 62, your monthly payments will be permanently reduced by 20 percent of what they would be if you waited until 65 to retire. However, if you wait until 65 to collect Social Security, your benefits will not decrease. If you work after 65, your benefits will increase by one-fourth of 1 percent for each month past age 65 that you delay retirement, but only up to age 70.

Because of longer life expectancies, the full retirement age will be increased in gradual steps until it reaches 67. This change started in 2003 and affects people born in 1938 and later. Look at Exhibit 18–7 on page 585 to determine your full retirement age.

ESTIMATING YOUR RETIREMENT BENEFITS   Beginning in 1999, the Social Security Administration automatically provides a history of your earnings and an estimate of your future monthly benefits. The statement includes an estimate, in today's dollars, of how much you will get each month from Social Security when you retire—at age 62, 65, or 70—based on your earnings to date and your projected future earnings. Use the accompanying Financial Planning for Life's Situations feature on page 585 to estimate your potential monthly benefits.

HOW TO BECOME ELIGIBLE   To qualify for Social Security retirement benefits, you must have the required number of quarters of coverage. The number of quarters you need depends on your year of birth. People born after 1928 need 40 quarters to qualify for benefits.

Financial Planning for Life's Situations

CHOOSING A SOCIAL SECURITY BENEFIT CALCULATOR

Use any of the three calculators below to estimate your potential benefit amounts using different retirement dates and different levels of potential future earnings. The calculators will show your retirement benefits as well as disability and survivor benefit amounts on your record if you should become disabled or die today.

- The Quick and Online calculators can be used from the screen. Mac users can use the Online Calculator.

- The Detailed Calculator must be downloaded. You can download the Mac version of the Detailed Calculator from ftp.ssa.gov/pub/oact/ anypiamac.sea.hqx.

- Calculator estimates will differ from those on your Social Security Statement if you use different assumptions.

- If you are eligible for a pension based on work that was not covered by Social Security, your benefit amount may be reduced.

1. **Quick Calculator.** Simple, rough estimate calculator. You input your date of birth and this year's earnings. (You must be over age 21 to use this calculator.)

2. **Online Calculator.** You input your date of birth and your complete earnings history. You may project your future earnings. (This calculation is similar to that shown on your Social Security Statement.)

3. **Detailed Calculator.** This program provides the most precise estimates. It must be downloaded and installed on your computer. (Includes reduction for WEP).

Source: www.socialsecurity.gov/planners/calculators.htm, April 15, 2005.

TAXABILITY OF SOCIAL SECURITY BENEFITS   Up to 85 percent of your Social Security benefits may be subject to federal income tax for any year in which your adjusted gross income plus your nontaxable interest income and one-half of your Social Security benefits exceed a base amount. For current information, telephone the Internal Revenue Service at 1-800-829-3676 for Publication 554, *Tax Benefits for Older Americans,* and Publication 915, *Tax Information on Social Security.*

Year of Birth	Full Retirement Age
1937 or earlier	65
1938	65 and 2 months
1939	65 and 4 months
1940	65 and 6 months
1941	65 and 8 months
1942	65 and 10 months
1943–54	66
1955	66 and 2 months
1956	66 and 4 months
1957	66 and 6 months
1958	66 and 8 months
1959	66 and 10 months
1960 and later	67

If your full retirement age is above 65 (that is, you were born after 1937), you will still be able to take your retirement benefits at age 62, but the reduction in your benefit amount will be greater than it is for people retiring now.

Exhibit **18-7**

Age to receive full Social Security benefits

Because of longer life expectancies, the full retirement age will be increased in gradual steps until it reaches 67.

Source: *Social Security: Understanding the Benefits* (Washington, DC: Social Security Administration, January 2005), p. 10.

585

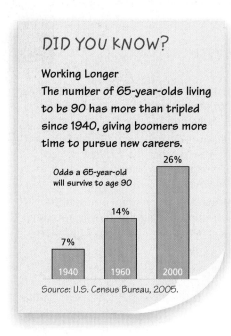

IF YOU WORK AFTER YOU RETIRE   Your Social Security benefits may be reduced if you earn above a certain amount a year, depending on your age and the amount you earn. You will receive all of your benefits for the year if your employment earnings do not exceed the annual exempted amount.

BENEFITS INCREASE AUTOMATICALLY   Social Security benefits increase automatically each January if the cost of living increased during the preceding year. Each year, the cost of living is compared with that of the year before. If it has increased, Social Security benefits increase by the same percentage.

SPOUSE'S BENEFITS   The full benefit for a spouse is one-half of the retired worker's full benefit. If your spouse takes benefits before age 65, the amount of the spouse's benefit is reduced to a low of 37.5 percent at age 62. However, a spouse who is taking care of a child who is under 16 or has a disability gets full (50 percent) benefits, regardless of age.

If you are eligible for both your own retirement benefits and for benefits as a spouse, Social Security pays your own benefit first. If your benefit as a spouse is higher than your retirement benefit, you'll get a combination of benefits equal to the higher spouse benefit.

INTERNET ACCESS   To view and print the Social Security Administration's publications, forms, reports, and program history, with links to information for employers, employees, children, parents, and teachers, visit the agency at www.ssa.gov.

THE FUTURE OF SOCIAL SECURITY   According to the Social Security Administration, the Social Security program is financially sound. The Social Security taxes received in recent years exceeded the Social Security benefits that were paid. Such surpluses are expected to continue until the year 2017, at which time a sizable reserve fund is expected to exist.

However, many people are concerned about the future of Social Security. They contend that enormous changes since Social Security started over 70 years ago have led to promises that are impossible to keep. Longer life expectancies mean retirees collect benefits over a greater number of years. More workers are retiring early, thus entering the system sooner and staying longer. The flood of baby boomers who will begin retiring early in the 21st century will mean fewer workers to contribute to the system. In 1945, 42 workers supported every recipient. By 2005, that number had dropped to three. The Social Security Administration estimates the number will drop to two workers by 2050 (see Exhibit 18–8).

Exhibit **18-8**

The number of workers per beneficiary has plummeted

Source: Social Security Administration, www.ssa.gov, May 23, 2005.

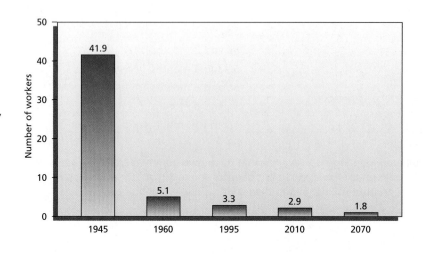

Financial Planning for Life's Situations

HOW TO FIX SOCIAL SECURITY

The many plans to deal with the predicted shortfall in promised Social Security benefits fall into three main categories.

RAISE TAXES, TRIM BENEFITS
Moderates and liberals alike figure the shortfall can be fixed with some combination of modest tax hikes coupled with some gradual reduction of the benefit.

Hiking Taxes. Lift the 6.2 percent rate workers and employers each now pay on the first $90,000 of wages. Or the taxable wage base could be raised to, say, $150,000, a step Bush and some Republicans may back. Some Democrats would use the estate tax, which expires in 2010, to help fund the shortfall, a nonstarter among Republicans.

Cutting Benefits. The retirement age is already due to rise to 67 for those born in 1960 or later and could be extended to 70. A variation: Adjust annual benefits to reflect longer life expectancy.

THE PRIVATE-ACCOUNT FIX
The idea: Tap the power of the stock market to fill Social Security's $3.7 trillion shortfall. Accounts would earn higher returns than the U.S. bonds that now fund the system.

Bush Model. Workers would reduce their payroll taxes by one-third and invest the money in individual accounts. The

promised basic benefit would be cut by indexing to inflation. Strongly backed by GOP and business; opposed by Democrats, labor, and senior groups.

Add-On-Accounts. All payroll taxes would still go to the Social Security fund, but workers would get incentives to save other income for retirement. Democrats like them, but such IRA-like savings plans would not fix Social Security's funding problem.

THE DO-NOTHING APPROACH
Optimists point out that the shortfall won't occur if the U.S. economy and population continue to grow at their historic rates over the next 75 years.

What Crunch? Some say the official projections are based on extremely conservative assumptions about economic growth that have been adjusted every year since the mid-1990s' economic and immigration booms. Each time, the crunch date for Social Security has been pushed into the future. Since any shortage wouldn't hit until 2042—or even 2052—why not wait to see what scenario plays out?

Source: *BusinessWeek*, January 24, 2005, pp. 66–67.

In early 2005 President George W. Bush suggested the most sweeping change to the Social Security program since its inception: Let the stock market help fix it. Is he right? Are private accounts really a good idea? Are there other options to fix Social Security? In the meantime, read the accompanying Financial Planning for Life's Situations feature as the debate continues.

OTHER PUBLIC PENSION PLANS

Besides Social Security, the federal government administers several other retirement plans (for federal government and railroad employees). Employees covered under these plans are not covered by Social Security. The Veterans Administration provides pensions for many survivors of men and women who died while in the armed forces and disability pensions for eligible veterans. The Railroad Retirement System is the only retirement system administered by the federal government that covers a single private industry. Many state, county, and city governments operate retirement plans for their employees.

Social Security is the most widely used source of retirement income.

The Economic Growth and Tax Relief Reconciliation Act (the EGTRRA) was passed by Congress in 2001. The act is the largest tax cut in two decades and is estimated to cut federal taxes by $1.35 trillion through 2011. Among other provisions, the act increases possible contributions to retirement accounts. However, as enacted, the entire act will expire after December 31, 2010. The new law introduces significant changes that affect retirement and estate planning.

EMPLOYER PENSION PLANS

Another possible source of retirement income is the pension plan your company offers. With employer plans, your employer contributes to your retirement benefits, and sometimes you contribute too. Contributions and earnings on those contributions accumulate tax free until you receive them.

Since private pension plans vary, you should find out (1) when you become eligible for pension benefits and (2) what benefits you will be entitled to. Most employer plans are defined-contribution or defined-benefit plans.

DEFINED-CONTRIBUTION PLAN   Over the last two decades, the defined-contribution plan has grown rapidly while the number of defined-benefit plans has generally dropped. A **defined-contribution plan** has an individual account for each employee; therefore, these plans are sometimes called *individual account plans*. The plan document describes the amount the employer will contribute, but it does not promise any particular benefit. When a plan participant retires or otherwise becomes eligible for benefits, the benefit is the total amount in the participant's account, including past investment earnings on amounts put into the account.

Defined-contribution plans include the following:

1. *Money-purchase pension plans.* Your employer promises to set aside a certain amount for you each year, generally a percentage of your earnings.
2. *Stock bonus plans.* Your employer's contribution is used to buy stock in your company for you. The stock is usually held in trust until you retire, at which time you can receive your shares or sell them at their fair market value.
3. *Profit-sharing plans.* Your employer's contribution depends on the company's profits.
4. *Salary reduction or 401(k) plans.* Under a **401(k) plan,** your employer makes nontaxable contributions to the plan for your benefit and reduces your salary by the same amounts. Sometimes your employer matches a portion of the funds contributed by you. If your employer is a tax-exempt institution such as a hospital, university, or museum, the salary reduction plan is called a *Section 403(b) plan.* Or, if you are a government employee, you may have a *Section 457 plan.* These plans are often referred to as **tax-sheltered annuity (TSA) plans.**

The EGTRRA of 2001 increased the employee contribution limit for 401(k) and other employer-sponsored retirement plans. For example, you can contribute $14,000 to your 401(k), 403(b), or Section 457(b) plan in 2005 ($18,000 if you are 50 or older). This new provision is intended to allow older workers to make up for lost time and catch up on their contributions. Notice that contribution limits increase, as shown in the table below.

Year	Maximum Contribution: Under 50	Maximum Contribution: Over 50
2005	14,000	18,000
2006	15,000	20,000
2007–2010	*	*
2011	10,500	10,500

*Indexed for inflation, rising in $500 increments.

defined-contribution plan A plan—profit sharing, money purchase, Keogh, or 401(k)—that provides an individual account for each participant; also called an *individual account plan.*

401(k) (TSA) plan A plan under which employees can defer current taxation on a portion of their salary.

AN EXAMPLE: HOW FUNDS ACCUMULATE

All earnings in a tax-sheltered annuity grow without current federal taxation. Dollars saved on a pretax basis while your earnings grow tax deferred will enhance the growth of your funds (see Exhibit 18–9).

TAX BENEFITS OF A TSA   With a TSA, your investment earnings are tax deferred. Your savings compound at a faster rate and provide you with a greater sum than in an account without this advantage. Ordinary income taxes will be due when you receive the income. The following table illustrates the difference between saving in a conventional savings plan and a tax-deferred TSA for a single person earning $28,000 a year. Notice how you can increase your take-home pay with a TSA.

> **DID YOU KNOW?**
>
> The median balance of the country's 60 million 401(k)s is just $50,000. And a staggering half of households headed by 50-to-60-year-olds have $10,000 or less in their accounts.
>
> Source: *BusinessWeek*, April 25, 2005, p. 110

	Without a TSA	With a TSA
Your income	$28,000	$28,000
TSA contribution	− 0	− 2,400
Taxable income	$28,000	$25,600
Estimated federal income taxes	− 5,319	− 4,647
Gross take-home pay	$22,681	$20,953
After-tax savings contributions	− 2,400	− 0
Net take-home pay	$20,281	$20,953
Increase in take-home pay with a TSA		$672

vesting An employee's right to at least a portion of the benefits accrued under an employer pension plan, even if the employee leaves the company before retiring.

What happens to your benefits under an employer pension plan if you change jobs? One of the most important aspects of such plans is vesting. **Vesting** is your right to at least a portion of the benefits you have accrued under an employer pension plan (within certain limits), even if you leave the company before you retire.

Financial Engines Inc. provides impartial investment advice, especially for those participating in 401(k) plans. Visit Financial Engines at **www.financialengines.com.** 401k.com provides investment education, market analysis tools, and resources for retirement investing. Visit their Web site at **www.401k.com.**

Exhibit 18-9

An early start + tax-deferred growth = greater savings

All earnings in a tax-sheltered annuity grow without current federal taxation.

Source: Massachusetts Mutual Life Insurance Company.

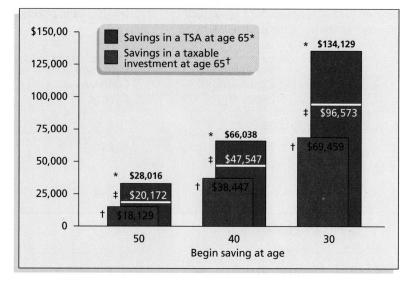

*Tax-deferred growth: Assumes a 28 percent tax bracket, a $100 contribution per month, and a 6 percent tax-deferred annual return.
†Taxable growth: Assumes a 28 percent tax bracket, a $72 contribution ($100 − $28 paid in taxes) per month, and a 6 percent taxable annual return (a 4.32 percent after-tax earnings rate). A 10 percent federal tax penalty may be due on amounts withdrawn before age 59½.
‡Net after 28 percent tax at retirement.

defined-benefit plan A plan that specifies the benefits the employee will receive at the normal retirement age.

DEFINED-BENEFIT PLAN   In a **defined-benefit plan,** the plan document specifies the benefits promised to the employee at the normal retirement age. The plan itself does not specify how much the employer must contribute annually. The plan's actuary determines the annual employer contribution required so that the plan fund will be sufficient to pay the promised benefits as each participant retires. If the fund is inadequate, the employer must make additional contributions. Because of their actuarial aspects, defined-benefit plans tend to be more complicated and more expensive to administer than defined-contribution plans.

Companies nationwide are switching their retirement plans to defined contributions from defined benefits. "Paternalistic employers are dying fast—if they're not already dead," says an actuary with an international consulting firm. The result is that "the shift to defined contributions has forced employees to take more responsibility for retirement. They have discretion as to how to invest the money and must make substantive decisions about their own financial futures." It is estimated that in 2005, employees managed $1.5 trillion of their own retirement money in 401(k) retirement plans. Exhibit 18–10 compares important features of defined-benefit and defined-contribution plans.

For retirement planning publications from the Pension Benefits Guarantee Corporation (PBGC), visit **www.pbgc.gov/retire/default.**

PLAN PORTABILITY   Some pension plans allow portability. This feature enables you to carry earned benefits from one employer's pension plan to another's when you change jobs.

The Employee Retirement Income Security Act of 1974 (ERISA) sets minimum standards for pension plans in private industry and protects more than 50 million workers. Under this act, the federal government has insured part of the payments promised to retirees from private defined-benefit pensions. ERISA established the Pension Benefit Guaranty Corporation (PBGC), a quasi-governmental agency, to provide pension insurance. The PBGC protects employees' pension to some degree if a firm defaults. For example, in 2005 United Airlines and U.S. Airways terminated their defined-benefit plans

Exhibit **18–10**   Comparison of defined-benefit and defined-contribution plans

	Defined-Benefit	Defined-Contribution—401(k)
Determined in advance	Benefit after retirement	Contributions while working
Payment in retirement	Determined by employer	Dependent on investment returns
Vesting period	Usually 5 years	Usually 0–2 years
When accrued	Greatest wealth accrues at end of career	Evenly, throughout career
Funding	Employer	Employees and some employer matching
Portability	Difficult to transfer assets when changing employers	Easy to transfer assets when changing employers
Control of assets	Employer manages investments	Employees manage investments among choices designated by employer
Investment risk	Employer bears investment risk	Employees bear investment risk
Administrative costs	Large administrative costs when employee turnover is high	Less costly for firms to administer with an increasingly mobile workforce
Risk of default	PBGC protects funds to some degree if firm defaults	Assets belong to employees and are protected from employer default

Source: Federal Reserve Bank of Dallas, *Southwest Economy,* September/October 2004, p. 8.

in bankruptcy. The PBGC will pay workers and retirees with high-paying jobs at airlines with reduced pension benefits. The PBGC's board of directors includes the secretaries of the U.S. Departments of Labor, the Treasury, and Commerce.

Use the checklist in Exhibit 18–11 to help you determine what your pension plan provides and requires.

PERSONAL RETIREMENT PLANS

In addition to the retirement plans offered by Social Security, other public pension plans, and employer pension plans, many individuals have set up personal retirement plans. The two most popular personal retirement plans are individual retirement accounts (IRAs) and Keogh accounts.

INDIVIDUAL RETIREMENT ACCOUNTS (IRAs)

The **individual retirement account (IRA),** which entails the establishment of a trust or a custodial account, is a retirement savings plan created for an individual. The Taxpayer Relief Act of 1997 included several provisions designed to help you save for retirement. The act expanded rules on traditional (classic) IRAs and created several new types of IRAs.

Furthermore, the EGTRRA of 2001 increased the amount of money you can contribute to an IRA from $2,000 in 2001 to

individual retirement account (IRA) A special account in which the employee sets aside a portion of his or her income; taxes are not paid on the principal or interest until money is withdrawn from the account.

DID YOU KNOW?

If you once worked for a company that offered a traditional pension and the company went out of business, merged with another firm, or closed its plan, it's possible that you may qualify for a "lost" pension. If you are unable to contact either your old firm or its pension plan administrator, try the Pension Benefit Guaranty Corporation's pension search service at www.pbgc.gov/search.

Exhibit **18-11**   Know your pension plan checklist

A. Plan Type Checklist

My plan is a:

Defined-benefit plan

☐ Integrated with Social Security.

☐ Nonintegrated.

Defined-contribution plan

☐ Integrated with Social Security.

☐ Nonintegrated.

My Social Security benefit:

☐ Will not be deducted from my plan benefit.

☐ Will be deducted from my plan benefit to the extent of _____ percent of the Social Security benefit I am due to receive at retirement.

B. Contributions Checklist

My pension plan is financed by:

☐ Employer contributions only.

☐ Employer and employee contributions.

☐ Union dues and assessments.

I contribute to my pension plan at the rate of $_____ per 1 month 1 week 1 hour or _____ percent of my compensation.

C. Vesting Checklist

My plan provides:

☐ Full and immediate vesting.

☐ Cliff vesting.

☐ Rule of 45 vesting.

☐ Other (specify).

I need _____ more years of service to be fully vested.

D. Credited Service Checklist

I will have a year of service under my pension plan:

☐ If I work _____ hours in a 12-consecutive-month period.

☐ If I meet other requirements (specify).

The plan year (12-month period for which plan records are kept) ends on _____ of each year.

I will be credited for work performed:

☐ Before I became a participant in the plan.

☐ After the plan's normal retirement age.

As of now, _____ [date], I have earned _____ years of service toward my pension.

My plan's break-in-service rules are as follows:

_____

_____

E. Retirement Benefit Checklist

I may begin to receive full normal retirement benefits at age _____.

Working beyond the normal retirement age ☐ will ☐ will not increase the pension paid to me when I retire.

I may retire at age _____ if I have completed _____ years of service. Apart from the age requirement, I need _____ more years of service to be eligible for early retirement benefits.

The amount of my normal retirement benefit is computed as follows: _____

The amount of my early retirement benefit is computed as follows: _____

My retirement benefit will be:

☐ Paid monthly for life.

☐ Paid to me in a lump sum.

☐ Adjusted to the cost of living.

☐ Paid to my survivor in the event of my death (see "Survivors' Benefit Checklist" on page 593).

F. Disability Benefit Checklist

My plan ☐ does ☐ does not provide disability benefits.

My plan defines the term *disability* as follows:

_____

_____

To be eligible for disability retirement benefits, I must be _____ years old and must have _____ years of service.

A determination as to whether my condition meets my plan's definition of disability is made by:

☐ A doctor chosen by me.

☐ A doctor designated by the plan administrator.

☐ The Social Security Administration in deciding that I qualify for Social Security disability benefits.

Continued

Exhibit **18-11**   Know your pension plan checklist (concluded)

I must send my application for disability retirement benefits to _____ within _____ months after I stop working.

If I qualify for disability benefits, I will continue to receive benefits:

☐ For life, if I remain disabled.
☐ Until I return to my former job.
☐ As long as I am eligible for Social Security disability benefits.

G. Survivors' Benefit Checklist

My pension plan ☐ provides ☐ does not provide a joint and survivor option or a similar provision for death benefits.

My spouse and I ☐ have ☐ have not rejected in writing the joint and survivor option.

Electing the joint and survivor option will reduce my pension benefit to _____.

My survivor will receive _____ per month for life if the following conditions are met (specify): _____
_____
_____.

H. Plan Termination Checklist

My benefits ☐ are ☐ are not insured by the Pension Benefits Guaranty Corporation.

I. Benefit Application Checklist

My employer ☐ will ☐ will not automatically submit my pension application for me.

I must apply for my pension benefits ☐ on a special form that I get from _____ within _____ months ☐ before ☐ after I retire.

My application for pension benefits should be sent to _____.

I must furnish the following documents when applying for my pension benefits:
_____.

If my application for pension benefits is denied, I may appeal in writing to _____ within _____ days.

J. Suspension of Benefits Checklist

☐ I am covered by a single-employer plan or by a plan involving more than one employer that does not meet ERISA's definition of a multiemployer plan.
☐ I am covered by a multiemployer plan as that term is defined in ERISA.

Source: *Know Your Pension Plan* (Washington, DC: U.S. Department of Labor, 2005).

$5,000 in 2008. As with 401(k), 403(b), and 457 plans, if you are 50 or older, you can contribute $500 more than the regular limits starting in 2002. As shown in the table below, the additional amount increases to $1,000 beginning in 2006.

Year	IRA Contribution Limit for 50 and Under	IRA Contribution Limit for 50 and Older
2005	4,000	4,500
2006–2007	4,000	5,000
2008 and after*	5,000	6,000

*Adjusted for inflation after 2008, rising in $500 increments.

To encourage lower-income workers, the new law provides a temporary credit for contributions to IRAs, 401(k)s, and other employer-sponsored retirement plans. This credit, depending on your income, ranges from 10 to 50 percent of the contribution and is available from 2002 to 2006. The maximum annual contribution eligible for the credit is $2,000. The credit is available only if your adjusted gross income (AGI) is $50,000 or less on a joint return, $37,500 for heads of households, and $25,000 for singles.

Sheet 64
Retirement plan comparison

Whether or not you are covered by a pension plan, you can still make nondeductible IRA contributions, and all of the income your IRA earns will compound tax deferred until you withdraw money from the IRA. Remember, the biggest benefit of an IRA lies in its tax-deferred earnings growth; the longer the money accumulates tax deferred, the bigger the benefit.

Exhibit 18–12 shows the power of tax-deferred compounding of earnings, an important advantage offered by an IRA. Consider how compounded earnings transformed the lives of two savers, Abe and Ben. As the exhibit shows, Abe regularly invested $2,000 a year in an IRA for 10 years, from ages 25 to 35. Then Abe sat back and let compounding work its magic. Ben started making regular $2,000 annual contributions at age 35 and contributed for 30 years until age 65. As you can see, Abe retired with a much larger nest egg—over $192,000 more than Ben's. Moral? Get an early start on your plan for retirement.

Your investment opportunities for IRA funds are not limited to savings accounts and certificates of deposit. You can put your IRA funds in many kinds of investments—mutual funds, annuities, stocks, bonds, U.S.-minted gold and silver coins, real estate, and so forth. Only investments in life insurance, precious metals, collectibles, and securities bought on margin are prohibited.

Regular (Traditional or Classic) IRA   This arrangement lets you contribute up to the amounts shown in the table on page 593. Whether the contribution is tax deductible depends on your tax filing status, your income, and your participation in an employer-provided retirement plan.

Roth IRA   With a *Roth IRA,* contributions are not tax deductible, but earnings accumulate tax free. You may contribute up to the amounts shown above (reduced by the amount contributed to a traditional IRA) if you are a single taxpayer with an AGI of less than $95,000 or less than $150,000 if you are filing jointly. You can make contributions even after age 70½. Five years after you establish your Roth IRA, you can take tax-free, penalty-free distributions if you are at least 59½ or will use the fund for first-time home buyer expenses.

Your Roth IRA is exclusively for you. Your interest in the account is nonforfeitable. You can't borrow from your Roth IRA. If you use your Roth IRA as collateral for a loan, the part you pledge as collateral will be taxed as a withdrawal.

fyi

Retirement and financial planning online resources, such as booklets and brochures from government and private sources, are available at **www.aoa.gov/retire.**

You may convert your traditional IRA to a Roth IRA. Depending on your current age and your anticipated tax bracket in retirement, it may be a good idea to convert. Is a tax-deductible IRA or a Roth IRA better for you? If you are saving for a first-time home purchase or retirement at age 59½, and these events are at least five years away, the Roth IRA allows for penalty-free withdrawals as well as tax-free distributions.

Spousal IRA   A *spousal IRA* lets you contribute up to the amounts shown in the table on behalf of your nonworking spouse if you file a joint tax return. As in the traditional IRA, whether or not this contribution is tax deductible depends on your income and on whether you or your spouse participates in an employer-provided retirement plan.

Rollover IRA   A *rollover IRA* is a traditional IRA that accepts rollovers of all or a portion of your taxable distribution from a retirement plan or from another IRA. A rollover IRA may also let you roll over to a Roth IRA. To avoid a mandatory 20 percent federal income tax withholding, the rollover must be made directly to a similar employer-provided retirement plan or to an IRA. If you receive the money yourself, you must roll it over within 60 days. However, you will receive only 80 percent of the

Exhibit **18-12**   Tackling the trade-offs (saving now versus saving later)

Get an early start on your plan for retirement.

	Saver Abe				Saver Ben		
Age	Years	Contributions	Year-End Value	Age	Years	Contributions	Year-End Value
25	1	$2,000	$2,188	25	1	$ 0	$ 0
26	2	2,000	4,580	26	2	0	0
27	3	2,000	7,198	27	3	0	0
28	4	2,000	10,061	28	4	0	0
29	5	2,000	13,192	29	5	0	0
30	6	2,000	16,617	30	6	0	0
31	7	2,000	20,363	31	7	0	0
32	8	2,000	24,461	32	8	0	0
33	9	2,000	28,944	33	9	0	0
34	10	2,000	33,846	34	10	0	0
35	11	0	37,021	35	11	2,000	2,188
36	12	0	40,494	36	12	2,000	4,580
37	13	0	44,293	37	13	2,000	7,198
38	14	0	48,448	38	14	2,000	10,061
39	15	0	52,992	39	15	2,000	13,192
40	16	0	57,963	40	16	2,000	16,617
41	17	0	63,401	41	17	2,000	20,363
42	18	0	69,348	42	18	2,000	24,461
43	19	0	75,854	43	19	2,000	28,944
44	20	0	82,969	44	20	2,000	33,846
45	21	0	90,752	45	21	2,000	39,209
46	22	0	99,265	46	22	2,000	45,075
47	23	0	108,577	47	23	2,000	51,490
48	24	0	118,763	48	24	2,000	58,508
49	25	0	129,903	49	25	2,000	66,184
50	26	0	142,089	50	26	2,000	74,580
51	27	0	155,418	51	27	2,000	83,764
52	28	0	169,997	52	28	2,000	93,809
53	29	0	185,944	53	29	2,000	104,797
54	30	0	203,387	54	30	2,000	116,815
55	31	0	222,466	55	31	2,000	129,961
56	32	0	243,335	56	32	2,000	144,340
57	33	0	266,162	57	33	2,000	160,068
58	34	0	291,129	58	34	2,000	177,271
59	35	0	318,439	59	35	2,000	196,088
60	36	0	348,311	60	36	2,000	216,670
61	37	0	380,985	61	37	2,000	239,182
62	38	0	416,724	62	38	2,000	263,807
63	39	0	455,816	63	39	2,000	290,741
64	40	0	498,574	64	40	2,000	320,202
65	41	0	545,344	65	41	2,000	352,427
		$20,000				$62,000	

Value at retirement*	$545,344	Value at retirement*	$352,427
Less total contributions	−20,000	Less total contributions	−62,000
Net earnings	$525,344	Net earnings	$290,427

*The table assumes a 9 percent fixed rate of return, compounded monthly, and no fluctuation of the principal. Distributions from an IRA are subject to ordinary income taxes when withdrawn and may be subject to other limitations under IRA rules.
Source: *The Franklin Investor* (San Mateo, CA: Franklin Distributors Inc., January 1989).

amount you request as a distribution (distribution minus the mandatory 20 percent withholding tax). Unless you add additional money to the rollover accumulation to equal the 20 percent withheld, the IRS will consider the 20 percent withheld to be taxable income. If you are under 59½, the 20 percent withholding will be considered an early distribution subject to a 10 percent penalty tax. The 80 percent you roll over will not be taxed until you take it out of the IRA.

The 2001 law made retirement savings more portable, permitting workers to roll money between 401(k)s, 403(b)s, and governmental 457s. That's especially good now for those with a 457. Before, you could not even transfer savings into an IRA when you left a job. You can now also roll regular deductible IRA savings into a 401(k). Beginning in 2003, employers can help workers set up IRAs at the workplace. Better yet, in 2006 employers may be able to offer Roth-style 401(k)s or 403(b)s. You can then split contributions between a regular 401(k) and one similar to a Roth.

Education IRA   The Education IRA, renamed the *Coverdell Education Savings Account* after the late Senator Paul Coverdell, has also been enhanced. You can now give $2,000 a year to each child—up from $500—for the Education IRA. These accounts grow tax-free and can be invested any way you choose. Coverdells can now be used for elementary and secondary school costs, including books, tuition, and tutoring. And more families can set up Coverdells, thanks to higher income limits. A married couple can contribute the full $2,000 if its AGI is $190,000 or less, up from $160,000 in 2001.[4]

Simplified Employee Pension Plans–IRA (SEP–IRA)   A *SEP–IRA plan* is simply an individual retirement account funded by the employer. Each employee sets up an IRA account at a bank or a brokerage house. Then the employer makes an annual contribution of up to $40,000. A glitch in the EGTRRA limits the deduction to 15 percent of the first $200,000 in self-employment, or $30,000, but Congress is expected to correct that.[5]

The SEP–IRA is the simplest type of retirement plan if you are fully or partially self-employed. Your contributions, which can vary from year to year, are tax deductible, and earnings accumulate on a tax-deferred basis. A SEP–IRA has no IRS filing requirements, so paperwork is minimal.

Exhibit 18–13 summarizes various IRA options.

IRA Withdrawals   When you retire, you will be able to withdraw your IRA in a lump sum, withdraw it in installments over your life expectancy, or place it in an annuity that guarantees payments over your lifetime. If you take the lump sum, the entire amount will be taxable as ordinary income and the only tax break you will have is standard five-year income averaging. IRA withdrawals made before age 59½ are subject to a 10 percent tax in addition to ordinary income tax, unless the participant dies or becomes disabled. You can avoid this tax if you roll over your IRA. Read the accompanying Advice from a Pro feature on page 598 to avoid pitfalls in taking IRA distributions.

You cannot keep money in most retirement plans indefinitely. Except for Roth IRAs, most tax-qualified retirement plans, including 403(b), 401(k), and other IRAs, are required by the IRS to begin what is known as "minimum lifetime distributions" at age 70½. If you have retired, you must either receive the entire balance of your tax-qualified plan or start receiving periodic distributions by April 1 of the year following the year in which you reach 70½ or retire, if later.

DID YOU KNOW?

Employees don't follow the rules of investing ... but they still manage to match the pros.

- The average employee has ten 401(k) investment options, but chooses fewer than three.
- 15 percent of employees have more than 90 percent of their 401(k) assets in their company's stock.
- 28 percent of workers in their 20s have no stock in their 401(k)s.

Average annual returns, 1990 to 1998:

- 401(k)s: 10.77 percent.
- Traditional pension plans: 10.84 percent.

Source: *BusinessWeek*, June 10, 2002, p. 12; using data from Watson Wyatt, Princeton Research Associates, and Employee Research Institute.

Type of Plan	Plan Features
Regular or Traditional IRA	• Tax-deferred interest and earnings. • Annual limit on individual contributions. • Limited eligibility for tax-deductible contributions.
Roth IRA	• Tax-deferred interest and earnings. • Annual limit on individual contributions. • Withdrawals are tax free in specific cases. • Contributions do not reduce current taxes.
Spousal IRA	• Tax-deferred interest and earnings. • Both working spouse and nonworking spouse can contribute up to the annual limit. • Limited eligibility for tax-deductible contributions.
Rollover IRA	• Traditional IRA that accepts rollovers of all or a portion of your taxable distribution from a retirement plan. • You can roll over to a Roth IRA.
Education IRA	• Tax-deferred interest and earnings. • 10% early withdrawal penalty is waived when money is used for higher-education expenses. • Annual limit on individual contributions. • Contributions do not reduce current taxes.
Employer-sponsored retirement plan (SEP–IRA)	• "Pay yourself first" payroll reduction contributions. • Pretax contributions. • Tax-deferred interest and earnings.

Exhibit 18–13

Summary of IRA options

Sources: Adapted from "12 Easy Retirement Planning Tips for Women," VALIC, An American General Company, April 1998, p. 20; and *BusinessWeek,* January 28, 2002, p. 111.

The amount of the minimum required distribution is based on your life expectancy at the time of the distribution. The IRS provides single- and joint-life expectancy tables for calculating required distribution amounts. The penalties for noncompliance in this case are severe. Insufficient distributions may be subject to an excise tax of 50 percent on the amount not withdrawn as required.

KEOGH PLANS   The new tax package of 2001 did not forget the self-employed. A **Keogh plan,** also known as a *self-employed retirement plan,* is a qualified pension plan developed for self-employed people and their employees. Generally, Keogh plans cannot discriminate in favor of a self-employed person or any employee. Both defined-contribution and defined-benefit Keogh plans have tax-deductible contribution limits, and other restrictions also apply to Keogh plans. Therefore, you should obtain professional tax advice before using this type of retirement plan. Whether you have an employer pension plan or a personal retirement plan, you must start withdrawing at age 70½ or the IRS will charge you a penalty.

Keogh plan A plan in which tax-deductible contributions fund the retirement of self-employed people and their employees; also called a *self-employed retirement plan.*

Advice from a Pro

HOW TO DODGE IRA PITFALLS

For years, you've been stashing money in 401(k)s and individual retirement accounts. But soon after you turn 70½, the Internal Revenue Service requires you to start taking it out. The rules are complex, and penalties can be stiff. To help you avoid costly mistakes, here's some advice from IRA expert Ed Slott.

WHAT ARE SOME COMMON MISTAKES?

For most people, the date you're required to begin taking withdrawals is April 1 of the year following the year in which you turn 70½. So if you turn 70½ this year, the IRS gives you until April 1 of 2005 to start. But it's a mistake to wait, because you'll have to take two distributions in 2005—one covering your first year of required distributions and the other covering your second. It's better to take your first distribution in 2004. That way you separate the distributions into two tax years and generally lower your income—and your tax bill—in each year.

CAN YOU DELAY DISTRIBUTIONS IF YOU'RE STILL WORKING AT 70½?

You don't have to take distributions from your employer's 401(k) plan. But when it comes to IRAs and 401(k)s from past employers, you can't escape.

IF YOU HAVE SEVERAL ACCOUNTS, DO YOU HAVE TO TAKE WITHDRAWALS FROM EACH?

If you have more than one IRA, add their balances. You can take a distribution from one account that covers all of them. Be careful not to mix 401(k)s and IRAs this way, though, since the rules require you to take money from each. Likewise, a married couple can't take money out of one spouse's account to cover the other spouse's distribution. And with more than one 401(k), you've got to take separate withdrawals from each.

ARE THERE ANY PROBLEMATIC INVESTMENTS?

Some people tie all their money up in certificates of deposit. As a result, they have to break into a CD early just to take their distribution and incur a penalty.

ANYTHING ELSE WE SHOULD KNOW?

You don't have to take distributions in cash. Say your required distribution is $10,000. If you own IBM stock in your IRA but want to hang onto it, you can transfer shares worth $10,000 to a taxable account and pay income tax on it. But when you sell the stock, remember that you already paid this tax, or you might accidentally pay the IRS twice.

Source: *BusinessWeek*, July 26, 2004, p. 84.

ANNUITIES

annuity A contract that provides an income for life.

In Chapter 12, you learned what an annuity is and how annuities provide lifelong security. You can outlive the proceeds of your IRA, your Keogh plan, or your investments, but an **annuity** provides guaranteed income for life. Who should consider an annuity? One financial planner uses them for clients who have fully funded all other retirement plan options, including 401(k), 403(b), Keogh, and profit-sharing plans, but still want more money for retirement.

You can buy an annuity with the proceeds of an IRA or a company pension, or as supplemental retirement income. You can buy an annuity with a single payment or with periodic payments. You can buy an annuity that will begin payouts immediately, or, as is more common, you can buy one that will begin payouts at a later date.

To the extent that annuity payments exceed your premiums, these payments are taxed as ordinary income as you receive them, but earned interest on annuities accumulates tax free until the payments begin. Annuities may be fixed, providing a specific income for life, or variable, with payouts above a guaranteed minimum level dependent on investment return. Either way, the rate of return on annuities is often pegged to market rates.

TYPES OF ANNUITIES
Immediate annuities are generally purchased by people of retirement age. Such annuities provide income payments at once. They are usually purchased with a lump-sum payment.

Exhibit **18-14**   Income annuity options

This exhibit gives you an approximate idea of how different income options compare. The amount of income you actually receive is based on factors such as how you invest, your age, your sex, and the income option you choose. Market conditions at any given time, especially interest rates, influence income amounts.

Income Option	Description	Common Uses	Typical Monthly Income*
Lifetime income. Also called *life income* or *life only*.	You receive income payments for the rest of your life. The income ceases upon your death.	Provides the most income per dollar invested of any lifetime option. Frequently used by single people with limited sources of additional income.	$923.71 per month for life.
Lifetime income with a minimum number of payments guaranteed. Also called *life with period certain*.	You receive income for the rest of your life. If you die before you receive a specific number of payments, your beneficiary will receive the balance of the number of income payments you choose.	Appropriate if you want a life income but dislike the risk of lost income in the event of premature death. People with heirs often consider this option.	$791.49 per month for life, 240-month minimum.
Lifetime income for two people. Also called *joint* and *survivor*.	Income payments are received for as long as either of the two people are alive. Upon the death of either person, income continues as a percentage of the original amount. Common percentages chosen for the survivor are 50, 66⅔, and 100%.	Often chosen by couples, who may choose the 100% option when there is little other income, or 50% or 66⅔% when there is other income. Lifetime income with period certain and installment refund† options are also available for joint-income plans.	$774.06 per month for as long as at least one of the people is alive, assuming the 100% option.

Note: The numbers above are hypothetical, and your actual income may differ. Only a portion of each payment would be taxable.
*Assumes a 65-year-old male with a 65-year-old spouse who invests $100,000 and begins receiving income immediately.
†In an installment refund annuity, you receive an income for the rest of your life. However, if you die before receiving as much money as you paid in, your beneficiary receives regular income until the total payments equal that amount.
Source: *Building Your Future with Annuities: A Consumer Guide* (Fidelity Investments and U.S. Department of Agriculture, August 1991), p. 12.

With *deferred annuities,* income payments start at some future date. Interest builds up on the money you deposit. Younger people often use such annuities to save money toward retirement.

A deferred annuity purchased with a lump sum is known as a *single-premium deferred annuity.* In recent years, such annuities have been popular because of the tax-free buildup during the accumulation period.

If you are buying a deferred annuity, you may wish to obtain a contract that permits flexible premiums. With such an annuity, your contributions may vary from year to year.

The cash value of your life insurance policy may be converted to an annuity. If you are over 65 and your children have completed their education and are financially self-sufficient, you may no longer need all of your life insurance coverage. An option in your life insurance policy lets you convert its cash value to a lifetime income.

OPTIONS IN ANNUITIES   You can decide on the terms under which your annuity pays you and your family. Exhibit 18–14 summarizes the major options and their uses.

Exhibit **18–15**

A comparison of variable and fixed annuities

The costs, fees, and other features of annuities differ from policy to policy.

	Variable	Fixed
Tax-deferred earnings	Yes	Yes
Variety of income options	Yes	Yes
Annual investment ceiling	No	No
Investment flexibility	Yes	No
Potential for higher returns	Yes	No
Increased investment risk	Yes	No
Hedge against inflation	Yes	No
Security of principal and earnings	No	Yes
Guaranteed interest rate	No	Yes
Control over type of investment in the annuity	Yes	No

WHICH ANNUITY OPTION IS THE BEST?   The straight life annuity gives more income per dollar of outlay than any other type. But payments stop when you die, whether a month or many years after the payout begins.

Should you get an annuity with a guaranteed return? Opinions differ. Some experts argue that it is a mistake to diminish your monthly income just to make sure your money is returned to your survivors. Some suggest that if you want to ensure that your spouse or someone else continues to receive annuity income after your death, you might choose the joint-and-survivor annuity. Such an annuity pays its installments until the death of the last designated survivor.

You have still another choice to make: how your annuity premiums are to be invested. With a fixed-dollar annuity, the money you pay is invested in bonds and mortgages that have a guaranteed return. Such an annuity guarantees you a fixed amount each payout period. With a variable annuity, the money you pay is generally invested in common stocks or other equities. The income you receive will depend on the investment results. Exhibit 18–15 compares variable and fixed annuities.

An annuity guarantees lifetime income, but you have a choice regarding the form it will take. Discuss all of the possible options with your insurance agent. The costs, fees, and other features of annuities differ from policy to policy. Ask about sales and administrative charges, purchase and withdrawal fees, and interest rate guarantees. Also, as explained in Chapter 12, be sure to check the financial health of the insurance company.

WILL YOU HAVE ENOUGH MONEY DURING RETIREMENT?

Sheet 65
Forecasting retirement income

Now that you have reviewed all the possible sources of your retirement income, estimate what your annual retirement income will be. Don't forget to inflate incomes or investments that increase with the cost of living (such as Social Security) to what they will be when you retire. (Use the inflation factor table in the Financial Planning Calculations box on page 579.) Remember, inflation is a major uncontrollable variable for retirees.

Now compare your total estimated retirement income with your total inflated retirement expenses. If your estimated income exceeds your estimated expenses and a large portion of your planned income will automatically increase with the cost of living dur-

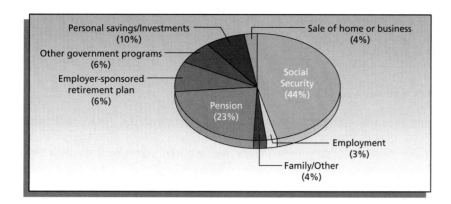

Personal savings/Investments (10%)
Sale of home or business (4%)
Other government programs (6%)
Employer-sponsored retirement plan (6%)
Social Security (44%)
Pension (23%)
Employment (3%)
Family/Other (4%)

Exhibit **18–16**

Sources of income in retirement

Social Security provides only 44 percent of the average retiree's annual income. On average, pension income accounts for about 23 percent, about half of what Social Security provides.

Source: Employee Benefit Research Institute, www.ebri.org/, May 2005.

ing your retirement, you are in good shape. (You should evaluate your plans every few years between now and retirement to be sure your planned income is still adequate to meet your planned expenses.)

If, however, your planned retirement income is less than your estimated retirement expenses, now is the time to take action to increase your retirement income. Also, if a large portion of your retirement income is fixed and will not increase with inflation, you should make plans for a much larger retirement income to meet your rising expenses during retirement.

Exhibit 18–16 summarizes the various sources of retirement income.

CONCEPT CHECK 18-5

1 What are possible sources of income for retirees?
2 What are examples of defined-contribution plans? How do they differ from defined-benefit plans?
3 What are the two most popular personal retirement plans?
4 What are annuities? What options are available in annuities? Which option is best?

Action Application   Survey retired individuals or people close to retirement to obtain information on their main sources of retirement income.

Living on Your Retirement Income

As you planned retirement, you estimated a budget or spending plan, but you may find your actual expenses at retirement are higher than anticipated.

The first step in stretching your retirement income is to make sure you are receiving all of the income to which you are entitled. Examine the possible sources of retirement income mentioned earlier to see whether you could qualify for more programs or additional benefits. What assets or valuables could you use as a cash or income source?

To stay within your income, you may also need to make some changes in your spending plans. For example, you can use your skills and time instead of your money. There are probably many things you can do yourself instead of paying someone else to do

Objective 6

Develop a balanced budget based on your retirement income.

them. Take advantage of free and low-cost recreation such as walks, picnics, public parks, lectures, museums, libraries, art galleries, art fairs, gardening, and church and club programs.

TAX ADVANTAGES

Be sure to take advantage of all the tax savings retirees receive. For more information, ask your local IRS office for a free copy of *Tax Benefits for Older Americans.* If you have any questions about your taxes, get free help from someone at the IRS. You may need to file a quarterly estimated income tax return beginning with the first quarter of your first year of retirement or arrange for withholdings on Social Security and pension payments.

WORKING DURING RETIREMENT

You may want to work part-time or start a new part-time career after you retire. Work can provide you with a greater sense of usefulness, involvement, and self-worth and may be the ideal way to add to your retirement income. You may want to pursue a personal interest or hobby, or you can contact your state or local agency on aging for information about employment opportunities for retirees.

Over 50 percent of recent retirees want to continue working part-time or even full-time after retirement, and only 11 percent are worried about outliving their financial resources. There is a rich talent pool of more than 46 million Americans in the 55 to 75 age range, over 50 percent of whom are retired—and many of them are interested in continued employment. These individuals, with their proven skills and abilities, provide a flexible, cost-effective resource that can sustain our productivity gains and economic growth. What drives many of them is the desire to remain productively engaged in life.[6]

If you decide to work part-time after you retire, you should be aware of how your earnings will affect your Social Security income. As long as you do not earn more than the annually exempt amount, your Social Security payments will not be affected. But if you earn more than the annual exempt amount, your Social Security payments will be reduced. Check with your local Social Security office for the latest information.

DID YOU KNOW?

More than half of Americans ages 65 to 74 are still in the workforce.

Completely retired (41%)
Not retired (20%)
Retired and working (38%)

Note: The chart does not add up to 100% due to rounding.

Source: National Council on the Aging, 2005.

INVESTING FOR RETIREMENT

The guaranteed-income part of your retirement fund consists of money paid into lower-yield, very safe investments. This part of your fund may already be taken care of through Social Security and retirement plans, as discussed earlier. To offset inflation, your retirement assets must earn enough to keep up with, and even exceed, the rate of inflation.

DIPPING INTO YOUR NEST EGG

When should you draw on your savings? The answer depends on your financial circumstances, your age, and how much you want to leave to your heirs. Your savings may be large enough to allow you to live comfortably on the interest alone. Or you may need to make regular withdrawals to help finance your retirement. Dipping into savings isn't wrong, but you must do so with caution.

How long would your savings last if you withdrew monthly income? If you have $10,000 in savings that earns 5.5 percent interest, compounded quarterly, you could take out $68 every month for 20 years before reducing this nest egg to zero. If you have $40,000, you could collect $224 every month for 30 years before exhausting your nest egg. For different possibilities, see Exhibit 18–17.

Exhibit 18–18 summarizes major sources of retirement income and their advantages and disadvantages. Finally, use Financial Planning for Life's Situations: Retirement Checklist on page 605 to assess your financial condition as you approach retirement.

DID YOU KNOW?

How do executives invest their retirement funds? Cautiously, according to Clark Consulting, the largest administrator of deferred compensation programs. Clark examined how 17,000 execs with $929 million in deferred-comp plans allocated their money. Approximately 67 percent was in conservative choices—fixed-rate investments, large-cap stocks, bonds, and money market. Less than 18 percent was in foreign, specialty, and other "riskier" options.

INVESTMENT OPTION	% OF ASSETS*
FIXED-RATE	26.3
LARGE-CAP STOCKS	24.9
SMALL-CAP STOCKS	10.9
BONDS	9.9
MONEY-MARKET	6.0
COMPANY STOCK	5.3
MIDCAP STOCKS	5.1
FOREIGN	4.6
BALANCED	4.2
SPECIALTY	1.5
WORLD	1.2

*Does not add up to 100% because of rounding.

BusinessWeek, March 14, 2005, p. 112.

Exhibit 18-17   Dipping into your nest egg

Dipping into savings isn't wrong; however, you must do so with caution.

Starting Amount of Nest Egg	You Can Reduce Your Nest Egg to Zero by Withdrawing This Much Each Month for the Stated Number of Years . . .					Or You Can Withdraw This Much Each Month and Leave Your Nest Egg Intact
	10 Years	15 Years	20 Years	25 Years	30 Years	
$10,000	$107	$ 81	$ 68	$ 61	$ 56	$ 46
15,000	161	121	102	91	84	69
20,000	215	162	136	121	112	92
25,000	269	202	170	152	140	115
30,000	322	243	204	182	168	138
40,000	430	323	272	243	224	184
50,000	537	404	340	304	281	230
60,000	645	485	408	364	337	276
80,000	859	647	544	486	449	368
100,000	1,074	808	680	607	561	460

Note: Based on an interest rate of 5.5 percent per year, compounded quarterly.
Source: Select Committee on Aging, U.S. House of Representatives.

Exhibit **18-18**   Major sources of retirement income: advantages and disadvantages

The income needed to live during retirement can come from various sources.

Source	Advantages	Disadvantages
Social Security		
In planning	Forced savings. Portable from job to job. Cost shared with employer.	Increasing economic pressure on the system as U.S. population ages.
At retirement	Inflation-adjusted survivorship rights.	Minimum retirement age specified. Earned income may partially offset benefits.
Employee Pension Plans		
In planning	Forced savings. Cost shared or fully covered by employer.	May not be portable. No control over how funds are managed.
At retirement	Survivorship rights.	Cost-of-living increases may not be provided on a regular basis.
Individual Saving and Investing *(including housing, IRA, and Keogh plans)*		
In planning	Current tax savings (e.g., IRAs). Easily incorporated into family (home equity). Portable. Control over management of funds.	Current needs compete with future needs. Penalty for early withdrawal (IRAs and Keoghs).
At retirement	Inflation resistant. Can usually use as much of the funds as you wish, when you wish (within certain requirements).	Some sources taxable. Mandatory minimum withdrawal restrictions (IRAs and Keoghs).
Postretirement Employment		
In planning	Special earning skills can be used as they are developed.	Technology and skills needed to keep up may change rapidly.
At retirement	Inflation resistant.	Ill health can mean loss of this income source.

RETIREMENT CHECKLIST

As you approach retirement, assess your financial condition using the following checklist. Don't wait too long, or you will miss one or more opportunities to maximize your future financial independence.

	Yes	No
1. Do you talk regularly and frankly to family members about finances and agree on your goals and the lifestyle you will prefer as you get older?	☐	☐
2. Do you know what your sources of income will be after retirement, how much to expect from each source, and when?	☐	☐
3. Do you save according to your plan, shifting from growth-producing to safe, income-producing investments?	☐	☐
4. Do you know where your health insurance will come from after retirement and what it will cover?	☐	☐
5. Do you review your health insurance and consider options such as converting to cash or investments?	☐	☐
6. Do you have your own credit history?	☐	☐
7. Do you have a current will or a living trust?	☐	☐
8. Do you know where you plan to live in retirement?	☐	☐
9. Do you anticipate the tax consequences of your retirement plans and of passing assets on to your heirs?	☐	☐
10. Do your children or other responsible family members know where your important documents are and whom to contact if questions arise?	☐	☐
11. Do you have legal documents, such as a living will or a power of attorney, specifying your instructions in the event of your death or incapacitating illness?	☐	☐

Source: Adapted from *Staying Independent,* American Express Consumer Affairs Office and IDS Financial Services Inc.

CONCEPT CHECK 18-6

1 What is the first step in stretching your retirement income?
2 How should you invest to obtain retirement income?

Action Application Outline the steps you must take to live on your retirement income and balance your retirement budget.

SUMMARY OF OBJECTIVES

Objective 1
Recognize the importance of retirement planning.
Retirement planning is important because you will probably spend many years in retirement; Social Security and a private pension may be insufficient to cover the cost of living; and inflation may erode the purchasing power of your retirement savings. Many young people are reluctant to think about retirement, but they should start retirement planning now, before they reach age 45.

Objective 2
Analyze your current assets and liabilities for retirement.
Analyze your current assets (everything you own) and your current liabilities (everything you owe). The difference between your assets and your liabilities is your net worth. Review your assets to ensure they are sufficient for retirement.

Objective 3
Estimate your retirement spending needs.
Since the spending patterns of retirees change, it is impossible to predict the exact amount of money you will need in retirement. However, you can estimate your expenses. Some of those expenses will increase; others will decrease. The expenses that are likely to be lower or eliminated are work-related expenses, clothing, housing expenses, federal income taxes, and commuting expenses.

Objective 4
Identify your retirement housing needs.
Where you live in retirement can influence your financial needs. You are the only one who can determine the location and housing that are best for you. Would you like to live in your present home or move to a new location? Consider the social aspects of moving.

Objective 5
Determine your planned retirement income.
Estimate your retirement expenses and adjust those expenses for inflation using the appropriate inflation factor. Your possible sources of income during retirement include Social Security, other public pension plans, employer pension plans, personal retirement plans, and annuities.

Objective 6
Develop a balanced budget based on your retirement income.
Compare your total estimated retirement income with your total inflated retirement expenses. If your income approximates your expenses, you are in good shape; if not, determine additional income needs and sources.

KEY TERMS

annuity 598

defined-benefit plan 590

defined-contribution plan 589

401(k) (TSA) plan 589

individual retirement account
   (IRA) 591

Keogh plan 597

reverse annuity mortgage
   (RAM) 573

vesting 589

FINANCIAL PLANNING PROBLEMS

1. *Preparing a Net Worth Statement.* Prepare your net worth statement using the guidelines presented in Exhibit 18–3. (Obj. 2)

2. *Comparing Spending Patterns during Retirement.* How will your spending patterns change during your retirement years? Compare your spending patterns with those shown in Exhibit 18–4. (Obj. 3)

3. *Evaluating Housing Options.* Which type of housing will best meet your housing needs in retirement? List the advantages and disadvantages of your choice. Choose two locations and compare the costs. (Obj. 4)

4. *Calculating IRA Contributions.* Gene and Dixie, husband and wife (ages 45 and 42), both work. They have an adjusted gross income of $40,000, and they are filing a joint income tax return. What is the maximum IRA contribution they can make? How much of that contribution is tax deductible? (Obj. 5)

5. *Calculating Net Pay and Spendable Income.* Assume your gross pay per pay period is $2,000 and you are in the 33 percent tax bracket. Calculate your net pay and spendable income in the following situations. (Obj. 5)

   a. You save $200 per pay period after paying income tax on $2,000.

   b. You save $200 per pay period in a tax-sheltered annuity.

6. *Calculating Monthly Withdrawals.* You have $50,000 in your retirement fund that is earning 5.5 percent per year, compounded quarterly. How many dollars in withdrawals per month would reduce this nest egg to zero in 20 years? How many dollars per month can you withdraw for as long as you live and still leave this nest egg intact? (Obj. 6)

FINANCIAL PLANNING ACTIVITIES

1. *Conducting Interviews.* Survey friends, relatives, and other people to get their views on retirement planning. Prepare a written report of your findings. (Obj. 1)

2. *Obtaining Information about Reverse Mortgages.* Obtain a consumer information kit from Senior Income Reverse Mortgage Corporation in Chicago (1-800-774-6266). Examine and evaluate the kit. How might a reverse mortgage help you or a family member? (Obj. 2)

3. *Using the Internet to Obtain Reverse Mortgage Information.*

   a. Visit the Web site of the American Association of Retired Persons (AARP) at www.aarp.org. Locate the AARP Home Equity Information Center, which presents basic facts about reverse mortgages. Then prepare a report on how reverse mortgages work, who is eligible, what you get, what you pay, and what other choices are available to borrowers.

   b. Visit Fannie Mae's Web site at www.fanniemae.com/ Homebuyer to find out about its reverse mortgage program.

4. *Determining Expenses during Retirement.* Read newspaper or magazine articles to determine what expenses are likely to increase and decrease during retirement. How might this information affect your retirement-planning decisions? (Obj. 3)

5. *Evaluating Retirement Housing Options.* Which type of housing will best meet your retirement needs? Is such housing available in your community? Make a checklist of the advantages and disadvantages of your housing choice. (Obj. 4)

6. *Writing Letters to Representatives in Congress.* Write a letter urging your representative in Congress to introduce or support legislation repealing the provisions of the present Social Security law that limit the earnings of Americans ages 65 to 69 who must work to provide for their needs. (Obj. 5)

7. *Requesting Personal Earnings and Benefits Statement.* Obtain Form SSA-7004 from your local Social Security office. Complete and mail the form to receive a personal earnings and benefits statement. Use the information in this statement to plan your retirement. (Obj. 5)

INTERNET CONNECTION

Planning for Your Retirement

Retirement planning can help you gain a sense of control over your financial future and security. Opening an individual retirement account (IRA) is a simple way to begin investing in your future.

Using an Internet search engine, find information on individual retirement accounts (IRAs). Complete the worksheet below and answer the questions that follow.

Net Results	
List three retirement information Web sites (site names and addresses)	
What is the difference between a traditional IRA and a Roth IRA?	
Describe the process involved in opening an IRA.	
List the eligibility requirements to opening an IRA.	
What are the penalties for withdrawal of IRA funds before age 59½?	
What is the age at which an investor is required to withdraw funds from an IRA?	

FINANCIAL PLANNING CASE

When He's Retiring but She Isn't

My husband is 53, and I am 10 years younger. During our 20-year marriage, I have been in and out of the workforce, raising children, and getting my Ph.D. in economics. Now, I plan to return to full-time employment. I am essentially just getting my career under way as my husband approaches the completion of his. None of the retirement seminars address the issue that not all husbands and wives are the same age, nor do they retire at the same time.

—e-mail from Worcester, Massachusetts

Couples with a wide age gap face a unique set of problems as they plan for retirement. They must often set aside the conventional wisdom about how much insurance they need, what they should invest in, and how to calculate their pension payouts. "Seldom do people have the same needs at the same time, but it's even harder to plan when there is a big age difference," says Deena Katz, a certified financial planner in Coral Gables, Florida.

A husband and wife approaching retirement might normally scale back their life insurance, especially if their kids are college age or older. But if the family will be depending on the income of the younger, still-working spouse, that would be a reason to increase his or her life insurance.

Spouses with big age gaps must also decide how to manage their pension money much earlier than couples who are the same age. With a younger spouse, the couple might have higher costs for a longer period of time, and their investment strategy must reflect that. "Couples must design their portfolio around their anticipated cash-flow needs, and then decide how to fund the expenses," says Stanley Ehrlich, a registered investment adviser in Clinton, New Jersey.

The husband in the Worcester couple has worked for 27 years as a computer-systems analyst at the same manufacturing company and is looking to retire within the next five years, while the wife is hoping to continue rising through the administrative ranks at the university where she works. They have paid off their mortgage and saved enough money through the husband's 401(k) to pay for college for their kids, ages 13 and 17, or retirement—but not both.

They hope to meet both financial goals by using the wife's salary to cover college costs and the husband's retirement funds to pay for day-to-day expenses. To protect her income, she will need to increase her life and disability insurance at the same time her husband decreases his. Now, she has no disability coverage, and he gets coverage through his job that protects 66 percent of his salary. They have $220,000 worth of life insurance, divided equally, but they will have to shift the balance in her favor.

Fortunately, health insurance will not be an issue, because the wife's policy will cover the husband until he qualifies for Medicare at age 65. They do both need to consider purchasing long-term care insurance, however.

As for their investment strategy, "They need to allocate their portfolio for the overall total return," and that means a high proportion of stocks, says Ehrlich. The wife must consider how long she intends to work and contribute the maximum amount to her existing retirement account. She plans to invest more aggressively than her husband—at least 60 percent in stocks. He has recently switched some money out of equities, and now more than half of his portfolio is in bonds.

When it comes to his pension payout, the husband should keep his 401(k) money in the company plan, even though he could move it to a rollover IRA. Why? Retirees from 55 to 59½ can withdraw from company plans at will and without penalties. With a rollover IRA, a retiree younger than 59½ must adhere to a strict withdrawal plan or get hit with penalties.

With his wife still working, the husband shouldn't have to draw down all his retirement stash. What's left when he's 70½ will be subject to the Internal Revenue Service's new distribution rules that took effect on January 1, 2002. These rules work to the advantage of spouses who are at least 10 years apart, says Sue Stevens, a certified financial planner in Deerfield, Illinois. They can choose a payout schedule that allows them to set up a withdrawal plan based on an average of their life expectancies instead of just his, which was previously the case. That allows the money to last longer—a comfort for anyone in this situation.

Questions

1. What unique problems do couples with a wide age gap face as they plan for retirement?

2. What are some solutions to their unique problems?

3. How does the couple in this case hope to meet both of their financial goals?

4. Do you think they both need to purchase long-term care insurance? Explain your answer.

5. What should be their investment strategy?

Source: Toddi Guttner, "When He's Retiring but She Isn't," *BusinessWeek*, December 3, 2001, p. 120.

FINANCIAL PLANNING CASE

Home Sweet Home

Last year, Inez Gardner noticed that her 87-year-old mother, Mamie, wasn't herself anymore. She would leave the phone off the hook, forget to turn off the oven, and get lost even in familiar places. Gardner, 43, an accountant with the State of Illinois, lived with her mother in Mamie's Evanston, Illinois, home. "My mother had made it clear to us years ago that she wanted to remain in her home," says Gardner. But how could she fulfill that wish and still ensure her mother's safety? It took months, but

Gardner and her brothers and sisters found a solution: a nearby adult day care center where their mother could spend each weekday engaged in a host of supervised activities, such as gardening or sculpting, then return home in the late afternoon. "I don't know how we could have helped her stay at home otherwise," says Gardner. "And she's really happy."

The following table lists several resources that can help people find services for aging family members who choose to live at home:

Resource	Description
Careguide.com www.careguide.com	Offers information and assistance in finding and paying for care.
Eldercare Locator 1-800-677-1116 www.aoa.dhhs.gov/elderpage/locator.html	Makes referrals for home care and community services.
Extendedcare.com www.extendcare.com	Search for providers and do research through its online geriatric library.
National Association for Home Care 202-547-7424 www.nahc.org	Features an extensive home care provider locator.
National Association of Professional Geriatric Care Managers 520-881-8008 www.caremanager.org	Find a member list on its Web site, or order a print directory for $15.

Questions

1. For most families, the options for elder care are so numerous that deciding which to use can be bewildering. Do you think Inez made the right choice for her mother?

2. Visit the Web sites listed in this case. What does each site offer for elderly individuals like Mamie who choose to remain at home?

Sources: Adapted from Anne Field, "The Best Old-Age Home May Be at Home," *BusinessWeek,* November 22, 1999, pp. 180–82. Reprinted by special permission. © 1999 McGraw-Hill Companies Inc.; and www.careguide.com/careguide/index.jsp, July 30, 2002.

VIDEO CASE

Planning for Retirement

Is a bad day fishing better than a good day at the office? Yes, according to a retired dad, Chuck. With his company pension, at least he didn't have to worry about money. In the good old days, if you had a decent job, you'd hang on to it, and then your company's pension combined with Social Security payments would be enough to live comfortably. Chuck's son, Rob, does not have a company pension and is not sure whether Social Security will even exist when he retires. So when it comes to retirement, the sooner you start saving, the better.

Take Maureen, a salesperson for a computer company, and Therese, an accountant for a lighting manufacturer. Both start

their jobs at age 25. Maureen starts saving for retirement right away by investing $300 a month at 9 percent until age 65. But Therese does nothing until age 35. At 35 she begins investing the same $300 a month at 9 percent until age 65. What a shocking difference! Maureen has accumulated $1.4 million, while Therese has only $553,000 in her retirement fund. The moral? The sooner you start, the more you'll have for your retirement. Women especially need to start sooner, because they typically enter the workforce later, have lower salaries, and, ultimately, lower pensions.

Laura Tarbox, owner and president of Tarbox Equity, explains how to determine your retirement needs and how your budget might change when you retire. Tarbox advises that the old rule of thumb that you need 60 to 70 percent of preretirement income is too low an estimate. She cautions that most people will want to spend very close to what they were spending before retiring. There are some expenses that might be lower, however, such as clothing for work, dry cleaning, commuting expenses, and so forth. Other expenses, though, such as insurance, travel, and recreation, may increase during retirement.

Questions

1. In the past, many workers chose to stay with their employers until retirement. What was the major reason for employees' loyalty?

2. How did Maureen amass $1.4 million for retirement, while Therese could only accumulate $553,000?

3. Why do women need to start early to save for retirement?

4. How is net worth determined?

5. What expenses may increase or decrease during retirement?

YOUR PERSONAL FINANCIAL PLANNER IN ACTION

Planning for Retirement

Long-term financial security is a common goal of most people. Retirement planning should consider both personal decisions (location, housing, activities) and financial factors (investments, pensions, living expenses).

Your Short-Term Financial Planning Activities	Resources
1. Identify personal and financial retirement needs for various stages of your life.	http://retireplan.about.com www.aarp.org www.mymoney.gov www.ssa.gov
2. Compare the benefits and costs of a traditional IRA, a Roth IRA, and other pension plans.	PFP Sheet 64 www.rothira.com www.pensionplanners.com www.401k.com www.403bwise.com
Your Long-Term Financial Planning Activities	
1. Research costs and benefits of various housing alternatives.	PFP Sheet 63 www.virtual-retirement.com
2. Estimate future retirement income needs and identify appropriate investments to meet those needs.	PFP Sheet 65 www.kiplinger.com/tools www.centura.com/tools
3. Develop a plan for expanding personal interests and increasing contributions to retirement accounts.	www.asec.org

CONTINUING CASE:

Retirement Planning

Life Situation

Pam, 48
Josh, 50
Children ages 21, 19, and 16

Financial Data

Monthly income $6,700
Assets $242,500
Living expenses $5,600
Liabilities $69,100

With two children in college, the Brocks once again find their life situation changing. Compared to five years ago, their total assets have declined due to college expenses. The Brocks' oldest child will graduate next year, but the youngest will enter college in a couple of years. The drain on the family's finances will continue.

While the family's finances are adequate, both Pam and Josh an beginning to think more about retirement. Over the years, Josh has taken advantage of different career opportunities. Today his annual salary is higher than ever. However, his employment changes have resulted in a smaller pension fund than would have been available had he remained with the same organization.

The current value of his pension plan is just over $115,000. The investment program he and Pam started almost 10 years ago is growing and is now worth about $62,000. But they still worry whether they will have enough money to finance their retirement when Josh retires in 15 years.

Questions

1. How would you assess the strengths and weaknesses of the Brocks' financial condition at this stage in their lives?

2. Since Pam is 48 and Josh is 50, what should be their major priorities as they continue planning for retirement?

3. Describe potential uses by the Brocks of *Personal Financial Planner* sheets 63–65.

19 Estate Planning

Key Concept

Identifying various kinds of wills and trusts will help you devise an estate plan that protects your interests as well as those of your family. Creating an effective estate plan will allow you to prosper during retirement and provide for your loved ones when you die.

www.mhhe.com/kdh

Digital Study Tools

Online Learning Center Study Tools for This Chapter

- Multiple-choice quiz
- Flashcards
- eLearning sessions
- Crossword puzzle
- Personal Finance Online: Retirement and Estate Planning

Student CD Study Tools for This Chapter

- Self-study software
- Narrated PowerPoint
- Personal financial planning software: Worksheets 66–69

Learning Objectives

1 Analyze the personal aspects of estate planning.

2 Assess the legal aspects of estate planning.

3 Distinguish among various types and formats of wills.

4 Appraise various types of trusts and estates.

5 Evaluate the effects of federal and state taxes on estate planning.

There's a Way—Where There's a Will

Face it: It's tough to own up to your mortality. Most of us haven't done so. Only 41 percent of all Americans have a will, and only a third of those with children have bothered to draw one up, according to a survey last year by FindLaw, a legal Web site. Even fewer have taken the time to do a full-fledged estate plan aimed at shielding heirs from the court costs, executors' fees, and estate taxes that death almost always triggers.

Of course, you already have a default estate plan, of sorts. It's a one-size-fits-all mishmash that varies according to where you live—and almost certainly won't result in what you intended. Think all of your property will be transferred naturally to your spouse when you die? In some states, only 30 percent to 50 percent goes to your spouse, and the rest is divided up among other relatives. Some may go to your kids—yes, even the financially irresponsible one. Some may go to your siblings, or even your parents, whether they need it or want it, or whether you want them to have it.

If you don't have a plan, now's a good time to get started. In 2001, Congress overhauled the estate tax law, with an eye toward repealing it, so you can at least reasonably predict that liability for the next few years. The new law, the Economic Growth and Tax Relief Reconciliation Act of 2001, gradually increases the estate tax exemption—the amount that can be passed along without paying estate tax—to $2 million in 2006 and $3.5 million in 2009. The law repeals the tax in 2010 but snaps it back to the original $1 million exemption in 2011—inviting a future Congress to make the repeal permanent.

Avoiding taxes isn't the main reason for estate plans, just a nice bonus. In fact, if you're in your 30s or 40s and in good health, you may want to stick with the basics: a will for your possessions and a living will and health care power of attorney to specify how medical decisions (such as ending life support) are to be made if you become incapacitated. It should cost $500 to $1,000.

The most pressing reason to write a will is to take care of minor children in case you and your spouse die simultaneously, or if you're a single parent. You'll want to name a guardian to bring them up—the probate court will do so if you don't—and perhaps someone else to oversee the finances this will require. You'll have to name an executor, too, to handle the estate's distribution. And your will must spell out as specifically as possible how you want your property divided.

If you know you'll keep putting it off, you can draw up a simple will in an evening using *Quicken Lawyer 2002*. This includes the software formerly known as *WillMaker* from Nolo (nolo.com). It also includes forms for living wills and medical powers of attorney. Or you can download the right forms for your state at partnershipforcaring.org.

Only 2 percent of Americans pay any estate tax at all. But don't be fooled into thinking that estate planning is only a rich person's concern or that the new laws make it unnecessary for you to address the important issues in advance. Without the basics in place, your even-modest estate could easily become a big problem for your family and heirs.

Source: Excerpted from Larry Armstrong, "There's a Way—Where There's a Will," *BusinessWeek,* April 8, 2002, pp. 81–82.

QUESTIONS

What Actions Should Be Taken?

1. What actions would you recommend for the 59 percent of Americans who have not prepared their wills?
2. What might be the major reasons for families to have a comprehensive estate plan?

What about Your Situation?

3. Have you prepared your will yet? If not, are you planning to draft your will? What type of will would you consider?
4. Does your family have an estate plan in place?

Learn More Online

Visit the National Association of Financial and Estate Planning Web site at www.nafep.com. What useful information is available that can help you with estate planning?

Why Estate Planning?

Objective 1

Analyze the personal aspects of estate planning.

estate Everything one owns.

Your **estate** consists of everything you own. While you work, your objective is to accumulate funds for your future and for your dependents. As you grow older, your point of view will change. The emphasis in your financial planning will shift from accumulating assets to distributing them wisely. Your hard-earned wealth should go to those whom you wish to support and not to the various taxing agencies.

Contrary to widely held notions, estate planning, which includes wills and trusts, is useful not only to rich and elderly people. Trusts can be used for purposes other than tax advantages, such as choosing a guardian for children and avoiding family fights over personal belongings. Furthermore, most people can afford the expense of using them.

This chapter discusses a subject most people would rather avoid: death—your own or that of your spouse. Many people give little or no thought to setting their personal and financial affairs in order.

As you learned in the previous chapter, most people today live longer than those of previous generations and have ample time to think about and plan for the future. Yet a large percentage of people do little or nothing to provide for those who will survive them.

Planning for your family's financial security in the event of your death or the death of your spouse is not easy. Therefore, the objective of this chapter is to help you initiate discussions about questions you should ask before that happens. Does your spouse, for instance, know what all of the family's resources and debts are? Does your family have enough insurance protection?

The question of whether your family can cope financially without your or your spouse's income and support is a difficult one. This chapter can't provide all of the answers, but it supplies a basis for sound estate planning for you and your family.

WHAT IS ESTATE PLANNING?

estate planning A definite plan for the administration and disposition of one's property during one's lifetime and at one's death.

Estate planning is a definite plan for the administration and disposition of one's property during one's lifetime and at one's death. Thus, it involves both handling your property while you are alive and dealing with what happens to that property after your death.

Estate planning is an essential part of retirement planning and an integral part of financial planning. It has two components. The first consists of building your estate through savings, investments, and insurance. The second involves transferring your estate, at your death, in the manner you have specified. As this chapter explains, an estate plan is usually implemented by a will and one or more trust agreements.

Nearly every adult engages in financial decision making and must keep important records. Whatever your status—single or married, male or female, taxi driver or corporate executive—you must make financial decisions that are important to you. Those decisions may be even more important to others in your family. Knowledge in certain areas and good recordkeeping can simplify those decisions.

At first, planning for financial security and estate planning may seem complicated. Although many money matters require legal and technical advice, if you and your spouse learn the necessary skills, you will find yourselves managing your money affairs more efficiently and wisely. Begin by answering the questionnaire in Financial Planning for Life's Situations: Estate Planning Checklist on page 615 to see how much you and your family know about your own money affairs. You and your family should be able to answer some of these questions. The questions can be bewildering if the subjects are unfamiliar to you, but after reading this chapter, you'll be able to answer most of them.

IF YOU ARE MARRIED

If you are married, your estate planning involves the interests of at least two people, and more if you have children. Legal requirements and responsibilities can create problems

Assets and possessions. Most people have various assets and many possessions that make up their estate.

Financial Planning for Life's Situations

ESTATE PLANNING CHECKLIST

Do you and your family members know the answers to the following questions?

1. Where are your previous years' income tax returns?

2. Where is your safe-deposit box located? Where is the key to it kept?

3. What kinds and amounts of life insurance protection do you have?

4. Can you locate your insurance policies—life, health, property, casualty, and auto?

5. Who are the beneficiaries and contingent beneficiaries of your life insurance policies?

6. What type of health insurance protection do you have, and what are the provisions of your health insurance policy?

7. Do you and your spouse have current wills? Who was the attorney who drafted them? Where are they kept?

8. Do you have a separate record of the important papers you keep in your safe-deposit box? Where is this record located?

9. Do you have a record of your spouse's and children's Social Security number?

10. Where is your marriage certificate and the birth certificates of all members of your family?

11. Do you know the name and address of your life insurance agent?

12. Do you know the principal financial resources and liabilities of your estate?

13. Are you knowledgeable about simple, daily, and compound interest rates? About retirement funds and property ownership?

14. Have you given any thought to funerals and burial arrangements?

15. What papers and records will be important to other people when you die?

16. Do you understand the functions of a bank trust department and the meaning of joint ownership?

Source: *Planning with Your Beneficiaries* (Washington, DC: American Council of Life Insurance, Education, and Community Services, n.d.), p. 2.

for married people that are entirely different from those of single people. Situations become more complex. Possessions accumulate. The need for orderliness and clarity increases.

Your death will mean a new lifestyle for your spouse. If you have no children or if the children are grown and lead separate lives, your spouse will once again be single. The surviving spouse must confront problems of grief and adjustment. Daily life must continue. At the same time, the estate must be settled. If not, catastrophic financial consequences may result.

If children survive you, making sure that your estate can be readily analyzed and distributed may be even more critical. If relatives or friends are beneficiaries, bequests have to be made known quickly and clearly.

Your desires and information about your estate have to be accessible, understandable, and legally documented. Otherwise, your beneficiaries may encounter problems and your intentions may not be carried out.

IF YOU NEVER MARRIED

Never having been married does not eliminate the need to organize your financial affairs. For people who live alone, as for married people, it is essential that important documents and personal information be consolidated and accessible.

The National Association of Financial and Estate Planning Web site at **www.nafep.com** includes free, useful information to help you with estate planning.

Remember that in the event of your death, difficult questions and situations will confront some person at a time of severe emotional strain. That person may not be prepared to face them objectively. Probably the single most important thing you can do is take steps to see that your beneficiaries have the information and the knowledge they need to survive emotionally and financially when you die.

Everyone should take such steps. However, the need to take them is especially great if you are only 5 or 10 years away from retirement. By then, your possessions will probably be of considerable value. Your savings and checking account balances will probably be substantial. Your investment plans will have materialized. If you stop and take a look at where you are, you may be pleasantly surprised at the value of your estate.

NEW LIFESTYLES

Millions of nontraditional households have unique estate planning problems. Nearly half of all American marriages end in divorce, creating difficulties for millions of adults contemplating estate planning. Single parents and other single persons all have formidable estate planning challenges. Financial planners and estate attorneys universally offer such households the following smart advice: Plan early, and get expert help. The law provides plenty of protection for married couples, but it is rife with pitfalls for almost everyone else.[1]

Single parents, divorced or not, must plan for their own death as part of retirement and estate planning. David Scott Sloan, chairman of trusts and estates at Sherburne, Powers & Needham, a law firm in Boston, says that simply leaving money to your children can result in a huge estate tax bill, sharply decreasing the funds available if your estate is worth more than $2,000,000 in 2006, 2007, and 2008. Sloan recommends setting up a trust for the children's benefit.

Unmarried couples face formidable retirement and estate planning challenges. A partner lacks any legal right to the companion's assets upon the companion's disability or death or upon the breakup of the partnership. Unmarried couples also cannot use the so-called marital deduction, which allows spouses to pass on everything they own to their surviving spouse tax free. Only the first $2,000,000 (in 2006, 2007, and 2008) of an unmarried partner's assets is exempt from estate taxes. Estate planning is even more important for unmarried couples. For example, if no beneficiary is named on your pension plan, the plan sponsor is required to give the proceeds to your closest blood relative. If you want your partner to receive the plan proceeds after you die, make sure he or she is named the beneficiary. Also, check to see whether the plan allows unmarried partners to receive joint-and-survivor benefits.

Sheet 66
Estate planning activities

THE OPPORTUNITY COST OF RATIONALIZING

Daily living often gets in the way of thinking about death. You mean to organize things that others need to know in case you die, but you haven't done this yet. One of your rationalizations may be that you are not sure what information you need to provide.

Think about the outcome of your delay. Your beneficiary will meet people who offer specific types of assistance—morticians, clergy, lawyers, insurance agents, clerks of federal government agencies, and so on. These people will probably be strangers—sympathetic, courteous, and helpful, but disinterested. Also, your bereaved beneficiary may find it difficult to reveal confidences to them. Today, however, the information survivors need is as close as the telephone. Call LIMRA International, a financial services research organization, at 1-800-235-4672 to order their booklet, *What Do You Do Now?*

The moral is to plan your estate while you are in good health and think through the provisions carefully. Last-minute "death-bed" estate planning may fail to carry out your wishes.

DEATH'S TOLL

What lives on after you die? The legacy of your work, your kind and generous acts, and the people you love, who will suffer the emotional toll, and possibly the financial toll, of your passing for a long, long time. How can you help? The care with which you prepare for your own death is a supreme act of love toward those you will one day leave behind. It can help your survivors a great deal emotionally, for dealing with chaos after a loss makes the loss itself more painful and frightening. It can also help your survivors a great deal financially, because with careful estate planning, you may save your loved ones thousands of dollars in pro-

bate fees, estate taxes, and attorneys' fees. Won't you take the actions necessary to protect the people you love, emotionally and financially? Will you please do it right away? Seeing to it that the people you love will always be safe is an expansive action, and once you've done so, you'll be the richer for it, closer to clarity, and all the more ready to receive all that you can, for the rest of your life.

Source: Suze Orman, *The Courage to Be Rich* (New York: Riverhead Books, 2002), p. 204.

CONCEPT CHECK 19-1

1 If you needed information about estate planning, would you go to the library or the Internet? Why?

2 Why is estate planning an important component of financial planning?

3 Why is estate planning important for single as well as married individuals? For "new" lifestyle individuals?

Action Application Develop a list of specific, long-term, estate-planning goals with your family. Discuss how those goals could be achieved even if you or your spouse died unexpectedly.

Legal Aspects of Estate Planning

When death occurs, proof of claims must be produced or the claims will not be processed. If no thought was given to gathering the necessary documents beforehand (with a sufficient number of copies), a period of financial hardship may follow until proof is obtained. If needed documentation cannot be located, irretrievable loss of funds may occur. Your heirs may experience emotionally painful delays until their rights have been established.

Objective 2

Assess the legal aspects of estate planning.

Important papers include the following:

1. Birth certificates—yours, your spouse's, and your children's.

2. Marriage certificates—always important, but especially important if you or your spouse were married previously—and divorce papers.

For pertinent laws about estate planning, visit Cornell University's Web site at **www.law.cornell.edu/topics/estate_planning.**

3. Legal name changes—judgment of court documents pertaining to any legal changes in the names that appear on birth certificates (especially important to protect the adopted children of a previous marriage or children who have been adopted through adoption agencies).

4. Military service records—the standard DD–214 (Armed Forces of the United States Report of Transfer or Discharge) or any other official statement of your military service details, if appropriate.

Here is a list of additional important documents:

- Social Security documents.
- Veteran documents.
- Insurance policies.
- Transfer records of joint bank accounts.
- Safe-deposit box records.
- Registration of automobiles.
- Title to stock and bond certificates.

You should have several copies of certain documents because when you submit a claim, the accompanying proof often becomes a permanent part of the claim file and is not returned. Remember too that in some circumstances, children may be required to furnish proof of their parents' birth, marriage, or divorce.

WILLS

will The legal declaration of a person's mind as to the disposition of his or her property after death.

One of the most vital documents every adult should have is a written will. A **will** is the legal declaration of a person's mind as to the disposition of his or her property after death. Thus, a will is a way to transfer your property according to your wishes after you die.

Whether you prepare a will before you die or neglect to take that sensible step, you still have a will. If you fail to prepare your own will, the state in which you legally reside steps in and controls the distribution of your estate without regard for wishes you may have had but failed to define in legal form. Thus, if you die **intestate**—without a valid will—the state's law of descent and distribution becomes your copy of the will, as shown in Exhibit 19–1.

intestate Without a valid will.

Consider the opportunity cost of a husband and father who died without a will. By default, he has authorized his estate to be disposed of according to the provisions of the fictitious document in Exhibit 19–1. The wording in this exhibit represents a pattern of distribution that could occur unless you prepare a valid will specifying otherwise.

This does not happen only to a husband. It could happen to anyone. To avoid such consequences, make a will! Consulting an attorney for this purpose can spare your heirs many difficulties, especially since the passage of the Economic Recovery Tax Act of 1981. This act created estate planning opportunities and problems for many people. It also created some difficult choices as to types of wills.

Peace of mind. Preparing a will can make things easier for your family after your death and ensure that your estate is distributed according to your wishes.

THE EFFECT OF MARRIAGE OR DIVORCE ON YOUR WILL   If you already have a will and are about to be married or divorced, review your will with an attorney for necessary changes. Upon divorce, only provisions favoring a former spouse are automatically revoked; provisions favoring family members of your ex-spouse, such as stepchildren, nieces, nephews, or in-laws, are not affected.

If you marry after you have made a will, the will is revoked automatically unless certain conditions are met. For example, marriage does not revoke a will if

- The will indicates an intent that it not be revoked by a subsequent marriage.
- The will was drafted under circumstances indicating that it was in contemplation of marriage.

Because your existing will's legal status may be uncertain, you are better off drawing a new will to fit your new circumstances.

Exhibit **19-1**

The opportunity cost of not making a will, or what the state will do to your property if you die intestate

If you die without a will, the state's law of descent and distribution becomes your will.

𝔐𝔶 𝔏𝔞𝔰𝔱 𝔚𝔦𝔩𝔩 𝔞𝔫𝔡 𝔗𝔢𝔰𝔱𝔞𝔪𝔢𝔫𝔱

Being of sound mind and memory, I, _____, do hereby publish this as my last Will and Testament.

FIRST

I give my wife only one-third of my possessions, and I give my children the remaining two-thirds.

A. I appoint my wife as guardian of my children, but as a safeguard I require that she report to the Probate Court each year and render an accounting of how, why, and where she spent the money necessary for the proper care of my children.

B. As a further safeguard, I direct my wife to produce to the Probate Court a Performance Bond to guarantee that she exercise proper judgment in the handling, investing, and spending of the children's money.

C. As a final safeguard, my children shall have the right to demand and receive a complete accounting from their mother of all of her financial actions with their money as soon as they reach legal age.

D. When my children reach age 18, they shall have full rights to withdraw and spend their shares of my estate. No one shall have any right to question my children's actions on how they decide to spend their respective shares.

SECOND

Should my wife remarry, her second husband shall be entitled to one-third of everything my wife possesses. Should my children need some of this share for their support, the second husband shall not be bound to spend any part of his share on my children's behalf.

A. The second husband shall have the sole right to decide who is to get his share, even to the exclusion of my children.

THIRD

Should my wife predecease me or die while any of my children are minors, I do not wish to exercise my right to nominate the guardian of my children.

A. Rather than nominating a guardian of my preference, I direct my relatives and friends to get together and select a guardian by mutual agreement.

B. In the event that they fail to agree on a guardian, I direct the Probate Court to make the selection. If the court wishes, it may appoint a stranger acceptable to it.

FOURTH

Under existing tax law, certain legitimate avenues are open to me to lower estate and inheritance taxes rates. Since I prefer to have my money used for government purposes rather than for the benefit of my wife and children, I direct that no effort be made to lower taxes.

IN WITNESS WHEREOF, I have set my hand to this, my LAST WILL AND TESTAMENT, this _____ day of _____ 20_____.

COST OF A WILL   Legal fees for drafting a will vary with the complexities of your estate and family situation. A standard will costs between $200 and $350. The price varies from place to place, but generally the cost of writing a will is less than that for writing a living trust (to be discussed later in the chapter). Look for an attorney experienced in drafting wills and in estate planning.

probate The legal procedure of proving a valid or invalid will.

Probate is the legal procedure of proving a valid or invalid will. It is the process by which an executor manages and distributes your property after you die according to your will's provisions. A probate court generally validates wills and makes sure debts are paid. You should avoid probate because it is expensive, lengthy, and public. As you'll read later, a living trust avoids probate and is less expensive, quicker, and private.

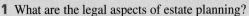

CONCEPT CHECK 19-2

1 What are the legal aspects of estate planning?
2 What is a will? Why is it an important estate planning tool?
3 How does marriage or divorce affect a will?

Action Application Contact several lawyers in your area to find out how much they would charge to prepare your simple will. Are their fees about the same?

Types and Formats of Wills

Objective 3

Distinguish among various types and formats of wills.

simple will A will that leaves everything to the spouse; also called an *I love you will.*

TYPES OF WILLS

A brief review of the types of wills will be helpful, since the tax effects of these wills differ. The four types of wills are the simple will, the traditional marital share will, the exemption trust will, and the stated dollar amount will.

SIMPLE WILL   A **simple will,** sometimes called an *I love you will,* leaves everything to the spouse. Such a will is sufficient for most smaller estates. However, if you have a large or complex estate, especially one involving business interests that you want to pass on to your children, a simple will may not meet your objectives. It may also create higher overall taxation, because everything would be taxed in your spouse's subsequent estate.

For example, in 2006, if your estate was $4 million and you left it all to your spouse, there would be no tax at your death. However, there would be a tax at your spouse's death, assuming the value of the estate remains constant. To avoid this, you could use a two-part marital will to split your estate into two halves, resulting in no tax at either death. If your spouse had separate property or if the value of your estate increased, the simple will would create higher taxation.

traditional marital share will A will in which the grantor leaves one-half of the adjusted gross estate to the spouse.

adjusted gross estate The gross estate minus debts and costs.

TRADITIONAL MARITAL SHARE WILL   The **traditional marital share will** leaves one-half of the **adjusted gross estate** (the gross estate minus debts and costs) to the spouse outright as a marital share. The other half of the adjusted gross estate might go to children or other heirs or be held in trust for the family. A trust can provide the spouse with a lifelong income and would not be taxed at the spouse's death.

Under this type of will, half of your estate is taxed at your death and half at your spouse's death. This results in the lowest overall amount of federal estate taxes on estates above a certain size (twice the exemption amount). However, there are other considerations. State inheritance taxes may be greater, especially at the first death, due to conflicting federal and state exemption and beneficiary classifications. Also, under this type of will, unlike a simple will or an exemption trust, federal estate taxes may have to be paid up front at the first death that will involve the loss of use of money. If your spouse has considerable assets in

For topics such as wills, trusts, living wills, and power of attorney, visit **www.nolo.com/lawcenter/index.**

his or her own right, it might not be prudent to increase your spouse's estate by any amount. In such a situation, a will that equalizes estates might be better. Finally, the nine community-property states severely limit your options as to how to allocate your money.

EXEMPTION TRUST WILL

The **exemption trust will** has been gaining in popularity due to its increased exemption. Under this type of will, everything passes to your spouse with the exception of an amount equal to the exemption, which would pass into trust. The amount passed to your spouse can be by will, trust, or other means. The exemption trust can provide your spouse with a lifelong income.

There would be little or no tax at your death due to the combination of the exemption and the marital deduction. The main advantage of the exemption trust will is that it eliminates future taxation of the exemption amount and any growth in it, which may be important if property values appreciate considerably.

exemption trust will A will in which everything passes to the spouse except the exemption ($2,000,000 in 2006).

STATED DOLLAR AMOUNT WILL

The **stated dollar amount will** allows you to pass on to your spouse any amount that satisfies your family objectives. These objectives may or may not include tax considerations. For example, you could pass on the stated amount of $2 million (in 2006, 2007, and 2008). However, the stated amount might instead be related to anticipated income needs or to the value of personal items.

State law may dictate how much you must leave your spouse. Most states require that your spouse receive a certain amount, usually one-half or one-third. Some states require that such interests pass outright, and others permit life interests. The stated dollar amount will may satisfy such requirements and pass the balance to others. You may, for example, decide to pass most of your estate to your children, thereby avoiding subsequent taxation of your spouse's estate. It may also make sense to pass interests in a business to children who are involved in the business.

Such plans may increase taxes at your death, since not all of your property passes to your spouse. However, the taxes at your spouse's subsequent death would be lower. You can also leave your spouse an outright amount equal to the exemption with a life estate in the balance, or a life estate in trust.

The stated dollar amount has one major shortcoming: The will may leave specific dollar amounts to listed heirs and the balance to the surviving spouse. Although these amounts may be reasonable when the will is drafted, they can soon become obsolete. What if estate values suddenly decrease due to a business setback or a drop in the stock market? Consider an individual with an extensive equities portfolio who drafted a will in 2000. After two years of bear markets, the value of the portfolio may have shrunk by one-third. None of that decrease will be borne by those who were left specific dollar amounts. The entire decrease will be borne by the surviving spouse. Therefore, you should use percentages instead of designated amounts.

stated dollar amount will A will that allows you to pass on to your spouse any amount that satisfies your family objectives.

WHICH TYPE OF WILL IS BEST FOR YOU?

The four types of wills just discussed are your basic choices. Which one is best for you?

Prior to the Economic Recovery Tax Act of 1981, many experts advocated the traditional marital share will. Today many attorneys believe the exemption trust will is best. However, there is no one ideal will. Which will is best for you depends on factors such as the size of your estate, the future appreciation of your estate, inflation, the respective ages of you and your spouse, cash on hand, and—most important—your objectives.

DID YOU KNOW?

According to a recent American Association of Retired Persons (AARP) survey, over 40 percent of Americans age 45 or older have not drawn up a will.

Source: *AARP Bulletin*, March 2004, p. 16.

FORMATS OF WILLS

Wills may be holographic or formal. A **holographic will** is a handwritten will that you prepare yourself. It should be written, dated, and signed entirely in your handwriting; no

holographic will A handwritten will.

formal will A will that is usually prepared with an attorney's assistance.

beneficiary A person who has been named to receive property under a will.

statutory will A formal will on a preprinted form.

printed or typed information should be on its pages. Some states, however, may not recognize a holographic will.

A **formal will** is usually prepared with an attorney's assistance. It may be either typed or on a preprinted form. You must sign the will and acknowledge it as your will in the presence of two witnesses, neither of whom is a **beneficiary** (a person you have named to receive property under the will). The witnesses must then sign the will in your presence.

A **statutory will** is one type of formal will. It is a preprinted form that may be obtained from lawyers and stationery stores. There are serious risks in using this or any other preprinted form. One risk is that such a form usually requires you to conform to rigid provisions, some of which may not be in the best interests of your beneficiaries. Also, if you change the preprinted wording, you may violate the law regarding wills, which may cause the changed sections or even the entire will to be declared invalid. There is also a risk that the form is out of date with respect to current law. It is always prudent to seek legal assistance in developing these documents.

WRITING YOUR WILL

The way to transfer your property according to your wishes is to write a will specifying those wishes. Joint ownership is no substitute for a will. Although jointly owned property passes directly to the joint owner and may be appropriate for some assets, such as your home, only a will allows you to distribute your property as a whole exactly as you wish. Select a person who will follow your instructions (your *executor* or *executrix*). By naming your own executor, you will eliminate the need for a court-appointed administrator, prevent unnecessary delay in the distribution of your property, and minimize estate taxes and settlement costs. See Financial Planning for Life's Situations: The 10 Commandments of Making Your Will on page 623 for guidance on important aspects of making a will.

SELECTING AN EXECUTOR   Select an executor or executrix who is both willing and able to carry out the complicated tasks associated with executing a will. These tasks are preparing an inventory of assets, collecting any money due, paying off any debts, preparing and filing all income and estate tax returns, liquidating and reinvesting other assets to pay off debts and provide income for your family while the estate is being administered, distributing the estate, and making a final accounting to your beneficiaries and to the probate court.

Your executor can be a family member, a friend, an attorney, an accountant, or the trust department of a bank. Fees for executors, whether professionals or friends, are set by state law. Exhibit 19–2 summarizes typical duties of an executor.

guardian A person who assumes responsibility for providing children with personal care and managing the deceased's estate for them.

trustee A person or an institution that holds or manages property for the benefit of someone else under a trust agreement.

SELECTING A GUARDIAN   In addition to disposing of your estate, your will should name a guardian and/or trustee to care for minor children if both parents die at the same time, such as in an automobile accident or a plane crash. A **guardian** is a person who assumes the responsibilities of providing the children with personal care and of managing the estate for them. A **trustee,** on the other hand, is a person or an institution that holds or generally manages property for the benefit of someone else under a trust agreement.

You should take great care in selecting a guardian for your children. You want a guardian whose philosophy on raising children is similar to yours and who is willing to accept the responsibility.

Most states require a guardian to post a bond with the probate court. The bonding company promises to reimburse the minor's estate up to the amount of the bond if the guardian uses the prop-

Financial Planning for Life's Situations

THE 10 COMMANDMENTS OF MAKING YOUR WILL

1. Work closely with your spouse as you prepare your will. Seek professional help so that your family objectives can be met regardless of who dies first.

2. Write your will to conform with your current wishes. When your circumstances change (for example, when you retire or move to another state), review your will and, if appropriate, write a new one.

3. Do not choose a beneficiary as a witness. If such a person is called on to validate your will, he or she may not be able to collect an inheritance.

4. If you are remarrying, consider signing a prenuptial agreement to protect your children. If you sign such an agreement before the wedding, you and your intended spouse can legally agree that neither of you will make any claim on the other's estate. The agreement can be revoked later, if you both agree.

5. Consider using percentages rather than dollar amounts when you divide your estate. For example,

if you leave $15,000 to a friend and the rest to your spouse, your spouse will suffer if your estate shrinks to $17,000.

6. Both you and your spouse should have a will, and those wills should be separate documents.

7. Be flexible. Don't insist that your heirs keep stock or run a cattle ranch. If you do so, they may suffer if economic conditions change.

8. Sign the original copy of your will and keep it in a safe place; keep an unsigned copy at home for reference.

9. Alter your will by preparing a new will or adding a codicil. Don't change beneficiaries by writing on the will itself; this may invalidate the will.

10. Select an executor or executrix who is both willing and able to carry out the complicated tasks associated with the job.

Executor's Duties

```
Takes control        Stocks          Cash          Safe-Deposit Box
of assets      ───   Bonds    ───            ───
   │
   ●
Files inventory
with court
   │
   ●
Liquidates selected  Stocks          Bills         Property
assets, if necessary, Bonds   ───            ───
and pays claims  ───
   │
   ●
                     Estate
Distributes estate   • Spouse
according to terms   • Children
of will        ───   • Grandchildren
                     • Other relatives
                     • Friends
                     • Charities
   │
   ●
Makes final
accounting to
the court
```

Exhibit 19-2

Major responsibilities of an executor

An executor is someone who is willing and able to perform the complicated tasks involved in carrying out your will.

Source: *Trust Services from Your Bank,* rev. ed. (Washington, DC: American Bankers Association, 1978), p. 9, American Bankers Association. Reprinted with permission. All rights reserved.

erty of the minor for his or her own gain. The bonding fee (usually several hundred dollars) is paid from the estate. However, you can waive the bonding requirement in your will.

Through your will, you may want to provide funds to raise your children. You could, for instance, leave a lump sum for an addition to the guardian's house and establish monthly payments to cover your children's living expenses.

The guardian of the minor's estate manages the property you leave behind for your children. This guardian can be a person or the trust department of a financial institution, such as a bank. Property that you place in trust for your children can be managed by the trustee rather than by the guardian of the minor's estate.

Each executor or a trustee has a fiduciary relationship to the beneficiaries of the will. This relationship dictates that beneficiaries' interests are paramount. The executor or trustee must not take advantage of his or her position.

ALTERING OR REWRITING YOUR WILL

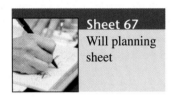

Sheet 67
Will planning
sheet

Sometimes you will need to change provisions of your will. Consider one change involving the marital deduction. The old law limited the amount you could pass to your spouse tax free to one-half of your adjusted gross estate. But the Economic Recovery Tax Act of 1981 created an unlimited marital deduction. You can now pass any amount to your spouse tax free.

If you do have a will, you should review it. This is necessary even if you have already done some planning and your will refers to the old 50 percent marital deduction. Why? The new 100 percent marital deduction is not automatic. Congress would not alter or rewrite your will; this task was left to you. Therefore, unless you change your will or unless your state passes a law making the new definition applicable, you will have to rewrite your will to make the unlimited marital deduction apply. Because many choices are of a personal nature, few, if any, states will get involved. For example, some people may not want to leave the entire estate to their spouse, perhaps for valid tax reasons.

You should review your will if you move to a different state; if you have sold property mentioned in the will; if the size and composition of your estate have changed; if you have married, divorced, or remarried; or if new potential heirs have died or been born.

Don't make any changes on the face of your will. Additions, deletions, or erasures on a will that has been signed and witnessed can invalidate the will.

If only a few changes are needed in your will, adding a codicil may be the best choice. A **codicil** is a document that explains, adds, or deletes provisions in your existing will. It identifies the will being amended and confirms the unchanged sections of the will. To be valid, it must conform to the legal requirements for a will.

codicil A document that modifies provisions in an existing will.

If you wish to make major changes in your will or if you have already added a codicil, preparing a new will is preferable to adding a new codicil. In the new will, include a clause revoking all earlier wills and codicils.

If you are rewriting a will because of a remarriage, consider drafting a **prenuptial agreement.** This is a documentary agreement between spouses before marriage. In such agreements, one or both parties often waive a right to receive property under the other's will or under state law. Be sure to consult an attorney in drafting a prenuptial agreement.

prenuptial agreement A documentary agreement between spouses before marriage.

LIVING WILL

living will A document that enables an individual, while well, to express the intention that life be allowed to end if he or she becomes terminally ill.

Wills have existed for thousands of years; the oldest known will was written by the Egyptian pharaoh Uah in 2448 BC. Recently a new type of will, called a living will, has emerged.

A **living will** provides for your wishes to be followed if you become so physically or mentally disabled that you are unable to act on your own behalf. A living will is not a substitute for a traditional will. It enables an individual, while well, to express the inten-

To My Family, My Physician, My Lawyer, My Clergyman;
To Any Medical Facility in Whose Care I Happen to Be;
To Any Individual Who May Become Responsible for My Health, Welfare, or Affairs:

Death is as much a reality as birth, growth, maturity, and old age—it is the one certainty of life. If the time comes when I, _____, can no longer take part in decisions for my own future, let this statement stand as an expression of my wishes, while I am still of sound mind.

If the situation should arise in which there is no reasonable expectation of my recovery from physical or mental disability, I request that I be allowed to die and not be kept alive by artificial means or "heroic measures." I do not fear death itself as much as the indignities of deterioration, dependence, and hopeless pain. I, therefore, ask that medication be mercifully administered to me to alleviate suffering even though this may hasten the moment of death.

This request is made after careful consideration. I hope you who care for me will feel morally bound to follow its mandate. I recognize that this appears to place a heavy responsibility upon you, but it is with the intention of relieving you of such responsibility and of placing it upon myself in accordance with my strong convictions that this statement is made.

Signed _____

Date   _____

Witness   _____

Witness   _____

Copies of this request have been given to _____

_____

_____

_____

Source: *Don't Wait until Tomorrow* (Hartford, CT: Aetna Life and Casualty Company, n.d.), p. 10.

Exhibit **19-3**

A living will: Example 1

A living will is not a substitute for a traditional will.

---

tion that life be allowed to end if he or she becomes terminally ill. Many states recognize living wills, and you may consider writing one when you draw a conventional will. Exhibits 19–3 and 19–4 are examples of typical living wills.

To ensure the effectiveness of a living will, discuss your intention of preparing such a will with the people closest to you. You should also discuss this with your family doctor. Sign and date your document before two witnesses. Witnessing shows that you signed of your own free will.

Money magazine's Web site at **money.cnn.com/pf/101/lessons/24** is an excellent source of information for topics related to estate planning.

Give copies of your living will to those closest to you, and have your family doctor place a copy in your medical file. Keep the original document readily accessible, and look it over periodically—preferably once a year—to be sure your wishes have remained unchanged. To verify your intent, redate and initial each subsequent endorsement.

Most lawyers will do the paperwork for a living will at no cost if they are already preparing your estate plan. You can also get the necessary forms from nonprofit advocacy groups. Aging With Dignity (www.agingwithdignity.org) lets you download a free, plain-English version called Five Wishes that's valid in 33 states. Partnership for Caring: America's Voices for the Dying is a national nonprofit organization that operates the only

Exhibit **19-4**

A living will: Example 2

Many states recognize living wills.

Source: *Don't Wait until Tomorrow* (Hartford, CT: Aetna Life and Casualty Company, n.d.), p. 11.

𝕷𝖎𝖛𝖎𝖓𝖌 𝖂𝖎𝖑𝖑 𝕯𝖊𝖈𝖑𝖆𝖗𝖆𝖙𝖎𝖔𝖓

Declaration made this _____ day of _____ (month, year)

I, _____, being of sound mind, willfully and voluntarily make known my desire that my dying shall not be artificially prolonged under the circumstances set forth below, do hereby declare

If at any time I should have an incurable injury, disease, or illness regarded as a terminal condition by my physician and if my physician has determined that the application of life-sustaining procedures would serve only to artificially prolong the dying process and that my death will occur whether or not life-sustaining procedures are utilized, I direct that such procedures be withheld or withdrawn and that I be permitted to die with only the administration of medication or the performance of any medical procedure deemed necessary to provide me with comfort care.

In the absence of my ability to give directions regarding the use of such life-sustaining procedures, it is my intention that this declaration shall be honored by my family and physician as the final expression of my legal right to refuse medical or surgical treatment and accept the consequences from such refusal.

I understand the full import of this declaration, and I am emotionally and mentally competent to make this declaration.

Signed _____

City, County, and State of Residence _____

The declarant has been personally known to me, and I believe him or her to be of sound mind.

Witness _____

Witness _____

---

national crisis and information hotline dealing with end-of-life issues. It also provides documents, such as living wills and medical powers of attorney, geared to specific states. You may download these documents free at www.partnershipforcaring.org. Working through end-of-life issues is difficult, but it can help avoid forcing your family to make a decision in a hospital waiting room—or worse, having your last wishes ignored.

A living will can become a problem. A once-healthy person may have a change of heart and prefer to remain alive even as death seems imminent. Living wills call for careful thought, but they do provide you with a choice as to the manner of your death.

ETHICAL WILL

ethical will A document that dispenses emotional and spiritual wealth to heirs.

Renewed interest in another type of will has emerged since the September 11, 2001, terrorist attacks. An **ethical will** is a way to pass on your values and beliefs to your heirs. Even though it is not a legally binding document, ethical wills help with estate planning (see the accompanying Financial Planning for Life's Situations feature on page 627).

POWER OF ATTORNEY

power of attorney A legal document authorizing someone to act on one's behalf.

Related to the concept of a living will is a power of attorney. A **power of attorney** is a legal document authorizing someone to act on your behalf. At some point in your life,

THE VIRTUES AND VALUES OF AN ETHICAL WILL

Before taking a trip to California shortly after September 11, 2001, Kim Payfrock, 42, wrote letters to her two sons and two stepsons, ages 11 to 17. The letters expressed her love for them as well as her joys and regrets in life. "I was nervous about flying and wanted them to open the letters if anything happened to me," says Payfrock, who is an activity coordinator at an assisted-living community in Minneapolis. "This was a way to leave them my thoughts, to give them a part of myself."

Payfrock didn't know it at the time, but she had written each of her children an *ethical will*. Whereas legal wills bequeath material wealth, ethical wills dispense emotional and spiritual wealth. "It's a way to pass on your values, share lessons learned, express love, and address any regrets," says Barry Baines, the medical director of a hospice in Minneapolis and author of *Ethical Will: Putting Your Values on Paper*. Preparing such a document is not easy, since it requires earnest self-examination. But writers and recipients of ethical wills say the result is an invaluable legacy.

Ethical wills go back to Biblical times. Today, there's renewed interest in leaving heirs a testament of values, due in part to the events of September 11, 2001. Although ethical wills vary widely in content, people who write them usually relate what they value most in life. They often express love for their survivors and tell them not to grieve. Some explain past actions or recount formative events. Many dispense advice. An example is a now-deceased doctor who wrote that he regretted giving up medical research for a more lucrative career as a surgeon. "There's no greater compensation than being happy in your work," he wrote to his children.

There is no single right way to draft an ethical will. "Just make sure it comes from the heart," says Baines, who also has a Web site, ethicalwill.com. And don't malign your heirs. "There's a temptation to try to criticize, cause guilt, or tell people how to behave," says Jack Riemer, a rabbi and coauthor of *So That Your Values Live On: Ethical Wills and How to Prepare Them*.

For more tips, you can check out a helpful online brochure coauthored by Robert Flashman, a professor at the University of Kentucky at Lexington (www.ces.ncsu. edu/depts/fcs/pub/1998/wills.html). People who have trouble expressing themselves in writing may opt to record their ethical will on audiotape or videotape, though a transcript is a good idea. You can also get professional help. "A lot of people don't have the time, or they may need help figuring out what they want to say," says Marcia Brier, whose company, Family Legacy Services in Needham, Massachusetts, helps clients write ethical wills, starting at $2,500.

Ethical wills are not legally binding, but many attorneys encourage clients to write them as codicils to their regular wills. They help with estate planning, says James Carolan, a trust and estates attorney in Port Huron, Michigan, because they clarify "what's important and what they really want to do with their money." Most important, says Flashman, the ethical will "is a way to leave something behind that goes way beyond any financial resources you may have." Indeed, Baines reads his father's every year on the anniversary of his death. One of its messages: "No father could be as proud as your father is of you. You have more than exceeded my greatest expectations." For most people, a bequest like that is more precious than gold.

Source: Excerpted from Kate Murphy, "The Virtues and Values of an Ethical Will," *BusinessWeek*, April 8, 2002, p. 83.

you may become ill or incapacitated. You may then wish to have someone attend to your needs and your personal affairs. You can assign a power of attorney to anyone you choose.

The person you name can be given limited power or a great deal of power. The power given can be special—to carry out certain acts or transactions—or it can be general—to act completely for you. A conventional power of attorney is automatically revoked in a case of legal incapacity.

LETTER OF LAST INSTRUCTION

In addition to your will, you should prepare a *letter of last instruction*. This document, though not legally enforceable, can provide your heirs with important information. It should contain the details of your funeral arrangements. It should also contain the names of the people who are to be notified of your death and the locations of your bank accounts, safe-deposit box, and other important items listed on pages 617–618.

CONCEPT CHECK 19-3

1 Distinguish among the four types of wills.
2 What are the two formats of wills?
3 What are the steps in writing your will?
4 What is an ethical will?
5 What is a power of attorney?
6 What is a letter of last instruction?

Action Application Draft your simple will, using Exhibit 19–1 as a guideline. Whom will you appoint as a trustee or guardian for your minor children? Why?

Types of Trusts and Estates

Objective 4

Appraise various types of trusts and estates.

trustor The creator of a trust; also called the *grantor.*

trust A legal arrangement through which one's assets are held by a trustee.

revocable trust A trust whose terms the trustor retains the rights to change.

irrevocable trust A trust that cannot be altered or ended by its creator.

A trust is a property arrangement in which a trustee, such as a person or a bank trust department, holds title to, takes care of, and in most cases manages property for the benefit of someone else. The creator of the trust is called the **trustor** or *grantor.* A bank, as trustee, charges a modest fee for its services, generally based on the value of the trust assets. All trust assets added together are known as an *estate.*

It is a good idea to discuss with your attorney the possibility of establishing a trust as a means of managing your estate. Basically, a **trust** is a legal arrangement through which a trustee holds your assets for your benefit or that of your beneficiaries. Trusts are used for everything from protecting assets from creditors to managing property for young children, disabled elders, or even the family pets (see Financial Planning for Life's Situations: Trust-Fund Babies with Wagging Tails on page 629).

Trusts are either revocable or irrevocable. If you establish a **revocable trust,** you retain the right to end the trust or change its terms during your lifetime. Revocable trusts avoid the often lengthy probate process, but they do not provide shelter from federal or state estate taxes. You might choose a revocable trust if you think you may need its assets for your own use at a later time or if you want to monitor the performance of the trust and the trustee before the arrangement is made irrevocable by your death. If you establish an **irrevocable trust,** you cannot change its terms or end it. The trust becomes, for tax purposes, a separate entity, and the assets can't be removed, nor can changes be made by the grantor. Irrevocable trusts often are used by individuals with large estates to reduce estate taxes and avoid probate. Therefore, an irrevocable trust offers tax advantages not offered by a revocable trust.

BENEFITS OF ESTABLISHING TRUSTS

Your individual circumstances dictate whether it makes sense to establish a trust. Here are some common reasons for setting up a trust. You can use a trust to

- Reduce or otherwise provide for payment of estate taxes.
- Avoid probate and transfer your assets immediately to your beneficiaries.
- Free yourself from management of your assets while you receive a regular income from the trust.
- Provide income for a surviving spouse or other beneficiaries.
- Ensure that your property serves a desired purpose after your death.

Trustee services are commonly provided by banks and, in some instances, by life insurance companies. An estate attorney can advise you about the right type of trust for you.

TRUST-FUND BABIES WITH WAGGING TAILS

Affluent pet lovers, take heart: Now you can get help setting up a trust fund to ensure that your pet gets quality care when you pass on. MassMutual is offering estate planning with creature comforts in mind. With pets in one-third of U.S. homes, businesses see opportunity in such planning—especially with trusts averaging $25,000. Since February, nearly 500 pet lovers have signed up for PetGuardian's $500 trust service, which takes into account factors such as life expectancy and potential chemotherapy costs. After all, some birds can live 80 years, and ensuring that they are comfy could take a lot of birdseed.

Patches and Chelsea are two golden retrievers set for life. They'll inherit $10,000 a year if their fiftyish Florida owners Bobbie and John Ford die before them. The Fords created a trust fund to care for their beloved dogs under a law passed in 2002 by Florida legislators.

Florida is following seven other states, including New York and California, that let pet owners create caretaking trusts for their animals. The idea is so hot that Representative Earl Blumenauer (D-Ore.) has introduced a bill to make the trusts legal nationwide.

Blumenauer wants to legitimize what many pet owners—including celebrities such as Oprah Winfrey, Betty White, and the late Doris Duke—have already done. In most states, leaving money to pets is not enforceable under law, so other heirs can challenge it.

Nearly 30 percent of the nation's 64 million pet owners mention animals in their wills anyway, according to Blumenauer's research. "People see pets as part of the family," says estate attorney Barbara Buxton, who set up the Fords' trust. Earning trust money, it seems, is a walk in the park.

Sources: Sheridan Prasso and Charles Haddad, "Trust-Fund Babies with Wagging Tails," *BusinessWeek,* June 3, 2002, p. 16; Jessi Hempel and Ira Sager, "Providing for Fido," *BusinessWeek,* May 17, 2004, p. 14.

TYPES OF TRUSTS

There are many types of trusts, some of which are described in detail below. Each of these types has particular advantages. Choose the type of trust that is most appropriate for your family situation.

CREDIT-SHELTER TRUST   A **credit-shelter trust** is perhaps the most common estate planning trust. It is also known as a *bypass trust,* a *"residuary" trust,* an *A/B trust,* an *exemption equivalent trust,* or a *family trust.* It is designed to allow married couples, who can leave everything to each other tax free, to take full advantage of the exemption that allows $2 million (in 2006, 2007, and 2008) in every estate to pass free of federal estate taxes.

The Economic Growth and Tax Relief Reconciliation Act of 2001 (EGTRRA) increased the exemption amounts to $3.5 million by the year 2009 as follows:

2006–2008	$2,000,000
2009	$3,500,000
2010	Repeal (No Estate Tax)
2011	$1,000,000

DISCLAIMER TRUST   A **disclaimer trust** is appropriate for a couple who do not yet have enough assets to need a credit-shelter trust but may need one in the future. For example, a newly practicing physician who will soon finish paying off college loans might want to take this approach. With a disclaimer trust, the surviving spouse is left everything, but has the right to disclaim some portion of the estate. Anything disclaimed goes into a credit-shelter trust. This

credit-shelter trust A trust that allows married couples to leave everything to each other tax free.

disclaimer trust A trust designed for a couple who do not yet have enough assets to need a credit-shelter trust but may need one in the future.

In whom we trust. For some people, setting up a trust is an effective way to organize and manage an estate.

approach gives the surviving spouse the flexibility to shelter any wealth from estate taxes. However, if the estate fails to grow as expected, the survivor isn't locked into a trust structure.

living trust A trust that is created and provides benefits during the trustor's lifetime.

LIVING, OR INTER VIVOS, TRUST

A **living trust,** or *inter vivos trust,* is a property management arrangement that you establish while you are alive. Well-structured estate plans often start with a living trust that becomes irrevocable at death, dividing itself into several other types of trusts, such as a credit-shelter trust. You simply transfer some property to a trustee, giving him or her instructions regarding its management and disposition while you are alive and after your death.

In the past several years, many people have opted for a living trust instead of a will, or in addition to one. But bare-bones living trusts, which start at $1,000, are overhyped and often misunderstood. (See Financial Planning for Life's Situations: Living Trust Offers—How to Make Sure They're Trustworthy on page 631.) They do not, for example, bypass estate taxes or protect you from creditors. What they do is avoid probate—which, in states such as Florida and California, can drag on for a couple of years and eat up as much as 5 percent or 10 percent of the estate's assets in administrative fees. With a living trust, you can change the terms while you're living, and your successor trustee, usually a family member, distributes the property without court interference when you die.[2]

Living trusts are a must if you own property in more than one state, since your heirs will not be subjected to multiple probate proceedings. Unlike wills, which become public as soon as they are filed with the probate court, living trusts are private documents. They can be handy for other situations as well, such as disinheriting estranged family members. The biggest mistake made in estate planning? You sign the documents setting up the trust, but don't follow through with the tedious task of retitling all of your property, such as real estate, stocks and bonds, and bank accounts, in the specific name of the trust.[3] A living trust has these advantages:

- It ensures privacy. A will is a public record; a trust is not.
- The property held in the trust avoids probate at your death. It eliminates probate costs and delays.
- It enables you to review your trustee's performance and make changes if necessary.
- It can remove management responsibilities from your shoulders.
- It is less subject to dispute by disappointed heirs than a will is.
- It can guide your family and doctors if you become terminally ill or incompetent.

However, a living trust involves higher costs than creating a will, and funding a trust can be time consuming.

testamentary trust A trust established by the creator's will that becomes effective upon his or her death.

TESTAMENTARY TRUST

A **testamentary trust** is established by your will and becomes effective upon your death. Such a trust can be valuable if your beneficiaries are inexperienced in financial matters or if the potential estate tax is substantial. Like a living trust, a testamentary trust provides the benefits of asset management, financial bookkeeping, protection of the beneficiaries, and minimizing of estate taxes.

Newly acquired property can always be added to your trust. But what if you forget to change the title on some of your assets? A simple pourover will, written when the trust agreement is drafted, is the answer. A *pourover* will is a simple document stating that anything you may have neglected to place in your trust during your lifetime should be placed in it at your death. While assets passing under a pourover will are generally probated, a small amount may be excluded from a probate.

life insurance trust A trust whose assets are derived at least in part from the proceeds of life insurance.

LIFE INSURANCE TRUST

In many families, the proceeds of life insurance policies are the largest single asset of the estate. A **life insurance trust** is established while you are living. The trust receives your life insurance benefits upon your death and

LIVING TRUST OFFERS: HOW TO MAKE SURE THEY'RE TRUSTWORTHY

Misinformation and misunderstanding about estate taxes and the length or complexity of probate provide the perfect cover for scam artists who have created an industry out of older people's fears that their estates could be eaten up by costs or that the distribution of their assets could be delayed for years. Some unscrupulous businesses are advertising seminars on living trusts or sending postcards inviting consumers to call for in-home appointments to learn whether a living trust is right for them. In these cases, it's not uncommon for the salesperson to exaggerate the benefits or the appropriateness of the living trust and claim—falsely—that locally licensed lawyers will prepare the documents.

Other businesses are advertising living trust "kits": consumers send money for these do-it-yourself products but receive nothing in return. Still other businesses are using estate planning services to gain access to consumers' financial information and to sell them other financial products, such as insurance annuities.

What's a consumer to do? It's true that for some people, a living trust can be a useful and practical tool. But for others, it can be a waste of money and time. Because state laws and requirements vary, "cookie-cutter" approaches to estate planning aren't always the most efficient way to handle your affairs. Before you sign any papers to create a will, a living trust, or any other kind of trust:

- Explore all your options with an experienced and licensed estate planning attorney or financial adviser. Generally, state law requires that an attorney draft the trust.
- Avoid high-pressure sales tactics and high-speed sales pitches by anyone who is selling estate planning tools or arrangements.
- Avoid salespeople who give the impression that AARP is selling or endorsing their products. AARP does not endorse any living trust product.
- Do your homework. Get information about your local probate laws from the Clerk (or Register) of Wills.
- If you opt for a living trust, make sure it's properly funded—that is, that the property has been transferred from your name to the trust. If the transfers aren't done properly, the trust will be invalid and the state will determine who inherits your property and serves as guardian for your minor children.
- If someone tries to sell you a living trust, ask whether the seller is an attorney. Some states limit the sale of living trust services to attorneys.
- Remember the *Cooling Off Rule*. If you buy a living trust in your home or somewhere other than the

seller's permanent place of business (say, at a hotel seminar), the seller must give you a written statement of your right to cancel the deal within three business days. The cooling off rule provides that during the sales transaction, the salesperson must give you two copies of a cancellation form (one for you to keep and one to return to the company) and a copy of your contract or receipt. The contract or receipt must be dated, show the name and address of the seller, and explain your right to cancel. You can write a letter and exercise your right to cancel within three days, even if you don't receive a cancellation form. You do not have to give a reason for canceling. Stopping payment on your check if you do cancel in these circumstances is a good idea. If you pay by credit card and the seller does not credit your account after you cancel, you can dispute the charge with the credit card issuer.

- Check out the organization with the Better Business Bureau in your state or the state where the organization is located before you send any money for any product or service. Although this is prudent, it is not foolproof: there may be no record of complaints if an organization is too new or has changed its name.

FOR MORE INFORMATION
To learn more about estate planning strategies, talk with an experienced estate planning attorney or financial adviser and check out the following resources:

AARP: 1-800-424-3410; www.aarp.org. Ask for a copy of *Product Report: Wills & Living Trusts*. AARP does not sell or endorse living trust products.

American Bar Association, Service Center, 541 N. Fairbanks Ct., Chicago, IL 60611; 312-988-5522; www.abanet.org/publiced/publicpubs.html.

Council of Better Business Bureaus Inc., 4200 Wilson Blvd., Suite 800, Arlington, VA 22203-1838; 703-276-0100; www.bbb.org/.

National Academy of Elder Law Attorneys Inc., 1604 North Country Club Rd., Tucson, AZ 85716; 520-881-4005; www.naela.org/.

National Consumer Law Center Inc., 18 Tremont St., Ste. 400, Boston, MA 02108-2336; 617-523-8010; www.consumerlaw.org/.

Source: www.ftc.gov, May 28, 2005.

OTHER TYPES OF TRUSTS

GRANTOR RETAINED ANNUITY TRUST (GRAT)

If you are worried about estate taxes, consider one of today's most popular alternatives. A grantor retained annuity trust (GRAT) not only shelters valuable assets that you can pass on to your heirs with minimal taxes but also lets you receive an annuity for as long as the trust lasts.

MARITAL-DEDUCTION TRUST

With a marital-deduction trust, you can leave to your spouse any money that doesn't go into a credit-shelter trust. Whatever the amount, it is free of estate tax when you die, since it qualifies for the marital deduction. Perhaps the most popular form of marital trust is the *qualified terminable interest property trust,* or *Q-TIP.* Here the surviving spouse gets all trust income, which must be distributed at least once a year, and sometimes receives access to the principal as well. When the spouse dies, the assets go to whomever you specified in the trust documents. The trust assets are then taxed as part of the surviving spouse's estate.

SELF-DECLARATION TRUST

A self-declaration trust is a variation of the living trust. Its unique feature is that the creator of the trust is also the trustee. The trust document usually includes a procedure for removing the creator of the trust as the trustee without going to court. Typically, one or more physicians or family members, or a combination of physicians and family members, have removal power. If the creator of the trust is removed, a named successor trustee takes over.

CHARITABLE REMAINDER TRUST

With a charitable remainder trust, you retain the right to the income but transfer that right to the charity upon death. If you have highly appreciated assets, it is a great way to improve your cash flow during your retirement and pursue a charitable interest at the same time. The biggest drawback is that you have to give away the asset irrevocably.

QUALIFIED PERSONAL RESIDENCE TRUST

A qualified personal residence trust (QPRT) lets you get your home or vacation home out of your estate. You give your home to a trust but live in it for a term of, say, 10 years. At the end of that time, the home belongs to the continuing trust or to the trust beneficiaries, depending on how the trust is written.

CHARITABLE LEAD TRUST

A charitable lead trust pays a specified charity income from a donated asset for a set number of years. When the term is up, the principal goes to the donor's beneficiaries with reduced estate or gift taxes. Such a trust has high setup and operating costs, however, which may make it impractical unless the assets involved are substantial. For this reason, it is a vehicle for very wealthy people, allowing them a way to keep an asset in the family but greatly reducing the cost of passing it on.

GENERATION-SKIPPING TRUST

A generation-skipping trust allows you to directly leave a substantial amount of money to your grandchildren or great-grandchildren. If you have a large estate, you should explore a generation-skipping (or dynasty) trust. Over time, it can save millions of dollars in taxes and can be used to help all of those family members who come after you.

SPENDTHRIFT TRUST

If your beneficiary is too young or unable to handle money wisely, consider a spendthrift trust. Here the beneficiary receives small amounts of money at specified intervals. It prevents the beneficiary from squandering money or losing it in a bad investment.

OTHER TYPES

There are still other types of specialized trusts. For example, a *pourover trust* is usually dormant during your lifetime, but can be activated if you become disabled. It can be used to manage your insurance, qualified pension or profit-sharing plan proceeds, and your probate estate. A *Q-DOT (qualified domestic trust)* is for spouses who are not U.S. citizens. It provides the same marital deduction benefit that is available to citizen spouses. A GRUT (grantor retained unitrust) and a *personal residence GRIT (grantor retained income trust)* permit grantors to use favorable rules for determining the amount of gift made to the trust.

Sheet 68
Trust comparison sheet

administers them in an agreed-on manner. Such a trust can be canceled if your family or financial circumstances change or if you wish to make new plans for the future.

Although common estate planning tools, life insurance trusts "aren't for the faint of heart," says one tax attorney. They require careful monitoring so that they don't run afoul of gift tax rules.

As you can see, trusts are complicated; therefore, you should seek a competent estate attorney in preparing this legal document. The purpose of all types of trusts is to preserve your estate for your heirs. Read the Financial Planning for Life's Situations: Other Types of Trusts feature for other types of trusts.

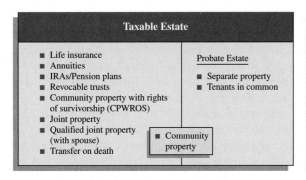

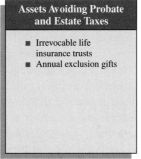

  Exhibit 19-5

What is your estate?

Your estate consists of everything you own.

Source: *Planning Your Estate* (A. G. Edwards, 1996), p. 6.

This exhibit shows which assets are included in your probate estate, the much larger number of assets included in your taxable estate, and the very few assets that can avoid both probate and estate taxes.

ESTATES

As mentioned earlier, your estate is everything you own (see Exhibit 19–5). It includes all of your property—tangible and intangible, however acquired or owned, whether inside or outside the country. It may include jointly owned property, life insurance and employee benefits, and property you no longer own. Thus, an important step in estate planning is taking inventory of everything you own, such as

1. Cash, checking accounts, savings accounts, CDs, and money market funds.
2. Stocks, bonds (including municipals and U.S. savings bonds), mutual funds, commodity futures, and tax shelters.
3. Life insurance, employee benefits, and annuities.
4. Your home and any other real estate, land and buildings, furniture, and fixtures.
5. Farms, grain, livestock, machinery, and equipment.
6. Proprietorship, partnership, and close corporation interests.
7. Notes, accounts, and claims receivable.
8. Interests in trusts and powers of appointment.
9. Antiques, works of art, collectibles, cars, boats, planes, personal effects, and everything else.

> **DID YOU KNOW?**
>
> In common-law states (most states), spouses are not considered co-owners of property unless it has been jointly titled. Surviving spouses are entitled to inherit a portion of the deceased spouse's property.

In the community-property states (Arizona, California, Idaho, Louisiana, Nevada, New Mexico, Texas, Wisconsin, and Washington), where each spouse owns 50 percent of the property, half of the community assets are included in each spouse's estate. **Community property** is "any property that has been acquired by either of the spouses during the marriage, but not by gift, devise, bequest or inheritance, or, often, by the income therefrom." In the other, non–community-property states, property is included in the estate of the spouse who owns it. The way you own property can make a tax difference.

community property Any property that has been acquired by either spouse during the marriage.

JOINT OWNERSHIP

Joint ownership of property between spouses is very common. Joint ownership may also exist between parents and children, other relatives, or any two or more persons. While joint ownership may avoid *probate* (official proof of a will), creditor attachment, and inheritance taxes in some states, it does not avoid federal estate taxes. In fact, it may increase them.

> **DID YOU KNOW?**
>
> In community-property states, spouses are generally considered co-owners of any property acquired during marriage. These states include Arizona, California, Idaho, Louisiana, Nevada, New Mexico, Texas, Wisconsin, and Washington.

There are three types of joint ownership, and each has different tax and estate planning consequences. First, if you and your spouse own property as *joint tenants with the right of survivorship (JT/WROS),* the property is considered owned 50-50 for estate tax purposes and will automatically pass to your spouse at your death, and vice versa. No gift tax is paid on creating such ownership, nor, due to the unlimited marital deduction, is any estate tax paid at the first death. However, this type of joint ownership may result in more taxes overall at the surviving spouse's later death than would be the case with a traditional marital share will, discussed earlier.

Second, if you and your spouse or anyone else own property as *tenants in common,* each individual is considered to own a proportionate share for tax purposes, and only your share is included in your estate. That share does not go to the other tenants in common at your death but is included in your probate estate and subject to your decision as to who gets it. While there are no gift or estate tax consequences between spouse joint owners, gifts of joint interests to children or others can create taxation.

Tenancy by the entirety, the third type of joint ownership, is limited to married couples. Under this type of joint ownership, both spouses own the property; when one spouse dies, the other gets it automatically. Neither spouse may sell the property without the consent of the other.

Joint ownership is a poor substitute for a will. It gives you less control over the disposition and taxation of your property. Your state laws govern the types and effects of joint ownership. Some states require that survivorship rights be spelled out in the deed, or at least abbreviated (for example, JT/WROS). Only your attorney can advise you on these matters.

LIFE INSURANCE AND EMPLOYEE BENEFITS   Life insurance proceeds are free of income tax, excluded from probate, and wholly or partially exempt from most state inheritance taxes. These proceeds are included in your estate for federal estate tax purposes if the policy contains any incidents of ownership such as the right to change beneficiaries, surrender the policy for cash, or make loans on the policy.

Assignment of ownership to your beneficiary or a trust can remove a life insurance policy from your estate. But if your spouse is the intended beneficiary, you do not need to assign ownership, since the proceeds will be free of estate tax due to the marital deduction.

Death benefits from qualified pension, profit-sharing, or Keogh plans are excluded from your estate unless they are payable to it or unless your beneficiary elects the special provision for averaging income tax in lump-sum distributions.

If there is "too much" money in your qualified retirement plan when you and your spouse die, your heirs could lose up to 80 percent in federal and state income taxes, estate tax, and the "excess accumulation" tax. Proper estate planning can minimize such confiscatory taxes.[4]

LIFETIME GIFTS AND TRUSTS   Gifts or trusts with strings attached, such as retaining the income, use, or control of the property, are fully included in your estate at their date-of-death value, whether your rights are expressed or implied. For example, if you transfer title of your home to a child but continue to live in it, the home is taxed in your estate. Or if you put property in trust and retain a certain amount of control over the income or principal, the property is included in your estate even though you cannot obtain it yourself. Also, if you are the beneficiary of a trust established by someone else and you have general rights to the principal during life or the power to appoint it to anyone at death, that amount is included in your estate.

SETTLING YOUR ESTATE

If you have had a will drawn, you are *testate* in the eyes of the law, and an executor (named in your will) will carry out your wishes in due time. If you have not named an executor, the probate court (the court that supervises the distribution of estates) will appoint an administrator to carry out the instructions in your will.

If you don't have a will, you become *intestate* at your death. In that case, your estate is put under the control of a court-appointed administrator for distribution according to the laws of the state in which you reside.

CONCEPT CHECK 19-4

1 Differentiate among the various types of trusts.
2 What is included in an estate?
3 What are the three types of joint ownership?

Action Application Discuss with your attorney the possibility of establishing a trust as a means of managing your estate.

Federal and State Estate Taxes

The tax aspects of estate planning have changed considerably due to recent major changes in the federal tax structure. The maximum tax rate on estates and gifts, for example, is gradually declining. As Exhibit 19–6 shows, estate settlement costs can quickly deplete an estate.

You can reduce your taxable estate by giving away assets to anyone during your lifetime. (But don't give away assets just to reduce your estate tax liability if you may need those assets in your retirement.) No gift tax is due on gifts of up to $11,000 to any one person in any one year. (A married couple, acting together, may give up to $22,000 to one person in one year.)

For example, suppose that on December 31, 2005, Michael gave $11,000 worth of shares of a stock mutual fund to his son. On January 2, 2009, these shares are worth $31,000. As a result of this gift in 2005, Michael has removed from his estate the $11,000 gift plus $20,000 of appreciation, for a total of $31,000. All of this has been accomplished at no gift tax cost.

TYPES OF TAXES

Federal and state governments levy various types of taxes that you must consider in planning your estate. The four major taxes of this kind are estate taxes, estate and trust income taxes, inheritance taxes, and gift taxes.

Objective 5

Evaluate the effects of federal and state taxes on estate planning.

DID YOU KNOW?

In 2006, 2007, and 2008, gross estates of $2 million or less will not owe federal estate taxes.

	Gross Estate	Settlement Costs	Net Estate	Percent Shrinkage
Elvis Presley	$10,165,434	$7,374,635	$2,790,799	73%
John D. Rockefeller	26,905,182	17,124,988	9,780,194	64
Clark Gable	2,806,526	1,101,038	1,705,488	39
Walt Disney	23,004,851	6,811,943	16,192,908	30

Source: Public court records, state probate courts.

Exhibit **19-6**

The erosion of probate and estate taxes

estate tax A federal tax on the right of a deceased person to transfer property and life insurance at death.

Death and taxes. Dealing with the financial aspects of a person's death can be a difficult burden.

ESTATE TAXES

An **estate tax** is a federal tax levied on the right of a deceased person to transmit his or her property and life insurance at death. Estate taxes have undergone extensive revision since the mid-1970s. The Economic Recovery Tax Act of 1981 made important tax concessions, particularly the unlimited marital deduction and the increased exemption equivalent.

Then, the Economic Growth and Tax Relief Reconciliation Act of 2001 brought important changes to the federal estate, gift, and generation-skipping transfer (GST) taxes, including a potential one-year repeal of the estate and GST taxes after 2009. However, the elimination of these taxes will be brief unless Congress considers legislation to permanently remove estate and GST taxes. As the act stands now, all of its provisions will be repealed as of December 31, 2010. Consequently, the estate, gift, and GST tax provisions in effect in 2001 will become the law once again on January 1, 2011—unless Congress takes intervening action.

Many changes in the estate, gift, and generation-skipping transfer taxes will be phased in gradually during this decade. For example, the amount exempt from estate tax rose to $1 million in 2002. The amount exempt from GST tax was adjusted for inflation in 2002 and 2003. Both exemptions (estate tax and GST tax) increased to $1.5 million in 2004 and to $2.0 million in 2006 and will increase to $3.5 million in 2009.

Under present law, with intelligent estate planning and properly drawn wills, you may leave all of your property to your surviving spouse free of federal estate taxes. The surviving spouse's estate in excess of $2 million (in 2006) faces estate taxes of 47 percent.

All limits have been removed from transfers between spouses during their lifetimes as well as at death. Whatever you give your spouse is exempt from gift and estate taxes. Gift tax returns need not be filed for interspousal gifts. There is still the possibility, however, that such gifts will be included in your estate if they were given within three years of your death.

ESTATE AND TRUST FEDERAL INCOME TAXES

In addition to the federal estate tax, estates and certain trusts must file federal income tax returns with the Internal Revenue Service. Generally, taxable income for estates and trusts is computed in much the same manner as taxable income for individuals. Under the Tax Reform Act of 1986, trusts and estates must pay quarterly estimated taxes, and new trusts must use the calendar year as the tax year.

inheritance tax A tax levied on the right of an heir to receive an estate.

INHERITANCE TAXES

An **inheritance tax** is levied on the right of an heir to receive all or part of the estate and life insurance proceeds of a deceased person. The tax payable depends on the net value of the property and insurance received. It also depends on the relationship of the heir to the deceased.

Inheritance taxes are imposed only by the state governments. Most states levy an inheritance tax, but the state laws differ widely as to exemptions, rates of taxation, and the treatment of property and life insurance. A reasonable average for state inheritance taxes would be 4 to 10 percent of your estate, with the higher percentages on larger amounts.

Over the past few years, many states have been phasing out their inheritance tax provisions, usually over a period of three or four years. This apparently reflects a desire to retain older and wealthy citizens as residents and to discourage them from leaving the states where they have lived most of their lives to seek tax havens in states such as Florida and Nevada. Increasingly, state legislatures have been questioning the equity of further taxes at death and are opting instead for sales and income taxes to provide state revenues.

GIFT TAXES   The federal and state governments levy a **gift tax** on the privilege of making gifts to others. A property owner can avoid estate and inheritance taxes by giving property during his or her lifetime. For this reason, the federal tax laws provide for taxes on gifts of property. The tax rates on gifts used to be only 75 percent of the tax rates on estates, but since 1976 the gift tax rates have been the same as the estate tax rates. Indeed, the tax rates are now called *unified transfer tax rates.*

Many states have gift tax laws. The state gift tax laws are similar to the federal gift tax laws, but the exemptions and dates for filing returns vary widely among the states.

As discussed earlier, the federal gift tax law allows you to give up to $11,000 each year to any person without incurring gift tax liability or having to report the gift to the IRS. Note that the Taxpayer Relief Act of 1997 increased this amount in $1,000 increments, depending on rates of inflation in future years. Gifts from a husband or a wife to a third party are considered as having been made in equal amounts by each spouse. Consequently, a husband and wife may give as much as $22,000 per year to anyone without incurring tax liability.

Even though estate and GST taxes are repealed in 2010, note that the gift tax is not scheduled to be repealed. Instead, the new law creates a $1 million lifetime gift tax exclusion, starting in 2002. In 2010, the maximum gift tax rate will be 35 percent, which will be the top individual federal income tax rate that year. Individuals are still allowed to give up to $11,000 annually to any person without paying a gift tax.

Exhibit 19–7 summarizes the important provisions of the Economic Growth and Tax Relief Reconciliation Act of 2001 pertaining to estate planning.

gift tax A federal and state tax on the privilege of making gifts to others.

TAX AVOIDANCE AND TAX EVASION

A poorly arranged estate may be subject to unduly large taxation. Therefore, you should study the tax laws and seek advice to avoid estate taxes larger than those the lawmakers intended you to pay. You should have a clear idea of the distinction between tax avoidance and tax evasion. *Tax avoidance* is the use of legal methods to reduce or escape taxes; *tax evasion* is the use of illegal methods to reduce or escape taxes.

CHARITABLE GIFTS AND BEQUESTS   Gifts made to certain recognized charitable or educational organizations are exempt from gift, estate, and inheritance taxes. Accordingly, such gifts or bequests (gifts through a will) represent one method of reducing or avoiding estate and inheritance taxes.

CALCULATING THE TAX

The estate tax is applied not to your total gross estate but to your net taxable estate at death. *Net taxable estate* is your testamentary net worth after subtracting your debts, liabilities, probate costs, and administration costs. These items, all of which are taken off your estate before calculating your tax, are cash requirements to be paid by your estate.

DEBTS AND LIABILITIES   In arriving at your taxable estate, the amount of your debts and other creditor obligations are subtracted. You are liable for the payment of these debts while living; your estate will be liable at your death. Your debts may include mortgages, collateralized loans, margin accounts, bank loans, notes payable, installment and charge accounts, and accrued income and property taxes. They may also include your last-illness and funeral expenses.

PROBATE AND ADMINISTRATION COSTS   Your estate administration costs will include fees for attorneys, accountants, appraisers, executors or administrators and trustees, court costs, bonding and surety costs, and miscellaneous expenses. These administration costs may run 5 to 8 percent of your estate, depending on its size and complexity. While the percentage usually decreases as the size of the estate increases, it may be increased by additional complicating factors, such as handling a business interest.

Next, deductions are made for bequests to qualified charities and for property passing to your spouse (the marital deduction). That leaves your net taxable estate, to which the rates shown in Exhibit 19–7 are applied to determine your gross estate tax.

Inheritance and estate taxes in your own state are additional costs, and these costs are not deductible in arriving at your taxable estate. In fact, you may have to pay inheritance taxes in two or more states, depending on the location of your property.

PAYING THE TAX

If, after having used various estate tax reduction techniques, you must still pay an estate tax, you should consider the best way to pay it. The federal estate tax is due and payable in cash nine months after your death. State taxes, probate costs, debts, and expenses also

Exhibit **19–7**   Estate tax law changes

The Economic Growth and Tax Relief Reconciliation Act of 2001 brought important and significant changes to the federal estate, gift, and generation-skipping transfer (GST) taxes, including a potential one-year repeal of the estate and GST taxes after 2009.

Tax Year	Highest Estate Tax Rate (%)	Gift Exemption ($ million)	Estate Exemption Unified or Credit Amount ($ million)	GST Tax Exemption ($ million)	Notes
2001	55	0.675	0.675	0.675	
2002	50	1.00	1.00	1.00*	Estate tax exemption is raised to $1 million; top estate tax is cut to 50 percent.
2003	49	1.00	1.00	1.00*	Top estate tax is cut to 49 percent.
2004	48	1.00	1.50	1.50	Estate tax exemption rises to $1.5 million; top estate tax rate is cut to 48 percent.
2005	47	1.00	1.50	1.50	Top estate tax is cut to 47 percent.
2006	46	1.00	2.00	2.00	Exemption rises to $2 million; top rate declines to 46 percent.
2007	45	1.00	2.00	2.00	Top rate declines to 45 percent.
2008	45	1.00	2.00	2.00	No change.
2009	45	1.00	3.50	3.50	Exemption rises to $3.5 million.
2010	0	1.00	Repeal	Repeal	Estate tax is completely repealed.
2011	55	1.00	1.00	1.00	The new tax law "sunsets" and all changes revert to before the new tax law, unless Congress amends the new law by this time.

*Adjusted annually for inflation.

usually fall due within that time. These often result in a real cash bind, because people rarely keep a lot of cash on hand. They derived their wealth from putting their money to work in businesses, real estate, or other investments. Estate liquidity—having enough cash to pay taxes and costs without selling assets or borrowing heavily—is often a problem.

Sheet 69
Estate tax projection and settlement costs

One way to handle the estate tax is to set aside or accumulate enough cash to pay it when it falls due. However, you may die before you have accumulated enough cash, and the cash you accumulate may be subject to income tax during your lifetime and to estate tax at your death.

Another way to handle the estate tax is for your family to sell assets to pay taxes. The first assets to be sold might be stocks, bonds, gold or silver coins, and similar liquid assets. However, these assets may be the source of your family's income after your death, and the market for them may be down. Assets such as real estate may also be sold, but prices on forced sales are usually only a fraction of the fair value.

Your family could consider borrowing; however, it is unusual to find a commercial lender that will lend money to pay back-taxes. If you do find one, it may require personal liability. In any event, borrowing does not solve the problem; it only prolongs it, adding interest costs in the process.

Borrowing from the IRS itself in the form of deferred payments or installments may be possible for reasonable cause. Tax extension and installment payment provisions are helpful, but they still leave a tax debt to be paid by your heirs at your death. Paying that debt, even over an extended period of time, could be a real burden and severely restrict their income and flexibility.

Life insurance may be a reasonable, feasible, and economical means of paying your estate tax. Instead of forcing your family to pay off the estate tax and other debts and costs by borrowing or selling, you can, through insurance, provide your family with tax-free cash at a fraction of the cost of borrowing.

CONCEPT CHECK 19-5

1 What are the four types of taxes to consider in planning your estate?
2 How is estate tax calculated?
3 What are the various ways to handle the payment of estate tax?

Action Application Ask your state department of revenue for brochures on state inheritance and gift taxes. What are the exemptions and rates of taxes? How are your property and life insurance treated for the purpose of inheritance tax? Of gift tax?

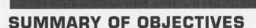

SUMMARY OF OBJECTIVES

Objective 1
Analyze the personal aspects of estate planning.
Estate planning is an essential part of retirement planning and an integral part of financial planning. The first part of estate planning consists of building your estate; the second part consists of transferring your estate, at your death, in the manner you have specified. The personal aspects of estate planning depend on whether you are single or married. If you are married, your estate planning involves the interests of at least two people, and more if there are children. Never having been married does not eliminate the need to organize your financial affairs.

Objective 2
Assess the legal aspects of estate planning.
In the event of death, proof of claims must be produced or the claims will not be processed. Among the papers needed are birth certificates, marriage certificates, legal name changes, and military service records. Every adult should have a written will, which is the legal declaration of a person's mind as to the disposition of his or her property after death. Thus, a will is a way to transfer your property according to your wishes after you die.

Objective 3

Distinguish among various types and formats of wills.
The four types of wills are the simple will, the traditional marital share will, the exemption trust will, and the stated dollar amount will. A will can be simple or complex depending on your personal and financial circumstances.

A *simple will,* sometimes called an *I love you will,* leaves everything to the spouse. Such a will is sufficient for most smaller estates. However, if you have a large or complex estate, a simple will may not meet your objectives. It may also create higher overall taxation, because everything would be taxed in your spouse's subsequent estate.

Objective 4

Appraise various types of trusts and estates.
Establishing a trust can be an excellent way to manage your estate. Trusts are revocable or irrevocable. Popular forms of trusts include credit-shelter trusts, grantor retained annuity trusts, disclaimer trusts, marital-deduction trusts, living trusts, self-declaration trusts, testamentary trusts, life insurance trusts, charitable remainder trusts, qualified personal residence trusts, charitable lead trusts, generation-skipping trusts, and spendthrift trusts. An attorney's help is needed to establish a trust.

If you establish a *revocable trust,* you retain the right to end the trust or change its terms during your lifetime. If you establish an *irrevocable trust,* you cannot change its terms or end it. However, an irrevocable trust offers tax advantages not offered by a revocable trust.

Objective 5

Evaluate the effects of federal and state taxes on estate planning.
The tax aspects of estate planning have changed considerably due to recent major changes in the federal tax structure. The four major federal and state taxes you must consider in planning your estate are estate taxes, estate and trust income taxes, inheritance taxes, and gift taxes.

The federal estate tax is due and payable in cash nine months after your death. State taxes, probate costs, debts, and expenses also usually fall due within that time.

KEY TERMS

adjusted gross estate 620	**gift tax** 637	**revocable trust** 628
beneficiary 622	**guardian** 622	**simple will** 620
codicil 624	**holographic will** 621	**stated dollar amount will** 621
community property 633	**inheritance tax** 636	**statutory will** 622
credit-shelter trust 629	**intestate** 618	**testamentary trust** 630
disclaimer trust 629	**irrevocable trust** 628	**traditional marital share will** 620
estate 614	**life insurance trust** 630	**trust** 628
estate planning 614	**living trust** 630	**trustee** 622
estate tax 636	**living will** 624	**trustor** 628
ethical will 626	**power of attorney** 626	**will** 618
exemption trust will 621	**prenuptial agreement** 624	
formal will 622	**probate** 620	

FINANCIAL PLANNING PROBLEMS

1. *Calculating the Gift Tax.* In 2006, Joshua gave $11,000 worth of Microsoft stock to his son. In 2009, the Microsoft shares are worth $23,000.

   a. What was the gift tax in 2006?

   b. What is the total amount removed from Joshua's estate in 2009?

   c. What will be the gift tax in 2009?

2. *Calculating the Gift Tax.* In 2006, you gave an $11,000 gift to a friend. What is the gift tax?

3. *Calculating the Gift Tax.* Barry and his wife Mary have accumulated over $4 million during their 45 years of marriage. They have three children and five grandchildren.

   How much money can they gift to their children and grandchildren in 2006 without any gift tax liability?

4. *Calculating the Gift Tax.* The date of death for a widow was 2006. If the estate was valued at $2,129,000 and the estate was taxed at 47 percent, what was the heir's tax liability?

5. *Calculating the Gift Tax.* Joel and Rachel Simon are both retired. Married for 50 years, they've amassed an estate worth $2.4 million. The couple has no trusts or other types of tax-sheltered assets. If Joel or Rachel dies in 2006–2008, how much federal estate tax would the surviving spouse have to pay, assuming that the estate is taxed at the 47 percent rate?

1. *Preparing a Written Record of Personal Information.* Prepare a written record of personal information that would be helpful to you and your heirs. Make sure to include the location of family records, your military service file, and other important papers; medical records; bank accounts; charge accounts; the location of your safe-deposit box; U.S. savings bonds; stocks, bonds, and other securities; property owned; life insurance; annuities; and Social Security information. (Obj. 1)

2. *Using the Internet to Obtain Information about Wills.* Visit Metropolitan Life Insurance Company's Web site at www.lifeadvice.com. Using this information, prepare a report on the following: (*a*) Who needs a will? (*b*) What are the elements of a will (naming a guardian, naming an executor, preparing a will, updating a will, estate taxes, where to keep your will, living will, etc.)? (*c*) How is this report helpful in preparing your own will?

FINANCIAL PLANNING ACTIVITIES

3. *Preparing the Letter of Last Instructions.* Prepare your own letter of last instructions. (Obj. 3)

4. *Determining Criteria in Choosing a Guardian.* Make a list of the criteria you will use in deciding who will be the guardian of your minor children if you and your spouse die at the same time. (Obj. 3)

5. *Using the Internet to Obtain Information about Estate Planning.* Visit the Prudential Insurance Company of America Web site at prudential.com/estateplan. Gather information on various estate planning topics such as an estate planning worksheet; whether you need an estate plan; when to update your plan; estate taxes, wills, executors, trusts, etc. Then prepare a report to help you develop your estate plan. (Obj. 4)

INTERNET CONNECTION

Estate Planning and Charitable Giving

Charitable gifts can be an important tool in estate planning. Giving to charity supports a cause and offers benefits such as reduced taxes and increased interest income.

To find ways to plan an estate and help your favorite charities at the same time, use the Internet to find at least three Web sites that suggest general ways to combine estate planning and charitable giving. At the Web sites, look for specific details about planned giving.

Keywords Used	Site Name	Web Site Addresses	Information Offered

1. What basic approaches to estate planning through charitable giving did you find?

_____

_____

_____

2. Which Web sites suggest using donations in estate planning?

_____

_____

_____

_____

3. Choose a charity that accepts donations from people's wills. How does the charity use these gifts?

_____

_____

_____

FINANCIAL PLANNING CASE

Don't Let Your Windfall Blow Away

Warren, a married entrepreneur who owns a successful promotions business in New York City, doesn't yet have kids, but he is already making plans. Last December, Warren received an unexpected inheritance of $1.4 million, after taxes, from his late grandfather. Instead of buying a Porsche or a new home, he did the right thing by his family-to-be and invested it all. "Warren is extremely fastidious," says Lesley Sommers, his financial planner.

Warren did what smart people do with sudden wealth: They decide not to blow it. "Letting your head rule your emotions lets you keep your money, not lose it," says Barbara Levin, director of the Forum for Investor Advice in Bethesda, Maryland, a research group for investment pros. A 1997 Forum survey found that 59 percent of 1,000 respondents who received cash payouts of $20,000 or more had sought professional advice. An equal number had invested every dime. When Warren got his windfall, Sommers invested all but $100,000. Warren says, "she taught me that this [windfall] should not change where I eat or go on vacation." So if you win the lottery, don't blow it on houses, cars, vacations, and luxury items. Even millions won't go far once the IRS takes its share. Instead, pay off high-interest credit card and other debts that offer no tax deductions. Then find a financial adviser. (A good source is the Certified Financial Planner Board of Standards at 1-888-237-6275; www.cfp-board.org.) This professional can help you find a competent estate planner and create an investment plan.

Questions

1. What did Warren do with his $1.4 million inheritance?

2. What do smart people do with sudden wealth?

Source: Adapted from Joan Oleck, "Don't Let Your Windfall Blow Away," *BusinessWeek On-line,* December 1999, p. 116. Reprinted by special permission. © 1999 McGraw-Hill Companies Inc.

VIDEO CASE

Estate Planning

A married couple, Linda and Charles, have just learned about the death of their friend, Lloyd, and wondered whether Lloyd had provided for his family. Charles admits he doesn't even have a will. What would happen to their children if Charles died today?

Rick Fenelli, an estate planning attorney, explains that the first step in estate planning is to identify all of your assets. He reminds us that most people forget that life insurance proceeds are fully taxable by Uncle Sam.

Linda and Charles believe their net worth is not much, even though they own a home, a savings account, 401(k)s, and a few IRAs. Their attorney friend calculates that Linda and Charles have a net worth of about $1 million. The couple is startled. The attorney friend explains that they already have a will even though they never wrote one. The will is written by the state and it's called "probate." Dying without a will is called "dying intestate."

Finally, Violet P. Woodhouse, an attorney and certified financial planner describes holographic, formal, and statutory wills. She explains that taxes—federal income taxes, gift taxes, estate taxes, and inheritance taxes—are relevant to estate planning.

Questions

1. What triggered Charles and Linda to start thinking about planning their estate?

2. According to attorney Rick Fenelli, what is the first step in estate planning?

3. Who writes your will if you don't?

4. According to attorney and certified financial planner, Violet P. Woodhouse, what are three kinds of wills?

5. What taxes are relevant in estate planning?

YOUR PERSONAL FINANCIAL PLANNER IN ACTION

Developing an Estate Plan

Most people do not think they have enough assets to do estate planning. However, the planned transfer of resources with the use of a will, trusts, and other legal vehicles is a necessary phase of your total financial plan.

Your Short-Term Financial Planning Activities	Resources
1. Investigate the cost of a will. Decide on the type of will and provisions appropriate for your life situation.	PFP Sheet 67 www.mtpalermo.com www.prudential.com www.nolo.com
2. Using the IRS and other Web sites, identify recent estate tax law changes that may affect your financial planning decisions.	www.irs.com www.banksite.com/calc/estate
3. Compare the benefits and costs of different trusts that might be appropriate for your life situation.	PFP Sheet 68 www.webtrust.com
Your Long-Term Financial Planning Activities	
1. Develop a plan for actions to be taken related to estate planning	PFP Sheet 66 www.naepc.org
2. Identify saving and investing decisions that would minimize future estate taxes	PFP Sheet 69 www.smartmoney.com

CONTINUING CASE

Estate Planning

Life Situation
Pam, 48
Josh, 50
Children ages 21, 19, and 16

Financial Data
Monthly income $6,700
Living expenses $5,600
Assets $242,500
Liabilities $69,100

Pam and Josh should also be concerned with various estate planning actions. They have talked about a will and investigated the benefits of several types of trusts. However, they have not taken any specific actions.

Questions

1. What types of estate planning activities might be considered by the Brocks at this time?
2. In what ways might *Personal Financial Planner* sheets 66–69 be used by the Brocks?

A Appendix: Financial Planners and Other Financial Planning Information Sources

"ATM fees rise."

"Global currency fluctuations may affect consumer prices."

"Mortgage interest rates remain constant."

These are just a few of the possible influences on personal financial decisions that occur each day. While this book offers the foundation for successful personal financial planning, changing social trends, economic conditions, and technology influence the decision-making environment. Your ability to continually update your knowledge is a skill that will serve you for a lifetime.

Various resources are available to assist you with personal financial decisions. These resources include printed materials, financial institutions, courses and seminars, the Internet, computer software, and financial planning specialists.

Current Periodicals

As Exhibit A–1 shows, a variety of personal finance periodicals are available to expand and update your knowledge. These periodicals, along with books on various personal finance topics, can be found in libraries.

Financial Institutions

Some financial advisers, such as insurance agents and investment brokers, are affiliated with companies that sell financial services. Through national marketing efforts or local promotions, banks, savings and loan associations, credit unions, insurance companies, investment brokers, and real estate offices offer suggestions on budgeting, saving, investing, and other aspects of financial planning. These organizations frequently offer booklets, financial planning worksheets, Web sites, and other materials and information.

Courses and Seminars

Colleges and universities offer courses in investments, real estate, insurance, taxation, and estate planning to enhance your knowledge of personal financial planning. The Cooperative Extension Service, funded through the U.S. Department of Agriculture, has offices located at universities in every state and in many counties (see your local telephone directory). Programs of these offices include community seminars and continuing education courses in the areas of family financial management, housing, consumer

Exhibit **A-1**   Personal financial planning periodicals

The area of personal finance is constantly changing. You can keep up with changes by reading the following periodicals. You can subscribe to them, read them at your school or community library, or access selected articles online.

Bloomberg Personal Finance

110 E. 59th Street

New York, NY 10022

(www.bloomberg.com)

BusinessWeek

1221 Avenue of the Americas

New York, NY 10020

(www.businessweek.com)

Consumer Reports

Consumers Union

101 Truman Avenue

Yonkers, NY 10703-1057

(www.consumerreports.org)

Forbes

60 Fifth Avenue

New York, NY 10011

(www.forbes.com)

Fortune

Time & Life Building

Rockefeller Center

New York, NY 10020-1393

(www.fortune.com)

Kiplinger's Personal Finance Magazine

1729 H Street, NW

Washington, DC 20006

(www.kiplinger.com)

Money

Time & Life Building

Rockefeller Center

New York, NY 10020-1393

(www.money.com)

Smart Money

224 West 57th Street

New York, NY 10019

(www.smartmoney.com)

U.S. News & World Report

2400 N Street, NW

Washington, DC 20037-1196

(www.usnews.com)

The Wall Street Journal

200 Burnett Road

Chicopee, MA 01020

(www.wsj.com)

Worth

575 Lexington Avenue

New York, NY 10022

(www.worth.com)

purchasing, health care, and food and nutrition. In addition, Cooperative Extension Service offices offer a variety of publications, videos, and software to assist consumers.

Civic clubs, libraries, and community organizations often schedule free or inexpensive programs on career planning, small-business management, budgeting, life insurance, tax return preparation, and investments. Financial institutions and financial service trade associations present seminars for current and prospective customers and members.

Personal Finance Software

Personal computer software is available to help you perform a variety of personal financial planning activities, from selecting a career to writing a will. These programs help you analyze your current financial situation and project your future financial position. Specialized computer programs are also available for conducting investment analyses, preparing tax returns, and determining the costs of financing and owning a home. Remember, a personal computer cannot change your saving, spending, and borrowing habits; only *you* can do that. However, your computer can provide fast and current analyses of your financial situation and progress.

SPREADSHEETS

A spreadsheet program, such as Excel, can assist with various financial planning tasks. Spreadsheet software can store, manipulate, create projections, and report data for activities such as

- Creating budget categories and recording spending patterns.
- Maintaining tax records for different types of expenses such as mileage, travel expenses, materials and supplies, and business-related costs.
- Calculating the growth potential of savings accounts and investments.
- Monitoring changes in the market value of investments.
- Keeping records of the value of items for a home inventory.
- Projecting needed amounts of life insurance and retirement income.

An Internet search for "personal finance spreadsheets" can help you locate various ready-to-use templates.

MONEY MANAGEMENT AND FINANCIAL PLANNING PROGRAMS

Integrated financial planning programs can help you maintain home financial records, create a budget, observe spending patterns, write checks, keep tax records, select and monitor investments, and project retirement needs. The most popular of these software packages are

MS Money	Quicken
Microsoft	Intuit
1-800-426-9400	1-800-446-8848
(www.microsoft.com/money)	(www.quicken.com)

TAX SOFTWARE

Each year the software available to prepare federal and state tax returns becomes more helpful. Besides preparation and printing of the various forms and schedules, programs include tax-planning tips (with audio and video clips), audit warnings, and the ability to file your tax return electronically. The most readily available tax software includes

TurboTax	TaxCut
Quicken	Kiplinger
1-800-446-8848	1-800-235-4060
(www.turbotax.com)	(www.taxcut.com)

INVESTMENT ANALYSIS PROGRAMS

Software designed for researching, trading, and monitoring an investment portfolio is also available. Most of these programs may be connected to online services to obtain current stock quotes and to buy and sell investments.

The Web and Personal Financial Planning

The Internet makes it possible to access more information from your home or office than libraries offer. You may use the Web for a variety of personal financial planning activities, including (1) researching current financial information; (2) obtaining programs to do financial planning calculations; (3) monitoring current stock and investment values; and (4) asking questions of experts and others through help lines, bulletin board services, and discussion forums. Some of the most useful Web sites providing current information on various personal finance topics include

- *Money* magazine at www.money.com; *Kiplinger's Personal Finance* at www.kiplinger.com; and *BusinessWeek* at www.businessweek.com
- The Motley Fool at www.fool.com
- "About Financial Planning" at financialplan.about.com
- Bankrate at www.bankrate.com
- Money Central at www.moneycentral.msn.com
- The Federal Reserve System at www.federalreserve.gov

Additional Web sites are offered at the end of each chapter in the Your Personal Financial Planner in Action feature.

Using Search Engines

A search engine is a Web site that allows you to locate information related to specific topics. Some of the most commonly used search engines include:

- www.altavista.com
- www.ask.com
- www.excite.com
- www.go.com
- www.google.com
- www.hotbot.com
- www.lycos.com
- www.northernlight.com
- www.search.com
- www.yahoo.com

Various search engines operate in different ways and provide various features. Some search engines look for topic areas; others seek specific words. When conducting Web searches, be precise with your descriptive words. For example, use "mortgage rates" instead of "interest rates" to obtain information on the cost of borrowing to buy a home. Use "resumes" instead of "career planning" for assistance on developing a personal data sheet.

Financial Planning Specialists

Various specialists provide specific financial assistance and advice:

- *Accountants* specialize in tax matters and financial documents.
- *Bankers* assist with financial services and trusts.
- *Certified financial planners* coordinate financial decisions into a single plan.
- *Credit counselors* suggest ways to reduce spending and eliminate credit problems.
- *Insurance agents* sell insurance coverage to protect your wealth and property.
- *Investment brokers* provide information and handle transactions for stocks, bonds, and other investments.

- *Lawyers* help in preparing wills, estate planning, tax problems, and other legal matters.
- *Real estate agents* assist with buying and selling a home or other real estate.
- *Tax preparers* specialize in the completion of income tax returns and other tax matters.

Many of these specialists offer services that include various aspects of financial planning. A financial planner's background or the company he or she represents is a good gauge of the financial planner's principal area of expertise. An accountant is likely to be most knowledgeable about tax laws, while an insurance company representative will probably emphasize how to use insurance for achieving financial goals.

WHO ARE THE FINANCIAL PLANNERS?

Many financial planners represent major insurance companies or investment businesses. Financial planners may also be individuals whose primary profession is tax accounting, real estate, or law. Over 250,000 people call themselves financial planners. Financial planners are commonly categorized based on four methods of compensation:

1. **Fee-only planners** charge an hourly rate that may range from $75 to $200, or may charge a fixed fee of between less than $500 and several thousand dollars. Other fee-only planners may charge an annual fee ranging from .04 percent to 1 percent of the value of your assets.
2. **Fee-offset planners** start with an hourly fee or an annual fee. This charge is reduced by any commission earned from the sale of investments or insurance.
3. **Fee-and-commission planners** earn commissions from the investment and insurance products purchased and charge a fixed fee (ranging from $250 to $2,000) for a financial plan.
4. **Commission-only planners** receive their revenue from the commissions on sales of insurance, mutual funds, and other investments.

Consumers must be cautious about the fees charged and how these fees are communicated. A study by the Consumer Federation of America revealed that more than half of financial planners who told "mystery shoppers" that they offer "fee-only" services actually earned commissions or other financial rewards for implementing the recommendations made to their clients.

DO YOU NEED A FINANCIAL PLANNER?

The two main factors that determine whether you need financial planning assistance are (1) your income and (2) your willingness to make independent decisions. If you earn less than $40,000 a year, you probably do not need a financial planner. Income of less than this amount does not allow for many major financial decisions once you have allocated for the spending, savings, insurance, and tax elements of your personal financial planning.

Taking an active role in your financial affairs can reduce the need for a financial planner. Your willingness to keep up to date on developments related to investments, insurance, and taxes can reduce the amount you spend on financial advisers. This will require an ongoing investment of time and effort; however, it will enable you to control your own financial direction.

When deciding whether to use a financial planner, also consider the services he or she provides. First, the financial planner should assist you in assessing your current financial position with regard to spending, saving, insurance, taxes, and potential investments. Second, the financial planner should offer a clearly written plan with different courses of action. Third, the planner should take time to discuss the components of the plan and help you monitor your financial progress. Finally, the financial planner should guide you to other experts and sources of financial services as needed.

HOW SHOULD YOU SELECT A FINANCIAL PLANNER?

You can locate financial planners by using a telephone directory, contacting financial institutions, or obtaining references from friends, business associates, or professionals with whom you currently deal, such as insurance agents or real estate brokers.

When evaluating a financial planner, ask the following:

- Is financial planning your primary activity, or are other activities primary?
- Are you licensed as an investment broker or as a seller of life insurance?
- What is your educational background and formal training?
- What are your areas of expertise?
- Do you use experts in other areas, such as taxes, law, or insurance, to assist you with financial planning recommendations?
- What professional titles and certifications do you possess?
- Am I allowed a free initial consultation?
- How is the fee determined? (Is this an amount I can afford?)
- Do you have an independent practice, or are you affiliated with a major financial services company?
- What are sample insurance, tax, and investment recommendations you make for clients?
- My major concern is _____. What would you suggest?
- May I see a sample of a written financial plan?
- May I see the contract you use with clients?
- Who are some of your clients whom I might contact?

Also, make sure you are comfortable with the planner and that the planner can clearly communicate. This type of investigation takes time and effort; however, remember that you are considering placing your entire financial future in the hands of one person.

HOW ARE FINANCIAL PLANNERS CERTIFIED?

While state and federal regulation of financial planners exists, the requirements for becoming a financial planner vary from state to state. For example, Kansas requires that new financial advisers pass an exam that measures knowledge of stocks, bonds, and other investment products. Some states license individual investment advisers; other states license firms but not individual advisers. A few states regulate neither individual advisers nor firms. Recent federal regulation requires that the Securities and Exchange Commission (SEC) monitor the largest financial advisers.

Many financial planners use abbreviations for the titles they have earned. Some of these abbreviations are quite familiar, for example, CPA (certified public accountant), JD (doctor of law), and MBA (master of business administration); others include CFP (certified financial planner), ChFC (chartered financial consultant, in the life insurance industry), PFS (personal financial specialist), AFC (accredited financial counselor), CFA (chartered financial analyst, handling stock and bond portfolios), AEP (accredited estate planner), CRP (certified retirement planner), RIA (registered investment adviser, registered with SEC), EA (enrolled agent, tax specialist), and RFC (registered financial consultant).

While these credentials provide some assurance of expertise, not all planners are licensed. The Better Business Bureau estimates that fraudulent planners take consumers for tens of millions of dollars in bad investments and advice each year. Financial planning activities such as insurance and investment security sales do come under regulatory control. Be wary of and investigate any financial planning action you are considering.

You may contact the following organizations and agencies for further information about certification and regulation of financial planners:

- National Association of Personal Financial Advisors at 1-888-333-6659 (www.napfa.org).
- Certified Financial Planners Board of Standards at 1-888-273-6275 (www.cfp.net).
- Financial Planning Association at 1-800-945-4237 (www.fpanet.org).
- North American Securities Administrators Association at 1-888-846-2722 (www.nasaa.org).
- National Association of Insurance Commissioners at 816-842-3600 (www.naic.org).
- Securities and Exchange Commission at 1-800-732-0330 (www.sec.gov).
- American Institute of Certified Public Accountants at 1-800-862-4272 (www.aicpa.org).

B Appendix: Consumer Agencies and Organizations

The following government agencies and private organizations can offer information and assistance on various financial planning and consumer purchasing areas. These groups can serve your needs when you want to

- Research a financial or consumer topic area.
- Obtain information for planning a purchase decision.
- Seek assistance to resolve a consumer problem.

Section 1 provides an overview of federal, state, and local agencies and other organizations you may contact for information related to various financial planning and consumer topic areas. Section 2 lists state consumer protection offices that can assist you in local matters.

Section 1

Most federal agencies may be contacted through the Internet; several Web sites are noted. In addition, consumer information from several federal government agencies may be accessed at www.consumeraction.gov

Exhibit **B-1**   Federal, state, and local agencies and other organizations

Topic Area	Federal Agency	State, Local Agency; Other Organizations
Advertising False advertising Product labeling Deceptive sales practices Warranties	Federal Trade Commission 600 Pennsylvania Avenue, NW Washington, DC 20580 1-877-FTC-HELP (www.ftc.gov)	State Consumer Protection Office c/o State Attorney General or Governor's Office (see Exhibit B-2) National Fraud Information Center Box 65868 Washington, DC 20035 1-800-876-7060 (www.fraud.org)
Air Travel Air safety Airport regulation Airline routes	Federal Aviation Administration 800 Independence Avenue, SW Washington, DC 20591 1–800–FAA–SURE (www.faa.gov)	International Airline Passengers Association Box 660074 Dallas, TX 75266 1–800–527–5888 (www.iapa.com)

Exhibit **B-1**   Continued

Topic Area	Federal Agency	State, Local Agency; Other Organizations
Appliances/Product Safety Potentially dangerous products Complaints against retailers, manufacturers	Consumer Product Safety Commission Washington, DC 20207 1-800-638-CPSC (www.cpsc.gov)	Council of Better Business Bureaus 4200 Wilson Boulevard Arlington, VA 22203 1-800-955-5100 (www.bbb.org)

Automobiles
New cars
Used cars
Automobile repairs
Auto safety
	Federal Trade Commission (see above)
	  National Highway Traffic Safety
	  Administration
	400 Seventh Street, SW
	Washington, DC 20590
	1-800-424-9393
	(www.nhtsa.gov)
		AUTOCAP/National Automobile
		  Dealers Association
		8400 Westpark Drive
		McLean, VA 22102
		1-800-252-6232
		(www.nada.org)
		
		Center for Auto Safety
		1825 Connecticut Ave., NW
		  (#330)
		Washington, DC 20009
		(202) 328-7700
		(www.autosafety.org)

Banking and Financial Institutions
Checking accounts
Savings accounts
Deposit insurance
Financial services
	Federal Deposit Insurance
	  Corporation
	550 17th Street, NW
	Washington, DC 20429
	1-877-275-3342
	(www.fdic.gov)
	
	Comptroller of the Currency
	15th Street and Pennsylvania
	  Avenue, NW
	Washington, DC 20219
	(202) 447-1600
	(www.occ.treas.gov)
	
	Federal Reserve Board
	Washington, DC 20551
	(202) 452-3693
	(www.federalreserve.gov)
	
	National Credit Union Administration
	1775 Duke Street
	Alexandria, VA 22314
	(703) 518-6300
	(www.ncua.gov)
		State Banking Authority
		
		Credit Union National
		  Association
		Box 431
		Madison, WI 53701
		(608) 232-8256
		(www.cuna.org)
		
		American Bankers Association
		1120 Connecticut Avenue, NW
		Washington, DC 20036
		(202) 663-5000
		(www.aba.com)
		
		U.S. savings bond rates
		1-800-US-BONDS
		(www.savingsbonds.gov)

Career Planning Job training Employment information	Coordinator of Consumer Affairs Department of Labor Washington, DC 20210 (202) 219-6060 (www.dol.gov)	State Department of Labor or State Employment Service

Exhibit **B-1**   Continued

Topic Area	Federal Agency	State, Local Agency; Other Organizations
Consumer Credit Credit cards Deceptive credit advertising Truth-in-Lending Act Credit rights of women, minorities	Federal Trade Commission 600 Pennsylvania Avenue, NW Washington, DC 20580 (202) 326-2222 (www.ftc.gov)	Consumer Credit Counseling Service 8701 Georgia Avenue, Suite 507 Silver Spring, MD 20910 1-800-388-2227 (www.nfcc.org)
Environment Air, water pollution Toxic substances	Environmental Protection Agency Washington, DC 20024 1-800-438-4318 (indoor air quality) 1-800-426-4791 (drinking water safety) (www.epa.gov)	Clean Water Action Project 4455 Connecticut Ave., NW (#A300) Washington, DC 20008 (202) 895-0420 (www.cleanwateraction.org)

Food
Food grades
Food additives
Nutritional information
	U.S. Department of Agriculture
	Washington, DC 20250
	1-800-424-9121
	(www.usda.gov)
	
	Food and Drug Administration
	5600 Fishers Lane
	Rockville, MD 20857
	1-888-463-6332
	(www.fda.gov)
		Center for Science in the Public
		   Interest
		1875 Connecticut Avenue, NW,
		   Suite 300
		Washington, DC 20009
		(202) 332-9110
		(www.cspinet.org)

Funerals Cost disclosure Deceptive business practices	Federal Trade Commission (see above)	Funeral Service Consumer Arbitration Program Box 486 Elm Grove, WI 53122 1-800-662-7666 (www.funeralservicefoundation.org)
Housing and Real Estate Fair housing practices Mortgages Community development	Department of Housing and Urban Development 451 Seventh Street, SW Washington, DC 20410 1-800-669-9777 (www.hud.gov)	National Association of Realtors 430 North Michigan Avenue Chicago, IL 60611 (www.realtor.com) National Association of Home Builders 1201 15th Street, NW Washington, DC 20005 1-800-368-5242 (www.nahb.com)
Insurance Policy conditions Premiums Types of coverage Consumer complaints	Federal Trade Commission (see above) National Flood Insurance Program 500 C Street, SW Washington, DC 20472 1-888-CALL-FLOOD (www.fema.gov/nfip)	State Insurance Regulator American Council of Life Insurance 1001 Pennsylvania Avenue, NW Washington, DC 20004-2599 1-800-942-4242 (www.acli.com) Insurance Information Institute 110 William Street New York, NY 10038 1-800-331-9146 (www.iii.org)

Exhibit **B-1**   Continued

Topic Area	Federal Agency	State, Local Agency; Other Organizations

Investments
Stocks, bonds
Mutual funds
Commodities
Investment brokers
	Securities and Exchange Commission
	450 Fifth Street, NW
	Washington, DC 20549
	(202) 942-7040
	(www.sec.gov)
	
	Commodity Futures Trading
	  Commission
	1155 21st Street, NW
	Washington, DC 20581
	(202) 418-5080
	(www.cftc.gov)
		Investment Company Institute
		1600 M Street, NW
		Washington, DC 20036
		(202) 293-7700
		(www.ici.org)
		
		National Association of Securities
		  Dealers
		1735 K Street, NW
		Washington, DC 20006
		(202) 728-8000
		(www.nasd.com)
		
		National Futures Association
		200 West Madison Street
		Chicago, IL 60606
		1-800-621-3570
		(www.nfa.futures.org)
		
		Securities Investor Protection Corp.
		805 15th Street, NW, Suite 800
		Washington, DC 20003
		(202) 371-8300
		(www.sipc.org)

Legal Matters Consumer complaints Arbitration	Department of Justice Office of Consumer Litigation Washington, DC 20530 (202) 514-2401 (www.usdoj.gov)	American Arbitration Association 140 West 51st Street New York, NY 10020 (212) 484-4000 (www.adr.org) American Bar Association 750 North Lake Shore Drive Chicago, IL 60611 (312) 988-5000 (www.abanet.org)
Mail Order Damaged products Deceptive business practices Illegal use of U.S. mail	U.S. Postal Service Washington, DC 20260-2202 1-800-ASK-USPS (www.usps.gov)	Direct Marketing Association 6 East 43rd Street New York, NY 10017 (212) 689-4977 (www.the-dma.org)

Medical Concerns
Prescription medications
Over-the-counter
  medications
Medical devices
Health care
	Food and Drug Administration (see
	  above)
	Public Health Service
	200 Independence Avenue, SW
	Washington, DC 20201
	1-800-336-4797
	(www.fda.gov)
		American Medical Association
		535 North Dearborn
		Chicago, IL 60610
		(312) 645-5000
		
		Public Citizen Health Research Group
		2000 P Street
		Washington, DC 20036
		(202) 872-0320

Exhibit **B-1**   Continued

Topic Area	Federal Agency	State, Local Agency; Other Organizations
Retirement Old-age benefits Pension information Medicare	Social Security Administration 6401 Security Boulevard Baltimore, MD 21235 1-800-772-1213 (www.ssa.gov)	American Association of Retired Persons 601 E Street, NW Washington, DC 20049 (202) 434-2277 (www.aarp.org)
Taxes Tax information Audit procedures	Internal Revenue Service 1111 Constitution Avenue, NW Washington, DC 20204 1-800-829-1040 1-800-TAX-FORM (www.irs.gov)	Department of Revenue (in your state capital city) The Tax Foundation One Thomas Circle Washington, DC 20005 (202) 822-9050 (www.taxfoundation.org) National Association of Enrolled Agents 6000 Executive Blvd. Rockville, MD 20852 1-800-424-4339
Telemarketing 900 numbers	Federal Communications Commission 445 12th Street, SW Washington, DC 20554 1-888-225-5322 (www.fcc.gov)	National Consumers League 815 Fifteenth Street, NW Washington, DC 20005 (202) 639-8140 (www.nclnet.org)
Utilities Cable television Utility rates	Federal Communications Commission 1919 M Street, NW Washington, DC 20554 (202) 632-6999 (www.fcc.gov)	State utility commission (in your state capital)

Information on additional government agencies and private organizations available to assist you may be obtained in the *Consumer Action Handbook,* available at no charge from the Consumer Information Center, Pueblo, CO 81009 or online at www.consumer-action.gov.

Section 2

State, county, and local consumer protection offices provide consumers with a variety of services, including publications and information before buying, as well as handling complaints. This section provides contact information for state consumer protection agencies. In addition to the primary offices listed here, agencies regulating banking, insurance, securities, and utilities are available in each state. These may be located through a Web search or by going to the *Consumer Action Handbook* at www.consumeraction.gov.

Many state consumer protection offices may be accessed through the Web site of the National Association of Attorneys General at www.naag.org or with a Web search for your state consumer protection office using "(state) consumer protection agency."

To save time, call the office before sending in a written complaint. Ask whether the office handles the type of complaint you have or if complaint forms are provided. Many offices distribute consumer materials specifically geared to state laws and local issues. Call to obtain available educational information on your problem.

State departments of insurance may be accessed online at www.naic.org or www.insurance.about.com/od/deptsofinsurance.

The Web sites of state tax departments are available at www.taxadmin.org or www.aicpa.org/yellow/yptsgus.htm.

Exhibit B-2   State consumer protection offices

Alabama
Office of Attorney General
Consumer Affairs Section
11 South Union Street
Montgomery, AL 36130
334-242-7335
Toll free in AL: 1-800-392-5658
www.ago.state.al.us

Alaska
Consumer Protection Unit
Office of the Attorney General
1031 West Fourth Avenue
Suite 200
Anchorage, AK 99501-5903
907-269-5100
www.law.state.ak.us

Arizona
Consumer Protection and Advocacy
   Section
Office of Attorney General
1275 West Washington Street
Phoenix, AZ 85007
602-542-3702
Toll free in AZ: 1-800-352-8431
www.azag.gov

Arkansas
Consumer Protection Division
Office of Attorney General
323 Center Street (#200)
Little Rock, AR 72201
501-682-2341
Toll free: 1-800-482-8982
E-mail: consumer@ag.state.ar.us
www.ag.state.ar.us

California
California Department of Consumer
   Affairs
400 R Street, Suite 3000
Sacramento, CA 95814
916-445-4465
Toll free in CA: 1-800-952-5210
www.dca.ca.gov

Colorado
Consumer Protection Division
Colorado Attorney General's Office
1525 Sherman Street (5th Floor)
Denver, CO 80203-1760
303-866-5079
Toll free: 1-800-222-4444

Connecticut
Department of Consumer Protection
165 Capitol Avenue
Hartford, CT 06106
860-713-6300
Toll free in CT: 1-800-842-2649
www.state.ct.us/dcp/

Delaware
Consumer Protection Division
Office of the Attorney General
820 North French Street (5th Floor)
Wilmington, DE 19801
302-577-8600
Toll free in DE: 1-800-220-5424
www.state.de.us/attgen

District of Columbia
Office of the Corporation Counsel
441 Fourth Street NW
Suite 450-N
Washington, DC 20001
202-442-9828 (consumer hotline)

Florida
Department of Agriculture &
   Consumer Services
2005 Apalachee Parkway
Tallahassee, FL 32399-6500
850-922-2966
Toll free in FL: 1-800-435-7352
www.800helpfla.com

Georgia
Governor's Office of Consumer
   Affairs
2 Martin Luther King, Jr., Drive
Suite 356
Atlanta, GA 30334
404-656-3790

Toll free in GA (outside Atlanta area):
   1-800-869-1123
www2.state.ga.us/gaoca

Hawaii
Office of Consumer Protection
Department of Commerce and
   Consumer Affairs
235 South Beretania Street (Room
   801)
Honolulu, HI 96813
808-586-2636
Fax: 808-586-2640
www.hawaii.gov/dcca/ocp

Idaho
Consumer Protection Unit
Idaho Attorney General's Office
650 West State Street
Boise, ID 83720-0010
208-334-2424
Toll free in ID: 1-800-432-3545
www.state.id.us/ag

Illinois
Consumer Protection Division of
   the Attorney General's Office
100 West Randolph Street (12th
   Floor)
Chicago, IL 60601
312-814-3580
Toll free in IL: 1-800-386-5438
www.illinoisattorneygeneral.gov

Indiana
Consumer Protection Division
Office of the Attorney General
Indiana Government Center South
402 West Washington Street (5th
   Floor)
Indianapolis, IN 46204
317-232-6201
Toll free in IN: 1-800-382-5516
www.in.gov/attorneygeneral

Iowa
Consumer Protection Division
Office of the Attorney General

Exhibit **B-2** continued

Director of Consumer Protection
   Division
1305 East Walnut Street, 2nd Floor
Des Moines, IA 50319
515-281-5926
E-mail: consumer@ag.state.ia.us
www.IowaAttorneyGeneral.org

Kansas
Consumer Protection Division
Office of Attorney General
120 SW 10th Street (4th Floor)
Topeka, KS 66612-1597
785-296-3751
Toll free in KS: 1-800-432-2310
E-mail: cprotect@ksag.org
www.ink.org/public/ksag

Kentucky
Consumer Protection Division
Office of the Attorney General
1024 Capital Center Drive
Frankfort, KY 40601
502-696-5389
Toll free in KY: 1-800-432-9257
E-mail: consumerprotection@law.
   state.ky.us
www.ag.ky.com

Louisiana
Consumer Protection Section
Office of the Attorney General
Box 94005
Baton Rouge, LA 70804-9005
Toll free nationwide:
   1-800-351-4889
www.ag.state.la.us

Maine
Attorney General
6 State House Station
Augusta, ME 04333
207-626-8800
www.maine.gov

Maryland
Consumer Protection Division
Office of the Attorney General
200 St. Paul Place (16th Floor)
Baltimore, MD 21202-2021
410-528-8662
E-mail: consumer@oag.state.md.us
www.oag.state.md.us/consumer

Massachusetts
Consumer Protection
Office of the Attorney General
One Ashburton Place

Boston, MA 02108
617-727-8400
www.mass.gov/ago

Michigan
Consumer Protection Division
Office of Attorney General
P. O. Box 30213
Lansing, MI 48909
517-373-1140 (complaint
   information)
1-877-765-8388

Minnesota
Consumer Services Division
Minnesota Attorney General's Office
1400 NCL Tower
445 Minnesota Street
St. Paul, MN 55101
612-296-3353
Toll free: 1-800-657-3787
E-mail: consumer.ag@state.mn.us
www.ag.state.mn.us/consumer

Mississippi
Consumer Protection Division
Office of Attorney General
P. O. Box 22947
Jackson, MS 39225-2947
601-359-4230
Toll free in MS: 1-800-281-4418
www.ago.state.ms.us

Missouri
Consumer Protection Division
P. O. Box 899
1530 Rax Court
Jefferson City, MO 65102
573-751-6887
573-751-3321
Toll free in MO: 1-800-392-8222
E-mail: attgenmail@moago.org
www.ago.state.mo.us

Montana
Consumer Affairs Unit
Department of Administration
1219 Eighth Avenue
Box 200151
Helena, MT 59620-0151
406-444-4500

Nebraska
Attorney General
Department of Justice
2115 State Capitol
P. O. Box 98920
Lincoln, NE 68509

402-471-2682
Toll free in state: 1-800-727-6432
www.nol.org/home/ago

Nevada
Nevada Consumer Affairs Division
1850 East Sahara (Suite 101)
Las Vegas, NV 89104
702-486-7355
Toll free: 1-800-362-5202
E-mail: ncad@consumer.org
www. fyiconsumer.org

New Hampshire
Consumer Protection and Antitrust
   Bureau
Office of Attorney General
33 Capitol Street
Concord, NH 03301
603-271-3641
www.doj.nh.gov/consumer/index
   .html

New Jersey
Division of Consumer Affairs
P.O. Box 45025
Newark, NJ 07102
973-504-6200
Toll free: 1-800-242-5846
E-mail: askconsumeraffairs@smtp.
   lps.state.nj.us
www.state.nj.us/lps/ca/home.htm

New Mexico
Consumer Protection Division
Office of the Attorney General
P.O. Drawer 1508
407 Galisteo
Santa Fe, NM 87504-1508
505-827-6060
Toll free in NM: 1-800-678-1508
www.ago.state.nm.us

New York
Bureau of Consumer Frauds and
   Protection
Office of the Attorney General
State Capitol
Albany, NY 12224
518-474-5481
www.oag.state.ny.us

North Carolina
Consumer Protection Division
Office of the Attorney General
9001 Mail Service Center
Raleigh, NC 27699-9001
919-716-6400
www.ncdoj.com

Exhibit **B-2** continued

North Dakota
Consumer Protection and Antitrust
    Division
Office of the Attorney General
4205 State Street (Box 1054)
Bismarck, ND 58502-1054
701-328-3404
Toll free in ND: 1-800-472-2600
E-mail: cpat@state.nd.us
www.ag.state.nd.us

Ohio
Ohio Attorney General's Office
10 West Broad Street (18th Floor)
Columbus, OH 43215
614-466-8574
E-mail: consumer@ag.state.oh.us
www.ag.state.oh.us

Oklahoma
Oklahoma Attorney General
Consumer Protection Unit
4545 N. Lincoln Avenue
    (Suite 104)
Oklahoma City, OK 73105
405-521-3653
Toll free: 1-800-448-4904
www.oag.state.ok.us

Oregon
Consumer Protection Section
Department of Justice
1162 Court Street, NE
Salem, OR 97310
503-378-4732
Toll free in OR: 1-877-877-9392
www.doj.state.or.us

Pennsylvania
Bureau of Consumer Protection
Office of Attorney General
14th Floor, Strawberry Square
Harrisburg, PA 17120
717-787-9707
Toll free in PA: 1-800-441-2555
www.attorneygeneral.gov

Puerto Rico
Department of Consumer Affairs
Minillas Station
P.O. Box 41059
Santurce, PR 00940-1059
787-721-0940
E-mail: Jalicea@Caribe.net

Rhode Island
Consumer Protection Unit
Department of Attorney General
150 South Main Street

Providence, RI 02903
401-274-4400
www.riag.state.ri.us

South Carolina
Department of Consumer Affairs
2801 Devine Street
P.O. Box 5757
Columbia, SC 29250-5757
803-734-4200
Toll free in SC: 1-800-922-1594
E-mail: scdca@infoave.net
www.scconsumer.gov

South Dakota
Division of Consumer Affairs
Office of the Attorney General
500 East Capitol
State Capitol Building
Pierre, SD 57501-5070
605-773-4400
Toll free in SD: 1-800-300-1986
www.state.sd.us/atg

Tennessee
Division of Consumer Affairs
500 James Robertson Parkway (5th
    Floor)
Nashville, TN 37243-0600
615-741-4737
Toll free in TN: 1-800-342-8385
www.state.tn.us/consumer

Texas
Consumer Protection Division
Office of Attorney General
P. O. Box 12548
Austin, TX 78711-2548
512-463-2185
www.oag.state.tx.us

Utah
Division of Consumer Protection
Department of Commerce
160 East 300 South
Box 146704
Salt Lake City, UT 84114-6704
801-530-6601
www.consumerprotection.utah.gov

Vermont
Consumer Assistance Program
Office of the Attorney General
104 Morrill Hall, UVM
Burlington, VT 05405
802-656-3183
www.atg.state.vt.us

Virgin Islands
Department of Licensing and
    Consumer Affairs
Property and Procurement Building
No. 1 Sub Base, Room 205
St. Thomas, VI 00802
340-774-3130
www.dlca.gov.vi

Virginia
Office of the Attorney General
Antitrust and Consumer Litigation
    Section
900 East Main Street
Richmond, VA 23219
804-786-2116
Toll free: 1-800-451-1525
Fax: 804-786-0122
E-mail: mail@oag.state.va.us
www.oag.state.va.us

Washington
Office of the Attorney General
1125 Washington Street, SE
Olympia, WA 98504-0100
Toll free in WA: 1-800-551-4636
www.atg.wa.gov

West Virginia
Consumer Protection Division
Office of Attorney General
812 Quarrier Street (6th Floor)
P. O. Box 1789
Charleston, WV 25326-1789
304-558-8986
Toll free in WV: 1-800-368-8808
E-mail: consumer@wvnet.edu
www.state.wv.us/wvag

Wisconsin
Division of Trade and Consumer
    Protection
2811 Agriculture Dr.
P.O. Box 8911
Madison, WI 53708-8911
608-224-4949
Toll free in WI: 1-800-422-7128
E-mail: datephotline@wheel.datep.
    state.wi.us
www.datcp.state.wi.us

Wyoming
Office of the Attorney General
Consumer Protection Unit
123 State Capitol Building
Cheyenne, WY 82002
307-777-7874
Toll free in WY only: 1-800-438-5799
attorneygeneral.state.wy.us

Source: www.consumeraction.gov.

Chapter 6

1. Peter Pae, "Credit Junkies," *The Wall Street Journal,* December 26, 1991, p. 1.
2. Joseph Weber, "Platinum vs. Platinum: The War over Fat Wallets," *BusinessWeek,* May 3, 1999, p. 152.
3. *Statistical Abstract of the United States: 2001,* Table 1189, p. 734.
4. Adapted from *Guide to Online Payments,* Federal Trade Commission, March 1999 (www.ftc.gov).
5. Adapted from William M. Pride, Robert J. Hughes, and Jack R. Kapoor, *Business,* 7th ed. (Boston: Houghton Mifflin, 2002), p. 568.

Chapter 7

1. Federal Reserve Bank of Cleveland, *Inside Vault,* Fall 2003, p. 4.
2. Judy Hammond, "Consumer Credit Counselors Say Debt Recovery Can Take Three to Five years," *Knight-Ridder/Tribune Business News,* February 16, 1999.
3. American Bankruptcy Institute, *Consumer Corner,* August 7, 1999, p. 4.

Chapter 11

1. Michael J. Mandel, "Health Care's Economic Payoff," *BusinessWeek,* April 29, 2002, p. 28; The Centers for Medicare and Medicaid Services; *BusinessWeek,* January 10, 2005, p. 115.
2. *Participant,* TIAA-CREF, May 2002, p. 18.
3. Eve Tahmincioglu, "The Catch-22 of Long-Term Care Insurance," *Kiplinger's Personal Finance,* May 1997, pp. 97–102.
4. "The New Power Play in Health Care," *BusinessWeek,* January 28, 2002, p. 90.
5. *U.S. Industry and Trade Outlook 2000,* p. 43–12.
6. "Mending Medicare: Washington's Real Hot Potato," *BusinessWeek,* March 1, 1999, p. 32.
7. *The Consumer's Guide to Disability Insurance* (Washington, DC: Health Insurance Association of America, September 1991), p. 1.
8. *Source Book of Health Insurance Data* (Washington, DC: Health Association of America, 1991), pp. 95–96.

Chapter 12

1. John Hillman, "Life Choices," *Best's Review,* June 2002, p. 88.
2. Carol Marie Cropper, "Paying a Premium," *BusinessWeek,* December 13, 2004, p. 148.

Chapter 13

1. Yahoo! Finance, finance.yahoo.com, April 7, 2005.
2. U.S. Bureau of the Census, *Statistical Abstract of the United States, 2004–2005* (Washington, DC: U.S. Government Printing Office), p. 448 (www.census.gov)
3. Motley Fool, www.fool.com, April 9, 2005.
4. Roger G. Ibbotson, "Predictions of the Past and Forecasts for the Future: 1976–2025," Ibbotson Associates website (www.ibbotson.com) April 9, 2005.
5. William J. Bernstein, "The Online Asset Allocator," *Efficient Frontier: An Online Journal of Asset Allocation,* www.efficientfrontier.com, April 9, 2005.
6. Ibid.
7. Motley Fool, www.fool.com, April 9, 2005.
8. Suze Orman, *The Road to Wealth* (New York: Riverbend Books, 2004), p. 371.

Chapter 14

1. Motley Fool, www.fool.com, April 9, 2005.
2. Roger G. Ibbotson, "Predictions of the Past and Forecasts for the Future: 1976–2025," Ibbotson Associates Web site (www.ibbotson.com) April 9, 2005.
3. Yahoo! Finance, finance.yahoo.com, April 18, 2005.
4. Ibid.
5. Investopedia.com, "Guide to Stock Picking Strategies," www.investopedia.com, April 20, 2005.
6. New York Stock Exchange, www.nyse.com, April 17, 2005.
7. Ibid.

Chapter 15

1. Motley Fool, www.fool.com, May 16, 2005.
2. G. Victor Hallman and Jerry S. Rosenbloom, *Personal Financial Planning* (New York: McGraw-Hill, 2000), p. 211.
3. Moody's Investors Service, www.moodysEurope.com, May 15, 2005.

Chapter 16

1. Mutual Fund Education Alliance, www.mfea.com, May 20, 2005.
2. Investment Company Institute, May 18, 2005.
3. Mutual Fund Education Alliance, www.mfea.com, May 20, 2005.
4. Prospectus for the Fundamental Investors Mutual Fund (American Funds, 1-800-421-0180 or www.americanfunds.com), March 1, 2005, p. 7.
5. "Index Investing: Index Funds," Investopedia, www.investopedia.com, May 21, 2005.
6. Vanguard Group, www.vanguard.com, May 21, 2005.
7. © 2005 Morningstar, Inc. All Rights Reserved. The information contained herein: (1) is proprietary to Morningstar and/or its content providers; (2) may not be copied or distributed; (3) does not constitute investment advice offered by Morningstar; and (4) is not warranted to be accurate, complete or timely. Neither Morningstar nor its content providers are responsible for any damages or losses arising from any use of this information. Past performance is no guarantee of future results. Use of information from Morningstar does not necessarily constitute agreement by Morningstar, Inc. of any investment philosophy or strategy presented in this publication.

Chapter 17

1. Kathleen Madigan, "After the Housing Boom," *BusinessWeek,* April 11, 2005, p. 78.
2. Carol Marie Cropper, "House Prices: More Down to Earth?" *BusinessWeek,* June 17, 2002, p. 88.
3. Kathleen Madigan, "After the Housing Boom," *BusinessWeek,* April 11, 2005, p. 78.
4. Joanne Lipman, "Land and Opportunity," *Wall Street Journal,* December 2, 1995, p. D22.
5. William M. Pride, Robert J. Hughes, and Jack R. Kapoor, *Business,* 8th ed. (Boston: Houghton Mifflin, 2005), p. 154.
6. Lewis Braham and Robert Berner, "The Wrong Time for REITs?" *BusinessWeek,* March 11, 2002. p. 86.
7. "Not Your Usual Real Estate Trusts," *BusinessWeek,* June 17, 2002, p. 96.
8. Lynn Asinof, "Real Estate Lures Investors Again after a Deep Slump," *Wall Street Journal,* October 22, 1992, p. Cl.
9. *Consumer Alert: Investing in Rare Coins* (Washington, DC: Federal Trade Commission, n.d.).

Chapter 18

1. Eric Schine, "There's Never Any Reason for Us to Be Bored," *BusinessWeek,* July 21, 1997, pp. 70–76.
2. Mary C. Hickey, "A Design for Senior Living," *BusinessWeek,* July 19, 1999, p. 136.
3. *Social Security: Fact Sheet* (Washington, DC: Social Security Administration, March 23, 2005.
4. Carol Marie Cropper, "The Ins and Outs of the New Tax Law," *BusinessWeek,* January 28, 2002, pp. 110–111.
5. Ibid.
6. William K. Zinke, "Retirees Are a Big Opportunity for Corporate America," *BusinessWeek,* August 16, 1999, p. 8.

Chapter 19

1. This section is based on Geoffery Smith, "Nest-Egg Planning for the Not-So-Average Joe," *BusinessWeek,* July 21, 1997, pp. 78–84.
2. Larry Armstrong, "There's a Way—Where There's a Will," *BusinessWeek,* April 8, 2002, pp. 81–82.
3. Ibid.
4. American Society of CLU and ChFC, *Looking beyond Your Current Estate Plan,* 1997.

Photo Credits

Index

Managed funds vs. indexed funds, 524–525
Management fees, 518
Management and human resources, 49
Mandel, Michael, N-1
Manufactured homes, 281–282
Manufacturing sector, 49
Margin, 469
Margin call, 469
Margin transaction, 470
Marginal tax rate, 112
Marital-deduction trust, 632
Market maker, 463
Market order, 466
Market risk, 417
Market timer, 523
Market value, 83
Market value calculations, 58
Mass media career information, 52
MasterCard, 174
Maturity, 499
Maturity date, 482
MBIA Inc. (Municipal Bond Insurance Association), 496
McCune, Jenny C., 281n
McIntyre, Warren, 399
McKinley, Robert B., 205
Mediation, 259
Mediator, 259
Medicaid, 358–359
Medical and dental expenses, 109, 125, 576
Medical payments coverage, 315, 322–323
Medical savings accounts (MSAs), 56–57, 340
Medicare, 107, 355–359
Medigap (MedSup) insurance, 358
Medium-priced loans, 206–207
MEDLINEplus, 359
Mental budget, 96
Mentor, 60
Mergent, 421, 451, 485–486
Michael, Jeff, 173n
Microsoft Money, 96
Midcap funds, 522
Midcap stock, 449
Minimum monthly payment trap, 217–218
Mobile homes, 282
Mobility, 276, 280
Money, 392, 430, 529, 625
Money-back term, 381
Money Central, 429
Money factor, 253
Money management; *see also* Budgeting; Personal financial planning
  activities of, 79
  components of, 78

Money management—*cont.*
  defined, 78
  financial goals and, 95–98
  opportunity cost and, 78
  personal financial records, 79–81
  planning for success, 78–79
  savings goals, 96–98
  Web sites for, 225
Money market account, 149
Money market funds, 145, 147, 149, 523
Money order, 159
Money-purchase pension plans, 588
Money supply, 15
Moody's Investors Service, 498, 500–501
Morningstar Investment Reports, 421, 451, 526
Mortality table, 373–375
Mortgage application process, 289, 297
Mortgage bond, 484
Mortgage brokers, 287
Mortgage companies, 145
Mortgage payment factors, 288
Mortgage rate, 143, 292
Mortgage REITs, 550
Mortgages, 83, 287
  adjustable-rate, variable-payment mortgages, 290–293
  adjustable-rate mortgages (ARM), 290–291
  application process, 289
  balloon mortgage, 290
  conventional mortgages, 289–290
  convertible ARMs, 292
  early payoff and prepayments, 295
  fixed-rate, fixed-payment mortgages, 289–290
  government financing programs, 290
  graduated-payment mortgages, 293
  growing-equity mortgages, 293
  investing in, 551
  payment cap, 292
  prequalification for, 282
  qualifying for, 286–288
  rate cap, 292
  refinancing, 294
  reverse mortgages, 293
  second mortgages, 293, 551
  shared appreciation mortgage (SAM), 293
  types of loans, 291
Motley Fool, 429, 450
Motor vehicle bodily injury coverages, 322–323
Motor vehicle property damage coverages, 323–324
Motor vehicle purchases
  certified pre-owned (CPO) vehicles, 251
  consumer buying matrix, 250

Motor vehicle purchases—*cont.*
  evaluating alternatives, 249–253
  financing alternatives, 254
  information gathering, 248–249
  leased cars, 251–253
  lemon laws, 255
  maintenance, 255–256
  new car bargaining, 253–254
  online car buying, 241
  operation and maintenance costs, 255
  postpurchase activities, 255–256
  preshopping activities, 248–249
  problem identification, 248
  purchase price, 253–254
  research-based approach to, 248
  selecting options, 249
  servicing sources, 256
  used cars, 249–251, 253
  vehicle options, 249
Moving expenses, 110
Mullaney, Timothy J., 335n
Multiunit dwellings, 280
Multiyear term life, 380
Municipal bond funds, 522
Municipal bonds, 128, 495–496
  taxable equivalent yield, 496
Murphy, Kate, 627n
Mutual Fund Education Alliance, 514
Mutual Fund Fact Book, 531
Mutual funds, 145, 423, 514
  advantages/disadvantages of, 533
  buy/sell decision, 524–532
  characteristics of, 516–520
  classifications of, 520–523
    balanced funds, 523
    bond funds, 522
    money market funds, 523
    other funds, 522–523
    stock funds, 520–522
  closed-end fund, 516–517
  diversification, 423, 515
  exchange-traded fund, 516–517
  fees/charges, 521
  financial publications, 529–531
  information sources, 513
    advisory services, 526–528
    annual reports, 529
    financial newspapers/publications, 528–531
    fund prospectus, 529
  Internet for information, 525–526
  load/no-load funds, 517–518
  managed vs. indexed funds, 524–525
  management fees and other charges, 518–520
  mechanics of transaction, 532–536
  net asset value, 517
  open-end fund, 517
  professional advisory services, 526–528

Preface

This *Personal Financial Planner* is designed to help you create and implement a personal financial plan.

Items to consider when using this Personal Financial Planner

1. Since these sheets are designed to adapt to every personal financial situation, some may be appropriate for you at this time, and not at other times in your life.

2. Most sheets are referenced to specific pages in the textbook. To help you use these sheets with the appropriate text material, the following textbook margin icon will refer you to the appropriate sheet.

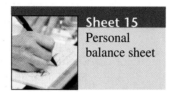

Sheet 15
Personal balance sheet

3. Some sheets will be used more than once (such as preparing a personal cash flow statement or a budget). You are encouraged to photocopy additional sheets as needed, or print additional copies from the CD-ROM.

4. To assist you with using the Internet for financial planning activities, suggested Web sites are listed on each sheet.

5. Finally, remember personal financial planning is an ongoing activity. With the use of these sheets, textbook material, and your efforts, an organized and satisfying personal economic existence can be yours.

Note: These sheets, along with other financial planning calculation tools, are available on the Windows® version of *Personal Finance,* Eighth Edition, CD-ROM.

Personal Financial Planner

Table of Contents

Personal Financial Planner

Personal Data

Purpose: To provide quick reference for vital household data.

Instructions: Provide the personal and financial data requested below.

Suggested Web sites: www.money.com   www.kiplinger.com

Name	_____	_____
Birth date	_____	_____
Marital status	_____	_____
Address	_____	_____
Phone	_____	_____
e-mail	_____	_____
Social Security no.	_____	_____
Driver's license no.	_____	_____
Place of employment	_____	_____
Address	_____	_____
Phone	_____	_____
Position	_____	_____
Length of service	_____	_____
Checking acct. no.	_____	_____
Financial institution	_____	_____
Address	_____	_____
Phone	_____	_____

Dependent Data

Name	Birth date	Relationship	Social Security no.
_____	_____	_____	_____
_____	_____	_____	_____
_____	_____	_____	_____
_____	_____	_____	_____

What's Next for Your Personal Financial Plan?

- Identify financial planning experts (insurance agent, banker, investment adviser, tax preparer, others) you might contact for financial planning information or assistance.
- Discuss with other household members various financial planning priorities.

Name: _____ Date: _____

Financial Institutions and Advisers

Purpose: To create a directory of personal financial institutions and financial planning professionals.

Instructions: Supply the information required in the spaces provided.

Suggested Web sites: www.quicken.com   www.bankrate.com

Attorney
Name _____
Address _____
_____
Phone _____
Fax _____
e-mail _____

Primary Financial Institution
Name _____
Address _____
_____
Phone _____
Fax _____
Checking acct. no. _____
Savings acct. no. _____
Loan no. _____

Insurance (Home/Auto)
Agent _____
Company _____
Address _____
_____
Phone _____
Fax _____
Policy no. _____
e-mail _____

Credit Card 1
Issuer _____
Address _____
_____
Phone _____
Fax _____
Acct. no. _____
Exp. date _____
Limit _____

Credit Card 2
Issuer _____
Address _____
_____
Phone _____
Fax _____
Acct. no. _____
Exp. date _____
Limit _____

Tax Preparer
Name _____
Firm _____
Address _____
_____
Phone _____
Fax _____
e-mail _____

Insurance (Life/Health)
Agent _____
Company _____
Address _____
_____
Phone _____
Fax _____
e-mail _____
Policy no. _____

Investment Broker
Name _____
Address _____
_____
Phone _____
Fax _____
e-mail _____
Acct. no. _____

Real Estate Agent
Name _____
Company _____
Address _____
_____
Phone _____
Fax _____
e-mail _____

Investment Company
Name _____
Address _____
_____
Phone _____
Fax _____
Acct. no. _____
e-mail _____
Web site _____

What's Next for Your Personal Financial Plan?

• Talk to various personal and professional contacts to determine factors to consider when selecting various financial planning advisers.

• Identify additional financial planning contacts that you might consider using in the future.

Setting Personal Financial Goals

Purpose: To identify personal financial goals and create an action plan.

Instructions: Based on personal and household needs and values, identify specific goals that require action.

Suggested Web sites: www.financialplan.about.com   www.moneycentral.msn.com

Short-Term Monetary Goals (less than two years)

Description	Amount needed	Months to achieve	Action to be taken	Priority
Example: pay off credit card debt	$850	12	Use money from pay raise	High

Intermediate and Long-Term Monetary Goals

Description	Amount needed	Months to achieve	Action to be taken	Priority

Nonmonetary Goals

Description	Time frame	Actions to be taken
Example: set up file for personal financial records and documents	Next 2–3 months	• Locate personal and financial records and documents. • Set up files for various spending, saving, borrowing categories.

What's Next for Your Personal Financial Plan?

- Based on various financial goals, calculate the savings deposits necessary to achieve those goals.
- Analyze current economic trends that might influence various saving, spending, investing, and borrowing decisions.

4

Name: _____ Date: _____

Monitoring Current Economic Conditions

Purpose: To monitor selected economic indicators that might influence your saving, investing, spending, and borrowing decisions.

Instructions: Using the *Wall Street Journal,* Internet searches, or other sources of economic information, obtain current data for various economic factors.

Suggested Web sites: www.bls.gov   www.federalreserve.gov

Economic Factor	Recent Trends	Possible Influences on Financial Planning Decisions
Example: Mortgage rates	*Decline in mortgage rates*	• *Consider buying a home.* • *Consider refinancing an existing mortgage.*
Interest rates		
Consumer prices		
Other: _____		
Other: _____		
Other: _____		

What's Next for Your Personal Financial Plan?

• Determine the economic factors that could affect your personal financial decisions in the next few years.
• Identify actions to take as a result of various current economic trends.

Making Career Contacts

Purpose: To create a guide of professional contacts.

Instructions: Record the requested information for use in researching career areas and employment opportunities.

Suggested Web sites: www.rileyguide.com   www.careerjournal.com

Name _____

Organization _____

Address _____

_____

Phone _____ Fax _____

Web site _____ e-mail _____

Date of contact _____

Situation _____

Career situation of contact _____

Areas of specialization _____

Major accomplishments _____

Name _____

Organization _____

Address _____

_____

Phone _____ Fax _____

Web site _____ e-mail _____

Date of contact _____

Situation _____

Career situation of contact _____

Areas of specialization _____

Major accomplishments _____

What's Next for Your Personal Financial Plan?

- Identify various people whom you might contact to obtain career information.
- Prepare specific questions to ask people about career fields and the application process.

Name: _____ Date: _____

Résumé Worksheet

Purpose: To inventory your education, training, work background, and other experiences for use when preparing a résumé.

Instructions: List dates, organizations, and other data for each of the categories given below.

Suggested Web sites: www.monster.com   www.rileyguide.com

Education

Degree/programs completed	School/location		Dates

Work Experience

Title	Organization	Dates	Responsibilities

Other Experience

Title	Organization	Dates	Responsibilities

Campus/Community Activities

Organization/locations		Dates	Involvement

Honors/Awards

Title	Organization/location		Dates

References

Name	Title	Organization	Address	Phone

What's Next for Your Personal Financial Plan?

• Create a preliminary résumé and ask others for suggested improvements.

• Conduct research to obtain samples of effective résumé formats.

Planning a Cover Letter

Purpose: To outline an employment cover letter.

Instructions: Prepare the preliminary draft of a cover letter for a specific employment position.

Suggested Web sites: www.monster.com   www.rileyguide.com

Name	_____
Title	_____
Organization	_____
Address	_____
Phone	_____
Fax	_____ e-mail _____
Information about employment position available	_____
Organizational information	_____

Introduction: Get attention of reader with distinctive skills or experience; or make reference to a mutual contact.

Development: Emphasize how your experience, knowledge, and skills will benefit the needs of the organization in the future.

Conclusion: Request an interview; restate any distinctive qualities; tell how you may be contacted.

What's Next for Your Personal Financial Plan?

- Research examples of effective cover letters.
- Prepare a preliminary cover letter and obtain comments from others for improvements.

Researching a Prospective Employer

Purpose: To obtain information about an organization for which an employment position is available.

Instructions: Use library research, informational interview, and other sources to obtain the information requested below.

Suggested Web sites: www.careerbuilder.com   www.businessweek.com/careers

Organization _____

Address _____

_____

Contact _____

Title _____

Phone _____

Fax _____ e-mail _____

Web site _____

Title of position _____

Major products, services, and customers

Locations of main offices, factories, and other facilities

Major historical developments of the company

Recent company and industry developments

Required skills and experience

Major responsibilities and duties

Employee benefits

Other comments

What's Next for Your Personal Financial Plan?

- Prepare a list of organizations and information you might obtain when researching these companies.
- Conduct library and online research about specific organizations in which you are interested.

Preparing for an Interview

Purpose: To organize information and ideas for a job interview.

Instructions: Prepare information for the items listed.

Suggested Web sites: www.rileyguide.com   www.careerbuilder.com

Organization _____

Address _____

_____

Contact _____

Title _____

Phone _____

Fax _____ e-mail_____

Web site _____

Title of position _____

Date/time/location
of interview _____

Required skills and experiences

Major responsibilities and duties

Questions you expect to be asked

Major ideas you plan to emphasize

Questions you plan to ask

Other comments

What's Next for Your Personal Financial Plan?

- Prepare preliminary answers for potential interview questions.
- Have others ask you questions in a practice interview setting.

Name: _____ Date: _____

Employee Benefits Comparison

Purpose: To assess the financial and personal value of employment benefits.

Instructions: When comparing different employment situations or when selecting benefits, consider the factors listed below.

Suggested Web sites: www.benefitnews.com   www.dol.gov/ebsa

Organization		
Location		
Phone		
Contact/title		
Health insurance		
Company/coverage		
Cost to be paid by employee		
Disability income insurance		
Company/coverage		
Cost to be paid by employee		
Life insurance		
Company/coverage		
Cost to be paid by employee		
Pension/retirement		
Employer contributions		
Vesting period		
Tax benefits		
Employee contributions		
Other benefits/estimated market value		
• vacation time		
• tuition reimbursement		
• child/dependent care		
• other		
Web site to access benefit information		

What's Next for Your Personal Financial Plan?

- Talk to various people about the strengths and weaknesses of their employee benefits.
- Conduct research to obtain information on various employee benefits required by law and those commonly provided in various industries.

Career Development and Advancement

Purpose: To develop a plan for career advancement.

Instructions: Prepare responses for the items listed.

Suggested Web sites: www.careerjournal.com   www.businessweek.com/careers

Current position _____

Address _____

_____

Phone _____

Fax _____ e-mail _____

Web site _____

Current responsibilities and duties

Accomplishments

Career goal within the next year

• Required skills and experience

• Plans to achieve that goal

Career goal within the next two years

• Required skills and experience

• Plans to achieve that goal

Career goal within the next five years

• Required skills and experience

• Plans to achieve that goal

What's Next for Your Personal Financial Plan?

• Talk with others about the career development activities in which they have participated.

• Prepare a list of formal and informal career development activities in which you might participate.

Name: _____ Date: _____

Financial Documents and Records

Purpose: To develop a system for maintaining and storing personal financial documents and records.

Instructions: Indicate the location of the following records, and create files for the eight major categories of financial documents.

Suggested Web sites: www.quicken.com   www.kiplinger.com

Item	Home File	Safe Deposit Box	Other (specify)
Money management records			
• budget, financial statements			
Personal/employment records			
• current résumé, Social Security card			
• educational transcripts			
• birth, marriage, divorce certificates			
• citizenship, military papers, passport			
• adoption, custody papers			
Tax records			
Financial services/consumer credit records			
• unused, canceled checks			
• savings, passbook statements			
• savings certificates			
• credit card information, statements			
• credit contracts			
Consumer purchase, housing, and automobile records			
• warranties, receipts			
• owner's manuals			
• lease or mortgage papers, title deed, property tax info			
• automobile title			
• auto registration			
• auto service records			
Insurance records			
• insurance policies			
• home inventory			
• medical information (health history)			
Investment records			
• broker statements			
• dividend reports			
• stock/bond certificates			
• rare coins, stamps, and collectibles			
Estate planning and retirement			
• will			
• pension, Social Security info			

What's Next for Your Personal Financial Plan?

- Select a location for storing your financial documents and records.
- Decide if various documents may no longer be needed.

Name: _____ **Date:** _____

Personal Balance Sheet

Purpose: To determine your current financial position.

Instructions: List the current values of the asset categories below; list the amounts owed for various liabilities; subtract total liabilities from total assets to determine net worth.

Suggested Web sites: www.money.com   www.lifeadvice.com

Balance Sheet as of _____

Assets

Liquid assets

Checking account balance	_____
Savings/money market accounts, funds	_____
Cash value of life insurance	_____
Other _____	_____
Total liquid assets	. . . . _____

Household assets & possessions

Current market value of home	_____
Market value of automobiles	_____
Furniture	_____
Stereo, video, camera equipment	_____
Jewelry	_____
Other _____	_____
Other _____	_____
Total household assets	. . . . _____

Investment assets

Savings certificates	_____
Stocks and bonds	_____
Individual retirement accounts	_____
Mutual funds	_____
Other _____	_____
Total investment assets	. . . . _____

Total Assets . . . . _____

Liabilities

Current Liabilities

Charge account and credit card balances	_____
Loan balances	_____
Other _____	_____
Other _____	_____
Total current liabilities	. . . . _____

Long-term, liabilities

Mortgage	_____
Other _____	_____
Total long-term liabilities	. . . . _____

Total Liabilities . . . . _____

Net Worth _____

(assets minus liabilities)

What's Next for Your Personal Financial Plan?

- Compare your net worth to previous balance sheets.
- Decide how often you will prepare a balance sheet.

Name: _____ Date: _____

Personal Cash Flow Statement

Purpose: To maintain a record of cash inflows and outflows for a month (or three months).

Instructions: Record inflows and outflows of cash for a one- (or three-) month period.

Suggested Web sites: www.asec.org   www.clevelandsaves.org

For month ending _____

Cash Inflows

Salary (take-home)	_____
Other income:	_____
Other income:	_____
Total Income	. . . . _____

Cash Outflows

Fixed expenses

Mortgage or rent	_____
Loan payments	_____
Insurance	_____
Other _____	_____
Other _____	_____
Total fixed outflows	. . . . _____

Variable expenses

Food	_____
Clothing	_____
Electricity	_____
Telephone	_____
Water	_____
Transportation	_____
Personal care	_____
Medical expenses	_____
Recreation/entertainment	_____
Gifts	_____
Donations	_____
Other _____	_____
Other _____	_____
Total variable outflows	. . . . _____
Total Outflows	. . . . _____

Surplus/Deficit   . . . .   _____

Allocation of surplus

Emergency fund savings	_____
Financial goals savings	_____
Other savings _____	_____

What's Next for Your Personal Financial Plan?

- Decide which areas of spending need to be revised.
- Evaluate your spending patterns for preparing a budget.

Name: _____ Date: _____

Cash Budget

Purpose: To compare projected and actual spending for a one- (or three-) month period.

Instructions: Estimate projected spending based on your cash flow statement, and maintain records for actual spending for these same budget categories.

Suggested Web sites: www.betterbudgeting.com   www.mymoney.gov

Income	Budgeted Amounts		Actual Amounts	Variance
	Dollar	**Percent**		
Salary				
Other _____				
Total income		100%		
Expenses	< < < < < < < < <	< < < < < < < <	< < < < < < < < < < <	< < < < < < < < <
Fixed expenses	< < < < < < < < <	< < < < < < < <	< < < < < < < < < < <	< < < < < < < < <
Mortgage or rent				
Property taxes				
Loan payments				
Insurance				
Other _____				
Total fixed expenses				
Emergency fund/savings	< < < < < < < < <	< < < < < < < <	< < < < < < < < < < <	< < < < < < < < <
Emergency fund				
Savings for _____				
Savings for _____				
Total savings				
Variable expenses	< < < < < < < < <	< < < < < < < <	< < < < < < < < < < <	< < < < < < < < <
Food				
Utilities				
Clothing				
Transportation costs				
Personal care				
Medical and health care				
Entertainment				
Education				
Gifts/donations				
Miscellaneous				
Other _____				
Other _____				
Total variable expenses				
Total expenses		100%		

What's Next for Your Personal Financial Plan?

- Evaluate the appropriateness of your budget for your current situation.
- Assess whether your budgeting activities are helping you achieve your financial goals.

Name: _____ Date: _____

Annual Budget Summary

Purpose: To see an overview of spending patterns for a year.

Instructions: Record the monthly budget amount in the first column and actual monthly spending in the appropriate column.

Suggested Web sites: www.mymoney.gov   www.bls.gov/cex

Expense	Monthly Budget	Jan	Feb	Mar	Apr	May	Jun
Savings							
Mortgage/rent							
Housing costs							
Telephone							
Food (at home)							
Food (away)							
Clothing							
Transportation							
Credit payments							
Insurance							
Health care							
Recreation							
Reading/education							
Gifts/donations							
Miscellaneous							
Other _____							
Other _____							
Total							

Expense	Jul	Aug	Sep	Oct	Nov	Dec	Year Totals Actual	Budget
Savings								
Mortgage/rent								
Housing costs								
Telephone								
Food (at home)								
Food (away)								
Clothing								
Transportation								
Credit payments								
Insurance								
Health care								
Recreation								
Reading/education								
Gifts/donations								
Miscellaneous								
Other _____								
Other _____								
Total								

What's Next for Your Personal Financial Plan?

- Decide which areas of spending need to be revised.
- Evaluate your spending patterns for preparing a budget.

College Education Cost Analysis and Savings Plan

Purpose: To estimate future costs of college and calculate needed savings.

Instructions: Complete the information and calculations requested below.

Suggested Web sites: www.statefarm.com/lifevents/lifevents.htm   www.centura.com/tools

Estimated Cost of College Education

Current cost of college education $_____

(including tuition, fees, room, board, books, travel, and other expenses)

Future value for _____ years until starting college at an expected annual
inflation of _____ percent (use future value of $1, Exhibit 1-A in
Chapter 1 Appendix) $_____

Projected future cost of college adjusted for inflation   (A) $_____

Estimated Annual Savings Needed

Projected future cost of college adjusted for inflation   (A) $_____

Future value of a series of deposits for _____ years until starting college and
expected annual rate of return on savings and investments of _____ percent
(use Exhibit 1-B in Chapter 1 Appendix)   (B) $_____

Estimated annual deposit to achieve needed education fund   A divided by **B** $_____

What's Next for Your Personal Financial Plan?

- Identify savings and investment plans that could be used to save for long-term goals.
- Ask others to suggest actions that might be taken to save for long-term goals.

Name: _____ Date: _____

Tax Planning Activities

Purpose: To consider actions that can prevent tax penalties and may result in tax savings.
Instructions: Consider which of the following actions are appropriate to your tax situation.
Suggested Web sites: www.irs.gov   www.taxlogic.com

	Action to be taken (if applicable)	Completed
Filing Status/Withholding		
• Change filing status or exemptions because of changes in life situation.		
• Change amount of withholding because of changes in tax situations.		
• Plan to make estimated tax payments (due the 15th of April, June, September, and January).		
Tax Records/Documents		
• Organize home files for ease of maintaining and retrieving data.		
• Send current mailing address and correct Social Security number to IRS, place of employment, and other sources of income.		
Annual Tax Activities		
• Be certain all needed data and current tax forms are available well before deadline.		
• Research tax code changes and uncertain tax areas.		
Tax Savings Actions		
• Consider tax-exempt and tax-deferred investments.		
• If you expect to have the same or lower tax rate next year, accelerate deductions into the current year.		
• If you expect to have the same or lower tax rate next year, delay the receipt of income until next year.		
• If you expect to have a higher tax rate next year, delay deductions because they will have a greater benefit.		
• If you expect to have a higher tax rate next year, accelerate the receipt of income to have it taxed at the current lower rate.		
• Start or increase use of tax-deferred retirement plans.		
• Other.		

What's Next for Your Personal Financial Plan?

• Identify saving and investing decisions that would minimize future income taxes.
• Develop a plan for actions to take related to your current and future tax situation.

Planning the Use of Financial Services

Purpose: To indicate currently used financial services and to determine services that may be needed in the future.

Instructions: List currently used services with financial institution information (name, address, phone) and services that are likely to be needed in the future.

Suggested Web sites: www.bankrate.com   www.creditunion.coop

Types of financial services	Current financial services used	Additional financial services needed
Payment services (checking, cash machine, money orders)	Financial Institution	
Savings services (savings account, certificate of deposit, savings bonds)	Financial Institution	
Credit services (credit cards, personal loans, mortgage)	Financial Institution	
Other financial services (investments, trust account, tax planning)	Financial Institution	

What's Next for Your Personal Financial Plan?

- Assess whether the current types of and sources of your financial services are appropriate.
- Determine additional financial services you may wish to make use of in the future.

Name: _____ Date: _____

Using Savings to Achieve Financial Goals

Purpose: To monitor savings for use in reaching financial goals.

Instructions: Record savings plan information along with the amount of your balance or income on a periodic basis.

Suggested Web sites: www.fdic.gov   www.savingsbonds.gov

Regular Savings Account

Acct. no. _____

Financial institution

_____

Address _____

_____

Phone _____

Web site _____

Savings goal/Amount needed/Date needed:

_____

Initial deposit: Date _____ $_____

Balance: Date _____ $_____

                  Date _____ $_____

                  Date _____ $_____

                  Date _____ $_____

                  _____   _____

Certificate of Deposit

Acct. no. _____

Financial institution

_____

Address _____

_____

Phone _____

Web site _____

Savings goal/Amount needed/Date needed:

_____

Initial deposit: Date _____ $_____

Balance: Date _____ $_____

                  Date _____ $_____

                  Date _____ $_____

                  Date _____ $_____

                  _____   _____

Money Market fund or account

Acct. no. _____

Financial institution

_____

Address _____

_____

Phone _____

Web site _____

Savings goal/Amount needed/Date needed:

_____

Initial deposit: Date _____ $_____

Balance: Date _____ $_____

                  Date _____ $_____

                  Date _____ $_____

                  Date _____ $_____

                  _____   _____

U.S. Savings Bonds

Purchase
location _____

_____

Address _____

_____

Phone _____

Web site _____

Savings goal/Amount needed/Date needed:

_____

Purchase date: _____   Maturity date: _____

Amount: _____   Maturity date: _____

Purchase date: _____   Maturity date: _____

Amount: _____   Maturity date: _____

What's Next for Your Personal Financial Plan?

- Assess your current progress toward achieving various savings goals. Evaluate existing and new savings goals.
- Plan actions to expand the amount you are saving toward various savings goals.

Savings Plan Comparison

Purpose: To compare the benefits and costs associated with different savings plans.

Instructions: Analyze advertisements and contact various financial institutions to obtain the information requested below.

Suggested Web sites: www.bankrate.com   www.fdic.gov

Type of savings plan (regular passbook account, special account, savings certificate, money market account, other)			
Financial institution			
Address/Phone			
Web site			
Annual interest rate			
Annual percentage yield (APY)			
Frequency of compounding			
Insured by FDIC, NCUA, other			
Maximum amount insured			
Minimum initial deposit			
Minimum time period savings must be on deposit			
Penalties for early withdrawal			
Service charges, transaction fees, other costs or fees			

What's Next for Your Personal Financial Plan?

- Based on this savings plan analysis, determine the best types for your current and future financial situation.
- When analyzing savings plans, what factors should you carefully investigate?

Name: _____ Date: _____

Payment Account Comparison

Purpose: To compare the benefits and costs associated with different checking/payment accounts.

Instructions: Analyze advertisements and contact various financial institutions (banks, savings and loan associations, or credit unions) to obtain the information requested below.

Suggested Web sites: www.bankrate.com   www.checkfree.com

Institution name			
Address			
Phone			
Web site			
Type of account (regular checking, interest-earning account, or other)			
Minimum balance for "free" checking			
Monthly charge for going below minimum balance			
"Free" checking accounts for full-time students?			
Online banking services			
Other fees/costs			
• printing of checks			
• stop payment order			
• overdrawn account			
• certified check			
• ATM, other charges			
Banking hours			
Location of branch offices and ATM terminals			

What's Next for Your Personal Financial Plan?

• Are your current payment activities best served by your current payment methods (checking account, cash card, online payments)?

• Talk with others about their online payment experiences.

Checking/Payment Account Cost Analysis

Purpose: To compare the inflows and outflows of a checking account.

Instructions: Record the interest earned (inflows) and the costs and fees (outflows) as requested below. *Note: Not all items will apply to every checking account.*

Suggested Web sites: www.bankrate.com   www.checkfree.com

Inflows (earnings)

Step 1

Multiply average monthly balance $_____ by average rate of return _____% to determine annual earnings

Outflows (costs)

Step 2

Monthly service charge
$_____ × 12 = $_____

Average number of checks written per month _____ × charge per check (if applicable) × 12 = $_____

Average number of deposits per month _____ × charge per deposit (if applicable) × 12 = $_____

Fee incurred when going below minimum balance _____ × times below minimum = $_____

Lost interest: opportunity cost _____% × required minimum balance $_____ = $_____

= [_____] +

Total estimated inflow

[$_____]

Total estimated outflow

[$_____]

> **Estimated inflows less outflows =**
> **Net earnings for account** _____
> **− Net cost for account** _____
> **+/−$** _____

Note: This calculation does not take into account charges and fees for such services as overdrafts, stop payments, ATM use, and check printing. Be sure to also consider those costs when selecting a checking account.

What's Next for Your Personal Financial Plan?

- What actions can you take to minimize checking/payment account costs?
- Talk to others about the actions they take to minimize checking account costs.

Personal Financial Planner

Name: _____ Date: _____

Checking Account Reconciliation

Purpose: To determine the adjusted cash balance for your checking account.

Instructions: Enter data from your bank statement and checkbook for the amounts requested.

Suggested Web sites: www.bankrate.com   www.checkfree.com

Date of bank statement _____

Balance on bank statement $ _____

Step 1

Subtract total of outstanding checks (checks that you have written but have not yet cleared in the banking system)

Check No.	Amount	Check No.	Amount
_____	_____	_____	_____
_____	_____	_____	_____
_____	_____	_____	_____
_____	_____	_____	_____

− $ _____

Step 2

Add deposits in transit (deposits you have made but have not been reported on this statement)

Date	Amount	Date	Amount
_____	_____	_____	_____

+ $ _____

Adjusted cash balance . . . . $ _____

Current balance in your checkbook   _____

Step 3

Subtract fees or other charges listed on your bank statement

Item	Amount	Item	Amount
_____	_____	_____	_____
_____	_____	_____	_____

− $ _____

Subtract ATM withdrawals, debit card payments, and other automatic payments.   − $ _____

Step 4

Add interest earned   + $ _____

Add direct deposits   + $ _____

Adjusted cash balance . . . . $ _____

(The two adjusted balances should be the same; if not, carefully check your math and check to see that deposits and checks recorded in your checkbook and on your statement are for the correct amounts.)

What's Next for Your Personal Financial Plan?

- Develop a plan to monitor your payment records.
- Select actions to reduce banking service costs.

Consumer Credit Usage Patterns

Purpose: To create a record of current consumer debt balances.

Instructions: Record account names, numbers, and payments for current consumer debts.

Suggested Web sites: www.finance-center.com   www.ftc.gov

Automobile, Education, Personal, and Installment Loans

Financial institution	Account number	Current balance	Monthly payment
_____	_____	_____	_____
_____	_____	_____	_____
_____	_____	_____	_____
_____	_____	_____	_____
_____	_____	_____	_____

Charge Accounts and Credit Cards

_____	_____	_____	_____
_____	_____	_____	_____
_____	_____	_____	_____
_____	_____	_____	_____
_____	_____	_____	_____

Other Loans (overdraft protection, home equity, life insurance loan)

_____	_____	_____	_____
_____	_____	_____	_____
_____	_____	_____	_____
_____	_____	_____	_____

Totals _____ _____

$$\text{Debt payment-to-income ratio} = \frac{\text{Total monthly payments}}{\text{net (after-tax) income}}$$

What's Next for Your Personal Financial Plan?

- Survey three or four individuals to determine their uses of credit.
- Talk to several people to determine how they first established credit.

Name: _____ **Date:** _____

Credit Card/Charge Account Comparison

Purpose: To compare the benefits and costs asociated with different credit cards and charge accounts.

Instructions: Analyze ads and credit applications and contact various financial institutions to obtain the information requested below.

Suggested Web sites: www.bankrate.com   www.banx.com

Type of credit/charge account			
Name of company/account			
Address/phone			
Web site			
Type of purchases that can be made			
Annual fee (if any)			
Annual percentage rate (APR) (interest calculation information)			
Credit limit for new customers			
Minimum monthly payment			
Other costs: • credit report • late fee • other _____			
Restrictions (age, minimum annual income)			
Other information for consumers to consider			
Frequent flyer or other bonus points			

What's Next for Your Personal Financial Plan?

• Make a list of the pros and cons of using credit or debit cards.

• Contact a local credit bureau to obtain information on the services provided and the fees charged.

Name: _____ Date: _____

Consumer Loan Comparison

Purpose: To compare the costs associated with different sources of loans.

Instructions: Contact or visit a bank, credit union, and consumer finance company to obtain information on a loan for a specific purpose.

Suggested Web sites: www.eloan.com   www.centura.com

Type of financial institution			
Name			
Address			
Phone			
Web site			
Amount of down payment			
Length of loan (months)			
What collateral is required?			
Amount of monthly payment			
Total amount to be repaid (monthly amount × number of months + down payment)			
Total finance charge/cost of credit			
Annual percentage rate (APR)			
Other costs • credit life insurance • credit report • other _____			
Is a cosigner required?			
Other information			

What's Next for Your Personal Financial Plan?

- Ask several individuals how they would compare loans at different financial institutions.
- Survey several friends and relatives to determine whether they ever cosigned a loan. If yes, what were the consequences of cosigning?

Name: _____   Date: _____

Unit Pricing Worksheet

Purpose: To calculate the unit price for a consumer purchase.

Instructions: Use advertisements or information obtained during store visits to calculate and compare unit prices.

Suggested Web sites: www.consumer.gov   www.consumerworld.org

Item _____

Date	Store/Location	Brand	Total price	÷	Size	=	Unit Price	Unit of Measurement
_____	_____	_____	_____		_____		_____	_____
_____	_____	_____	_____		_____		_____	_____
_____	_____	_____	_____		_____		_____	_____
_____	_____	_____	_____		_____		_____	_____
_____	_____	_____	_____		_____		_____	_____
_____	_____	_____	_____		_____		_____	_____

Highest unit price

Store _____

Date _____

Lowest unit price

Store _____

Date _____

Difference: _____

_____
Wisest consumer buy/best overall store

_____
Reasons

What's Next for Your Personal Financial Plan?

• Talk to others about actions they take to get the most for their money.

• Prepare a list of local and online shopping locations that provide the best value.

Consumer Purchase Comparison

Purpose: To research and evaluate brands and store services for purchase of a major consumer item.

Instructions: When considering the purchase of a major consumer item, use ads, catalogs, the World Wide Web, store visits, and other sources to obtain the information below.

Suggested Web sites: www.consumerreports.org   www.cairo.com

Product

_____

Exact description (size, model, features, etc.)

_____

Research the item online and in consumer periodicals with information regarding your product

source _____   source _____

date _____   date _____

_____

What buying suggestions are presented in the articles?

_____

Which brands are recommended in these articles? Why?

_____

Contact or visit two or three stores that sell the product to obtain the following information:

	Store 1	Store 2	Store 3
Store name			
Address			
Phone/Web site			
Brand name/cost			
Product difference from item above			
Guarantee/warranty offered (describe)			

Which brand and at which store would you buy this product? Why?

What's Next for Your Personal Financial Plan?

- Which consumer information sources are most valuable for your future buying decisions?
- List guidelines to use in the future when making major purchases.

Current and Future Transportation Needs

Purpose: To assess current and future transportation.

Instructions: Based on current needs and expected needs, complete the information requested below.

Suggested Web sites: autoadvice.about.com   www.kbb.com

Current situation: Date _____

	Vehicle 1		**Vehicle 2**
Year/Model	_____	Year/Model	_____
Mileage	_____	Mileage	_____
Condition	_____	Condition	_____
Needed repairs	_____	Needed repairs	_____

Estimated annual costs   **Estimated annual costs**

gas, oil, repairs	_____	gas, oil, repairs	_____
insurance	_____	insurance	_____
loan balance	_____	loan balance	_____
Estimated market value	_____	Estimated market value	_____

Expected and projected changes in transportation needs

_____

Personal desires and concerns regarding current transportation

Analysis of Future Desired Transportation Situation

_____

Description of new vehicle situation

_____

Time when this situation is desired

_____

Financing resources needed

_____

Available and projected financial resources

_____

Concerns that must be overcome

_____

Realistic time when transportation of choice may be achieved

_____

What's Next for Your Personal Financial Plan?

- Talk to others about their experiences with public transportation.
- Identify financial and personal factors that affect your transportation spending decisions.

Name: _____ Date: _____

Used-Car Purchase Comparison

Purpose: To research and evaluate different types and sources of used cars.

Instructions: When considering a used-car purchase, use advertisements and visits to new and used car dealers to obtain the information below.

Suggested Web sites: www.carbuyingtips.com   www.kbb.com

Automobile (year, make, model)			
Dealer name			
Address			
Phone			
Web site			
Cost			
Mileage			
Condition of auto			
Condition of tires			
Radio			
Air conditioning			
Other options			
Warranty (describe)			
Items in need of repair			
Inspection items: • any rust, major dents?			
• oil or fluid leaks?			
• condition of brakes?			
• proper operation of heater, wipers, other accessories?			
Other information			

What's Next for Your Personal Financial Plan?

- Maintain a record of automobile operating costs.
- Prepare a plan for regular maintenance of your vehicle.

Personal Financial Planner

Name: _____ Date: _____

Buying versus Leasing an Automobile

Purpose: To compare costs of buying and leasing an automobile or other vehicle.

Instructions: Obtain costs related to leasing and buying a vehicle.

Suggested Web sites: autoadvice.about.com   www.leasesource.com

Purchase Costs

Total vehicle cost, including sales tax ($_____)

Down payment (or full amount if paying cash) $ _____

Monthly loan payment $_____ times _____ month
loan (this item is zero if vehicle is not financed) $ _____

Opportunity cost of down payment (or total cost of the vehicle if
bought for cash)

$_____ times number of years of financing/ownership times
_____ percent (interest rate which funds could earn) $ _____

Less: estimated value of vehicle at end of loan term/ownership $ _____

Total cost to buy . . . . $

Leasing Costs

Security deposit $ _____

Monthly lease payments $_____ times _____ months $ _____

Opportunity cost of security deposit:

$_____ times _____ years times _____ percent $ _____

End-of-lease charges (if applicable*) $ _____

Total cost to lease . . . . $

*With a closed-end lease, charges for extra mileage or excessive wear and tear; with an open-end lease, end-of-lease
payment if appraised value is less than estimated ending value.

What's Next for Your Personal Financial Plan?

• Prepare a list of future actions to use when buying, financing, and leasing a car.
• Maintain a record of operating costs and maintenance actions for your vehicle.

Comparing Cash and Credit for Major Purchases

Purpose: To compare the costs and benefits of cash and credit.

Instructions: When considering a major consumer purchase, complete the information requested below.

Suggested Web sites: www.consumerreports.org   www.pricescan.com

Item/Description _____

Cash Price

Selling price	$ _____
Sales tax	$ _____
Additional charges (delivery, setup, service contract)	$ _____
Discounts (employee, senior citizen or student discounts, discounts for paying cash)	$ − _____
Net cost of item times percent interest that could be earned times years of use to determine opportunity cost	$ _____
Total financial & economic cost when paying cash	$

Credit Price

Down payment	$ _____
Financing: monthly payment times months	$ _____
Additional financing charges (application fee, credit report, credit life insurance)	$ _____
Product-related charges (delivery, setup)	$ _____
Discounts that may apply	$ − _____
Total financial & economic cost when using credit	$

Other Considerations

Will cash used for the purchase be needed for other purposes?

Will this credit purchase result in financial difficulties?

Do alternatives exist for this purchasing and payment decision?

Note: Use Sheet 33 to compare brands, stores, features, and prices when making a major consumer purchase.

What's Next for Your Personal Financial Plan?

- Develop a plan to save for major purchases in the future.
- Create a list of personal factors to consider when comparing cash and credit purchases.

Name: _____ Date: _____

Auto Ownership and Operation Costs

Purpose: To calculate or estimate the cost of owning and operating an automobile or other vehicle.

Instructions: Maintain records related to the cost of categories listed below.

Suggested Web sites: www.consumerreports.org   www.autobytel.com

Model year _____   Make, size, model _____

Fixed Ownership Costs

Depreciation*

Purchase price $_____ divided by estimated life of _____ years $ _____

Interest on auto loan

Annual cost of financing vehicle if buying on credit $ _____

Insurance for the Vehicle

Annual cost of liability and property $ _____

License, registration fee, and taxes $ _____

Cost of registering vehicle for state and city license fees $ _____

Total fixed costs . . . . $ _____

Variable Costs

Gasoline

_____ estimated miles per year divided by _____

miles per gallon of _____ times the average price

of $_____ per gallon $ _____

Oil changes

Cost of regular oil changes during the year $ _____

Tires

Cost of tires purchased during the year $ _____

Maintenance/repairs

Cost of planned or other expected maintenance $ _____

Parking and tolls

Regular fees or parking and highway toll charges $ _____

Total variable costs . . . . $ _____

Total costs $ _____

Divided by miles per year $ _____

Equals cost per mile $ _____

*This estimate of vehicle depreciation is based on a straight-line approach—equal depreciation each year. A more realistic approach would be larger amounts in the early years of ownership, such as 25–30 percent in the first year, 30–35 percent in the second; most cars lose 90 percent of their value by the time they are seven years old.)

What's Next for Your Personal Financial Plan?

- Talk to others to obtain suggestions for reducing auto operation costs.
- Prepare a list of local businesses that provide the best value for motor vehicle service.

Legal Services Cost Comparison

Purpose: To compare costs of services from different sources of legal assistance.

Instructions: Contact various sources of legal services (lawyer, prepaid legal service, legal aid society) to compare costs and available services.

Suggested Web sites: www.ftc.gov   www.fraud.org   www.nolo.com

Type of legal service			
Organization name			
Address			
Phone			
Web site			
Contact person			
Recommended by			
Areas of specialization			
Cost of initial consultation			
Cost of simple will			
Cost of real estate closing			
Cost method for other services—flat fee, hourly rate, or contingency basis			
Other information			

What's Next for Your Personal Financial Plan?

- Determine the best alternative for your future legal needs.
- Maintain a file of legal documents and other financial records.

39

Personal Financial Planner

Name: _____ Date: _____

Current and Future Housing Needs

Purpose: To assess current and future plans for housing.

Instructions: Based on current and expected future needs, complete the information requested below.

Suggested Web sites: homebuying.about.com   houseandhome.msn.com

Current situation _____   Date _____

Renting

Location _____

Description _____

_____

Advantages _____

_____

Disadvantages _____

_____

Rent $ _____

Lease expiration _____

Buying

Location _____

Description _____

_____

Advantages _____

_____

Disadvantages _____

_____

Mortgage payment $ _____

Balance $ _____

Current market value _____

Expected and projected changes in housing needs
_____

Personal desires and concerns regarding current housing situation
_____

Analysis of Future Desired Housing Situation

Description of new housing situation	
Time when this situation is desired	
Financing resources needed/available	
Concerns that must be overcome	
Realistic time when housing of choice may be achieved	

What's Next for Your Personal Financial Plan?

• List personal factors that would affect your decision to rent or buy.

• Talk with various people about factors that affect their housing decisions.

Renting versus Buying Housing

Purpose: To compare cost of renting and buying your place of residence.

Instructions: Obtain estimates for comparable housing units for the data requested below.

Suggested Web sites: www.homefair.com   www.newbuyer.com/homes

Rental Costs

Annual rent payments (monthly rent $_____ × 12)	$ _____
Renter's insurance	$ _____
Interest lost on security deposit (deposit times after-tax savings account interest rate)	$ _____
Total annual cost of renting	$

Buying Costs

Annual mortgage payments	$ _____
Property taxes (annual costs)	$ _____
Homeowner's insurance (annual premium)	$ _____
Estimated maintenance and repairs	$ _____
After-tax interest lost because of down payment/closing costs	$ _____
Less: financial benefits of home ownership	
Growth in equity	$ − _____
Tax savings for mortgage interest (annual mortgage interest times tax rate)	$ − _____
Tax savings for property taxes (annual property taxes times tax rate)	$ − _____
Estimated annual depreciation	$ − _____
Total annual cost of buying	$

What's Next for Your Personal Financial Plan?

- Determine whether renting or buying is most appropriate for you at the current time.
- Prepare a list of circumstances or actions that might change your housing needs.

Name: _____ Date: _____

Apartment Rental Comparison

Purpose: To evaluate and compare rental housing alternatives.

Instructions: When in the market for an apartment, obtain information to compare costs and facilities of three apartments.

Suggested Web sites: apartments.about.com   www.taa.org

Name of renting person or apartment building			
Address			
Phone			
E-mail, Web site			
Monthly rent			
Amount of security deposit			
Length of lease			
Utilities included in rent			
Parking facilities			
Storage area in building			
Laundry facilities			
Distance to schools			
Distance to public transportation			
Distance to shopping			
Pool, recreation area, other facilities			
Estimated utility costs: • electric • telephone • gas • water			
Other costs			
Other information			

What's Next for Your Personal Financial Plan?

- Which of these rental units would best serve your current housing needs?
- What additional information should be considered when renting an apartment?

Housing Affordability and Mortgage Qualification

Purpose: To estimate the amount of affordable mortgage payment, mortgage amount, and home purchase price.

Instructions: Enter the amounts requested, and perform the required calculations.

Suggested Web sites: www.centura.com/tools   loan.yahoo.com/m/

Step 1

Determine your monthly gross income (annual income divided by 12).

$ _____

Step 2

With a down payment of at least 10 percent, lenders use 28 percent of monthly gross income as a guideline for TIPI (taxes, insurance, principal, and interest), 36 percent of monthly gross income as a guideline for TIPI plus other debt payments (enter 0.28 or 0.36).

× _____

Step 3

Subtract other debt payments (such as payments on an auto loan), if applicable.

− _____

Subtract estimated monthly costs of property taxes and homeowners insurance.

− _____

Affordable monthly mortgage payment

$ _____

Step 4

Divide this amount by the monthly mortgage payment per $1,000 based on current mortgage rates (see Exhibit 9–9, text p. 288). For example, for a 10 percent, 30-year loan, the number would be $8.78).

÷ _____

Multiply by $1,000.

× $1,000 _____

Affordable mortgage amount

$ _____

Step 5

Divide your affordable mortgage amount by 1 minus the fractional portion of your down payment (for example, 0.9 for a 10 percent down payment).

÷ _____

Affordable home purchase price

$ _____

Note: The two ratios used by lending institutions (Step 2) and other loan requirements are likely to vary based on a variety of factors, including the type of mortgage, the amount of the down payment, your income level, and current interest rates. If you have other debts, lenders will calculate both ratios and then use the one that allows you greater flexibility in borrowing.

What's Next for Your Personal Financial Plan?

- Identify actions you might need to take to qualify for a mortgage.
- Discuss your mortgage qualifications with a mortgage broker or other lender.

Name: _____ Date: _____

Mortgage Company Comparison

Purpose: To compare the services and costs for different home mortgage sources.

Instructions: When obtaining a mortgage, obtain the information requested below from different mortgage companies.

Suggested Web sites: www.bankrate.com   www.hsh.com

Amount of mortgage
$_____

Down payment
$_____

Years
_____

Company		
Address		
Phone		
Web site		
Contact person		
Application fee, credit report, property appraisal fees		
Loan origination fee		
Other fees, charges (commitment, title, tax transfer)		
Fixed rate mortgage		
Monthly payment		
Discount points		
Adjustable rate mortgage		
• time until first rate charge		
• frequency of rate charge		
Monthly payment		
Discount points		
Payment cap		
Interest rate cap		
Rate index used		
Commitment period		
Other information		

What's Next for Your Personal Financial Plan?

- What additional information should be considered when selecting a mortgage?
- Which of these mortgage companies would best serve your current and future needs?

Mortgage Refinance Analysis

Purpose: To determine savings associated with refinancing a mortgage.

Instructions: Record financing costs and amount saved with new mortgage in the areas provided.

Suggested Web sites: www.interest.com   www.mortgage-net.com

Costs of refinancing:

Points	$ _____
Application fee	$ _____
Credit report	$ _____
Attorney fees	$ _____
Title search	$ _____
Title insurance	$ _____
Appraisal fee	$ _____
Inspection fee	$ _____
Other fees	$ _____

Total refinancing costs . . . . (A) $ _____

Monthly savings:

Current monthly mortgage payment $ _____

Less:

New monthly payment $ _____

Monthly savings . . . . (B) $ _____

Number of months to cover finance costs

Refinance costs (A) divided by monthly savings (B)

(A) _____ ÷ (B) _____ = _____ months

What's Next for Your Personal Financial Plan?

- Monitor changing mortgage rates to determine if any actions are necessary.
- Talk with a mortgage broker about expected trends in mortgage rates.

Name: _____ Date: _____

Current Insurance Policies and Needs

Purpose: To establish a record of current and needed insurance coverage.

Instructions: List current insurance policies and areas where new or additional coverage is needed.

Suggested Web sites: www.insurance.about.com   www.iii.org

Current Coverage	Needed Coverage
Property insurance	
Company _____	
Policy no. _____	
Coverage amounts _____	
Deductible _____	
Annual premium _____	
Agent _____	
Address _____	
Phone _____	
Web site _____	
Automobile insurance	
Company _____	
Policy no. _____	
Coverage amounts _____	
Deductible _____	
Annual premium _____	
Agent _____	
Address _____	
Phone _____	
Web site _____	
Disability income insurance	
Company _____	
Policy no. _____	
Coverage _____	
Contact _____	
Phone _____	
Web site _____	
Health insurance	
Company _____	
Policy no. _____	
Policy provisions _____	
Contact _____	
Phone _____	
Web site _____	
Life insurance	
Company _____	
Policy no. _____	
Type of policy _____	
Amount of coverage _____	
Cash value _____	
Agent _____	
Phone _____	
Web site _____	

What's Next for Your Personal Financial Plan?

- Talk with others to determine the types of insurance they have.
- Conduct a Web search for various types of insurance on which you need additional information.

Home Inventory

Purpose: To create a record of personal belongings for use when settling home insurance claims.

Instructions: For areas of the home, list your possessions including a description (model, serial number), cost, and date of acquisition.

Suggested Web sites: www.quicken.com/insurance   www.iii.org

Item, description	Cost	Date acquired
Attic		
Bathroom		
Bedrooms		
Family room		
Living room		
Hallways		
Kitchen		
Dining room		
Basement		
Garage		
Other items		

What's Next for Your Personal Financial Plan?

- Determine common items that may be overlooked when preparing a home inventory.
- Talk to an insurance agent to determine how best to document your property in the event of an insurance claim.

Determining Needed Property Insurance

Purpose: To determine property insurance needed for a home or apartment.

Instructions: Estimate the value and your needs for the categories below.

Suggested Web sites: www.insurance.about.com   www.insure.com   www.iii.org

Real Property

(this section not applicable to renters)

Current replacement value of home $ _____

Personal Property

Estimated value of appliances, furniture, clothing, and other
household items (conduct an inventory) $ _____

Type of coverage for personal property

       actual cash value   ☐

       replacement value   ☐

Additional coverage for items with limits on standard personal property coverage such as jewelry, firearms, silverware, photographic, electronic and computer equipment

Item	Amount
_____	_____
_____	_____
_____	_____

Personal Liability

Amount of additional personal liability coverage desired for
possible personal injury claims $ _____

Specialized Coverages

If appropriate, investigate flood or earthquake coverage excluded
from home insurance policies $ _____

Note: Use Sheet 49 to compare companies, coverages, and costs
for apartment or home insurance.

What's Next for Your Personal Financial Plan?

- Talk to others about the amount of coverage of their home and property.
- Research the main factors that affect home insurance costs in your region.

Name: _____ Date: _____

Apartment/Home Insurance Comparison

Purpose: To research and compare companies, coverages, and costs for apartment or home insurance.

Instructions: Contact three insurance agents to obtain the information requested below.

Suggested Web sites: www.quicken.com/insurance   www.iii.org

Type of building: ☐ apartment   ☐ house   ☐ condominium

Location: _____

Type of construction _____ Age of building _____

Company name			
Agent's name, address and phone			
E-mail, Web site			
Coverage:	Premium	Premium	Premium
Dwelling $			
Other structures $ (does not apply to apartment/ condo coverage)			
Personal property $			
Additional living expenses $			
Personal liability Bodily injury $ Property damage $			
Medical payments Per person $ Per accident $			
Deductible amount			
Other coverage $			
Service charges or fees			
Total Premium			

What's Next for Your Personal Financial Plan?

- Conduct a survey to determine common reasons that renters do not have renter's insurance.
- Determine cost differences for home insurance among various local agents and online companies.

Name: _____ Date: _____

Automobile Insurance Cost Comparison

Purpose: To research and compare companies, coverages, and costs for auto insurance.

Instructions: Contact three insurance agents to obtain the information requested below.

Suggested Web sites: personalinsure.about.com   www.insquote.com

Automobile (year, make, model, engine size) _____

Driver's age _____ Sex _____ Total miles driven in a year _____

Full- or part-time drive? _____ Driver's education completed? _____

Accidents or traffic violations within the past three years? _____

Company name			
Agent's name, address and phone			
E-mail, Web site			
Policy length (6 months, 1 year)			
Coverage:	**Premium**	**Premium**	**Premium**
Bodily injury liability			
Per person $			
Per accident $			
Property damage liability per accident $			
Collision deductible $			
Comprehensive deductible $			
Medical payments per person $			
Uninsured motorist Per person $			
Per accident $			
Other coverage			
Service charges			
Total Premium			

What's Next for Your Personal Financial Plan?

• Research actions that you might take to reduce automobile insurance costs.

• Determine cost differences for auto insurance among various local agents and online companies.

Name: _____ Date: _____

Assessing Current and Needed Health Care Insurance

Purpose: To assess current and needed medical and health care insurance.

Instructions: Assess current and needed medical and health care insurance. Investigate your existing medical and health insurance, and determine the need for additional coverages.

Suggested Web sites: www.insure.com   www.life-line.org

Insurance company
_____

Address
_____

Type of coverage   ☐ individual health policy   ☐ group health policy

☐ HMO   ☐ PPO   ☐ other

Premium amount (monthly/quarter/semiannual/annual)
_____

Main coverages
_____

Amount of coverage for
_____

• Hospital costs
_____

• Surgery costs
_____

• Physician's fees
_____

• Lab tests
_____

• Outpatient expenses
_____

• Maternity
_____

• Major medical
_____

Other items covered/amounts
_____

Policy restrictions (deductible, coinsurance, maximum limits)
_____

Items not covered by this insurance
_____

Of items not covered, would supplemental coverage be appropriate for your personal situation?
_____

What actions related to your current (or proposed additional) coverage are necessary?
_____

What's Next for Your Personal Financial Plan?

• Talk to others about the impact of their health insurance on other financial decisions.

• Contact an insurance agent to obtain cost information for an individual health insurance plan.

Disability Income Insurance Needs

Purpose: To determine financial needs and insurance coverage related to employment disability situations.

Instructions: Use the categories below to determine your potential income needs and disability insurance coverage.

Suggested Web sites: www.ssa.gov   www.insuremarket.com

Name: _____ Date: _____

Monthly Expenses

	Current	When Disabled
Mortgage (or rent)	$_____	$_____
Utilities	$_____	$_____
Food	$_____	$_____
Clothing	$_____	$_____
Insurance payments	$_____	$_____
Debt payments	$_____	$_____
Auto/transportation	$_____	$_____
Medical/dental care	$_____	$_____
Education	$_____	$_____
Personal allowances	$_____	$_____
Recreation/entertainment	$_____	$_____
Contributors, donations	$_____	$_____
Total monthly expenses when disabled		$_____

Substitute Income

Monthly Benefit*

	Monthly Benefit*
Group disability insurance	$_____
Social Security	$_____
State disability insurance	$_____
Worker's compensation	$_____
Credit disability insurance (in some auto loan or home mortgages)	$_____
Other income (investments, etc.)	$_____
Total projected income when disabled	$_____

If projected income when disabled is less than expenses, additional disability income insurance should be considered.

*Most disability insurance programs have a waiting period before benefits start, and they may have a limit as to how long benefits are received.

What's Next for Your Personal Financial Plan?

- Survey several people to determine if they have disability insurance.
- Talk to an insurance agent to compare the costs of disability income insurance available from several insurance companies.

Determining Life Insurance Needs

Purpose: To estimate life insurance coverage needed to cover expected expenses and future family living costs.

Instructions: Estimate the amounts for the categories listed.

Suggested Web sites: www.insure.com   www.kiplinger.com/tools/

Household expenses to be covered

Final expenses (funeral, estate taxes, etc.)   (1) $_____

Payment of consumer debt amounts   (2) $_____

Emergency fund   (3) $_____

College fund   (4) $_____

Expected living expenses:

    Average living expense $ _____

    Spouse's income after taxes $ ⁻_____

    Annual Social Security benefits $ ⁻_____

    Net annual living expenses   (a) $ _____

    Years until spouse is 90   _____

    Investment rate factor (see below) (b)   _____

Total living expenses (a × b)   (5) $ _____

Total monetary needs (1 + 2 + 3 + 4 + 5) $ _____

Less: Total current investments $ ⁻_____

Life insurance needs $ _____

Investment rate factors   Years until Spouse Is 90

	25	30	35	40	45	50	55	60
Conservative investment	20	22	25	27	30	31	33	35
Aggressive investment	16	17	19	20	21	21	22	23

Note: Use Sheet 54 to compare life insurance policies.

What's Next for Your Personal Financial Plan?

• Survey several people to determine their reasons for buying life insurance.

• Talk to an insurance agent to compare the rates charged by different companies and for different age categories.

Name: _____ Date: _____

Life Insurance Policy Comparison

Purpose: To research and compare companies, coverages, and costs for different insurance policies.
Instructions: Analyze ads and contact life insurance agents to obtain the information requested below.
Suggested Web sites: www.quotesmith.com   www.accuquote.com

Age: _____

Company			
Agent's name, address, and phone			
E-mail, Web site			
Type of insurance (term, straight/whole, limited payment, endowment, universal)			
Type of policy (individual, group)			
Amount of coverage			
Frequency of payment (monthly, quarterly, semiannual, annual)			
Premium amount			
Other costs: • Service charges • Physical exam			
Rate of return (annual percentage increase in cash value; not applicable for term policies)			
Benefits of insurance as stated in ad or by agent			
Potential problems or disadvantages of this coverage			

What's Next for Your Personal Financial Plan?

- Talk to a life insurance agent to obtain information on the methods they suggest for determining the amount of life insurance a person should have.
- Research the differences in premium costs between a mutual and a stock company.

Setting Investment Objectives

Purpose: To determine specific goals for an investment program.

Instructions: Based on short- and long-term objectives for your investment efforts, enter the items requested below.

Suggested Web sites: www.fool.com   www.americanbank.com

Description of financial need	Amount	Date needed	Investment goal (safety, growth, income)	Level of risk (high, medium, low)	Possible investments to achieve this goal

What's Next for Your Personal Financial Plan?

- Use the suggestions listed in Chapter 13 to perform a financial checkup.
- Discuss the importance of investment goals and financial planning with other household members.

Name: _____ **Date:** _____

Assessing Risk for Investments

Purpose: To assess the risk of various investments in relation to your personal risk tolerance and financial goals.

Instructions: List various investments you are considering based on the type and level of risk associated with each.

Suggested Web sites: www.investor.nasd.com   www.fool.com

Level of risk	Loss of market value (market risk)	Type of Risk		
		Inflation risk	Interest rate risk	Liquidity risk
High risk				
Moderate risk				
Low risk				

What's Next for Your Personal Financial Plan?

- Identify current economic trends that might increase or decrease the risk associated with your choice of investments.
- Based on the risk associated with the investments you chose, which investment would you choose to obtain your investment goals.

Name: _____   Date: _____

Evaluating Investment Information

Purpose: To identify and assess the value of various investment information sources.

Instructions: Obtain samples of investment information from at least three sources that you might consider to guide you in your investment decisions.

Suggested Web sites: www.kiplinger.com   www.money.com

	Item 1	Item 2	Item 3
Location (address, phone)			
Web site			
Overview of information provided (main features)			
Cost			
Ease of access			
Evaluation: • reliability • clarity • value of information compared to cost			

What's Next for Your Personal Financial Plan?

• Based on the information that you provided on this form, choose one source that you feel is not only easy to use, but also provides quality information that could help you obtain your financial goals.

• Choose one specific investment and use your "best" source that was just identified to conduct a more thorough evaluation of the chosen investment alternative.

Personal Financial Planner

Name: _____ Date: _____

Evaluating Corporate Stocks

Purpose: To identify a corporate stock that could help you obtain your investment goals.

Instructions: Use Internet research or library materials to answer the questions on this personal financial planning sheet.

Suggested Web sites: finance.yahoo.com   www.smartmoney.com

Note: No checklist can serve as a foolproof guide for choosing a common or preferred stock. However, the following questions will help you evaluate a potential stock investment. Use stock Web sites on the Internet and/or use library materials to answer these questions about a corporate stock that you believe could help you obtain your investment goals.

Category 1: The Basics

1. What is the corporation's name?_____
   _____

2. What are the corporation's address and telephone number? _____
   _____

3. Have you requested the latest annual report and quarterly report? ☐ Yes ☐ No

4. What information about the corporation is available on the Internet? _____
   _____

5. Where is the stock traded? _____
   _____

6. What types of products or services does this firm provide? _____
   _____

7. Briefly describe the prospects for this company. (Include significant factors like product development, plans for expansion, plans for mergers, etc.)
   _____

Category 2: Dividend Income

8. Is the corporation currently paying dividends? If so, how much? _____
   _____

9. What is the current yield for this stock? _____
   _____

10. Has the dividend payout increased or decreased over the past five years? _____
    _____

11. How does the yield for this investment compare with those for other potential investments?
    _____

Category 3: Financial Performance

12. What are the firm's earnings per share for the last year? _____
    _____

13. Have the firm's earnings increased over the past five years? _____
    _____

14. What is the firm's current price-earnings ratio?
    _____

15. How does the firm's current price-earnings ratio compare with firms in the same industry?
    _____

16. Describe trends for the firm's price-earnings ratio over the past three years. Do these trends show improvement or decline in investment value? _____
    _____

17. What are the firm's projected earnings for the next year? _____
    _____

18. Have sales increased over the last five years?
    _____

19. What is the stock's current price? _____

20. What are the 52-week high and low for this stock?
    _____

21. Do the analysts indicate that this is a good time to invest in this stock? _____
    _____

22. Briefly describe any other information that you obtained from Mergent, Value Line, Standard & Poor's, or other sources of information.

A Word of Caution

When you use a checklist, there is always a danger of overlooking important relevant information. This checklist is not all-inclusive, but it does provide some questions that you should answer before making a decision to invest in stock. Quite simply, it is a place to start. If you need other information, *you* are responsible for obtaining it and for determining how it affects your potential investment.

What's Next for Your Personal Financial Plan?

• Identify additional factors that might affect your decision to invest in this corporation's stock.
• Develop a plan for monitoring an investment's value once a stock is purchased.

Investment Broker Comparison

Purpose: To compare the benefits and costs of different investment brokers.

Instructions: Compare the services of an investment broker based on the factors listed below.

Suggested Web sites: www.fool.com   www.scottrade.com

Broker's name		
Organization		
Address		
Phone		
Web site		
Years, type of experience		
Education and training		
Areas of specialization		
Certifications held		
Professional affiliations		
Employer's stock exchange and financial market affiliations		
Information services offered		
Minimum commission charge		
Commission on 100 shares of stock at $50/share		
Fees for other investments: • corporate bonds • mutual funds • stock options		
Other fees: • annual account fee • inactivity fee • other		

What's Next for Your Personal Financial Plan?

- Using the information you obtained, choose a brokerage firm that you feel will help you obtain your investment goals.
- Access the Web site for the brokerage firm you have chosen and answer the questions on page 467 in your text.

Personal Financial Planner

Name: _____ Date: _____

Evaluating Corporate Bonds

Purpose: To determine if a specific corporate bond could help you obtain your financial goals.

Instructions: Use the Internet or library sources to answer the questions below.

Suggested Web sites: bonds.yahoo.com   www.bondsonline.com

Category 1: Information about the Corporation

1. What is the corporation's name? _____
_____

2. What are the corporation's address and telephone number? _____
_____

3. What type of products or services does this firm provide? _____
_____

4. Briefly describe the prospects for this company. (Include significant factors like product development, plans for expansion, plans for mergers, etc.)
_____
_____
_____

Category 2: Bond Basics

5. What type of bond is this? _____
6. What is the face value for this bond? _____
7. What is the interest rate for this bond? _____
8. What is the dollar amount of annual interest for this bond? _____
9. When are interest payments made to bondholders?
_____
10. Is the corporation currently paying interest as scheduled?   ☐ Yes   ☐ No
11. What is the maturity date for this bond? _____
12. What is Moody's rating for this bond? _____
13. What is Standard & Poor's rating for this bond?
_____
14. What do these ratings mean? _____
_____
_____
15. What was the original issue date? _____
_____
16. Who is the trustee for this bond issue? _____
_____
17. Is the bond callable? If so, when? _____
_____

18. Is the bond secured with collateral? If so, what?
☐ Yes   ☐ No
19. How did the corporation use the money from this bond issue? _____
_____

Category 3: Financial Performance

20. What are the firm's earnings per share for the last year? _____
21. Have the firm's earnings increased over the past five years? _____
22. What is the firm's current price-earnings ratio?
_____
23. Describe trends for the firm's price-earnings ratio over the past three years. Do these trends show improvement or decline in investment value? _____
_____
24. What are the firm's projected earnings for the next year? _____
25. Have sales increased over the last five years?
_____
26. Do the analysts indicate that this is a good time to invest in this company?
_____
_____
27. Briefly describe any other information that you obtained from Moody's, Standard & Poor's, or other sources of information.
_____
_____

A Word of Caution

When you use a checklist, there is always a danger of overlooking important relevant information. The above checklist is not a cure-all, but it does provide some questions that you should answer before making a decision to invest in bonds. Quite simply, it is a place to start. If you need other information, *you* are responsible for obtaining it and for determining how it affects your potential investment.

What's Next for Your Personal Financial Plan?

• Talk with various people who have invested in government, municipal, or corporate bonds.

• Discuss with other household members why government, municipal, or corporate bonds might be a logical choice for your investment program.

Evaluating Mutual Fund Investment Information

Purpose: To identify and assess the value of various mutual fund investment information sources.

Instructions: Obtain samples of several investment information sources that you might consider to guide you in your investment decisions.

Suggested Web sites: www.morningstar.com   www.mfea.com

	Item 1	Item 2	Item 3
Location (address, phone)			
Web site			
Overview of information provided (main features)			
Cost			
Ease of access			
Evaluation • Reliability • Clarity • Value of information compared to cost			

What's Next for Your Personal Financial Plan?

- Talk with friends and relatives to determine what sources of information they use to evaluate mutual funds.
- Choose one source of information and describe how the information could help you obtain your investment goals.

Evaluation of a Mutual Fund

Purpose: To determine whether a specific mutual fund could help you obtain your investment goals.

Instructions: Use the Internet or library sources to answer the questions below.

Suggested Web sites: www.morningstar.com   www.mfea.com

Category 1: Fund Characteristics

1. What is the fund's name?
   _____

2. What is this fund's Morningstar rating?
   _____

3. What is the minimum investment?
   _____

4. Does the fund allow telephone or Internet exchanges? ☐ Yes ☐ No

5. Is there a fee for exchanges? ☐ Yes ☐ No

Category 2: Costs

6. Is there a front-end load charge? If so, how much is it?
   _____

7. Is there a redemption fee? If so, how much is it?
   _____

8. How much is the annual management fee?
   _____

9. Is there a 12b-1 fee? If so, how much is it?
   _____

10. What is the fund's expense ratio?
    _____

Category 3: Diversification

11. What is the fund's objective?
    _____

12. What types of securities does the fund's portfolio include?
    _____

13. How many different securities does the fund's portfolio include?
    _____

14. How many types of industries does the fund's portfolio include?
    _____

15. What are the fund's five largest holdings?
    _____

Category 4: Fund Performance

16. How long has the fund manager been with the fund?
    _____

17. How would you describe the fund's performance over the past 12 months?
    _____

18. How would you describe the fund's performance over the past five years?
    _____

19. How would you describe the fund's performance over the past 10 years?
    _____

20. What is the current net asset value for this fund?
    _____

21. What is the high net asset value for this fund over the last 12 months?
    _____

22. What is the low net asset value for this fund over the last 12 months?
    _____

23. What do the experts say about this fund?
    _____

Category 5: Conclusion

24. Based on the above information, do you think an investment in this fund will help you achieve your investment goals? ☐ Yes ☐ No

25. Explain your answer to question 24.
    _____

A Word of Caution

When you use a checklist, there is always a danger of overlooking important relevant information. This checklist is not a cure-all, but it does provide some questions that you should answer before making a mutual fund investment decision. Quite simply, it is a place to start. If you need other information, *you* are responsible for obtaining it and for determining how it affects your potential investment.

What's Next for Your Personal Financial Plan?

• Identify additional factors that may affect your decision to invest in this fund.

• Develop a plan for monitoring an investment's value once a mutual fund(s) is purchased.

Retirement Housing and Lifestyle Planning

Purpose: To consider housing alternatives for retirement living and to plan retirement activities.

Instructions: Evaluate current and expected needs and interest based on the items below.

Suggested Web sites: www.aarp.org   www.lifenet.com

Retirement Housing Plans

Description of current housing situation (size, facilities, location)

_____

_____

Time until retirement _____ years

Description of retirement housing needs

_____

_____

Checklist of Retirement Housing Alternatives

_____ present home	_____ professional companionship arrangement
_____ house sharing	_____ commercial rental
_____ accessory apartment	_____ board and care home
_____ elder cottage housing	_____ congregate housing
_____ rooming house	_____ continuing care retirement community
_____ single-room occupancy	_____ assisted-living facility
_____ caretaker arrangement	_____ nursing home

Personal and financial factors that will influence the retirement housing decision

_____

Financial planning actions to be taken related to retirement housing

_____

Retirement Activities

What plans do you have to work part-time or do volunteer work?

_____

What recreational activities do you plan to continue or start? (Location, training, equipment needs)

_____

What plans do you have for travel or educational study?

What's Next for Your Personal Financial Plan?

- Survey local senior housing facilities to determine the types of services available to seniors.
- Make a list that suggests the best housing options for seniors.

Name: _____ **Date:** _____

Retirement Plan Comparison

Purpose: To compare benefits and costs for different retirement plans (401K, IRA, Keogh).

Instructions: Analyze advertisements and articles, and contact your employer and financial institutions to obtain the information below.

Suggested Web sites: www.lifenet.com   www.aarp.org

Type of plan			
Name of financial institution or employer			
Address			
Phone			
Web site			
Type of investments			
Minimum initial deposit			
Minimum additional deposits			
Employer contributions			
Current rate of return			
Service charges/fees			
Safety insured? By whom?			
Amount			
Payroll deduction available			
Tax benefits			
Penalty for early withdrawal: • IRS penalty (10%) • Other penalties			
Other features or restrictions			

What's Next for Your Personal Financial Plan?

- Survey local businesses to determine the types of retirement plans available to employees.
- Talk to representatives of various financial institutions to determine their suggestions for IRA investments.

Forecasting Retirement Income

Purpose: To determine the amount needed to save each year to have the necessary funds to cover retirement living costs.

Instructions: Estimate the information requested below.

Suggested Web sites: www.ssa.gov   www.pensionplanners.com

Estimated annual retirement living expenses

Estimated annual living expenses
if you retired today $_____

Future value for _____ years until
retirement at expected annual
income of _____% (use future
value of $1, Exhibit 1–A of the
Chapter 1 Appendix)   × _____

**Projected annual retirement living
expenses adjusted for inflation** . . . . (A) $_____

Estimated annual income at retirement

Social Security income $_____

Company pension, personal
retirement account income $_____

Investment and other income $_____

Total retirement income . . . . (B) $_____

Additional retirement plan contributions (if B is less than A)

Annual shortfall of income after
retirement (A − B) $_____

Expected annual rate of return
on invested funds after retirement,
percentage expressed as a decimal $_____

Needed investment fund after retirement A − B . . . . (C) $_____

Future value factor of a series of deposits for _____ years until
retirement and an expected annual rate of return before
retirement of _____ % (use Exhibit 1–B of the Chapter 1 Appendix)

(D) $_____

**Annual deposit to achieve needed investment fund
(C divided by D)** . . . . $_____

What's Next for Your Personal Financial Plan?

- Survey retired individuals or people close to retirement to obtain information on their main sources of retirement income.
- Make a list that suggests the best investment options for an individual retirement account.

Personal Financial Planner

Name: _____ Date: _____

Estate Planning Activities

Purpose: To develop a plan for estate planning and related financial activities.

Instructions: Respond to the following questions as a basis for making and implementing an estate plan.

Suggested Web sites: www.nolo.com   www.webtrust.com

Are your financial records, including recent tax forms, insurance policies, and investment and housing documents, organized and easily accessible?	
Do you have a safe-deposit box? Where is it located? Where is the key?	
Location of life insurance policies. Name and address of insurance company and agent.	
Is your will current? Location of copies of your will. Name and address of your lawyer.	
Name and address of your executor.	
Do you have a listing of the current value of assets owned and liabilities outstanding?	
Have any funeral and burial arrangements been made?	
Have you created any trusts? Name and location of financial institution.	
Do you have any current information on gift and estate taxes?	
Have you prepared a letter of last instruction? Where is it located?	

What's Next for Your Personal Financial Plan?

- Talk to several individuals about the actions they have taken related to estate planning.
- Create a list of situations in which a will would need to be revised.

Name: _____ Date: _____

Will Planning Sheet

Purpose: To compare costs and features of various types of wills.

Instructions: Obtain information for the various areas listed based on your current and future situation; contact attorneys regarding the cost of these wills.

Suggested Web sites: www.netplanning.com   www.estateplanninglinks.com

Type of will	Features that would be appropriate for my current or future situation	Cost Attorney, Address, Phone

What's Next for Your Personal Financial Plan?

- Create a list of items that you believe would be desirable to include in a will.
- Obtain the cost of a will from a number of different lawyers.

Name: _____ **Date:** _____

Trust Comparison Sheet

Purpose: To identify features of different types of trusts.

Instructions: Research features of various trusts to determine their value to your personal situation.

Suggested Web sites: www.webtrust.com   www.lifenet.com

Type of trust	Benefits	Possible value for my situation

What's Next for Your Personal Financial Plan?

- Talk to legal and financial planning experts to contrast the cost and benefits of wills and trusts.
- Talk to one or more lawyers to obtain information about the type of trust recommended for your situation.

Estate Tax Projection and Settlement Costs

Purpose: To estimate the estate tax based on your financial situation.

Instructions: Enter the data requested below to calculate the tax based on current tax rates.

Suggested Web sites: www.irs.gov   www.lifenet.com/estate

Gross Estate Values

Personal property	$_____
Real estate	$_____
Joint ownership	$_____
Business interests	$_____
Life insurance	$_____
Employee benefits	$_____
Controlled gifts/trusts	$_____
Prior taxable gifts	$_____
Total estate values	$_____

Deductible Debts, Costs, Expenses

Mortgages and secured loans	$_____
Unsecured notes and loans	$_____
Bills and accounts payable	$_____
Funeral and medical expenses	$_____
Probate administration costs	$_____
Total deductions	– $_____
Marital deduction	– $_____
Taxable estate	= $_____
Gross estate tax*	$_____

Allowable Credits

Unified credit	$_____
Gift tax credit	$_____
State tax credit	$_____
Foreign tax credit	$_____
Prior tax credit	$_____
Total tax credits	– $_____
Net Estate Tax	$_____

*Consult the Internal Revenue Service (www.irs.gov) for current rates and regulations related to estate taxes.

What's Next for Your Personal Financial Plan?

• Research the history of the estate tax law to find out when the law was first implemented and how it has changed over the years.

• Research the inheritance and gift tax laws in your state.

Personal Financial Planner

Name: _____ Date: _____

Financial Data Summary

Date >>>>>>>>>>					
Balance sheet summary					
Assets					
Liabilities					
Net worth					
Cash flow summary					
Inflows					
Outflows					
Surplus/deficit					
Budget summary					
Budget					
Actual					
Variance					
Date >>>>>>>>>>					
Balance sheet summary					
Assets					
Liabilities					
Net worth					
Cash flow summary					
Inflows					
Outflows					
Surplus/deficit					
Budget summary					
Budget					
Actual					
Variance					

Savings/Investment Portfolio Summary

Description	Organization contact/phone/ Web site	Purchase price/date	Value/ date	Value/ date	Value/ date	Value/ date

Personal Financial Planner

Progress Check on Major Financial Goals and Activities

Some financial planning activities require short-term perspective. Other activities may require continued efforts over a long period of time, such as purchasing a vacation home. This sheet is designed to help you monitor these long-term, ongoing financial activities.

Major financial objective	Desired completion date	Initial actions and date	Progress checks (date, progress made, and other actions to be taken)

Summary for Money Management, Budgeting, and Tax Planning Activities

As you complete the various sheets in this *Personal Financial Planner,* transfer financial data, goals, and planned actions to the following summary sheet. For example:

Sheet	Actions to be taken	Planned completion date	Completed (✓)
14 (Financial documents and records	Locate and organize all personal financial documents	Within 3-2 months	
20 (Current income tax estimate)	Sort current tax data, compute estimate to determine tax amount	February 15	✓

(Text Chapterters 3–4)

Sheet	Actions to be taken	Planned completion date	Completed (✓)

Name: _____ **Date:** _____

Summary for Banking Services and Consumer Credit Activities

(Text Chapters 5–7)

Sheet	Actions to be taken	Planned completion date	Completed (✓)

Name: _____ Date: _____

Summary for Consumer Buying and Housing Activities

(Text Chapters 8–9)

Sheet	Actions to be taken	Planned completion date	Completed (✓)

Personal Financial Planner

Name: _____ Date: _____

Summary for Insurance Activities

(Text Chapters 10–12)

Sheet	Actions to be taken	Planned completion date	Completed (✓)

Summary for Investment Activities

(Text Chapters 13–17)

Sheet	Actions to be taken	Planned completion date	Completed (✓)

Name: _____ Date: _____

Summary for Retirement and Estate Planning Activities

(Text Chapters 18–19)

Sheet	Actions to be taken	Planned completion date	Completed (✓)